D1568010

The Shakespeare Name Dictionary

Garland Reference Library of the Humanities
Vol. 976

MR. WILLIAM SHAKESPEARES

COMEDIES, HISTORIES, & TRAGEDIES.

Publiſhed according to the True Originall Copies.

LONDON

Printed by Iſaac Iaggard, and Ed. Blount. 1623.

The Shakespeare Name Dictionary

J. Madison Davis
A. Daniel Frankforter

Garland Publishing, Inc.
New York & London
1995

Ref.
PR
2892
.D33
1995

Copyright © 1995
J. Madison Davis and A. Daniel Frankforter
All rights reserved

Library of Congress Cataloging-in-Publication Data

Davis, J. Madison.
The Shakespeare name dictionary / by J. Madison Davis and A. Daniel Frankforter.
p. cm. — (Garland reference library of the humanities ; vol. 976)
Includes bibliographical references.
ISBN 0-8240-6341-4
1. Shakespeare, William, 1564–1616—Dictionaries. 2. Names, Geographical, in literature—Dictionaries. 3. Names, Personal, in literature—Dictionaries. I. Frankforter, A. Daniel. II. Title. III. Series.
PR2892.D33 1995
822.3'3—dc20 94-13784
CIP

Printed on acid-free, 250-year-life paper
Manufactured in the United States of America

30318620

Contents

Introduction

This dictionary attempts, by cataloguing the names and collecting the accumulated facts and speculations regarding Shakespeare's use of them, to define the contexts of the times in which Shakespeare—or those who may have co-authored the plays usually attributed to him—created his magnificent body of plays and poems. In the following pages we have listed every name, proper adjective, official title, literary and musical title, and place name which appears in the text of the complete plays and poems of William Shakespeare. We have attempted to be as thorough and as inclusive as possible. Where there is a question about whether a word is intended as a name or merely as a common word, we have included it. We have allowed ourselves latitude in including some terms that may not be considered proper nouns in most quarters ('football' and 'pia mater,' for example) but which may provide some insight into the culture and the man whose remarkable writings were produced by it. We have also cross-referenced a number of common editorial spellings which were not used in the edition which served as our standard, *William Shakespeare: The Complete Works*, ed. by Stanley Wells and Gary Taylor (Oxford University Press, 1986). 'Imogen,' for example, the most common editors' choice for *Cymbeline*, is listed, but refers the reader to Wells and Taylor's choice, 'Innogen.' Similarly, 'Nym' refers the reader to 'Nim.' Sometimes these seemingly superficial spelling variations have been seen to have significance in interpreting the playwright's intentions, pronunciation, or sources. A few actors are also listed whose names survived from the manuscripts into the early editions.

We have not, however, included any name or term which does not appear in the texts of the plays and poems. It was our intention from the beginning to adhere rigorously to what appeared only in the oeuvre. For example, Elizabeth I is mentioned in *Henry VIII*, and therefore receives an entry. James I, despite his importance in the time period, is never mentioned by name within the plays and poems and is therefore omitted. There is a short poem which was reported as a reply to a witticism of Ben Jonson—who is entered—but in the oeuvre there is no mention of Thomas Middleton or George Wilkins, who may have collaborated with Shakespeare, so they receive no entry.

An entry for a fictional character usually contains a description of the character and, if he or she is major, a few words about how the character is usually interpreted. We also discuss what scholars have considered the likely interpretation which Shakespeare and his audience may have had—which in many instances may have been quite different from the interpretation of the character many centuries later. We also discuss possible sources for the name, and any meanings which might reflect upon interpretation. One cannot know, in many instances, whether Shakespeare was aware of the meaning of a particular name, whereas in others it seems impossible that he is not alluding to the meaning. If it is known that a name had a particular implication in the time period—it was upper- or middle-class, or associated with prostitutes—we discuss the possibilities.

Historical characters are listed with the details of their lives as is known by modern historians. Shakespeare's deviations from what is now accepted as the historical record are pointed out, as well as the origin of these deviations, if known. The manipulation of the record in the cases of Macbeth and Richard III are well known, but, it is important to know that the histories available to the playwright already contained many of these manipulations, and we considered it important to identify them. Mythological and legendary characters are similarly treated. How Shakespeare appears to have understood classical mythology and Biblical stories, as opposed to what modern readers know about them, may also be significant in gaining greater insight in Shakespeare's work and times.

Places are located on the contemporary and modern maps, and a brief history of the nation or area up to the seventeenth century is given. Other facts of which people of Renaissance England may have been aware are also given, such as the meaning of the name, common prejudices relating to the place or nation, and misconceptions associated with the broad and ever more complex world that was unfolding before them.

Finally, each entry contains line citations based upon Wells and Taylor's edition. When there is only a single reference to a name, this citation appears at the beginning. If there are multiple citations, they are listed at the end of the entry. As it was not our intention to duplicate the many fine concordances to Shakespeare, when a name appears frequently in a play, the citations refer to the play as a whole. There is little point in listing each use of 'Richard' in *Richard III*; however, a single reference to him in another play may have significance.

When we began this work seven years ago, we severely underestimated the magnitude of it. In a sense, a project like this can never be finished. It is merely another chapter in a lengthy process of attempting to understand and appreciate a particularly remarkable man and his extraordinary times. On occasion in this process we have been privileged to peek behind the curtain of the centuries and have received an inkling of how this genius of four centuries ago lived and worked, what amused him, what angered him, and what troubled him. Many more times the curtain remained down and the dim shadows played about its edges as we squinted to make them out and consulted with the many great scholars whose lifetimes of work make our effort tiny indeed. What we hope to have done is to have collected their wisdom wisely enough that future scholars may use our work as a means to gain other significant glimpses into the era in which our modern world was born.

—J. Madison Davis and A. Daniel Frankforter

Abbreviations

The Writings

1H4: The History of Henry the Fourth.
1H6: The First Part of Henry the Sixth.
2H4: The Second Part of Henry the Fourth.
2H6: The First Part of the Contention of the Two Famous Houses of York and Lancaster (Henry the Sixth, part 2).
3H6: The True Tragedy of Richard Duke of York and the Good King Henry the Sixth (Henry the Sixth, part 3).
Ado: Much Ado About Nothing.
Ant: The Tragedy of Antony and Cleopatra.
AWW: All's Well That Ends Well.
AYLI: As You Like It.
Cor: The Tragedy of Coriolanus.
Cym: Cymbeline King of Britain.
Err: The Comedy of Errors.
H5: The Life of Henry the Fifth.
H8: All is True (Henry the Eighth).
Ham: The Tragedy of Hamlet Prince of Denmark.
JC: The Tragedy of Julius Caesar.
Jn: The Life and Death of King John.
LC: A Lover's Complaint.
LLL: Love's Labour's Lost.
Lr: The Tragedy of King Lear (Folio Text).
Lr Q: The History of King Lear (Quarto Text).
Luc: The Rape of Lucrece.
Mac: The Tragedy of Macbeth.
MM: Measure for Measure.
MND: A Midsummer Night's Dream.
MV: The Comical History of the Merchant of Venice, or Otherwise Called the Jew of Venice.
MWW: The Merry Wives of Windsor.
Oth: The Tragedy of Othello, the Moor of Venice.
Per: Pericles Prince of Tyre.
PhT: The Phoenix and the Turtle.
PP: The Passionate Pilgrim.
R2: The Tragedy of King Richard the Second.
R3: The Tragedy of Richard the Third.
Rom: The Most Excellent and Lamentable Tragedy of Romeo and Juliet.
Shr: The Taming of the Shrew.
Son: Sonnets.
STM: Sir Thomas More.
Tmp: The Tempest.
TGV: The Two Gentlemen of Verona.
Tim: The Life of Timon of Athens.
Tit: The Most Lamentable Tragedy of Titus Andronicus.
TN: Twelfth Night, or What You Will.
TNK: The Two Noble Kinsmen.
Tro: Troilus and Cressida.
Var: various poems.
Ven: Venus and Adonis.
WT: The Winter's Tale.

Other Abbreviations

AD: *anno domini*
Add.: additional lines (from other editions)
BC: before Christ
c.: circa, if preceding a date; century, if following an ordinal number.
Du.: Dutch
epi.: epilogue
F1: the First Folio
ff.: and following
fl.: flourished
Fr.: French
Ger.: German
Gr.: Greek
Heb.: Hebrew
Ind.: Induction
It.: Italian
l., ll.: line, lines
L.: Latin
mi.: miles
n.: noun
OE: Old English (Anglo-Saxon)
OED: *The Oxford English Dictionary*
pl.: plural
pro.: prologue
Q: quarto edition
Q1, Q2, etc.: first quarto, second quarto, etc.
q.v.: which see
qq.v.: see all
rptd.: reprinted
sd: stage direction
Sh.: Shakespeare or his work
sing.: singular
Sp.: Spanish
sq. mi.: square miles
trans.: translated
v.: verb
vol.: volume

Acknowledgements

We would like to thank the following students for their assistance in some of the initial work in compiling the dictionary: Kristina Kierzek, Matthew Gregoroff, Dana Grudzien, Susan Holder, A. Mamaux, Ann Pollard, Rebecca Radish, Caroline Poniatowski, Anissa Wardi, and Vail Weller. We would also like to thank Dr. Jack S. Shreve, linguist and scholar, for his assistance in matters of Romance etymology.

A

Aaron, the Moor, *Tit,* adulterous lover of the emperor Saturninus' wife Tamora, father of her illegitimate child, and author of plots to destroy the family of Titus Andronicus. Aaron is a thoroughly evil character unredeemed by any trace of remorse. Sh.'s source for *Tit* is uncertain, but an 18th c. chapbook preserves a version of a tale that Sh. may have known. The Moor in the chapbook is unnamed and is less important to the plot of its story than he is to Sh.'s tragedy. It is likely, therefore, that Sh. fleshed out the character and chose its Hebrew name. The Biblical Aaron was Moses' elder brother and the first Hebrew high priest. By linking a black man with the 'blasphemous' Jews, Sh. invoked common prejudices of his day to establish Aaron as an archetypal villain, an alien creature devoid of moral scruples.

Abbey, *H8 4.1.58,* see Westminster 2).

Abel, second son of Adam and Eve (Genesis 4:2–16). Abel was a herdsman; his brother Cain a farmer. Each offered the product of his labors to God, who accepted the animal brought by Abel, but rejected the grain provided by Cain. Jealousy enraged Cain and drove him to commit biblical history's first murder, the slaughter of his brother Abel. *1H6 1.4.39. R2 1.1.104.*

Abergavenny, Lord, *H8,* George Neville (1471–1535), youngest son of the first earl of Westmorland and heir to the estate of his maternal grandfather, Richard Beauchamp. Although Abergavenny had served Henry VII loyally, Henry VIII suspected him of participating in treasonous conversations with his father-in-law, Edward Stafford, the third duke of Buckingham. Buckingham and Abergavenny were both arrested in 1521. Abergavenny was soon pardoned and restored to his hereditary ceremonial offices at court, but he never recovered Henry's full confidence.

Abhorson, *MM,* executioner. In *4.2* he resists instructing the bawd Pompey as his assistant because his trade is a 'mystery.' The Provost, however, finds little difference between the men and after some quibbling by Pompey, Abhorson agrees. In *4.3* he sets about to execute Barnardine, but the murderer refuses. This comic relief reflects the corruption of justice in Vienna. The name is obviously composed of 'abhor,' and 'whoreson.'

Abraham, 1) son of Terah, father of Isaac and Ismael, husband of Sarah, and founding father of the Hebrew nation. Genesis 12 records an agreement between God and Abraham that guarantees the Jews a unique place in history. In exchange for Abraham's vow of exclusive loyalty, God decrees that Abraham's descendants will become a nation through whom all the families of the earth will bless themselves (12:3). *R3 4.3.38:* 'A.'s bosom,' an allusion to Luke 16:22, where it is said that the righteous dead rest with Abraham. In the Middle Ages the expression had come to mean where souls who were not damned waited to enter Heaven. Later, through the influence of Augustine, this developed into the concept of Purgatory, which was formalized by the Roman Catholic church in the 16th c. *R2 4.1.95.*

2) *Rom,* a servingman of the Montagues. He fights with the Capulet servants in the first act, demonstrating the extent of the feud.

3) *Rom 2.1.13,* see Adam 5).

4) *MWW,* see Slender, Abraham.

Abram, *MV 1.3.71, 159,* see Abraham 1).

Absey book, *Jn 1.1.196,* from 'ABC's,' a primer or introductory text, alluded to at *TGV 2.1.21* and *LLL 5.1.45-46.* It was usually a single page covered with horn to protect it and attached to a handle. Besides the alphabet, it would have the Lord's Prayer and some catechism.

Absyrtus, *2H6 5.3.59,* Medea's brother, a minor figure in the legend of Jason and the Argonauts. After Jason seduced Medea and persuaded her to help him steal the golden fleece, the thieving lovers fled, pursued by Medea's father. She resorted to a heartless strategy, murdering her brother and strewing pieces of him in the wake of Jason's ship. Medea's distraught father stopped to pick up the fragments of the corpse, and Medea and Jason escaped. Sh. implies that the passions that divided the houses of York and Lancaster during the War of the Roses inspired brutality equal to the worst found in Greek mythology.

Accost, Mistress Mary, *TN 1.3.49, 52,* Aguecheek's confused name for Maria. He doesn't understand Sir Toby's urgings to 'accost' the woman.

Acheron, the 'river of woe' in ancient Greek and Roman mythology that must be crossed to enter the underworld. Charon ferried the dead across for a small fee. It was one of the five rivers of Hades. Acheron was a god punished for giving sustenance to the Titans in the war against the Olympian gods. The term is used in the more general sense of 'the realm of the dead.'

Tit 4.3.45. MND 3.2.358, 'black as A.' *Mac 3.5.15,* 'pit of A.,' the witches have named their meeting place after the entrance to the infernal regions.

Achilles, son of Thetis the sea-nymph and Peleus, he is the figure around whom the plot of Homer's *Iliad* revolves. Educated by Chiron the centaur, he was granted invulnerability except for a small area on his heel. Upon the opening of the Trojan conflict he was disguised as a girl in Lycomedes' palace. There he impregnated Deidameia with Neoptolemus. Ulysses saw through his disguise by noting that one of the girls was interested in weaponry. As leader of the Myrmidons, Achilles was the most renowned of the Greek soldiers who gathered to fight the Trojan war. The *Iliad* is the story of a quarrel he had with his overlord, Agamemnon. The difficulty began in the tenth year of the war as a dispute over the division of some loot, particularly the slave girl Briseis. Agamemnon forced him to yield, and he, feeling dishonored, withdrew from combat. This decision set in motion a chain of events that cost the life of his closest friend, Patroclos. Patroclos' death forced him to weigh his desire to vindicate his honor against his obligation to avenge his slaughtered companion. When he concluded that the duty owed to friends outweighed the obligation to self, he made his peace with Agamemnon and returned to the battlefield to confront Hector, the Trojan who killed Patroclos. He killed and mutilated him. Near the war's end he was killed by an arrow shot by Paris into his vulnerable heel.

2H6 5.1.100: a comparison between a king's glance and A.'s spear because both have the ability 'to kill and cure.' The reference is to a legend narrated by Ovid (*Metamorphoses,* 12.12, 112; 13.171–172; *Amores,* 2.9.7). He says that when Telephus, Priam's son-in-law, tried to prevent the Greeks from landing at Troy, he was wounded by Achilles' spear. The Greeks soon regretted their victory, for an oracle revealed that they would not reach Troy if Telephus died. Achilles saved the day by treating Telephus' wound with rust from the weapon that had caused it.

Luc 1424. LLL 5.2.625.

Tro: In line with the kinship felt by the British towards their fictional ancestors, the Trojans, Sh. gives Achilles one of the most uncomplimentary depictions in literature. It is perhaps implied that he is the cause of all the chaos which informs the play when Ulysses points out that Achilles' mockery of his commanders encourages others to do likewise. His killing of Hector is anything but an heroic deed. The *Iliad* provides some of the raw material to portray him in his petulance and his desecration of Hector's body. However, Achilles drags Hector's corpse behind his chariot in the *Iliad,* not by his horse's tail as in Sh. This is a detail derived from William Caxton's *Recuyell of the Historyes of Troye* (c. 1474) or possibly John Lydgate's *Troy Book* (1412-20). *Tro 1.3.211,* 'A.'s horse,' a comparison to show impossibility. A.'s horses were, however, immortal children of Boreas and a Harpy: Balius and Xanthus.

Achitophel, *2H4 1.2.35,* Ahithophel the Gilonite, councilor to David, king of the Jews. Ahithophel betrayed David and joined a band of rebels led by David's son, Absalom (II Samuel 15:12).

Actæon, hunter in classical mythology who fell afoul of the goddess Diana (Artemis). Actæon accidentally blundered into Diana's presence as she and her nymphs bathed in a forest pool. The modest virgin goddess destroyed the hapless voyeur by changing him into a stag and setting his own dogs on him.

Tit 2.3.63. MWW 2.1.113, 'Sir A.,' the parallel to Falstaff's victimization is obvious. Both fall afoul of a woman and are 'torn' by 'hounds.' Here, however, Pistol compares Ford to A., about to be torn by his own hounds. *3.2.38,* 'secure and wilful A.,' Ford will show Page to be overly confident.

Actium, *Ant 3.7.51,* promontory thrusting into the Ionian Sea off the western coast of Greece (Acarnania) between the gulf of Corinth and the island of Corcyra. In 31 BC it was the site of a naval engagement that decided the struggle between Mark Antony and Octavius (Augustus) for control of the Roman empire. It is not certain what transpired at Actium. Only Octavius' description of the battle survives, and it is part of an elaborate propaganda campaign. Octavius was determined to convince Rome that Cleopatra, the wicked queen of Egypt, had made Antony her helpless puppet, and Actium, allegedly, confirmed Octavius' charge that Antony had been unmanned by love for Cleopatra. Octavius' historians claimed that Cleopatra insisted on accompanying Antony, but, as a woman, she was not able to endure the sight of battle. She panicked and fled at the start of the engagement, and Antony, her infatuated slave, abandoned his men to follow her. The woman meant more to him than honor and empire. Sh. dramatizes this romantic tale, but there is a more mundane explanation of what might have happened at Actium. The armies that met were both composed of soldiers who had been devoted to Julius Cæsar. Since the troops regarded both Antony and Octavius as Cæsar's heirs, it was difficult for them to work up much enthusiasm for fighting among themselves. Antony's men were also demoralized by losses they had suffered on a recent campaign in Parthia. When things came to a head, Antony may have discovered that his soldiers were reluctant to fight and that he and Cleopatra had no choice but to flee to Egypt.

Adallas, *Ant 3.6.71,* Adullas, Sadales or Sadala, a king of Thrace who Plutarch ('Antony,' 61.2) says sided with Mark Antony against Octavius at the battle of Actium. In 48 BC, a son of King Cotys of Thrace, named Sadales, joined the army that Pompey led against Julius Cæsar. After Cæsar defeated Pompey at Pharsalia, Sadales was pardoned. When Sadales died in 42 BC (long before the battle fought at Actium in 31 BC), he bequeathed Thrace to Rome. Antony's Adallas may have been one of Sadales' relatives and a pretender to his throne, or simply an anachronism.

Adam, 1) the first man. The name comes from the Hebrew for 'man,' which in turn derives from the word *adhamah,* 'earth,' or 'ruddy' in Hebrew, and the term is rooted in an early Akkadian word for 'creature.' Genesis says that Adam was formed out of clay in the 'image of God' and given dominion over the earth. In Genesis, there are three accounts of the Creation. In the first (Chapter 1-2.3, the 'Creation Hymn'), man and woman are created 'in God's image' on the sixth day and they are created together. Similarly in Chapter 5, God creates male and female together. In Chapters 2, 3, and 4 God creates man from the dust of the ground, places him in the garden of Eden and then decides it is not good for him to be alone. He puts Adam into a sleep, takes a rib from Adam, and makes woman. God had forbidden Adam to eat the fruit of the tree of the knowledge of good and evil, but his wife Eve succumbs to the serpent's temptation that the fruit will make Adam and Eve wise as gods. To prevent them from also eating from the tree of life and becoming immortal, God drives them from Eden to the punishment that their disobedience merited—the struggle to earn bread by the sweat of hard labor. Eve later bore Cain and Abel, and afterwards Seth as a replacement for the slain Abel. In Ch. 5, the Eden story is omitted, as well as Cain and Abel, and Adam is said to be a hundred and thirty years old when he begets Seth, living on another eight hundred years after Seth's birth and begetting unnamed sons and daughters. In the other religions of the world there are many parallels to this ancient Hebrew version of the creation of Adam.

2H6 4.2.133. LLL 4.2.40, 5.2.322. AYLI 2.1.5, 'the penalty of A.,' winter, the punishment for sin. *R2 3.4.74. 1H4 2.5.95, 3.3.166. Ado 2.1.236, 2.1.57,* 'A.'s sons,' ordinary men. *H5 1.1.30. Ham 5.1.31, 37.*

2) *Shr 4.1.122,* one of Petruccio's servants.

3) *Err 4.3.14-16,* name of a jailer or a comic nickname applied to a jailer who is compared to the first man because a jailer wears a leather jacket just as the first man wore animal skins (Genesis 3.21).

4) *AYLI,* old servant of the family of Sir Rowland de Bois. There is an 18th c. tradition that Sh. himself once acted the part. In Sh.'s source, Lodge's *Rosalynd,* and in *The Tale of Gamelyn* the corresponding character is named Adam Spencer.

5) celebrated archer Adam Bell. He was as famous in the north of England as was Robin Hood in the midlands and did many feats which have been borrowed from or mingled with the Robin Hood legend. Adam Bell was given an annuity by Henry IV, but lost it when he joined with rebellious Scots. His home was either Sherwood Forest or Inglewood in Cumberland. In ballad, he is a poacher who is pardoned by the king and made yeoman of the queen's chamber. *Rom 2.1.13:* F1 says 'Abraham' here, but many critics think it to be an error. Cupid (q.v.), as simultaneously the youngest and the oldest of the gods, might inspire the contradiction of 'Young Abraham,' but so might 'Young Adam,' if it referred to the biblical Adam. It has also been suggested that 'Abraham' is a corrupted form of 'auburn,' but then it becomes necessary to explain why Cupid should be regarded as having this color. An 'Abraham-man' meant a cheater or a roving thief and it has been argued that this describes Cupid. Since it is in the context of archery, however, the reference is most likely to Bell. This is much simpler than trying to justify Abraham in this context. *Ado 1.1.242,* most likely the archer, but possibly Adam in the sense of 'the first man' (to hit the target).

Adon, metrical shortening of Adonis. *Ven 769,* 1070 ('Adons,' pl.); *PP 6.5, 9.4.*

Adonis, beloved of Venus, son of Cinyras and Myrrha, or Cinyras and either Cenchreis or Metharme, or of Phoenix and Alphesiboea. His name has become synonymous with perfect male beauty and his story symbolizes nature's cycle of birth, death, and regeneration. Adonis bears some resemblance to the ancient Middle Eastern fertility deities, Tammuz and Osiris. Like them, he is associated with plants more than animals. According to Ovid's *Metamorphoses,* 10.503-555, 680-736, Myrrha was struck with a passion for her father Cinyras and went to his bed in the guise of another woman while her mother Cenchreis was celebrating the festival of Ceres. After intercourse, Cinyras recognized his daughter and chased her from his house. After nine months of wandering she came to the land of Sabæa, where her pleas to the gods were answered by her being transformed into the myrrh tree, whose bark weeps fragrant sap. Adonis, the child within her, however, was struggling to be born. The trunk split and he was saved by nymphs and grew rapidly. Venus leaned to kiss her son Cupid one day and the arrow in his quiver grazed her. When she saw handsome Adonis afterwards, she became lovesick over him, preferring his company to that of the gods. Normally languid she even accompanied him hunting, hiking up her clothes for running like the huntress Diana. One day Adonis speared a boar but failed to kill it. The boar chased him down, tearing into Adonis' groin with his teeth. When Venus found his body, she created the delicate flower, the anemone, from his blood.

Shr Ind. 2.49: Venus and Adonis as symbols of perfect beauty were frequent subjects in Renaissance painting. *1H6 1.8.6,* 'A.'s garden,' possibly alludes to a cultic practice of the ancient Athenians. During Adonis' annual festival they decorated their homes with plants whose growth had been forced. The artificially stimulated foliage, which withered as rapidly as it sprang up, represented the annual miracle of spring. The image has also been thought to be a confusion with the garden of King Alcinous in the *Odyssey,* 7; however, Edmund Spenser has a long description of Adonis' garden in *Færie Queene,* 3.6.29 or 42. *Ven. Son 53.5. PP 4.2, 6.4, 9.6.*

Adrian, 1) *Cor,* Hadrian, name Sh. gives the Volscian citizen who first learns of Coriolanus' banishment from Rome. Adrian does not appear in the source, Plutarch's 'Coriolanus,' but Sh. may have come across the name while browsing in Plutarch's works. An Adrian is mentioned in Plutarch's 'Lucullus' 17.1–2. Hadrian and Adrian are prominent names in Roman and papal history. They derive from a town in northern Italy 'Hadria' or 'Adria' which also gives its name to the Adriatic sea.

2) *Tmp,* a lord in the service of Alonzo. Although present in a few scenes, he speaks very little. This has been taken by some critics as evidence that the play was revised and in an earlier version his part was more substantial. This is highly conjectural. 'Spear carriers' as they are called in opera are often part of the scenery in drama.

Adriana, *Err,* wife of Antipholus of Ephesus, sister of Luciana. Jealous and independent, she nonetheless has a deep affection for her husband and thereby becomes the most interesting character in what might be Sh.'s earliest play. The various confusions between the twin Antipholuses lead her first to suspect her husband is cheating again, then that he is insane. Her intent pursuit of her husband, however, eventually leads to the sorting out of the characters. The shrewish aspect of her character derives directly from the wife of Menæchmus in the source, Plautus' *Menæchmi,* though he makes her more than simply a shrew.

Adriatic, *Shr 1.2.73,* the sea between Italy and modern Croatia and Albania, about 500 mi. long and 60-140 mi. wide. Its name derives from the ancient city of Atria, between the Adige and Po rivers, and originally applied only to the northernmost part of the sea near the city. Gradually Atria's harbor silted up and it lost its importance as a trading city by the Middle Ages. In Sh.'s time, the major port on the Adriatic was Venice.

Æacides, *Shr 3.1.50,* Ajax. The name refers to any descendant of Æacus, king of Ægina. His sons were Peleus, Telamon, and possibly Polycrates. His grandsons were Achilles, Ajax, and Teucer. Æacus himself was son of Jupiter and Ægina, husband of Endeis. He helped build the walls of Troy and repopulated the island of Ægina with the Myrmidons, ants turned into men by Jupiter (Ovid, *Metamorphoses,* 7). Æacus became one of the three judges of the dead in Hades.

Æacus, *2H6 1.4.59,* son of Jupiter and Ægina (daughter of a river god) and judge of the dead in the underworld. He was famous for the fairness of his decisions and was often called on to arbitrate disputes among the gods. Pyrrhus, the Illyrian king who received the oracle that Sh. cites as a model of ambiguity, listed Æacus among his ancestors.

Ædile, *Cor,* an officer of the Roman Republic who had police functions. Æditles supervised markets, ensured supplies of food and water, and maintained order at public gatherings.

Ægles, *MND 2.1.79,* Ægle, daughter of Panopeus and Neæra, a nymph for whom Theseus deserted Ariadne. Theseus' love life is recounted in Plutarch.

Æmilia, *Err,* see Emilia.

Æmilius, *Tit,* Roman nobleman and minor character whose primary function in *Tit* is to carry messages. Sh.'s choice of a name for him may have been entirely arbitrary. The Æmilii were a prominent patrician family in ancient Rome, and many of them are mentioned in the works of Plutarch from which Sh. drew much of his knowledge of Rome's history.

Æneas, the son of Anchises and Venus and a relative of Priam, king of Troy. In English medieval legend he was also the grandfather of Brut, from whom Britain was supposedly named. After the fall of Troy, Æneas wandered the Mediterranean searching for a new home. He spent some time in Carthage as the guest of the Phoenician queen, Dido, the city's founder. Dido fell in love with Æneas and offered to share her throne with him, but the gods had a different destiny in store for the last of the Trojans. Venus ordered Æneas to continue his wanderings, and Dido leapt into the flames of a funeral pyre as his ship left Carthage. Æneas ended his travels in Italy where he married the daughter of King Latinus. Their descendants founded Rome, and Rome fought the Punic wars that inflicted Dido's fate on all Carthaginians. His story was portrayed in great detail in Virgil's *Æneid,* a poem which was a tremendous influence upon Sh. and all of Renaissance culture.

2H6 5.3.62, 5.3.64: Sh. refers to a scene from the *Æneid* 2.804, that was popular with painters: Æneas flees the burning city of Troy carrying his aged father on his back. *Tit 3.2.27. JC 1.2.114.*

Tro: 'Lord A.,' the fictional kinship of the Britains to the Trojans (which appears as early as Geoffrey of Monmouth's *Historia Regum Britanniæ,* c. 1136) makes Sh. portray Æneas more sympathetically than any of the Greeks; however, Æneas is little more than a messenger for most of the play. He is a proper person on the whole, noble and mannered. *Ant 4.15.53. Cym 3.4.58,* 'false A.,' the betrayer of Dido. *Tmp 2.1.84. TNK 4.3.15.*

Æolus, king of the Æolian islands and master of the winds (*Odyssey,* 10). Æolus extended hospitality to Odysseus and his men as they tried to find their way home to Ithaca after the Trojan war. To permit them to continue their journey, Æolus gave Odysseus all the contrary winds tied up in a bag. Odysseus' men, thinking that their commander was hiding a treasure from them, opened the bag to see what it contained. The winds were loosed, and the ship was blown back to Æolus' kingdom. Æolus then washed his hands of the greedy Greeks and left their fate to the sea. *2H6 3.2.92.*

Æschines, *Per,* 'Escanes,' 'Eschines,' and 'Escenes' in original texts; a lord of Tyre. The name is probably borrowed from the Athenian orator (c. 390-c. 314 BC) who viciously attacked Demosthenes. Æschines favored Philip II of Macedon while Demosthenes favored Athenian independence. Æschines is mentioned several times in Plutarch's life of Demosthenes. Diogenes Lærtius in his *Lives and Opinions of Eminent Philosophers* (c. 3 AD) describes a student of Socrates' by the same name and states that eight notable men bore the name, including a sculptor, a rhetorician, and a pupil of Isocrates.

Æsculapius, god of physicians, son of Apollo and Coronis. Coronis was pregnant with the god's child when she betrayed him for a mortal. Apollo angrily slew her, but as she was placed upon the funeral pyre he rescued the unborn child and gave it to Chiron the centaur to raise. The child Æsculapius was so skilled that he surpassed his teachers in medical skills and for a large fee raised a dead man, Hippolytus (Theseus' son), to life. Jupiter became afraid that men might cheat death altogether so he struck down doctor and patient with thunderbolts. Æsculapius became a god. Ovid tells in *Metamorphoses* 15 how Æsculapius came to Rome in a time of great sickness by assuming the form of a giant serpent. Cicero also recounts the myth of Æsculapius in *Natura Deorum,* and Spenser mentions him in *The Færie Queene,* 1. The staff of Æsculapius—snakes twisting around a wooden staff—is still a symbol of the science of medicine. *MWW 2.3.26. Per 12.108.*

Æson, *MV 5.1.14,* mythological son of Cretheus and Tyro, and the father of Jason. Æson ruled a kingdom in Thessaly, but turned his crown over to his half-brother Pelias until Jason should reach majority. Upon Jason's return from the quest for the Golden Fleece, Æson was so decrepit he was unable to attend the victory feast. Jason then begged his wife Medea to restore Æson's vitality. She mixed a complicated potion of herbs and took forty years off his age. The story is told in Ovid's *Metamorphoses,* 7.

Æsop, *3H6 5.5.25,* (620–560 BC), Greek freedman, reputed author of fables in which animal characters act out morally edifying lessons.

Ætna, see Etna.

Afric, 1) (n.) *Cor 1.9.3, Cym 1.1.168, Tmp 2.1.74,* see Africa.
2) (adj.) African, *Tro 1.3.363.*

Africa, *2H4 5.3.101,* continent south of Europe. The Romans were first to call the continent Africa, but did not include Egypt or Ethiopia, nor sub-Saharan Africa, which they knew little about. The Greeks called the continent Libya, so the word is thought to have been borrowed by the Romans from the natives east of Carthage in some way. Among suggestions are the Berber tribe of the Aourigha (pronounced Afarika) who comprised much of the population of Carthage; a word meaning 'country of fruit'; and a Phoenician word meaning 'separate,'as the Carthaginians were separated from their homeland. After the Roman provinces dissolved, the name came to apply to the entire continent. Although the exploration of the perimeter of the African continent had begun in Sh.'s day, he and his audience viewed Africa as the ancient Greeks and Romans had—i.e., as a Mediterranean country that supplied Europe with gold and exotic substances from fabulous, unknown lands.

African, (n.) *Tmp 2.1.131,* a native of Africa.

Agamemnon, king of Argos and Mycenæ and general of the Greeks who fought the Trojan war, son of Atreus and Aërope. He led the Greeks to Troy to avenge Paris' abduction of Helen, his brother Menelaus' wife. Cursed by the bloody history of his family, his life consisted of one horror after another. To obtain his wife Clytemnestra, he murdered her husband and her newborn child. When the fleet is detained at Aulis, he sacrificed his daughter Iphigenia in order to receive a favorable wind. Upon the destruction of Troy, he took Cassandra as his mistress and returned to be butchered by Clytemnestra as he bathed.

3H6 2.2.148: Sh. sees a parallel between the story of Agamemnon and Helen and the history of Henry VI and his queen, Margaret. In both cases troublesome women caused men to go to war. *2H4 2.4.221. H5 3.6.7.*

Tro: By the Middle Ages, the Greeks were considered the bad side of the Trojan War and Hector had come to symbolize the most chivalrous of heroes. This was particularly so in England, where the myth that Britain was founded by Brutus, grandson of Æneas, was current. Despite this, the Greek leader is not the most reprehensible of his group. In fact his characterization is a bit pale. His main trait seems to be his propensity for augustan language. Perhaps the ambiguity is the result of Sh.'s feeling that Agamemnon, as the general, is due more obeisance than he is getting from his troops. Ulysses makes remarks to the effect that the whole enterprise is endangered by willfulness.

Agenor, son of Neptune and Libya, king of Phoenicia, father of Cadmus, Europa, and others. *Shr 1.1.166,* 'daughter of A.,' Europa. After she was kidnapped, Agenor sent his sons to find her, thus in some myths creating the traditional antipathies between Asia and Europe, which was named after the kidnapped girl. In Ovid's *Metamorphoses* 2, Europa is referred to only as 'daughter of Agenor.'

Agincourt, *H5 pro. 14, 4.0.52, 4.7.87, 88,* French village in the county of Artois near Boulogne and Calais. It was the scene of one of the most famous battles in medieval history. In August, 1415, Henry V attacked the French port at Harfleur and rekindled the Hundred Years' War. Since no French army could be organized in time to come to Harfleur's aid, the city quickly surrendered. But Henry was unable to follow up his victory and press farther into France. Disease ravaged his troops, and he was compelled to order them north to Calais, an English held port that provided a secure base from which to ship soldiers across the Channel. A French army materialized in time to block Henry's retreat, and Henry dodged inland to outflank his enemies. The French followed and forced Henry to stand his ground at Agincourt. Although the English were greatly outnumbered, their skillful use of archery devastated the French on 25 October 1415 and carried the day. The battle set in motion a chain of events that culminated in the recognition of Henry V as heir to the throne of France.

Agrippa, *Ant,* Marcus Vipsanius A., (63–12 BC), Roman general on whom Octavius (Augustus) relied for the military expertise needed to conquer and rule the Roman empire. He was a man of obscure origins who, in his youth, became one of Octavius' close friends. He served Octavius loyally all his life and made a major contribution to Octavius' remarkably successful career. When Julius Cæsar was assassinated, Agrippa followed Octavius to Rome and helped Octavius raise the army Octavius needed to lay claim to his adoptive father's legacy. Octavius was not a skillful general, and he depended on him to fight the battles that overwhelmed his rival, Mark Antony. After Antony's defeat, Agrippa became Octavius' chief aide in the task of running the Roman empire. He married Octavius' daughter, Julia, and Octavius recognized Agrippa's sons as his heirs. Octavius survived him by almost twenty-five years, and Agrippa's sons did not live to claim their inheritance. Agrippa had descendants in the female line, however, who ascended Octavius' throne, the emperors Caligula and Nero.

Agrippa, Menenius, *Cor,* see Menenius Agrippa.

Aguecheek, Sir Andrew, *TN,* foolish gentleman who attempts to court Olivia, friend of Sir Toby Belch. Aguecheek is an example of the 'gulled gentleman' whom we also see in the character of Roderigo in *Oth* and may have been played by the same actor. He is pompous and stupid, confusing words. He is cowardly, frivolous, and easily misled. Sir Toby has been milking him for money in his courtship and his being led into a duel with Viola results in the thrashing he deserves. A good actor will draw on the poignancy of his stupidity for a small measure of sympathy; however, he primarily demonstrates the corruption and weakness of Sir Toby's circle, regardless of their amusing qualities. He is described as a thin man, which by pairing him with Sir Toby produces a Laurel and Hardy type of comedy couple long standard in the theater. The 'ague' is a fever, such as malaria, which causes much shivering and sweating. He would therefore be a quaking, nervous figure, high-strung and uncertain. The ague would make one thin, also (see *JC 2.2.113*). Initially the word referred to the high fever which preceded the shakes, which would mean 'hot-cheek,' and which applies to Aguecheek's quarrelsome enthusiasm, but by Sh.'s time 'ague' generally implied the quaking of the disease.

Agueface, Sir Andrew, *TN 1.3.41,* Sir Toby's mocking name for Sir Andrew Aguecheek, no more ridiculous than his real name. Possibly Sh. considered this as the name and failed to change it in the papers from which F1 was set.

Ajax, F1 'Aias,' 'Aiax,' Ajax the Greater, Telamonius, hero of the Trojan War famed for his strength, size, and courage, but hindered by his slowness of mind. Son of Telamon and either Periboea or Eriboea, he was named after an eagle which appeared as an omen to his father.

Ajax was a suitor of Helen and as a consequence took twelve ships from Salamis against Troy. He fought Hector in an impressive single combat concluding in a draw, and assumed upon Achilles' death that the armor would be awarded to him as a symbol of his stature as the second mightiest warrior of the Greeks. Achilles' armor was, however, awarded to Odysseus because wisdom is greater than valor. Blinded by Athena with a mad rage Ajax slaughtered dozens of sheep and cattle thinking he was avenging himself on Odysseus and his men. When the madness lifted, he saw what he had done and threw himself on his sword. From his blood a hyacinth sprang and in its petals one can see the letters 'AI' which are both his name (Greek, Aias) and the Greek cry of sorrow. The story appears in many ancient sources such as Ovid's *Metamorphoses,* 13; Homer's *Odyssey,* 11.541; and Sophocles' *Ajax.* Coincidentally, his name, as pronounced in Renaissance England sounded like 'a jakes,' which was slang for a privy, and this made it difficult to use the character for anything other than a comic purpose. Sir John Harington's *Metamorphosis of Ajax* (1596) used the term 'jax' for a toilet.

Shr 3.1.51. 2H6 5.1.26. Tit 1.1.376. Luc 1394, 1398. LLL 4.3.6, 'mad as A.' *5.2.572:* In the Middle Ages Alexander the Great was given a coat of arms which had a lion sitting on a throne holding a battle axe. Costard turns the throne into a 'close-stool' (enclosed chamberpot) or a 'jakes' in order to make it the coat of Ajax.

Tro, 'Lord A.': in line with the general attitude to the Greeks and to Ajax in particular, Sh. depicts him as bestial and stupid. He may be associated to a degree with the braggart soldier, a stock comic part after which Sh. patterned his Falstaff, although his Ajax is a substantial, if brutish, warrior. He is also described as being melancholy without reason, which may be an odd way of playing on the privy humor, as foul smells were said to induce melancholy. It has been said that Sh. creates his character by conflating Ajax the Greater and Ajax the Lesser (of Locris, son of Oïleus). The two often battled in concert in Homer, but the latter was famed in mythology for his boastfulness, a thing which resulted in his being struck dead by Poseidon. John Lydgate's *Troy Book* (1412-20) mentioned the boastful Oïleus, but Telamonides is also a braggart in claiming Achilles' armor, in Ovid's *Metamorphoses,* 13.1-122, while Oïleus (12.622) doesn't dare to claim it.

Lr 2.2.122 (Q 7.120): Kent calls Cornwall an Ajax (cowardly braggart, with the pun on 'privy' to boot), which Cornwall then confirms by raging. *Ant 4.15.38,* 'seven-fold shield of A.,' shield described in Homer's *Iliad,* 7.251-258. A full-body shield, it consisted of seven layers of oxhide covered with bronze and was made by Tychius of Hyle. *Cym 4.2.253.*

Alarbus, *Tit,* eldest son of Tamora, queen of the Goths. Titus Andronicus, a Roman general, sacrifices Alarbus at the funeral of one of his sons who was a casualty of a war with the Goths. Sh.'s source for the plot of *Tit* is uncertain. An 18th c. chapbook preserves a later version of a tale that might have been known to Sh., but it does not mention Alarbus or the sacrifice of the queen's son. Its plot revolves around Tamora's determination to avenge the death of her husband. The chapbook gives Tamora a son named Alaricus, but he is her co-conspirator, not her motivation. (In *Tit* the sons who assist the queen in taking revenge on Titus Andronicus are named Demetrius and Chiron.) No Alarbus appears in the ancient histories Sh. consulted, but Sh. probably knew the famous Gothic king Alaric who sacked Rome in 410 AD. Sh. may have distorted the spelling of 'Alaric' or invented a name that sounded similarly Gothic.

Alban, St., *2H6 2.1.66, 110, 136,* first native of Britain to suffer martyrdom and achieve canonization. He probably died during the persecution of Christians decreed by the Roman emperor Diocletian (286–303). He was venerated in Christian churches on the continent as early as 429, and references to him appear in the works of the early English authors Gildas and Bede. Alban was a resident of Verulamium, a town north of London that has been renamed in his honor. His witness to the Christian faith began while he was still a pagan. When the persecution of Christians commenced in Verulamium, he hid a priest in his home. The Roman authorities tracked the man to Alban's doorstep, and Alban helped his guest to escape by dressing in the priest's clothes and leading his pursuers on a wild goose chase. When he was caught, he was accused of being a Christian and, much to his surprise, he discovered that he had acquired faith. He doomed himself at his trial by refusing to affirm the divinity of the Roman emperor. At his passion he performed two miracles. He converted one of his executioners and caused the eyes to fall out of the other.

Albany, *Lr,* a dukedom of the northern part of the island of Britain. According to Holinshed, it was originally allotted to Albanacte and was called Abanactus or Albania (as it is called by Geoffrey of Monmouth). Later a smaller area retained the name and the rest of it was called Scotland from the Scots immigrants from Ireland. The hilly country of west Perthshire is still called Albainn. According to Bullough, Albany is Scotland east of Stratspey and north of a line between Edinburgh and Fort William. Other sources say it is Scotland north of the Firths of Forth and Clyde. Holinshed says it was originally all of Scotland north of the Humber to Caithness. The Celts may have called all of Britain Albany. The name is believed to derive from the Celtic *alp,* 'rock' or 'cliff.' It may have been politically astute for Sh. as a subject of King James to show that in ancient times the entire island had been united under King Lear and then broken up by evil manipulations.

Albany, Duke of, *Lr,* husband of Goneril. He is ignorant of the depths of his wife's evil until he learns of Gloucester's blinding by Cornwall and reacts more strongly than one would have expected from his weak responses early in the play. This may be regarded as flawed characterization, but it is not of major consequence as his part is secondary. At play's end he asks Edgar and Kent to rule the shattered kingdom. In Geoffrey of Monmouth's version of the story, the Duke of Albania is named Maglaunus (Maglanus in Holinshed and Maglan in Spenser's *Færie Queen,* 2.10). The title of duke of Albany went through several creations and extinctions. The first was created by King Robert III in 1398. The third was Henry Stuart (Lord Darnley) and was granted by Mary, Queen of Scots in 1565. From him it passed to King James VI (later I of England). He then passed the title to his son Charles on his birth in 1600. This may explain why Albany undergoes a change of heart near the end of the play.

Albion, name ancient Greek geographers gave to Britain. It may mean 'white land' in Greek and derive from the chalk cliffs at Dover. Since they overlooked the narrowest part of the English channel, it was probably the spot on the coast of Britain toward which most sailors aimed. The name may also derive from the Celtic *alp,* which means 'cliff' or 'rock.' One myth says that a giant, Albion, son of Neptune and Amphitrite, discovered and ruled Britain, introducing astrology and shipbuilding. Another has it being the home of Albia, daughter of the King of Syria and eldest of forty-nine sisters. Michael Drayton's *Poly-Obion* (1613) has England's first martyr who came from Rome named Albion, though this is probably just a confusion with St. Alban. *2H6 1.3.48, 3.2.113. 3H6 3.3.7, 3.3.49. H5 3.5.14. Lr 3.2.85.*

Alcibiades, major political and military figure in the Peloponnesian War. Born about 450 BC to Clinias and Deinomache, Alcibiades was the kinsman of Pericles and became his ward after his father died in 447. Wealthy, handsome, athletic, intelligent, courageous, of aristocratic ancestry, and utterly lacking principles, he married well and squandered his money by ostentatious public displays, such as at the Olympic Games in 420. However, he developed a political following among the common people and exploited the Athenian discontent with the peace negotiated with Sparta by Nicias in 421 BC. He got himself appointed a commander of an army in 415 and lost a battle at Mantinea in 418, but his impassioned speeches led to a disastrous expedition against the Spartan colony of Syracuse. Nicias, curiously, was commissioned to command the expedition and just before the fleet sailed, Alcibiades was indicted for sacrilege done to the statues of the god Hermes. Called home for trial, he went to Sparta and advised his former enemies on defending against the Sicilian venture. He was sentenced in absentia to death and his properties were seized.

In August 413 the Syracusans captured the Athenians and imprisoned them in stone quarries to die of exposure and starvation. Alcibiades also helped the Spartans revive the war on the mainland. They established a base of operations on the north coast of Attica to harry the Athenians and received Persian aid in building a fleet to challenge the Athenians' sea monopoly. In 414, he travelled with the Spartans to Chios and incited an Ionian rebellion against the Athenians. Athens was in desperate trouble, but ironically the traitor Alcibiades came to their aid. He was forced to flee Sparta in 413 after an embarrassing affair with the Spartan queen and a plot on his life. He went to Tissaphernes, a Persian governor, and used his Persian contacts to get his exile revoked. He suggested that the Athenian Empire might get the assistance of the Persians if the government were stabilized by becoming more oligarchic.

After an attempted coup and some civil disorder, Alcibiades got himself elected admiral of a fleet. He commanded it well, winning a major victory in 410 and recapturing Byzantium in 408. In 407 he returned to Athens and was given a fleet of 100 ships for an expedition in Asia. Some of his ambitious associates turned a foraging expedition into a disaster by directly engaging the Spartans at Notium in 406. The heavy losses resulted in Alcibiades' being sent back into exile, this time in Phrygia, where, at the request of the Athenian government and the instigation of Lysander, the Spartan commander, he was assassinated in 404. Alcibiades died in a hail of arrows as he fled from his burning house. Plutarch wrote his biography and compared him to Coriolanus. Alcibiades also appears in Plato as a friend of Socrates.'

Tim: Timon's last friend, he avenges the ingratitude of the Athenians. After attempting to defend a veteran who has killed a man while drunk, Alcibiades is exiled by the Senate and takes arms against Athens. Timon finances Alcibiades' attack on the city, which succeeds. Although there is little historical accuracy in these events, the character of Alcibiades does have several traits derived from the Plutarchan portrayal.

Al'ce Madam, *Shr Ind. 2. 107:* Sly is asking what his wife is called. The humor is that he imagines a lady has this common name, as if a duchess were named 'Boopsy.'

Alcides, 'son of Alcæus,' Hercules, deriving from his grandfather Alcæus son of Perseus and Andromeda. Alcæus was also Hercules' name at birth, before the oracle at Delphi revealed his destiny and granted him a new appellation.

Shr 1.2.258, 'A.'s twelve,' the labors of Hercules. *Tit 4.2.94. 1H6 4.7.60. Jn 2.1.144. MV 2.1.35. 3.2.55,* a reference to Ovid's *Metamorphoses,* 11. When Hercules rescued the virgin Hesione from the sea monster sent by Apollo to punish Troy, he did it for the horses he was promised and not for love. *Ant 4.13.44. TNK 5.3.119.*

Alecto, *2H4 5.5.37,* one of the three Furies. She is a demonic creature crowned with venomous serpents: Virgil, *Æneid,* 7.341–352.

Alençon, duchy 100 mi. west of Paris on the border between Normandy and Maine. It was purchased in 1220 by King Philip Augustus and added to France's royal demesne. Louis IX gave it to his fifth son, Peter as an appanage, a property reserved for the support of a member of the royal family. At Peter's death in 1284 it passed to the second son of Charles I, count of Valois, the founder of the last house of Alençon. The county was elevated to a duchy in 1414. Henry V occupied it in November 1417, when he advanced on Paris. See Alençon, Duchess of, *H8*; Duke of, *H5*; *2H6*; *LLL.*

Alençon, Duchess of, *H8 3.2.86,* Margaret of Navarre (Marguerite d'Angoulême, 1492-1549) sister to Francis I (1494–1547) and grandmother to Henry IV of France (see Ferdinand, king of Navarre). Her first husband was Charles, duke of Alençon (d. 1525). Holinshed (3.906) says that it was rumored that Henry VIII wanted to divorce Katherine of Aragon to marry her, but she refused him. In 1527 she married Henry d'Albret, king of Navarre. She was a literary patron and the accomplished author of *The Heptameron* (1558), inspired by Boccaccio's *Decameron*.

Alençon, Duke of, 1) John II (1404–1476), second duke of Alençon and Joan of Arc's advocate. The dukes of Alençon belonged to the Armagnac or Orléanist party that opposed the duke of Burgundy's efforts to make himself regent for the mad king of France, Charles VI. John's father was a casualty of the battle at Agincourt (1415) where the Armagnacs tried in vain to destroy the army that Henry V had brought to France. John married into the family of Charles of Orléans, a leader of the Armagnac faction. He joined the armies defending the Dauphin, when Henry V's occupation of Paris forced the Dauphin to seek refuge in Orléans. John was taken prisoner at the battle of Verneuil (17 August 1424) by Sir John Fastolf, and his ransom paid for the construction of Fastolf's Caister Castle in Norfolk. Alençon was the first Frenchman of high rank to endorse Joan of Arc, and he arranged her initial interview with the Dauphin at Chinon. He was Joan's patron and advocate at the Dauphin's court, and he helped her organize the expedition that ended the English siege of Orléans.

Once the English retreated from France and the Dauphin was crowned Charles VII, Alençon grew disillusioned with the monarch he had helped to the throne. He joined a plot (the *Praguerie*) to purge the court of the king's favorites. Its failure led to his conviction in 1455 on a charge of treason. The duchy of Alençon was confiscated by the crown, but the duke's sentence of death was commuted to a term of imprisonment in the dungeons of Loche. A reference to a 'duke of Alençon' might have reminded Sh.'s audience of events more recent than those of the Hundred Years' War. In 1566 the duchy of Alençon was assigned to one of the sons of Catherine de Médicis, queen of France. The boy was a seriously considered, if unpopular, suitor for Elizabeth I's hand. *1H6. 2H6 1.1.7.*

2) *LLL 2.1.61, 195:* in the first passage, Catherine speaks neutrally about the duke, but in the second, Boyet indicates she is his heir, and therefore probably his daughter. This may be the usual Shakespearean imprecision, or in the first instance Catherine is taking a highly formal tone. This Alençon does not seem to be based upon a real person.

3) *H5 3.5.42, 4.7.152, 154, 4.8.19, 28, 38, 96,* Jean, (d. 1415), first count of Alençon to be elevated to the rank of duke. He died at the battle of Agincourt after having slain the duke of York, Edward of Norwich (Aumerle). Sh. found his name on Holinshed's list of casualties (3.555).

Aleppo, city in northern Syria on the Koeik river 71 mi. east of the Meditteranean. It dates back to about 2000 BC and was known in ancient times as Berea or Beroea. It lay on the main caravan route to Baghdad, about halfway between the sea and the Euphrates. It was the center of a Hittite kingdom, prospered under Byzantine rule and at various times was taken or besieged by the Arabs, Seljuk Turks, Mongols, Crusaders, and Saladin. In Sh.'s time it was part of the Ottoman empire (conquered 1517) and would remain in Turkish hands until 1920, except for a brief period under Egyptian rule. After the Turkish conquest, the British were quite involved in trade through the city. An outpost of the British Levant Company was established there during the Jacobean period. The city declined because of the new trade routes to India and internal dissension. Sh. seems to have borrowed the episode he mentions here from Hakluyt's *Voyages,* which has an account of a ship called the Tiger in 1583 sailing to Tripoli, where the crew continued to Aleppo by caravan; or Sh. may have known of the voyage firsthand from gossip or the participants themselves. Ben Jonson's *Every Man in his*

Humour 2.4 (1598), in which Sh. acted, also mentions the city. *Mac 1.3.6. Oth 5.2.361.*

Alexander, 1) Pl.: *H5 3.1.19,* warriors equal to Alexander the Great (q.v.)

2) *Tro 1.2,* Cressida's servant. He satirically describes the brutish Ajax. Alexander (Alexandros) was a name for Paris in mythology, so it may have been convenient to borrow.

3) *Ant 3.6.15,* (b. 40 BC), Antony's son by Cleopatra. Antony's public acknowledgement of the boy and his twin sister, Cleopatra, caused adverse comment in Rome, but it was part of Antony's strategy for unseating his fellow triumvir, Octavius. Antony hoped to overwhelm Octavius by winning a stunning victory over Rome's largest neighbor, Parthia. Antony's Parthian campaign depended on the resources of Egypt, and his personal tie with Cleopatra was promoted to give Egypt a stake in his success. Antony promised Armenia, Media, and Parthia to Alexander and Syria and Cilicia to Ptolemy-Cæsarion, a son Cleopatra had by Julius Cæsar. The failure of the Parthian campaign doomed Antony and gave Octavius the edge he needed to destroy both Antony and Cleopatra. Octavius killed Ptolemy-Cæsarion, but he sent the children Cleopatra had borne Antony to Rome to be raised by Antony's wife, Octavius' sister Octavia.

Alexander the Great, (356–323 B.C), king of the northern Greek state of Macedon and conqueror of the Persian Empire. Alexander's father, Philip, conceived the idea of attacking the Persians and built the army that Alexander used against them with stunning success. Philip believed that a war with Persia would distract the Greeks from fratricidal quarrels that threatened their survival and force them to work together. The Greeks had entered a Golden Age of achievement a century before Philip's birth when they repulsed an invasion from Persia. But, as events unfolded, it became clear that Greeks were better at self-defense than self-government. Athenian and Spartan military leagues were organized to protect the Ægean from the Persians. These organizations polarized the Greek world and spawned a civil war (the Peloponnesian War). Fratricidal conflict destroyed the great city-states that had policed Greece and set each town free to indulge its grudges against its neighbors. Philip hoped to correct this situation and bring peace to Greece by persuading the Greeks to cooperate against their common enemy, Persia. Philip was assassinated on the eve of the war he planned, and it fell to his son, Alexander, to realize his dream.

In 334 Alexander marched into Asia Minor and never saw Macedon again. During the remaining eleven years of his life he led the Greeks on an adventure that more than fulfilled their wildest expectations. Alexander triumphed over incredible odds to conquer Egypt, Persia and all their possessions. Then he moved beyond Persia's frontiers, and led his armies through the Himalayas, down the Indus Valley to the Indian Ocean, and back across the Gedrosian desert to Babylon. Having conquered 'the world' by the age of 34, he died of a fever shortly after his return to Babylon.

LLL 5.2.531, 558-578: in the pageant of the Nine Worthies (q.v.), Nathaniel assumes the role of Alexander, although earlier Holofernes wanted him to be Joshua. *H5 4.7.12/13,* Fluellen's 'A. the Pig' is a comic pun created by Fluellen's Welsh pronunciation of 'A. the Big.' *H5 4.7.19, 21, 30, 32, 43. Cor 5.4.22. WT 5.1.47,* 'Great A.' did not succeed his throne by heredity, but by merit, Leontes argues. An echo of the line occurs in Quintus Rufus Curtius as translated by John Brende in 1602. Though there is a similar passage in Arrian's *Anabasis Alexandri,* it was available only in French and Latin at the time of *WT.*

Alexandria, *Ant 1.4.3, 2.2.76, 3.6.2, 3.13.171, 4.9.30,* capital of Egypt during the Hellenistic era and one of the ancient world's largest cities. Alexander the Great founded it to celebrate his conquest of Egypt in 332 BC. After Alexander's death in 323 his friend Ptolemy seized Egypt and buried Alexander's body in the city named for him. Ptolemy founded a dynasty of rulers, the last of whom was the famous Cleopatra. In addition to its commercial and political importance, the city boasted the largest library in the ancient world. A fire that ravaged its collections in 48 BC did not diminish the city's reputation as an intellectual center. The schools of Alexandria flourished into the early Middle Ages.

Alexas, *Ant,* 'the Laodicean,' one of Cleopatra's attendants. Sh.'s source for the character was Plutarch's 'Antony' 72.2–3. Plutarch says that Antony trusted Alexas more than any other Greek and that he was instrumental in reviving Antony's interest in Cleopatra after Antony's wedding to Octavius' sister, Octavia. When Antony's fortunes began to decline, he sent Alexas to the court of Herod the Great to persuade Herod to stand by him in his struggle with Octavius. Alexas, who sensed that Antony's days were numbered, betrayed him in the hope of toadying favor with Octavius. The sacrifice of his honor earned him nothing, for Octavius chose the high road. He refused to deal with a traitor and ordered his execution.

Alfonso, *TGV 1.3.39,* a gentleman of Verona. Don Alfonso is going with a group of men to offer their services to the Emperor (Duke of Milan). This presumably Italian gentleman's being titled 'Don' is a heritage of the occupation of the kingdom of Naples by the Spanish. The use of 'Don' is still current in southern Italy. It is used in the Spanish source of the story, Jorge de Montemayor's *Diana Enamorada* (1559). The Don could be a Spaniard resident in Italy, also, although Antonio is also referred to as 'Don Antonio' by the Duke (*2.4.52*).

Algiers, *Tmp 1.2.263, 266,* 'Argier' in F1, the place from which Sycorax the witch is exiled, located on the Mediterranean coast of Africa on the Bay of Algiers. Algiers was established by the Phoenicians about 1200 BC and was taken after the Punic Wars by Rome in 146 BC. In the 5th c. it was captured by the Vandals, who were replaced by the Byzantines in the 6th c. and then the Arabs in 650. It virtually disappeared after the collapse of the Roman empire, but was reestablished by Berbers in 950. Ownership of the city changed hands many times after that. The Spanish in 1510 seized the island in the harbor, but in 1518 Algiers joined the Ottomans in expelling the Spaniards and the city fell under Turkish rule for three centuries as capital of the Barbary Coast. The famous fortress called the Casbah was built there in the 16th c. by the Turks. The name Algiers comes from the Arabic for 'islands.' Before 1525, four islands lay off the coast, but afterwards they were connected to the mainland.

Alice, the name of a common woman in Sh.'s day. 1) *Shr,* see Al'ce Madam.

2) *MWW,* see Ford, Alice.

3) *H5,* lady attendant on Catherine of Valois, the French princess who wed Henry V. Sh. invents amusing lessons in the English language for her to give to Catherine replete with French double entendres.

Aliena, *AYLI,* false name used by Celia as shepherdess, likely adapted from the name of Celia's counterpart Alinda in Lodge's *Rosalynde,* the source of *AYLI.*

Alisander, *LLL 5.2.560, 565, etc.,* mispronunciation of Alexander by Nathaniel and Costard, picked up for mockery by Boyet and Biron.

All Hallow Eve, *MM 2.1.121,* F1 'Allhallond Eve,' Halloween, the night before All Saint's Day. In Celtic days it was the last night of the calendar year, when witches roamed. Like many pagan customs, this was adopted by the Christians.

Allhallowmas, *MWW 1.1.187,* All Saint's Day, 1 November. This day to honor all of the martyrs was originally held on 1 May upon Pope Boniface IV's dedication of the Pantheon (q.v.) to a church in 610. In 834 it was changed to the first day of the Celtic calendar year. OE *halig,* 'holy man,' is the word source.

Allhallown summer, *1H4 1.2.156,* the equivalent of 'Indian summer,' a period of mild weather that often occurs in late autumn near All Saints Day.

All-Souls' day, *R3 5.1.10, 12, 18,* religious festival commemorating the dead. In the current ecclesiastical calendar it falls on 2 November. The custom of devoting a special day to prayers for the souls of the dead was instituted by the church in the 11th c. The Christian ceremony had roots in an ancient pagan belief that at a certain time of the year the dead might rise to walk abroad in the land of the living. At such seasons it was necessary to placate the spirits of the deceased with prayers and offerings of food and drink. The pagan festival survives as the secular holiday Halloween.

Almain, *Oth 2.3.76,* a German, from the Latin *Allemania,* the country of the Allemanni tribe. French for 'Germany' is *Allemagne.*

Alonso, *Tmp,* king of Naples, brother of Sebastian. There is an Alphonso or Alonzo of Naples in Dent's translation of the *History of Philip de Comines* (1526), along with parallels of other characters' names. An Alonso also appears in Robert Eden's *History of Travaile* (1577), a likely source of some material for the play.

Alps, mountains that cross Switzerland and southern Germany and divide Italy from northern Europe. They run from France to Albania for nearly 700 mi. The highest peak is Mont Blanc at 15,781 ft. They have always served as an obstacle to the invasion of the peninsula, which is why Hannibal's crossing the Alps was viewed with such alarm by the Romans and later as one of the major military feats of ancient history. *Jn 1.1.202. R2 1.1.64:* a remote and uninhabitable place. *H5 3.5.52. Ant 1.4.66.*

Althæa, *2H6 1.1.234,* mother of the Argonaut Meleager who led the Calydonians against the Curetes. When Meleager killed his uncle, Althæa's brother, in battle, he created a moral dilemma for his mother. Althæa's duty as a sister was to avenge the death of her brother, but in this instance vengeance required her to assassinate her son. Since the defense of one family tie required the violation of another, Althæa was forced to choose the lesser of two evils. Althæa concluded that a sister's bonds were stronger than a mother's, and she murdered her son. She used an unusual weapon. When Meleager was born, the Fates announced that his life would last only as long as a stick that was blazing on the hearth in his mother's room. Althæa saved her infant by snatching the brand from the fire. She kept the talisman safe from destruction until she concluded that family honor required Meleager's death. She then burned the object that preserved her son's life. Sh. read the story in Ovid's *Metamorphoses,* 7.445–545.

Althea, *2H4 2.2.80, 2.2.82,* see Althæa. Sh. confuses myths about visions had by two different expectant mothers. In *2H4* he has a page compare Prince Harry to the 'firebrand' to which Althea dreamed she gave birth. Hecuba, the mother of Paris (the Trojan who provoked his city's tragic war with the Greeks), dreamed that she would give birth to a 'firebrand' (Ovid, *Heroides,* 16.45–46). The life of Althea's son was linked to the survival of a magical firebrand whose significance the gods revealed to her at his birth.

Alton, *1H6 4.7.65,* Alverton castle, Staffordshire.

Alton, Lord Verdun of, *1H6 4.7.65,* title among the many that Sh. lists as belonging to the English hero of the Hundred Years' War, John Talbot. Verdun (Verdon) was the name of the Norman family William the Conqueror established at Farnham Royal in Buckinghamshire and Brandon Castle in Warwickshire. Their principle residence was Alton Castle (Alverton) in Staffordshire. The direct male line of the family ended in 1316 with the death of Theobald de Verdon.

Amaimon, *MWW 2.2.286,* high-ranking demon, one of Satan's emissaries. He ruled the eastern part of hell, according to medieval demonology.

Asmodeus (see Asnath) was his lieutenant. Sh. borrowed the name from Reginald Scot's *Discoverie of Witchcraft* (1584), which spells it in various ways, as he did the other demon names here.

Amamon, *1H4 2.5.339,* see Amaimon.

Amazon, tribe of warrior women in Greek mythology. The term may derive from a Greek word meaning 'breast-less.' Some legends claimed that Amazons cut off their right breasts to make it easier for them to use bows and other weapons. Theseus, king of Athens, was believed to have defeated the Amazons and married their queen, and a battle between Greeks and Amazons was a popular motif for the decoration of Greek temples.

3H6 1.4.115, 4.1.104. 1H6 1.3.83. MND 2.1.70, 'bouncing A.,' Hippolyta. *Jn 5.2.155. Tim.*

Amazonian, *TNK 1.1.78,* Hippolyta. The passage about her slaying the boar may be a confusion with Atalanta who in Chaucer's *Knyghtes Tale* (A 2070) 'hunted the wild boar.' It is also Atalanta who hunts the Calydonian boar in Ovid's *Metamorphoses,* 8.

America, *Err 3.2.136,* location on the 'globe' that is Nell, the continents and islands of the western hemisphere. Although there may have been earlier European contact with the Americas, particularly by the Norse, the memory of these voyages seems to have been lost until Columbus' voyage in 1492. America was thus in Sh.'s time literally a New World and the stories which circulated about it and its inhabitants were often as reasonable as drive-in movies about Martians. Remote, filled with animals in numbers and types hitherto unknown and people whose cultures were totally different from any previously known, America was a place of fantastic wonder and the projection of European fears and fantasies ('O brave new world/ That has such people in't!' *Tmp 5.1.186-7*). At first the new continent was not an objective in itself, but was of interest only as a gateway to the riches of Asia, hence the application of 'West Indies' and 'Indians' to the place and its inhabitants. Ultimately the continents were recognized as such, largely through the explorations of Amerigo Vespucci (1454-1512), an Italian who discovered the mouth of the Amazon and made significant contributions in calculating longitude. His first name was soon applied to the new world.

Amiens, *AYLI,* singing nobleman attending Duke Senior. The name may be a borrowing of the name of the capital of Picardy, where a treaty was concluded between the English and the French in 1264.

Amphimacus, *Tro 5.5.12,* Greek warrior, one of the suitors of Helen of Troy. He joined the war with the Eleian forces and was slain by Hector. In William Caxton's *Recuyell of the Historyes of Troye* (c. 1474), the first English printed book, and Sh.'s major source for the play. A 'Duc Amphymacus' is with the troops of Ajax. There is also an Amphymacus from Calydonia and a 'Duc Amphimacus of Rusticane.' Later, the 'kynge Amphymacus' is slain by Æneas. In the *Iliad* 2.713, he is described as the son of Cteatus, grandson of Poseidon, and commander of the Epeans.

Ampthill, *H8 4.1.28,* Bedfordshire town 45 mi. northwest of London. Its castle was Katherine of Aragon's home after Henry VIII sent her from court and began proceedings to dissolve their marriage.

Amurath, *2H4 5.2.48,* Murad, sultan of the Ottoman empire. When he succeeded to his father's throne in 1574, he slaughtered all his brothers to prevent one of them from becoming his rival.

Amyntas, *Ant 3.6.74,* king of Lycaonia and Galatia who Plutarch ('Antony' 61.2) says sided with Mark Antony against Octavius at the battle of Actium in 31 BC. He died in 25 BC, and his domain was absorbed into the Roman empire.

Anchises, father of Æneas and human mate of the goddess Venus. Venus crippled him to punish him for revealing the fact that she was Æneas' mother. Anchises was an old man when Troy, his home, fell to the Greeks. His son carried him from the doomed city on his back, and the two men set out in search of a land where they could make a new start. He died in Sicily before Æneas discovered that his destiny was to sire Italy's Roman race. *2H6 5.3.62. JC 1.2.116. Tro 4.1.22.*

Ancus Martius, *Cor 2.3.239,* (640–616 BC), fourth king of Rome and the grandson of its second king, Numa Pompilius. Legend credits him with conquests among the Latins and the settlement in Rome of the ancestors of the Republic's plebeian families.

Andrew, *MV 1.1.27,* name of a ship, possibly derived from the Italian admiral Andrea Doria (c. 1467–1560), though there is no particular reason to believe so.

Andrew, Sir, *TN,* see Aguecheek, Sir Andrew.

Andromache, *Tro,* wife of Hector. Achilles slew her father Eëtion, her husband, and her seven brothers. Her son Astyanax was taken from her at the fall of Troy and thrown to his death. She became the concubine of Neoptolemus, bore him three sons and then was cast off for Hermione. After the death of Neoptolemus, she became the wife of Helenus and queen of Epirus. She is the title character of a play by Euripides and plays a large role in both his and Seneca's versions of *The Trojan Women.* Her sorrows are generally symbolic of the sorrows of all women caught up in war. In Sh. she vainly tries to talk Hector out of fighting Achilles and is reminiscent of Calpurnia warning Cæsar. As in *JC,* this humanizes the great man to establish sympathy for his death.

Andronici, *Tit 2.3.189, 5.3.130, 175, Add. Q1 A.1.1.35,* family to which Titus Andronicus belonged. Sh.'s Andronici are creatures of fiction. Several men named Andronicus achieved prominence in ancient history, but none founded a noble Roman family.

Angelica, *Rom 4.4.5,* either Capulet's Wife, the Nurse, or a servant. The latter is not identified as being on stage at this point, but there is no reason why a servant would not be. The remark 'Spare not for cost' might, some critics have asserted, be something which could only be in the control of Capulet's Wife, yet it might also be a general expression of joy and attitude. There is also no reason why the Nurse or a housekeeper might not have financial responsibilities. The name was common and appears in Ariosto, Sannazaro, and many other places. It derived from lithurgical L. *angelicus,* 'angelic.'

Angelo, 1) *Err,* goldsmith. He makes a carcanet (necklace) for his friend Antipholus of Ephesus and then tries to collect the debt from Antipholus of Syracuse. A necklace serves a similar function in the source, Plautus' *Menæchmi,* although a cloak is also involved.

2) *MM,* 'Lord A.,' the Duke of Vienna's kinsman, placed in charge of the state to clean up some of the corruption that has infected the city. Angelo, however, proves too zealous in his prosecution of Claudio and then undermines all that he stands for in his attempt to force Isabella to his will. Even more despicable, after trading Claudio's life for Isabella's virginity, he attempts to renege on the deal by ordering Claudio's prompt execution. This last bit of viciousness is prevented only by extraordinary machinations by the Duke, who reveals Angelo's hypocrisy and forces Angelo's marriage to Mariana, whom Angelo abandoned. The extreme cruelty of Angelo's acts reflect his own incapacity to deal with sexuality, particularly his own. Lacking the capacity to forgive, he is an inflexible, marred man who—like many another Sh. character—needs to be taught a lesson about being an adult. Usually a woman engineers the torments that are intended to enlighten, but in this case the Duke does so. Angelo's name may have been borrowed from Sh.'s sources. In Cinthio's play *Epitia* (published 1583) a drama-

tization of a tale he had already recounted in *Hecatommithi* (1565), Angelo is called Juriste, but his sister is Angela. There may be some ironic suggestion related to 'angel' but it is not exploited.

3) *Oth 1.3.16,* 'Signor A.', an otherwise unmentioned gentleman of Venice who has a sailor report that the Turks are moving towards Rhodes. A few moments later this movement is proven to be a feint whose actual intention is Cyprus. It is thought that the specificity of this name might imply a lost source for the play.

Angers, *Jn,* capital of the French province of Anjou, situated 220 mi. southwest of Paris on the Mayenne river.

Angleterre, *H5 3.4.1, 4.4.55, 5.2.335,* Fr. 'England.'

Anglia, *H5 5.2.336,* L. 'England.'

Angus, 1) former earldom and sheriffdom in eastern Scotland, named after the eldest of seven brothers who supposedly ruled the country in the times of the Picts, or possibly after a hill east of the church of Aberlemno. The area is currently called Forfarshire and is located on the North Sea above the Firth of Tay, east of Perthshire, and south of Aberdeen and Kincardine. When the first parliament convened after the defeat of Macbeth it met in the chief town of the county, Forfar. When Matilda, countess of Angus, married Gilbert de Umfravill in 1243, the Celtic line of succession was broken, and ultimately (in 1761) the title went to the dukes of Hamilton. *1H4:* Angus was the seat of the Douglas family.

2) *Mac,* nobleman who brings word that Macbeth has been made Thane of Cawdor and who later joins Malcolm's rebellion against Macbeth's rule. The character is based upon Gilchrist, Thane of Angus. In 1056, he was elevated to Earl of Angus for his services to Malcolm. Sh. likely borrowed the name from the list of Malcolm's allies in Raphael Holinshed's *Chronicles.* William Douglas (d. 1611), the Roman Catholic 10th earl of Angus, was very active in Sh.'s day and adamantly refused to recant his faith. Excommunicated in 1608, he spent his final years in Paris. His career may have made his name familiar to Sh.'s audiences.

Angus, Earl of, *1H4 1.1.73,* George Douglas (d. 1403), earl by right of his mother, Margaret Stewart, and husband of Mary Stuart, daughter of Robert III, king of Scotland. He was captured at the battle at Holmedon in 1402 and died of plague while imprisoned.

Anjou, feudal state in the Loire valley, bordered by Maine on the north and Poitou on the south. Geoffrey Plantagenet, count of Anjou, married Matilda, daughter and heir of Henry I of England. Their son, Henry II, inherited the kingdom of England and a sprawling collection of French fiefs historians have dubbed 'the Angevin (from Anjou) empire.' Henry controlled more French territory than the king of France, but his sons, Richard I and John, lost most of England's continental possessions to Philip (II) Augustus of France. Philip's son, Louis IX, made Anjou an appanage (an estate reserved for the support of a member of the royal family) for his brother, Charles, count of Provence and king of Naples and Sicily. In 1290 the property passed by marriage to Charles of Valois, son of Philip III. When Charles's heir, Philip of Valois, became King Philip VI in 1328, he assigned Anjou to his son, John the Good. When John succeeded to the throne in 1350, he elevated Anjou from a county to a duchy and gave it to his second son, Louis. It remained in the hands of his descendants until the death of René of Anjou in 1480, when it reverted to the direct control of King Louis XI.

2H6. Jn 1.1.11, 2.1.152, 488, 529. See René, duke of Anjou.

Anjou, Duke of, *1H6,* see René, duke of Anjou, king of Naples.

Anna, *Shr 1.1.152:* sister of Dido and Pygmalion, daughter of either Belus, king of Tyre; Agenor; or Mutto. Extremely devoted to Dido she unwittingly helped her sister commit suicide over the loss of Æneas (Virgil's *Æneid,* 4).

Anne, 1) *2H6 2.2.38,* see Mortimer, Anne.
2) *MWW,* see Page, Anne.
3)*H8 3.2.403, 4.1.43,* see Boleyn, Anne.

Anne, Lady, *R3,* (1452–1484), younger daughter of Richard Neville, earl of Warwick ('the Kingmaker') and pawn of her father's shifting political alliances. She was with her father in France in 1464 when he tried to negotiate an alliance between Edward IV and Louis XI. The failure of that project and the revelation of Edward's secret marriage to Elizabeth Woodville Gray turned Warwick against his king. Warwick turned to Louis XI for help in deposing Edward, and Louis induced him to join forces with his former enemies, the house of Lancaster. In 1470 Warwick promised to help restore Henry VI to the throne, and Henry's son, Edward, pledged to marry Anne. Although Sh. assumes that a marriage was consummated, the historical record is unclear. Warwick and Edward met their deaths at the battles of Barnet (14 April 1471) and Tewkesbury (4 May 1471), respectively, and Anne came under the protection of her sister's husband, Edward IV's brother George, the duke of Clarence. Anne did not, as Sh. claims, preside at Henry VI's funeral, for Clarence kept her in hiding until his younger brother Richard of Gloucester tracked her down and married her in 1473. When Richard usurped the throne in 1483, she was crowned at his side. Their only child, a son named Edward, died in 1484 at the age of eight. Consumption carried Anne off a year later. There were rumors that she was poisoned by her husband, but this is one of the few slanders that Sh. neglects to repeat about Richard III. The historical king appears to have been genuinely fond of his wife.

Anne, St., mother of the Virgin Mary. Anne is not mentioned in Christian literature until the 4th c. and all the information about her derives from Apocryphal gospels. The stories greatly resemble other stories in the Bible. Her husband was named Joachim. Having had no children, he fasted and prayed in the desert for 40 days, after which an angel announced the upcoming birth to Anne. There was an early cult of Anne in Eastern Orthodox churches. Justinian dedicated a church to her. Yet, Anne developed a particularly strong following in England. In 1382, in England alone, a feast was begun in her honor. In 16th c. the celebration spread through the entire western church. Her feast day is July 26. *Shr. 1.1.248. TN 2.3.112.*

Anselme, *Rom 1.2.65,* count invited to Capulet's feast along with his 'beauteous sisters.' The frequent mention of the attractiveness of the women who will be accompanying the male guests leads one to suspect that old Capulet, rather like the president of a fraternity house, is trying to insure enough female companionship at his feast. Though if, as some commentators have speculated, Romeo is not reading Capulet's invitation literally, but is editorializing, these remarks on the pulchritude of the guests would indicate Romeo's frivolous nature.

Antenor, *Tro,* elderly Trojan seer, advisor to Priam, and father of Polydamas and Laocoön (among many others). He advised the Trojans to make peace by returning Helen to her husband. During the war, he maintained contact with Menelaus and Ulysses and suggested the wooden horse stratagem. He was protected at the fall of Troy by a panther skin posted on his door and migrated with his family to the Adriatic. He was the subject of a lost drama by Sophocles and is present in the memorable scene in the *Iliad* in which Helen walks the walls and surveys the Greek armies. In Sh. he is, curiously, a non-speaking character who is often spoken of as a valued counsellor. After his capture by the Greeks, he is exchanged for Cressida which ironically sets up the future fall of Troy. He is an important character in William Caxton's *Recuyell of the Historyes of Troye* (c. 1474), the first English printed book, and Sh.'s major source for the play.

Antenorides, *Tro Prol.17,* one of the six gates of Troy, presumably named after Antenor. These are not in the *Iliad* which appears to give Troy only one double gate, but in William Caxton's *Recuyell of the Historyes of Troye,* 3 (c. 1474), the first English printed book, and Sh.'s major source for the play, the six gates are listed, Antenorides being the last. In the French book by Raoul Lefevre which Caxton translated, Antenorides is called 'Aminorides.'

Anthony, *Rom 1.5.9,* F1 'Anthonie,' a servant in Capulet's house. Some editors prefer Antony.

Anthropophagi, *Oth 1.3.143,* cannibals. The name comes from the Greek for 'man-eaters.' Sources for the anthropophagi and for the men whose heads are between their shoulders include Sir John Mandeville's *Travels* (late 14th c.), Sir Walter Raleigh's *Discoverie of the Large, Rich, and Beautiful Empire of Guiana*, and Pliny the Elder's *Naturalis Historia.*

Anthropophaginian, *MWW 4.5.8,* cannibal savage. Possibly the joke relates to the expression, 'He'll bite your head off.' See Anthropophagi.

Antiates, *Cor 1.7.53, 1.7.59, 5.6.80,* people of the city of Antium who helped the Volscian tribes in their battles with the armies of the infant Roman Republic. See Antium.

Antic, *1H4 1.2.60,* 'stage name' for buffoons and comedians.

Antigonus, *WT,* lord of Sicilia, husband of Paulina. Setting out to expose the infant Perdita in the 'deserts of Bohemia,' he is killed in perhaps Sh.'s most famous stage direction: 'Exit pursued by a Beare.' Discussion has centered around how this was accomplished on the stage and also for the convenient, if unimaginative way it removes Antigonus from the subsequent action. The name occurs in Plutarch from which Sh. got most of his names for the play. Antigonus is described as the most powerful among the captains and successors of Alexander. Antigonus was also mentioned in the translations of Josephus available in 1602 and 1609.

Antioch, *Per 1.17,* capital of the Greek kings of Syria, located on the Orontes river about 21 mi. from its harbor Seleucia on the Mediterranean. it was founded about 300 BC by Seleucus I Nicator and named after his father Antiochus. Later enlarged by Antiochus (III) the Great and his son Antiochus Epiphanes, it was one of the largest cities of the Middle East between 200 BC and 300 AD and has the distinction of being the first place in which the followers of Jesus were called Christians. A magnificent city, it was a resort for wealthy Romans and a trade center between East and West. Besides being subject to major earthquakes, the city changed hands in many conquests. The Persians raided the city in 260 AD and sacked it in 538. The Arabs captured the city in 637 AD. in 969 the Byzantines took it, and then the Seljuk Turks in 1084. The First Crusade recaptured it in 1098 and it became a powerful principality under Bohemond I when he broke with Byzantine Emperor Alexius I. Later, he was forced to accept Alexius' control. The city remained under Christian control until 1268, when the Egyptians inflicted great destruction and slaughter. It never recovered from this blow. It was absorbed by the Ottoman Empire in 1516, and is now the Turkish city called Antakyah.

Antiochus III, *Per,* called 'the Great,' king of Antioch (242-187 BC). He ascended the throne of Greek Syria in 223. He subdued Parthia and Bactria and wrested control of Palestine and Lebanon from Ptolemy V of Egypt in 198. He was drawn into conflict with Rome by Philip of Macedon and the Greek states but was defeated at Thermopylæ in 191 by Marcus Cato. He was eventually crushed by Scipio Africanus the Elder in 190 at Magnesia. Severe terms of surrender were imposed on him. He was killed while looting a temple in Elymais to obtain money for the Romans. The story of Antiochus' love for his daughter appears in John Gower's *Confessio Amantis* (1390) a major source for the play, but it dates back to Apollonius of Tyre (see Pericles). Plutarch describes the incestuous love of Antiochus I for his father Seleucus' wife Stratonice, which might have been confused and associated with Antiochus III. Antiochus' death as described by Helicanus at *8.5-13* is reminiscent of a passage beginning at 2 Kings 1.10, a scene in Robert Greene and Thomas Lodge's *A Looking-Glass for London* (1594), and the death of Antiochus Epiphanes in 2 Maccabees 9. It also recalls a passage in Acts 12:20-23 describing Herod's death and mentioning Tyre in this chapter and Antioch in the first chapter of the next. Like a number of things in the play, Antiochus appears in Plutarch, particularly in his life of Demetrius.

Antiopa, *MND 2.1.80,* Antiope, queen of the Amazons and one of Theseus' conquests. He abducted her and precipitated an Amazon invasion of Attica. In mythology, she is often the same as Hippolyta, but is also often Hippolyta's sister. In some versions she married Theseus and bore him Demophon, only to be killed by him when she interfered with his plans to marry Phædra. Sh. distinguishes between Hippolyta and Antiopa but does not make them sisters. Theseus' love life is recounted in Plutarch. See Hippolyta.

Antipholus, *Err,* the two brothers separated in infancy, twin sons of Egeon, masters of the two Dromios. It may derive directly from the Greek *antiphilos,* 'mutual love,' but is more likely borrowed from the character Antiphilis in Sir Philip Sidney's *Arcadia,* 2, a polygamist who is killed by women.

1) A. of Ephesus, husband of Adriana. In the F1 stage directions at *2.1,* he is called 'Antipholis Sereptus,' which likely echoes the prologue of Plautus' *Menæchmi* from which the play is derived in its use of *surreptum* (l. 38) and *subreptus* (l. 41) from the verb *surripio* 'to secretly take away.' The corresponding character in the source is Menæchmus the Citizen. In the *Amphitryon* by Plautus, Jupiter takes Amphitryon's place with his wife similar to the way in which Antipholus of Syracuse dispossesses Antipholus of Ephesus.

2) A. of Syracuse, man who arrives in Ephesus after five years of searching for his brother. Mistaken for his twin, he dines in his brother's home. When he finds himself attracted to Luciana, Adriana assumes that her husband's adultery has reached a new level. In F1, he is called 'Antipholis Erotes' *1.2.sd* and 'Antipholis Errotis' *2.2.sd,* which might refer to Erotium, the mistress of Menæchmus the Citizen in Plautus. Much more likely, however, it is a corruption of Latin *erraticus* 'wandering.' in Plautus he is called Menæchmus the Traveller.

Antipodes, the directly opposite place on the planet, figuratively the ends of the earth. There are a group of islands near New Zealand called the Antipodes for this reason. The word literally means those whose feet are opposed to ours. *MND 3.2.55:* the passage means, 'I'll believe it when the earth has a hole drilled through it, big enough so that the moon (Diana) can creep through to join the sun (her brother Apollo) and join noon with its opposite (the Antipodes).' *MV 5.1.127,* when Portia walks at night, compliments Bassanio, he shares day with the Antipodes. *R2 3.2.45. Ado 2.1.248.*

Antium, *Cor 3.1.11, 18, 19, 4.4.1, 8,* town on the coast of ancient Latium. It was founded by Etruscans and allegedly conquered by the last Roman king, Tarquinius Superbus. Antium resisted Roman domination and assisted the Volscian tribes in their wars with the young Roman Republic. Rome sent expeditions against Antium in 468 BC and in 338 BC. Following the latter, Rome stripped Antium of its ships and brought their prows (i.e., *rostri*) to Rome to be displayed on the speakers' platform in the forum. This prompted the use of the word 'rostrum' for a podium.

Antoniad, *Ant 3.10.2,* Egyptian flagship at the battle of Actium. The battle was allegedly lost when Cleopatra turned the vessel around and fled for home. Her hasty departure supposedly alarmed Antony (q.v.) so much that he abandoned his men to follow her.

Antonio, 1) *TGV,* father of Proteus. Sternly he orders his son to the court of the Emperor (Duke of Milan) for the boy's education. He is referred to as 'Don Antonio' by the Duke (*2.4.52*). This presumably Italian gentleman's being titled 'Don' is derived from the Spanish source, Jorge de Montemayor's *Diana Enamorada* (1559) and is not a confusion of Sp. with It. In fact, the use of 'Don' has long been common in southern Italy because of the period of Spanish control over the kingdom of Naples and the Two Sicilies.

2) *Shr 1.2.53, 189; 2.1.68,* Petruccio's deceased father, a prominent man. According to Petruccio he left a substantial estate which Petruccio has enlarged. He was known to Baptista Minola, which makes his son not only a willing husband for Katherine but an excellent prospect to insure her future.

3) *MV,* 'Anthonio' in F1, the merchant of Venice, an older man of substantial wealth. Antonio's friendship with the younger Bassanio knows no limit as he borrows on credit in order to finance the young man's attempt to win Portia. *MV* seems to provide through Antonio an ideal view of true friendship, as there seems little rational reason for the merchant to risk any more of his money on Bassanio—who has already wasted previous loans on other ventures—especially on a cockamamie scheme to get rich by marrying the faraway Lady of Belmont. For that reason some critics have suggested that the relationship between the older man and the younger is deeper than friendship; however, this view utterly ignores the obvious and intentional fabulism of the play and Antonio's allegorical significance as the good Christian. While he has mistreated the Jew Shylock, he pays for it, accepting his fate in a Job-like manner, never begging for a special dispensation from the law of Venice, nor when the tables have turned, failing to exercise mercy upon Shylock as Graziano urges him. He refuses Shylock's money and insists the Jew become a Christian.

In modern times, one may find Shylock's forced conversion distasteful at best, but in Sh.'s England, where, by law, Jews did not exist, it was most likely regarded as saving the man's soul in spite of himself. Though Shylock is such a dominant character in the play that he is often mistaken for the title character, the play can be seen as a progression from Antonio's initial mysterious depression to a rebirth of his spirit through an encounter with death. The story is of such wide and ancient provenance that Sh. may have chosen the name for any number of reasons. The corresponding merchant in Ser Giovanni Fiorentino's *il Pecorone* (1558), the likely source, is Ansaldo. In the earliest dramatic analogue, *Le miracle de un marchant et un juif* (1377) he is called Audry. Antonio is common in Sh.'s plays, so it may merely have been a convenient Italianate name. The allusion to Rodrigo Lopez at *4.1.131-137,* who was hanged for an alleged assassination attempt upon Elizabeth I and the pretender for the crown of Portugal, Antonio Perez, has suggested to some that the name is from the Pretender.

Another suggestion is that it relates to the story of one of the saints Anthony. Anthony the Great (251-356 AD) was reared in a wealthy home in Egypt, but gave it all away to take up the life of a hermit. He lived in some ruins on a mountain, seeing only one man a year who brought him bread. At age 54 he came down and founded an ascetic monastery. He went to Alexandria in 311 to encourage resistance to the persecutions of Maximus, and later to refute Arianism. His body was buried secretly on Mt. Kolzim near the Red Sea. A life of St. Anthony was written by Bishop Athanasius of Alexandria (d. 373) which was particularly influential in the hagiography of England. Anthony's giving of all he had without regret is sometimes seen to parallel Antonio's. St. Anthony of Padua (1195–1231) was born in Lisbon as Ferdinand de Bulhoes and became the patron saint of the poor. He was a great preacher of the Franciscan order who did missionary work among the Muslims of Morocco, and died quite young in Padua. Many miracles were attributed to him and the church recognized him, despite his age, as one of the Doctors of the Church because of his extraordinary knowledge of Scripture. In art he is usually depicted as a young man with the baby Jesus on his arm—a reference to one of the miracles attributed to him. Alms given in his honor were called 'St. Anthony's bread.'

4) *Ado,* 'Antony,' 'Anthonio,' the spirited brother of Leonato, who flirts in disguise despite the palsy in his head and dryness of his hand. He challenges Don Pedro of Aragon and Claudio to a duel over the death of his niece Hero. In this he must be relying on Claudio's noble nature as he would die for nothing knowing Hero is still alive. Antonio is one of the better character roles in Sh. In Matteo Bandello's *Novelle* (1554), the primary source, the corresponding character is Girolamo, but there are many contemporary versions of the plot.

5) *TN,* F1 'Anthonio,' an accomplished military man, rescuer of Sebastian during the shipwreck. He offers to serve the young nobleman and is rejected. Nonetheless he goes on into illyria at his peril because Orsino is an old enemy of his from when Antonio was a raiding sea captain. Because of the confusion of Viola with Sebastian, Antonio endures a test to the face of death of his loyalty to the young man. Commentators have therefore tried to link this Antonio with the good friend of Bassanio in *MV.* In *Gl'ingannati* (1538), a possible source for the play, Fabrizio (corresponding to Sebastian) arrives in Modena accompanied by Master Piero, a pedant, but he bears no resemblance to Antonio except as he assists the boy and there is a similar exchange about where they will stay. There may be some suggestion of Malvolio in Piero's criticism of Stragualcia's drinking.

6) *JC, Ant 2.2.7, 2.5.26,* see Antony, Mark.

7) *AWW 3.5.77* the Duke of Florence's eldest son, mentioned only as he passes by in a parade.

8) *Tmp,* 'Anthonio' in F1, usurping brother of Prospero. Ferdinand says (*1.2.441-2*) that Antonio has a son, but this appears to be either a simple mistake or a survival from a source or earlier play. It is possible it is meant that Antonio has lost his son in the shipwreck. The name may come from the Antony Adorno who replaced his brother Prospero Adorno as ruler of Genoa in 1488 (see Prospero). An 'Anthonio' also appears in Robert Eden's *History of Travaile* (1577), along with several other names from *Tmp.* Some critics feel that the 'th' in Anthonio is intentional by the playwright, not merely the vagary of Renaissance spelling.

Antonius, *Ant 1.1.56, 3.1.25,* see Antony, Mark.

Antony, Mark, Marcus Antonius, (83–30 BC), member of the second triumvirate and chief competitor of Octavius for control of the Roman empire. His career was fostered by Julius Cæsar (to whom he was related through his mother). He served in Cæsar's army, and during the later phases of Cæsar's campaign to overthrow Pompey, he was Cæsar's second in command. In the year 44 BC, Cæsar and Antony shared the consulships, the chief executive offices of the Roman Republic. Cæsar's assassination in March of that year made him (the sole surviving consul) the logical man to lead Rome. He presided at Cæsar's funeral and kept Cæsar's angry soldiers from tearing Rome apart. His assumption of the prerogatives of Cæsar's heir was, however, quickly challenged by Octavius, a nephew whom Cæsar had adopted shortly before his death. The orator Cicero persuaded the Senate to support Octavius. He argued that this would divide Cæsar's followers and set them fighting among themselves. He was wrong. Soldiers pledged to both men were loyal to Cæsar's memory and reluctant to shed each other's blood. Consequently, Antony and Octavius were compelled to work together to avenge Cæsar by killing the Senators who had plotted his assassination. The Senators fled to Greece and recruited troops that had once served Cæsar's enemy, Pompey.

The approach of civil war gave Antony, Octavius, and Lepidus (another of Cæsar's officers) an excuse to suspend constitutional government and declare a state of emergency. They proclaimed themselves a 'triumvirate' (a committee of three dictators) empowered to do whatever was necessary to restore the Republic. In 42 BC Antony and Octavius won a decisive victory at the battles of Philippi, and the triumvirate assumed control of the empire. Since the army was not yet persuaded of the necessity of choosing among its commanders, the triumvirs were compelled to continue to appear to cooperate. Lepidus, the weakest of the three, was shunted off to deal with a minor crisis in Africa while Antony and Octavius plotted strategies that each hoped would someday permit him to destroy the other. Antony, the stronger military man, won the most dangerous, but promising, assignment. He was commissioned to make war on Parthia, the only major civilized nation on the borders of Rome's empire. A victory over the huge Parthian state would have brought him the troops and popular support he needed to force Octavius from power. To Octavius, meanwhile, fell the important, but far less glamorous, task of governing Italy. It was difficult for Octavius to find things to do at home that would generate the kind of support that Antony would win from a successful foreign war. The work of an administrator rarely excites a wildly enthusiastic following, but Octavius was adept at exploiting his one advantage: direct access to the people of Rome. Octavius launched a propaganda campaign designed to undercut confidence in Antony and to turn the Roman world against him.

Antony played directly into his rival's hands when he developed a relationship with Cleopatra, queen of Egypt. He met her in 41 BC, summoning her to his headquarters at Tarsus to inform her he intended to take from Egypt whatever he needed to support his invasion of Parthia. Egypt was a sovereign state, and a Roman commander had no right to order its monarch to do his bidding, but Cleopatra knew that her homeland was flanked by Roman territory and that an impatient Roman general might simply annex her kingdom. To prevent that, she maneuvered Antony into visiting Egypt as her guest. He spent the winter of 41 BC in Egypt, but hastened back to Italy when news reached him that his wife, Fulvia, and his brother, Lucius, had raised a rebellion against Octavius. Since he did not want to risk a showdown with Octavius before he was finished with his Parthian campaign, he repudiated responsibility for his wife's actions. Fulvia fled Italy and died en route to his headquarters. Her death gave him an opportunity to repair the diplomatic damage she had done. He sealed a new agreement with Octavius by marrying Octavius' sister, Octavia, who accompanied him when he returned to the east to resume preparations for the Parthian war. For several years they lived in apparent harmony. In 37 BC Antony went to Italy to renew the legal arrangement on which the authority of the triumvirate rested. He then established a base in Syria from which to march on Parthia and made a second trip to Egypt.

In Egypt he shocked the Roman world by marrying Cleopatra, whom he had not seen for over three years, and by declaring his intent to bestow Parthian territory on a son she had conceived by him during his visit in 41 BC. This marriage was not binding in Rome, and the ceremony did not mean that he divorced Octavia. His alliance with Egypt's queen may have had more to do with diplomacy than romance, but it troubled the Romans and gave Octavius a weapon against him. Octavia inadvertently helped her brother by conducting herself with conspicuous loyalty to her husband. Octavius contrasted his sister's virtue with her husband's vices and warned the Roman people that Antony had been bewitched by a foreign woman who planned to use him to conquer them. Although Antony understood the danger, he ignored Octavius and marched into Parthia. He believed that Rome's elation at a Parthian victory would easily dispel the anxiety created by Octavius' propaganda. He was unable, however, to defeat the Parthians. They retreated into their vast land, drew him deep into unknown territory, cut off his supplies, and surrounded him. He demonstrated superb generalship by rescuing a portion of his army from the trap into which he had led them, but a successful retreat did not win him many friends in Rome.

Octavius sensed that the time had come to challenge Antony. He terminated the triumvirate, declared him a threat to the Republic, and sent an army into Antony's territory. Events were decided by a naval skirmish off the coast of Actium. Octavius' explanation of what happened at Actium was designed to support his contention that love had made Antony Cleopatra's slave. Octavius claimed that Cleopatra, a woman, had no stomach for battle and fled at the start of the engagement. Antony saw her ship retreat and abandoned his men to follow the woman who had infatuated him. Octavius' story is not convincing, for it is unlikely that a woman as intelligent, experienced, and audacious as Cleopatra lacked courage. It is probable, however, that Antony's troops were so dispirited by Octavius' propaganda and by their losses in Parthia that the battle was lost before it began. When Cleopatra and Antony reached Egypt, he may have suffered a brief collapse. By the time he roused himself to fight, it was too late to organize a defense for Egypt. In a fit of despair, he mortally wounded himself, but survived long enough to be carried to Cleopatra to die in her presence. Almost all of what Sh. knew about Antony he got from the biographies in Plutarch.

H5 3.6.14. JC. Mac 3.1.58: supposedly, Antony's spirit was weak in the presence of Octavius (see *Ant 2.3.16-20*). This is mentioned in Plutarch's 'Antony.' *Ant.*

Apemantus, *Tim,* surly man who warns the wealthy Timon against flattery and later mocks him in his poverty. Timon drives him away. The ancient Apemantus, according to Plutarch, celebrated the feast of the dead with the real Timon, who insulted him for violating his solitude. See Timon.

Apennines, *Jn 1.1.202,* mountain range that runs 800 mi. down the length of the Italian peninsula, reaching a maximum height of 9,560 feet at Mt. Corno.

Apollinem, *Tit 4.3.54,* L., objective case, for Apollo.

Apollo, Greek god of the sun, music, prophecy, and medicine, son of Jupiter and Latona (Gr. Leto), born on Delos as twin brother of Diana. The lyre was sacred to him and the Muses were his attendants. His oracle at Delphi was considered one of the most sacred in the ancient world. He spent part of each year among the Hyperboreans who were blessed by warmth and fecundity, and his return to Delphi was a metaphor for the coming of spring. Apollo killed Python, a serpent sprung from the slime which covered the Earth after the flood, and therefore archery was also sacred to him. His sacred tree was the laurel (because of his ill-fated love for Daphne, q.v.) and his bow was decorated with its leaves. His sacred animals were the raven, swan, wolf, goat, ram, mouse, and dolphin.

Shr Ind. 2.34, 58. Tit 4.1.65, 4.4.15. LLL 4.3.319, 'A.'s lute strung with his hair.' *5.2.914,* 'songs of A.,' the intellectual pleasures of the sonnets and other poetry of the court, interrupted by the messenger. *MND 2.1.231,* alludes to his pursuit of Daphne.

Lr: Cæsar said the gods of the Druids were Apollo, Mars, Jupiter, and Minerva, but Sh. probably relied more on William Harrison's *Historical Description of the Iland of Britain,* which was published in vol. 1 of Holinshed's chronicles. Lear's father Bladud, according to Geoffrey of Monmouth, attempted to fly and was killed by falling on the temple of Apollo. The story is repeated in Holinshed and *Mirror for Magistrates. 1.1.159, 160 (Q 1.151, 152):* as Apollo is the all-seeing God, this exchange seems particularly apropos to the theme of the failure to see the truth.

Per 12.65. Tro 1.1.98, 1.3.322, 2.2.78, 3.3.294, 'fiddler A.'

WT, passim. 2.1.185, 'A.'s temple,' the oracle at Delphi. *3.1.19,* 'A.'s great divine,' the priestess at Delphi. *4.4.30,* 'Golden A.,' a reference to A. as sun god and his living as a herdsman in the service of Admetus. *4.4.25-31:* Ovid's *Metamorphoses,* 6, describes Arachne's tapestry and contains a non-specific reference to A. in peasant garb, as well as to Neptune as ram and Jupiter as bull, and is therefore the obvious source of the passage. *TNK 1.4.46,* 'great A.'s mercy,' *5.2.15,* the god as physician.

Apollodorus, *Ant 2.6.70,* 'the Sicilian,' one of Cleopatra's friends and servants. It was he, Plutarch ('Cæsar' 49.1) says, who wrapped the young Cleopatra in a blanket and smuggled her into Julius Cæsar's presence. The audacious scheme amused Cæsar and was the first step in

Cleopatra's plan to seduce the Roman general into promoting her dynastic ambitions.

Apostle, the, *STM Add. II.D.104,* Paul (q.v.) in Romans 13:1-5.

Apostle Paul, *R3 5.5.170,* see Paul, St.

April, fourth month of the year in the Gregorian calendar. Its name derives from the Latin *aperire* 'to open,' describing the flowering of spring. *Tit 3.1.18. Luc 395. Jn 4.2.120. MWW 2.3.62. Tro 1.2.170:* as April is the month of spring showers and of the zodiac symbol Aquarius, Pandarus implies that a man born then should be capable of great weeping. *Ant 3.2.43.*

Aquilon, *Tro 4.6.9,* Roman name for the north wind, possibly related to the word for eagle, and therefore associated with Jupiter and his lightning.

Aquitaine, one of the old provinces of southwestern France, originally named by Julius Cæsar, probably from a local tribe, the Auscetani. After the Roman period, it became a bone of contention between Visigoths and Franks, and among various Frankish rulers. It was also threatened by the Saracens in the 7th c. It began as a duchy in 660, but was styled a kingdom from 781, when Charlemagne granted it to his son Louis. In 845, it was reestablished as a duchy. The last duke, William X, married his daughter, Eleanor of Aquitaine to Louis VII and the duchy was her dowry. Upon her remarriage in 1152 to Henry II of England, however, it became an English possession. After the treaty of Paris in 1259, 'Guienne' (a corruption of Aquitaine) began to be applied to the land north of the Garonne river, and 'Gascony' to the land south. In 1451, France regained control of the former Aquitaine. After Henry IV united his hereditary lands with the crown, the history of Aquitaine is essentially the same as France.

LLL 1.1.135, 2.1.8, 145, 148, 159, 248: Ferdinand is approached by the Princess of France about giving up Aquitaine, part of which was held in collateral for a loan by Ferdinand's father to the king of France. After some confusion about whether the debt has been paid, Ferdinand agrees to give up the land as soon as Boyet reveals the payment. The dispute about the province is reminiscent of the long struggles for it, as an English, French, or Navarrese possession, and the allusion to it as a dowry cannot but have reminded the English of Eleanor; however, the province was also part of the dowry of Marguerite de Valois, and when she and Catherine de Médicis came to Nérac in 1578 to discuss the separation with Henry of Navarre, Aquitaine was part of the negotiation. Furthermore, Charles of Navarre secured a debt of 200,000 crowns by the king of France with significant land holdings in 1425. Both of these incidents seem to have provided Sh.'s inspiration for the Princess' embassy.

Arabia, largest peninsula on earth (about a million sq. mi.), located in southwest Asia and surrounded by the Red Sea, the Persian Gulf, and the Indian Ocean. Although usually thought of as inhospitable, there are areas which are fertile. In the traditional division made by Ptolemy the peninsula consists of three areas Arabia Felix (the fertile areas of the south: Yemen, Oman, the Hadramaut), A. Petræa (the stony areas of the north), and A. Deserta (the great central desert, the Rub al Khali or Empty Quarter). Long occupied by nomads, it was also the site of Sheba (Saba or the Sabæan kingdom) and the birthplace of Islam. In Sh.'s time, Arabian power had been superseded by the Ottomans and the area was another mysterious place of the East, famed for perfumes, magic, exotic inhabitants, and wealth. Besides the daunting climate, much of the peninsula was forbidden to non-Moslems, so the information available was mostly from Greek and Roman sources or from the rumors of travellers. Like many of Sh.'s geographical place names, 'Arabia' was probably not very precise. Part of Egypt from the Nile to the Red Sea is called the Arabian desert even now.

MV 2.7.42, 'the vasty wilds of wide A.' *Cor 4.2.26. Mac 5.1.49,* 'perfumes of A.' *Ant 3.6.72. Tmp 3.3.22.*

Arabian, (adj.) of Arabia. *PhT 2,* 'A. tree,' *Oth 5.2.359,* 'A. trees,' the Arabian myrtle (*Balsamodendron myrrha*), which produces the fragrant myrrh (the 'medicinable gum' of the next line). It can in this context be associated with incense and therefore atonement. *Ant 3.2.12,* 'A. bird,' the Phoenix. *Cym 1.6.17,* 'A. bird': Giacomo is saying that if Innogen's mind is equal to her beauty, she is a unique creature.

Aragon, F1 'Arragon,' kingdom located in northeast Spain on the Pyrenees. It is divided by the Ebro river. After the Punic Wars, Aragon became part of the Roman province of Hispania Tarraconensis when Augustus reorganized the peninsula's administration. It fell to the Visigoths in the 5th c. and to the Moors on their way into France in the 8th c., but its genesis as a power begins in the Christian resistance to the Moorish conquerors. Later, it became part of the kingdom of Navarre, whose king Sancho the Great attempted to unite Spain. At his death, however, he scattered the various kingdoms among his sons. Aragon's history as a significant independent kingdom begins with Ramiro I, Sancho's son, in 1035. It grew, annexing Navarre and various Moorish lands, though Navarre would later be released. Marriage joined Aragon with Catalonia and Barcelona to the east in 1137, which immediately increased its power because of access to the sea. The Moorish stronghold of Valencia, the Balearic islands, Sardinia, Naples, and Sicily (conquered by Pedro III) all fell under the power of Aragon. When Ferdinand II of Aragon and Isabella I of Castile married in 1469, Aragon ceased to exist as an independent kingdom. The formal union of Aragon and Castile occurred in 1516 on the accession of Charles I. *MV. Ado,* Don Pedro's kingdom.

Aragon, Prince of, *MV,* F1 'Arragon,' suitor of Portia. After rejecting the lead casket as unworthy of him and the gold casket as being what other (inferior) people would desire, he choses the silver casket in his attempt to win her and learns that his vanity doesn't pay. Partly he represents the stock comic caricature of Spanish pride, but primarily his role is to develop the theme of the need for sacrifice in love.

Arcas, *TNK 2.3.38,* rural man coming to the fair, described as a fine dancer. 'Arcas' is used by Arthur Golding in his translation of Ovid's *Metamorphoses* 3 to mean 'Arcadian' in the episode in which Actæon is torn by hounds, a scene which is known to have influenced Sh. elsewhere. *3.5.49,* the Second Countryman seems to be addressing Arcas, which must mean he is the Fifth Countryman, a non-speaking part. Possibly, too, the commas are wrong and he is saying that an offstage Arcas can be told.

Archdeacon, *1H4 3.1.69,* host of the meeting at which Edmund Mortimer, the Percies, and Owain Glyndŵr planned a rebellion to unseat Henry IV. Sh.'s source for the scene was Holinshed (3.522), who may have had erroneous information. The Bangor cleric whom Henry IV outlawed for his support of the rebels was the dean of the canons of Bangor cathedral, not the archdeacon.

Archelaus, *Ant 3.6.69,* last king of Cappadocia and one of the monarchs who Plutarch ('Antony' 61.1) says sided with Mark Antony against Octavius at the battle of Actium. Archelaus was a descendant of a general who served Mithridates of Pontus in his wars with Rome. Mark Antony recognized him as king of Cappadocia in 36 BC, and after Actium, Octavius confirmed him in possession of his throne and increased the size of his kingdom. Octavius' successor, Tiberius, summoned him to Rome to answer a charge of treason. He died there in 17 AD, and Cappadocia became a Roman province.

Archibald, *1H4 1.1.53,* see Douglas, Earl of.

Archidamus, *WT,* a lord of Bohemia. The name occurs in Plutarch, from which Sh. got most of his names for the play. This Archidamas is described as king of the Lacedæmonians and son of Zeuxidamus. He opposed the Athenian Pericles.

Arcite, *TNK,* 'Lord A.,' one of the two kinsmen of the title. Originally intending to leave Thebes, he recognizes his duty to defend his homeland with his cousin Palamon. As a wounded prisoner of war, however, he falls into a love triangle with his cousin and duels over Emilia. Arcite is victorious but is killed by a runaway horse. Arcite is more of a leader than his cousin and petitions Mars for assistance when Palamon petitions Venus. They are not terribly different, however, and both characters are vague in delineation, the result of multiple authorship or general carelessness. The name is borrowed from the source, Chaucer's *Knyghtes Tale.* Chaucer also wrote a poem about the Theban knight entitled *The Compleynt of feire Anelida and fals Arcite.* Richard Edwards (c. 1523–1566) also wrote a play called *Palamon and Arcite,* which was performed in 1566, but is no longer extant.

Ardea, *Luc 1, 1332,* town in ancient Latium that was the seat of the Rutulian tribe. Rome conquered it in 442 BC and made it a colony.

Arden, *AYLI,* the more traditional sp. of Ardenne, appearing in Thomas Lodge's *Rosalynd,* the source of the play. Wells and Taylor point out that the context of the play rules out the forest of Arden in Warwickshire as the setting. This, however, as well as the fact it was Sh.'s mother's maiden name, may have appealed to the playwright and his later editors.

Ardenne, the Ardennes, a forest and hill area located in southeast Belgium between the Moselle and Meuse rivers and extending into France, Luxembourg, and the Rhineland. The hills gradually slope towards the Flanders plain. This is the spelling preferred by Wells and Taylor, though it is Arden in F1. *AYLI:* Although Sh. obviously has France in mind, the lower class characters are particularly English, as his comedy required and the forest of the play is more imaginary than specific, as with his Italian cities, illyria, etc. Sh.'s source, Lodge's *Rosalynd,* is set in 'Arden,' and though Lodge's geography is confused at best, he intends the Ardennes.

Ardres, *H8 1.1.7,* or Andren, a district in the French province of Picardy.

Argus, called 'Panoptes,'(many-eyed), son of inachus, a creature with a hundred eyes. When Jupiter transformed his lover Io into a heifer in order to conceal her, Juno suspected the ruse and wiled the heifer out of her husband as a gift. She also set Argus, whose eyes never slept simultaneously, to watch over the heifer. Jupiter, however, sent Mercury, who disguised himself as a shepherd and used his sleep-producing caduceus and a lullaby on the pan pipes to put the monster asleep and slay him. Juno scattered the eyes of Argus upon the peacock and satisfied her jealousy by driving Io over the earth with a tormenting fly. The story is recounted in detail in Ovid's *Metamorphoses,* 1.568-750. One interpretation of this myth is that it is an allegory for the many-starred (eyed) sky being swept away by the morning breeze (Mercury's music). *LLL 3.1.194. MV 5.1.230. Tro 1.2.28.*

Ariachne, *Tro 5.2.155,* metrical variation on Arachne, a weaver. Daughter of Idmon of Colophon, she had earned a great reputation and bragged she wove better than Minerva. The goddess appeared and they competed. Minerva could find no flaw in Arachne's tapestry, and angrily destroyed it. She further tormented the girl with a headache until she hanged herself. In remorse, Minerva lifted her, saving her life, and transformed her into a spider so that she could go on weaving throughout eternity. The story is told in detail in Ovid's *Metamorphoses,* 6.1-145.

Ariadne, daughter of Minos and Pasiphæ; sister of Phædra, Crateus, Deucalion, Glaucus, and others; mother of Thoas, Ceramus, Œnopion, Staphylus and others. She was living in the palace at Cnossos while her father exacted the tribute of Athenian youths and maidens to be fed to the monster Minotaur in the Labyrinth, a prison of such complex passageways that there was no finding one's way out after entering. Theseus arranged to become one of the doomed youths. On his arrival Ariadne fell in love with him and asked Dædalus, who had built the maze (and a dance floor for her), for the secret of it. She provided a ball of thread which Theseus could unwind as he entered the Labyrinth. He slew the Minotaur, escaped with her, and then abandoned her on Naxos on his voyage home. Dionysus rescued and married her, placing the crown from their wedding in the stars as the *corona borealis.* In another version, Theseus put in at Naxos because she was very seasick, a storm blew his ship away, and by the time he got back, she was dead. In other variations, she died of heartbreak for Theseus, in the birth of twin sons, or during a fight between Dionysus and Perseus. The story was widely known throughout the Renaissance, appearing in Ovid, Catullus, Plutarch, and other authors. *MND 2.1.80. TGV 4.4.164.*

Ariel, *Tmp,* spirit servant of Prospero. The name appears to be traditional in the literature of magic, though it is used for widely different spirits. There is an Ariel in the Faust-books, who resists pacts and has to be coerced. The name appears in Isaiah 29, but the relationship, if it exists, is rather forced by critics. Ariel is a man's name in Ezra 8.16. Ariel compares in many ways with Hermes (Mercury) of classical mythology and as she raises St. Elmo's fire on the ships, it is worth noting that the Italians occasionally call the phenomenon St. Hermes' fire. Robert Eden's *History of Travaile* (1577) mentions St. Elmo's fire twice near the mention of Setebos (q.v.), reinforcing the idea that it was used as a source.

Aries, *Tit 4.3.71,* L. 'the Ram,' astrological symbol for a constellation in the northern hemisphere.

Arion, *TN 1.2.14,* F1 'Orion,' Arion of Methymna, legendary poet and singer of the 8th or 7th c. BC. He was supposedly the first to use the dithyramb and play a cithara. He travelled to Sicily to enter a competition and won several prizes. In returning to the court of Periander of Corinth, pirates seized him and threatened to pitch him overboard. As a last request he asked to sing and when he was cast into the sea, a dolphin charmed by his singing bore him safely to land. The story is mentioned in Ovid's *Artis Amatoriæ,* 3.325-26, and Virgil's *Eclogues,* 8.56, but it was widely known. Chaucer's *Hous of Fame* calls the constellation Lyra, 'Arion's harp.'

Aristotle, (384-322 BC), one of the most influential of Greek philosophers, often considered the greatest thinker who has ever lived. Bertrand Russell wrote that it was two thousand years after Aristotle's death before the world would produce a philosopher that was his equal. Born in Stagira, Thessaly as the son of a court physician, he became Plato's student in about 366 and remained at the Academy until his master's death, nearly two decades later. After moving to Assos, he married Pythias, the sister or niece of a tyrant named Hermias, who was later killed by the Persians. Aristotle then fled to Macedonia and became the teacher of Alexander the Great until the boy's sixteenth year. Aristotle lived in Athens from 335 to 323 and headed the Peripatetic school of philosophy at the Lyceum there. In the year of Alexander's death the Athenians revolted, indicted Aristotle for impiety (as they had Socrates), and he withdrew to an estate in Euboea, where he died a year later.

After the fall of Rome, his works were lost to the West, but were introduced in the 9th c. AD to the Islamic world. By the 13th c. he was again familiar to the Latin world, particularly through the works of Thomas Aquinas. His scientific concepts remained official doctrine until the Renaissance and his philosophic concepts and methods are still with us. Most of his extant writings come from his Athenian period and include such works as *Constitution of Athens, Eudemian Ethics, Metaphysics, Nicomachean Ethics, On the Soul, Organon, Physics, Politics,* and *Rhetoric.* His *Poetics,* an essay primarily upon drama, was rediscovered at the beginning of the 16th c. and exerted a powerful influence upon the creation of tragedy thereafter, though it is unclear to what extent this work and commentary upon it may have affected Sh. There is little in the plays to indicate that Sh. was particularly familiar with anything written by Aristotle. *Shr 1.1.32. Tro 2.2.165:* the passage alludes to the *Nicomachean Ethics,* 1.3, and is a blatant anachronism.

Armado, Don Adriano de, 'Señor A.,' a Spanish braggart, pompous and exaggerated in his language. Ferdinand finds him so ridiculous, he enjoys having him in his court. His competition with Costard for the common woman Jaquenetta, however, does end in his success as she is revealed to be pregnant by him in the last act after he has played the role of Hector in the pageant of the Nine Worthies. Like Falstaff or Captain Bobadill of Ben Jonson's *Every Man in His Humour,* Armado belongs in the tradition of the *miles gloriosus* of ancient Roman drama and the Capitano of the *commedia dell'arte.* In the latter, the braggart soldier was often a Spanish enemy of Italy. He has also been described as a satire of the melancholy lover, sharing some characteristics with Malvolio. Some critics have asserted he is based on Sir Walter Raleigh, but this is dubious at best. His name is an obvious mockery of the great Armada which the English defeated in 1588.

Armagnac, feudal district in the south of France between Gascony and Toulouse. At the death of Louis of Orléans in 1407, the count of Armagnac became the leader of the party of French nobles that opposed the duke of Burgundy's ambition to become regent for the mad king, Charles VI. The quarrel that blossomed between the Burgundians and the Armagnacs (or Orléanists) divided France and made it vulnerable to attack from England. The French army that Henry V defeated at Agincourt in 1415 was composed largely of Armagnacs. Vicious mercenary soldiers recruited from the district of Gascony were also called 'Armagnacs.' See Armagnac, Earl of, *1H6.*

Armagnac, Earl of, *1H6 5.1.2, 5.1.17, 5.7.44,* John IV, (fl. 1418), count of Armagnac, leader of a faction of French nobles at Charles VII's court. When madness incapacitated Charles VI, a struggle for control of France erupted between the king's uncle, the duke of Burgundy, and his brother, the duke of Orléans. In 1407 Burgundy assassinated his opponent, Louis of Orléans. Louis' young son, Charles of Orléans, had married the daughter of Bernard VII, count of Armagnac. Bernard succeeded to Louis' position as leader of the Burgundian opposition, a faction subsequently known as 'the Armagnacs.' The Armagnacs were severely weakened in 1415, when Henry V slaughtered their army at Agincourt. Charles of Orléans was carried captive to England, and in 1418 his father-in-law Bernard was killed. The Burgundians joined the English in an assault on northern France, and the Armagnacs were forced to retreat from Paris to their territories in the south. The deaths of Henry V and Charles VI in 1422 began a slow reversal of fortunes. England steadily lost ground on the continent. Burgundy abandoned its alliance with England, and in 1440 the inept young king of England, Henry VI, released Charles of Orléans from captivity—hoping that Orléans could bring about peace with France. When Charles VII, king of France, refused to accept Orleans' mediation, Orléans tried to compel the French king's cooperation by forming a coalition with the dukes of Brittany and Alençon and John IV, count of Armagnac. Henry VI was urged to marry one of John's daughters to cement a bond with his French allies. Charles VII divided his opponents, captured John IV, and confiscated his domain.

Armenia, *Ant 3.6.14, 3.6.35,* ancient nation east of Asia Minor at the headwaters of the Tigris river and south of the strip of land that separates the Black and Caspian seas. Its history is a sad tale of a small nation caught as a pawn between great powers and it is still a site of ethnic conflict. The Medes conquered it c. 521 BC and ruled until Cyrus the Great absorbed it in 549. After Alexander the Great had conquered Persia and weakened it, Armenia became independent, but about a century later it fell to Antiochus the Great. Again it became independent under Tigranes the Great in the 1st and 2nd c. BC, but he was defeated by the Romans in 69 and once again Armenia became a puppet of Rome. In the conflict between the Parthians and the Romans, Armenia tried to remain neutral. In the 3rd c. AD the Persians again captured the country but it was later liberated with the assistance of the emperor Diocletian. The country was converted to Christianity in 303. When the Arabs conquered it in the 7th c., an Armenian prince was retained on the throne and Armenia had a period of prosperity and growth in the 9th and 10th c. Caught between the Byzantines and the Seljuks, however, the country was ravaged and many of its inhabitants fled. Later it was victim of the Mongols, and as an island of Christianity became a bone of contention among the Turks, Persians, and Russians.

Armigero, *MWW 1.1.8, 9,* L. ablative *armiger* 'bearing arms,' and therefore 'esquire': a man owning a coat of arms, a gentleman. Sh. mocks the snobbery that minor gentlemen often developed over their status. 'Nobility' was often purchased by a well-placed bribe in the College of Heralds. It has also been suggested that this is the Italian word for 'valiant at arms,' but that is not in the style of the humor here and there is nothing warlike about Shallow.

Art to Love, The, *Shr 4.2.8,* Ovid's *Artis Amatoriæ.* It was this poem which got the ancient Roman poet exiled. It is a humorous manual on how to develop relationships with the opposite sex. The first book tells men how to find and win a mistress. The second, how to keep her. The third book similarly advises women.

Artemidorus, *JC,* A. of Cnidos, teacher of rhetoric who Plutarch ('Cæsar' 65.1–2) says tried to warn Cæsar of the plot against his life. Artemidorus' post as an instructor in Greek literature would have given him access to aristocratic households where he would have heard rumors of what was afoot in Rome.

Artesius, *TNK 1.1 sd, 1.1.158,* follower of Theseus who is ordered to mobilize the army for the conquest of Thebes. After the first scene he no longer appears. The character does not exist in Chaucer's *Knyghtes Tale,* Sh.'s source, but an 'Artesia' is a female character in Philip Sidney's *Countesse of Pembrokes Arcadia* (1590).

Arthur, legendary Celtic monarch who was said to have reigned over Britain sometime between the departure of its Roman defenders in the 5th c. and the triumph of its Anglo-Saxon conquerors in the 7th. The Celtic peoples of Wales were the first to evolve cycles of tales about an Arthur, and some scholars believe that their ancient legends contain shreds of historical information. He may have been a Roman general from the family Artorius—or a Celtic chieftain with a similar name—who rallied the native Britons to defend their homeland from Anglo-Saxon invaders. The myth of his utopian kingdom of Camelot and the quests of the ideal Christian knights gathered at his round table did not emerge full blown until the 12th c. In 1147 an Oxford scholar, Geoffrey of Monmouth, wrote a fanciful history of ancient Britain (*Historia Regum Britanniæ*) that introduced Arthur to the literary public. In 1155 a Norman chronicler, Robert Wace, used verse (*Roman de Brut*) to popularize and augment Geoffrey's work. Thereafter the production of Arthurian romances became a major medieval industry. *2H4 2.4.32:* Falstaff's reference to Arthur is a jumbled quotation from a ballad entitled 'Sir Lancelot du Lac.' *H5 2.3.9, 10.*

Arthur, duke of Brittaine, *Jn,* (1187–1203), 'Plantagenet,' claimant to the throne of England. By the rule of inheritance that governed succession to feudal estates Arthur had the best claim to the throne vacated by the death of England's childless king, Richard the Lionhearted. Richard was Henry II's third son. Arthur was the son and heir of Geoffrey Plantagenet, Henry's fourth son. It was, however, Henry's fifth son, John, who seized the crown. Brittany refused to acknowledge John's authority, and John knew that so long as Arthur was at liberty his nephew would be a focal point for trouble. Arthur and his mother, Constance, sought help from the king of France, but their Breton subjects were leery of the French and any deal that might compromise Brittany's independence. In 1201 Constance died and left Arthur, at the age of 14, to manage his own affairs. In 1202 John captured Arthur, who was besieging his grandmother at Mirabeau castle. Arthur died while he was in John's keeping, and it was rumored about Europe that John murdered him. The circumstances of his death are unknown. Some sources claim that John lost his temper and killed the boy with his own hands. Others say that John simply ordered Arthur's death. Sh.'s claim that Hubert de Burgh failed to carry out John's orders to blind Arthur is based on a tale from the chronicle of Ralph of Coggeshall. Sh.'s account of Arthur's death takes liberties with history. Arthur died in France, not England, and by medieval standards he was an adult, not a child.

Arthur, Prince, *H8 3.2.71,* (1487-1502), Henry VII's eldest son and heir to his throne. On 14 November 1501, young Arthur wed Katherine of Aragon, daughter of Ferdinand and Isabella of Spain. The prince died five months later, and his brother Henry succeeded to his offices and to his wife (June 1509). Arthur's youth and ill health had probably prevented the consummation of his marriage with Katherine, but a papal dispensation was obtained to settle doubts about the propriety of a wedding between Henry and his former sister-in-law. Katherine's failure, after eighteen years of marriage, to bear Henry VIII a son determined Henry to separate from her. He argued that their union was, despite the pope's blessing, contrary to God's law (Leviticus 20:21) prohibiting sexual congress between a man and his brother's wife. When the papal court rejected Henry's argument and refused to grant him a divorce from Katherine, he withdrew England from the Roman Catholic communion.

Artois, *1H6 2.1.9,* county near the city of Calais, the port on the English channel that was the only continental property remaining in English hands at the end of the Hundred Years' War. Disputes over the ownership of the county of Artois caused tensions between Burgundy and France.

Arviragus, *Cym,* son of Cymbeline, kidnapped as a baby with his brother Guiderius by Belarius and reared in the wilderness of Cambria as Cadwal. When the brothers encounter their sister Innogen in disguise, they immediately develop a strong liking for her, but their true identities are not revealed until they become heroes in the battle between the British and the Romans. The lost prince or princess who is rediscovered is a standard ingredient of romance. Sh. may have borrowed the name from Harrison's *Description of Britaine* (1587), in which an Arviragus' son Marius is mentioned. Juvenal's *Satires,* 4.127, uses Arviragus as the name of a famous soldier from Britain. In Spenser's *Færie Queene,* 2.10.50, Arvirage, the brother and successor of Kimbeline, wars mightily against the Romans. Arveragus is also mentioned in Chaucer's *Frankeleyns Tale.*

Ascanius, *2H6 3.2.116,* son of the Trojan hero, Æneas. In classical mythology several incompatible claims are made for him. According to one legend Ascanius remained in Asia Minor after the fall of Troy and established a new kingdom on its ruins. Another tale says that he accompanied his father to Italy. Yet another version of this story makes him a son born to Æneas and the Italian princess, Lavinia, daughter of King Latinus. This was the tradition favored by the Julians, the family that produced Rome's first emperors. The Julians believed that Ascanius was also known as 'ilus,' the root of their name, and that he was their eponymous ancestor.

Ascension Day, *Jn 4.2.151, 5.1.22, 26,* annual Christian festival that commemorates the resurrected Christ's entrance into heaven. It is celebrated forty days after Easter, which means that, like Easter, it is a moveable feast whose date is determined by the first full moon of the spring equinox.

Ash Wednesday, *MV 2.5.26,* first day of Lent, seven Wednesdays before Easter, a day when Catholics smear ashes on their foreheads as a sign of penitence. Lancelot in this scene seems to be speaking nonsense to mock his master.

Asher House, *H8 3.2.232,* or Esher House, a country house belonging to the bishop of Winchester. It was about 15 mi. west of London near Cardinal Wolsey's palace at Hampton Court.

Ashford, *2H6 3.1.357,* town in the county of Kent, 14 mi. southwest of Canterbury. It was one of the places at which the rebellion named for Jack Cade erupted.

Asia, name Greek geographers gave to the district between the eastern shore of the Mediterranean and India and China. It derives from ancient Akkadian for 'place of the rising sun.' Sh. and his contemporaries thought of it as an exotic place rich in gold, jewels, and wonders. *Ado 2.1.250. Err 1.1.133. 2H4 2.4.161. Ant 1.2.94.*

Asnath, *2H6 1.4.39,* F1 'Asmath,' the demon whom Sh. says necromancers contacted during a seance attended by Eleanor Cobham, duchess of Gloucester. The name may be a scrambled version of 'Satan' (spelled 'Sathan' by many of Sh.'s contemporaries). The mixing of letters in names was a common magician's technique. He could also be Asmodeus of the Book of Tobit in the Apocrypha. Because of his love for Sara, daughter of Raguel, he successively causes the death of seven of her bridegrooms on their wedding nights. Because of this, Asmodeus is a demon of marital unhappiness, which might relate thematically to the disruptive marriage between Henry VI and Margaret of Anjou. Asmodeus derives from the Avestan *Aeshma,* 'spirit of anger.' At the end of his appearance Asnath is dismissed to hell, the place from which he presumably came.

Aspinall, Alexander, *Var,* schoolmaster at the Stratford grammar school from 1582 to his death in 1624. His name appears in a 'posy' ascribed to Sh. in a manuscript compiled by Sir Francis Fane of Bulbeck (1611-1680). The manuscript is in possession of the Shakespeare Birthplace Trust Records Office (MS ER.93). The little poem 'Shaxpaire upon a peaire of gloves that maser sent to his mistris' was possibly intended to accompany a gift of gloves purchased from John Shakespeare to be given by Aspinall to his second wife, Anne Shaw, whom he married in 1594. Aspinall was born in Lancashire and received a B.A. at Oxford in 1575 and an M.A. in 1578. In the original, for unknown reasons the name is given 'A shey ander Asbenall,' possibly an inside joke. E. I. Fripp argued in 1938 that the schoolmaster was the inspiration for Holofernes.

Assurance, Sir. *Shr 5.2.67,* Petruccio's mocking name for Baptista Minola.

Astræa, daughter of Zeus. She lived among human beings during the Golden Age that Greek mythology postulated as the first era in world history. When the blessedness of the original state of humanity faded, Astræa was the last of the gods to leave the earth. She symbolizes innocence and purity. Virgo is her constellation in the heavens. Astræa's mother, Themis, is the goddess who is often depicted holding the scales of justice. According to legend, the reappearance on earth of these divine females will herald the return of the Golden Age. *1H6 1.8.4:* Joan, the 'maid' of Arc, reminded her friends of the virgin goddess, for she, they hoped, was the harbinger of a glorious future for her homeland. *Tit 4.3.4.*

Atalanta, mythological daughter of Schoeneus of Boeotia, famed for her fleetness. An oracle warned her that marriage would be the end of her happiness so she announced that any suitor would have to race her. If he defeated her, they would wed. If not, he would be put to death. Hippomenes, judge of one of her races, offered himself and appealed to Venus for help. The goddess gave him three golden apples from

Cyprus, the island sacred to her. Each time Atalanta gained ground on Hippomenes he dropped one of the apples and Atalanta stooped to pick it up. This slowed her enough for him to win. In their celebration, however, they neglected to honor Venus, who contrived to make them yield to their sexual desires in a holy grotto, defiling the place. They were changed into lions and forced to draw Cybele's chariot. The story is told in Ovid's *Metamorphoses,* 10. Atalanta was also a participant in the Calydonian boar hunt with Meleager (q.v.) *AYLI 3.2.144, 3.2.271,* 'A's heels,' swiftness.

Ate, daughter of Zeus and Eris (Roman Discordia), a minor Greek goddess who inspired human beings and gods to rash, morally blind, or ill-considered deeds. In some stories she resembles Nemesis, a deity whose advice caused her victims to bring disaster on their own heads. *LLL 5.2.681,* 'more Ates,' more provocation. *Jn 2.1.63. Ado 2.1.239,* 'infernal A. in good apparel,' the reference seems to be to an episode in Edmund Spenser's *Færie Queene* (4.1.19-30) in which Ate and the false Duessa enter 'in good apparel' to hide 'vile treason and foul falsehood.' *JC 3.1.274.*

Athenian, 1) (n.) native of Athens. *MND 2.2.73, 3.2.41, 352, 4.1.27. Tim. Lr 3.4.169 (Q 11.166):* Lear is calling the Fool his philosopher, like Plato and Aristotle of the School of Athens. *TNK 3.1.3,* (pl.).

2) (adj.) Of or pertaining to Athens. *MND. Tro Prol.6,* 'A. bay': Piræus is the port of Athens and has three natural harbors on its promontory. The largest was the Cantharus on the west, with the Zea and Munychia on the southwest and southeast. The promontory overlooks the bays of Salamis and Faliron which are parts of the Saronic gulf.

Athens, capital of ancient Attica and frequently capital of Greece. It is located in the central plain of Attica about 4 mi. from the Gulf of Ægina, a part of the Ægean sea enclosed by the Peloponnese peninsula and mainland Greece. In mythology it was founded in 1550 BC by Cecrops, the son of Gæa, who had the body of a man and the lower parts of a dragon. He named Zeus as supreme god and instituted marriage rites and monogamy. He also decided that the patronage of the city (and thus its name) would go to Athena, goddess of wisdom, rather than Poseidon, because she gave the olive tree to the city. It was also important as the city of Theseus, the great hero. In fact, the Acropolis (a plateau at the center) has been occupied since Neolithic times and was fortified during the Bronze Age. Early Athens somehow resisted the Dorian invasions and remained an Ionic Greek speaking city (linking it with the islands and Asia Minor) and it enters history as an aristocracy already moving towards democracy under the various rulerships of Cylon, Draco, Solon, Peisistratus, and Cleisthenes. The political situation had stabilized somewhat when Athens was threatened from outside, as were all the Greek peoples, by the Persian Empire under King Darius. The incredible victory at Marathon, only 14 mi. from Athens, preserved Greek independence (490 BC), but led to the punitive invasion by Darius' son Xerxes. During these wars Athens was twice captured and looted, but in 479 BC the Persians were routed at Platæa.

Gradually the Delian League, set up to protect Greece from the Persians, evolved into an Athenian Empire. Under Pericles (443-429 BC), Athenian culture exploded and the city grew into the center of classical civilization. Walls were built to the seaport of Piræus; the Parthenon, the temple of Athena Nike, and the Erectheum were built. The theater of Dionysius presented the great plays of Greek antiquity. All of this happened in an extraordinarily brief period, but its legacy is still with us. Athens' power began to decline during the Peloponnesian War with Sparta from 431-404 BC. Sparta was unable to maintain its control, but the empire was gone and Athens fell under the rule of Philip of Macedon in 338 BC. Rome captured the city in 146 and it was sacked in 86. Despite all this the schools established by Plato and Aristotle continued, symbolizing Athens' preeminent position as a seat of learning throughout the ancient period. The Visigoths damaged the city in 395 AD and in 529 Justinian closed the pagan schools, thus destroying what glory the city had left. The Byzantine Empire left it a cultural backwater. In 1204, the Crusaders sacked Constantinople and Athens became a French duchy. In 1311, Catalans captured it only to be replaced by a Florentine dynasty. In 1458, the Turks gained control of it and turned the Parthenon into a mosque. In Sh.'s time this was the status of the city, just another town under Ottoman control. It would remain so for nearly four centuries, until the 1830's. The very name of Athens, however, excited in the Renaissance, as now, the vision of the beautiful, intellectually vibrant city of the 5th c.

MND, setting. Though Theseus is shown as king, Sh. is thinking of the city as a seat of civilization, more Renaissance than Classical. Like most of Sh.'s comedic settings, it bears no particular resemblance to the historical (or even mythologic) place. The fairies' remark that the 'weeds of A.' (clothes) are recognizable, but whatever Sh. thought was distinctive about them is unknown. It may only mean city clothes as distinct from rustic garb, or as distinct from fairy garb. *Tro Prol.3,* 'port of A.,' the city is inland and uses Piræus as a port. By the Peloponnesian war, there were attempts to connect Athens to Piræus by means of three walls called the 'Long Walls.' The original Piræus was destroyed by the Romans in 86 BC, but was rebuilt when Athens became the capital of a revived Greece. Piræus went from a few hundred inhabitants in 1834 to near 50,000 by the turn of the century.

Tim, setting. *Ant 3.1.35, 3.6.64, 3.12.15. Per 6.34.* 'a knight of A.,' one of Thaisa's suitors *TNK 1.1.222, 1.4.49, 2.1.38, 2.3.49, 5.6.55,* Theseus' dukedom.

Athol, Scottish earldom named for a district in northern Perthshire. See Athol, Earl of, *1H4.*

Athol, Earl of, *1H4 1.1.72,* Walter Stuart or Stewart (d. 1437), second son of Robert II, king of Scotland. Sh.'s reference to an earl of Athol among the prisoners the Percies captured at the battle of Holmedon may be an anachronism. The earldom of Athol had escheated to the crown in 1341 and may not yet have been bestowed on Walter when he fought at Holmedon in 1402. After being ransomed, Walter returned to a Scotland that was in turmoil. By 1406 Robert III concluded that he could no longer guarantee the safety of his son and heir, the future James I, and he directed that the boy be sent to France. The scheme miscarried. The English captured the boat on which the prince sailed, and Robert died of grief at the news of the fate that had befallen his son. Robert's brother, the duke of Albany, became regent for the absent James I and did nothing to win his nephew's release. James grew up in England as Henry IV's ward, and Albany ruled Scotland for eighteen years.

When Albany died, Walter (Athol) negotiated a truce with England that permitted James to return to Scotland. The new king soon came to a parting of the ways with his sponsors. The Scottish barons were accustomed to a freedom that bordered on license. But James had spent most of his life in England, and he looked to the example of the English monarchy to provide him with models to guide his administration of Scotland. When James tried to impose a strong royal government on the Scots, he forfeited their support and was assassinated (1437). Walter was one of the conspirators against James. He hoped to win the throne for his grandson, Robert Stuart, but his scheme failed. He was captured, tortured, and executed by members of a rival faction.

Atlas, one of the Titans, the class of gods who, according to Greek mythology, ruled the world before the birth of Zeus and the Olympians. As punishment for joining his fellows in a war against Zeus, Atlas was condemned to hold aloft the weight of the heavens. In some stories Atlas was transformed into a mountain that served as the pillar supporting the sky. Artists often depict him as a giant carrying the world on his shoulders, and his name became equivalent to a book of maps when such an image was placed on the title page of Rumold Mercator's edition of his father's maps in 1595. A similar image of

Hercules substituting for Atlas in the labor of the golden apples of the Hesperides has long been believed to have been on the sign of the Globe theater, built in 1599. *3H6 5.1.36. Ant 1.5.23.*

Atropos, *2H4 2.4.196,* one of the Fates, the female divinities who in classical mythology determine human destiny. The name means 'inflexible.'

Audrey, *AYLI,* goatherd married by Touchstone. The name is a drastically reduced form of Etheldreda, who was the founder of Ely church but called St. Audrey by the locals. The name was not unusual in Sh.'s time in England or France.

Aufidius, Tullus, *Cor,* leader of ancient Italy's Volscian tribe and a resident of the city of Antium. Sh. found the character in Plutarch's 'Coriolanus' 22. Plutarch says that Aufidius was a man renowned for his courage who recognized the same virtue in his former opponent, Coriolanus. Aufidius persuaded the Volsci to shelter Coriolanus, when he was driven out of Rome, and to use him to avenge themselves on Rome. *Cor 5.6.128,* pl.

Augustus, *Cym 2.4.11, 5.6.83. 3.1.1, 63,* 'A. Cæsar.' See Octavius Cæsar.

Aulis, *TNK 1.1.211,* Q 'Anly,' 'at the banks of A.,' port on the coast of Boeotia northeast of Thebes, located between two bays and on the Euripus river. It is most famous as the site where the invasion force for Troy assembled and was stalled by unfavorable winds. Agamemnon then sacrificed his daughter Iphigenia to placate the gods.

Aumerle, Aumale, Albemarle, or Aubemale, originally a territory in Normandy. Odo of Champagne, brother-in-law of William the Conqueror, founded the first line of counts. When Philip Augustus annexed Normandy to France, the title was continued by William de Fortibus and his heirs in England as 'earl of Albemarle.' Aumale became part of various French noble houses' lands. The name is from L. *Alba Marla.*

Aumerle, Duke of, *R2,* Albermarle, Edward of Norwich (1373–1415), earl of Rutland, second duke of York, grandson of England's King Edward III. As a young courtier, Rutland (not yet the duke of Aumerle) enjoyed the favor of his cousin, Richard II, at whose coronation he was knighted. Richard appointed him admiral of the fleet and constable of the Tower of London, and in 1394 he fought in the king's first campaign in Ireland. He negotiated a peace with France that was ratified by Richard's second marriage (to Isabella, daughter of Charles VI). Rutland sided with Richard against the 'lords appellant,' a party of nobles who wanted to limit the king's freedom of action. In July 1397, the earl helped Richard carry out a plan to destroy his opponents. Thomas of Woodstock (the duke of Gloucester), Thomas Arundel (the bishop of Ely), and Thomas Beauchamp (the earl of Warwick) were arrested and executed or exiled. Rutland's reward was the dukedom of Aumerle (a part of Gloucester's estate) and Gloucester's office as constable of England. In the later capacity, Aumerle was scheduled to preside at a trial by combat that Richard ordered Henry (IV) Bolingbroke and Thomas Mowbray to fight in September, 1398. The duel did not take place, for Richard decided instead to exile both men.

In 1399, while Aumerle and Richard were in Ireland mounting a second expedition for its conquest, word arrived that Henry had returned from exile and was raising a rebellion. Aumerle returned to England with Richard. And although Richard's men defected and the king's situation quickly deteriorated, Aumerle encouraged Richard to fight and remained with him until he capitulated to Henry. At Henry's first parliament Aumerle was accused of complicity in the murder of his uncle, Thomas of Woodstock, one of the 'lords appellant.' Aumerle had been sent by Richard to arrest the duke of Gloucester in the coup of 1397, and Gloucester had subsequently died or been killed while in prison in

Calais. As punishment for the crime, Henry stripped Aumerle of his ducal title and degraded him to his former rank of earl of Rutland. Sh.'s story of Rutland's implication in a plot to kill Henry is not supported by any historical evidence or by Henry's subsequent behavior toward him. Henry gave Rutland a full pardon in 1401 and entrusted him with the defense of England's French possessions in Aquitaine. In 1402 Henry allowed Rutland to succeed to his father's duchy of York. The new duke of York was not, however, firmly committed to Henry.

In 1405 York concluded that he had been inadequately reimbursed for expenses incurred carrying out his duties in France and Wales, and he joined the barons of northern England in an attempt to overthrow Henry. The uprising failed, but again York suffered only mild punishment. At the start of Henry V's reign, York was assigned an important military post on the Scottish border, and the duke joined Henry's expedition to France in 1415. York was among the very few English nobles who died on the field at Agincourt.

Aurora, Roman goddess of the dawn (Greek: Eos), child of either Uranus and Gaia or Hyperion and Theia, mother of Memnon. Aurora had a penchant for loving mortals which usually was disastrous. In Ovid's *Metamorphoses,* 7, she carries away Cephalus against his will and when he remains in love with his wife Procris, Aurora plants the ideas that bring about his accidentally killing Procris. In the writings of Horace and Apollodorus, she also fell in love with Tithonus, son of Laomedon, snatching him away and begging Jove to grant him immortality. She forgot, however, to ask that Tithonus not age. He faded physically and was closed up in a chamber from which his weak voice emerged. Ultimately she turned him into a grasshopper. Ovid also tells (Bk. 13) of Aurora's grief at the death of Memnon (her son by Tithonus). Memnon, king of the Ethiopians, went to the Trojan War and performed bravely until killed by Achilles. Aurora pleaded with Jove to grant her son some honor. The ash from Memnon's fire became birds called Memnonides which circled and fought, dying back in the fire. Each year this spectacle would be repeated. Aurora's many tears for Memnon became the dew.

MND 3.2.381, 'A.'s harbinger,' the morning star, Venus. *Rom 1.1.133,* 'A's bed,' the seat of dawn. An image of Aurora may have been in Sh.'s mind from his source Arthur Brooke's *Tragicall Historye of Romeus and Juliet* (1562), where Aurora clears the sky and chases shade from the earth on the morning after Romeo and Juliet consummate their marriage (l. 1707-08). At this point in his play Sh. substituted the passage about the lark and the nightingale.

Austria, *Jn 3.1.40,* nation surrounded by Germany, Czechoslovakia, Hungary, Yugoslavia, Italy, and Switzerland. In Sh.'s day it was a duchy belonging to the Holy Roman Empire and the seat of the empire's Hapsburg rulers, but at the time of King John it was a minor state and its margrave was vassal to the duke of Bavaria. The nation derived its name from the Eastern March (Ostmark) which Charlemagne established at the end of the 8th c. to stop further invasions from the east. Eventually the area became known as the Österreich (Eastern Kingdom). Since it commanded the Danube valley, a highway into Europe from the east, Austria was Europe's bulwark against invasion by the Ottoman Turks. See Austria, Duke of.

Austria, Duke of, 1) *Jn,* character Sh. formed by combining two of Richard the Lionhearted's enemies into one: Guidomar, viscount of Limoges (d. 1200); and Leopold of Babenberg, duke of Austria (d. 1195). The former was a vassal of Richard's. He and the king disputed ownership of a buried treasure found on one of the fiefs granted to Guidomar, and in 1199 Richard died besieging Guidomar's castle. The latter was Richard's ally on the third crusade. He and Richard quarreled at the siege of Acre, and Leopold avenged himself in 1192 by capturing and imprisoning Richard as Richard headed home to England through Austrian territory. Leopold was already dead when the events in *Jn* transpired. The confusion of the characters originated in a play (*The Troublesome Raigne of John, King of England*) that Sh. may have used as a source for *Jn*.

2) *AWW 1.2.5,* kinsman of the king of France. He has requested that the French refuse any requests for aid from the duke of Florence. The Austrians (Hapsburgs, Holy Roman Emperors) often had designs on Tuscany.

Austringer, *AWW 5.1.6, 5.3.129,* F1 'a gentle Astringer,' a gentleman who raises goshawks (short-winged hawks) for falconry. The sport is never mentioned nor is it relevant to the plot, so the designation is probably a matter of making him more colorful, perhaps with a hawk on his arm or some other emblem on his costume. The title is derived from the Old Fr. *hostur* or *ostour,* 'goshawk.'

Authority, *MM 1.2.112, Add'l 1.2.37,* personification of official power, as 'demigod' implies, originating in God and implemented by divinely appointed human agents.

Autolycus, *WT,* delightful cony-catcher ('con man'), onetime servant to Florizel. His cynical manipulations add a more down to earth quality to the pastoral romance of the play, while his songs and humor make an audience forgive his deceitfulness. Autolycus in mythology was the son of Hermes (Mercury) and Chione who gave birth to both Autolycus and Philammon (by Apollo) in the same day. As one of the Argonauts, Autolycus taught Hercules how to wrestle, took Amyntor's helmet, and stole cattle by changing their identifying marks. Sh.'s Autolycus is a character slightly based upon Capnio in the source story, Robert Greene's *Pandosto,* or the Triumph of Time (1588; rptd. 1607 as *Dorastus and Fawnia*), and draws on materials from Robert Greene's various pamphlets on cony-catching (confidence games), 1591-92. Greene was also the author of the main source of *WT.*

It is most likely Sh. took the name from the mythological thief whose birth is described in Ovid's *Metamorphoses,* 11, where his cleverness is stated. Martial (*Epigrams* 8.59) also mentions Autolycus' prowess as a thief. It has also been suggested that the name may have been taken from a work by Lucian, but this is less likely. The name also occurs in Plutarch (from whom Sh. frequently borrowed) in his biography of Lucullus. This Autolycus is said to be a son of Deimachus who accompanied Hercules on the expedition against the Amazons. Autolycus is also the name of Odysseus' grandfather in the *Odyssey* and a passage in Bk. 19 calls him an incomparable liar and thief with a special relationship to Hermes. It is questioned, though, whether Sh. could have read a translation of this by the time of his writing *WT.* The meaning of Autolycus is 'All-wolf' or 'Wolf's self,' reflecting his predatory business.

Auvergne, former province and countship in Aquitaine. At one point it became part of the English crown under Henry II because of his marriage to Eleanor of Aquitaine. It was later disputed and divided into four feudal territories that evolved in south central France during the early Middle Ages: the county of Auvergne, the dauphiné of Auvergne, the duchy of Auvergne, and the episcopal county of Clermont. The fief from which the dauphin, the heir to the French throne, took his title was not the dauphiné of Auvergne, but the dauphiné de Viennois. The area was named for the Celtic tribe of the Arverni, whose most famous warrior was Vercingetorix, Cæsar's opponent. See Auvergne, Countess of, *1H6.*

Auvergne, Countess of, *1H6,* character invented by Sh. The story of an interview between a French noblewoman and Lord Talbot does not appear in any of the historical sources used by Sh. Folk tales (like the Robin Hood narratives) might have provided Sh. with a model for the episode, and there were two women who might have suggested the Auvergne name to him. John II, duke of Bourbon, was count of Clermont, one of the four lordships of Auvergne, when he married Charles VII's daughter, Jane. Jane might have been the countess Sh. had in mind. By having the sister of the king of France acknowledge Talbot's prowess Sh. testified to the stature of the hero of his play. The queen of France at the start of Sh.'s career was Catherine de Médicis (1519–1589), a former countess of Auvergne. Three of her sons succeeded to the throne, and Catherine had considerable influence in formulating policies that were of concern to Elizabethan England. By having 'the countess of Auvergne' capitulate to Talbot, Sh. suggested France's implicit acknowledgement of England's invincibility.

Ave Maries, term for the Rosary, a pious discipline that entails the recitation of sequences of prayers: 15 'Pater Nosters' and 'Glorias' and 15 'Aves.' L. *Ave Maria* 'Hail Mary' is the beginning of the recitation. *2H6 1.3.59. 3H6 2.1.162.*

B

Babion, *TNK,* Q 'Bavian,' a character in the morris dance. The word is an archaic spelling of 'baboon.' The rural fellow dressed as the Babion says nothing except when taking instructions from Gerald the Schoolmaster at *3.5,* when he is warned not to offend the ladies in a passage somewhat reminiscent of the lion passage in *MND 1.2.60-78.* He is described (*134*) as having a 'long tail and eke long tool,' meaning a long phallus. Besides the fact that real baboons—creatures of great wonder to Renaissance Englishmen—have a tendency to indelicate displays, this detail of the costume was also characteristic of ancient Greek satyr plays. It is usually assumed that there was also a She-babion in the morris dance, as in Francis Beaumont's antimasque to *The Masque of Grayes-Inn and the Inner Temple* (1613).

Babylon, city on the Euphrates river founded in the second millennium BC by the Amorites, capital of several ancient Mesopotamian empires. *H5 2.3.36,* 'whore of B.,' allusion to an image from Revelation 17:5: 'Babylon the great, mother of harlots and of earth's abominations.' Babylon owed its unfortunate reputation in the Bible to its king, Nebuchadnezzar, who in 587 BC sacked Jerusalem, destroyed its temple, and forced the Jews into exile. The name of the city remains a sobriquet for any place of remarkable decadence, such as Hollywood. 'Whore of B.' was also frequently used in the Reformation as a Protestant epithet for the Roman pope, curia, or church. Luther frequently refers to Rome as Babylon, for example. *TN 2.3.75,* a fragment from a song called 'the godly and constant Wyfe [wise?] Susanna.'

Bacchanals, *MND 5.1.48 (add. 31),* Bacchæ, worshippers of Bacchus who killed and mutilated Orpheus.

Bacchus, Roman name for the Greek deity Dionysos, god of wine, ecstacy, and inspiration. 'Bacchus' derives from a Gr. epithet meaning 'raucous,' and was a description of the god's characteristic behavior, for he was habitually intoxicated and accompanied by a band of drunken revellers. Classical mythology contains strange stories about the origin and adventures of Bacchus. The god Jupiter sired him by a human female, Semele, the daughter of Cadmus king of Thebes. Semele burst into flame when she insisted on seeing her divine lover in his full glory, and Jupiter took drastic steps to save the child she carried. He sewed the fetus into a gash in his thigh and created a surrogate womb where it could come to term. Jupiter's spouse, Juno, harbored a deep hatred for her husband's love child. She persecuted Bacchus, drove him mad, and forced him to wander the earth seeking refuge. Bacchus ultimately vindicated his claim to a place in the company of the gods on Olympus. His cult was particularly popular with women. 'Bacchants' were rumored to hold midnight orgies at which live animals and men were torn limb from limb. See Orpheus.

LLL 4.3.315, 'dainty B.' *Ant 2.7.111.*

Bagot, *R2,* William, (d. 1407), sheriff of Leicester and one of Richard II's unpopular ministers. In 1397 he helped the king bring down his enemies, the 'lords appellant,' by proposing their condemnation in parliament. He was one of the regents Richard left in charge of England when the king embarked on his second Irish expedition in 1399. Bagot came to Ireland to bring Richard news of Henry (IV) Bolingbroke's invasion, and he returned to England with Richard to fight Henry. He was imprisoned when Richard surrendered, and he was the only one of Richard's intimates to survive to stand trial. At the inquest into his conduct in office he accused the duke of Aumerle of murdering his uncle Thomas of Woodstock, duke of Gloucester. The charge led to Aumerle's demotion to the rank of earl of Rutland. Bagot served a term of imprisonment in the Tower of London before being freed to live out the remainder of his life on his rural estates.

Bajazet, *AWW 4.1.42,* 'B's mute,' F1 'Baiazeth's Mule.' Bayezid I (c. 1360-1403) was sultan of the Ottomans (1389-1402). After several major victories in the Balkans, he was very close to destroying what was left of the Byzantine Empire. He attempted to starve out Constantinople by means of a blockade that lasted a decade, but the Mongol Tamburlaine (Timur Khan) attacked Anatolia and Bajazet was decisively beaten at Ankara. He died a prisoner. Bajazeth is a character in Christopher Marlowe's *Tamburlaine* (c. 1587, published 1590). He is imprisoned in a mobile iron cage drawn by Moors. Most of the time he spends cursing Tamburlaine, but ultimately brains himself against the cage bars. The meaning of Sh.'s passage is obscure. The sense is that Paroles regrets his quickness to boast, but how this relates to Bajazet is a mystery. Possibly there is some lost story about the sultan cutting the tongue from someone, or Tamburlaine's cutting out the sultan's. Perhaps the line is related to *H5 1.2.231-2:* 'or else our grave,/Like Turkish mute, shall have a tongueless mouth.'

Balthasar, 1) *Err,* merchant friend of Antipholus of Ephesus. When his friend is locked out of his own house, Balthasar persuades him that breaking in will serve no purpose but ruining his and his wife's reputation.

2) *Rom,* Romeo's servant. In the first act he joins Abraham in squabbling with the Capulets. In the final act he serves largely as a messenger, telling Romeo that Juliet is dead, then goes with Romeo to Juliet's tomb and is given a letter to Romeo's father which he later gives to the Prince of Verona. In early editions at *5.2.22* the stage direction says Peter, but most editors believe Balthasar is meant. One explanation for the confusion might be that Kemp doubled the roles (see Peter).

3) *MV 3.4.45,* Portia's servant sent to acquire the legal advice and robes of her cousin, the eminent doctor of laws Bellario.

4) *MV 4.1.152, 163,* Portia in her disguise as a young judge. Perhaps she adopts the name from her servant, or Sh. is not being particularly inventive in this situation.

5) *Ado,* attendant to Don Pedro. In *2.3,* he is forced to sing, despite protestations of his poor voice. If the actor were indeed a poor singer, there is an opportunity for humor in it, but later he sings at Hero's 'rites,' which is less easy to imagine as a moment of parody. If the actor were a popular singer with Sh.'s audience, his protestations might be a kind of toying with the audience and Don Pedro's remarks about his mere adequacy, ironic—as if, for example, Luciano Pavarotti were making a cameo appearance. Benedick's remarks about his 'bad voice' would either confirm the poorness of his singing or the irony, however it was played.

In F1, the stage directions call Balthasar 'Iacke Wilson,' indicating the actor or musician who played the role at some point. There are two main candidates, a singer who is recorded as having been hired by the city on occasion, and a John Wilson (1595-1674) who was a composer. The latter, however, was much too young to have appeared in the earliest performances. There is always the possibility of a 'Jack Wilson' otherwise unknown to us. Many editors feel that Balthasar's flirting with Margaret at the masked ball (*2.1.90-101*) which is shared with Benedick in F1 and Q should be attributed to Borachio who is later proven to have a relationship with her.

Banbury, *MWW 1.1.119,* town in Oxfordshire on the Cherwell river, known for its Puritans, its cheese, and a type of currant cake. It was also the site of the famous Banbury cross of nursery rhyme which was destroyed by the Puritans in 1602 as being too heathen. The cheeses were only an inch or so thick. Calling Slender a 'Banbury cheese' would refer primarily to his gauntness, but also to his disapproval of Falstaff's friends.

Banister, *H8 2.1.110,* Ralph, trusted agent who betrayed Buckingham to Richard III. When the rebellion led by Henry Stafford, second duke of Buckingham, collapsed, the duke fled for his life. He asked Banister, one of his retainers, to hide him from the king, but Banister betrayed him for the price that Richard had put on his head.

Richard rewarded Banister with one of the manors confiscated from Buckingham's estate.

Banquo, *Mac,* Macbeth's companion in arms, later murdered by him and tormenting him in the form of a ghost, father of Fleance. In the mythology of Stuart descent, James I was supposedly a descendant of Lord Banquo; however, modern historians have found no evidence for this and few of them believe Banquo was an historical person at all, though he may have been based upon some ancient Scottish leader. Raphael Holinshed's *Chronicles* (Sh.'s source) have Banquo as a co-conspirator against Duncan who is killed by Macbeth for what he knows. Why Sh. sanitized the king's supposed ancestor is obvious, but Banquo's failing to act on the witches' prophecy that he will father a line of kings counterbalances Macbeth's immediate fascination with his future as king.

Baptista 1) *Shr,* see 2) below, see Minola, B.

2) *Ham 3.2.228,* wife of Gonzago in the play presented by Hamlet to entrap Claudius. As a man's name it is usually part of *Gianbattista,* 'John the Baptist.' Predominantly a male name in It., it has a common feminine ending and has often been used by women. For example, the wife of Federico da Montefeltro, one of the most celebrated dukes of Urbino, was Battista Sforza. See 'Murder of Gonzago.'

Bar, seat of the duchy of Bar, a medieval feudal state located 125 mi. east of Paris. See Bar, Edouard, duke of, *H5.*

Bar, Edouard, duke of, *H5 3.5.42, 4.8.98,* (d. 1415), one of the important French nobles whom Holinshed (3.555) lists as casualties of the battle at Agincourt.

Bar'son, *2H4 5.3.91,* possibly a reference to either Barston or Barcheston, towns in Warwickshire.

Barabbas, 'stock of B.,' *MV 4.1.293,* the Jews. Barabbas is a thief in the New Testament. Upon being offered by Pontius Pilate the release of either Jesus or him, the mob demanded Barabbas' release, thus assuring Jesus' crucifixion. Sh. would also have been very much aware that the main character of Christopher Marlowe's *Jew of Malta,* the competing 'Jew play' which provided the commercial impetus for *MV,* was 'Barabas.'

Barbara, *TNK 3.5.26,* Q 'Barbery,' one of the morris participants.

Barbary, 1) northern coast of the African continent between Egypt and the Atlantic. The Barbary States were semi-autonomous under Ottoman rule beginning in the 16th c., including Algeria, Tunisia, Tripolitania, and Morocco. The name comes from the Greek for a foreigner, one whose speech sounds like 'bar bar,' a barbarian, a Berber. Much of the sugar consumed in Europe in Sh.'s day was produced there. The district was also famous for its horses, but exported many other things. See Barbary 2).

1H4 2.5.74. MV 3.2.267, one of Antonio's failed ventures was bound from Barbary. *AYLI 4.1.142,* 'B. cock-pigeon.' *2H4 2.4.96,* 'B. hen,' a Guinea fowl or harmless barnyard bird. *Oth 1.1.113-14,* 'B. horse': some of the most expensive horses were imported from stud farms in Barbary. A 'Barb' was one of medieval Europe's valuable equine breeds. Iago is nastily comparing Othello to an animal. *TNK 3.5.61,* 'Barbary-a,' a song effect.

2) *R2 5.5.78,* Richard II's favorite horse which, Sh. claims, Henry IV rode to his coronation. Since no historical source is found for this story and some chroniclers report that Henry walked in his coronation procession, it is possible that Sh. invented the tale of the faithless horse. Richard was known for his enthusiasm for fine horses (see 'B. horse,' *Oth,* above).

3) *Oth 4.3.25, 32,* F1 'Barbarie,' Desdemona's mother's maid, perhaps named for her country of origin.

Barbason, demon derived from 'Barbas,' who appears in the shape of a lion and is mentioned in Reginald Scot's *Discoverie of Witchcraft* (1584), and 'Barbason,' a French warrior who met Henry V in single combat at the siege of Melun (Holinshed, 3.577). The change from Barbas to the French warrior's name may be either a confusion of memory or an attempt to make three syllables to parallel the other demons mentioned. *H5 2.1.52. MWW 2.2.287.*

Bardolph, Lieutenant, one of Prince Harry's youthful companions, a coward. He is red-faced, apparently from drinking, and is hanged for robbing a church during Henry V's French campaign. This death sentence is one way in which Henry establishes that he is not corrupted by his old friendships. Bardolph is the same character who bears the name 'Rossill' in *1H4* Q1-6. Sh. changed the name when he transformed Oldcastle into Falstaff. In 1597 Oldcastle's descendants, the family of William Lord Brooke, objected formally to Sh.'s lampooning of their ancestor. Having offended one troop of courtiers, Sh. was alert to the danger of insulting William Russell, earl of Bedford. His original reason for choosing the name may have been a desire to make a private joke for his circle of intimate companions. *The Famous Victories of Henry V,* an anonymous play from which Sh. took material for *1H4,* lists a 'Tom' as one of the thieves who plotted the robbery at Gadshill. Sh. had a good friend, one of the executors of his will, named Tom—Thomas Russell. Sh.'s final name for the character is puzzling, for another Bardolph (Lord Bardolph) appears in the play. Sir John Fastolf, the probable model for 'Falstaff,' at one time had a soldier called Bardolph in his company, but it is doubtful that Sh. knew that. John Florio's Italian-English dictionary of 1598, *A Worlde of Wordes,* says *bardo* means 'light, nimble, bould, saucie' and may have been in Sh.'s mind, particularly given the possible Florio connection with Peto and Stefano (q.q.v.)

2H4. H5. MWW: Falstaff has rejected Bardolph, and he makes his living as a tapster at the Garter.

Bardolph, Lord, *2H4,* Thomas, (1368-1408), English baron who sided with the Percies against Henry IV. Since Bardolph's estates, like those of the Percies,' lay in northern England and Bardolph had ties by marriage with the household of Henry Percy, earl of Northumberland, it is not surprising that he followed the lead of his powerful neighbors. In 1399, when the Percies decided to help Henry (IV) Bolingbroke overthrow Richard II, Bardolph joined them. He subsequently served in an expedition Henry led into Scotland, but Henry did not come to trust him. Henry suspected Bardolph of complicity in the rebellion that Henry Percy, 'Hotspur,' raised in 1403. After Hotspur's defeat and death at Shrewsbury, he and the king were reconciled, but bad feelings must have remained. In 1405 he refused to obey Henry's summons to military service and fled to Scotland with Hotspur's father, Northumberland. They visited Wales and Flanders, and in 1408 they returned to Scotland to organize a raid into northern England. Bardolph was mortally wounded at the skirmish at Bramham Moor, Yorkshire, where Northumberland was killed.

Bargulus, *2H6 4.1.108,* Bardylis or Bardulus, king of ancient Illyria who owed his power over his men to his reputation for impartially sharing booty. In the opinions of the Romans and the Macedonians on whom he preyed, Bardulus was little more than the leader of a band of robbers. Cicero (*De Officiis,* 2.11, 40) recounted Bardulus' story to buttress his argument that a reputation for justice confers authority on a leader. Fair dealing, Cicero noted, creates a sense of loyalty even among thieves. There were several Illyrian warlords named Bargulus. Cicero's was a warrior whose depredations were curtailed by the Roman general Gaius Lælius (d. 160 BC).

Barnardine, *MM,* comic murderer who refuses to be executed because he has a hangover and is not in a fit state to die. The Duke declines to force the execution because it will kill the man without possibility of redemption. Later in the play Barnardine is pardoned to emphasize the general theme of mercy, but it is almost as if Sh. could not bring himself to execute the character after its creation and fabricated Ragusine as

Claudio's stand-in. A Claudio substitute is part of George Whetstone's *Promos and Cassandra* (1578), one of Sh.'s sources, but he is an anonymous felon. Barnardine may have come from Erasmus' *Funus* where Sh. may have gotten material about holy orders and adapted several other names. Erasmus mentions a Franciscan named Bernardine (Bernardino). Another possibility is that it comes from Barnaby Barnes, a poet charged with attempted murder in 1594.

Barnardo, *Ham,* one of Elsinore's sentinels. He comes to relieve Francisco at the play's outset, and sees the ghost.

Barnes, George, *2H4 3.2.19,* one of the companions of Justice Shallow's youth whose school boy escapades at Clement's Inn Shallow nostalgically recalls.

Barnet, *3H6 5.1.113, 5.3.20,* village about 10 mi. northwest of London, site of the battle on Easter Sunday, 14 April 1471, at which the Yorkist king, Edward IV, decisively secured his hold on England. Edward had assumed royal authority in 1461 by capturing and deposing his Lancastrian predecessor, Henry VI. In 1470 the defection of Edward's ally, the powerful earl of Warwick, restored Henry to the throne, but Warwick's death at Barnet doomed the Lancastrian resurgence. Edward quickly reclaimed the crown and executed Henry.

Bartholomew, *Shr,* page of the lord in the induction, he disguises himself as Sly's wife and dodges his sexual advances with an expression of concern for Sly's health. His few lines on a wife's obedience (*Ind. 2.104-5*) and his feigned concern foreshadow the subject of the play, as well as the deception of Sly for his own moral health.

Bartholomew boar-pig, *2H4 2.4.232,* medieval fairs were annually held on St. Bartholomew's Day, 24 August. Since the late summer festival marked the start of the season for slaughtering and putting up meat, Doll Tearsheet may be comparing Falstaff to an animal that sees its end approaching.

Bartholomew-tide, *H5 5.2.306,* the late summer season. St. Bartholomew's day is 24 August.

Barthol'mew, *Shr Ind. 1.103,* Bartholomew, for meter.

Basan, Hill of, *Ant 3.13.128,* Bashan, place mentioned in the Scriptures, famous for its huge cattle. It lay east of the sea of Galilee in an agriculturally rich mountainous district. Sh.'s allusion to a 'horned herd' roaring on the hills of Basan recalls Psalm 22:12.

Basilisco, *Jn 1.1.244,* character that Sh.'s audience would have recognized from another play, *Solyman and Perseda* (c. 1588, possibly by Thomas Kyd). Basilisco was a boastful, cowardly knight in the *miles gloriosus* tradition, who was dominated by his servant Piston.

Basilisk, *2H6 3.2.52, 328,* (Gr. *basileus* 'king') mythological king of serpents. It could kill its enemies with a glance. Spenser mentions it in *The Færie Queene,* 4.8.39.7.

Basimecu, Monsieur, *2H6 4.7.26,* pun on the Fr. *Baise mon cul!* ('Kiss my ass!'). Sh.'s reference is to the dauphin, the heir to the French throne. Jack Cade, who coins the term, is of the opinion that the dauphin has made fools of the English and tricked them out of their conquests in France.

Basingstoke, *2H4 2.1.171,* a town about 45 mi. south west of London.

Bassanio, *MV,* callow young man, friend of Antonio. After having been wasteful with his inheritance, he imposes upon the friendship of the older Antonio for money to finance his scheme to marry the Lady of Belmont. A major aspect of the play is Bassanio's development from a wasteful young man through the unselfish sacrifices of his friend and through the manipulation of him by Portia in the final act. Like many another Shakespearean male lover, Bassanio thus follows the pattern of having his love tested by the beloved one in a manner that teaches him the nature of true love as opposed to playing the role of the lover. At first, it is not at all clear that Bassanio is worth the sacrifices being made for him, but since the play ends happily one assumes he has learned his lesson, or at the least that Portia will keep him on a short leash. The origin of the name is L. *bassus* 'low.' 'Bassanius' was a Roman name for a man of short stature or low morals. The low terrain of Lombardy leads to the town Bassano in Venetia and to St. Bassano, a colleague of St. Ambrose and patron of Lodi. As a somewhat low character raised by his association with Antonio and Portia, Bassanio would draw comparison to Shylock, an even lower character, 'raised' (in the view of the time) by his Christian tormentors. Attempts to link the name to the L. *basio* 'to kiss' and the Gr. *basanos* 'touchstone,' (alluding to the caskets) are farfetched contrivances. The corresponding character in Ser Giovanni Fiorentino's *Il Pecorone* (1558), a probable source, either direct or indirect, is Gianetto and in Masuccio's *Il Novellino,* he is Giuffredi Saccano. In Anthony Munday's *Zelauto or the Fountaine of Fame* (1580) he is Strabino. Possibly Sh. got the name from the mysterious lost play *The Jew,* mentioned by Stephen Gosson in his *Schoole of Abuse* (1578), which may have been his primary source.

Basset, *1H6,* possibly Peter Basset (fl. 1421), Henry V's chamberlain and a chronicler of his reign. Basset's full name is not given in the play, and the incident that features him is not historical. He and Vernon, the character with whom he is paired, respectively represent the followers of the houses of Lancaster and York. In the play their exchange of challenges symbolizes the War of the Roses that was soon to set the Lancastrian and Yorkist factions at each other's throats. The fact that Basset's biography of Henry was a source for one of Sh.'s sources, Edward Hall's chronicle, may have suggested Basset to Sh. as the perfect man to represent the Lancastrian party.

Bassianus, *Tit,* brother to the Roman emperor, Saturninus. He disputes Saturninus' right to the throne and challenges his claim to the hand of Titus Andronicus' daughter, Lavinia (whom he abducts and marries). Saturninus subsequently weds the Gothic queen, Tamora whose sons, Demetrius and Chiron, murder Bassianus. Sh.'s source for *Tit* is uncertain, but the events he dramatizes are not historical. An 18th century chapbook preserves a later version of a tale about a Titus Andronicus that was probably known to Sh., but it does not mention Bassianus. If Sh. chose the name, he may have had the infamous emperor Caracalla (211-217 AD) in mind. Caracalla's birth name was Bassianus. He changed Bassianus to the more imperial Marcus Aurelius Antoninus, but he was popularly known as Caracalla—a nickname that derived from a distinctive kind of Gothic cloak he favored. Like Sh.'s Bassianus and Saturninus, Caracalla and his brother fought over their father's throne.

Bastard of Orleans, *1H6,* see John, count of Dunois.

Bates, John, *H5,* fictional character with a solidly English name, a soldier on whom Henry V eavesdrops on the eve of the battle of Agincourt.

'Battle with the Centaurs, to be Sung By an Athenian Eunuch to the Harp, The.' *MND 5.1.44-45 (add't'l ll. 27-8),* one of the possible entertainments offered to Theseus. He declines it because he has already told Hippolyta of his participation with Pirithous in the battle at the Lapith wedding.

Baynard's Castle, *R3 3.5.96,* fortress on the banks of the Thames at London's western end. It was built by Ralph Baynard, one of William the Conqueror's Norman knights. Henry VI granted the castle to Richard of York, and it was the headquarters for Yorkist activities in London. Edward IV launched his campaign for Henry's throne from Baynard's, and Richard III resided there while carrying out his plans for the disinheritance of Edward's sons. The Tudor kings remodeled the fortress and used it as a royal residence.

Bayonne, Bishop of, *H8 2.4.169,* French cleric who, Sh. says, negotiated an engagement between the duke of Orléans, Francis I's second son, and Henry VIII's daughter Mary (May 1527). When Henry subsequently raised doubts about Mary's legitimacy by questioning the validity of his marriage to her mother, Katherine of Aragon, the engagement was broken. Grammont, bishop of Tarbes, was the French ambassador who handled discussions of the alliance, but Sh. followed Holinshed in erroneously reporting that the bishop of Bayonne, Jean du Bellay, had a hand in the affair.

Bayonne, *H8 2.4.169,* city on the Atlantic coast of southern France just north of the Pyrenees. It was the administrative center of a diocese of the same name.

Bead, *MWW 5.5.48,* Q1-2 'Pead' to reflect Evans' Welsh accent, F1 'Bede,' the assumed fairy name of one of the tormentors of Falstaff. The name perhaps suggests the beads of a rosary, as the next line mentions prayers, and 'Bede' might also be associated with the venerable church historian and therefore prayer, etc. Most likely it simply implies the smallness of a bead, as the fairy names of *MND* often imply and the specific use of 'bead' in this meaning at *MND 3.2.331.*

Bear, *Oth 2.1.14,* 'burning B.,' Ursa major, the constellation also known as the 'Big Dipper.' It could also refer to Ursa minor because of the reference to Polaris in the next line.

Beatrice, *Ado,* 'Lady B.,' niece of Leonato, a quick-witted and sharp-tongued woman who seems to have little use for men, especially her antagonist Benedick. Ultimately, however, their verbal fencing becomes love with the Cupid-playing of her friends and relations. This is not portrayed as an imposition upon the young couple, but rather as a bringing out of the true nature of their affection: they are a good match whether they know it or not. There is a resemblance to the relationship of Katherine and Petruccio, though Beatrice is not a shrew. The story of Beatrice and Benedick does not seem to derive from an earlier source and therefore may be Sh.'s invention. Her name, shared with the beloved of Dante, comes from the Latin *beatrix,* 'she who blesses,' and is counterpoint to Benedick, *benedictus,* 'he who is blessed.'

Beauchamp, Richard, (1382-1439), earl of Warwick, the son of one of the 'Lords Appellant,' who opposed Richard II. His family endorsed Henry IV's usurpation of Richard's throne and loyally served Henry's Lancastrian house. Beauchamp succeeded to the earldom in 1401. As a young man he campaigned in Wales against Owain Glyndŵr and acquired a reputation for military prowess. He then travelled widely, making a pilgrimage to the Holy Lands and serving Henry V as ambassador to France and Germany. He also represented England at the council that convened at Constance, Switzerland, in 1414 to resolve the 'Great Schism,' a quarrel over possession of the papacy. Beauchamp took part in Henry V's wars in France and served as commander of the port of Calais. On Henry's death bed the king charged Warwick with the responsibility of educating the infant heir to the crown. Warwick held a seat on the regency council that governed England during Henry VI's minority, and he ran the boy king's household. In 1430 Warwick escorted Henry to France for his coronation, and he presided at the trial of Joan of Arc. At the time of his death he was the king's lieutenant for Normandy. *1H6. 2H4, passim;* at *3.1.61,* Sh. confuses Beauchamp with the man who succeeded to his title in 1449, his son-in-law, Richard Neville. *H5.*

Beaufort, family name adopted by the descendants of John of Gaunt (the fourth son of King

Edward III) and his mistress/wife, Katherine Swynford. Before their marriage in 1396 Gaunt and Swynford had four children: John, Henry, Thomas, and Joan. These offspring were named 'Beaufort' for a castle their father owned in Anjou. The Beauforts were declared legitimate by Richard II in 1397. Henry IV confirmed their standing in 1407, but he excluded them from the succession to the throne. John Beaufort had two sons, John and Edmund, who were active at Henry VI's court. The Beaufort male line was extinguished during the War of the Roses. The second John Beaufort, however, had a daughter, Margaret, who married Edmund Tudor and gave birth to Henry VII, the first of the Tudor kings and Elizabeth I's grandfather. See Somerset, Duke of (1) *1H6, 2H6*; (2) *3H6*; Exeter, Duke of, *1H6*; Winchester, Bishop of, *1H6, 2H6.*

Beaufort, Cardinal, *2H6,* see Beaufort, Henry.

Beaufort, Edmund, 1) (ca. 1404-1455), second duke of Somerset. Sh.'s plot for *1H6* condenses twenty years of Henry VI's life into a few weeks of action. This creates an anachronism for the character known as the duke of Somerset. There was no duke of Somerset when Henry V died in 1422, but Sh. brings such a character on stage at Henry's funeral. In 1397 Richard II had granted an earldom of Somerset to John Beaufort (1373-1410), the eldest son of John of Gaunt and Katherine Swynford. John's son, also named John, became the first duke of Somerset in 1443. Duke John could not have been the Somerset Sh. had in mind in *1H6.* John earned a dismal record as a commander in the French wars and took his own life in 1444. The duke of Somerset who appears in *1H6* is a champion of the Lancastrian cause and a participant in the events leading up to the War of the Roses. He must, therefore, be John's brother and heir, Edmund. Early in his career Edmund served with some distinction in France. He recaptured the port of Harfleur in 1440. In 1442 he relieved the siege of Calais, and in 1448 he succeeded to the duke of York's post as Henry's regent for France. This did not please York, who was forced from office because of his objection to Henry's decision to buy peace by ceding Maine and Anjou to Charles VII. Somerset abused his office so badly that he became an easy target for York and others who resented his influence with the king.

When Somerset violated the terms of a truce that Henry hoped would become a peace, the Hundred Years' War moved swiftly to its conclusion. The English army crumbled before a French offensive. Rouen fell, and all of Normandy was lost. Somerset was blamed for the catastrophe and tried to recoup his reputation by a fruitless raid on Gascony. In 1453 England was compelled to sue for peace, and the crisis probably contributed to Henry VI's nervous breakdown. York took charge of England's government and used his power as regent to punish his personal enemies. Somerset was sent to the Tower, and more drastic punishment was forestalled only by Henry's timely recovery. Henry never lost confidence in Somerset. When the king resumed control of his government, he forgave Somerset his recent military failures and assigned him the task of defending England's last continental possession, the port of Calais. York was infuriated by Somerset's return to royal favor, and in May 1455, he killed Somerset at the first battle of St. Albans, the engagement that began the War of the Roses. *2H6. 1H6.*

2) *3H6* (1438-1471), fourth duke of Somerset, brother of the third duke, Henry Beaufort. Henry Beaufort was one of Queen Margaret's chief allies in her struggle to restore her husband, Henry VI, to the throne of England. In 1464 Beaufort was captured and executed with the Lancastrians who fought at Hexham. Although Beaufort's title was suspended by Edward IV, his heir, Edmund, ignored that technicality and called himself duke of Somerset. Edmund remained in France with the exiled Lancastrian party until 1471, when Warwick drove Edward IV from the throne. The duke survived the rout of the Lancastrians at Barnet, only to be captured and beheaded at the battle of Tewkesbury. The death of his brother John at the same time extinguished the male line of the Beaufort succession. The 'Somerset'

that Sh. creates in *3H6* is a composite of the third and fourth dukes. The third enjoyed a brief period of reconciliation with Edward IV in 1464 before reverting to the family's traditional Lancastrian allegiance. The fourth remained staunchly Lancastrian throughout his career.

Beaufort, Henry, (ca. 1377-1447), bishop of Winchester, the grandson of King Edward III. Henry's father, John of Gaunt, did not marry his mother, Katherine Swynford, until twenty years after his birth, but in 1397 he and his siblings were declared legitimate by Richard II. Henry IV confirmed their status in 1407, but excluded them from succession to the throne. Henry was one of the great political churchmen of medieval England. He became bishop of Lincoln in 1398 and was translated to the more prestigious and lucrative diocese of Winchester in 1404. He served terms as chancellor under kings Henry IV, Henry V, and Henry VI. He was a member of the council that governed England during Henry VI's minority. Henry's uncle, Humphrey of Gloucester, disliked Beaufort, and the problems of the regency were compounded by frequent quarrels between the two royal relatives. In 1427 Beaufort turned his back on English politics in order to pursue a personal objective. He became a cardinal and leapt into international ecclesiastical politics. He hoped ultimately to win the papacy. He served as papal legate for Germany, Hungary, and Bohemia from 1422 to 1431, and he organized a Central European crusade to halt the spread of the Hussite heresy of Bohemia.

In 1429 Beaufort forfeited the hope of advancement in the service of the papacy by diverting the crusading army he had raised in England to the defense of Paris. Men were desperately needed to stem the tide of French victories that had begun with Joan of Arc's rescue of Orléans. In recognition of his services, Beaufort was given the honor of presiding at Henry's coronation as king of France (1431) and reappointed to the king's council. After the death of the duke of Bedford in 1435, Beaufort angered Humphrey of Gloucester by advocating an end to the war with France. Henry VI sided with him, but Beaufort did not remain at court to savor his triumph. In 1443 he retired to spend the four remaining years of his life in his diocese, and the earl of Suffolk inherited the leadership of the bishop's party. Sh. delivers a far harsher verdict on Beaufort than most historians. The bishop was a talented politician, and after his departure Henry VI's government went steadily down hill.

1H6. 2H6.

Beaufort, Thomas, (d. 1426/27), duke of Exeter, third and last son of John of Gaunt and his wife/mistress, Katherine Swynford. Although he was a grandson of Edward III whom Richard II declared legitimate in 1397, he was excluded from succession to the throne by Henry IV (1407). He began his career at sea. He took charge of Harfleur after a crucial naval engagement helped deliver that French port into English hands (1415). Beaufort later governed Gascony and Normandy for Henry V. He was made earl of Dorset in 1412 and duke of Exeter in 1416. In 1420 he helped negotiate the Treaty of Troyes by which the duke of Burgundy and regents for Charles VI of France recognized Henry V's claim to the French throne. He was an executor of Henry's will, one of the infant Henry VI's guardians, and a member of the council that ruled England during the king's minority. *1H6. H5.*

Beaumont, 1) *R2 2.2.54,* Henry Beaumond (1396-1413), fifth baron, and one of Henry IV's life-long companions. In 1390 he accompanied Henry (IV) Bolingbroke on his first crusade to Lithuania. In 1399, as constable of Dover Castle, he rendered valuable service to Henry in the rebellion that overthrew Richard II. He spent the rest of his life at Henry's court.

2) *H5 3.5.44, 4.8.100,* (d. 1415), French lord listed by Holinshed (3.555) among the casualties of the battle at Agincourt.

Beaumont Castle, *R2 2.2.54,* Beaumond (Fr. 'beautiful mountain') on the Rille river in Normandy about 80 mi. west of Paris. Its title was claimed by Henry Beaumond, a baron who took part in Henry (IV) Bolingbroke's campaign to overthrow Richard II. A later owner of Beaumont died at Agincourt fighting for the French (Holinshed, 3.555).

Bedford, Duchy of, feudal domain located in Bedfordshire, in the English Midlands between Cambridge and Oxford. The duchy was created for Henry IV's third son, John (1389-1435). See John, duke of Bedford.

Bedford, Duke of, *1H6, H5 4.3.53,* see John, duke of Bedford.

Bedlam, 1) London hospital for the insane. The term was a contraction for 'St. Mary of Bethlehem,' the name of an inn established in 1247 outside Bishopsgate by a religious order that provided hospitality for clergy visiting London. By the middle of the 14th century Bedlam had undertaken the care of the sick, and by the early 15th century it had begun to specialize in the treatment of mental illnesses. Henry VII gave the hospital to the City of London in 1547. Its contemporary connotation of chaos is particularly derived from its becoming an amusement in the 17th c., when a cruel management charged admission to people who wished to watch the mad doing mad things.

2H6 3.1.51, 'B. brainsick.' *5.1.129. Jn 2.1.183. Lr. 1.2.133,* see 'Tom o' B.' *2.2.177 (Q 7.180),* 'B. beggars,' mad beggars. *3.6.6 (Q 13 sd), 4.1 sd (Q 15 sd),* 'B. beggar.' *Q 2.131.*

2) *Q 14.101,* madman, the Old Man who leads Gloucester.

Beelzebub, name the New Testament (Matthew 12:24, Luke 11:19) sometimes gives the supernatural leader of the forces of evil. Baalzebub, 'lord of flies,' was originally a Philistine god. The Pharisees thought of him as the prince of demons and accused Jesus of drawing power from him. In ordinary use the term is interchangeable with the Hebrew 'Satan' and the Gr. 'Diabolos.' *H5 4.7.135. TN 5.1.282. Mac 2.1.4.*

'Beggar and the King, The,' *R2 5.3.78,* see Cophetua.

Bel, idol worshipped in Babylon, the same as Baal (Hebrew for 'master' or 'lord.') *Ado 3.3.130,* 'B's priests,' a reference to a stained glass depiction of a story in the Apocrypha, *Bel and the Dragon,* written in Gr. about 100 BC. In it, Daniel destroys the idol.

Belarius, *Cym,* kidnapper of Arviragus and Guiderius. Belarius was unjustly accused by king Cymbeline and stole away with the king's infant sons. He reared them in the wilds of Cambria while using the name Morgan. At play's end he is forced to reveal the royal identity of Guiderius in order to save him from execution for killing the nobleman Cloten. Cymbeline then forgives Belarius for the capital offense of stealing his sons. In assuming the Welsh disguise, Belarius also assumes some of the Renaissance stereotypes of a Welshman. The episode in which Belarius and his foster sons defeat the Romans derives from an account in Holinshed's *Chronicles* (*History of Scotland*) of the battle of Loncarty in 976 AD. In it the Danes are marching against King Kenneth, but are routed by the valiant battling of Haie and his sons.

The name 'Belarius' seems to be related to the L. *bello, bellare,* 'to wage war.' Bellerium was the Roman name for the Land's End promontory in Cornwall. There is also, in Holinshed, mention of a general of Cassibelan's named Belinus. In Byzantine history, Belisarius (d. 565) was a great general of Justinian's who took north Africa from the Vandals, and Sicily and Italy from the Ostrogoths. He also fought the Persians, the Bulgarians, and suppressed a rebellion in Constantinople. Valerius was also the name of an important Roman family and could be the source. This family had a province (Valeria) named after it.

Belch, Sir Toby, *TN,* relative of Olivia (either uncle or the vague Elizabethan 'cousin'), a wastrel gentleman. The resemblance to John Falstaff is obvious: he trains Sir Andrew in debauchery, tricks him out of his money, sets up a duel no one wants, and drinks mightily. Like Falstaff—or for that matter, the old Vice figure mentioned in the play—Sir Toby is unable to deceive anyone who is without obvious weakness. Sir Andrew is begging to be conned, and Malvolio is humiliated through his own weakness, also. Falstaff is, however, a more compelling character than Sir Toby, partly because he is valued by Hal—Toby has no equivalent admirable character who loves him. Furthermore, the main scheme of the subplot is not devised by Sir Toby, the king of Fools, but by Maria. What we see, then, is a drunken, braggart, pompous hanger-on who sponges off his niece and gulls his best friend. Nonetheless, he is so unabashedly joyous and unrestrained by conventional morality without being truly dangerous that the audience cannot help but enjoy his revels. Sh. did not derive any of the names in this play from any of the sources of which we are aware. In *Gl'Ingannati* (1538), a possible source for the play, Stragualcia, a servant of Fabrizio (corresponding to Sebastian) is fond of food and drink and resents Master Piero, a pedant, who may have suggested Malvolio. Belch is descriptive of the drunkard; Toby is a common jolly name. Though it is often wrongly assumed to be the case, Sh.'s character has nothing to do with the jolly 'Toby mug,' an 18th c. invention. It was based on a drunkard, Toby Philpot, in a poem.

Belgia, L. 'Belgium' or Flanders. In the 16th c. many Englishmen, including Ben Jonson and Sir Philip Sidney, served in the wars in the Low Countries. It has been argued, on scant evidence, that Sh. served there too. *3H6 4.9.1:* When Warwick the 'Kingmaker' won the support of France for his campaign to drive Edward IV out of England and restore Henry VI to the throne, Edward fled to Flanders. Flanders was ruled by Charles the Bold, duke of Burgundy. Charles, who was eager to do what he could to frustrate the plans of the king of France, helped Edward raise the army that defeated Warwick and restored the Yorkist dynasty. *Err 3.2.142,* here the Low Countries, Belgium and the Netherlands, are equated, for the pun that Dromio could not look so low on the 'globe' that is Nell.

Bellario, *MV,* Portia's cousin, an eminent doctor of laws in Padua, a city renowned for its learning. Though he never appears on stage, he provides the legal argument for overturning Shylock's demand when Portia sends to him for his notes and the clothes with which to disguise herself as a judge. The source of the name is unknown, but it could be of the same origin as Belarius (q.v.) or from Valerius, an important Roman gens or patrilineal clan sharing a common land, cult, burial ground, and name.

Bellona, Roman goddess of war. She is variously described as the sister, wife, or friend of Mars. She is sometimes identified with the Greek goddess Enyo, daughter of Ares and Aphrodite, who accompanied Ares into war. *Mac 1.2.54,* 'B.'s bridegroom,' Macbeth, or possibly Mars. Sh. is likely comparing Macbeth to Mars himself, in that the Scot is worthy to be the goddess' groom. He could also mean figuratively that Mars, or war itself, rebuffed Cawdor. There is a possibility that this passage was inspired by the end of the second scene of *The Misfortunes of Arthur* by Thomas Hughes and others, which was presented on 8 February 1587. Bellona, Mars, and the word Cador are all part of the passage. *TNK 1.1.75, 1.3.13.*

Belman, *Shr Ind. 1.20,* a dog. The dog's names in this section seem to come from their physical or behavioral traits. Since a belman or 'bellman' was a town crier, this name likely refers to the dog's bark.

Belmont, *MV 1.1.161, 171, 182, 4.1.454, 5.1.17,* Portia's home, from It. 'beautiful mountain.'

Benedick, *Ado,* 'Signor B. of Padua,' amusing young man who serves in the war with his friend Claudio. Posing as indifferent to women, he verbally spars with Beatrice until his friends play Cupid with the couple. Common to Sh. is the theme a young man coming to maturity through the discomforts of love. Although Beatrice does not torture her man as much as Rosalind, for example, she does test his love by urging him to turn against his friends to avenge Hero. The jolly Benedick thereby shows a depth of feeling which rescues him from being merely another witty nobleman. When they marry, a good match has been well made with one of Sh.'s best couples. Their story seems to have no origin in the source materials of the Hero and Claudio plot, and it may well be Sh.'s invention. Benedick derives from the L. *benedictus,* 'blessed,' as counterpoint to Beatrice, *beatrix,* 'she who blesses.' In the 19th c. the name Benedict was borrowed as a term for a newly married man, especially one who had been a confirmed bachelor. Walter Scott is cited by the *OED* as having used the name as a term in his *Lockhart,* 6.313 (1839).

Benedictus, *Ado,* see Carduus benedictus.

Bentii, *AWW 4.3.170,* commander in the Duke of Florence's army, possibly shortened from Bentivolii.

Bentivolii, *Shr 1.1.13,* F1 'Bentiuoly,' Lucentio's family name. It is a version of 'good will' (like Benvolio), an appropriate name for a successful merchant. The meaning 'well desired' may refer to a son who was particularly hoped for at birth. Bentivòglio and Bentivògli are common names in the region of Emilia-Romagna and in the province of Bologna. Giovanni Bentivoglio became lord of Bologna in 1401, but was killed in 1402. His heirs recaptured control in 1438, but were driven out by Pope Julius II in 1506. There is also a place name for a town founded in the 15th c., named after the distinguished family.

Benvolio, *Rom,* nephew of Montague. He is a sensible person who tries to prevent the fights between the families, but cannot. His name derives from the It. for 'good will.'

Bergamask, *MND 5.1.347,* 'b. dance.' The rustic people of the province of Bergamo in the Venetian Republic were considered buffoons. A ridiculous dance in imitation of these people was a staple of Italian comedy. From It. *Bergamasco,* 'of Bergamo.'

Bergamo, town in Lombardy in the foothills of the Alps. Ancient Bergomum was founded by Gauls, then granted rights as a city by Julius Cæsar. Attila's Huns destroyed the city in the 5th century, but it was rebuilt. By Sh.'s time it had been ruled by Venice since 1427 and would continue as part of the Venetian Republic until 1797. *Shr 5.1.71,* 'a sailmaker in B.' (Tranio's father). Bergamo in the *commedia dell'arte* was the traditional home of the Harlequin, who, like Tranio, is a servant. Bergamo is more than 100 mi. from Genoa and the sea, but textiles have long been a major industry there.

Berkeley, *R3 1.2.209,* gentleman of the court. Since Sh. has invented his own account of Henry VI's funeral and has Berkeley appear as an attendant to Anne Neville, who was not there, it is impossible to identify the character with any certainty. There were several sons of the Lancastrian family that held Berkeley Castle. Any or all of them might have helped to bury their former king.

Berkeley Castle, fortress in Berkeley, a town in Gloucestershire about 115 mi. west of London. Sh. takes care to point out to his audience that Henry (IV) Bolingbroke headed there after his landing in England in 1399. Edward II, England's first deposed king, was allegedly murdered in the dungeons, and Sh. appreciated the drama of history's ironic repetition of itself in Richard's case. *R2 2.2.119, 2.3.1, 33, 51. 1H4 1.3.246.*

Berkeley, Lord, *R2,* Thomas, (d. 1417), fifth baron of Berkeley Castle. Berkeley had a successful career in the service of both Richard II and the man who usurped Richard's throne, Henry IV. In 1399, when Henry (IV) Bolingbroke ignored the sentence of exile Richard imposed on him and returned to England, Richard's regent, the duke of York, sent Berkeley to ask Henry to declare his intentions. When, shortly thereafter, Richard surrendered to Henry and Henry claimed the crown, Berkeley was charged by parliament with the duty of carrying out Richard's formal deposition.

Henry IV subsequently gave Lord Berkeley a commission with the army that fought in Wales.

Bermudas, *Tmp 1.2.230,* 'Bermoothes' in F1, seeming to approximate the Spanish pronunciation ('Bermudez'). Also known as Somers Islands, they are a group of over 300 small coral islands on a volcanic base in the Atlantic stretching about 20 mi. northeast to southwest and lying about 600 mi. southeast of the Carolinas. The largest islands are Bermuda, St. George, Somerset, and Ireland islands. Lying on the route between Europe and the West Indies, they possess good shelter for ships and an extremely amiable climate, although without any potable wells or standing supplies they depend upon rain for the water supply. Discovered by the Spaniard Juan de Bermudez in 1503 when he shipwrecked there, they were first settled in 1609 by Sir George Somers and Sir Thomas Gates. With nine ships and 500 colonists Somers was bound for the Jamestown colony. A storm on July 25 forced his ship the *Sea-Adventure* ashore. All 150 on board survived, as well as much of their equipment. In May 1610 Somers set out for Virginia, and arrived safely. In 1612 a new group of colonists arrived placing the administration under the Virginia Company. In 1684, the islands became a crown colony.

Because of its history of settlement by storm, so to speak, the Bermudas occupied a vivid place in the imaginations of Jacobean Englishmen. By the end of 1609 news of the wreck had gotten to England and in 1610 several works were published describing the wreck either in fiction or nonfiction. Of these many available sources, scholars agree that Sh. seems to have borrowed from three for *Tmp: Discovery of the Bermudas, otherwise called the Isle of Divels* by Sylvester Jourdain (1610), *True Declaration of the state of the Colonie in Virginia, with a confutation of such scandalous reports as have tended to the disgrace of so worthy an enterprise* by the Council of Virginia (1610), and a letter by William Strachey dated 15 July 1610, but not published until 1625. The geography of the events in *Tmp* indicate that it takes place in the Mediterranean; however, Sh. borrowed material from these accounts of the Bermudas in order to create Prospero's island.

Berowne, *LLL,* F1, Q for Biron.

Berri, Duke of, *H5,* John (1340-1416), son of King John II of France. Berri and his brother, Philip of Burgundy, ruled as regents during the minority of Charles VI, but Berri had little ambition for political power and no talent for government. His most important contribution to the Renaissance world was his lavish patronage of art. For example, he commissioned the beautiful *Très Riches Heures du Duc de Berry* (1413–1416) an illuminated book done by Flemish artists Pol de Limbourg and his two brothers. His passion for art collecting was, however, merely another way he flaunted his ostentatious life-style, as depicted by the Limbourg brothers' in their January calendar painting of the duke at a banquet. The oppressive taxes that financed his sybaritic self-indulgence earned him the hatred of his subjects and, on occasion, forced the royal government to dismiss him from office and intervene in the administration of his estates.

Berri had spent six years of his youth living in England as a hostage for his father's treaties, and he favored a policy of peace with England. In 1396 he was instrumental in arranging a marriage between Richard II and Charles VI's daughter, Isabella. Three years later Charles VI's government loudly protested Henry (IV) Bolingbroke's deposition of the king's son-in-law, but Charles's mental illness created problems that prevented France from intervening in the affairs of England. Two factions within the royal family—the Burgundians led by the king's uncle, Philip, and the Orléanists headed by his cousin, Louis—fought for control of the regency. Berri mediated between them and tried to head off civil war. When the assassinations of both Philip and Louis made reconciliation impossible, Berri aligned himself with the Orléanists. His death in Paris on 15 June 1416, spared him the pain of witnessing Henry V's triumph over the divided French nation.

Bertram, *AWW,* Count of Roussillon, a young nobleman of the French court. Helen requests he be made her husband as a reward for her having cured the king. Bertram momentarily acquiesces, but at Paroles' urging, flees to fight in Tuscany, despite the king's having forbidden it. Later he is tricked by Helen into consummating the marriage and the play ends rather hesitantly reuniting the couple. Bertram is sufficiently reprehensible that many critics have wondered why Helen goes to such extraordinary lengths. His bad traits are somewhat mitigated by his being under the evil influence of Paroles, his callowness, and his courage in the wars. In adapting the character from Beltramo in Boccaccio's *Decameron* (as translated through William Painter's *Palace of Pleasure,* 1566), Sh. softened him somewhat and makes him another of his men—Orlando, Claudio—who must go through adversity (particularly a test created by a strong woman) to find their true moral natures. The problem with Bertram is that his lying, etc., seems to most readers to be more than mere indiscretion.

Berwick, the town of Berwick-upon-Tweed, which is situated at the eastern end of the border between England and Scotland. During the medieval era the district around Berwick was the scene of much skirmishing between the Scots and the English. On occasion the Scots occupied Berwick, but at the end of the Middle Ages the town was an important English base protecting Northumberland from raids. *2H6 2.1.85, 161. 3H6 2.5.128.*

Besonians, *2H6 4.1.136,* beggars or low lifes, a term of derision. A *bisogno* (It.) was an impoverished man who sought employment as a soldier of fortune. It was a common practice during the late medieval period for entrepreneurs to recruit companies of destitute individuals and sell their military services to cities and nations. The appearance of soldiers like the Besonians was a sign of the decline of feudalism. The new weapons that appeared on late medieval battlefields restored the importance of infantry and required combatants to field larger armies than the feudal system could provide. Since governments did not have incomes that permitted them to maintain large standing armies, they occasionally supplemented traditional feudal levies with 'free companies' (groups of men not bound by feudal obligations). Since the free companies were motivated by economic self-interest, not patriotism or duty, their loyalty was uncertain. They often turned on their employers in battle and preyed on defenseless civilian populations in peacetime. During the Hundred Years' War they devastated parts of France. They were a problem for Renaissance Italy, and they provided manpower for England's War of the Roses.

Bess, *3H6 5.7.15,* affectionate nickname that Sh. has Edward IV use in conversation with his queen, Elizabeth Woodville Gray. See Gray, Lady.

Bessy, *Lr. Q 13.21,* name in a song sung by Edgar and dated to at least 1558. In it, Bessy and Poor Tom are companions, with Bessy described as a harlot.

Best, *WT 1.2.419,* the best of all men, Jesus Christ.

Best 's son, *2H6 4.2.23,* soldier in Cade's army and one of the 'honest workers' (a tanner from Wingham) to whom Cade's revolutionaries compared England's aristocrats—to the great disadvantage of the latter.

Betts, George, *STM,* one of the commoners working himself up to riot. According to Holinshed, the 'Bets' brothers (George and Ralph) were sentenced to be hanged on May 7, 1517, but were reprieved just before their turn.

Bevis, 1) F1 *1H6,* name given to one of Cade's rebels. This is probably the name of an actor, rather than the character. He is usually thought to be the same as 'George' who enters with Lord Saye at F1 *4.7.21.* See John, *1H6.*

2) *H8 1.1.38,* of Hampton (Southampton), a legendary hero whose stupendous feats at arms are celebrated in medieval romance.

Bianca, 1) *Shr,* see Minola, Bianca.

2) *Oth,* courtesan who loves Michael Cassio. Her jealousy parallels Othello's in that Cassio is not guilty of betraying her. However, she is far from an unattractive character. The meaning of her name, 'white,' seems to have no particular significance, though it could be intended to be ironic, or an obscure play on Othello's blackness. 'White' is, of course, traditionally associated with purity and moral correctness and it is possible to parallel Bianca's situation to that of Desdemona, in that she is called a whore despite acting 'fair': bravely and loyally. It is curious that Ludovico Sforza, ruler of Milan, was nicknamed 'the Moor,' had a mistress Bianca, and that his first name is used for one of the minor characters. There is no indication, however, that these are anything other than coincidences.

Bigot, Lord, *Jn 4.2.162,* Roger Bigot (Bigod), earl of Norfolk (d. 1221), close friend of Richard the Lionhearted's and steward of his estates. He opposed the schemes John, the king's brother, devised to undermine Richard's authority while Richard was abroad on the third crusade. After Richard's death Bigot acquiesced to John's ascension to the throne, but he had little confidence in the new king. Bigot was one of the lords who forced Magna Carta on John and whose continuing suspicions made it difficult for John to rule. When pope Innocent III absolved John from the oath he had taken to abide by the terms of Magna Carta, Bigot and other disaffiliated barons urged the heir to the French throne to invade England and depose John. John's unexpected death changed the political situation completely. Bigot and his party turned on their French ally and rallied to the defense of John's 9-year-old son, Henry III.

Billingsgate, *2H6 4.7.124,* docking facility on the Thames near London Bridge.

Biondello, *Shr 1.1.42,* servant of Lucentio. He pretends to be the servant of Tranio, another servant of Lucentio's, so that his master can pretend to be a Latin teacher and get close to Bianca. The name implies 'fair-haired.'

Birnam, *Mac,* 'Great B. Wood,' 'B. Forest,' a forest on a hill near Dunkeld. It is 12 mi. from Dunsinane. When Macduff's troops approach Macbeth's castle they use branches from the woods as camouflage and it appears that the woods are marching on Dunsinane, fulfilling the prophecy. Macbeth was killed in Birnam Wood by Malcolm Canmore.

Biron, *LLL,* 'Berowne,' a courtier in service to the king of Navarre, wooer of Rosaline. He has the self-awareness to know that he cannot resist the attractions of love and initially opposes the king's oath of asceticism. When in love, he knows his own foolishness and accepts it. This dimension of character and his wit make him the most interesting and rounded character in the play. Later recognizing the artificiality of courtly love talk he vows to express himself more plainly. Offended by his mockery of the crude pageant of the Nine Worthies, Rosaline agrees to accept him if he spends a year amusing the ill in hospitals. The exchanges between the two lovers are suggestive of the verbal fencing between Beatrice and Benedick. The name is thought to have been borrowed from the liaison officer of Henry of Navarre at the siege of Rouen in which the Earl of Essex participated in 1591. In 1595, the son of Maréchal de Biron, also became prominent in assisting the rebellion of Burgundy against its Spanish masters. See Ferdinand, king of Navarre.

Bishop, Lord, *2H4 4.1.241,* see, Scrope, archbishop of York.

Black Monday, *MV 2.5.24-5,* Easter Monday. According to the Renaissance chronicler John Stow, in the siege of Paris by Edward III in 1360, Easter Monday was dark with mist and hail and bitter cold, so much so that men died on horseback from exposure. Lancelot's reference to it is apparently nonsense to mock his master Shylock.

Black Prince, *R2 2.3.100. AWW 4.5.42:* Lavatch compares him to the devil. See Edward, the Black Prince.

Blackamoor, black-skinned Moor, or any black-skinned person. The word perhaps distinguished the darker of the mixed races of the Moors, but was more often probably a synonym for Negro. It seems to have evolved from 'black Moor,' which was descriptive and apparently not pejorative. The *OED* dates the first use of 'b.' to 1581. Blacks were well-known by then and many had been in London. *LLL 5.2.157* (pl.): several are part of the pageant—probably musicians in costume. *Tro 1.1.77:* this use has a negative connotation.

Blackfriars, London convent constructed by the Dominican order in 1276 on a tract of land near Baynard's Castle. During the Reformation the property was divided and sold. The Gatehouse became an investment property for Sh. Another building was used for the Blackfriars Theatre, an indoor facility, which had smaller audiences than the Globe and a more upscale clientele. Part of the building was used as a theater between 1576 and 1584, then the Children of the Chapel, a boys' theatre group, took over. In 1609, the King's Men (Sh.'s company) acquired it. The Dominicans' dark robes caused them to be nicknamed the 'black friars.' The Franciscans, the other major order of friars, wore brown, and the Carmelites, white. *R3 1.2.214. H8 2.2.139:* Holinshed also sets this meeting there.

Blackheath, *H5 5.0.16,* large field about 5 mi. east of London between the royal palaces at Eltham and Greenwich. It was a convenient place for large bodies of men (e.g., armies serving on the continent, or bands of rebels planning assaults on London) to assemble.

Blackmere, fief near Whitchurch in Shropshire. See Blackmere, Lord Strange of, *1H6.*

Blackmere, Lord Strange of, *1H6 4.7.65,* one of the many titles that Sh. says belonged to England's warrior hero, John Talbot. The lords Strange were descendants of John le Strange (d. 1269), a baron of the Welsh March. Talbot's mother, Ankaret, was heiress to the last lord Strange of Blackmere. Talbot succeeded to the title in 1421 after the deaths of his elder brother and his brother's only child.

Blanch, *Lr. 3.6.21 (Q 13.57),* dog whom Lear imagines barking at him, or a formerly faithful dog that has turned against him. The comparison to his three daughters is obvious. Fr. *blanch* means 'white.'

Blanche of Spain, *Jn,* 'of Castile' (d. 1252), granddaughter of Henry II of England by his daughter Eleanor, wife of Alfonso IV of Castile. In 1200 her marriage with Louis (VIII), heir to the French throne, sealed a treaty between her uncle, John, king of England, and Philip Augustus of France. When the English barons turned against John in 1215, they declared their allegiance to her and invited her husband to depose John and claim the English throne by right of his wife. John's sudden and unanticipated death ended England's enthusiasm for French rule, and nothing came of the effort to make her queen of England. As events unfolded, however, she had sufficient work to occupy her in her husband's homeland. Louis VIII died in the third year of his reign (1226), and she became regent for their young son, Louis IX. Had it not been for her astute political maneuvering, the French nobility might have set the boy aside in favor of an adult. Blanche prevented this by keeping France's great lords distracted and at odds with each another until Louis came of age in 1236. Throughout her life she remained one of Louis' most important advisors, and it was to her that he entrusted his kingdom when he departed on crusade in 1248.

Blithild, *H5 1.2.67,* Blichilde, a Merovingian princess. Holinshed (3.545-546) identified her as the daughter of Clotaire I and an ancestress of the first king of the Carolingian dynasty, Pepin the Short. During the Middle Ages genealogies were freely invented to serve the needs of political propagandists, and the information they contained was not always historically accurate. If Pepin had royal connections, he did not invoke them to legitimate his usurpation of the crown. Pepin was the product of a union between the children of Arnulf of Metz and Pepin of Landau, two nobles who served as advisors to Clotaire II (613-628) and Clotaire's son, Dagobert. In 751 Pepin used the power acquired by his family to depose the last of the Merovingian kings, Childeric III (743-751)—and to disinherit Childeric's son, a man with a hereditary claim to the throne far stronger than any that Pepin could have made. It was the papacy's endorsement of this act and its acknowledgement of Pepin's demonstrated fitness for royal office, not a hereditary right, that established Pepin's dynasty.

Blois, *1H6 4.3.45,* town and district on the Loire river south of Orléans. It was purchased from the last of its hereditary counts, Guy II, by Louis I, duke of Orléans. Louis' son, Charles of Orléans, made it his chief residence when he returned to France in 1440 from a long period of captivity in England.

Bloody Parliament, *3H6 1.1.39,* see Parliament.

Blunt, James, *R3,* (d. 1493), third son of Sir Walter Blunt, Baron Mountjoy, and friend and supporter of William, Lord Hastings. Blunt commanded Hammes Castle, a fortress that the English possessed in Picardy, 70 mi. northeast of Paris. Richard III's execution of Hastings may have alienated him, for in 1484 he defected to Richard's opponent, Henry, earl of Richmond. He turned Hammes over to Henry and followed Henry to England. He helped Henry defeat Richard at the battle of Bosworth Field, and he prospered from the patronage of the new Tudor dynasty.

Blunt, John, *2H4,* (d. 1418), character who appears on stage only to conduct someone else (Coleville) off (*4.2.72*). He has no lines of his own. John's father Walter died defending Henry IV at Shrewsbury. Sh. says that both father and son were rumored to have died in that battle (*1.1.16*). John, however, survived to fight in Henry V's wars in France. He was governor of Calais, and he assisted Henry at the successful siege of Harfleur. He died with the English forces that took Rouen in 1418.

Blunt, Thomas, *R2 5.6.8,* Blount, (d. 1400), knight loyal to Richard II who refused to acquiesce to Henry IV's usurpation of the crown. He was a member of a group of conspirators who worked out a plan to murder Henry at a tournament at Windsor Castle in January 1400. Someone (Sh. claims that it was the duke of York's heir, the earl of Rutland) leaked information about the plot to the king. Blunt fled, but was captured at Oxford and executed.

Blunt, Walter, *1H4,* renowned soldier who served in the armies of the Black Prince and John of Gaunt, duke of Lancaster. An executor of Gaunt's estate, he rallied to the side of Gaunt's son, Henry (IV) Bolingbroke when Richard II tried to confiscate Gaunt's legacy. After Henry took the crown from Richard, Blunt entered the new king's service. He bore Henry's standard at the battle of Shrewsbury where he was killed by Archibald, earl of Douglas.

Blunts, *2H4 1.1.16,* see Blunt, Walter; Blunt, John.

Bocchus, *Ant 3.6.69,* king of Libya and one of the monarchs who Plutarch ('Antony' 61.1) says sided with Mark Antony in his battle with Octavius at Actium. A Bocchus was king of the African nation of Mauretania at that time, but he was Octavius' ally. His brother Bogud, who challenged his right to the crown, was in Antony's camp. When Bocchus died in 33 BC, Bogud may have begun to style himself king of Libya in the hope of reclaiming his homeland. He died fighting for Antony as Octavius advanced on Egypt after the battle at Actium. Rome declared Libya a province of its empire.

Bodykins, *MWW 2.3.41,* oath, 'by God's body.'

Bohemia, country located in what is now the Czech Republic and bordered by Germany, Austria, Poland and Moravia. Its natural borders are mountains which once surrounded a prehistoric sea about the size of Lake Michigan. The mountains also served as a defense against Germanic invaders protecting the Czechs, providing only two passes through the Bohemian Forest which divides Germany and Bohemia. The mountains separating it from Moravia, however, are much lower. The traditional capital of the kingdom was Prague. After confusing origins, Bohemia emerged as a kingdom in the ninth century under the Premysl dynasty. It became part of the Holy Roman Empire in 950 and a kingdom within that empire in 1198. The country gained great influence and ruled over large sections of central Europe, by the end of the 1200s from Saxony to the Adriatic. Vienna was called its second capital. It became seat of the Holy Roman Empire under Charles IV from 1355 to 1378 and was said to be the freest, most progressive, most powerful and wealthy nation on earth. The wars against the Hussite religious reformers in the 1400s weakened the nation and after 1526, when a treaty with Austria and Hungary put it under Hapsburg domination, it declined. Two years after Sh.'s death, the Thirty Years' War began (1618) as a revolt in Bohemia when the Catholic king was removed in favor of a Protestant. By the peace of Westphalia (1648), the Hapsburgs were in decline and the Holy Roman Empire disintegrating, but Bohemia and the Czechs would remain in subjugation for many centuries afterwards. *MM 4.2.132,* Barnardine's birthplace.

WT, country of King Polixenes and partial setting of the play, also used as the name of Polixenes. Sh.'s Bohemia is a fantasy land much like his Ardenne or his Illyria and has little connection with the real other than its name. The major discussions of Sh.'s Bohemia revolve around the geographical error of attributing to it a sea-coast. Ben Jonson was the first on record to point out the error in his talks with William Drummond of Hawthornden in 1619 and the example is often used to prove Sh.'s geographical ignorance. Editor Thomas Hanmer was so vexed by this error that he substituted Bithynia throughout, which allowed Charles Kean in 1856 to do the entire play as a Greek costume pastoral. The whole issue, however, is another of those pointless Shakespearean controversies. No one suspects that Sh.'s intention in *WT* was to write a realistic play and certainly not that his Bohemia is anything more than a vague distant kingdom populated, like Ardenne and Illyria, with extraordinarily English types of people. His Bohemia is no more literal than Anthony Hope's Ruritania or James Hilton's Shangri-La, and an audience would not have been in Sh.'s time, nor would be now, disturbed by any factual errors about remote kingdoms. A novelist now might easily write about a shipwreck on the coast of Bolivia or Laos or Zimbabwe—all land-locked—without testing the patience of most American readers.

Secondly, the detail of the sea-coast is borrowed directly from his source, Robert Greene's *Pandosto,* or the Triumph of Time (1588; rptd. 1607 as *Dorastus and Fawnia*), although Sh. has reversed the settings of Sicilia and Bohemia as they are used in Greene. Other defenders of Sh. have pointed out that in its most powerful periods the lands of Bohemia did indeed go to the shores of the Adriatic at what is now northeast Italy and northwest Yugoslavia. Finally, there is the theory that Bohemia means the coast of Apulia in southeast Italy which is sometimes called Bohemia in fifteenth century documents, possibly from Bohemund I of Tarentum, a famous Crusader. This possibility would place the geography of the play in a more contained area. These fustian attacks and counters may be interesting, but ignore the obvious implications of the title of the play which tells us it is a fantasy.

Bohemian Tartar, *MWW 4.5.18,* nonsense expression which would imply a wild or uncivilized man.

Bohun, Edward, *H8 2.1.104,* name used by Edward Stafford, duke of Buckingham, to affirm his claim to the office of Lord High Constable of England—an honor to which he believed that he was entitled because of his connection with the extinct family of the de Bohuns, the earls of Hereford.

Boleyn, Anne, *H8,* F1 'Anne Bullen,' (1507-1536), second wife of Henry VIII and mother of Elizabeth I. Her parents, Sir Thomas Boleyn and Elizabeth Howard, daughter of the earl of Surrey and duke of Norfolk, were ambitious Tudor courtiers. In 1519 they won places for both their daughters, Mary and Anne, in the entourage of Henry VII's daughter Mary, when she went to France to wed Louis XII. Anne remained abroad until 1522, when the Boleyns brought her home to be presented at court. By 1520 her sister, Mary, had become the king's mistress, and the Boleyns were basking in royal favor. Anne was poised to make a good marriage, and her hand was sought by a worthy candidate, Henry Percy, heir to the earldom of Northumberland. Percy was, however, a member of Cardinal Wolsey's household, and Wolsey had a politically more advantageous alliance in mind for him. The cardinal separated Anne from her suitor, and Percy married the earl of Shrewsbury's daughter. Anne blamed Wolsey for her disappointment, and developments she could not have anticipated brought her opportunities for revenge. By the year 1526 the king had tired of Anne's sister and begun to court her. Anne was reluctant to become a royal mistress, and her show of virtue both increased Henry's infatuation and strengthened his resolve to separate from his aging queen, Katherine of Aragon. When Wolsey failed, after many tries, to obtain papal approval for the king's divorce and remarriage, the cardinal was deprived of his political offices and sent from court (October 1529).

Henry separated from Katherine in July 1531, and Anne openly lived with him. In January of 1533 she informed him that she was pregnant, and he married her. They wed in secret, for Henry had not yet won legal acknowledgement of his claim that his marriage to Katherine was invalid. On 30 March, Thomas Cranmer, Anne's chaplain, was consecrated archbishop of Canterbury, and on 23 May Cranmer used the power of his office to grant Henry an annulment. The announcement that Katherine and Henry had never been married meant Henry had been legally free to wed when he and Anne took vows in January. In September, 1533, she gave birth to the princess Elizabeth. Henry was disappointed by the child's sex, and he completely lost confidence in his second wife when she was delivered of a stillborn male on 30 January 1536. Katherine of Aragon had died (7 January) a few weeks before Anne's confinement, and Henry realized that, if he were a widower, he would be free to contract a marriage of undoubted validity. On 2 May 1536, Anne was accused of adultery and sent to the Tower of London. Five men, including her own brother, Lord Rochford, were named as co-respondents, and they were convicted by a court presided over by her uncle, the duke of Norfolk. On 17 May Cranmer declared her marriage with Henry invalid and her daughter illegitimate. She was beheaded on 19 May. The next day Henry married her successor, Jane Seymour.

Boleyn, Thomas, *H8 1.4.95,* (d. 1539), father of Henry VIII's second wife, Anne Boleyn. Thomas was the scion of a family of London merchants whose wealth made them acceptable suitors for the hands of daughters of the aristocracy. Thomas' mother, Margaret Butler, belonged to the Irish house of Ormonde, and Thomas married the daughter of Thomas Howard, earl of Surrey and duke of Norfolk. Boleyn held posts of some importance at Henry VIII's court. He participated in Henry's campaigns in France and helped arrange the famous meeting between the kings of England and France on the 'Field of the Cloth of Gold' (1520). His rank and prestige increased as his daughters, one after the other, became romantically involved with the king. Mary Boleyn, Lady Carey, became the king's mistress about 1520, and in 1525 her father was named viscount Rochford. By 1526 Henry had fallen in love with Boleyn's second daughter, Anne, and in 1529 he became the earl of Wiltshire and Ormonde.

Henry married Anne in 1533, and her execution in 1536 ended her father's career.

Boleyns, *H8 3.2.90,* see Boleyn, Anne.

Bolingbroke, Henry (Harry), F1 'Bullingbrooke,' *1H6 2.5.83, 2H6 2.2.39, R2, 1H4, 2H4,* see Henry IV. Henry was called by that name because of his birth at Bolingbroke, Lincolnshire.

Bolingbroke, Roger, *2H6,* man convicted of practicing sorcery in the service of Eleanor Cobham, duchess of Gloucester. He is mentioned by both Edward Hall (*Union of the Two Noble and Illustre Famelies of Lancaster and Yorke,* 202) and Holinshed (3.623), who note, as Sh. does not, that he died professing his innocence. He was charged with constructing a wax figure that was to be manipulated magically to bring about the death of Henry VI. In Sh.'s version of the story his crime was to conjure up a demon that the duchess quizzed about the king's future.

Bon, Monsieur le, *MV 1.2.52-53,* French suitor to Portia; 'Mr. Good.' She describes him as lacking character and imitating those around him, presumably in order to seem agreeable. Sh. is mocking gentlemen whose manners are better than their integrity.

Bona, Lady, of Savoy (d. 1485), younger sister of Louis XI's queen, Charlotte. In June, 1463, Edward IV and Louis XI met at St. Omer to conclude a treaty between England and France. The earl of Warwick, the most powerful man at Edward's court, may have proposed sealing the deal with a royal wedding between Edward IV and one of Louis XI's daughters. Some historians have doubted the story that follows, but it provided Sh. with a dramatic motive for Warwick's subsequent break with his protege, Edward. The French king was supposedly agreeable to a marital alliance, but not between Edward and a French princess. Louis' daughters were, he insisted, too young to be engaged. In their place he offered Louis' sister-in-law, Bona, daughter of Louis, duke of Savoy. Warwick's plan to bind England to its traditional enemy, France, was not popular in England—particularly since other nations were eager to side with England in efforts to contain France. Both Burgundy and Castile, fearing that the balance of power would be disturbed by an Anglo-French dynastic tie, hastened to offer Edward brides. Edward played along with these negotiations even though he knew that they were in vain. Edward had already secretly married an English woman, Elizabeth Woodville Gray.

When the news of the royal wedding became known at the French court in October of 1464, it acutely embarrassed Warwick. Louis XI may have exploited Warwick's anger at his home government by encouraging Warwick to break with the Yorkist king. Louis reconciled Warwick and Queen Margaret and gave them money for an army to invade England and restore Henry VI to the throne. Sh.'s suggestion that Bona felt herself a wronged woman was a dramatic invention. Bona played no part in Warwick's plot against Edward. She married the duke of Milan.

3H6. R3 3.7.172.

'Bonny Robin,' *TNK 4.1.108,* popular song, one line of which is sung by Ophelia at *Ham 4.5.185.* 'Robin' was probably a reference to the penis then, as 'John Henry,' and 'Dick' are today. The song is included in Chappell's *Popular Music of The Olden Time.*

Bonville, Lord, William Lord Harrington and, *3H6 4.1.56,* (d. 1461), wealthy supporter of the Yorkist cause whose heir, Cecily, was obtained by Elizabeth Woodville Gray as a marriage prize for her second son, Thomas Gray. The wedding was one of several that Sh. says were resented by the enemies of the Woodvilles. Edward IV's queen was vulnerable to the charge that she used her influence with her husband to enrich her family beyond the bounds of ordinary greed.

Book of Riddles, *MWW 1.1.184, 186,* unidentified anthology of the sort that was popular in the period. One such, *The Booke of Merry Riddles, together with proper Questions and Witty Proverbs to make pleasant pastime* was available in 1575 and 1629, for certain. Another such book was available as early as 1511, and there were likely others. Possibly Slender is still referring to *Songs and Sonnets* (q.v.).

Book of Trespasses, *TNK 1.1.33,* the metaphorical book in heaven listing each person's sins.

Bo-peep, *Lr. Q 4.170,* informal game for young children in which players cover their eyes or hide themselves, then uncover or spring out to surprise or startle, 'peek-a-boo.' 'Bo!' is an old equivalent of 'Boo!' and to peep is to look. The image is of deliberately covering one's sight. It therefore evokes the theme of blindness. This is not a reference to the girl in the nursery rhyme, though she cannot see her sheep.

Borachio, *Ado,* follower of Don John, he plots to defame Hero by having Margaret appear at Hero's window. Claudio and Don Pedro mistake her for Hero, whom they then assume to be promiscuous. Later, the watchman overhears Borachio's description of the plot. At the end of the play, he assumes all the blame for Hero's death and is willing to take full punishment. This improves the impression of his basic character, particularly if Margaret is more than a dupe. His name derives from the name of a goatskin wine container (It. *borraccia*) or from the Sp. *borracho,* 'drunk,' or 'drunkard,' which derives from Arabic. The name may imply that his judgment has been impaired, particularly by Don John, whom he equates with the devil. Many editors feel that Balthasar's flirting with Margaret at the masked ball (*2.1.90-101*), which is attributed to both Benedick and Balthasar in F1 and Q, should be attributed to Borachio who is later proven to have a relationship with her.

Bordeaux, capital of the French province of Guienne (Gascony). It is about 375 mi. southwest of Paris. Its site on the Garonne river gives it access to the sea and made it a major center for trade between medieval England and France. For much of the medieval period Guienne and Bordeaux belonged to England. *R2 5.6.33. 2H4 2.4.61. 1H6 4.2.1, 4.3.4, 8, 22. H8 1.1.95.*

Boreas, *Tro 1.3.37,* Greek god of the north wind (L., Aquilo). Son of Astræus the Titan and Eos the dawn. He lived in a cave in Mount Hæmus in Thrace and was the father of many famous horses, including those of Achilles, Ares, Dardanus, Erectheus, and Danaus. He carried off the nymph Orithyia and fathered Zetes and Calaïs, the winged Argonauts (Ovid's *Metamorphoses,* 6.675-721).

Bosworth, *R3 5.3.1,* town in Leicestershire, about 100 mi. northeast of London. The last battle of the War of the Roses was fought near there. The armies of Richard III and Henry Tudor, earl of Richmond, met about a mile south of town on what subsequently came to be called 'Bosworth Field.'

Bottom, Nick, *MND,* a weaver. In the rustics' play before Theseus, he takes on the role of Pyramus, though he offers to do every part as it is discussed. During the rehearsal, Robin Goodfellow turns his head into that of an ass and Titania, bewitched, falls in love with him. He alone among the characters is allowed to experience the supernatural realm directly. Although he is ignorant and has a great opinion of himself, he is not arrogant but gentle with those around him. These traits combined with his enthusiasm, make him one of Sh.'s most endearing characters. His name derives not from the more recent (18th c.) use of 'bottom,' to refer to the anatomy, but to the spindle or spool upon which a weaver wound thread. 'Bottom' also means a skein or ball of thread. His translation into an ass is likely to have been borrowed from Lucius Apuleius' *Golden Ass* (2nd c. AD) in which the hero is transformed into a jackass.

'Bottom's Dream,' *MND 4.1.212.* Although he cannot recall exactly what has happened to him, Bottom feels he has had a vision which should be memorialized in a ballad of this title by Peter Quince. He thinks it should be called this also because the dream was totally inexplicable in the mortal sphere—it had no core or foundation and is therefore infinite in meaning. 'Bottom' was also in use at the time to mean the underlying reality. Bottom's fumbling to characterize his dream seems to come from the passage 1 Corinthians 2:9 as rendered in the Bishop's Bible (1568).

Boucicault, Duke of, *H5 3.5.45, 4.8.77,* Jean le Meingre (1366-1421), son of one of the marshals of France, and a career soldier. Although he spent most of his life in the east fighting the Turks, he happened to be in France in 1415 when Henry V invaded. He was captured at the battle of Agincourt and taken to England. He died there six years later awaiting the payment of his ransom.

Boult, *Per,* a 'leno' (pimp) who buys Marina for his master the pander. In Gower, Leonin is the 'maister of the bordel' who buys Thaisa (Marina) in Mytilene. The name seems first to appear in *Per* and does not appear in the sources, even *The Painfull Adventures of Pericles, Prince of Tyre* (1608) by George Wilkins, who may have been Sh.'s co-author.

Bourbon, Duke of, *H5,* Jean, (d. 1433), brother to Joan of Bourbon, mother of Charles VI of France. When Charles went insane, his uncle, John the Fearless of Burgundy, tried to take control of France. Bourbon joined the dukes of Berri, Brittany, and Orléans (the Armagnac faction) in a campaign to frustrate Burgundy's plan. In September, 1413, he and his allies forced the Burgundians from Paris. In 1415 the Burgundians took their revenge by refusing to intervene when Henry V invaded France. Bourbon was captured at Agincourt in 1415 and spent the rest of his life in England awaiting payment of his ransom.

Bourbon, Lord, *3H6,* Louis (d. 1487), count of Rousillon and admiral of France. He was the natural son of Charles I, duke of Bourbon, and the son-in-law of Louis XI, king of France. He wed Louis' natural daughter, Joan. Louis bestowed legitimacy on him in 1463 and made him admiral of France in 1466. Bourbon fought in the battles that restored Brittany to French allegiance, and he helped to negotiate the treaty of Picquigny that established peace between Edward IV and Louis XI.

Boyet, 'Lord B.,' *LLL,* slick courtier accompanying the Princess of France. A sycophant, he reveals the Princess' essential level-headedness in his first scene as he lavishes copious praise and she reprimands him for it. Otherwise, he delivers messages and tells the Princess about the Russian disguises the Navarrese court will wear. The name appears in contemporary records of the career of Henry of Navarre. See Ferdinand, King of Navarre.

Boys, *AYLI,* F1 for 'Bois.' It may reflect pronunciation.

Brabant, duchy in the Lowlands between the Meuse river and Flanders. Joanna, the daughter of John III, the last native duke of Brabant, bequeathed the duchy to Antony, second son of her niece, Margaret of Flanders, and Margaret's husband, Philip the Bold of Burgundy. *LLL 2.1.114, 115:* Rosaline receives Biron's question exactly like it sounds, as a cheap pick-up line. *H5,* see Brabant, Antony, duke of.

Brabant, Antony, duke of, *H5 2.4.5, 3.5.42, 4.8.96,* (d. 1415), second son of Philip the Bold, duke of Burgundy. He inherited Brabant from his great-aunt, Joanna, daughter of John of Brabant. When Antony's brother, John the Fearless, refused to help Burgundy's enemies, the Armagnac party, defend France against Henry V, Antony was scandalized. He hastened to Agincourt to uphold the honor of his family and was killed in the battle.

Brabanzio, *Oth,* F1 'Brabantio,' Desdemona's father, an important Venetian senator. While he has been happy to have the heroic general Othello to his house, he is outraged over the secret marriage to his daughter. He charges

Othello with bewitching her. This failing, his spirit is broken by the marriage, and he dies. Although there is plenty that sounds racial in his tirades, he might likely, in that time, to have been more upset by Othello's low birth and by his daughter's disregarding him in marrying. He warns Othello that a girl who would deceive her father would deceive her husband. In that sense perhaps he is intimating that the social order has been disrupted. In Sh.'s source for the plot, Giraldi Cinthio's *Hecatommithi* (1566), 3, 7, he is unnamed and vague 'relatives' oppose Disdemona's [*sic*] marriage to the Moor. Brabantio's name is an Italianate version of Brabant. Less likely is that it relates to 'brabble,' which meant a petty quarrel or a frivolous lawsuit.

Brabbler the hound, *Tro 5.1.88,* a quarrelsome, noisy dog. 'To brabble' is to engage in a loud squabble. It is related to the Du. *brabbelen,* 'to jabber.'

Brach, Lady, *Lr.1.4.111,* a dog. 'Brach' meant bitch. It was also the name of a short-tailed setter, usually spotted. The figure of speech suggests that the stinking dog of falsehood drives out the truth. Gonoril herself is also suggested by the remark. Compare *Lr. Q 4.108,* 'L. the brach.'

Brackenbury, Robert, *R3,* (d. 1485), commander of the Tower of London during Richard III's reign. He was a member of an ancient family settled in Durham, a district from which Richard drew many followers. Richard entrusted the Tower to him in 1484, and although he allegedly refused to participate in the murder of Edward IV's sons, he remained loyal to Richard to the end. He helped put down Buckingham's rebellion, and he died fighting for Richard at the battle of Bosworth Field. One commentator thinks his name implies 'break and bury' because of his role in the Tower, but this is reaching.

Bracy, John, *1H4 2.5.337,* man sent by Henry IV to alert Prince Harry to the rebellion raised by the Percies in July 1403. A Bracy family held lands in Worcestershire, but nothing is known about John.

Brandon, *H8,* man whom Sh. says Henry VIII sent to arrest Edward Stafford, the duke of Buckingham, on 16 April 1521. Holinshed (3.863) identifies the arresting officer as Sir Henry Marney, captain of the Tower guard, but there was a Brandon at Henry's court. Charles Brandon was the duke of Suffolk and one of the king's closest friends. Brandon supported Henry's decision to separate from his wife, Katherine of Aragon, and to nationalize the English church. Sh. may have considered him an appropriately distinguished agent for the king to use in bringing about the fall of one of England's greatest peers.

Brandon, William, *R3 5.4.4,* 5.8.14, (d. 1485), Lancastrian partisan who shared the earl of Richmond's exile in Brittany. When Richmond invaded England, Brandon carried Richmond's standard into battle. He was one of the men whom Richard III killed by his own hand during the battle of Bosworth Field.

Brecon, *R3 4.2.125,* Brecknock, chief town of Brecknokshire in Wales and site of a Norman castle belonging to the dukes of Buckingham. Henry Stafford, second duke of Buckingham, retreated to Brecon to raise an ill-fated rebellion against Richard III.

Brentford, fat woman of, *MWW 4.2.67, 77. 89,* 'witch of B.' *157,* 'maid's Aunt of B.' *4,5.25,* 'wise woman of B.' In the first two quartos, this woman is called Gillian of Brainford. She kept a tavern in Brentford, and was well known because of a poem *Jyl of braintford's Testament* by Robert Copland (c. 1560). In it she bequeathes 'a score of farts among her friends.' Brentford is a village about a dozen mi. from Windsor, at the junction of the Brent and Thames rivers. One of Sh.'s actors, John Lowin, kept an inn called the Three Pigeons there. The town had a reputation in Sh.'s time as an extremely dirty place.

Bretagne, *2H6 1.1.7, R3 4.4.458, 5.6.54,* see Brittany.

Bretagne, Duke of, *2H6 1.1.7,* see Francis I, duke of Bretagne.

Breton, 1) (n.) F1 'Britaine,' anyone from Brittany. *R3 4.3.40,* Since Henry Tudor, the young earl of Richmond, took refuge in Brittany when the last Lancastrian attempt to unseat Edward IV failed in 1471, Richard dubbed him a Breton. Henry remained in Brittany until he returned to England to challenge Richard III in 1485. *R3 5.6.47, 5.6.63* (pl.), Henry Tudor's allies. Early in Edward IV's reign, Brittany had looked to England for help in its efforts to resist the French crown's encroachments on the duchy's traditional liberties. Edward promised aid to the duke of Brittany, but failed to honor his commitments in time to prevent the duke from having to come to terms with Louis XI. Brittany, under French influence, turned against Edward and provided a place of refuge for the house of York's Lancastrian enemies.

2) (adj.) of Brittany. *R3 4.4.452,* 'B. navy.'

Briareus, *Tro 1.2.27,* 'the strong,' also called Ægæon, giant son of Uranus and Gæa, one of the Hecatonchires (the Hundred-Handed) with his brothers Cottus the Striker and Gyges the Crippler. He was father of Ætna and one of Zeus's allies against the Titans. He is mentioned in Virgil's *Æneid,* 6, as a giant under an enormous elm on the path to the river Cocytus.

Bridget, name implying commonness, as the three uses show. 1) *Err 3.1.31,* F1 'Briget,' a house servant of Antipholus of Ephesus.

2) *MM 3.1.345,* Pompey's woman, a prostitute. Lucio asks why she can't help Pompey, but he seems to do it to mock him.

3) *MWW 2.2.13,* 'Mistress B.,' a woman known by Falstaff, otherwise unmentioned. The fan handle mentioned would have been of silver or some other valuable material.

Bridgnorth, *1H4 3.2.175, 178,* town on the Severn river in Shropshire 140 mi. northwest of London.

Bristol, the major port on the Bristol channel, the waterway that provides southwestern England with access to the Atlantic ocean. Bristol was, after London, medieval England's chief commercial center. *2H6 3.1.328, Add. C.9. R2 3.2.138. 1H4 1.3.265.*

Bristol Castle, *R2 2.2.135, 2.3.163,* one of medieval England's strongest fortresses. It protected England's second most important port, Bristol.

Britain, island encompassing England, Scotland, and Wales. The Romans called the province they established on the island 'Britannia,' and medieval legend derived the name from 'Brut,' a Trojan warrior who allegedly fled west after his homeland fell to Homer's Greeks. The origin of the word is more likely to be found in Greek and Latin transliterations of a Celtic term. *LLL 4.1.122. Cym, passim. 3.1.12-13, 3.4.138-39:* The island was often described as being part of the world and yet not part of it because of its watery separation from the continent. The concept goes back to a line in Virgil's *Eclogues* 1.67 (which Holinshed quotes), but is also in Florus, Claudian, and Horace. It provided the British with a conception of their own unique place in the world, which informs John of Gaunt's famous speech in *R2 2.1.31-68,* and to this day affects even the negotiations for the European Economic Community. *H8 1.1.21.*

Britains, people of Britain. *Cym 4.4.5.*

British, (adj.) of or pertaining to the island of Britain or its people. *Lr. 3.4.172 (Q 11.169),* 'B. man': the rhyme is more commonly 'Englishman,' and this may be an attempt to approximate Lear's kingdom or to remind everyone of the United Kingdom of James I. *4.3.21 (Q 18.22),* 'B. powers,' Gonoril's and Regan's armies. *Cym 3.5.65, 5.6.481.*

Briton, 1) (n.) F1 'Britaine,' a person of Britain. *Cym 4.2.371, 5.5.75.* Pl.: *3.1.33, passim.*
2) *Cym 1.4.26, 1.6.68:* Posthumus.
3) (adj.) British, of or pertaining to Britain and its people. *Cym.*

Briton Reveller, the, *Cym 1.6.62,* Giacomo's characterization of Posthumus in Rome.

Brittaine, *Jn 2.1.156, 2.1.301, 2.1.311, 2.1.552,* see Arthur, Duke of; *R2 2.1.279,* see Brittany; Brittaine, Duke of.

Brittaine, Duke of, *R2 2.1.287,* John IV de Montfort (d. 1399), Henry (IV) Bolingbroke's host during part of the time he spent in exile. John died in November 1399, shortly after Henry claimed the English throne. On 3 April 1402, Henry married John's widow, Joan of Navarre, who was regent for the young heir to Brittany.

Brittany, *3H6 2.6.97, 4.7.97, 101,* (Bretagne, Brittaine) medieval duchy situated on the peninsula that comprises the northwestern corner of France. The district was bound on the south by the bay of Biscay and on the north by the English channel. On the landward side it shared borders with Maine, Anjou, and Normandy. Brittany may have been named for British Celts who fled to the continent in the 6th century to escape the Anglo-Saxon invasion of Roman Britain. Although the duke of Brittany was a vassal of the king of France, Brittany was frequently aligned with England against France. During the 12th century the dukedom was surrounded by fiefs belonging to the English king, Henry II, and Henry eventually brought it into his 'Angevin Empire' by marrying his son Geoffrey to its heiress. In the early 14th century the kings of England and France supported rival claimants to the duchy, but the people of Brittany fought to maintain their independence of both monarchs. In 1491 the French scored a coup when Anne, heir to the duchy, married King Charles VIII. In 1532 a treaty tied Brittany to France while granting it limited provincial autonomy. To this day Brittany has retained a unique culture that distinguishes it from the rest of France.

Brocas, *R2 5.6.14,* Bernard, (d. 1400), one of the men implicated in a plot to assassinate Henry IV at the start of his reign. Brocas came from a family of Frenchmen who cooperated with the English forces that occupied Gascony. His father fought beside Richard II's father, Edward the Black Prince, and Brocas inherited the post of chamberlain to Richard's queen. Brocas and others who were not willing to acquiesce to Richard's deposition planned to assassinate Henry while he watched a tournament at Windsor Castle early in 1400. News of the conspiracy was leaked to the king, and he eluded entrapment. Some of the would-be assassins were lynched by an angry mob in Cirencester, but the king's men brought Brocas to trial. He was convicted and executed.

Brook, Edmund (Edward), Lord Cobham, *3H6 1.2.40, 56* Kentish nobleman who was consistently loyal to the Yorkist cause and a personal friend of Richard, duke of York. He fought at the first battle of St. Albans and at Northampton. Sh. has him rally the men of Kent for the battle of Wakefield at which Richard was killed.

Brooke, *MWW,* 'Master B.,' disguise assumed by Frank Ford. It is interesting that this is the name of the lord William Brooke, Lord Cobham (or his son Henry) who objected to the use of his ancestor Sir John Oldcastle's name, so Sh. changed it to Falstaff. The use of Brooke is perhaps a way of mocking the puritanical arrogance of Lord Cobham. In F1, Brooke becomes 'Broome' which indicates a change since the 1602 Quarto. The reason would be unclear for this but may be related to Henry and his brother George Brooke's treason against King James in 1604. George was executed and Henry was jailed for life.

'Broom, The,' *TNK 4.1.107,* popular song of the period. It is included in William Chappell's *Popular Music of the Olden Time* (1859).

Brownist, *TN 3.2.30,* member of a Separatist Puritan religious sect which is mocked in many writings of the time. The controversy is typical of the freewheeling religious discussion which characterizes the period. The founder Robert Browne (1550-1633) was born at Tolethorpe in Rutland and educated at Corpus Christi College of Cambridge. He began his attacks upon the Church of England about 1580. He soon had gathered enough followers to get the attention of the Bishop of Norwich. Insolent at his trial he was remanded into custody of the sheriff's officer, but soon released at the urging of his relative Lord Burghley. He took refuge in Middelburg, Holland, but his congregation there gradually fell apart. In the religious freedom of the Netherlands he published several books, including *A Treatise of Reformation Without Tarying for Anie* and *A Booke Which Sheweth the Life and Manner of All True Christians.* In 1583 two men were hanged for distributing his works.

He went to Scotland and preached against the Presbyterian system of church governance. A year later he was back in England, was cited by the bishop of Peterborough and, after ignoring the summons to trial, was apparently frightened enough to seek absolution and rejoin the Church of England, sorely disappointing his followers. Controversy continued to swirl about him, but in 1591 he became a rector of Achurch-cum-Thorpe Waterville, Northamptonshire, and might have died in peace except that the irritable octogenarian got in an argument with a parish constable and beat him. Arrogant in court, he was put in Northampton jail and spent his last years there. He bragged on his death bed that he had been in 32 prisons. Despite his unpredictable behavior, he had many followers. In 1592 Sir Walter Raleigh estimated there were 20,000 Brownists. Their beliefs contributed to the Puritan movement and developed in a milder form into Congregationalism. Brownists believed that priests should be elected and removed by the congregation, that marriage was a civil—not religious—contract, and that no obedience should be owed by any church to a larger jurisdictional body. They also opposed the recitation of all given forms of prayer.

Brundisium, *Ant 3.7.21,* Brundusinus, Brindisi, city near the entrance to the Adriatic sea. It was ancient Rome's most popular port of embarkation for journeys to Greece and the eastern Mediterranean. Its name came from an Illyrian word for 'deer' which must have once been plentiful there. In ancient times the peninsula on which Brundisium was located was called Calabria, but in modern times it is Apulia. Strangely, now Calabria is the western peninsula, rather than the eastern.

Brute, or Bruté, L. vocative for 'Brutus.' Sh.'s allusion is to the Brutus who betrayed his friend Julius Cæsar by taking part in the plot to assassinate Cæsar. The famous phrase 'Et tu, Brute!' seems to be Sh.'s invention. *3H6 5.1.81:* the phrase is quoted as a proverb by Edward IV, who uses it to encourage his brother George (Clarence) to renounce Warwick and return to the Yorkist party. *JC 3.1.77:* it purports to be Cæsar's last words.

Brutus, 1) Lucius Junius Brutus (fl. 510 BC), man who, according to legend, raised the revolution that drove the hated king, Tarquinius Superbus, from Rome. As a youth Brutus feigned stupidity to protect himself from Tarquinius' jealousy, which earned him the nickname *brutus,* 'stupid.' An oracle, which only he interpreted correctly, prepared him for the role he was destined to play in Rome's history. When Tarquinius' son, Sextus, raped a virtuous matron, Lucretia, Brutus roused the Romans to overthrow the tyrant. He refused the offer of the crown and suggested that the Romans establish a republic. Although the story of his adventures was accepted as history by the ancient Romans, modern scholars believe that the Brutus family did not exist at Rome at the start of the republican period. The tales that sprang up about the exploits of the first Brutus may have evolved as a reflection of the reputation his family earned in later years in the service of the Republic. He is mentioned in Plutarch's 'Poplicola'; however, the tale of his interpreting the oracle is only in Livy's fragmentary *History of Rome,* 1.56, and it may have influenced the creation of Hamlet. *Luc 1734, 1807, 1847. H5 2.4.37. JC 1.2.160. Cor.*

2) Marcus Junius Brutus (78-42 BC), one of the Roman aristocrats who carried out the assassination of Julius Cæsar. Brutus was Cæsar's friend, but felt his duty to Rome compelled him to destroy Cæsar. Cæsar had acquired great power by exploiting the weaknesses of Rome's archaic republican institutions. In Cæsar's day Rome was still governed by political traditions it had evolved when it was a tiny city-state. These were designed to prevent any individual from monopolizing power, but they established so many checks and balances that they made it impossible for the duly elected magistrates to maintain order throughout Rome's far-flung empire. As a result, ambitious men exploited their offices to create huge military machines. Clashes among them developed into a civil war that no one was able conclusively to win. Like other Roman strongmen, Cæsar ingeniously exploited the situation to his own advantage. He won public office, used it to acquire an army, and turned that army to the destruction of rival generals. Cæsar was, however, different from others in the sense that he understood the situation into which his nation had blundered and he had a plan to break the cycle of conflicts that endangered the stability of the empire.

Once in power Cæsar hoped to persuade the Romans to accept a tightly centralized form of government that would prevent the rise of other persons like himself. He proceeded cautiously, but he failed to convince Rome's conservative aristocracy of the wisdom of his program. They accused him of aspiring to monarchy and scoffed at the idea that their republican institutions were inadequate. In their opinion it was Cæsar who threatened the Republic with failure, not the failure of the Republic that gave Cæsar his opportunity. The solution to the problem, from their point of view, was not the reform of the Roman system of government, but the destruction of the man who was urging changes in Rome's institutions. A plot to murder Cæsar was conceived by Gaius Cassius Longinus. He recruited Brutus and a host of other senators. On 15 March 44 BC, they surrounded Cæsar at a meeting of the Senate and stabbed him to death. The assassins had no desire to take responsibility for the government of Rome. They naively assumed that the Roman republic would automatically flourish once Cæsar was gone. This hope faded quickly. Claimants to Cæsar's power gained control of portions of his army, and civil war returned. Brutus fled to Greece and raised an army to oppose Cæsar's heirs, Octavius and Antony. When Brutus' men were defeated at the battle of Philippi, he chose to die by his own hand.

2H6 4.1.138. MV 1.1.166, 'B's Portia,' the daughter of Cato.

JC: Sh., like many poets and historians, struggled with the ambiguity of Brutus' career. Because of Brutus' betrayal of his friend, Dante made him and Cassius companions of Judas Iscariot in the deepest pit of Hell (*Inferno,* 34.65), but Brutus' patriotic motives and his advocacy of republican ideals were not without appeal to many Renaissance intellectuals. On the whole, he is portrayed as selfless and honest, unlike his conspirators, but unable to lead by galvanizing men to his purpose.

Ham 3.2.100. Ant 2.6.13, 16, 3.2.57, 3.11.38.

Buckingham, town in the county of Buckinghamshire, a district in south central England on the Thames between Oxford and London. Edward III licensed its merchants for participation in England's 'staple,' the nation's crucial international trade in wool. An earldom of Buckingham may have existed at the time of the Norman conquest. In the 12th century that honor was claimed by members of the Clare family, and in 1377 Richard II bestowed it on his uncle, Thomas of Woodstock. After the death of Thomas' son Humphrey, the earldom passed to Thomas' daughter Anne. Her son by Edmund

Stafford, Humphrey Stafford, was created duke of Buckingham in 1444. See Buckingham, Duke of.

Buckingham, Duke of, (1) *2H6, 3H6 1.1.10, 4.9.14,* see Humphrey, earl of Stafford and duke of Buckingham.

2) *R3,* see Henry, earl of Stafford and duke of Buckingham.

3) *H8,* see Edward, earl of Stafford and duke of Buckingham.

Buckingham, Henry of, *H8 2.1.108,* see Henry, earl of Stafford and duke of Buckingham.

Buckingham's Surveyor, *H8,* Charles Knevet (Knivet), steward, at one time, of the estates of Edward Stafford, duke of Buckingham, and witness against him at his trial for treason. Knevet was a distant relation of Stafford's, but a blood tie did not prevent him from bearing his former employer a grudge. Knevet may have believed that Stafford had unfairly dismissed him from his job or cheated him out of an inheritance. If he sought vengeance, he got it by testifying that he had often heard Stafford discuss the possibility of making a bid for Henry VIII's throne.

Bucklersbury, *MWW 3.3.67,* street in Cheapside where medicines and herbs were sold. One can assume it was fragrant in season.

Bullcalf, Peter, *2H4,* comic name that describes a stalwart young buck who would have made an excellent recruit for an army. A bribe persuades Falstaff to dismiss him and press less qualified men into service.

Bullen, Anne, see Boleyn, Anne.

Bulmer, William, *H8 1.2.191,* knight identified by Holinshed (3.863) as one of the sources for the bad feeling that developed between Henry VIII and Edward Stafford, duke of Buckingham. Although Bulmer had sworn allegiance to Henry, Buckingham ignored the man's oath to the king and took him into his own service. Henry cited this incident as one of several indications of Buckingham's presumption.

Bum, *MM 2.1.207,* Pompey says this is his name, though he could mean it in the sense in which we now say, 'my name is mud.' It leads to jokes about his large buttocks, which has long been British slang for 'arse.' The word was also, as now, applied to a disreputable person, but also then referred to a drink, which is appropriate to a tapster.

Bunch of Grapes, *MM 2.1.124,* room in an inn, or possibly a café-like inn open at the front. The name may have suggested the wine sold within; however, some critics believe 'bunch of grapes' to have been slang suggestive of male organs. The name could then be another way of suggesting the moral decay of Vienna.

Burgundy, 1) Duchy of, remnant of a kingdom established by German barbarians in the upper Rhine valley in the 5th century. The emerging nations of France and Germany pulled the Burgundian kingdom apart, and in 1032 the Burgundian royal title lapsed. The Carolingian kings of France established a duke in Burgundy to guard their frontier with Germany, and in 1015 the Capetian successors to the Carolingians assigned the duchy to a prince of the royal house. In 1361 John the Good, king of France, inherited the duchy, and in 1363 he transferred it to his son, Philip the Bold. Philip married the heiress to the wealthy county of Flanders and acquired other territories that turned his sprawling domain into a major power. When Philip's nephew, Charles VI, went mad, Philip fought Charles's brother, Louis of Orléans, for control of France's regency government. Under Philip's heir, John the Fearless, the quarrel between the Burgundians and Orléanists escalated into civil war, and Henry V of England seized the opportunity to attack a divided France. In 1419 efforts to unite the warring French nobles in defense of their nation foundered when John the Fearless was assassinated by the Orléanists. His son, Philip the Good, joined the English and nearly succeeded in putting Henry V on the throne of France. Henry's premature death in 1422 halted the English advance.

In 1435 Charles VII, king of France, detached Philip the Good from his alliance with England by freeing him from the obligation of doing feudal homage for his lands. In the hands of Philip's son, Charles the Bold, Burgundy expanded to the point where it endangered the balance of power on the continent. Charles the Bold's hope was to create a sovereign kingdom out of his far-flung collection of fiefs. King Louis XI of France seized the opportunity of Charles's death in battle in 1477 to block the expansion. By annexing the lands that had belonged to the original duchy, he prevented a Burgundian nation from evolving. A politically important portion of the ducal domain succeeded, however, in retaining its independence. Charles's daughter, Mary, relied on her husband, Maximilian of Austria, to help her hold Flanders, and, to the dismay of France and England, Flanders was annexed by the huge Hapsburg empire. The most dramatic historical event of Sh.'s life may have been an attempt in 1588 by the Spanish Hapsburg king, Philip II, to use a portion of Flanders as a base for an invasion of England.

3H6 2.1.143, 4.7.79, 4.7.90, 4.8.6. R3 1.4.10. Lr 1.1.258 (Q 1.249), 'wat'rish B.,' although this may be a phrase of contempt, the Low Countries are criss-crossed by rivers and are very well-watered. Whatever the setting of *Lr* may be, B. is an anachronism, existing as a nation long after the supposed reign of Lear.

2) *Lr,* the duke of Burgundy.

Burgundy, Duchess of, *3H6 2.1.146,* possibly Isabel, daughter of John I of Portugal and John of Gaunt's daughter, Philippe of Lancaster. She married Philip the Good, duke of Burgundy (d. 1464). She was Edward IV's distant cousin, not, as Sh. says, his aunt. Sh. may have intended the title 'aunt' to indicate respect for an older relative, not a literal relationship. Isabel was not the only Burgundian duchess with a link to the house of York. Edward's sister, Margaret, married Charles the Bold, and in 1471, when Warwick forced Edward to flee England, the desperate monarch won back his throne with Burgundy's help.

2) *Lr. 1.1.244,* Cordelia's proposed title.

Burgundy, Duke of, 1) *1H6.* Sh. took some liberty with history in describing a conference chaired by the king of France and attended by a duke of Burgundy on the eve of the battle of Agincourt (*H5 3.5.42*). The duke whose brother died at Agincourt (*H5 4.8.97*) was John the Fearless (1371-1419). But by 1415, the date of Agincourt, mental illness had forced King Charles VI to yield the reigns of government, and the duke of Burgundy was no longer in his entourage. In 1392 John's father, Philip the Bold (1364-1404), one of Charles's uncles, had tried to take over France as Charles's regent. Philip's enemies created the party of the 'Armagnacs' to stop him, and the Armagnacs forced the Burgundians from Paris. Sh.'s duke of Burgundy is a patriotic nobleman who convinces the kings of England and France to make peace by uniting their families and their nations.

The motives of the real dukes who reigned over Burgundy during this period were different. The help Burgundy gave England was a by-product of its fight with the Armagnacs. Burgundy refused to cooperate with the Armagnac army that engaged Henry at Agincourt, and most of those who died at Agincourt were allies of the Armagnacs. The decimation of the Armagnacs allowed Burgundy to regain control of Paris and of its invalid king. Once in power, however, Duke John had no desire to see the English conquer France, and he was as alarmed as the Armagnacs when Henry V returned to the continent with an army in 1417. Both parties of French nobles knew that they ought to work together against the English, but passion prevailed over reason. When John appeared at a ceremony at Melun in July, 1419, to make peace with the Armagnacs, they assassinated him. This drove John's son, Philip the Good (1396-1464), the duke of Burgundy who appears as a speaking character in *H5 5.2,* into the arms of the English. With Philip's help, Henry V seized Paris and Charles VI. Henry married Charles's daughter, Catherine, disinherited her brother, and asserted his right—through his own blood lines and those of his wife—to be Charles VI's successor. See Philip the Good.

2) *Lr,* ruler who drops his suit of Cordelia as soon as it becomes obvious she will not receive a dowry. The lack of a dowry caused many a Renaissance woman to be less desirable as a mate, and so modern readers should not regard him with too much revulsion, although sympathy is clearly with the romantic willingness of the King of France to accept Cordelia with no reward but herself. There is no equivalent character in Sh.'s sources and the duke was apparently created to dramatize all that Cordelia gives up in her perseverance. 'Divers Peeres' are said to be interested in her in *The True Chronicle History of King Leir* (1605), but none of them appears on stage but Gallia (France).

Burton, *1H4 3.1.93,* town on the Trent river in Staffordshire 130 mi. northwest of London.

Burton Heath. *Shr Ind. 2.17,* either Barton on the Heath, a village about 16 mi. from Stratford, or Barton, 8 mi. distant.

Bury, or Bury St. Edmunds, town in the county of Suffolk. It was the site of a monastery dedicated to the memory of Edmund, an Anglo-Saxon king slaughtered by the Danes in 869. After the Norman conquest Bury St. Edmunds became one of England's largest and richest cloisters. The institution was so commodious and well endowed that it could afford to offer hospitality to the entire royal entourage. The court often visited Bury, and parliaments sometimes convened there. Bury St. Edmunds was the site of the fateful parliament at which the Yorkist party induced Henry VI to consent to the arrest of his uncle, Humphrey of Gloucester. *2H6 2.4.72, 3.2.241. Jn 4.3.114.*

Bushy, *R2,* Bushey, Bussy, John, speaker of parliament's house of commons and one of Richard II's councilors. Some of his contemporaries considered him a base flatterer who fostered an unhealthy lust for power in the king. He may have helped Richard plan the coup that overthrew the 'lords appellant' in 1397. In 1398 he maneuvered parliament into delegating its power to a standing committee composed of the king's men. Since it was treason to attack the person of the king, criticism of the royal government usually took the form of hostile comments about the king's advisors, and Bushy was a convenient target for the anger Richard's tyrannical policies stirred up among his subjects. When Henry (IV) Bolingbroke invaded England to unseat Richard in 1399, Bushy comprehended the danger and fled for safety to Bristol Castle. His asylum was poorly chosen. Bristol quickly surrendered to Henry and turned Bushy over for execution without the formality of a trial.

Butler, *1H4 2.4.67, 72,* man Hotspur employs to help organize a rebellion against Henry IV.

Butts, Doctor, *H8,* William, Henry VIII's physician (d. 1545). He was a Cambridge graduate and one of the founders of the Royal College of Physicians. Although attracted to Protestantism and a friend of Thomas Cranmer's, he interceded with Henry for Cardinal Wolsey when Henry punished Wolsey for the failure of his plan to obtain papal approval for termination of the king's marriage with Katherine of Aragon. Butts stood by Wolsey in his disgrace and attended him during his terminal illness.

Byzantium, *Tim 3.6.59,* allusion to Alcibiades' recapture of Byzantium, although the history bears no real resemblance to the drama. Byzantium was the ancient name of Constantinople (modern Istanbul), located at the entry to the Black Sea in Thrace. Founded by Greeks in 667 BC, it became a center of power when Constantine I, emperor of Rome, chose it as the location for Constantinople, his capital, in 330 AD. In 395, the Roman Empire divided into east and west, with the eastern portion claiming the entire empire after the fall of Rome. The last emperor to attempt to reunite the Roman Empire was Justinian in the 6th c. and though he had limited success, his reign brought a great flourishing of art and architecture, as well as the codification of Roman law. The Roman and Eastern Orthodox churches separated in the time of Charlemagne. The Byzantine Empire was renowned for its internal dissension, complex administration, and corruption, yet while absorbing many oriental influences, it nonetheless maintained a position as the center of western culture and most important city in Christendom for centuries. Constantly assailed by invaders, the empire was nibbled away. Asia Minor was lost to the Seljuk Turks in 1071 and the city was sacked by Christian Crusaders in 1204. Reduced to a wraith of its former splendor, the Byzantine Empire was destroyed by the Ottomans under Muhammed II when the city fell in 1453, a date often given as the beginning of the modern era. Its fall removed the last obstacle for a Turkish invasion of Europe and the constant threat of the Ottomans, who once nearly captured Vienna, was an obsession with the Europeans throughout Sh.'s lifetime.

C

Cacaliban, *Tmp 2.2.183,* Caliban, the extra syllable for the sake of the music or to indicate drunkenness.

Cade, Jack, *2H6,* (d. 1450), leader of a popular uprising aimed at the ouster of Henry VI's advisors and the reform of the fiscal policies of his government. Cade's identity is uncertain. Some sources say that he was an Irishman, but the name 'Cade' was relatively common in Sussex where Cade first appeared as a member of the household of a Sir Thomas Dacre. An indictment on a charge of murder prompted him to flee to the continent. For a short time he earned his living by fighting for the French. Adopting the name 'Aylmer' and claiming to be a physician, he returned to England and settled in Kent. He married and became a leader among the rural gentry, a class of propertied people who were upset about the taxes imposed by Henry VI's government. Henry was unable to make peace or war successfully, and it seemed to those who paid the bills that the king drained money from England to no good purpose. The merchants and farmers of Kent, Sussex, and Surrey were also angered by their government's inability to protect them from French adventurers who preyed on their ships and raided England's coast. Cade's rebellion was, at the start, a protest by the commercial classes against bad government. Its political objectives were essentially conservative. The rebels wanted better royal government, not the abolition of monarchy. The leader of the revolt demonstrated its royalist sympathies by claiming to be John Mortimer, an alleged cousin of the duke of York. This man may have been Cade, or Cade may have taken his place as the uprising spread.

Whoever the first captain of the rebels was, he had significant executive skills. The rebellion began at the end of May 1450 and spread rapidly across England's southern counties. In early June companies of armed men advanced on London and established a fortified camp at Blackheath, a crossroads 6 mi. southeast of the city. To avoid the appearance of treason, Cade's followers claimed that their target was not the king, but the royal advisors who, they said, had misled Henry. They proved their loyalty to Henry by obeying his order to withdraw from their camp, but when Henry unwisely sent soldiers after them, they defended themselves and routed the royal army. Feeling betrayed and confirmed in the justice of their cause, the rebels wheeled about and marched on London. Henry retreated from the city to the distant castle of Kenilworth, and Cade set up headquarters in Southwark at the entrance to London bridge. Londoners cherished many of the same grievances as the rebels, and on 2 July 1450, they permitted Cade to enter their city. Lord Saye, Henry's treasurer, was taken from the Tower and beheaded, and Saye's son-in-law, William Cromer, the sheriff of Kent, was apprehended at his home and executed. The enthusiastic rebels paraded the heads of their victims through the streets. Success tempted Cade to increase his demands and his men to loosen their discipline. The Londoners began to feel less secure—and, consequently, less enthusiastic for the revolt.

On 6 July Matthew Gough, captain of the Tower, seized London Bridge and prevented Cade from returning to town from his camp in Southwark. This challenge culminated in a bloody, but militarily inconclusive, confrontation. Henry's councilors took advantage of the confusion created by the incident and intervened. A committee of clergy promised royal pardons to all who would lay down their arms, and the rebels, having vented their anger and tired of their adventure, melted away. By promising mercy the government emerged victorious, but there was a limit to its willingness to forgive and forget. Cade, like his fellows, had received a pardon, but Henry's judges declared it void because it had been issued to a fictitious 'John Mortimer,' not a Jack Cade. Cade fled into the forests near Lewes, Sussex. Alexander Iden, the sheriff of Kent, tracked him to Heathfield, where he was mortally wounded resisting arrest. His death did not prevent Henry from taking revenge. Cade's corpse was beheaded, quartered, and displayed to the public as a warning to any who might challenge the king's authority.

Cadmus, founder of Thebes, son of Agenor and Telephassa, brother of Europa. After Jupiter abducted Europa, Cadmus searched for her. In the process he killed a dragon while attempting to found Thebes and sowed its teeth. An armed man grew out of the earth from each. The dragon was sacred to Mars and Cadmus served the god for eight years as penance. Later he married Harmonia, but the misfortunes of his children led him to say that since the gods so valued the serpent, he wished he were one. He was then transformed with Harmonia into a harmless crested snake. The stories appear in Ovid's *Metamorphoses,* 3, 4. *MND 4.1.111:* Hippolyta's story of hunting with Cadmus seems to have no mythological precedent.

Caduceus, *Tro 2.3.12,* golden magical rod of the god Mercury. Topped by wings its rod was entwined by two snakes. It had power over wealth, happiness, and dreams. Mercury received it from Apollo in exchange for the lyre, which he had invented from a tortoise shell. The name comes from the Greek 'karukelon' for 'herald's wand,' as Mercury (Hermes) was the gods' messenger. The staff became an emblem equivalent to the 'peace pipe' symbolizing an end to conflict and was also the protective symbol of messengers and ambassadors. The serpents on the rod have been associated with Æsculapius (serpents were ancient symbols of restorative health because of their moulting) and by Sh.'s time the Caduceus had become a symbol of the medical profession.

Cadwal, *Cym,* name given to Arviragus by his foster father Belarius. It is probably borrowed from the famous Welsh hero Cadwallader.

Cadwallader, last of the native British kings to offer serious resistance to the Anglo-Saxons who invaded Britain after the fall of the Roman empire. He was the ruler of Gwynedd in northern Wales and the mortal enemy of his neighbors, the Saxons of Northumbria. In 633 he joined Penda, the Saxon king of Mercia, in a raid on Northumbrian territory. The Northumbrians were routed, and Cadwallader launched a campaign to drive them from Britain. Oswald, a Northumbrian prince, rallied his people and killed Cadwallader in a battle near Hexham. *H5 5.1.27,* C.'s 'goats' are the Welsh people, an unflattering characterization.

Cælius, *Ant 3.7.73,* probably Cornelius Sossius, consul for 66 BC and Mark Antony's partisan. Antony appointed him to a governorship in Syria, and Cælius commanded the left wing of Antony's fleet at the battle of Actium. Sossius survived Actium and in due time found favor with Antony's victorious opponent, Octavius. Sh. took the corrupted spelling of Cornelius Sossius' name from Thomas North's translation of Plutarch's works that was his major source for *Ant* ('Antony' 65.1).

Cærnarfonshire, *H8 2.3.48,* county in northwestern Wales, site of some of the highest mountains in Britain. Since the district was a natural refuge for Welsh rebels, Edward I tried to bring it under control by building a castle at Cærnarvon. His son, Edward II, who was born at Cærnarvon, was the first heir to the English throne to use the title 'prince of Wales.'

Cæsar, 1) see Cæsar, Caius Julius, or Octavius Cæsar.

2) *Tit 1.1.10,* unnamed Roman emperor, father of Saturninus and Bassianus. At the start of *Tit,* Bassianus contests his brother's right to their father's throne, but the Roman people side with Saturninus. Although Sh. chose appropriate Roman, Greek, and Gothic names for the characters in *Tit,* he was not dramatizing events or persons from history.

Cæsar, Caius Julius, (c. 102 BC–44 BC), in legend and fact one of the greatest of Roman generals, statesmen, and authors. In the Renaissance his name was synonymous with 'conqueror.' Early in his career he aligned himself with the popular political party of Marius as opposed to the Senatorial party of Sulla. Later Crassus also helped advance Cæsar's career. After a successful campaign in Spain, Cæsar joined Crassus and Pompey to form the First Triumvirate, driving the leaders of the Senatorial opposition (Cato and Cicero) into exile. When his consulship ended Cæsar set about building a base of military power equal to Pompey's. He did so by becoming governor of Rome's modest provinces in Gaul and provoking a war with the Gauls to the north. His successes, including an invasion of Britain, provoked his writing *De Bello Gallico* ('The Gallic Wars') whose clear, direct language has made it a superior text for the study of elementary Latin in schools of the Renaissance. Sh. and his literate contemporaries were all familiar with it.

In 53 BC Crassus was killed in battle and the triumvirate unravelled. Pompey assumed a sole consulship in Rome and in 49 BC, Cæsar committed treason by crossing the Rubicon river dividing Gaul and Italy. Pompey and the Senatorial party retreated to Greece where Cæsar defeated him at Pharsalus in 48 BC. Pompey retreated to Egypt where he was murdered. Cæsar was sent Pompey's embalmed head as a gesture, but Cæsar invaded Egypt to avenge Pompey. During this campaign he impregnated Cleopatra who bore him a son, Cæsarion. Cæsar recognized her as queen of Egypt and placed a statue to her in a new temple of Venus. In 46 BC she visited Rome to see him. Cæsar chased down most of his enemies and set about reorganizing Rome into a monarchical government. In order to prevent Cæsar's assumption of sole political power, Brutus and Cassius organized about 60 conspirators who ganged up on Cæsar on the Ides of March and assassinated him. His death caused a revival of the civil wars that had raised him to power.

2H6 4.1.139. 4.7.59, 'commentaries' of JC, alludes to *De Bello Gallico,* 5.14. *3H6 5.1.81, 5.5.52. 1H6 1.1.56. 1.3.118,* 'C. and his fortune,' a reference to a passage in Plutarch's lives (3.429) that describes C.'s crossing of the Adriatic Sea at Brundisium in pursuit of Pompey and the battle that decided the fate of the empire.

R3 3.1.69, 3.1.84. LLL 5.2.608, 'pommel of C.'s falchion,' the knob at the handle of C.'s curved broadsword. The pommel is commonly decorated and is therefore compared to Holoferne's face. *R2 5.1.2. 2H4 1.1.23, 2.4.163. JC. AYLI 5.2.30* 'C.'s thrasonical brag': *Veni, vidi, vici,* his statement after an easy victory over Pharnaces II in Pontus. Rosalind is saying that this is a brag in the style of the soldier Thraso in Terence's *Eunuch* (161 BC).

Ham 3.2.99. MM 2.1.238, 3.1.312. Oth 2.3.114. AWW 3.6.54. Ant 1.5.66, 1.5.67, 1.5.68, 1.5.70, 2.6.72, 3.13.118. Cym 2.4.21, 3.1.2, 6, 12, 23, 48; 3.1.31, 'C.'s sword,' an allusion to a story repeated by Holinshed that Nennius, brother of Cassibelan, captured this weapon when Cæsar imbedded it in Nennius' shield. After Nennius died of a wound inflicted by it, Cassibelan buried it with his brother.

2) 'C.' as a title for a conqueror. *3H6 3.1.18. H5 5.0.28,* a flattering allusion to Robert Devereux, earl of Essex, whom Elizabeth sent to Ireland in the spring of 1599 to suppress a rebellion led by the earl of Tyrone. The name was frequently used as a synonym for 'conqueror' referring to Julius, or 'emperor/ruler' referring to Octavius and his successors. *2H4 2.4.163,* (pl.) vigorous military commanders who, like Julius Cæsar, could cover a great deal of ground quickly and in good order. *MWW 1.3.9. Cym 3.1.11, 36,* emperors of Rome or military geniuses of the prowess of Julius Cæsar.

Cæsar, Octavius, see Octavius Cæsar (he adopted the name Cæsar from Julius). *JC 5.1.24. Ant. Cym 2.4.11. 3.1, passim. 3.5.102, 3.7.10, 5.6.82, 461, 475. Mac 3.1.58.*

Cæsarion, *Ant 3.6.6, 3.13.165,* (47–30 BC), son of Julius Cæsar and Cleopatra. He was also called Ptolemy after one of his mother's ancestors, the Macedonian general who founded the last Egyptian dynasty. Part of Antony's strategy for overthrowing Octavius, his rival for control of the Roman empire, was the conquest of Parthia. The acquisition of the huge Parthian empire would have tipped the balance of power in Antony's favor and won him the enthusiastic support of the Roman people. The resources of Egypt were essential to the success of the Parthian war, and on the eve of the campaign Antony promised Egypt's queen, Cleopatra, that he would establish kingdoms in the lands he conquered for her sons. Ptolemy was promised Phoenicia, Syria, and Cilicia. In 42 BC, Cleopatra proclaimed Cæsarion king of Egypt, and Antony accorded him the title 'king of kings' in 34 BC. His expectations were never realized, for Antony failed to conquer Parthia and Octavius destroyed Antony's army at the battle of Actium. Antony and Cleopatra committed suicide, and Octavius executed Cæsarion. The Julian blood in his veins may have made it too dangerous for Octavius to allow him to live. The boy's status as Cæsar's natural child made him a potentially dangerous rival to Octavius, Cæsar's adopted son.

Cain, the first murderer in biblical history, Genesis 4:2–16. Cain and his younger brother Abel were born to Adam and Eve after their expulsion from the Garden of Eden. Cain became a farmer and Abel a herdsman. Both men offered God the fruits of their labors. God accepted Abel's, but rejected Cain's. This humiliation enraged Cain and prompted him to slay his brother. Cain also has symbolic significance as the first man to be born of woman.

1H6 1.4.38. LLL 4.2.35, 'at C.'s birth,' in extreme antiquity. *R2 5.6.43. Jn 3.4.79. MWW 1.4.21,* 'C.-coloured beard': like Judas, C. was represented as having reddish (or, as here, yellow) hair. Red hair often has a lot of yellow in it, especially in the beard. Other less convincing possibilities are that this should read 'cane-coloured,' the color of a cane or of the dye of the wild arbutus (Anglo-Irish 'cane' from Irish *caithne*). *2H4 1.1.157.*

Caithness, 1), *Mac,* region on the northeastern tip of Scotland, its rocky coast jutting out toward the Orkneys. It is surrounded on three sides by water and bordered to the west by Sutherland. Picts, Norwegians, and Danes have all left archaeological remains in the area. It was named after the local Celtic tribe, the 'Cat people' of whom nothing is known.

2) *Mac,* F1 'Cathness,' a nobleman who joins the rebellion against Macbeth. He seems to be used by Sh. to demonstrate that the Scots from end to end of the country now oppose Macbeth. The historical earl was named Thorfinn Sigurdsson. He was a Viking ruler whose domains included Caithness, the Orkney Islands and the Hebrides. He and Macbeth joined forces to defeat Duncan in 1040, when the king attempted to grant Thorfinn's lands to his nephew Moddan. Either Thorfinn's daughter or his sister became the first wife of Malcolm. He appears in the Norse epic *King Harald's Saga* as Thorfinn the Mighty.

Caius, 1) *MWW* French physician in love with Anne Page. Although her mother arranges for him to abduct and marry her, the fairy disguises make him run off with the wrong person. Caius is a foul-mouthed, excitable, stereotypical Frenchman challenging Sir Hugh to a duel and his comeuppance is a great source of humor. His character type survives in the John Cleese portrayal of the nasty French soldier in *Monty Python and the Holy Grail* and numerous comically obnoxious French waiters.

The name is a common Roman one which Sh. borrowed. Scholars are uncertain whether Caius is pronounced with one syllable ('keez') as Caius College at Cambridge has been pronounced for many centuries, or two syllables ('kay-us'), or three ('ka-ee-oos'). Many, however, incline to believe it was one syllable because of the antiquity of that pronunciation in England.

2) *Lr. 5.3.259,* Kent's name in disguise, used nowhere else in the play. Lear describes him as dead, then seems to recognize him.

3) *JC,* see Cassius, Caius.

4) *JC,* see Ligarius, Caius.

5) *Cym,* see Lucius, Caius.

Caius Marcellus, *Ant 2.6.111,* C. Claudius Marcellus, (d. 41 BC), first husband to Octavia, sister of Octavius. Marcellus was consul for the year 50 BC. Although he was related to Julius Cæsar by marriage, he supported Cæsar's rival,

Pompey. When war broke out between Pompey and Cæsar, Marcellus, like his friend Cicero, was too timid to commit himself to a specific course of action. Octavia was carrying his child when Marcellus died in 41 BC. In compliance with her brother's wishes, the heavily pregnant Octavia promptly wed Mark Antony. In 25 BC Octavius adopted the son his sister bore Marcellus and wed the boy (Marcus) to his only child, Julia. He was intended to be Octavius' heir, but he did not live beyond the age of twenty.

Caius Martius, *Cor,* see Coriolanus.

Calaber, Duke of, *2H6 1.1.7,* duke of Calabria, the district that occupies the 'toe' of Italy's boot-shaped peninsula. It was part of the Norman kingdom of Sicily and Naples to which Henry VI's father-in-law, René of Anjou, had a claim.

Calabria, southwestern portion of the peninsula of Italy, one of the provinces of the medieval kingdom of the Two Sicilies (i.e., Naples and Sicily). In ancient times, the eastern peninsula of southern Italy was called Calabria, but after the Middle Ages it is called Apulia. The area now called Calabria was called Bruttium. See Calaber, Duke of, *2H6.*

Calais, F1 'Callice,' French port opposite the English city of Dover. Calais and Dover commanded the narrowest point on the English channel. Calais was the last continental possession left to England at the end of the Hundred Years' War. During the War of the Roses it had special significance, for it was a safe haven outside England to which combatants in England's civil war could retreat to regroup. It was staffed by England's largest standing garrison. Warwick 'the Kingmaker' used Calais as a base for organizing the coup that nearly unseated Edward IV. France did not reclaim it until 1558. *1H6 4.1.9, 170. Jn 3.3.73. R2 1.1.126, 4.1.12, 73. H5 3.2.46, 3.3.139, 3.6.141, 4.8.125, 5.0.7.*

Calais, Lord of, *3H6 1.1.239,* title for the commander of England's last outpost in France, in this case, Warwick. See Neville, Richard.

Calchas, *Tro,* father of Cressida, a Trojan priest who has defected to the Greeks before the beginning of the play because he foresees the downfall of Troy. He suggests the trade of Antenor for his daughter, thereby inadvertently setting up the treason of Antenor and Cressida's betrayal of Troilus. In Homer, Calchas is a Greek soothsayer. He is the son of Thestor and prophesizes four things: Iphigenia must be sacrificed, the war will drag out for a decade, Achilles is required for the fall of Troy, and the Greeks will be relieved of their plague only after the return of Chryseis to her father. Calchas' rival in soothsaying was Mopsus. He challenged him to a contest, but when Mopsus was able to predict the exact number of figs on a tree and Calchas was not, he died of disappointment. Calchas' transformation to Sh.'s character occurred in the Middle Ages. He first seems to have become a Trojan in the apocryphal Dares Phrygius' *De Excidio Trojæ Historia* (circa 6th c. AD) and the father of Briseïda (Cressida) in Benoît de Sainte-More's *Le Roman de Troie* (1184).

Caliban, *Tmp,* deformed native of the island of Prospero, son of Sycorax the witch. The origin of the name is uncertain. It may be a variation on Carib, the tribe which gave the Caribbean its name. Virgil and Pliny mention the Chalybeates, who are cannibals. In Spenser's *Færie Queene,* 6.4, the knight Calepine encounters the 'saluage man.' There are a number of resemblances between this Savage Man and Caliban and the similarity of the knight's name seems more than a coincidence. Most critics favor the theory that the name is an anagram of 'cannibal,' particularly since Michel de Montaigne's essay 'Of Cannibals,' translated by John Florio, is evident as a source throughout the play. 'Cannibal' seems to derive from Taino, through 16th c. Sp., and is a doublet of 'Caribe' a tribal name which survives in 'Caribbean.' Another possibility is the town of Calibia, located on the African coast between Tunis and Hammamet on Diego Ribeyro's map of 1529. In Thomas Malory's *Le Morte d'Arthur* there is a 'paynyme of Perse' named Calleborne who is killed by Sir Broce. Another suggestion has been that Caliban is modeled on a West African prince living in London. His name was Dedery Jaquoah, son of King Caddibiah of the river Cetras in Guinea. The prince was baptized John on 1 January 1611. Why this converted prince should inspire the creation of a monster is not clear. Also offered as origins are 'kalebon,' Arabic slang for 'vile dog,' 'cauliban' a Gypsy (Romany) word for 'black,' a Greek word for 'drinking cup,' and 'Kalee-ban,' the satyr of Kalee in Hindo scripture. This latter suggestion sets a standard for nutty Shakespearean criticism.

'Calin o custure me,' *H5 4.4.4,* F1 'calmie custure me,' possibly an Irish song. Other critics think the words may be mere nonsense.

Calipolis, *2H4 2.4.176,* wife of Muly Mahamet, the hero of *The Battell of Alcazar,* a play by one of Sh.'s contemporaries, George Peele (1588). The reference is to a scene in which the protagonist offers his starving wife lion's meat impaled on a sword.

Callice, F1 for 'Calais.' It may reflect pronunciation.

Calpurnia, *JC,* Julius Cæsar's last wife. She was the daughter of Lucius Calpurnius Piso, consul for the year 58 BC. Cæsar wed her in 59 BC. They had no children.

Calydon, *2H6 1.1.235,* town in Ætolia, the district on the northwestern shore of the gulf of Corinth. In Greek legend it was the place where a hunt caused a dispute that led to a tragic feud between kinsmen, the Calydonians and the Curetes. See Althæa.

Cambio, *Shr,* Lucentio's disguise as a Latin teacher.

Cambria, *Cym 3.2.43, 5.6.17,* medieval Latin for Wales, where Belarius lived in exile with Cymbeline's sons. According to Spenser (*Færie Queene,* 2.10.14), it was named after an ancient king, Camber, who ruled the western quarter of Britain.

Cambridge, *H5 2.2.13,* county seat of Cambridgeshire, situated on the Cam river about 50 mi. northeast of London. It boasted one of the two universities that existed in England in Sh.'s day. See Richard, earl of Cambridge, *H5, 1H6.*

Cambridge, Earl of, *H5, 1H6,* see Richard, earl of Cambridge.

Cambyses (d. 522), son of the founder of the Persian empire, Cyrus the Great. He succeeded to his father's throne in 529 and subsequently added Egypt to his family's vast domain. He was alleged to have had a violent temper that may have been a symptom of mental illness. He died under mysterious circumstances that spawned rumors of suicide. *1H4 2.5.390,* 'C.'s vein' is not to the king, but to the florid style of a play about the king: *The Life of Cambises, King of Percia* by Thomas Preston (1569).

Camelot, *Lr. 2.2.84 (Q 7.82),* legendary site of King Arthur's court and the Round Table. It was traditionally said to have been located at three places. First, Cærleon-on-Usk in South Wales, was the site of one of the three great forts of the Roman legions in Britain. Cærleon may derive from *Castra legionem,* 'legion fort.' The Second Augusta Legion garrisoned it. The ruins there probably caused it to be associated with Arthur. Tintagel, on the north coast of Cornwall near Camelford, is also a candidate. Sir Thomas Malory in his *Le Morte d'Arthur* clearly identifies Camelot with Winchester. However, Sh.'s passage probably refers to Cadbury castle in Somerset, an area where geese were bred. Cadbury is about 9 mi. northwest of Yeovil and is the site of an Iron Age fort which is about 300 feet above the surrounding fields and looks across the plain to the northwest toward Glastonbury Tor. Badbury Rings, an iron age fortress near Wimborne, Dorset, is considered a possible site for the battle at 'Mons Badchicus' where the Saxons drove back the British in 486. In 552 they defeated them again at Old Sarum, and in 556 at Barbury (Swindon). All of these battles are near Salisbury Plain, moving in order to the north and the second and third might be sources for the idea that Arthur was driven from the plain.

Camillo, *WT,* lord of Sicilia. In Sh.'s source, Robert Greene's *Pandosto,* or the Triumph of Time (1588; rptd. 1607 as *Dorastus and Fawnia*), Camillo's equivalent is the character Franion, with some touches derived from Capnio. Sh. expands and deepens Camillo's role. Furius Camillus is one of the lives discussed by Plutarch, from whom Sh. got most of his names for the play; however, the name was well known. John Webster's *White Devil* (1612) has a character Camillo and there were several books authored by one Camillus or another before 1611. A St. Camillus de Lellis established the ecclesiastical order of Fathers of a Good Death in 1584, and was succeeded as its head by a Roger—a name also used in *WT.* A fearsome Camilla is described in Virgil's *Æneid,* 11.690–698, and is mentioned by Spenser (*Færie Queene* 3.4.2.8).

Campeius, Cardinal, *H8,* Lorenzo Campeggio (1461–1539), the papal commissioner who presided with Cardinal Wolsey at an ecclesiastical court convened to consider Henry VIII's request for a divorce from Katherine of Aragon. Campeggio was an Italian nobleman who had begun his career as a married professor of canon law at the university of Padua. After the death of his wife in 1510, he was ordained to the priesthood and, in 1517, named a cardinal. He was also consecrated bishop of Salisbury to recompense him for serving as England's agent at the papal curia. In May 1529 the pope yielded to pressure from Cardinal Wolsey and sent Campeius to England to begin divorce hearings. Henry leapt to the conclusion that he would soon receive the permission he had long been seeking to separate from Katherine. The troops that Katherine's nephew, Charles V, had stationed in Italy meant, however, that Pope Clement was not free to grant Henry his wish. Rather than offend either party, the pope instructed Campeggio to stall the proceedings as long as possible, and in July 1529 he transferred the case to Rome. Henry was infuriated at what he perceived to be a crass political trick. He dismissed Cardinal Wolsey in disgrace and terminated England's relationship with the Roman church.

Canary, 1) sweet white wine from the Canary Islands, similar to Madeira. The Canary islands had become a Spanish possession by the 16th c. They were originally named for the wild dogs of the island (L. *canaria*), so, curiously, the wine and the songbird both bear the name of the dog. The first use of the word for wine (according to *OED*) is in *2H4* in 1597, though *MWW* may predate it. *MWW 3.2.89. 2H4 2.4.25. TN 1.3.78, 81.*

2) sprightly dance originating in the Canary Islands. *LLL 3.1.11. MWW 2.2.60, 63:* the peculiar use of the word by Mistress Quickly is considered by most commentators to be a pun on 'quandary,' though it could also be some sort of play on the dance: 'You have put her into a wild dance.' *AWW 2.1.73.*

Cancer, *Tro 2.3.194,* astrological sign, L. 'crab.' It appears at the summer solstice when the sun has reached the zenith of its move to the north. It moves sideways like a crab. When Hercules fought the Lernean Hydra, Juno sent the crab to torment him. It managed to bite Hercules' foot, but was killed. Juno placed it in the sky.

Candy, *TN 5.1.57,* Candia (Greek: *Herakleion*), the major port of Crete located on the gulf of Candia. Coincidentally, Candavia was a mountainous region of Illyria in Roman times, but this could not be meant.

Canidius, *Ant,* Lucius Canidius Crassus, (d. 30 BC), one of Antony's soldiers. At the time of Julius Cæsar's assassination he was serving under Lepidus' command with Cæsar's army in

Gaul. He helped Lepidus negotiate a place with Antony in the second triumvirate, and he was appointed to Antony's staff. Canidius directed important campaigns for Antony in Armenia, and he was one of the officers who counseled Antony on preparations for the battle at Actium. Plutarch ('Antony' 63.3) says that Canidius tried to persuade Antony to send Cleopatra away from the army and to take his stand in Thrace or Macedon rather than at Actium. Although Antony rejected his advice and chose to fight at Actium, he entrusted him with command of his infantry. The day was decided, as Canidius had feared, at sea, and he was compelled to watch from the sidelines as his party went down to defeat. Antony fled to Egypt, but Canidius kept the army intact for a week hoping that its commander would return. When he realized that this would not happen, he went to Egypt to bring Antony the news that many of the men had defected to his rival, Octavius. Antony committed suicide. Octavius conquered Egypt, and Canidius was captured and executed.

Canterbury, *1H4 1.2.124,* city 55 mi. southeast of London in the county of Kent. At the start of the Middle Ages it was the capital of the Anglo-Saxon kingdom of Kent and a base for missionaries the pope sent to Christianize Britain. Since the diocese was the first see established in Britain, it supervised the development of the English church and its archbishop became England's 'primate,' the nation's pre-eminent churchman. In addition to the prestige that it enjoyed as the seat of the primate, in the 12th c. it acquired a unique sacred treasure. In 1170 Henry II's soldiers broke into the cathedral and murdered Archbishop Thomas Becket. Three years later Becket was canonized, and his tomb began to attract pilgrims. By the end of the medieval era it had become the most venerated shrine in England. Henry VIII decreed its destruction in 1538 as part of his religious reform program. See Canterbury, Archbishop of, *Jn*; *R2*; *H5*; *H8*.

Canterbury, Archbishop of, 1) office of primate or head of the English church. The diocese of Canterbury was created at the end of the 6th century when Pope Gregory the Great established a mission among the pagan Saxons of Britain. At that time the city was the capital of the kingdom of Kent, and Æthelbert of Kent provided a home for the Benedictine monks who worked among his people. St. Augustine, leader of the mission, founded the diocese and was consecrated its first bishop. He and his successors directed the work of other bishops as more sees were organized in Britain. The province managed by the archbishop during the high Middle Ages contained all the English dioceses south of Cheshire and Yorkshire. A second province, headed by an archbishop of York, evolved in northern England. York has occasionally challenged the supremacy of Canterbury, but with no lasting effect.

2) *Jn 3.1.69–70,* see Langton, Stephen.

3) *R2 2.1.283,* Thomas Arundel (1352–1414), brother of Richard, earl of Arundel. In 1386 parliament forced Richard II to dismiss his chancellor, Michael de la Pole, and appoint Arundel, then bishop of Ely, to the post. After Arundel became archbishop of York in 1388, Richard deprived him of the chancellery, but he returned to that office to serve from 1391 to 1396. In 1396 he was translated from the see of York to Canterbury. As primate of England, he vigorously combatted the proto-Protestant heresies of the Oxford professor, John Wycliff. In 1397 Richard executed Arundel's brother, the earl, who was one of the 'lords appellant' charged with plotting to diminish the king's power. Arundel fled to Rome where he received a cool welcome. Richard persuaded Pope Boniface IX to translate Arundel from Canterbury to a remote see in Scotland that an English bishop could not hope to occupy. When Richard banished Henry (IV) Bolingbroke in 1398, Arundel joined the Lancastrian heir in exile and assisted him in raising the army that drove Richard from the throne. Arundel reclaimed Canterbury and helped negotiate terms for Richard's abdication. He presided at Henry IV's coronation and served briefly as the new king's chancellor. He devoted most of his energy thereafter to prosecuting 'Lollards,' Wycliff's followers. Shortly

before his death, he tried and condemned for heresy Sir John Oldcastle, the person after whom the character of Falstaff is modeled.

4) *H5,* Henry Chichele (1362–1443), Oxford scholar and Carthusian monk who rose from a humble background to become the primate of England. Despite his monastic calling, Chichele had an active political career. He served for a time as England's ambassador to the papal court, and he led several missions to France on behalf of the English king. In 1414 Henry V designated Chichele successor to Archbishop Arundel. Sh. follows Holinshed (3.545), but exceeds the historical evidence, in making Chichele the chief advocate for Henry's war with France. He was not yet archbishop when Henry began to plan the invasion of France with his councilors, and it is doubtful Chichele had the influence at court that Sh. assumes. He did support the war and was ardently nationalistic. In 1419 he helped negotiate Rouen's surrender to Henry, but Chichele's greatest concern was the defense of the English church from Lollard heresies and from papal encroachments. To protect the privileges of Canterbury, he persuaded Henry V to force the king's uncle, Henry Beaufort, bishop of Winchester, to decline the cardinalate and the legatine powers that Pope Martin V offered him (1417). After Henry's death Chichele sided with the duke of Gloucester in the struggles among the regents who ruled for the infant Henry VI. Chichele's lasting memorial was All Soul's College, the school he endowed at Oxford.

5) *H8 2.4.215, 3.2.403, 4.1.24–25, 88, 5.1.81, 5.2.22, 193,* see Cranmer, Thomas.

Capaneus, King, *TNK 1.1.59,* husband of Evadne, the unnamed First Queen who appeals to Theseus for vengeance. Capaneus of Argos was the son of Hipponous and Astynome and became one of the seven warriors who besieged Thebes on behalf of Polyneices against his brother Eteocles. According to the First Queen, the body of Capaneus has been left rotting in the fields by Creon, who regards the Seven Against Thebes as traitors. According to mythology, Capaneus bragged that the gods could not prevent his burning the city, whereupon Zeus struck him dead with a thunderbolt as he climbed a scaling ladder—the very siege instrument the ancients credited Capaneus with inventing. Upon Capaneus receiving his funeral rites, Evadne flung herself upon his pyre. The mentioning of Capaneus alone among the Seven Against Thebes is exactly as in Chaucer's *Knyghtes Tale.* Chaucer also mentions Capaneus in *The Compleynt of feire Anelida and fals Arcite.*

Capel, *Rom 3.1.2,* (pl.) *5.1.18, 5.3.127,* 'C.'s monument,' the Capulet tomb. Capel and Capulet are both used in Sh.'s source, Arthur Brooke's *Tragicall Historye of Romeus and Juliet.* One critic asserted that the Scaliger monument at Santa Maria Antiqua in Verona is the setting which Sh. or his antecedents had in mind, but insufficient evidence exists to prove it.

Caper, Master, *MM 4.3.9,* mocking name for one of the impoverished criminals Pompey knows. As prisoners paid for their own food, many were forced to beg passers by. To 'caper' is to frolic, to leap, or to dance, deriving from L. *caper* 'goat.' It implies the satyrical nature well known to Pompey.

Caphis, *Tim,* servant of one of Timon's creditors, the Senator. Caphis the Phocian is a friend of Sylla's (q.v.) in Plutarch.

Capilet, *AWW 5.3.161,* 'the ancient C.,' a surname. As Diana Capilet indicates, Sh. thought of it as an old name long present in Italy. He had already used it in *Rom* and as the name of Andrew Aguecheek's horse (*TN 3.4.27-8*), see Capulet.

Capilet, Diana, *AWW,* daughter of the Widow Capilet, a virginal woman of Florence whom Bertram attempts to seduce. She participates in a 'bed trick,' at Helen's request. She makes an appointment for an assignation with Bertram, but Helen takes her place. Her first name is symbolic of her chastity.

Capilet, Widow, *AWW,* mother of Diana. She helps Helen recover Bertram. Her worldliness is demonstrated by her recognition of Bertram's character.

Capitol, pertaining to the Capitoline hill at the western end of the Roman forum. The Capitoline was crowned by the *Capitolium,* the temple of Jupiter Optimus Maximus, and the *Arx,* a citadel that had been the defensive heart of early Rome. Consuls took their oaths of office in the Capitoline temple. Generals ended their triumphal processions there. But the Capitol was not, as Sh. seems to have believed, the political center of Rome. The Senate had a meeting house, the *Curia,* in the forum. It burned in 52 BC and was being reconstructed by Julius Cæsar at the time of his death. (Since the *Curia* was not finished, the Senate was meeting in Pompey's theater, south of the forum, on the day that Cæsar was assassinated, so he was not killed at the Capitol as Sh. assumes.) In front of the *Curia* there was a podium and an open space where crowds could gather to hear speeches. During a political emergency, the Roman mob would have convened here rather than on the Capitoline hill. *Luc 1835, JC. Ant 2.6.18, Cor Tit. Ham 3.2.100. Cym 1.6.107,* possible reference to the flight of stairs for travellers on foot from the Arch of Septimus Severus to the C.

Cappadocia, *Ant 3.6.70,* ancient kingdom in the heart of eastern Asia Minor. During the era of the second triumvirate, it was surrounded by the Roman provinces of Asia, Galatia, Pontus, Armenia, Commagene, and Cilicia. Its kings were clients of the Roman empire.

Capulet, 1) *Rom,* Juliet's family, one of the feuding families of the play. Sh. got this name, like most in the play, from his source Arthur Brooke's *Tragicall Historye of Romeus and Juliet* (1562), where it appears as 'Capelet' and 'Capilet.' The name remains fairly consistent in earlier forms of the story. It appears in Luigi da Porto's *Istoria novellamente ritrovata di due Nobili Amanti* (c. 1530) as 'Capelletti.' The Capelletti of Cremona are mentioned in Dante's *Inferno* for causing disorder, along with the Montecchi of Verona. In a masque by Gascoigne, they are referred to as the 'Capels' (see Montague). In Verona there is a 13th c. building that used to be an inn called 'Il Capello' ('the hat'). Because of the resemblance to the name it has been popularly identified as the setting for the play and performances have been given there. The balcony from which it is said Juliet pledged to Romeo has suffered greatly from the thousands of tourists who have broken off pieces as souvenirs.

2) *Rom,* Juliet's father. Because of his discussion with old Capulet at *1.5.30–40* he seems to be at least fifty, though his wife may be as young as twenty-eight. He has been accused of being an inconsistent character, but if we accept that he is volatile in his emotions, quick to anger, yet capable of consideration of his daughter's feelings and joy at the festivities arranged for her wedding, most of his changes of temper may be seen to be justified. He first appears on stage in his gown rushing to the fight between the servants and calling for his sword, an idea his wife mocks. He seems willing to give up the feud in *1.2* when he resists Paris' offer of marriage for Juliet, urging the young man to be patient and to woo her. Later, in accordance with the obligations of a host he orders Tybalt not to make a scene at the presence of Romeo at the masque.

By *3.4,* in the wake of Tybalt's death, he decides to persuade his daughter to marry Paris immediately. The reason is not clear, but would be logical if he has a suspicion about his daughter and Romeo, or simply that he recognizes or has been told, say by her Nurse, that she is now ready for mature relationships and is in danger of ruining her reputation. This, too, would help justify his anger when he presents the news to Juliet. Even though a father of the time had the right—even obligation—to secure a proper marriage for his daughters, his anger at being rebuffed betrays a violent temper or deeper cause. We later see him happily involved in the wedding preparations, then immediately cast down by her apparent death. He is quite overcome, ranting, until calmed down by Friar

Laurence. In the climax he offers to reconcile with Montague and to match the offer of Montague's statue to Juliet with one of Romeo.

3) *Rom 1.2.69,* uncle of Juliet's father, invited to the feast at which Romeo meets Juliet. To avoid confusion some editors call him 'Old Man.'

4), *TN 3.4.278,* F1 'gray Capilet,' Sir Andrew Aguecheek's horse. 'Capul' was a northern dialect word for 'horse' and C. may be a diminutive of it.

Capulet, Juliet, *Rom,* star-crossed lover and wife of Romeo. She is said to be only fourteen, though at least sixteen in the sources. Perhaps Sh. intended her age to reveal the fallibility of her judgement in matters of love or related to the actor who played her. Although it has been said that Juliet's name derives from the month of her birth—the Nurse says she was born at Lammastide—her name varies little in the sources, regardless of the language. In Sh.'s direct source, Arthur Brooke's *Tragicall Historye of Romeus and Juliet* (1562), she is Juliet. In Bandello's *Le Novelle del Bandello* (1554), which Brooke translated, it is 'Julietta,' as she is in the French versions. In Luigi da Porto's *Istoria novellamente ritrovata di due Nobili Amanti* (c. 1530), she is 'Giulietta,' though in Masuccio's *Il Novellino* (1476), the character corresponding is named 'Giannozza,' meaning 'big Joan.'

Capulet's Wife, *Rom,* often called Lady Capulet by modern editors, though there is no particular indication that the family is a noble one. *4.4.5* probably indicates that her first name is Angelica (q.v.). A steely woman, she calls for revenge upon Romeo for killing Tybalt and threatens to arrange to have him poisoned. She is unsympathetic to Juliet's distress at the arranged marriage and only gains a small sympathy when she laments Juliet's death. She may be the much younger wife of a much older man, a not uncommon situation in those days. She tells Juliet she bore her when she was Juliet's age (*1.3.73–75*). This would make her about twenty-eight, though Capulet and his cousin discuss the last time they were in a masque, twenty-five or thirty years ago (*1.5.32–40*). The general conception of age may be consequential, but Sh. was generally careless in the consistency of such details throughout his career.

Caputius, Lord, *H8,* Eustachius Chapuys, Spanish nobleman who served as ambassador from Charles V to Henry VIII. Caputius staunchly supported Charles's aunt, Katherine of Aragon, as she desperately battled to prevent her husband from winning a divorce. When Henry banished her from court, Chapuys kept in touch with her. He attended her on her deathbed and brought Henry her last message—a declaration of affection.

Car, John de la, *H8 1.1.218, 1.2.163, 2.1.21,* duke of Buckingham's chaplain and confessor. He was arrested with Buckingham (Edward Stafford), and he gave damaging testimony at the duke's trial. His name appears as John de la Court in proceedings of the trial, and Holinshed (3.863) lists him as Car alias Court.

Cardinal, 1) title given the highest ranking officials in the Roman Catholic hierarchy. Cardinals are the pope's chief administrative assistants, and they govern the church when the papal throne is vacant. Cardinal status began to be conferred during the 5th century to identify Roman clergy who served posts directly under papal control. The rank, therefore, indicates administrative, not sacramental, authority, and it is supplementary to the clerical offices ('bishop,' 'priest,' 'deacon,' etc.) conferred by ordination and consecration. Since it was customary during the early medieval period for the clergy of a diocese to choose the man who was to be their bishop, the cardinal clergy of the Roman see found themselves in a peculiar position. The bishop who ruled them was also the head of the Latin church. Consequently, the cardinal clergy were not often permitted the luxury of an election free from external influences. During the early medieval period, German kings intervened in Italian politics and dictated the choice of popes. In the 12th century reforms were enacted to secure the cardinals' exclusive right to elect popes. Since that time cardinals have consistently shown a strong preference for candidates from within their 'college.' *2H6 1.3.64.* 1H6 1.3.36, 49, F1 'c's hat,' see 2). *Jn 3.1.64. H8.*

2) F1 'C. of Winchester,' *1H6 1.3.19,* see Beaufort, Henry. The F1 citation is in error as he is not yet a cardinal at this point in the play.

3) *R3,* Thomas Bourchier (1404–1486), descendant through his mother, Anne, of Thomas of Woodstock, Edward III's youngest son. Bourchier's royal connections won him rapid advancement to high office in the English church. At the age of thirty, he became bishop of Worcester. Nine years later he was moved to the diocese of Ely, and in 1454 he became archbishop of Canterbury and Henry VI's Lord Chancellor. As befitted the primate of England, Bourchier tried to mediate between the factions of York and Lancaster during the War of the Roses. He helped negotiate terms for peace after the first battle of the war at St. Albans. Although he did not urge Edward of York to stake a claim to Henry VI's crown, he accepted York's decision to do so and presided at his coronation.

He helped Edward weather the earl of Warwick's attempt to depose him in 1471, and he was instrumental in persuading Edward's brother, Clarence, to repudiate his ties with Warwick and to assist Edward in regaining the throne. In 1473 Bourchier was granted a cardinal's hat, but events in England gave him no leisure to involve himself in the affairs of the international church. After Edward IV's death, he favored Richard of Gloucester as regent for Edward's son, and he acquiesced when Richard set his nephew aside and usurped the throne. But the disappearance of Edward's sons, for whose safety Bourchier had pledged his honor, may have embarrassed him and turned him against Richard. He welcomed Henry Tudor's victory over Richard III at Bosworth Field, and he presided at Henry (VII)'s coronation and his marriage to Edward IV's daughter, Elizabeth. Bourchier died a few months after the royal wedding that, by uniting the remnants of the houses of York and Lancaster, ended the dispute that had preoccupied his generation.

4) *H8,* see Wolsey.

Carduus benedictus, *Ado 3.4.69, 72, 73,* the blessed thistle, a plant believed to have many beneficial medicinal properties.

Carlisle, seat of the English county of Cumberland. It is located at the western end of the border between England and Scotland. There is also a diocese of Carlisle. See Carlisle, Bishop of, *R2.*

Carlisle, Bishop of, *R2,* Thomas Merke (d. 1409), a churchman who owed his see to the patronage of Richard II and who remained conspicuously loyal to Richard to the end. Richard persuaded the pope to give Merke the diocese of Carlisle in 1397, the year Richard destroyed the 'lords appellant' and filled government offices with his own men. Merke was so actively employed on the king's business that he seems to have taken no part in ecclesiastical affairs. Merke was with the army Richard led to Ireland in 1399, and he returned to England with the king to confront Henry (IV) Bolingbroke's invasion. He was the only person to speak out in parliament against Richard's forced abdication, and he may have had knowledge of the conspiracy to assassinate Henry IV in 1400. After exposure of that plot, Henry confined Merke to the Tower and stripped him of his diocese. Henry subsequently pardoned Merke and in 1403 provided a benefice for his support.

Carlot, *AYLI 3.5.109,* former cottage-owner, name derived from 'carl' (churl).

Carthage, ancient city on a peninsula on the Bay of Tunis in North Africa, not far from modern Tunis. According to legend it was founded by Dido with Phoenician colonists from Tyre, and historians have surmised it was founded about 850 BC as a trading post by merchants of Utica and Tyre. From its birth the city grew to become a major commercial center controlling trade in the western Mediterranean. In 149 BC the city had a population of about 700,000. The Carthaginians possibly imported tin from Britain and traded in Atlantic Africa and Europe. There is even the likelihood that the Carthaginian explorer Hanno circumnavigated Africa. Carthage was frequently in conflict with other trading empires. Initially (when Rome had little naval power) Rome and it were allies against Greek expansionism. Finally, however, Rome intervened in Sicily, where the Greeks and Carthaginians had struggled for years, and the Punic Wars followed. The great general Hannibal succeeded in invading Italy in the second Punic war, but was ultimately defeated at the battle of Zama in Africa in 202 BC by Scipio Africanus. After a remarkable revival under Hannibal's leadership, Hannibal was forced to flee to the East, and Carthage was totally destroyed by the Romans in 146 BC, one story being that the site was sown with salt to destroy all vestiges of life. Caius Gracchus attempted unsuccessfully to rebuild the city 24 years later. When Augustus succeeded in doing so, it became one of the major cities of the empire and subsequently capital for the Vandal kingdom (439--533 AD). The Arabs destroyed this city in 698.

Shr 1.1.152, 'Queen of C.,' Dido. *MND 1.1.173,* 'C. queen,' Dido. *MV 5.1.12. Tmp 2.1.87–90,* Tunis and Carthage are the same place, Gonzalo wrongly insists. It has been noted, however, that Æneas' voyage in Virgil, goes from Carthage to Cumæ (Naples) as does that of Alonso's party, with an instructive visit to the underworld which could be paralleled to the visit to the island of Prospero.

Casca, *JC,* Publius Servius Casca, (d. 42 BC), one of Cæsar's assassins, the man who Plutarch ('Cæsar' 64.4) says struck the first blow. He was a plebeian tribune for the year 44 BC. He fought at Philippi in 42 BC and died shortly thereafter.

Cassado, Gregory de, *H8 3.2.322,* or Cassalis, English ambassador to the papal court. Holinshed (3.912) mentions him when he details the abuses of power with which Henry VIII charged Cardinal Wolsey. Henry accused Wolsey of sending Cassado to the duke of Ferrara to negotiate a treaty that the cardinal intended to conceal from the king.

Cassandra, *Tro,* Alexandra, Trojan soothsayer, daughter of Priam and Hecuba. In mythology she was given the power of prophecy by Apollo, but she spurned the god's advances, and he caused her predictions never to be believed. Dragged from the temple of Athena and raped by Ajax the Lesser during the pillaging of Troy, she is awarded to Agamemnon as his booty. This version of her story is later in origin than the *Iliad,* in which she is not a seer, but merely another member of Priam's huge family. By the 5th c. BC, however, Æschylus gives her a major role in the tragedy *Agamemnon,* as she enters the city of Argos in a chariot and psychically experiences the curse of the house of Atreus. Her frenzy is followed by the slaughter of Agamemnon and her own death at the hands of Clytemnestra and her lover Ægisthus. She is also in Euripides' *Trojan Women* and Seneca's *Agamemnon.* Sh.'s Cassandra is true to the classical model, a frenzied prophetess who is described as brainsick. She predicts the fall of Troy and Hector's death. Her name is still applied to anyone who consistently predicts gloom and doom.

Cassibelan, *Cym 1.1.30, 3.1.5, 30, 41,* said to be an uncle of Cymbeline's. Sicilius fought with him against the Romans. As described in Cæsar's *Gallic Wars,* Cassivelaunus was the leader of the resistance against the invasion of Britain in 54 BC. His territory is described as being in the interior, towards the Thames. Unable to directly confront the Roman force, he fought a hit and run guerrilla war until the devastation forced him to sue for peace. Cæsar accepted hostages and tribute in order to end the war before winter. In Spenser's *Færie Queene* 2.10.47, Cassibalane is Lud's brother and regent to Androgeus and Tenantius, the sons of Lud. He assumes the crown and resists the Romans until betrayed by Androgeus. He is succeeded by

Tenantius and is therefore Kimbeline's great uncle, which is the descent adopted by Sh.

Cassio, Michael, *Oth,* soldier of Florence whom Iago maneuvers into being the object of Othello's jealousy. He has been promoted to lieutenant, a position Iago wanted for himself, but Iago exploits his susceptibility to drink by getting him drunk and into a cheap brawl. Later Iago fills Othello's head with unlikely stories about Cassio's speaking of Desdemona in his sleep and uses Desdemona's handkerchief as proof. Iago and Othello plot to get Cassio killed by Roderigo, but the scheme fails. Cassio is depicted as being more noble in blood than Iago, but easily manipulated by the vulgar Iago. Cassio's relationship with the courtesan Bianca contributes to the general impression of a frivolous side to the young nobleman's character, which is all the weakness Iago needs to degrade him. He survives all this to be given command of Cyprus by play's end, thereby loosely fitting the pattern in Sh. of a man who suffers in order to be cleansed. *1.1.19:* it has been argued at great length whether Cassio is really a Florentine, since there is no indication otherwise he has a wife. It has been argued (rather unconvincingly) that Florentine refers not to the town, but to Cassio's arithmetical (merchant) background, since the Italian Bookkeeping method originated in Florence. The wife could be merely be another instance of carelessness, as well as the Florentine reference. In Sh.'s source for the plot, Giraldi Cinthio's *Hecatommithi* 3.7, (1566), Cassio is unnamed and called 'the Corporal.' Perhaps Sh. Italianized the Roman name. Cassio's name may also relate to 'cassia,' a fragrant plant, or come from Richard Knolles' *General Historie of the Turkes* (1602) in which a Lucas Michaell is a commander sent into Crete.

Cassius, Caius, *JC, Ant 2.6.15, 3.11.37,* Caius Cassius Longinus, (d. 42 BC), chief conspirator in the plot to assassinate Julius Cæsar. Cassius served in the ill-fated army that the triumvir Crassus led into Parthia in 53 BC. When the Parthians captured and killed Crassus, Cassius took charge and organized a retreat that saved what was left of Crassus' expedition, preventing the Parthians from exploiting the situation and moving into Roman territory. In 49 BC, after he had stabilized the empire's eastern frontier, he returned to Rome and entered politics as a plebeian tribune. In the war between Pompey and Cæsar, he commanded Pompey's fleet. After Pompey's death, Cæsar pardoned him and allowed him to resume his political career. At the time of Cæsar's death, he had been promised the governorship of Syria. He looted Syria to raise the money he needed to fight Cæsar's heirs, Mark Antony and Octavius, and he brought an army to Philippi in 42 BC. When Antony routed his men, Cassius, who did not know that his companion Brutus had evened the score by driving Octavius from the field, despaired prematurely and committed suicide.

Castalian King Urinal, *MWW 2.3.31,* F1 'Castalion-king-Vrinall,' obscure expression. It could mean a 'Castilian-king urinal,' a urinal appropriate for one of the most powerful kings in Europe, the king of Castile. 'Castalion' is also a common spelling of Castiglione, whose *Book of the Courtier* (written 1528, translated 1561) was widely read. The sense might then be a 'courtly king's urinal.' Castalia was also the sacred spring of the Muses and might relate in the joking. The three words may be an overblown ironic adjective modifying Hector, meaning something like 'you're a pissoir Hector.'

Castiliano vulgo, *TN 1.3.40,* obscure expression. It may be a misreading of *Castiliano volto,* but even that doesn't clarify it. It seems to mean 'keep a Castilian face.' Sir Toby seems to be urging Maria to be polite. Castilians were thought to be well mannered, sedate, serious, but no particular Castilian attribute stands out in this context. It could just as well be a lost drinking expression, or refer to some such expression, and we mustn't forget that much of the humor in this play is based on corrupting words and phrases.

Castle, The, *2H6 5.2.3,* alehouse in the town of St. Albans. During the first battle of St. Albans the duke of Somerset was cornered and killed when he took refuge there. Sh. claims that Somerset's death in the tavern was the fulfillment of an ironic prophecy. During a seance arranged for the duchess of Gloucester, a conjured spirit had warned Somerset to avoid 'castles.'

Castor, *TNK 3.6 136,* 'By C.,' oath. Castor was one of the Gemini or Dioscuri, the twin sons of Leda. He was the son of Tyndareus, whereas his brother Pollux (Gr. Polydeuces) was the son of Zeus. Helen of Troy was similarly his half-sister by Zeus and Clytemnestra his full sister. An Argonaut, he taught Hercules fencing, was a horse tamer, and participated in the Calydonian boar hunt which is alluded to in *TNK.* He and his brother captured Talus, a man of brass made by Hephæstus, and rescued Helen from her abductor Theseus. Castor was killed in battle by Idas over either cattle or the daughters of Leucippus. Pollux offered to ransom Castor's life with his own, so Zeus placed them in the heavens. They were considered patrons of travellers and in Rome, where they had a temple in the Forum, patrons of knighthood, which is quite appropriate to the story of *TNK.*

Catesby, William, *R3,* (d. 1485), Richard III's close friend and advisor. He had training in the law, and he may have begun his career as one of Lord Hastings' clerks. Richard, while still only duke of Gloucester, used him to discover what Hastings thought about Richard's plan to dispossess Edward V's heirs and claim the throne for himself. When Hastings proved uncooperative, Catesby helped Richard do away with Hastings. He was rewarded with Hastings' office of chancellor of the exchequer, and he was speaker of the house in the only parliament that met during Richard III's reign. He was captured and beheaded at the battle of Bosworth Field.

Cathayan, F1 'Catayan,' a Chinese, from Cathay, an old name for China. In the contexts it is used in Sh., it seems to mean a liar, a tricky person, or possibly a thief, though it may merely be drunken nonsense by Toby to pun on Maria's use of 'caterwauling' at *TN 2.3.72. MWW 2.1.136.*

Catherine, 1) *Shr,* see Minola, Katherine.

2) *LLL,* lady in waiting of the Princess of France, wooed by Dumaine. Her most memorable moment is when she recalls the death of a sister. Emilia has a similar recollection scene in *TNK.* The inspiration for the passage may have come from a woman in attendance on Marguerite de Valois who died of love for an absent nobleman in 1577. It may also have influenced the creation of Ophelia in *Ham.* Catherine was a common name in French history. Catherine de Médicis was mother of Marguerite of Valois, who may have vaguely inspired the role of Princess of France.

3) *H5,* C. of Valois (1401–1437), Henry V's wife, youngest daughter of Charles VI, king of France, sister of Isabella, Richard II's second wife. Before his ascension to the throne, Henry had bid unsuccessfully for Catherine's hand, but his victory at Agincourt and his subsequent alliance with the duke of Burgundy made him an irresistible suitor. In June 1420 Henry ratified the treaty of Troyes, in which Burgundy acknowledged Henry's claim to the throne of France, by wedding her. In December 1421, at Windsor castle she bore Henry his only child, Henry (VI). After Henry V's death in 1422, she remained in England. In 1428 she defied convention by secretly marrying without her government's consent. The husband she chose was one of her late husband's squires, a poor but handsome Welshman named Owen Tudor. Owen and she kept their enemies at bay until 1436, when he was imprisoned and she was compelled to take refuge at Bermondsey Abbey. She died there a year later. Despite the political complications created by the sons she bore Owen, Henry VI treated his half-brothers generously. He made Jaspar Tudor earl of Pembroke and Edmund Tudor earl of Richmond. Edmund wed Margaret Beaufort, in whose veins flowed the royal blood of John of Gaunt, son of Edward III. Their son Henry (VII) usurped the

throne from Richard III and established the Tudor dynasty, of which Sh.'s queen, Elizabeth, was the last monarch.

4) *H8,* see Katherine of Aragon.

Catherine of France, *2H4 epi. 27,* see Catherine, 2) *H5.*

Cato, Marcus Porcius Cato Uticensis, 'the younger,' (95–46 BC), great-grandson of Marcus Porcius Cato Censorius, or 'the elder,' who is remembered for his hatred of Greek culture, Carthage, immorality and indolence. Cato the Younger was a student of Stoic philosophy, and followed his great-great grandfather's devotion to the harsh disciplines that Romans liked to believe were the customs of their remote ancestors. He enjoyed an exemplary military reputation. His first important command was a commission to help end the slave revolt begun by the gladiator Spartacus in 72 BC. In 67 BC he became a military tribune in Macedonia, and in 65 BC he returned to Rome to begin his political career. He campaigned against corruption in government and protested misappropriation of state funds. He endorsed Cicero's dubiously legal means for the suppression of the Catilinarian conspiracy. He opposed the first triumvirate (Pompey, Julius Cæsar, and Crassus), which he believed to be a threat to the traditions of the Republic. When civil war broke out, he decided that Pompey was the lesser of the available evils and enlisted in his army. He commanded Pompey's base camp during the battle of Pharsalus and led the remnants of Pompey's forces to Africa after Pompey's defeat. When Cæsar's victory at Thapsus (6 April 46) made continued resistance useless, he chose to die rather than surrender. The gash he inflicted to his abdomen was not immediately mortal, and friends tried to save him by binding up his wound. He spurned their efforts, tore off his bandages, and let his entrails spill out. Shortly after Cato's death, Cicero wrote his biography and began the process of his canonization as a hero of the Republic. Cæsar was offended by the swelling tide of praise and tried to tell his side of the story by publishing a less laudatory account of Cato's life.

MV 1.1.166, 'C's daughter' his daughter, Portia, married Cæsar's assassin, Marcus Brutus. *JC 2.1.294, 5.1.101, 5.4.4, 6. Cor 1.5.28,* 'to C.'s wish,' a soldier who would please Cato.

2) *JC 5.3.106, 5.4.9, 11,* 'young C.,' the son of Cato the Younger and Atilia. Plutarch tells us he was present at his father's suicide, but he fell into an idle existence, chasing women and lingering in the house of Marphadates of Cappadocia, who had a beautiful wife. His courageous death at Philippi, however, restored his reputation.

Caucasus, *Tit 2.1.17,* chain of mountains between the Black and Caspian seas. For the ancient Greeks they marked the edge of the known world and in mythology became the place to which the gods exiled their enemies. Zeus, for instance, chained the Titan, Prometheus, to a peak in the Caucasus.

Cavaliero, variously spelled title applied to a gentleman. It was fabricated by anglicizing It. *cavaliere,* or possibly derived from Sp. *caballero,* as it seems to have gained currency in England about the time of the Spanish Armada. The word is used in Ben Jonson's *Every Man in his Humour* 2.2 (1598) in which Sh. acted. *MWW 2.1.188,* 'C. Justice,' Shallow. *2.1.199,* 'guest-c.,' Ford. *2.3.67,* 'C. Slender.' *MND 4.1.22,* 'Cavaliery Peaseblossom.' *2H4 5.3.60,* pl.

Cawdor, 1) *Mac,* castle and thaneship located in the north of Scotland a short distance from the Moray and Inverness firths in the present county of Nairnshire. Sh. sets the killing of Duncan in the castle, though Duncan was actually killed in battle. Furthermore, the death of Duncan occurred about 1040. The castle at Cawdor was first erected in 1454 and overlooks a tributary of the Nairn.

2) *Mac,* traitorous thane who supports the king of Norway against Duncan. He accepts his death, according to the second-hand reports, quite nobly. His title is given to Macbeth. Raphael Holinshed's *Chronicles* do not mention

any thane of Cawdor at the battle, so the traitor's inclusion is an obvious dramatic device.

3) *Mac,* Macbeth, see 2).

Cedius, *Tro 5.5.11,* king, ally of the Greeks, slain by Margareton. In William Caxton's *Recuyell of the Historyes of Troye,* 3 (c. 1474), the first English printed book, and Sh.'s major source for the play, a 'Cedus' (also 'Cedeus') has his arm cut off in his angry attack to avenge his brother Epistrophus and is killed by Hector.

Celia, *AYLI,* friend of Rosalind, daughter of Duke Frederick. Celia is one of the short, dark women playing counterpoint to the tall, blonde friend (Rosalind). This pairing is common in Sh.'s comedies and despite its useful dramatic and symbolic overtones, likely derived from the physical characteristics of two of his boy actors.

Censorinus, *Cor 2.3.243,* Caius Marcius Rutilus, granted the cognomen 'Censorinus' in 265 BC in recognition of the unusual honor of having twice served the Roman Republic in the office of censor. Plutarch ('Coriolanus' 1.1) says that one of the pieces of legislation Censorinus drafted during his second term was a law that made it illegal for anyone else to do what he had done.

Centaur, 1) race of mythological beings who were half human and half equine. They were alleged to have lived on mount Pelion in Thessaly until Hercules, or a group of native people called the Lapiths, drove them to Mount Pindus in Epirus. Chaucer in his *Monkes Tale* mentions Hercules' killing 'Centauros.' The word 'centaur' means 'killer of bulls' and may recall a blood sport practiced by prehistoric horsemen. *Tit 5.2.201,* 'C.'s feast': a Greek myth. Centaurs attended a Lapith wedding (Pirithous was groom), became drunk, and caused a ferocious battle by attempting to abduct female guests. Theseus and his companions slaughtered the creatures. *MND 5.1.44 (add. 27):* Theseus declines to see a play on the Lapith wedding because he has already told Hippolyta about it. It hardly seems like an auspicious subject for a nuptial feast.

2) *Err 1.2.9, 104; 2.2.2, 9, 16; 4.4.150; 5.1.413,* an inn.

Cephalus, *MND 5.1.197–8,* mythological hunter. The goddess Aurora fell in love with him and tried her best to please him. He, however, remained in love with his wife Procris and returned to her. Aurora warned him he would be sorry for it. Procris had received a dog and a javelin from Diana, which she gave to Cephalus. The dog (Lælaps), as well as his quarry (a wild beast loosed on the countryside by Themis), was changed to stone. It was Cephalus' habit to call out to command the breeze to cool his sweaty body. This, being overheard, was taken by some busybody to be Cephalus calling out to a nymph lover. Procris concealed herself in the bushes to find out. When he called out as usual, she sobbed. He mistook the noise for an animal and killed his wife with the javelin. The story ends Ovid's *Metamorphoses,* 7.

Cerberus, in Greek mythology a dog born of Typhon and Echidna (or of Medusa) with three heads with serpents and a mane around his head and a serpent's tail. It guards the entrance of Hades, eating the dead who tried to escape and the living who tried to enter. In Ovid's *Metamorphoses,* 7.409–419, the dragging of Cerberus out of Hades is one of the labors of Hercules. As the dog's foam hits the earth, the poisonous plant aconite springs up. At 10.65, Ovid also gives Cerberus the power to turn a man to stone with a look. *Tit 2.4.51. LLL 5.2.583,* Holofernes says Hercules killed C. *2H4 2.4.165. Tro 2.1.34.*

Ceres, a goddess of grain and harvest worshiped by the Romans. Her name survives in the word 'cereal.' Although she is often equated with the Greek earth-mother, Demeter, Ceres was originally a native Italian deity. She was among the earliest of the gods venerated by the Latin tribes. One rationale for the seasonal changes was contained in the myth of her daughter Proserpina's kidnapping by Dis (Pluto). In the part of the year Proserpina resides in the Underworld, Ceres is unhappy and the grain will not grow.

Tmp: the goddess appears in a masque celebrating the betrothal of Miranda and Ferdinand. She tells Iris she will not continue if Cupid and Venus are present. She blames them for Proserpina's kidnapping as she does in Ovid's *Metamorphoses,* 5.346–571. Later she sings a blessing with Juno. *2H6 1.2.2. TNK 5.1.52,* 'teeming Ceres' foison,' the abundant crop provided by the goddess.

Cerimon, *Per,* physician who saves Thaisa. Cerimon is one of many of Sh.'s character names that appear in John Gower's *Confessio Amantis* (1390) and in Lawrence Twine's *Patterne of Painefull Adventures* (1594). See Pericles. The name's resemblance to the word 'ceremony' may have been in Sh.'s mind, also, since he is involved with ceremonial scenes.

Cesario, *TN,* name assumed by Viola in disguise. It may have been suggested by Cæsar, Cæsarion, or the It. Cesare. The names assumed by the Viola character in *Gl'Ingannati* (1538) is Fabio, in Niccolo Secchi's *Gl'Inganni* (1562) Ruberto, and in Barnabe Riche's 'Apolonius and Silla,' from *His Farewell to the Military Profession* (1581), Silvio, her brother's name. In a second *Gl'Inganni* (1592) by Curzio Gonzaga, a girl in disguise assumes the name Cesare. We also hear the echo of Hamlet's *Murder of Gonzago* in the author's name; however, not much about this *Gl'Inganni* seems to have affected either *TN* or *Ham* other than this possible coincidence of names.

Chairbonne the puritan, *AWW 1.3.52,* F1 'Charbon,' a name for any Puritan. The French would mean 'good meat' and contrasts with the Roman Catholic practice of avoiding meat on holy days.

Cham, king of the Mongols, the Khan. *Ado 2.1.251,* 'the Great C.'s beard,' fetching a hair from the beard of the Cham was a Herculean task and seems to have worked its way into the popular jargon of the time.

Chamberlain, Lord, officer of the royal household whose title derived from his duty to attend the king in his bed chamber. The chamberlain was not a domestic servant, but a highly ranked administrator who had charge of the royal household, the king's finances, and the king's schedule. His ability to influence the flow of royal patronage gave him great power. The chamberlain occupied a prominent place in the royal entourage on state occasions. *R3 1.1.77, 124, 1.3.38, 3.2.108,* see Hastings, William, Lord. *H8 1.4.57, 73, 93. 2.2.12, 62:* during the period covered by the action here described two men held the office. Charles Somerset, earl of Worcester, presided over the arrangements for the meeting between Henry VIII and Francis I on the 'Field of the Cloth of Gold,' and he took part in the duke of Buckingham's treason trial. When Worcester died in 1526, William Sands (q.v.) succeeded to the office.

Chambermaid, *TNK 3.5.128,* character in the morris dance before Theseus. She parallels a character in Francis Beaumont's antimasque for *The Masque of Grayes-Inne and the Inner Temple* (1613).

Champ, *Cym,* see Richard du Champ.

Chancellor, Lord, king's secretary, the official charged with the government's correspondence and the keeper of the seal that authenticated royal documents. He was one of the most important royal councilors and administrators. *3H6 1.1.239,* see Warwick, earl of, 2). *H8:* several men held the post during the period covered by the action. Cardinal Wolsey served as chancellor until October 1529, when Sir Thomas More replaced him (*3.2.395*). More resigned in 1532, and Thomas Audley, keeper of the Great Seal, took his place. Audley participated in Anne Boleyn's coronation, and at his death in 1544 he was followed in office by Thomas Wriothesley—one of Thomas Cranmer's most determined enemies.

Chanticleer, rooster's name in *Reynard the Fox,* the name of a loose cycle of animal stories of the 12th c., that seems to have originated in northeastern France and Flanders, although the earliest names used for the animals are German (Reinhardt, Bruin the Bear, Baldwin the Ass, and Tibert the Cat). They seem to have come from various folk origins and Æsop. They parody the institutions of chivalry, the clergy, the wealthy, and the courts. Very popular in France, they came into England as early as the 13th c. Chaucer used the cycle for his *Nonnes Preestes Tale* and Chanticleer appears in the story. The name derives from Fr. *chanter clair,* 'to sing clearly or brightly.' *AYLI 2.7.30. Tmp 1.2.388.*

Chaos, void which existed before the creation in Greek mythology, sometimes referred to as a god. The name has become a synonym for 'disorder.' In Hesiod, Chaos is the yawning abyss of void, mass and darkness. Gaia then came into being as well as Eros, while Erebus and Nyx (night) issued directly from Chaos. Other versions have Time preceding Chaos and Tartarus issuing from Chaos *3H6 3.2.161. Ven 1020. Luc 767. Rom 1.1.177. Tro 1.3.125. Oth 3.3.93.*

Charing Cross, *1H4 2.1.25,* location between London and Westminster where there was a memorial to Edward I's queen, Eleanor. Eleanor died at a village in Lincolnshire. When her coffin was brought to Westminster for burial, Edward erected a cross in her memory at each place where her funeral procession rested.

Charity, St., *Ham 4.5.58,* saint in Ophelia's song. Charity was probably not a real person, but allegorical. Supposedly she and her Faith and Hope were the daughters of Wisdom (Sophia), a widow in Rome. They were persecuted in the rule of Hadrian and the young daughters tortured in horrible ways. Each was protected from the initial torment. Charity, for example, was beheaded after emerging unscathed from being thrown into a furnace. Another saint, Charita, was martyred at Rome with Justinus the Philosopher on 12 June 167. Spenser mentions St. 'Charitee' in *The Shepheardes Calender,* "May," 247.

Charlemagne, *AWW 2.1.76,* F1 'Charlemaine,' see Charles the Great.

Charlemain, *H5 1.2.75,* mistake by Holinshed (3.545) that Sh. replicates. The 'Charlemain' whom Sh. identified as 'son to Louis the Emperor'—usually known as 'Louis the Pius' (814–840)—was 'Charles II, the Bald' (d. 877), or his brother Carloman, king of Bavaria and Carinthia (b. 828, r. 876–80), not 'Charles the Great' (i.e., 'Charlemain' or 'Charlemagne').

Charles, 1) *LLL 2.1.162,* father of Ferdinand, king of Navarre. He loaned money to the king of France and received part of Aquitaine as collateral. Ferdinand is often thought a parallel to Henry of Navarre, whose father was Antoine de Bourbon, who became king of Navarre in 1554, several years after marrying Jeanne d'Albret, queen of Navarre. Perhaps 'Charles' was suggested by Charles, duke of Bourbon (1490–1527), constable of France, who was not paid the debts owed him by King Francis I for the Italian campaigns. He allied himself with Henry VIII after being sued by Louise of Savoy (Francis I's mother) and having some of his lands seized. He died in the successful siege of Rome, supposedly shot by Benvenuto Cellini—or so the imaginative autobiographer claimed.

2) *AYLI,* the Duke's wrestler. G. B. Shaw once remarked he enjoyed *AYLI* because it was easier to find a good wrestler than a good actor. In Sh.'s source (Lodge's *Rosalynde*) the wrestler is simply called 'the Norman.'

3) *H8 5.1.59, 5.1.72,* Charles Brandon. See Suffolk, Duke of; also see Brandon.

Charles, Dauphin, *1H6,* see Charles VII.

Charles, duke of Lorraine, *H5 1.2.70, 1.2.83,* (d. 992), Charlemagne's descendant in the male line via the emperor's French grandson, Charles the Bald. After the death in 987 of Lorraine's childless nephew, Louis V, the duke claimed the throne of France. The French nobles passed over him and gave their allegiance to Hugh Capet, count of Paris. Charles contested Hugh's election. But Hugh captured him, and Charles died a prisoner in Orléans. His daughter Adelaide provided him with heirs, and her descendant, Isabella, wife of René of Anjou, bore Margaret of Anjou, wife to Henry VI and queen of England.

Charles the Emperor, *H8 1.1.176, 185, 188, 2.1.162, 2.2.24,* Charles V (1500–1558), head of the Hapsburg empire and most powerful monarch of his generation. In 1520 he inherited a sprawling domain that included the dukedom of Austria, its central European dependencies, the 'Holy Roman Empire' (Germany and Italy), Flanders, Spain, and Spain's possessions in the Mediterranean and the western hemisphere. His potential strength alarmed many of his contemporaries, who hastened to try to block the consolidation of his power. The Ottoman Turks threatened his eastern domains and Mediterranean bases. The German principalities and self-governing cities embraced the Reformation in their eagerness to form a common front against the Catholic emperor. The French invaded Italy to prevent encirclement by Hapsburg lands. The English, however, were not immediately drawn into these conflicts. They had a tradition of cooperating with Spain against France, and their king, Henry VIII, had married Charles's aunt, Katherine of Aragon. Charles paid a state visit to England at the start of his reign to court Henry's friendship.

While the English king had no sympathy for German Protestants and no love for the French, he saw advantages in playing the field. Henry maneuvered freely until 1527, when his decision to terminate his marriage with Katherine severely curtailed his options. Katherine refused to acquiesce to an amicable separation and turned to Charles for help in blocking Henry's efforts to divorce her. The Hapsburg emperor used the army he had stationed in Italy to prevent the pope from granting Henry's request for an end to his marriage, and his intervention in Henry's domestic affairs had dramatic consequences. The English parliament concluded that the pope was Spain's puppet, and it endorsed Henry's decision to withdraw the English church from allegiance to Rome. Katherine's death in 1536 removed the chief bone of contention between Henry and Charles and permitted Henry to return to his earlier policy of exploiting the tensions that existed between France and Spain.

Charles the Great, *H5 1.2.46, 61, 71, 77, 84,* Charlemagne (742–814), eponymous monarch of the Carolingian dynasty. Charlemagne's father, Pepin the Short, deposed the last of the Merovingian rulers and, with papal approval, assumed the title 'king of the Franks.' Charles and his brother Carloman divided their father's kingdom at his death in 768, and war between them was averted only by Carloman's death in 771. Charles restored the unity of the Frankish state and embarked on a series of conquests that made him master of Europe from the Pyrenees to the Elbe river. On Christmas day, 800, Pope Leo III bestowed the Roman imperial title on him. The gesture, which invoked the memory of Rome and its civilization, was appropriate, for during his reign Europe emerged from the Dark Ages. His patronage supported an effective program to revivify Europe's schools and rescue the tools of literacy. Increasing intellectual sophistication strengthened Europe's awareness of its unique cultural identity, and a connection with Charlemagne, the man who restored the west, became a means for later rulers to legitimate the authority of the kingdoms they created from fragments of his empire. Medieval royal families resorted to imaginative reconstructions of their genealogies to establish links with the Carolingian line.

Charles VI, *H5,* (1368–1422), king of France. Charles was son and heir to Charles V, the monarch who, in the midst of the Hundred Years' War, pulled France back from the brink of disaster. During Charles VI's reign most of the ground Charles V had gained was lost, and England came very close to conquering France. Charles was only twelve when he inherited his father's throne, and he was no match for a gaggle of powerful uncles: the dukes of Anjou, Berri, Burgundy, and Bourbon. The situation changed in 1385, when Charles married Isabel, the daughter of the duke of Bavaria. Isabel was a willful woman with a large number of ambitious relatives. She encouraged Charles to assert his independence, but the period of his personal rule ended dramatically in 1392 when the king suffered an attack of mental illness. For the rest of his life Charles was subject to fits of violent insanity that sometimes required his confinement. Charles's increasing incapacity necessitated the appointment of a regent, and a struggle for the office broke out between the king's uncle, the duke of Burgundy, and his brother, the duke of Orléans. In 1396 France made an effort to end the simmering hostilities of the Hundred Years' War by agreeing to a marital alliance between Charles's daughter, Isabel, and King Richard II of England. The union failed to secure lasting peace, for in 1399 Henry IV usurped Richard's crown, and Isabel's marriage ceased to have diplomatic significance.

The French refused to recognize the legitimacy of Henry's government, but they were in no position to intervene in England's internal affairs. Quarrels among Charles's relatives were inching France toward civil war. In 1407, following a ceremony of reconciliation, John the Fearless, duke of Burgundy, murdered his rival, Louis of Orléans. Bernard VII, count of Armagnac, whose daughter had married Orléans' son, rallied the Orléanist faction, and in 1413 the 'Armagnacs' took control of the king and drove the Burgundians from Paris. In 1415 Henry V invaded France, and Burgundy refused to cooperate with the Armagnacs in defending the nation. John the Fearless was delighted when Henry's dramatic victory at Agincourt devastated the Armagnac forces, but Burgundy had no wish to see Henry conquer France. In 1419 he agreed to join the other French nobles against the English, but at the conference that was to formalize a truce between the parties of Burgundy and Orléans, an Armagnac avenged Louis of Orléans by assassinating John. John's son, Philip the Good, entered into negotiations with the English, and in 1420 he, Queen Isabel, and Henry V ratified the Treaty of Troyes. Henry V was proclaimed heir to Charles VI. Charles's son, the dauphin, was disinherited, and Henry wed Charles's daughter, Catherine. The union of France and England for which Troyes prepared the way seemed to be assured when Catherine bore Henry a son late in 1421. Things did not, however, develop as planned. In 1422, Henry V and Charles VI died within a few months of each other. Although the infant Henry VI was recognized as heir to the thrones of his father and grandfather, there was no tradition strong enough to hold France and England together during the long minority of a child king. When Joan of Arc appeared and breathed new life into the French, Charles VI's son, Charles VII, fought his way to Rheims and claimed the French crown. Henry VI's regents slowly lost their grip on England's continental possessions, and the Valois dynasty returned to power.

Charles VII, (1403–1461), king of France (1429–1461) and the Dauphin or heir apparent whom Henry V sought to dispossess of the French crown. The death in 1328 of Charles IV, the last of Philip IV's sons, extinguished the senior branch of the Capetian family that had ruled France since the 9th c. Charles's cousin, Philip VI, succeeded to the throne and founded the Valois dynasty. The Valois claim to the French crown was challenged by Edward III, king of England. Edward's mother was Philip IV's daughter, and Edward argued that his rights as Philip's grandson took precedence over those of the Valois claimant who was only a nephew of the former king. His argument was not taken seriously in France, for the French nobles had asserted in 1316 (following the death of Louis X) that a woman could neither succeed to the French throne nor transmit title to it. Edward protested this decision and in 1346 led raids into French territory. This began the Hundred Years' War, a long period of intermittent conflict. The English won major battles at Crécy (1346) and Poitiers (1356), but they were not strong enough to exploit their victories by annexing land. In 1415 Henry V revived the lagging war by launching a highly successful raid on Normandy. Unlike his predecessors, Henry was able to build on the battles he won, for the France he invaded was at war with itself.

The king of France, Philip VI's great-grandson Charles VI (1380–1422), was incapacitated by mental illness, and two factions at his court disputed the right to rule his nation for him. His uncle, the duke of Burgundy, and his brother, the duke of Orléans, quarreled, and in 1407 John the Fearless of Burgundy assassinated Louis of Orléans. Louis' Orléanist (or Armagnac) party declared war on the Burgundians, and Henry V took superb advantage of the confusion. An alliance with the Burgundians allowed Henry to take Paris and the person of the French king. Henry married Charles VI's daughter, Catherine, and was recognized as heir to the throne. Charles's son, the Dauphin, who had retreated to the Orléanist camp, was slow to react, but the deaths of Henry V and Charles VI in 1422 revived his faction's hopes. Henry V's estate passed to an infant, Henry VI, his son by Catherine. The baby's interests in France were guarded by his uncle, the duke of Bedford. Bedford tried to preserve the momentum of England's campaign on the continent, but his efforts were hampered by the fact that the regents who ran England for Henry VI expected France to finance the expenses of its own conquest.

The turning point in the war came in 1428. Joan of Arc, a peasant girl, convinced Charles that God had sent her to deliver France from the English. Joan sparked the Dauphin into action, forced the English to abandon their siege of Orléans, and in 1429 led the Dauphin to the cathedral of Rheims to be crowned Charles VII of France. In 1435, when the duke of Bedford died, Philip the Good, duke of Burgundy, broke with the English. Charles steadily advanced on the English, and by 1453 English possessions on the continent had been reduced to the port at Calais.

2H6 1.1.39. 1H6.

Charles's Wain, *1H4 2.1.2,* group of seven stars in the constellation of Ursa Major. A wain is a large, open wagon, and the Charles in question is the Frankish emperor Charlemagne.

Charmian, *Ant,* Cleopatra's faithful attendant and a member of the Egyptian queen's inner circle. Charmian committed suicide with Cleopatra. Sh. found the character in Plutarch's 'Antony' 60.1; 85.4.

Charolais, *H5 3.5.45,* see Philip the Good, duke of Burgundy. Philip was duke of Charolais before he inherited the duchy of Burgundy from his father in 1419. Charolais is a region of east-central France whose principal town is Charolles.

Charon, son of Erebus and Night, the ferryman over the Styx and Acheron into the land of the dead. For the price of a silver obolus (which the Greeks placed in the mouth or hand of the dead), he carried people across. If there was no fare, the dead were forced to wander the shore for a century. He was depicted as an old, gray, strong, and dirty man with a beard, a short cloak, and an appropriately grumpy attitude. *Tro 3.2.9. R3 1.4.46:* Clarence alludes to Charon but does not name him.

Chartreux, *H8 1.1.221, 1.2.149,* site 15 mi. north of Grenoble, France, where the motherhouse of the Carthusian monastic order was established in 1084.

Charybdis, *MV 3.4.15,* mythological daughter of Poseidon and Gæa. It was a whirlpool which sucked down three times a day and disgorged three times. Located in the Strait of Messina between Italy and Sicily, it was narrowly escaped by the hero Odysseus. It is mentioned in many ancient works and paired with the Scylla on the opposite shore, becomes symbolic of a dilemma.

Chatham, *2H6 4.2.86,* port on the Medway river, a tributary of the Thames, situated about

30 mi. southeast of London. See Emmanuel, Clerk of Chatham, *2H6*.

Châtillon, *Jn,* probably Hugh de Châtillon-St. Pol (d. 1248), one of the great lords active at the court of France's king, Philip Augustus. He would have been an appropriately distinguished person to serve as Philip's ambassador to John of England.

Châtillon, Jaques, *H5 3.5.43, 4.8.93,* (d. 1415), admiral of France and lord of Dampier. Holinshed (3.555) lists him among the casualties of the battle of Agincourt.

Chaucer, Geoffrey, *TNK Pro. 13,* (c. 1343–1400), greatest poet of Middle English, author of *The Canterbury Tales, Troilus and Criseyde,* and other works. He was the son of a wine merchant and became an important civil servant. He served in the household of the wife of Lionel, Duke of Clarence. He fought in France (1359–60) was captured, and ransomed. He married the sister of Katherine Swynford, mistress and third wife of John of Gaunt in 1366 and by 1367 was an esquire to Edward III. He served on diplomatic missions to France, Spain, and Italy and may have met Petrarch. Having made contact with the early Renaissance culture, he began writing by translating *Le Roman de la Rose.* From 1374–86, he held customs posts and represented Kent in Parliament in 1386. In 1389 he was appointed Clerk of the King's Works, a post in which he was assaulted and twice robbed. In 1391 he took a position as deputy forester in the royal forest of Petherton in Somerset. Frequently in debt, he received grants from Richard II and Henry IV. He died in a house he had rented in the garden of Westminster Abbey, where he was buried. This was a great honor for one who was common born, and he was first of those occupying what would become Poets' Corner.

The Book of the Duchess (c. 1369), an elegy for John of Gaunt's first wife, is his earliest extant original work. He later wrote *The Hous of Fame* (c. 1379), a translation of Boethius, and *The Parliament of Fowls.* He also wrote an essay on the astrolabe for his ten-year-old son Lewis in 1390. He seems to have begun the Prologue to his *Canterbury Tales* in 1387, though he likely composed a few of the tales earlier. The loose structure of the *Tales* allows Chaucer to portray the range of people in his society with humor and wisdom. The tales of the Wife of Bath and the Pardoner are usually considered to be the masterpieces of the collection, building on the psychological insight he had already demonstrated in *Troilus and Criseyde* (c. 1385). By Sh.'s time, English was well into its major shift from Middle to Modern English and some of the magic of Chaucer's language was being lost; however, his stature was still significant as the *TNK* Prologue demonstrates. Chaucer is here praised in a manner similar to the praise of Chaucer's friend, poet John Gower, by the Prologue in *Per. The Knyghtes Tale* upon which *TNK* is based was adapted from Giovanni Boccaccio, whose works Chaucer had likely first encountered on his diplomatic missions.

Cheapside, *2H6 4.2.70,* London's most prestigious commercial district, home to goldsmiths' shops and other expensive establishments. By having Cade threaten to turn Cheapside into pasture, Sh. suggests that the revolutionary leader planned the destruction of the propertied classes and the economic order on which their power depended.

Chertsey, *R3 1.2.29, 1.2.202, 1.2.213,* Benedictine monastery located in the town of Chertsey, in Surrey, 20 mi. southwest of London. Henry VI was buried at Chertsey until Henry VII moved his remains to Westminster Abbey.

Cheshu, *H5 3.3.8, 3.3.15, 3.3.24,* dialect; see Jesus Christ.

Chester, *2H4 1.1.39,* chief town in Cheshire, 180 mi. north west of London. Its location at the northern end of England's frontier with Wales made it a place of considerable military importance when wars raged between the Welsh and English.

Chetas, *Tro pro. 16,* one of the six gates of Troy. These are not in the *Iliad* which appears to give Troy only one double gate, but in William Caxton's *Recuyell of the Historyes of Troye,* 3 (c. 1474), the first English printed book and Sh.'s major source for the play, the six gates are listed, Chetas being the fourth.

Chief Justice, Lord, *2H4,* William Gascoigne (1350–1412/19), lawyer who became a member of young Henry (IV) Bolingbroke's household in the early 1390's. In 1400, shortly after Henry ascended the throne, Gascoigne was appointed England's chief justice. He quickly earned a reputation for probity in the conduct of his office. Gascoigne was one of the judges who tried the rebels Henry captured at the battle of Shrewsbury. Although Gascoigne was loyal to Henry, in 1405 he may have protested the actions of the court that convicted Archbishop Scrope of crimes similar to those for which Gascoigne had condemned prisoners from Shrewsbury in 1403. Few medieval lawyers were willing to concede the state's right to try an archbishop in a secular court, and Henry's decision to execute Scrope shocked his subjects. The story that Prince Harry insulted Gascoigne and was sent to prison is first found in Thomas Elyot's *Governour* (1531). Scholarly opinion is divided as to the truth of the tale.

Child Roland, see Roland.

Childeric (III), *H5 1.2.65,* last king of the Merovingian dynasty (743–751). He was deposed by Pepin the Short who, with papal permission, usurped the Frankish throne and founded the Carolingian royal house. Childeric and his son Theoderic were confined to monasteries where enforced celibacy extinguished their family.

Chiron, *Tit,* one of Queen Tamora's sons. He and his brother Demetrius rape and mutilate Titus Andronicus' daughter, Lavinia. They also bring about the deaths of Titus' sons for a crime the boys did not commit. Titus kills Tamora's wicked spawn and serves their flesh to their mother in a feast of mock reconciliation. No source for Sh.'s play is known, but an 18th century chapbook preserves a version of a tale that might have been familiar to him. It, however, calls Tamora's sons Alaricus and Abonus. A centaur called Chiron must have been familiar to Sh. from classical mythology, but there is no apparent connection between that virtuous and learned creature and the villain of Sh.'s play. Since Chiron and his brother Demetrius, although Goths, have Greek names (as does Andronicus, the Roman hero of the play), Sh.'s source may have been a Greek legend.

Chitopher, *AWW 4.3.169,* commander in the Duke of Florence's army. Possibly 'Christopher' is intended, or 'Achitophel,' the general in 2 Samuel 16–17 and 1 Chronicles 27 who assisted Absalom in his attempted overthrow of his father, King David.

Chorus, character who directly comments to the audience on the action, though he does not participate in it. Occasionally a character involved in the action will make remarks similar to a Chorus, but the line between this and soliloquy is quite thin. Sh. and his contemporaries borrowed the device from Seneca, who borrowed it from the ancient Greeks to reassert the links between their culture and his own. Greek choruses had different purposes than Roman or English ones. They consisted of groups whose function was either to represent a group of people observing the action or not directly involved in the primary action. The Greek word meant 'dance group' and the chorus long dominated the dramatic performances before Æschylus 'invented' the single actor, as part of theater's evolution from the religious rituals of Dionysos.

What Sh. knew about ancient Greek drama is debatable, but it doesn't seem to have been much. The Senecan model, however, would powerfully influence drama until the Romantic period. In two instances, Sh. designated a Chorus: *Rom* and *H5,* but only in the later is he effective, calling the audience to open their minds' eyes to the spectacle and glory of the history which lay behind the play. In *Rom* the notion of using one seems to have been aborted. The opening Chorus is omitted in F1 (though in Q), possibly, critics have speculated because it was not by Sh. F1 does include the Chorus' lines at the end of act 1, which might instead indicate that the opening Chorus was on a separate page which was misplaced or left off by a printer's error. After the Chorus disappears, the Prince serves a choral function at play's end by announcing the moral of the story. In *Per,* Time functions as Chorus, as does Gower in *WT,* both speaking in artificially antique language. It has been said that the secular nature of Renaissance English drama made the Chorus irrelevant; however, Choruses are dramatically effective in *H5, Per,* and *WT.* They set the mood and raise audience expectations. See also Prologue.

Chrish, *H5 3.3.36, 49, 53, 56,* dialect; see Jesus Christ.

Christ, *1H6 1.3.85,* 'C.'s mother.' *R3 1.4.185,* 'C.'s dear blood.' *R2 4.1.90, 161. 1H4 1.1.19, 3.2.111,* see Jesus Christ.

Christendom, 1) territories of western Europe where Christianity was the received religion. The term's primary association is, however, not with religion, but with culture. For Sh. it was a synonym for 'the civilized world.' *2H6 2.1.131. R3 3.4.51. Jn 2.1.75. 1H4 1.2.97, 3.1.160. Mac 4.3.193. H8 1.3.14, 3.2.67, 4.2.63.*

2) any Christian name. *AWW 1.1.170,* 'adoptious christendoms,' adopted names.

Christian, 1) member of the Christian religion, a follower of the 'Christos,' the Greek term for the Hebrew word 'messiah' or 'anointed one.' The word connotes religious attitudes and moral values appropriate to followers of Christ, but for Sh. it also had a secular meaning. By the 16th century Europe had been an exclusively Christian society for over a thousand years. Since the few Jews who lived in Europe were ignored, Christian faith was assumed to be a fundamental trait of European identity. 'Christian,' therefore, came to mean 'everyone'—or at least every 'civilized' person.

TGV 2.5.47, 3.1.270, 'bare C.,' Lance is preoccupied with the Jews, indicating a kinship between *TGV* and *MV. 2.5.50,* a reference to a church-ale, a fundraiser featuring the sale of ale. *Err 1.2.77. R2 4.1.74.*

MV: frequently used by Shylock, for example at *2.5.14–15* where he announces his bitter intention 'to feed upon/The prodigal C.' (Antonio). The word reverberates throughout as Shylock's behavior is contrasted with the merciful ideal of Christianity. *1H4 5.5.9. MWW 1.1.94,* pl. *2H4 2.2.64.*

Ado 2.3.184, 'Christianlike fear,' Benedick is as afraid of women as a saint. *AYLI 4.3.34. Ham 3.2.31,* sing. and pl.

TN 1.3.82, 3.2.66. MM 2.1.54, pl. *Oth 4.2.85. H8 2.1.65,* pl. *5.2.213.*

2) (adj.) of or pertaining to Christianity, European civilization, and therefore by implication, goodness and honesty. *Shr. 3.2.68,* 'C. footboy.' *2H6 4.7.38,* 'C. ear.' *1H6 4.2.30,* 'C. soul.' *R3 1.4.4, 3.7.96, 103, 116. R2 2.1.54, 4.1.84, 85, 121. Jn 5.2.37. MV. MWW 3.1.86, 4.1.65. 2H4 4.1.341. H5 1.2.241. Ham 4.5.198, 5.1.1. AWW 4.4.2,* 'C. world.' *Oth 2.3.165,* 'C. shame.' *H8 2.2.93, 131, 3.1.98, 3.2.245, 4.2.157.*

Christmas, 'Christ's Mass,' the celebration of Jesus' birth. Though the exact date is unknown, the church in 440 AD attached it to the day of the winter solstice, which was a time of festivity. The Romans celebrated Saturnalia about then and the Anglo-Saxons, New Year's. Many pagan symbols are associated with Christmas celebrations, such as the pine tree. The general merriment of the celebrations has often been considered irreverent by stricter religious groups, such as the Puritans, who outlawed many of the traditional festivities. *LLL,* according to the title page of Q, was performed for Queen Elizabeth at Christmas in 1597, which is supported by the two mentions. Supposedly *Lr.* was performed for James I on 26 December 1606, which indicates not all Yule entertainment was mirthful or perhaps explains why the play does not seem to have been much of a success until the late 1600s.

Shr Ind. 2.134. LLL 1.1.105. 5.2.462, 'To dash it like a Christmas comedy': mocking the performances at Christmas seems to have been part of the entertainment, as we can see in the pageant of the Nine Worthies, or in the Pyramus and Thisbe of *MND.* This may, however, allude to a specific incident at the Christmas revels held by the lawyers at Gray's Inn in 1594/5, later called the 'Night of Errors.' On December 28, the crowd became unruly and serious entertainment was suspended in favor of dancing and a performance of a 'Comedy of Errors (like to *Plautus* his *Menechmus*),' probably Sh.'s. The account of the evening was reported in the *Gesta Grayorum* (1688). A masque of Russians was also part of the festivities and likely also inspired the similar masque in *LLL.*

Christopher, *R3,* Christopher Urswike, a priest who carried messages from the countess of Richmond to her son, Henry Tudor, the earl of Richmond. The countess remained in England during the period of her son's exile in Brittany and fomented schemes to put him on England's throne. Urswike, an unswervingly loyal Lancastrian, was a trusted agent who kept important people in touch with each other during the dangerous days leading up to the battle at Bosworth Field.

Chronicles, *Shr Ind. 1.4,* Sly claims his ancestry is recorded here. It is possibly a reference to Raphael Holinshed's *Chronicles of England, Ireland and Scotland* (1577; rptd. and enlarged 1587), upon which Sh. relied so heavily, or to Edward Hall's chronicles, published as *The Union of the Two Noble and Illustre Famelies of Lancastre and Yorke* (1547), which, it is now thought, Sh. borrowed heavily from for his earlier histories. Many editors do not consider this use of 'Chronicles' to be specific and it might very well be a general use of the term with the capital letter in F1 not indicating a specific book.

Church, the Christian community. The term derives from a Greek word meaning 'lord's house.' In many contexts it denotes only the clergy, the leaders of the faith, the Church of England, or the papacy.

2H6 1.1.184. 1H6 1.1.32, 'C's prayers.' *1.1.33, 1.4.49,* 3.1.47. *Rom 2.5.37,* 'Holy C.' *Jn 3.1.67, 181, 182, 193, 3.4.172. 2H4 2.2.141. MWW 1.1.29. H5 1.1.10, 24. H8 5.2.151.*

Cicely, 1) *Err 3.1.31,* F1 'Cisley,' a house servant of Antipholus of Ephesus.

2) *TNK 3.5.45,* seamstress' daughter who does not show up as promised for the morris dancing. She is taken by Gerald the Schoolmaster to be a typically fickle woman, slippery as an eel. Her typically English country name is an anachronism in the play, but also typical of the dramatic practices of Sh.'s time in which the name is used to imply the lower class context.

Cicero, *JC,* see Tully.

Ci'cester, Cirencester or Ciren, *R2 5.6.3,* town in Gloucestershire about 90 mi. west of London. It was burned in the fighting that took place in 1399, when Henry (IV) Bolingbroke forced Richard II from the throne.

Cilicia, *Ant 3.6.16,* district on the southeastern coast of Asia Minor.

Cimber, *JC,* see Metellus Cimber.

Cimmerian, *Tit 2.3.72,* member of a race that Greek mythology alleged to live along the coast of the great ocean that marked the western edge of the world. Since the Cimmerian homeland was supposed to be swaddled in mists, the Cimmerians were associated with places of darkness.

Cinna, 1) *JC,* Lucius Cornelius Cinna, one of the Senators implicated in the conspiracy to assassinate Julius Cæsar. He came from a politically active family. His father was prominent among the opponents of the dictator Sulla, and Cinna carried on a struggle against Sulla's successor, Pompey. As a youth, he fled to Spain to join a rebel army led by Sertorius, one of Pompey's enemies. After Sertorius' defeat,

Cæsar persuaded Pompey to allow Cinna to return to Rome, but Cæsar's kindness failed to win Cinna over. Cinna's deeply inbred fear of leaders who might become dictators and threaten his vision of the Roman Republic made it impossible for him to trust Cæsar. Sh. drew his knowledge of Cinna's career and character from Plutarch's 'Brutus.'

2) *JC,* Gaius Helvius Cinna, Latin poet and friend of Cæsar's. After Cæsar's assassination, a frenzied mob mistook the poet for the Cinna who was Cæsar's assassin and tore the innocent man limb from limb. Plutarch ('Cæsar' 68.2–3) claims that it was Cinna's fate that frightened Brutus and Cassius into leaving Rome.

Cinque Ports, *H8 4.1.49,* five port cities on England's southeastern coast: Sandwich, Dover, Hythe, Hastings, and Romney. They were grouped together because they shared an obligation to provide ships for their homeland's defense. The barons of these districts enjoyed the honor of carrying the canopy under which England's kings and queens walked to their coronation ceremonies. The use in Sh.'s day of a French title for English cities was a relic from the high Middle Ages. French had for many generations been the preferred language of England's ruling class, which was composed largely of descendants of Norman soldiers.

Circe, daughter of the sun-god Helios and Perseis. Her magical powers are described in Homer's *Odyssey,* 10. As Odysseus struggles to find his way home from the Trojan War, he lands on Ææa, Circe's island, where she is the only human inhabitant. With a potion, she turns his men into swine and holds him captive for a year. She also turned Scylla (q.v.) into a monster. *1H6 5.4.6. Err 5.1.271,* 'C.'s cup.'

Clare, St., *MM 1.4.5,* 'votarists of St. C.,' the Franciscan nuns, sworn to a life of austerity, named after the saint to whom Isabella's order is dedicated. Her selection of the order is perhaps a manifestation of her extreme attitudes. In Erasmus' *Funus* ('The Funeral,' 1526), a dying man dedicates his eldest daughter to St. Clare. There are many parallel names (such as 'Bernardine') in the dialogue, and it is believed Sh. may have resorted to it for information about holy orders. St. Clara (1194–1253) founded the Franciscan nuns. Born in Assisi of a noble family, she was moved at age 18 by a sermon of St. Francis (q.v.). After testing her commitment to the vows of poverty, she was accepted into the order and the nuns became the Second Order of St. Francis. She was the abbess of St. Damian's for forty years and rigorously resisted any attempts to weaken the life of poverty to which the nuns were committed. Her efforts in maintaining Franciscan values resulted in the pope's recognition of their regulations two days before her death. Franciscan nuns became known as Poor Clares or Clarisses. They spread into England around 1293 and were established outside Aldgate, where they were known as the Minoresses. The tension between the desire for an austere rule of poverty and a more moderate one continued long after Clara's death and led to the Coletine and the Capuchin reforms.

Clarence, earldom and duchy, possession of the earls and dukes of Gloucester. It was named for the Clare family whose name derived from the town of Clare (L. *Clarentia*) in Suffolk. The family were descendants of one of William the Conqueror's companions, Godfrey, the eldest illegitimate son of Richard the Fearless, duke of Normandy. In 1342 Edward III's son, Lionel of Antwerp, married Elizabeth, the Clare heiress and was proclaimed first duke of Clarence. The title died out at the time of his death in 1368, but Henry IV revived it for his son Thomas (1389–1421). When Thomas died without an heir, the title lapsed again until Edward IV bestowed it on his younger brother George (1499–1478). See Clarence, Duke of, *1H6, 2H6*; *3H6, R3*; *2H4, H5.*

Clarence, Duke of, 1) *2H6 2.2.13, 34, 50, 56, 4.2.135, 4.4.28, 1H6 2.4.83, 2.5.75,* see Lionel, duke of Clarence.

2) *3H6, R3,* see George, duke of Clarence.

3) *2H4, H5,* see Thomas, duke of Clarence.

Claribel, *Tmp,* queen of Tunis, daughter of Alonso, from whose marriage the Neapolitans are returning when they wreck on Prospero's island. In Edmund Spenser's *Færie Queene,* 6.12, Claribell is 'the fayrest lady then of all that living were.' Her father, the Lord of Many Ilands, opposed her love for Bellamoure. Married quietly, she gives birth to a child who is reared by a shepherd and later identified because of a rosy birthmark. The story is a cliché of romance and it seems likely that Sh. may have been thinking of it in choosing the name. It derives from the Fr. *clair et belle,* 'bright and beautiful.'

Claudio, 1) 'Count C.,' 'County C.,' *Ado,* young nobleman who returns from the wars to fall instantly in love with Hero. Later duped by Don John into believing Hero unchaste, he emphatically rejects her at the altar, causing (he believes) her death. After the girl's guiltlessness is proved, he penitently agrees to marry an unseen cousin of Hero's. She, in the fashion of the typical Shakespearean romance, turns out to be Hero in disguise. In Claudio we see the pattern common from the earliest of Sh.'s comedies: a young man's hastiness or self-righteousness must be tempered by the fire of an emotional trauma inflicted by a more mature young woman. Thus, he learns the nature of love. In this, Claudio's situation is parallel to that of his comrade Benedick's. In modern times, however, Benedick is almost invariably seen as the more interesting of the two young men, for it is possible to see Claudio as shallow and a little cruel. His chastening seems more necessary and therefore, he is much less likable. Claudio, after all, marries on the basis of love at first sight, makes a public spectacle of rejecting the girl, and then agrees to marry to lessen his guilt. There is little indication, however, in the text that Claudio is anything other than one of the finest young men of his generation, and it must be recalled that an Elizabethan would find few complaints with his behavior. In the context of the time, the Benedick/Claudio parallel is one of 'high love' versus low, comic love, though Benedick is far from the buffoon who usually represents this type of love. Claudio's lesson in life is certainly also similar to that undergone by many noble characters in the late romances. Hero's resurrection is very much like that of Hermione, for example. In Sh.'s apparent source for the play (there are many contemporary versions of the plot), Matteo Bandello's *Novelle* (1554) Claudio is called Don Timbreo di Cardona.

2) *JC,* Claudius, one of Brutus' soldier-servants. He is a minor character with a common Roman name. Sh. probably had no historical individual in mind as a prototype for him.

3) *MM,* 'Signor C.,' brother of Isabella, betrothed to Juliet who is pregnant with his child. Despite his willingness to marry her, he is condemned to death by Angelo for violating the law on fornication. His finest scene is when he is visited by Isabella and suggests to her that she might be willing to yield to Angelo's blackmail to save his life. She responds to his fear of death by humiliating him for thinking of such a thing, leading some critics to say it proves her as inflexible as Angelo. In Cinthio's *Hecatommithi* (1565), one of Sh.'s sources, Claudio is called Vico and is a condemned rapist who is executed. In George Whetstone's *Promos and Cassandra* (1578) he is called Andrugio and his crime has been mitigated to consensual rape and as in Sh., a felon's head is substituted for Andrugio's and he is saved.

Claudius, *Ham,* king of Denmark, husband of Gertrude, and murderer of his brother King Hamlet. Although Hamlet gets most of the attention for his characterization, Claudius is also fascinating, an evildoer suffering genuine remorse, but pursuing no penance. Out of illicit passion he has committed a heinous crime and he now knows it, but he does not hesitate to commit further crimes to protect what he has won. At times he is more sympathetic than his adversary. In Belleforest's *Histoires tragiques* (1576), he is called Fengon, after the early version in Saxo Grammaticus' *Historiæ Danicæ* (c. 1200) in which he is Feng. In *Der Bestrafte Brudermord* (1710), which seems to be a German rendition of an old version of the play, Claudius is called Erico in the Dramatis Personæ, but 'King' in the text. It is likely that Sh. himself changed the name, though it may have been Claudius in a lost play. One suggestion is that it is an allusion to the emperor Claudius who divorced his wife Messalina to marry Agrippina, his niece. This incest was rewarded with his poisoning by Agrippina in order to place her son by a previous marriage, Nero, on the throne. Claudius and Claudio, however, are used elsewhere in Sh. and it may have been simply convenient.

Cleitus, *H5 4.7.37, 4.7.43,* (d. 328 BC), Macedonian officer with whom Alexander the Great had a quarrel that marked a turning point in the Greek king's career. Macedon was a feudal state, and the aristocratic officers of its army expected their monarch to lead them as a first among equals. Consequently, Alexander's soldiers treated him with the kind of familiarity appropriate to comrades-in-arms. When Alexander conquered Persia, he discovered that eastern tradition ranked kings with gods, and Alexander's Persian subjects could not comprehend the legitimacy of a king who did not inspire awe. Alexander, therefore, found it politically expedient to conform to the expectations of the Persians, and he asked his Macedonians to observe the rules of Persian court etiquette. Cleitus and others considered Persian customs humiliating. They rejected them outright and accused Alexander of trampling on the dignity of the men who had won him his empire. In 328 Cleitus got drunk at a feast and heaped ridicule on men whom Alexander had persuaded to take the lead in introducing a Persian ceremony to the court. Alexander lost his temper, grabbed a weapon from a guard, and killed him. An assault on an officer by his commander might have sparked mutiny, but Alexander mastered the volatile situation. He threatened to kill himself with the weapon with which he had murdered. When his men spontaneously reacted to disarm him, he retreated to his tent and sank into an ostentatious orgy of remorse. Finally, the Macedonians, realizing that they were deep in alien territory and lost without his leadership, begged Alexander to forget the incident and resume command. Alexander emerged from the crisis stronger than ever and a step closer to reconciling the disparate cultures of his empire.

Clement's Inn, *2H4 3.2.13, 206, 277, 304,* one of the London Inns of Court that lodged young men training for the law. It was connected with the Inner Temple. See Temple, The.

Cleomenes, *WT,* lord of Sicilia. The name occurs in Plutarch from which Sh. got most of his names for the play. Cleomenes is one of the major figures Plutarch discusses, comparing Agis and Cleomenes with Tiberius and Caius Gracchus. He was son of Leonidas, king of Sparta and succeeded him. Several of the names Sh. borrowed from Plutarch in *WT* appear in the lives of Agis, Cleomenes, and Camillus.

Cleon, *Per,* governor of Tarsus. He is called Strangulio in John Gower's *Confessio Amantis* (1390) and Stranguilio in Lawrence Twine's *Patterne of Painefull Adventures* (1594). The name is common in classical literature. One Cleon appears in Plutarch's biography of Nicias. Yet another was the Athenian tanner who ruled Athens after Pericles' death and who was mocked by Aristophanes in his *Wasps.*

Cleopatra, (69 BC–30 BC) daughter of Ptolemy XI Auletes, queen of Egypt. In legend the most beautiful woman in the world. After the death of her father, according to Egyptian custom she married her brother Ptolemy XII, and the Egyptian court split into two factions, one supporting the 12-year-old Ptolemy, and the other the 17-year-old Cleopatra. They ruled jointly until Ptolemy forced Cleopatra into exile in Syria. After Pompey was defeated by Julius Cæsar at Pharsalus, he fled to Egypt, expecting help (he had helped Ptolemy's father secure the throne). In an attempt to placate Cæsar, Ptolemy's faction killed Pompey, and inadvertently gave Cæsar a pretext for invading Egypt. Cleopatra joined with the Romans, led a revolt, and in 47 BC Ptolemy was drowned. Cæsar proclaimed her queen of Egypt and she married her 11-year-old brother Ptolemy XIII. In 46 BC she went to Rome as Cæsar's mistress, bearing him Cæsarion (Ptolemy XIV). After Cæsar's assassination she may have poisoned Ptolemy XIII to secure sole rulership of Egypt.

In 41 BC Marc Antony summoned Cleopatra to his military headquarters in Tarsus to explain her reluctance to take sides in the Roman power struggle which had developed between Octavius Cæsar and himself. He wanted Egypt's resources for his war and Cleopatra wanted more security in her position. She evidently charmed him and he went to live with her in Egypt for a while. After Antony was forced by political developments to return to Italy, she bore him twins. He married Octavius' sister Octavia in Rome to try to settle the conflict, but when he went on another expedition against the Parthians in 36 BC, Cleopatra rejoined him at Antioch and he celebrated his victory over the Parthians in Alexandria. He married her and acknowledged her children. Octavius declared war on them both and after some preliminary fighting in Greece defeated them at Actium in 31 BC. Although it is not clear what happened in the sea battle, it was said that Cleopatra lost her nerve in the battle and as her ship fled, her navy fled with her. Antony killed himself. Unable to entice the calculating Octavius, Cleopatra chose suicide to avoid being dragged through the streets of Rome as a slave. She arranged to be bitten by the sacred asp, whose fatal bite was said to confer immortality.

Rom 2.3.39, 'C. a gypsy': a strange figure of speech, since 'gypsy' derives from 'Egyptian.' *AYLI 3.2.143.*

Ant: Sh.'s depiction of her is powerfully ambiguous. He allows her a magnificent ability to fascinate a man as great as Antony: 'Age cannot wither her, nor custom stale her infinite variety,' says Enobarbus (she was quite mature by ancient standards when she charmed Antony). On the other hand, she is called a strumpet in the first scene and it is insistently implied that she is a decadent force in Antony's life. His pathetic pleading for a kiss while being lifted to Cleopatra who refuses to leave her tomb is perhaps the most stunning visual representation of their relationship. Yet her refusal to degrade herself ennobles her, and she dies well, like many another Sh. character, evil or good. The portrayal of Antony as corrupted by her is transmitted to Sh. through Plutarch who was repeating the Octavian version of events. It was much to Octavius' advantage to portray a Roman Antony on an Egyptian leash and it no doubt contributed to swinging public sympathy to Octavius.

Cym 2.4.70.

Clifford, 1) the elder, *2H6,* Thomas, Baron Clifford (1414–1455). Lord Clifford was Henry 'Hotspur's' grandson, and he trained with others of the Percy family in the raids and skirmishes that were a way of life in the borderlands between England and Scotland. He was the sheriff of Westmorland, and he served on Bedford's staff in France in 1435 and 1439. Sh.'s Clifford is a paradigm of loyalty to the Lancastrian party. His death at the hands of the duke of York in the first battle of the War of the Roses (St. Albans) prompts his son to swear an oath of vengeance against the house of York. The incident represents the passionate personal feuds that developed among the English nobility as the war progressed. The Cliffords survived the extinction of Lancaster and York to enjoy appointment to important posts at the Tudor court.

2) the younger, *2H6, 3H6,* John, Baron Clifford (1435–1461), son and heir of Thomas, Baron Clifford. The death of John's father at the first battle of St. Albans prompted John to join a revolt led by Somerset and Northumberland. The rebels demanded compensation from the house of York for their losses at St. Albans and convinced the king and his council to discipline York, Salisbury, and Warwick. Although Clifford's Percy ancestors had not been remarkable for their loyalty to the Lancastrians, Clifford adhered firmly to the king's

party. He fought for Henry VI at Wakefield, where he beheaded the corpse of the duke of York. After the battle, he presented Queen Margaret with York's head decked with a paper crown. He died in a skirmish at Ferrybridge on the eve of the battle of Towton.

Cliffords, *3H6 5.7.7,* see Clifford, 1) and 2).

Clifton, *1H4 5.4.45, 5.4.57,* John, (d. 1403), knight from the shire of Nottingham and one of Henry IV's officers at the battle of Shrewsbury.

Clitus, *JC,* Cleitus, one of Brutus' soldier-servants. Sh. found the story of Clitus' refusal to help his master commit suicide in Plutarch's 'Brutus' (52.1).

Clotaire, *H5 1.2.67,* Clothaire II (584–629), Merovingian king, father of Blithild, ancestress through whom Sh. says that Pepin the Short claimed the Frankish throne. Pepin's ancestors, Arnulf of Metz and Pepin of Landau, were highly placed officials at Clotaire's court, but Pepin did not rely on a blood connection with the Merovingian house to justify his usurpation of the crown. The case he made for his actions rested on political reality, not genealogy. The Merovingians had impoverished themselves by the pursuit of foolish campaigns and self-destructive vendettas, and the responsibility for the defense of their kingdom had shifted to Pepin's ancestors. Since the impotent Frankish kings had long been shunted aside and ignored in the conduct of daily affairs, Pepin persuaded his people that the man who had the duties of the king ought also to have the king's title. Pepin deposed the last Merovingian and his son, and the pope bestowed divine approval on Pepin's usurpation of the throne. The English politicians whose arguments influenced the histories Sh. read were not interested in ancient Frankish history for its own sake. They sought precedents that bore on current issues of public policy. In the 14th century the king of England had asserted a right to the throne of France inherited from his mother. The French had denied his claim by insisting that ancient custom prevented women from possessing or transmitting title to France's crown. The English responded by searching history for occasions on which French kings had based their legitimacy on the rights of women. The genealogies that English propagandists produced in the course of this debate did not always contain reliable information.

Cloten, *Cym,* cloddish son of Innogen's evil stepmother. An arrogant and contemptible dolt, his foolishness becomes very pernicious when he sets out to kill Posthumus and rape Innogen. He is beheaded by Guiderius before this happens and his death is regarded as being of little consequence until the legal technicality arises that Guiderius, disguised as a commoner, should be executed for killing a nobleman. When Guiderius is revealed to be the king's son, apparently Cloten can be forgotten. Cloten is not a memorable villain. His irregular character lacks the panache of other Sh. villains, almost as if the playwright were uncertain of what Cloten's function should be, other than to prod along the perplexing plot. Sh. may have borrowed the name from Harrison's *Description of Britaine* (1587), which identifies him as the inheritor of Britain after the deaths of Ferrex and Porrex. This Cloten was the father of Dunwallo Mulmutius.

Clotharius, *H8 1.3.10,* Clothar, or Clotaire, one of four kings of the Franks who reigned in the period between the 6th and the 8th centuries. Sh. pairs Clotharius with Charlemagne's father, Pepin, as examples of monarchs of great estates. He may have had either of two of the four Clothars in mind. The most powerful of them was Clothar I (d. 561), the son of the founder of the Merovingian empire, Clovis. But Clotar II (584–629) was more closely associated with Pepin. He was the father of the woman through whom Pepin claimed the kingdom of the Franks. See Clotaire.

Clowder, *Shr Ind. 1.16,* a dog's name. The other dog's names in this section generally suggest that they are named for their characteristics. The *OED* provides a couple of possibilities. One meaning might derive from the word 'claw.' There is a Somerset dialect word 'clow' referring to a fork-like farm implement for dragging manure out of cow stalls. Clowder could then mean the dog is a fervent digger or clawer. More likely is the 16th c. use of 'cloy' or 'clow' to mean nail, or wound with a nail or spike. It could then be a dog so wounded, or a reference to nail-like teeth. A 'cloyer' was a thief in some of the cony-catching pamphlets who took part of the proceeds. In this sense the dog could be one who snatches things that other dogs have caught. There might be the sense implied of 'cloy' meaning satiate, in the sense that the dog is annoying in not being independent. The obsolete form 'clowder' meaning 'clutter' does not seem to apply.

Clown, in several plays, comic characters (particularly the comic lead) are merely dubbed 'clown' in the stage directions and dialogue attributions. This indicates that a stock character was in the playwright's mind, indeed that a particular actor was in mind. Beginning with Richard Tarleton, the stage clown was a popular ingredient of the English Renaissance drama. Sh. used two primary clowns: William Kempe until 1599, and Robert Armin afterwards. The latter was famed for his singing ability, his improvisations, and his quick verbal wit. These are shown in the roles in *Ham, TN, Lr,* etc. He is more of a jester. Kempe leaned more toward physical humor. He is more of a sturdy, but uneducated, peasant type, a bumbler prone to malapropism, but well-meaning. The earlier clown roles are more remote from the main plots, as if Kempe were given set-pieces to exercise his humor (Lance and his dog Crab, for instance), whereas the later, or jester types are more integrated into the plot (Feste, for example). *Tit. TN. AWW. Oth Ant WT.*

2) *TNK 3.5.133,* 'beest-eating C.,' a character in the morris dance before Theseus. He parallels the 'Country Clown or Shepherd,' in Francis Beaumont's antimasque for *The Masque of Grayes-Inne and the Inner Temple* (1613). 'Beest' (or 'beestings') is the milk which a cow gives for several days after giving birth. It was sometimes considered unhealthy for either calf or man, but the implication may here be that the Clown is a hick.

Cobham, Eleanor, duchess of Gloucester, *2H6,* (d. 1446), last wife of Humphrey of Gloucester. Eleanor, daughter of Lord Cobham of Sterborough, first came to Humphrey's attention as lady in waiting to his wife, Jacqueline of Bavaria. Eleanor's star rose as Jacqueline's faded. Gloucester had wed Jacqueline in 1422 intending to exploit her hereditary claim to the lordships of Hainaut and Holland. Gloucester's personal ambitions in the Lowlands were contrary to the interests of his nation's most important ally, the duke of Burgundy, and the English government opposed the duke's efforts to win control of his wife's estates. In 1425 Burgundy captured Jacqueline, and Gloucester abandoned her to her fate. In 1428 he successfully petitioned the pope for an annulment of their marriage and promptly wed Eleanor. Gloucester was no more successful in domestic politics than in foreign policy. His opposition to Henry VI's plan for restoring peace with France cost him influence at court, and his enemies used Eleanor, a vain and extravagant woman, to undercut his position. Humphrey was a patron of learning and a collector of books. His interest in arcane scholarship spawned rumors that he and Eleanor dabbled in the black arts. On 23 July 1441, two priests of Eleanor's acquaintance, Roger Bolingbroke and Thomas (Sh. calls him 'John') Southwell, were charged with practicing witchcraft for Eleanor. It was alleged that Eleanor asked them to perform rituals that would end Henry VI's life and clear a path to the throne for her husband. Cardinal Beaufort, Gloucester's enemy, indicted Eleanor, and she fled to sanctuary in Westminster Abbey. The duchess was convicted of heresy and ordered to do penance. She was forced to parade bareheaded through London carrying a candle and making offerings at various churches. The men tried with her were condemned to death, while she was committed to prison for life on the Isle of Man. Gloucester was powerless to do anything for his wife, and his own situation became increasingly precarious. In 1447 the king assented to his uncle's arrest at the parliament at Bury, and Gloucester's death four days later may have been a result in part of impotent anger at the humiliation of his family. Sh.'s eagerness to cast a good light on the Lancastrian family disposed him to judge Eleanor harshly. Sh. represents Gloucester as a beloved popular leader whose nemesis was a vain and foolish wife.

Cobham, Lord, *3H6 1.2.40, 56,* see Brook, Edmund (Edward), Lord Cobham.

Cobham, Reinhold Lord, *R2 2.1.280,* Rainold or Reginald, friend of Henry (IV) Bolingbroke and Henry's ally against Richard II. Cobham was the son of a Reginald Cobham who fought at the battles of Crécy and Poitiers.

Cobweb, *MND,* a fairy. To increase the humor, Bottom addresses the fairy deferentially as Master and Monsieur, makes reference to the practice of using a cobweb to staunch the bleeding of small cuts, and sends him to fetch the honeybag from a bee. The simplicity of the role, in which Cobweb seems almost to be led around the stage by the primary actors and has only to answer a question for his line, suggests that the part may have been for a small child. This could have been darling, and if the play was done for a noble festivity, as has been suggested, perhaps small children of the nobility were dressed up for the cameo role. It is also convenient in production to double the other 'rude mechanicals' in these fairy parts.

Cock, euphemism for God. *Shr 4.1.105,* 'C.'s passion,' an oath: 'by the suffering and death of Christ.' *Ham 4.5.61,* 'by C.,' oath. *MWW 1.1.283, 2H4 5.1.1,* 'by c. and pie,' 'by God and a pastry dish,' possibly 'by rooster and magpie' or 'by God and piety' or 'by God and the service book of the Church.'

Cockney, effeminate, affected, childish, or spoiled person. This should not be confused with the more-limited meaning of a lower-class native of London, which originally began as a rural person's insult for city dwellers or a person born within the sound of the bells of St. Mary le Bow, though this meaning was in use in Sh.'s time. The word derives from an old name for a misshapen egg, or a child that does not wean as quickly as normal. Also in the middle ages an imaginary country of idleness was called Cokaigne; this land was jokingly related to London. *TN 4.1.14. Lr. Q 7.283.*

Cocytus, *Tit 2.3.236,* river in Epirus that the ancient Greeks believed was a route to the underworld. In classical mythology it was a tributary of the Styx, the stream that flows by Hades. Sh. thought of the Cocytus as the mouth of hell.

Coeur de lion, Fr. 'lion-heart,' *1H6 3.5.42, Jn 1.1.54, 85, 136, 2.1.12,* see Richard (I) the Lion-hearted.

Coint, Francis, *R2 2.1.286,* one of the companions in exile who returned to England with Henry (IV) Bolingbroke to try to force Richard II from the throne. Holinshed (3.498) claims that there were not many men like him at Henry's disposal. In 1399, when Henry sailed for England to challenge its king, he had no more than fifteen 'lances' (men-at-arms) in his company.

Colbrand, wicked Danish giant who is killed by Sir Guy, earl of Warwick, the hero of an English romance written about 1240. His death relieved England from tribute payments to the Danes. *Jn 1.1.225. H8 5.3.21.*

Colchis, *MV 1.1.171,* kingdom on the Black Sea from which the Argonauts took the Golden Fleece. Strabo, the ancient geographer, describes it as being at the foot of the Caucasus mountains and bordering Armenia and Cappadocia.

Coldspur, *2H4 1.1.50,* ironic play on Henry Percy's nickname 'Hotspur' made when his death at Shrewsbury is reported.

Coleville, John, *2H4,* possibly a descendant of one of Edward III's soldiers and the warden of Wisbeach Castle. A knight with this name is mentioned by Holinshed (3.38) as having been beheaded at Durham (not York as Sh. has it) for rebelling against Henry IV. There was also a John Coleville in the army that Henry V took to France.

Collatine, *Luc 7,10, 33, 82, 108, passim,* see Collatinus.

Collatinus, *Luc 218, 232, 256, 829,* Tarquinius Collatinus, nephew of the Roman king, Tarquinius Superbus, and husband of Lucretia. While encamped at the siege of the city of Ardea, Collatinus and his royal cousins fell to boasting about the virtues of their wives. They put their claims to the test by paying surprise visits on their women. In Rome the royal princesses were found banqueting and revelling in an unseemly manner. In Collatium, Collatinus' wife Lucretia was discovered seated at her loom ruling a peaceful, decorous household. The sight of her virtue inflamed the passions of Collatinus' cousin, Sextus. After Sextus and his companions returned to camp, he sneaked back to rape her. Lucretia revealed his crime and, despite her innocence, killed herself. The wrong done her inspired such rage in the Roman people that they drove Sextus and his father from Rome, abolished the monarchy, and established a Republic. Sh. probably knew the story from several sources—including Ovid and Chaucer.

Collatium, *Luc 4, 50,* Sabine town in ancient Latium on the Anio river. It was conquered by the Roman king Tarquinius Priscus.

College, *AWW 2.1.116,* the society or 'guild' of physicians.

Colmekill, *Mac 2.4.34,* Icolmkill or Iona, a small island of the Inner Hebrides on which all the kings of Scotland from Kenneth III to Macbeth (973–1040) were interred. It is only 3.5 by 1.25 mi. in size. A monastery there and a cathedral dated from the times of St. Columba (c. 563), who converted the Scottish. It appears to have been a sacred island to the Druids even earlier. It was an important religious center until 1561 when it was pillaged upon Henry VIII's separation from the Roman church. It was said that 48 Scottish, 8 Norwegian, 4 Irish, and 1 French king were buried there, as well as numerous island lords, but this cannot be verified with certainty. Many pilgrims came to die on Iona in order to lie in the sanctified soil. 'Icolmkill' means the 'island of St. Columba's Cell (Chapel).' Protestant desecrations of the 16th c. make it impossible to identify the graves of Duncan and Macbeth; however, the chapel of St. Oran built by Margaret, wife of Malcolm, constitutes the oldest ruins on Iona.

Colnbrook, *MWW 4.5.73,* F1 'Cole-brook,' a small town east of Windsor.

Colossus, *JC 1.2.137,* huge bronze statue of the god Apollo, one of the wonders of the ancient world. The sculptor Chares erected the Colossus at the port of Rhodes in the early 3rd century BC, and it was destroyed by an earthquake in 224 BC. The legends with which Sh. was familiar claim that the legs of the statue straddled the entrance to Rhodes' harbor. For reasons both of aesthetics and engineering, this design is improbable.

Comagene, *Ant 3.6.74,* Syrian kingdom between the Euphrates river and the Taurus mountains. It shared borders with Cilicia, Cappadocia, and Armenia. Prior to the reign of the Roman emperor Vespasian (69–79 AD), Comagene was ruled by descendants of one of Alexander the Great's generals, Seleucus (I) Nicator.

Combe, John, *Var,* usurer and friend of Sh.'s for whom Sh. is alleged to have composed an epitaph extemporaneously. Sh. is also credited with having composed a second, less humorous epitaph for Combe after his death. The extemporaneous epitaph is similar to many others from the time and may have been borrowed by Sh. as a witticism or may merely have been attributed to him. The more serious epitaph, though there is only one source for it, seems to fit what we know about Combe. When he died in 1614, he left a generous £1000 to the poor, as the epitaph suggests, as well as £5 to Sh. Combe was the wealthiest man in Stratford and appears in many records suing to recover debt. John's brother Thomas was involved in business with Sh. and Thomas' epitaph has also been attributed to Sh. Two years after Thomas' death, Sh. was a plaintiff in a suit against Thomas' son William. Thomas' second son (also Thomas) is in Sh.'s will as the inheritor of his sword.

Comedy, see Old Comedy.

Comfit, Count, *Ado 4.1.317,* 'a goodly Count, Comfect,' F1. Beatrice's exact words are disputed by editors, but the meaning is fairly clear. She is calling Claudio a sugar-candy or confectionary count. 'Count' itself might have been pronounced like the French *conte,* a 'story' or 'fiction,' doubling the insult.

Cominius, *Cor,* Roman general who granted Caius Martius (Marcius) the agnomen 'Coriolanus.' It was meant to acknowledge his bravery in a war Rome had waged against the Volscian city of Corioli. Sh. found the story in Plutarch's 'Coriolanus' (8.1–2, 11.1). If a Cominius really existed, he may have been a Roman of Samnite ancestry. There was a town by the name of Cominium in Samnite territory.

Commandments, Ten, see Ten Commandments.

Commons, lower house of Parliament representing the untitled propertied classes. During the 13th century England's kings acquired the habit of summoning influential commoners from various parts of the country to meet with the clergy and feudal barons who customarily attended the royal council. John held several courts that included persons from many regions of his kingdom, but the first national assembly that represented all the propertied classes was the invention of a revolutionary. In 1264 Simon de Montfort, Henry III's brother-in-law, raised a revolt that ended with the capture of the king. Simon hoped to avoid the appearance of treason by soliciting the nation's approval for his coup. He was concerned only about the opinions of persons on whom the state depended for financial support, so he only invited men of substance to his meeting: the clergy, the nobility, the landowners from the shires of the English countryside, and the merchants from England's chartered towns or 'boroughs.' Since the medieval parliament's chief function was to grant subsidies to the government, the only persons who took part in it were those who had money. Simon did not long outlive the parliament he convened in 1265. Edward (I), Henry's son, routed Simon's army and assumed responsibility for his incompetent father's government.

Edward was not bound to follow Simon's example, but he continued to call parliaments like the one Simon had invented because they were useful sources of revenue. Since these early parliaments were expanded versions of the feudal councils attended by the king's vassals, there was no tradition to govern the role commoners might play in them. The forty-eight parliaments that Edward III convened over a period of 50 years—all involving commoners—changed this. The frequency of Edward's meetings encouraged the growth of assumptions about how many men should be sent to parliament from each district and how these men should be chosen. Regular assemblies also accustomed the members of parliament to work together and helped them discover interests they shared. In 1339 the knights of the shires and the burgesses from the towns agreed to deal with the king through a single spokesman. This decision created a 'house of commons' that quickly discovered the advantages of solidarity. In 1340 the Commons carried the point on which their political future depended: The principle that the king could levy taxes only with the approval of Parliament.

R2 4.1.145, 262. H5 1.1.72.

Compiègne, *1H6 1.1.60,* French city about 50 mi. north of Paris. Joan of Arc's military career ended there when she was captured by the duke of Burgundy's soldiers.

'Concolinel,' *LLL 3.1.3,* apparently the title of Mote's song, with the lyrics omitted from the text. There is much speculation on it. It may be a Fr. song that begins '*Quand Colinelle.*' There is an Irish lyric, '*Can cailin gheal*' ('Sing, Fair Maiden') which is not unlikely if Pistol is mentioning an Irish song, '*Calin o custure me*' at *H5 4.4.4.*

Conrad, *Ado,* a minor character in the retinue of Don John. His banter with Don John illuminates the melancholy evil in his lord, and he listens to Borachio's explanation of the plot to defame Hero, which the watch overhears. He appears in a later scene, but does not speak. Pretty much Conrad is a plot device, though his character is somewhat revealed by Don John's remark that he was born under Saturn. In the confusion of actor's names with character's names which is common in F1, Conrad is often given additional lines, such as the outburst against Dogberry in *4.2,* but this scene has led to many disputes among editors. Charles I became king of the Two Sicilies in 1266 by killing Manfred, the son of Holy Roman emperor Frederick II. Manfred was possibly illegitimate, though Frederick seems to have treated him as if legitimate. When Conrad IV, Manfred's half-brother, died, Manfred became regent in the name of Conradin, Conrad's son. In 1258, Manfred heard that Conradin had died. He was crowned king of the Two Sicilies only to discover Conradin was still alive. He refused to give up his crown and Charles of Anjou received the blessings of Pope Urban IV in deposing Manfred. Conradin led a revolt against Charles, but was captured and executed on November 29, 1268, and Charles brutally punished the nobility who had supported him. Since it is Charles who was later defeated by Pedro of Aragon (son-in-law of Manfred and the 'prince' of *Ado*), the use of the name Conrad for a rebellious nobleman seems more than coincidence. See Pedro.

Constable, Lord High, *H8 2.1.103,* chief military officer in the royal household. Edward Stafford, duke of Buckingham, held the post until Henry VIII indicted him for treason.

Constable of France, *H5,* see Delabret, Charles.

Constance, Lady, *Jn,* (d. 1201) heiress to Brittany, wife of Henry II's son, Geoffrey, and mother of Arthur. Since her son was heir to Geoffrey, Henry's fourth son, Constance believed that Arthur had a better claim to Richard I's estate than his uncle John, who was Henry's fifth son. Constance worked very hard to win converts to her son's cause. In *Jn* she appears as the widowed, beleaguered mother of a defenseless child. In reality, she was at the time of the events in the play the wife of Guy, viscount of Tours, and her son was old enough, by the standards of the day, to be considered an adult.

Constantine 'the Great,' *1H6 1.3.121,* (c. 288–337), Roman emperor who ended the persecution of the Christian religion. His patronage hastened Christianity's triumph over paganism and laid the foundation for medieval Europe's Christian culture.

Constantinople, *H5 5.2.206,* original name for modern Istanbul. The city perpetuated the memory of its founder, Constantine, the first Christian emperor of Rome. Constantine chose it to be the capital of his empire, for it was better situated than Rome to guard the empire's endangered frontiers. When the western half of the Roman empire fell to German invaders in the 5th century, Constantinople preserved its hold on Rome's eastern provinces. During the Middle Ages most of these were lost to the Muslims, and Constantinople's culture changed dramatically. The term 'Byzantine,' from the Greek name for the site where the city stands, distinguishes the medieval from the ancient phases in the city's history. In 1453 the Ottoman Turks dispersed the ghosts of old Rome by conquering Constantinople, renaming it, and transforming its churches into mosques.

Cook, William, *2H4 5.1.9, 13, 20, 24,* one of the many fictional characters in Sh.'s plays whose names reflect their occupations. He is Justice Shallow's untrustworthy chef.

Cophetua, legendary African king of great wealth, who fell in love with Penelophon (Sh. 'Zenelophon') a beggar. He married her and lived happily ever after. The story was memorialized in a contemporary ballad, 'A Song of a Beggar and a King' (also known as 'King Cophetua and the Beggar Maid'), later printed in Richard Johnson's *Crown Garland of Golden Roses* (1612). Cophetua is also mentioned in Ben Jonson's *Every Man in his Humour* 3.4, (1598) in which Sh. acted.

LLL 4.1.65. Rom 2.1 14. 2H4 5.3.103: it is conjectured that there may have been a play on this story quoted and mocked by Pistol (*2H4 5.3.100–101*) for its bombast. In the three contexts in which King Cophetua is cited, however, comic effect is always predominant, so the ballad or the conjectured play or both must have been regarded as ridiculous. The song is also mentioned at *LLL 1.2.104–5* and *R2 5.3.78.*

Copperspur, Master, *MM 4.3.13,* mocking name for one of the impoverished criminals Pompey knows. As prisoners paid for their own food, many were forced to beg passers by. Possibly a play on coppernose, a red nose caused by acne or heavy drinking with 'spur' referring to the sexual organ.

Coram, *MWW 1.1.5,* corruption of L. *quorum,* 'of whom.' It is not a title, though Slender uses it as such. The word began one of the clauses in the document appointing a magistrate and indicates one of a select group of justices whose presence was necessary for a legal proceeding.

Corambus, *AWW 4.3.167,* commander in the Duke of Florence's army. Corambis was the original name of Polonius in *Ham.*

Cordelia, *Lr,* daughter of Lear, sister of Goneril and Regan, wife of the king of France. Cordelia refuses to flatter her father as her sisters do and Lear flies into a rage, disinheriting her. France marries her saying she is a treasure in herself. Later, when the sisters mistreat Lear, Cordelia returns with an army, is defeated and assassinated. Her love for her father never fails, though she is treated very badly by him. Some commentators find her refusal to humor the old man a parallel to Lear's stubbornness and find them jointly responsible for the tragedy, if not simply an indication that Cordelia is more Lear's daughter than her sisters. In Geoffrey of Monmouth's and Holinshed's versions of the story, she is named Cordeilla. In John Higgin's *Mirror for Magistrates* (1574), Cordile or Cordell. Cordeill or Cordelia in Spenser's *Færie Queen,* 2.10. Apparently Sh. chose to use the daughters' names from Spenser, and both writers would have appreciated the resemblance to the Latin *cor, cordis,* 'heart,' and also *cordatus,* 'prudent, wise.' A most interesting parallel exists in a legal matter of 1603 when a Mrs. Cordell Annesley resisted an attempt to have her aged father Bryan Annesley declared incompetent by his son-in-law. Annesley had three daughters. Cordell succeeded and inherited most of her father's property when he died in 1604. There is no proof Sh. knew any of these people, though one of the estate's executors Sir William Harvey, was a husband of the Countess of Southampton, who was mother of Sh.'s patron. Harvey later married Cordell in 1607 and is considered by some to be a candidate for the mysterious 'Mr. W. H.' of the sonnets. Bullough speculates that, if the case were widely discussed, perhaps it inspired the revival of *The True Chronicle Historie of King Leir* in 1605, which in turn inspired Sh.

Corin, 1) *MND 2.1.66,* common name for a shepherd in the pastorals of the time. In *Tottel's Miscellany* (1557) is the pastoral poem entitled 'Harpalus' Complaint of Phillida's Love bestowed on Corin that loved her not, and denied him that loved her.' This may be the first English use of the name in a pastoral context. Corineus is mentioned in Spenser's *Færie*

Queene 2.10.10.9, but Sidney's *Countesse of Pembrokes Arcadia* frequently refers to Helen, queen of Corinth. Coridon or Corydon is a similar name used by Virgil and Spenser, among many others.

2) *AYLI,* a shepherd. The corresponding character in Thomas Lodge's *Rosalynde* (1590) is Coridon, providing evidence that Sh. was familiar with the shepherd Corin from *Sir Clyomon and Clamydes* (1599, anon.), Lodge's source.

Corinth, city of ancient Greece located near the southern end of the Isthmus of Corinth which connects the mainland with the Peloponnesian peninsula. The city was about 48 mi. west of Athens and lay between the Gulf of Corinth (or Lepanto) to the west and the Saronic gulf to the east. The city's origins are lost in prehistory, but archæologists tell us it was settled in pre-Mycenæan times. After the Dorian invasion (sometime before 1000 BC) it developed, by 650, into the major trading city of Greece and a colonial power, founding Corcyra and Syracuse (8th c.) and Potidæa (7th c.). In the center of the city stood a citadel, the Acrocorinthus, and between its harbors at Lechæum and Cenchreæ vast amounts of materials were shipped in both directions. Even ships were moved between the gulfs. As Athens expanded as a power, it envied Corinth's access to the western Mediterranean and began a series of actions to acquire a toehold on the Gulf of Corinth. In 433 BC Athens helped Corcyra fend off the Corinthian navy. In revenge, Corinth helped Potidæa (which had become part of the Delian League) secede from the Athenian alliance. Sparta came to the aid of Corinth and invaded Attica in 431 BC, thus beginning the costly conflict of the Peloponnesian War (which Sparta won in 404 BC). From 395 to 386 BC, Corinth allied with Athens and fought Sparta in the Corinthian War, but in 338 the city fell under the rule of Philip of Macedon. After the Fourth Macedonian War (149–148 BC) the Romans broke Greek resistance to their rule by razing the city. It was rebuilt by Julius Cæsar in 44 BC. It later became the capital of the province of Achæa. St. Paul was temporarily in residence there and addressed two of his epistles to the Corinthians. The Visigoths captured the city in 395 AD. It fell into Turkish hands in 1458, where it remained until 1687 when it was briefly held by the Venetians. It then reverted to the Ottomans until Greek independence. In 1858 the ancient city was leveled by an earthquake and the city relocated a mile and a half to the east.

Err 1.1.87, 93, 111; 5.1.364, 367. Tim 2.2.69. Per 6.39, one of the suitors of Thaisa is from C.

Corinthian, *1H4 2.5.12,* a good companion in revelry. The ancient city of Corinth was a thriving port known for its wealth, its wine and its prostitutes.

Coriolanus, *Cor, Tit 4.4.68,* Caius Martius (Marcius) 'Coriolanus,' Roman soldier who earned his agnomen in battle with the Volsci of the city of Corioli. The contempt the aristocratic Coriolanus openly expressed for the common man offended the voters of the Roman republic and cost him a consulship. He fought back by attempting to exploit a famine. He proposed withholding supplies of food from the people until they surrendered their right to elect tribunes (magistrates empowered to protect commoners). The Romans exiled their difficult hero, and he defected to the Volscian camp. He persuaded the Volscians to place themselves under his command, and he led them to victory over the Roman army. Various distinguished Roman officials pleaded with him to spare their city, but he refused until his mother, wife, and children appeared before his tent. When they reproached him for the shame he was bringing on his family, he pulled the Volscian forces back from Rome. Legends supply him with two fates. One story is that he retired to live out his final years among the Volsci. Another legend claims that the Volsci killed him because he cost them their chance to destroy Rome. Almost all of Sh.'s inspiration for *Cor* was Plutarch's biography 'Coriolanus.'

Corioles, *Cor,* town in ancient Latium inhabited by people from the tribe of the Volsci. Caius Martius, an aristocratic Roman soldier, earned the agnomen 'Coriolanus' by conspicuous bravery in battle with Volscian troops from Corioles.

Cornelia, 1) *Tit 4.1.12,* mother of Tiberius and Gaius Gracchus, liberal politicians who were martyred while trying to reform the Roman Republic. The Cornelian family was one of the most distinguished in Rome. All its female members were, according to Roman custom, named Cornelia. The woman to whom Sh. refers was a daughter of Publius Scipio Africanus, the conqueror of Carthage. She was respected for her learning and for her efforts to educate her sons. Their dedication to the service of the common people of Rome was assumed to be the result of her influence, and she was honored in her own right as a champion of the Republic. Sh. probably drew what he knew of her life from Plutarch's biographies of her sons.

2) *Tit 4.2.140,* midwife who helps Tamora with the birth of a child who was conceived as a result of the empress's adulterous affair with Aaron the Moor. Sh.'s source for *Tit* is uncertain. An 18th c. chapbook preserves a later version of a tale that might have been known to Sh., but it does not supply all the names that he used for the play's characters. It is likely that Sh. arbitrarily chose a Roman name for the minor figure of the midwife. 'Cornelia' may have come to mind, because Sh. had, in a previous scene, alluded to a story about the mother of Tiberius and Gaius Gracchus.

Cornelius, 1) *Ham,* courtier in the service of Claudius. Along with Valtemand, he is sent on a mission to the king of Norway to request that he restrain his nephew Fortinbras from demands he has been making on Denmark. Later they return to report that Norway has rebuked Fortinbras for his designs on Denmark, but requests free passage for him to make war on the Poles. The purpose of the scenes seems to be to establish the threat of Fortinbras, who perceives the Danish kingdom to be in disorder, and perhaps to demonstrate Claudius' competence as king. Cornelius is a weighty name in Roman history. In Plutarch, Caius Cornelius, for example, is an augurer who predicts Cæsar's victory over Pompey. Members of the Cornelius family included Scipio Africanus, Scipio Æmilianus Africanus, Sulla, and Cornelia (q.v.), mother of the Gracchi.

2) *Cym,* physician to Cymbeline's evil queen. He is asked by her to provide a poison, but he gives her a sleeping potion instead, thwarting her plans. Later, he reveals her deathbed confession. Cornelius is hardly an unusual name, though a famous physician of Charles V was so named, as was the classical A. Cornelius Celsus (1st c. AD).

Cornwall, *Lr,* peninsula of southwest England, lined with rocky cliffs. The climate is pleasant and there are excellent harbors. Tin was mined there from ancient times and may have been traded to the Phoenicians. Queen Elizabeth imported German miners to revive that industry during her reign. Though Christianity came to Cornwall in the 5th c., the Cornish held out until the 11th c. against the Saxon invasions, being the last area of England to be taken. Other than an occasional rebellion such as the one in 1497 against a tax and in 1549 in favor of Latin services and against the Book of Common Prayer, Cornwall has had a relatively quiet history. As a result, there are a great number of ancient ruins still surviving there. One heritage of the Celts, the Cornish language, survived on the peninsula nearly to the 19th c. and there are still a few diehard Cornish nationalists who want to secede from England. It is thought the name derives from the peninsula's shape, 'like a horn,' from the Celtic *corn, cornu* or the Latin *cornu.* A legend also has it being named after Corineus, who defeated a giant and received the area as his reward. This story is mentioned in Spenser's *Færie Queen,* 2.10.

Cornwall, Duke of, *Lr,* husband of Regan. A consummate villain, his most horrible act is the blinding of the Duke of Gloucester, for which an outraged servant kills him. In Geoffrey of Monmouth's version of the story, the Duke of Cornwall is named Henuinus (Henninus in Holinshed). In John Higgin's *Mirror for Magistrates* (1574), Hinnine is duke of Cambria and Cornwall; in Spenser's *Færie Queen* simply Cambria, and in *The True Chronicle Historie of King Leir,* Cornwall marries Gonorill, while Cambria replaces Albany. The title was created in 1337 for Edward the Black Prince (thus making it another anachronism in *Lr*) and has traditionally gone to the king's son.

Corydon, *PP 17.35,* ancient name for a typical shepherd of Arcadia. The name appears in the works of Theocritus (*Idyl* 4), Virgil (*Bucolics* 7), and Calpurnius Siculus. There is a Coridon in Edmund Spenser's *Færie Queene,* 6 (1596), and one in Thomas Lodge's *Rosalynde* (1590) from which Sh. derived his *AYLI.*

Cosmo, *AWW 4.3.168,* commander in the Duke of Florence's army. The name was perhaps suggested by Cosimo de Medici (1389–1464), ruler of Florence.

Costard, *LLL,* clown. He misdelivers two love letters and plays Pompey the Great in the pageant of the Nine Worthies. His humor consists largely of his malapropism and he fits rather nicely as a stock *commedia dell'arte* character among Armado, Holofernes, and Nathaniel. Early in the play he is sentenced to fast for pitching woo at Jaquenetta, and later he reveals that she is pregnant by Armado. A 'costard' was a large, ribbed apple and Sh. frequently uses the word as a metaphor for head (*R3 1.4.151, MWW 3.1.14, Lr 4.5.240*) in common speech.

Cotswold, range of hills running through Gloucestershire and separating the basins of the Thames and Severn rivers. The Cotswolds are near Sh.'s birthplace at Stratford-on-Avon, and Sh. knew them as a rough country more suited to sheep ranching than farming. *R2 2.3.9. 2H4 3.2.20. MWW 1.1.83,* F1 'Cotsall.'

Cotus, *Cor 4.5.3, 4,* servant of the Volscian general Tullus Aufidius. The name does not appear in Sh.'s source, Plutarch's 'Coriolanus,' but Sh. may have found it while browsing through other works by Plutarch. A Cotys, king of Thrace (383–385 BC) and an uneasy ally of the ancient Athenians, is mentioned in Plutarch's 'Agesilaus' (11.1).

Council, in the narrow sense, a committee of secular and ecclesiastical authorities composed of the king's chief advisors. During periods of royal incapacity (such as Edward III's old age and Henry VI's long minority) a regency council could be appointed to act in the king's name. In the broader sense the council was a class of persons who swore a special oath to serve the English monarch. In the late medieval era a hundred or more of the royal servants were at any given time recognized as councilors. Different councilors met in different groups to handle special items of business, and they promoted the evolution of departments of administration within a governmental bureaucracy. Henry VIII's chief administrators constituted a kind of high court called the Council of the Star Chamber. After Cardinal Wolsey's fall, the Star Chamber devoted itself to legal business, and the responsibility of guiding the ruler's political thinking passed to an organization known as the Privy Council. Councils and courts evolved from a feudal custom that required a vassal to come to consult with his lord when summoned. Councils were originally occasions for kings to demonstrate their power by commanding the obedience of their barons, but during the latter part of the medieval era councils provided a way for influential men to block the development of autocracy in England. Similar institutions evolved in France, but, without the support of an organization like the English parliament, they failed to halt the evolution of absolutism.

2H6 1.1.86, 3.1.27, 4.2.15. R3 2.3.13, 3.2.9, 17, 73, 3.5.36. R2 1.3.24. 1H4 1.1.32, 102, 3.2.32, 4.3.101. MWW 1.1.31, 32, 33, 110. H5 5.2.79, 276. H8 3.2.318, 5.1.43, 51, 5.2.170.

Councillor [sic], *H8 5.2.16, 83, 177,* see Council.

Counter gate, *MWW 3.3.73,* prison gate. In common parlance, a 'counter' was a prison, though this allusion is almost certainly to Counter or Compter prison south of the Thames in Southwark. Debtors were held here. Prisons stank terribly.

County Palatine, *MV 1.2.44, 57,* suitor to Portia, a melancholy gentleman. Counts palatine were high officials throughout the Middle Ages and the term came in England to mean a count with exceptional powers. There were several palatine counties in England, including Durham, Chester, and Lancashire. Even some of the American colonies were ruled as palatine provinces. Portia's suitor could well be from anywhere in Europe, then, though the Palatinate most frequently refers to an area of the kingdom of Bavaria west of the Rhine. There has been an attempt to link Portia's suitor to Albertus a Lasco (or Count Alasco) of Poland who was visiting London in 1583 and ran into debt.

Court, Alexander, *H5,* fictional character, a common soldier with whom Henry V converses in disguise before the battle at Agincourt.

Courtenay, Edward, *R3 4.4.431,* (d. 1509), supporter of Henry Tudor, earl of Richmond, in his struggle to depose Richard III. Although the Courtenay family had been loyal to Richard's brother, Edward IV, and to the house of York, Edward joined his cousin, the bishop of Exeter, in the duke of Buckingham's rebellion against Richard. When the coup failed, Courtenay fled to Brittany and joined Richmond in exile. He returned to England in Richmond's army and shared in the largess with which the victorious Tudor king rewarded those who helped him to the throne. After the battle at Bosworth Field, Courtenay was named earl of Devonshire and, in 1490, inducted into the Order of the Garter.

Courtesan, *Err,* woman with whom Antipholus of Ephesus dallies. She also tries to claim a necklace which he promised her. She corresponds to the character of Erotium in the source, Plautus' *Menæchmi.*

Coventry, major city in the county of Warwickshire, 90 mi. northwest of London. During the Middle Ages it was a wealthy center for the wool trade. It was within the earl of Warwick's domain, and Sh. has 'the Kingmaker' establish his headquarters at Coventry as he prepares for his last stand against Edward IV at the battle of Barnet. *3H6 4.10.26, 32. R2 1.1.199, 1.2.45, 56. 1H4 4.2.1, 39. 2H4 4.1.133.*

Cowley, Richard, one of the 'Principal Actors' listed in F1. His name appears in the speech prefixes in *MND* and *Ado,* indicating that he played Peter Quince and Verges—straight man to William Kemp's Bottom and Dogberry. His other roles are uncertain. He is thought to have been an original member of the Lord Chamberlain's Men (formed 1594) after having appeared with Lord Strange's Men in the early 1590s. He also appears to have stayed with that group until his death because the witnesses of his will in 1618 include several of the King's Men (the title of the Chamberlain's Men after falling under the patronage of James I).

Cox, *AWW 5.2.40,* 'C. my passion!,' Cock's my passion!: by the suffering of God.

Crab, *TGV,* Lance's little dog, the subject of two very funny monologues by Lance (*2.3.1–32* and *4.4.1–38*). The name may refer to the dog's supposed motion, lowness to the ground, or, most likely, temperament in the sense of sourness, since a 'crab' was also a crab apple. The comparison of Proteus' dog gift to Silvia with Crab and with a squirrel gives us the size of Crab. Evidently there was at least one lady in London in that time period who sported a squirrel on a leash in public and this might have been a source of topical humor. Crab is ten times larger than the squirrel-sized lap dog Proteus wished to give. The imagery of dogs in this play (like the imagery of dogs in *Tim,* strangely enough) drops in from point to point, yet never becomes consistent as overall imagery, as, for example, monkeys and goats become so central to *Oth.* In both plays (*TGV* and *Tim*) this incomplete imagery is taken as one of many signs of the imperfect state of the only available texts (F1).

Cranmer, Thomas, *H8,* (1489–1556), archbishop of Canterbury during the reigns of Henry VIII and his son Edward VI. He entered Cambridge University intending to prepare for the priesthood, but an impulsive decision to marry one of his landlady's kin cost him his fellowship. The death of his wife in childbed enabled him to return promptly to school and to apply for ordination, but thereafter his career made little progress. He was over forty before he got an opportunity to win high office and a place in history. In 1529 he was in Waltham, Essex, serving as tutor to the sons of a nobleman. The court passed through the neighborhood, and he struck up a conversation with two of Henry VIII's men about the hot issue of the day: the problem of determining the validity of Henry's marriage with Katherine of Aragon. He suggested that the opinions of the university professors and the canon lawyers be sought and that the case be decided in the ordinary ecclesiastical courts, not in Rome at the papal curia. His ideas were reported to Henry who commissioned him to present the king's case to the faculties of the universities of Oxford and Cambridge. He subsequently travelled to Rome to explain the consensus reached by the English academicians and to Germany to seek support from Protestant authorities.

While in Nuremberg he was befriended by a Lutheran theologian, Andreas Osiander, and in 1532 he married Osiander's niece. He kept his marriage a secret, for England and its king were not yet ready to join the Protestant campaign against clerical celibacy. He may not have feared exposure, for at the time of his marriage he was well into middle age and had spent most of his life in relative obscurity. He had every reason to expect that he would pass the remainder of his days safely in the shadows. He must, therefore, have been somewhat dismayed when an unanticipated development thrust him suddenly into the spotlight. In August 1532 William Warham, the archbishop of Canterbury, died, and Henry decided to make Cranmer England's primate. He was known to hold two convictions that Henry found politically convenient. He believed that England had a right to manage its own ecclesiastical affairs without papal interference, and he believed that the king should be released from his barren marriage. Although initially reluctant to accept the post Henry thrust on him, he acquiesced in the hope that he could encourage the Reformation in England.

Following his consecration on 30 March 1533, he did all that Henry asked. On 23 May he annulled Henry's marriage with Katherine. On 28 May he announced that a valid wedding had taken place between the king and Anne Boleyn the previous January. On 1 June he crowned Anne queen of England, and in September he stood godfather to her daughter Elizabeth. When Anne fell from Henry's favor, he interceded for her life. His appeal fell on deaf ears, and he was forced to humiliate her and himself by reversing his previous judgment declaring her marriage with Henry legal. He had little leverage in dealing with Henry, for in 1534 the king had, with the blessings of parliament, declared himself the head of the church in England. The most that Cranmer could do was to use his access to the king to persuade him to implement some Protestant reforms. This proved a formidable task. Henry's repudiation of the authority of the pope did not entail the king's approval of any other items on the Protestant agenda. Henry was, to the contrary, eager to defend himself against charges of heresy by preserving most of the doctrines and trappings of traditional Catholicism. He believed that his quarrel with the pope was political, and he did not want theology to confuse the issue.

Despite Henry's lack of enthusiasm for reform, Cranmer was able to implement a few modest changes in the practice of Christianity in England. An English translation of the Bible was authorized and made available to the public in each parish. Some revisions of liturgies and creeds were approved, and priests were permitted to recite portions of the Mass in English. Nothing more radical was attempted until Henry died in 1547. The king's death increased the archbishop's power, for he became one of the regents who ruled England during the minority of Henry's heir, Edward VI. Edward, who had been educated by Protestant tutors, was genuinely enthusiastic for the Reformation. During the boy's short reign Cranmer abolished the laws under which heretics were prosecuted and issued a new liturgy that transformed the Latin Mass into an English communion service.

The Protestant cause and Cranmer's hopes for the future were dealt severe blows by Edward's premature death in 1553. Edward tried to protect England's Reformation by excluding his Catholic half-sister, Mary, from the royal succession. But the English people refused to allow the most obvious royal heir to be set aside. Mary was proclaimed queen, and on 14 September 1553, she had the pleasure of imprisoning the archbishop who had slandered her mother's marriage and declared her illegitimate. He was convicted of treason, but, as a clergyman, he could not be punished by a secular court. Mary kept him in prison until she persuaded parliament to restore papal authority in England. On 14 February 1556, a Catholic ecclesiastical tribunal condemned him for heresy and ordered his execution. He weakened under torture and recanted his Protestant faith, but a troubled conscience cleared his mind, and at the end he found the courage to die bravely—proclaiming confidence in the reformed religion that he had helped establish in England.

Crassus, *MM 4.5.8,* friend or vassal of the duke, obviously borrowed from Cæsar's political sponsor.

Creator, God. *3H6 4.7.44. Tro 2.3.66.*

Crécy, *H5 2.4.54,* French town near the mouth of the Somme river approximately 100 mi. north of Paris and 30 mi. south of Calais. The first major battle of the Hundred Years' War was fought at Crécy on 26 August 1346. On that occasion Edward III routed a much larger French force. Ten years later his son, Edward the Black Prince, continued the war by winning a similar victory at Poitiers.

Creon, *TNK 1.1.40, 149, 1.2.62, 99, 2.2.105,* king of Thebes, last ruler of the Cadmean dynasty, brother of Jocasta (wife of Oedipus), and father of Hæmon. In both Sophocles' and Seneca's *Oedipus* he brings word from Delphi that the murder of Laius has polluted Thebes, and Oedipus suspects him of trying to usurp the throne. Upon Oedipus' ruin, Eteocles and Polyneices agree to rule jointly, but this arrangement falls apart and Polyneices leads the 'Seven Against Thebes.' When both sons of Oedipus die in combat, Creon takes the throne and forbids the burial of Polyneices because he is a traitor. Antigone defies him and is executed by being buried alive, causing Hæmon to commit suicide. Creon is finally killed by Theseus or, in alternative legend, by Lycus. He appears in numerous ancient plays, both extant and not, mostly hovering threateningly at the edge of the action, a vulture ready to pick over the soon-to-die. In *TNK* he is described as a corrupt and immoral ruler and the uncle of Palamon and Arcite. The details derive almost entirely from the source, Chaucer's *Knyghtes Tale.*

Cressid, 'Lady C.,' variant of Cressida. *MV 5.1.6. H5 2.1.74. Tro. AWW 2.1.97,* 'C.'s uncle,' Pandarus, a pimp or go-between.

Cressida, daughter of Calchas, beloved of Troilus. She is not a character from Greek or Roman mythology but an invention of the Middle Ages. Her name was adapted, possibly, from Chryseis, a Trojan woman who became Agamemnon's concubine, although in the original versions of the tale of Troilus and Cressida, she is called Briseïda in Benoît de Sainte-Maure's *Le Roman de Troie* (1184) and Griseida in Boccaccio's *Filostrato* (1338), indicating that Briseis, the slave that Agamemnon and Achilles squabble over in the *Iliad,* is being thought of, although this woman has nothing to do with Troilus. Chaucer's *Troilus and Criseyde,* a direct source for Sh., may have settled the name, and afterwards Cressida's reputation declined rapidly.

TN 3.1.51, 55. Tro: generally vilified as the epitome of the fickle woman and certainly an opportunist in love, Sh.'s Cressida is more passive than might be expected and more self-aware. This makes her somewhat sympathetic, another example of Sh.'s ability to mingle the yarn of human character. Her lack of force, however, makes her a rather pale character to be central to the plot.

Crete, large island in the eastern Mediterranean south of Greece by about 60 mi., north of Africa by about 230 mi. Crete is about 160 mi. long and varies in width from 7 to 35 mi. Civilization appeared on Crete before it developed on the mainland of Greece, and early myths preserve dim recollections of a time when the Greeks were subject to the 'Minoans,' so-called from Crete's legendary king Minos. About 1600 BC, Minoan civilization abruptly collapsed. Some believe that this is the source of the myth of Atlantis. Crete became a major prize in struggles between Islam and the West.

Shr 1.1.167, 'the Cretan strand,' where Europa came ashore. *3H6 5.6.18. 1H6 4.6.54,* 'sire of C.,' Dædalus. *MND 4.1.112, 125. H5 2.1.71,* 'hound of C.,' possibly a bloodhound. Others think it is a lapdog similar to the Iceland dog mentioned a few lines previous. Others have seen it as a reflection of Pistol's embellishments, akin to his distortion of foreign phrases, and that both types of dogs are fabrications. However, the phrase appears in Golding's translation of *Metamorphoses* 3, in the scene in which Actæon's dogs viciously attack him.

Cricket, *MWW 5.5.42,* name of a fairy who, appropriately, makes certain the hearths are well-kept.

Crispian, *H5 4.3.43, 4.7.89,* Crispinian, a Gallic Christian who was beheaded in 287 in the company of a similarly named colleague (Crispin) by the Roman emperor Maximian. The two martyrs share the same feast day.

Crispian, Feast of, *H5 4.3.40, 46, 48, 57,* Christian church's annual commemoration on 25 October of the deaths of the martyrs Crispin and Crispinian.

Crispin, *H5 4.3.57, 4.7.89,* Gallic Christian who was beheaded in 287 in the company of a similarly named colleague, Crispian (q.v.) or Crispinian, by the Roman emperor Maximian.

Cromer, James, *2H6 4.7.108–109,* Crowmer, (d. 1450), son-in-law of James Fiennes, Lord Saye, and sheriff of Kent at the time of Cade's rebellion. He was among those responsible for collecting the heavy taxes levied by Henry VI's government. Cade and his rebels blamed him and Saye for the king's fiscal policies and demanded the deaths of the royal agents. Both men were executed on 4 July 1450, and their heads were paraded through London on pikes.

Cromwell, Lord, *1H6 4.7.66,* see Wingfield, Lord Cromwell of.

Cromwell, Thomas, *H8,* (1485–1540), close advisor to Cardinal Wolsey and to Henry VIII. Cromwell, the son of a blacksmith and brewer, rose from humble origins to become one of the most powerful men in England. Cromwell left home at a young age to seek his fortune. He travelled on the continent, and he may have served a term as a mercenary with the French army. For several years he lived in Antwerp, where he prospered as a merchant. He returned to England, and in 1524 won admission to Gray's Inn, London. This entitled him to practice law, and in 1525 Cardinal Wolsey hired him to handle the dissolution of some monasteries whose properties were to be transformed into endowments for colleges. Cromwell remained with Wolsey until Henry dismissed the cardinal from his service in 1529. The loss of his powerful patron forced Cromwell to scramble to rescue his career. He won election to parliament, where his conduct attracted the king's attention. In 1530 he took the oath of a royal councilor, and his skill as an administrator earned him rapid advancement. By 1536 he had acquired the office of keeper of the privy seal and a peerage. Cromwell delighted Henry by devising legal arguments that validated Henry's break with the papacy and the king's decision to nationalize the English church. Cromwell drafted the various decrees of parliament that culminated in the Act of Supremacy of 1534, the bill that made the king the head of the church in England.

Henry used his newly won ecclesiastical authority to commission Cromwell to conduct an inquiry into the conduct of England's monks and nuns. Cromwell's documentation of monastic abuses provided the evidence Henry needed to justify the dissolution of England's monasteries and the government's confiscation of their endowments. From 1537 to 1540 Cromwell directed this huge and profitable project. As Henry's agent for ecclesiastical affairs, Cromwell also supervised the process of reforming religious life in England. He tried to implement higher standards for the clergy and to curtail the popular medieval entertainment of making pilgrimages to shrines. Cromwell's downfall was the failure of the foreign policy he advocated. Convinced that Catholic Spain and France constituted the greatest threat to England's security, Cromwell urged Henry to develop ties with German Lutheran lords. The result was an alliance sealed by the king's fourth marriage, a union with Anne of Cleves. Henry found his bride distasteful and his Lutheran allies unreliable. Both relationships were quickly annulled, and Cromwell was blamed for their failure. He was accused of heresy and executed on 28 July 1540.

Crosby House, *R3 1.2.200, 3.1.187,* mansion built in 1479 by Sir John Crosby near Bishopsgate in north London. After Crosby's death in 1475, the building was rented to Richard, duke of Gloucester, who occupied it until he became King Richard III.

Crosby Place, *R3 1.3.343,* see Crosby House.

Crusadoes, *Oth 3.4.26,* Portuguese coins worth about 3 shillings each. It was named for the cross which decorated it.

Cubiculo, *TN 3.2.50,* possibly the name of a specific room, but likely more posturing in foreign languages, the equivalent of using *chambre à coucher* for 'bedroom.'

Cumberland, county situated at the western end of England's border with Scotland. The Irish Sea is to the west. The area called by the name included Cumberland, Westmorland, and Northern Strathclyde. The Romans left many ruins in the area and after their departure, it was long a disputed territory, conquered by Angles, Danes, Scots, and Norman and English lords, until the union of Scotland and England under James I. There is a reference to a kingdom of the Cumbri in a 9th c. document, which would imply that the name derives from an ancient people. *Mac:* C. was held as a fiefdom by the Scots under the ownership of the English crown. For 'Clifford of Cumberland' *(2H6 5.3.1, 5.3.6)*, see Clifford, the elder.

Cumberland, Prince of, *Mac 1.4.39, 48,* heir to the throne of Scotland, usually used in the play to mean Malcolm. Although the crown was not hereditary in old Scotland, this title was bestowed upon the man each king designated to succeed him. Duncan's naming his son prince would force Macbeth's hand.

Cupid, Roman god of love corresponding to Gr. Eros, son of Mars and Venus, or Mercury and Diana, or Mercury and Venus. He had the ability to cause anyone to fall totally in love with the first person they saw by shooting them with a golden arrow—or out of love if nicked with a leaden missile. He was also usually depicted blindfolded to indicate the randomness of his hits. The classical attitude that such love made fools of people, or even destroyed them, is reflected in Sh.'s often mocking or pointing up the disasters that follow from impetuous love matches. He was also called the youngest and the oldest god because he was in the form of a child and yet was either born of the creation of the universe or, as Love, caused the creation of the gods by making material things male and female.

Ven 581, 'C.'s bow,' Venus takes an oath on it. *LLL 1.2.62. 1.2.167,* 'C.'s butt-shaft,' this type of arrow was used in target practice. It had a point, but was without barbs. It could therefore be pulled from the target—the 'butt'—without tearing it up. *2.1.255,* 'C.'s grandfather': the joke combines Saturn, the aged and morose god, and Boyet's being an 'old love-monger.' *3.1.175,* 'Dan C.,' Lord C.: Dan is a variant of *don,* a shortened *dominus* which is Latin for 'master.' Spenser uses 'Dan C.' in *The Færie Queen* 3.9.46, and Chaucer 'daun Cupido,' in *The Hous of Fame,* l. 137. *3.1.197, 4.3.21. 4.3.55,* 'C.'s hose.' *4.3.342, 5.2.87,* 'Saint C.' *5.2.9,* 'C.'s name.'

MND 1.1.169, 'C.'s strongest bow.' *1.1.235. 2.1.157, 161, 165:* a story designed blatantly to flatter Elizabeth I, the Virgin Queen, whom not even C.'s arrow can affect. Some critics take this as evidence that the play was performed for her, or at a wedding which she attended. *3.2.103,* 'C.'s archery.' *3.3.28. 4.1.72,* 'C.'s flower,' love-in-idleness or the wild pansy. *Rom 1.1.206,* 'C.'s arrow.' *1.4.4,* C. 'hoodwinked with a scarf,' blindfolded. *1.4.17* and *2.4.8,* 'C.'s wings.'

MV 2.6.5. 2.9.99, 'quick C.'s post,' love's messenger. *MWW 2.2.131,* 'C.'s carriers,' go-betweens. *5.5.27.*

Ado 1.1.38, 39. 1.1.174, 'C. is a good hare-finder,' an unclear passage, it seems to mean that Benedick is asking Claudio if he is speaking nonsense or mocking him. C. is the archer, not the locater of the hunted hares. *1.1.236–7,* 'sign of blind C.,' the usual sign in front of a brothel depicted this, implying the indifference of the selection in such places and possibly the discreetness. *Ado 1.1.253, 2.1.360. 3.1.22,* 'C.'s crafty arrow.' *3.1.106. 3.2.10,* 'C.'s bowstring.'

AYLI 1.3.1, 4.1.45. Son 153.1, 14, C. fell asleep and a maid of Dian stole his fire, later he found new fire. The episode is allegorical and is repeated in *Son 154,* without the gods' names.

Tro 3.1.107, 3.2.13. 3.2.71–2, 'C.'s pageant': Curiously, monsters do appear in a 'maske of Cupid' in Spenser's *Færie Queene,* 3.12. *3.2.206, 3.3.215. Oth 1.3.269,* 'light-winged toys/ Of feathered C.,' the amusements of love. *AWW 1.1.171,* 'blinking C.,' poor-sighted C. *3.2.15.*

Tim 1.2.119–124, a woman appears as C. to begin a masque for Timon. *Lr 4.5.134 (Q 20.133),* 'blind C.' *Ant 2.2.209* (pl.). *Per 1.81,* 'C.'s wars,' the struggles for love. *Cym 2.4.89,* 'winking Cupids,' 'blind C.'s.' *3.2.39,* 'C.'s tables,' C.'s writing book. *TNK 2.2.31.*

Curan, *Lr,* follower of the Duke of Gloucester. He speaks of rumors of trouble between Albany and Cornwall, but has no other part in the play. He may also appear elsewhere in the play, but is named only at *2.1 (Q 6).* Possibly it is the name of the actor who had the part. No equivalent character exists in Spenser's or Holinshed's version of the Lear story.

Curio, *TN,* servant of Orsino. There is a Curio in John Lyly's *Euphues.*

Curtal, *AWW 2.3.60,* bay horse. This may be the horse's name or simply descriptive. A curtal, 'curtail,' was a horse whose tail was cut short.

Curtis, *Shr,* Petruccio's servant. The name derived from a nickname meaning 'courteous,' refined (as from the court), or from a nickname for a short person, one who wore 'curt hose.'

Cush, *MV 3.2.283,* F1 'Chus,' Jew, a 'countryman' of Shylock. In the Old Testament, Cush was the son of Ham, cursed son of Noah, and also the father of Nimrod, the mighty hunter. The Land of Cush is usually associated with Ethiopia, though scholars disagree whether it was located in Arabia or Africa.

Custalorum, *MWW 1.1.6,* corruption of the L. *custos rotulorum,* 'the keeper of the rolls,' the most important county magistrate.

Cyclops, *Tit 4.3.47,* race of giants mentioned in classical mythology. They were sometimes described as having a single eye positioned in the center of their foreheads. It has been suggested that the myth was inspired by the skulls of elephants, which have a large hole for the trunk in the center. In Homer's *Odyssey* 9, Odysseus finds an ingenious way to help his men escape the Cyclops Polyphemus, who intends to eat them. The classical Greeks credited the mysterious ruins of ancient Mycenæan buildings to Cyclops who they said were a branch of a prehistoric race of divine beings called Titans.

Cydnus, river that flows through Cilicia to empty into the Mediterranean at the city of Tarsus. Cleopatra came to Tarsus for her first meeting with Mark Antony, and the fabulously equipped barge on which she seduced Antony sailed the Cydnus. Sh. took the detail from Plutarch's 'Antony' (26.1). *Ant 2.2.194, 5.2.224. Cym 2.4.71.*

Cymbeline, *Cym,* king of Britain, father of Innogen. In many ways Cymbeline is the typical wrongheaded patriarch of the late romances. He is mislead by his second wife and her evil son Cloten. He rejects his innocent daughter and Posthumus, after having earlier unjustly condemned Belarius. Because of such acts, he loses his sons for most of their lives, his daughter, and very nearly his kingdom. There are obvious parallels to Leontes in *WT,* and Pericles, prince of Tyre. Similarly, all that he has lost is restored to him. A major difference is that Cymbeline is almost a minor character in his own play. He is more often acted upon than acting, and events resolve themselves rather than being resolved by activity on his part. After having been defeated by the Romans, Cymbeline is saved only by the intervention of his lost sons, for example. Some critics have suggested various allegorical elements in the play, particularly since it has so little to do with the historical Cymbeline, about whom little is known. Jupiter's appearance has suggested to some critics the union of Scotland with the crown of England brought about by the ascension of James. There is some possibility that Renaissance playgoers felt there was an internecine tinge to the conflict between the Britains and the Romans as it was believed that both groups were descendants of the Trojans. In that way there is also a suggestion that the peace which ends the conflict is like the Jacobean union of Scotland and the English realm.

The historical Cymbeline was more commonly known as Cunobelinus, whose shadowy reign is described in Raphael Holinshed's *Chronicles* as the son of Theomantius. He is said to have come to the throne in 33 BC, to have reigned 35 years, and to have been buried at London. Holinshed is uncertain what caused the break between the Romans and Cymbeline, who was brought up in Rome and knighted in Augustus' court. At some point the tribute to Rome was denied, but Augustus was too busy with the rebellious Pannonians to enforce the payments. Thus Holinshed has no war between Cymbeline and the empire. Cymbeline appears as Cinobellinus in the Roman historian Suetonius' biographies of the Cæsars. Cinobellinus' son Adminius who was exiled, submitted to Caligula in Germany in 40 AD. The mad emperor then sent flamboyant letters to Rome claiming the total subjection of Britain. Three years later, the emperor Claudius sent Aulus Plautius to assert authority over Britain. The Romans were opposed by Cunobelinus' sons Togodumnus and Caractacus. Ostorius Scapula was ultimately victorious and Caractacus was brought to Rome in chains. Suetonius describes Caractacus' proud speech asking for clemency, which states the necessity of resistance to Roman power though it implies some regret. That aspect of Cymbeline's resistance is certainly in the play, though there is no historical mention of Cunobellinus in conflict with the Romans. In Spenser's *Færie Queene,* 2.10, Kimbeline is described as the successor of Tenantius. He resists paying the tribute, is slain by a traitor, and succeeded by his brother Aruirage.

Cynthia, 1) *Ven 728,* Roman epithet for Diana, goddess of the moon, who was born as twin of Apollo on Mount Cynthus on the island of Delos. *Rom 3.5.20. Per 9.10.*

2) *TNK 4.1.151,* the moon, or a woman mentioned in a song which is now unknown. Thomas Sackville borrows the same line in his induction to 'Complaint of Henry Duke of

Buckingham' in *The Mirror for Magistrates* (1563). The moon shines from light 'borrowed' from the sun as the song says, but it is not clear that this scientific fact is what is alluded to.

Cyprus, large island south of Turkey. Its location has made it a battleground for the military powers of the eastern Mediterranean and a center for trade. It was advanced in the Neolithic and Bronze ages. Egypt conquered part of it c. 1450 BC and Greeks founded a colony there some 50 years later. Phoenicians set up colonies about 800 BC, as well as other peoples before and after. At various times in its history it has been under the rule of the Assyrians, Persians, Alexander the Great, the Ptolemies of Egypt, the Romans, and the Byzantines. It was extremely prosperous until the Arab conquests when it changed hands several times. The local Byzantine rulers were very despotic, but in 1191 Isaac Comnenus made the mistake of mistreating the crusaders. Richard the Lionheart captured Isaac and sold the island to the Knights Templar. They then sold it to Guy of Lusignan, crusader king of Jerusalem. His dynasty ruled until Caterina Cornaro, widow of James II, yielded power to Venice in 1489. Selim II invaded in 1570 and though Famagusta heroically withstood its siege for nearly a year, Cyprus was turned over to the Turks in 1571, who held it for three centuries. After the annihilation of the Turkish fleet at Lepanto in 1571, a Turkish ambassador is said to have remarked that the Christians had singed the Ottoman Empire's beard, but that the Turks had cut off Venice's arm—they had captured Cyprus. The recent history of the island has been a nasty struggle between the Greek majority in the south and the Turkish occupation of the north.

Oth: Sh.'s mention of a joint invasion of Rhodes and Cyprus never happened, but associating Othello with the general struggle of Venice against the Ottomans enlarges his stature as a general. The Turks threatened, in Sh.'s lifetime, to subject Europe to Islam, with the Venetian Republic the primary seapower standing in their way. The city which Sh. had in mind as the setting for the play would most likely be Famagusta. *Ant 3.6.10.*

Cyrus the Great (559–529 BC), conqueror who founded the Persian Empire. He was Alexander the Great's inspiration and the ancient world's model for empire-builders. An account of 'Cyrus's death,' (*1H6 2.3.6*), is found in Herodotus' *Histories,* 1.214. When Cyrus invaded the territory of the Scythian queen Tomyris and killed her son, Tomyris counterattacked, destroyed the Persian army, and took imaginative revenge on her foe. She tossed Cyrus' head into a vat of human blood and invited him to drink his fill.

Cytherea, epithet for Venus, from the island Cythera, sacred to her as the place she first came ashore after being born from the sea's foam. About 109 sq. mi., Cythera is south of the Peloponnese peninsula, outside the Gulf of Laconia. *Shr Ind. 2.50.* 'C.'s breath,' *WT 4.4.122. PP 4.1, 6.3. Cym 2.2.14.*

D

Dædalus, architect and inventor employed by the legendary King Minos of Crete. Dædalus built a labyrinth to contain the Minotaur, a beastly offspring of Minos' queen. When Minos refused to allow Dædalus to leave Crete and return to his home in Athens, Dædalus mused on the fact that Minos ruled the land and the sea, but not the air. Dædalus made wings out of wax and feathers, and he and his son, Icarus, took flight. Dædalus' ingenious escape from Crete was marred by tragedy. Icarus, intoxicated by the experience of flying, forgot his father's order to steer a middle course between the realms of fire and water. He soared too near the sun, his wings melted, and he plunged to his death in the sea (Ovid, *Metamorphoses,* 8.183–235). *3H6 5.6.21. TNK 3.5.117.*

Dagonet, Sir, *2H4 3.2.277,* fool or jester at the court of the legendary King Arthur of Britain. His story is found in Thomas Malory's *Le Morte d'Arthur* (1485).

Dale, *2H4 4.2.4, 6, 9, 38,* a deep place. Sh. has Falstaff pun on the name of his prisoner, 'Sir John Coleville of the Dale,' as a way of threatening his captive with incarceration in a dungeon.

Dalmatians, *Cym 3.1.73, 3.7.3,* ancient peoples of the Adriatic coast. Roman Dalmatia roughly corresponded to modern Croatia, Bosnia-Herzegovina, and Montenegro, and extended some distance inland to Serbia. Afterwards the name usually refers only to the coastal area. Greek colonies had been established on the coast in the 4th c. BC. The Romans conquered the area in the 1st c. AD, but there were several revolts against them, in conjunction with other Illyrian peoples, such as the Pannonians. It successively fell to the Avars, the Croats, and Hungary, which fell into numerous conflicts with Venice. Dalmatia had become part of the Venetian Republic in Sh.'s time, and from 1797 to World War I incorporated into Austria-Hungary.

Damascus, *1H6 1.4.38,* ancient city in Syria on the border of modern Lebanon not far from Israel's northern frontier. St. Paul was converted to the Christian faith while on the road from Jerusalem to Damascus, but in medieval legend the city had an association with a much earlier event in Biblical history. The widely circulated compendium of travel tales that John Mandeville compiled in the 1360's claimed that Damascus was the place where Cain slew Abel.

Dame Partlet, see Partlet.

Dan Cupid, see Cupid.

Danaë, mother of Perseus. While imprisoned in a tower she was impregnated by Jupiter when he came to her as a shower of gold. Although this is usually taken literally and she is often depicted being buried in an avalanche of coins, many critics of ancient literature think that the gold mentioned is actually sunlight. She is mentioned in Ovid's *Metamorphoses,* 4. *Rom 1.1.211:* some critics say this is an allusion to Danaë, but it is more likely a simple reference to bribery.

Dane, 1) native of Denmark. The Renaissance English stereotype was of a hard-drinking, crude people. *Ham 5.1.255, 5.2.293. AWW 4.1.72,* a speaker of Danish. *Oth 2.3.71, 75.*

2) king of Denmark, Hamlet's father. *Ham 1.1.12, 1.2.44, 1.4.26.*

3) king of Denmark, Claudius, *Ham 5.2.277.*

Daniel, *MV 4.1.220, 330, 337,* prophet of the Old Testament. Of noble birth, he grew famous for his wisdom at a young age and therefore is an appropriate comparison for Portia in the role of Balthasar the judge. Daniel was one of the talented children given special treatment by Nebuchadnezzar after his capture of Jerusalem. He made a number of prophecies for the king and rose to an eminent position. After the capture of Babylon by Darius, he was made the ruler of Babylon. The most famous story of Daniel concerns his being placed in a lion's den by Darius and being protected from the animals by God. See Bel.

Danish, (adj.) of or pertaining to Denmark. *Ham 4.3.63,* 'D. sword,' a reference to English\Danish warfare. *4.4.1. 4.5.108,* 'D. dogs,' the rabble calling for Lærtes to be king. King Eric V had been forced to sign a charter in 1282 which made the crown subordinate to law. The monarchy would be dependent upon the nobility for its power until 1660 when it became hereditary. The situation caused great difficulties for many Danish monarchs, including Christian II (1513–23). Perhaps this scene alludes to some of the disorder which resulted from the power of the Danehof (legislature). Sh. shows himself in many plays to be very much against mob rule, which he apparently sees as the inevitable result of democratic institutions. *5.2.51, 125.*

Da'ntry, *3H6 5.1.6,* Daintry, or Daventry, Northamptonshire town situated south of Coventry and about 70 mi. northwest of London.

Daphne, beloved of Apollo, daughter of Peneus the river god or Ladon. After slaying the Python, Apollo mocked Cupid for his childlike bow. Cupid struck Apollo with a golden arrow of love, but struck Daphne with the lead arrow of disdain. Daphne took to the woods, avoided men, and ignored her father's pleas to marry. Apollo pursued her, but she fled. During the chase she begged her father to save her from the beauty which had enraptured Apollo and she was transformed into a laurel. Because of Apollo's love for the tree the laurel decorated Apollo's hair, bow, and quiver. In the ancient world, the laurel wreath was symbolic of victory. The story is in Ovid, *Metamorphoses,* 1. *Shr Ind. 2.56. MND 2.1.231. Tro 1.1.98.*

Dardan, 1) land of Troy in northwest Asia Minor, named for Dardanus, the son of Zeus and Electra (one of the Pleiad sisters). He founded the city of Troy and migrated to Hesperia, a land which Virgil identifies with Italy for Æneas' escape west. *Tro pro. 13,* 'D. plains,' the Troad. *Luc 1436,* the shores of the Dardanelles, or the Hellespont, the waterway that connects the Black and Ægean seas.

2) *Tro pro. 16,* one of the six gates of Troy. These are not in the *Iliad* which appears to give Troy only one double gate, but in William Caxton's *Recuyell of the Historyes of Troye,* 3 (c. 1474), the first English printed book and Sh.'s major source for the play, the six gates are listed, Dardan being the first.

Dardanian wives, *MV 3.2.58,* Trojan wives, in this image standing upon the great walls of the city to watch the conflict.

Dardanius, *JC,* Dardanus, Brutus' shield bearer and a friend who was with him when his defeat at the battle of Philippi prompted him to commit suicide (Plutarch, 'Brutus' 52.1).

Darius III (336–330 BC), Persian emperor whom Alexander the Great supplanted. Darius' first encounter with Alexander took place in October, 333 BC, at the Issus river, which empties into the Mediterranean sea near the frontier that modern Turkey shares with Syria. *1H6 1.8.25:* 'rich-jewelled coffer of Darius' recalls anecdotes found in Plutarch's *Lives,* 7.2; 26.1–2. Plutarch says that Alexander considered Homer's *Iliad* to be a general's best textbook. Since Alexander wished always to have it at hand, he kept a special edition, which Aristotle made for him, in a box under the pillow on his bed. Alexander's victory at Issus brought him a very grand container for the 'pillow *Iliad.*' The Persians fled in such haste that Darius had to abandon his camp, his family, and his personal possessions. Alexander's agents went through the loot and brought Alexander a small coffer that was alleged to be the richest object in the emperor's possession. Alexander put the *Iliad* into it—claiming that Homer's poem was the only thing he possessed that was worthy of such splendor.

Datchet Lane, *MWW 3.5.92–3,* street in Windsor, evidently where the laundries were.

The lane led eventually to the Thames crossing to Datchet, a village on the east bank of the river.

Datchet Mead, *MWW 3.3.13, 124, 142,* field between the Little Park of Windsor and the Thames.

Dauphin, 1) title for the heir to the French throne. It may derive from the name of the family of the 12th c. counts of Albon, whose heraldic emblem was the dolphin. The English often used 'Dolphin' and 'Dauphin' interchangeably. In Greek mythology dolphins were guardians of the souls of the dead, and early Christians used the dolphin as a symbol for immortality. By the early 13th c. the man who held the county of Viennois, the dauphiné de Viennois, was known as the 'dauphin.' It was not until 1349, when Charles of Valois purchased Viennois for his eldest son, that its title was linked with the office of crown prince. Sh. (*Jn*) is incorrect, therefore, in assuming that Philip Augustus' heir, Louis VIII, was called 'dauphin.' Although the dauphin appears as a single character in *H5,* three men succeeded to the office of France's heir-apparent during the period of time covered by the play. Charles VI's eldest son, Louis, was dauphin at the start of Henry V's reign. He died in 1415 not long after Henry's victory at the battle at Agincourt. Louis' brother John succeeded to the title, but lived to enjoy it for only a year. In 1416 their younger brother became dauphin and eventually ascended the throne as Charles VII. *Lr. 3.4.93:* the Dauphin was sometimes equated with the devil, as he seems to be here in this line which is apparently from an old song urging the D. to pass by.

2) *H5, 1H6, 2H6 1.3.128, 173, 4.7.27, 3H6 1.1.108, 2.2.151,* see Charles VII, King of France.

Dauphin, Guiscard, *H5 4.8.94–95,* (d. 1415), 'Great-Master of France,' one of the French generals whom Holinshed lists (3.555) among the casualties of the battle at Agincourt. He was the 'prince dauphin' of Auvergne, a title that distinguished him from the 'king dauphin,' the heir to the throne whose eponymous fief was the dauphiné de Viennois.

Daventry, *1H4 4.2.47,* see Da'ntry.

Davy, *2H4,* Justice Shallow's steward, one of the many clever servants who, in the comedic tradition, dominate foolish masters.

Death, personification of mortality, usually clearly thought of as male. *1H6 4.7.18,* 'antic d.' *Ven 930, 932. LLL 5.2.607,* 'a death's face.' *Rom 4.1.75, 5.3.87, 92. R2 3.2.158. Jn 2.1.352, 457, 459, 3.4.25, 5.2.177, 5.7.15. MV 2.7.63. 2H4 5.4.27,* 'Goodman death,' an insult for the skinny beadle.

Tro 4.5.62, 'I will throw my glove to D. himself': Troilus is willing to challenge Death to a duel. Throwing down the gauntlet was a medieval way to challenge. If the glove was picked up, the fight was on. *Son 18.11, 32.2,. 107.10. MM 3.1.11. WT 5.3.102. Cym 5.5.69.*

Deborah, sole female judge whose exploits are described in the Hebrew Scriptures (Judges 4:4–5:31). In the days before the establishment of a Hebrew monarchy, the Jews were ruled by charismatic leaders called 'judges.' Judges were appointed by God and charged with the protection of his people. They settled disputes and oversaw the defense of the twelve tribes of Israel. She did not lead men in battle, but she appointed the general who did, accompanied him in the field, and was credited with his victories. Since she was the first female in biblical history to exercise military authority, medieval people saw her as a precursor of Joan of Arc. *1H6 1.3.84:* 'sword of D.' is a poetic invention. She, unlike Joan, is not said to have engaged directly in personal combat. Spenser's *Færie Queene* 3.4.2.7-8, however, might leave this impression when it remarks how 'Debora strake/ Proud Sisera.' Jael actually did the killing (Judges 4).

December, first month of winter. Its name derives from the Latin for ten, as it was the tenth month in the Julian calendar. It was also the tenth month in Sh.'s day, as the New Year began in March. *R2 1.3.261. Ado 1.1.182. AYLI 4.1.139. TN 2.3.81,* 'twelfth day of D.,' a line from a lost ballad. *Son 97.4. WT 1.2.170. Cym 3.3.37.*

Decius Junius Brutus, *JC,* (84–43 BC), 'Albinus' (from the name of his adoptive father Postumius Albinus), member of the conspiracy to assassinate Julius Cæsar that was led by Marcus Junius Brutus and Cassius. D. Brutus served in Cæsar's army in Gaul, and he sided with Cæsar against Pompey in the Roman civil wars. Despite a debt of gratitude to Cæsar for numerous acts of patronage, he entered enthusiastically into the plot to murder him. Plutarch ('Cæsar' 64.1) claims that he was instrumental in persuading Cæsar to ignore evil omens and attend the Senate meeting where he was to be killed. After Cæsar's death, D. Brutus struggled with Mark Antony for control of the province of Cisalpine Gaul. He was betrayed into Antony's hands and executed.

Decretas, *Ant,* Dercetæus, one of Antony's guards. Plutarch says that he was the first to bring Octavius news of Antony's death ('Antony' 78.1).

Deepvow, Master, *MM 4.3.12,* mocking name for one of the impoverished criminals Pompey knows. As prisoners paid for their own food, many were forced to beg passers by.

Deiphobus, *Tro,* valiant Trojan warrior, son of Priam and Hecuba. He forced himself on Helen after Paris' death, but was slain in the fall of the city after Helen took his weapons and led Menelaus into their bedroom. Menelaus mutilated his body. He is only a minor character in Sh. but is mentioned frequently as 'Deyphebus' in William Caxton's *Recuyell of the Historyes of Troye* (c. 1474), the first English printed book, and Sh.'s major source for the play. In the *Iliad* 12.115, he is first mentioned striding beside his brother Helenus in the assault on the Greek camp. He is prominent in the battle among the ships (13). Later, Athena deceives Hector by assuming the form of Deiphobus (22.270 ff), and he is insulted by Priam in his despair over the death of Hector (24.293 ff).

Delabret, Charles, *H5 3.5.40, 4.8.92,* de la Bret or Breth, (d. 1415), constable of France and son of Charles, king of Navarre. He commanded the French forces at Agincourt and died during the course of the battle (Holinshed, 3.55).

Delay, *Err 4.3.40,* a ship. This doesn't seem a particularly promising name for a real vessel, but serves the humor of the context by contrast to the ship *Expedition.*

Delphos, *WT 2.1.185, 2.3.196, 3.2.125,* Delphi, ancient site of the temple of Apollo, located in Phocis in a valley west of Mt. Parnassus. Possibly originally a site sacred to Gæa, the earth, Delphi became the principal place of the worship of Apollo. In a temple built in the 6th c. BC a priestess called the Pythia (after a python slain by Apollo) sat upon a tripod and delivered the oracles in a trance. Her words were interpreted in verse by a priest. History records a number of interesting but very ambiguous prophesies delivered by the oracle which influenced such events as the Persian Wars. There was also some influencing of the interpretations by party factions. The Pythian Games, sacred to Apollo, were held in Delphi, and the Amphictyonic League also met there. The fame of the oracle spread throughout the ancient world and it was consulted by Greeks and non-Greeks until the time of Constantine the Great, who took the sacred tripods to decorate the hippodrome of Constantinople. In Sh. the oracle is represented incorrectly as being on an island; however, it is so represented in Sh.'s source, Robert Greene's *Pandosto, or the Triumph of Time* (1588; rptd. 1607 as *Dorastus and Fawnia*). This is the result of a confusion, common in the English Renaissance with Delos, the island birthplace of Apollo. Also, the oracle's reply to Leontes' question is atypically specific, with its only ambiguity about the lost child, Perdita. The description of Delphos in *WT* has also been linked to Virgil's *Æneid,* 3.

Delver, Goodman, *Ham 5.1.14,* 'Mister Digger,' Hamlet's mocking name for the gravedigger, possibly not intended as a nickname and therefore often edited to lower case.

Demetrius, 1) *Tit,* wicked son of Tamora, queen of the Goths and empress of Rome. He and his brother Chiron helped their mother avenge herself on the Roman general, Titus Andronicus. Titus had sacrificed Tamora's eldest son at the funeral of one of his sons who died in battle with Tamora's people. Demetrius and Chiron responded by raping and mutilating Titus' daughter, Lavinia, and by tricking the emperor into executing two of Titus' sons for a crime they did not commit. When, at the end of the play, Titus turns the tables on his enemies, Demetrius and Chiron are killed and their flesh is served to their mother at a feast of mock reconciliation. The source for Sh.'s play is uncertain, but an 18th c. chapbook preserves a version of a tale that might have been familiar to him. It calls Tamora's sons Alaricus and Abonus. Since Sh. gave the Gothic boys (and their Roman enemy, Andronicus) Greek names, he may have had a Greek source for the story of *Tit.*

2) *MND,* young nobleman described as spotted and inconstant. He has made love to Helena, though he expects to marry Hermia. When she elopes into the woods, he pursues her and Lysander only to be affected by Robin Goodfellow's love potion and find himself in love with Helena. In the sorting out of who loves whom, he ends up betrothed to her. The name is borrowed from Plutarch who wrote a biography of Demetrius Poliorcetes, king of Macedonia and a warrior in the struggles after Alexander the Great's death. Plutarch's interpretation of the biography is that great natures can produce great vices as well as virtues, a lesson plainly applicable to Sh.'s Demetrius.

3) *Ant,* Mark Antony's friend. The character's name does not appear in the dialogue of Sh.'s play, but is supplied by the folio edition from which all extant texts of *Ant* derive. No friend of Antony's named Demetrius is found in the sources that Sh. is known to have used. Since Demetrius appears only in the opening scene of the play, has no development as a distinct character, and makes no contribution to the action of the plot, Sh. may have invented him and his colleague Philo, but borrowed the name of Demetrius Poliorcetes (see *MND* above) whom Plutarch compares with Antony. Sh. uses their conversation to illustrate the Roman attitude toward Antony's relationship with Cleopatra and to set the stage for the story he wants to tell.

Denis, F1 'Dennis,' common French name. *AYLI,* Oliver's servant.

Denis, St., first bishop of Paris and the patron saint of France. Denis (Dionysius) was martyred when the emperor Decius (249–251) launched Rome's first universal persecution of the Christian religion. By the 5th c. his grave near Paris had become the site of a major church, and his fame grew as Paris evolved into the capital of the Frankish kingdom. Medieval authors usually identified Dionysius of Paris with Dionysius Areopagiticus, one of the few converts to the Christian faith that St. Paul made in the city of Athens (Acts 17:34). In the 9th c. the emperor of Constantinople presented Charles the Bald of France with an ancient Greek manuscript that was believed to contain the teachings of Dionysius Areopagiticus. The work was translated by John Scotus Erigena and helped renew interest in the study of philosophy in medieval Europe. The church of St. Denis became the burial place of France's kings, and in the 12th c. Suger, abbot of St. Denis and chief minister to Louis VI, rebuilt the shrine to reflect the increasing prestige of the French monarchy. Suger's work at St. Denis accelerated the development of the Gothic style that was the supreme achievement of medieval architects. *1H6 1.8.28, 3.3.1. LLL 5.2.87. H5 5.2.182, 204.*

Denmark 1), *Ham,* Scandinavian country in northern Europe. Most of the country consists of islands, except for the Jutland peninsula, which is attached to the European mainland at northern Germany. Roman writer Pliny the Elder first mentions the area and Procopius first calls its people the Danes, a name which derived from the legendary first settler of Jutland, Dan. The Danes originated in the southern Scandinavian peninsula, but moved into the area of Denmark in the 5th and 6th c. AD. In the Middle Ages, Denmark was one of the homes of the Vikings who made frequent attacks on England, beginning in 787. Part of England was set aside as the 'Danelaw,' and through its existence the culture and language of Britain were affected. Several English maritime words, such as 'ship,' derive from Danish and the Danes are prominent in the Anglo-Saxon epic *Beowulf.*

According to legend, Scyld was the ancestor of both the English and Danish royal houses. Rollo took Normandy in 911, whose ruler a century and a half later, William the Conqueror, seized England from the Anglo-Saxons. Harold Bluetooth was the first Christian Danish king and unifier of his people. His son Sweyn conquered England by 1014. Canute unified England, Denmark, and Norway from 1018 to 1035. The Danes also held large parts of Sweden until 1658 and expanded to the east in the 12th and 13th c. In 1397, Denmark was united with Sweden and Norway, which included Iceland and the Færoe islands. Sweden broke away in 1523, but Norway remained until 1814. By the 17th c., Denmark entered several failing military campaigns and was in decline despite gaining some colonial territories. In Sh.'s day, however, it was still a significant world power and its king Christian III (1534–59) had brought it, with some considerable resistance, into the Lutheran camp. The relationship between the English and the Danes also continued to be significant because of trade through the Baltic, whose gates were largely Danish and controlled by tolls. There was suspicion of the Danes because of their alliance with Scotland and their trading with the Spaniards, and the Danes filed a diplomatic protest against the seizing of Danish ships by English ships. When Anne of Denmark became queen of England in 1603, these difficulties were smoothed over.

2), *Ham,* king of Denmark.

Denny, Anthony, *H8,* (1500–1549), one of Henry VIII's life-long friends. He was a member of the king's Privy Council, executor of the royal will, and a regent for Henry's heir, Edward VI. Denny was an enthusiastic Protestant who used his influence to promote the reform of the English church.

Derby, Earl of, *R2 1.3.35,* one of Henry (IV) Bolingbroke's titles. Bolingbroke was heir to the duchy of Lancaster which acquired the earldom of Derby from the Ferrers family during Henry III's reign. Derby is the county seat of Derbyshire in the British Midlands about 110 mi. northwest of London.

Derby, Lord, *R3,* apparently Thomas Stanley. Since Stanley received the earldom of Derby as a reward for helping Henry VII depose Richard III at the battle at Bosworth Field, he would not, as he is in *R3,* have been addressed by this title during Richard's reign. In *R3 1.3.17* Lord Gray announces the approach of Lord Derby, and the character who speaks is identified as Stanley. Stanley's name may have been changed to Derby in an early edition of the play to make certain that Tudor audiences recognized him, and the modern text could be an imperfect combination of versions that used different names. See Stanley, Lord, earl of Derby.

Desdemon, *Oth 3.1.56, 4.2.43, 5.2.211,* shortening of Desdemona, in the first two instances for meter. In the third (Graziano's speech) it may create ten syllables if 'I am' is contracted.

Desdemona, *Oth,* wife of Othello, daughter of Brabanzio. A relatively passive figure, Desdemona is smothered by her husband after Iago carefully orchestrates a rising jealousy in the Moor. Desdemona is the quintessential victim, pure and absolutely good, which has led some critics to see her as almost an allegorical figure representing goodness in the face of evil, of acceptance of God's will, and of sacrifice. As in a morality play, she can be seen as the angel who struggles with Iago the devil for Othello's soul. She is less innocent than she appears, however. For example, Brabanzio accuses Othello of bewitching Desdemona, but when Othello defends himself, he describes how Desdemona fell in love with him because of the exciting stories he told her. Further, she disregarded her father's wishes in her relationship with Othello, an important violation of the societal order in that time, and Brabanzio plants the notion that she may betray her husband as she has betrayed him. Although the audience's sympathies are with her love for the Moor, the outcome may be seen as deriving from this sin against patriarchy, which is not to say that 'she gets what she deserves,' any more than one would say it about Romeo and Juliet. In Sh.'s source for the plot, Giraldi Cinthio's *Hecatommithi* (1566), 3.7, Disdemona is the only named character. The name has been argued to be from Gr. *dusdaimon* 'the unfortunate' and not *deisdaimon,* 'superstitious,' as sometimes alleged.

Deucalion, the Noah of ancient Greek mythology, son of Prometheus and Hesione, king of Pheræ in Thessaly, husband of Pyrrha, father of Amphictyon, Hellen, Pandora, Protogeneia, and Thyia. Angry with the crime and bloodshed on earth, Jupiter decided to drown humanity and create a new, more worthy race. Deucalion and Pyrrha, both guiltless, alone survived in a little boat which came to rest on Mt. Parnassus. Jupiter took pity on them and caused the waters to recede. In their loneliness they prayed to Themis for help in restoring the human race. Advised by the oracle to throw the bones of their mother over their shoulders, Deucalion interpreted it to mean they should cast stones (the 'bones' of Mother Earth). The stones thrown by Deucalion became hardy men, those by Pyrrha became women. The story is told in Ovid's *Metamorphoses,* 1. *Cor 2.1.90. WT 4.4.431,* Polixenes will make his errant son's claim to the throne by ancestry as remote as the ancestry of D.

Devil, character that personifies the principle of evil. Used throughout the plays, in some contexts the term 'devil' signifies the chief enemy of God (*1H6 1.1.125*); in others it suggests a lower ranking denizen of wickedness. 'Devil' derives from a Greek verb, 'to throw across,' and evolves from the idea of crashing into something for the purpose of destroying it. *MM 2.4.16,* 'd's horn,' *2.1.17,* 'd's crest': depicted as horned, the Devil should be, as Angelo reasons, a good angel because lust is a natural thing. The horn also implies an erection. A crest is a heraldric device above the shield on a coat of arms, but also a decoration on the upper part of a helmet. The sense of the passage is that Angelo is embracing his lust as a good thing.

Devonshire, *R3 4.4.429,* county in southwestern England bordered by both the English and the Bristol channels. Its seat is the cathedral city of Exeter.

Dew, *H5 4.4.8,* dialect; see Dieu.

Diablo, *Oth 2.3.154,* Sp. 'the devil,' an oath.

Dian, 1) 'Diane,' shortening of Diana, usually metrical. *Shr 2.1.253, 255–6. 3H6 4.9.21. Tit 2.3.57, 61. Ven 725. MND 4.1.72,* 'D.'s bud,' chastity. *Rom 1.1.206,* 'Dian's wit.' *Ado 4.1.57. Son 153.2,* 'A maid of D.'s,' a symbol of chastity, for she stole Cupid's fire. The story is retold in *Son 154,* but the names are omitted. *AWW 1.3.111, 208, 2.3.75. Tim 4.3.389,* 'the consecrated snow/ That lies on Dian's lap,' virginity. *Per. Cor 5.3.67. Cym 2.4.82, 2.5.7, 5.6.180. TNK 2.5.51,* 'D.'s wood,' a specific sacred wood may be intended, or all woods as they are sacred to her.

2) *AWW 4.3. 216, 232,* see Capilet, Diana.

Diana, 1) daughter of Jupiter and Latona, chaste goddess of the hunt and of the moon. A primitive Italian deity whom the Romans of the classical period equated with the Greek goddess, Artemis. In the Olympic pantheon she was Apollo's twin sister. Her cult may have been rooted in veneration of a paleolithic earth mother who was the patroness of the animals on which hunting cultures depended for their survival. Although she had fertility functions, she was a virgin goddess with a reputation for hostility to men. She could bring sudden death (like her brother Apollo), but she was also a protector of life, the guardian of pregnant humans and animals. The moon was her symbol, and ancient poets described her hunting by its light in the company of a troop of nymphs. References to her modesty recall a tale in which she destroyed a young hunter, Actæon, who accidentally blundered into her presence while she bathed in a forest pool. She transformed him into a stag so that his dogs would mistake him for their quarry and tear him apart.

MND 1.1.89, 'D.'s altar.' *MV 1.2.104, 5.1.66. 1H4 1.2.25.*

AYLI 3.4.14, 'Cast lips of D.,' chaste or dispassionate lips. *4.1.145,* 'like D. in the fountain': Diana's statue was commonly used in fountains, though this line has been taken by some to date the play to refer to the erection of a particular fountain in Cheapside in 1596. It may also refer to the story of Actæon. *TN 1.4.31,* 'D.'s lip.' *Tro 5.2.94,* 'D.'s waiting--women,' the stars, the moon's attendants.

Per: Diana descends from heaven in Sc. 21. She is not referred to in the sources for *Per* as frequently as in the play, which perhaps says something about the playwright's (or playwrights') intentions. *9.9,* 'D.'s liv'ry,' maidenhood. *14.12,* 'D's temple': Ephesus was a particularly sacred spot for her. *Cym 1.6.134,* 'D.'s priest,' a chaste being. D. had priestesses not priests; however, in *Per 21.227,* 'maiden priests' also refers to women. Sh. also used witch to refer to males. *2.3.67,* 'D.'s rangers,' the protectors of the huntress goddess' animals.

2) *AWW,* see Capilet, Diana.

Dick, 1) generic name for any ordinary man. *LLL 5.2.464, 898. Cor 2.3.116.*

2) *3H6 5.5.35,* belittling nickname for 'Richard.' See Richard Crookback; Richard III.

3) *1H4 2.5.8,* one of three bartenders whom Prince Harry considered personal friends.

Dick Surgeon, *TN 5.1.195,* any surgeon. In Sh.'s time, barbers performed surgical procedures. The traditional barber's pole with its red stripes represents bloody bandages and the gold knob at the top, the basin used to shave customers. Surgery was not taken from barbers until 1745, and was considered one of the lowest forms of medical practice until the 20th c. British surgeons today still call themselves 'Mister,' instead of 'Doctor,' but the title has become a mark of distinction.

Dick the Butcher, *2H6,* character Sh. invented to represent the kind of person attracted to Cade's rebellion. Sh. depicts Cade's followers as illiterate members of the laboring classes. Sh. may not have known that Cade had many supporters among the rural gentry.

Dickie, *3H6 1.4.77,* belittling nickname for 'Richard.' See Richard Crookback; Richard III.

Dickon, *R3 5.6.35,* belittling nickname for Richard III. It had long been in use as a nickname. Its relationship to 'the dickens' as an alliterative substitute for 'the devil' is not clear. The first use of 'what the dickens!' occurs in *MWW 3.2.16.* This may imply that Dickon was similarly used, which fits well with the suggestion of the context.

Dictynna, *LLL 4.2.36,* the nymph Britomartis, a follower of Artemis, inventor of fishermen's nets. After being pursued by Minos for nine months, she threw herself into the sea. She then became patron goddess of hunters and fishermen. The name also became synonymous with Diana and was so used by Ovid and others, the way Holofernes uses it here.

Dido, or Elissa, legendary founder and queen of Carthage, niece and widow of Sychæus (Sicharbas) or Acherbas (Acerbas), daughter of Mutto, king Belus of Tyre, or Agenor. Several versions of Dido's story exist. The one found in Virgil's *Æneid* is the best known. According to Virgil, Dido, a princess from the Phoenician city of Tyre, fled her homeland when her brother Pygmalion murdered her husband Sychæus. She and her followers settled in Libya, where they built Carthage. Carthage appeared just as the

Greeks brought the Trojan war to a conclusion, and Æneas, a refugee from Troy, spent some time in the new African state. Dido became enamored of Æneas and offered to share her throne with him, but Æneas' mother, the goddess Venus, refused to permit the alliance. Æneas accepted his destiny and abandoned Dido. As he sailed from Carthage, she committed suicide by leaping onto a blazing funeral pyre. Æneas subsequently settled in Italy, took a Latin wife, and established the line that was to found the city of Rome. Virgil's account of Dido's death was a symbolic anticipation of Rome's destruction of Carthage in the Punic wars.

2H6 3.2.117. Tit 2.2.22, 5.3.81. Rom 2.3.39. MV 5.1.10. Ant 4.15.53. Tmp 2.1, the humor in this passage is obscure, but may have come from the playing on 'die, do' and 'any ass' (Æneas) as in Thomas Middleton's *Roaring Girl. TNK 4.3.14.*

Dieu, *H5 3.4.28, 37, 48, 3.5.5, 15, 4.4.6, 39, 5.2.116,* Fr. 'God.'

Dighton, John, *R3 4.3.4, 9, 17,* groom to Sir James Tyrrell. In Thomas More's account of Richard III's crimes, he appears as one of two servants whom Tyrrell sent to murder Edward IV's sons in the Tower. More's source for the story was allegedly a confession given by Tyrrell in 1502, when he was executed by Henry VII for another crime. More claimed that Dighton confirmed Tyrrell's confession by admitting to his role in the murder. The story is, however, suspect. If Tyrrell confessed to murdering the princes, that fact was never published by the king, who had everything to gain from proving that the princes were dead. Dighton was also still at liberty and unpunished when More wrote in 1513. Sh. follows a popular and near contemporary source for his account of the fate of Edward IV's heirs, but historians have yet to agree on what happened to them and who was responsible for their disappearance.

Diomed, 1), see Diomedes. *Tro,* 'Sir D.' This spelling is much more common in the play, excepting stage directions, perhaps indicating pronunciation. *3H6 4.2.19:* Sh. chooses a particular incident from the *Iliad,* 10, as a prototype for daring military raids carried out under cover of darkness: Diomedes and Odysseus sneak into the Trojan camp at night to steal the horses of the Thracian king, Rhesus.

2) *Ant,* Diomedes, Cleopatra's secretary. According to Plutarch ('Antony' 76.5), Diomed brought word to Mark Antony that Cleopatra was, despite rumors to the contrary, alive. He arrived too late to prevent Antony from mortally wounding himself.

Diomedes, *Tro 1.3 sd, 2.3.67 sd, 3.3 sd; 30, 4.4 sd.,* 'Diomed' in spoken lines, a Greek warrior, king of Ætolia, son of Tydeus and Deipyle. In Homer, Diomedes is nearly as great a warrior as Achilles. Much of the *Iliad* is devoted to the description of Diomedes' feats at arms. He wounded Aphrodite and Ares, nearly killed Æneas, and slew Pandarus, Rhesus, and Dolon. A suitor of Helen, he often engages in exploits with Odysseus, including the theft of the statue of Athena that was supposed to protect Troy. In one version, Odysseus attempts to murder him to get sole credit for the theft, but Diomedes ties him up and beats him all the way back to the Greek camp. Diomedes also was one of the men concealed in the Trojan Horse. A later tradition has him emigrating to Italy after unhappy marital experiences and founding several cities. He was made immortal by Athena and worshipped on the Adriatic. In Sh. he conveys Cressida from Troy to her father Calchas and easily seduces her. He fights with Troilus to no conclusion. He is a cynical character, without apparent conscience. In William Caxton's *Recuyell of the Historyes of Troye* (c. 1474), the first English printed book, and Sh.'s major source for the play, Diomedes is more prominent as a lover of Breseyda (Cressida) than is Troilus, whom he fights several times.

Dion, *WT,* a lord of Sicilia. The name occurs in Plutarch, from which Sh. got most of his names for the play, where Dion of Syracuse is compared to Brutus. Dion opposed tyranny and toppled Dionysius the Younger.

Dionyza, *Per,* Cleon's wife, who orders the murder of Marina. Dionyza is one of many of Sh.s character names that appears in John Gower's *Confessio Amantis* (1390). Dionisiades appears in Lawrence Twine's *Patterne of Painefull Adventures* (1594). See Pericles. The resemblance to the name Dionysus is attractive because of the many instances of madness the god inflicted.

Dis, the god Pluto (q.v.) The name is a contraction of L. *dives* 'rich man,' which is a translation of Gr. *ploutos* 'wealth.' *WT 4.4.121,* 'D.'s wagon.' *Tmp 4.1.89. TNK 3.5.117.*

Disdain, Lady, Ado *1.1.112,* Benedick's mocking name for Beatrice.

Ditis, *2H6 B.4,* Dis, the 'City of Satan' to which Dante is guided by Virgil on their journey through hell (*Inferno,* 9). 'Dis' was a Roman name for Pluto, god of the underworld.

Dives, *1H4 3.3.31,* name that legend has invented for the anonymous rich man who is the subject of one of Jesus' parables: Luke 16:19–31. It derives from the Latin *dives,* 'rich man.' Dives dies and goes to hell while heaven welcomes Lazarus, a beggar who spent his life languishing in misery at the entrance to Dives' house. The point of the story is that Dives chose the lesser heaven of earthly pleasures and thereby forfeit ed his claim to the greater heaven of eternal bliss.

Dizzy, *MM 4.3.12,* a mocking name for one of the impoverished criminals Pompey knows. As prisoners paid for their own food, many were forced to beg passers by.

Doctor of Physic, *MWW 3.1.3-4,* Caius' self-proclaimed title, 'Medical doctor.'

Doctor She, *AWW 2.1.78,* Lafeu's mocking name for Helen, who has come to heal the king.

Dog-fish, *1H6 1.6.85,* small ugly sharks that live in coastal waters. Sh. mentions them in order to make a pun on 'dauphin,' the title of the heir to the French throne. The crown prince of France came to be called 'the Dauphin' in the 14th c. when his office was endowed with a feudal territory that used the dolphin as a heraldic emblem. The dolphin had noble associations, but the dog-fish was despised by medieval people as a worthless form of life, although it is not only edible but quite tasty. Recently in England there was marketing ploy to rename it the 'rock salmon' to make filets of it more commercial. In Greek mythology dolphins were benign creatures who guided the spirits of the dead to the next world. Their association with life after death led Christian artists to transform them into symbols of immortality.

Dogberry, *Ado,* 'Master Constable,' chief constable of the watch, one of Sh.'s most celebrated clowns. A master of malapropism, Dogberry delays the revelation of the plot against Hero by being so longwinded that the importance of what he is saying is overlooked. A lovable buffoon, Dogberry resembles Falstaff, though lacking the knight's complexity because of his naiveté. The broad comedy of Dogberry and the watchmen tends to mitigate the nastiness of Don John's plot against Hero and Claudio's humiliation of the girl and lighten the tone of what would otherwise be more melodramatic than comic. In F1 *4.2,* Dogberry is labeled 'Kemp.' or 'Kem.' indicating that the part was played and probably originated for William Kempe, Sh.'s chief clown before 1599. The name Dogberry likely derives from the fruit of a common English shrub, *Cornus sanguinea,* the common dogwood, prick-wood, prick-timber, cornel, houndberry, or dogberry. The fruit of this shrub is a dark, small, bitter berry sometimes used in oil and soap. The 'dog' in the plant's name is generally thought to mean 'inferior,' although the wood has been used for various purposes. Another theory, probably fanciful, is that since 'berry' also referred to 'roe' then, it may be a play on 'dog roe,' 'dog eggs.'

Doit, John, *2H4 3.2.18,* companion of Justice Shallow's youth. Shallow remembers him as a participant in the riotous games he played during his student days at Clement's Inn. Since a doit was a tiny Dutch coin, Sh. was no doubt implying that John was a person of little consequence or stature.

Dolabella, *Ant,* Publius Cornelius Dolabella, son of a man by the same name whom Antony had appointed governor of Syria. The elder Dolabella committed suicide in 43 BC to avoid punishment for the murder of another Roman governor. Plutarch ('Antony' 84.1) provides most of what is known about the younger Dolabella. He was a friend of Octavius, but also one of Cleopatra's acquaintances. After Antony's death, Dolabella handled the negotiations for Cleopatra's surrender to Octavius. He lived to become consul in 10 AD.

Doll, 1) see Tearsheet, Doll.

2) *STM,* one of the commoners working herself up to riot, sister of Arthur Watchins. She has no equivalent in Holinshed's version of events.

Dolphin, see Dauphin. *Lr. Q 11.90:* the 'Dolphin' was sometimes equated with the devil, as he seems to be here in this line which is apparently from an old song urging the D. to pass by.

Dolphin chamber, *2H4 2.1.89,* the name of a room in an inn, probably referring to the decorations on its walls or ceiling.

Dominie, *TNK 2.3.41, 3.5.137,* nickname or title for Gerald the Schoolmaster, from the L. *dominus,* 'lord.' Recipients of the Bachelor of Arts were given the title, and also used the knightly 'sir' before their names in Sh.'s time.

Domitius Enobarbus, *Ant,* see Enobarbus, Domitius.

Don John, *Ado,* see John.

Don Pedro, *Ado,* see Pedro.

Donalbain, *Mac,* second son of Duncan. He flees into exile in Ireland after the murder of the king and never reappears in the play. The historical Donald Bain or Donald Ban (the name means 'Donald the White,' likely referring to blonde hair) was a child when his father was killed in 1039 and was taken into exile in the Hebrides. Donald supported the goals of the Celtic nobility in the north and opposed the English orientation of his brother Malcolm's rule. When Malcolm was killed at Alnwick in 1093 along with his eldest son Edward, there were several claimants to the throne: Duncan, a hostage in England, son of Malcolm by his first wife; Edmund, son of Malcolm and Margaret; and Donald. Duncan and Donald ruled jointly for three years. The dispute was not settled until Duncan was killed. Edgar, another son of Malcolm and Margaret, was placed on the throne by Edgar Ætheling, a claimant to the throne of England. Edgar blinded Donald and imprisoned him until his death soon after in 1099. This struggle for the throne oriented Scotland towards England, since Margaret and her brother Edgar Ætheling were of ancient English nobility pushed out by the Normans. Margaret forced the Celtic church to conform to the rest of western Christendom and died quite unpopular. Donald Ban was the last Scottish king to have a Gælic surname (other than Malcolm IV, 'the Maiden,' c. 1141–1165) and possibly the last to speak Gælic.

Doncaster, *1H4 5.1.42, 58,* town in Yorkshire on the Don river 160 mi. north of London. After Henry (IV) Bolingbroke landed at Ravenspurgh in July 1399, he met his allies at Doncaster to plan an attack on Richard II. The Percies later claimed that Henry had taken an oath at Doncaster not to depose Richard, but only to insist on the restoration of Henry's patrimony, the duchy of Lancaster. Historians are uncertain whether Henry made such a promise or whether the Percies invented the story to justify their rebellion against Henry in 1403.

Doomsday, final judgment decreed by God at the end of history. 'Doom' derives from an early German term for a law or a court. *R3 5.1.12. Err 3.2.100. LLL 4.3.272. Rom 3.3.9, 5.3.233. 1H4 4.1.135. JC 3.1.99. Ham Add'l Q2 A.1.1.13, 2.2.240, 5.1.59. Ant 5.2.228.*

Dorcas, *WT,* shepherd. Dorcas is a Biblical name (Acts 9.36, 39) for a woman, from Gr. 'gazelle.' She was raised from the dead by St. Peter. In Sidney's *Countesse of Pembrokes Arcadia,* there is a prince of Thessalia, named Musidorus or Dorus, who may have suggested the pastoral association.

Doreus, *Tro 5.5.8,* Greek warrior captured by Margareton. In William Caxton's *Recuyell of the Historyes of Troye,* 3 (c. 1474), the first English printed book, and Sh.'s major source for the play, Doreus is a king slain by Hector in his anger over the death of 'kynge philis.' There is also an earl, Dorius, who accompanies Ajax. There is no Doreus in the *Iliad,* but Dorion is a city in Nestor's kingdom in the southwestern Peloponesus.

Doricles, *WT 4.4,* name assumed by Florizel in disguise. The name appears in Virgil's *Æneid,* 5.620 and in the *Iliad* 11.577, where he is killed by Ajax. There are similar names, such as Doreus, Dorastus, and Dorilaus in Caxton, Sidney, and a variety of sources.

Dorothy Although several saints bore the name *Dorotheus,* Gr. 'gift of God' (a reversal of 'Theodore'), it fell out of use in the Middle Ages, but resurfaced in its feminine form in the 16th c. and remained popular thereafter. Perhaps the revival resulted from the Renaissance's increased awareness of the Greek language. Sh.'s uses imply that it was a name used by commoners.

1) Mistress D., *2H4 2.4.123,* see Tearsheet, Doll.

2) *Cym 2.3.135,* servant of Innogen's.

Dorset, county just west of the center of England's southern coast. See Dorset, Lady Marquis of, *H8*; Marquis of, *R3*; *H8.*

Dorset, Lady Marquis, *H8,* 'Marchioness D.,' Margaret, mother of Henry Gray, third marquis of Dorset, grandmother of Lady Jane Gray, and godmother to Elizabeth I.

Dorset, Marquis of, 1) *R3,* Thomas Gray (1451–1501), Elizabeth Woodville Gray's elder son by her first husband, John Gray. In 1461 Thomas succeeded to his father's title and became the ninth Lord Ferrers. His mother's marriage to Edward IV in 1464 greatly enhanced his prospects. He was named earl of Huntingdon in 1471, and he was granted the hand of a wealthy heiress who brought him the honors of Harrington and Bonville. In 1475 he became marquis of Dorset—ranking higher than an earl, but lower than a duke. Dorset served his royal stepfather well. He fought at Tewkesbury and may have collaborated in the murder of one of its captives, Prince Edward, Henry VI's heir. When Richard III's usurpation of the throne dashed the Woodvilles' hopes of becoming regents for the youthful Edward V, Dorset plotted against Richard. The failure of the duke of Buckingham's revolt forced Dorset to flee to Brittany and offer his services to Henry Tudor, earl of Richmond. Richmond, leader of the Lancastrians, was not inclined to trust a man who was implicated in the murder of Henry VI's son. Consequently, Dorset played no role in the crucial battle at Bosworth Field that won Richmond Richard's crown. Henry VII, however, bore no grudges. He confirmed Dorset's titles and possessions and gave him military assignments.

2) *H8 4.1.38,* Henry Gray (d. 1554), husband to Henry VIII's niece, Frances Brandon. The Grays were descendants of Edward IV's queen, Elizabeth Woodville, by her first marriage with John Gray. Elizabeth's son

Thomas, was the first marquis of Dorset, and Henry Gray was his grandson. Dorset took part in Anne Boleyn's coronation, and his mother served as godmother to Anne's daughter, Elizabeth. In 1551 Dorset was named duke of Suffolk. He presided at Henry VIII's funeral and was a regent for Edward VI. When Edward died, Suffolk plotted to dispossess Edward's Catholic sister, Mary, and place his own Protestant daughter, Jane, on the throne. Jane Gray had a claim to the throne through her maternal grandmother, Mary Tudor, Henry VIII's sister. The attempt to persuade the people to accept Henry's grandniece in place of his eldest child failed almost as soon as it began. After a reign of only nine days Suffolk persuaded his daughter to renounce the royal title he had forced on her and to throw herself on Mary's mercy. Suffolk was permitted to retire from court, and he lived in obscurity until 1554. In that year Mary's unpopular decision to wed Philip of Spain sparked a rebellion. Sir Thomas Wyatt, son of a knight who had been one of Henry VIII's favorites, rallied the men of Kent and demanded Mary's abdication. Wyatt's actions doomed Suffolk and his daughter. Mary put Jane and her family to death to prevent them from becoming rallying points for further challenges to her authority.

Double, *2H4 3.2.39, 51,* old man whose death is reported to Justice Shallow by his friend Justice Silence. Sh. may have chosen the name to suggest an old man doubled over by the weight of years.

Douglas, Earl of, *1H4, 2H4 Ind. 31, 1.1.17, 77, 82, 127,* Archibald, (1369–1424), one of many important Scotsmen Hotspur (Henry Percy) took prisoner at the battle of Holmedon Hill on 14 September 1402. (Douglas served his father-in-law, Robert III of Scotland, as commander of the Scottish marches, and he led numerous raids into English territories.) After Holmedon, Hotspur and Henry IV quarrelled over who had the right to the ransom that was to be paid for Douglas and the other prisoners. Rather than yield to the king, Hotspur organized a rebellion and enlisted Douglas' help in overthrowing Henry. At the battle of Shrewsbury Hotspur was killed and Douglas was again captured. The earl paid Henry a large ransom, returned to Scotland, and devoted himself to issues of foreign policy. In 1412 he went to France to negotiate a treaty with the Burgundians. And when hostilities broke out between England and France, he fought for the French. Charles VII rewarded him with the dukedom of Touraine. He died fighting the battle of Verneuil and was buried in Tours.

Dover, English port situated at the narrowest point on the English channel. It is famous for its chalky white cliffs, which have given England one of its ancient names, Albion, and come to symbolize the nation. Since ancient times it was the trading gateway to the continent by way of Whitsand and, later, Calais. In 1465, it was made the only legal departure point for France. It was defended by a fort as early as the 4th c. AD. It was a frequent bone of contention in various wars. Its most celebrated defenses were in 1216, when Hubert de Burgh held the castle against a French force, and a naval battle in 1217 which solidified Henry III's hold on the throne.

1H6 5.1.49. H5 3.0.4. Lr.: several events revolve around Dover, including Cordelia's invasion and Gloucester's attempted suicide.

Dover Castle, *Jn 5.1.31,* fortress at the eastern end of the English port at Dover. It had special military significance, for it guarded the narrowest point on the English channel.

Dowsabel, *Err 4.1.110,* from the French *douce et belle* ('sweet and beautiful'), a name of affection. Dromio is here applying the name humorously to his Nell.

Dragon's tail, *Lr. 1.2.127 (Q 2.124),* the constellation Draco. It is located near Ursa Major and Minor, and therefore would have, as Edmund is saying, little difference in the effect of being born under U. Major.

Dromio, 1) of Ephesus and 2) of Syracuse, *Err,* twins separated in infancy, servants to the Antipholus twins. Primarily clowns, they become the focus of much slapstick as they are beaten in confusion for one another. The name may derive from the Dromio in John Lyly's *Mother Bombie* (1594), which has mistaken identities and some other minor features in common with *Err.* Dromo, however, is a common name for a slave in the plays of the Roman comedian Terence, so either Sh. or Lyly might have adapted it. The plot of the duplicate servants and masters, however, derives from the *Amphitryon* of Plautus, in which Jupiter and Mercury disguise themselves as Amphitryon and Sosia his servant, in order to accomplish another Jovian seduction. Dromio of Syracuse would therefore correspond to Mercury in this source.

Drop-hair, *MM 4.3.14,* F1 'Drop-heire,' mocking name for one of the impoverished criminals Pompey knows. As prisoners paid for their own food, many were forced to beg passers by. This is likely a joke on hair loss due to venereal disease. Possibly it means someone who has lost an inheritance.

Drum, *AWW,* see John D. and Tom D.

Duchess, wife of a Duke.

1) *2H6,* Eleanor Cobham, D. of Gloucester.

2) *R2 2.2.97,* Eleanor de Bohun, D. of Gloucester.

3) *MND 1.2.6, 71,* Hippolyta.

4) *Lr. 1.1.244,* D. of Burgundy, Cordelia's proposed title.

Duff, *Mac 2.3.88,* Banquo's emotional shortening of Macduff.

Duke, ruler of a duchy, one of the most powerful ranks of the nobility. It derives from the Latin *dux,* 'ruler.' As the examples below demonstrate, Sh. sometimes uses the term for kings. Although monarchs often were also dukes, he frequently uses the term in its original Latin generic sense.

1) *TGV 4.1.47:* though the outlaw is banished from Verona, he is later pardoned by the Duke of Milan. Either duke may be meant, though there is no reason to introduce a second duke into the story. *4.4.18, 22, etc.,* d. of Milan.

2) *LLL 1.2.36, 120,* Ferdinand, king of Navarre. Perhaps an indication of the play's revision or else the use of duke to mean 'ruler.'

3) *MND,* Theseus.

4) *MV 2.8.4, 3.2.278,* the Doge. Venice was not a dukedom of the usual type. The Doge was an elected ruler whose power was severely restrained by an oligarchical constitution putting real power in the hands of the Council of Ten, the Senate, and the administrative Collegio. Sh.'s 'duke' is similar to many of Sh.'s rulers in that he cannot set aside the letter of the law simply because of his own sympathy for Antonio. Fully prepared to allow the death of Antonio to uphold the law, he begs Shylock not to persist in his suit and is greatly relieved when Portia reveals the loophole that can save the merchant's life. Furthermore, he has absorbed Portia's famous speech for mercy because he extends what mercy he can to Shylock, something which contrasts with Graziano's mood of vengeance.

5) *MWW 4.3.2, 4.5.66,* leader of the visiting Germans whom Evans accuses of stealing the Host's horses. This seems to allude to Frederick, Duke of Württemberg, who was elected a Knight of the Garter. As Count Mömpelgard in 1592, he had visited England and begun an unseemly campaign for the Garter which included sending emissaries in 1595. For foreign policy reasons, it seemed appropriate to grant the Duke his wish in 1597. He did not attend the Garter Feast, which seems to be part of the joke on the Host, who does not know there is no duke at court.

6) *Ado 3.5.19,* 'D.'s officer's': the duke here is evidently Don Pedro, actually the king of Aragon, but maybe also duke of Messina. It seems sloppy to say that there is an offstage duke of Messina.

7) *Ham 3.2.228,* D. of Vienna, the Player King.

8) *MM,* see Vincentio.

9) *Oth,* wise ruler of Venice. He adjudicates Brabanzio's complaint against Othello and frets about the Turkish military plans. He does not appear in Sh.'s source, Cinthio's *Hecatommithi.* The complaint brought by Brabanzio before the duke, however, dramatizes the opposition of the vague 'relatives' mentioned by Cinthio.

10) *Tmp 1.2.103,* D. of Milan.

11) *TNK,* see Theseus.

Duke Frederick, *AYLI,* father of Celia, uncle of Rosalind, usurper of his brother Duke Senior's throne, but who is conveniently converted offstage by a meeting with an old religious man.

Duke Senior, *AYLI,* father of Rosalind, exiled to Ardenne. He mainly sets the tone for the green world by praising the simple life away from the city.

Duke's oak, *MND 1.2.103,* site in the woods, otherwise unidentified.

Dull, Anthony, *LLL,* constable who appears several times in the play, first when Costard is sentenced for consorting with women. Later he serves as counterpoint for the false erudition of Holofernes and Nathaniel. His name reflects his mental capacity.

Dumaine, 1) *LLL,* 'Dumain,' a courtier of Navarre. He falls in love with Catherine as the men's vows of asceticism crumble. The name is thought to have been borrowed from Charles of Lorraine, Duc de Mayenne (1554–1611), an enemy of Henry of Navarre until 1590, when he was defeated at Ivry and thereafter became his supporter. Another possibility is the Maréchal Jean D'Aumont (d. 1595), one of Henry's allies. Maine is also a former French province in the north and the lord could be from there, however unlikely it would be that he would be a courtier of Navarre. See Ferdinand, King of Navarre.

2) First and Second Lords D., *AWW,* 'Captains D.', two French noblemen who join the war in Tuscany and assist in opening Bertram's eyes by revealing Paroles' cowardice. Other than in this important action, they serve as interchangeable gentlemen of the Solario/Solanio type, who reveal the nature of other characters by their commentary or behavior towards them. In F1 they are referred to as 'G.' and 'E.' which is usually thought to be the initials of the actors which played the roles, William Ecclestone and either Samuel Gilburne and Robert Gough. The name Dumaine is rarely used in F1 *AWW.* Its use here is thought to derive from the same sources as *LLL.*

Dumb, Master, *2H4 2.4.85,* Mistress Quickly's pastor. His comic name recalls a passage from Isaiah 54:10 that Puritans often applied to lax and stupid clergy: 'His watchmen . . . are all dumb dogs, they cannot bark; dreaming, lying down, loving to slumber.'

Dumbleton, Master, *2H4 1.2.29,* merchant from whom Falstaff has ordered satin for his cloak. Sh. may have derived the name from 'dummel,' a term meaning 'dumb' in the sense of 'stupid.' The merchant was, however, not so foolish as to extend easy credit to Falstaff.

Dump, sad song, a tear-jerker. *TGV 3.2.84. Luc 1127. Rom 4.5.132, 134, 153* (pl): Peter's 'merry dump' is an oxymoron. *Ado 2.3.70.*

Dun *Rom 1.4.41,* name of a draft horse in a Christmas game in which people tried to pull a log as if they were pulling Dun from being stuck in the mud. The fun came from the disorganization of the pulling and attempts to make it fall on other participants' toes. From the color of a mouse: grayish brown.

Dun Adramadio, *LLL 4.3.197,* Costard's muddling of Don Adriano de Armado, perhaps playing on 'dun,' brown.

Duncan, *Mac,* (d. 1040), king of Scotland, son of Crinan (Cronan) lay abbot of Dunkeld, maternal grandson of Malcolm II, and father of Malcolm III and Donalbain. Portrayed by Sh. as a saintly, elderly ruler, Duncan I was, according to what history is known, as dubious a claimant to the throne as Macbeth and approximately the same age. The truth is obscure, but one explanation is that Duncan ruled south of Forth and Clyde, Macbeth ruled Moray, and Thorfinn Sigurdsson (earl of Caithness) ruled the north. Duncan had been granted his crown as king of Scots by his grandfather and thus became the first person to inherit the Scottish throne. He gave Thorfinn's lands to his nephew Moddan, who was defeated when he went to seize them. In assisting Moddan, Duncan was killed in battle by Thorfinn's ally Macbeth. All this is uncertain except that the historical Macbeth did not murder him while he was a guest. The murder scene in *Mac* is based upon Donwald's murder of King Duff in 972 and is possibly intended to remind King James of the murder of his father.

Dunsinane, *Mac,* 'D. Hill,' small mountain (1012 ft.) about 7 mi. northwest of Perth in the Sidlaw Hills. It overlooks the Tay valley and the Carse of Gowrie. It is the supposed site of Macbeth's castle and indeed there are vestigial ruins there from an old fortress. Although the prophecy makes Birnam Wood come to Dunsinane for the final battle, in fact Malcolm Canmore slew Macbeth at Lumphanan as Macbeth fled from Birnam Wood, according to Holinshed.

Dunsmore, *3H6 5.1.3,* heath that lies halfway between Daventry and Coventry. The earl of Oxford's army, having arrived at Dunsmore, was only 10 mi. from its rendezvous with Warwick 'the Kingmaker's' forces at Coventry. Warwick was marshalling troops for the battle of Barnet. At Barnet Warwick died and Edward IV regained England's throne.

Dunstable, *H8 4.1.27,* town 30 mi. northwest of London, near Ampthill, the castle where Henry VIII's queen, Katherine, was housed during their divorce proceedings. After Henry failed to get a ruling on the validity of their marriage from the papacy, he directed Thomas Cranmer, archbishop of Canterbury, to hear the case. Cranmer convened an ecclesiastical court at the priory of the Black Canons at Dunstable, which, on 23 May 1533, granted the king an annulment.

Dutch, 1) *2H6 4.7.56,* western Germanic language of the Lowlands at the mouth of the Rhine river. 'Dutch' derives from *dietsch,* meaning the vernacular (as opposed to Latin). It may be considered a language in between English and High German both geographically and in its characteristics. The Rhine links the Lowlands with western Germany and accounts for the powerful influence that German culture has had on the area and also for the fact that 'Dutch' in some contexts meant 'German'. See Low Dutch, *AWW.*

2) (adj.) of or pertaining to the Dutch nation. *MWW 3.5.110,* 'D. dish,' their cuisine was heavy with butter and grease.

Dutchman, 1) native of the Netherlands. *LLL 5.2.247,* a mockery of a Dutchman's pronunciation, playing on 'well,' 'veil,' and '-ville' in Longueville. *Ado 3.2.31,* the passage mocks the stylish Englishman's mixing of national fashions. *TN 3.2.26,* 'icicle on a D.'s beard,' probably an allusion to the explorations of Willem Barents in the Arctic (1594, 1595, and 1596). Searching for a passage to India he discovered Novaya Zemlya and Spitsbergen. On the third expedition, Barents was trapped by ice north of Novaya Zemlya and suffered through a brutal winter. Barents died shortly after making a June escape in an open boat. Other members of his crew were rescued in Lapland. From exactly where Sh. drew his simile is unknown. There was an account of the voyage by Gerrit de Veer registered for publication in 1598, but the story of Barents' expeditions would have been common gossip in their time.

2) *AWW 2.3.42:* 'Dutchman' here is usually taken to mean a speaker of German, a 'Deutsch man,' because *lustig* is German for

'lustily' or 'merrily.' However, the word means virtually the same in Dutch.

3) *Cym 1.4,* nonspeaking character who listens in on Giacomo's wager with Posthumus. He is probably present only for the sake of his distinctive costume to add a worldly flavor to the first scene in Rome, for the sake of ethnic parody, or possibly to show Filario's hospitality to people of all nations. The character appears in one of Sh.'s sources, *Frederyke of Jennen* (anonymous, 1560). Unidentified gentlemen are present at the wager in Boccaccio's *Decameron* (2.9), the major source of the love plot.

E

Earl, a highly ranked noble. Sh. is careless in distinguishing earls from dukes and counts, and often seems to use the term in the old Anglo-Saxon sense of 'lord,' or 'chieftain.' In *Lr.*, for example, the duke of Gloucester is called 'the old Earl.' Many noblemen, of course, bore both titles in their various roles.

East, *Ant 1.5.45, 2.3.38, 2.6.50,* in this context, only the lands at the eastern end of the Mediterranean, the modern Middle East.

East Indies, *MWW 1.3.64,* fabled wealthy lands of the Orient, the spice islands, etc. Falstaff here means a place in which to get rich: Mistresses Ford and Page shall serve this purpose as his Indies.

Eastcheap, London street straddling Bridge Street and ending at Tower Street. Sh. follows an earlier anonymous play, *The Famous Victories of Henry V* in making it the location of the tavern where Falstaff (Oldcastle), Prince Harry, and their cronies met. *1H4 1.2.129, 155, 189, 2.5.14, 446. 2H4 2.1.71, 2.2.139.*

Easter, Christian holy day commemorating the resurrection of Jesus. It derives from OE *eastre,* a spring equinox celebration in honor of Eostre, the Teutonic dawn goddess. In western Christianity, it is the first Sunday after the full moon on the vernal equinox or thereafter. Its earliest date would be March 22, its latest April 25. *Rom 3.1.27:* as Easter is the last day of Lent, Benvolio is accused of criticizing a tailor for wearing new garments before the end of Lent.

Ebrew Jew, see Hebrew Jew.

Echo 1), one of the Oreads (nymphs of the mountains and grottoes). Often when Jupiter dallied with the nymphs, Juno would try to catch him. Echo delayed the angry goddess, so that the nymphs could escape, by chattering. Juno punished Echo by giving her the ability to speak only when spoken to and to say only what was said to her. Later Echo fell in love with Narcissus. He rejected her and she withered away until only her voice remained. The tale is in Ovid's *Metamorphoses,* 3. *Rom 2.1.206,* 'the cave where E. lies,' Echo supposedly lives in caves or in the mountains.

2), *Shr Ind. 1.24,* a dog, the name referring to its deep, carrying bark. The dog's names in this section seem to come from their physical or behavioral traits.

Eden, *R2 2.1.42,* earthly paradise that God created for the first human beings, Adam and Eve (Genesis 2:8–3:23). The name may derive from a Sumerian term for 'plain.' Ancient Mesopotamians associated fertile gardens with plains, for the farmers of Sumer sought out flat land that could be irrigated.

Edgar, *Lr.,* son of Gloucester, half-brother of Edmond. Accused by his brother of plotting against their father, he is unjustly exiled, but in his disguise as a Bedlam beggar, returns to save his blinded father's life. All of this is in parallel to Cordelia, wronged by her father. Edgar does not die, however, but ends the play sharing power with Albany. It is not known if Sh. borrowed the name from any specific source. One important Edgar was king Edgar (944–975), son of Edmund the Magnificent and father of the Ætheling Edmund. The Ætheling Edgar (c. 1050–c. 1130) was grandson of king Edmund Ironside, and was nearly chosen Saxon king to resist William the Conqueror. He submitted, however, and retreated to Scotland, where his sister Margaret married Malcolm Canmore. He took part in a rising against William and was imprisoned for backing Robert of Normandy against Henry I. After his release he disappears from history. There are interesting coincidences in Edgar's link to Scotland. This would give both rulers of England upon Lear's death, Albany and Edgar, links to King James through marriage or title. Both historical Edgars are associated with Edmunds also, and both suggest the era before the Conquest.

Edmond, *Lr,* Q 'Edmund,' 'the Bastard,' son of Gloucester, illegitimate half-brother of Edgar. Sh. may have borrowed the name from Samuel Harsnett (see Flibbertigibbet) who discusses Edmund Campion, a priest who was hanged in 1581 and whose girdle was used in exorcism. William Weston, who used the alias Edmunds, was an exorcist and chief villain of Harsnett's book, specifically mentioned in Harsnett's lengthy title. Weston went into exile in 1603 and was made Spiritual Father of the English College at Seville. See Edgar.

Edmund, 1) duke of Rutland, *2H6 4.8.39,* Richard of York's second son (d. 1460). He and his father died at the battle of Wakefield. Edmund was killed by John Clifford, who hacked the head from Richard's corpse and brought it, decked with a paper crown, to Queen Margaret. Sh. claims that Clifford's grisly vengeance was inspired by York's murder of Clifford's father at the first battle of St. Albans.

2) *Lr Q,* see Edmond.

Edmund Langley, (1341–1402), fifth son of Edward III and first duke of York. At the age of 18 he joined his father's armies in France and spent much of his life fighting abroad. In 1367 he and his brothers Edward the Black Prince and John of Gaunt led troops into Spain. By helping Pedro the Cruel of Castile recover his throne, they hoped to ensure Spain's support for England's wars in France. Gaunt married Pedro's heiress, Constance, and Edmund wed her younger sister Isabel. In 1376 and 1377 the deaths of the Black Prince and of Edward III created a crisis for England's royal family. Since the heir to Edward's throne, the Black Prince's son, Richard II, was too young to rule, his uncles jockeyed for control of a regency government. York was far less ambitious than his brothers, John of Gaunt (duke of Lancaster) and Thomas of Woodstock (duke of Gloucester). Consequently, he took little part in public affairs until both of them were dead.

In 1381, after another term of military service in France, he was sent to Portugal to assist its king, Ferdinand. Ferdinand's daughter, Beatrice, wed his son, Edward. York's most historically significant assignment was his last and least successful. In 1399 Richard left his uncle in charge of England while Richard led an expedition to Ireland. To York, therefore, fell the responsibility of dealing with Henry (IV) Bolingbroke's rebellion. Henry was Richard's cousin, John of Gaunt's son. In 1398 Richard had exiled him, and in 1399 the king had confiscated his inheritance, the duchy of Lancaster. On 4 July 1399, Henry landed in England with a small continent of soldiers to demand the restoration of his patrimony. York tried to organize a response to Henry's challenge, but Richard had taken most of the royal army to Ireland and the great baronial families of northern England rallied to Henry's side. York could do little but yield to the inevitable. On 27 July he surrendered to Henry at Berkeley Castle and urged Richard to abdicate. York withdrew from court after Richard's deposition and lived out the rest of his days in the house in which he had been born, King's Langley in Hertfordshire.

2H6 2.2.15, 2.2.46. 1H6 2.5.85.

Edmund York, *R2 1.2.62,* see Edmund Langley.

Edward, *Mac 3.6.27,* 'most pious E.,' see Edward Confessor.

Edward III, (1312–1377), English king who began the Hundred Years' War and whose heirs, the houses of York and Lancaster, waged the War of the Roses. Edward's reign began under very peculiar circumstances. Edward II (1284–1327), his father, behaved so irresponsibly that he forfeited the confidence of his men and the loyalty of his wife, Isabella. With the help of an exiled English baron named Roger Mortimer, Isabella staged a coup and forced her husband to abdicate in favor of their son. At the age of fifteen Edward III was thrust onto the throne to serve as a figurehead for a government run by his mother and her lover. He did not tolerate this indignity for long. In 1330 a coalition of nobles helped him kill Mortimer and force Isabella into retirement. The young king's highest priority was to undo the damage his parents had done to the reputation of the monarchy. He first tried to prove himself to his subjects by resuming a war with Scotland that had been left unfinished at the death of his grandfather, Edward I, but he soon turned his attention to a far more challenging enemy, France.

French aid enabled the impoverished Scots to carry on their struggle with England, and France contested Edward's right to fiefs in Aquitaine (Gascony) that the English had held since the days of Henry II. It also threatened England's financial stability by making war on Flanders, where England marketed the wool that was its chief export, and by raiding English shipping. Edward hoped to weaken France by challenging the legitimacy of its king. His weapon was an argument based on genealogy. His mother, Isabella, was the daughter of Philip the Fair, king of France. In 1328 the death of Isabella's last brother extinguished the senior branch of the French royal family. Isabella might have been in line to inherit the crown had the French courts not decreed in 1316 that ancient custom prevented a woman from exercising or transmitting the right to royal authority in France. Isabella was, therefore, ignored and her cousin, Philip VI, was offered the throne of France. Edward took issue with this. He argued that since he was the grandson of the French king, he had a better right to the throne than Philip who was only the ex-king's nephew. England was much smaller than France, and Edward knew that he had no hope of taking France by storm. But simply by lodging a claim to the throne, he handicapped Philip. Philip could not risk doing anything that would alienate his vassals for fear that they would repudiate him and endorse Edward's claim.

Edward wanted to put pressure on Philip by leading a foray into French territory, but he had difficulty raising money for a war. In 1340 a naval battle near Sluys deprived the French of most of their ships, but it was not until 1346 that Edward was able to take advantage of France's vulnerability and invade Normandy. He planned nothing more than a quick raid, but his venture became a much larger and more dangerous enterprise than he had anticipated. A vastly superior French army cornered him at Crécy. Although numbers favored the French, Edward's longbowmen turned the tide of battle by slaughtering France's unsophisticated feudal cavalry. The surprising victory caused a lot of comment, but it left the political situation unchanged. He lacked the means to exploit his triumph and had no choice but to return to England. A year later he seized the French port at Calais. This proved to be his only lasting achievement. His war failed in its foreign policy objectives, but it was a success on the domestic front. England, in the 14th c., was infatuated with the legends of King Arthur, and Edward's subjects revelled in the romantic illusion that their valiant monarch was the reincarnation of England's mythical hero. He entered into the game with unrestrained enthusiasm. He gathered knights at a round table and enacted the feasts and tournaments of Camelot.

England's confidence in its monarchy was restored, and in 1357 its faith in the prowess of the royal blood was vindicated by another victory over France. Edward's son, the Black Prince, destroyed a huge French army at Poitiers and brought the king of France, John the Good, captive to England. The great battles of Edward's reign enhanced the reputation of tho English monarchy, but they brought England no control over France and no new resources. In 1360 a deteriorating situation at home forced him, despite his record of military victories, to make peace with France. His reign, which had begun so forcefully, trailed off to a dismal end. In 1369 Charles V of France, who was a far more capable ruler than his father John, broke the truce by attacking England's fiefs in Gascony. Edward, feeling the effects of age, turned for help to his son, the Black Prince. The prince was a vigorous soldier in whose hands England's future seemed to be safe, but in

1367 the heir to the throne contracted an illness that slowly deprived him of the strength to lead his father's government. Edward, who had become senile, could do nothing for himself. His mistress exploited his weakness, and his sons dissipated their energies by fighting among themselves. In 1376 a scandalized and desperate parliament insisted that the royal government be reorganized. Little was achieved, however, for no leader had enough authority to do more than try to hold things together.

The deaths of the Black Prince in 1376 and Edward a year later did nothing to help the situation. The heir to the throne was the Black Prince's young son, Richard II. Since he was not yet old enough to rule, England continued to labor under the burden of a weak regency government. Despite Edward's military achievements, kingly virtues, and great popularity, his reign set England on a disastrous course. The fight that Edward had picked continued for a hundred years, and in the end it profited nothing. Descendants of his sons fought over the throne, and civil war plagued the nation until 1485. Stability did not return until Henry Tudor exterminated the last of Edward's line and established a new dynasty in England.

2H6 2.2.10, 46. 1H6 1.3.10, 2.4.84, 2.5.66, 76. R2. 2H4 4.3.128. H5 1.1.90, 1.2.162, 248, 2.4.93.

Edward IV, (1442–1483), Edward, earl of March, Edward of York, first king from the Yorkist branch of England's royal family. Edward was the beneficiary of a long struggle between his father, Duke Richard of York, and King Henry VI. Richard was ten years older than the king, his cousin, but he was the more vigorous, competent man. When Henry lapsed into a catatonic depression in 1453, Richard, his nearest relative, became his guardian. Since Henry was in failing health and had no children, Richard expected soon to accede to Henry's throne. His plans were complicated by Henry's queen, Margaret, who bore Henry a son in the midst of his illness. When Henry recovered his health and reclaimed his authority, Richard was left in a difficult position. An infant prince blocked York's path to the throne, and Queen Margaret was determined to end any threat York posed to her family. In May 1455 Richard's men clashed with members of the king's Lancastrian party at St. Albans, and the skirmish at St. Albans began a generation-long civil war that historians have dubbed the War of the Roses. Henry's health broke under the strain of the conflict. His illness returned, and Richard resumed control of England's government until Henry recovered in February, 1456. Margaret and Henry then established a base at Kenilworth castle and waged a campaign to undercut Richard.

On 10 July 1460, the Yorkists scored a major victory in a battle fought at Northampton, and Richard seized the opportunity to convene a parliament and put forward his claim to the throne Henry occupied. The deposition of a king—even an incompetent one—seemed too drastic an action to the leaders of parliament. They induced Richard to accept a compromise whereby Henry would remain king but disinherit his son, Edward, in Richard's favor. Richard did not live long enough to enter on the office that was dangled before him. He was killed in a skirmish at Wakefield on 30 December 1460, and his claim to the throne passed to his 18-year-old son, Edward. His mother was a Neville, and the Nevilles became the young duke of York's chief backers. In the 1450s the Nevilles had triumphed over their chief competitors, the Percies, and quarrels with Henry VI's favorite, the duke of Somerset, had estranged them from the house of Lancaster. Edward's cousin, Richard Neville, the earl of Warwick, was one of the richest and most ambitious men in England. Warwick was fourteen years older than Edward, and his age and resources made him the natural leader of the Yorkist faction. Warwick drove Henry VI from England and helped Edward to the throne.

Edward owed a great debt to Warwick, but, as the king matured, he became his own man and worked to distance himself from 'the Kingmaker.' He was particularly at odds with Warwick on questions of foreign policy. Warwick favored an alliance with Louis XI of France.

Edward preferred to maintain England's traditional posture of hostility to France and to help the dukes of Burgundy and Brittany contain Louis XI. He also ignored what Warwick considered to be an invaluable diplomatic opportunity. Since the king was a bachelor, he could have bartered marriage for an important foreign alliance. Edward, however, chose his heart's desire over politics. On 1 May 1464, he secretly wed an English widow, Elizabeth Woodville Gray—without consulting Warwick or his other advisors. The union made no political sense, and it embarrassed Warwick. He was in France when it took place, suing for the hand of a French princess for his king. When news of Edward's marriage reached France in October, 1464, Warwick was humiliated. He grew angrier when he returned to England to find the court filling up with his natural enemies, the queen's relatives. Warwick continued to urge Edward to make peace with France, but the Woodvilles were related to the dukes of Burgundy and wanted England to help Burgundy and Brittany against France.

On 3 July 1568, Edward made a commitment to Burgundy and pledged his sister, Margaret, to Duke Charles the Bold. Louis XI tested Edward's commitment to his new friends by attacking Brittany. When Edward failed to come to Brittany's rescue, its duke capitulated. Burgundy lost confidence in its ally, and Louis convinced Burgundy to stand aloof if war broke out between England and France. Warwick concluded that he had little hope of steering England in the direction that he thought it should go so long as Edward remained king. Having helped him to the throne, Warwick saw no reason why he should not replace him with a more obliging prince. Edward's younger brother, George, duke of Clarence, was willing to be Warwick's instrument, and he bound himself to Warwick by marrying the earl's daughter. Edward got wind of the plot and indicted Warwick for treason. Warwick defied the king and refused to present himself for trial. Tempers cooled when both sides realized that they were not yet prepared for a showdown. A ceremony of reconciliation was staged on 16 January 1468, but the peace was short lived.

In April of 1470, Edward expelled Warwick from England. Louis XI offered to help the earl against Edward, but insisted that Warwick avoid the appearance of treason by embracing the Lancastrian cause. Warwick joined forces with the exiled Lancastrian queen, Margaret, and in September of 1470 he returned to England at the head of a Lancastrian army. Edward was taken by surprise and fled to the continent. Henry VI was liberated from captivity and restored to the throne. Edward found temporary refuge in the Lowlands, but those to whom he turned for help were slow to take his side for fear of offending France. It was not until Louis revealed his hostile intentions toward Burgundy that its duke concluded that he had nothing to lose by helping him. In March of 1471, Edward and a small army landed in the north of England. The Percies, who had no love for Warwick and the Nevilles, helped him organize his campaign, and Edward had no trouble persuading his shifty brother, Clarence, to defect from the Neville camp. Clarence had sided with Warwick because Warwick had promised him the throne. Once Warwick became a Lancastrian, the throne was no longer his to offer. On 11 April 1471, Edward occupied London and recaptured Henry VI. Three days later he killed Warwick at the battle of Barnet. Queen Margaret and her son Prince Edward arrived in England too late to help Warwick. They took their own stand at Tewkesbury where the Lancastrian prince was executed and his mother captured. Edward marched to London to celebrate his victories, and on the night of his arrival Henry VI died. The circumstances surrounding Henry's passing are unknown, but his death left Edward the undisputed king of England.

Once secure at home, he undertook to punish France for its intervention in his affairs. Burgundy suggested a joint venture against Louis, but lack of funds prevented Edward from dispatching an army to his continental port at Calais until July 1475. By that time Duke Charles had become involved in serious fighting on the eastern frontiers of his domains and was not able to be of much help against the French. Louis preferred diplomacy to battle and seized the opportunity to invite the English to parley. The resulting Treaty of Picquigny (29 August 1475) was a coup for Edward. Louis agreed to pay him a large annual annuity in exchange for peace. The French money enabled Edward to court popularity at home by reducing the tax burden on his English subjects. In 1477 Charles the Bold was killed in battle, and Louis XI annexed a great part of Burgundy. This caused a foreign policy crisis for Edward's government. England lost its strongest potential ally against France, and France became the largest and best organized nation on the continent. Louis pressed his advantage by urging England's perennial enemies, the Scots, to take up arms. Edward had tried to negotiate a peace with Scotland by arranging a marriage between one of his daughters and the heir to the Scottish throne, but James III of Scotland was not firmly enough in control of the feisty Scottish clans to guarantee that treaties could be kept. In the midst of Edward's negotiations with Scotland his brother, Clarence, created a serious complication.

The Neville wife whom Clarence had wed in the hope of winning England's throne died in 1476, and Clarence was eager for a new bride who would advance his political ambitions. Edward, who had ample reason to distrust Clarence, forbade him the two richest prizes available: the heiress of Burgundy and the sister of the king of Scotland. Clarence accused him of tyranny, and Edward ordered his arrest on suspicion of treason. On 19 January 1478, Clarence was convicted before parliament and quietly executed in the Tower of London. England's relationship with Scotland deteriorated, and in 1479 Edward considered a declaration of war against Scotland. Charles the Bold's heirs, Mary and Maximilian of Burgundy, confused the situation by requesting his help against France. Edward was unable to support two major campaigns and unable to choose between them. While he delayed trying to decide what to do, events sorted themselves out without him. On 27 March 1482, Mary of Burgundy died, and her country concluded a separate peace with France. Louis, freed from the fear of an Anglo-Burgundian alliance, stopped payment of the annuity and sent money to Scotland to fund raids into English territory. Edward had no time to work out a solution to these problems.

Late in March 1483, he fell ill. Reports of his symptoms are too vague to permit a secure diagnosis of the malady to which he succumbed on 9 April 1483. On his death bed he vainly tried to make peace between the warring factions at his court, but he delayed too long in making arrangements to secure the future of his dynasty. Since he was only 41 and had always enjoyed robust health and enthusiastic appetites, he had not contemplated an early death and had not made plans for the succession of an underage son. The unstable situation at his court guaranteed that his demise would be followed by a vicious struggle for control of Edward V, the 13-year-old heir to the throne, and resumption of the War of the Roses that had brought Edward to power. In the fighting that ensued his family was exterminated and England's aristocracy decimated.

The Tudors, who wrested the crown from the hands of his brother, Richard III, earned the gratitude of their subjects by bringing much needed stability to English affairs. Tudor historians regarded the Yorkist past with disdain and had little affection for Edward IV. They accused him of being indolent, irresolute, avaricious, self-indulgent, and much more inclined to drift than lead. Modern historians have moderated the harsh Tudor portrait. In Edward's defense it can be said that he kept England out of wars, maintained a difficult truce among powerful factions of the nobility, and found sources of income that freed his subjects from burdensome taxes. Sh. treated him kindly, but primarily because Sh. wanted to cast Richard III, the king whom the Tudors killed for usurping Edward's throne, in the blackest possible light.

2H6. 3H6. R3.

Edward V, *R3,* (1470–1483), elder of Edward IV's two sons by Elizabeth Woodville Gray.

Young Edward was England's king for only about two months, during which time his mother's family carried on a power struggle with Edward IV's brother, Richard Crookback, duke of Gloucester. Richard captured Edward when the boy's Woodville uncles tried to bring him to London for his coronation, and the duke confined him and his younger brother (another Richard) in the Tower of London. Parliament succumbed to Gloucester's argument that Elizabeth's marriage to Edward IV was invalid, declared her sons illegitimate, and deprived Edward V of his title. This cleared the way for Gloucester, the boy's uncle, to be crowned Richard III. The unwillingness of important nobles to submit to a regency dominated by the unpopular Woodvilles may have had something to do with the speed with which Edward IV's sons were shoved aside. The boys were last observed playing in a courtyard in the Tower of London in July of 1483.

Many of their contemporaries believed that Richard ordered their deaths and had them secretly buried in unmarked graves on the Tower grounds. Rumors that the boys had escaped were also current, and various pretenders appeared from time to time to claim their inheritance. The mystery of what happened to them remains unsolved. In 1647 bones were discovered in the Tower that at the time were believed to be those of the princes. These relics disappeared, but Charles II gave a second set that came to light in 1674 a royal burial in Westminster Abbey. They were exhumed and subjected to scientific examination in 1933. The forensic evidence was consistent with the possibility that the fragments are the remains of the ill-starred princes. It is unlikely that the boys escaped death in the Tower. Elizabeth Woodville Gray, their mother, tried to marry her daughter Elizabeth to Henry Tudor and to make him king in Richard's place. She would not have done that had she believed her sons to be alive. Richard III's responsibility for the princes' fate cannot be proved, but it is unlikely that anyone would have taken it upon himself to murder them without Richard's consent.

Edward Confessor (d. 1066), Edward the Confessor, last English king of the Anglo-Saxon dynasty of Wessex, son of Ethelred II. He lived much of his early life in Normandy, but in 1041 Hardecanute invited his return and he was crowned the following year. Most of his reign was spent juggling his power relationship with Godwin, earl of Wessex. Edward had married Godwin's daughter and was supported for the throne by him, but he sometimes resisted Godwin's influence. His appointment of Tostig, Godwin's son, as earl of Northumbria resulted in a rebellion because of Tostig's oppression and Edward was forced to exile him. Shortly after, he died and was succeeded by Godwin's son Harold, who would lose his kingdom to William the Conqueror. As his sobriquet implies, Edward was considered to be a pious king. He founded Westminster Abbey and was canonized within a century of his death. *Mac:* Edward supported the military actions by Malcolm Canmore against Macbeth, thus helping keep the Celtic claimants from the throne of Scotland.

H8 4.1.90: The crown of Edward Confessor was used at the coronations of medieval England's kings and queens. In 1649 Oliver Cromwell beheaded Charles I, established a republican government for England, and destroyed the ancient crown that was the symbol of monarchy. The 'St. Edward's crown' currently displayed in the Tower of London is a reconstruction made in 1660 for the coronation of Charles II.

Edward, earl of March, *2H6, 3H6,* see Edward IV.

Edward, earl of Stafford and duke of Buckingham, *H8,* (d. 1521), eldest son and heir of Henry, the earl of Stafford and duke of Buckingham who was executed in 1483 for raising a revolt against Richard III. The estates and titles that Richard confiscated as punishment for Henry's treason were restored to Henry's son by King Henry VIII, and the king appointed his new duke of Buckingham Lord High Constable. Edward had more good fortune than good sense. His arrogant conduct made him an enemy in Cardinal Wolsey, and Wolsey engineered his downfall. Edward, who gloried openly in his royal descent through John of Gaunt, might have been indiscreet in discussing his place in the line of succession to the throne. An anonymous letter from a member of his household to Cardinal Wolsey set in motion the events that culminated in Henry's decision to behead him for treason.

Edward of York, *2H6, 3H6,* see Edward IV.

Edward Plantagenet, *3H6 2.2.61, R3 1.2.118,* see Edward, Prince, (1).

Edward, Prince, 1) (1453–1471), Henry VI's son. In 1460 Henry VI was captured by Richard of York at the battle of Northampton. Prince Edward and Queen Margaret fled to Scotland and abandoned Henry to the mercy of his enemies. Richard contemplated usurping the crown, but he was persuaded by parliament, which had respect for the tradition that the king's person was sacred, to allow Henry to live out his reign. Henry remained nominal king, but was compelled to disinherit his son and acknowledge Richard of York as his heir. Richard did not survive to profit from this arrangement, for he was killed at Wakefield two months after capturing Henry. Queen Margaret reorganized the Lancastrian forces in Scotland, and on 17 February 1461, at the second battle of St. Albans, she rescued her husband. Margaret failed to press her advantage, and York's heir, Edward, persuaded London to acknowledge him as king. On 29 March 1461, at the battle of Towton, Edward IV drove the Lancastrians back into exile. Henry took refuge in Scotland, while Margaret and Prince Edward went to France to search for allies. When Henry was captured during a foray into England in 1465, what little enthusiasm Margaret had been able to generate for her husband's cause faded. She and the prince retired to live in obscurity on one of her relative's estates.

In 1470, their fortunes suddenly took a turn for the better. The earl of Warwick broke with Edward IV and declared himself Lancaster's champion. Warwick raised an army, invaded England, and liberated Henry from the Tower of London. Despite this encouraging beginning, the Lancastrian revival faltered. Warwick was killed at the battle of Barnet on Easter Sunday, 1471, and Margaret and Prince Edward landed in England just in time to be overwhelmed by Yorkist forces at Tewkesbury (4 May 1471). He was captured and killed at Tewkesbury, and his death removed the last reason Edward IV had for allowing Henry VI to live. On 22 May 1471, Edward extinguished the Lancastrian male line by murdering Henry in his prison in the Tower.

3H6, R3: Sh. says that Richard Crookback arranged the deaths of Henry and Prince Edward to clear his own path to the throne (*3H6 3.2.130*), and Sh. follows Edward Halle's *Union of the Two Nobel and Illustre Famelies of Lancastre and York* in reporting that Richard and his brothers, Edward and George, murdered the Lancastrian prince in cold blood. One contemporary source, however, acquits Richard of personal involvement in Prince Edward's death, and it seems unlikely that Richard could have plotted his own succession so far in advance.

2) *3H6 5.7ff., R3,* Edward IV's son, see Edward V.

Edward shovel-boards, *MWW 1.1.142–3,* shillings from the reign of Edward VI. They were large and when smoothed out by wear were used in a game. Players slid them on a board marked with lines. The game plainly evolved into shuffle-board, or to the desk-top football children play with triangles of paper or a broken Popsicle stick.

Edward, the Black Prince, (1330–1376), Edward of Woodstock, King Edward III's eldest son. His sobriquet derived from the black armor that became his trademark. The large ruby that is set in the front of Britain's Imperial State Crown is alleged originally to have adorned the prince's helmet. The same gem is also said to have been worn later by Henry V at the battle of Agincourt. In 1346, when he was only sixteen, the Black Prince inaugurated what was to be a brilliant military career. He held a command at Crécy, where his father won England's first great victory in the Hundred Years' War. Edward III granted his stalwart son the first duchy created in England (Cornwall, 1337), and the prince was among the first group of royal companions to be inducted into Edward's exclusive organization for the practice of chivalry, the Order of the Garter. The heir to the throne deserved the honors he collected, for he had all the knightly virtues his father cherished. In 1355 the Black Prince assumed command of the English armies in Gascony, and in 1356, at Poitiers, he won a victory that was the equal of his father's triumph at Crécy. He returned to England the following year with John the Good, king of France, among his captives. Edward dubbed his son 'Prince of Aquitaine' and sent him back to France to try to recover the vast duchy of Aquitaine that had once belonged to England.

The prince established a court at Bordeaux and threw himself into struggles with the Gascon nobles. In 1367 he fought in Spain as an ally of Pedro the Cruel of Castile. During the campaign he contracted an illness from which he never recovered. In 1371, finding himself unequal to the increasingly difficult physical challenge of maintaining order in Gascony, he relinquished his post to his brother, John of Gaunt. He died in England on 8 July 1376. His father, who by then had lapsed into senility, outlived him by a year and bequeathed the throne to the Black Prince's 9-year-old son, the ill-fated Richard II.

2H6 2.2.11. 1H6 2.5.64. H5 1.2.105, 2.4.56, 4.7.91–92.

Egeon, *Err,* merchant of Syracuse, father of the twins Antipholus. In F1 he is called the 'Merchant of Siracusa' initially and not named until *1.1.140.* Captured in Ephesus during a dispute between the two cities, he pleads to the duke that he is searching for his son who went in search of his brother five years past. During a shipwreck his sons were separated, he raising one and the mother disappearing with the other. This speech serves as a prologue to establish the comic premise so that the play can 'hit the ground running.' Despite his plea, he is to pay a ransom or die. The Duke, however, does allow the merchant a day's freedom to gather the ransom. He reappears at play's end in imminent danger of execution, but is saved as the confusions over who is who are resolved. Egeon has no equivalent in Sh.'s source, Plautus' *Menæchmi,* though resemblances have been noted between Egeon and Apollonius in John Gower's *Confessio Amantis.* Ægeus, father of Theseus, or the Ægean sea, may have provided the name of the merchant.

Egeus, *MND,* father of Hermia. Early in the play he demands his daughter be put to death under the ancient law of Athens for willfully disobeying him. Later, when Demetrius has come to love Helena, he relents and allows his daughter to marry Lysander. The name is borrowed from Plutarch's biography of Theseus, whose father was Ægeus, ruler of Athens.

Eglamour 1) *TGV,* courtly nobleman who helps Silvia escape from Milan. She seems to think he is brave and courageous, but when the outlaws capture her, he flees, never to reappear. Some critics think that this is an inconsistency of character, yet it could easily be yet another of Sh.'s playings with fair face and false heart, this time for humor's sake. The name may have had a humorous implication. In Thomas Malory's *Le Morte d'Arthur,* 'Merlin,' there is a runaway knight named Egglame.

2) *TGV 1.2.9,* 'Sir E.,' prospective husband for Julia, probably not the same man as Silvia's friend. If he is not, the use of the same name for both is a large oversight, or perhaps indicative of the state of the text as a revision. If he is, then he changes affections as easily as Proteus.

Egypt, 1) ancient north African nation whose territory is defined by the valley and delta of the Nile river. Unique natural advantages permitted civilization to evolve in Egypt and neighboring Sumer before it appeared elsewhere in the west.

Annually flooding rivers constantly renewed the fertility of the soil in both countries. This made it possible for primitive agriculturalists to support large populations in permanent settlements and to marshal the resources to create sophisticated cultures. Since Egypt was nearly self-sufficient and separated from other nations by huge expanses of desert, it had little contact with the outside world. That situation changed about 1750 BC, when a Semitic tribe crossed the Sinai and conquered the delta. The Egyptians endured a century and a half of foreign domination before they drove out the invaders and embarked on their own program of empire building. Egypt's influence spread as far east as the Euphrates river and endured into the 12th c. BC. In the 8th c. the Assyrians dominated Egypt. After Assyria's fall, the Persians made Egypt a satrapy within their empire.

Alexander the Great conquered Persia and Egypt in the 4th c. BC. After Alexander's death his friend Ptolemy set himself up as a pharaoh and restored Egypt's independence and power. Ptolemy's dynasty endured until 30 BC, and it was only after a long and ingenious fight that his descendant, Cleopatra, yielded its prerogatives to the Roman conqueror Octavius-Augustus. Augustus ended the succession of pharaohs and made Egypt a province ruled by a Roman governor. Sh.'s vague description of the country suggests that he had read little about it. His impression of its appearance probably derived from the Bible.

MND 5.1.11 (Add. 7), 'a brow of E.,' a pagan or dark face, a gypsy face (they were believed to have originated there). *AYLI 2.5.58,* 'the firstborn of E.,' an obscure reference to the killing of the Egyptian firstborn by God in order to force Pharaoh to release the Israelites (Exod. 11; 12). Possibly a particular preacher is being mocked by Jaques. *Ant:* Egypt is portrayed as a decadent kingdom where splendor, riches and the indulgence of personal pleasure corrupts the Romans. *H8 2.3.93.*

2) *Ant,* Cleopatra as queen and therefore personification of the nation.

3) *Ant 2.1.37,* 'E.'s widow,' Ptolemy XIII's widow, Cleopatra. She was earlier the widow of Ptolemy XII.

Egyptian, 1) (n.) F1 'Ægyptian,' native of Egypt. *TN 4.2.45,* 'the Egyptians in their fog,' a reference to Exodus, 10:21, in which Moses brings thick darkness onto Egypt for three days, making it impossible for them to move about. Only the Isrælites had light in their homes. This curse was part of his campaign to persuade Pharaoh to release the Israelites. *Oth 3.4.56:* as Egypt was considered a land of magic, Othello ascribes a mystic origin to the handkerchief. A gypsy could also be meant here.

Per 12.83: it is argued that this passage was intended to refer to the skill of Egyptian physicians and not to an Egyptian patient. The story may have come originally from the *Philopseudes* ('The Lover of Lies') by Lucian. In folklore, Egyptian priests and physicians have always been said to have occult powers. The word Gypsy derived from Egyptian because of the racial resemblance and the Romany people's perceived interest in magic. It is possible that E. means 'Gypsy' here. Pl.: *Ant 3.7.63, 3.13.167.*

2) *Ant 2.2.225, 4.13.10,* Cleopatra.

3) (adj.) of or pertaining to Egypt. *TN 5.1.116,* 'th' E. thief,' an allusion to a story in which the thief, finding his life endangered, killed his beloved in order to have her available to him in the next life or to prevent other men from enjoying her as the thief had. In Heliodorus' *Ethiopica,* which was translated by 1570 and appeared in a second edition in 1587, the thief is Theagenes and the woman Chariclea. In Herodotus' *Persian Wars,* 2, 121, an Egyptian thief is forced to behead his brother to escape identification, but this is less likely to be the allusion. One is also reminded of the tyrant Sardanapalus in Byron, who destroyed every thing he loved in order to prevent its being loved by anyone else. Variations of the story are widespread, but Sh.'s allusion seems to be specific to Heliodorus and familiar to his audience. *Ant 1.2.110, 2.6.64, 126, 2.7.100, 3.10.2, 5.2.204.*

Elbe, *H5 1.2.45, 1.2.52,* river that flows from Prague to Hamburg where it empties into the North Sea west of the Danish peninsula.

Elbow, *MM,* the bumbling duke's constable. He is patterned on Dogberry: he mispeaks himself and is urged by Escalus to hire other law officers as Dogberry did. However, his role in the drama is even more peripheral to the plot than Dogberry's. Probably this is an attempt to reprise the foolish constable without a comic actor like William Kempe to make it memorable and it is therefore abbreviated to a mere thematic overtone to the main plot. At *2.1.165,* for example, Escalus compares Elbow to justice and Pompey to iniquity. This may refer to morality play characters, but it certainly illustrates the unequal match between the corruption in Vienna and the shabby institutions that are supposed to ferret it out. Possibly the name suggests a constable's taking by the elbow in an arrest, as 'bum-baily' referred to a bailiff's coming up behind those he would arrest. It could also refer to a physical trait. Pompey says he is 'out at elbow' (*2.1.58*), meaning he has worn-out sleeves, is poor, or in bad condition.

Eleanor, *2H6 2.2.38,* see Mortimer, Eleanor.

Eleanor, Queen, *Jn,* (1122–1204), usually called 'Eleanor of Aquitaine,' duchess of Aquitaine and, successively, queen of France and queen of England. In 1137, when the death of her father, William X, duke of Aquitaine, made her the richest heiress in France, Louis VI, king of France, claimed her as his ward and arranged for her to marry his son, Louis VII. She and Louis were not compatible, and in 1151 they persuaded the pope to annul their union on the grounds of consanguinity. She promptly remarried—choosing young Henry of Anjou, heir to the kingdom of England and to a great many French fiefs. Her estates sprawled over much of the south of France, and when they were added to Henry's possessions, the English royal family controlled more French land than her ex-husband, the king of France. She had given Louis two daughters, and she bore Henry five sons. Two of them, Richard I 'the Lionhearted' and John, succeeded to the throne. Throughout her long life she searched for a political role. When Henry thwarted her ambition, she encouraged her sons to try to overthrow him. Henry survived the crisis and kept her confined for the rest of his life—fifteen years. After his death she emerged again as a public figure. She helped both Richard and John to the throne and actively opposed the barons who contemplated unseating John in favor of her grandson Arthur of Brittany. Arthur was captured by John while the youth was besieging his 80-year-old grandmother in the castle at Mirabeau. She died two years later, just as John's empire began to crumble.

Elephant, The, *TN 3.3.39, 48, 4.3.5,* inn supposedly in the 'south suburbs.' Sh. likely means in London, as he certainly has no knowledge of inns in Illyria. It was a common name, though 'The Elephant and the Castle' was more common. There was one in Fleet street in 1610, one in Newington (a south suburb) at least from the mid-1600s, and one in Cornhill in 1681. The specificity of the mention would seem to be another local allusion to an establishment well known to the Globe's patrons.

Elizabeth, *R3 4.3.41, 4.4.204,* 4.5.18, 5.8.29, (1465–1503), 'E. of York,' eldest daughter of Edward IV. Edward contemplated several important matches for her, but the political implications of her marriage were greatly increased after his death. The disappearance of her two brothers made her heir to her father's legacy, and contestants to the throne sought her hand to confirm the legitimacy of their succession. After Richard III's wife, Anne, died in 1485, it was rumored that he was tempted to flout public opinion and marry Elizabeth—even though she was his niece. If it was in his mind, he had not yet acted on it when the earl of Richmond killed him at the battle of Bosworth Field. Richmond, as king Henry VII, claimed Elizabeth. Their marriage united the houses of Lancaster and York and made her the mother of a Tudor dynasty.

Elizabeth I, *H8 5.4.3, 9,* (1533–1603), queen of England, the second of Henry VIII's daughters, the product of his union with Anne Boleyn. She was preceded on the throne by a younger half-brother, Edward VI, who died without issue in 1553, and an older half-sister Mary, who died childless in 1558. Elizabeth herself, by refusing to wed, willed the extinction of the Tudor dynasty. She guided England through a precarious period in history. The religious reformation that had spread across Europe in her father's day created bloody civil wars in France and Germany, but she kept England at peace. The queen was a Protestant, but was as strict with Puritan extremists as with 'papists' and punished religious dissenters only when their activities verged on treason. Since she was the most prominent European monarch to embrace Protestantism, religious considerations entered into most of her foreign policy decisions. France was torn by wars of religion that invited her intervention, but the French Protestant lords were a quarrelsome, unstable lot—as difficult to deal with as their Catholic kings. Philip of Spain proposed marriage, but, although she flirted to stall for time, she had no intention of falling into the clutches of the most rabidly Catholic monarch in Europe. England's relationship with Spain deteriorated badly when her councilors persuaded her to assist Protestant rebels trying to liberate the Netherlands from Spain.

In 1588 Philip went on the offensive, dispatching a great armada with orders to conquer England. The threat of invasion by a superior foreign power rallied Elizabeth's subjects, and when they defeated the Armada, they experienced a surge of patriotic feeling that swelled their confidence in their nation and their pride in its emerging culture. Sh. arrived in London to begin his career just before the Armada sailed, and the Elizabeth he came to know was the mature queen who headed a victorious state. Several of Sh.'s early plays were performed for her. According to legend, she was particularly taken with the character of Falstaff, which Sh. introduced in *1H4* under the name Oldcastle. *MWW* may have been written in response to Elizabeth's request for amorous adventures of the popular buffoon. Sh. is not known to have taken an active role in politics, but his plays were exploited by those who did. In 1601 the earl of Essex sponsored a revival of *R2.* The dramatization of the deposition of a king may have been intended to marshal support for Essex, who contemplated making a bid for Elizabeth's throne. She was aware of the political implications of the play, but she did not prohibit its performance or punish its author and players.

Sh. was at the height of his powers when she died in 1603, but at that time he wrote no known tribute to her, though he had earlier alluded to her with lavish praise in *MND* (see Cupid). His patron, the earl of Southampton, had been involved in Essex's treasonous projects, and Southampton spent the last two years of Elizabeth's reign in prison. His faction rejoiced at her demise and welcomed her successor, James I, the son of her cousin, Mary Queen of Scots. Southampton became one of James's favorite courtiers, and the new monarch's patronage extended to Sh.'s company. These circumstances have often been interpreted to mean that Sh. was a supporter of Essex against Elizabeth, but this is conjecture. *H8* ends with Elizabeth's baptism and a claim that her birth was an omen forecasting a glorious future for England—a future that had been Sh.'s youth.

Elizabeth, Queen, *R3,* see Gray, Lady.

Ellen, *2H4 3.2.6,* Justice Silence's daughter and Justice Shallow's god-daughter. Her father laments that she is a 'black ouzel,' a 'black bird.' Brunettes and dark complexions were not the fashion at the court of the red-headed Elizabeth I.

Elsinore, *Ham 1.2.173, 2.2.272, 371, 549,* setting for *Ham,* Helsingør, a seaport on the east coast of the island of Zealand (Sjaelland) in east Denmark, a little more than 20 mi. from Copenhagen. Helsingborg, Sweden is opposite the town and it has changed hands between Denmark and Sweden several times in its history. It was a trading port as early as the 8th c., but was burned in 1522 by troops from the city of Lübeck, capital of the Hanseatic League. Christian III, king of Denmark and Norway, recaptured it in 1535. The Kronborg castle, wherein most of the play takes place, was built in the latter part of the century. Its turrets served as a lighthouse and it served as a collection point for the tolls on ships passing into or out of the Baltic. English theater companies are known to have travelled there in 1585 and 1586. Some speculation exists that Sh. may have accompanied them, but there is no evidence supporting it. His descriptions of the castle have been accused of being inaccurate. It was damaged by fire in 1637, but restored by Christian IV. It is now a naval museum which holds frequent performances of Sh. Saxo Grammaticus, author of the *Historica Danica* (c. 1200), upon which *Ham* is based, was born in Elsinore.

Eltham, *1H6 1.1.170, 3.1.160,* royal residence south of London. Henry VI spent much of his childhood there.

Ely, cathedral city in Cambridgeshire about 70 mi. northeast of London. See Ely, Bishop of, *H5*; *R3*; *H8*.

Ely, Bishop of, 1) *R3* , John Morton (1420--1500), Oxford trained lawyer whose conspicuous talents early earned him the patronage of Thomas Bourchier, a relative of the royal family who rose to become archbishop of Canterbury and chancellor of England. Morton favorably impressed Henry VI, and after the rout of the Lancastrian forces in 1461 he followed Queen Margaret and Prince Edward into exile. In 1470 he helped to reconcile Margaret with her nemesis, the earl of Warwick. After the failure of Warwick's campaign to restore the Lancastrian monarchy, Morton made his peace with Edward IV and the house of York. Edward sent him on diplomatic missions and in 1479 presented him for consecration as bishop of Ely. Following Edward's death Richard ordered Morton's imprisonment, but Morton escaped by encouraging his jailor, Buckingham, to rebel against Richard. When Buckingham's coup failed, Morton fled to Flanders and provided the earl of Richmond with information that helped him avoid a trap that Richard had set for him. Henry of Richmond repaid the favor. Once he ascended the throne as Henry VII, he recalled Morton and made him a trusted advisor. In 1486 Morton succeeded his patron, Bourchier, as archbishop of Canterbury and in 1487 as Lord Chancellor. He became a cardinal in 1493 and served a term as chancellor of the university of Oxford.

2) *H5,* John Fordham (d. 1425), canon of the cathedral at York and Richard II's secretary. He was consecrated bishop of Durham in 1382, and in 1386 Richard appointed him treasurer of England. As one of Richard's intimates, he was a convenient target for those who sought for ways (short of direct, treasonous attacks on the king) to express their disapproval of the king's policies. In 1388 Richard's enemies forced Fordham from his government office and persuaded the pope to transfer him from Durham to the less prestigious see at Ely.

3) *H8,* Nicholas West (1461–1533), chaplain to Katherine of Aragon. West supported the queen in her fight to prevent her husband from divorcing her. He died shortly after England separated from Rome and Henry wed Anne Boleyn.

Ely House, *R2 1.4.57, 2.1.217,* London residence of the bishops of Ely. It was in the district of Holborn west of the city wall. John of Gaunt's presence in Ely House at the time of his death is explained by the fact that the bishops rented the facility when they were not in residence.

Elysium, the Elysian Fields, a fabled land, just beyond the horizon, to which the heroes of Greek mythology were translated without dying to spend eternity under the beneficent rule of Rhadamanthus. The name derives from Gr. *eleusis* 'arrival,' a place where people gather. Homer describes it as blessed islands in the Western Ocean where the weather is always moderate. As other Greek sources set Elysium on the Fortunate Isles, the myth may have influenced or been the source of the myth of Atlantis. In Latin sources it resembles the Christian heaven, an abode for the spirits of the blessed. Tartarus was its opposite.

TGV 2.7.38. 2H6 3.2.403. 3H6 1.2.30. Ven 600. H5 4.1.271. TN 1.2.3. Cym 5.5.191, 'shadows of E.,' spirits of the dead. *TNK 5.6.95.*

Emilia, 1) *Err,* F1 'Æmilia,' abbess of Ephesus, former wife of Egeon, and mother of the Antipholuses. She does not appear until the last act when she lectures Adriana on jealousy and a woman's role and unknowingly orders her long lost son to leave the sanctuary of the priory. when she recognizes Egeon, however, she explains how kidnappers stole Antipholus of Ephesus and Dromio from her after the shipwreck that separated her from her husband and Antipholus of Syracuse. The choice of making her an Abbess may have been inspired by memory of the temple of Diana in Ephesus, as well as that city's reputation as a center for the practice of magic mentioned in *Ephesians.* There are also instructions on marital obligations in Paul's epistle.

2) *Oth,* Iago's wife and attendant of Desdemona. A worldly woman with a sharp tongue, Emilia is loyal to her mistress, but unwittingly provides her husband with the handkerchief which will drive Othello into jealous murder. Iago seems to suspect her of betraying him with Othello, but this is not followed up. Though she admits her willingness to commit adultery, this seems merely to contrast Desdemona's purity with a more cynical view. Emilia is much like such characters as Juliet's nurse, who accentuates the nobility or purity of the person she serves. Emilia becomes most interesting when Iago's monstrosity is revealed, instantly exposing him and setting aside all pretense of wifely loyalty. The enraged Iago stabs her for this and Emilia dies requesting she be laid beside her mistress.

3) *WT,* lady-in-waiting for Hermione. The name Æmilia appears in Plutarch, from which Sh. got most of his names for the play. Most suggestive is Plutarch's life of Æmilius Paulus, which, with a little tinkering would provide the names of two female characters in the play.

4) *TNK,* 'Queen E.,' sister of Hippolyta. Both Palamon and Arcite fall in love with her, destroying their friendship and running headlong into tragedy. She is not a particularly interesting love object, seeming to have no preference for either man and totally accepting everything that happens to her as the gods' will. She is somewhat sympathetic as fate buffets her, but very passive, possibly the result of the play's likely dual authorship. Her name and character, however, do derive almost entirely from the source Chaucer's *Knyghtes Tale,* in which she is similarly pale.

Emily, *TNK,* see Emilia 4).

Emmanuel, clerk of Chatham, *2H6,* character whom Sh. invents to illustrate his belief that Cade and his rebels were fools and enemies of civilization. Emanuel is indicted before Cade on a charge of being able to read, write, and keep account books. Cade's men did try to disrupt the machinery of royal taxation by destroying government records and looting lawyers' offices, but their actions were crude attempts at economic and political reforms, not a condemnation of literacy. The term 'clerk' could be applied in medieval England to any man who had some formal education, and it did not necessarily imply priestly status. Medieval schools were under the control of the church, and boys admitted to them routinely underwent tonsuring, the first of the seven ceremonies that led to full ordination. Tonsured men could claim some of the legal privileges of clergy, but they could also marry and have secular careers. Many were office workers for whom the title 'clerk' had much the same meaning that it has today.

Emperal, *Tit 4.3.93,* comic mispronunciation of 'emperor.'

Emperor, 1) ancient Roman title. During the period of the Roman Republic an *imperator* (from which 'emperor' derives) was a man who held an important military command. Octavius

Augustus created the Roman empire by acquiring military authority in key Roman provinces. Octavius became known as 'the' *imperator* because he held *imperium* over most of the empire. Since he delegated the management of armies to his assistants, his title lost some of its military aura and became a term designating the state's chief executive. *Tit 1.1.229.*

2) *Tit 1.1.283, 292, 296,* see Saturninus.

3) *Ant 2.7.99, 3.7.61, 79, 4.6.28, 4.8.1, 4.15.90, 127, 5.2.75,* see Antony, Mark.

4) *Ant 5.2.110,* see Octavius (later Augustus) Cæsar.

5) *Cym 1.6.188, 3.5.21, 3.7.1,* Augustus Cæsar.

Emperor (Holy Roman), medieval royal title. The office of emperor of Rome lapsed in western Europe in 476 with the deposition of Romulus Augustulus. In 800 the papacy revived it for the Frankish king Charlemagne, and it passed to the heirs of the eastern portion of his empire. For much of the medieval period the title was used by men who were little more than German kings. See Emperor 3), 4), 8).

1) *TGV 1.3.27, 38, 41, 58,* ruler to whose court Proteus has gone and to which Antonio sends Valentine for his education. Apparently the Duke of Milan is meant, though he is not called Emperor after this scene. Charles V, crowned Holy Roman Emperor in 1530, was also ruler of Milan as the heir to the Spanish throne, after the defeat of Francis I at Pavia in 1525 and after the Peace of Cambrai in 1529. A puppet ruler of the Sforza family ruled locally until 1535, when Francesco Sforza died and Milan remained under Spanish jurisdiction until the War of the Spanish Succession in 1714.

2) *1H6 5.1.2. H5 4.1.43, 5.0.38.* Sigismund (1368–1437), Holy Roman Emperor (1411–1437). The imperial title gave Sigismund nominal precedence, but no real power, over the kings of Europe. Sigismund hoped that by finding opportunities to function as an international leader he could create precedents that would add substance to his office. A crisis within the church gave him an excellent excuse to exercise imperial leadership. In 1378 a challenge to the validity of a papal election had led to the establishment of rival popes at Rome and Avignon—and, ultimately, at Pisa. The 'Great Schism' defied solution for thirty years. The longer it lasted, the more it endangered the practice of religion, and every nation in Europe was equally affected. Since papal claimants could only be taken seriously if they attracted followers, Sigismund's plan was to convince the leaders of Europe to agree to support one candidate and ignore all others. An international congress provided the most convenient forum for negotiating a pan-European consensus, and in 1415 Sigismund presided at the opening of a meeting of representatives of kings, universities, and ecclesiastical institutions at Constance, Switzerland. By chairing such a council, Sigismund at least appeared to preside over Europe. If his council provided the long-sought end to the schism, it would bolster the prestige of his imperial office. As peace among the nations represented at the council was crucial to its success, Sigismund paid state visits to France and England in May 1416 to mediate an end to the Hundred Years' War. Many things worked against his success, but he did not help his cause by insisting that his hosts take part in ceremonies acknowledging the superiority of his rank to theirs.

3) *Jn 1.1.100,* Henry VI (1165–1197), second emperor of the Hohenstaufen dynasty. Henry's father, Frederick Barbarossa (d. 1190), died leading troops into Asia Minor for the third crusade. Henry spent most of his reign consolidating his hold on Italy and Sicily, his wife's patrimony. English missions to the German imperial court, like the one Sh. mentions, were common. England and Germany shared a dislike for their common neighbor, France, and their ruling families intermarried to foster good diplomatic relations.

4) *H8 3.2.319, 4.2.110,* see Charles the Emperor.

Empress, 1) *Tit 1.1.317,* title for the wife of the head of the ancient Roman state.

2) *Tit,* see Tamora.

3) *H5 5.0.30,* Sh.'s flattering allusion to his queen, Elizabeth I. When *H5* was first performed, nationalistic passions were high. England was waiting for news from a campaign led by Elizabeth's 'Cæsar,' the earl of Essex. Essex had been sent to Ireland to suppress a rebellion headed by the earl of Tyrone.

4) *Ant 3.11.33, 4.16.74, 5.2.70,* see Cleopatra.

Enceladus, *Tit 4.2.92,* one of the Titans, a race of divine giants who, according to Greek mythology, made war on the Olympian gods. Either Jupiter, Hercules, or Minerva struck down Enceladus. He was buried under Mt. Etna and it was thought that when he moved there was an earthquake. Eruptions were the hissing of his breath. He is mentioned in the passage about Rumour (q.v.) in Virgil's *Æneid* 4.179, in Ariosto's *Orlando Furioso* and Sannazaro's pastorals. He is also mentioned (along with Capaneus) in the ancient Greek *Batrachomyomachia* 'Battle of the Frogs and Mice' l. 283, a mock epic poem anciently attributed to Homer but dating to about 480 BC.

Endymion, *MV 5.1.109,* son of Æthlius or Zeus and Calyce. The moon (Selene, identified with Diana) looked down upon the handsome man sleeping as he tended his flocks on Mt. Latmos. She fell in love, descended, kissed him, and watched over him. In some versions he is the father of fifty children by her. Her repeated absences from the sky provoked Jupiter to give the man a choice between death or perpetual sleep. Thus he slept eternally, never aging in his cave. The story comes from Ovid, Pausanias, Apollonius, and Apollodorus. John Lyly's comedy *Endimion, the Man in the Moon* (1588) is thought to have influenced Sh. Modern readers are more familiar with John Keats' poem based on the myth.

England, 1) Sh.'s native land. Since Sh. wrote for an English audience composed largely of Londoners and courtiers, it is not surprising that his history plays are blatantly nationalistic and attentive to sensitive issues of party politics. Sh.'s England was not the modern nation of Britain. Tudor England ruled Wales, but Ireland resisted English occupation, and Scotland was an independent, hostile country. The people of Wales, Scotland, and Ireland shared a Celtic heritage that distinguished them from the English. 'Angle-land' was established in the 6th c. when Germanic tribes of Angles, Saxons, and Jutes crossed the English channel to occupy the old Roman province of Britain. The newcomers evicted or assimilated the older Romano-Celtic populations. Scotland and Ireland, which had never been part of the Roman empire, defended themselves against the newcomers and provided a haven for refugees. Wales, which had been loosely integrated into the Roman system, asserted its independence as a Celtic nation.

The Anglo-Saxons divided Roman Britain into a number of independent kingdoms, and fought among themselves until the Viking invasions of the 8th c. altered the political landscape. The Vikings destroyed all of the Saxon states but Wessex, modern Devon and Cornwall. After a brief period of Viking dominance, the kings of Wessex re-emerged to unite England under a single Anglo-Saxon monarch. The death of Edward the Confessor in 1066 extinguished the native dynasty and precipitated a struggle for the throne. William, duke of Normandy, whose ancestors had been Vikings, conquered England and added French feudal institutions to the island's culture. The Normans established strong military zones, or 'marches,' along England's borders with Wales and Scotland, where fighting was virtually continuous. In 1283 Edward I beat the Welsh into temporary submission. He hoped to assimilate the Welsh by exterminating native leaders and appropriating the title 'prince of Wales' for the heir to England's throne. His strategy was only partially successful, and rebellions continued to percolate in Wales until the 16th c.

In 1485 a Welsh nobleman, Henry Tudor, unseated England's Plantagenet dynasty and seized England's throne. As a Welshman, Henry VII had a unique advantage in negotiating with the Welsh, and Wales and England were officially joined by statute in 1536. During

Sh.'s lifetime another heir to the English throne was able to move Scotland and England toward a rapprochement. Under the command of Edward I (1272–1307) the English came close to conquering Scotland, but Edward's untimely death elevated a bumbling heir, Edward II, who allowed the Scots to regain their freedom. During the Hundred Years' War France was eager to help the Scots stir up trouble for the English. The War of the Roses that followed the Hundred Years' War gave the Scots another situation they could exploit to good advantage. Scotland became a retreat for ousted Lancastrians who used it as a base from which to mount attacks on their Yorkist enemies. When the Tudor dynasty brought the civil war to an end, the Tudors tried to reach an understanding with Scotland. In 1503 Henry VIII's sister, Margaret, wed James IV of Scotland. The alliance had an unanticipated outcome. Henry's last child, Elizabeth, died without issue in 1603, and Margaret's descendant, James VI of Scotland, inherited England's throne. James VI of Scotland became James I of England and began the process of reconciling his two kingdoms. Traditions of animosity were hard to overcome, and union of the parliaments of the two nations did not take place until 1707.

England was less successful in dealing with Ireland than with Wales and Scotland. Henry II (1154–1189) urged English barons to conquer Ireland, and they carved out an English sphere of influence around Dublin. In 1171 Henry went to Ireland to receive the homage of its kings, but Ireland was more a coalition of warring tribes than a nation. It was difficult to pin its people down and identify effective leaders with whom meaningful treaties could be made. Ireland had no centralized government with which the English could deal, and endless numbers of tribal chiefs promoted rebellion. England was usually too preoccupied with projects elsewhere to give Irish affairs the attention they needed. The result was the development in Ireland of powerful, quarrelsome oligarchies of Celtic and Norman families. The survival of a strong Catholic element in Ireland complicated the country's relationship with England after Henry VIII's break with the papacy. In 1599 Sh. witnessed a major contest in Ireland between the armies of Hugh O'Neill, the earl of Tyrone, and Elizabeth's favorite, the earl of Essex. The passions the campaign excited are reflected in the fervent nationalism of the play that Sh. wrote that season, *H5.* Elizabeth failed to reach an accommodation with the Irish, and the unresolved problems of her era have created a legacy of bloody conflict for our generation.

1H6. R3. Err 3.2.128, a location on the 'globe' that is Nell. *Jn 2.1.26, 2.1.89, 2.1.90. R2 1.3.200, 1.3.269, 1.4.34, 2.1.50. MV 1.2.64, 1.3.20, 2.7.55, 3.2.266. 1H4. MWW 1.1.271. 2H4. H5. TN 3.2.46. Ham:* Claudius intends to get Hamlet out of his hair by sending him on a mission to England. Later, he also includes letters to the king ('E.') to kill Hamlet.

STM Add. II.D.82, 144. Oth 2.3.81, Iago toasts the nation of hardest drinkers. *Mac:* Malcolm flees to England to escape Macbeth, later returning with military aid in dethroning him. *Tmp 2.2.28. H8 1.1.134, 2.3.46, 2.4.9.*

2) king of England. *Jn 1.1.4, 2.1.52, 56. H5. Ham.*

3) *Mac 4.3.44, 19,* see Edward Confessor.

English, 1) language that evolved in the parts of Britain occupied by the Anglo-Saxons at the start of the Middle Ages. English is one of the Indo-European tongues. Its distinct identity can be traced to the 6th c. and the word for the language appears before the country is called England. The Teutonic dialect spoken by the Anglo-Saxons, 'Old English,' prevailed until the middle of the 12th c., but not as the preferred speech of all Britain's people. The conquest of England by Normans in the 11th c. made French the language of the court. For generations aristocrats spoke French and commoners English. Numerous French words crept into ordinary speech as a consequence of their use in law and government, but the court's preference for French slowed the development of a native literary language. The situation changed in the 14th c. as 'Middle English' emerged. The loss of the lands that England had occupied on the continent, the outbreak of the Hundred Years'

War between England and France, and the growth of a literate English middle class promoted a clearer sense of national identity. The underlying structures of Old English held up in general, while the incorporation of French vocabulary enriched the language. English began to be used in official documents and by the writers who depended on the generosity of wealthy patrons. Since life in late medieval England centered on the country's only major city, London, it was inevitable that the dialect spoken in London should set the standard for the national tongue. Printing also advanced the standardizing of the written language. Modern English began to evolve in the 16th c. when Sh. and his colleagues gathered in London to demonstrate the vernacular's potential as a medium for art and subtle thought.

R2 1.3.154. MV 1.2.69. 1H4 2.5.24, 3.1.118, 189. MWW 1.3.45; 1.4.5, 'King's E.'; *2.1.131,* 'frights E. out of his wits': changes the meaning of the language; *3.1.72, 4.3.6, 5.5.133, 142. H5 5.1.72, 5.2.242, 5.2.243, 5.2.280, 5.2.282. H8 3.1.45, 3.1.49, 5.4.14.*

2) (n.) people subject to the English monarchy. *Jn 2.1.322. 1H4 1.1.22. 2H4 4.3.98. H5 1.2.111, 3.1.17. Oth 2.3.73. AWW 2.3.95. Mac 5.3.58. H8 1.1.20.* See Englishman(-men)

3) (adj.) of or pertaining to England or its people. *MV 2.8.29,* the sea referred to is the English Channel. *MWW 2.3.55. MM 2.2.33,* 'E. kersey,' a thick cloth of wool from Kersey in Suffolk. It is being contrasted here with thin French velvet (the hairlessness caused by venereal disease). *AWW 4.5.39. Mac 2.3.13,* 'E. tailor,' a joke about the aping of foreign fashions; *5.2.1. 5.3.8,* 'E. epicures,' weak noblemen. *5.3.20.*

4) (v.) *MWW 1.3.42,* 'to be Englished': to be made plain.

Englishman(-men), *Jn 5.2.145. R2 1.1.66, 1.3.272, 3.3.43. MV 1.2.77,* see Falconbridge. *R3 2.1.70. MWW 2.3.57. H5 3.7.153, 4.7.121, 5.2.362. PP 15.3. Oth 2.3.74:* several contemporary sources brag that the English are better at holding their liquor than the Danes and Dutchmen from whom they learned the custom of toasting. *H8 3.1.83.* See English 2).

Enobarb, *Ant 2.7.119,* see Enobarbus, Domitius.

Enobarbus, Domitius, *Ant,* Cnæus Domitius 'Ahenobarbus' ('Brass-bearded'), consul of the Roman Republic, 32 BC. As a youth he followed his father's lead in the Roman civil wars and sided with Pompey against Julius Cæsar. When Pompey was defeated, Cæsar pardoned Enobarbus. He was in Italy at the time of Cæsar's assassination, but he was not involved in Cæsar's murder. He joined Mark Antony's staff and was a member of the ill-fated expedition that Antony led into Parthia in 36 BC. Antony's defeat by the Parthians and his relationship with Cleopatra alienated Enobarbus. Some of Antony's soldiers may have tried to persuade him to organize a mutiny against Antony, but he chose simply to defect to Octavius. He died before the battle of Actium (31 BC) decided Antony's fate.

Ephesians, congregation to which St. Paul addressed one of his epistles. Paul warned them not to 'get drunk with wine, for that is debauchery' (Ephesians 5:18) and admonished them: 'Put off your old nature which belongs to your former manner of life . . . and put on the new nature, created after the likeness of God' (Ephesians 3:22–24). Ephesians 'of the old church' were the unreformed degenerates whose behavior called forth this advice. Sh. used them to illustrate the kind of people with whom Falstaff preferred to associate. *2H4 2.2.141. MWW 4.5.16,* (sing.): this allusion may also include Romans 16:23.

Ephesus, ancient city on the Ægean sea at the mouth of the Cayster river in Asia Minor, one of the 12 Ionic cities. Founded in the 11th c. BC by Ionian Greeks—in legend by Androcles, last king of Athens—it was a gateway for trade into Asia. It was conquered by a succession of invaders: the Cimmerians (7th c.), the Lydians under Croesus (6th c.), and the Persians under Cyrus the Great. In the rebellion against the Persians at the end of the 6th c. BC, the Ionic cities appealed to Sparta for help, but got none, so after Persia's defeat in the Persian Wars, Ephesus became an ally of Athens. In the Peloponnesian War (431–404), however, it allied with Sparta against Athens. After the war, the Spartans ceded it to the Persians. Alexander the Great conquered the city in 333 BC and the Hellenistic period saw it flourish. It was briefly renamed Arsinoe. The Romans took control of it in 189 BC and made it the capital of the province of Asia.

Christianity came to Ephesus in 1 AD with the apostle Paul. The Epistle to the Ephesians has been attributed to him based on a tradition that he wrote to the city because of its important role in early Christendom, though some think the work may be misattributed. In 262, Ephesus began a precipitous decline when the Goths destroyed it. Its last great moment in history was as the site of the Council of Ephesus in 431, which condemned the doctrine of Nestorianism and declared Mary to be the mother of God. The Byzantine Empire neglected the city, its harbor silted up, and in the 14th c. it was abandoned. There was no city there by Sh.'s time. The site is south of the present city of Izmir, Turkey, and northeast of Samos.

Err, setting for the play. Sh. changed it from his source Plautus' *Menæchmi* which used Epidamnum. Paul's epistle alludes to the city as a center for witchcraft, which perhaps contributes to the characterization of Pinch. It was also famed for its temple of Diana, which may have suggested the priory. This temple was one of the Seven Wonders of the Ancient World and was burned by an obscure Ephesian named Erostrate on the same night in 356 BC as Alexander the Great was born. Furthermore, Ephesus is the setting for John Gower's tale of Apollonius in the *Confessio Amantis* which is considered a source for Egeon's story. Gower mentions Diana's temple.

Per: Ephesus is important in this play as the site of the temple. The story of Apollonius in Gower is the major source of the play.

Epicure, *Mac 5.3.8, Ant 2.7.51,* see Epicurus.

Epicurean, (adj.) *MWW 2.2.277, Ant 2.1.24,* see Epicurus.

Epicurism, *Lr 1.4.222 (Q 4.238),* the supposed practices of Epicurus (q.v.): excessive seeking of pleasure, particularly in food and drink.

Epicurus, *JC 5.1.76,* (342–270 BC), Greek philosopher. Epicurus was born on the island of Samos to a family of Athenian origin, and in 306 BC he founded a school in Athens. Epicurus (like his famous contemporaries, the Stoics and the Cynics) was a philosophical materialist. He taught that the universe was nothing but a machine that obeyed the laws of physics. It had no consciousness and no capacity to intend harm or good to any individual. Enlightened people did not, therefore, expect the world to conform to their wishes—or waste time lamenting the seeming injustices of personal misfortune. Epicurus urged his students to find peace of mind in the knowledge that life had no meaning beyond simple existence, and he advised them to be content with the natural pleasures of the healthy body and rational conduct. Epicurus dismissed common religious beliefs of his day (e.g., oracles and sacrifices) as pernicious superstitions. He insisted that the gods, if they existed, were as much a part of the material world as human beings and as limited in their sphere of operation as men and women. His name has traditionally, though unjustly, been associated with debauchery, excessive good living and particularly food and drink.

Epidamnum, Epidamium, or Epidamnus, ancient seaport on the Adriatic coast of modern Albania, about 50 mi. south of Shkodër (Scutari), 22 mi. from Tirana. In more recent history it has been known as Durazzo, and currently, Durrës. In ancient times it would have been a center for trade from Illyria. It was founded by Corcyra and Corinth about 625 BC. Their squabble over it precipitated the Peloponnesian War in 431. Renamed Dyrrachium, like the peninsula upon which it was located, it fell under the rule of Epirus c. 300, then of Rome in 229, which made it an important naval base. As part of the Byzantine Empire from the 8th c. AD, it was often captured by foreign powers. The Angevin kings of Naples made it a duchy in 1267 and the Venetians held it from 1392 until 1501. It was then conquered by the Turks, who held it for more than 400 years.

Err 1.1.41, 62; 1.2.1; 4.1.85, 94; 5.1.357, 361, references to Epidamnum as an important trading port. Epidamnum is the setting of Plautus' *Menæchmi,* Sh.'s source for *Err,* but Sh. changed it to Ephesus (q.v.).

Epidaurus, *Err 1.1.93,* important seaport in ancient Greece, located in Argolis in the northeast Peloponnese on the Saronic Gulf. It was not far from Corinth. It was named after Epidaurus, son of Argus and Evadne and is described by Strabo as being surrounded on all sides by mountains, making it a natural fortress. Its 4th c. BC temple of Æsculapius (Asclepius) on a prominence just outside the city was known for its beautiful sculpture and its inscription over the entrance that declared it open only to the pure of heart. The ill often went there to seek cures and treatments were kept on tablets there. Annual festivals honored the god. In the area of Epidaurus Theseus supposedly slew Periphetes, a club-carrying son of Hephæstus, and adopted the club for his own weapon. It has also been argued that Sh. here might mean the modern port of Dubrovnik, north of Epidamnum, but the mention of Corinth seems to make the Greek Epidaurus more likely.

Epilogue, speech at play's end which directly addresses the audience about what they have just seen. It may have been a common device of players in open venues in order to commence 'passing the hat,' but also to provide a notice that the play was ended. Epilogues appear at the ends of *MND, 2H4, H5, AYLI, TN, Tro, AWW, Per, Temp, H8,* and *TNK.* In several plays, characters turn to the audience to speak the epilogue, such as Robin Goodfellow in *MND,* Rosalind in *AYLI,* Feste in *TN* (sung), Pandarus in the Q version of *Tro,* and Prospero in *Temp.* In *H5, Per,* and *H8,* the prologue and epilogue are spoken by the same person, who is not a part of the play's action. In *2H4* and *TNK,* timid actors who are not part of the play speak it. In *AWW,* an anonymous actor. Where the epilogue was not spoken by a character in the play, it is possible that the man who delivered it was garbed in a special costume as was done with Rumor, Prologue, or other allegorical characters.

Epistropus, *Tro 5.5.11,* Epistrophus, Greek king, son of Iphitus, killed at Troy by Margareton. In William Caxton's *Recuyell of the Historyes of Troye,* 3 (c. 1474), the first English printed book, and Sh.'s major source for the play, Epistropus is a brother of Cedius and king of 'Focyden' who breaks a spear on Hector and insults him. Hector then slays him. In Raoul Lefevre's book which Caxton translated from French, Epistropus is called Epicropus. In the *Iliad,* Epistrophus is commander of the Phocians.

'Erc'les, *MND 1.2.25, 36,* Bottom's corruption of Hercules, whom he would like to play.

Erebus, in classical mythology a place of darkness between the earth and the underworld through which the dead must pass. It sprang from Chaos and Darkness. *2H4 2.4.153. MV 5.1.87. JC 2.1.84.*

Ermengarde, *H5 1.2.82,* daughter of Charles of Lorraine, the Carolingian heir to the throne of France whose rights were ignored in 987 when the nobles elected Hugh Capet king. In *H5* Sh. has the archbishop of Canterbury develop an elaborate refutation of the 'Salic' law, a custom that French authorities said prevented women from inheriting France's throne or transmitting title to it to male relatives. The archbishop assures Henry V that the scrupulous Capetian monarch, Louis IX (Saint Louis), doubted his right to throne until he discovered that he had Carolingian blood inherited from his grandmother, Isabel, one of Ermengarde's descendants. Louis apparently knew no rule that prevented men, like Henry V, from tracing rights to thrones through female ancestral lines. Holinshed (3.545–546) gave Sh. the outline of the argument that Henry used to justify his claim to the French crown.

Eros, *Ant,* Antony's slave. When Antony orders Eros to kill him, the slave refuses and kills himself. Plutarch describes the incident in his 'Antony.' Romans preferred Greeks as household slaves in order to appropriate their culture. *Eros* is Greek for 'love' and also the name of Cupid. Since love was Antony's weakness, it seems very appropriate, almost allegorical, to have a person so named present at his death.

Erpingham, Thomas, *R2 2.1.284, H5,* (1357–1428), Lancastrian knight who began his career in the service of John of Gaunt and lived long enough to fight in the famous battles led by Gaunt's grandson, Henry V. Gaunt assigned Erpingham to the household of his son, Henry (IV) Bolingbroke, when the heir to the duchy of Lancaster was still a boy. Erpingham stayed at Henry's side for the rest of Henry's life. He shared in Henry's crusades and pilgrimages in the 1390's, and in 1398, when Richard II banished Henry from England, he followed his lord into exile. After Gaunt's death, he returned to England with Henry to help him win possession of the Lancastrian legacy which Richard had appropriated. When Henry discovered that Richard no longer had the support of his subjects, Henry forced Richard from the throne. Erpingham was one of the commissioners sent to witness the king's formal abdication. Henry claimed the crown and rewarded faithful followers with prestigious posts. Erpingham became warden of the Cinque Ports and commander of Dover Castle, the 'door' to England. In 1401 Henry sent him to Ireland on the staff of the king's second son, Thomas, duke of Clarence, and in 1404 he became the king's steward and a member of his Privy Council. Henry V showed as much confidence in Erpingham as his father had. In 1415 Henry took the aging soldier along on his raids into France, and the king entrusted him with the responsibility of deploying the army for the crucial battle fought at Agincourt. Erpingham may have given the signal that began the famous fight that proved to be his last great adventure. He left royal service in 1416 and spent the last decade of his life in retirement. His loyalty to the crown did not prevent him from having a mind of his own. He was a friend of Sir John Oldcastle whose heretical opinions and treasonous proclivities stirred up a great deal of trouble for Henry IV and Henry V. Oldcastle was convicted of Lollardy in 1413 and executed in 1417.

Error, *JC 5.3.66, 67,* allegorical figure representing judgment prejudiced by melancholy emotions.

Escalus, 1) *Rom,* prince of Verona. He breaks up a street brawl in the first act, punishes Romeo with exile in the third, and oversees the end of the feud in the fifth. Although he seems to be respected for his authority, he admits to not having intervened in the disorder soon enough. The name appears in Arthur Brooke's *Tragicall Historye of Romeus and Juliet* (1562), Sh.'s source, though Sh. uses it only once, in the stage direction in which he first enters. The name is a Latin version of Della Scala (also known as Scaliger), a family which ruled Verona from 1260 to 1389. The most illustrious Della Scala was Can Grande I, Francesco della Scala, a patron of Dante. The city lost its independence with the extinction of this dynasty and was thereafter controlled by Milan, Padua, and Venice.

2) *MM,* 'Old E.,' counselor to the duke. He shows wisdom in most of his dealings and advises Angelo not to pursue the execution of Claudio. He serves mainly to comment on the action and point up the excessive behavior of the others. He is also ineffective, however, and resembles Polonius, Antonio, and other elderly men who can comment on crises but do little about them. On the other hand, he is patient about getting to the truth—which Angelo is not—in the scene with Pompey and Elbow, demonstrating that the seeking of justice involves some considerable wallowing in the real

world. His name could be derived from the ancient playwright Æschylus or indirectly from Sh.'s Italian sources, but Sh. likely simply remembered it from 1). Another excellent possibility is the old knight Æschylus in Sir Philip Sidney's *Arcadia* (1590).

3) *AWW 3.5.78,* a Florentine warrior mentioned only as he passes in a military parade.

Esperance, *1H4 2.4.71, 5.2.96,* the Percy battle cry from their family motto *Esperance ma comforte* ('Hope, my comfort').

Esquire, courtesy title accorded professional men. In the original medieval sense the term referred to young apprentice soldiers who were preparing for knighthood, but by Sh.'s day squires were understood to be men of property separate from the feudal class of knights. *2H6 4.9.42, 5.1.75. MWW 1.1.3, 100. 2H4 3.2.56, 4.2.125. H5 4.8.104.*

Essex, *3H6 1.1.157,* county on England's eastern coast. The Thames marks its southern border. It derives from 'land of the East Saxons.' See Essex, Earl of, *Jn.*

Essex, Earl of, *Jn,* Geoffrey Fitzpeter (d. 1213), earl by right of his wife, Beatrice, sister of Geoffrey Mandeville. He was one of the men to whom the government of England was entrusted while Richard the Lionhearted was absent on the third crusade. After William Longchamp's death in 1197 Essex was the highest ranking royal official in Richard's kingdom. He earned a lamentable reputation for efficiency in raising money to support Richard's foreign wars. When Richard died, he helped engineer John's succession. He was John's regent in England during John's campaigns in France.

Ethiop, or Ethiope, 1) a person of the black race, or simply of a race of dark skin, deriving from the Greek *Aithiops,* which may have meant 'burnt face' or else was a corruption of the name of a foreign peoples. It was not used in ancient times to apply exclusively to Africans. Homer applies it to those peoples which live at the ends of the planet both east and west. Later Ethiopia is localized to the land of Cush, as the Hebrews called it, or south Arabia. Herodotus and some other sources describe two races as Ethiopians, one straight-haired and one woolly-haired. Around the 1st c. the name became equivalent to Habashat (Abyssinia). The founder of the kingdom, according to chronicles, was Menelek, son of Solomon and Sheba. As a Coptic Christian kingdom supposedly converted by a black man who encountered St. Paul, it was frequently a target in the expansion of Islam, but somehow maintained the faith. It therefore attracted some attention from the Europeans and may be the source of the legend of Prester John. Sh. seems to have little knowledge of, or interest in Ethiopia as a country and uses Ethiop figuratively as an image of swarthiness in comparison to fairness. Ethiop curiously never appears in *Oth* for example, which might support the contention that Sh. has the mixed Moorish race in mind more explicitly than the black African races. The figurative use dates back to Roman times, where it often has a negative connotation as in Sh.

TGV 2.6.26, 'swarthy E.': this is comparable to *Rom.* The wordings are similar and both plays were influenced by Arthur Brooke's *Tragicall Historye of Romeus and Juliet* (1562). *LLL 4.3.116, 266 (pl.) MND 3.2.258. Rom 1.5.45,* 'E.'s ear': Juliet is as bright against the night as a jewel is against the dark skin of an Ethiopian. *Ado 5.4.38. Per 6.20,* 'swarthy E.'

2) (adj.) *AYLI 4.3.36,* 'E. words,' angry words, dark words.

Ethiopian, 1) (n.) *MWW 2.3.25,* dark-skinned or ugly man, a wild man.

2) (adj.) *WT 4.4.362,* 'E.'s tooth': an image of whiteness by contrast.

Etna, or Ætna, active volcano at the eastern end of Sicily. It overlooks the Straits of Messina and is over 11,000 ft. high. It now covers over 600 sq. mi. and has changed throughout a long history of continual eruption, often doing serious damage, as when it wiped out Catania in

1169 AD. In ancient times, the strange noises that emerged from it were attributed to the Cyclops and the ironworking of Vulcan's forge. The giant Enceladus (q.v.) was also supposed to have been buried under the volcano after the uprising of the Titans against Jupiter was suppressed, and his attempts to escape were also supposed to be sources of the noise, as well as the noises of Typhon (q.v.). The name of the mountain derives from the Greek word for 'burn,' *aitho.*

Luc 1042. Tit. 3.1.240. MWW 3.5.117.

Eton, *MWW 4.4.74, 4.5.63, 4.6.24, 5.5.180,* town in Buckinghamshire on the north bank of the Thames across the river from Windsor. Eton is the site of the most celebrated of English public schools, King's College of Our Lady of Eton Beside Windsor—Eton College—founded by Henry VI (1440/1441) and connected in various arrangements to King's College, Cambridge, also founded by the unfortunate Henry. The original buildings were not completed until about 1521, and many additions were made later. It has a long history of distinguished graduates.

Euphrates, *Ant 1.2.94,* river that with the Tigris defines the district that the Greeks called Mesopotamia (i.e., 'the land between the rivers'). It originates in Turkey and flows 2,200 mi. southeast to the Persian Gulf. Sumer, the first of the west's civilizations, flourished along its banks. The Persian empire, which Alexander the Great conquered, extended from the Mediterranean to the Indus, but during the Roman era the Euphrates marked the frontier of the western world.

Euriphile, *Cym 3.3.103, 4.2.235, 239, 5.6.341,* nurse of the infants Arviragus and Guiderius, who stole the babies for Belarius and later reared them as her own children after marrying Belarius. A 'Eruphylus' is one of the Greek kings in William Caxton's *Recuyell of the Historyes of Troy* (1474), Sh.'s major source for *Tro.* An 'Eriphile' is a widow in one of Henry Pettie's stories in *A Petite Pallace of Pettie His Pleasure* (1574). Erphilem is also mentioned in Chaucer's *Wyves Tale of Bathe,* 743. She marries for money and betrays her husband for his wealth; however, he goes into hiding to avoid the wars, which may have suggested the name for *Cym.* There is a 'Euripil' and a 'Ewrypyle' in Golding's translation of *Metamorphoses,* and 'Eurypulus' in Spenser's *Færie Queene.* The *Iliad* has two characters named Eurypylus: one is king of Cos and son of Hercules, the other a commander of Thessaly.

Europa, 1) beautiful daughter of Agenor, king of Sidon. Jupiter fell in love with her and, while she was at the seashore, assumed the form of a great white bull. Seeming gentle, he thus enticed Europa upon his back and eased out into the water until it was impossible for her to dismount (Ovid, *Metamorphoses,* 2). He carried her to the island of Crete and fathered Minos, Rhadamanthys, and Sarpedon by her. After she was kidnapped, Agenor sent his sons to find her, thus in some myths creating the traditional antipathies between Asia and Europe, which was named after the kidnapped girl. *Ado 5.5.46. MWW 5.5.3.* See also Agenor, *Shr 1.1.166.*

2) *Ado 5.5.45,* L. 'Europe' (q.v.)

Europe, continent that stretches from the Atlantic ocean to the Ural mountains and from the Baltic and North seas to the Mediterranean. In very early Greek texts the term seems to apply only to mainland Greece as opposed to Asia Minor and the Greek islands but it is used in the modern way by classical times. According to mythology it was named for Europa; however, the name may derive from ancient Akkadian *ereb,* 'land of the setting sun,' as Asia derives from *asu* 'land of the rising sun.'

2H4 2.2.125, 4.2.22. H5 2.4.133, 3.7.5. WT 2.2.3. Tmp 2.1.130. Cym 2.3.141.

Evans, Sir Hugh, *MWW,* 'Master Parson,' Welsh parson and teacher. He begins the play trying to negotiate an end to the trouble between Falstaff and Slender, only to be drawn into a duel with Dr. Caius. When the Host of the Garter keeps Caius and him apart to prevent the fight, they then turn on the Host and scheme revenge. After the comic interlude of Evans' Latin lesson with William Page, apparently he and Caius steal the Host's horses and blame it on the Germans, though this comic business seems not fully borne to its conclusion. Finally Evans plays the role of a fairy in the tormenting of Falstaff. Evans represents the long tradition of ethnic humor with his heavy accent. Both his Christian name and surname are very common in Wales. His song in *3.1* alludes to the Welsh interest in singing and, possibly, the disappearance of the Host's horses relies on the audience's suspicion of Welshmen as thieves (though the plot is hatched with the Frenchman), which is why what exactly happened to the horses is never explicit. It has been argued that the use of the Welsh stereotype in several plays implies that Sh. had one or more Welsh actors, but in the absence of other evidence, this assertion is silly. Utilitarian Irish, German, Southern, or 'Jewish' accents have long been the staples of various performers of ethnic humor in vaudeville and other theater, and frequently from the same performer. Al Jolson had no need to be African-American. It has also been appealing to attribute the scene with William to Sh.'s personal memories of learning his 'little Latin,' as his instructor in Stratford, Thomas Jenkins, may have been Welsh. The evidence is extremely thin, however. Latin lessons were a general experience for anyone schooled at the time.

Eve, in the Bible, the first woman, wife of Adam, blamed for the first violation of God's orders and for tempting Adam to do likewise. Her name derives from a Hebrew word for 'life' and describes her function as the primal mother, the 'giver of life.' Although Genesis 1:27–28 seems to posit a simultaneous origin for males and females, Genesis 2:21–24 says that God formed Eve from a rib taken from Adam, the first man, and that Eve's appearance completed the process of divine creation. Genesis 3 records the story of the human species' fall from divine favor. Eve, tempted by a serpent, persuades Adam to eat the fruit of a tree that God has ordered them not to touch. This act of disobedience, which is grounded in a freedom of will that makes them the 'image of God,' changes their relationship with God and their destiny. God drives them from Eden, an earthly paradise, and they endure the hardships of the perennial human condition. Eve's special punishment was the burden of bearing children in pain.

TGV 3.1.329, 'E.'s legacy,' the sin of pride. *LLL 1.1.255, 5.2.322. R2 3.4.76. TN 1.5.26,* 'E.'s flesh,' womanhood. *Son 93.13,* 'E.'s apple,' the symbol of external attractiveness masking falsehood or corruption.

Evil Angel, *Err 4.3.19,* possibly an allusion to the Bad Angel in Christopher Marlowe's *Doctor Faustus,* or to the opposite of the good angel that released Peter from jail in Acts 12: 6–11. It could simply be a general expression.

Exeter, *R3 4.2.105,* seat of Devonshire and cathedral city of the diocese of Exeter, located on the river Exe. A duchy of Exeter was created for John Holland (d. 1400), Richard II's half-brother. See E., Bishop of; E., Duke of.

Exeter, Bishop of, *R3 4.4.432,* Peter Courtenay (d. 1492), scion of a powerful Devonshire family and a churchman who was deeply involved in secular politics. Courtenay was educated at Oxford and in Italy and made his career in the service of the house of York. In 1478 Edward IV approved his consecration as bishop of Exeter, the Devonshire see. Although Courtenay initially acquiesced to Richard III's usurpation of the crown, he was not one of Richard's firm allies. He joined the duke of Buckingham's ill-fated rebellion and was forced to flee England when it failed. After Richard's death at the battle of Bosworth Field, the new king, Henry VII, restored Courtenay's honors and estates and made the bishop keeper of the Privy Seal at the Tudor court. Sh. errs in asserting that Courtenay was the elder brother of another of Buckingham's conspirators, Sir Edward Courtenay. Sir Edward was Peter's cousin.

Exeter, Duke of, 1) *1H6, H5,* see Beaufort, Thomas.

2) *3H6,* see Holland, Henry.

3) *R2 2.1.282,* John Holland (1352--1400), member of a conspiracy to murder Henry IV and restore Richard II to the throne. He was Richard's half-brother. After the death of his father, his mother had married Edward the Black Prince and given birth to Richard. Exeter also had a close connection with the Lancastrian house. He had fought under John of Gaunt's command in Spain and had wed Gaunt's second daughter—Henry (IV) Bolingbroke's sister. Made earl of Huntingdon in 1387, he became admiral of the fleet and chamberlain of England. He earned the duchy in 1397 by helping Richard defeat the 'lords appellant,' the barons who tried to curtail the king's freedom of action. He was a member of the expedition Richard led to Ireland in 1399 and was the man Richard trusted to handle negotiations with the rebel army raised by Henry (IV) Bolingbroke. After Richard's abdication and Henry's enthronement, he was accused of involvement in the murder of the duke of Gloucester, one of the 'lords appellant.' When Henry punished him by depriving him of his duchy, he and other dissident barons concocted a plan to assassinate Henry while the king witnessed a tournament that was held at Windsor early in January 1400. When news of the plot leaked out, Exeter tried to escape, but he was captured at Pleshey, Essex, and beheaded. His titles and lands were forfeited.

Expedition, *Err 4.3.38,* name of a ship. Since 'expedition' also means 'speed' there is a play on the ship *Delay.*

Exton, Piers, *R2,* alleged murderer of Richard II. Holinshed (3.517) claims that Richard was killed as a result of a casual remark made by Henry IV. Henry supposedly lamented that he had no friend to rescue him from the threat of Richard's resurgence. Exton heard the king and, on his own initiative, undertook to slaughter Richard to prove his loyalty to Henry. The story, which originated in France and is not mentioned by any of the contemporary English chroniclers, may be a fabrication. There is no record of a knight at Henry's court named Piers or Peter Exton, but historians cannot be sure that he did not exist. 'Piers Exton' could be a garbled spelling of Piers Bukton, the soldier who served as Henry's standard bearer. There might also have been a Piers who was a relative of Nicholas Exton, the sheriff and mayor of London who headed a contingent of persons hostile to Richard in parliament.

Eye, *2H6 1.2.75,* town near Winchester, home of a Margery Jordan who was executed for practicing black magic in the service of Eleanor, duchess of Gloucester.

F

Fabian, *TN,* 'Signor F.' He seems to be Olivia's servant, although he often acts as if he is the equal to Sir Toby and Sir Andrew. If he, indeed, is of a lower class, it degrades the knights in comparison to his lack of crudity. It is possible that he is meant to be an impoverished nobleman, forced to sponge off Olivia, maybe because of gambling. Malvolio tattled on Fabian's bear-baiting, a cruel sport that the Puritans disapproved of, but which was linked to the theater. Often plays were presented in the bear-baiting arenas. Fabian has been out of favor with his mistress, so he takes part in the scheme to humiliate Malvolio, but he restrains Toby from beating Malvolio, and protects Maria from blame for the letter scheme. The Fabii were a prominent family and Fabius was a common Roman name. Cicero's wife was named Fabia, also.

Fairy King, *MND 4.1.92,* see Oberon.

Fairy Queen, 1) *MND 2.1.8,* see Titania.

2) *MWW 5.5,* disguise of Mistress Quickly (q.v.) in the humiliation of Falstaff. The role does not seem to suit the character, and many have argued that the text indicates a doubling by an actor, rather than that Quickly is capable of simulating the speech and manner of the Fairy Queen.

Falconbridge, 1) *Jn 1.1.134, 1.1.251,* Faulconbridge, English earldom established after the Norman conquest. In Sh.'s day the title belonged to the Belasyse family, whose properties were in Yorkshire. There is no known connection between them and the Falconbridge characters in *Jn.* Some scholars believe that Sh. took the name from an earlier play, *The Troublesome Raigne of John, King of England,* and that it is a corruption of Falcasius de Brente (Fawkes de Brent), the name of a knight of illegitimate birth whose story is told in Matthew Paris' *Chronica Majora* (c. 1259), a chronicle of English history.

2) *3H6 1.1.240,* William Neville, earl of Kent (d. 1463); second son of Ralph Neville, earl of Westmorland; Lord Falconbridge by right of his wife, Joan. Although Falconbridge's mother, Joan Beaufort, was John of Gaunt's daughter and kin to the house of Lancaster, Falconbridge sided with York against Henry VI. Falconbridge was a soldier who fought in France, and the loss of England's lands in France may have turned him against Henry. Richard of York gave Falconbridge a seat on the regency council that governed England during Henry VI's first bout with mental illness. Falconbridge fought for Edward at Towton, and Edward granted him the earldom of Kent. When Falconbridge's nephew, the earl of Warwick, became lieutenant of Calais, Falconbridge was given command of the English ships patrolling the channel. In 1462 he was appointed admiral of England and was ordered to prevent Queen Margaret from crossing from France to England. He died in 1463, before the struggle between York and Lancaster reached its conclusion.

3) *MV 1.2.63,* suitor to Portia, a baron of England. Portia sees him as a man of no education and poor behavior who cannot even match the elements of his wardrobe. As the only English suitor, Falconbridge is not a good representative of the author's nation, but implies oppositely the desired qualities of a noble husband.

Falconbridge, Lady, *Jn,* alleged mistress of Richard the Lionhearted and mother of his illegitimate son, Philip the Bastard. Early versions of her story give her different names: Marian, Margaret, Margery, etc. No historical source is known for Sh.'s Falconbridge tales, which may derive from an anonymous play, *The Troublesome Raigne of John, King of England.*

Falconbridge, Lord of, *1H6 4.7.67,* one of the titles Sh. lists belonging to England's hero of the Hundred Years' War, John Talbot. The baronage of Fauconberg belonged to the Neville family and was claimed by Talbot as the inheritance of his first wife, Maud, daughter of Thomas Neville.

Falconbridge, Robert, 1) *Jn,* husband of a woman by whom Richard the Lionhearted allegedly fathered a son called Philip the Bastard. In *Look about You,* an anonymous play that was probably written after *Jn,* a Lord Falconbridge appears as 'Richard,' not 'Robert.' But the names may be entirely arbitrary, for no historical evidence has been found for Sh.'s Falconbridge stories. Some scholars believe their source is an anonymous play, *The Troublesome Raigne of John, King of England.* The rumored link between Richard the Lionhearted and a Falconbridge may have originated in folk tales. A Fawkes de Brent, a warrior of illegitimate birth, was a thorn in the side of Richard's unpopular heir, John. In the imagination of story tellers he, Richard's avenger, became Richard's son, and English accents compressed his name into Falconbridge.

2) *Jn,* younger half-brother to Philip the Bastard. Sh. has him assert a right to Philip's Falconbridge estates when Philip wins recognition of his claim to be the natural son of Richard the Lionhearted. Neither a historical source for this story nor a definite historical prototype is known.

Falstaff, Sir John, Sh.'s most popular comic character, lecherous, gluttonous, cowardly, and yet lovable enough that Henry's righteous rejection of the old man seems cruel. When he was first introduced to the stage in *1H4,* Sh. called him Sir John Oldcastle. The name was probably adopted from one of Sh.'s sources, an anonymous play entitled *The Famous Victories of Henry the Fifth,* in which he is often called 'Jockey,' a nickname for John. Although Oldcastle was an instant hit with Sh.'s audience and *MWW* may have been written in response to Elizabeth I's request to see more of the character, 'Oldcastle' created a controversy. William Brooke, Lord Cobham, was a descendant of the Lollard sympathizer, Sir John Oldcastle. In 1597 he or his son Henry accused Sh. of slandering their ancestor. Sh. tried to avoid difficulty by changing Oldcastle's name to Falstaff and by explicitly denying any connection between his character and the real Oldcastle in the epilogue of *2H4.*

His efforts were futile, for Henry Brooke's enemies, the friends of Elizabeth's young favorite, the earl of Essex, found the association all too amusing. 'Falstaff' is probably a distorted version of the name of Sir John Fastolf (1378–1459), one of Henry V's generals. Fastolf appeared in *1H6,* a play written before *2H4.* For the folio edition of *1H6* 'Fastolf' was spelled 'Falstaff.' The real Fastolf, like the real Oldcastle, bore little resemblance to Sh.'s character. Fastolf was only about ten years older than Prince Harry (b. 1387), and he was no buffoon. Fastolf, however, offered Sh. a safe target, for Sh.'s contemporaries were prejudiced against his memory and happy to see him lampooned. In 1429 Fastolf had escaped from a battle with the French in which the popular English hero, John Talbot, had been killed. Although Fastolf was probably not at fault, he was accused of cowardice and his reputation never recovered.

MWW. 2H4. H5 2.3.5, 4.7.49.

Fame, personification of renown, the goddess reputation or rumor. Fama was the Roman goddess of fame and rumors (Gr. *Pheme*). She was ejected from Olympus by Jupiter. It is often difficult to distinguish Sh.'s use of Fame as a personification, from fame as a synonym for renown or rumor (L. *Fama,* who is prominently described in the *Æneid*—see Rumour). *3H6 3.3.63. Tit 2.1.127:* Sh.'s reference to fame's house recalls the title of Geoffrey Chaucer's *Hous of Fame,* but Sh. may also have had in mind Ovid's *Metamorphoses,* 12, where fame is said to live in a tower with many doors. *1H6 2.3.68. LLL 2.1.21. Ado 2.1.200-1,* 'Lady F.' *Tro 3.3.203, 4.7.27. Per 10.22, 22.118.*

Fang, Sergeant, *2H4,* descriptive name Sh. invents for an officer of the law. A 'fang' was a slang term for the capture or seizure of someone or something. Fang and his aide, Snare, attempt to take Falstaff into custody.

Far, Monsieur la, *Lr. Q 17.9,* Maréchal of France, general of the forces of Queen Cordelia in her attempt to rescue her father. The invasion fails. It would have been politically unwise to show a successful French invasion of England, as Sh.'s sources tell the story—not to mention destroying the tragic thrust Sh. gave the legend. The fabrication of Far also spares the noble King of France from humiliation, it being explained that important matters of state forced him to return to his kingdom. The source of the general's name is not known. There is a Fer mentioned in *H5,* whose name may have popped into Sh.'s mind.

Farewell, *Tro 3.3.163,* personification of leave-taking.

Fastolf, John, *1H6,* (1378–1459), professional soldier from the district of Norfolk. In 1413 he joined the English forces in Gascony. Henry V's decision to rekindle the Hundred Years War guaranteed him employment, and he earned a good record in the field. By 1423 he was commanding garrisons in Maine and Anjou, and in 1426 he was inducted into the Order of the Garter. On 18 June 1429, his career suffered a setback. Forces led by Fastolf and John Talbot were routed by Joan of Arc in a battle near a French village called Patay. Talbot was captured; Fastolf escaped. The debacle may have been caused by Talbot's rashness and Fastolf may have left the field only when all hope was lost, but the fact that Talbot stayed and Fastolf fled made one look good and the other bad. A malicious story that Fastolf was stripped of the Order of the Garter for conduct unbecoming a knight at Patay was recorded in Enguerrand de Monstrelet's chronicle whence it passed into the English histories Sh. read. In reality, Fastolf remained on duty in France after Patay and enjoyed honorable appointments to the staffs of the dukes of Bedford and York. In 1440 Fastolf left the military and returned to England, where he subsequently had considerable financial success. His avaricious conduct as a businessman did nothing to increase his popularity. Gossips delighted in casting aspersions on his war record and comparing him unfavorably to Talbot. The result was a legend ready-made for Sh.'s drama—in which Fastolf serves as a cowardly foil for the heroic Talbot.

Fate, personification of destiny, or the goddess of destiny. The Greeks called her Moira, but Sh. may not have known this. In many references it is unclear whether Sh. is thinking of a goddess or of the general concept of destiny. See Fates.

1H6 4.6.8. MND 3.2.92. MWW 3.5.97. 2H4 3.1.44. TN 1.5.300. Mac 1.5.28. Ant WT 3.3.27. Tmp 1.1.29, 3.3.61.

Fates, in classical mythology, three female divinities (Klotho, Lachesis, and Atropos) who determine the destinies of individual human beings. They are often depicted holding spindles on which they spin threads that represent the continuity of mortal lives. The word derives from the L. *fari,* to speak, to ordain. In some references it is not clear whether Sh. has the goddesses in mind or a more general conception of destiny.

3H6 4.4.32. Err 1.1.140. MND 1.2.34, 'foolish F.' *5.1.196, 280. MV 2.2.58. 2H4 2.4.155. JC 1.2.139, 2.3.16, 3.1.99. TN 2.5.141. Ham 3.2.202. Per 13.8, 17.14. WT 4.4.20.*

Fauconbridge, *H5 3.5.44, 4.8.99,* Fauconberg, (d. 1415), one of the many prominent French nobles whom Holinshed (3, 555) lists as a casualty of the battle of Agincourt.

Fauconbridge, Jaques, *LLL 2.1.42, 205,* a nobleman. Maria says that she witnessed a marriage between Lord Périgord and the beauteous heir of Fauconbridge, although Boyet describes Maria later as an heir of Fauconbridge. Either there was more than one female heir or this is another example of textual carelessness. The name appears in Holinshed. See also Falconbridge.

Faustuses, Doctor, *MWW 4.5.65,* evil magicians, based upon Dr. Georg or Johann Faust or Faustus (d. 1538?). An astrologer and alchemist, he supposedly taught at various German universities (Heidelberg, Erfurt, Wittenberg) and was thought a conscienceless fraud. In some accounts he became a prosperous and upright citizen after coming under the patronage of the Archbishop of Cologne in 1532. He made grandiose claims for his ability to raise the spirits of Homeric heroes and to affect the outcome of Italian wars. Although his contemporaries often reviled him, they also feared him, and when he was supposedly found dead face down, this confirmed his demonic powers. The actual man is inconsequential. He was soon the subject of stories of his unholy powers and bad deeds. Within a couple of decades a Latin work appeared describing his life. In 1587 a book by Johann Spies, *Historia von Dr. Johann Fausten,* was published in Frankfurt. In it Faust makes a pact with the devil. It exploded into the Renaissance imagination and was soon translated into most European languages. An English verse version appeared in 1587, and a prose version in 1592. The same year, Christopher Marlowe's play (written as early as 1588), was a major success and probably Marlowe's last. Unfortunately, the text survives in a mutilated form. Restored, it is frequently staged. Since the Renaissance, the story has been used as the inspiration for some of the greatest works of literature, art, and music, including efforts by Berlioz, Gounod, and Mann, among many others, though most of these derive their inspiration from Goethe's great poem of 1808 and 1832.

Feeble, Francis, *2H4,* descriptive name Sh. invents for a character, who despite his manifest lack of qualifications, is impressed into military service by the unprincipled Falstaff. The bribes Falstaff has accepted to exempt better candidates force him to meet his quota of recruits by impressing the sickly poor. The fact that Feeble is a ladies' tailor would also have implied effeminacy, similar to the way modern comedy stereotypes hair dressers.

Fenton, Master, *MWW,* young suitor of Anne Page. He is not a very impressive person and his suit is not favored by Anne's parents. He is said to have been one of wild Prince Hal's companions and, being without money, he seeks to marry it. George Page also feels that the marriage would be a bad one because Fenton is higher born and would view his wife as property. Although Fenton admits he initially was after money, he says that upon wooing her he found her of more value than gold. This situation depicts a social pattern that caused considerable tension in the late Middle Ages and Renaissance as wealth shifted to the merchants and tradesmen of the middle class and away from the landed nobility. It was not just for love that many nobility married 'beneath their station.' They needed bourgeois money to sustain their lifestyles. The use of 'master' might indicate the level to which he has fallen, or that he occupies a rather low branch on the tree of nobility.

Fer, Master or **Monsieur,** *H5 4.4.25, 4.4.26, 4.4.27,* fictional French soldier who is captured by Pistol at Agincourt. His name, which means 'iron' in English, is an ironic comment on his eagerness to bend to Pistol's will and beg for his life.

Ferdinand, traditional name among Spanish royalty with Visigothic origins. It made its way to England's Catholics during the reign of Mary I, whose husband was Philip, the king of Spain.

1), *Shr 4.1.137,* Petruccio's cousin. Though Petruccio wants Katherine to know him, he never appears. Either this is an oversight in the text, or is intended merely as further evidence of Petruccio's irrationality.

2) King of Navarre, *LLL.* Ordering an ascetic lifestyle for his court, Ferdinand prohibits all entertainment, banquetting, and dalliances with women as a means to learning and wisdom. He says he will create a little academe which will be the wonder of the world. This all falls apart, however, when his kingly duties require him to greet the embassy from the king of France led by the Princess of France. Cupid proves his power over good intentions by making Ferdinand fall in love and the play demonstrates that (as with Lear) a king cannot withdraw from the world. At play's end, the King of

France dies and the Princess exacts the promise of a year of asceticism before their marriage. It is one of the most odd things about this comedy that it does not end with the usual Shakespearean wedding festivities.

The play has no specific source and as one of the few original works by Shakespeare seems to have been created out of a number of suggestions from contemporary events. Although he was a celebrated womanizer, Henry IV of France seems to have suggested Ferdinand. He was king of Navarre and a Protestant hero until 1593 when he converted to Catholicism in an act of political expediency to become the first Bourbon king of France. Soon after, he issued the Edict of Nantes to establish religious tolerance. He was a patron of learning. His distant and curious marriage to Marguerite de Valois (who was allied with the Catholics) also suggests the separation of Ferdinand from the Princess of France at the end of the play, as well as Henry's having to go through a trial period before the Church was convinced of his 'sincerity.' The meeting of the princess and her ladies in waiting with Ferdinand likely was inspired by the meeting at Nérac in 1578 in which Marguerite (now separated from Henry), her mother Catherine de Médicis and a group of ladies attempted to resolve the questions remaining about the disposition of the dowry of the failed marriage. Furthermore, the names of many of the other characters are prominent from the career of Henry IV. The loan described in *2.1* seems to be derived from a similar deal between King Charles of Navarre and the king of France.

Ascetic withdrawal was long a way to attain spiritual refreshment and wisdom; however, the particular description of Henry III of France's academy in the ethical essay by P. de la Primaudaye *Académie Française* (1577, trans. 1586) seems a most likely source (see Solomon). The particular strictness of *LLL*'s monarch may have been suggested by Ferdinand V, 'the Catholic,' king of Castile, annexer of Navarre, and husband of Isabella. He began the Holy Brotherhood in 1476 to enforce religious orthodoxy and to control the power of the nobility. He also instituted the Spanish Inquisition in 1478.

3) *Tmp,* Alonso's handsome son. He falls in love with Miranda after undergoing hardship under Prospero and fits with the many Shakespearean males who must suffer to achieve the wisdom of mature love. (See the reference to Ferdinando, king of Naples, under Prospero) There is a Ferdinand, the son of Alphonso or Alonzo of Naples in Dent's translation of the *History of Philip de Comines* (1526), along with parallels of other characters' names. A Ferdinand also appears in Robert Eden's *History of Travaile* (1577), along with several other names from the play.

4) *H8 2.4.45,* (1373–1416), king of Aragon whose marriage with Isabella of Castile unified Spain. Henry VIII's first wife, Katherine of Aragon, was Ferdinand and Isabella's daughter. Katherine's elder sister, Juana 'the Mad,' inherited the family's crowns and passed them to her son, Charles V.

Ferrara, *H8 3.2.324,* Italian duchy on the coast of the Adriatic sea at the mouth of the Po river, bordered by the Republic of Venice and the Papal States. In 1450 the Este family came to power in Ferrara, and their lavish patronage of artists and intellectuals made the duchy a center for the development of the Italian Renaissance. The dukes of Ferrara were also deeply involved in the convoluted plots and schemes for which Renaissance politicians became infamous. Cardinal Wolsey even envisioned a role for Ferrara to play in Henry VIII's divorce proceedings. Wolsey's plan was to enlist the support of Ferrara to weaken Charles V's position in Italy, to liberate the papacy from Charles's domination, and to induce a grateful Clement VII to grant Henry VIII a divorce from Charles's aunt, Katherine of Aragon.

Ferrers, Lord, *R3 5.8.14,* Sir Walter Devereux (d. 1485), Lord Ferrers by right of his wife, Anne, and a Yorkist partisan. He died fighting for Richard III at the battle of Bosworth Field.

Feste, *TN,* 'the Clown,' jester to Olivia. Witty and clever, he seems to be another example of the 'wise fool,' one who mocks everything vigorously and yet in whose mockery much wisdom is revealed. He is a catalyst for revealing true natures throughout. His songs are also important in establishing the mood in various parts of the play. Feste was tailored for Robert Armin, whose particular talents suited the role well. In the original copies of the play, Feste is usually referred to as 'Clown,' indicating the name is merely an afterthought. Feste implies the festive, superficially frivolous nature of the character and the play, though neither is ultimately superficial.

Fidele, *Cym,* name assumed by Innogen in disguise. Its meaning, 'faithful one,' compares to the symbolic names of other daughters in the late romances, such as Perdita, Marina, and Miranda.

Fife, county on Scotland's eastern coast. Located between the Firths of Forth and Tay, it was enclosed to the west by the Ochil hills. It was once an independent Pictish realm and was referred to affectionately by its inhabitants as 'The Kingdom.' The name itself is thought to come from a Frisian word for 'forest.' Both Frisians and Danes immigrated into Fife. *1H4:* see Mordake. *Mac 1.2.48,* possibly the thane of Fife, Macduff, but more likely the county. The later reference in the play to Saint Colum's inch (Inchcolm) places the scene of the battle in Fife. *2.4.37.*

Fife, Earl of, *1H4 1.1.71, 1.1.94,* see Mordake.

Fife, Thane of, *Mac 4.1.88, 5.1.40,* see Macduff.

Filario, *Cym,* F1 'Filorio,' 'Philario,' friend of Cymbeline's in Rome. Posthumus stays with him there, though he has never met him. Filario is a generous host who serves as a sounding board for various bits of exposition. There is no definite source for the name. Plutarch records a Philargyrus as a freedman of Cato's and Philarus as a stream, but maybe it is an adaptation of the Gr. *philein* 'to love (as a friend).'

Finsbury, *1H4 3.1.248,* open field north of London's wall between Cripplegate and Moorgate. In Sh.'s day it was a popular place for Londoners to stroll. The name would imply that some named Finn had a manor there in remote times.

Firedrake, *Mac 4.1.47,* spirit called forth by the witches in a song not appearing in F1, but which appears in Thomas Middleton's play *The Witch* (c. 1609, but not printed until the 18th c.). William Davenant's version of *Mac* (printed 1674), however, contains the song and it has been argued that he may have had access to an earlier text. A 'fire-drake' was a dragon. It was applied to meteors. The name was taken from Reginald Scot's *Discoverie of Witchcraft* (1584).

Fish Street, *2H6 4.7.155,* New Fish Street in the Billingsgate district of London. It led to St. Magnus Church near the entrance to London Bridge.

Fitzwalter, Lord, *R2,* Walter, (d. 1407), leader of a group of barons who, according to Holinshed (3.512), accused the duke of Aumerle of complicity in the murder of Thomas of Woodstock, duke of Gloucester. Gloucester had been one of the 'lords appellant' arrested by Richard II. Although Aumerle maintained his innocence and accepted Fitzwalter's challenge to a duel, Henry IV stripped him of his duchy.

Flaminius, *Tim,* one of Timon's servants. The name may have been suggested by Titus Flamininus, the subject of one of Plutarch's lives. Flaminio Scala, another possibility, was a comedian for the Duke of Mantua. His *Flavio Tradito, Comedia* was published in 1611, but the comedies were probably known before that and may have been a source or analogue to *TGV.* Flaminia is also a female character in the comedy that resembles *TGV.*

Flanders, the district on the continental side of the English channel between Calais and the

Scheldt river. Although Flanders was small, it was rich and powerful. Its towns were centers for a highly profitable cloth industry, and its ports, particularly Bruges and Antwerp, were hubs of medieval Europe's commerce. Flanders' wealth made it a prize for which feudal lords (particularly, the kings of France and the dukes of Burgundy) frequently contested. From time to time Flanders' prosperous merchant and working classes also rallied behind popular leaders who advocated independence and native self-government. England watched developments in Flanders very closely, for the English economy depended upon access to the Flemish wool markets. Flanders was also a convenient staging area for armies that planned to invade England. *3H6 4.6.22. STM Add. II.D.142. H8 3.2.320.*

Flavina, *TNK 1.3.54, 84,* girlhood friend of Emilia, who admits to Hippolyta that she may never love a man as much as she loved her friend. The story is intended to enlighten the close relationship of Theseus and Pirithous, and Hippolyta's acceptance of their bond. Also because Emilia lost Flavina to death, it suggests the theme of Emilia's acceptance of what the gods decree. It also emphasizes the theme that Platonic love between friends should transcend sexual love, as in *TGV.* Palamon and Arcite fail in that as they allow their love for Emilia to come between them. The source of the name is probably the many Flaviuses in Plutarch, though there is a Flavia in Spenser's *Colin Clouts Come Home Againe* (1591) l. 572.

Flavio, 1) *JC 5.3.107,* see Flavius 2).

2) *MM 4.5.6,* friend or vassal of the duke.

Flavius, 1) *JC,* Lucius Cæsetius Flavius, plebeian tribune (44 BC) deposed by Julius Cæsar. Plutarch ('Cæsar' 61, 1–5) says that on the feast of the Lupercalia Mark Antony offered Cæsar a crown and invited Cæsar to declare himself king of Rome. When a crowd of bystanders failed to respond enthusiastically to Antony's suggestion, Cæsar saved face by spurning the idea. Subsequent events imply that if Cæsar had not urged Antony to his audacious gesture, he was also not reluctant to receive royal honors. When someone decked Cæsar's statues with crowns, Flavius and his colleague in the tribunate, Marillus (Murellus), protested. They removed the offending symbols of royalty and arrested some men who had cheered when Antony tempted Cæsar to overturn the Republic. Although some citizens hailed Flavius as a second Lucius Junius Brutus (the patriot who had driven the last king from Rome), Cæsar was offended and had him removed from office.

2) *JC,* Caius Flavius, (d. 42 BC), Marcus Junius Brutus' chief military engineer. He died in the battle of Philippi. Plutarch ('Brutus' LI, 2) says that Flavius was one of the men recalled and mourned by Brutus as Brutus contemplated suicide.

3) *MM 4.5.10,* see Flavio, 2).

4) *Tim,* Timon's steward, who warns him against his financial profligacy. The name appears in Plutarch's 'Mark Antony,' which contains a passage about Timon, and in his 'Cæsar.' This is the same tribune as 1).

Fleance, *Mac,* son of Banquo. Though Macbeth plans his murder along with Banquo's, Fleance escapes leaving the line prophesied to bear future kings (such as James I, Sh.'s patron) intact. There is no real historical evidence that a Fleance existed. Sh. got the name from Raphael Holinshed's *Chronicles* (1577), his source, which derived from Hector Boece's *Scotorum Historiæ* (1526), which, though highly respected, incorporated many legends in order to provide a complete history of Scotland up until 1488.

Fleet, *2H4 5.5.89,* London prison near Ludgate on the edge of the Fleet, a stream that flowed along medieval London's western wall. In Sh.'s day the lock-up was a relatively benign facility to which disgraced members of the nobility were sent.

Fleming, native of Flanders, an area in the Low Countries now overlapping northern France and western Belgium. It existed as a state from the times of Frankish ruler Charles the Bald until its absorption into Burgundy in the late 14th c. Bruges and Ghent were the primary cities of the region. The Flemish language is essentially the same as Dutch (Netherlandic) and there was essentially no cultural difference in the peoples. Many English soldiers fought in the Low Countries in Sh.'s time and Flanders was devastated by the wars against the Spanish rulers of the Netherlands. Attempts to suppress Flemish language and culture in favor of French is still a source of acrimony in the nation of Belgium. *MWW 2.2.291,* the joke refers to the Dutch diet, heavy in butter.

Flemish, (adj.) of or pertaining to Flanders and the Flemings. *MWW 2.1.22,* 'Flemish drunkard': the heavy-drinking Dutch stereotype is the allusion.

Flibbertigibbet, *Lr. 3.4.108 (Q 11.104); Q 15.59,* 'Stiberdegebit,' a devil. Sh. got the name from a book attacking Jesuit exorcists by Samuel Harsnett, *A Declaration of egregious Popish Impostures, to with-draw the harts of her Majesties Subjects from their allegeance, and from the truth of the Christian Religion, professed in England, under the pretence of casting out devils. Practised by Edmunds, alias* Weston *a Jesuit, and divers Romish Priests his wicked associates* (1603). Chaplain to the Bishop of London, Harsnett had earned his reputation by debunking the celebrated exorcisms of John Darrell and followed that success with this book. Harsnett lists the names of the demons driven out primarily to mock them as 'non-significant' names. His book is quite amusing as he ridicules what the various demons are alleged to have said about themselves in their possessions of various people. Harsnett's spirit of skepticism is, unfortunately, uncommon even today. Flibbertigibbet, described by Edgar as prince of 'mocking and mowing' and possessor of chambermaids and waiting-women, was previously used as the name of a mischievous spirit similar to a puck, and derives from a mockery of meaningless chatter. He is mentioned in Bishop Latimer's sermons and Thomas Heywood's *Proverbs and Epigrams.* The name is still applied to anyone who is flighty and chatty.

Flint Castle, *R2 3.2.205,* fortress built by Henry II in the town of Flint, the seat of the Welsh shire of Flint. Holinshed (3.500–501) says that Richard II surrendered to Henry (IV) Bolingbroke there. Richard's army had already melted away in the face of Henry's insurrection, but Richard may have come believing that he would be permitted to retain the crown. Only later did he realize that he had become Henry's captive and was not likely ever to be set at liberty.

Flora, *WT 4.4.2,* Roman goddess of flowers and gardens, wife of Zephyrus (the west wind). In the source, Robert Greene's *Pandosto,* or the Triumph of Time (1588; rptd. 1607 as *Dorastus and Fawnia*), Fawnia (Sh.'s Perdita) is described: 'shee seemed to bee the Goddesse Flora her selfe for beauty.'

Florence, (It. *Firenze*) city of central Italy, located on both banks of the Arno river about 170 miles northwest of Rome in a beautiful valley encircled by the Apennines. Florence was perhaps the major center of Renaissance culture and many of its greatest leaders worked there—by Sh.'s time including Galileo, Dante, Machiavelli, Michelangelo, Petrarch, Boccaccio, Leonardo da Vinci, Giotto, Savonarola, Raphael, Amerigo Vespucci, Benvenuto Cellini, Andrea del Sarto, and a variety of popes. It became for the Renaissance what Athens had been for 5th c. BC Greece. Its gold coin, the florin, was a standard throughout Europe. Its architectural splendors completed by Sh.'s time include the Campanile (begun 1332, designed by Giotto), the Duomo (designed by Brunelleschi), the Pitti Palace (begun 1458), the Ponte Vecchio (c. 1350), the Palazzo Vecchio (begun 1298, finished 1550), the church of Santa Croce, and the Uffizi.

Of obscure origin, probably Etruscan, the city first became known when Sulla established a Roman colony there in the late 2nd or early 1st c. BC. It was named for the abundant flowers in the area in Roman times when it was called *Colonia Florentia* 'flowering colony.' During Tiberius' reign (14-37 AD) it was distinguished for its writers and orators. In 541 Totila, king of the Goths, almost entirely destroyed the city, but it was restored by Charlemagne around 250 years later. In the 12th c. it gained autonomy and grew immensely as the chief city of a republic, despite the Guelph and Ghibelline conflict of the 13th c., and the civil war between Guelph factions which began in 1300. Rival to Milan through the 14th and 15th c., Florence's acquisition of the seaport Pisa in 1406 was a major step in its development as a power. A conflict between the aristocrats and the merchant-bankers resulted in Cosimo de' Medici in 1434 exiling his upper class opponents and seizing virtual control of the city, though he was ostensibly a private citizen. From that point until the 18th c., with brief interruptions from 1494-1512 and 1527-30, Florence was a Medici domain. In 1537, they officially made it their dukedom and the title of grand duke of Tuscany was conferred by the pope in 1569.

Shr 1.1.14: Lucentio has been brought up in Florence, indicating his high education. *4.2.92,* the Pedant has bills for money from Florence, a hint of the city's financial importance. *AWW 3.2.68, 4.3.16, 218, 5.3.94, 127,* setting for much of the play as the young men volunteer to fight in Florence's war with Siena. *Oth 1.3.45.*

2) *AWW 1.2.12,* the duke of F.

Florence, Duke of, *AWW,* relation of the king of France. In his war with Siena he uses volunteers from France. There is no particular indication that any specific ruler was in Sh.'s mind in creating this character. Florence and Siena struggled frequently during the Guelf/Ghibelline conflicts of the 12th and 13th c. and Florence used French troops against Siena. French meddling in Tuscany was a constant factor, however. By 1557 Siena fell to the rule of Florence under Cosimo I de' Medici, (1519-74) grand duke of Tuscany, who may be suggested by Sh.'s duke. The Medicis were related to the French royal family because of the marriages of Catherine and Marie de Medicis to French kings.

Florentine, 1) (n.) native of Florence. *Shr 1.1.202. Ado 1.1.10. AWW 5.3.132, 160. Oth 1.1.19, 3.1.39:* see Cassio, Michael. Pl.: *AWW 1.2.1, 3.6.24.*

2) *AWW 1.2.6, 4.1.74,* duke of Florence.

3) (adj.) of or pertaining to Florence. *AWW 2.1.0.*

Florentius, 'F.'s love,' *Shr 1.2.68.* Florentius appears in John Gower's *Confessio Amantis,* 1 (1390). He swore to marry a deformed hag so that he could receive from her the solution of a riddle upon which his life depended. The story has been compared with Geoffrey Chaucer's *Wife of Bath's Tale.*

Florizel, *WT,* prince of Bohemia, son of Polixenes. He disguises himself as Doricles the shepherd to the consternation of his father, but wins the love of Perdita. The name may come from Don Florisel, who is hero of *Amadis de Grecia* by Don Feliciano de Silva. Florisel disguised as a shepherd wins the love of a princess disguised as a shepherdess. The tale was widely translated, though its availability in English is uncertain. A French version, *Champenois* by Charles Colet (1564) may have been known to Sh., as Greene, who uses the story in Sh.'s primary source *Pandosto,* or the Triumph of Time (1588; rptd. 1607 as *Dorastus and Fawnia*), borrowed the name of his character Garinter from it. Florizel would suitably imply the pastoral nature of the play with its origin in the word for flower. In *Pandosto,* Florizel's equivalent is Dorastus.

Flower de luce, *1H6 1.1.80, 1.3.78,* Fr. *fleur-de-lis,* heraldic symbol derived from the lily. It first appeared as a royal emblem in France when Louis VII used it at the coronation of his son, Philip Augustus (1180–1223). Heraldic symbols were just beginning their evolution in the late 12th century, and the rules governing their interpretation were not yet fully developed. Louis may have intended the *'fleur de Loys'* to be a pun on his own name. The fully developed arms of France (the light blue shield with three golden *fleurs de lis*) does not appear on the royal seal until the reign of Louis VIII (1223–1226). English kings added it to their lion rampant shield when they laid claim to the French crown in the 14th century.

Fluellen, Captain, *H5,* fictional character, a dour Welshman quick to take offense at everything. Sh. may have found his inspiration for Fluellen in a member of Elizabeth's court. Roger Williams (one of Essex's companions) or a certain Ludovic Lloyd have both been suggested as suitable prototypes. It is also possible that Sh. modeled Fluellen's colorful personality on a real soldier who has his own role in the play: David Gam, Dafydd ab Llewelyn (i.e., Fluellen). See Gam, Davy.

Flute, Francis, *MND,* young bellows-mender who is forced into the role of Thisbe in the rustics' performance before Theseus, even though he protests he has a beard coming. His name may represent the sound of his voice, thin and reedy or in puberty's embarrassing process of breaking. It also refers to the snout of a bellows, called the flute.

Foix, County of, feudal domain on France's border with Spain. During the 13th century it belonged to the duchy of Aquitaine and was part of the Angevin empire of England's King Henry II. In 1398 it passed by marriage to the family of the counts of Graiily. See Foix, Earl of, *H5.*

Foix, Earl of, *H5 3.5.45, 4.8.99,* John, (1382–1436), French nobleman whom Sh., following Holinshed (3.555), lists as a casualty of the battle at Agincourt. In reality Foix survived that conflict and joined the victorious English. Since he had previously been involved in the schemes of both the Burgundian and Armagnac (Orléanist) factions, neither French party had much confidence in him. His commitment to England ended in 1422 when Henry V died. He reasserted his allegiance to his homeland and spent the rest of his life in the south of France chasing marauding bands of outlaws and dabbling in the wars between the Spanish kingdoms of Aragon and Castile.

Fontibel, *AWW 4.2.1,* F1 'Fontybell.' Bertram has been told that this is Diana's name. There is no explanation why. It likely derives from OFr. *fon et belle,* 'doting and beautiful.'

Fool, 1) *Lr.,* Lear's jester. In the tradition of the 'wise fool,' he warns the king about the senselessness of his action, even offering to exchange Lear's crown for his coxcomb. Unlike Kent, he gets away with it because he is expected to say foolish things. Most critics have long argued that court fools or jesters served an important social role in allowing a ruler to see outside his circle of noble flatterers. While this may overestimate the wisdom of comics and grossly underestimate the inability of most rulers and noblemen to profit from a joke, it is a commonly held critical view that Lear's fool has his latitude because of playing this social role. Given the great variety of personalities at the various courts, it seems generous to refer to the fool as an 'institution.' Comedy always implies some sort of social criticism.

There is no equivalent for the Fool in any of Sh.'s sources for the play. It is generally thought that the role was written for and created by Robert Armin, a superb verbal comedian and singer, who joined the Lord Chamberlain's Men after William Kemp (q.v.) left in 1599. A play by him survives, *Two Maids of Moreclacke* (c. 1598) and joke books, *Fool Upon Foole* (1600) and *Quips Upon Questions* (1600). It is very likely that many of the quips were Armin's own inventions and were incorporated into Sh.'s text.

A most interesting legend is that Armin might have doubled the roles of the Fool and Cordelia. They do not appear on the stage at the same time and Lear compares his daughter to the Fool late in the play. If so, Armin, already one of the most famous actors of his time, would also have been one of the most brilliant. Even though it has always been difficult for modern playgoers to understand how boys were convincing as women in the original productions, and they clearly were, a counter argument to the doubling theory is that Armin was too recognizable to pull off Cordelia, unless he regularly assumed women's roles, which is not known to be the case. He originated the roles of Feste, Touchstone, and Thersites, as well as reviving Kemp's Dogberry (q.q.v.) among his other roles.

2) *TNK 3.5.128,* a stock character in the morris dance before Theseus.

Football, game played with an inflated cow bladder covered with leather. According to legend, the inspiration for it was provided by some workmen who entertained themselves by kicking the skull of a Dane they had discovered while digging. However the idea came about, it became popular in the late 11th c. Adjacent towns would attempt to kick the bladder over the countryside to the center of the opposition town. Sometimes there would be dozens of participants and the game became so rowdy that authorities were forced to confine it to playing fields with end lines. It thereby evolved toward what Americans now call soccer. By the reign of Henry II (1154–1189), the sport was so popular that the king ordered an end to it—he was worried that the players were neglecting their archery. The game was suppressed and only occasionally permitted until the early 16th c. when Dubliners defied the ban and Englishmen began playing on the sly. In the early 17th c., since firearms had supplanted archery, King James was asked to set aside the old laws against it. He not only did so, but expressed his enthusiasm for its manly healthfulness. It once again became wildly popular, but was also played quite roughly.

Err 2.1.82: Dromio's remarks here imply the nature of the ball, as he complains about being abused. *Lr. 1.4.84 (Q 4.83),* 'thou base football player': Kent says this when he trips Oswald, an indication of the rough style of the game.

Ford, Master Frank, *MWW,* husband of Alice, a highly temperamental man whose anger over Falstaff's intention towards his wife can hardly be contained. He at first refuses to believe in the knight's plot because his wife is too old. Later, however, he accepts the notion much more easily than the restrained Page. He disguises himself as Brooke and tries to encourage Falstaff's attack on his wife in order to expose the knight's relations with Alice, and to demonstrate to Page what he sees as the sad reality of female infidelity. There is, in his story, the pattern of the male whose lack of confidence in his wife leads to a painful chastening, as in *Ado, WT,* and other plays. He may have learned something about his wife and women in general at play's end, but he is not so changed that he is the one who initiates the overtures of reconciliation. It is Page who invites Falstaff to dinner. Ford is a common English name and when he assumes the name Brooke to deceive Falstaff, it is likely a quibble referring to water.

Ford, Mistress Alice, *MWW,* wife of Frank. Her husband is more inclined to jealousy than George Page is of his wife and Alice's friend, Margaret, so Alice gets a double pleasure out of deceiving Falstaff as it torments her husband and gives him a lesson about the consequences of his quick anger. In the first humiliation of Falstaff, he is invited to the Ford house and forced to escape in a malodorous pile of laundry. In the second humiliation, Falstaff attempts to escape the angry Ford in the disguise of the old woman of Brentford, whom Alice knows her husband despises. Her situation with her husband contrasts with the happier marriage of the Pages and she knows it. However, there is hope at the conclusion that Ford has learned something about her and life, though his excitable nature has likely not changed and she will have to endure it. This difference in characterization between the two couples would have been deemed unnecessary by lesser writers, but adds much depth to what is basically a farce. *2.1.48,* 'Sir Alice Ford,' another allusion to the ritual granting of the Garter at Windsor.

Forest, *R3 4.3.4, 4.3.10, 4.3.15,* Miles F., one of the jailers who looked after Edward IV's sons after Richard III sent them to the Tower. James Tyrrell supposedly recruited him to murder the boys, and he and John Dighton, a groom, allegedly carried out the crime. Richard later appointed Forest keeper of the wardrobe at Baynard Castle, and Forest was reported to have died shortly thereafter from a loathsome disease that rotted his flesh. The historical evidence relating to the disappearance of the princes is so confused that the identities and relative responsibilities of those involved will probably always remain a mystery.

Forres, *Mac 1.3.37,* town near the coast on Moray Firth in northern Scotland. It lies about halfway between Elgin and Nairn in the modern county of Elgin, and is not far from Cawdor. The Gælic name means 'near water.' A very ancient town, it is the site of the murder of King Duff, which provided most of the details of the murder of Duncan in Sh.'s play. A local tradition holds that Duncan was killed by Macbeth on Castlehill, though that structure was destroyed in 1297. Nearby is a carved monolith known as Sueno's stone, which is of uncertain origin but may celebrate a victory by Sueno, son of Harald king of Denmark, or the driving of the Danes from Moray in 1014. In any case, the tradition of the struggle between the inhabitants and Scandinavian invaders is quite obvious. There is another stone nearby which tradition calls the Witches' Stone because it is supposed to be where Macbeth met the witches. These traditions would place the battle far from where it seems to take place in other references, but details of that time period are obscure and Sh. is always rather careless with his geography.

Forthright, Master, *MM 4.3.15,* F1 'Forthlight the tilter,' a mocking name for one of the impoverished criminals Pompey knows. As prisoners paid for their own food, many were forced to beg passers by. There is perhaps an obscene joke in his being a straight-ahead jouster.

Fortinbras 1), *Ham,* son of the king of Norway. He is intent upon winning back the lands lost by his father, who was killed by Hamlet's father. Although he is on a mission of revenge much like Hamlet, his straightforward military actions are portrayed as noble and heroic in a way that Hamlet's vacillations are not. Hamlet seems to measure himself against Fortinbras, although the moral morass in which Hamlet finds himself is not really parallel to Fortinbras' situation. As Hamlet dies, he passes his kingdom on to Fortinbras who enters much like Richmond at the end of *R3,* to purge the kingdom. Like Richmond, Fortinbras is so adamantly noble that he is more a symbol than a character. Even the meaning of his name is straightforward, deriving from the French for 'strong arms.' A less likely argument is that it is a form of *fierumbras,* or 'iron arms,' which is to be read 'iron-side,' a name applied to a Norse king. The implication of the meaning would be no different. A Niccolò Fortebraccio was also a known leader of mercenaries in Italy

2), *Ham 1.1.81, 85, 91,* old F., king of Norway killed by Hamlet's father. The thrones of Norway and Denmark were united for much of history, though they were frequently contested by various Scandinavian factions.

Fortune, Fortuna, Roman goddess of destiny, particularly associated in Sh.'s time with the image of Fortune's wheel, to which a person's life was metaphorically attached, to rise or fall as the wheel inevitably turned. She is generally portrayed as a fickle goddess, a 'Lady Luck.' She is often referred to as a loose woman who changes her affections on whim.

Jn 2.1.391, 2.2.61, 3.1.44, 3.4.119, 5.2.58. 1H4 1.1.82. H5 3.6.26, 3.6.36, 3.6.37. PP 17.10, 'frowning fortune, cursèd fickle dame.' *Cym 4.1.23. AYLI 1.2.30-54,* 'Lady F.,' *2.7.16. MV 2.1.36,* 'blind F.,' *2.2.160, 4.1.264.*

TN 2.2.18. Tro 3.3.82, 129, 'skittish F.'s hall.' *Ham 2.2.230,* 'F.'s cap.' *2.2.236,* 'private parts of F.,' the genitalia of the goddess. *2.2.243. 2.2.495,* 'Strumpet F.': see also *2.2.236-237. 2.2.513,* 'F.'s state.' *3.2.65,* 'F.'s buffets.' *3.2.68,* 'F.'s finger.' *Lr. 2.2.227,* 'F., that arrant whore.' *5.1.36 (Q 23.47). 5.3.6 (Q 24.6),* 'false fortune's frown.'

AWW 1.3.108, 3.3.7, 5.2.4-33. Oth 3.4.120, 'F.'s alms.' *Per 18.42. WT 4.4.51, 668.*

Tim 1.1.65-95, the Poet and Painter discuss their depictions of the goddess. *Ant 4.13.19, 4.16.46, 5.2.3. TNK 3.1.16,* 'Lady F.' *5.6.17, 20.*

France, 1) country in western Europe. For much of its history, all or part of it was claimed as belonging to the English monarchy by virtue of descent from William the Conqueror, and therefore many of the events in Sh.'s histories take place in the context of trying to solidify these claims. By his own times, France was largely a battlefield for Catholicism and Protestantism. French nobles are often portrayed as being too fashion-conscious and decadent, leading to their weakness in the face of British sturdiness. Whether Sh. may ever have been to France remains conjectural. He seems to have known the language somewhat, but there is nothing particular in his works that indicates any special familiarity with the country or language that could not have been learned from secondary sources. His Ardenne, *AYLI,* for example, is no more a representation of France than his Illyria is of that land.

3H6. R3 3.1.92, 3.7.6, 3.7.10, 4.4.115, 5.6.58. Err 3.2.125, 131, a location on the 'globe' that is Nell: there is an allusion to the civil war in which the Catholic nobles refused to allow Henry of Navarre to take the throne, though Henry II had designated him heir.

LLL 4.1.6, 104, 119, 4.3.347, 5.2.550, the Princess of France comes with her retinue to settle a debt. *MV 1.2.72. R2 1.1.131, 5.1.22, 37, 54, 78, 87. Jn 1.1.150, 2.1.22, 90. MWW 3.3.49, 163, 164,* references to the stylishness of French society. *2H4 5.5.105, epilogue.27. STM Add. II.D.142.*

Ham 1.2.51, 55, 1.3.73, 4.5.86, 5.2.156: France is portrayed as a country in which Lærtes can learn sophistication (dressing well) and fencing. *AWW,* setting for much of the play. *Lr., passim. Q 7.370,* 'hot-blood in F.,' compare France 5). *2.2.385. Cym 1.4.10, 60, 65, 1.6.190. H8.*

2) *LLL 2.1.152,* father of the Princess of France.

3) *Jn,* see Philip (II) Augustus.

4) *AWW,* the king. *3.1.7,* 'our cousin F.'

5) *Lr., passim,* the king. *2.2.385,* 'hot-blooded F.,' see France 1).

France, King of, 1) *LLL 2.1.30,* father of the Princess of France (q.v.). He borrowed money from Ferdinand of Navarre's father to carry out a war. Word of his death interrupts the merry-making in the final act.

2) *AWW:* a kindly, yet authoritative ruler, he is ill as the play begins and is cured by Helen, rewarding her with Bertram's hand in marriage. As is normal for the wise rulers in Sh., he also sorts out the misunderstandings that have imperilled the various characters. It is doubtful that Sh. had a particular king in mind, only a typical wise ruler. In Sh.'s source, Boccaccio's *Decameron,* 3.9, as translated by William Painter in *The Palace of Pleasure* (1566), the corresponding character is the Count of Rossiglione and the equivalent of Bertram is the count's son.

3), *Lr.,* husband of Cordelia. He marries her despite her lack of dowry and attempts to help her re-establish her father upon the throne. Pressing matters in his country, however, keep him away from the final struggles which result in his wife's and Lear's death. To show the ruler of France as being chivalrous and noble might be one thing, but to have him participating in an invasion of England, even on behalf of Lear was politically unwise. In Geoffrey of Monmouth's *Historia Regum Britanniæ,* Holinshed's *Chronicles,* and in John Higgin's *Mirror for Magistrates* (1574), the King of the Franks is named Aganippus; Aganip in Spenser's *Færie Queen,* 2.10. These are all possible sources for Sh.

Frances, *LLL 3.1.118,* any whore. The name seems to have been used much in the same way that 'John' has become the name of a prostitute's customer.

Francesca, *MM,* F1 'Francisca,' nun in the order that Isabella intends to join. In *1.4* Isabella complains to her that the restrictions for the order are not strong enough and when Lucio approaches, Francesca says she is not permitted to speak to men except in the presence of the prioress. Even then she would not be permitted to show her face. If revealing the face, she could not speak. Her name is given only once in the stage direction opening the scene and it is believed to have been chosen from St. Francis (Latin, *Francisco*) in Erasmus' *Funis* (as were St. Clare, Barnardine, and Vincentio) which seems to have been used by Sh. as a source of information about the orders.

Francia, *H5 5.2.337,* L. 'France.'

Francis, *1H4,* one of three bartenders whom Prince Harry considered personal friends.

Francis I, duke of Bretagne, *2H6 1.1.7,* (d. 1488), heir to John V, the duke of Brittany, who died on 28 August 1442. Francis' political situation and family life were complicated by the fact that the kings of England and France disputed the overlordship of Brittany. Francis' father, John, had won the dukedom with England's help. France had backed Charles of Blois against him. Despite reliance on England, Brittany had a tradition of independence that John was careful not to compromise. He was astute at pitting the French and English against each other. John's younger son, Giles, was raised at the English court as one of Henry VI's companions, and this established a bond between Giles and Henry that subsequently shaped English diplomacy. In 1443 the inept conduct of Somerset, England's commander in France, created a military situation that threatened Brittany and forced its new duke, Francis, into the French camp.

Giles, Francis' brother, was unhappy with the inheritance that had been assigned him, and he encouraged England to intervene. In 1446 Giles openly opposed an oath of limited vassalage that Francis offered Charles VII of France. Francis reacted by charging Giles with treason and arresting him. Henry demanded the release of his friend, and the incident gave the French an excuse to declare war. Henry refused to participate in any meetings where the duke of Brittany was listed among the vassals of France, and his firmness on this point was cited by Charles VII as a reason for resuming hostilities between the two nations. On 31 July 1449, the Hundred Years' War flared up for the last time. The French quickly overran Normandy, and the English found that they were powerless to protect Giles who was murdered on 24 April 1450. In 1488 Francis died without a male heir, and in 1491 the marriage of his daughter Anne to Charles VIII brought Brittany indisputably within the orbit of the French throne.

Francis, Friar, *Ado,* priest who presides over Hero's abortive wedding. Not believing in her guilt, he persuades Leonato to let her feign death in order to make Claudio see the cruelness of his immediate acceptance of her alleged promiscuity. One of the criticisms leveled at the play is that this plan does not prove Hero's innocence and it is only happenstance which brings about the joyous ending in which the friar marries the young couples. Sh. likely had the Franciscan order in mind (see St. Francis).

Francis, St., of Assisi (1182-1226). Born Giovanni Francesco Bernardone, son of a wealthy merchant, he lived comfortably until a battle between Assisi and Perugia resulted in his imprisonment. He nearly died of an illness and resolved to lead a more holy life. His charity work so infuriated his father that he was rejected by the family. He took up residence on Mt. Subasio caring for lepers and other outcasts and restoring the chapel of S. Maria degli Angeli. In 1208 he returned to Assisi, preached, and gathered twelve disciples who became the first brothers of the Franciscan order (Order of Friars Minor). The order was officially approved by Pope Innocent III in 1209 and was sworn to poverty and acts of charity everywhere. In 1212 Francis established a female Franciscan order, the Clares (q.v.). He went to the Holy Land, preached among the Moors in Spain and to the sultan in Egypt. He suffered great pain and blindness in his final years. Among the miracles associated with him were the appearance of stigmata on his body and his ability to preach to animals, who had no fear of him. After his death the order he had founded built a convent and basilica at Assisi and suffered much dissension. It grew to be second only to the Dominicans and was divided by Pope Leo X in 1517 into the Conventuals and the Observants. Later, the Capuchins were also separated from the order. The order produced four popes. It also was the primary force in bringing Christianity to the New World.

Rom 2.2.65: Friar Laurence is clearly intended to be Franciscan, as his oath implies. His interest in learning was also considered a Franciscan trait by Sh.'s time, the order having produced in England many prominent university scholars such as William of Ockham, Duns Scotus, and Roger Bacon. Laurence is said to be Franciscan in Arthur Brooke's *Tragicall Historye of Romeus and Juliet* (1562), Sh.'s source, and much of the action takes place in 'Saint Frauncis church.'

Francisco, 1) *MWW 2.2.26,* Dr. Caius: the Host's grandiloquent way of saying 'Frenchman.' In Q1-2, the word is 'francoyes,' an attempt to correct it to a more French sounding word.

2) *Ham,* one of the sentinels at Elsinore. He is relieved by Bernardo and his comments establish the time, setting, and mood—an important task in the outdoor theater of Sh.'s day. Francisco is named in the German curiosity *Der Bestrafte Brudermord* (1710) which is often thought to be based on an earlier version of *Ham,* possibly written by Thomas Kyd. If the theory is correct, then Francisco has long been part of the story. He is officer of the guard and swears loyalty to Hamlet's plans for revenge, the equivalent of Marcellus' taking an oath of secrecy in Sh.'s play. The name is common in the Italian literature which influenced Sh. so much. Possibly it was suggested by the murder of Francisco Maria della Rovere, duke of Urbino (see 'Murder of Gonzaga').

3), *Tmp,* lord who is shipwrecked with Antonio and the others. He enters three times *2.1.1, 3.3.1,* and *5.1.57*; speaks twice *2.1.119, 3.3.39*; and falls to sleep at *2.1.119.* Like many another minor Shakespearean gentleman he is a witness to offstage events, but otherwise has no role in the plot. The character helps fill the stage like a good prop and kept one of the King's Men from being idle. The name was common and chosen for its Italian sound.

Frankfurt, *MV 3.1.79,* F1 'Franckford,' where Shylock bought a diamond which Jessica stole. A central German city located on the north bank of the Main river, 24 mi. above its confluence with the Rhine, and therefore in an excellent trading location. It was known for several centuries for its very successful fairs. It was founded by the Romans in the first century AD and later occupied by the Franks, who gave it their name 'the ford of the Franks.' It was one of the seats of Charlemagne's empire in the 8th c. Louis I surrounded it with walls in 838 and it was the site of many important councils during the Middle Ages. It was also the place where elections for the office of Holy Roman Emperor were held and it became the coronation site for the emperors two years before Sh.'s birth. At the onset of the Reformation, Frankfurt sided with the Protestants and was occupied by imperial soldiers. A popular rising called the Fettmilch insurrection (1612-1616) was directed against the oligarchical families in control of the city and the Jews. In 1616, however, the Jews were restored to their previous position and were compensated for their losses. Shylock's reference to Frankfurt is therefore more than just coincidental: the city had a strong Jewish population and a major international market.

Frateretto, *Lr. 3.6.6 (Q 13.6),* a demon. It may mean 'little brother' from the L. *frater,* but is more likely 'little flatterer' with the L transposed to R in Sara Williams' account of her exorcism in Harsnett's *Declaration of Popish Impostures.* See Flibbertigibbet.

Frederick, 1) *AYLI,* see Duke Frederick.

2) *MM 3.1.211, 218,* soldier. When he was drowned in a shipwreck, his sister Mariana's dowry was lost and Angelo heartlessly abandoned his plans to marry her. Frederick is otherwise unmentioned and is probably only drawn into this discussion to demonstrate that

Mariana comes from good stock. This was an uncommon name in Sh.'s England and considered Germanic, though it had been used in Britain during the Norman era.

Freetown, *Rom 1.1.99,* place where the Prince intends to try to make a settlement of the feud between the families. The name comes from Arthur Brooke's *Tragicall Historye of Romeus and Juliet* (1562), Sh.'s source, where Juliet's father says it is the castle of the Capulets (l. 1974). 'Free towne' is Brooke's translation of the Italian 'Villafranca' in *Le novelle del Bandello* (1554) from which he borrowed the story.

French, 1) (n.) modern language that evolved from the Latin originally spoken in Roman Gaul. During the Middle Ages many dialects developed within the confines of what became France, but the 'francien' spoken in Paris emerged as the national tongue. There were several reasons for its success. Paris was the seat of France's royal government and of Europe's most important university. The French monarchy began to use French in addition to Latin for official documents in the 13th century, and as the power of the kings spread to the provinces of France so did the language of the court. By the 15th century Francien had become France's language of literature as well as law. In Sh.'s day the French kings abandoned Latin entirely and made their vernacular mandatory for all official purposes.

2H6 4.3.164. LLL 3.1.9. R2 5.3.117, 5.3.122. MV 1.2.67. H5 4.4.22, 29, 30. 5.2.185, 186, 216, 218, 334: one of the most interesting scenes in Sh. regarding the author's intended audience or his expectations of all or part of his audience occurs at *3.4,* in which Catherine of France gets an English lesson from Alice. A number of the jokes depend for their humor upon knowing that the English sound of words such as 'foot' and 'gown' sound very much like French obscenities. Are these dirty jokes for the multilingual nobility, or could Sh. assume a larger share of his audience would catch the humor?

2) (n.) people whose culture and language evolved in the early Middle Ages in the territories that had been Roman Gaul. Their name derives from the German tribes of Franks who reorganized Gaul after the fall of the Roman empire. Since France had not achieved political unification under a centralized monarchy by the end of the Middle Ages, use of the term was not always limited to persons who were directly subject to the authority of the French king. The French were often mocked for their changeable, indecisive natures, noted for their excellence in sports such as falconry, riding, and fencing, and in amusements such as dancing.

2H6. 1H6. R2 2.1.179, 2.3.101. Jn 2.1.214, 4.2.161, 5.1.5. MV 2.8.29, a reference to the English Channel. *MWW 3.1.89. 2H4 1.3.71, 84. H5 5.2.362. Ham 4.7.69, 5.2.124. AWW 2.1.20, 2.3.95, 4.1.73 (a F. speaker). H8.*

3) (adj.) of or pertaining to France, often used as a term of contempt. *2H6 4.2.156,* 'F. crowns': the *écu,* a gold coin worth about six shillings; however, the phrase also had an obscene connotation meaning a bald head produced by the venereal disease syphilis, the 'F. disease.' *R3 1.3.49,* 'F. nods,' the use of foreign mannerisms implied deceit.

LLL 1.1.133. 1.2.61, a mockery of French courtiers' fashion consciousness. *3.1.7,* 'F. brawl,' a dance originating in France which was similar to a cotillion. Hands were held and the dancers moved side to side together. *3.1.138,* 'F. crown,' see above.

MND 1.2.88, 'F.-crown-colour beard,' gold-coloured beard. *1.2.90,* 'F. crowns,' see above. *Rom 2.3.41. 45,* 'F. slop,' loose trousers. *MV 1.2.52,* 'F. lord,' a suitor of Portia. *MWW 1.3.79,* 'F. thrift': there is no particular sense in Sh. or his contemporaries that the French were thought thrifty. Possibly this refers to some particular instance of a French nobleman with a single page. It may be an attempt at the ever-popular venereal disease joke, or French fickleness, or falseness (meaning no thrift at all). None of these explanations is convincing. *3.1.57.*

2H4 3.2.219, and *H5 4.1.222, 225,* 'F. crowns,' above. *H5 3.6.52,* 'F. hose,' padded, wide, short breeches worn below the doublet. 'Hose' did not mean 'stockings' and included a variety of garments. *Ham 2.2.433,* 'F. falc'ners,' they were reputed to be among the best at this sport. *5.2.114,* 'F. rapiers'; *5.2.123,* 'F. swords,' the French were reputed to excel at fencing and their swords were considered very high quality.

MM 1.2.34, 'F. velvet,' the pile of velvet would be thin compared to kersey and therefore akin to the hair on someone infected with syphilis. There is also a pun on 'pile,' a tumor on the private parts. *1.2.50,* 'F. crown,' above. *AWW 1.1.157-58,* 'F. withered pears.' *2.2.21,* 'F. crown,' see above. *3.5.3, 3.5.12.*

Mac 2.3.13, 'F. hose,' see above. The joke here is about aping foreign fashions or stealing from the extra cloth in 'F. hose.' There is an obscene connotation in that a 'needle' is sneaking out of breeches to cook a 'goose' (whore). *Per 16.101,* 'F. knight,' Monsieur Veroles, a brothel customer afflicted with syphilis.

H8 1.3.41, 'F. song and a fiddle': the ladies are said to have a particular weakness for their tunes. There is also likely a joke on 'fiddle,' meaning 'trifle with,' a usage dating back at least to the 16th c.

Frenchman, any male native of France.

1) *1H6 3.7.85. Ado 3.2.31,* the passage mocks the stylish Englishman's mixing of national fashions. *AWW 4.5.38.* Pl.: *2H6 1.1.89, 4.2.167. 1H6. Jn 2.1.42, 316. H5 3.6.150. AWW 2.1.12, 4.2.74.*

2) *MV 1.2.79,* see Bon, Monsieur le.

3) *MV 2.8.27,* anonymous informant of Salerio's.

4) *MWW 2.1.208,* see Caius.

5) *Ham 4.7.106,* see Lamord.

6) *AWW 3.5.78,* see Bertram.

7) *AWW 4.3.181,* see Dumaine 2).

8) *Cym 1.4, 1.6.65, 77,* minor character who has met Posthumus on a previous visit to Orléans. In recalling a conflict over the relative virtues of women, he provokes the wager between Giacomo and Posthumus. His being present with the non-speaking Dutchman and Spaniard, presumably in distinctive costumes, demonstrates the cosmopolitan nature of Filario's home. Later, Giacomo contrasts Filario with the jolly Posthumus in order to deceive Innogen of the depth of Posthumus' love.

Frenchwoman, see Margaret of Anjou. *2H6 1.3.143. 3H6 1.4.150.*

Friar, member of one of the religious orders, particularly the four orders that were sworn to live by alms: the Dominicans, Augustinians, Carmelites, and Franciscans. From Fr. *frere* 'brother.'

1) *Rom,* see Laurence, and John.

2) *Ado,* see Francis.

3) *MM,* see Lodowick, and Peter.

Friday, sixth day of the week, named after the Norse god Freya by comparison to Venus, for whom the day was named in Latin. In the Christian tradition, it is the worst day of the week because it is the day of the Crucifixion and traditionally a day to refrain from the eating of meat. *Tro 1.1.76:* [Cressida would] 'be as fair o' Friday as Helen is on Sunday'; Cressida would be as beautiful on her worst day as Helen is on her best. *MM 3.1.440,* a reference to Friday fasting, but also to refraining from sex—'mutton' was slang for 'prostitute.' *AYLI 4.1.108.*

Friz, *TNK 3.5.25,* morris dance participant.

Frogmore, *MWW 2.3.68, 78, 3.1.31,* area and possibly a village within the forest of Windsor, 1 mi. south of the castle on the road to Staines. A small residence for members of the royal family was located there in later times. Its name would mean 'a pool or swampy area frequented by frogs.'

Froissart, *1H6 1.3.8,* (c. 1338–1410), major chronicler of the events of his own generation (concluding with the deposition of England's Richard II). Although a native of Hainaut, a district spanning the border between modern Belgium and France, Froissart had considerable first-hand knowledge of English affairs. In his youth he acquired an important patron at the English court: Edward III's wife, Philippa, also a native of Hainaut. Froissart travelled in the entourage of England's Black Prince, and went to Italy to witness the marriage of Lionel, duke of Clarence, to Violante Visconti. He returned to his homeland after Philippa's death (1369) to begin the composition of the chronicle that has earned him his reputation. He paid a last, extended visit to England in 1395, where he was again received at court. Although Froissart took Holy Orders and held livings in the church, his values were those of an aristocratic warrior. He patterned his historical narratives on the romances that were the favorite entertainments of his noble patrons, and he was a sincerely enthusiastic publicist for the elaborate codes of chivalry that fascinated the upper classes. He delighted in colorful descriptions of battles, tournaments, feasts, and feats of valor.

Froth, *MM,* 'Master F.,' one of the customers of Mistress Overdone's brothel. In the comic scene at *2.1* he is brought in by Elbow and his officers. He admits having eaten some of Mistress Overdone's prunes, which, as they were then believed to help cure venereal disease, implies his corruption. As 'Froth' is only a customer, Escalus eventually releases him with a warning. As he exits, the joke is made that he is 'drawn in' to bars—as froth appears in a taphouse when a beer is drawn. As Froth is a native of Vienna, he serves to show the corruption that Pompey promotes in the city.

Fulvia, *Ant,* wife of Mark Antony and self-appointed defender of his interests in Italy. Fulvia, the daughter of Marcus Fulvius Bambalio, had several politically significant marriages. To her first husband, Publius Clodius, she bore a daughter, Clodia, who became the first wife of Antony's chief competitor, Octavius (Augustus). Fulvia's second husband was Caius Scironius Curio, and Antony was her third. Fulvia was a stereotypical Roman matron—hard and ruthless in the pursuit of her family's political objectives. Antony's intent was to maneuver himself into a position of power that would permit him to oust Octavius, his colleague in the second triumvirate, and assume sole command of the Roman empire. Although Octavius was her son-in-law, Fulvia was entirely committed to her husband's interests. When Antony took up his post in the east, Fulvia stayed in Italy to intrigue against Octavius. In 41 BC she persuaded Antony's brother, Lucius, to declare war on Octavius, and Octavius assaulted their stronghold at Perugia. Antony was not pleased by his wife's well-intentioned initiative. His plan was to conquer Parthia before precipitating a showdown with Octavius, and he did not want to be distracted by a war in Italy. Antony must have been particularly upset when he learned that Fulvia and Lucius had bitten off more than they could chew. Octavius compelled Lucius to surrender. (Lucius subsequently made his peace with Octavius and joined Octavius' army.) Fulvia fled to Greece to seek her husband's protection, but she became ill and died without seeing him again. Her death atoned for her political failures. The widowed Antony made peace with Octavius and sealed a truce by accepting the hand in marriage of Octavius' sister, Octavia.

Furies, the Eumenides or the Erinyes, the avenging deities of classical mythology. They issued forth from the underworld to enforce curses and plague persons who violated nature's moral laws. *2H4 5.3.107. AWW 5.3.264.*

Furnival, Lord, *1H6 4.7.66,* see Sheffield, Lord Furnival of.

Fury, 1) *Tit 5.2.82, Ant 2.5.40,* see Furies.

2) *Tmp 4.1.255,* spirit in the shape of a hound, named after the Greek goddesses or the animal's temperament.

G

Gabriel, *Shr 4.1.119,* servant of Petruccio. His shoes weren't suitable for meeting his master as requested. He is otherwise unmentioned. His name may be intended merely as evidence that Petruccio is indeed wealthy, with many servants.

Gad, *H5 2.1.28:* 'Gad's lugs,' 'God's lungs,' an oath.

Gads Hill, rise in the road between London and Rochester, about 2.5 mi. west of Rochester. A favorite haunt of robbers, it was a desolate spot on a busy commercial highway. *1H4 1.2.123, 3.3.36. 2H4 1.2.150, 2.4.311.*

Gadshill, *1H4,* one of the low life companions of Prince Harry and Sir John Oldcastle. Sh. may have borrowed the character from an earlier anonymous play, *The Famous Victories of Henry V.*

Galathe, *Tro 5.5.20,* Hector's horse. It is mentioned in William Caxton's *Recuyell of the Historyes of Troye,* 3 (c. 1474), the first English printed book and Sh.'s major source for the play. It is described as one of the strongest horses in the world. Menon tries to take Galathe after Hector slays Patroclus, but Hector prevents it. Galathe is killed out from under Hector in a battle with Menelaus and Ajax, but in a later conflict Achilles tries to take the horse. In Raoul Lefevre's French version from which Caxton translated, it is spelled 'Galate' and 'Galateam.'

Galen, (130–200 AD), physician from Pergamon in Asia Minor. After pursuing the study of medicine at various centers of Greek learning, Galen settled in Rome (c. 164). There he made the acquaintance of a number of its leading citizens—including the emperor, Marcus Aurelius. Galen rejected the magical or mystical approach to healing, which was favored by many of his contemporaries, and he relied on experimentation and the careful study of physiology to develop methods of treatment. His medical treatises became the standard textbooks used for the training of physicians well into the 19th c.

MWW 2.3.27 (referring to the physician Caius), *3.1.62. 2H4 1.2.119. AWW 2.3.11. Cor 2.1.114,* an anachronism. The characters lived centuries before Galen.

Gallia, L. for the land of the Gauls (the Celts). During the early Middle Ages Roman Gallia was settled by tribes of Germanic Franks. Their presence caused 'Gallia' to fall out of fashion in favor of the more accurately descriptive 'France.' *3H6 5.3.8. 1H6 4.6.15, 4.7.48, 5.6.139. MWW 3.1.89:* in this context (see Gaul) the word either means France—as Sh. uses it elsewhere—or Wales. Possibly it is an attempt at Gwalia, a pseudo-Welsh word for Wales, though that is more likely with the following word 'Gaul.' Possibly also, Sh. took Gallia to mean land of the Celts which would make it apply to both France and Wales and in this context mean Wales. That might work in some plays, but not really in the histories.

H5 1.2.216, 5.1.85, Cym 1.6.202, 2.4.18, 3.5.24, 3.7.4, 12, 4.2.335.

Gallian, *Cym 1.6.67,* of or pertaining to Gaul or France.

Galloway nags, *2H4 2.4.187–88,* popular breed of small riding horses developed on the Galloway peninsula in southwestern Scotland, the district between the Solway Firth and the Clyde.

Gallus, *Ant,* Caius Cornelius Gallus, (66–26 BC), ally of Octavius and opponent of Mark Antony. Son of an obscure family from Gaul, he used his talent as a poet to win admission to Rome's most important houses. His works have disappeared, but the praise showered on him by the eminent artists of his day witnesses to the quality of his writing. When the young Octavius came to Rome to fight for his rights as Cæsar's heir, Gallus took up Octavius' cause and became one of his most intimate counselors. Octavius entrusted him with important administrative duties in Italy and assigned him a military command at Actium. After Antony's flight from Actium, Gallus was dispatched with troops to occupy Egypt. Plutarch ('Antony' 79.1–2) says that Gallus handled Octavius' negotiations with Cleopatra. After Cleopatra's death, Gallus became the first prefect of the new Roman province of Egypt. His conduct as prefect somehow offended Octavius, and at the end of a term of four years Octavius stripped him of his property and sent him into exile. Rather than accept this humiliation, he committed suicide.

Gam, Davy, *H5 4.8.104,* Dafydd ab Llewelyn (d. 1415), Welshman who sided with Henry IV in England's struggle with the Welsh nationalist, Owain Glyndŵr. Gam joined Henry V's expedition to France and was slain at Agincourt. 'Gam' was a nickname meaning 'squint.' The word has also been used to mean 'bow-legged.'

Ganymede, 1) (Roman, Catamitus), Zeus's boy lover taken to Olympus by an eagle to succeed Hebe as the gods' cupbearer. *TNK 4.2.15,* 'wanton G.'

2) *AYLI,* name assumed by the disguised Rosalind in Ardenne. The name plays on the idea of the boy who is girl/girl who is a boy.

Gar, by, *MWW,* 'by God,' Doctor Caius' favorite oath.

Gardiner, *H8,* Stephen G. (1483/90–1555), bishop of Winchester and, in succession, private secretary to Cardinal Wolsey and Henry VIII. The university and church gave him, like other men of humble origins, opportunities to rise to positions of wealth and power. At Cambridge he was tutor to the duke of Norfolk's son. Norfolk recommended him to Wolsey, who sent him to Rome with the deputation that argued Henry VIII's case for a divorce from Katherine of Aragon. Henry subsequently employed him as his private secretary and relied on him to carry out delicate assignments. He served on the panel of judges that granted the king an annulment of his marriage with Katherine, and he rallied clergy to support the king's decision to withdraw England from obedience to the papacy. Despite his commitment to the nationalization of the church (which he defended in a pamphlet), he was no Protestant. Thomas Cromwell's attacks on church property and tradition alarmed him, and, since he could do nothing about them, he withdrew from court until Cromwell fell from power. Although he returned to the inner circle of royal advisors at the end of Henry's life and was chosen to say the Mass at the king's funeral, his conservative religious opinions disqualified him for appointment to the board of regents that governed England during the minority of Henry's heir, Edward VI.

When Gardiner refused to accept the reforms the new government mandated, he was deprived of his see and confined to the Tower. Edward's death and Mary's ascension reversed his fortunes. Mary had good reason to hate him. He had helped Henry VIII separate from her mother, Katherine of Aragon, and he had favored severing the ties between England and the papacy that Mary intended to restore. But Mary needed allies, and Gardiner's recent sufferings at the hands of radical Protestants helped the Catholic queen think of him as a defender of orthodoxy. He quickly became one of the most prominent figures at Mary's court. He presided at her coronation and served as her Lord Chancellor. He wrote pamphlets refuting Protestant doctrines, and he urged Mary to the harsh policies that earned the queen a reputation as a bloody persecutor of religious dissenters. He was particularly hostile to Mary's sister Elizabeth, for he understood that her succession would mean the revival of the religious practices he hoped to stamp out. He died three years before Mary's death cleared Elizabeth's path to the throne.

Gargantua, giant with enormous appetites from François Rabelais' *Vie inestimable du grand Gargantua* and *Faits et Prouesses du très renommé Pantagruel.* These satiric romances written between 1532 and 1562 allowed the author to explore philosophy, politics, and other subjects in his vigorous, humanistic, and tolerant manner. They were instantly popular, and translated quickly into English. *AYLI 3.2.220,* 'G's mouth.'

Gargrave, Thomas, *1H6,* (d. 1428), knight mentioned in Edward Hall's *Union of the Two Noble and Illustre Famelies of Lancastre and Yorke* (1542) as the earl of Salisbury's companion at the siege of Orléans. When he and the earl climbed a tower on the Orléans bridge to survey the city's defenses, they were killed by the same cannon shot.

Garmombles, *MWW 4.5.72,* F1 'Cozen-Iermans,' the Germans in service of the Duke. Garmombles comes from Q and is probably a play on the name Mömpelgard (see Duke, *MWW*). 'cozen-German' would be a joke on 'cousin german' or 'first cousin.' The word 'geremumble' is used by Thomas Nashe and seems to mean 'to clean fish.' The *OED* suggests Scottish 'jurmummle,' 'to crush, disfigure; to bamboozle,' might be related. The latter meaning might well apply here. 'Jerrycummumble,' 'to shake, towzle, or tumble about' is cited in Francis Grose's dictionary of 18th c. slang.

Garter, the, *MWW 2.1.170,* an inn. Windsor was celebrated for the number of its inns. Seventy were reported in 1650. This one was obviously named in honor of the Order of the Garter (q.v.), whose seat was Windsor.

Garter King-of-Arms, *H8,* one of the three 'kings-of-arms' who served in the office of the Earl Marshall. The Garter King-of-Arms had the right to proclaim the accession of a new monarch. He functioned as a herald.

Garter, Order of the, England's most prestigious chivalric organization. It was created by Edward III, but the year of its institution and its original purpose are uncertain. Since Edward and the Black Prince each headed teams of twelve knights within the Order, it may have been a tournament club. Women were, however, involved with the order as early as the 14th c., though not accorded full membership. They were granted robes, permitted to wear insignia, and were present at ceremonies. Women were later banned during the reign of Henry VIII. According to legend its title began when either the Countess of Salisbury, Joan of Kent, or Queen Philippa lost her garter, always a problem in the age before elastic. The king found it and when attempting to return it noticed the smirks and glances of his courtiers. The king then tied the garter on his own knee and said '*Honi soit qui mal y pense,*' (Fr. 'Shame on him who thinks evil'), which became the motto of the order. The knights of the Garter wore distinctive robes (and garters) and had rights to special seats in the company of the king. Their society was also known as the Order or Confraternity of St. George, the warrior saint whom Edward III chose as England's patron. The headquarters of the organization was St. George's chapel, Windsor Castle. *1H6 4.1.15, 4.1.34.*

Gaul, *MWW 3.1.89,* France in ancient times. In this passage the Host of the Garter contrasts names for the Frenchman and the Welshman. Though Gallia and Gaul should mean the same thing, elsewhere Sh. always uses Gallia to mean France, so 'Gaul' here should mean Wales. Various theories link the Q spellings of 'gawle' and 'gawlia' to Gwalia, a pseudo-Welsh name of Wales, or to the French name for the Welsh, *les Galles.*

Gaultres Forest, *2H4 4.1.2,* royal forest north of York.

Gaunt, Ghent (Fr. *Gand*), one of medieval Europe's major ports and the birthplace of Edward III's son, John of Gaunt. It is near Brussels at the confluence of the Scheldt and Lys rivers. Because of its location it has been a trading center since at least the 7th c. AD. Baldwin I of Flanders built a fortress there in the 9th c. and the Cathedral of St. Bavon has parts dating to the 10th. By the 15th c. it was a major production center for fabrics. See John of Gaunt, *R2, 1H4, 2H4, 1H6, 2H6, 3H6.*

Gawsey, Nicholas, *1H4 5.4.44, 57,* (d. 1403), Goushill, knight from Nottinghamshire who died with his son fighting for Henry IV at the battle of Shrewsbury.

Gemini, *MWW 2.2.10,* the constellation representing Castor (q.v.) and Pollux, sons of Leda, from the L. 'twins.'

General, commander of an army.

1) *TGV 4.1.59,* commander of the outlaw band.

2) *2H6 4.2.110, 4.4.13,* see Cade, Jack.

3) *3H6 1.2.68:* 'woman's general' is more likely an indefinite expression of contempt rather than a reference to a particular commander. It is not known who was Margaret of Anjou's overall commander at Wakefield. Holinshed reports that 'the dukes of Excester and Summerset, the earle of Devonshire, the lord Clifford, the Lord Ros, and in effect all the lords of the north parts. . .marched from York to Wakefield.' Contrary to Holinshed's description, however, modern historians do not believe Margaret was present at the battle but was still in Scotland. It was not Margaret who placed the paper crown on Richard of York's decapitated head, but Clifford the younger.

4) *1H6 1.1.73* (pl.) *4.2.2,* the defender of Bordeaux. *5.2.8,* the Dauphin.

5) *LLL 3.1.180,* figurative.

6) *Rom. 5.3.218,* figurative.

7) *2H4 4.1.27, 139,* see John, duke of Bedford.

8) *H5 5.0.30,* usually thought to be an allusion to the Earl of Essex and his attempt to subdue the rebellion in Ireland.

9) *JC 4.2.180* (pl.), see Cassius and Brutus.

10) *Tro 4.6.20. 4.7.111. 5.1.70,* see Agamemnon.

11) *Son 154.7,* see Cupid.

13) *AWW 3.3.1,* see Bertram. *4.1.89, 4.3.130.*

14) *Lr. 5.3.67 (Q 24.73),* see Edmund. Regan offers him herself and all her rights after his victory over the French.

15) *Ant 1.1.1,* see Antony, Mark.

16) *Cor. 4.1.24,* see Menenius Agrippa.

Genoa, seaport in northwest Italy at the foot of the Ligurian Alps. It flourished under the Romans and after the collapse of the empire of Charlemagne became a republic. In the Middle Ages it developed a mercantile empire of its own with foreign possessions and an extensive trade network, particularly in the Middle East, and was a rival of Venice and Pisa, leading to warfare. Gradually Genoa lost its power and came under the control of France and Milan. In the 16th c. there was a brief revival of Genoese power under Andrea Doria (died 1560), but the city was subsequently ruled by the Spanish, the French, the Austrians, and the Kingdom of Sardinia until it was united with Italy. In Sh.'s time, Genoa was still one of the major trading cities in Europe.

Shr 4.4.4. MV 3.1.74, 92, 99, 100, where Tubal searched unsuccessfully for Jessica.

Geoffrey, *Jn 1.1.8, 2.1.99, 102–106, 126, 3.4.46, 4.1.22,* G. Plantagenet,(1158–1186), fourth son of Henry II, king of England, and Eleanor of Aquitaine. He married Constance, heiress to the duchy of Brittany, who, after his death in a tournament in 1187, bore him a son, Arthur. Had Geoffrey lived, he would have been next in line to his brother Richard the Lionhearted for the English crown. When Geoffrey died, his right of succession passed to Arthur. But the boy was unable to claim his patrimony. His uncle, John, Geoffrey's younger brother, seized the throne when Richard was killed in 1199.

George, 1) F1 *1H6,* rebel who enters with Lord Saye at *4.7.21.* This is usually thought to be the actor's name, rather than the character's, and the same actor as Bevis at *4.2.*

2) emblem of St. George worn by those who had been inducted into the Order of the Garter. The honor was awarded only to persons of very high rank. Sh. has the duke of Suffolk display his 'George' in a futile attempt to convince the pirates who kidnapped him that it was in their interest to spare his life for ransom.

2H6 4.1.30. R3 4.4.297, 300. See Garter, Order of the.

3) *Jn 1.1.186,* arbitrarily chosen male name. It originally derives from Gr. meaning 'farmer.'

George Alow, *TNK 3.5.60,* a ship in a song which is similar to 'The George Aloo and the Swifte-stake,' a ballad entered in the Stationers' Register on 19 March 1611.

George, duke of Clarence, (1449–1478), third of Richard of York's four sons, Edward IV's brother. After York's death at Wakefield on 30 December 1460, Richard Neville, earl of Warwick, assumed command of the Yorkist forces on behalf of his young cousin Edward. Warwick dispersed the Lancastrian army, imprisoned Henry VI, and won recognition for Edward as England's king. Warwick 'the Kingmaker' intended to be the power behind Edward's throne, but as Edward matured, he fought for his independence from his patron. Warwick's disillusionment with Edward inspired a scheme to depose the king in favor of his brother Clarence. Clarence pledged allegiance to Warwick by marrying Warwick's daughter, Isabel Neville, and he sided with Warwick in the coup that forced Edward to flee England in 1470. He soon discovered, however, that he had made a bad deal. Warwick turned to France for the backing he needed to depose Edward, and France insisted that Warwick ignore him and restore Henry VI to England's throne. Edward raised an army in Burgundy and returned to England in 1471 to fight for his crown. Clarence, having nothing to hope for from Warwick and the Lancastrians, made peace with his brother and fought for him at the battles of Barnet and Tewkesbury.

Once the Lancastrians were decisively defeated, Clarence's record of dubious loyalty and unsatisfied ambition made it difficult for Edward to trust him. In 1472 he was suspected of treason and given a warning. Two of his wife's kin (George Neville, archbishop of York, and John de Vere, earl of Oxford) were accused of plotting and imprisoned. Since Clarence was the most viable alternative to Edward, the plans laid by Edward's enemies often involved deposing the king in his brother's favor. Clarence could not always control what others said they wanted to do in his name, but he could have conducted himself in such a way as to try to win Edward's confidence. Instead, he ignored Edward's warnings, made a spectacle of himself at court, kept questionable company, and virtually forced the king to discipline him. In 1476 following the death of his Neville wife, he pushed Edward to the breaking point. He sought a new bride who would bring him an estate that would improve his chance to seize Edward's throne. First, he convinced Edward's sister, Margaret, the dowager duchess of Burgundy, to support his request for the hand of Mary of Burgundy, heiress to the lands of Charles the Bold. When Edward prudently refused to allow him to acquire control of a rich nation from which the duke might launch an assault on England, he tried for an equally dangerous match. He asked permission to marry the sister of the king of Scotland. Edward also denied him this, and Clarence took his disappointment very badly.

He began openly to flaunt Edward's authority. In the spring of 1477, Edward may have tried to give him a fright that would teach him discretion. Edward accused John Stacy, an astronomer, of using magic to predict the date of the king's death. Stacy confessed under torture to plying the black arts in the service of one of the duke's men, Thomas Burdett. Stacy and Burdett were both executed on 20 May 1477. Their deaths were meant to be a warning, but the duke refused to be intimidated. He accused Edward of tyranny and began to preach sedition. By June of 1477, Edward had had enough. He ordered Clarence's arrest and imprisoned him in the Tower. On 19 January 1478, the duke was indicted for treason before parliament. He was convicted and returned to the Tower for a quiet execution that was intended to avoid further scandal to the royal family. The secrecy that surrounded his death encouraged rumors, and colorful stories circulated about his execution. It was believed by some that Clarence was drowned in a barrel of wine. A less sensational tale claimed that he was submerged in his bath. Sh. preferred the wine story and added to it the unsubstantiated claim that Richard (III), duke of Gloucester, was to blame for Clarence's troubles. In *R3* Richard clears his way to Edward's throne by setting Edward against Clarence and personally ordering Clarence's execution. There is no historical evidence to support the belief that Richard aspired to the throne at such an early date or had a hand in determining the fate that the duke worked so hard to earn for himself.

3H6. R3.

George, Order of St., *1H6 4.7.68,* see Garter, Order of the.

George, St., patron saint of England, Portugal, Aragon, Catalonia, Lithuania, and numerous medieval communes and corporations. Despite his popularity, little is known about him. He may have been a native of Palestine and a highly ranked soldier who witnessed for the Christian faith during the Emperor Diocletian's persecution (c. 303). A tomb containing the relics of a St. George was attracting pilgrims to Lydda in Palestine as early as 530. The cult of St. George, like the veneration paid other early Christian saints, may have assimilated aspects of pagan culture. The famous story of St. George battling the dragon recalls another tale set in Palestine: Perseus' rescue of Andromeda from a sea monster. St. George was known to the popes of the 5th c., but it was the crusades of the 12th and 13th c. and the flowering of chivalry and the romance that made the saintly knight a European hero. In 1222 the Synod of Oxford made his feast a national festival in England, and Edward III named him England's special intercessor. Since England claimed George as its patron, English soldiers used his name as their battle cry: *3H6 2.1.204, 2.2.80, 4.2.29* (Lancaster), *3H6 5.1.116* (York). *Shr 2.1.233,* 'by Saint G.,' an oath. *1H6 1.1.154, 2.1.39, 4.2.55, 4.6.1. R3 5.5.224, 5.6.31, 79. LLL 5.2.610,* 'Saint G.'s half-cheek,' his profile. *Jn 2.1.288. R2 1.3.84. H5 3.1.34, 5.2.204.*

Gerald the Schoolmaster, *TNK,* pedantic organizer of the morris dance to be performed before Theseus. The inspiration for his character may have derived from Francis Beaumont's antimasque in *The Masque of Grayes-Inne and the Inner Temple* (1613), which features a morris led by a pedant, though his comic type was very popular (see Holofernes, and Quince, Peter).

Gérard de Narbonne, *AWW 1.1.25, 35, 2.1.100,* father of Helen, a great physician. Gerardo of Narbona is the name in the source, Boccaccio's *Decameron* 3.9, as translated in William Painter's *Palace of Pleasure* (1566). Narbonne, on the western shore of the Gulf of Lions, was the first Roman colony beyond the Alps and was an important port. Among others, the Saracens held the city for some time until Charlemagne made it the capital of the duchy of Gothia. For a while it rivaled Marseilles, but an economic decline brought about by the silting of the harbor in the early 1300s and the expulsion of the Jews was never reversed. Medicine was regarded as a specialty of the Saracens and Jews and so Narbonne would have had a reputation for it. The city was brought under the French crown in 1507.

German, 1) (n.) a native of Germany, often stereotyped as a drunkard. *3H6 4.9.2,* pl., mercenary soldiers recruited from German speaking lands. Many German soldiers were for hire in the late medieval period, for the political situation in Germany encouraged militarization and limited opportunities for employment. By the 15th c. the feudal nobility had defeated the attempts of several royal dynasties to pull the German people together as a single nation. Germany had evolved hundreds of petty states whose governments were constantly at war among themselves. Political confusion created problems for the economy, retarded the evolution of German society, and spawned large armies that maintained themselves by selling their services abroad. Their reputations were not good. They were accused of being ruder and less civilized than soldiers from more sophisticated nations.

MV 1.2.81, a suitor of Portia's. *MWW 4.3.1, 4.5.67,* see Duke 5). *AWW 4.1.72,* a German speaker. *Ado 3.2.31,* the passage mocks the fashionable Englishman's indiscriminate mixing of national fashions. *Oth 2.3.71.*

2) (adj.) of or pertaining to Germany. *LLL 3.1.185,* 'like a German clock,' a complicated machine, with dancing figures, etc., very likely to break down. *MWW 4.5.65. STM Add. II.D.143,* 'G. province.' *Cym 2.5.16,* F1 'a Iarmen on': it isn't clear what a boar's being German has to do with this passage. There is some possibility that it means 'german' (germane), or 'a true one.'

Germany, large European country that, by the end of the Middle Ages, shared frontiers with France, Italy, Hungary and Poland. Medieval Germany evolved a distinctive language and culture, but it was not a nation in the political sense of the term. A successful scheme for uniting the various independent duchies, ecclesiastical principalities, and free cities of Germany was not devised until 1871.

MV 1.2.72. Jn 1.1.100. H5 1.2.44, 53. Lr. Q 21.89. H8 5.2.64: 'upper' Germany—Saxony (q.v.) in particular—was the northern part of the country where the Protestant Reformation was most successful.

Gertrude, *Ham,* Hamlet's mother, wife of her husband's brother Claudius. The question of whether it was incestuous to marry your deceased spouse's sibling was a prominent one in the debate over whether Henry VIII was entitled to divorce Katherine of Aragon, who had been married to his brother Arthur when the heir to the Tudor throne had been a boy, and would have been familiar to Renaissance audiences. There are conflicting passages in the Bible. It is not clear in the play whether Gertrude's hasty marriage is considered reprehensible by anyone other than Hamlet and his father's ghost, though it is likely a part of the general 'rotten' state of Denmark. There are certainly signs that the succession of Claudius is dubious, as the mob shouts for Laertes to be king, but one must recall that the Danish succession was not strictly hereditary until after Sh.'s lifetime. No great affection is shown between Gertrude and Claudius, although Claudius seems a man whose passion for her maddened him to fratricide and Hamlet's imaginings of the relations between his mother and Claudius are revolting to him to the extent that an Oedipal interpretation invites itself.

Gertrude is apparently not guilty of murdering her husband, nor of taking part in the plots against Hamlet. It is not even clear that she was Claudius' lover before the murder. The ghost seems to say so, but he may be referring to the period after his death, and he is not explicit. His use of the word 'adulterate' may not in the parlance of the time mean 'adultery.' The 'black and grainèd spots' she sees on her soul likely refer only to her incest. This makes her a bit too shadowy for many critics. She is kind of a bone to be fought over by the two main adversaries. Even her death is an ironic accident, denying Claudius what he has tried so hard to keep and Hamlet what he has defended. Possibly she is treated delicately because Anne of Denmark had been the wife of king James since 1589. An evil Danish queen might have been as problematic as mocking a Scotsman (which James was) for Ben Jonson, who saw his play *Every Man in His Humour,* shut down. In Sh.'s source, François de Belleforest's *Histoires tragiques* (1576), Gertrude is called Geruth. She and Hamlet's names are the only ones Sh. directly borrows. In *Der Bestrafte Brudermord* (1710) which seems to be a German rendition of an older version of the play, Gertrude is called Sigrie.

Ghost, *Ham,* see Hamlet 2).

Giacomo, *Cym,* F1 'Iachimo,' playful acquaintance of Posthumus in Rome. Represented as an Italianate gentleman, Giacomo sets about to prove that the virtuous Innogen is as vulnerable to his charms as any other woman. His bet with Posthumus is distasteful on both their parts, but when Giacomo fails in his seduction, he has himself carried into her chamber in a chest and collects enough evidence to prove to Posthumus that he has been intimate with her. The wager resembles that in *MV* and even involves a ring as Giacomo's prize; however, this game becomes much more serious. Giacomo is more of a frivolous character than a malicious one. He later fights with the Romans and when he recognizes his slander nearly resulted in Innogen's murder, he accepts death as his punishment. Posthumus forgives him. Giacomo has come to an understanding of the serious consequences of his frivolity, thus illustrating the common Sh. pattern of a young man coming to maturity.

Some parallels have been argued as existing between Iago, who slanders a woman until she is murdered, and Giacomo, though Giacomo cannot really be described as evil. He is often compared to Autolycus in *WT*. By using this common Italian name for a character who should be a Roman, Sh. exacerbates the linguistic muddle of *Cym* in which a Latin name is assumed by a Welsh outlaw (Polydore), a British name by his brother (Cadwal), and a French name by their sister (Fidele). It has been pointed out that there is a Giacomo in William Painter's *Palace of Pleasure* (1567) in the story *Two Gentlemen of Venice,* following that of Romeo and Juliet; however, Giacomo is very common, leaving no particular reason to believe it was chosen from Painter. The story of Posthumus' wager on Innogen's chastity is from Boccaccio's *Decameron* 2.9, though the corresponding character to Giacomo is Ambrogiuolo of Piacenza.

Gilliams, *1H4 2.4.65,* messenger serving Hotspur as the Percies prepare their rebellion against Henry IV in 1403.

Gillian, *Err 3.1.31,* house servant of Antipholus of Ephesus.

Ginn, *Err 3.1.31,* house servant of Antipholus of Ephesus.

Gipsy, see Gypsy.

Giraldo, *TNK 4.3.12,* Jailer's Daughter's mocking name for Gerald the Schoolmaster.

Gis, *Ham 4.5.58,* probably a shortening of 'Jesus,' as in the modern 'Jeez!' and 'Gee!' Another possibility is that it means 'Cis,' St. Cecily.

Gisors, *1H6 1.1.61,* town about 45 mi. northwest of Paris, capital of the Vexin, a district on the frontier of Normandy over which the kings of England and France frequently quarreled.

Giulio Romano, *WT 5.2.96,* F1 'Iulio Romano,' the great artist who is supposed to have created the lifelike statue of Hermione. Critics have objected to the statue's being painted in lifelike colors, actually a common practice since ancient times, and to the anachronism of Giulio Romano in the ancient Greek setting, though anachronisms are a hardly relevant accusation against a 'winter's tale.'

More interesting is the question whether, and if so, how, Sh. knew of the artist's work. Giulio Romano (c. 1492–1546) was an Italian artist, architect, and engineer. Real name Giulio Pippi de' Giannuzzi, he became the favorite pupil of Raphael and was a founder of Mannerism. He assisted Raphael in the completion of many frescoes, including *The Battle of Constantine* and *Apparition of the Cross* in the Vatican Palace. After Raphael's death he succeeded him as head of the Roman school. After Federigo Gonzaga duke of Mantua became his patron, Giulio Romano designed the Church of San Benedetto, rebuilt the Palazzo del Te, and reworked the drainage of the marshes. His frescoes *Psyche, Icarus,* and *The Titans* adorn the Te palace. His best works are considered *The Martyrdom of St. Stephen,* and *Mary and Jesus.*

It has been proposed by several that Sh. had traveled in Italy but there is no substantial evidence for it. One critic in 1894 argued that Sh.'s *Rape of Lucrece* describes paintings based upon Giulio Romano's frescoes in Mantua. There may have been some of his paintings in England, as there are records of them in the collection of Charles I. More simply, Sh. may have gotten his knowledge of the painter from Giorgio Vasari's very famous *Lives of the Artists* (1550) who not only praises the lifelike qualities in Giulio's art, but also mentions his epitaph alluding to his ability in sculpture, something which is not delineated in any detail. Since, so far as we know, Vasari was not translated in Sh.'s lifetime, this would imply that Sh. either read Vasari in the original or received the specific information second hand.

Glamis, 1) *Mac,* castle and thaneship in Forfarshire, Scotland. Most of the existing structure dates from the 17th c.; however, the older part goes back to at least the 11th. It was occasionally used as a royal residence by early Scottish kings, and became the seat of the earl of Strathmore and Kinghorne. The widow of the 6th Lord Glamis was burned as a witch in 1537 for plots against James V and the property was forfeit to the crown. Six years later, she was cleared and her son was restored to the lordship. The name is Gaelic in origin and means 'gap' or 'vale.'

2) *Mac,* Macbeth.

Glasdale, William, *1H6,* Glansdale, commander of an important post at the siege of Orléans in 1429. When the English first assaulted Orléans, the city's defender, the Bastard of Orléans, charged out to meet them. The French were forced back and in the process lost the tower that commanded the bridge into the city. The victorious English entrusted the tower and the maintenance of a blockade around Orléans to Glasdale. He was escorting the earl of Salisbury on a tour of the tower when a cannon lobbed a shot through a window and killed Salisbury.

Glendower, Owen, see Glyndŵr, Owain.

Globe, *Tmp 4.1.153,* the world. It has long been a tradition that *Tmp* may have been Sh.'s farewell to the theater and that when Prospero gives up his magic it represents Sh. giving up the magic of playwrighting. This is appealing but impossible to know. However, the use of the word 'globe' here is likely one of the double entendres Sh. was so fond of, since it was also the name of his primary theater. Some critics find other coy references in other passages, also.

The Globe was erected by Cuthbert Burbage in 1599 from timbers removed from the site of the Theater and opened the same year with Sh. as part owner. Located south of the Thames outside the jurisdiction of the city of London, it was nonetheless conveniently reached by boat. According to contemporary drawings it was a polygon of three stories with a small structure on top. There are several disagreements about the layout of the inside of the structure, which had an open roof, except over the galleries. Recently, a construction project in London uncovered the foundations of the building and the excitement over this gave great impetus to the late American actor Sam Wanamaker's long-fought battle to have the Globe reconstructed on its original site. The original structure burned in a performance of *H8* on June 29, 1613. The thatch on its roof caught fire when the hot wadding of a cannon used for sound effects landed in it. It was rebuilt with a tile roof, but was ultimately razed during the Puritan regime of the 1640s.

Gloster, see Gloucester.

Gloucester, 1) frequently spelled 'Gloster' or 'Glo'ster' in old editions to reflect pronunciation, shire lying in the west of England at the head of the Bristol channel. Its main features are the Severn valley and the Cotswald hills. Sh.'s Avon also flows into the Severn in Gloucester. It became a shire probably in the 10th c. and was part of Harold's earldom at the time of the Norman invasion. The earldom of Gloucester was created for Robert (son of Henry I) in 1121, who later rebelled against his half-brother King Stephen. His success in placing his sister Mathilda on the throne was eaten away by her behavior, which inspired the antipathy of the church to her cause and a revival of Stephen's party. The ducal title was created for Edward III's youngest son, Thomas of Woodstock in

1385. The title died out several times, but it was revived for Humphrey in 1414 and for Richard (later III) in 1461. *MWW 1.1.4,* 'county of G.' See Gloucester, Duchess, *R2*; Gloucester, Duke, *R2, 2H4, H5, 1H6, R3.*

2) city and port on the east bank of the Severn river. There was likely a Celtic settlement there (Gleucastre) which became a Roman colony founded by Nerva about 97 AD. Its importance rose after the founding of the Abbey of St. Peter in 681 and the castle became an occasional royal residence and a mint. Richard III gave the city the status of a county in 1483. Sea trade in iron, corn, and wine, as well as products of the cloth, pin, and bell making trades, were all sources of Gloucester's importance in Sh.'s time. *Lr. 1.5.2,* the city or castle is here often mistaken for the duke.

Gloucester, Duchess of, *R2,* Eleanor de Bohun (d. 1399), heiress to the last de Bohun earl of Hereford, Essex, and Northampton. Her status as one of the richest marriage prizes in England won her a husband from the royal family: Edward III's son, Thomas of Woodstock, the future duke of Gloucester (q.v.). In 1397 Gloucester was arrested by his nephew, Richard II, and murdered while in captivity. Eleanor's only son, Humphrey, died two years later and left no descendants. These tragedies may have hastened her death, which occurred either at her chief residence, Pleshey Castle, or at Barking Abbey.

Gloucester, Duke of, 1) *R3,* see Richard (III) Crookback.

2) *R2 1.1.100, 132, 1.2.1, 16, 2.1.129,* Thomas of Woodstock (1354–1397), youngest son of Edward III. He opposed the efforts of his nephew, Richard II, to establish an absolute monarchy in England. He distrusted men, like Michael de la Pole, whom Richard chose as friends, and he accused them of unduly influencing the king. In 1386 he assaulted Richard in parliament and forced him to dismiss Pole from the chancellorship. When Richard objected to this trespass on his royal prerogative, Gloucester was said to have reminded him that there was precedent for the deposition of kings in England (e.g. Edward II). In 1388, when Richard tried to overturn acts of parliament, Gloucester came close to implementing this threat. He, Arundel, Warwick and others took up arms against the king and might have deposed him had they been able to agree upon his successor. Gloucester believed that he was entitled to the crown, but his nephew, Henry (IV) Bolingbroke, claimed it by right of descent from Gloucester's elder brother, John of Gaunt. The inability of the barons to maintain a united front gave Richard the chance to regain control of his government. Once he was back in power he waited for a chance to avenge himself on the 'lords appellant' (Gloucester's associates who had 'appealed' or 'lodged' a charge of treason against the king's advisors). Gloucester continued to speak out against the king and vehemently opposed Richard's policy of pursuing peace with France. His open contempt for the king's decision to marry Charles VI's daughter, Isabella, in 1396, may have pushed Richard to the breaking point. In July 1397 Richard arrested him, Arundel, and Warwick and charged them with treason. By the time the courts reached a verdict in the case, Gloucester was already dead in his prison in Calais. An inquiry conducted by Henry IV's government produced a witness who claimed that Richard had ordered Gloucester's murder and that men sent by the duke of Aumerle, Gloucester's nephew, had done the deed.

3) *2H4, H5, 1H6,* see Humphrey, duke of Gloucester.

4) *Lr.,* chief lord under Lear, father of Edmund and Edgar. Like Lear he is confused about the loyalty of his sons, rejects Edgar, and is usurped by Edmund as a result of the mistake. Later he is blinded by Cornwall, attempts suicide, and is rescued by Edgar disguised as a madman. However, his heart fails when he discovers the true identity of the madman who has saved him. The parallel of Gloucester's story to Lear's is obvious and though there is no antecedent for his character in the sources of Lear's story, it reinforces the tragic theme of human weakness and 'blindness.'

Gloucester, Earl of, *Lr. 3.5.17–18 (Q 12.17–18),* title to be assumed by Edmund. Sh. makes no distinction between the duchy and the earldom, though the former would be an anachronism before 1385. See Gloucester, *Lr.*

Gloucestershire, *R2 2.3.3, 5.6.3. 1H4 1.3.241, 3.2.176. MWW 3.4.43, 5.5.177. 2H4 4.2.79, 4.2.124.* See Gloucester.

Glyndŵr, Owain, Owain Glyn Dwr, Owain Glyndyvrdwy, Owen ab Gruffydd, or Owen Glendower (1359–1416), Welsh nobleman who led a rebellion against Henry IV. He was thoroughly familiar with his English enemy. He studied law at Westminster, served as squire to the earl of Arundel, and was one of Henry's acquaintances before Henry deposed Richard II and seized the crown. Despite Sh.'s allusion (*R2 3.1.43*), no battle is known to have taken place between Henry (IV) Bolingbroke and he before Richard II's deposition. The long struggle between Henry and Glyndŵr, the last of the great native leaders of Wales, began in 1400. Sh. may invoke Glyndŵr's name in *R2* because Richard relied on the Welsh for soldiers with which to fight Bolingbroke and Holinshed (3.518) says that Glyndŵr was with Richard when Richard surrendered to Bolingbroke at Flint Castle in Wales. His revolt began as a dispute between him and his English neighbor, Reginald Grey of Ruthin. Their squabble over property rights escalated into a war for Wales's independence from England. Since Wales was much smaller and poorer than England, England ought to have been able to crush Glyndŵr without difficulty, but he fought skillfully and solicited help from important allies, such as France and some members of the great baronial families of the marches. The Percies courted his support in their effort to unseat Henry IV. Edmund Mortimer, the champion of the house of York, married Glyndŵr's daughter and joined him in plotting fantastic schemes for the conquest of England.

Henry IV led several forays into the mountains of Wales, but rugged terrain and pressing duties elsewhere prevented the English king from concentrating his forces. Glyndŵr's success in prolonging the campaign spawned rumors that he was a magician who used the supernatural to frustrate his enemies. Among his powers, allegedly, was the ability to make himself invisible. Paucity of resources eventually undercut his campaign and lessened the threat he posed to England. Young Henry V, who wished to concentrate all his attention on a war with France, offered him a pardon, but the aging rebel refused to make a formal peace with his enemies. The circumstances surrounding his death are uncertain.

2H6 2.2.41. R2 3.1.43. 1H4. 2H4 1.3.72, 3.1.98.

Gnæus Pompey, *Ant 3.13.119,* see Pompey the Great.

Gobbo, 'old G.,' *MV,* nearly blind father of Lancelot. Gobbo is It. for hunchback, which may mean Sh. intended the part to be played so. In Venice there was a statue 'Gobbo di Rialto' which supports a granite pillar from which the laws were published. The name, however, is not an unusual Italian name, particularly in Venice.

Gobbo, Lancelot, *MV,* clown, a merry devil who dislikes his position as servant in Shylock's house. He assists Jessica in her flight with Lorenzo and gets himself in the employ of Bassanio. His speech implies that he has a rather high opinion of himself. He is also a trickster who takes advantage of his sand-blind father. There is an obvious resemblance between this character and that of Lance in *TGV* in style of humor. They both have comic monologues that run to puns and malapropisms. Lance brings up Jews in a way not particularly relevant to his own plot which suggests Lancelot, also. In F1, Lancelot refers to Shylock's calling him 'Iobbe' several times, which may be Shylock's confounding of Lancelot's name with Job's and a mocking of the Jew's accent. The Job comparison can then also be made with Lancelot's suffering in Shylock's service. It may also merely be a compositor's error. If there is an intention to refer to the Arthurian hero

Lancelot du Lac in the choice of this name, it is obscure.

Goblin, 1) mischievous spirit who pinches and plays tricks on people. He could assume different forms and chase people through the woods. The word is of unknown origin but came into English through French and Latin, and is probably related to the surname Gobelin (of tapestry fame). In the 12th c. a spirit named Gobelinus supposedly haunted the area of Évreux. The name may derive from the Gr. *kybalon,* 'a rogue.' *Err 2.2.193. Temp 4.1.256,* (pl.).

2) demonic spirit, more evil than playful. *Ham 1.4.22, 5.2.23. Tro 5.11.29. WT 2.1.28.*

3) *MND 3.2.400,* see Goodfellow, Robin.

God, *passim,* Judeo-Christian deity, the Supreme Being. Sh.'s characters often invoke the divine name to witness to the veracity of their statements or the justice of their causes. God was also viewed in a political sense as the ultimate authority in the hierarchy of rulers or 'great chain of being.' A 1606 act of Parliament made the use of 'God' and 'Jesus Christ' illegal on the stage, so various euphemisms were substituted such as 'Zounds!' for the oath 'by God's wounds!'

Shr 4.6.1, 19. Tit 4.4.42. Luc 1345. MV 2.2.41, 'God's sonties,' an oath, 'by God's saints,' possibly related to the Scottish 'sauntie' (saint). It may also be 'by God's health' from the French *santé* or 'by God's sanctity.' 'God's santy' occurs in Dekker and Middleton's *Honest Whore* (1604) and 'God's santie' in *The Longer thou Livest the More Fool thou Art.*

Rom 3.5.176, 'G.'s bread,' another way of saying 'G.'s body,' derived from the Eucharist. *MWW 1.4.5,* 'G's patience.' *Ado 1.1.263,* 'the tuition of God,' the teachings of the Lord, part of a standard letter closing. *Ham 2.2.532,* 'G.'s bodykins,' by G.'s little body. *PP 17.6. Lr. 5.3.17 (Q 24.17),* 'G.'s spies.' *Cym 1.7.170,* 'descended God' (like a god come to earth). The phrase alludes to Greek and Roman mythology, but also to Acts 14.11. F1 has 'defended G.' which makes no sense.

God's mother, *1H6 1.3.57,* the Virgin Mary, the 'mother of God' (Gr. *theotokos*) by virtue of Christ's incarnation through her and his participation in triune deity. The appropriateness of this title was hotly debated in the east in the 5th c. At issue was the question of the relationship between Christ's human and divine natures. Orthodox Christians in the east and in Europe supported the use of the title as an affirmation of Christ's full humanity and divinity.

Gog, variation of 'God' to avoid a direct oath. *Shr 3.3.33:* 'G.'s woun's.'

Golden Fleece, Order of the, *1H6 4.7.69,* fraternity of knights created in 1430 by Philip the Good of Burgundy to celebrate his marriage to Isabella of Portugal. Although no one knows why, the order took its symbols from the Greek legend of Jason and the Argonauts, who left home to seek treasure and adventure in fabulous lands and bore an obvious resemblance to the knights whose quests in exotic locales are among the most popular subjects treated in medieval romances. Since the wealth of Burgundy was based on the European wool trade, a golden fleece was a uniquely appropriate emblem for a Burgundian order. The order was, despite its allusion to pagan mythology, thoroughly Christian and devoted to the special veneration of the Virgin and St. Andrew.

Golgotha, or Calvary, place where Christ was crucified outside the walls of Jerusalem. The name derives from an Aramaic word for 'skull.' *R2 4.1.135. Mac 1.2.40.*

Goliases, *1H6 1.3.12,* (pl.) Goliaths.

Goliath, *MWW 5.1.22,* giant warrior whose final battle is described in the Hebrew scriptures. He came from the city of Gath and was a mercenary soldier in the employ of the Philistines, the enemies of the ancient Hebrews. He was slain either by David, King Saul's young squire (1 Samuel 17:2–51), or by Elchanan, son of Jair (2 Samuel 21:19).

Goneril, *Lr.,* Q 'Gonoril,' daughter of Lear, wife of Albany, sister of Regan and Cordelia. After extravagantly declaring her love for the king, she divides the kingdom with Regan and proves the more villainous of the two in her treatment of her father. She also begins a relationship with Edmond and plots against her husband. When the plot fails, she poisons her sister and stabs herself. Goneril is conjectured to derive from Gwenar, the British form of Venus, but Sh. borrowed it directly from his sources, changing only the spelling. In John Higgin's *Mirror for Magistrates* (1574), she is Gonerell. In Geoffrey of Monmouth's version of the story, she is named Gonorilla, as in Holinshed. She is Gonorill in Spenser's *Færie Queen,* 2.10.

Gonzago, *Ham 2.2.540, 3.2.227, 250, 252,* duke of Vienna, murdered by his brother in a play designed by Hamlet to entrap Claudius into revealing his guilt. The name may derive from the supposed murder of Francisco Maria della Rovere, duke of Urbino, in 1538 by Luigi Gonzaga (see *Murder of Gonzago, The*). The Gonzaga family was powerful and prominent in Renaissance Mantua. Their name derived from the town in which they originated. The original line ruled Mantua from 1328–1627. It was succeeded by another line which also became extinct in 1708 when it came under the power of Austria. In Q1, Gonzago is called Albertus. In *Der Bestrafte Brudermord* (1710), which seems to be a German rendition of an older version of *Ham,* Gonzago is called Pyrrus, which suggests the influence of the speech about Pyrrhus and the fall of Troy in Sh.'s *Ham.*

Gonzalo, *Tmp,* honest old councilor of Naples. He has notable affinities with Polonius in that he speaks wisdom, while often being ridiculous. A Gonzalo appears in Robert Eden's *History of Travaile* (1577), along with several other names from *Tmp.* It is, however, a common Spanish name, chosen probably for its sound, which might have been appropriate to the Italian characters because of Spanish influence in southern Italy.

Good Friday, Christian festival that commemorates the crucifixion of Christ. Since it is celebrated on the Friday that precedes Easter Sunday, its date changes annually with the date of Easter. *Jn 1.1.235. 1H4 1.2.114.*

Goodfellow, Robin, *MND,* prankster spirit in the service of Oberon. He fetches the love-in-idleness flowers to make Titania fall in love with the first thing she sees, transforms Bottom into a creature with the head of an ass, and places the love potion drops into the eyes of the wrong Athenian youth causing chaos among the four lovers. He also chases them through the forest, assuming various forms. He is a 'puck' (a word related to 'pixie' from Old Norse *puki*) and the term has often been substituted for his name. A puck was a nasty household sprite who did such things as pinch girls when they weren't looking, pull off bed-clothes, make people spill things, trip them, and so forth. These attributes were widely known—Spenser, for example, mentions the 'Pouke' in *Epithalamion* (1595)—but Sh. seems to have made his fairies less demonic than they were represented earlier and is credited by some critics with having created a literary fad in fairies which led to their being regarded as benign and innocent creatures of nature.

Reginald Scot's *Discoverie of Witchcraft* (1584) tells of the custom of leaving a bowl of milk for the Incubus or Robin Goodfellow, but said that the belief in the puck was in decline. King James (then of Scotland) in his *Dæmonology* (1593) discusses this decline and the fanciful royal court of the 'Phairy.' Scot also describes how spirits can assume other forms to terrorize people. Thomas Nashe in *Terrors of the Night* (1593) also mentions Robin Goodfellow and describes his pranks. The puck was very similar to Hobgoblin and usually equated with him. The character of Robin Goodfellow also contributed substantially to the original persona of Robin Hood, likely even being the outlaw's antecedent. One might argue that a number of things involving the 'jolly old elf' Santa Claus: his playfulness, his creeping into the house, and the cookies and milk left for him derive from the folklore of the puck.

Goodman, any middle-class head of household, a 'mister.'

Goodman Delver, see Delver.

Goodman, John, *2H6 1.3.18,* character Sh. invents to illustrate the abuses of power allegedly perpetrated by the followers of Cardinal Beaufort (Winchester), Humphrey of Gloucester's enemy. Sh. has a petitioner hand the queen a request for redress of grievances. The plaintiff charges John Goodman, 'my lord Cardinal's man,' with depriving him of everything: house, lands—and wife.

Goodrich, *1H6 4.7.64,* F1 'Goodrig,' castle dating from 1102 in Herefordshire about 12 mi. south of the county seat at Hereford.

Goodrich, Lord Talbot of, *1H6 4.7.64,* one of the titles which Sh. lists as belonging to John Talbot. Talbot's father was Richard Talbot of Goodrich Castle in the Welsh march.

Goodwin Sands, *Jn 5.3.11, 5.5.13,* shoal between the Isle of Thanet and the coast of Kent, near the mouth of the Thames. It had disappeared beneath the sea by the end of the 11th c., but its name recalled the fact that it had once been part of the estates of Godwin (Good win), the Saxon earl of Kent.

Goodwins, the, *MV 3.1.4,* see Goodwin Sands.

Gorboduc, *TN 4.2.15,* legendary British king. He divided his country between his sons Ferrex and Porrex, causing civil war. Porrex killed Ferrex, then his mother with the assistance of her ladies in waiting, tore Porrex apart. Geoffrey of Monmouth reported the legend and the characters are mentioned in Spenser's *Færie Queene,* but the story was most well known to Renaissance Englishmen because of Thomas Norton and Thomas Sackville's Senecan tragedy (1562), a popular and impressive step towards the more sophisticated drama of the later part of the century. It is possible the accounts of the play's success made Sh. grasp onto the story of Lear. The 'niece of King G.' is an invention.

Gordian Knot, symbol for an extraordinarily complicated or difficult problem. In Plutarch's life of Alexander the Great, he says that at the end of the first year of Alexander's campaign for the conquest of the Persian empire Alexander camped near the city of Gordium in Asia Minor. There he was shown a chariot that had allegedly belonged to Midas, king of ancient Lydia. Midas' father Gordius had risen from farmer to king and had tied the vehicle's shaft and yoke with a rope of bark twisted into a complex knot. Alexander was told that the man who could loose the knot was destined to rule the east. Plutarch records two different versions of what ensued. The more colorful is that Alexander sliced through the knot with his sword—claiming that he would loose the knot in the same way that he would rule the east. *H5 1.1.47. Cym 2.2.34.*

Gorgon, one of a family of female monsters described in Greek myth. The most famous of the clan was Medusa, a creature so hideous that the sight of her turned people into stone. Medusa was beheaded by Perseus, one of Zeus's mortal sons. The goddess Athena is often depicted bearing a shield ornamented with the head of a snake-haired Gorgon. *Mac 2.3.72. Ant 2.5.117.*

Gospel, one of the first four books of the New Testament (Matthew, Mark, Luke, and John). 'Gospel' derives from OE *godspell,* 'good news,' a translation of L. *evangelium. TN 5.1.285* (pl.). *STM Add. II.D.97:* this leads into Lincoln's awful joke on 'mark.'

Got, *H5 3.3.60, Gott,* Ger. 'God.'

Goths, ancient people descended (according to tradition) from the Gotar of Sweden. By 3 AD they had settled north of the Black Sea. In the

4th c. they divided into the Ostrogoths (eastern Goths) and Visigoths (western Goths) who were the first tribe of barbarians to mount a successful challenge to the Roman empire. In the year 410 AD a group of Visigoths under the leadership of a young king named Alaric sacked the city of Rome. Although Rome was by that time no longer the seat of the empire's administration, the event proclaimed that Rome's power was waning. Since the western half of Rome's empire never recovered its integrity, some historians have chosen 410 as a convenient date to mark the end of the ancient world. *Tit. AYLI 3.3.6,* the crude people among whom Ovid was exiled.

Gough, Matthew, *2H6,* Goffe, (d. 1450), scion of a Welsh family and career soldier in the service of Henry VI. Gough acquired his early military experience in the company of the most popular general of Henry VI's minority, John Talbot, earl of Shrewsbury. Henry trusted Gough with a number of sensitive assignments in France. While negotiations were underway for a truce that was to follow Henry's marriage to Margaret of Anjou, Gough was given permission to lead a company of unemployed English soldiers into German territory to fight for the French. After the wedding, Gough was charged with the unpopular task of carrying out Henry's orders to surrender the county of Maine to Charles VII. Gough was also deeply involved in the affairs of his and Henry's friend, Giles of Brittany. Giles, who had been raised in England, quarreled with his brother Francis I, the duke of Brittany, over the issue of Brittany's allegiance to France. In October, 1445, Henry sent Gough to reconcile the brothers. When it proved impossible for them to come to terms, Gough encouraged Giles to renounce his French ties in the hope of receiving the English earldom of Richmond to which the Bretagne ducal family had a claim. Francis promptly accused Giles of treason and arrested him. Gough tried unsuccessfully to raise an army to go to his rescue, and Giles was murdered on 24 April 1450. Gough was back in England by 1450, and he and Lord Scales were commissioned to hold the Tower of London against Cade's rebels. Gough died on 6 July 1450, in the bloody fight for London Bridge that marked the turn in Cade's fortunes.

Governor of England, Lord, *R2 2.1.221,* see Edmund Langley. The title describes the duke of York's assignment in 1399 when he ruled England for his nephew Richard II who was campaigning in Ireland.

Gower, Captain, Fluellen's friend and confidant, possibly Thomas Gower, a Yorkshire knight who served with Henry V in France and governed the city of Mans for the regents who ruled for Henry's infant heir, Henry VI. *2H4 2.1.135–197,* 'Master G.': this Gower merely brings a message to the Lord chief Justice and is often thought to be an entirely different character than the captain. He has only a few lines, making the question unanswerable, though there seems no particular reason to think he is different. *H5.*

Gower, John, *Per,* chorus or 'presenter' of the play. He bridges large intervals in the plot, often speaking in a deliberately archaic style to simulate the real poet's verse. His role as Chorus is most like that of Chorus in *H5,* but also bears a strong resemblance to the use of the Chorus in *The Divil's Charter* by Barnabe Barnes and *The Travailes of Three English Brothers* by John Day, William Rowley, and George Wilkins. Day and Wilkins have often been cited as possible coauthors of *Per.* John Gower (d. 1408) was from a prosperous family of Kent, was a property owner in Norfolk and Suffolk, a member of the society of the Inner Temple, and a benefactor of churches. He was in the service of Henry Bolingbroke (later Henry IV) and his fortune rose with his master's. He wrote in Latin, French, and English and his works all have a moral purpose. *Speculum meditantis* or *Mirour de l'homme* (1376–9) explores the effects of sin on society. *Vox clamantis* (c. 1382) attacks the government of Richard II and includes much material on the violence of the Peasants' Revolt of 1381. *Confessio amantis* (1390, mostly in English) is 33,000 lines long and was written at the request of

Richard II, though it was rededicated to Henry IV in 1392. Important not only for its Bk. 8, 'Unlawful Love' as one of the sources for *Per,* it tells a series of stories demonstrating the Seven Deadly Sins applied to love. Known for his plain style in Middle English, he used eight syllable couplets in the work and achieves a romantic flavor which even his friend Geoffrey Chaucer, who called him 'the moral Gower' in his *Troilus and Criseyde,* could not surpass. Before his death, he became blind and thus became associated in the Renaissance with blind Homer. Although the opinion of his work declined appreciably, Sir Philip Sidney honored him with Chaucer as one of the first English poets. The contents of his poetry was valued, but the verse was considered old-fashioned and unsophisticated.

Grace, *WT 1.2.82, 101,* goddess Charis or Aglaia, one of the three Graces (along with Thalia and Euphrosyne), the daughters of Jupiter and Eurynome. She presided over social accomplishments, politeness, banquet, and dance. She was a wife of Hephæstus (Roman Vulcan), as was Aphrodite. Homer added a fourth sister Pasithea. The Graces were also known as the Charites, and the coincidence of the similarity of the theological grace, associated the sisters with Faith, Hope, and Charity. They were commonly depicted in art as nude, with Faith and Hope (for the afterlife) facing away from the viewer and flanking Charity (an act of this world), who faced the viewer.

Grandpré, French village on the Aisne river about 120 mi. northeast of Paris. See Grandpré, Lord, *H5.*

Grandpré, Lord, *H5,* duke of, (d. 1415), one of the most prominent of the French nobles whose deaths at the battle at Agincourt Sh. found reported in Holinshed (3.555).

Gratii, *AWW 4.3.168,* commander in the Duke of Florence's army. In Golding's translation of *Metamorphoses,* 'Grayes' (Graii) is used to mean 'Greeks.' Spenser has a 'Gratian' in his *Færie Queene* 2.10.61.5, and there was a minor Lating poet of the Augustan period named Grattius, whose writings on hunting were republished in Venice in 1534 and elsewhere later. Gratii could also be some sort of pun on the It. *grazie* 'thank you,' similar to the invention of Bentivolii (q.v.).

Gray, Lady, *3H6, R3 1.1.64,* Elizabeth Woodville (1431–1492), Edward IV's Queen Elizabeth. *R3* Elizabeth was the daughter of Richard Woodville and Jacquetta of Luxemburg, widow of John, duke of Bedford. Her first husband was Sir John Gray (Grey), the son of Edward Gray, Lord Ferrers of Groby. Sh., for an unknown reason, departed from his source (Edward Hall's *Union of the Two Noble and Illustre Famelies of Lancastre and Yorke,* 264) and called her husband Richard rather than John (*3H6 3.2.2*). John died fighting for Henry VI at the second battle of St. Albans (1461), and Elizabeth was one of Queen Margaret's ladies of the bed chamber. Sh. noted the Lancastrian allegiance of the Gray family in *R3 1.3.127–128,* but in *3H6 3.2.6–7* he ignored history and declared that John fell fighting for the house of York.

The distortion of the record made it possible for Sh. to invent an entertaining bit of action. Since no one knew how Edward first made Elizabeth's acquaintance, Sh. imagined a romantic scene to explain the origin of their relationship. He has them meet when Gray's beautiful young widow comes before her king to request the defense of her right to her loyal husband's estate. In reality, Edward's courtship of her was as secret as their marriage. The king probably made her acquaintance at her parents' home in Grafton Regis. His decision to marry her may have been impulsive and self-indulgent. Edward had a reputation for being easily swayed by his sexual appetites, and she may have been unobtainable outside marriage. The alliance brought Edward no political advantages and created some problems. The wedding probably took place late in May, 1464. The new queen, who was presented at court in September of that year, was not popular. She was ambitious for a very large crowd of relatives: two sons by her first marriage, five brothers, and seven unmarried sisters. Edward's efforts to provide gifts, titles, and wealthy alliances for all the Woodvilles and Grays naturally angered other nobles who saw the queen's gains as their losses. The Woodvilles and Grays did not, however, acquire estates to rival those of the Nevilles, and they may have been resented more for the swiftness of their rise than the scope of their greed. The queen's influence at court increased as the fortunes of Warwick, the Nevilles, and Clarence declined. Ultimately, even Richard of Gloucester (Sh.'s 'Crookback'), the king's sole surviving brother, withdrew from court to duties in the north of England.

The queen's most active opponent at the end of Edward's reign was William, Lord Hastings. On his death bed Edward attempted unsuccessfully to reconcile his wife and Hastings, who had been his friend since youth. The bad feeling between Hastings and the queen had serious political consequences, for Hastings was instrumental in frustrating Elizabeth's plan to install herself and her kin as the power behind her son's throne. Hastings blocked her attempt to have young Edward V brought to London at the head of a large army. Consequently, the young king's uncle, Richard of Gloucester, was able to take him away from his Woodville guardians. Queen Elizabeth, who intuited Gloucester's intent, fled to sanctuary in Westminster Abbey with the second of Edward IV's sons, Richard. When Gloucester persuaded parliament to declare her marriage to Edward invalid and her children illegitimate, the church induced her to surrender her son and to leave sanctuary. Her boys were sent to the Tower of London and never heard from again. She must have believed them dead, for her continued resistance to Richard III (Gloucester) focused on schemes to marry her eldest daughter, Elizabeth, to Henry Tudor, the leader of what was left of the Lancastrian faction. After Henry defeated Richard III at the battle of Bosworth, she was briefly recognized as the dowager queen, but she quickly fell from favor with the new government and was compelled to retire to the abbey of Bermondsey. She spent the remainder of her life in obscurity.

Gray, Lord, *R3,* Richard Gray (d. 1485), younger son of John (Richard) Gray and Elizabeth Woodville Gray, step-son of Edward IV. Gray assisted his uncle, Lord Rivers, in caring for Edward IV's sons. While conducting young Edward V to London to claim his father's throne, Gray, Rivers, and Sir Thomas Vaughan were captured by Richard of Gloucester. Richard accused them of undue influence over the young king, imprisoned them at Pontefract Castle, and executed them without benefit of trial.

Gray, Richard, *3H6 3.2.2,* first husband of Edward IV's queen, Elizabeth Woodville Gray. Edward Hall's *Union of the Two Noble and Illustre Famelies of Lancastre and Yorke* (264) records his name as John, not Richard. John Gray inherited his title, Lord Ferrers of Groby, from his father, Edward, who held it by right of his wife. John married Richard Woodville's daughter, Elizabeth, in 1450. They had two sons, Thomas and Richard, who profited a great deal from their mother's second marriage with the king. The lavish royal patronage Elizabeth solicited for her relatives caused much ill feeling at Edward's court. Although Elizabeth wed the leader of the house of York, her family had Lancastrian connections. John, her first husband, died at the second battle of St. Albans (17 February 1461) fighting for Henry VI. Sh. acknowledged this fact in *R3 1.3.127–128,* but in the earlier *3H6 3.2.6–7,* he revised history by having Edward IV say that Gray fell in the service of York.

Gray's Inn, *2H4 3.2.31–32,* one of the London Inns of Court that lodged young men training for the law. It was on the Holborn road just west of London's wall.

Graziano 1), *MV,* 'Gratiano' in F1, friend of Antonio's. He accompanies Bassanio on his quest for Portia, but is made to promise he will behave himself. He is the most nasty and least merciful of the Venetians in his mocking of

Shylock in the trial scene, thus forming a contrast with Antonio's acceptance of his fate. Later he is paired with Nerissa to complete the round of marriages that end the comedy. The name is a common Italian one, but might allude to It. *gratiano* in John Florio's *A Worlde of Wordes Or Most copious and exact Dictionary in Italian and English* (1598): 'a foole or clownish fellowe in a play or comedie.' Since its etymological meaning via a saint who was martyred at Amiens during the reign of Diocletian means 'pleasing' (as in 'gratify') Florio's comic definition may be ironic. The name is also used in the *commedia dell'arte* for the comic doctor.

2) *Oth,* F1 'Gratiano,' Brabanzio's brother and Desdemona's uncle. He has little function in the play other than to bring the news from Venice that his brother has died of a broken heart over his daughter's marriage. Otherwise he merely observes the attack on Cassio and the climax of the play and comments upon it.

Grecian (adj), Greek. *MV 5.1.5,* 'G. tents.' *AYLI 4.1.92* 'G. club.' *Son 53.8,* 'G. tires,' ancient Greek clothing. *Tro.*

Grecians, *AWW 1.3.70,* the Homeric Greeks.

Greece, nation that occupies the southeastern portion of the peninsula of the European continent that extends into the Mediterranean between Italy and Turkey. In Sh.'s day it was dominated by the Ottoman Turks, who ruled it until 1821. But the Greece to which Sh. most often alludes is the ancient community that produced the myths, legends, and anecdotes he cites from classical literature.

Shr Ind. 2.92, see Greet. *3H6 2.2.146. 1H6 5.7.104. Luc 1368. Err 1.1.132,* Egeon searches there five years without finding his son, then is shipwrecked and brought to Ephesus. *MWW 2.3.31,* 'Hector of G.,' a joke. Hector was enemy of the Greeks. *Tro 4.5.123,* 'lord of G.,' Diomedes. *Cor 3.1.110, 118. Per 4.96, 105.*

Greek 1) (n.) *JC 1.2.279, 284,* language of Greece.

2) (n.) a native of Greece, usually, the warriors who attacked Troy. *TN 4.1.17,* 'foolish G.,' possibly alluding to the stereotype, possibly to Pandarus (to whom Feste later compares himself) because he is asking Sebastian to visit Olivia. *Tro; 4.5.55,* 'merry G.': the Romans stereotyped Greeks as fond of food, drink, and sensual pleasures. *Ham 2.2.472. Cym 4.2.315.* Pl.: *3H6 2.1.52. Luc 1384, 1402, 1470.*

3) (adj.) of or pertaining to Greece. *AYLI 2.5.56,* 'a G. invocation,' a nonsense word. Since Roman times, saying something was Greek meant it was unintelligible.

Greekish, *Tro,* of or pertaining to Greece.

Green, Henry, *R2,* (d. 1399), son of one of Edward III's royal justices and a favorite of Richard II's. After Richard destroyed the 'lord appellant' in 1397, he assumed absolute power and relied on men like Green to do his bidding. Green, therefore, took the blame for many of the king's unpopular policies. When Henry (IV) Bolingbroke raised England against Richard in 1399, Green fled to Bristol Castle. Bristol turned him over to Henry who executed him without benefit of trial.

'Greensleeves,' popular song still sung as a Christmas carol with the words 'What Child Is This?' It was listed in the Stationer's Register in September 1580 as 'a new northern ditty of the Lady Greensleeves.' Other incarnations of the tune include its use for Royalist political ballads during the Civil War and as a song entitled 'The Blacksmith,' mentioned in Samuel Pepys' diary in April 1660.

MWW 2.1.60: the comic contrast intended by Sh. is between the sacred quality of the Psalms and the secular nature of 'Greensleeves.' *5.5.19.* See Hundredth Psalm.

Greenwich, *H8 1.2.189,* town in the county of Kent on the Thames river. In Sh.'s day it was the site of a much used royal residence. Henry VIII and both his daughters were born there. English monarchs frequented Greenwich until Charles II gave the facility to the royal navy. In the late 17th c. an important institute for the study of astronomy was established in the park of the former royal palace.

Greet, *Shr Ind. 2.92,* F1 'Greece,' a small village in Gloucestershire, not far from Stratford. Sh. seems to have used the names of people from his home area in this passage.

Gregory, common name which derives from the Gr. 'vigilant.'

1) *Shr 4.1.108,* one of Petruccio's servants.

2) *Rom,* member of the house of Capulet. He participates in the brawl in the first scene.

Gremio, *Shr,* old man who wishes to marry Bianca for her money. A comic dolt, everything he tries goes against him. He is too obsequious, he lies about his own wealth, and he even hires his rival Lucentio (in disguise) to tutor Bianca in Latin, thereby guaranteeing Lucentio's success. He is the only one of the three suitors of Bianca who ends the play unmarried. At his first entrance in F1, Gremio is described as 'a Pantelowne' (*1.1.47*), establishing that his character is derived almost entirely from the *pantalone* of the *commedia dell'arte,* though Sh. gives him a trifle more humanity. The pantaloon was said to originate as a parody of a Venetian merchant, named from the popular Venetian saint Pantaleone, a patron of physicians. He was depicted as lean, wearing spectacles, slippers, and loose pants (compare *AYLI 2.7.157–63*). In later forms the pantaloon was not necessarily a merchant or Venetian, and in some areas he became equivalent to the Dottore, the aged pedant, the character type which influenced the creation of Holofernes and Gerald the Schoolmaster. Eventually Pantalone's lower garment became known as 'pantaloons' or 'pants.'

Grey, Thomas, *H5,* (d. 1415), one of three men whom Henry V paused to execute on a charge of treason before launching his invasion of France from Southampton. Grey came from Berwick, and he had connections with northern lords who were not conspicuous for their loyalty to Henry's family. Grey's mother was a Mowbray, and Grey married a Neville, the daughter of the earl of Westmorland.

Griffith, Richard, *H8,* attendant who accompanied Katherine of Aragon to the court that inquired into the legitimacy of her marriage with Henry VIII. He appears in government records as a member of Katherine's household during the period of her residency at Ampthill castle. Nothing is known about his family or background.

Grimalkin, *Mac 1.1.8,* F1 'Gray-Malkin,' a gray cat, a name applied to a spirit who calls the witches. 'Malkin' is a diminutive of 'Mary.' Grimalkin was a common name for a cat, like 'Tabby' or 'Puss.' Witches were supposed to keep spirits in the form of a cat.

Grindstone, Susan, *Rom 1.5.9,* woman, along with 'Nell,' invited to the servants' part of Capulet's feast. The surname is an obvious pun on the order of 'Doll Tearsheet.' Tearsheet also appears with a Nell. Both the pun and the comparison suggest what particular attraction Susan holds.

Grissel, *Shr 2.1.290,* Griselda, a patient and obedient wife. Married to Walter, Marquis of Saluces (Saluzzo), she endures much abuse, including the possibility of bigamy until the nobleman is convinced of her loyal devotion. They then live happily ever after. The testing through abuse may have suggested Petruccio's treatment for shrewishness. Her story is told in the last tale in Boccaccio's *Decameron.* Boccaccio may have gotten it from a Provençal tale. It was later translated by Boccaccio's friend Petrarch into Latin (*De Obidentia ac Fide uxoria Mythologia*). Chaucer subsequently used Petrarch's version as the basis for his *Tale of the Clerk of Oxenford.* There were also many ballads using the story. The first dramatic use occurs in 1395 and later plays include one written by Ralph Radcliffe during the reign of Henry VIII and

Patient Grissil (1603) by Thomas Dekker, Henry Chettle, and W. Haughton.

Grumio, *Shr 1.2.5.* Petruccio's chief servant, mocked for his small stature. His lack of comprehension is clownish, but it seems to be a ruse to manipulate others. He frequently comments on the action, revealing a native intelligence he otherwise conceals. There is a Grumio who is a servant in Plautus' *Mostellaria* ('The Haunted House'). The name could also be an Italianizing of 'groom,' a word long in use in its meaning of 'servant.'

Gualtier, *2H6 4.1.38,* Fr. 'Walter.' Sh. has Suffolk translate Walter Whitmore's name into French in order to avoid an ominous pun. Suffolk had been told by an astrologer that he would die 'by water.' An Elizabethan would have pronounced 'Walter' so that it sounded like 'water.' Consequently, when Suffolk was confronted by a 'Walter' who threatened his life, Suffolk tried to fend off the omen by calling him 'Gualtier.'

Guiana, *MWW 1.3.62,* region on the northern coast of South America. The legendary city of El Dorado (also called Manoa or Omoa) with its fabulous wealth was supposed to lie in the interior. Many expeditions attempted to locate it, the most famous of which were by Francisco de Orellana for the Spanish in 1540 and Philip von Hutton for a German company in 1541. The area of Guiana in Sh. is South America north of the Amazon and Rio Negro, now roughly French Guiana, part of Brazil, Surinam, Guyana, Venezuela, and part of northern Colombia. Sir Walter Raleigh published *The Discoverie of the Large, Rich, and Beautiful Empire of Guiana* in 1596 after his voyage to South America. It claimed that the city of gold was located on an island in the middle of a lake called Parimá. This fiction was so well accepted the lake appeared on maps for two centuries, though it does not exist. Sh. was likely thinking of Raleigh's book when he gives Falstaff the remark.

Guiderius, *Cym,* son of Cymbeline, kidnapped as a baby with his brother Arviragus by Belarius and reared in the wilderness of Cambria as Polydore. When the brothers encounter their sister Innogen in disguise, they immediately develop a strong liking for her, but their true identities are not revealed until they become heroes in the battle between the British and the Romans. The lost prince or princess who is rediscovered is a standard ingredient of romance. Holinshed says that Guiderius succeeded his father in 17 AD and resisted Roman power, refusing to pay the empire's tribute and raising rebellions.

Guildenstern, *Ham,* boyhood friend of Hamlet now in the service of Claudius. Along with Rosencrantz, with whom he is indistinguishable, he is an opportunistic courtier who cannot be trusted by his old friend. How guilty they are in Claudius' plots is never clear; however, they are certainly guilty of acquiescing to the general corruption of the state. When Hamlet switches papers on them, they go unknowingly to their deaths. Guildenstern was a noble name common at the Danish court in the late 16th c. and at the university of Wittenberg. The name came into prominence with Tom Stoppard's existential play *Rosencrantz and Guildenstern Are Dead* (1967) in which the two befuddled characters are in a play neither can comprehend.

Guildford, Henry, *H8,* (d. 1553), soldier who served as Henry VIII's Master of the Horse and standard-bearer. He was a scion of an ancient Kentish family that sided with the Tudors in the last phase of the War of the Roses.

Guildfords, *R3 4.4.434,* family long resident in the county of Kent. Sir John Guildford managed Edward IV's household. He and his son, Sir Richard, refused to acquiesce to Richard III's assumption of Edward IV's crown, and in 1483 they raised a rebellion in Kent to support the candidacy of Henry Tudor, earl of Richmond. Sir Richard fled to Brittany to join Richmond and returned to England with the Tudor pretender in 1485 to fight at Bosworth Field. He became one of Henry VII's privy councilors and enjoyed a distinguished military career.

Guildhall, *R3 3.5.71, 100, 3.7.35,* building where London's governing council met. Medieval London was run by an oligarchy of merchants. Since its mayor and alderman were chosen by and from the leadership of the city's major guilds, it was natural for them to use the guildhall for their assemblies. A modest 12th c. building on the north side of London housed the guilds until 1411, when a much grander facility, which still serves the people of London, was erected.

Guillaume, *AWW 4.3.168,* Fr. 'William', F1 'Guiltian,' a commander in the Duke of Florence's army.

Guiltian, *AWW,* see Guillaume.

Guinea-hen, F1 'Gynney Hen,' *Oth 1.3.315,* old term for a prostitute.

Guinevere, *LLL 4.1.122,* wife of King Arthur. She is mentioned to evoke the remote past. Her name was Guanhumara in Geoffrey of Monmouth's *Historia Regum Britanniæ* (one of the most important Arthurian sources) derived from the Welsh *Gwenhwyfar.* From a noble Roman family, she was an extraordinary beauty who retreated to a nunnery after Mordred defeated Arthur. It was Chrétien de Troyes, however, who first introduced the tale of the adulterous love between Guinevere and Lancelot du Lac, a story very similar to that of Tristan and Isolde.

Guisnes, *H8 1.1.7,* castle in France near the port of Calais. During Henry VIII's reign it and the small district it commanded were held by the English king. In 1520 Henry and Francis I met near Guisnes. The lavish displays of wealth with which they sought to impress each other caused their encampment to be dubbed 'the Field of the Cloth of Gold.' In January 1557, Guisnes and Calais were conquered by a French army led by Francis, duke of Guise. A treaty of peace between England and France was negotiated at Cateau-Cambrésis in March 1559. It called for the return of Guisnes and Calais to England in 1567, but the provision was never carried out. The king of France repudiated the treaty and retained possession of the territories to punish England for encouraging Huguenot rebels.

Gurney, James, *Jn,* name Sh. gives to one of Lady Falconbridge's attendants. The Falconbridge episodes in *Jn* may have been invented by Sh. or copied from another play (*The Troublesome Raigne of John, King of England*), and it is unlikely that Sh. based their characters on historical persons. There was a baronial family named Gurney (Gourney, Gorney) that held fiefs in both England and France. King John of England seized a castle belonging to a Norman lord, Hugh Gurney, in 1202, and Hugh is recorded as a witness to treaties between John and Philip Augustus.

Guy, Sir, *H8 5.3.21,* legendary earl of Warwick whose combat with a giant named Colbrand is described in a 13th c. English romance.

Guyenne, *1H6 1.1.60,* district on France's southern Atlantic coast near Bordeaux. Guyenne, Guienne, and Gascony all refer to the same area. Guyenne was the last fragment of the great medieval duchy of Aquitaine that sprawled over much of southern France. Aquitaine came under English control in 1152 when Eleanor of Aquitaine married Henry II of England. A portion of the old duchy was still occupied by England at the start of the Hundred Years' War, and the English maintained a presence there until 1450.

Gypsy, nomadic race of people, originating in India probably in the lower castes. They migrated from northern India beginning in the 5th c., but most heavily beginning with the 11th c. Moslem invasions. They migrated to Persia and Asia Minor, then on to Greece in the 14th c. They arrived in France and Germany in the 15th c. and in England, Scandinavia, Russia, and Spain in the 16th. In their own language, which is Indo-European, they are called *Rom,* or *Romani,* but the Europeans thought they were from Egypt because of their swarthy complexions and Egyptian became shortened to Gypsy. Close-knit, with strong cultural traditions, they traditionally regarded the influence of outsiders as 'polluting,' though they frequently adapted local religions to their own worship. They have long been stereotyped as fortune-tellers, musicians, and itinerant tinkers and smiths. The slang verb 'to gyp' derives from their supposed propensity for crooked dealing. They have also suffered from strong prejudice. They were expelled from Paris in 1539 and England in 1563. In the 20th c. they became the target of Nazi genocide and many were exterminated. Though there were theoretically no gypsies allowed in England in Sh.'s day (as there were no Jews), the term was used as equivalent to wandering musician, vagabond, thief, or con artist.

Rom 2.1.39: Cleopatra is a mere gypsy to Romeo's current love. *AYLI 5.3.14. Ant 1.1.10,* 'gipsy's lust,' Cleopatra's lust. *4.13.28. TNK 4.2.44,* perhaps an allusion to the old myth that gypsies steal children.

H

Hacket, Cicely, *Shr Ind. 2.88,* household maid for whom Sly has called out, presumably a common woman. Hackets are recorded in the parish records of the 1590s as living in the village of Wincot (q.v.), and they are likely to be the source of the name. Less likely, but possible, is that Hacket might be related to 'haggard,' a falcon allowed to hunt on its own before training, and thus, a whore. A 'hack' was a board on which the bird's meat was laid and was applied to a state of partial liberty allowed to haggards before training. 'Hack' was also used to mean a gash, a hoe, a mattock, or pick-ax. All of these could have obscene implications.

Hacket, Marian, *Shr Ind. 2.20,* 'the fat ale-wife of Wincot,' a person who is supposed to know Sly quite well. The common type of woman with whom Sly would associate suggests both lewdness (see Marian) and such later characters as Luce or Nell (*Err*), Mistress Quickly, and others. See Hackett, Cicely.

Hagar's offspring, *MV 2.5.43,* Ishmael. Hagar was an Egyptian whom the barren Sarah gave to her husband Abraham as a concubine. Hagar became pregnant, for which Sarah treated her roughly. She fled but God told her that she would have a son, Ishmael, and her descendants would be numberless. God also told her Ishmael would be a 'wild man,' his hand against everyone and everyone's against him. When Isaac was later born of Sarah, the enmities of the mothers became the rivalry of their sons. The story is told in Genesis 16. The descendants of Ishmæl are traditionally the Arabs. In this reference, Shylock is associating Lancelot with the enemies of the Jews.

Hal, *1H4, 2H4 5.5.41,* see Henry V.

Half-can, *MM 4.3.16,* 'wild H.,' mocking name for one of the impoverished criminals Pompey knows. As prisoners paid for their own food, many were forced to beg passers by.

Half-moon, *1H4 2.5.27,* name for a room in an inn.

Halidom, 'by my h.,' an oath, 'by the Virgin Mary,' the Holy Dame. It may also mean either ' holy-dom,' the realm of holiness, salvation; or a holy relic. *TGV 4.2.132. Shr 5.2.104. Rom 1.3.45,* 'holidam.' *H8 5.1.117.*

Hallowmas, feast of All Hallows or All Saints. A festival in celebration of all the saints was added to the Christian calendar by pope Gregory IV in 834. *TGV 2.1.24,* reference to the custom of begging on this day, similar to our Halloween custom. *R2 5.1.80:* the calendar in use in England in Sh.'s day would have brought Hallowmas (1 November) about two weeks closer to the winter solstice than it is today—hence Sh.'s reference to the shortest day of the year. *MM 2.1.120.*

Hames Castle, Hammes, fortress near Calais. Its isolated location in an English military district on the continent made it an excellent place to confine political prisoners who were too dangerous to keep in England. In 1472 George Neville, archbishop of York, was sent there under suspicion of treason. His kinsman, John de Vere, earl of Oxford, joined him in 1473, after a failed attempt to raise a rebellion against Edward IV in Cornwall. *3H6 5.5.2.*

Hamlet, 1) *Ham,* the melancholy prince of Denmark. He has been attacked, indeed, criticizes himself, for his vacillations in pursuing vengeance for his father. He kills old Polonius, seemingly without justification (although he doesn't dismember him and feed him to the pigs as he does in Sh.'s source, François de Belleforest's *Histoires tragiques,* 1576). He drives Ophelia to suicide, and tricks his old friends Rosencrantz and Guildenstern into their deaths. Despite all this, Hamlet is one of the most compelling creations of literature and his name is well known throughout the world. To some extent this is due to the abilities of great actors (and actresses) to interpret him and the melancholy in him. Everyone has likely experienced the kind of self-doubt and depression that Hamlet suffers, if not the degree, and therefore, as in other major literary characters caught in incredible situations (such as Oedipus), one nonetheless identifies with his tragedy. It is a mystery exactly how he evolved. Sh. got the story from Saxo Grammaticus' *Historiæ Danicæ* (c. 1200) by way of Belleforest, or possibly also a Thomas Kyd *Hamlet* (c. 1594 or earlier) which is no longer extant. Kyd's *Spanish Tragedy* influenced *Ham* quite a bit, or Kyd's *Hamlet* was very much like his other play. It is possible there was a previous version by Sh. himself.

In the extant sources, one is reminded of Sh.'s immeasurable talent for taking excessive tales and charging them with insight and subtlety. Part of Hamlet's character is derived from Timothy Bright's *Treatise of Melancholie* (1586). His hesitation may be his own questioning of the morality of revenge or a sensible caution in believing the Ghost, who, in Elizabethan thinking, was as likely to have been sent by the devil as by God. Sh. took Hamlet's name as well as Gertrude's from Belleforest with little change. Amleth is the prince in both Saxo Grammaticus and in Belleforest, but there is little evidence that Sh. directly used Saxo. It may derive from an ancient Norse legend in which a hero, Amlothi, feigns madness. The name means 'desperate (mad) in battle'—perhaps in the same dunderheaded way that the Greek hero Ajax was mad. Amlothi is mentioned in a quote from a poet named Snaebjorn in the *Prose Edda* by Snorri Sturluson (1179–1241). From the Roman historian Livy, both Sh. and Saxo would have known how Lucius Junius Brutus escaped the murderous Tarquin by feigning idiocy, which may also have influenced the creation of Sh.'s Hamlet as well as Saxo's Amleth. It is particularly interesting that Sh. named his son Hamnet. The boy died young and some psychological critics see Hamlet's talking to his father's ghost as a mirror of Sh. trying to deal with his son's death.

2) *Ham 1.1.83, 94,* old king Hamlet. The use of identical names for Hamlet and son, and Fortinbras and son is confusing, even if one wishes to say that a comparison is drawn between Fortinbras, Jr., the decisive avenger and Hamlet, Jr., the indecisive. In Belleforest, the old king is called Horvendile, from Saxo Grammaticus' Horwendil. The murder of the old king may have come from the alleged murder of Francisco Maria della Rovere, duke of Urbino, in 1538. It has even been suggested that Hamlet's description of his father's portrait may be derived from a portrait of the duke engraved by Titian. Another parallel is that the duke of Urbino had been married to Eleonora Gonzaga for 30 years at his death. In the play within the play the king has been married for either thirty (Q2, F1) or forty (Q1) years.

Hampton, *H5 2.2.88,* see Southampton.

Hannibal, (247–183 BC), Carthaginian general, son of Hannibal Barca and brother of Hasdrubal. In the 1st Punic War, he took command of Carthaginian forces in Spain from another Hasdrubal (his brother-in-law). The 2nd Punic War, however, built his great reputation. With crack troops he terrified Italy by invading it. He made an heroic crossing of the Alps with elephants and wiped out Roman resistance in the Po valley. Rome had no general to equal him, and the Romans suffered horrendous losses whenever they met the Carthaginians in battle. The Romans were finally forced to adopt the strategy of avoiding direct engagements and waiting for shortages of supplies to weaken their enemy. In 216 he inflicted a crushing defeat on the Romans at Cannæ, but was unable to exploit it because of insufficient Carthaginian support, though he had acquired a number of allies in southern Italy. Hasdrubal, who had defended Spain against Roman attack, invaded Italy also, but was defeated and killed at the Metaurus river in 207. This forced Hannibal to withdraw. Leading the defense of Carthage against Scipio Africanus Minor, he was defeated in 202 at Zama. He ruled Carthage after peace was concluded, but the Romans demanded he be turned over to them. In exile, he took poison to avoid their revenge. For Sh. and his contemporaries, Hannibal typifies the invincible general.

1H6 1.7.21. LLL 5.2.662. MM 2.1.168, 172, 'wicked H.,' possibly a malapropism for 'cannibal,' though Hannibal might represent a dreaded pagan. The joining of Pompey to Hannibal would also be humorous.

Harcourt, *2H4,* possibly Sir Thomas Harcourt of Stanton, Oxfordshire. Sh.'s character sides with Henry IV against the Percies. The real Thomas Harcourt must have remained loyal to the king during the revolts led by the Percies, for in 1407 Henry appointed him sheriff of Berkshire.

Harfleur, *H5 3.0.17, 27, 3.3.91, 110, 135, 140, 3.5.49, 3.6.123,* French town on the estuary of the Seine river. During the Hundred Years' War the English coveted it as a base for operations in France. It opened the way to Rouen, the capital of Normandy, and to Paris. The Black Prince took Harfleur in 1346, and in 1415 Henry V reoccupied it as a prelude to his victory at Agincourt.

Harfleur, Governor of, *H5,* chief administrator of the French port that was Henry V's first target in his campaign for the conquest of France. At the time of Henry's investure, Jean, Lord D'Estouteville was in charge, but when the French reinforced the city with 300 men, Raoul, Sieur de Gaucourt seems to have become the governor.

Ha'rfordwest, *R3 4.5.7,* Haverfordwest, administrative center of the Welsh county of Pembrokeshire, 250 mi. west of London.

Harlechly Castle, *R2 3.2.1,* Harlech, built by Edward I about 1270 in northern Wales on the shore of the Cardigan bay. It was the place where Richard II landed in 1399 when he returned to England from Ireland to confront the rebellion raised by Henry (IV) Bolingbroke.

Harpier, *Mac 4.1.3,* apparently the spirit in service to the third witch, as Grimalkin and Paddock serve the others. It is most likely from 'Harpy.' Other suggestions have included the Hebrew *habar,* 'an incantation'; a crab on the east coast of Scotland called the 'Harper crab'; and an animal so named because its cry is like the sound of a harp.

Harpy, one of the three monsters with the body and claws of a bird and a woman's head with a face pale with hunger. They were extremely foul-smelling. The Harpies were daughters of Thaumas by Electra, or of Poseidon and Gæa, and sisters of Iris. One myth tells of Phineus who enraged Zeus with his prophecy (or because of his cruelty). He was blinded and whenever he tried to eat, the Harpies befouled his food, making it inedible, or stole it. Two of the Argonauts, Calais and Zetes, nearly cut the Harpies to pieces but Iris intervened and swore that Phineus would never be tormented by them again. In another version they killed the monsters and were given their wings. Virgil has Æneas on his voyages landing on the Strophades (their islands) where they had gone after being driven from Phineus. Æneas and his men killed the cattle and sat to eat when the Harpies snatched the food away. After a second time the men tried to battle them but the feathers were too hard to penetrate. One of the Harpies, Celæno, perched on a rock and predicted great suffering for the men.

Ado 2.1.253. Per 17.47. Tmp 3.3.52, the action on this stage direction seems to be an allusion to Virgil's *Æneid,* 3.225–8, where the Harpies steal the food from Æneas.

Harry, nickname for Henry.

1) *3H6 3.1.15, 1H6 4.2.4, R3 4.4.25, 59, 5.5.83,* see Henry VI.

2) *R2 1.1.162, 2.1.193, 280, 2H4 intro.23, 5.2.14, 49, 59, 5.3.115, 116,* see Henry IV (Bolingbroke).

3) also 'Prince H.' *1H4, 2H4, H5,* see Henry V.

4) *1H4 2.4.39, 78, 85, 2.5.106, 2H4 2.3.12, 43,* see Hotspur.

5) *H8 1.4.9,* see Guildford, Henry.

Harry groat, *STM Add. II.D.2,* small silver coin struck during Henry VIII's reign.

Harry of Monmouth, *H5 4.7.31, 44,* see Henry V.

Harry Percy, *2H4 1.1.42, 49,* see Hotspur.

Harry ten shilling, *2H4 3.2.218,* coin minted by Henry VII, worth only five shillings in Sh.'s day. It was familiar to Sh.'s audience, but an anachronism during the reign of Henry IV.

Harvey, *1H4,* one of Oldcastle's disreputable companions. He helps plot the robbery at Gadshill. This character seems to be identical with Bardolph in *2H4.* Sh. may have found it expedient to change the name, for in 1598 Mary, the widowed mother of Sh.'s patron, the earl of Southampton, married William Lord Harvey of Kidbrooke.

Hastings, Lord, 1) William (1430–1483), a life-long adherent to the Yorkist cause. He served both Richard of York and his son Edward IV. In Edward's government he held the posts of master of the mint, royal chamberlain, ambassador to both France and Burgundy, and captain of Calais (the largest of England's standing garrisons). In 1471, when Warwick 'the Kingmaker' defected to the Lancastrian camp and forced Edward to flee England, he stayed behind to organize resistance. He convinced Edward's brother, George, duke of Clarence, to repudiate Warwick, his father-in-law, and cast his lot with Edward. He also played prominent roles in the battles at Barnet and Tewkesbury and may have been personally involved in the murder of Henry VI's son, Edward. The major complication for his career was his inability to get along with Edward's queen, Elizabeth Woodville Gray. As Edward lay dying, the king tried to force a reconciliation between Hastings and the queen, but the gesture failed to secure the future of Edward's dynasty. Hastings was loyal to Edward's sons, but he prevented the Woodvilles from raising an army to solidify their hold on the heir and his throne. As a result, Edward's brother, Richard of Gloucester, won control of the young princes and convinced parliament to disinherit them. When Hastings refused to support Richard's proposal, Richard called him to a council meeting, accused him of treason, and beheaded him without benefit of trial (13 June 1483).

3H6 4.1.46–47: Sh. says that Edward IV rewarded his loyalty by giving him the hand of Thomas Hungerford's heiress. In reality Hastings' son Edward, another Lord Hastings, had the privilege of wedding this wealthy lady. *R3.*

2) *2H4,* Ralph Hastings, a participant in the rebellion that Archbishop Scrope initiated to overthrow Henry IV. The sources disagree as to whether or not he was executed with his co-conspirators following the failure of the revolt in 1405. Despite the title Sh. accords him, he was a knight, not a baron.

Hastings, the Pursuivant, *R3,* a servant or officer of a court of law ranking below a herald. Sh. dramatized a story told by Holinshed (3.723) in which Lord Hastings misinterprets an omen. Just before Hastings' condemnation, he meets an agent of justice who bears his name. Since he had run across the man once before when he faced danger and had, on that occasion, come off well, he concludes that he will be lucky a second time.

Hatfield, *2H6 2.2.12,* town in Hertfordshire about 20 mi. north of England, the site of a royal palace that had originally been the property of the bishops of Ely. Edward III's second son, William of Hatfield, was born there. Henry VIII used the estate as a nursery for his children, and Sh.'s sovereign, Elizabeth I, spent much of her youth there.

'Heart's Ease,' *Rom 4.4.128–130,* popular song requested by Peter. It is mentioned in *Misogonus* by Thomas Rychardes, a play dating to before 1570.

Heaven, the sky, the Christian Paradise, or as a personification of God. In the latter case it may have been used to avoid censorship. It was pronounced as one syllable or two. Although some instances in which it seems to be monosyllabic may be the result of substituting it for 'God.'

Hebrew, (n.) a Jew. The word is from Eber (mentioned Genesis 10: 24–25), great grandson of Shem son of Noah. As Shem is the father of the Semites, Eber is the ancestor of Abraham, and therefore the Jews. His name is thought to be related to the Hebrew *'avor* 'to cross over.' The association may have been with nomadic ancestors of the Jews who crossed over Palestine's eastern frontier. To the civilizations of Mesopotamia, Canaan was the land over the Euphrates where Abraham went. Ironically, the word Arab is likely to be linguistically related to Hebrew, also. *TGV 2.5.46,* the line is reminiscent of Falstaff's 'H. Jew' (q.v.) *MV 1.3.55.*

Hebrew Jew, *1H4 2.5.180,* F1 'Ebrew Iew,' a redundancy. The expression was used as an emphatic term of contempt to mean, 'absolute Jew' or 'utter Jew.'

Hecate, ancient Thracian goddess of witchcraft who took a variety of forms in Greek mythology. Sometimes she was associated with Proserpina, queen of the Underworld, and sometimes with Diana or Luna, the moon goddess, though Hecate represented the dark of night and Diana the moonlight. Hecate was present at crossroads and graveyards and she roamed at night, her coming seen only by dogs, who barked at her. She was often depicted carrying a torch. Medea was her priestess and best student. Sh. knew her as a powerful underworld creature who inspired witches and sent men nightmares and oracles.

1H6 3.5.24. Ham 3.2.246, 'H.'s ban,' Hecate's curse. *Mac:* she appears with the witches in a section of the play often attributed to some writer other than Sh., usually Thomas Middleton. *MND 5.2.14,* 'triple H.'s team': Hecate as Diana the moon in the sky (Cynthia or Luna), as Diana on earth, and as Proserpine in the Underworld. *Lr. 1.1.110 (Q 1.103).*

Hector, warrior who was Troy's greatest defender, oldest son of Priam and Hecuba, husband of Andromache. The plot of Homer's *Iliad* turns on Achilles' determination to avenge himself on Hector for the death at Hector's hands of Achilles' friend Patroclos. The *Iliad* opens with a quarrel between Achilles and Agamemnon, the Greek commander. Agamemnon forces Achilles to give up a woman who was his share from the spoils of battle, and Achilles, who takes this as an assault on his honor, resigns from the Greek army. To make sure that Agamemnon is punished for his arrogance, Achilles persuades the gods to give the Trojans the power to defeat the Greeks. Patroclos sympathizes with Achilles' anger, but he is distressed at the slaughter of his countrymen. Patroclos, therefore, devises a plan. He asks Achilles for the loan of his armor. He knows that if Achilles armor is seen on the field of battle, the Trojans will flee—believing that the Greeks' invincible hero has finally come out to fight. Events unfold as Patroclos expects until Hector recognizes and kills him. Patroclos' death affects Achilles so deeply that he sets aside his anger at the slight Agamemnon has done to his honor. He returns to battle and avenges Patroclos by killing Hector. Achilles vents his rage on the corpse, but at the end of the *Iliad* his sense of common decency returns and he permits Priam to ransom his son's body for burial.

LLL 5.1.121, 5.2.530, 'H. of Troy.' *5.2.625–632:* in the pageant of the Nine Worthies, Armado the braggart plays Hector. *3H6 4.9.25. Tit 4.1.87. 1H6 2.3.19. Luc 1430, 1486. MWW 1.3.11,* 'bully H.'; *2.3.31,* 'H. of Greece,' a joke: he was enemy of the Greeks. *2H4 2.4.220. Ado 2.3.181,* an allusion to the great hero's running away from Achilles.

Tro, 'Lord H.,' 'the Prince': in line with the tradition that had developed over the Middle Ages, Hector is the chivalrous, valiant, and wise prince of Troy, while the Greeks are scheming, immoral bullies. While he supports returning

Helen to her husband, Menelaus, in order to end the war, he goes along with the prevailing opinion. His insistence upon fighting when he has received so many warnings is reminiscent of Julius Cæsar's insistence upon going to the Senate in defiance of all the warnings he has received. Interestingly, this makes the comparison even more similar as critics either take the view that doing so is foolhardy or vain, or that great men have no choice but to accept their destinies. Dying well rather than skittering away from the rantings of soothsayers seems to be an important virtue for Sh., whether in his Cæsar or Hector. The ambush of Hector by the Myrmidons is little different from the conspirators' nasty slaughter of Cæsar, except that Hector, more in tone with the bitter quality of *Tro,* is vulnerable to the Myrmidons because he disarms to steal the sumptuous armor from a Greek he has killed. He does not seem to understand that Achilles will take advantage in a way Hector would not. Keeping in mind that looting was a normal part of war (much of the reason for it, in fact), Sh. may have viewed Hector's going after this armor as being much less tainting to his character than moderns do. It is exactly Hector's looting which has, at least partly, made him a great man. The great man coming to ruin because of his doing what made him great is the essence of tragedy.

Ant 4.9.7, pl. *Cor 1.3.43, 44, 1.9.11.*

Hecuba, Thracian princess who through marriage with Ilium's king Priam became queen of Troy, mother of Paris, Cassandra, Hector, Helenus, Deiphobus, Polyxena, and Troilus. She is attributed various mothers and fathers (many of the latter are river gods). She had the misfortune of witnessing the destruction of her homeland and the deaths or enslavements of all her children and thus became a symbol of the tragedies war inflicts upon women. At the fall of Troy she was made a slave to Ulysses and ultimately was turned into a dog for killing the sons of Polymestor the Thracian tyrant and blinding him. Homer's *Iliad* is the original and earliest source of information about Hecuba. Euripides wrote a play that describes what befell her after the Trojan war, but Sh. probably drew what he knew of her after the fall of Troy from Ovid's *Metamorphoses,* 13.

Tit 4.1.20. 1.1.136 (mentioned, but not named). *Luc 1447, 1485. Tro 1.2.1, 1.2.138, 5.1.36, 5.3.56, 5.11.15. Cor 1.3.42. Ham 2.2.504, 560, 561:* she is mentioned in a speech from a play, possibly a lost play on Dido and Æneas. *Cym 4.2.315.*

Helen, 1) see Helen of Troy.

2) *1H6 1.3.121,* (c. 247–347), Helena, mother of the Roman emperor Constantine. She is credited in medieval legend with the discovery of the burial place of the true cross and the various implements used at Christ's crucifixion. A legend without foundation circulated in the Middle Ages in Britain that she had been born in England. Actually she was likely a native of Bithynia.

3) *MND,* see Helena.

4) *MND 5.1.196,* the rustic's confusion of Helen with Hero.

5) *AWW,* F1 'Hellen,' 'Helena,' daughter of Gérard de Narbonne. She cures the king's fistula with her deceased father's remedies and asks for Bertram's hand in return. The King grants it, Bertram flees, and she follows him to Tuscany. She tricks him unknowing into her bed and then, later, in Paris reveals that the marriage has been consummated and they are reconciled. Helen is another plucky Sh. heroine who puts her callow man to some difficulty before he comes to his senses. She says that instead of looking for divine intervention, we ought more often to find our remedies in ourselves. The problem for many critics has been that Bertram seems an unworthy fellow for such an admirable woman to expend so much effort, and the reconciliation seems forced. Her name is chosen by analogy to Helen of Troy to whose beauty hers is compared. In Sh.'s source, William Painter's *Palace of Pleasure* (1566), which translates a story from Boccaccio's *Decameron,* 3.9, she is Giletta and has been reared with Beltramo (Bertram). The only other large differences are that she is wealthier than Helen and

spends some time ruling Rossiglione while Beltramo is in Tuscany.

6) *Cym,* servant to Innogen.

Helen of Troy, in Marlowe's words 'the face that launched a thousand ships,' sister of the mortal Clytemnestra and of the gods Castor and Pollux, wife of Menelaus, mother of Hermione, Pleisthenes, and possibly Nicostratus. She was most famously born of the seduction of Leda (wife of Tyndareus) by Zeus in the form of a swan, though some myths have her as the daughter of Nemesis, whose egg Leda cared for. When young, she was kidnapped by Theseus and Peirithous and rescued by Castor and Pollux. She is sometimes credited with being the mother by Theseus of Iphigenia. The story of her being the cause of the Trojan War begins at the wedding of Peleus and Thetis. Discord, or Eris, irritated at not being invited, tossed a golden apple into the celebration. On it was written 'To the Fairest' and each of the goddesses Hera, Aphrodite, and Athena claimed it. Zeus put the judgement upon Paris, a prince of Troy. Hera promised Paris wealth and power if he chose her, Athena promised fame in war, but Aphrodite promised the most beautiful woman in the world, Helen. She had many suitors before her marriage to Menelaus, but each had taken an oath to defend her choice of a husband by force, if necessary. With the aid of Aphrodite, Paris sailed to Sparta, seduced her, and took her to Troy. (In some versions only an image of Helen is seduced and taken to Troy, the real Helen is concealed in Egypt.) Menelaus called upon those who had sworn to defend his marriage, a fleet was assembled, and the Greeks attacked Troy. Helen spent most of this time in seclusion weaving a tapestry of her sad life, though from the walls she watched a duel between her husband and Paris.

After nine long, bloody years, Troy fell. Menelaus and she set out for home, were driven by storms to Cyprus, Phoenicia, and Egypt, but ultimately settled back in Sparta where they lived out the rest of their lives. In some versions Polyxo, mother of Tlepolemus (killed at Troy), conspired to have her hanged. In another version she escapes the hanging as a servant is mistaken for her. Although Homer says that Priam, king of Troy, did not blame her for the war that destroyed his people, Sh. was less generous. He saw her as the prototype for all the meddlesome queens in history who caused bloody confrontations among nations. The story of her beauty and its consequences has been a powerful inspiration in literature and art over the centuries and particularly in the Renaissance.

Luc 1369 and *3H6 2.2.146,* 'H. of Greece.' *MND 5.1.11 (Add. 7). Rom 2.3.39. 2H4 5.5.33. AYLI 3.2.142,* 'H.'s cheek, but not her heart': H.'s beauty, but not her fickleness.

Tro 3.1.44–155: constantly maligned as a poor reason for war, Helen only appears in this scene. She seems rather bubble-headed, only interested in music while the world burns about her. She is clearly symbolic of the general sense of disordered values in the play. *2.1.82,* 'H.'s needle,' a bawdy metaphor for Paris. *Son 53.7,* 'H.'s cheek.' *AWW 1.3.69–71:* alluded to, but not named.

Helena, 1) *MND,* daughter of the deceased Nedar, she is madly in love with the 'spotted and inconstant' Demetrius who has earlier made love to her. This puts her into a situation with him similar to that of Mariana of *MM* with Angelo, and she desperately follows him into the woods when he pursues the eloping Hermia. When Robin Goodfellow confuses who should receive the love potion, both Lysander and Demetrius pursue her, much to her consternation. When all is settled, she becomes Demetrius' betrothed, but her self-humiliation is another uncomfortable comment on the madness of love. The fairer of the two female lovers, she was played by a boy actor who commonly assumed the fair roles to contrast with the boy actor playing the dark Hermia. In similar contrasts he might have played Rosalind or Beatrice opposite Celia or Hero.

2) *Rom 1.2.72,* 'lively H.,' woman invited to Capulet's feast. See Anselme.

3) *AWW,* see Helen. As in *MND,* both forms occur in F1 and editors usually standardize it throughout the play.

Helenus, *Tro,* son of Priam and Hecuba, Cassandra's twin, a priest of Troy. He argues that returning Helen would be the sensible thing to do. Troilus is very nasty with him, since it is quite clear that Helenus is not much of a warrior (*1.2.215–219, 2.2.32–49*), although he goes forth to battle while Paris, Troilus, and Pandarus are playing love games (*3.1.132*). His debate with Troilus is an episode Sh. borrowed from his sources, William Caxton's *Recuyell of the Historyes of Troye* (1474) and John Lydgate's *Troy Book* (1412–20). In mythology, he was gifted with prophecy and the only son of Priam to survive the war. He became the slave of Neoptolemus along with Andromache. After she had borne three sons by her master, he tired of her and gave her to Helenus. After Neoptolemus' death he became king of Epirus and married her (described in Virgil's *Æneid,* 3).

Helias, *Tro pro. 16,* one of the six gates of Troy. These are not in the *Iliad* which appears to give Troy only one double gate, but in William Caxton's *Recuyell of the Historyes of Troye,* 3 (c. 1474), the first English printed book, and Sh.'s major source for the play, the six gates are listed, Helias being the third. In the French version by Raoul Lefevre, which Caxton translated, Helias is called 'Elias,' and 'Clias.'

Helicane, *Per,* Helicanus.

Helicanus, *Per,* a lord of Tyre. 'Hellican' appears in John Gower's *Confessio Amantis* (1390). See Pericles.

Helicons, *2H4 5.3.105,* residents of a range of mountains in the Greek district of Boetia. The area was sacred to the Muses, and they fostered poetic talent in those who drank from its fountains.

Hellespont, ancient name for the Dardanelles, the narrow strait dividing Asia Minor from European Turkey or the Greek peninsula, and therefore one of the boundaries between East and West. About 40 mi. long and 1–4 mi. wide, it connects the Sea of Marmara to the Ægean. It was named after the mythological Helle, who drowned in it after falling from the back of a golden ram provided by Hermes to enable her to flee with her brother Phrixus from her stepmother Ino. The city of Troy was near its west mouth. It is also the body of water in which Leander drowned. *TGV 1.1.22, 26. AYLI 4.1.97. Oth 3.3.459.*

Hellwain, *Mac 3.5.44,* spirit called forth by the witches in a song not appearing in F1, but which appears in Thomas Middleton's play *The Witch* (c. 1609, but not printed until the 18th c.). William Davenant's version of *Mac* (printed 1674) and Q (1673), however, contain the song and it has been argued that he may have had access to an earlier text. In Davenant's version, the spirit is 'Helway.' A wain is a wagon. A hellwain was a spirit wagon seen in the sky at night. The name came from Reginald Scot's *Discoverie of Witchcraft* (1584).

Henricus, *H5 5.2.336,* L. 'Henry,' see Henry V.

Henry III, *Jn 5.6.35,* see Henry, Prince.

Henry IV, (1367–1413), duke of Lancaster who took England's crown from Richard II. Henry, called 'Bolingbroke' from the place of his birth in Lincolnshire, was the son of John of Gaunt, Edward III's fourth son. Henry was the earl of Derby, and in 1380 he acquired the earldom of Hereford by marrying Mary de Bohun. As heir to his father's duchy of Lancaster, one of the richest estates in England, his prospects were bright, but not as bright as those of his slightly younger cousin Richard. In 1377 Richard, at the age of ten, inherited the throne of England from the grandfather he shared with Henry. Gaunt, as the senior member of the young king's family, helped hold Richard's kingdom together, but as Richard matured, he rebelled against his councilors and made things increasingly uncomfortable for Gaunt. In July 1386 Gaunt bowed out of England's politics and went to Spain to press a claim to the throne of Castille. His departure hastened the inevitable showdown between Richard and his advisors, and Richard lost. In October 1386 the barons and the commons formed a united front in the 'Wonderful Parliament,' forced Richard to dismiss his favorites from office, and created a parliamentary commission to watch over the king. Richard fought parliament's decrees in the courts—arguing that they were an illegal transgression on royal prerogatives. His uncle, Thomas of Woodstock, duke of Gloucester, with the backing of the earls of Arundel and Warwick, sought to intimidate him by accusing (or in technical legal terms, 'appealing') his advisors of treason. Robert de Vere, one of Richard's most unpopular cronies, raised an army to go to the king's defense, and in December 1387 the 'lords appellant,' assisted by Henry Bolingbroke, routed de Vere in a battle at Radcot Bridge, Oxfordshire.

De Vere fled England, and Richard had no choice but to sue for terms. The lords may have flirted with the idea of deposing Richard, but a practical problem dissuaded them from taking action. Richard had no children. If he vacated the throne, it was not certain who should succeed him. Gloucester wanted the crown, but Henry insisted that he, the son of Gloucester's elder brother, had a better claim to Richard's legacy. There was yet a third candidate, Roger Mortimer, a descendant of a branch of the royal family senior to Henry's whom Richard had recognized as his heir presumptive in 1385. The lords fell to squabbling among themselves. Henry broke with them, and Richard regained the upper hand. In May 1389 Richard dismissed the officials appointed by parliament and assumed sole responsibility for England's government. Later the same year Gaunt came home and began again to exert his influence as the senior royal relative. This situation left Henry, at the age of 27, with nothing much to do, so he decided to see the world. In 1390 he led a troop of 70 men to Lithuania to fight a crusade organized by the order of Teutonic Knights. In March 1391 he went home to prepare a second expedition, and in July 1392 he landed in Prussia with another company of soldiers bound for Lithuania. He was dismayed to discover that during his absence the combatants had called off the war. Disappointed in one crusade, he sought another. He marched his men south to Venice and took ship for the Holy Lands. These adventures helped him pass the time, but time did not improve the situation that awaited him in England.

When he came home on 1 July 1393, he found that the tensions within the royal family were worse than ever. Richard had decided to make peace with France. Gaunt supported him, but Gloucester raised stiff opposition. In October 1396 Gaunt and Henry accompanied Richard to France to witness Richard's marriage to Charles VI's daughter, Isabella of Valois. Gloucester was contemptuous of the match, and in July 1397 Richard learned that his feisty uncle was again discussing the possibility of his deposition. Richard took sudden, decisive action. He arrested Gloucester and the other 'lords appellant' and intimidated parliament into acquiescing to their executions or banishments. Since Henry had broken with Gloucester, he was not implicated in the plot, but Richard had a long memory for grudges, and, having begun so successfully, he was eager to sweep England clean of anyone who had an association with the disgraced lords. In December he got a chance to move against him. Henry quarreled with Thomas Mowbray, duke of Norfolk, and Richard ordered the two knights to settle their dispute by combat. The duel was scheduled to take place at Coventry on 16 September 1398, but at the last moment Richard called it off and exiled both parties. Norfolk's banishment was for life and Henry's for only ten years, but it is possible that Norfolk's sentence was a sham. Norfolk may have helped Richard entrap Henry, and Richard may have intended, after a decent interval, to pardon Norfolk. If so, he never got the chance. Norfolk set out for the Holy Lands and died in

Venice in 1399. The care Richard took to appear to deal with Henry fairly and legally may have been motivated by fear of Gaunt, but Gaunt's death on 3 February 1399, freed Richard from anxiety about the powerful house of Lancaster.

On 18 March Richard exiled Henry for life and confiscated the Lancastrian estate. Henry and other English nobles Richard had exiled gathered in Paris to consider their options, and two months later Richard gave them the opening they had been hoping for. Richard left England to campaign in Ireland. On 4 July 1399, Henry defied his sentence of banishment and landed a small company of soldiers on the coast of northern England. The heir to the duchy of Lancaster headed for districts traditionally loyal to his house to recruit allies, for he did not yet have enough men with whom to confront the king. The success he met with was partly owing to Richard who had inadvertently prepared the ground for him. Richard had quarreled with the heads of the powerful Percy and Neville families, and on 13 July they came to meet Henry at Doncaster and offered him their help. Richard had appointed his uncle, the duke of York, regent for England during his absence, but York organized no resistance to Henry. York was not a vigorous man, and Richard had left him few soldiers. York sensed that momentum was building for Henry, and on 27 July he gave up the pretext of opposition. Richard was slow to grasp the significance of what was shaping up in England and reluctant to break off the campaign he had just begun in Ireland. By the time he crossed from Ireland to his camp in southern Wales his army had lost heart and dispersed. Richard found that he had no option but to seek to come to terms with Henry. At first he may have assured Richard that his throne was safe. If that promise was made, it was one that he could not afford to keep. The deaths of the 'lords appellant' were sufficient warning to him of the risk of giving Richard a second chance. He shut Richard up in the Tower of London on 1 September and spread the word that a parliament would meet on 1 October. On 29 September, just days before parliament convened, Richard abdicated.

Richard's decision was reported to parliament, and Henry announced that he was ascending the throne. His explanation of his right to Richard's legacy was purposefully vague, for his was not the best claim that could have been put forward. Parliament may have accepted him because there was no one to champion the cause of the alternative heir. Gloucester had been murdered when Richard attacked the 'lords appellant,' but he was not Henry's only competitor for the throne. Richard had designated his own successor: Roger Mortimer, earl of March—a descendant of Edward III's second son, Lionel of Clarence. Roger had died on 20 July 1398, almost a year before Henry unseated Richard, but Roger's claim to the throne passed to his son, Edmund. At the time of Richard's deposition, however, Edmund was only 8 years old, and without Henry's cooperation there was no possibility that a regency government could hold England together until the boy matured. Richard's reign and its troubled conclusion had created a dangerous, unstable situation, and it was not certain that even Henry could rise to the challenge of keeping order in England. English kings had been deposed before Richard was forced from the throne, but only in favor of their sons and unquestioned heirs. Henry's ascension smacked of usurpation and set an unfortunate precedent. The English noble class was small and intricately intermarried. There were many men who had links with the royal family, and many who considered him no better qualified than themselves. If he crossed them, they would not hesitate to do to him what he had done to Richard. Given these circumstances, it is not surprising that his authority was challenged almost immediately.

Early in January 1400 the earls of Rutland, Kent, and Huntingdon conspired to assassinate him at a tournament held at Windsor. He learned of the plot in time to escape, and the rebel earls were tracked down and executed. The failure of the 'earls' plot' may have precipitated the very thing it was supposed to prevent. Richard was still alive and under close guard in a remote castle, but the earls had proven that his existence was a danger. So long as Richard lived, rebels could dignify treason by claiming that it was necessary to restore England's rightful king. On 14 February 1400, six weeks after the defeat of the earls' plot, it was announced that Richard had starved himself to death. Henry brought Richard's body to London and displayed it to the people to squelch rumors that Richard had escaped and might some day reappear to reclaim his throne. Richard's death may have simplified Henry's life, but it did not end challenges to his authority. His reign was plagued by crises. France refused to recognize the legitimacy of his government, and wars broke out with Scotland and Wales. The Welsh conflict, under the leadership of Owain Glyndŵr, stretched into a long and grueling campaign. Although Glyndŵr was forced back into the hills by 1408, he outlived Henry and survived to cause trouble as a guerrilla fighter for Henry V.

Henry's foreign wars were fought while the king struggled with powerful rivals at home. English monarchs had rarely risked interfering with the activities of the powerful lords of the marches—the military districts that defended England's borders with Scotland and Wales. The Percies, as wardens of the Scottish marches, were heads of a great military machine that had helped him to the throne. They were aware of their strength, and they assumed that he would not dare to cross them. In September 1402 the Percy earl of Northumberland and his belligerent son Henry 'Hotspur' inflicted major losses on the Scots at the battle of Holmedon Hill. Henry was glad to see the Scots weakened, but he could not afford to let the Percies become invincible. When he stepped in to claim the fruits of Holmedon Hill, they objected and recruited Glyndŵr for a campaign to overthrow him in favor of the Mortimer heir. He moved before his opponents could gather their forces, and he dealt the Percies a severe blow by killing Hotspur at the battle of Shrewsbury on 21 July 1403. Northumberland concluded a reluctant peace, and in 1405 he attempted a second rebellion. When it failed, he fled to France. He continued to raid England from bases in Scotland until 1408, when he was killed skirmishing with the sheriff of Yorkshire. In 1405 Thomas Mowbray, the eldest son of the duke of Norfolk whom Richard had banished for fighting with Henry, joined the Percy archbishop of York in another uprising. Both rebel leaders were captured and beheaded. Henry's decision to execute an archbishop shocked his contemporaries and cost him considerable political capital.

As a military leader he had numerous successes, but few campaigns that roused the patriotic passions of his subjects. His wars were expensive, and the lengths to which the king went to raise money lessened enthusiasm for his administration. In 1406 parliament humiliated him by compelling him to submit to an audit of his books and to accept supervision by a group of councilors it appointed. As he aged, his subjects' impatience to make a fresh start with a new ruler strained the king's relationship with his heir. Although he refused to listen to suggestions that he abdicate in favor of his son, illness forced him into semi-retirement. Prince Henry (Harry, Hal) and his allies, Henry IV's Beaufort half-brothers, took control of the royal council, and in 1411 the prince convinced the council to override the king's wishes and declare war on France. Henry was not so tired that he was prepared to let such a challenge pass. In November 1411 he reorganized the council and Harry's seat was given to his younger brother, Thomas. Henry resumed the duties of the chief executive, but his health proved unequal to the burdens of the office. On 20 March 1413, he collapsed while praying in Westminster Abbey. He was carried into a side room, the 'Jerusalem Chamber,' and lingered for only a few hours.

2H6 2.2.21–23. 3H6 1.1.133, 140, 3.3.83. R2. 1H4. 2H4. 1H6 2.5.63.

Henry V, 'Harry,' 'Hal,' (1387–1422), second king of England from the house of Lancaster. Henry, called 'Monmouth' from the place of his birth, was the eldest son of Henry (IV) Bolingbroke and Mary de Bohun. Two years after his birth in 1387, his father deposed Richard II and ascended the throne. At the age of 13 Monmouth (the prince of Wales) was made governor of Wales. Since the Welsh were not yet reconciled to English rule, the post provided the boy with plentiful opportunities to hone his military skills. In 1403 Prince Harry commanded troops at the battle of Shrewsbury and helped his father put down a revolt raised by the Percy family. In 1408, the elder Henry's health began to fail, and the king turned to his son for help with the government of England. Serious tensions soon developed between the ambitious 21-year-old and his aging parent. The stories that circulated in Sh.'s day about Prince Harry's dissolute behavior may derive from political propaganda generated by the quarrel between the partisans of the old king and those of his eager successor. There is no truth to the charge that Sir John Oldcastle, a knight who served the prince of Wales, led the prince on romps through taverns and bawdy houses. Oldcastle was a religious fanatic, not a rake.

Harry's troubles with his father were rooted in something more serious than a young man's wild oats. Henry IV was aware of his declining popularity with his heavily taxed subjects and of his son's impatience to come into his inheritance. The uneasy situation encouraged plotting and the formation of factions at court. Henry IV's half-brothers, John of Gaunt's Beaufort sons (Thomas, admiral of England, and Henry, bishop of Winchester), took the prince's side, and in 1411 they persuaded the royal council to end the peaceful relationship that Henry had established with France. This infuriated the king, who emerged from semi-retirement to reclaim control of his government. He dismissed the prince and the Beauforts from the royal council and promoted Harry's younger brother Thomas, duke of Clarence, to his place. Henry repaired relations with France by sending an army under Thomas' command to help the French king make war on the duke of Burgundy. The campaign was cut short by Henry IV's death on 20 March 1413.

Since the crown that Henry V inherited from his father had been usurped from Richard II, the new monarch was eager for projects that would promote public confidence in the legitimacy of his dynasty. He took pains to look like a king who had no doubt about his rights and no reason to fear a challenge to his title. He gave Richard II's body honorable reburial. He demonstrated confidence in the security of his position by treating with kindness the man who had the strongest counter-claim to the throne, Edmund Mortimer, and he tried to win over the enemies of his Lancastrian house by restoring their confiscated estates. His strategy of reconciliation was successful, but only partially. In January 1414, Sir John Oldcastle, who had been indicted for heresy, recruited a band of religious radicals and tried to kidnap him. The coup failed, but Oldcastle escaped and remained at large for three years. A second threat to the young king materialized within the court circle. In July 1415, Richard, earl of Cambridge (Edmund Mortimer's brother-in-law), Henry, Lord Scrope of Masham (nephew of Richard Scrope, the archbishop of York who had led a rebellion against Henry IV), and Sir Thomas Grey of Heton (Hotspur's cousin and a partisan of the rebellious Percies), plotted his death. Responding to a timely warning from Mortimer, he seized and executed the would-be assassins at Southampton.

Their deaths cleared the way for him to begin the great adventure of his life—a project that captured the affections of his subjects and increased their confidence in the house of Lancaster. On 11 August 1415, he rekindled the Hundred Years' War, renewed England's claim to the throne of France, and lay seige to the port of Harfleur. The time for the attack was well chosen. In 1392 Charles VI, king of France, had gone insane. His relatives fought among themselves for control of a regency government, and their squabbles paralyzed France. Since no French leader was prepared to respond to Harfleur's plea for help, the city surrendered to the English on 19 August 1415. Henry was not able to exploit his victory, for he had lost a large number of men to disease during the siege. Consequently, he ordered his troops to march north to the English port of Calais, where he intended to ship them back to England. A tardy French army materialized in time to force him to change his plans. The Armagnac faction at the French court forced their opponents, the

Burgundians, to retreat from Paris and hastily organized an expedition to punish Henry for his assault on Harfleur. He tried to outflank them, but they blocked his path to Calais and forced him to take a stand at a Norman village called Agincourt. There on 25 October 1415 (the feast of the saints Crispin and Crispinian), one of the most famous battles of the Middle Ages was fought. Henry's longbowmen slaughtered the French feudal cavalry, and England suffered very few losses while sweeping a vastly larger army from the field. So overwhelming was the English victory at Agincourt that he issued a controversial order to avert the danger of being undone by success. In contravention of the codes of chivalry, he executed many of his prisoners.

Europe was shocked, but England was deliriously happy with its young king. His victories over France resembled the glorious triumphs of Edward III and his son, the Black Prince. They revived dreams of an English continental empire that had been fading for two generations. England's problem during the opening year of the Hundred Years' War had not been winning battles, but mustering sufficient manpower to exploit victories. England was a much smaller nation than France, and it had too few soldiers to occupy France—even when France's defenses were in disarray. But Agincourt promised a different sequel. In September of 1416, Henry received assurances of neutrality from the Armagnacs' enemy, the duke of Burgundy, and on 23 July 1417, he led a second army to the continent. The English landed at their recently won port at Harfleur and moved up the Seine. On 19 January 1419, the fall of Rouen, the capital of Normandy, opened their way to Paris. His progress alarmed the Burgundians as well as the Armagnacs, but efforts to unite the French nobility for the defense of their nation failed. John the Fearless, duke of Burgundy, was murdered while negotiating a truce with the Armagnacs, and Burgundy's son avenged his father's death by entering the war on England's side. The Burgundians seized the mad French king, Charles VI, and Charles's son, the dauphin (Charles VII), fled to the Armagnac camp at Orléans. On 19 April 1420, at the city of Troyes, Henry negotiated a treaty with Charles VI that proposed to end the Hundred Years' War by uniting France and England. He married Charles's daughter, Catherine. Charles's son, the dauphin, was disinherited, and Henry was named Charles VI's heir. He and his bride entered Paris on 1 December 1420. In February 1421 they visited England where Catherine was crowned queen.

At the end of March 1421, the death in battle of his brother, Thomas, duke of Clarence, prompted him to return to France. He advanced on the city of Orléans where the dauphin was ensconced, but he could not tempt its defenders into battle. He moved off to beseige Meaux. It fell to him on 2 May 1422, and it was his last victory. During the campaign he contracted dysentery. Failing health forced him to return to Paris where Catherine awaited him with an infant son, Henry (VI). When it became apparent that he would not live much longer, he retired to a castle at Vincennes to organize a regency government. Thomas Beaufort and Walter Hungerford were assigned responsibility for the care and education of the heir to the throne. Throughout his reign Henry had relied heavily on his brother, John, duke of Bedford. Bedford had held England for him during his sojourns in France, and Bedford had commanded the French forces when Henry was in England. He probably intended Bedford to be chief regent and hoped that his youngest brother, Humphrey, duke of Gloucester, would provide Bedford with the same sort of assistance that Bedford had given him. His death on 31 August 1422, was followed a few months later (21 October) by that of his father-in-law, Charles VI. At the age of 10 months, Henry VI had become king of England and France. Henry V's well thought out arrangements for his son's minority failed to prevent the new king's reign from becoming one of the saddest and bloodiest in England's history.

Because of the youthfulness of Henry V and the great promise of his reign, many critics have suspected that Sh.'s portrayal is meant to remind his contemporaries of the Earl of Essex, who was executed for his ill thought out attempt to overthrow the aging Queen Elizabeth. Since much of Sh. is more topical than one can know after 400 years, this is appealing, but it would have been extremely dangerous for the Lord Chamberlain's Men, especially since Essex's men commissioned a special performance of *R2* just before the attempted coup. There seems to have been no retribution for having been an Essex sympathizer, either. As such, it is impossible to determine for certain whether Sh. was sympathetic to Essex's cause and portrayed Henry with Essex in mind. If he did, he was careful to do it only by suggestion.

2H6 1.1.75, 93, 2.3.34, 4.2.155, 4.7.189, 4.8.211. 3H6 1.1.107, 3.3.85, 90. 1H6 1.1.5, 6, 4.3.52. 1H4. 2H4. H5.

Henry VI, (1421–1471), son of Henry V and Catherine of France, the last Lancastrian king of England, reigned at the end of the Hundred Years' War and the beginning of the War of the Roses. Sh.'s portrait of Henry reflects the influence of a popular cult that developed not long after the king's death. In the early Tudor period, the English government asked the papacy to canonize Henry, and the church collected reports of miracles credited to his intercession. Veneration for him grew to the point where he rivaled Thomas Becket as England's most beloved martyr. The Tudor monarchs encouraged this, for it vindicated their usurpation of the throne from the Yorkist family that had murdered him. Belief in his saintliness made the Tudor dispossession and destruction of York an act of divine retribution. Modern historians have cast a less charitable light on his career. His right to England's throne was shaky, and his conduct invited challenges to his authority. His grandfather, Henry (IV) of Lancaster, became king by deposing his cousin, Richard II. Since Henry IV was heir to John of Gaunt, King Edward III's fourth son, he had a right to the throne, but it was inferior to that of his cousins of Clarence and York, who were descendants of John of Gaunt's elder brother, Lionel of Antwerp.

At the time of the Lancastrian usurpation, Lionel's heiress raised no objection, and no one contested Henry V's right to succeed his father, but his son's promising future was imperiled by Henry's premature death. There was no precedent in England for a regency government of the kind that was required to hold Henry VI's patrimony until he came of age. At the time of his death Henry V tried to make provision for his infant son's kingdoms and designated his brothers, Bedford and Gloucester, regents for France and England respectively. The compromise failed to please a faction of the English nobility opposed to Humphrey of Gloucester. He was named 'protector,' not 'regent,' and forced to exercise his authority through a council of nobles. The arrangement did not work and quarrels among the councilors kept the government in a state of turmoil. The situation deteriorated rapidly after Bedford's death in 1435. By then, Henry had reached adolescence, and his advisors were eagerly anticipating an end to the unwieldy regency. In 1437 they granted the 16-year-old king full royal authority, and he began to play a role in affairs of state. He had no experience of war and no desire to acquire any.

Although England still had armies in France, little was being achieved on the military front. Since the French war was expensive and further conquests were unlikely, he decided to be content with the lands he held in Normandy and Gascony and to sue for peace. His older and more experienced opponent, Charles VII of France, was not as pleased as he was with the status quo. Much French territory was still in English hands, and Henry angered Charles by refusing to agree to cease using the title 'king of France.' He conceived the romantic notion that he might win Charles over if he married a French princess and surrendered some land. Although this scheme was hotly opposed by his uncle, Gloucester, and by many of his subjects, he persevered. Charles VII denied him the hand of one of his daughters, but in 1444 Henry wed Margaret of Anjou, Charles's niece. Margaret cost Henry a great deal and brought him little. As part of the marriage and truce arrangements, he agreed to give up the county of Maine, the key to the defense of his other possessions. The result was disaster. After the marriage Charles increased his demands for concessions, picked a quarrel, terminated the truce, and occupied Normandy (1450). The loss of Normandy cost England control of the channel and exposed the English coast to attack. The English economy was severely shaken, and pressure mounted on the royal government to do something. Since direct criticism of the king was considered treason, malcontents expressed their anger by demanding the punishment and replacement of the king's advisors. Henry's favorite, the duke of Suffolk, was impeached and ordered into exile. The ship on which Suffolk was sent from England was boarded at sea, and the duke was beheaded by unknown assailants.

When Henry ordered retaliation for the murder of his friend, a rebellion erupted in England's southeastern counties. A horde of armed men, under the command of a certain Jack Cade, marched on London and demanded the punishment of more politicians. Henry's unwillingness to talk frustrated Cade's men, who began on their own initiative to seek out and execute unpopular royal officials. The promise of a pardon finally induced the tired rebels to go home, but the incident had serious consequences. Cade's men, when they lost faith in Henry, had openly discussed the possibility of deposing him in favor of his cousin, Richard of York. The failure of the rebellion prompted York to return to England from his post in Ireland to profess his innocence of involvement in the uprising. Once home, Richard joined Henry's critics and pushed for the punishment of yet another of Henry's favorites, the duke of Somerset. Henry was so preoccupied with domestic problems that he paid scant attention to France. Charles VII made the most of his opportunities. By July, 1451, the French had taken Gascony, as well as Normandy, and all that remained of Henry's huge French patrimony was a single port, the city of Calais. Henry pondered schemes for winning back what he had lost, but he failed to implement any consistent policy. He insisted upon his right as king to make decisions, but his hesitancy, vacillation, and unrealistic frame of mind fatally handicapped his government.

The pressures of an office for which he was unfit may have contributed to the mental breakdown he suffered in 1453. His maternal grandfather, Charles VI of France, had gone mad, but Charles's symptoms differed from Henry's. Charles became a violent, murderous maniac. Henry slipped into a depression bordering on catatonia. For over a year he had no ability to communicate or to control his limbs and no awareness or memory of what was happening around him. During his illness York became his protector. York had good reason to care for his kingdom and to wait patiently for his death. York was his nearest male relative, and he was the presumed heir to the throne. Two months after the illness began, this situation changed. Margaret, who had been barren for eight years, bore her husband a son. York's hopes for an easy and imminent succession were dashed, and Margaret concluded that there would be no security for her husband and son so long as York lived. When Henry recovered sufficiently to resume the reins of power, Margaret insisted that York be driven from court. Supporters lined up behind the leaders of the two branches of the royal family, and the stage was set for civil war. The first blood was shed on 22 May 1455, at St. Albans, a town just north of London. York killed Somerset and captured Henry, who at the age of thirty-three witnessed his first military action. The shock of events caused him to suffer a relapse, and York once again became his protector.

When he recovered in February 1456, he may have been amenable to a compromise with York. Margaret, however, would have none of it. She retreated with the king to the Lancastrian stronghold at Kenilworth, and for almost four years there was little government in England. From time to time the two factions probed at each other. Then, at Northampton on 10 July 1460, York scored a major victory and captured Henry. York's plan was to convene a parliament at which he would put forth his claim to the throne, but his allies, who feared the appearance of treason, convinced him to settle for something short of deposition. It was agreed that Henry should be permitted to live out his days as king, but that he should dispossess his son and recognize York as his heir. This arrangement was never put to the test, for two months after it was ratified York was killed in a skirmish at Wakefield Bridge. Queen Margaret, who had taken refuge in Scotland, descended upon England with a mixed band of soldiers. At a second battle at St. Albans, on 17 February 1461, she defeated the Yorkists and liberated her husband. The resurgence of the Lancastrian party did not last long. Richard of York's son, Edward, entered London and was proclaimed king. On 29 March 1461, at Towton he defeated the Lancastrians in the largest engagement of the war. Margaret and Henry fled to Scotland, and in England the reign of Edward IV began. While Henry remained in Scotland, Margaret and Prince Edward went to the continent to beg for help from the French. In April, 1464, Henry accompanied a group of raiders into England. The band was caught and crushed near Hexham, but he eluded capture and remained at large in northern England for over a year.

Edward finally tracked him down in July 1465 and consigned him to the Tower of London. For the next five years Henry remained quietly out of sight. Events beyond his control brought him fatally back into the limelight. Edward and his most powerful advisor, the earl of Warwick, quarreled over the issue of Edward's marriage. Warwick was compelled to flee to France to seek help from Charles VII's heir, Louis XI. Louis was delighted to assist the English in tearing themselves apart. Warwick repudiated Edward, proclaimed Henry VI the true king of England, and raised an army to free him from the Tower. Events took Edward by surprise, and he, in his turn, fled to the continent. Warwick liberated Henry, and from 13 October 1470 to 11 April 1471, he was again nominally England's ruler. Edward appealed to the duke of Burgundy for help. Since Burgundy feared the alliance that Louis and Warwick had forged between England and France, he was persuaded to assist Edward. Edward raised an army and returned to England to destroy Warwick at the battle of Barnet. Shortly thereafter (4 May 1471) Henry's 17-year-old son, Edward, was killed at the battle of Tewkesbury. The death of the Lancastrian heir meant that Edward IV had no reason to keep Henry alive, and on 22 May 1471, he was put to death in the Tower. Although his reign was virtually devoid of political achievements, his tragic end won him the sympathy of the people. The legend of 'Good King Henry,' the mild-mannered and saintly martyr, quickly developed, and pilgrims began to pray at his grave. Enduring memorials of his reign survive at the schools which he founded at Eton and King's College, Cambridge.

2H6. 3H6. 1H6. R3 (as corpse and ghost). *H5 epi. 9.*

Henry VII, (1457–1509), Henry Tudor, earl of Richmond, founder of the Tudor dynasty. The Tudors were of Welsh origin, tracing descent from a steward who served Llywelyn, prince of North Wales, in the mid-13th c. They entered English history in the person of Owen Tudor (d. 1461), a young squire who occasioned a scandal at Henry VI's court. Owen, a clerk of the wardrobe to Henry V's widow Catherine, was an exceptionally handsome man, and the young dowager queen fell in love with him. It is uncertain whether they were ever formally married, but they lived together long enough to produce five children. An alliance with the king's mother was, of course, an affair of state, and the regency council was furious at Owen's presumption in acting without authorization. Owen and Catherine may have been protected by the king's uncle, John, duke of Bedford, for after Bedford's death in 1435, their household was broken up. The queen entered a nunnery. Her children became wards of the state, and Owen was twice imprisoned—and twice escaped. When Henry VI achieved his majority, the vendetta against Owen ceased. Owen repaid Henry's kindness by taking his side in the War of the Roses. In 1461 Owen's loyalty to his royal step-son cost him his life. The king's Yorkist enemies captured and beheaded the Welsh adventurer following a skirmish at Mortimer's Cross. Henry VI treated Owen's sons, Edmund and Jasper Tudor, as close relatives. He acknowledged their legitimacy and granted them earldoms: Richmond for Edmund, and Pembroke for Jasper. In 1455 Edmund improved the Tudors' standing by marrying Margaret Beaufort, daughter of the duke of Somerset, John Beaufort. Margaret, a descendant of Edward III's son, John of Gaunt, brought her only son by Edmund, Henry Tudor, a bit of royal blood.

Edmund died before Henry's birth, and the young earl of Richmond was placed in the custody of his uncle Jasper. The murder of Henry VI and his son Edward by the Yorkists in 1471 left Henry heir to the leadership of the house of Lancaster and compelled Jasper to send his nephew to safety in Brittany. Henry could do little to advance his claim to the throne so long as England was content with its Yorkist kings, but after Edward IV's death, the Yorkist party split over the issue of Richard III's dispossession of Edward's sons. In 1483 the strongest of the malcontents, the duke of Buckingham, rebelled. When he failed to unseat Richard, his backers pledged their allegiance to the earl of Richmond. Henry proposed an alliance between Lancaster and York to be sealed by his marriage with Edward IV's eldest daughter, Elizabeth. France gave him aid, and in 1485 he invaded England via Wales. Richard met him at the battle of Bosworth Field, where Stanley's timely defection turned the tide in Henry's favor. Richard died in combat, and he claimed England's throne. Henry VII was crowned on 30 October 1485, and on 18 January 1486, he married Elizabeth. The wedding was intended to legitimate the new Tudor dynasty, but it did not guarantee the peace. Unreconciled Yorkists fomented plots in the names of remote heirs of their house: in particular, Edward, earl of Warwick, the son of Edward IV's brother, Clarence; and John de la Pole, earl of Lincoln, a nephew whom Richard III had designated his successor. Henry kept the earl of Warwick under lock and key in the Tower of London, but in 1487 a Lambert Simnel posed as Warwick and raised a rebellion. Simnel was captured and the earl of Lincoln, who had collaborated with him, was killed.

From 1492 to 1497 Henry pursued a Perkin Warbeck, who claimed to be Edward IV's long vanished younger son, Richard. France, Burgundy, Scotland, and Ireland all assisted the pretender, but in 1497 Henry scored a coup that gave his dynasty enhanced standing in the international community. He negotiated a treaty with Spain and engaged his heir, Arthur, to marry Katherine of Aragon, the daughter of Ferdinand and Isabella. Two years later he further secured his position by capturing and executing Warbeck and ordering the murder of the earl of Warwick, who had spent most of his days in the Tower. Two of the earl of Lincoln's younger brothers ended their lives in the Tower, and the last died in 1525 fighting for the king of France in Italy. The elimination of Yorkist heirs helped to stabilize the situation in England, and Henry's foreign policy lessened the risk of foreign invasion. Spain become an ally. Charles VIII of France undertook the conquest of Italy and wanted to avoid antagonizing England. In 1503 Henry secured his northern frontier by arranging a marriage between his sister, Margaret, and James IV, king of Scotland. These developments were welcomed, for England desperately needed an era of peace and responsible government. Henry made great strides toward the restoration of order and prosperity to a nation ravaged by a generation of civil war. He was helped by the fact that the War of the Roses had extinguished, impoverished, or decimated many of the old aristocratic families. The depletion of the ranks of the nobility meant that the king had fewer potential rivals and more opportunities to employ loyal, talented members of the middle class in government.

Henry paid close attention to the petty, but important, details of administration. He supported the work of local officials—such as the justices of the peace who were trying to quiet a countryside where enforcement of the law had been sporadic for over a generation. He also took an interest in finances and budgets that proved to his haughty critics that he lacked the dignity of a true prince. He increased the crown lands by confiscating the properties of Yorkist opponents and defunct noble families. He improved his income from customs dues by promoting English trade. He negotiated treaties with foreign powers that expanded the market for England's chief export, woolen cloth, and he endorsed the voyages of John Cabot, an Italian explorer with an anglicized name, whose discoveries gave England title to the lands it subsequently colonized in North America. Henry's careful management made possible the 'Golden Age' framed by the reigns of his son, Henry VIII, and his granddaughter, Elizabeth, and it lay the foundation for Sh.'s England.

R3. H8 2.1.113.

Henry VIII, *H8,* (1491–1547), second king in England's Tudor dynasty. Henry was the second son of Henry VII, the victor in the War of the Roses, and of Elizabeth of York, daughter of Edward IV. The Renaissance made its influence felt in England during his youth, and he and his siblings received the sorts of educations recommended by the humanist scholars of the age. Henry was trained in languages, classical literature, and music—as well as wrestling, jousts, and field sports. The prince had a gift for music and poetry, and he was vigorous and athletic. Over the long haul he would probably have found it difficult to sustain the self-effacing role of the second son, but in 1502 the death of his sickly elder brother, Arthur, solved that problem. Arthur's demise promoted a better candidate to the throne, but it created a crisis in foreign policy. A few months before his death Arthur had married a Spanish princess, Katherine of Aragon. England was not eager to return her dowry or lose the dynastic alliance that she represented. Henry VII was a widower, and he briefly entertained the thought of marrying his 16-year-old daughter-in-law. His proposal was unacceptable to Katherine's father, and for several years the young woman languished in England uncertain of her fate. Prince Henry was willing to marry her, but his prescient father feared that the match would threaten the future of the dynasty.

By the standards of the age, sexual congress between a brother-in-law and sister-in-law smacked of incest, and grounds could be found to challenge the legitimacy of the offspring of such a union. Much hinged on the question of whether or not Katherine and Arthur had been truly married. They had gone through the ceremony, but Katherine claimed that youth and ill health had prevented the consummation of the relationship. If that was true, no marriage had taken place and there was no impediment to her wedding with Henry. The English authorities considered the princess's word an insufficient guarantee and insisted upon a papal dispensation as a precondition for the marriage. The much discussed and controversial wedding took place a few months after Henry ascended the throne. Katherine, at age 23, apparently fell in love with her 17-year-old husband, and years passed before he expressed any dissatisfaction with her. While youth lasted, he had no anxiety about the future of his dynasty. He assumed that he had plenty of time to breed heirs. More urgent was his desire to win the respect and affection of his people by leading them in battle with their traditional foe, France. He persuaded his Spanish in-laws to join him, but after Spain achieved what it wanted, it made a separate peace with France. Henry, humiliated and left holding the bag, had no choice but to do the same. On 13 August 1514, he ratified a treaty with France and bestowed the hand of his young sister, Mary, on the aged Louis XII. Mary was relieved when her doddering husband survived his wedding by a mere 83 days.

Having once been used as a pawn in her brother's diplomatic games, the young widow had no intention of allowing Henry to choose her another unattractive husband. She ignored the law that required her to seek the king's permission to marry and eloped with her sweetheart, Charles Brandon, the duke of Suffolk. Henry's second sister, Margaret, also acquired a colorful marital history. Margaret was first wed to James IV of Scotland. James died in battle with the English on 9 September 1513, and Margaret became regent for their 17-month-old son, James V. When, within a year of her husband's death, she married Archibald Douglas, the earl of Angus, the Scots nobles deprived her of the regency and gave the office to John Stewart, duke of Albany. Margaret fled to England where she gave birth to the future countess of Lennox. The children of both of Henry's sisters had children who laid claim to the English throne. Mary's granddaughter was Jane Gray, the girl whom the Protestants at Edward VI's court hoped to crown in place of his Catholic sister, Mary. Margaret's grandson, Lord Darnley, married James V's daughter, Mary queen of Scots, and their son, James, inherited the English crown from Elizabeth I. If Henry's wife, Katharine, had been as successful at producing children as the king's sisters, English history would have evolved quite differently. The royal couple's reproductive problems were not for want of trying. Katherine was frequently pregnant, but prone to miscarriages. She conceived five times in the first seven years of her marriage, but it was not until 1516 that she bore a child that lived: the princess Mary.

Henry welcomed Mary's birth as proof that Katherine was capable of giving him children, but he was not prepared to pin his hopes for England's future on a daughter. He believed that only a male heir could guarantee a peaceful succession to the throne and preserve the nation's stability. England had only recently emerged from a generation-long civil war that could erupt again if there was no acceptable candidate for the royal office. History suggested that a woman would have a difficult time establishing herself as a reigning queen in England. In the early 12th c. Henry I had bequeathed his throne to his daughter, and the result had been two decades of strife that nearly obliterated royal government. Even if Tudor England had evolved to the point where it would accept a queen, her accession would create problems that Henry and his advisors did not want to contemplate. A queen would have to marry to perpetuate her dynasty. If she chose one of England's nobles over the others, disappointed candidates were likely to rebel. If she chose a foreign prince, her nation might be dominated by his or be combined with his as an inheritance for their child. England was a small country in comparison with its neighbors, France and Spain. It could not risk a succession that would render it vulnerable to invasion or assimilation. As the years passed and he pondered these issues, events conspired to urge him to take action to secure the future of his line. On 10 November 1518, Katherine was delivered of yet another stillborn girl. A few months later Henry's mistress, Elizabeth Blount, gave birth to a boy whose paternity was proclaimed by his name, Henry 'Fitzroy' ('King's-son'). Fitzroy reassured Henry that with the proper female assistance he could sire healthy boys.

In 1519 the death of the Hapsburg emperor, Maximillian, created opportunities for forging new alliances, and Henry embarked on a risky venture. Both Charles V, the Hapsburg heir (and Katherine's nephew), and Francis I, king of France, wanted an alliance with England. Charles courted Henry by visiting him in England, and Francis met Henry at an extravagantly staged conference on the frontier of the marches of Calais (the Field of the Cloth of Gold). In the end, Henry's dream of recovering England's lost continental fiefs led him to side with Charles. His plan was to invade France while Charles pinned Francis down in Italy. The scheme fell afoul of the English parliament which refused to provide adequate funding for the war. Francis had some initial success in Italy, but in 1525 Charles decisively defeated the French king and forced him to make peace. The resolution of the war between France and Spain robbed Henry of his clout in international politics. Charles made that clear by breaking an engagement to wed Henry's daughter in order to marry a Portuguese princess. These events forced Henry to come to terms with the fact that England did not have the resources to compete against the great nations of the continent, and they increased his conviction that he had to have a strong heir. Katherine offered scant hope of assistance, for she turned 40 in the crucial year 1525. Her age and reproductive history made it highly unlikely that she would bear more living children. Consequently, Henry concluded that he had no choice but to replace her with a younger wife.

Cardinal Wolsey, his chief advisor, helped him apply to Pope Clement VII for an annulment of his marriage. The papacy had often done such favors for kings, but Katherine was unwilling to cooperate and the situation in Italy made it impossible for Clement to risk alienating her. In 1527, the year in which Henry appealed to the pope, armies belonging to Katherine's nephew, Charles V, sacked Rome. Clement could not afford to offend anyone, so he stalled for time. This frustrated Henry, who believed that he was being denied justice because the pope respected the power of Spain more than the law of God. Henry had no sympathy with the Protestant Reformation which erupted in Germany early in his reign. When Martin Luther was excommunicated in 1520, Henry rallied to the pope's side by publishing a defense of the Catholic sacraments (1521). There was, however, a Protestant principle that he found useful in arguing the case for his annulment. Luther had declared that the pope had no power to contravene the word of God contained in Scripture, and Henry believed that Scripture was on his side in his fight to rid himself of Katherine. Leviticus 20:21 forbade a man to take his brother's wife. A papal dispensation had removed earthly impediments to Henry's union with Katherine, but he claimed that their infertility was proof of God's displeasure and his unwillingness to seal the sacrament of marriage between them.

Arguments of this nature failed to elicit the desired response from a beleaguered Rome, but they carried the day at home. Parliament supported his decision to seek an annulment, and it connived with him to frighten the pope into granting the king what he wanted. By stages the English government curtailed Rome's privileges in England. The strategy was clever, but timing robbed it of effect. Charles's army was a far greater threat to Clement than the loss of privileges in England. Parliament could not sway the pope, but its willingness to support the state against the church may have encouraged Henry to take action. On 10 July 1531, Henry banished Katherine from his presence and never saw her again. Her place was taken by Anne Boleyn, the daughter of one of Henry's courtiers. In January 1533 Anne found that she was pregnant, and he took a bold step. He withdrew England from the jurisdiction of the papal courts and began the process of nationalizing its church. Thomas Cranmer, a newly appointed archbishop of Canterbury who harbored Protestant sympathies, held an inquiry and ruled that Henry and Katherine had never been truly married in the sight of God. This cleared the way for Henry to announce that he had secretly wed Anne in January. He also declared Mary, the daughter Katherine had borne him, illegitimate and illegible to inherit the throne. A very few prominent persons (among them: Sir Thomas More, the king's chancellor; and John Fisher, bishop of Rochester) objected to these developments, but there was no mass uprising to protest the king's actions.

In 1534 parliament recognized Henry as the head of the church in England and severed all ties with Rome. Henry wanted the world to understand his reasons for breaking with the papacy. He claimed that the pope had become Spain's tool and had allowed himself to be used to endanger England's security. Henry's quarrel with the pope was political, not theological, and he eschewed any connection with Protestant heresies. Henry's church ceased to be Roman Catholic, but it did not become Lutheran. The king followed the impulses of his humanist education and sanctioned the translation of the Bible, the use of English in some parts of services of worship, the suppression of monasticism, the closing of shrines, and the banning of pilgrimages, but he affirmed the Catholic sacraments and executed persons accused of holding opinions that he branded excessively Protestant. His ecclesiastical reforms were designed to bring the English church into line with his assumptions about the sovereign rights of nations, and his church fulfilled his expectations by carrying out his orders. It gave him the queen he felt he needed, and when she proved a disappointment, it helped him exchange her for more promising candidates. Anne Boleyn bore a child—another daughter, Elizabeth. Then Anne, like Katherine, suffered miscarriages that undercut his confidence in her. In 1536 developments led him to consider changing mates again. Anne was delivered of a stillborn male infant, and Katherine died. He realized that if Anne, like Katherine, were out of the way, he would at last be free to contract a marriage whose legality no one could question.

On 1 May 1536, he indicted Anne on a charge of adultery, an act of treason for a queen. On 19 May she was beheaded, and the next day he wed another lady of his court, Jane Seymour. A year later Jane died giving birth to the long awaited son, the future Edward VI. The pliant archbishop of Canterbury announced that Henry's marriage to Anne had been irregular and that Elizabeth, like Mary, was illegitimate. The year 1536 also witnessed a reaction to Henry's religious revolution. His decision to close England's 530 monastic houses and confiscate their endowments had alarmed many of his pious subjects. Their concern spontaneously erupted in 'the Pilgrimage of Grace,' a popular revolt in northern England which was brutally suppressed by the duke of Norfolk. Henry's ambiguous attitude toward religious reform was as confusing to his advisors as to the rank and file of his people. Some of England's leaders, like Bishop Gardiner, were conservative Catholics; others inclined to various Protestant camps. Henry protected his authority by playing parties against each other, and he had no reluctance, when it suited him, to switch from side to side. In 1539, after publicly condemning Protestants as heretics, he married a Protestant princess, Anne of Cleves. When neither the bride nor the alliances she represented proved satisfactory, both were discarded. His obvious dislike for Lutheranism was not enough to convince the pope that he could be reclaimed for the Catholic church, and in December of 1538 the pope branded him a heretic and called on the Catholic kings of Europe to depose him. The pope's impeachment of Henry's orthodoxy angered him, and he set out to prove to Europe that he was a victim of papal politics, not a theological innovator.

On 16 May 1539, Henry endorsed the Act of Six Articles which spelled out his commitment to traditional Catholic dogma—particularly to the Mass and the doctrine of transubstantiation. He also made an example of the man who had carried out his orders to dissolve England's monasteries. Thomas Cromwell was executed on a charge of heresy. Catherine Howard, a member of a prominent aristocratic family, took Anne of Cleves' place as Henry's queen, but by this time his enthusiasm for the marriage bed was waning. Catherine's flagrant sexual indiscretions prompted her execution in 1542, and Henry chose as his last wife, Catherine Parr, an intelligent, mature woman with decided Protestant leanings. Catherine, who was wise enough to conceal some of her opinions, brought much needed order to the royal household. She had a great deal of influence on the education of Henry's children and gave them a taste of stable family life.

Although he was aging, he had not yet given up all the dreams of his youth. In 1544 he was tempted into yet another attack on France. France's greater concern with Spain and England's limited resources kept the conflict from blossoming into a major war. The failure of the venture forced him to give up the hope of recovering the land that England had once ruled in France. In the end, his schemes did not yield much fruit on the continent, but he had success in reorganizing the British Isles. He integrated Wales into England's administrative system. He arrived at an agreement with the Irish and assumed their crown. And he intimidated the Scots into keeping the peace. When he died on 28 January 1547, he left his successors a more powerful throne than he had inherited, but he also left a legacy of problems that remained troublesome into Sh.'s generation. His only son was consumptive and did not live long enough to produce children. The cloud Henry had cast on the legitimacy of his daughter Mary kept her unmarried until it was too late for her to have children. His daughter Elizabeth avoided the political complications inherent in the marriage of a reigning queen by refusing to wed. As a result, the dynasty whose future Henry had gone to such lengths to secure died with his children. Ironically, the religious tensions Henry's dynastic aspirations generated had much greater longevity. His son, Edward VI, was attracted to Protestantism, and his government accelerated the pace of the English Reformation.

Mary, Edward's heir, was an embittered Catholic who devoted her reign to obliterating everything that her brother and father had done. She restored the power of the pope over the English church and burned at the stake Protestants who refused to recant their faith. Elizabeth, who followed Mary to the throne, carefully steered a course between the extremists of both camps. As a result, there were many vital issues unresolved in Sh.'s England, and he and his contemporaries found religion and Tudor history touchy subjects.

Henry Bolingbroke, *2H6 2.2.21,* See Henry IV.

Henry, earl of Stafford and duke of Buckingham, *R3,* (d. 1483), leader of an unsuccessful revolt against Richard III. Buckingham inherited his duchy from his grandfather, Humphrey, in 1460. As an orphaned youth of high birth, he became a ward of the royal family and was welcomed to its inner circle. Edward IV had him knighted at the coronation of Edward's queen, Elizabeth Woodville, and he married Elizabeth's sister, Catherine. Despite these connections, he did not become a member of the queen's party at court. He remained in the political background until Edward IV's death and then emerged as Richard of Gloucester's chief ally in his campaign to dispossess Edward's heirs. When Richard III was not greeted by a spontaneous show of affection from his subjects, the new king's uncertain future may have encouraged Buckingham to reflect on his own chance of winning the throne. Since he descended from Edward III through Edward's youngest son, Thomas of Gloucester, his blood qualified him for royal office. In the fall of 1483 he attempted to overthrow Richard, but a spate of foul weather was enough to disperse his small army. Realizing that there was no popular support for his cause, he tried to flee England. The man he turned to for help betrayed him to the king, and Richard ordered his immediate execution.

Henry, Lord Scrope of Masham, *H5,* (1376–1415), third baron Scrope of Masham, nephew of Richard Scrope, the archbishop of York who led a rebellion against Henry IV; son of Stephen Scrope, a baron who refused to join Henry IV in his campaign to overthrow Richard II and who was implicated in the revolt against Henry IV led by the Percies. Toward the end of Henry IV's reign the Scropes appeared to make their peace with the Lancastrian dynasty. Henry Scrope became a close friend of Henry IV's son, Prince Harry. Scrope was treasurer of England when Henry V ascended the throne. Henry removed him from that office, but employed him on embassies to France and Denmark. While abroad on these missions, the earl of Cambridge recruited him for a conspiracy against the king's life. Scrope's motives are uncertain. He was related to Cambridge, and Cambridge may have offered him a large sum of money in exchange for his help. When the plot was revealed to Henry on the eve of his invasion of France, he executed its leaders.

Henry of Lancaster, *3H6 1.1.165,* see Henry VI.

Henry, Prince, *Jn 5.6.35,* Henry III (1207–1272), king of England. Henry had a long, disastrous reign. He was not a competent ruler, but many of the problems that plagued his administration were not of his making. England's confidence in the throne was shaken by the erratic conduct, abrasive personality, and disastrous foreign policy of his father, King John. In 1215, after years of mismanagement, John's barons forced him to accept limits on royal authority spelled out in a document called Magna Carta. Magna Carta permitted various groups to vent their anger, but it did not create a basis for a new working relationship between John and his men. Civil war erupted, and some of John's vassals invited the heir to the French throne to help them liberate England from John's tyranny. John's sudden and unexpected death changed their minds. Henry, John's heir, was only 9 years old, and England's barons were quick to realize the advantages to the nobility of a long period of minority government. The French were compelled to retreat, and the nobles appointed regents to rule for the young king. When Henry came of age and tried to reclaim what he considered to be the rightful prerogatives of a monarch, he faced deeply entrenched opposition. A gifted politician or a great general might have been able to restore the power and prestige of the monarchy, but Henry was neither. He blundered into one foolish difficulty after another, and his reign, like that of his father, ended in a baronial revolt. He was imprisoned by his vassals and effectively deposed in favor of his son, Edward I.

Herald, servant of a warrior. The title derives from an ancient German term for war, but a comparable office existed in the armies of the early Greeks and Romans. The herald carried messages between combatants and handled such vital functions as declarations of war and arrangements for conferences and truces. The herald's function required that he be granted a kind of diplomatic immunity so that he could cross battle lines. At the end of the 12th c. the kings of Europe and their knights began to paint their shields with symbols by which they could be identified. The interpretation of these armorial bearings was a skill associated with heralds, for heralds had to be able to locate specific individuals for whom they had messages. The rules governing the design and use of armorial bearings consequently came to be known as heraldry.

R2. Jn. H5. 1H6. 2H6. Cor. Oth. Lr. TNK.

Herbert, Walter, *R3,* second son of Sir William Herbert. Sir William served as the young earl of Richmond's guardian when the Yorkists took the boy from his Lancastrian relatives in 1468. The Herberts were created earls of Pembroke in place of Richmond's attaindered uncle, Jasper Tudor. Sir Walter married the duke of Buckingham's second daughter, Anne Stafford, and joined his father-in-law in an attempt to overthrow Richard III. After the failure of Buckingham's revolt, Walter joined Richmond in exile on the continent. He returned to England with Richmond in 1485 to fight in the battle of Bosworth Field.

Hercules, (Gr. *Herakles*), son of Jupiter and Alcmene, one of the greatest of mythological heroes, and the father of an exceptional number of children. Precociously strong, in his cradle he strangled two serpents sent by the jealous Juno to kill him. His short temper or various madnesses brought on by Juno caused him to be involved in various broils which led him into exploits such as killing the Nemean lion, the twelve labors, killing the Hydra, wrestling the giant Antæus, and capturing Troy. He was eventually killed by a robe poisoned with the blood of a centaur, but the divine part of his being (from Jupiter) was raised to immortality and was married to Hebe.

3H6 2.1.53. 1H6 2.3.18. Shr 1.2.257.

LLL 1.2.64, 65. 1.2.168, 'H.'s club,' symbolic of a warrior's skill. *4.3.165. 4.3.316,* one of the twelve labors was to acquire the golden apples of the Hesperides. *5.1.123,* Mote, despite his stature assumes the role of Hercules in his minority in the pageant of the Nine Worthies. *5.1.128–33,* allusion to Hercules' strangling Juno's serpents in his cradle. *5.2.531, 582. MND 4.1.111:* this incident seems to be a fabrication mixing Hercules' 7th labor, capturing the Cretan bull, and Cadmus' search for his sister Europa. Mythology does not tell of Hippolyta hunting with either hero. *5.1.47 (add. 30),* 'my kinsman H.': both Theseus and Hercules are descended from Jupiter, but given the god's appetites, few mythological heroes weren't.

MV 2.1.32, allusion to Ovid's *Metamorphoses,* 9, in which the weak Lichas hands Hercules the poisoned garment which kills him. Chance, the Prince of Morocco is saying, may allow the weak to defeat their betters. *3.2.60,* Bassanio is compared with Hercules, who rescued Hesione, not for love, but for horses. *3.2.85,* 'beard of H.,' the emblem of courage. Possibly an equating of Samson, whose strength derived from his hair, with Hercules. *MWW 1.3.6,* 'bully H.' *1H4 2.5.273.*

Ado 2.1.342, 'H.'s labours.' *3.3.131,* 'shaven H.,' a reference to a depiction in a tapestry. Why the hero is shaved is unclear. Possibly it depicted Hercules when he was punished for flinging Iphitus, the son of King Eurytus, from the walls of Tiryns in a fit of madness. Zeus made him for three years a slave to Queen Omphale of Lydia who made him dress as a woman and weave or spin. Other conjecture is that Hercules is confused with Samson. *2.1.237,* 'would have made H. have turned spit': would have transformed Hercules into the lowest ranking cook (the one who cranked the spit).

AYLI 1.2.198. Ham 1.2.153. 2.2.362, the globe rested on Hercules' shoulders on the sign of the Globe playhouse. *5.1.289. AWW 4.3.257. Ant 3.7.67, 4.3.14. Cor 4.1.18, 4.6.104.*

Cym 4.2.115, 313. TNK 1.1.66, 'H. our kinsman': according to Plutarch Theseus was a cousin of Hercules on his mother Æthra's side. The connection appears to be rather loose, however, going back six generations to Hercules' oversexed father Jupiter. *2.5.2.*

Hereford, Earl of, 1) *2H4 4.1.129, 4.1.136,* see Henry IV.

2) *H8 1.1.200,* see Edward, earl of Stafford, duke of Buckingham.

Hereford, Earldom of, *R3 3.1.192, 4.2.93,* crucial post for the defense of England's border with southern Wales. The county of Herefordshire was the scene of much fighting between the Saxons and the Celts prior to the Norman conquest of England in the 11th c. The military importance of the district was such that the Norman kings erected their first castles there and vested its earls with special responsibilities. William the Conqueror granted the honor to William FitzOsbern in 1067. It passed to the family of Henry DeBohun in 1200. In 1397 Henry (IV) of Lancaster married the DeBohun heiress, and in 1550 Edward VI established a viscountcy of Hereford for Walter Devereux, a descendant of the DeBohun family.

Hereford, Henry, (Harry) *R2,* Harry, see Henry IV. The earldom of Hereford was one of the honors that came to Henry (IV) Bolingbroke, heir to the duchy of Lancaster, by right of his wife, Mary de Bohun, younger daughter of the last de Bohun earl of Hereford. Her elder sister was married to Henry's uncle, Thomas of Gloucester.

Herefordshire, *1H4 1.1.39,* English county sharing a border with south central Wales.

Hermes, Greek god, son of Zeus and Naia, equated with the Roman Mercury. Hermes appeared in classical mythology as the messenger of the gods. In this role, he brought prophetic dreams from gods to human beings and ruled over the realm of sleep. He was the patron of travellers, and conducted the souls of the dead on their last trip to Hades. The boundary stones and markers on which travellers depended were sacred to him, and his name is linked with Gr. *herma* 'prop' or 'pillar,' the word used for milestones or markers which were later topped with his bust. His guardianship of frontiers led to the belief that he was the divinity that watched over treaties and contracts. Like many of the denizens of the open road who are forced to live by their wits, he was cunning. He committed fraud and theft, but his facile mind was also the source of useful inventions. Music was among the many arts and technologies credited to his ingenuity. He made the first lyre, the favored instrument of poets and the god Apollo. *H5 3.7.18,* 'pipe of H.,' recalls a passage in Ovid's *Metamorphoses* (1.677) where he uses a flute to lull the monster Argus to sleep.

Hermia, *MND,* daughter of Egeus. She refuses to marry the 'spotted and inconstant' Demetrius at her father's command, despite the possibility of execution and flees into the woods with her love Lysander, pursued by Demetrius. After the confusion of the love potion, when neither man wants her, her father relents and she is betrothed to Lysander. Described as dark of complexion and hair, she was likely played by the boy actor with those attributes who also played Celia and Hero.

Hermione, *WT,* wife of Leontes, unjustly accused of adultery. Hermione was a common enough name and was even used for males, although it has been asserted that it was borrowed from Menelaus and Helen's daughter who was married to Neoptolemus and later Orestes, who killed her first husband to recover his kingdom. Hermione means 'pillar-like' (see Hermes), related to Gr. *herma,* which would conveniently be reflected in both her staunch character and her appearance as a statue in the melodramatic conclusion. There was also a Hermione (Harmonia) who was wife of Cadmus in ancient mythology. In Illyria, she was transformed with her husband into a pair of beautiful snakes, not as a punishment but as a relief from suffering. The story of Cadmus was often used as a Job-like illustration that the innocent suffer as well as the guilty, which makes a loose thematic relation with *WT.* This myth is told in Ovid's *Metamorphoses,* 4, but the name of the wife is omitted. In Sh.'s main source, Robert Greene's *Pandosto,* or the Triumph of Time (1588; rptd. 1607 as *Dorastus and Fawnia*), the character who corresponds to Hermione, Bellaria, dies. The change truly makes *WT* a fairy tale—a 'winter's tale'—and the idea of the statue of Hermione coming to life may have derived from the famous story of Pygmalion and Galatea in Ovid's *Metamorphoses,* 10. The name Hermione appears in North's translation of Plutarch, from which Sh. got most of his names for *WT.*

Herne the Hunter, *MWW 4.4.27, 37, 42, 5.5 s.d., 26,* ranger of Queen Elizabeth's who having met her disapproval hanged himself from an oak in Windsor Great Park. His spirit supposedly haunted the woods, wearing a chain.

Herne's Oak, *MWW 4.4.39, 4.6.19, 5.1.11, 5.3.14, 23, 24,* haunted tree upon which Herne the Hunter hanged himself in Windsor Great Park. The tree was alleged to be 650 years old when it fell in 1863.

Hero, *Ado,* 'Lady H.,' daughter of Leonato, niece of Antonio, and beloved of Claudio. Claudio loves her at first sight, but not enough to disbelieve the accusations against her chastity engineered by Don John and Borachio. Humiliated at the altar by Claudio, Hero faints or feigns death, deliberately or not is not clear; however, her innocence is later revealed by Dogberry and his watch, and she masquerades as a cousin of hers who Claudio penitently has agreed to marry unseen. Like many of Sh.'s romantic heroines, Hero is paired with a devoted friend Beatrice. She is also described by Benedick as being dark and little (*1.1.163–5*), and short (*200–1*). She takes a less active role in events, however, than Rosalind, for example, or Hermia. She does not do anything to prove her innocence and the lesson Claudio learns about love is not of her doing, so she is intrinsically less heroic and less interesting than many of the other heroines. The source materials for the play do not use the name Hero. In Matteo Bandello's *Novelle* (1554), the primary source, the corresponding character is Fenicia, 'phoenix' who dies and comes back to life. Fenicia assumes the name Lucilla when feigning death. There are many other contemporary versions of the plot. Sh. obviously chose Hero for the mythological resonance. See Hero (of Sestos).

Hero (of Sestos), mythical priestess of Aphrodite. Leander saw her at a festival and fell instantly in love with her. In order to meet her each night, he swam the Hellespont from Abydos on the Asian side to Sestos on the European side, guided by a torch she placed in a tower. He drowned one night in a storm, his body was washed up on the European shore, and she threw herself into the sea in despair. Marlowe made the story the subject of his poem *Hero and Leander,* incomplete at his death on May 31, 1593, but completed by Chapman and published in 1598. There are several quotations from Marlowe's poem in Ben Jonson's *Every Man in his Humour* 4.2 (1598) in which Sh. acted. A direct quotation from this poem at *AYLI 3.5.82–83* has been used for dating Sh.'s play. The romantic appeal of this tale later caused

Lord Byron to swim the Hellespont in one hour and ten minutes. *TGV 3.1.119,* 'H.'s tower.' *Rom 2.3.39. AYLI 4.1.94, 99.* Leander unromantically died of a cramp, not love, says Rosalind.

Herod, 'the Great' (37–4 BC), king who ruled Judea and neighboring territories as a client of the Roman empire. He was adept at keeping his subjects under control while ingratiating himself with their enemies, the Romans. Octavius Augustus recognized him as king of the Jews in 40 BC and rewarded his loyalty over the years by adding to his sprawling Palestinian domain. Herod was eager to promote closer relations between Hebrew and gentile cultures. The splendid port he built at Cæsarea and named for Cæsar Augustus was intended to open his nation to Roman goods and influences. He equipped the cities he ruled with theaters, pagan temples, gymnasiums, and all the amenities of Greco-Roman civilization. His fondness for the gentile way of life did nothing to foster his popularity with his Jewish subjects, but he courted their favor by giving Jerusalem one of the most magnificent temples in the Roman empire—the sanctuary frequented by Jesus and his disciples. According to the gospels of Luke and Matthew, Jesus of Nazareth was born at the end of Herod's reign. Matthew (2:16–18) claims that Herod was aware of Jesus' birth and anxious about prophecies that predicted the appearance in Bethlehem of a messiah who would establish a new royal line in Jerusalem. Matthew says that Herod tried to head off a challenge to his dynasty by ordering the murder of all the male babies recently born in Bethlehem.

MWW 2.1.19, 'H. of Jewry.' *H5 3.3.124:* Matthew's 'slaughter of the innocents' became a favorite subject for illustration by medieval artists, and Sh.'s words would have reminded his audience of many paintings and sculptures. *Ham 3.2.14,* 'out-Herods Herod,' a reference to actors ranting and raving in the role of Herod, the braggart tyrant. The tradition of a blustering Herod went all the way back into the era of the Chester Plays and other mysteries. *Ant 1.2.24, 3.3.3, 4, 3.6.73, 4.6.13.*

Hesperides, goddesses who protected the Golden Apples of the sunset which grew at the end of the earth on a golden tree with golden leaves. The goddesses' parentage is variously attributed. Usually Atlas is said to be their father, but Zeus, Phorcys, and Erebus are also named. Their mother was said to be either Pleione, Hesperis, Ceto, or Nyx. They were four in number in most versions, but seven in others. In Sh. and other writers of his time, the daughters were often confused with their garden. *LLL 4.3.317:* one of the twelve labors of Hercules was to acquire the apples. *Per 1.70.*

Hesperus, *AWW 2.1.164,* 'Moist H.,' the evening star, also called Vesper. He was the son of Eos (Dawn) and either Astræus or Cephalus. The king of the Western Land, the wind, carried him into the sky to become a star. Actually the planet Venus, Hesperus was called Phosphorus or Lucifer as the morning star. Sh. confuses Hesperus with the goddess Hesperis, wife of Atlas and mother of the Hesperides.

Hibbocrates, *MWW 3.1.61,* Evans' Welsh mispronunciation of Hippocrates (c. 460–c. 377 BC), the great ancient Greek physician often called the 'Father of Medicine.' He was thought to be descended from Æsculapius. He probably traveled widely but set up a school of medicine on the island of Kos and died in Larissa in Thessaly. Although held in enormous esteem, the details of his life, as they have come down to us, are extremely obscure. Many ancient works of medicine are attributed to him, though it is not clear how many were by his hand. The *Hippocratic Collection* examines illness as the result of natural causes and his teachings did much to free medicine of belief in supernatural causation. The essays concern such subjects as predicting the course of a disease, the cause of epilepsy, gynecology, and head wounds. The renowned Hippocratic Oath, which physicians have ascribed to in various forms over the centuries, is also part of the collection, though it may have originated in a Pythagorean school of the 4th c. BC.

Hiems, L. 'winter,' a personification. *LLL 5.2.876:* he appears at the end of the pageant and sings. *MND 2.1.109,* 'old H.'s crown.'

Hill, *2H4 5.1.33,* possibly Stinchcombe Hill in Gloucestershire, place of residence Sh. gave the Clement Perks who brings a case against a William Visor in Justice Shallow's court. Shallow's steward, Davy, tries to influence the outcome of the suit.

Hinkley Fair, *2H4 5.1.21,* annual market held at Hinkley, a town in Leicestershire about 30 mi. northeast of Sh.'s home at Stratford-on-Avon.

Hipparchus, *Ant 3.13.151,* freedman who Plutarch ('Antony' 67.7) says was the first of Antony's men to swear allegiance to Octavius after Antony's flight from the battle of Actium. Hipparchus was the son of Theophilus, Antony's steward, and Plutarch claims that Antony took his defection very hard. When Octavius sent a legate to Cleopatra, Antony whipped the man and sent him back to Octavius with the suggestion that Octavius equal the score by similarly abusing Hipparchus.

Hippocrates, *MWW 3.1.61,* see Hibbocrates.

Hippolyta, Amazon queen. In some mythology, sister of Antiope and Penthesilea, daughter of Mars and Otrera. In many versions she is the mother of Hippolytus, and Antiope is another name for her. One of the labors of Hercules was to steal the girdle which Mars had given her. After he succeeded, she died of a broken heart. In another version, she agreed to give him the girdle, but Juno convinced the Amazons that Hercules intended to abduct their queen. When attacked, Hercules thought Hippolyta was being treacherous and killed her. In yet another variant, Theseus abducted her and upon the birth of Hippolytus, the Amazons unsuccessfully invaded Attica, though they entered Athens itself. For both plays in which she is a character, the playwright seems to have gotten all the information he needed from Chaucer's *Knyghtes Tale,* where she is depicted as a pleasant fiancée sympathetic to the sufferings of others—hardly a war-loving Amazon at all. In both plays also (as in Chaucer) the opening situation is much the same as Theseus and she prepare for their wedding. Her name (and her son's) would imply a relationship with horses (Gr. *hippos*). Hippolytus was dragged to his death by his chariot horses. *MND. TNK.*

Hiren, *2H4 2.4.156, 172,* pun on the name of a Greek harlot, Hyrin, who would have been known to members of Sh.'s audience from plays his contemporaries staged in London. When the initial 'h' is dropped, as it would have been in the London dialect of Sh.'s day, Hiren sounds like 'iron' and brings to mind the sword that Pistol draws at this point in the action of *2H4.*

Hirtius, *Ant 1.4.58,* (d. 43 BC), consul for the year 43 BC, friend of Julius Cæsar and opponent of Mark Antony. Hirtius worked with Cæsar in Gaul and aided Cæsar in Cæsar's struggles with Rome's Senate. Hirtius became consul following Cæsar's assassination. Initially he supported Antony in an attempt to maintain order in the city, but he did not like Antony, and Cicero persuaded him to help Cæsar's adopted son Octavius mount a challenge to Antony. Sensing the shift in the political winds, Antony retreated from Rome to Mutina to attack Brutus, one of Cæsar's assassins. Since control of the province of Cisalpine Gaul was at stake, Hirtius and his co-consul, Pansa, raised an army to force Antony to lift his seige of Mutina. Pansa was killed in battle, and Hirtius, who prevented Antony from winning the day, died leading a charge on Antony's camp. Octavius buried the bodies of the fallen consuls with conspicuous honors, but he could not have regretted their fates. Their deaths cleared the way for him, despite his youth, to claim a consulship and command of the Senate's army.

Hisperia, *AYLI 2.2.10,* 'the Princess' [Celia's] gentlewoman.' The name is from Hesperia, one of the Hesperides.

Histerica passio, *Lr. 2.2.232 (Q 7.226),* hysteria so intense it causes choking. It was also known as 'the mother,' because it was supposedly what happened to a woman who longed for her mother. One supposedly felt it beginning in the abdomen and rising to the brain.

Hob, *Cor 2.3.116,* from 'Rob,' short for 'Robin,' a generic name for a vulgarian or a fool. In *Cambises, King of Percia* by Thomas Preston (c. 1569), a popular play of the period, Hob is the husband of Marian-May-Be Good, for example, an obvious allusion to the Robin Hood skits.

Hobbididence, *Lr. Q 15.57,* see Hoppedance.

Hobgoblin, mischievous sprite often synonymous with the puck, though sometimes mentioned separately. Hob (q.v.) also was used to imply a fool. See Goblin.

1) *MND 2.1.40,* see Goodfellow, Robin.

2) *MWW,* role assumed by one of the people of Windsor in their humiliation of Falstaff.

Holborn, *R3 3.4.31,* road leading into London from the west via Newgate. The bishop of Ely's palace and gardens lay along its northern side just outside the city walls next to the guild of lawyers housed at Furnival's inn.

Holdfast, *H5 2.3.48,* reference to a proverb: 'Brag is a good dog, but Holdfast is a better.'

Holidam, *Rom 1.3.45,* 'by my h.,' see Halidom.

Holiness, his, term of respect for the pope, the vicar of Christ on earth. Medieval theologians held that God had established two kinds of government on earth: a priestly hierarchy that culminated in the papacy, and a secular hierarchy of feudal magnates commended to the service of a king. In theory the sacred and secular realms were separate. In practice it was very difficult to keep them apart. The pope was deeply involved in secular politics, and he used the same instruments of earthly power as kings. In some medieval contexts, therefore, the title 'his Holiness' was intended to have mocking or ironic overtones.

1H6 5.1.53. Jn 5.1.6. MM 3.1.478. H8 2.4.118, 3.2.32, 223.

Holland, modern European nation bordering Belgium, Germany, and the North Sea. Trade along the Rhine river brought German (*deutsch,* or 'Dutch') influence to bear on the culture of Holland, but the district was ruled during the late medieval era by the French dukes of Burgundy. In 1420 Burgundy's properties passed by inheritance to the Hapsburg emperor, Charles V, and to his son, Philip II of Spain. Philip's attempts to curtail the spread of Protestantism in the Lowlands alienated the Dutch and sparked a war for national independence. During Sh.'s youth, Holland was locked in combat with Spain. To prevent the Spaniards from solidifying their hold on a coastal district that would have given them a base from which to invade England, Sh.'s queen, Elizabeth, was motivated, despite her dislike for radical Protestants, to help the Dutch. Holland's independence from Spain was not formally recognized until 1648, when an international treaty acknowledged the right of the Dutch people to self-government. The cities of Holland and Belgium were famous for the cloth they manufactured. Good quality linen was called 'holland.' *1H4 3.3.70. 2H4 2.2.22.*

Holland, Henry, *3H6,* (1430–1473), duke of Exeter, brother-in-law to Edward IV, but loyal supporter of Henry VI. He fought for the Lancastrians at Wakefield, Towton, and Barnet, and he accompanied Queen Margaret into exile. Edward stripped him of his lands and honors, and he died in poverty. Sh. makes him a witness to a debate between York and Lancaster about the merits of their respective rights to the crown. Implausibly, Sh. has him side with York.

Holland, John, 1) *1H6,* see John 1).

2) *R2,* see Exeter, Duke of.

3) *H5,* see Huntingdon.

Hollander, 1) *Oth 2.3.72, 77,* person from Holland, stereotyped as fond of drink.

2) (pl.) *3H6 4.9.2,* men from the Lowlands who often served as mercenaries in wars among the English, French, Burgundians, and Bretons. A group of Hollanders accompanied Edward IV when he returned to England for his final confrontation with Warwick and Henry VI.

Holmedon Hill, *1H4 1.1.55, 65, 70, 1.3.23, 5.3.14,* Homildon, at the eastern end of the Cheviot range near the boundary between Northumberland and Scotland. Scene of a victory that Hotspur (Henry Percy) won over the Scots on 14 September 1402.

Holofernes, 'Master H.,' pedant schoolmaster. He is a stock comedy type, based on Dottore in *commedia dell'arte* and his name is borrowed from Dr. Tubal Holofernes in François Rabelais' *Gargantua and Pantagruel.* He babbles in Latin unintelligibly and condescends to the other characters as he directs their pageant of the Nine Worthies. Mercilessly mocked by the nobility as he plays the role of Judas Maccabeus, when he withdraws he nonetheless arouses some sympathy in a way similar to Malvolio when he withdraws in *TN.* His directing the pageant also suggests the similar function of Peter Quince, though the latter is less of a caricature. Some critics have tried to link him with contemporaries of Sh.—John Florio, Gabriel Harvey, and others—but it is highly dubious the playwright would parody someone by using such a stock character.

Holy Church, *Jn 5.2.71,* see Church.

Holy Father, *Jn 3.1.71,* term of respect for the pope or a priest.

Holy Land, *R2 5.6.49, 1H4 1.1.48, 2H4 3.1.103, 4.3.339, 367,* Palestine, modern Israel, a country medieval Europeans considered sanctified because its history was the source of the divine revelation recorded in the Bible. Although Palestine and most of the Middle East passed into Muslim hands in the 7th c., hordes of European Christians continued to make pilgrimages to the sites mentioned in the Bible. They and the leaders of their church considered it a scandal that Christ's homeland was controlled by persons who did not acknowledge his divinity. At the end of the 11th c. an army was sent out from Europe to rectify that situation. This 'first crusade' was fortunate in its timing. The Muslims were divided among themselves and unable to organize an adequate defense. They fell back, and triumphant European knights staked claims to a gaggle of 'crusader states' composing a loosely organized 'kingdom of Jerusalem.' Although there was a steady trickle of knights who visited the Holy Lands to polish their reputations for chivalry or escape embarrassments at home, the Christians could not recruit the manpower needed to maintain the beachhead they had established in Muslim territory. In 1144 the Muslims recovered a large part of the land they had lost, and the cry went up in Europe for a second crusade. It achieved nothing but the embarrassment of its leader, Louis VII of France. In 1187 Jerusalem surrendered to the Muslims, and Europe was roused to a monumental third crusade. It enlisted the services of the kings of England, France, and Germany, but it, too, was a failure. Experience should have convinced the Europeans that they had no hope of winning a war in the east, but expeditions and calls for crusades continued until the rise of the powerful Ottoman Empire in the 15th c. made all such ventures patently hopeless.

Holy Mother, *Jn 3.1.67,* the church, the institution charged by God with maternal responsibility for nurturing the human spirit.

Holy Rood, *R3 3.2.72, 4.4.166,* cross of Christ as used in Christian worship. In English churches the choir and the nave were often separated by an elaborately carved screen on which a crucifix, or 'rood' was mounted.

Holy Writ, *R3 1.3.335,* the Judeo-Christian Scriptures. The version that Sh. favored was the

Geneva Bible, a scholarly English translation published in 1560 by William Whittingham, Anthony Gilby, and Thomas Sampson. Its name derived from the fact that it was financed by the Calvinist congregations of Geneva. Although it was not approved for use in England's churches, its handy size and legible type won it a wide readership and made it the version of the Bible most often found in the homes of lay persons. The more enduring 'authorized' or, as it is commonly known, 'King James' version of the Bible did not appear until 1611, about the time that Sh. retired.

Holy-rood day, *1H4 1.1.52,* 14 September, feast in honor of the Cross of Christ, the Holy Rood or 'wood.'

Honour, *AWW 4.2.51,* a personification.

Hoodman, *AWW 4.3.122,* Paroles under his hood, a blindfolded person. The game of Blind Man's Buff was once called Hoodman Blind.

Hopkins, Nicholas, *H8 1.1.222, 1.2.148, 149, 2.1.23,* Carthusian monk who served as the duke of Buckingham's confessor. He was accused of posing as a seer to urge Edward Stafford, duke of Buckingham, to rebel against Henry VIII. When Buckingham was indicted for having aspired to the throne, Hopkins gave evidence against him.

Hoppedance, *Lr. Q 13.26,* name of a demon. Sh. borrowed it from Samuel Harsnett's 'Hoberdidance.' See Flibbertigibbet for details. Presumably the name describes the demon's frenetic dancing, though Edgar describes him as 'prince of dumbness.'

Hoppo, *Mac 3.5.44,* spirit called forth by the witches in a song not appearing in F1, but which appears in Thomas Middleton's play *The Witch* (c. 1609, but not printed until the 18th c.) William Davenant's version of *Mac* (printed 1674) and Q (1673), however, contains the song and it has been argued that Davenant may have had access to an earlier text. In Davenant's version, the spirit is 'Hopper.' 'Hop-o'-my Thumb,' was a dwarf so small it could hop on one's thumb. He is referred to in *Taming of A Shrew* and other contemporary works. The name came from Reginald Scot's *Discoverie of Witchcraft* (1584). In Middleton's play, Hoppo is one of the witches.

Horace, Quintus Flaccus Horatius (65–8 BC), one of the greatest of the ancient Latin poets. His father, an enterprising freedman, scraped together the money to send him to Rome and Athens for an excellent education. He was in Athens when Brutus, Cæsar's assassin, came to Greece to raise an army to fight Mark Antony and Octavius. Horace accepted a commission from Brutus and took part in the battle at Philippi. The experience taught him that he was no warrior, and he returned to Rome to seek civilian employment. A clerkship in a government office enabled him to survive while he polished his literary skills. The poet Virgil was impressed by his work and introduced him to the most munificent patron of the arts of the day, Caius Cilnius Mæcenas. In 34 BC Mæcenas gave him a farm that produced enough income to permit the poet to devote himself entirely to writing. Through Mæcenas, he met Octavius and won admission to Rome's most exalted circles. *Tit 4.2.22, 24:* Sh. quotes from Horace's *Odes* 1.22, 1–2.

Horatio, *Ham,* Hamlet's friend and fellow university student. He is the only one the prince trusts with his secrets. The name may be borrowed from Thomas Kyd's *Spanish Tragedy,* which had a tremendous influence on the play. In it, another Horatio plays an important role as best friend of the protagonist. Its origin may for both plays be in the legend of the Horatii, loyal brothers who defended Rome.

Horner, Thomas, *2H6,* the name Sh. gives to an unidentified armorer whom Edward Hall (*Union of the Two Noble and Illustre Famelies of Lancastre and Yorke,* 207–208) says was indicted for treason against Henry VI. Horner was accused by his apprentice of saying that the duke of York had a better claim to the crown than the king. Since the armorer arrived at his trial too drunk to defend himself, he was convicted. Sh. embellished Hall's account by having Horner confess to his treason with his dying breath.

Hortensio. *Shr,* friend of Petruccio's and suitor of Bianca. He disguises himself as a lute teacher in order to gain access to her. Katherine, however, breaks the lute over his head. As he cannot gain Bianca's affection, he conveniently finds a widow to marry and is proven to be more the fool when she handles him shrewishly and Hortensio is said to be afraid of her. The name may be borrowed from Plutarch, like Hortensius (q.v.), but the Quintus Hortensius in Plutarch's 'Cato the Younger' tries to bargain for a wife.

Hortensius, *Tim 3.4,* one of Timon's creditors. The name appears in Plutarch's 'Mark Antony' which contains a passage about Timon. Hortensius the lawyer also appears in Plutarch's 'Lucullus.' There is a commander with the name in Plutarch's 'Sulla' (see Sylla) and in his 'Cæsar.' A Quintus Hortensius appears in 'Cato the Younger.'

Host of the Garter Inn, *MWW,* jolly keeper of the inn at Windsor, with a flamboyant speaking style. He tries to settle the disagreement between Falstaff and Shallow and tricks Hugh Evans and Dr. Caius to prevent their duel. He is rewarded for his good deeds by having his horses stolen from him, probably by Evans. Even though he is depressed over the theft, he helps Fenton to marry Anne Page by finding a vicar for the ceremony. See Garter Inn.

Hostess, *H5,* see Quickly, Mistress.

Hostilius, 1) *Tim 3.2.63,* name of the second stranger.

2) *Cor 2.3.240,* Tullus Hostilius, (673--642 BC), legendary third king of Rome in succession to Numa Pompilius and Romulus. His chief claim to fame was his record of success in wars with Rome's Sabine and Latin neighbors.

Hotspur, Henry Percy (1364–1403), eldest son of the earl of Northumberland. Percy's relentless dashing from fight to fight in border wars with the Scots earned him his frenetic nickname. Sh. portrays him as Prince Harry's contemporary, but he was actually the same age as Harry's father, Henry IV. Hotspur and Northumberland were co-wardens of the Scottish Marches for Richard II, but they were not fond of the king and refused to obey his order to join the army he assembled in 1399 for war in Ireland. When Henry (IV) Bolingbroke landed in England in July 1399 to demand the restoration of his estates, Hotspur and Northumberland rallied to his side. Their support tipped the balance in Henry's favor and helped Henry force Richard's abdication. Henry IV rewarded Hotspur by sending him to Wales to deal with a revolt raised by Owain Glyndŵr. The honor proved to be more expensive than Hotspur had anticipated, for Henry failed to reimburse him for the expenses of the campaign. Hotspur concluded that he had been made a fool of, resigned his office, and rejoined his father in northern England. In 1402 Archibald, earl of Douglas, led a large Scottish raiding party into Northumberland.

The Percies saved the day by decisively defeating the invaders at the battle of Holmedon Hill. They expected their king to reward them for this service to the nation, but Henry was less than generous. He demanded custody of the prisoners for whom the Percies expected to collect rich ransoms. Furthermore, he refused to sanction the ransom of Hotspur's brother-in-law, Edmund Mortimer, who had fallen into Glyndŵr's clutches. Henry's actions were expressions of his lack of confidence in the Percies and the Mortimers and his eagerness to contain them. In 1403 the showdown Henry hoped to avoid occurred. The Percies allied with Douglas and Glyndŵr against Henry and proclaimed Edmund Mortimer (son of Richard II's heir presumptive), England's legitimate ruler. Henry saved himself by quick action. He forced a battle before the rebel forces could assemble, and on 21 July 1403, at Shrewsbury an unknown soldier killed Hotspur. Prince Harry was only 16 when Shrewsbury was fought. Although Holinshed (3.522) records his presence at the battle, there is no historical evidence for Sh.'s claim that he killed Hotspur.

1H4. 2H4 ind. 25, 30, 36, 1.1.50, 121, 1.3.26, 2.3.37, 44.

Hubert, *Jn,* H. de Burgh (d. 1245), one of the most powerful nobles at the court of King John of England. Since Hubert was among John's few friends, the king relied heavily on his assistance and gave him frequent and profitable promotions. Hubert was custodian of numerous castles and of the important royal prisoners in their dungeons. John turned his nephew, Arthur of Brittany, over to him after Arthur's capture at the siege of Mirabeau in 1202. Sh.'s claim that John ordered Hubert to put out Arthur's eyes but he could not bring himself to do so is based on a rumor recorded by Ralph of Coggeshall. The tale is probably false, for nothing in Hubert's subsequent relationship with John suggests that the king found him disobedient. He became warden of the Welsh Marches and acquired the revenues of numerous English counties and French castles. At Runnymede he sided with John against the barons who forced the king to accept the limitations on royal power spelled out in Magna Carta. After Runnymede Hubert became John's justiciary, and John entrusted Dover castle to him. Dover was of great importance, for it guarded the narrowest point on the English channel—a stretch of beach along which John expected a French assault. When the French attacked, Hubert repulsed them and won a decisive battle against their fleet. He survived John to become the chief regent for the king's young heir, Henry III. After Henry declared his majority in 1227, Hubert continued to serve as one of the king's advisors. Henry made him earl of Kent and sanctioned a prestigious fourth marriage for him—with the sister of the king of Scotland.

Hugh, *MWW,* see Evans, Sir Hugh.

Hugh Capet, *H5 1.2.69, 78, 87,* (938–996), founder of France's Capetian dynasty. Hugh, heir to fiefs at Paris and Orléans, exploited the weakness of the waning Carolingian dynasty to make himself the strongest man in northern France. When Louis V died childless in 987, Hugh commanded sufficient support to wrest the throne away from the dead king's uncle and heir, Charles of Lorraine. Although Hugh was Louis V's remote cousin, his claim to the throne of France was not, as Sh.'s sources led him to believe, based on his blood lines. At the time of Hugh's succession he and his supporters argued that the French crown was an elective, not a hereditary, office. It was many generations before the Capetians secured a firm hold on the throne and established the tradition of hereditary succession.

Hume, John, *2H6,* priest who was charged with helping the duchess of Gloucester practice the black arts. Sh. has Henry VI send him to the gallows, but the chronicles of Hall (202) and Holinshed (3.623) record his pardon.

Humphrey, duke of Gloucester, (1391–1447), fourth son of King Henry IV of England. His brother, Henry V, made him duke of Gloucester in 1414 and reportedly saved his life when they fought at Agincourt the following year. Gloucester took part in the early phases of Henry's campaign for the conquest of France, but in 1420 he was sent home to England to serve as Henry's regent. Henry probably wanted him to retain that office during the minority of Henry's heir, Henry VI, but influential barons did not trust Gloucester and forced him to accept the less powerful post of royal protector. Gloucester did not inspire confidence. He quarreled with his colleagues in domestic government and pursued private projects that were at odds with England's foreign policy. Two years after Henry V's death Gloucester invaded the county of Hainaut, which he claimed by right of his wife, Jacqueline of Bavaria. Philip the Good of Burgundy, England's most important ally in its war with France, also laid claim to Hainaut. When Philip routed Gloucester's men, Gloucester abandoned Jacqueline. His marriage was quickly annulled, and he created a scandal by wedding his mistress, Eleanor Cobham. The defeat of his foreign ambitions prompted him to seek a larger role in the government of England, but here he was frustrated by his uncle, Bishop Beaufort.

Gloucester tried to make up for his lack of support among the barons by courting a popular following. On one occasion he went so far as to raise the city of London against the royal council. Gloucester continued to be a disruptive influence even after Henry VI achieved his majority and commenced personal rule. In 1435 Charles VII detached Burgundy from its alliance with England, and Henry decided that the time had come to end the Hundred Years' War. The truce with France and the royal marriage with Margaret of Anjou that were part of it were both unpopular with the masses. By condemning Henry's policy and pushing for renewed hostilities with France, Gloucester exploited the people's nationalistic passions for his own advantage. Henry VI resented criticism by his uncle, and in 1447 he ordered Gloucester arrested on suspicion of treason. Gloucester died four days after his confinement. In politics he had done little more than cause trouble, but his other endeavors were more constructive. Gloucester was England's leading patron of scholars and the most ardent book collector of his generation. His huge library was entrusted to Oxford University, and the Italian authors it contained may have provided many English scholars with their first experience of the Renaissance. *2H6. 1H6. 2H4.*

Humphrey, earl of Stafford and duke of Buckingham, *2H6,* (1402–1460), grandson of Edward III's youngest surviving son, Thomas of Woodstock, and owner of one of the largest estates in England. He served in France under Henry V, who knighted him in 1421, and he sat on the council that governed England during the minority of Henry V's son, Henry VI. He was constable for England's French territories in 1430 and captain of Calais in 1442. Buckingham took a prominent part in the political maneuvers that resulted in the arrest of Henry VI's uncle, Humphrey, duke of Gloucester. He tried in vain to head off Cade's rebellion by negotiating with the rebels. And although he supported Henry and Queen Margaret in their struggle against Richard of York, he tried to keep communications open between the two camps. When compromise failed, he stood by the Lancastrians. He was wounded at St. Albans and killed defending Henry at the battle of Northampton.

Humphrey Hewer, *R3 4.4.176,* 'the Humphrey Hour,' possibly a reference to a custom that developed in connection with a tomb in London's cathedral of St. Paul. Paul's was a place where the people of London gathered to do business as well as to worship. Unemployed servants walked its aisles seeking jobs. Lawyers and their clients staked out places for conferences within its bays. And gentlemen who were down on their luck could stand by 'Duke Humphrey's' tomb to signal their hope of being invited somewhere for dinner. The grave actually held the remains of a Sir John Beauchamp (d. 1358), and it is not clear how it came to be associated with 'Duke Humphrey.'

Hundred Merry Tales, The, *Ado 2.1.120,* book of coarse stories, *A C. Mery Talys,* first published in 1526 and still popular in Sh.'s time. There is a tradition that Queen Elizabeth was entertained by it on her deathbed. Beatrice is insulted that Benedick claims she got her wit from the Renaissance equivalent of *1001 Dirty Jokes.*

Hundredth Psalm, *MWW 2.1.60,* F1 'hundred Psalms.' Wells and Taylor edit F1 to 'hundred and fifty psalms' since Sh. certainly knew how many Psalms there were. Many others, however, prefer the reading that the metrical version of Psalm 100, which was well known, was intended to be incongruously linked to the popular tune 'Greensleeves' (q.v.). This metrical version of Psalm 100 begins, 'All people that on earth do dwell,/Sing to the Lord with cheerful voice.'

Hungarian, (adj.), *MWW 1.3.19,* 'base H. wight.' Here the word is probably punning on 'hungry,' and may also be mocking a line from another play or poem.

Hungary, country east of Austria in central Europe. The region had been a Roman province then passed through the hands of Germanic tribes, the Huns, the Avars, the Moravians and the Franks. In the late 9th c., the Magyars took control and after a century became Christian. They were a powerful nation for many centuries, but after the Mongol invasion of the early 13th c., the Magyar kingdom was weakened and subject to much foreign interference. In the 15th c. when an Angevin dynasty was in place, Turkish invasions threatened the existence of the country. János Hunyadi's brilliant military skill saved it and subsequently his son, Matthias Corvinus, was elected king (1458). He gained control of Hapsburg Austria as well. After his death there was a severe decline. In 1526, after inflicting several defeats on the disorganized Hungarians, Sultan Suleiman I inflicted a severe defeat on the army at Mohács and for a century and a half Hungary was squabbled over by the Turks, the Hapsburgs, and its local lords. The Magyars joined the Protestant cause, provoking the Hapsburgs even more. This was the situation in Sh.'s day and a duke of Austria placing demands on the king would have been common. By the end of the 17th c. the crown of Hungary was a hereditary possession of the Hapsburgs and the country would not regain independence until after World War I. The name of the country derives from the Old Russian name for the people, *Ungari* or *Ugri,* which seems to have a Turkic origin.

MM 1.2.2, 5: Lucio and the gentlemen gossip about some disagreement between the Duke of Vienna and the king. It seems to be merely a rumor begun by the duke's leaving. Possibly there is a pun on 'hunger.' Hungary was the setting of George Whetstone's *Promos and Cassandra* (1578), which was one of Sh.'s sources for *MM.*

Hungerford, town on the border between the English counties of Berkshire and Wiltshire about 60 mi. west of London. See Hungerford, Heir of Lord, *3H6*; Lord *1H6, 3H6.*

Hungerford, Lord, Robert Hungerford (1431–1464), third Baron Hungerford and Baron Moleyns by right of his wife, heiress to Sir William Moleyns. Hungerford accompanied John Talbot to Aquitaine in 1452 and was captured while trying to raise the siege of Castillon. Henry VI first summoned him to parliament, and he remained a staunch supporter of the Lancastrian cause to the end. In 1461 he joined Henry and Margaret on their flight to Scotland, and he accompanied Margaret on the continent while she sued for help. From his bases in Scotland Hungerford tried to raise northern England against Edward IV. The Yorkists captured him at Hexham on 15 May 1464, and promptly executed him at Newcastle. His son, Thomas, who participated in Warwick's conspiracy to restore Henry VI to the throne, was executed in 1469.

1H6 1.1.146. 3H6 4.1.48, 'heir of Lord H.,' Mary, only child of Sir Thomas Hungerford (d. 1469). Her father was executed by Edward IV for his part in Warwick's uprising. Sh. mistakenly believed that she was married by her guardian, Lord Hastings. In reality, she married Hastings' son, Edward, the second Lord Hastings.

Huntingdon, 1) *H5 5.2.85,* seat of the county of Huntingdonshire, situated about 58 mi. north of London.

2) *H5 5.2.85,* John Holland (1395–1447), second son of the earl of Exeter who was executed in 1400 for his role in the 'earls' conspiracy,' a plot to overthrow Henry IV before he became firmly established on the throne. Huntingdon's loyal service to the Lancastrian dynasty wiped out the memory of his father's treason and earned him the restoration of his family's estates and titles. He joined the first expedition Henry V led against France, and he took part in the campaigns that culminated in Henry's triumphant entry into Paris in 1420. In 1421 he

fell into the hands of the Orléanists (or Armagnacs) and remained in captivity in France for four years. During his ordeal Henry V died, but Huntingdon was not forgotten. After his release, he was assigned a prominent position at the court of the young Henry VI. He was one of the men commissioned in 1435 to negotiate a treaty of peace between England and France.

Hunts-up, *Rom 3.5.34,* allusion to a song played in the early morning to awaken and gather the hunters, or to any morning song. It may allude to a specific tune entitled 'The Hunt's Up.' One such tune was said to be a favorite of Henry VIII's.

Hybla, town 10 mi. north of the Sicilian city of Syracuse. The ancient Romans praised the quality of its honey. *1H4 1.2.41. JC 5.1.34.*

Hydra, monster destroyed by the Greek hero Hercules. The hydra was a beast with nine heads that roamed the countryside near the city of Argos. Eurystheus of Tiryns, whom the gods had ordered Hercules to obey, set the strongman the task of destroying the hydra. This proved more difficult than expected, for each time he knocked off one of the monster's heads, it grew two new ones. He finally prevailed by singeing the stumps as he performed each decapitation. *1H4 5.4.24. 2H4 4.1.264. H5 1.1.36. Cor 3.1.96. Oth 2.3.297.*

Hymen, god of the marriage ceremony or wedding feast, attendant of Aphrodite, son of Aphrodite and Dionysus, or of Urania and either Apollo or Dionysus. Some versions say that he was a mortal who was killed in a tragic accident on his wedding day. Some recount tales of adventure in which he earns a bride by rescuing a group of maidens from kidnappers. His name is linked with the 'hymeneal,' a hymn Greeks and Romans sang at weddings.

AYLI 5.4: Hymen appears in a masque-like scene as a *deus ex machina* to sort out the lovers. *Ado 5.3.32. Ham 3.2.152. Tim 4.3.386,* 'H.'s purest bed,' marriage.

Tmp 4.1.23, 'H.'s lamps,' *97,* 'H.'s torch,': if the flame of H.'s torch burned clear, the marriage was predicted to be a happy one. If the flame was smoky, the opposite. The plural of lamp could be an error. *TNK 1.1 sd,* H. enters with a burning torch, but does not speak.

Hymenæus, *Tit 1.1.322,* L. 'Hymen' (q.v.).

Hyperion, Helios, the sun god. Actually Hyperion was father of the sun god, a Titan born of Uranus and Gæa, husband of Thea, and also father of Selene (the moon), and Eos (the dawn; Roman: Aurora). The name means 'the one on high.' As with 'Titan,' however, Sh. uses Hyperion only to refer to the sun, not the Titan who fathered it. Using Hyperion as a patronymic was also done in classical literature.

Tit 5.2.56. H5 4.1.272. Tro 2.3.195. Ham 3.4.55, 'H.'s curls,' the comparison to the sun seems to imply blondeness. *Tim 4.3.185,* 'H.'s quik'ning fire,' the sun's life-giving warmth.

Hyrcan tiger, *Mac 3.4.100,* a wild beast, see Hyrcania.

Hyrcania, remote country southeast of the Caspian sea, bounded by the Oxus river (modern Amu Darya) on the east. The area is now mostly in Turkestan (the former Soviet Union) and northern Iran. The ancient geographer Strabo describes it as fertile, covered with oak forests, and boasting notable cities. Xenophon mentions its conquest by the Assyrians. For generations the ancient Greeks assumed that the Caucasus mountains, which extend from the Black to the Caspian seas, marked the eastern perimeter of the habitable world. Because of their location they were reputed to be earth's wildest, most inhospitable region. *3H6 1.4.156,* 'tigers of H.' is drawn from Virgil's *Æneid* (4.367), where Dido curses Æneas for abandoning her. Dido claims that Æneas' hardness of heart is inhuman and appropriate only to a creature spawned on the rocks of the Caucasus and nurtured by the ferocious tigers of that harsh land. When York hears of the death of his young son, the earl of Rutland, he curses Lord Clifford, the boy's murderer, as ten times more ruthless than Æneas.

Hyrcanian, (adj.), of Hyrcania. *MV 2.7.41,* 'H. deserts,' desert implies only wilderness, not aridness. *Ham 2.2.453,* 'H. beast,' tiger.

I

Iachimo, *Cym,* see Giacomo.

Iago, *Oth,* husband of Emilia, the manipulative villain who leads Othello to the murder of Desdemona. He is one of Sh.'s most fascinating characters, clearly a literary cousin of Richard III, who is generally seen by the people around him as good and honest, but who leads people to their doom because of their own weaknesses. Only his wife seems to see him clearly although she does not recognize his plot until it is too late. His evil seems motiveless to many critics, although there is a clear susceptibility to envy in him when Cassio is promoted and there is an elusive line (*2.3.298*) which suggests he thinks Othello has slept with his wife. If this is intended, it is underdeveloped. In Sh.'s time, audiences may not have been as concerned with motive as much as they are now. That he was disposed to evil might be sufficient, especially in a context deriving from medieval drama when a devil or Vice went after a soul. His relish in doing evil certainly makes him comparable to Vice. His gulling of Roderigo has a comic quality which allows Iago to become almost likable, in a manner similar to Richard. Cassio says that Iago is more kind and honest than any of his Florentine countrymen (*3.1.39*), even as Iago is engineering his ruin (a possible other reading is that Iago is a Florentine, but this is very unlikely). Iago is Spanish for 'James,' and the name may have been chosen to evoke the patron saint of Spain, England's enemy. It may just as easily have been chosen for its Mediterranean sound, as Sh. was not particular about the differences among Romance languages. The equivalent character is called 'The Ensign' but is otherwise unnamed in Sh.'s source, Giraldi Cinthio's *Hecatommithi* (1566).

Icarus, son of Dædalus, mythical Greek architect who built the labyrinth that imprisoned the Minotaur. He and his father fled Crete on wings that Dædalus made from feathers and wax. Icarus was so intoxicated by the experience of flight that he forgot his father's instructions and soared too near the sun. His wings melted, and he plunged to his death in the sea (Ovid, *Metamorphoses,* 8.183–235). *3H6 5.6.21. 1H6 4.6.55, 4.7.16.*

Iceland, *H5 2.1.39, 2.1.40,* island between Norway and Greenland on the edge of the Arctic circle. It may have been settled by Irish monks in the 8th c. AD; however, the great influx of population began c. 870 with Vikings from Britain and Scandinavia. The Danes, who ruled the island from 1380, gradually limited trading with England, and in 1602 established a monopoly. In Sh.'s day Iceland exported a breed of dogs that was popular in England.

Iden, Alexander, *2H6,* (fl. 1450), the man who tracked down the Jack Cade who raised a rebellion against Henry VI's government. Iden may have had a personal grievance against Cade. Iden became sheriff of Kent in succession to William Cromer, whose widow he married. Cromer was one of the royal officials Cade murdered. Cade's revolt ended when the rebels agreed to disperse in exchange for a royal pardon. Cade subsequently discovered that the general amnesty did not apply to him. The king's justices declared that the pardon issued Cade was invalid, for it was registered in the name of 'John Mortimer,' an alias under which Cade had fought. Cade tried to escape into the forests of Sussex, but Iden cornered him at Heathfield. Cade was mortally wounded resisting arrest.

Ides, see March.

Ilion, Gr. 'Ilium' (q.v), the city of Troy (q.v.) *Luc 1370, 1524. LLL 5.2.646. Tro.*

Ilium, Ilion, the city of Troy. An oracle told Ilus, son of Dardanus, to found a city wherever a cow he had won at the Phrygian games lay down. It did so on a hill sacred to Ate. The city and the kingdom were later called Troy, though

Ilium was the city's name into classical times. *Tro. Ham 2.2.477.*

Illyria, region roughly encompassing modern Dalmatia, Bosnia, and Croatia. After settlements by Indo-European tribes in the 14th c. BC, the Greeks established colonies along the coast beginning in the 7th c., but the Illyrians maintained their independence. The Greeks regarded them as barbarous people who tattooed their bodies and made human sacrifices. They were always a threat to the Greeks, particularly in Macedonia. About 383 BC they united under Bardylis and inflicted major defeats on Macedonia. By the end of the century, however, Philip the Great had crushed them and appropriated part of their country. The Illyrian royal family allied itself with the rising power of Macedon, shared in the glory of Alexander the Great's conquests, and played a major role in the wars that raged among Alexander's heirs. In the 3rd c. the last Illyrian kingdom was ruled from what is now Shkodër, Albania. Pirates from the kingdom were always harrying Adriatic shipping and the Greeks requested Roman assistance. After the queen of the Illyrians murdered the Roman ambassadors, the Romans made successful war against them in 228 and 219 BC. After the Dalmatians split the kingdom, the last Illyrian king surrendered his capital to Rome in 168 BC. By the 1st c. all of the kingdom was a Roman possession, which Rome split into the provinces of Pannonia and Dalmatia.

Although the locals caused Rome much trouble until Tiberius finally ended all rebellion in 9 AD, the area prospered under Roman rule and several of the later emperors were natives of Dalmatia. Extensive Roman ruins still decorate the coast, especially in the modern town of Split. Several ethnic invasions swept through the area including the Huns, Ostrogoths, and Avars. After the fall of the western Roman empire, Illyria was absorbed into the Byzantine Empire. Slavic peoples (the Serbo-Croatians) absorbed most of what was left of the Illyrians beginning in the 7th c., although islands of Latinized populations (the Vlachs) and some of the mountain tribes which had never been absorbed in Albania maintained their independence. Most of the area was later seized by the Ottomans. In Sh.'s day, Dalmatia was in the hands of Venice, while most of the interior of what had been Illyricum remained subject of the Turks.

TN: Sh.'s Illyria is a fantasy land, much like his Arden or Prospero's Island. He uses Italian names for most of the characters, and yet the names of inns and lowlifes like Sir Toby, are distinctly English. Because of the Italian aspect of the play, however, it has often been presented with Venetian costumes and settings to simulate a Dalmatian dukedom. *2H6 4.1.108.*

Imogen, *Cym,* see Innogen.

Ind, India, but in a general sense which includes the subcontinent itself and all the Indies, possibly even east and west. *LLL 4.3.220,* 'man of Ind,' a disrespectful savage. *AYLI 3.2.86,* 'western I.,' the furthest extremity of the west. Ind is a parody of overrhyming here. *Tmp 2.2.58,* 'men of I.,' this phrase occurred in Miles Coverdale's translation of Jeremiah 13.23, which refers to dark skin. The King James translation gives us 'Ethiopian' for the phrase.

India, the Asian subcontinent. Although Indian trade goods had been available in Europe since the days of the Roman empire, Sh. and his contemporaries had little accurate information about the East. Their 'India' was a land of fantasy, a place of exotic spices, miraculous occurances, and fabulous jewels—such as the 'Indian stone' that might adorn a royal crown (*3H6 3.1.63*). *MND 2.1.69,* Oberon's normal habitation seems to be India.

MV 3.2.267. 1H4 3.1.165. TN 2.5.13, 'my metal of I.': 'my rare, precious thing,' 'my gold.' *Tro 1.1.100, 1.2.71. H8 1.1.21.*

Indian, 1) (n.) native inhabitant of America. *AWW 1.3.200,* 'I.-like,' like a heathen. *H8 5.3.32:* Sh.'s allusion to the Indian's 'great tool' is the kind of racist humor that lies behind modern bawdy stories about the size of the sexual organs of non-Caucasians. *Oth 5.2.356:* F1

'Iudean,' a reference to many stories of an Indian who threw away a precious jewel, not recognizing its worth. The alternative reading of F1, Judean, may refer to Judas (l.368 may carry the allusion further, to Judas' kiss, or may be only literal). It may also refer to Herod the Great who caused the death of his wife Mariamne in a jealous fit. *Tmp 2.2.33,* 'dead I.': a dead Indian was likely exhibited in London after Sir Martin Frobisher's expedition searching for the Northwest Passage in 1577. This particular unlucky native was later buried in Bristol. It is likely others were commonly shown, as various exotic mummies filled sideshows into the 20th c.

2) (adj.) of or pertaining to the subcontinent of India or to Asia. *MND 2.1.22,* 'I. king.' *2.1.124,* 'I. air.' *3.2.376,* 'I. boy,' the changeling over which Oberon and Titania argue. *MV 3.2.99,* 'I. beauty,' the meaning is obscure. Bassanio's preceding words seem to imply a contrast in which, one would expect, the 'beauteous scarf' to conceal something not beautiful. Either Indian is negative here—an 'I. beauty' being anything but beautiful—or the passage was printed wrongly. It sounds most like a Sh. figure of speech to interpret Indian as pejorative here and the various substitutions for 'beauty' suggested by scholars are, at best, unconvincing. Perhaps the intention is 'heathen beauty.'

Indies, islands of the Caribbean or the islands of south Asia, both fabled to be rich lands, the names deriving from the initial confusion by the early Renaissance explorers of the western hemisphere with the eastern. *Err 3.2.136,* the West Indies, here equated to America, a location on the 'globe' that is Nell, her face speckled with pimples as the Caribbean is with islands. There is a possible topical allusion in that a carrack (merchant vessel) was captured in September 1592 with such a large cargo that the pepper on board wreaked havoc on the market in that commodity for some time. *MV 1.3.18. TN 3.2.75,* 'the new map with the augmentation of the I.': this passage is usually thought to date the play to Edward Wright's map of 1598–1600, which was the first English map employing the Mercator projection and was published in an edition of Hakluyt's *Voyages.* It says a great deal about the time that the publication of a map detailing the Indies was a subject of public discussion, just as the photographs of Jupiter's moons caused so much excitement in our time: it was a brave new world they were discovering.

Iniquity, *1H4 2.5.459,* Prince Harry's characterization of the aged Oldcastle: 'grey Iniquity.' The Prince's point is that Oldcastle has none of the virtuous character and wisdom appropriate to a dignified elder.

Innocent III, *Jn 3.1.65, 72,* (1198–1216), most powerful of the medieval popes. Innocent was destined by talent and family connections to have a brilliant career in the church. After he took doctorates in theology and canon law at the universities of Paris and Bologna, his uncle, Pope Clement III, made him a cardinal. At the unusually young age of 38 he ascended the papal throne and launched a program for the political reorganization of Europe and the reinvigoration of its Christian culture. He centralized the government of the church and subjected the clergy to effective papal control. His legislation (particularly the decrees of the IV Lateran Council) redefined the practice of Christianity and set the church on a path that remained unchanged until the 16th c. and the Council of Trent. His dream was to bring the same order to the state that he established within the church. To that end, he tried to persuade the kings of Europe to recognize him as their feudal overlord. His intention was not to dominate them, but to acquire the right to mediate their disputes. Since all the nations of Europe were Christian, he hoped to promote peace among them by bringing them together on the common ground of their church. Innocent could not compel kings to become his vassals, but by making ingenious use of difficulties into which kings got themselves he maneuvered some of them into recognizing the authority of the papacy. He won his most famous victory in a fight with John of England, for no king of

Innocent's generation rendered himself more vulnerable than John.

In 1205 an archbishop of Canterbury died, and a dispute erupted over the choice of his successor. Innocent proposed a compromise, but John refused to negotiate. For five years the king and the pope squabbled. He closed the churches of England, excommunicated John, and, ultimately, invited Philip Augustus of France to invade England and depose its obdurate king. John ignored the pressure Innocent brought to bear on him until 1213, when the pursuit of important political and military objectives persuaded John that it was in his interest to make peace with the church. John permitted the enthronement of Innocent's archbishop and took an oath of vassalage to the papacy. John was the most significant European ruler to take this step, but his capitulation was an astute political maneuver, not an admission of weakness. John transformed the church from an enemy into an ally and used it to defend the prerogatives of his crown. When John's mismanagement of England's affairs pushed his barons to the brink of revolution, they met him at Runnymede and forced him to agree to rule in accordance with principles they set forth in a document called Magna Carta. Magna Carta scandalized Innocent who believed that ordinary people had no right to dictate terms to the rulers God set over them. He, therefore, released John from his oath to uphold Magna Carta and supported the king in war with his barons. Technically, John submitted to him and became his vassal, but the relationship was more profitable to the king than to his overlord. Innocent's support for an unpopular monarch and his advocacy of an absolutist theory of royal government that was at odds with English tradition won the papacy few friends in Britain.

Innogen, 1) *Ado,* wife of Leonato. Mentioned in the opening stage direction in F1, Innogen neither speaks, nor plays an active part in the plot. Editors usually drop the character. This mention of her, however, is another example of the confusion in the names in the text of the play from which F1 was set. Hero's mother is frequently mentioned in Sh.'s primary source, Matteo Bandello's *Novelle* (1554), so possibly he intended to have her in his play, but abandoned the idea.

2) *Cym,* daughter of Cymbeline, wife of Posthumus. The victim of several plots against her purity and her life, she manages by the use of disguise to survive all assaults until the flood of reconciliations that closes the play. Although she has been highly praised by various commentators in the past, her character, as difficult as the general thrust of the play, is perplexing. At times she seems to be moving in the path of Rosalind (*AYLI*), taking control of her destiny. At other times she is a feather in a hurricane of fate. She escapes murder because Pisanio takes pity on her and because the physician Cornelius distrusts the Queen, not because of any knowledge or action on her part. This pull between the kind of passive spiritual purity which protects Marina (*Per*) and the pluck which protects Rosalind seems to indicate an unclear perception of her by Sh. The traditional spelling of 'Imogen' is thought to be a misreading by the compositors of F1, who thought the two n's were an m. Simon Forman, an astrologer and contemporary of Sh., describes the play in his diary and calls her Innogen. Innogen is also the wife of Leonato in *Ado,* although she only appears in a stage direction. Furthermore, in Holinshed's *Chronicles,* 'Innogen' is the wife of Brute, king of Britain ('Ignogen' in Layamon's *Brute*). Imogen is therefore without precedent and was either invented by Sh. or a printer's mistake. The story of Posthumus' wager on Innogen's chastity is from Boccaccio's *Decameron* (2.9), though the wife is Lady Ginevra and assumes a disguise as Sicurano da Finale.

Inns of Court, London schools for the training of lawyers. By the 14th c. the law in England had evolved to the point where persons involved in litigation needed professional advice. Medieval lawyers, like the practitioners of many other trades, trained by watching masters of their craft at work. The king's judges were in session four times each year. Since they used the halls at Westminster that also sheltered parliaments, men who aspired to careers in the law came to Westminster to observe the conduct of those who sat on the royal bench. The London inns where the judges and their students lodged evolved into institutions analogous to the colleges of medieval universities. The inns of court supervised students, acquired the right to license lawyers, and housed practicing attorneys. The earliest of these establishments was either Lincoln's Inn (c. 1350) or the Temple. By the 15th c. analogous institutions were functioning at Gray's, St. George's, Thavie's, Barnard's, Staple, Furnival, and Clifford's inns.

2H6 4.7.2. 2H4 3.2.12, 3.2.21.

Inverness, *Mac 1.4.42,* town and county in northwest Scotland, site of Macbeth's castle in Sh., where he murders Duncan. The town lies on the Ness river and Moray Firth about 100 mi. north of Perth. Its name means 'mouth of the Ness' in Gaelic. In a strategic location, it was an early fortress for the Picts. St. Columba visited it in 565 in an attempt to convert king Brude. According to tradition Macbeth's castle was destroyed by Malcolm, who built a new stronghold about a half mile to the southwest. This castle was added to but in 1746 it was blown up by the Jacobites. It is possible that the area of Inverness is meant here rather than the town and that the King intends to go to Cawdor, which is quite near Inverness. Where Sh. has Duncan killed is not very important, as the real Duncan fell in battle.

Ionia, *Ant 1.2.96,* ancient name for the western coast of Asia Minor. At the start of the classical era it was colonized by Greeks speaking the Ionian dialect.

Ionian Sea, *Ant 3.7.22,* portion of the Mediterranean between Greece and Italy south of the entrance to the Adriatic. Its sea lanes linked the Greek (Ionian) and Latin worlds.

Iovem, *Tit 4.3.54,* L. 'Jove,' objective case.

Ipswich, *H8 1.1.138, 4.2.59,* port city that is the seat of the English county of Suffolk. It is on the channel coast 70 mi. northeast of London. The name derives from the river Gipping which joins the Orwell there. Cardinal Wolsey was born at Ipswich, and he tried to found a college there as a memorial to himself. The project failed, for Henry VIII closed the school and confiscated its endowments shortly after Wolsey's fall from royal favor.

Iras, *Ant,* one of Cleopatra's maids. Plutarch ('Antony' 60.1) says that Octavius tried to convince the Roman people that Mark Antony was so bewitched by Cleopatra that he allowed her eunuchs and maids to govern for him. Plutarch also says (85.3) that Iras and Charmion were the only witnesses to Cleopatra's suicide and that they elected to die with their queen.

Ireland, the large island to the west of England, Wales, and Scotland. Its native cultures and languages were those of the Celtic peoples that settled it in the 4th c. BC. The Romans, who conquered Britain, never ventured into Ireland, but in the 5th c., the British missionary, Patrick, brought Roman learning and Christian faith to the Irish. His work had more ramifications than he could have imagined. Safe on the periphery of the known world, Ireland was spared the worst consequences of the fall of the Roman empire. The migrating Germanic tribes that fatally undermined the institutions of civilization in Britain and on the continent did not settle in Ireland. As a consequence, classical culture degenerated everywhere but there, and by default it sustained the best schools and libraries in the west. When the worst of the upheavals of the Dark Ages subsided, Irish missionaries began to restore Christian culture to Anglo-Saxon England and Merovingian Europe. The Roman popes sponsored similar projects, but they were not comfortable with the Irish as allies. During the years when the two centers of western Christianity had been cut off from each other, Irish and Roman Catholics had evolved different customs. Disagreements about the dates of religious festivals and appropriate systems for the exercise of ecclesiastical authority caused conflicts and confusion in the mission field. In the 7th c. the Irish lost interest in the fight and turned their backs on the outside world.

They were not permitted the luxury of uncontested isolationism. During the 9th and 10th centuries Viking raiders made strenuous efforts to establish toeholds, and in 1155 Pope Adrian IV gave the English king, Henry II, title to Ireland—on condition that he force the Irish to conform to Roman religious practices. Henry left the work of fighting the Irish to fortune-hunting Norman entrepreneurs, but in 1171 he visited Ireland to validate their conquests and accept the submission of Irish chieftains. A district known as the English 'pale' evolved around Dublin, but most of the island eluded England's grasp. Native clan organizations successfully resisted efforts by Anglo-Norman lords to seize new lands, and English immigrants showed, in the opinion of their home government, an alarming tendency to acculturation. In the early 14th c. a massive revolt nearly forced the English out, and Edward III was left with little more than nominal sovereignty over the eastern counties. In 1394 Richard II bolstered the English cause by visiting the island in person, but the agreements he negotiated with the native chiefs were violated after his departure. He was compelled to return in 1399 to patch things up. Richard's soldiers had little success against the Irish guerrilla fighters, and Richard himself was soon called away to more urgent business. In the summer of 1399 Richard's cousin, Henry of Lancaster, sparked a rebellion that forced Richard from the throne.

The Lancastrian kings, who succeeded Richard, were far too busy with projects at home and in France to pay much attention to Ireland. Their habit of benign neglect dispelled even the illusion of central government. The fragmented political situation grew increasingly chaotic, but the Hundred Years' War and the ensuing War of the Roses prevented the English authorities from intervening. When at the end of the 15th c. the long fight over the English throne ended with the establishment of the Tudor dynasty, the English were finally free to turn back their attention. Henry VII restored royal authority in the 'pale,' and by 1541 Henry VIII had maneuvered the Irish into recognizing him as nominal king over the whole land. Henry's pretensions to reign far exceeded his power to rule. The English authorities believed that their control depended on their success in abolishing Celtic tribal institutions and imposing England's quasi-feudal system of land tenure. The Irish resisted this attack on their culture and fought both for their political independence and their identity as a people. In the past the initiative in the struggle had been with the English, for England had always been able safely to ignore Ireland when more interesting projects developed elsewhere. Henry VIII's break with the Roman church changed that. In Ireland, as on the continent, the Reformation blended issues of nationalism, patriotism, and faith. The Irish expressed their determination to fend off English influences by clinging to Catholicism, and religion gave the Irish a strong hand to play in international politics. Catholic Spain was eager to help Ireland defend itself.

An alliance was a serious threat to England, for it would have permitted Spain to sandwich England between Ireland and bases Spain already operated in the Netherlands. England's security depended on the Tudor monarchs' discovery of a quick solution to the Irish problem. Neither Edward VI nor Mary made any progress, and it fell to Sh.'s queen, Elizabeth I, to resolve the situation. Fortunately for Elizabeth, the confusion that reigned among the Irish made it difficult for the Spaniards to assist their allies. Spanish resources either failed to reach Ireland or were misappropriated. In 1588 the defeat of Philip II's great armada was a further, but not fatal, setback for an Iberian-Hibernian alliance. The turning point came in 1594 when the Irish at last found a leader for their war for independence. The earl of Tyrone, whose center of operations was the northern province of Ulster, organized a major uprising, and Spain prepared a fleet to go to his aid. A daring raid on Cadiz by the earl of Essex destroyed many of the Spanish ships in their home port, but in 1598 Tyrone slaughtered an English army. His success disheartened the English and rallied the Irish. Spain prepared yet another fleet to bring Tyrone reinforcements, but foul weather prevented its landing. Although Elizabeth was appalled at estimates of the cost, she finally commissioned an army to subdue Tyrone. The earl of Essex was appointed its commander.

Essex had been Elizabeth's favorite, but her relationship with him had cooled and scholars debate whether Essex sought the assignment or had the risky post thrust on him by his political enemies. At the start of the venture he was the hero on whom the hopes of a nation were pinned. The imminence of war stirred deep patriotic emotions in England and inspired the moving speeches on the themes of glory and honor for which *H5* is famous. Essex was unable to live up to the exaggerated expectations of his people and his queen. He led his men on timid forays that trained them in fighting on the Irish terrain, but he avoided an assault on Tyrone's stronghold. Ultimately he and Tyrone patched up a truce, and Essex went back to England. Elizabeth was furious with him and ordered his confinement. In February 1600 Charles Blount, Lord Mountjoy, was sent to Ireland to continue the fight against Tyrone. Blount contained Tyrone in Ulster, but the assault he planned on the rebel's territory was delayed when he learned that the Spaniards had finally succeeded in landing an army. Mountjoy skillfully organized a blockade to isolate the Spanish troops in their port of entry. He prevented Tyrone from linking with his allies, and on 23 December 1601 he launched a surprise attack that routed the Irish. The Spanish gave up and sued for terms. A year later Tyrone surrendered, and Ireland submitted to English rule.

Err 3.2.19, a reference to the local moisture or to the foul odors of the bogs. *2H6. 3H6 4.8.72. R3 4.2.108. R2.. Jn 1.1.11, 2.1.152. H5 3.7.52, 5.0.31, 5.2.237. Mac 2.3.137, 3.1.32:* to avoid Macbeth's murderous designs, Donalbain escapes to Ireland as Malcolm escapes to England, making the royal line safer by separation. *H8 2.1.43, 3.2.261.*

Iris, messenger of Juno and goddess of the rainbow, daughter of Thaumas and Electra (daughter of Oceanus). She is the messenger commonly employed by the Olympian gods in the *Iliad.* (In the *Odyssey* her function is performed by Mercury.) Iris also spread rumors and panics among the forces assembled for the Trojan war. She usually sided with Zeus's wife (Hera) in the political squabbles of the gods. Because she moved back and forth between heaven and earth, poets associated her with the rainbow, the bridge that links the two realms. Her most prominent place in mythology is in summoning Somnus to give a dream to Alcyone (Ovid's *Metamorphoses,* 11) and Helen to the battlements of Troy (*Iliad*). In Ovid, she also draws water up to the clouds for the Great Flood and summons Hersilie to join her husband Romulus as an immortal.

2H6 3.2.411. Tro 1.3.373, 'blue I.,' likely a rainbow even though it is many colors. It is thought possible this might refer to the flower (family *Iridaceæ*), although critics argue that Sh. elsewhere calls it the 'flower-de-luce' (*fleur de lis*), which referred to a white blossom (*Iris germanica*) or the yellow blossom (*I. pseudacorus*) favored in French heraldry. 'Blue I.' might therefore have been intended to be another flower than the 'flower-de-luce.' *AWW 1.3.148,* 'many-coloured I.' *Tmp 4.1,* Iris begins the masque and acts as master of ceremonies. *TNK 4.1.87.*

Irish, 1) (n.), *1H4 3.1.232,* native speech of Ireland: the only living language representing the Goidelic branch of the ancient Celtic tongue. The earliest specimens of Irish are 300 short inscriptions preserved from the 4th and 5th centuries. The modern form of the language evolved about 1200. Although English has long predominated in Ireland, Irish has survived as a vehicle for a large and growing body of literature.

2) (adj.) of or pertaining to Ireland and its people. *AYLI 3.2.173,* 'I. rat.' Rosalind is mocking Orlando's poems. According to myth Irish rats could be killed by rhyming. An allusion to this appears in Sidney's *Defense of*

Poesy (1595) and many other contemporaries. *5.2.105,* 'I. wolves.' The image may have been borrowed from Lodge's *Rosalynde* in which the howling of Syrian wolves is mentioned. Why Sh. particularly chose Irish wolves is unclear. Was there something peculiar about the howl of these now extinct animals or is it merely a reference to a wild country? It seems possible given these two Irish references in the play that Ireland was on his mind for some reason—possibly because he was reading the manuscript of Edmund Spenser's *Veue of the Present State of Ireland* (written 1595–7, but not published until 1633).

Irishman, native of Ireland. 1) *MWW 2.2.292,* the old stereotype: an Irishman can't be trusted with liquor.

2)*H5 3.3.11,* see MacMorris, Captain.

Isabel, 1) *H5,* Elizabeth of Bavaria (1370–1435), daughter of Stephen II of Bavaria and, after her marriage to Charles VI in 1385, queen of France. Although the onset of Charles's mental illness in 1392 created an opportunity for Isabel to take an active part in the government of France, she was of little help to her husband or children. She sought distraction from the personal problems created by her husband's infirmity in dissolute amusements and flagrant luxuries, and she exacerbated quarrels among the king's relatives. For some time she sided with the Armagnac (Orléanist) faction, but when her life-style became an embarrassment to them and they tried to restrain her, she switched her allegiance to John the Fearless, duke of Burgundy. After Burgundy's murder by the Orléanists, she turned to the English for protection. In 1420 she agreed to the Treaty of Troyes which disinherited her son and recognized Henry V of England as heir to her husband's throne. She sealed the agreement by giving Henry the hand of her daughter, Catherine. By committing herself so completely to the English, Isabel burned her bridges with France—a step she ultimately had reason to regret. The deaths of Henry V and Charles VI in 1422 reversed the fortunes of war, and as the English retreated from the continent, Isabel was abandoned to a lonely old age in poverty.

2) *MM,* var. for Isabella, used familiarly.

Isabella, *MM,* 'Gentle I.,' a novice nun. When her brother Claudio is sentenced to death for licentiousness, Angelo offers to exchange her virginity for her brother's life. She is uncompromising, however, so uncompromising that many critics consider her as extreme in her own way as Angelo is in his. The duke arranges a 'bed trick' as in *AWW,* which saves her from the evil Angelo. Later she pleads mercy for Angelo, which emphasizes one of the play's themes, and then, curiously, Isabella is immediately willing to marry the duke. Sh. altered his source stories to create her. In Cinthio's *Hecatommithi* (1565), Isabella is Epitia, who yields to Juriste, who kills her brother nonetheless. She then demands justice of the Emperor. Juriste marries her and after she pleads for his life, they are happy ever after. In George Whetstone's *Promos and Cassandra* (1578), Isabella is Cassandra, and the story is essentially the same as Epitia's. In Whetstone's second version of the tale, his *Heptameron of Ciuill Discourses* (1582), she is narrator of her story.

Isbel, *AWW 1.3.18, 23, 3.2.12–14,* the clown Lavatch's woman. He intends to marry her merely to contain his lust and says he is quite indifferent to being cuckolded. Later at court he says he has lost interest in her altogether. This vague offstage subplot perhaps serves as a commentary on love and marriage which is based upon lust, an emotion which dissipates.

Iscariot, *LLL 5.2.592,* see Judas Iscariot.

Isidore, *Tim 2.1.1, 2.2,* one of Timon's creditors.

Isis, *Ant 1.2.58, 61, 63, 67, 3.3.15, 42, 3.6.17,* Egyptian goddess, wife of Osiris and mother of Horus. She and Osiris were ancient eastern fertility deities whose cults flourished during the Hellenistic era. The legend of Isis and Osiris symbolized nature's cycle by describing Osiris' death and resurrection. An enemy killed Osiris, dismembered his body, and scattered it (like seeds) over the earth. Isis recovered the pieces of her husband's corpse, reunited them, and revived him to become the king of the dead. Horus, Osiris' son by her, was incarnated in the persons of Egypt's pharaohs and given dominion over the world of the living. The cult of Isis and Osiris (Serapis) spread to Greece and thence to Rome. There was resistance to it from the Roman Senate, which was suspicious of many eastern things. Octavius forbade the construction of temples to the goddess within the city of Rome, but the prohibition quickly lapsed and Isis was granted a large temple on the Campus Martius.

Israel, *Ham 2.2.404,* the northern kingdom of the Jews, located in Palestine. The name seems to come from the Hebrew for 'he contended with God' which was a name given to Jacob as father of the Twelve Tribes after he wrestled with the angel. Some linguists have argued that it means either 'man friend of God,' or 'God rules.' Israel was distinct from the southern kingdom of Judah, in ancient times, but later came to be applied to the concept of Jewish nationality more than a place. In Sh.'s time, Palestine was under the rule of the Ottomans. The nation of Israel disappeared in 721 BC with the deportation of the northern Jews to Assyria by Sargon II.

Italian, 1) (n.) the language of Italy. *MV 1.2.67. Ham 3.2.251:* besides many of the choice tales of Renaissance England having come from Italy, this tale deals with poison, a supposed Italian specialty.

2) (n.) native of Italy. *AWW 4.1.73,* a speaker of Italian. *Cym 2.1.37, 2.1.48,* a visitor to court with whom Cloten gambles and loses; *3.2.4,* 'false I.'

3) (adj.) of or pertaining to the country of Italy and its people. *Shr 2.1.399,* 'I. fox,' a crafty old man like myself wouldn't be that stupid, says Gremio. *AWW 2.3.287. Cym 5.6.196,* 'mine I. brain': Italians were supposed crafty, deceptive, and skilled in the use of poisons. *5.1.18, 23, 5.6.210.*

Italy, nation occupying the peninsula of the European continent that extends south from the Alps into the center of the Mediterranean. The ancient Romans thought of Italy proper as the territory south of the Po valley cradled by the Apennine mountain chain. The Apennines run down the peninsula's eastern side, and Italy's primary agricultural plains and ports are on its western coast. Three different civilizations shared it at the start of its recorded history. The northern district, later known as Tuscany, was home to the Etruscans, a people of uncertain origin and mysterious language. In the 8th c. BC Greeks colonized the southern coast and the plain of Campania (the area around Naples). Between the lands settled by the Etruscans and the Greeks lay Latium, a small territory whose northern frontier was the Tiber river. The Latins were a primitive people when the Greeks settled, and the people of Latium acquired civilization through trade contacts with their more advanced neighbors to the north and south. The growing importance of Italy's inland trade routes in the 8th c. led the Latins to found Rome. The city commanded a crucial ford on the Tiber, and its location astride Italy's lines of communication meant that the Romans were frequently called upon to defend themselves from attack. From the 5th to the 2nd centuries BC Rome was involved in virtually continuous warfare with a succession of enemies. By the time of the birth of Christ, however, Rome's struggle for self-preservation had won it hegemony over most of the Mediterranean.

In the early Christian era Rome evolved imperial institutions that brought order and stability to the whole of the ancient world. Rome spread Hellenistic civilization throughout its empire, and it pacified and educated the primitive peoples of northern Europe. In the 5th c. a host of economic and political problems sapped Rome's ability to deal with the responsibilities of world government, and large numbers of German migrants flooded across its Rhine and Danube frontiers. Roman civilization declined as Rome struggled to assimilate the newcomers, and the empire's central government faded as German kings carved tribal domains from its territory. After the invasion of the Huns in the mid-5th c. sapped the last of the strength of the western Roman empire, the Lombards occupied Italy. In the 8th c. their regime was overthrown by Charlemagne, heir to a kingdom of the Franks that was based in Roman Gaul. When Charlemagne's successors split up his empire, Italy emerged again as a distinct political entity, but it did not rebuild a centralized government like the one it had enjoyed in the Roman period. As in the rest of feudal Europe, independent local governments replaced nation states. This was not necessarily a step backwards, for in some parts of the western world it marked a transition to new and more effective forms of government. France and England, for instance, coalesced as strong countries under the leadership of their feudal monarchies.

Italy, however, had special problems that complicated its political evolution. It was tied to the memory of the west's original 'empire,' and its imperial legacy linked it fatally with Germany and with the Christian church's supreme leader. The kings of Germany had claimed the legacy of Charlemagne and the right to style themselves 'Holy Roman Emperors.' They believed that their title gave them the right to rule Italy. It was also, however, home to another imperial heir, the bishop of Rome. The man who presided over the diocese of Rome was something more than a bishop—or even a king or an emperor. Early in the Middle Ages Rome's bishop, the pope, won recognition as the head of the church in the Latin west. The pope knew that he would lose this distinction if he came under the dominance of the German 'emperors.' Despite the grandeur of their titles, the Germans did not preside over the kings of Europe, and a pope who was their puppet would not be able to command the allegiance of Christians of all nations. The papacy, therefore, did everything that it could to frustrate the ambitions of the Germans, and the struggle between pope and king prevented anyone from pulling Italy together as a nation. In the absence of a central government, the Italian cities extended their influence into the countryside and evolved city-states. These began as republics, but by the 16th c. the pressures of incessant warfare had forced most of them to establish more efficient political systems.

Families like the Medici, Sforza, Este, and Visconti came to power and transformed free city-states into autocratic duchies. The Italian duchies were small, but they generated enough wealth from trade and banking to make their dukes the equals of Europe's kings. Late in the medieval period a cultural awakening called 'the Renaissance' began in Italy's cities and spread throughout Europe. For several generations the most advanced art and thought in the west was inspired by Italian example. Italy's products, great and trivial, were imitated by artists and intellectuals from all parts of Europe. (Sh. thought of it as the place from which most fads and novelties came. *R2 2.1.21.*) The combination of fame, wealth, and political confusion proved disastrous for the Italians. They had powerful neighbors for whom the divided nation was too rich and vulnerable a prize to be left to its own devices. In the 16th c. the kings of France and the Hapsburg emperors sent armies into Italy. They succeeded only in ruining the treasure they coveted. At the same time, Italy suffered two additional blows to its prosperity. The Ottoman Turks closed the eastern end of the Mediterranean to Christian shipping, and the Spaniards, Portuguese, and Dutch began to develop Atlantic trade routes to which Italy had no access. The Mediterranean lost its place as the center of the civilized world, and Italy faded with the importance of the sea that had made it great. It was not unified under a central government until late in the 19th c.

Shr 1.1.4, 2.1.69. Luc 107. R2 4.1.88. MV 1.2.71, 2.2.153, 3.2.294. Ado 5.1.169. JC 1.3.87, 3.1.267. AWW 2.1.12, 'higher I.,' northern Italy on the Adriatic side, or, more likely, 'noble Italians.' *2.1.19, 2.2.256.*

Ant 1.2.86, 1.3.44, 1.4.51, 2.5.23, 3.5.19. Cor 5.3.34, 5.3.209. Cym 1.3.30, 1.4.64, 92, 3.4.49, 5.6.161, the women of Italy were considered skilled lovers. *3.4.15, 5.5.158,* 'drug-damned I.,' Italians were supposed to be crafty and skilled with poisons and other drugs. *3.6.59, 4.2.340.*

Ithaca, small island in the Ionian sea off the coast of Epirus. It was the kingdom of the legendary Odysseus (L. Ulysses, q.v.), one of the *Iliad*'s Greek heroes. Odysseus left Ithaca in the charge of his wife Penelope when he went off to fight the Trojan war. He was gone for twenty years, and Homer's *Odyssey* tells the story of Odysseus' journey home. *Tro 1.3.69,* 'Prince of I.,' Ulysses. *Cor 1.3.86.*

Iudean, *Oth 5.2.356,* see Indian.

J

Jack, 1) first name, often implying low social status. *2H6,* see Cade, Jack.

2) diminutive of John: *1H4,* John Oldcastle. *MWW 2.2.134,* John Falstaff.

3) *MWW 1.4.54,* John Rugby. It has been argued that the meaning here is 'knave Rugby,' but Caius may just be showing wonderment at the English language. Later in the play there seems no insult intended by Caius against Rugby: *2.3.1, 3, 8, passim.*

4) generic name for any common man, often used with contempt for arrogant young men, as we now use 'guy.' Richard III, for example, remarks that the world is topsy-turvy, wrens have displaced eagles and 'Since every Jack became a gentleman,/There's many a gentle person made a Jack' (*R3 1.3.72–3*). *Shr 2.1.158, 284. 4.1.36:* Grumio is fond of catches or rounds and this is the first line of one. *R3 1.3.53. Rom 2.3.142, 3.1.11. MV 3.4.77,* 'bragging Jacks,' arrogant young men. *1H4 2.5.11, 3.3.85, 139, 5.3.137. Ado 1.1.173, 5.1.91. Ant 3.13.93, 103. Cor 5.2.63. Tmp 4.1.197.*

5) *Shr 4.1.44* (pl.), play on the different meanings of J.: boys, leather jugs, or a drinking measure of about a quarter pint, against Jills/gills (girls, drink containers, or a measure of about half a pint).

6) Jill's lover in nursery rhymes. *LLL 5.2.861. MND 3.3.45.* See also *Rom 2.3.142-4.*

7) *Rom 4.5.170,* term of contempt, or, possibly, the name of the 1st Musician or the actor who portrayed him.

8) plectra of a virginal, though in *Son 128.5, 14,* Sh. uses it to mean the keys, and puns on 'saucy jacks,' a phrase the Welshman Fluellen maybe confuses into 'Jack-sauce' in *H5 4.7.138.*

9) target ball in lawn bowling, *Cym 2.1.2.*

10) figure striking the bell on antique clocks. *R3 4.2.117. R2 5.5.60. Tim 3.7.96,* 'minute-jacks,' someone who marks every minute, a toady.

Jack-a-Lent, *MWW 3.3.23, 5.5.126,* figure which was the target in a throwing game at Lent. It therefore came to mean 'blockhead,' or the docile subject of abuse.

Jack-dog, *MWW 2.3.57,* 'Scurvy j. priest!' an insult.

Jack-out-of-office, *1H6 1.1.175,* slang expression. A 'Jack' is any man, and one who is 'out of office' has lost his job.

Jack-priest, *MWW 1.4.113, 2.3.29,* 'knave-priest,' an insult referring to Evans.

Jack-sauce, *H5 4.7.138,* a saucy rascal. The compound also occurs in *How a Man May Choose a Good Wife from a Bad, 5.1.8* (1602), which may mean this is not a confusion by Fluellen of 'saucy Jacks.' The play, possibly by Joshua Cooke, was very popular. It was acted many times by the Earl of Worcester's Men and published at least eight times between 1602 and 1634.

Jackie of Norfolk, F1 'Iockey of Norfolke,' *R3 5.6.34,* condescending name for John Howard, duke of Norfolk (q.v.). This note contains the same message as Edward Hall's *Union of the Two Noble and Illustre Famelies of Lancastre and Yorke* reports was painted on his gate as a warning not to support king Richard.

Jacob, 1) son of Isaac and Rebecca, twin brother to Esau, grandson of Abraham, and father of the twelve tribes of Israel. The name has been linked with Hebrew words for 'heel' and 'usurp,' which relate to his story. God told Rebecca that the elder of her sons would serve the younger and Esau was born first, with Jacob holding his heel. Esau—who though a hunter was weak in character—sold his birthright to Jacob for a mess of pottage. Later, when Isaac was old and nearly blind, Jacob disguised himself as the hairy Esau, and received his blessing. To protect

Jacob from his angry brother, Isaac sent him to Laban. Jacob worked for Laban for seven years to earn the right to marry Rachel, but on the wedding night, Laban sent his elder daughter Leah to Jacob's bed. Afterwards he gave him Rachel, also. A competition developed between the sisters about who should give Jacob the most children, even to the extent that they used their handmaids as surrogate mothers. After suffering under Laban for twenty years, Jacob returned to his homeland and was reconciled with Esau. He also wrestled with an angel and received the name Israel, which seems to mean 'he contended with God.' Ultimately Jacob went into Egypt because of his son Joseph and prospered. On his deathbed he blessed his sons and exacted Joseph's promise that he would not be buried in Egypt.

MV 1.3.70, 71, 76, 79, 87, 90. MV 2.5.36, 'J.'s staff,' Jacob was a shepherd. He mentions his staff at Genesis 32:10. A pilgrim's staff was also known as Jacob's staff in the Renaissance because the patron saint of pilgrims, St. James (or Jacob), was pictured as carrying one, but Shylock could not be swearing by St. James unless some kind of ironic humor is intended, as when Communist Soviet atheists used to use the common Russian expression, 'My God!'

2) *MM 3.1.461,* see Philip and Jacob.

Jakes, *Lr. 2.2.66 (Q 7.65),* a privy. See Ajax.

James, Elias, *Var,* brewer with premises in the Blackfriars district, the subject of an epitaph attributed to Sh. in John Stow's *Survey of London* (1633). Elias took over his father Dericke James' business in 1600. His burial is recorded in the parish of St. Andrews for September 24, 1610 and mentions the man's charity to the poor, something also mentioned in the epitaph. Another possible connection to Sh. was that John Jackson, who had close business dealings with Sh., married Elias James' sister-in-law. The tomb itself was destroyed in the Great Fire of London (1666) or in the restorations afterwards.

James of Arc, *1H6,* father of Joan of Arc. Sh.'s picture of him as a poor, bumbling shepherd may not be accurate. James was a farmer, but he was probably a man of some standing in his hometown of Domrémy. He appears in court records as a representative of his village and was probably one of its presiding elders.

Jamy, Captain, *H5,* James, fictional Scottish soldier, whose service in Henry V's army alongside comrades from Wales and England symbolizes the solidarity of support in the British Isles for Henry V's French wars. During Henry's lifetime Scotland was an independent nation usually allied with France against England, but Sh. may have had historical inspiration for the character of Jamy. At least one Scot named James fought for Henry. James I, heir to the throne of Scotland, was raised at the court of Henry IV and remained in England throughout Henry V's reign. Young James fell into English hands when civil disturbances in Scotland prompted his father to try to send him to safety in France. At the English court Henry IV's stepmother took a maternal interest in the foreign prince, and she arranged for him to be set at liberty in exchange for his oath to serve in the English army. After Henry V's death, he was tied by marriage to the English royal family and permitted to return to Scotland (1423). There his dead father's intuitions proved true. His subjects murdered him.

Jamy, St. *Shr 3.2.80,* James the Great, one of the twelve apostles, son of Zebedee, brother of John, patron saint of Spain. See Jaques, St.

Janus, Roman god of beginnings and endings, elevated from being an ancient king of Italy. He was the son of Apollo and Creusa. His name, related to the L. for 'going' and the word for door, *janua,* survives in the name of the month of January. *MV 1.1.50,* 'two-headed J.,' the god was depicted as facing two directions at once, illustrating that a beginning is also an ending. The circularity of this conception seems quite relevant to the jesting surrounding this oath. *Oth 1.2.33.*

Japhet, Japheth, third son of Noah, reputed ancestor of the Greeks and the Europeans. Prince Harry jokes that thanks to him, a universal common ancestor, every man in England can claim kinship with the king. *2H4 2.2.110.*

Jaquenetta, *LLL,* country wench whom both Costard and Armado love. Biron's love letter to Rosaline is mixed up with Armado's and Jaquenetta turns it over to Ferdinand, exposing Biron's failure to keep his oath. Later Costard says that Armado has made Jaquenetta 'quick' with child. Armado then swears he will be loyal to her. Her name is a feminization of Jaques, perhaps bringing along its attendant pun on 'jakes.'

Jaques, 1) *AYLI,* melancholic nobleman in exile with Duke Senior. He is the most articulate spokesman for the real world against the pastoral. His often gloomy view of human existence has been frequently championed as Sh.'s own attitude. His 'seven ages of man' speech is one of Sh.'s finest and is one of the most quoted passages ever written. While mocked by the other characters as puritanical, Jaques is often wise in his observations about the moral appropriateness of what is going on. He is thus simultaneously wise and foolish in a way that bears comparison to Polonius. Countering this view is the association of his name with 'a jakes,' or 'jax,' a privy, and his hypocrisy spoken of by the Duke (*2.6.64–9*). His disposition could even be a joke, as foul odors were thought to induce melancholy and his name is the same as a toilet's.

Metrics usually indicate the name had two syllables or at least suggested two syllables as in the word aches; however, there are also a number of indications that the word was commonly pronounced with one syllable in Sh.'s time. Possibly Sh. had two syllables in mind to suggest the foreign setting, though the situation is analogous to that of Arden itself (which is the Ardennes and also a forest in Warwickshire). The name Jaques was a common Warwickshire name at the time. Likely Sh. is, as usual, having it both ways. The name may also have been suggested by the shepherd's son in *Sir Clyomon and Clamydes* (1599), a probable source, but there is nothing particular to support it.

2) *AWW 4.3.167,* commander in the Duke of Florence's army.

Jaques de Bois, *AYLI,* brother of Orlando and Oliver. He is 'kept at school,' mentioned only at the very beginning and appearing only at the end of the play to present Duke Frederick's miraculous change of heart. The name is an unnecessarily confusing choice considering the large role played by the other Jaques and possibly in the original drafts they were intended to be the same character. In Act 5 of F1 he is referred to merely as 'Second Brother.' In the source, Lodge's *Rosalynde,* his counterpart is named Fernandyne, a name not shared by any other characters. See Rowland de Bois.

Jaques, St., *AWW 3.4.4,* St. James the Great (Heb. Jacob), one of the twelve apostles, son of Zebedee and Salome, and brother of John the Evangelist. As one of the most prominent disciples, he was present with Peter and John at Jesus' request at the transfiguration and at the agony in Gethsemane. Jesus called him and his brother the 'sons of thunder' either because of their voices or their impetuous temperaments. James was a martyr, beheaded by Herod Agrippa I, c. 44 AD. in Palestine and supposedly removed to the shrine at Compostela, because of the legend, current before 400 AD, that he preached in Spain before his death. Many pilgrims have visited the shrine over the centuries. Pilgrims of the Middle Ages sewed his symbol, the scallop shell, to their garments for a safe journey. Sir Walter Raleigh mentions the scallop shell in the poem he wrote the night before his beheading, 'The Pilgrimage.' See Saint Jaques le Grand.

Jason, mythological hero, leader of the Argonauts on the quest for the Golden Fleece, son of Æson and either Alcimede or Polymede. It had been predicted to King Pelias of Iolcus that his nephew Jason would succeed him, so Pelias persuaded the youth to seek the Fleece, in hopes that the young man would be killed. Jason organized the Argonauts, which included many great heroes, and took the fleece, returning with the sorceress Medea as his wife. She was instrumental in the death of Pelias and Jason became king, but after ten years of marriage he divorced her. Medea then gave his second wife (Glauce or Creusa) a gown which burst into flames when she put it on. She also slaughtered her children by Jason. In his dotage, Jason took to sitting in the Argo, where he was killed by a falling beam. *MV 1.1.172, 3.2.239,* (pl.): Bassanio's quest for Portia is compared to Jason's quest.

Jephthah, one of the charismatic leaders or 'judges' who provided a primitive form of government for the early Hebrew nation. A rash oath compelled him to make a horrible sacrifice. He begged God to help his people win a battle and promised God a burnt offering of whatever he saw when he stepped from the door of his house. As he left his home, his eye fell on his only child. His story appears in *Judges* 11. *3H6 5.1.94:* George of Clarence recalls the story of Jephthah's sacrifice to justify his decision to violate his oath of loyalty to the earl of Warwick and to return his allegiance to his brother Edward IV. Clarence claims that the keeping of oaths like Jephthah's, which run counter to the obligations of nature and family, is a greater impiety than their repudiation. *Ham 2.2.404, 411, 412,* Hamlet compares Polonius to Jephthah in his having a beautiful daughter.

Jeronimy (St.). *Shr Ind. 1.7.* This is an allusion to a line in Thomas Kyd's very popular *Spanish Tragedy* (printed c. 1592): 'Hieronimo, beware; go by, go by.' Sly, however, is confusing the main character of Kyd's play with St. Jerome (L. *Hieronymus*).

Jerusalem, 1) a city sacred to Jews, Christians, and Muslims. Its site was inhabited during the paleolithic era, but it was not until the early 10th c. BC that it became an important political and cultural center. David, the second Hebrew king, made it the capital of the first Jewish state. David's son, Solomon (961–922), brilliantly exploited the potential of Jerusalem's location astride the crossroads of Near Eastern trade. He acquired great wealth and commissioned monumental buildings. His most notable project was the first of the Hebrew temples. At Solomon's death, the Jewish state split apart. The larger and richer northern portion of the kingdom, Israel, seated its government at Schechem. Jerusalem became the capital of a small, countrified district called Judah. Israel was destroyed by Assyria in 721 BC, but Jerusalem maintained its independence until 587. In that year the Chaldeans of Babylon overwhelmed Judah and exiled its citizens. In 538 the Chaldeans were conquered by the Persians, who permitted some Jews to return to Jerusalem to rebuild its temple. Thereafter, with the exception of brief periods of quasi-autonomy, Jerusalem existed as a client state within various gentile empires. The city had little importance during the era of Alexander the Great and his successors, but the first Roman emperor, Octavius Augustus, entrusted Herod the Great with the city and a large stretch of contiguous territory. Herod built the last and the most magnificent of Jerusalem's temples. Rome destroyed the building in 70 AD as punishment for a revolt against the authority of the empire. In 638 AD the Muslims occupied Jerusalem.

Since the Arab peoples claimed descent from Abraham, the ancestor of the Jews, and Islamic tradition held that the Prophet Muhammad ascended to heaven from the site of the ancient Hebrew temple, Jerusalem was accorded the dignity of a sacred city. A major mosque, the Dome of the Rock, was erected on the temple mount, and it survives today as one of Islam's most important shrines. Since all the Christian nations of the early medieval period were either culturally backward or politically chaotic, no challenge was mounted to the Muslim control of the Holy Lands until the end of the 11th c. In 1099 Europe launched the first of many crusades designed to bring Palestine under Christian control. The soldiers of the first crusade conquered Jerusalem, but the west lacked the men and the communications necessary for maintaining a permanent presence in

Palestine. It was reclaimed by the Muslims in the 12th c., and in Sh.'s day it was part of the powerful Ottoman Empire. Sh. sometimes uses the term 'Jerusalem,' as does the Bible, as a metaphor for a divine place. The meaning of 'Jerusalem' is uncertain. It may mean (ironically) 'town of peace.' Others believe it may be named for a river god, 'Salem' who predates Judaism.

2H6 1.1.46. 3H6 5.5.8. Jn 2.1.378. 1H4 1.1.101.

2) *2H4 4.3.363, 366, 369,* hall built in the late 14th c. for the dean of Westminster Abbey. It was named for the biblical verses describing the holy city of Jerusalem that ornamented its walls. It was predicted to Henry IV that he would die only in Jerusalem. Though he longed to go on a crusade, as he had in his youth, he never came near the city. His death in the Westminster Abbey hall was seen to fulfill the prophecy.

Jerusalem, King of, title established by the crusaders who conquered the Holy Lands in 1099. In 1187 the Muslims regained control of Jerusalem, but Europe's hope of restoring its fortunes in the east was slow to die. Its royal title symbolized the Christian claim to the Holy Lands, and it continued to be used by members of various European families. A king of Sicily and emperor of Germany, Frederick II (d. 1250), was the last Christian monarch to exercise any authority there. When Charles of Anjou conquered Naples and Sicily, late in the 13th c., the claim passed to the French. The king of Jerusalem to whom Sh. refers was Henry VI's French father-in-law, René of Anjou. Since René never succeeded in winning control of Naples, much less the Holy Lands, his English opponents ridiculed his pretensions to monarchy. *2H6 1.1.108–109. 3H6 1.4.122–124, 5.7.39. 1H6 5.7.37–38.*

Jeshu, *H5 4.7.109,* see Jesus Christ.

Jessica, *MV,* beautiful daughter of Shylock. Bored with the stern solemnity of her father's house, she falls in love with Lorenzo and escapes with him to Belmont. Her stealing of her father's wealth creates, to say the least, ambiguous feelings about her character. Her wishing to become a Christian, would have made her intentions good, maybe even despite her doing it out of love rather than out of a desire for salvation. On the other hand, she is frivolous enough to exchange a valuable turquoise of sentimental value to her father for a monkey. Perhaps the intention was to show the kind of daughter that Shylock would bring upon himself, and despite the marvelously lyrical passage which she shares with Lorenzo at the outset of Act 5, her behavior would send shudders through any father. In her final line of the play she is demonstrating a melancholy streak by not liking music, which Lorenzo tries to eradicate. Perhaps the intention is to show that she has not yet changed enough. The name occurs in the King James Bible (Genesis 11:29) as Ischa, though in earlier editions it is Jesca, a niece of Abraham's. The present form of the name occurs first in Sh.

Jesu, *2H6 1.1.159. R3 1.3.136, 5.5.132. Rom 2.3.27. R2 5.2.17. 1H4 2.5.287, 394, 399, 3.3.83. 2H4 2.4.46, 296, 3.2.32, 42. H5 5.1.38.* See Jesus Christ.

Jesu Christ, *2H6 5.1.212. R2 4.1.84. H5 4.1.66.* See Jesus Christ.

Jesu Maria, *Rom 2.2.69,* 'Jesus, son of Mary!' a mild oath.

Jesus, *3H6 5.6.75. 1H4 2.2.80. 2H4 3.2.215. Var,* 'Jesus' sake,' Sh.s famous epitaph against moving his body. See Jesus Christ.

Jesus Christ, (d. c. 30 AD), the founder of the Christian religion. Luke 1:31 maintains that the angel of the annunciation instructed the Virgin Mary to call her son 'Jesus,' a variant of the common Hebrew name 'Joshua' ('the Lord is salvation'). 'Christ' is a title, not a name. It is a Greek translation of the Hebrew and Aramaic terms transliterated by the English word 'messiah.' 'Messiah' means 'anointed.' Anointing was a solemn ritual that created a commissioner with special authority. The desire for a messianic deliverer uniquely empowered by God was very strong among Jews who fought assimilation to the Greco-Roman world. Many Jews of Jesus' generation feared that God's 'chosen people' could not retain their identity without the help of an agent sent them by God. Different groups of Jews had different expectations of the messiah, but the Christian claim that Jesus of Nazareth was the anticipated savior was not, as St. Paul acknowledged, easy for either Jew or gentile to accept. It is impossible to do more than suggest a probable outline for the events of his life. The Christian scriptures are the only sources available for the study of his history, and they do not provide the kind of information that historians require. According to tradition, he was born in Bethlehem during the reign of the first Roman emperor, Octavius Augustus. At about the age of 30 he was baptized by a charismatic orator named John. Jesus immediately abandoned his home and career and, like John, became an itinerant preacher. During the period of his ministry he spent most or all of his time in Galilee. He died in Jerusalem during a visit to celebrate the festival of Passover. The Roman authorities crucified him as punishment for the crime of treason. Some of his followers came to believe that he rose from the dead, and this convinced them that he was the messiah. Their proclamation of the resurrection inaugurated a religious movement that swept the western world. His name was commonly used as an oath by Sh.'s contemporaries (e.g., *3H6 5.6.75*).

Jew, descendant of the Hebrew peoples or a follower of Judaism. The word derives from Judah, one of the twelve tribes of ancient Israel named for the twelve sons of the patriarch Joseph. Judah was also the name for the southern portion of the nation established by King David. Following the death of his son, Solomon, the Hebrew state split into two competing kingdoms: Judah and Israel. In the 8th c. Israel was swept away by the Assyrians, and Judah survived as the last anchor for the identity of the Hebrew people. In many instances in Sh., reflecting the mores of the time, the word is used more generally in the sense of a non-believer, and therefore, someone who cannot be trusted. A convert to Judaism would have been an unlikely imagining in the Renaissance English view and it seems that the conception of the Jew is more of a dispossessed nation or race that refuses to believe in Christianity, than of a group of religious adherents. To be Jewish was not legal in the England of Sh.'s time, so it has been argued that what appears as anti-Semitism in *MV, Jew of Malta,* and other works of the time is more of an attack upon a fantasy race—not unlike the supposed men with tails or with heads between their shoulders—that refuses redemption and is greedy, superstitious, deceitful, and somber. In any case, Sh.'s portrayal of Shylock allows much more human possibility than that of Marlowe, for instance.

There is a popular performing baboon referred to in numerous late 16th c. documents (Guilpin, Marston, and Jonson all mention him) whose name was 'Gew' or 'Gue.' This may well be a direct insult to the Jews and would have lent a whole different implication to the Elizabethan listeners to Shylock's famous speech, 'Hath not a Jew eyes?,' particularly as 'Gew' was blind. The substantial possibility of the allusion points out the difficulty in ascertaining after 400 years both the playwright's intentions and the nature of topical humor and prejudice.

TGV 2.3.11, a heartless man. *2.5.46:* Lance seems overly interested in Jews, perhaps indicating (along with the similarity of his name to Lancelot Gobbo's) some kinship between *TGV* and *MV. LLL 3.1.132,* 'my incony J.,' obscure phrase of affection. 'Incony' was popular around the early 17th c. appearing in Christopher Marlowe's *Jew of Malta,* for example, and seems to mean 'darling,' 'rare,' 'sweet,' or 'fine.' It may be related to the Fr. *inconnu,* 'unknown,' or 'uncanny,' but it is hard to make the connection. 'Jew' in this phrase is equally obscure and may be a shortened 'jewel,' or 'juvenal' (which see).

MND 3.1.89, see *LLL. MV 2.5.42,* 'J.'s eye': 'worth a J.'s eye.' denoting something valuable, dates from a tale from King John's reign. A Jew of Bristol resisted paying a tax of

10,000 marks. As punishment it was ordered that one tooth should be ripped from his mouth each day until he paid. Seven teeth were pulled until he gave up, whereupon the king is supposed to have joked, 'A Jew's eye may be a quick ransom, but a Jew's teeth give the richer harvest.' Extorting money by threatening mutilation was common in the Middle Ages. Some editors of Sh. turn F1's spelling 'Jewes' into 'Jewess' to refer to Jessica's looking out the window; however, it is more likely that the possessive was being pronounced in an old-fashioned manner.

1H4 2.5.180, 'Hebrew J.,' a term of contempt meaning a total J. *Ado 2.3.251:* the phrasing here is similar to Falstaff's. *Mac 4.1.26.*

2) *MV 1.3.152, 176, 2.2.2, passim,* see Shylock.

Jewel House, *H8 4.1.113, 5.1.34,* repository for the royal plate and other valuable ornaments of monarchy. Jewels and items of gold and silver were purchased to permit a monarch to make a display appropriate to the dignity of high office. Such treasures were also used as surety for the loans that funded governmental projects.

Jewish, of or pertaining to the Jews. *MV 1.3.111,* 'J. gaberdine': there is no particular knowledge that Jewish garments were markedly different in the case of Venetian merchants, though perhaps Sh. imagined it might be so. *4.1.79,* 'J. heart,' a hard heart.

Jewry, land of the Jews, Judea or all of Palestine. *R2 2.1.55. MWW 2.1.19,* 'Herod of J.' *H5 3.3.123. Ant 1.2.24, 3.3.3, 3.6.73, 4.6.11.*

Jezebel, wife of Ahab, a foreign born queen of witchcraft and loose morals (2 Kings 9). When Jehu saw her dressed up with a painted face to seduce him on his entrance into Jezreel, he had her thrown from a window by her eunuchs and her body trampled. Later, when he decided to bury her, there were only skull, hands and feet left and he was reminded God had decreed she should be eaten by dogs. *TN 2.5.39,* Sir Andrew remembers Jezebel was shameless, but forgets she was a woman.

Jill, any young woman. *Shr 4.1.44* (pl.), the servant girls. In some editors, this is 'Gills' to emphasize the pun on Jacks (boys, leather jugs, or a drinking measure of about a quarter pint) and Jills/gills (girls, drink containers, or a measure of about half a pint). *Rom 2.3.144,* 'flirt-jills,' F1 'flurt-gils,' loose women.

2) Jack's lover. *LLL 5.2.861. MND 3.3.45.*

Joan, general name for a low-class woman. *Shr Ind. 2.107,* 'J. Madam': Sly is asking what his wife is called. The humor is that he imagines that a lady would have this name, often associated with prostitutes. *LLL 3.1.200, 4.3.180. 5.2.904, 912,* 'greasy J.' *Jn 1.1.184.*

Joan la Pucelle, *1H6,* see Joan of Arc.

Joan of Arc, *1H6,* (1412–1431), peasant girl who miraculously turned the tide of the Hundred Years' War. By inspiring the French armies with a sense of divine purpose at a moment when the English leadership was faltering, she tipped the scales decisively in favor of France. She was a native of Domrémy, a village west of Paris on the border between Champagne and Lorraine. Her father was a farmer, but not an abjectly poor peasant. James of Arc had modest personal property and a position of leadership in his community. At the age of thirteen Joan began to hear voices that she believed were those of angels and saints. In her sixteenth year she decided that these voices were ordering her to go to the Dauphin to help him rescue France. In May of 1428, against her father's will, she sought an interview with the French commander at Vaucouleurs. He was unimpressed and sent her home. That summer Domrémy and the surrounding countryside was harassed by English soldiers, and by October the English siege of Orléans had begun. She again sought help at Vaucouleurs, and again her request for an audience with the Dauphin was refused. In desperation she disguised herself in male clothing and travelled to Nancy. There she made contact with Charles II of Lorraine and his son-in-law, René of Anjou. They gave her a horse and a small escort and sent to Chinon, where the Dauphin was in residence.

The Dauphin conferred with her at length, but he was unwilling to trust her orthodoxy until she had been examined by a board of theologians. She was sent to the university at Poitiers where inquiries were made into her opinions and her background. When Charles received a good report of her, he ordered her to Tours to equip herself for battle. The French expedition left Tours for Orléans on 28 April 1429, and on May 7 she led an assault that evicted the English from a key position blocking the bridge into Orléans. The English retreated from Orléans and suffered several significant defeats in the weeks that followed. At her urging the French army moved on to Rheims and the coronation of the Dauphin, Charles VII (16 July 1429). Instead of following her advice and pressing on toward Paris, Charles opted for a truce. He hoped to win an easy victory by detaching Burgundy from its alliance with England. Joan presided over the capitulation of a few more towns, but was frustrated by Charles's passivity. When the English launched a campaign to secure the territory around Paris and prepare for Henry VI's arrival and coronation, she organized a raiding party to liberate Compiègne. There, on 23 May, as a result of a bungled retreat, she was captured by a Burgundian soldier. The Burgundians sold her to their English allies. Bedford, the English commander, believed that it was necessary to discredit her before killing her, so she was sent to Rouen to be tried for heresy. Ten theologians from the university of Paris sat on the board that heard her case. Their verdict was a foregone conclusion, and Charles VII did nothing to help her. The court convened on 21 February 1431, and the proceedings culminated in her execution at the stake on 30 May 1431. England used her conviction to try to discredit Charles VII and circulated accounts of the trial to the courts of Europe. Charles took no steps to defend her reputation until the 1450's. In 1456 the papacy decreed that her condemnation had been an error, but her canonization waited until 1920. Sh.'s claim that she was a witch and a whore derives entirely from English propaganda.

Joan, Old, *2H6 2.1.4,* hawk whose flight Queen Margaret discusses with Henry VI and the duke of Suffolk. Edward Hall in his *Union of the Two Noble and Illustre Famelies of Lancastre and Yorke* (236) claims that the hunting expedition that Sh. describes was part of a plot by Margaret to bring about the death of the duke of York.

Job, a model of faith whose trials are described in the biblical book that bears his name. Although Job is stripped of his wealth, his family, and his health, he resists the temptation to question God's judgment. He affirms that the will of God is beyond human understanding, and admonishes God's people to cling by faith to confidence in divine justice. *MWW 5.5.154–5,* alludes to Job's wife urging him to curse God (Job 2:9). *2H4 1.2.128,*

Jockey of Norfolk, *R3,* see Jackie of Norfolk.

Johan, *Ham 5.1.60,* F1 'Yaughan.' The general drift seems to be that the First Clown is sending the Second to get him a drink, possibly at a nearby tavern. It may be a simple attempt to duplicate the Danish 'John.' It may be for humorous effect a topical allusion to a tavern keeper near the Globe named Vaughn, or Yaughan (a Welsh name) or a foreign-born tavern-keeper named Johan. Other suggestions are that it is a misspelling of 'tavern,' or a confused stage direction in which the Clown was supposed to 'yawn.'

John, 1) *1H6,* one of Cade's rebels, identified as John Holland at *4.2* in F1. Since an actor with this name is known to have been associated with Lord Strange's Men, it is usually thought that this refers to the actor playing the part of the rebel, not the name of the rebel himself. Similarly in this scene in F1 his compatriot is identified as 'Bevis,'which is likely to be an actor's name also.

2) *Rom 1.1.30, Tmp 2.2.27,* 'poor-John,' dried and salted hake, the poorest fish. It was a staple for the lower classes, especially during Lent.

3) *R3 3.2.105,* 'Sir J.,' the name Sh. provides for the unidentified priest with whom Holinshed (3.723) says William, Lord Hastings was conversing when a messenger came to hurry him to the council meeting at which Richard III had him arrested and condemned to death. Educated clergy (recipients of the Bachelor of Arts) used the knightly 'sir' in Sh.'s time.

4) *1H4 5.4.128,* John of Lancaster. See John, duke of Bedford.

5) *Ado,* 'Don J.,' 'Count J.,' 'J. the Bastard,' and 'Sir J.,' brother of Pedro of Aragon, and implementer of the plot to defame Hero. John describes himself as melancholic, while his follower Borachio refers to him as the Devil (3.3). John thereby resembles Iago, Richard III, the bastard Edmund, and other of Sh.'s characters who exploit the weaknesses of others to bring about evil—a Vice figure. While it might be argued that John's character has derived from his being denied his rightful heritage because of his illegitimacy and his envy of Claudio, this is not much emphasized in the text and his nastiness comes close to the 'motiveless malignity' attributed to Iago. Despite his inability to hide his feelings about failing in his revolt against his brother, John successfully dupes Don Pedro and humiliates Claudio. His cruel machinations deserve a serious punishment; however, he runs away before the play's end, allowing the misguided Borachio to be caught in his stead. Borachio's repentance maintains the happiness of the ending, whereas the capture and punishment of John might have been too serious, even though he would be getting what he deserved. John's offstage capture doesn't occur until nearly the last line of the play and his punishment is put off until 'tomorrow,' which very awkwardly ties up the loose end.

In the primary source novel (there are many contemporary versions of the plot) by Matteo Bandello, the corresponding character who hatches the plot against Hero is Signor Girondo Olerio Valentiano. He is not Pedro's brother, but merely a rival for the woman's hand. When he believes the woman is dead, he repents and ultimately marries her sister. It is curious that Sh. complicates this with John's bastardy and evil, the addition of Borachio, and the apparent doom awaiting John offstage as the play ends. Bandello's plot seems much more Shakespearean than Sh.'s, strangely. As he borrowed the name of Don Pedro from Pedro II of Aragon, Sh. may have borrowed the name Don John from Don John of Austria whose fleet assembled in Messina in 1571 before his triumph over the Turks at Lepanto. As with Don Pedro, there is little more than the borrowing of a name associated with Messina. There was also a Don John who was governor-general of the Netherlands for Philip II in the late 16th c.

6) Little John, Robin Hood's lieutenant. On first encountering the outlaw, unceremoniously dumped him in a stream. He then became Robin's lieutenant. Because of his enormous height, Robin Hood supposedly inverted his name from John Little. His last name was also said to be Nailor. He appears in one of the earliest mentions of Robin, *The Original Chronicle of Scotland* by Andrew of Wyntoun (1420). *2H4 5.3.104. MWW 1.1.158.*

7) *MWW,* servant of the Fords.

8) *H5 2.1.113, 2.3.15,* see Falstaff.

John, count of Dunois, *1H6,* (1403–1468), called the 'Bastard of Orléans,' the illegitimate son of Charles VI's brother, Louis, the duke of Orléans, and one of the most talented French generals of his generation. Dunois came to public attention in 1427 when he drove off an English army that was assaulting Montargis. The action created excitement, for the French had enjoyed few victories since the rout of the Orléanist forces at Agincourt in 1415. Dunois was in command of Orléans when the English siege began in 1428. He joined forces with Joan of Arc at Orléans and shared several expeditions with her. After the deaths of Henry V and the duke of Bedford, Dunois led the armies that forced the English out of Normandy and Gascony.

John Drum, *AWW 3.6.39,* 'J. D.'s entertainment,' a beating. *The Three Ladies of London* (1584) uses the expression. John Marston wrote a play entitled *John Drum's Entertainment* (1600), mocking Ben Jonson.

John, duke of Bedford (1389–1435), Henry IV's third son, an able contributor to Henry V's campaigns and the dominant member of the regency council that governed during the minority of Henry VI. In 1413 Henry V gave John the duchy of Bedford, and in 1415 Henry left Bedford in charge of England while he launched his first attack on France. In 1416 Bedford got a taste of the action. He commanded the fleet that destroyed the French navy at Harfleur. In 1417 he returned to his post in England and led an expedition against the Scots. He saw further service in France in 1419, but in 1421 he was sent back to England once again to serve as Henry's regent. When Henry came home, Bedford took the king's place in France, and at Henry's death, parliament accorded Bedford, the king's elder surviving brother, chief responsibility for the care of the kingdom and its infant heir. Bedford tried to strengthen England's crucial alliance with Burgundy by marrying Anne, Philip the Good's sister. Relations between the two powers were, however, strained when Bedford's brother, Humphrey of Gloucester, tried to take Hainaut away from Burgundy. Gloucester's frequent quarrels with his uncle, Bishop Beaufort, and other members of the regency council forced Bedford into the role of mediator and peace-keeper. In 1426 Bedford journeyed to England to prevent its government from coming apart. After knighting young Henry and recruiting more soldiers, he returned to France where he renewed the Burgundian alliance.

All went well until the failure of the siege of Orléans in 1429. In 1430 Bedford tried to mitigate the effect of Charles VII's coronation at Rheims by having young Henry crowned in Paris. For a short time England held its ground against Charles, but it was difficult to ignore proliferating signs of trouble. In 1432 the death of Bedford's wife, Anne, severed an important link between England and Burgundy, and Bedford began to worry about rumors that he was mishandling the affairs of the kingdom. In 1433 he insisted on returning to England to defend himself. Parliament gave him a vote of confidence and confirmed his position as the king's chief councilor. In 1434 he went back to France to prosecute the war while negotiating peace. A conference was held at Arras in 1435. When it failed to reconcile the antagonists, Burgundy concluded a treaty of its own with France. The loss of Burgundian support made the English position in France untenable, but Bedford did not live long enough to witness the collapse of his life's work. He died in Rouen on 14 September 1435, at the age of 46.

1H6. 2H6 1.1.80, 93.

John, Friar, *Rom,* friar dispatched by Friar Laurence with a letter to warn Romeo of the deception of Juliet's death. He is also John in Arthur Brooke's *Tragicall Historye of Romeus and Juliet* (1562), Sh.'s source.

John, king of England, *Jn,* (1167–1216), successor to his brother, Richard (I) 'the Lionhearted' (d. 1199). He was the fifth son Eleanor of Aquitaine gave her husband Henry II. Henry nicknamed him 'Lackland,' for, when he was born, most of the Angevin empire had already been parcelled out as appanages for his older brothers. Given the circumstances, John might have been expected to blend quietly into the background and play the self-effacing role of the redundant prince, but whatever his faults, laziness and timidity were not among them. The premature deaths of his brothers, William, Henry, and Geoffrey cleared major obstacles from his path, but it seemed almost certain that his surviving sibling, Richard, who became king in 1189, would keep him from the throne. Richard departed for the third crusade shortly after his coronation, and the arrangements he made for the care of his kingdom during his absence suggest that he did not trust John. The king's brother was not designated his regent—or even assigned a place on the council appointed to govern in the king's name. Richard, who did not marry until the eve of the crusade, also declared an heir presumptive to secure the succession until he had a child of his own. Here, too, he passed over John, the most mature candidate, and favored an infant nephew, Arthur, son of his deceased elder brother Geoffrey.

Richard clearly intended John to sit idly by on the sidelines, but he exploited the opportunity of Richard's long absence in the Holy Lands to claw his way to a position of power. He undercut the authority of Richard's regents and allied himself with Richard's most dangerous enemy, Philip Augustus of France. When word arrived in 1192 that Richard had been taken captive by a fellow crusader, John and Philip made plans to divide up his estates. Queen Eleanor saved Richard by intervening through the papacy to negotiate terms for his release, and Richard returned to his kingdom in 1194. John sought asylum in France until Eleanor persuaded Richard to forgive him. For the remainder of Richard's life he and John got along so well that on Richard's deathbed in 1199, the king changed his mind about the arrangements he had previously made for the succession. He proclaimed John his heir—despite the fact that their nephew Arthur was on the brink of manhood and in possession of the better hereditary right. Arthur's duchy, Brittany, and the county of Anjou refused to acquiesce to John's succession, and a small war broke out.

In 1202 John captured Arthur at Mirabeau, where the young duke was besieging a castle defended by his grandmother. Arthur died after a few months in prison. It was generally believed that John ordered his death, and there was a rumor that he had killed the boy with his own hands. Such a murder would have been a violation of feudal law, but John's behavior was not constrained by respect for legal niceties. In 1200, for example, he divorced his wife, Isabella of Gloucester, to marry a richer heiress, Isabella of Angoulême. The relatives of the English Isabella were infuriated—as were those of the French Isabella's fiancé, Hugh of Lusignan. John freely trampled on these and other powerful persons until he pushed them to take advantage of a peculiarity in his legal position. He was king of England in his own right, but his continental lands were fiefs granted him by the French king. He was simultaneously the monarch of an independent nation and a vassal of France. According to feudal custom a baron who had a grievance against one of his fellows could appeal to their overlord for justice. Since Philip Augustus was his overlord, John's disgruntled men called him to account in Philip's court. In 1200 he and Philip had linked their houses by a marriage between John's niece, Blanche of Castile, and Philip's heir, Louis (VIII). But his alliance did not prevent Philip from exploiting John's quarrel with his barons.

Philip summoned him to Paris to stand trial on the charge of having violated feudal contracts. John, of course, refused to compromise his royal dignity by submitting to Philip's judgment. Philip, therefore, ruled him in contempt of court and declared his lands in France forfeit. The nobles of northern France seized on this as an excuse to repudiate John and declare their allegiance to Philip. John beat a hasty retreat to England, and it took him a long time to devise a strategy to recover what he had lost. He may, in part, have been distracted by a quarrel with the papacy. In 1205 John and the monks who served the cathedral at Canterbury disagreed about the choice of a new archbishop. When the dispute could not be resolved in England, the rival candidates for the post hastened to Rome to demand consecration from Pope Innocent III. Innocent dismissed both of them and proposed that the king and the monks accept a worthy compromise: Stephen Langton, a distinguished English scholar and cardinal. John preferred to risk a war between church and state. He refused Langton permission to enter England, and his direct challenge to papal authority forced Innocent to hurl every weapon in the church's arsenal. The pope closed England's churches, excommunicated John, and invited the French to depose him.

The battle lasted for five years, and then, suddenly, in 1213 John did an abrupt about face and submitted to the pope. John was moved neither by faith nor by conscience, but by an opportunity to win back the territory he had lost in France. Otto of Brunswick, the Holy Roman Emperor, agreed to join him in an assault on France that he and John hoped would destroy Philip Augustus. The contending armies met at Bouvines in 1214, and Philip repulsed the invaders. With the exception of Gascony, a part of Queen Eleanor's duchy of Aquitaine, John lost everything his family had once held in France. The defeated and unpopular monarch fled back to England to face a crowd of angry barons. In June 1215 they met him at Runnymede outside London and forced him to accept limits on the use of his power. The principles that were to govern the conduct of the king were spelled out in a document called Magna Carta. Despite the great charter's subsequent importance in English constitutional history, Magna Carta failed to achieve the purpose for which it was drafted. Civil war broke out. The pope released John from the oath he had taken at Runnymede, and his disillusioned barons invited the heir to the French crown to invade England and claim its throne. John defended himself vigorously until his time ran out. He died on 18 October 1216, a victim, apparently, of dysentery. By dying he organized a better defense for his dynasty than he could have devised if he had lived. England's barons had every reason to prefer the weak rule of John's 9-year-old son, Henry III, to government by a powerful French king. Once John was out of the way and they were free to act in their own best interests, they turned against the foreign armies they had invited into England and united to defend the young Plantagenet heir.

John of Gaunt, (1340–1399), duke of Lancaster, Edward III's fourth son. He was named for the place of his birth, the Flemish city of Ghent (Gaunt). His ducal title derived from estates brought him by his first wife, Blanche of Lancaster. Gaunt began his career in 1355, campaigning in Spain with his brother Lionel, duke of Clarence. Spanish politics preoccupied him for much of his life. In 1367 Gaunt joined an army led by his eldest brother, Edward the Black Prince. Its mission was to restore Pedro the Cruel to the throne of Castile. Pedro regained his crown, but England did not profit from his success. An epidemic devastated the English army, the Black Prince contracted an illness from which he never recovered, and Aquitaine, a French duchy ruled by England, rebelled to protest the taxes that had been levied to cover the cost of the Spanish war. When ill health forced the Black Prince to return to England in 1371, he charged Gaunt with the restoration of English authority in Aquitaine. Dreams of triumphs in Spain distracted Gaunt from his responsibilities in France. After the death of his first wife, Gaunt had married Pedro of Castile 's heir, Constance. Constance had been dispossessed of her patrimony by Henry of Trastamara. Gaunt hoped to drive Trastamare from Castile, but Gaunt was, unfortunately, not a skillful soldier. In 1373 his pointless maneuvers squandered an English army that had been sent to rescue Brittany and Aquitaine from French raiders. Within a year Gaunt lost everything but the cities of Bordeaux and Bayonne.

A deteriorating domestic political situation then forced him to abandon his continental projects and go back to England. The royal family was fast falling into disarray. Lionel of Clarence had died in 1368, the Black Prince's health was broken, Edward III had become senile, and the heir to the throne, the Black Prince's son Richard II, was too young to assume any responsibility. The various incapacities of Gaunt's relatives made him the most viable member of the royal family. Parliament, although it had little confidence in Gaunt, had no choice but to grant him a prominent place on the council that governed England for the aged king and his minor heir. Since some of England's clergy were among Gaunt's most active opponents, Gaunt was attracted to the cause of the church's most prominent critic, the religious reformer, John Wycliffe (1325–1384).

Gaunt's liberal religious policy was not in the best long range interest of the crown, for the arguments that Wycliffe developed to undercut the authority of ecclesiastical princes could also be turned against secular rulers. Wycliffe's followers launched a proto-Protestant movement called Lollardy, and the Lollards fomented plots and rebellions that plagued the English monarchy for the remainder of the medieval era. In 1378 Gaunt was sent back to France to defend England's interests on the continent, but he again failed to achieve anything of note. In 1381 he was in Scotland trying to negotiate a peace treaty when Wat Tyler's 'Peasants' Revolt' nearly overthrew young Richard II's government.

Richard did not trust his uncle, and in 1386 he got him out of England by financing Gaunt's long contemplated bid for the throne of Castile. The campaign failed as a military venture, but Gaunt's rival, Juan of Castile, made peace on generous terms. He married Gaunt's daughter and pledged Gaunt an annuity in exchange for Gaunt's renunciation of claims to the Spanish crown. In 1389 Richard assumed sole power in England and welcomed Gaunt home as a check to Richard's other surviving royal uncle, Thomas of Woodstock, duke of Gloucester. Gaunt was proclaimed duke of Aquitaine and given the job of negotiating a truce with France. In 1396 Richard ratified a treaty of peace with France by marrying a French princess. At about the same time Gaunt scandalized England's court by taking a third wife, his children's governess and his long term mistress, Katherine Swynford. Richard bestowed his blessing on the union and legitimized its offspring. The three sons and one daughter Katherine bore Gaunt were known as the Beauforts from a castle Gaunt owned in Anjou. Their status was greatly enhanced when their half-brother, Henry, Gaunt's son by an earlier marriage, usurped Richard's throne. Richard II was an unpopular king whom insecurity drove to tyrannical acts. In 1398 he accused his cousin Henry of breaking the peace and exiled him from England. When Gaunt died on 3 February 1399, Richard seized the opportunity of Henry's absence to destroy the powerful house of Lancaster. He disinherited Henry and declared the Lancastrian estates forfeit to the crown. This was a political blunder of major proportions. Richard's autocratic behavior alarmed the nobility, and the landed classes were not prepared to stand by while the king abolished the rights of family and property.

Henry defied Richard by returning to England, and England's barons rallied to his side to protest royal tyranny. Richard's soldiers deserted him, and he was forced to abdicate in Henry's favor. Richard died shortly after surrendering the crown, and his death extinguished the senior branch of the royal family. Gaunt's heirs were completely triumphant, but their coup set an unfortunate precedent. Within a few years the Lancastrian kings were forced to defend themselves against their cousins, the dukes of York. The result was England's long and bloody 'War of the Roses.'

2H6 2.1.41, 2.2.14, 22, 54, 56. 3H6 1.1.19, 3.3.81, 83. 1H6 2.5.77. R2. 1H4 2.2.65. 2H4 3.2.43, 310–311, 314.

John of Lancaster, *1H4, 2H4,* see John, duke of Bedford.

John-a-Combe, see Combe, John.

John-a-dreams, *Ham 2.2.570,* 'John the dreamer,' an idle, sleepy man. Robert Armin's *Nest of Ninnies* (1608) uses the term. It is similar to usages such as 'John-a-nokes,' 'John-a-stiles,' 'Jack-a-Lent' and 'Jack-a-lantern.' 'John-a-droynes' is mentioned by Thomas Nash in 1596 and George Whetstone's *Promos and Cassandra* (1578) has a character with the name, which probably means a peasant drudge.

Jonson, Ben, *Var,* 'On Ben Jonson': this witticism was supposedly improvised by Sh. in one of the verbal tavern duels between Sh. and Jonson (1572–1637), a playwright, poet, man of letters, and one of the giants of Renaissance English literature. Born in Westminster, he attended the school there and was trained to be a bricklayer like his stepfather. He served in the

Low Countries with the English army, then joined Philip Henslowe's theater company in 1592. He revised plays and acted. He was jailed with Thomas Nashe for having been part-author of *The Isle of Dogs* (1597), which was suspected of having seditious and slanderous content. He was also imprisoned in 1598 for having killed Gabriel Spencer, a fellow actor, in a duel, but was released after pleading benefit of clergy and being branded on the thumb. *Every Man in His Humour,* his first original play was presented in 1598 by the Lord Chamberlain's Men with Sh. in the cast. This 'comedy of humours' was so successful, he followed it with *Every Man Out of His Humour* (1599). His reputation as a playwright today, however, primarily rests upon *Volpone* (1606), *Epicene, or the Silent Woman* (1609), *The Alchemist* (1610), and *Bartholomew Fair* (1614). His tragedies *Sejanus His Fall* (1603), which also had Sh. in the cast, and *Catiline His Conspiracy* (1611) were much less successful. His later comedies, *The Devil Is an Ass* (1616), *The Staple of News* (1626), *The New Inn* (1629), and *A Tale of a Tub* (1633) were also not as successful as his early plays.

He was appointed Poet Laureate in 1619 which gave him yearly a salary and a butt of canary wine from the royal cellars. He also had a pension from the city of London, but he was careless with his money and died in poverty. A man of strong opinions, Jonson used his erudition in classical literature to put forth theories of playwrighting as a literary form and he never held back in expressing his ideas about the works of other writers. Though he valued Sh. as perhaps the only man who was his equal or better—all evidence indicates that they were friends—he criticized him for writing without careful thought and leaving many a bad line. Most famously he accused Sh. of having 'little Latin and less Greek,' but he also attacked *WT, Per,* and *Tit* in various ways. Nonetheless, many sources report Sh. was godfather to his child and there is a credible story that Sh., after he retired, took fever after drinking too hard with his guests, Jonson and Michael Drayton. Jonson's comedies satirizing other playwrights, such as *Cynthia's Revels* (1600) and *Poetaster* (1601) produced the so-called War of the Theaters and a counterattack in the form of *Satiromastix or the Untrussing of the Humorous Poet* (1600) by Thomas Dekker and John Marston. Despite the 'war,' Jonson was later jailed with Marston and George Chapmen for sharing authorship of *Eastward Ho!* because of a joke at the expense of the king. Holding forth at the Mermaid Tavern in Cheapside, he proposed that drama should adhere to Aristotelian principles and avoid such practices as the blending of comedy and tragedy, something which the less theoretical Sh. exploited to great effect.

His seriousness about drama as an art form, however, led him to produce his First Folio collecting his own plays in 1613, and led to the collection of Sh.'s plays in the First Folio of 1616. Without either of these collections, a large and incredibly valuable number of plays would have been lost. The flavor of Jonson's conversations were recorded by William Drummond of Hawthornden whom he visited from December 1618 to January 1619. Jonson also wrote masques for the court of King James including *The Satyr* (1603), *The Masque of Beauty* (1608), and *The Masque of Queens* (1609). He also invented the antimasque, the first success being *The Masque of Blackness* (1605). These masques were elaborately staged with settings designed by architect Inigo Jones, with whom he later quarreled because he thought the stagings were interfering with his words. As a result Jonson was replaced. The masque, however, also gave vent to Jonson's great talent for lyric poetry, which he had expressed elsewhere as well. His most famous lyric is undoubtedly 'Drink To Me Only With Thine Eyes' which was published in *The Forest* (1616), a collection of epigrams, epistles, and lyrics. Another collection was published posthumously.

Jordan, Margery, *2H6,* woman condemned for practicing witchcraft in the service of Eleanor Cobham, duchess of Gloucester. Medieval custom usually accorded witches and heretics a single opportunity to repent, and Jordan exhausted the patience of her judges. A charge of dabbling in magic first brought her before the bar in 1433. On that occasion she was released to the custody of her husband, but following her second trial, she was condemned to be burned at the stake. The sentence was carried out at Smithfield, a meadow on London's north side.

Joseph, *Shr 4.1.79,* one of Petruccio's servants.

Joshua, *LLL 5.1.120,* the successor to Moses, leader of the Israelites who conquered the land of Canaan, and most famously sacked Jericho. Later he divided his conquests among the Twelve Tribes and entered into a new covenant with God. His exploits are described in the Book of Joshua. In recent times archaeologists have attempted to verify Joshua's historical existence in order to certify the claim of the Jews upon the area that is now Israel. The name means 'the Lord is salvation.' In the pageant of the Nine Worthies, Holofernes originally instructs Nathaniel to take the role of Joshua, but later we find him as Alexander.

Jove, Roman name for Jupiter (Gr. Zeus) the chief Indo-European sky god. *TGV 4.4.200. Shr 1.1.167,* reference to Jove's disguise as a bull to win Europa. *2H6 4.1.49, 50. 3H6 5.2.14:* as he dies, the earl of Warwick compares himself to an oak—felled after sheltering a brood of royal beasts. *Tit 2.3.70, 4.1.65, 4.3.41, 4.4.14. R3 4.3.55. Ven 1015. Luc 568.*

LLL 4.3.115, 117, 139, 142, 5.2.494. MND 5.1.176. Rom 2.1.135: that Jove laughs at lovers' perjuries is from Ovid's *Artis Amatoriæ,* 1, possibly Marlowe's translation. Some critics (ignoring Sh.'s dependence on Ovid) think he may have gotten the line from Robert Greene's *Metamorphosis* or even Boiardo's *Orlando Innamorato. MWW 5.5.3, 9, 10, 14,* references to the god's many disguises in search of love. *2H4 2.2.166, 5.5.46. Ado 2.1.88, 5.5.46,* 'lusty Jove.'

H5 2.4.100, 4.3.24. AYLI 1.3.123, 'J.'s own page,' Ganymede. *2.4.56,* an oath: Jove is often substituted for the proscribed 'God.' *3.2.231,* 'J.'s tree,' the oak was sacred to the god. *3.3.7. Ham 3.2.271, 3.4.55. TN 1.5.109, 2.5.95, 166, 171, 3.4.73, 81, 4.2.12:* as Malvolio falls foolishly in love, he abandons his Puritanism for more courtly practices, perhaps indicated by his frequent invocation of the pagan god. *Tro 1.3.19, 236,* 'great Jove's acorn [accord],' *2.2.44, 126, 2.3.10 3.3.270, 4.1.18, 26, 4.7.13, 5.2.45, 52, 107. PP 6.14. MM 2.2.114. Oth 2.1.78,* 'Great J.' *2.3.17. 3.3.361,* 'Jove's dread clamours.'

AWW 4.2.26, 5.3.289. Tim 4.3.109. Ant 1.2.143, 2.7.66, 3.4.29, 3.13.85, 4.6.29, 4.16.37. Per 1.50, 147, Antiochus' daughter is fit for Jove's embracements (not that Jove shows himself very particular in mythology), and therefore for her own father's. Neither Jove nor kings need follow ordinary mores; *7.26.*

Cor 2.1.263, 3.1.89, 110, 257, 294, 5.3.71. WT 2.3.126; 4.4.16. Cym 3.3.88, 4.2.208, 350, 'J.'s bird,' the eagle. *Tmp 1.2.202,* 'J.'s lightning,' and *WT 3.1.10,* 'J.'s thunder': Jove threw thunderbolts. *Tmp 5.1.45* 'J.'s stout oak.' *TNK 1.1.29, 137, 175. 4.2.16,* see Ganymede. See Jupiter.

Jovial, (adj.) like the god Jove: cheerful, exuberant. *Cym 4.2.313,* 'his J. face.'

Judas, see Judas Iscariot. In *LLL,* also see Judas Maccabeus.

Judas Iscariot, one of the twelve men whom the Gospels say that Jesus invited to travel with him as personal companions. Judas may have been the only one of the group who was not a Galilean. He was said to have been from Kerioth. His special assignment was to handle financial affairs for Jesus and the disciples. Judas may have belonged to the party of Jews who hoped for a messiah who would destroy Rome and create a Hebrew empire on earth. When Jesus disappointed him, he lost faith and sold him to his enemies. For thirty pieces of silver he agreed to lead the servants of the High Priest of the Hebrew temple to Jesus' camp in the garden of Gethsemane. There, according to Mark 14:43, he identified Jesus by kissing him—betraying the God of love with love's symbol. Later he tried to return the silver to the priests, cast it on the floor of the temple, and hanged himself; in an alternate version he fell and burst asunder. The silver was used to buy a potter's field, Aceldama, the Field of Blood. He was traditionally portrayed as having red hair. He was also supposed to have hanged himself from an elder. *3H6 5.7.33:* Sh. saw a direct parallel between Judas' cynical kiss and the signs of affection Gloucester bestowed on the young Yorkist princes whom he planned to murder. *LLL 5.2.590–625:* Holofernes' portrayal of Judas Maccabeus in the pageant of the Nine Worthies is deliberately confused by the nobles with J. Iscariot. *R2 3.2.128, 4.1.161. AYLI 3.4.7, 8,* alludes to J.'s hair and the kiss of betrayal.

Judas Maccabeus, greatest of the five sons of Mattathiahs Maccabee of the Hashmonaean family and general of the wars for Jewish independence in the 2nd c. BC. Although outnumbered, he inflicted several defeats upon the Seleucid rulers of Palestine and in 165, liberated the temple in Jerusalem and purified it from the Greek religious practices imposed by Antiochus IV Epiphane. This purification is commemorated by Hanukkah. After subsequent warfare, Syria acknowledged Jewish religious independence, but Judas continued the war for political independence, even seeking Roman help. He was killed in battle in 161. 'Maccabeus' derives from Aramaic for 'the hammerer.' The history of the Maccabee family is told in the four books of the Maccabees, which are variously regarded in the different Christian sects as Old Testament or Apocrypha. *LLL 5.1.120,* in the pageant of the Nine Worthies, Holofernes assumes the role of Judas Maccabeus. *5.2.532, 589–598:* the nobles mock him by confusing Maccabeus with Judas Iscariot.

Jude, *LLL 5.2.619, 621,* Holofernes as Judas Maccabeus.

Judgement, *Err 4.2.40,* Judgement Day, the end of history.

Jug, *Lr. 1.4.217 (Q 4.219),* term of endearment, or nickname for Joan or Jane, possibly from an old song, 'Jug's Jugg.' It was often synonymous with 'whore.'

Jule, *Rom 1.3.45, 49, 59,* Juliet. This is either the nurse's husband's affectionate nickname, or an error. The context implies the former and produces an image of attachment between the servant and the child while her parents are away. It is also a possible play on 'jewel.'

Julia, *TGV,* one of the two female leads. Betrothed to Proteus, she disguises herself as a page when Proteus abandons her for Silvia. Later she wins him back. This shuffling of partners and the pursuit in the woods is reminiscent of *MND* and perhaps Julia is a prototype for Helena, wildly chasing the cad she loves, or even for the Helena of *AWW.* Her name as a page, Sebastian, is the same as Viola's brother in *TN,* which also features a woman in disguise as a servant. Interestingly, however, in a German analogue to *TGV* derived from an English play (*Tragædia von Julius und Hyppolita*), the main male character (who steals his best friend's betrothed) is named Julius. This would mean nothing were it not for a number of other resemblances, though not in the naming.

Juliet, 1) *Rom,* see Capulet, Juliet.

2) *MM,* 'Madame J.,' betrothed of Claudio and pregnant by him. She has a tiny role in the play and is merely a victim of Angelo's insane way of dealing with her fiancé's supposed licentiousness. There is an equivalent for her, Polina, in George Whetstone's *Promos and Cassandra* (1578).

Julietta, *MM 1.2.71, 134,* 'Madame J.,' see Juliet, *MM.*

Julius, see Cæsar, Caius Julius. *JC 3.1.205, 4.2.71. Ham, add't'l ll., Q2, A. 1.1.7,* 'the mightiest J.'

Julius Cæsar, *JC, Ant 2.6.12, 65, 3.2.55,* see Cæsar, Caius Julius.

July, seventh month of the year, named after Julius Cæsar. *Ado 1.1.265,* 'sixth of J.,' Midsummer's Day, a day for madness. *H8 1.1.154:*

Sh.'s reference is to the clarity of the fresh water that flows from springs in summer.

June, sixth month of the year, named for the goddess Juno. *1H4 2.5.365, 3.2.75. Ant 3.10.14.*

Junius Brutus, *Tit 4.1.90, Cor,* see Brutus, Decius Junius.

Juno, (Gr. Hera), queen of the Olympian gods; daughter of Saturn (Cronos); sister and wife of Jupiter and consequently goddess of marriage and protector of wives; mother of Mars, Discord (Eris), Arge, Eleithyia, Hebe, and Vulcan. Her name is a L. feminine form of 'Jove.' She married Jupiter after he had disguised himself as a cuckoo to seduce her. Most of the classical myths involve her jealousy over Jupiter's numerous seductions. Roman wives held a festival in her honor called Matronalia on the first of March (then New Year's).

LLL 4.3.116. AYLI 1.3.74, 'like J.'s swans,' evidently a confusion: Venus' chariot was drawn by swans, not Juno's. *5.4.139,* 'Wedding is great J.'s crown.' *Tro 1.2.116.*

AWW 3.4.13. Lr 2.2.198, 'By J.' *Ant 3.11.28, 4.16.35. Per 7.28, 21.100:* the image is reminiscent of Enobarbus' great speech on Cleopatra (*Ant 2.2.242*). *Cor 2.1.99, 4.2.56.*

WT 4.4.121, 'Juno's eyes,' Samuel Johnson argued that this was a mistake akin to 'J.'s swans' in *AYLI* and that Pallas Athena's eyes were meant, as she was the goddess of blue eyes. However, the peacock was Juno's sacred bird and the allusion may be to the Argus eyes on the feathers. Furthermore, Homer called Hera (Gr. Juno) as 'ox-eyed,' so there is no reason not to think of her eyes or eyelids as 'sweet' in the sense of delightful, soft, etc. *Cym 3.4. 166,* 'You made great Juno angry': Innogen's beauty has aroused Juno's jealousy; *4.2.52, 5.5.126.*

Tmp 4, Prospero calls up the vision of Juno as a lesson for Ferdinand and Miranda. *TNK 1.1.63,* 'J.'s mantle': in Homer's *Iliad,* 14, the robe which the goddess wears to arouse Zeus is described. *1.2.21:* Jupiter's last mortal love was a Theban—Alcmene, mother of Hercules. As a result Juno had a great hatred for the city. This line resembles Arcite's remark in Chaucer's *Knyghtes Tale,* A 1543–44, the most important source of *TNK. 4.2.20,* 'great-eyed J.'s.'

Jupiter, (Gr. Zeus), supreme god of the Romans often called upon to resolve disputes among the other gods, son of Saturn (Cronos), husband of Juno, he became king of the Olympian gods by castrating his father and overthrowing the Titans. Jupiter means 'God the father.' His tree was the oak—the giant of the forest that was frequently struck by the god's preferred weapon, the lightning bolt. He had a lighter and less dignified side. Many of his appearances in mythology involve his assuming various forms to gratify his enormous sexual appetites, and the plenitude of his seductions have often caused them to be cited in humorous contexts, though these dalliances often have serious consequences because of Juno's wrath against the offspring. On one occasion he transformed himself into a bull in order to abduct a princess who inspired his lust. When Europa, daughter of King Agenor of Phoenicia, was seduced into climbing onto his back, he swam with her to Crete where he made her the mother of several children. Sh. often seems to use Jupiter or Jove to avoid violating the censors' restrictions against the use of 'God.'

Tit 4.3.67, 79, 83, 84. MWW 5.5.6. AYLI 2.4.1, 3.2.152. Tro 1.2.60, 158, 2.3.196 4.7.75, 5.1.50. Lr 1.1.177 (Q 1.168), 2.2.197 (Q 7.201), 'By J.' *Ant 2.2.6, 3.2.9, 10. Cor 1.3.40, 1.10.89, 2.1.102, 4.5.104. WT 4.4.27,* refers to Jupiter's rape of Europa. Ovid's *Metamorphoses,* 6, describes Arachne's tapestry and contains a reference to Neptune as ram, to Apollo in peasant garb, and Jupiter as bull and is therefore the obvious source of the passage *4.4.25–31.*

Cym 5.5: the god appears as a *deus ex machina* in a vision of Posthumus promising Sicilius that his son's ill fortunes will be reversed. Jupiter leaves a tablet which is interpreted within the play, but has also been seen as praise of the uniting of the kingdoms by the crowning of James I. If this was intended, then Jupiter may be symbolic of James himself. From the stage directions it seems that a mechanical contrivance was used to lower Jupiter upon an eagle to the stage. *2.3.122,* 'son of Jupiter,' a possible allusion to Hercules, though likely to mean any son of Jupiter. *2.4.121, 3.5.84, 3.6.42,* Jupiter used as an oath. *2.4.122, 5.5.84, 5.6.428, 483. Tmp 4.1.78. TNK 4.3.32.*

Justice, allegorical figure or goddess of equity or fairness. Justice has been depicted as a virgin blindfolded and holding scales, a common legal symbol. The Greeks called her Dike, or Praxidice, daughter of Zeus and Themis (who was also a goddess of justice). The Romans worshipped her as Astræa or Justitia. *Tit 4.3.40, MM 1.3.29, 32, 3.1.511.*

Justice of the Peace, country gentleman charged with maintaining the king's peace. Originally the justices assisted the itinerant judges who presided at the king's circuit courts. In the 15th c. they were empowered to convene courts of their own and render verdicts in certain kinds of cases. An appointment as a justice was often a stepping stone to a higher governmental office. *2H6 4.7.39,* (pl.) *2H4 3.2.57. MWW 1.1.4, 254.*

Juvenal, term of endearment used by Falstaff, Flute, and Armado. If it refers to the great Roman satirist Decius Junius Juvenalis (c. 60–c. 140 AD), it is not clear how. Possibly it is a pun on his name although it seems to mean merely 'boy' or possibly 'jewel.' The three characters who use it commonly mistake one word for another for humorous effect and Juvenal would have been a familiar author to Sh.'s audience. Although pessimistic on the whole, Juvenal had a remarkable capacity for the felicitous phrase, many of which are still in current use, such as *Mens sana in corpore sano,* ('A healthy mind in a healthy body') and his observations about hypocrisy and corruption must have seemed as relevant in the Renaissance city as they do in our own.

LLL 1.1.8, 12, 13, 'tender juvenal.' *3.1.64. MND 3.1.89,* 'juvenile,' F1 'Iuvenall.' *2H4 1.2.19.*

K

Kate, nickname for Katherine or Catherine, often punning on 'cate,' a choice morsel or dainty.

1) *Shr,* nickname for Katherine Minola, used almost exclusively by Petruccio. His first use of it (*2.1.181*) is considered an impudence by her as it is too familiar. He plays on 'cate,' (*2.1.188–89*) and 'cat' (*2.1.271*), and as in much early Sh., the joke goes on far too long. Even Gremio gets into the act: 'Petruccio is Kated' *3.3.117. 2.1.188,* 'Kate Hall': possibly Petruccio means that Kate is held in such repute that the Minola home has acquired her name.

2) *LLL 4.3.80,* see Catherine 1).

3) *1H4, 2H4,* see Percy, Lady.

4) *H5,* Henry's affectionate term for Catherine of France.

5) *MM,* see Keepdown, Mistress Kate.

6) *Tmp 2.2.48,* common woman in Stefano's drinking song who staved off sailing men with a strong tongue (a suggestion of Petruchio's Kate in *Shr*?) but who had a weakness for tailors.

7) *H8 2.4.130,* affectionate nickname that Sh. has Henry VIII use in intimate conversations with his wife, Katherine of Aragon. Sh. ignores the fact that Henry treated Katherine roughly when she opposed his decision to end their marriage. There was a prospect of war with the Holy Roman Emperor Charles V (Katherine's nephew) if Katherine refused to recognize the divorce. Though Henry seems to have held affection for Katherine and his daughter Mary, Anne Boleyn arranged a number of humiliations to which Henry acquiesced.

Katherina, variation of Katherine, *Shr 1.1.52, 100; 1.2.98, 123; 2.1.1.sd, 43–4, 181.sd; 5.2.7.* Usually used to accommodate the meter, though it also appears in the stage directions. See Minola, Katherine.

Katherine, 1) *Shr,* see Minola, K.

2) *LLL,* see Catherine.

3) *H5,* see Catherine.

Katherine of Aragon, *H8,* (1485–1536), Henry VIII's first wife and mother of Queen Mary. Katherine was the daughter of Ferdinand and Isabella of Spain. At the age of 16 she was wed to Henry VII's 15-year-old son, Arthur, the heir to the English throne. Arthur died five months after their marriage. Henry VII was reluctant to return Katherine's dowry and to lose her as a tie with Spain, but he did not know how to justify keeping her in England. Since he was recently widowed, he flirted with the idea of marrying her himself. The plan was unacceptable to her father, who preferred a union with the new heir to the throne, Arthur's brother, Henry. Henry VII was not initially enthusiastic about the idea. The validity of a marriage between a man and his former sister-in-law could be questioned and doubts raised about the legitimacy of their children. Such suspicions could imperil the future of a dynasty. Although Katherine claimed that Arthur's youth and ill health had prevented the consummation of their union and that, therefore, no valid marriage had taken place, English authorities insisted on a papal dispensation to permit her to wed Henry. Julius II issued the required documents on 26 December 1503, but Henry did not marry Katherine until 11 June 1509, two months after he had inherited the throne. He may have been urged to this step by his dying father who regretted the way Katherine had been treated. Henry was six years Katherine's junior, but differences in age created no obvious impediment to domestic harmony. Henry was affectionate with his wife and conducted his extramarital affairs with a great deal more discretion than most of his fellow kings.

The only problem with their marriage was her difficulty in bearing children. In the first seven years of their life together Katherine was pregnant five times before she bore a child who lived (1516). Henry was delighted, but not content. The infant was a girl (the future queen, Mary). No woman had ever successfully ruled England, and the strong prejudices of the age led many to doubt that a woman could or should lead a nation. Henry was convinced that the security of England depended on his siring a male heir. Katherine's last pregnancy ended with the stillbirth of another female in 1518. And, as the years passed, the queen's increasing age made it less and less likely that she could give Henry the son he wanted. By 1524 it was rumored about Europe that the king of England was considering a divorce, and in 1526 events prompted him to act. Henry fell in love with Anne Boleyn, the daughter of one of his courtiers. His desire to have legitimate children by her brought him early in 1527 to ask Katherine for a divorce. Henry hoped that Katherine would submit to an amicable separation. He tried to convince her that their union had been unfruitful because it contravened God's law. Katherine found his argument less than convincing. Leviticus 20:21 prohibited a man from taking his brother's wife, but Deuteronomy 25:5 laid out circumstances under which such relationships were permissible. More importantly, the pope had given them his blessing, and Katherine was not about to submit to an annulment that would brand her daughter illegitimate and destroy Mary's claim to England's throne.

Cardinal Wolsey, Henry's chief advisor, persuaded him to seek papal approval for a separation from Katherine There was ample precedent for the dissolution of royal marriages, but in this instance the timing was unfortunate. Katherine's nephew, Charles V (Holy Roman Emperor, ruler of Burgundy and the Netherlands, and king of Spain), was waging a successful war in Italy. Charles supported his aunt's campaign to preserve her marriage, and Clement VII could not risk offending him. Clement's strategy was to delay as long as possible. In October 1528, Cardinal Wolsey won papal permission to convene a court in England to hear the king's case, but when Katherine refused to recognize its jurisdiction and appealed to Rome, the pope terminated the proceedings (July 1529). Henry vented his rage on those within reach. He dismissed Wolsey from his service, and on 14 July 1531, he sent Katherine from court. He never saw her again, refused to receive letters from her, and denied her the company of her daughter. The king began openly to live with Anne Boleyn, and by January 1533, Anne was pregnant. Henry secretly married Anne, and on 23 May 1533, Thomas Cranmer, a Protestant sympathizer who had recently been consecrated archbishop of Canterbury, declared that Henry had never been validly wed to Katherine. She was ordered to cease using the title 'queen' and to style herself 'princess dowager,' the rank due her as the widow of her husband, Arthur, prince of Wales. When she refused to comply, her household was reduced and her life made physically and psychologically difficult.

In December 1533, Henry repudiated the authority of the papacy, and on 23 March 1534, Clement, having nothing to lose from the gesture, announced a verdict in Katherine's favor. The pope's action did her and her Catholic faith no good. She considered leaving England, but Charles V persuaded her to stay, and there was a possibility of war over Henry's actions. In November 1534, parliament recognized Henry as the head of the English church. Katherine's health broke under the strain of her situation, and she died on 8 January 1536. Her last act was to dictate an affectionate letter to Henry beseeching him to be kind to their daughter. Although foreign born, Katherine earned the affection of the English people. They admired her courage, respected her reputation as an honorable woman, and were shamed by the treatment she received which was often instigated by Henry's temper or Anne Boleyn's vengeance. She cast a long shadow from which Anne never escaped.

Katherine, St., *1H6 1.3.79,* one of the heavenly figures with whom Joan of Arc believed herself to be in contact. The voices Joan heard directed her to go to St. Katherine's church at Fierbois to find the sword she was to use to drive the English from France. It was allegedly the weapon Charles Martel (714–741) had used to defend France from Saracen invaders. St. Katherine of Alexandria was a 4th c. martyr who was executed for the crime of converting the Empress Faustina to the Christian faith. St.

Katherine was tortured on the wheel and decapitated. Her cult became popular in Europe in the 10th c. Since she was the guardian of maidens, she was an ideal patroness for young Joan.

Keech, Goodwife, *2H4 2.1.96,* comical name for a butcher's wife. A 'keech' is a lump or roll of fat harvested from a slaughtered animal.

Keepdown, Mistress Kate, *MM 3.1.458,* Lucio's mate, according to Mistress Overdone. She claims Kate had a child of Lucio's a bit more than a year ago and that she cares for it. This may be a fabrication to help her own case, but Escalus believes it and orders Lucio's arrest. Kate's name reflects her profession.

Keighley, Richard, *H5 4.8.104,* Ketly, Kelly, (d. 1415), English casualty of the battle at Agincourt. Only three other English gentlemen died winning Henry V's great victory over the French. French losses, on the other hand, were said to have numbered in the thousands.

Kemp, William, also 'Kempe,' (fl. 1583–1602) one of the most celebrated performers in the company called the Lord Chamberlain's Men. His name appears in older editions of *Ado F1 4.2* and *Rom Q2, s.d. 4.5.99* in place of the characters he is portraying, Dogberry and Peter. As principal clown, his roles involve malapropisms, earthiness, and physical humor, and critics argue that he performed the roles of Lance, Costard, Lancelot Gobbo, Bottom, and Falstaff. He was one of the original shareholders of the Lord Chamberlain's Men and the Globe, but he was already known as a comic. He was a fool for the Earl of Leicester in the mid-1580s and performed in Netherlands and Denmark. By 1593, he was in Lord Strange's Men. In 1599, however, he left the company. Exactly why is unknown, but the possibility that he had been involved in the pirated editions of several plays—he passed copies of plays to unauthorized printers—has been argued convincingly by James Forse. Shortly thereafter in February 1600, perhaps to raise money, he morris danced from London to Norwich (100 mi.) in 9 stages, and published a book on the feat, *Kemps nine daies wonder.* This seems to have been the peak of his career. He travelled on the continent. In 1602, he was with the Earl of Worcester's Men, joining Thomas Heywood in a royal performance. The next year he disappears from history and was said to be dead by 1608.

Kendal green, *1H4 2.5.236,* rough woolen fabric produced in the town of Kendal in Westmorland. Since Robin Hood and his men were alleged to wear uniforms made of the durable cloth, it was associated with highway robbers.

Kenilworth, *2H6 4.4.38, 4.4.43,* a great castle in Warwickshire whose construction began in the 12th c. The stronghold was acquired and enlarged by John of Gaunt, ancestor of the Lancastrian kings. The royal family used it as a retreat during the War of the Roses. It remained in royal hands until the Tudor queen, Elizabeth I, gave it to Robert Dudley. Near Sh.'s home town of Stratford, it was the site in 1575 of a three-week spectacular with masques and other entertainment honoring Elizabeth. The boy Sh. would likely have been among the crowds who saw it.

Kent, county at the southeastern tip of England. It commands the British side of the narrowest portion of the English channel and is, therefore, a natural focal point for communications between Britain and the continent. Both the Roman and Saxon conquests of Britain were directed from beachheads established there. At the start of the medieval period it was an independent Anglo-Saxon kingdom that had strong ties with the continent and the papacy. Its organization as a shire may date from the times of King Ecgbert of Wessex in 839, when he gave the county to his son Æthelstan. After the Norman Conquest, the first earl was Odo, the Bishop of Bayeux. When there was war between France and England, it was uniquely vulnerable. On several occasions the threat of invasion or raids on ports and shipping caused the people to march on nearby London to protest the ineffectiveness of a weak royal government. Kentishmen were active in Wat Tyler's Rebellion (1381), Jack Cade's Rebellion (1450), and the revolt of Sir Thomas Wyatt (1554), son of the sonneteer, against the marriage of Mary Tudor to Philip of Spain. One of the oldest place names in Britain, the geographer Strabo mentions it in the 1st c. BC. It probably derives from a Celtic word meaning 'edge' or 'border.' Canterbury is in the county and its name has the same origin.

Jn 4.2.201, 5.1.30. R2 5.6.8. 1H4 2.1.55. 2H6 4.1.100, 4.2.121, 4.4.56, 4.7.51, 52, 59. 3H6 1.1.157, 4.9.12. R3 4.4.434.

Kent, Earl of, 1) *R2 5.6.8,* Thomas Holland (1375–1400), duke of Surrey, one of Richard II's faithful allies. He took part in the coup of 1397 that enabled Richard to destroy the 'lords appellant,' the barons who had tried to limit the king's freedom to govern independently. He helped with the arrest and execution of his uncle, the earl of Arundel, and he profited personally from the destruction of Arundel and his allies. The fall of the 'lords appellant' left Richard free to fill posts with his own men. He rewarded Kent with the dukedom of Surrey and appointed him Earl Marshal of England. In the later capacity, Surrey (Kent) was to have presided at a trial by combat between the hereditary marshal, Thomas Mowbray, duke of Norfolk, and Henry (IV) Bolingbroke, heir to the duchy of Lancaster. The duel was cancelled when Richard decided to banish both men from England, and Norfolk's exile left Surrey (Kent) in uncontested possession of the marshal's title. The marshal was with Richard's army in Ireland in 1399 when Henry defied his sentence of banishment and returned to England with armed companions. Surrey attempted, but failed, to mediate between Richard and Henry, and when Richard yielded the throne to Henry, Surrey was imprisoned for some offense against the new king. (He may have received land belonging to Henry's duchy of Lancaster—an estate Richard had confiscated following the death of John of Gaunt.) He was also accused of involvement in the murder of the duke of Gloucester, one of the 'lords appellant.' Henry stripped him (and other men whom Richard had recently promoted) of the rank of duke. Late in 1399, Surrey (no longer Kent) joined a conspiracy to assassinate Henry IV and restore Richard. When news of the scheme leaked out, Surrey and his fellow conspirators fled to Cirencester. They were captured and killed by a mob loyal to the king.

2) *Lr,* an honest nobleman who suffers banishment for urging his king not to make the horrible mistake of rejecting Cordelia. His loyalty is in sharp contrast to the self-aggrandizement practiced by so many others in the play. Though under threat of death by a confused monarch, he disguises himself to remain in England and help Lear's cause. Lear never recognizes his devotion and is incapable of knowing him at the end. When Albany asks Kent to share power with Edgar, Kent says that he will soon join the Lear and serve him in death. In *The True Chronicle Historie of King Leir* (1605), Sh. found his model for the selfless nobleman in the chracter of Perillus, who stays by Leir's side and protects him from murder. Because of the verbal echoes of Perillus in Kent, it has been argued that Sh. himself may have played Perillus for the Lord Chamberlain's Men in the late 1500s. It has also been speculated that the Cordell Annesley affair, which took place in Kent, might have provoked Sh.'s use of the name (see Cordelia).

Kentishmen, residents of the county of Kent. During the medieval era the men of Kent were a source of political unrest in England, for they often had reason to be angry at their king. Since Kent occupied the corner of England that most closely approached the continent, it was unusually vulnerable to attack. When England's royal government was weak, England's enemies roamed the channel harassing the shores of Kent and looting the ships of its merchants. *2H6 3.1.356. 3H6 1.2.41.*

Kersey, coarse woollen cloth, usually ribbed. It was associated with simplicity or plainness. Its name derives from the village of Kersey west of Ipswich on a tributary of the river Brent in

Suffolk in eastern England, where it was thought to have originated. *Shr 3.2.65,* 'k. boot-hose.' *LLL 5.2.413,* 'honest k. noes.' *MM 1.2.33.*

Kildare, Earl of, *H8 2.1.42,* Gerald Fitzgerald (d. 1534), ninth earl and Henry VIII's deputy in Ireland. Kildare is an Irish town and county southwest of Dublin. In Henry's day England had direct control only over the 'English Pale,' a small area (60 mi. across) supervised from Dublin. Order in the rest of the country was maintained by native family organizations whose heads were vassals of the English king. The most powerful of these was the Fitzgerald clan led by the earls of Kildare. The commitment of the Irish nobles to their English overlord was shaky, and Henry's quarrel with the pope provided them with an excuse to repudiate his authority. In 1534 Henry induced Kildare to leave the safety of Ireland and come to court. Once in England, Kildare was arrested and sent to the Tower. The charge against him was conspiracy to permit the pope's agents to establish a base in Ireland. He died of natural causes a few months later, and his case never came to trial. Kildare's son took revenge by instigating a revolt that nearly drove the English into the sea. An English army under the command of Lord Leonard Grey suppressed the rebellion and captured young Kildare in the summer of 1535. In 1541 Henry reached an agreement with the Irish clans and celebrated the event by assuming the title 'king of Ireland.' The title implied greater authority than he or any of his heirs was able to exercise.

Kimbolton, *H8 4.1.34,* town in Huntingdonshire, 65 mi. north of London. Katherine of Aragon was housed in its castle following her separation from Henry VIII. She died there on 8 January 1536.

King, monarch of a single land or people, in rank usually inferior only to an emperor.

1) *Tit.* see Saturninus.

2) *LLL 2.1.2, 137, 153, 5.2.712,* the king of France, father of the Princess.

3) *LLL 4.1.1, 4.2.136, 140, 5.2.815, Add. B 2,* see Ferdinand, king of Navarre.

4) *LLL 4.1.70, 74, 77, 78,* see Cophetua.

5) *MND 2.1.18,* see Oberon.

6) *MWW 1.1.103,* see Henry V. There is no sign that Falstaff has been rejected by Henry, as he is in *2H4,* yet Fenton's life with the wild prince (*3.2.66–67, 3.4.8*) is spoken of in the past tense, indicating that Henry has reformed. Regardless of when written, this should mean that the action of *MWW* is set before *2H4,* though one should never expect Sh. to be consistent in such matters.

7) *STM,* Henry VIII, mentioned, but not appearing.

8) *Ant 3.1.3,* see Orodes.

9) *TNK 1.2.107,* see Creon. *1.4.16:* this description would make Palamon and Arcite the children of sisters and nephew of Creon and therefore the sons of Jocasta (by Oedipus) and Hipponome (by Alcæus). It is not likely that this was intended. Nephew probably is equivalent to the Renaissance sense of 'cousin,' meaning 'relative,' and Creon's sisters are not meant.

King and the Beggar, *LLL 1.2.104–5,* see Cophetua.

King of Cats, *Rom 3.1.76,* see Tybalt.

King of Heaven, *R3 1.2.105,* the Christian God.

King of Kings, *1H6 1.1.28, R3 1.4.190, 2.1.13,* the Christian God. The title is found in Revelation 17:14; 19:16.

King's English, *MWW 1.4.5,* proper English, reminding one that the word 'grammar' is related to 'glamour,' implying that the high-born speak properly, though several English kings spoke a dialect or no English at all. The expression (King's or Queen's E.) had been in use for some time before Sh.

King's King, *R3 4.4.277,* see King of Kings.

King's peace, *1H6 1.4.73,* concept in English law. The early Anglo-Saxons assumed that each head of a household had the right to maintain peace within his establishment. A fight among guests was a violation of their host's 'peace,' and the higher the rank of the householder, the more serious the crime of breaching his peace. The king's peace prevailed wherever he was present, and it included places, like courts, where royal agents represented him. The jurisdiction of the peace slowly spread to institutions (e.g., churches) and localities (e.g., roads) that transcended local governmental authority. Finally, the peace was understood to encompass the entire realm with respect to certain kinds of crimes.

Knight of the Burning Lamp, *1H4 3.3.25-26,* parody of the kinds of names often given to heroes in medieval romances.

Knight, Sir, *TN 3.4.264,* name for Sir Andrew, or a personification of duelling. Viola seems to be saying, 'I would rather engage in peaceful practices than warlike ones.'

L

Laban, brother of Isaac, father of Leah and Rachel, uncle and father-in-law of Jacob. *MV 1.3.70, 77,* the story alluded to is that in Genesis 30 in which Jacob caused Laban's sheep to become weaker and his own stronger thus enriching himself at the expense of his uncle (who had exploited Jacob's labor for twenty years).

Labienus, *Ant,* Quintus L., (d. 39 BC), Roman soldier whose free-lance activities threatened Mark Antony's control of the eastern half of the Roman empire. Labienus' father, a plebeian tribune who defected from Cæsar's party to Pompey's, died in the wars between Cæsar and Pompey. Labienus joined the army raised by Cæsar's assassins, Brutus and Cassius. They sent him to Parthia to negotiate an alliance with its king, Orodes. Orodes was so impressed by him that he allowed him to share command of a Parthian army with one of Orodes' sons. In 40 BC Labienus' Parthian troops broke through Mark Antony's lines, captured the city of Antioch, and entered Asia Minor. (This is the disaster that is reported to Antony in *Ant 1.2.92.*) A year later Antony's general, Publius Ventidius, drove the Parthians back. Labienus fled into Cilicia where he was captured and executed.

Labio, *JC 5.3.107,* Quintus Antistius Labeo, (d. 42 BC), Roman legal scholar and one of the men who Plutarch says ('Brutus' 13.4–5) helped Brutus and Cassius plot Julius Cæsar's assassination. He committed suicide following the loss of his party's cause at the battle of Philippi.

Labyrinth, *1H6 5.5.144,* a maze. The term may derive from a Greek word for the twisted passages of a mine. Stories about a number of labyrinths appear in classical mythology. The best known is that of a maze designed by an Athenian architect, Dædalus, for Minos, king of the island of Crete. According to the myth as it is narrated by Ovid (*Metamorphoses,* 8.155), Minos' wife had intercourse with a bull and conceived a monster. Minos ordered Dædalus to build an enclosure from which the creature and the human beings who were fed to it could not escape. Some scholars have speculated that the great palace at Knossos on the northern shore of Crete might have suggested the idea of the Minoan labyrinth to the early Greeks. Complexly built with a confusing series of hallways and rooms, it also was decorated, the archeologist Sir Arthur Evans discovered, with the motif of a double-headed axe called a *labrys.* Labyrinths never passed out of fashion. They were outlined on the floors of medieval cathedrals, and pilgrims did penance by exploring them on their knees. Gardeners in Sh.'s day designed labyrinths of hedges for the amusement of people who enjoyed the challenge of wandering through a geometric puzzle.

Lacedæmon, alternative name for Sparta, which was founded in legend by the hero Lacedæmon. See Sparta. *Tim 2.2.148,* Timon's lands extended all the way to the borders of Attica; *3.6.59,* an allusion to Alcibiades' battles against Sparta.

Lackbeard, Lord, *Ado 5.1.188,* Benedick's insulting name for Claudio. He is calling him a boy.

Lacys, *2H6 4.2.45,* one of England's great noble families. In 1232 John de Lacy, son of Robert de Lacy (d. 1212), justiciar of England, became, by right of his wife's inheritance, earl of Lincoln. Henry de Lacy (1251–1311), the third earl (one of the 'Lords Ordainers,' the group of barons that dominated Edward II's government), bequeathed Lincoln to his daughter Alice. From her mother Alice inherited another earldom, Salisbury. Both honors passed to Alice's husband, Thomas of Lancaster, and became part of the huge patrimony of the Lancastrian dukes and kings.

Lady, 1) 'Our L.,' the Virgin Mary. 'By our Lady!' was a common, mild oath. *Tit 4.4.48. 1H6*

1.3.53. R3 2.3.4. LLL 2.1.98. Rom 1.5.33. 1H4 2.5.44, 2.5.301, 2.5.427. 2H4 5.3.90. TN 2.3.61. Oth 3.3.75. H8 1.3.46.

2) *Lr. Q 4.108,* 'L. the brach,' name of a female dog. Compare *Lr. 1.4.111,* 'L. Brach.'

Lady [of May], *TNK 3.5.127,* character in the morris dance before Theseus. Also known as the Queen of May, she was usually represented in the costume of Maid Marian.

Lady of the Strachey, *TN 2.5.37,* see Strachey.

Lærtes, 1) legendary king of Ithaca and father of Odysseus (Ulysses). In his youth Lærtes was said to have sailed with Jason and the Argonauts. Lærtes' name is very ancient. It appears in Cretan linear B tablets and derives from Greek meaning 'to urge on.' Sh.'s allusion (*Tit 1.1.377*) is to a story about Odysseus in which Odysseus persuades the Greek king Agamemnon to give honorable burial to Ajax's corpse. The rites appropriate to the occasion were uncertain, for Ajax had gone mad and killed himself. The tale is told in Sophocles' *Ajax,* but Sh. may have known it from a commentary on Horace's *Satires.*

2) *Ham,* son of Polonius, brother of Ophelia. He studies fencing in France and returns to avenge his sister's mistreatment by Hamlet by being drawn into Claudius' scheme. He dies in the duel which closes the play and his repentance at his imminent death redeems his character somewhat. The name has no precedent in the sources for Sh.'s play. In *Der Bestrafte Brudermord* (1710) which seems to be a German rendition of an older version of the play, Lærtes is called Leonhardus. Both he and his sister have names with Greek origins.

Lafeu, *AWW,* F1 'Lafew,' 'Lord L.,' elderly noble of the court of France, a man of wisdom, though also of anger. He advises Bertram to accept the marriage to Helen and furiously berates Paroles. He provides a contrast to the immature behavior of Bertram. His name means 'fire' in French and refers to his quick temper. He does not exist in Sh.'s sources for the play.

Lammas Eve, *Rom 1.3.19, 23,* Juliet's birthday, July 31. See Lammastide.

Lammastide, *Rom 1.3.16,* August 1. It commemorated the deliverance of St. Peter from prison and celebrated the first harvests of the year. Bread was made with the new grain and used in the Eucharist. The name derives from OE *hlafmæsse,* 'mass of the loaf.' It was the Puritan custom to avoid popishness by substituting '-tide' for '-mas' in holy day constructions. Sh. moved the season of the play from Easter in his source to summer.

Lamond, common editorial alternative for Lamord, based on F1.

Lamord (Q spelling), *Ham 4.7.78,* F1 'Lamound,' a Norman who praises Lærtes to Claudius. There is a possibility that all of this is a fabrication to manipulate a popular candidate for Claudius' throne into a duel with his second enemy, Hamlet. Note that it is Lærtes who supplies the name, although Claudius does describe him until Lærtes recognizes him. It has been suggested that this is an allusion to Pietro Monte (in English translation, Peter Mount), a famous swordsman who was instructor of Louis VII's Master of Horse. He was master of military exercises at the court of Urbino and served in the Venetian army. He is mentioned in the influential *Book of the Courtier* (1.5, 25; 2.16) by Baldassare Castiglione, but little is known about him.

Lancaster, 1) *1H4 5.1.45,* duchy and dynasty whose name derived from that of a Roman camp (*castra*) on the river Lune in northern England on the coast of the Irish Sea. The duchy was the patrimony of the English kings Henry IV, Henry V, and Henry VI. An earldom of Lancaster was created in 1267 for Edmund Crouchback, the second son of King Henry III. Edmund's grandson, Henry Wryneck, became the second duke created in England. The first was Edward III's heir, Edward the Black Prince. Henry's daughter, Blanche, brought the family lands and titles to her husband, John of Gaunt, Edward III's fourth son. Gaunt's son, Henry Bolingbroke, established the house of Lancaster by forcing the abdication of his cousin, Richard II. Henry founded a Lancastrian dynasty that included himself (1399–1413), his son, Henry V (1413–1422), and his grandson, Henry VI (1422–1461). The Lancastrians were forced from the throne by their cousins, the dukes of York. Since the heraldic emblems of the houses Lancaster and York were red and white roses respectively, their fight over the throne came to be known as the 'War of the Roses.' The direct line of male descent within the house was extinguished during the War of the Roses, but the Tudor kings who replaced the Yorkists after the battle of Bosworth in 1485 based their claim to the throne on vague connections with the Lancastrians. Henry VI's mother, Catherine of France, took Owen Tudor as her second husband. Her sons by Owen, Edmund (earl of Richmond) and Jasper (earl of Pembroke), were Henry's half-brothers. Edmund reinforced the Tudor-Lancaster tie by marrying Margaret, daughter of John Beaufort (duke of Somerset and grandson of John of Gaunt). Their only son, Henry (VII), established the Tudor dynasty, whose last queen, Elizabeth, was reigning over England at the start of Sh.'s career. It was to Sh.'s advantage to treat the history of the house of Lancaster with respect. *2H6 1.1.257, 2.2.66, 4.1.52. 3H6. 1H6 2.5.102. R3 1.2.6, 1.3.128, 1.4.15, 199, 5.5.90, 5.8.27.*

2) used as a name for a member of the house of Lancaster. *R3 1.2.4,* see Henry VI. *1H4 5.4.16,* see John, duke of Bedford.

3) the duke of L. *R2 1.1.1., 5.5.2,* see John of Gaunt. *1H4 3.1.8, 4.3.63,* see Henry IV.

Lance, *TGV,* F1 'Launce,' dull-witted clown. The part was probably a vehicle for the comedian William Kempe and a number of similarities between this play and *MV* imply that Lance is a prototype for Lancelot Gobbo. The jesting between Lance and Speed may have been suggested by that between Daris and Samias in John Lyly's *Endimion* (1591). There is also a resemblance between Lance and Grobianus Pickelhering (in that he speaks about a dog) in Jakob Ayrer's *Tragædia von Julius und Hyppolita,* a German analogue to *TGV* which was taken from an English play performed in Germany by an English company.

Lancelot, *MV,* see Gobbo, L.

Langley, King's Langley, village in Hertfordshire about 20 mi. northeast of London. It was the site of the royal palace at which Edward III's son, Edmund Langley was born. See Edmund Langley, *1H6, 2H6.*

Langton, Stephen, *Jn 3.1.69,* (d. 1228), archbishop of Canterbury whose consecration inaugurated a lengthy battle between Pope Innocent III and John, king of England. The death of Hubert Walter in 1205 necessitated the choice of a new primate for the church in England, but there was confusion about the procedure for the appointment of his successor. The monks who staffed the cathedral at Canterbury had papal permission to conduct an election, but custom dictated that candidates for important ecclesiastical offices be acceptable to the kings of the nations where they served. The choice of an archbishop called for negotiation between church and state, but the monks did not trust John and feared that he intended to force a man on them they did not like. Their strategy, therefore, was to present the king with a *fait accompli.* They sent the prior of their cloister to Rome in the hope that he would be consecrated before John could do anything about it. When John learned of their ploy, he dispatched his own candidate to Rome and ordered the pope to ignore the man sent by the monks. Innocent, hoping to avoid a choice that would impugn the privileges of either the king or the church, suggested a compromise. He rejected both candidates that had been sent to him from England and consecrated a neutral party who had no involvement in the fight: Stephen Langton.

Langton was an Englishman who had distinguished himself as a theologian and politician. He and Innocent had become friends during their student days in Paris, and Innocent had given him a post at the papal court. Although he was in every respect worthy of Canterbury, John refused to accept him and forced the showdown between church and state that the pope had tried to avoid. Once the contest began, Innocent used all the spiritual weapons at his disposal. In March 1208 he closed the churches of England and deprived John's subjects of the sacraments. When that failed to move John, the pope excommunicated the king (November 1209). John proved indifferent to threats to his soul, and Innocent was compelled to go the limit and call for his deposition (on the grounds that a man who had shut himself out of the church had no right to rule a Christian nation). The pope did not have the power to force a king to lay down his crown, but by declaring a government illegitimate, the pope could encourage rebels to take up arms. In 1213 self-interest succeeded where religious duty had failed. John's evolving political agenda persuaded him to make peace with the church. John wanted to organize an international coalition against France and win back the lands he had lost on the continent. That project required him to make sure that England was united behind him and that the church was publicly committed to the rightness of his cause.

John won the church's support by giving Innocent more than he expected. John welcomed Langton to England in July 1213, and he took an oath of fealty to the papacy. When John's elaborate plan for the conquest of France foundered in 1214 at the battle of Bouvines, Langton joined the king's enemies. He was a leader among the English barons who forced John to the conference at Runnymede, and he helped draft Magna Carta. Langton's behavior shocked Innocent, who had no sympathy with rebellious subjects who presumed to dictate terms to the kings and popes God appointed to lead them. Innocent suspended the archbishop and committed the church to John's defense. The deaths of both Innocent and John in 1216 ended the crisis. Langton returned to Canterbury, and at the start of Henry III's reign he carried out a thorough reorganization of the English church.

Lapland, area of northern Europe comprising northern Scandinavia and the Kola Peninsula in what is now Russia. Mostly above the Arctic circle it is largely tundra with some areas of mountain and forest and has a harsh climate. The summer is short and relatively hot because the sun remains above the horizon for most of the three months. During this time mosquitoes fill the air. In winter the sun does not rise for seven to eight weeks and the aurora borealis is often the only light. The area draws its name from the Lapps who are descendants of a central Asian people who were pushed northward by the Finnish, Gothic, and Slavic migrations. Their language belongs to the Finnic group of the Uralic family of languages, relating it to Estonian and Finnish. They were under the nominal control of Sweden and Norway in the Middle Ages, but were not entirely Christianized until the 18th c. Their traditional economy and daily lives are built around the nomadic herding of reindeer, although many Lapps have settled down and taken up fishing or more sedentary modes of life. In Sh.'s time they would have been a mysterious people at the top of the world; however, the English did have considerable trade through the northern Russian ports, so would have had contact with the Lapps fairly regularly. *Err 4.3.11,* 'L. sorcerers': Lapland was notorious for its sorcery, because its inhabitants spent so much time in the dark.

Lartius, Titus, *Cor,* Roman hero and Coriolanus' companion in his battle for the Volscian city of Corioli. Lartius is alleged to have been the first man appointed to the office of dictator by the citizens of the Roman Republic. The Lartian family, which was of Etruscan origin, took a prominent part in the affairs of the early Republic, but it had no descendants of note in later Roman history. Sh.'s source for the character was Plutarch, 'Coriolanus' (8).

Latin, language of the ancient Romans. It spread throughout the west with the expansion of their empire and survived as a living vernacular into the early medieval period. The migrations of illiterate Germans into Roman territories in the 5th c. encouraged the evolution of separate languages for scholarship and common discourse. As the Roman empire was replaced by more primitive societies that had little use for reading and writing, the speech of ordinary men and women drifted away from the standard preserved in books. Modern European vernaculars evolved on the streets, while the few persons who retained literacy continued to work in Latin—the only language in which books were available. At the start of the medieval period, Europe had very few resources, and a literary education was reserved for those for whom it was a necessity. The clergy needed to know how to read and write, for it was their duty to interpret the word of God preserved in the Latin Scriptures. They also had the responsibility of maintaining the sacraments of the Latin liturgy which contemporary Christians believed to be the only channels of God's grace. For much of the medieval period literacy and formal education remained the prerogative of clergy and the hallmark of their profession. Consequently, students spoke Latin at their schools and preserved it as a living language that grew in response to the needs of scholars. There was little motivation to invent systems for transcribing the Germanic tongues and Romance languages used by ordinary persons, for these men and women could not read.

Throughout the Middle Ages Latin was the vehicle for serious books and learned conversations. The students who flocked to the medieval universities from all corners of Europe had no other language in common, and they made it the common medium for international communications. Latin's dominance of law, literature, and diplomacy was unchallenged until a new class of literate persons appeared at the end of the medieval era. The revival of trade in Europe created an urban middle class that, like the clergy, needed to be able to read and write. Merchants and tradesmen had to keep records and send messages. Some learned Latin, but it was easier for most to write the language they spoke. The literacy they acquired in their professions was, of course, used to enrich their idle hours. It spawned an appetite for vernacular literature that artists and scholars learned to feed. One of the achievements of the Renaissance was the creation of respect for Europe's national languages. Renaissance scholars loved Latin—but the Latin that had been the vernacular of classical civilization and ancient secular culture, not the instrument of the medieval schools. The humanistic values of the Renaissance accorded dignity and significance to the lives and languages of ordinary people. Far-sighted artists, like Dante Alighieri, urged intellectuals to use languages that would make their work accessible to the masses. The Protestant reformers insisted that every person had a right to a Bible in a language that he or she could understand. The appearance of translations of the Scriptures and of major works composed in vernaculars broke the monopoly that Latin had enjoyed in Europe for a thousand years. Sh., Cervantes, and their lesser contemporaries heralded the start of the modern world where art, science, and ordinary conversation share the same tongue.

LLL 3.1.134, 5.1.75: Holofernes arrogantly uses his Latin, often badly, to prove his erudition. *MV 1.2.66. MWW 1.1.164, 4.1.43. H5 5.2.335. H8 3.1.41.*

Launce, *TGV,* see Lance.

Laura, *Rom 2.4.39,* see Petrarch.

Laurence, Friar, 1) *TGV 5.2.35,* never mentioned anywhere else, this is perhaps a mistake for Friar Patrick. It is also another obvious link to *Rom* and the common influence on *Rom* and *TGV* of Brooke (see 2).

2) *Rom,* Franciscan friar skilled in herbs who marries and then assists the star-crossed lovers in order to end the broil between their families. He is directly borrowed from Arthur Brooke's *Tragicall Historye of Romeus and Juliet* (1562), Sh.'s source, and is 'Lorenzo' in Luigi da Porto's *Istoria novellamente ritrovata di due Nobili Amanti* (c. 1530).

Lavache, *AWW,* see Lavatch.

Lavatch, *AWW,* 'Clown,' jester to the Countess of Rousillon. Not at all central to the plot, he nonetheless comments on the events of the play and provides a counterpoint to such issues as the nature of a proper married love. He is not a very happy jester and he often annoys other characters. Although he has some good lines, he often seems to have been wedged into the play mostly to provide employment for his first interpreter, Robert Armin. His name appears in F1 only in the words of Lafeu, which may mean that this is not a name at all, but some kind of joke. Editors usually, however, interpolate it for Clown. Its meaning is probably the French *lavache,* 'cow,' and it is often edited to that spelling. Another theory is that *lavage* 'washing' is meant and relates to Lavatch's frequent use of metaphors of smell to describe the corruption about him. He does not exist in Sh.'s sources for the play.

Lavinia, *Tit,* daughter of Titus Andronicus. Sh.'s source for *Tit* is unknown—if he used one—but it is clear that the play was not inspired by historical persons or events. There is an 18th c. chapbook that preserves a late version of a Titus legend that was probably known to Sh., and it calls Titus' daughter Lavinia. Lavinia's misadventures parallel those of a mythological heroine, Philomela, whom Sh. knew from Ovid's *Metamorphoses,* 6.

Lazarus, *1H4 4.2.25,* beggar whose fate illustrates one of Jesus' parables: Luke 16:19–31. Lazarus and a rich man (before whose door he has begged) both die at the same time. Lazarus is recompensed for a lifetime of suffering by admission to heaven. The rich man, judged to have had his share of blessings while on earth, is condemned to the torments of hell.

Le Beau, *AYLI,* (Fr. 'handsome'), one of Duke Frederick's courtiers. He has little purpose in the play other than exposition.

Leah, *MV 3.1.113,* woman from whom Shylock, as a bachelor, received a turquoise ring which Jessica steals. Leah is perhaps implied to have been Shylock's wife, though she is mentioned nowhere else. In Genesis, from which Sh. borrowed many of the Jewish names for this play, Leah is the first wife of Jacob.

Leander, lover of Hero who swam the Hellespont nightly to be with her. See Hero. *AYLI 4.1.93. TGV 1.1.22, 3.1.120. Ado 5.2.29.*

Lear, *Lr.,* aged king of Britain, father of Cordelia, Goneril, and Regan. He is Sh.'s most genuinely tragic figure. His error of judgment in failing to recognize Cordelia's worth destroys his entire family, turns his old age to misery and brings him a horrible death, yet his error arises from a weakening of the mind brought on by age or a desire to be loved, things which could happen to anyone. He thereby represents the closest manifestation of Aristotelian pity and terror in Sh., who saw that the happy ending which appeared in all other versions of the legend was inadequate. Stories of children's ingratitude and father's misjudgments can hardly be unusual on this planet, so there may be many independent sources of the legend itself and many Indo-European parallels. Sh. anachronistically sets the play in the time after Charlemagne in which Burgundy and France had separated; however he portrays Lear as a pre-Christian. The story of Lear and his daughters had been circulated for centuries in various folkloric forms, but the direct descent to Sh. begins with Geoffrey of Monmouth's *Historia Regum Britanniæ* (c. 1136), which drew on earlier materials and embellished them freely.

Whether there was a real king upon whom Lear is based is unknown and to speculate upon it is pointless. Geoffrey describes him as son of the builder of Bath, Bladud, and builder of Kærleir or Leicester (once said to be Leir Castre, 'Leir's town'). He was supposed to have reigned 60 years. Four centuries later, Holinshed described Leir as the son of Baldud, who ruled the Britons in the year of the world 3105, when Joash reigned in Judah. Despite the particulars, this is little better than 'once upon a time.' In fact, Lir was the name of a Celtic sea-god, which is likely the actual source of Leicester. In *The Fate of the Children of Lir* (an Irish romance and one of the *Three Sorrows of Storytelling),* he is the father of Fionnuala, one of four daughters changed into a swan by Lir's evil second wife, Aoife, and forced to wander the ocean for 900 years until retranslated by St. Mochaomhog. In the *Mabinogion,* a collection of Welsh tales composed from the 11th to the 13th c., he appears as Llyr and there are vague similarities between the fate of Branwen and that of Cordelia. William Camden's 1606 attribution of a similar tale to Ina, king of the West Saxons, may be borrowed from the Lear story or, like the story itself, based upon Celtic mythology.

Leda, *MWW 5.5.6,* mythological mother of Castor and Clytemnestra by her husband Tyndareus. Zeus came to her in the form of a beautiful swan in order to seduce her and she then became mother of Helen of Troy and Pollux. The seduction of Leda has been a subject of art since classical times and according to Ovid (*Metamorphoses* 6) since Arachne contested with Athena in skill of weaving.

Legion, *TN 3.4.84,* all the devils of Hell. The term derives from Mark 5:9. When Jesus confronts a possessed man, he asks, 'What is thy name?' The devils reply, 'My name is Legion, for we are many.' Jesus drives the devils into a herd of swine, freeing the man.

Leicester, county seat of Leicestershire, located about 100 mi. northwest of London. Richard III spent a night in an inn at Leicester on his way to the fateful battle at Bosworth Field that cost him his throne and his life. According to Geoffrey of Monmouth's *Historia Regum Britanniæ,* Leicester 'Leir Castre' is named from King Lear. It is more likely named from a tributary of the Soar river called the Leire. L. *castra* means a military camp or town. *R3 5.2.12, 5.8.10. H8 4.2.17.*

Leicestershire, *3H6 4.9.15,* county at England's center.

Lemander, *MND 5.1.195,* Bottom's corruption of Leander.

Lennox, *Mac,* F1 'Lenox,' thane who speaks against the evil of Macbeth's reign. Since King James was the grandson of the 4th Earl of Lennox, Sh. may have intended his presence in the play as a compliment. For a short period while he was king of Scotland, James held the title himself and granted it to his uncle Charles. The three previous earls had all met violent ends. The domain of Lennox is in Dumbartonshire and Stirlingshire in central Scotland north of Glasgow and includes all the lands around Loch Lomond. The first recorded earl of Lennox, Alwin, was invested in the second half of the 12th c. and died sometime before 1217. This follows the historical episodes in Macbeth by nearly two centuries.

Lent, one of the seasons of the Christian liturgical year, a period of forty days of fasting culminating in the feast of Easter. The discipline of fasting in the Middle Ages involved abstinence from meat. *2H6 4.3.6:* butchering was allowed during Lent in Elizabethan England only with a special license. *Rom 2.3.127,* see Lenten. *2H4 2.4.351:* Mistress Quickly has been in legal trouble for being casual about the fasting laws.

Lenten, (adj.) of or pertaining to Lent, used figuratively to mean spare, lean. *Rom 2.3.123,* 'l. pie': it should have no meat, unless one sneaked in an old hare. Mercutio teases the Nurse, punning on 'hoar,' 'hare,' 'whore,' and abstention. *Ham 2.2.317. TN 1.5.8,* 'l. answer,' a brief answer.

Leonardo, *MV 2.2,* servant to Bassanio. He speaks and is mentioned in this scene only. In F1 the stage direction has him exit before he actually leaves and has been said to indicate that the manuscript used for F1 had been used as a stage copy.

Leonati, *Cym 5.1.31, 5.5.124, 154,* family of Sicilius Leonatus, 'the lion-born.'

Leonato, *Ado,* 'Signor L.,' father of Hero, brother of Antonio, governor of Messina. Sh. took the name from his primary source, Matteo Bandello's *Novelle* (1554) in which Leonato is a gentleman (not the governor) named Lionati de'Lionati, who also knows that his daughter is not dead fairly early in the plot and decides to ship her discreetly out of town. Lionati works out the reunion as does Leonato. Sh. would have been quite aware of the 'born of the lion' meaning behind the name. Of all his 'Leo's,' Leonato is the most decent man. His angry fit over Hero's debasement *(4.1)* is nothing compared to Leontes' (*WT*) irrational jealousy, though both may play on the supposed fiery temperament of the lion.

Leonatus, *Cym,* honorary surname of Sicilius inherited by his son Posthumus.

Leonine, *Per,* sworn by Dionyza to murder Marina, he allows the pirates to take her instead. The murderer in John Gower's *Confessio Amantis* (1390) is named Theophilus as he is in Lawrence Twine's *Patterne of Painefull Adventures* (1594). In Gower, Leonin is the 'maister of the bordel' to which the girl is sold in Mytilene. It is interesting that characters in Sh. whose names begin with Leo- are generally weak in character, though the name would imply 'lion.'

Leontes, *WT,* king of Sicilia. In Sh.'s source Robert Greene's *Pandosto, or the Triumph of Time,* (1588; rptd. 1607 as *Dorastus and Fawnia*), Leontes' equivalent is Pandosto. In Plutarch, Leonidas is a king of Sparta who is responsible for the deaths of three people. There are also the variations Leonatus, Leontidas, and Leontini. Also in Plutarch, Leontes is the name of a tribe. There are also a Leon, Leonatus and Leontius in Sir Philip Sidney's *Arcadia.* The resemblance between Leontes and Postumus Leonatus of *Cym* is quite obvious and other characters in Sh. with names beginning in Leo- are usually weak or criminal characters, despite the name's deriving from 'lion.'

Lepidus, Marcus Æmillius (d. 13 BC), weakest member of the second triumvirate. He was one of Cæsar's allies in Cæsar's struggle with Pompey. When many of Rome's Senators fled to Greece to join the army Pompey raised against Cæsar, Lepidus was the highest ranking official to remain in Italy. Cæsar relied on him to hold Italy while Cæsar went abroad to confront Pompey. After his victory over Pompey, Cæsar rewarded him with an important military assignment in Spain. This enabled him to qualify for a triumph in 47 BC and to stand for a consulship with Cæsar in 46 BC. At the time of Cæsar's assassination he was near Rome recruiting troops to take to the empire's western provinces. He retreated to his proconsular post in Gaul to watch the progress of the struggle between Cæsar's heirs, Mark Antony and Octavius (Augustus). In 43 BC he threw in his lot with Antony, and the Senate declared him an enemy of the Republic. He and Antony marched into Italy and came to amicable terms with Octavius, whom the Senate had erroneously believed to be its puppet and Antony's implacable enemy. In October, 43 BC, Octavius, Antony, and Lepidus shunted the Senate aside, formed the second triumvirate, and vested themselves with the authority of a shared dictatorship. Their declared purpose was the punishment of Cæsar's assassins, Brutus and Cassius, and the restoration of the Roman Republic. Lepidus held Italy while Octavius and Mark Antony went to Greece to deal with Brutus and Cassius. Following their triumph at Philippi, the triumvirs divided responsibility for the empire. Lepidus, by far the weakest member of the alliance, was assigned a command in Africa that relegated him to the periphery of events. In 36 BC Octavius ordered him to Sicily to deal with a rebellion raised by Pompey's son, Sextus. Lepidus made a desperate grab for power, but he underestimated Octavius. Octavius captured him, stripped him of his political offices, and held him under house arrest until his death in 13 BC.

JC. Ant.

Lestrelles, *H5 3.5.45, 4.8.100,* (d. 1415), the earl of Lestrake whom Holinshed (3.555) lists among the French casualties of the battle at Agincourt.

Lethe, (Gr. 'oblivion') in classical mythology, a river in the underworld. The spirits of the dead drank its waters to obliterate the memories of the lives they had lost. Souls that were to be incarnated also sipped from it to wipe out the knowledge that they had existed before birth. *2H4 5.2.71. R3 4.4.237. Ham 1.5.33,* 'L. wharf.' *Ant 2.7.105. TN 4.1.61.*

Leviathan, huge sea monster mentioned in the Bible (Job 41:1, Psalms 74, 104, and Isaiah 27:1), possibly the crocodile, whale, or a sea serpent. The name derives from Heb. 'writhe' or 'curl.' *TGV 3.2.79,* (pl.) *MND 2.1.174. H5 3.4.109.*

Liard, *Mac 4.1.48,* spirit called forth by the witches in a song not appearing in F1, but which appears in Thomas Middleton's play *The Witch* (c. 1609, but not printed until the 18th c.). William Davenant's version of *Mac* (printed 1674), however, contains the song, and it has been argued that Davenant may have had access to an earlier text. Middleton's text is usually adapted to 'Liar Robin,' as was done by Davenant. Another possibility is 'Laird R.,' 'Lord Robin.' But a *liard* was also a tiny French coin worth a fourth of a sou. It may, therefore, mean something like 'Hop-o'-my-Thumb' (see Hoppo). That this is an invocation of two different spirits, however, is obvious given what Hecate says in *The Witch 1.2.1 ff.* The names are taken from Reginald Scot's *Discoverie of Witchcraft* (1584).

Liberty, *MM 1.3.29,* personification of licentiousness.

Libya, area in north Africa vaguely distinguished from Egypt to the east and Morocco (the country of the Moors) to the west. The name appears as early as 2000 BC in Egyptian hieroglyphics and possibly in the Old Testament in the name of Lehabim and in the people called the Lubims (2 Chronicles 12.3). Originally, the name seems to have been used to mean Africa, though Egypt was not included in it because it was considered part of Asia until Ptolemy divided Asia from Africa at the Red Sea. Homer's *Odyssey* (4.85) describes it as a very fertile land. The early Greeks knew little of the interior and climatological changes have now increased the desert. Strabo, the ancient geographer, describes the coast as fertile, but the interior rocky, sandy, and full of wild beasts. He lists many tribes of inhabitants. The territory which is now the nation of Libya has been occupied by the Phoenicians, Greeks, Carthaginians, Romans, Vandals, Arabs, Normans, Moroccans, Egyptians, and Spaniards. In its Roman period it was usually called Cyrenaica, until the emperor Diocletian divided it into *Libya inferior* and *L. superior.* It was absorbed by the Ottoman Empire in 1551 and remained under the Turks until the Italian seizure in 1911.

Tro 1.3.322, 'banks of L.,' the dunes of the Libyan desert. *Ant 3.6.69. WT 5.1.156, 165.*

Lichas, in mythology, the servant of Hercules, who brought his master the garment stained with Nessus the Centaur's blood and tainted with the poison of the Lernæan hydra. Neither Lichas nor Hercules' wife Deianira who sent the garment were aware of its toxic nature. Hercules, his flesh being eaten away, saw Lichas cowering in terror in a cave. He spun him and threw him. So terrified was Lichas all his moisture drained from his body and he turned into a reef as he fell into the sea off Cape Cenæum in Euboea. The story is in Ovid's *Metamorphoses,* 9.

MV 2.1.32: the allusion Morocco makes to Lichas is simply that chance may favor the undeserving. At random contests, rather than merit, Lichas may beat his great master. *Ant 4.13.45.*

Lichorida, *Per,* see Lychorida.

Licio, *Shr,* Hortensio's assumed name so that he may woo Bianca. There is a Licio in John Lyly's *Midas,* but a more likely source is the servant 'Lytio' in George Gascogne's *Supposes* (1566), the source of *Shr*'s wooing of Bianca plot, with its many disguises.

Ligarius, Caius, *JC,* Quintus Ligarius, (d. 43 BC), one of the men who plotted Julius Cæsar's assassination. Ligarius had sided with Pompey's party in the Roman civil war and had been banished by Cæsar. During his exile he was accused of malfeasance by Quintus Ælius Tubero and defended by Cicero. Although Cæsar was persuaded to pardon him, he felt no loyalty to Cæsar and readily joined the conspiracy against him. After Cæsar's death he was executed by order of the second triumvirate. Sh. knew Ligarius from Plutarch's 'Brutus' (11.1). Plutarch claims that Ligarius was so eager to witness Cæsar's death that he ignored the effects of a debilitating illness in order to participate in the plot.

'Light o' Love,' popular song from the period, mentioned in many sources beginning about 1578. The music is preserved, but not the lyrics. *TGV 1.2.83. Ado 3.4.40. TNK 5.4.54.*

Limbo, from L. *limbus,* 'edge' or 'border,' area on the border of Hell in which souls who were prevented by circumstance from entering Heaven were confined. The unbaptized for example, or the Old Testament prophets who preceded Christ's coming would be held there. Often it was used in the sense of Hell itself. In the Middle Ages the term came to mean the place where souls who were not damned waited to enter heaven, but through the influence of Augustine, this developed into the conception of Purgatory, which was formalized by the Roman Catholic church in the 16th c.

Tit. 3.1.149. Err 4.2.32, 'Tartar l.,' jail. *AWW 5.3.264. H8 5.3.63, limbo patrum,* slang for a prison, was actually the afterlife residence for the just who died before the coming of Christ (L. 'limbo of the fathers').

Limehouse, *H8 5.3.60,* district on the northern shore of the Thames east of London. It was named for a lime production industry that thrived there throughout the medieval period. Since Limehouse was a dockside community inhabited by rowdy men, Sh.'s 'limbs of Limehouse' may refer to gangs of ruffians—the 'limbs' or 'agents' of the devil.

Limoges, *Jn 3.1.40,* French city on the Vienne river, 240 mi. south of Paris. Richard the Lionhearted died from a wound received while besieging a castle belonging to Vidomar of Limoges, one of his vassals. The king and his man were quarrelling over rights to a treasure found on Vidomar's land. Sh. blended two of Richard's enemies into a single character: Vidomar, whose soldiers killed the king, and Leopold VI, archduke of Austria, who took Richard prisoner as he returned from the third crusade.

Lincoln, *Jn 5.6.42,* county seat of Lincolnshire and site of the cathedral of the diocese of Lincoln. It is situated about 130 mi. northwest of London. Its name derives from the combination of a Celtic word for the marshes in the area and the L. *colonia* 'colony.' See Lincoln, Bishop of, *H8.*

Lincoln, Bishop of, or **Lord of,** *H8,* John Longland (1476–1547), Henry VIII's confessor. Henry claimed that it was Longland who first caused him to have doubts about the validity of his marriage with Katherine of Aragon. It was probably Henry, however, who raised this sensitive subject. Longland supported Henry's decision to nationalize the English church, but, like Henry, he accepted the validity of the Catholic sacraments and opposed Lutheranism.

Lincoln, John, *STM,* rabble-rouser who stirs the crowd against foreign laborers. According to

Holinshed, he was a broker in London who was later hanged in Cheapside on May 7, 1517, although the other ringleaders were pardoned by the king at the last moment. M. M. Mahood argues that the insertion of 'Linco' as a speech heading in the handwritten Manuscript indicates that Sh. had a habit of writing the dialogue first and labeling the speakers later, which might explain the number of misattributions throughout the works.

Lincoln Washes, *Jn 5.6.42, 5.7.63,* marshy bay southeast of the English city of Lincoln. While retreating from the attack of rebel barons in 1216, King John lost his baggage train to the treacherous tides of the washes.

Lincolnshire, *1H4 1.2.76,* county at the midpoint of England's eastern coast.

Lingard, Lady, *H5 1.2.74,* Lingare, daughter of Charles the Bald, alleged ancestress of Hugh Capet. French authorities cited a tradition known as the Salic (or Salian) law to refute England's argument that its kings had a right to the throne of France. England's claim rested on the fact that its kings were the last direct descendants of the senior branch of the Capetian house. In 1328 the death of Philip IV's last son ended the unbroken line of father-son successions to the French throne that had begun in the 10th c. with Hugh Capet. No woman had ever ruled France, and on one occasion the French nobles had asserted that a king's brother took precedence over a king's daughter in the order of succession. When Charles IV died in 1328, France ignored the English kings who were descendants of Philip IV through his daughter, Isabella, and recognized as their king Charles's cousin, a son of Philip IV's brother, the duke of Valois. England objected, but French lawyers justified the action by insisting that the customs of the Salian Franks, from whom the French derived their laws, prevented women from inheriting or transmitting title to the throne.

The English responded to this argument by producing genealogies that showed that at various times in the past female blood lines had been used to legitimate French dynasties. The historians on whom Sh. relied (to construct the argument that he has the archbishop of Canterbury use to persuade Henry V to invade France) drew on this material. Most of it was political propaganda and untrustworthy as a source for history. If Hugh Capet did have Carolingian blood inherited from Lingard, it did not bring him the crown of France. Hugh was elected to the royal office by the French nobility, and it was not until 1223 that the Capetians were able to dispense with the formality of an election and treat the throne as heritable property.

Lion, *MND,* role assumed by Snug in the rustics' play before Theseus. The humor primarily revolves around a topical incident of August 30, 1594. Various members of Elizabeth's court attended the christening of James' son in Edinburgh. In the festivities a chariot was drawn by a blackamoor. It was originally, however, intended that it should be drawn by a lion, but it was feared that the animal might react violently to the torches or frighten the ladies.

Lionel, duke of Clarence (1338–1368), Edward III's third son, also known from the place of his birth as Lionel of Antwerp. His first wife was Elizabeth of Burgh, heiress to the earldom of Ulster and to the estates of the wealthy Clare family. The duchy of Clarence was created for Lionel in recognition of his succession to the Clares. Elizabeth died in 1362 leaving a single child, a daughter named Philippa. In 1368 Philippa married Edmund Mortimer, and she provided their descendants, the dukes of York, with a claim to the throne that they believed was superior to that of their cousins from the house of Lancaster. (Since Lionel was the older brother of the founder of the Lancastrian line, John of Gaunt, he took precedence over Gaunt in the order of succession.) Lionel spent most of his life in a futile struggle to subdue the Irish. In 1366 he gave up that project and entered a very different political arena. He went to Italy to wed Violante Visconti, daughter of Galeazzo II, co-ruler with his brother Bernabo of the small, but wealthy, city-state of Milan. The English diplomatic schemes that depended on this alliance were dashed by his death five months after his marriage.

2H6 2.2.13, 34, 50, 56, 4.2.135, 4.4.28. 1H6 2.4.83, 2.5.75.

Lipsbury pinfold, *Lr. 2.2.8 (Q 7.8),* obscure expression meaning a place where Kent could chastise Oswald. A pinfold is an enclosure for stray animals, but there is no known place called Lipsbury. It could be an expression meaning 'in the teeth,' playing on 'lips.' Some have argued that a boxing ring or something similar is meant, an enclosure from which two combatants could not escape, or that it is an expression parallel to the slang 'Lob's pound,' (the stocks, jail, any place of confinement). It has also been suggested that Finsbury is meant on the slim assumption that there must have been a pinfold there.

Lisbon, *MV 3.2.267,* capital of Portugal. Located on the Tagus river about 7 mi. from the Atlantic, it was at its height as a major trading city in the 16th c., thanks to the explorations begun by Henry the Navigator and the flourishing Portuguese Empire in Africa, Asia, and Brazil. The name derives from that of Ulysses and a legend he founded a city in Iberia. The Romans took the city in 205 BC, then Alaric in 407 AD and the Visigoths held it until the Moors conquered in 714. In 1147 it was wrested from them by Alphonso I and became the capital of the nation about 1260. From 1580 to 1640, it was under Spanish rule and was the port from which the Armada sailed on England.

Livia, 1) *Rom 1.2.70,* woman invited to Capulet's feast.

2) *Ant 5.2.165,* Livia Drusilla, (d. 29 AD), wife of Octavius and one of his most important political advisors. When Octavius met her, she was the pregnant spouse of Tiberius Claudius Nero. Octavius induced her husband to divorce her so that he might marry her, and she bore Tiberius' second son, Drusus, in her new husband's home. Although the fact that she gave Octavius no children of his own created dynastic difficulties, he never appears to have entertained the thought of putting her aside. The mysterious deaths of numerous heirs to Octavius' estate spawned rumors that she was murdering people to clear a path to the throne for her sons. It was even whispered about that Octavius himself met death at her hands. His successor was her son, Tiberius. If Tiberius believed that he owed his fortune to his mother, he felt no gratitude to her. Tiberius ordered her from court, refused to visit her during her terminal illness, and took no part in her funeral rites.

Lodovico, *Oth,* Venetian nobleman. He is present at the attempt on Cassio and at the end of the play he takes charge of the murder scene, reveals the incriminating letters which were in Roderigo's pockets, and gives the closing lines denouncing Iago. A curious set of coincidences is that Ludovico Sforza, ruler of Milan, was nicknamed 'the Moor' and had a mistress Bianca, but there doesn't seem any other relation to the play and the name is otherwise common in northern Italy. It was Ariosto's first name, for example.

Lodowick, *AWW 4.3.168,* commander in the Duke of Florence's army.

Lodowick, Friar, *MM 5.1.125, 126, 142, 259,* name adopted by Vincentio, duke of Vienna, in disguise. In Cinthio's *Hecatommithi,* the equivalent of Claudio is called Vico, a shortening of Lodovico (q.v.).

Lombard Street, *2H4 2.1.27,* London street not far from Falstaff's favorite haunts in Eastcheap. It took its name from the Italian merchants and bankers who lived along it in the 13th c. So many of medieval Italy's businessmen came from the district of Lombardy that northern Europeans called all Italians engaged in commerce 'Lombards.'

Lombardy, region of about 9300 sq. mi. in northern Italy, comprising the southern Alps and land north of the Po river. Cities in the region include Bergamo, Milan, Pavia, and Mantua. The Romans conquered the area from the Gauls in 222 BC and made it the province of Cisalpine Gaul. In 568 AD the Lombards under King Alboin invaded the region giving it its name. In 774 Charlemagne absorbed the kingdom. After the death of the last duke of Milan in 1447 and the wars afterward, Lombardy passed into the control of Spain under Charles V who defeated Francis I of France at Pavia in 1525 and took Milan in 1535. Spain held Lombardy until 1713. *Shr 1.1.3:* 'fruitful L./The pleasant garden of great Italy.' Lombardy has always been a fertile region. Lucentio is either saying he is on his way there after Padua, has arrived in Lombardy, or even is coming from Lombardy (Tranio, his servant, is said to have his father in Bergamo, central Lombardy).

London, England's largest city. Since 'London' is a Celtic name, possibly even pre-Celtic, there was likely a settlement at the city's site on the north bank of the Thames before the Roman conquest. If so, it was of little importance, for it remained a modest town throughout the Roman period. It owed its later growth to the trade medieval England developed with the continent. It came of age in 1191, when it won royal recognition of its right to function as a self-governing commune. Its chief magistrates were a mayor and twenty-five aldermen. As the leaders of the largest city in the British Isles, they wielded considerable influence in national politics, and London was more a quasi-independent state within the English kingdom than a seat of royal power. Although some departments of the royal administration (in particular, the judiciary and finance) showed an early tendency to establish permanent headquarters, the medieval government of Britain was largely itinerant. It moved with the monarch from one royal castle, manor, or hunting lodge to another. Traditions that went back to Alfred the Great (871–899) favored Winchester as England's symbolic capital, and the eagerness with which Londoners guarded their independence discouraged kings from becoming too dependent on the city. As it evolved into the center of England's trade and communications, its attraction as a home for an increasingly centralized system of national administration became irresistible. By Sh.'s day it had begun to function as England's capital, and as the British empire grew it became and remained the largest city in the world until the 20th c.

2H6 2.1.213, 4.3.17, 5.4.10, 5.5.29. 3H6 1.1.208, 1.2.36. 1H6 3.1.80. R3 2.2.110, 3.2.79, 4.5.14. Jn 5.1.31. R2 3.3.206, 3.4.91, 98, 5.2.3, 5.3.5, 5.5.77, 5.6.7, 13. 1H4 1.2.126, 2.1.42, 2.3.3, 5.3.30. 2H4 1.3.104, 2.2.135, 160, 2.4.295, 4.3.51, 5.3.60, 61, H5 2.0.34, 3.2.12, 3.6.70, 5.0.24, 35. H8 2.2.5.

London Bridge, only bridge giving access to medieval London from the south bank of the Thames. London was situated 50 mi. inland from the English channel on the Thames estuary. Until 1894 no bridge spanned the Thames down river of London Bridge, and London Bridge was the city's only bridge until 1750. The bridge was a vitally important communications link, and battles were often waged at the bridge as armies tried to force entrance to the city. The bridge that Sh. knew was built in the 13th c. and was an elaborate stone structure that carried a double row of buildings as well as a road. *1H6 3.1.23. 2H6 4.4.48, 4.6.14, 4.7.123.*

London Stone, *2H6 4.6.2,* stone that stood in Cannon Street near the entrance to London Bridge. Cade, according to Sh., enthroned himself on the stone while asserting a claim to jurisdiction over the city. Early English kings were sometimes acclaimed while seated on sacred stones. The English throne now, as in Sh.'s day, encloses the 'stone of Scone,' a block on which the kings of Scotland once sat.

London Tower, see Tower of London.

Londoners, *H8 1.2.155,* people of the city of London. By far the largest city in England (almost four times greater than its nearest competitor, Norwich), and England's chief window on the world, London had great influence. The Londoners swayed the policies of the national government, and England's monarchs often solicited support for national programs from them.

Long Lane, *Shr 4.3.183,* street in London near Pie Corner and West Smithfield. It constituted the northern boundary of St. Bartholomew's Priory, which was dissolved in 1538 by Henry VIII. Long Lane was known for its second-hand dealers in old linen, pawnbrokers, and moneylenders. Obviously, this street is a great distance from the Italian setting of the play, but Sh. frequently mixed local references with his 'foreign' settings.

Longaville, *LLL,* see Longueville.

Longueville, *LLL,* 'Longaville,' courtier in the service of Ferdinand, king of Navarre. He embraces the vow of asceticism wholeheartedly, but has his intentions destroyed by his love for Maria. At play's end Maria promises to return to him after a year's mourning for the late king of France. The Duc de Longueville appears in contemporary records of the career of Henry of Navarre as one of Henry's chief supporters. See Ferdinand, King of Navarre.

Lord Mayor, title of the mayor of London. It may date back to 1354. Within the city he was considered second in power only to the king. *2H6 4.5.4. R3 3.5.14, 71. 3.7.55:* he supports the crowning of Richard. *STM:* he attempts to persuade the commoners to give up their intention to riot. *H8 2.1.151, 5.5.sd, 70.* See Mayor.

Lord of Hosts, *1H6 1.1.31,* title for God signifying his function as leader in the fight against the forces of evil. It appears first in the Hebrew Scriptures in reference to God as the head of the armies of Israel (1 Samuel 17:45).

Lord of May, *TNK 3.5.127,* character in the morris dance before Theseus. Also called the Lord of Misrule, he was usually represented by Robin Hood.

Lord, our, *R3 3.7.2,* see Jesus Christ.

Lord, the, *1H4. 2H4 3.2.298, 4.2.46. H5 2.4.102,* 4.1.289, 5.2.152. *Mac 2.3.67,* 'L.'s anointed temple,' the body of the king. See God, or Jesus Christ.

Lorenzo, *MV,* beloved of Jessica. He elopes with her and though the stealing of Shylock's money taints their relationship in the modern view, the lyrical passage between them at the opening of Act 5 establishes a much more favorable tone to the relationship. A parallel might be seen in Lorenzo's seeking out Jessica because of her wealth, in the same way that Bassanio seeks Portia, but love soon seems to conquer whatever initial venality began the seduction. Portia's entrusting Belmont to Lorenzo and Jessica reflects favorably upon him also.

Lorraine, dukedom on the border between Germany and France, defined geographically as the territory drained by the Moselle river. The name evolved from Lotharingia, the kingdom of Lothar II, great-grandson of Charlemagne. See Charles, duke of, *H5.*

Lou, *1H6 1.6.44,* 'lords,' possibly recalling old variant spellings: 'lourde,' 'hloured,' 'lurd.'

Louis, King, *3H6,* see Louis XI.

Louis X, *H5 1.2.77, 1.2.88,* Louis IX (1226–1270), French king, member of the Capetian dynasty. In identifying this monarch Sh. replicates an error made by Holinshed (3.546). The 'Saint Louis' to whom Holinshed referred was not Louis X, but Louis IX. As a saint, the scrupulousness of Louis' conscience was beyond question. Sh. has the archbishop of Canterbury use this assumption to good rhetorical advantage. In *H5* the archbishop develops an elaborate argument to convince Henry V of the legitimacy of his claim to the throne of France. The sticking point was the 'Salic' law which the French insisted denied women the right to transmit title to the throne. Henry's claim to France was through the female line, and the archbishop is eager to prove to him that the French kings themselves occasionally cited ancestresses to demonstrate the legitimacy of their claim to royal authority. The archbishop alleges that the saintly Louis was uncertain of his right to rule until he discovered that his grandmother was a descendant of a female member of the unquestionably legitimate Carolingian line.

Louis XI, *3H6 3.1.34,* (1423–1483), king of France. He had a very unhappy relationship with his father and predecessor, Charles VII. As a youth, he was all too eager to come into his inheritance. At the age of sixteen he took part in a rebellion to unseat his father. When the coup failed, Charles banished him to the Dauphiné in the south of France. Exile did nothing to curb Louis' appetite for plots, and his behavior pushed his father to the breaking point. In 1456 Louis fled France and sanctuary in Burgundy under the protection of Philip the Good. He remained abroad until his father's death brought him the throne in 1461. Louis was a king with a plan. He intended to add territory to France and to strengthen and centralize his nation's royal government. France's feudal lords, who resented royal initiatives that curtailed their freedoms, reacted by leaguing against him. Charles the Bold, heir to the dukedom of Burgundy, assisted the French rebels, for it was in his interest to weaken Louis. He dreamed of annexing parts of France and having his expanded duchy elevated to the status of a kingdom. From 1465 to 1472 the situation remained highly volatile. Louis weathered crisis after crisis by exploiting the personal weaknesses and misfortunes of his enemies. His gift for devious diplomacy led his contemporaries to dub him 'the Spider.'

Although his elaborate schemes were often expensive and laid a heavy burden on France's tax paying subjects, the urban and middle classes remained loyal to their king. Louis, unlike the avaricious nobles, saw to it that the commons got value for their money. He tamed the aristocracy and kept Burgundy, France's most dangerous enemy, at bay. His struggles forced him to pay considerable attention to England, for England's entrance into the fray might have tipped the balance against him. Fortunately for him, the English were distracted by the dynastic turmoil of the War of the Roses. The French king, therefore, did what he could to keep alive the dispute between the English houses of York and Lancaster. In 1470 he persuaded the earl of Warwick, who had fled England, to join Henry VI's exiled queen, Margaret, in a campaign to overthrow Edward IV. When that project failed and Edward decisively defeated the Lancastrians, Louis bought peace with his former enemy by agreeing to pay Edward IV a large annual pension. Louis also kept Edward distracted by stirring Scotland up against England. 'The Spider' was ultimately successful in all that he set out to do. England was neutralized. Charles of Burgundy died in battle in 1477, and Louis annexed enough of his duchy to bring the frontiers of France to something approximating their modern configuration. The French nobles were subjected to tighter control. By the end of his reign, he had become one of the most powerful monarchs in Europe. Success brought him no sense of increased personal security. He lived out his last years in seclusion—plagued by fears of assassination and burdened by irrational anxieties and superstitions.

Louis the Dauphin, *Jn,* Louis VIII (1187–1226), French prince whom the barons of England asked to lead the rebellion they mounted against King John in 1216. Sh. committed an anachronism by referring to him as a 'dauphin.' The province of Auvergne, to which that title was attached, was not acquired by the French royal family until 1349, and the custom of calling the heir to the French throne 'the dauphin' evolved late in the 14th c. The barons of England turned to Louis because he had a claim to England through his wife, Blanche of Castile, Henry II's granddaughter and John's niece. Louis invaded England with a small army that he expected to be augmented by volunteers, but John's death cost him the welcome he had anticipated. Once John was out of the way, the

English lords had no reason to prefer Louis' potentially strong hand to the weak rule of John's 9-year-old heir, Henry III. He sensed the change in the wind and withdrew from England to devote his energies to a more promising project. He began a war with the Albigensian heretics that ultimately extended royal authority over the south of France. He promised to be a worthy successor to his great father, Philip Augustus, but he never had a chance to prove himself. He died after a reign of only three years (1223–1226) and left his kingdom to a son who was far too young to govern it. The power of the French monarchy had grown dramatically under Philip Augustus, and Louis' barons seized the opportunity of his death to turn back the clock. Louis' dynasty owed its survival to the political skill of his widow, Blanche. She adroitly played the nobles off against each other and distracted them until her son, Louis IX, was old enough to defend his rights.

Louis the Emperor, *H5 1.2.76,* (814–840), Louis the Pious, only surviving son of Charlemagne and, as sole heir to his estate, fount of legitimacy for the dynasties ruling the nations that were subsequently carved out of the Carolingian domain. The speech that Sh. puts in the mouth of Henry V's archbishop of Canterbury alleges that the kings of France based their royalty on their connection with Louis through the female line. His point is that the French had never observed the 'Salic' law that they cited as a reason for denying Henry V's claim to their throne. Henry was related to the Capetian family through his great-grandmother Isabella, wife of Edward II and daughter of Philip IV of France. French authorities maintained that the customs of their ancestors, the Salian Franks, prevented women from inheriting the throne or transmitting title to it.

Louvre, palace in Paris on the northern bank of the Seine river. It was begun by Philip Augustus (1180–1223) and rebuilt by Henry VIII's contemporary, Francis I. In Sh.'s day it was the seat of the French court. *H5 2.4.132. H8 1.3.23.*

Love, 1) personification of the emotion: either an allegorical figure; a reference to Venus (Aphrodite), the goddess of sexual passion; or to Cupid. *LLL 4.3.100, 303–341* (Biron's meditation about love). *MND 1.1.233, 234. 241,* Cupid. *2.2.52. Rom 2.4.7,* Cupid. *MWW 2.1.5,* personification of emotion opposed to reason. It may allude to Sir Phillip Sidney's sonnet 10 from *Astrophel and Stella. AWW 1.3.209,* here masculine gender. *2.3.76, 83, 86,* Venus or Juno, marital love. *MM 3.1.411. Ant 1.1.46. TNK 2.6.88,* Cupid.

Love, Lord, *MV 2.9.100,* possibly Portia's sobriquet for Bassanio. However, the punctuation of the early editions may make 'love' an imperative verb and some editors make the line read 'Bassanio, lord, love if thy will it be' or something similar.

Love, Monsieur, *Ado 2.3.34,* Benedick's mocking name for the lovesick Claudio.

Love, Signor, *AYLI 3.2.285–6,* mocking name applied to Orlando by Jaques, exploiting the pretensions of the Italianate lover.

Love-in-Idleness, *MND 3.1.168,* magic flower struck by Cupid's arrow, the wild pansy (*Viola tricolor*). Compare *Shr 1.1.149.*

Lovell, Thomas, (d. 1524), soldier whose fortunes rose with those of the Tudor dynasty. As a young man, he was one of the earl of Richmond's squires. He took part in the battle at Bosworth Field that won Richmond the throne of England, and the new king (Henry VII) appointed him Chancellor of the Exchequer. He served the second Tudor monarch, Henry VIII, as marshal and constable of the Tower. He was the jailor responsible for Edward Stafford, duke of Buckingham, when the duke was confined in the Tower awaiting the outcome of his trial for treason against Henry VIII. Lovell retired from court in 1516—caring neither for Cardinal Wolsey nor for Protestants. He was fortunate to die just as his sovereign set foot on the road to England's reformation. *R3 4.4.449. H8.*

Low Dutch, *AWW 4.1.72,* possible reference to Plattdeutsch or Low German, which is spoken in the area of the Netherlands and has many similarities to the many dialects of Dutch.

Lubhard's Head, *2H4 2.1.27,* F1 'Lubbars head,' the sign that advertised the shop belonging to a silk merchant to whom Sh. gave the descriptive name, 'Master Smooth.' It depicted a leopard. Mistress Quickly mispronounces 'leopard' as 'lubhard' (i.e., 'oaf'). A less likely argument is that she is mispronouncing 'Lombard,' a merchant (see Lombard Street).

Luccicos, Marcus, *Oth 1.3.44,* man whom the Duke wishes to contact immediately, evidently about the Turkish threat to Cyprus. It is thought that the specificity of this name might imply a lost source for the play.

Luce, woman's name, possibly 'Lucy.' 1) *Err,* Adriana's kitchen maid. Since Nell is also described as a kitchen maid (at *3.2.96* and *5.1.417–18*) many editors assume that both Nell and Luce are the same character. It might indeed be one of those careless confusions of names that is so common in Shakespearean texts, or 'Nell' might be used in the sense of a common or sluttish woman as a nickname. In the early plays, however, there often seems an unnecessary proliferation of characters, so it is entirely possible Sh. intended to give Adriana more than one 'kitchen wench' to imply Antipholis' prosperity.

2) *TNK 3.5.26,* one of the morris dance participants.

Lucentio, 1) *Shr,* son of Vincentio, young man in love with Bianca Minola. In order to woo her, he disguises himself as a Latin teacher and has his servant Tranio, disguised as Lucentio, negotiate with her father. His courtship successful, he runs away with Bianca, and his father reassures Baptista Minola with a financial settlement. Later in the feast ending the play, he discovers that Bianca is not as he idealized her. Lucentio is depicted early in the play as the typically overboard young lover. He may pine and burn as he tells Tranio, but it blinds him to Bianca's true nature, which is shown to be slightly manipulative during his wooing.

2) *Rom 1.5.35:* Capulet remarks that he was last in a masque at Lucentio's nuptial, twenty-five or thirty years before. Lucentio is not otherwise identified.

Lucetta, *TGV,* Julia's witty servant. Her role is reminiscent of that of the nurse in *Rom* which has many kinships with this play. The name is fairly unusual in Sh.'s day, even in Italy, and may derive from Lucilla who abandons the title hero in John Lyly's *Euphues, or the Anatomy of Wit* (1579), or from a number of minor early saints.

Luciana, *Err,* sister of Adriana. She argues with her sister about the proper role for a wife, telling her that a woman should be pliant to her husband's will. This attitude quite resembles Katherina's speech in *Shr* and may foreshadow, or possibly echo it. Later Antipholus of Syracuse makes advances to her and she, believing him to be Antipholus of Ephesus, is revolted by them. At play's end Antipholus of Syracuse announces his intention to continue his pursuit of her. She has no equivalent in Sh.'s primary source, Plautus' *Menæchmi.*

Lucianus, *Ham 3.2.232,* murderer in the play presented by Hamlet (*The Murder of Gonzago*) to trap his uncle Claudius. Lucianus murders Gonzago in exactly the way that Claudius is supposed to have murdered his brother, although Lucianus is the nephew of the king, like Hamlet. In *Der Bestrafte Brudermord* (1710), which seems to be a German rendition of an older version of the play, the chief player is called Carl, possibly the German actor's name. Lucian was a well-known Greek satirist of the 2nd c. He mocked mythology in his dialogues and adventure stories in his *True History.* A similar mockery seems appropriate to Lucianus' function in *Ham.* The alleged murderer of Francesco Maria della Rovere (see 'Murder of Gonzago') was Luigi Gonzaga. Possibly Lucianus is an adaptation of Luigi.

Lucifer, name commonly accorded Satan, the prince of demons. The term, which means 'bringer of light,' was originally a Latin title for Venus, 'the Morning Star,' the brightest of the planets. Venus' appearance on the horizon signals the imminent rise of the sun. Early Christian theologians associated the planet with the enemy God cast from heaven. Isaiah 14:12 celebrated the defeat of a king of Babylon, the arch enemy of the people of God, by comparing his lost glory to the fate of a fallen star. In Luke 10:18 Jesus was reported saying, 'I have seen Satan falling as lightning from heaven.' Christian scholars assumed that Jesus here had the Isaiah passage in mind and that his 'Satan' was Isaiah's 'day star'—the 'bringer of light.'

Jn 4.3.123, 1H4 2.5.340, MWW 1.3.70. 2.2.286: here the name comes from Reginald Scot's *Discoverie of Witchcraft* (1584), as do the other demon's names. *2H4 2.4.337. H5 4.7.135. H8 3.2.372.*

Lucillius, 1) *JC,* Lucilius, Roman soldier who demonstrated a capacity for fierce loyalty. Plutarch ('Brutus' 50.1–5) says that he saved Brutus from capture at Philippi by convincing the troops Antony sent to take Brutus that Lucillus was the man they were looking for. Antony, impressed by his willingness to sacrifice himself for his commander, pardoned him and won his friendship. He remained Antony's intimate companion to the end of his life. After Actium, when things went badly for Antony, Lucillus prevented Antony from acting on thoughts of suicide and brought him to temporary safety in Alexandria (Plutarch, 'Antony' 69.1–2).

2) *Tim,* Timon's servant. Wishing to marry the daughter of an old Athenian, he is provided with money by Timon. The name appears in Plutarch's lives of Mark Antony (which contains a passage about Timon) and of Marcus Brutus.

Lucina, Roman goddess of childbirth, associated with Juno. The Greek equivalent was Eleithyia, daughter of Zeus and Hera. Mentions of the goddess may have come to Sh.'s mind from the works of Terence, in which women in childbirth call out to her. She is also mentioned in Sannazaro's pastorals. *Per 1.51:* Pericles' wife Thaisa is called Lucina in Lawrence Twine's *Patterne of Painefull Adventures* (1594). *Cym 5.5.137.*

Lucio, 1) *Rom 1.2.72,* man invited to Capulet's feast. See Anselme.

2) *MM,* 'Signor L.,' degenerate gentleman of Vienna. He is a brothel customer, has deserted his pregnant mistress, informs on Mistress Overdone, and slanders the duke. He is sentenced to be whipped and hanged. He receives mercy, however, in the swell of generosity which closes the play. Like most of Sh.'s villains, he is not without redeeming qualities. He tries to help Isabella plead for her brother's life, and accuses her of being cold, which she often appears to be. The name is probably derived from Lucius but may hint at Lucifer.

Lucius, 1) *Tit,* eldest son of Titus Andronicus who avenges the wrongs done his family by the Roman emperor Saturninus and Saturninus' wife, Tamora. Sh.'s source for the plot of *Tit* is uncertain. An 18th c. chapbook preserves a version of a tale about a Titus Andronicus that may have been known to Sh., but it makes no mention of a son like Lucius. In Sh.'s play he survives his father and Saturninus to restore just government to Rome. The story has no basis in history, and Lucius may be Sh.'s invention.

2) Lucius the younger, *Tit,* Titus Andronicus' grandson. His aunt Lavinia, following her rape and mutilation by the sons of the empress Tamora, struggles to explain what has befallen her. Deprived of both tongue and hands, she communicates by opening Lucius' copy of Ovid's *Metamorphoses* to the story of Philomela, a heroine from Greek mythology who suffered a fate similar to Lavinia's. Sh.'s source for the plot of *Tit* is uncertain, and the events it drama-

tizes are not historical. It is probable that he invented young Lucius.

3) *JC,* Brutus' young servant. The character has no historical prototype. Sh. invents him in order to give Brutus a chance to reveal his essential gentleness and nobility. Brutus treats the boy with paternal affection and shows concern for his welfare even in the midst of pressing business.

4) *Tim,* a lord to whom Timon appeals for help. The name appears in Plutarch's life of Mark Antony, which contains a passage about Timon.

5) *Ant 1.2.83,* Lucius Antonius, youngest brother of Mark Antony. In 41 BC he obtained a consulship and used the post to try to undercut Mark Antony's fellow triumvir, Octavius. Lucius and Antony's wife, Fulvia, raised an army and tried to drive Octavius from Italy. Although Octavius had little difficulty routing them from their base at Perugia and Antony denied any responsibility for the affair, the episode was a serious political embarrassment for Antony. Lucius was pardoned by Octavius and given a military post in Spain. Fulvia died before she had an opportunity to be reconciled with her husband.

Lucius, Caius, *Cym,* ambassador of Rome to Britain and later general of the invading army. He is an extremely noble man, representative of all that was considered finest in Roman character. He helps protect Innogen and courageously faces execution upon his defeat. His lack of animosity for his opponents brings about not only Cymbeline's reprieve of his execution, but also the general reconciliation ending the play. The name was a common Roman one which Sh. used on several other occasions. The combination 'Caius Lucius,' however, has been said to be irregular, as both are *prænomen* and one should not follow the other. This is something only the owlish should fret about. It has been pointed out that there was a tradition in the Renaissance that the first Roman soldier who became Christian was named Lucius and that perhaps this was an influence on the creation of the character, although one of Sh.'s characters so named (*Tim*) is anything but noble. Lucius also suggests 'enlightenment,' from the L. *lux* 'light.' When the emperor Claudius subdued the sons of the historical Cymbeline, his generals were Aulus Plautus and Ostorius Scapula, and Cymbeline apparently never warred with the Romans. In Sh.'s source for the love plot, Boccaccio's *Decameron,* (2.9), the gentleman who accepts the service of the disguised Ginevra (Innogen's equivalent) is called Senor Encarach, a Catalan.

Lucius Pella, *JC 4.2.54,* Roman prætor whom Brutus condemned for embezzling public funds. Sh. found Pella's story in Plutarch's 'Brutus' (35.1–3). Plutarch says that when Brutus refused to intervene to prevent Pella's prosecution, Brutus' friend Cassius was upset. Pella was one of Cassius' cronies, and Cassius was of the opinion that defense of the law was less important than the defense of political allies. Brutus justified himself to Cassius by reminding Cassius that they had slain Cæsar, not for Cæsar's faults, but for the abuses perpetrated by men who sheltered behind Cæsar's patronage. Brutus felt compelled, therefore, to hold himself and his followers to the most honorable standards of conduct.

Lucrece, wife of Lucius Tarquinius Collatinus. Her rape by Sextus Tarquinius, the son of Rome's last king, Tarquinius Superbus, led to the establishment of the Roman Republic. Lucrece's fate unfolded when her husband boasted of her virtue to a group of his companions in arms. When the men broke camp and hastened home to see if each of their wives was behaving as she ought, they discovered that only Lucrece presided over an orderly, sober household. Her noble demeanor excited lust in Sextus Tarquinius, who devised an elaborate plan to rape her. After Collatinus and his friends returned to the field, Sextus took the first opportunity to sneak back to her house. Since Sextus was her husband's friend, she offered him hospitality. He seized the opportunity to assault her and warned her that if she resisted him, he would kill her and place her naked body in bed with the corpse of a male slave. It would then appear to the world that he had discovered her in an act of base adultery and had treated her as Roman law permitted. Realizing she was trapped, she submitted to Sextus, but when he departed, she did not, as he expected, keep the assault secret. She summoned her husband and revealed everything. Although Collatinus believed her and wished her to remain his honored wife, she refused. After making him promise to punish Sextus, she committed suicide by stabbing herself. Collatinus' friend Brutus and the Roman people were so moved by her behavior that they drove Sextus and his father from the city and vowed never again to submit to the authority of kings.

Shr 2.1.291. 'Roman L.' *Luc. Tit 2.1.109, 4.1.90. TN 2.5.91. 2.5.104,* 'L. knife,' a fatal weapon.

Lucretia, *Luc 317, 510, AYLI 3.2.145,* see Lucrece.

Lucretius, *Luc 1751, 1773, 1800,* father of the noble matron Lucrece whose rape and suicide led to the establishment of the Roman Republic. Plutarch ('Publicola' 12.4) says that Lucretius shared a consulship with Publius Valerius Publicola, one of the men who helped Brutus drive the Tarquinian kings from Rome. He did not long survive his election to the Republic's highest office. His term was finished by a Marcus Horatius.

Lucullus, *Tim,* lord to whom Timon appeals for help. He tries to bribe Flaminius, Timon's servant, to say that he could not be found. Lucian Licinus Lucullus was a Roman consul notorious for his extraordinary banquets in the 1st c. BC and from whom we have the adjective 'lucullan.' He is most likely whom Sh. had in mind. Plutarch devotes one of his 'Lives' to Lucullus, whom he compares with Cimon. There is also a Marcus Lucullus, prætor of Macedonia, in Plutarch's Cæsar.

Lucy, Lady, *R3 3.7.5, 169,* Elizabeth Lucy, the daughter of a certain Wyat Lucy of Southampton. Edward IV was rumored to have been engaged to her before his marriage with Elizabeth Woodville Gray. Edward had a son, Arthur Plantagenet (d. 1542), by Elizabeth Lucy, but Sh. may be wrong in assuming that Edward contracted to marry her. The engagement to wed that Richard III cited before parliament as an impediment to Edward's marriage with Elizabeth Woodville Gray was an agreement between Edward and Eleanor Butler, the daughter of the earl of Shrewsbury. It did not involve Elizabeth Lucy.

Lucy, William, *1H6,* (d. 1460), Lancastrian partisan, descendant of an Anglo-Norman family that settled in England in the 12th c. William's father, Thomas, was one of John of Gaunt's retainers and held the office of sheriff of Worcestershire in 1406. William was employed by Henry VI to negotiate peace between the warring Neville and Percy families in 1453, and he died fighting for Henry at the battle of Northampton.

Lud's town, London. King Lud, according to Holinshed's *Chronicles,* substantially strengthened the defenses of Troynovant ('New Troy,' supposedly from the Trojan hero who escaped to establish the British race) with new walls and a strong gate called Ludgate. Because of the people's love for the king, the town began to be known as Cærlud, or Lud's town, which Holinshed supposed had been corrupted to London. The etymology won't pass muster, and the gate, on the west of the City of London was first mentioned in the 12th c. and used as a prison for several centuries. Located halfway up Ludgate Hill, it was renovated in 1586 and razed in the 1760s. Lud was a mythical king who was probably derived from the name of a Celtic river god. The son of Helie and the father of Tenantius and Androgeus, and either brother or father to Cassibelan, Lud was Cymbeline's grandfather. He was supposedly buried by his gate. *Cym 3.1.32; 4.2.101, 124:* the public display of the heads of criminals on prominent landmarks such as London Bridge or Ludgate was considered a deterrent to crime; *5.6.482.*

Ludlow, *R3 2.2.109, 112, 124,* castle in Shropshire about 140 mi. west of London. Edward IV's sons were housed there at the time of his death.

Lupercal, Feast of, *JC 1.1.67, 3.2.96,* festival that the ancient Romans celebrated in mid-February. It honored no particular god, but was probably a continuation of primitive rituals that had been associated with Rome's earliest settlement on the Palatine hill. The Luperci, the priests after whom the rite was named, were young men who raced round the walls of the city lashing out at people with strips cut from the skins of sacrificed animals. Barren women who were whipped by the Lupercal racers were believed to be rendered fertile. Originally there were two colleges of Luperci, and a third was founded in 44 BC to honor Julius Cæsar. Mark Antony was the new organization's first presiding officer.

Lutheran, *H8 3.2.100,* strictly, a follower of Martin Luther, but in Henry VIII's day the term was casually applied to anyone who was anti-clerical. Anne Boleyn's enemies accused her of Lutheranism because she fought with Cardinal Wolsey and favored England's break with the papacy, but the charge did not imply that Henry's queen accepted Luther's interpretation of the sacraments or endorsed other Protestant doctrines.

Lycaonia, *Ant 3.6.75,* district in Asia Minor surrounded by Galatia, Cappadocia, Cilicia, and Isauria. It was ruled by Amyntas, the king of Galatia who aided Mark Antony at the battle of Actium. When Amyntas died in 25 BC, his lands were assimilated into the Roman empire.

Lychorida, *Per,* Thaisa's nurse. 'Lichorida' is one of many of Sh's character names that appear in John Gower's *Confessio Amantis* (1390). See Pericles.

Lycurguses, *Cor 2.1.54,* pl. 'Lycurgus.' The most famous Lycurgus was the legendary author of Sparta's constitution. Different stories have been handed down about him. Some say that he was a Minoan scholar whom the Spartans employed as a consultant to redesign their state. Other tales make him a Spartan prince who travelled to Crete and Egypt in search of the wisdom that enabled him to invent a new way of life for his people. Lycurgus allegedly persuaded the Spartans to accept a rigid discipline that kept them in a state of permanent, total military mobilization.

Lydia, *Ant 1.2.96, 3.6.10,* territory in the heartland of Asia Minor. At the start of the Hellenic era, it was the seat of a kingdom that dominated all of Asia Minor. Its borders fluctuated from generation to generation, and the Lydia Mark Antony knew was a small territory defined by the valleys of the rivers Caister and Hermus.

Lynn, *3H6 4.6.21,* town of Lynn Regis or King's Lynn, a port in Norfolk on the Ouse river. It was a center for trade with Flanders.

Lysander, *MND,* beloved of Hermia, he elopes into the woods with her only to be driven by Robin Goodfellow's love potion into a madness for Helena. Later, when the potion is reversed, he becomes betrothed to Hermia. Sh. borrowed the name from the ancient Spartan naval commander who defeated Athens and brought an end to the Peloponnesian War. His biography appears in Plutarch. That Lysander is described as having grown up in poverty outside the royal bloodlines. His virtues, however, overcame his background. Sh.'s Lysander is comparable in that, despite his virtues, Egeus does not consider him a suitable husband for his daughter.

Lysimachus, *Per,* governor of Mytilene. He is called Athenagoras in John Gower's *Confessio Amantis* (1390) and Lawrence Twine's *Patterne of Painefull Adventures* (1594). There are a few Lysimachus' in Plutarch. The most interesting is in the life of Demetrius. He does not compare with the Lysimachus in the play except that there is an echo of an anecdote from the book at

Per 3.5–6. A passage in Barnabe Riche's *Souldiers Wishe to Britons Welfare* (1604) has also been suggested as a direct source for the name, though this is a retelling of Plutarch's anecdote. Mytilene, on Lesbos, was ruled for some time by a Lysimachus, and there is an aged one in Plautus' *Mercator* ('The Merchant').

M

Mab, Queen, *Rom 1.4.54–55,* fairy who brings on dreams and inspires in Mercutio one of Sh.'s finest speeches. The name probably derives from Mabh, the chief of the Irish fairies, though 'queen' may not necessarily indicate sovereignty. *Mab,* in Welsh and in Breton dialects, is also a child or infant, which fits well with Mercutio's descriptions of her tininess. Other suggestions of the name have been that it is a contraction of 'Dame Abunde' (or Habunde) who supposedly ruled over the fairies, to 'Dame Ab' to 'Mab.' It may simply be a diminutive of Mabel, from L. *amabilis,* 'lovable,' or (less likely) It. *mabella* 'my beautiful daughter.'

Macbeth, *Mac,* warrior and king of Scotland (1040–1057), thane of Glamis and Cawdor. The tragic hero of one of Sh.'s most popular plays, Macbeth has been interpreted as a man driven by his ambition but filled with doubt, or as a man driven by his wife's ambition and therefore hesitant. There is much about him that is reminiscent of Richard III. They both override decency in order to fulfil their personal ambitions, they are both tormented by ghosts, and they both rise warrior-like to the occasion of their deaths, spitting defiance into the face of fate. Macbeth, however, is much more human a character than Richard. He has more self-doubt, he is less effectively a manipulator, and he is much less demonic. Like Richard, also, the historical Macbeth has been distorted by the historians Sh. relied upon, and then further distorted to suit the drama. The Gaelic name Macbeth implies a religious man: *Mac Beatha* means 'son of life,' and the historical Macbeth, though far from a saint, was much less a villain than the play makes him.

He was the son of Finlæch, hereditary ruler of Moray and Ross. He was grandson of Malcolm II and husband of the granddaughter of Kenneth III, whose throne had been usurped by Malcolm II. Macbeth's father had been murdered by nephews in 1020, and in 1029, Macbeth likely assumed his titles upon the death of one of the murderers, named Malcolm. According to the *Saxon Chronicle,* Macbeth may have been one of the lords who swore loyalty to Canute in 1031. In placing his grandson Duncan on the throne, Malcolm II also usurped the claims of Lulach, son of Gruach (Lady Macbeth) and Gilcomgain, and Macbeth seems to have become the defender of those claims. Among the Celtic Scots in particular, Duncan was regarded as the usurper, not Macbeth. When Duncan awarded the lands of Thorfinn Sigurdsson to his nephew Moddan, Macbeth allied himself with the Scandinavian and led a rebellion against Duncan around 1040. Duncan was killed in a battle at Dunsinane and Macbeth seized the throne, ruling for fifteen to seventeen years until the second invasion supported by Siward's army, which was not the first rebellion. Crinan, lay abbot of Dunkeld, had rebelled in 1045. In contrast to the play, old records say that the reign of Macbeth was a happy one. He was generous to the church and possibly made a pilgrimage to Rome in 1050. Siward won a victory at Dunsinane in 1054 and the war ended when Macbeth was killed in battle against Malcolm Canmore at Lumphanan (according to Holinshed) in 1057 or 1058.

Macbeth, Lady, *Mac,* wife of Macbeth and one of Sh.'s greatest female characters. Her vigor and ambition overlays a weakness which drives her mad once her goals have been achieved. She calls upon demons to help her overcome any feminine instincts which might make her hesitate in urging the murder of Duncan on her husband and she even participates in setting up the murder scene when Macbeth becomes befuddled, but in the end, she wanders the palace raving about the blood on her hands. The emphasis upon exactly how much culpability she has in persuading Macbeth to murder provides a range of interpretation for various actors through the centuries and legendary performances in the role have been given by Sarah Siddons, Ellen Terry, Sybil Thorndike, and other great actresses. The character is based upon Donwald's wife, in Holinshed, who urges the murder of King Duff. Otherwise, her character is entirely a creation of Sh.'s imagination, as there is no historical record portraying Macbeth's wife. The historical Lady Macbeth was named Gruach and she was the granddaughter of Kenneth III. She had married Gilcomgain by whom she had a son, Lulach, and as a widow married Macbeth, who seems to have advanced the claims of the Celtic bloodlines of Lulach against the bloodlines of Malcolm II, who was regarded as having illegitimately placed his grandson Duncan on the throne.

Maccabeus, see Judas Maccabeus.

Macdonald, *Mac 1.2.9,* F1 'Macdonwald,' rebel leader against Duncan. Sh. may have constructed the name from Donwald, who murdered King Duff. *Mac* is Scottish Gaelic for 'son of.' The description of this murder in Raphael Holinshed's *Chronicles* (1577) provided the details of Macbeth's murder of Duncan in the play, although Holinshed uses the name 'Macdowald.'

Macduff, *Mac,* thane of Fife, avenger of King Duncan and his family, and slayer of Macbeth. Macduff has the power to undermine Macbeth's magical protection by being 'not of woman born' (birth by cesarean section). His character, however, is not particularly vivid beyond his aspect as the avenger. His finest scene occurs when he has been told of the slaughter of his innocent wife and children, and this saves him from being as unremittingly God's agent of retribution as is the Earl of Richmond in *R3.* There is, however, no evidence for his existence in history. The name derived from Sh.'s source, Raphæl Holinshed's *Chronicles* (1577) by way of Hector Boece's *Scotorum Historiæ* (1526), which contains many legendary elements. The cesarean section is an interesting detail and it is plainly regarded as being somehow unnatural and therefore an omen of greatness, much like Othello's and Julius Cæsar's epilepsy. There has been a legend that the term cesarean derives from Cæsar who was also allegedly born in this way; however, since this practice in ancient Rome, and later, resulted in the death of the mother, the long life of Cæsar's mother makes it extremely unlikely. The origin of the word is now assumed to be the Latin verb *cedere,* 'to cut,' which reflects Sh.'s use of 'ripped' to describe it.

Macduff, Lady, *Mac,* wife of Macduff. When Macduff flees the villainous Macbeth to join Malcolm, Macbeth orders that she and her children be killed. She has an appropriate sympathy-building scene and the account of their deaths becomes the vehicle for Macduff's finest scene and the motivation for his revenge. There is virtually no historical evidence for the existence of a real Lord and Lady Macduff, though he appears in Raphael Holinshed's *Chronicles* (1577) and Hector Boece's *Scotorum Historiæ* (1526).

Macedon, Macedonia, the most northern of the states on the mainland of ancient Greece. The name, according to myth, comes from the name of a son of Zeus, Macedon, but that seems to derive either from Gr. *makednos* 'tall,' referring to the mountains, or an Illyrian word *maketia* 'cattle.' Throughout much of classical Greece's history it was a remote, isolated region ignored by its more highly civilized southern neighbors. The situation changed dramatically during the reign of Philip II (359–336 BC). Philip subdued the feudal nobility who had kept Macedon at war with itself and enlisted them in the service of the most sophisticated military machine the Greek world had ever assembled. Philip's army enabled him to impose his will on the Greek city-states and to plan the conquest of the Persian empire. Philip died on the eve of his Persian campaign, but his son, Alexander the Great, carried the project through to completion.

H5 4.7.19, 21, 24, 25. Per 6.24: a prince of Macedon (with an Italian motto—perhaps he is ruler of a Venetian colony), is one of Thaisa's suitors.

Machiavel, Niccolo Machiavelli (1469–1527), government official, diplomat, and Italian political scientist. He reorganized the defense system of Florence to lessen its dependence on mercenaries, then worked among the most powerful rulers of Italy. In 1512 Giuliano de Medici was placed in power in Florence by the Holy League. Machiavelli was removed from office, imprisoned and tortured. His apparent fall became his vehicle to greatness as he retired to the country to write. His *Discourses on the First Ten Books of Livy* (written 1513–21, published 1531) lay out his conceptions of republican government. He also wrote *On the Art of War* and *The History of Florence,* as well as the play *Mandragola,* poems, and other literary works. His most notorious work, however, is a slim textbook dedicated to a young ruler from the Medici family. *Il Principe* ('The Prince,' written 1513, published 1532) argued that the art of politics was primarily the pursuit and preservation of power. Despite the republican attitudes that he had expressed in most of his work, his name became associated with amoral expediency, and his ideas were much debated and usually reviled by Sh.'s contemporaries.

3H6 3.2.193: Richard of Gloucester (1452–1485) was a contemporary of Machiavelli's, but could have read nothing by him—the books weren't written until after Richard's death. *1H6 5.6.74:* it is, of course, a flagrant anachronism for Sh. to have Richard of York (1411–1460), refer to a man who was born nine years after Richard's death. *MWW 3.1.93.*

MacMorris, Captain, *H5,* fictional character, an allegedly typical Irishman. Sh. uses his presence in the English army alongside comrades from Wales and Scotland to symbolize the solid support of the people of the British Isles for Henry's venture in France. Relations between the Irish and English were very poor in Sh.'s day, and *H5* was probably written during the summer of 1599 while the earl of Essex was engaged in a less than successful campaign to put down a rebellion in Ireland. Sh.'s contemporaries considered the Irish to be crude barbarians, and MacMorris is a quarrelsome warrior distinguished by his lust for blood.

Madam. *Shr Ind. 2. 106, 108,* the lord tells Sly a lord's wife should be addressed with this title. There is humor in that 'Madam' was sometimes applied to a woman who put on airs, to a courtesan, for example, so that Sly's understanding of the word comes from the gutter as opposed to the lord's. See Al'ce Madam and Joan Madam.

Madeira, *1H4 1.2.115,* sweet white wine from Madeira, the largest of a group of islands in the Atlantic west of Morocco. *Madeira* is the Portuguese for 'wood' or 'log'—timber covered the islands.

Madeline, *TNK 3.5.25,* Q 'Maudline,' one of the morris participants. Possibly the name refers to the role of Malkin the Clown (Maid Marian). The name derives from Fr. for Magdalen from Mary Magdalen which was often said to mean 'of the town of Magdala.' However, no such town has been discovered and experts now think the name may derive from Heb. *magdal* 'great' or 'large'—thus 'Mary the Great' or 'Big Mary.'

Mæcenas, *Ant,* Caius Cilnius Mæcenas, (c. 73 BC–8 BC), friend of Octavius and patron of Roman artists. He was the descendant of an ancient and very wealthy family of equestrian rank. About 40 BC he became one of Octavius' intimates, and he handled the delicate negotiations between Octavius and Mark Antony that were occasionally required to preserve the second triumvirate. When the triumvirs dissolved their relationship, he held Italy for Octavius while Octavius went to Greece for a showdown with Antony. He helped Octavius reorganize Rome after Antony's defeat, and for about a decade he was part of the empire's inner circle of policy makers. About 20 BC, he retired from public service to spend the rest of his life in literary pursuits. He provided financial support for the great Latin poets, Virgil and Horace, and brought them to the attention of Rome's literati.

Magnifico, 1) title given to important men in Venice, members of the ruling oligarchy. *MV 3.2.278* (pl.).

2) *Oth 1.2.12,* see Brabanzio.

Magnus, St., *2H6 4.7.155,* Christian missionary who worked among the people of southern Germany and Switzerland at the start of the Middle Ages. His mission was supported by the Carolingian monarchs who hoped that the spread of Christianity and civilization would augment the effectiveness of their rule. The London church dedicated to him was among the city's wealthier houses of worship.

Mahu, *Lr 3.4.135. (Q 11.132), Q 15.58,* name of a demon, the prince of stealing, according to Edgar. Sh. borrowed it from Samuel Harsnett (see Flibbertigibbet for details). Perhaps it suggests Mahoun, deriving from Mohammed and sometimes a synonym for the devil.

Maidenhead, *MWW 4.5.73,* town upstream on the west bank of the Thames northwest of Windsor. The town is very old and served as a crossing point on the road to London. Its name implies that young women regularly met here for some reason. As early as 1297, Edward I acted to repair the bridge and subsequent monarchs arranged for guilds to maintain it.

Maidenliest star, *Lr 1.1.129 (Q 2.127),* probably the constellation Virgo, representing Erigone, who hanged herself out of grief at her father's murder and was transported to the heavens. This would fit with Edmund's mockery of the influence of astrology. The moon, associated with Diana, the chaste huntress, might also be suggested to Sh.'s audience, although Edmund is probably speaking generally.

Maine, French province between Normandy and Orléans. Its name may derive from the local Gallic tribe the Cenomani. In 1126 it passed by marriage to the house of Anjou. When the English crown was inherited by Henry II, who was count of Anjou as well as king of England, Maine became part of England's Angevin empire. Philip Augustus reclaimed it for France from Henry's son, John, and the English won it back again after their victory at Agincourt in 1415. Henry VI alienated some of his subjects by voluntarily surrendering Maine to France in 1444. Henry hoped by means of this gift and his marriage with Margaret of Anjou to induce the French to make peace. The scheme failed, for the acquisition of Maine simply made it easier for the French to assault Normandy and to deprive the English of all their fiefs in northern France.

2H6. 1H6 4.3.45, 5.5.110. Jn 1.1.11, 2.1.152, 488, 528.

Malchus, *Ant 3.6.72,* king of Arabia Petræa and one of the men who Plutarch ('Antony' 61.2) says sided with Mark Antony against Octavius at Actium. Since his nation was threatened with absorption into the Parthian empire, he tried to stay on good terms with any Roman general who established himself as a power in the eastern Mediterranean.

Malcolm, *Mac,* son of Duncan I, prince of Cumberland, and ultimately Malcolm III. When his father is murdered, he flees to the safety of England and organizes an army against the usurper. The historical Malcolm was given the sobriquet Canmore, which means 'large-headed.' Malcolm itself means 'a follower of St. Columba,' the 6th c. missionary who converted many of the Scots. His name is thus conveniently pious for the play. In 1040 when Macbeth seized the throne in battle, Malcolm first lived with his uncle Siward and then lived in safety at the court of Edward the Confessor, as in the play. In July 1054, he returned to defeat Macbeth and was crowned at Scone in April 1057. This ended the dynastic struggle that had begun when Malcolm II had usurped the claims of the Celtic line in granting his succession to Duncan. Macbeth seems to have been defending the claims of Lulach, Lady Macbeth's son by a previous marriage, and shortly after Macbeth's death, Lulach was killed, too, certifying Malcolm III's claim.

Because of his time in the English court, his reign was marked by a reorienting of Scottish culture towards England and the rest of Europe. His second wife, Margaret, was the sister of Edgar Ætheling, a claimant to the English throne driven out by the Normans.

Margaret was particularly involved in changing the Celtic church to conform with the Roman Catholicism of the rest of Europe, and died so unpopular she was buried in secret. She was later made a saint. In 1070 Malcolm invaded England in support of Edgar's claims, but William the Conqueror counterattacked in 1072. Malcolm made peace with William at Abernethy, but broke the truce by reinvading the north of England repeatedly, until William Rufus forced his submission. Later Rufus ordered him to do homage to the Norman king at Gloucester. Malcolm refused in an attempt to maintain the independence of the Scottish crown. On November 13, 1093, he was killed at Malcolm's Cross, near Alnwick. Four of his sons became kings of Scotland and his daughter united the Saxon and Norman royal houses by her marriage to Henry I.

Mall, *Tmp 2.2.47,* common woman who loved sailing men, mentioned in Stefano's drinking song. In June 1600, there was a prominent scandal in which a woman named Mall Fowler plotted with her lover William Haynes to get rid of her husband by framing him for treason. After some time the plot was revealed. Mall was sentenced to a whipping and life in prison. Much of the scandal revolved around her brother Henry Boughton's encouragement of her adulterous relations.

Mall, Mistress, *TN 1.3.122,* woman whose portrait is referred to by Sir Toby. Some early critics identified her with Mary Frith, a. k. a. Moll Cutpurse, a notorious woman. However, this has been rejected on account of Frith's age at the time the play was written, though the reference may have been a later insertion. Another suggestion was that the reference is to one Mary Ambrée who fought at Ghent in 1584. Yet a third is that it refers to a portrait of Maria. A good possibility is Mistress Mall Fowler, a notorious woman who plotted to kill her husband (see Mall). It is thought that the Clown's lines at *3.1.16–20* may allude to this case as well. Most critics, assuming that if it is a topical allusion it is unclear or forever lost, now take it to refer to any woman, Mistress Mall being on the order of 'Jane Doe.'

Malmsey, sweet, fortified white wine originally produced in Greece. It was named after the port of Monembasia, called Malmasia in Medieval Latin. *R3 1.4.152, 265. LLL 5.2.233. 2H4 2.1.39,* 'm.-nose,' an inflamed nose from excessive drinking.

Malvolio, *TN,* 'Monsieur M.,' steward of Lady Olivia. He is described as 'some kind of puritan,' is melancholic and too righteous. He has made his enemies by revealing their sins to his lady. They, in turn, catch him up in his own ego by making him think he is beloved by his lady, and humiliate him by tricking him into wearing outlandish yellow hose cross-gartered and treating him as if he were insane. His treatment is so severe, however, he earns some audience sympathy. One critic has suggested that the name derived from a character 'Malevolti' from the play *Il Sacrificio* which preceded *Gl'Ingannati* (1538), Sh.'s probable source. In *Gl'Ingannati* (1538), Fabrizio (corresponding to Sebastian) arrives in Modena accompanied by Master Piero, a pedant, who is resented by Stragualcia because of his criticism of Stragualcia's carousing. There may be a suggestion of Malvolio in this, though it is slight. One critic wished to connect him with John Marston's Malevole in *The Malcontent,* but the dating is wrong. The name is an opposite of Benvolio ('good will') and implies 'ill will'; however, it seems more appropriate to link it with L. *mage-volo,* 'I wish for more.'

Mamillius, *WT,* prince of Sicilia, son of Leontes. A pleasant child, Mamillius sickens upon the accusation against his mother and dies in Act III over his mother's torment. Leontes takes the boy's death as punishment by Apollo for the injustice he has done to his wife and daughter. The name was probably taken from Robert Greene's two *Mamillia* (1583, 1593). In Sh.'s source, Robert Greene's *Pandosto, or the Triumph of Time,* (1588; rptd. 1607 as *Dorastus and Fawnia*), Mamillius' equivalent is Garinter.

It has been suggested that there may be a connection between Leontes' reference to nursing in *2.1.58* and the name which would imply in L. *mamilla* 'breast.'

Man i'th' Moon, the differing shadings of the lunar surface have traditionally been seen as a face, identified at differing times with Endymion, Cain, and the sabbath-breaker of Numbers 15: 32–36. *MND 5.1.240, 242–3, 253,* see Moonshine. *Tmp 2.2.137–8.* Stefano means to impress the savage Caliban by saying he has dropped from the moon, a ruse similar to many played on primitive peoples by explorers.

Man, Isle of, island in the Irish Sea at the center of a circle defined by the coasts of Ireland, Scotland, England, and Wales. Julius Cæsar recorded its name as Mona in his *Gallic Wars,* from the L. *mons* 'mountain' or a Celtic cognate meaning the same. England and Scotland both claimed Man until Edward III brought it indisputably within England's orbit. Edward granted it and its traditional title of 'king' to William Montague, first earl of Salisbury. Montague's heirs passed the property to William le Scrope, and in 1406, Henry IV transferred it to John Stanley, England's lieutenant for Ireland. The Stanleys eschewed the royal title and styled themselves simply 'lords' of Man. Since the Isle of Man was both remote and secure, it was an ideal place for the confinement of internal exiles. Henry VI's government banished his aunt, Eleanor Cobham, there. *2H6 2.3.13, 2.4.79, 95.*

Mandragora, *Ant 1.5.3,* sleeping potion concocted from mandrake root. Machiavelli's best play *La Mandragola* revolved around the same potion.

Manningtree ox, *1H4 2.5.457,* a fatted ox from the Essex town of Manningtree. Some now-forgotten joke or gossip that circulated in London in Sh.'s day probably prompted him to make a reference to Manningtree. The context for the term has been lost, but it seems to imply that the people of Manningtree had reputations as drunkards or gluttons.

Mantua, city protected on three sides by the Mincio river (a tributary of the Po) in south Lombardy. It was an Etruscan and Roman city, later passing to the Lombards. It became a free commune in 1115, but the Gonzaga family gained control in 1328, making it a duchy in 1530. Under the Gonzagas, it was a prosperous center of Renaissance culture. Its name may derive from the Etruscan lord of the underworld, Mantus. *TGV 4.1.48,* the Second Outlaw murdered a man in Mantua; *4.3.23, 5.2.45,* Valentine and Silvia flee there; this recalls Romeus' exile there in Arthur Brooke's *Tragicall Historye of Romeus and Juliet* (1562), Sh.'s primary source for *Rom.*

Shr 2.1.60, Licio (Hortensio in disguise) is from M.; *4.2.78–9, 82,* the Pedant is from M. *Rom,* city to which Romeo flees in banishment. *1.3.30,* the nurse says that Juliet's parents were away at Mantua when Juliet was weaned, at just under age 3. *5.1.51:* Spain, Portugal, and Italy all had laws against the sale of poisons.

Mantuan, *LLL 4.2.94, 98,* Mantuanus, or Baptista Mantuan (Johannes Baptista Spagnolo, 1448–1516). A scholar and humanist, he was the author of Latin eclogues in imitation of Virgil which were often taught in English schools. Erasmus held him in enough esteem to dub him the 'Christian Maro' from Virgil's full name. Holofernes quotes Mantuan's first eclogue, perhaps incorrectly.

Marcade, see Mercadé.

Marcellus, 1) See Marseilles.

2) *Ham,* one of the sentinals at Elsinore. Along with Bernardo, he sees the ghost. His most memorable moment is when he says 'Something is rotten in the state of Denmark' (*1.4.67*). In the speculation about who pirated Q1 (known as the 'Bad Quarto' of 1603), the actor who played this part is usually accused of the thievery because his lines are accurately reproduced. As he is a military man, his name

might be associated with Mars, but it is, given no particular source, likely to come from the famous Roman general of the second Punic War, Marcus Claudius M. (d. 208 BC) who captured Syracuse and Capua, and whose biography appears in Plutarch's lives.

3) *Ant 2.6.111,* see Caius Marcellus.

March, 1) third month of the year, named for the god Mars. Sh.'s assumption about the ill effects of the March sun may reflect folk wisdom. People seem to have a greater susceptibility to illness during the changing of the seasons. *1H4 4.1.112. Ado 1.3.52,* 'M. chick,' an early chick, a precocious boy.

JC 2.1.59, 4.2.70. 1.2.20, 21, 25, 2.1.40, 3.1.1, 4.2.70, 5.1.114, 'Ides of M.,' from the Latin *Idus,* (pl., *Ides*) the name for the day at the middle of a month. The fifteenth days of March, May, July, and October were Ides. The term, when used in association with the eight shorter months of the year, referred to the thirteenth day. The ancient Romans considered the mid-month day important enough to be deserving of its own name, for it was a date when fiscal obligations commonly came due.

TNK 3.5.74, 'mad as a March hare.' During the mating season, hares are jittery. 'March' might not mean the month but refer to marshy areas or borderlands on which there is little brush in which a hare could hide—hence making it skittish.

2) earldom or fief of special military importance on England's Welsh and Scottish frontiers. 'March' derives from an early French word for borderlands, and in feudal terminology it was used to designate an area requiring development as a strong military base. The Welsh marches descended in the family of Roger Mortimer (1286–1330). The Scottish marches were the domain of the earls of Dunbar.

3H6 2.1.140 (pl.), see ff. M., Earl of,: *2H6 2.2.37, 2.2.48, 3H6 1.1.106,* see Mortimer, Roger; *1H6, 2H6 2.2.49, 4.2.134,* see Mortimer, Edmund, 1); *3H6 2.1.179,* see Edward IV; *1H4,* see Mortimer, Edmund 2).

Marcus, *Cor 5.6.123,* common first name for a Roman male. No reference to a historical person is intended. There were few first names (about a dozen) to choose from in Roman times. 'Marcus' may be related to the god Mars or to *mas, maris* 'male,' or 'masculine.'

Marcus Andronicus, *Tit,* Roman tribune and Titus Andronicus' brother. Although Sh.'s source for *Tit* is uncertain, an 18th c. chapbook preserves a later version of a tale that he might have known. The chapbook does not mention Titus' brother, who may be one of Sh.'s inventions.

Marcus Antonius, *Ant 2.6.112,* L. for 'Mark Antony.'

Marcus Brutus, *JC,* see Brutus, Marcus.

Marcus Crassus, *Ant 3.1.2, 3.1.5,* 'the Rich,' (d. 53), member of the first triumvirate. Crassus, a gifted entrepreneur, built one of the largest fortunes in ancient Rome and spent it pursuing ambitious political goals. His first major office, a prætorship, brought him the task of ending a slave revolt led by the gladiator, Spartacus. His reward was a consulship that he shared with Rome's most famous general, Pompey. He was jealous of Pompey and willing to spend whatever was necessary to out bid him for the attention of the Roman electorate. Rivalry between the two created an opportunity for a political newcomer, Julius Cæsar. Cæsar persuaded Crassus and Pompey to join him in forming the first 'triumvirate,' a private alliance that brought together enough power to permit the three men to impose their wills on the Roman Republic.

Each member of the triumvirate got something from it that he coveted for the advancement of his career. Pompey was able to compel the Senate to ratify treaties he had negotiated during his wars in the east and to obtain land in Italy on which to retire his veteran soldiers. Cæsar got proconsular authority in Gaul and an opportunity to start a war that gave him an excuse to build an army as large as Pompey's. Crassus, who knew that he could not survive politically unless he equaled the military exploits of his colleagues, won the right to lead an expedition against the only major civilized state still outside the Roman empire, Parthia. It was Crassus' misfortune that he did not share the military talents of his colleagues. The vast Parthian state was also a very difficult target. In 54 BC he led a brief foray across the Euphrates into Parthian territory. Encouraged by this venture, he returned a year later, but this time a large Parthian force blocked his retreat, and he was compelled to accept an invitation from the Parthians to negotiate a truce. The Parthians violated a promise of safe conduct, seized Crassus, and killed him. His head was sent to the Parthian emperor who allegedly poured molten gold into its mouth to punish Crassus for his greed.

Marcus Justeius, *Ant 3.7.72,* officer who Plutarch says ('Antony,' 65.2) shared the command of the central unit of the army that fought for Mark Antony at Actium in 31 BC.

Marcus Octavius, *Ant 3.7.72,* distant relative of Octavius, but an ally of Octavius' opponent, Mark Antony. Marcus Octavius sided with Pompey when the civil war erupted, and he fled to Africa after Pompey's defeat at the battle of Pharsalia. In the fight between Cæsar's heirs, he favored Antony and commanded part of Antony's fleet at Actium. It is not known what happened to him after the defeat of Antony's forces. Sh. knew Marcus Octavius from Plutarch's description of the disposition of Antony's forces at Actium ('Antony,' 65.1–2).

Mardian, *Ant,* eunuch who is mentioned by Plutarch ('Antony,' 60.1) as one of Cleopatra's servants. Plutarch says that Octavius told the Roman people that Mardian and Cleopatra's maids were running Mark Antony's affairs. Octavius convinced the Romans that Cleopatra had established complete mastery over Antony and that they had to destroy Antony to prevent her from using him to win control over them. Mardian's name might indicate that he was born among the Amardi, a tribe of warriors native to the area of the Caspian Sea. An Amardi or 'Mardian' gave Antony information that helped him plan the invasion of Parthia ('Antony' 41). When Cleopatra and Antony quarreled after their defeat at Actium, Plutarch says that Cleopatra precipitated Antony's suicide by sending him the false report that she had died. Plutarch does not name Cleopatra's messenger ('Antony' 76.3), but Sh. assigns this fatal errand to Mardian.

Maréchal, 1) *1H6 4.7.70,* Marshal, a military rank. A marshal was originally a servant entrusted with the care of a warrior's horses, but by the end of the Middle Ages the title implied the highest command responsibilities. Marshals led crusades and oversaw the military affairs of nations. See Marshal, Earl; Talbot, Lord.

2) 'M. of France,' *Lr,* see Far, Monsieur la.

Margaret, *Ado,* 'Meg,' attendant to Hero. Margaret comes to Hero's window for a liaison with Borachio and according to the witnesses speaks in a way that reveals her lusty nature. The witnesses, however, have been fooled into thinking they are listening to Hero. Fortunately Borachio clears her name when he confesses, but earlier, he makes it sound as if she is in on the plot, for she will call him 'Claudio' (which makes no sense; Claudio is a witness) and he will call her 'Hero' (*2.2.36–37*). In his confession he says she was in Hero's garments (*5.1.230*). If this is a figure of speech (she is in the 'guise' of Hero), she is innocent. Whether she is in on the deception or not, it enhances Borachio when he takes all the blame. If it is literal (she is wearing her mistress' clothes), it is hard to make her innocent unless she enjoys dressing as her mistress.

The promiscuous nature revealed by her overheard talk seems to bother no one. Her sexual openness, the use of the nickname, the banter with Beatrice and Hero, and her interest in the misguided Borachio implies that Sh. is contrasting common people or low love with nobility and ideal love. Meg is not made bad by the comparison, Hero is elevated. Similarly, her name makes her ordinary, while Hero's brings mythological reference. Her flirting with Balthasar (or Borachio, as some editors prefer) at *2.1.90–101* could be fairly innocent or her wish for a 'good dancer' might imply something more randy. The latter seems more likely. When Balthasar/Borachio says 'The clerk is answered,' has he been refused or accepted? Possibly that hinges on the editorial question of whether Balthasar or Borachio should have the lines.

Margaret, Queen, (1430–1482), Margaret of Anjou, wife of Henry VI and mother of his only child, Edward (1453–1471). Henry's marriage with Margaret was part of a diplomatic strategy that he hoped would end the Hundred Years' War and bring peace to England and France. Henry first asked Charles VII for the hand of one of his daughters, but Charles persuaded the English king to accept a lesser bride. Although royal princesses were often pledged in marriage in their cradles, Charles insisted that none of his daughters was of appropriate age to be wed. In their place he proposed his kinswoman, Margaret of Anjou. She was a descendant of King John of France, and her father's sister, Mary, had married Charles VII. Charles was both her uncle and her distant cousin. She had some royal blood, but many of Henry's subjects believed that she was a poor match for their king. Her father styled himself 'king of Sicily,' but he never ruled the land he claimed and was too poor to provide Margaret with a dowry befitting a queen. She brought Henry little and cost him a great deal. In a naive attempt to induce the French to make peace Henry ceded the county of Maine to her father. The loss of Maine made the defense of other English continental possessions difficult and hastened the loss of all the land in France that Henry had inherited from his predecessors.

Margaret cannot be blamed for originating her husband's foolish foreign policy, but she pressed him to carry it out and dabbled disastrously in England's internal affairs. Henry was a weak man who could not hold a consistent course or make up his mind about important issues. He was vulnerable to manipulation by false friends. Margaret was stronger than her husband, but she was no more astute. By making personal enemies of important men and entering into the private quarrels of the nobility, she and Henry hastened the outbreak of the civil war that cost them their thrones. Events came to a head in 1453, when Henry was incapacitated by his first attack of mental illness. She hoped to be allowed to govern during his convalescence, but parliament and England's magnates turned instead to Henry's nearest male relative, Richard of York. The use which York made of his power as 'protector' frightened her. He imprisoned Henry's chief councilor, the duke of Somerset, and replaced Henry's appointees with friends of his own. She concluded that York was a threat to the future of the Lancastrian dynasty, and her growing determination to destroy York inched England into open war. Her hand was greatly strengthened on 13 October 1453, when she bore her husband a son. The birth of a prince distanced York from the throne and deprived him of his chief reason for propping up Henry's government. In January of 1455, York's fortunes declined further. Henry recovered his senses, restored personal rule, freed the duke of Somerset, and purged the court of York's men.

These acts exacerbated tensions between the partisans of the two houses, and on 22 May 1455, fighting broke out at St. Albans, a town north of London. The so-called 'War of the Roses' began well for the house of York. At the first battle of St. Albans Richard killed Somerset and captured Henry. The disaster caused a recurrence of Henry's mental illness, and York regained the office of 'protector.' When Henry recovered a few months later, he might have been persuaded to compromise with York and continue him as chief royal councilor. Margaret, however, convinced Henry that York was too dangerous to be allowed to play any role in government, and Henry ordered York to Ireland. York reorganized his forces, and on 10 July 1460, he captured Henry at the battle of Northampton. York was inclined to depose Henry, but his followers persuaded him to adopt a strategy that would seem less treasonous to the kingdom's subjects. York proposed that Henry remain king for the rest of his life, but that he disinherit Prince Edward and name York his heir. Margaret refused to accept this compromise. She and Edward fled to Wales and then to Scotland. Mary of Geldenland, regent for Scotland, gave them shelter while Margaret plotted ways to win back her son's inheritance. News of York's death in a fight at Wakefield on 30 December 1461, prompted her to lead a band of Scots into England. She defeated the Yorkists under the command of Richard Neville, earl of Warwick, at a second battle at St. Albans on 17 February 1461, and rescued her husband. She chose not to press on to London, which would have defended itself vigorously against her Scottish troops. She and Henry retreated to northern districts traditionally loyal to the Lancastrians, and on 4 March 1461, London opened its gates to the Yorkist forces. Richard of York's son, Edward, was proclaimed king, and a few weeks later Edward confirmed his title by destroying the Lancastrian army in a battle at Towton.

Henry took refuge in Scotland, while Margaret and Prince Edward hastened to France to beg Louis XI for aid. Louis promised them help, but only after they agreed to mortgage to the French the only English property remaining on the continent (the port of Calais). She came back to Scotland to raise yet another army. Her efforts were frustrated by the refusal of the English Lancastrians to join the Scots in raids on English territory. She turned to the duke of Burgundy for assistance, but Burgundy was worried about France and determined to stay on good terms with the man who was in power in England. Having exhausted all options, she had no choice but to give up the struggle and return to her family lands in Anjou. In 1464 Henry, left to his own resources, accompanied a small band of soldiers on a raid into England. They were routed near the town of Hexham, but Henry went underground and eluded capture until July of 1465. For five years, while his wife and son endured poverty in France, Henry remained a prisoner in the Tower of London. In 1470 events beyond his control conspired to give him another chance. Edward IV quarreled with Warwick. Warwick fled to France to ask Louis XI for help in overthrowing Edward. Since Warwick needed Henry to provide a legitimating pretext for his war, Louis XI patched up a peace between Warwick and Margaret.

In September of 1470, Warwick invaded England, liberated Henry, and restored him to the throne. Margaret, who may not have trusted her old enemy, was slow to respond to Warwick's call to bring Prince Edward to England. On the day she landed, Edward IV used troops acquired in Burgundy to destroy Warwick at the battle of Barnet. She again rallied men to the Lancastrian cause, but on 4 May 1471, at Tewkesbury Edward killed her son and captured her. The death of the Lancastrian heir meant that the Yorkists no longer had any reason to let Henry live. A few weeks after the death of his son, Henry was murdered by his captors. Margaret remained in an English prison until 1475, when Louis XI negotiated her release and allowed her to return to France. She lived out the rest of her life in retirement as Louis' pensioner.

2H6. 3H6. 1H6. R3.

Margareton, F1 'Margarelon,' probably a printer's error. *Tro 5.5.7,* one of many bastard sons of Priam. He is usually referred to as 'Bastard' in early editions of the play, but he is presumably the same person. He confronts Thersites in *5.8.* Sh. got the name from his sources, William Caxton's *Recuyell of the Historyes of Troy* (1474), in which Margareton is slain by Achilles, and John Lydgate's *Troy Book* (1412–21).

Margery, 1) *MV 2.2.84, 86,* Gobbo's wife, mother of Lancelot. She is mentioned only after the joking about the dubious certainty of fatherhood and never mentioned again.

2) *Tmp 2.2.47,* common woman who loved sailors in Stefano's drinking song.

Margery, Lady, *WT 2.3.160,* term of contempt for the lord who with Antigonus defends Hermione's child. It may relate in imagery to the earlier use of Dame Partlet, since 'margery-prater' was also a slang term for hen.

Maria, 1) *LLL,* lady-in-waiting of the Princess of France. She is wooed by Longueville and at play's end promises to return to him after a year's mourning. Maria was common in contemporary French history, from which Sh. selected the names for this play.

2) *TN,* 'Mistress Mary,' 'Mary,' attendant on the Lady Olivia. Witty and energetic, it is she who develops the plot to humiliate Malvolio. She forges the love letter that entraps him and arranges his imprisonment as a madman. At play's end she marries Sir Toby, though she clearly deserves better.

Marian, the name of any common woman.

1) *Err 3.1.31,* house servant of Antipholus of Ephesus.

2) *LLL 5.2.908,* woman in Winter's song, 'M.'s nose.'

3) *TN 2.3.13,* Maria, a possible allusion to the Robin Hood legend.

4) *Tmp 2.2.47,* woman who loved sailors in Stefano's drinking song.

Marian, Maid, *1H4 3.3.114,* character depicted in May day celebrations, morris dances, and Robin Hood plays (qq.v.). She was not initially a character in the old Robin Hood poems and apparently came into the legends by way of the May day plays around the early 16th c. The part was taken by a man in woman's clothing who was a butt for ribald jokes. In these performances, Maid Marian was anything but a maid. *Cambises, King of Percia* by Thomas Preston (c. 1569), a popular play of the period, has the character 'Marian-May-Be Good,' for example, and her companion 'Hob' (an old form of Robin). There are numerous other examples. Only in later centuries did she evolve into a noble romantic heroine of the age of chivalry.

Mariana, 1) *MM,* betrothed of Angelo. Abandoned by Angelo when her brother Frederick was lost at sea along with her dowry, at play's beginning she resides at the 'moated grange,' a farmhouse surrounded by a ditch. Sh. created her character from the sources by dividing Epitia of Cinthio's *Hecatommithi* and Cassandra of George Whetstone's *Promos and Cassandra* into Mariana and Isabella, but her love for Angelo despite his nasty treatment, and her forgiveness of him have special thematic importance in the play. Since this Mariana consents to a 'bed trick' similar to that in *AWW,* her name may have been borrowed from Diana's neighbor in *AWW.*

2) *AWW,* friend and neighbor of the Widow Capilet. She has no plot function except to warn Diana Capilet of the dubious morality of Paroles and Bertram.

Marina, *Per,* Pericles and Thaisa's daughter. Named from being born at sea, she is typical of the daughters in Sh.'s late romances (Perdita and Miranda) by being named according to her function in the plot, and in the name's originating with Sh. She is called Thaisa in John Gower's *Confessio Amantis* (1390) and Tharsia in Lawrence Twine's *Patterne of Painefull Adventures* (1594). See Pericles.

Mark, attributed author of the Gospel bearing his name. *STM Add. II.D.98:* this is possibly a pun on the Gospel and 'mark' or 'listen.'

Marle, Earl of, *H5 4.8.100,* (d. 1415), one of the French nobles whom Sh. found listed by Holinshed (3.555) as a notable casualty of the battle at Agincourt. Marle is a town near the city of Laon.

Marquis, or marquess, title accorded a count or, in England, an earl who is responsible for a 'march,' a military district on a difficult frontier. The honor was first awarded in England late in the 14th c. In English court protocol a marquis is superior to an earl but inferior to a duke.

1) *2H6 1.1.59,* see Suffolk, duke of, William de la Pole.

2) *R3 1.3.253, 259,* see Dorset, Marquis of, 1).

Marry, a mild oath or expletive derived from Mary, the mother of Christ.

Mars, 1) Roman god of war corresponding to the Greek Ares. *LLL 5.2.637, 644,* 'armipotent M.' *MV 3.2.85,* 'frowning M.,' a warlike demeanor. *MWW 1.3.96. Ham 2.2.493,* 'M.'s armor,' Vulcan forged it with the assistance of his Cyclops. *3.4.56. Tro 2.1.55,* 'M. his idiot!': possessive—Ajax is the idiot of M. *2.3.240. 3.3.184,* possible reference to the *Iliad* 5, in which M. takes the side of the Trojans. *4.7.61, 82. 4.7.139,* an oath on Vulcan's forge, which 'stithied' M.'s helmet. *5.2.167.*

Son 55.7. AWW 2.1.46. 2.3.280, 'M.'s fiery steed,' a warhorse. *3.2.9. Tim 4.3.386. Ant 1.1.4, 1.5.18, 2.2.6, 2.5.118, 4.15.48. Cor 1.4.10, 4.5.119, 4.5.197, 5.6.102. Cym 5.5.126. Tmp 4.1.98,* 'M.'s hot minion,' the god's lustful darling, Venus.

TNK 1.1.62, 'M.'s altar.' *1.1.226. 1.2.20,* 'M.'s so-scorned altar.' *1.4.17,* 'By th' helm of M.,' an oath. *5.1.35, 59. 5.2.12,* 'M.'s drum.' *5.6.106.*

2) fourth planet from the sun. Its unusual red glow and extreme orbit caused astrologers to conclude that it had dangerous characteristics. Since Mars was believed to be an ominous influence promoting violence and confusion, the Romans saw it as the appropriate symbol for the god of war. The redness of the planet was sometimes said to be the blood of soldiers who had fallen in battle. Sh.'s 'Mars' was a term for the fate that brings victory in battle.

R2 2.1.41, 2.3.100, 1H4 3.2.112, 4.1.117, H5 pro. 6, 4.2.43, 1H6 1.2.1. AWW 1.1.188–90, 92, Parolles brags he was born under it.

Marseilles, F1 'Marcellus,' 'Marcellæ.' F2 'Marsellis.' French city on the Gulf of Lyons, 219 mi. southeast of Lyons. Long a trading center, Phocæan Greeks settled there about 600 BC and called it Massalia. Greek is said to have been spoken there until well into the Roman period AD. Julius Cæsar captured the city in 49 BC, and after the Romans it fell to the Goths, Burgundians, Franks, and Saracens. In the 1100's it became part of the dominions of the counts of Provence. During the Crusades, the city was often a departure point for the Holy Land. It was bequeathed to the French crown in 1481.

Shr 2.1.371. Gremio refers to the trading of M. in offering a merchant ship in 'Marcellus roade' (F1): M. harbor. *AWW 4.4.9, 4.5.80.*

Marshal, Earl or **Lord,** 1) *R2, 1H4 4.4.2, H8 4.1.19,* officer of the English court who was entrusted with the management of the monarch's military establishment. The title derived from a term for a man charged with responsibility for cavalry, the most important component of a feudal army. In England the office of Earl Marshal originated in the 12th c. when William the Marshal married the heiress to the earldom of Pembroke. The honor descended through their line to the Bigod family and was inherited in 1306 by Edward I. In 1316 Edward II bestowed it on his brother Thomas, earl of Norfolk, and in 1385 Richard II gave it to his friend Thomas Mowbray, duke of Norfolk (1397). In 1398 Richard II banished Mowbray and Henry Bolingbroke for quarreling and granted the marshal's office to Thomas Holland, duke of Surrey (*R2*). Mowbray died in exile before Bolingbroke returned to England to depose Richard and ascend the throne as Henry IV, but Mowbray's son, also named Thomas (1386–1405), took up his father's fight. In 1405 he joined Northumberland and the archbishop of York in a plot to overthrow Henry. The revolt they initiated collapsed, and those associated with it were arrested and executed. The Mowbray estate passed to John Howard, husband of Thomas' sister, Margaret. Richard III appointed him marshal in 1483, and he died with the king at the battle of Bosworth Field. The Tudor and Stuart monarchs passed the office of Lord Marshal from hand to hand, but in 1672 Charles II returned it to the Howards who still have it in their keeping.

2) *1H4 4.4.2, 2H4 1.3.4, 2.3.42, 4.1.218,* see Thomas, Lord Mowbray.

Marshalsea, *H8 5.3.84,* prison attached to the court of the marshal of the royal household. In

1372 Edward III established it in Southwark opposite London. This angered the Londoners, who believed that the Marshalsea impinged on the jurisdiction of their courts.

Martem, *Tit 4.3.55,* L. objective case, 'Mars.'

Martext, Sir Oliver, *AYLI,* village vicar. The pun 'mar text' is an obvious allusion to a lack of religious orthodoxy or to his intelligence. As Touchstone's and Jaques' remarks (*3.3.75–98*) indicate, Martext is intended as a sincere, but unsanctioned or inadequate, country preacher. Such preachers proliferated as the Reformation eroded the powers of official church structures. The 'Sir' is a comparison of the priesthood to the knighthood (see Dominie). It is only a title of respect for a clergyman, not in this case an indication of nobility (see Sir Hugh Evans).

Martial, (adj.) of or pertaining to the god Mars. *Cym 4.2.312,* 'his M. thigh,' his warrior's thigh.

Martians, House of, *Cor 2.3.238,* patrician family that claimed descent from Rome's fourth king, Ancus Marcius. Coriolanus is the only member of the family who played a prominent role in the early history of the Republic.

Martin, St. *1H6 1.3.110,* (316–397 AD), Roman soldier who became bishop of the French city of Tours and the founder of one of Europe's earliest monasteries. He supposedly divided his cloak with a naked beggar. 'St. Martin's summer,' was the benign autumnal season that Americans call 'Indian summer.' The feast of St. Martin, which is celebrated on 11 November, often corresponds with the warm spell that precedes the onslaught of winter. As it was also the Feast of Bacchus, M. became the patron saint of recovering alcoholics, as well as innkeepers.

Martino, *Rom 1.2.64,* one of the guests invited to Capulet's feast, along with his wife and daughters. See comment at Anselme.

Martius, 1) *Tit,* one of Titus Andronicus' sons. He and his brother were framed for the murder of the emperor Saturninus' brother, Bassianus, and executed. Their deaths were among the many wrongs that caused Titus Andronicus to take fearful revenge on his arch enemies, the empress Tamora and her Moorish servant Aaron. Sh.'s source for *Tit* is unknown, but a later version of a tale that might have inspired him survives in an 18th c. chapbook.

2) 'M. the younger,' *Cor,* Coriolanus' son. Coriolanus' children are mentioned, but not named, in Sh.'s source for the play, Plutarch's 'Coriolanus.' Sh. probably inferred the son's name from the father's: Caius Martius 'Coriolanus.'

Martius, Caius, *Cor,* see Coriolanus.

Martlemas, *2H4 2.2.95,* feast of St. Martin celebrated on 11 November. It ended the season of harvest when fatted cattle were slaughtered and the meat put up for the winter.

Mary, 1) Virgin Mary, mother of Christ. *R2 2.1.56. H8 5.2.32:* in having Henry VIII use Mary's name as an oath, Sh. is not guilty of an anachronism. Henry's Protestantism consisted primarily in his belief that he, not the pope, should lead the church in England. In most matters of faith and practice, he was content to abide by the traditions of medieval Catholicism.

2) *TN 1.3.51. 1.5.10, 2.3.117,* 'Mistress M.,' see Maria.

Mary I, *H8 2.4.172,* (1516–1558), elder daughter of Henry VIII and first woman to reign in England. Mary was the only viable child produced by Katherine of Aragon, Henry VIII's first wife. Since Mary was for many years her father's chief heir, the choice of her husband was a matter of major diplomatic importance. Various engagements were negotiated for her, but her youth passed without any of them leading to a marriage. When she was only 2 years old, she was promised to the dauphin of France. This agreement was abrogated in 1522 in favor of a more prestigious match with her cousin, the Hapsburg emperor, Charles V. In 1525 Charles, who had broken ten previous engagements, jilted her and wed Isabella of Portugal. Charles's victory over Francis I in 1525 made France desperate for allies and revived the possibility of a French husband for Mary. It was suggested that she might marry Francis himself or his second son, Henry, the duke of Orléans (*H8 2.4.172*). This arrangement fell afoul of Henry's decision to repudiate his marriage with Katherine, her mother. Henry based his request for an annulment on the argument that his union with Katherine had been contrary to Scripture and, therefore, invalid. If Henry was correct, he had never been married to Katherine and her daughter was illegitimate. A royal bastard was a far less attractive fiancée than a potential heir to the throne. Consequently, as Henry's marital plans prospered, his daughter's declined.

In 1533 Anne Boleyn bore Henry a second daughter, Elizabeth, whom Henry acknowledged as his heir. Mary was stripped of the title 'princess' and of a place in the order of royal succession. She objected loudly to her loss of status, and Henry took a hard line with her. She was separated from her mother and forced to accept the humiliation of being appointed lady-in-waiting to her baby half-sister. She refused to bend to her father's will, and Henry punished her by denying her permission to visit her mother during Katherine's terminal illness. Mary blamed her misfortunes on Anne Boleyn, Protestantism, and the Reformation. Like her mother, she remained an ardent Catholic and an opponent of her father's religious policies. After Boleyn's execution, Elizabeth joined Mary on the roster of the king's illegitimate children, but Henry's will restored legitimacy to both his daughters and named them heirs to Henry's only son, Edward VI. The Protestant faction at court knew that she was the implacable enemy of their religion, and when Edward died without issue in 1553, they tried to dispossess her and bestow England's crown on her cousin, Jane Gray. The people of England frustrated their efforts to set aside Henry's daughter in favor of his niece. Mary ascended the throne, and Jane was executed in 1554. As Mary's enemies anticipated, she tried to reverse the course set by her father and brother. Papal authority was restored in England.

Orthodox Catholic clergy were appointed to episcopal sees, and she sought out and destroyed Protestants. About 300 men and women were burned at the stake by 'Bloody Mary.' Despite the ferocity of the queen's religion, it was less troubling to her subjects than her foreign policy. Her advisors urged her to marry an Englishman, but she wed her cousin, Philip II, Charles V's son. Passionately loyal to her Spanish kin who had supported her and her mother in their difficulties, Mary wanted the help of the strongest Catholic power in Europe to rebuild England's church. Although her subjects feared that the queen's foreign marriage might cost them their national independence, she wed Philip in July 1554. She was 38, and he was 27. Philip was not prepared to dally long in England, where his wife's subjects made it clear that he was not welcome. He lived with her for a year and returned to visit her only once (1557). Despite her age, she was desperate to have a child who would follow her to the throne and secure the future of English Catholicism. So certain was she that God would give her an heir that she convinced herself that she was with child and began to display the physical signs of pregnancy. She ordered services of thanksgiving in England's churches and made a great show of her expectations. In due time it became apparent that she was mistaken and that her pregnancy was hysterical. She was humiliated and depressed by the knowledge that her heir would be the hated Anne Boleyn's daughter, Elizabeth. Mary had forced Elizabeth to conform to the Catholic faith, but Elizabeth, as the child of her father's first Protestant marriage, had no enthusiasm for the papacy. When Mary died of ovarian cancer on 17 November 1558, Elizabeth ascended the throne. The new queen was a religious moderate. She had no sympathy with radicals of either camp, but she was firm in her father's conviction that the head of England was the head of England's church.

Mary-buds, *Cym 2.3.23,* most likely, the marigold (*Calendula officinalis*). It opens with the rise of the sun and closes at dusk. There has also been some discussion of the daisy (*Bellis perennis*) and the lesser celandine (*Ranunculus ficaria*); however, *WT 4.4.105* mentions the opening and closing of the marigold, which would seem to settle it. The marigold is named after the Virgin Mary.

Masham, *H5 2.2.13, 145,* town 30 mi. northwest of the city of York.

Mass, Christian ritual, 'the Eucharist,' the commemoration of the 'Last Supper.' It derives from L. *missa,* 'dismissal,' and referred to the dismissal of the unbaptized before the actual Eucharist. Later, however, the term came to refer to the entire service. 'By the Mass' is used as an oath throughout the plays, though for reasons of decency it was omitted in some editions.

Master gunner, *1H6,* trained practitioner of a highly specialized military craft. By the end of the 13th c. medieval scientists knew how to make gun powder, but explosives were not successfully employed in military weapons until the mid-14th c. At that time, gun powder had to be mixed at the site where it was used, and its effectiveness as a propellant depended upon the skill of the man who compounded, packed, and fired it. The word 'gun' in the 14th c. referred to a variety of different kinds of machines for launching projectiles. Those that employed explosives were a novelty, and they were provided by civilian military contractors who were not bound by the aristocratic traditions of the feudal military establishment.

Maud, *Err 3.1.31,* house servant of Antipholus of Ephesus. Maud is a medieval form of Mathilda.

Mauritania, *Oth 4.2.229,* African country, 'land of the Moors.' Roughly it comprised the areas at the north west of Africa, including parts of modern Morocco, Algeria, and Mauritania. The original Berber inhabitants had established kings when they first entered Roman history around 110 BC. In 25 BC, Augustus granted sovereignty over M. to Juba II, king of Numidia. In 40 AD, Caligula executed Ptolemæus, son of Juba and absorbed M. as two provinces, Mauritania Tingitana (west of the Mulucha river) and M. Cæsarea (east of the river). The Vandals destroyed the kingdom in 429, and the area was conquered by the Arabs in the 7th c. As a Muslim power it attempted to expand both north into Europe in the Middle Ages and south into Africa. The modern nation of Mauritania acquired independence from France in 1960, but does not include the main area of historical Mauritania. See also Moor.

May, fifth month (third in Sh.'s day) of the year. Since it is the month when full spring erupts in England, poets associated it with youth, beauty, and pleasure. The name comes from the Roman goddess Maia, also called Fauna or Bona Dea, a fertility goddess.

LLL 1.1.106, 'M.'s new-fangled shows.' *4.3.100. MND 1.1.167,* to celebrate May Day. *4.1.132,* 'rite of M.,' this remark would seem to change the setting of the play from midsummer night (around the summer solstice, June 21) to May Day, but both times were associated with festivities, lunacy, and the supernatural. Though the theme of marriage is traditionally viewed as having been occasioned by the play's performance as part of a wedding celebration, it might as likely be related to the customs of the May Day and the summer solstice.

R2 5.1.79. 1H4 4.1.102. MWW 3.2.62. H5 1.2.120. Tro 1.2.172, 'a nettle against M.,' a play on the old saw 'April showers bring May flowers.' *TN 3.4.140,* 'a M. morning,' a day for frivolity, as on May-day. *TNK 2.5.51,* 'flow'ry M.' *3.1.5. 3.1 sd,* 'a-Maying,' celebrating May Day. *3.1.3,* 'bloomed M.' See Lord of May, Lady of May, May Day.

May Day, popular medieval festival that marked the beginning of the growing season. Some of the colorful, and often bawdy, customs associated with its celebration, such as the morris dance and the May-pole, originated in the fertility religions of pre-Christian Europe. *AWW 2.2.23. H8 5.3.14.* See May.

Mayor, the head of a city government. The title 'mayor' derives from the Latin word *maior,* 'greater,' and was often used during the Middle Ages to indicate the highest official in an administrative hierarchy. Medieval cities were not part of the feudal system. They were founded and inhabited by persons who were on the margins of medieval society—by people who were not commended to anyone by feudal oaths of personal loyalty and who, therefore, had no title to land. Townsmen lived by trade, not by farming or by rendering military service, and were neither vassals nor serfs. During the 11th c. a revival of European trade and industry created a large 'middle' class between the traditional feudal castes of the lords and peasants. These people banded together, set up legal communes, and negotiated with feudal authorities for charters that recognized their right to manage their own affairs. Cities generated wealth, and kings came to rely on cities for taxes to support royal government. Consequently, the officials who ran cities acquired political influence and were treated with deference.

'M. of London,' as the head of the largest community in England, he wielded considerable power in national politics. *2H6 4.3.12:* no particular mayor seems to be referred to by this passage, though the mayor's sword that the wicked Mr. Cade intends to appropriate would have been the mayor of 1450, Thomas Chalton. *1H6:* John Coventry. *R3 3.1.17:* Sir Edmund Shaw or Shaa. A prominent goldsmith, he became mayor in 1482. A strong supporter of Richard III, he may have been financially linked to the house of York. He was rewarded by being made a privy councillor. He died in 1487, leaving many generous donations in his will. *H5 5.0.25:* the passage refers to Henry's triumphant return from Agincourt on 23 November 1415. The Lord Mayor at that time was Thomas Fawcomer. He was flanked in the procession by mayors William Cromer and Nycholas Wotton. *H8 2.1.151, 5.4.69:* Sir Stephen Pecocke.

Mayors of other towns also appear in Sh.'s plays: e.g., mayor of St. Albans, *2H6*; mayor of York, *3H6* ; mayor of Coventry, *3H6* (in 1471, he is listed as 'Joh. Bette').

Mede, *Ant 3.6.75,* see Media.

Medea, witch from Greek mythology who committed horrifying crimes in the service of love. She was the daughter of Æetes, king of Colchis, the land at the eastern end of the Black Sea to which Jason and the Argonauts journeyed. She fell in love with Jason and helped him steal her nation's treasure, the Golden Fleece. When Æetes learned of the theft and set off in pursuit of his faithless daughter and her lover, he discovered just how ruthless she could be. She had kidnapped her young brother, Absyrtus, so that she could kill him and scatter bits of his corpse in the wake of Jason's ship. She knew that her father, who had a much stronger sense of family obligation than she did, would stop to gather up his son's remains for burial.

Jason and she shared many epic adventures, most of which gave her an opportunity to demonstrate her magical powers and lack of moral scruples. When she and Jason returned to his home, they discovered that Jason's throne was occupied by an aging man named Pelias. She realized that Pelias' children feared his decline, and she skillfully exploited their affection and anxiety. She promised to teach Pelias' daughters a magic ritual that would rejuvenate their father. To demonstrate the effectiveness of her therapy, she dismembered an aged animal, boiled its parts in a pot with magic herbs, and resurrected it in the full bloom of youth. Eager to restore their father's vigor by the same means, Pelias' daughters promptly butchered him for the kettle. Without her magic, the well-intentioned girls discovered that they were powerless to raise the father they had slaughtered. She succeeded in destroying Pelias, but her scheme failed to restore Jason to the throne.

The wrath of Pelias' heirs forced her and Jason to flee, and they sought refuge in Corinth.

There Jason seized an opportunity to make a new life for himself without her. He repudiated her and announced his intention to marry Glauce, daughter of Creon, king of Corinth. Medea avenged herself in her usual style. She sent Glauce a gorgeous robe dipped in poison. When the girl put it on, her flesh dissolved. Her father died trying to pull the deadly garment from her body. Medea punished Jason by killing their sons and depriving him of the heirs that were a Greek male's only hope of immortality. Having done her utmost to punish Jason, she moved to Athens and began a new life with Ægeus, the city's king. She bore Ægeus a son, Medeus, but Medeus never ruled Athens. Ægeus was ignorant of the fact that he already had an heir, Theseus. When Theseus appeared in Athens, Medea divined his identity and tried to save the throne for her son by tricking Ægeus into killing Theseus. The plot was discovered, and she returned to Colchis. Medeus became the eponymous ancestor of the people the Greeks called the Medes. The Medes joined forces with the Persians to build a great empire that continued into the 3rd c. BC Medea's tradition of endangering Greek lives. Medea herself went on to greater glories. Hera, wife of Zeus, was an admirer of female initiative—and no stickler for moral niceties. She bestowed immortality on her and sent her to reign over the Elysian Fields as Achilles' queen.

2H6 5.3.59. MV 5.1.13.

Media, *Ant 3.1.7, 3.6.14,* ancient kingdom occupying the western highlands of Iran. Its people were descendants of Indo-Europeans who appeared there in the 2nd millennium BC. In 559 BC, they allied with their Persian neighbors and, led by Cyrus the Great, created one of the ancient era's largest empires.

Mediterranean, body of water enclosed by Africa, Europe, and Asia, consisting of several smaller seas, including the Ægean and the Adriatic. The primary rivers feeding it are the Nile, Rhone, Po, and Ebro. It covers approximately 1,150, 000 sq. mi., with narrow natural openings into the Atlantic at Gibralter and into the Black sea at the Dardanelles. It became the 'pond' upon which much of classical history was played out. The Romans called it *Mare Internum,* the internal or inland sea, and it was not called by its present name which means 'in the middle of land' or 'at the center of the earth' until the 3rd c. AD in the works of C. Julius Solinus (see Solinus, duke of Ephesus). The anglicized name was uncommon even in Sh.'s day, most writers adhering to the L. form *Mediterraneum* (q.v.) if using it at all. The earliest *OED* citation is 1594, although 'Mediterrany' is used as early as the 15th c. *Tmp 1.2.235,* 'M. float'.

Mediterraneum, *LLL 5.1.55,* L. for Mediterranean (q.v.). Apparently this form was not as pompous as it might seem, as the Latin was in more common use than 'Mediterranean.' It nonetheless contributes to Armado's pomposity.

Meg, nickname for Margaret. 1) *2H6 3.2.26,* Margaret of Anjou. Henry VI uses the endearment to indicate the saintly king's honest affection for his unworthy mate.

2) *MWW 2.1.139,* Margaret Page. George Page's use of it contrasts with Ford's cool treatment of Mistress Ford.

3) *Ado,* see Margaret.

4) *Tmp 2.2.47,* common woman who loved sailors in Stefano's drinking song.

Mehercle, *LLL 4.2.77,* oath, 'by Hercules.'

Meissen, *H5 1.2.53,* district drained by the Saale and Elbe rivers and encompassing parts of Bohemia and Silesia.

Melancholy, *JC 5.3.66,* allegorical figure representing the state of depression.

Melancholy, Monsieur, *AYLI 3.2.288,* name applied to Jaques by Orlando, mocking Jaques's prevailing humour.

Meleager, *TNK 3.5.18,* son of Œneus and Althæa, an Argonaut most celebrated for killing the Calydonian boar. The Fate Atropos predicted he would die when a certain stick in the fire was consumed. Althæa, his mother, plucked it from the fire, quenched it and preserved it. When Œneus neglected proper homage to Artemis, she sent a vicious boar to ravage Calydon. Meleager organized the greatest heroes of Greece, including Castor, Pollux, Theseus, Pirithous, Jason, Peleus, Telamon, Nestor and Atalanta, to kill it. Upon killing the boar, he granted the trophies to Atalanta, but his uncles took them away and Meleager, in a rage, killed the two of them. Althæa, to avenge her brothers, thrust the stick which she had protected into the fire and her son died in horrible pain. She then committed suicide. The story is told in Ovid's *Metamorphoses,* 8.

Melford, Long Melford, village in Suffolk where Sh. says that the duke of Suffolk was accused of appropriating common lands for his personal use. The issue of enclosing commons was hotly debated in Sh.'s day. Changes in the English economy and increasing opportunities for profits in the wool trade encouraged entrepreneurs to acquire vast tracts of land for pasturing sheep. This led to the eviction of tenants from unproductive small farms and the private expropriation of lands that villagers had traditionally shared in common. The rich and enterprising benefited, but the new agricultural industries and property laws cost many poor people their only means of earning a living. *2H6 1.3.23.*

Melun, Count, *Jn,* French nobleman whom Sh. says accompanied Louis (VIII) when he invaded England to depose King John. Melun is a town situated on the Seine river about 30 mi. southeast of Paris near the forest of Fontainebleau, but it is not certain that Sh.'s character had a historical prototype. A French count de Melun is mentioned in a treaty between France and England in 1194. Sh.'s character claims to have had an English grandfather, and there was an English family bearing the de Melun name. A Robert de Melun was bishop of Hereford from 1163 to 1166. Since many English nobles were descendants of Norman soldiers who followed William the Conqueror to England, many had family connections in Normandy. Melun's role in Sh.'s play is that of a French insider who has English sympathies, and it may be that Sh. invented his English ancestry to give him a motive for betraying the Dauphin's confidences.

Menaphon, *Err 5.1.370,* duke, famous warrior, uncle of Solinus duke of Ephesus. He brought Antipholus and Dromio of Ephesus to Ephesus.

Menas, *Ant,* Menodorus (d. 35 BC), freedman who changed sides several times in the struggle between Sextus Pompey and Octavius. He held a command in Sextus Pompey's fleet, and he objected to the peace Sextus made with Octavius and Mark Antony in 39 BC. He was alleged to have urged Sextus to kidnap and murder Octavius and Antony when they came aboard Sextus' vessel for a feast to celebrate their truce. By scorning his advice, Sextus lost his best opportunity to destroy his enemies and forfeited Menas' confidence. When hostilities broke out a year later, Menas defected to Octavius' camp. In 36 BC he reverted briefly to the Pompeians, but he returned to Octavius and died fighting for him.

Menecrates, *Ant,* (d. 38 BC), one of Sextus Pompey's freedmen military commanders. When Sextus' colleague Menas defected to the service of Octavius in 38 BC, Menecrates was assigned the task of capturing and punishing him. Fleets led by the two men met off Cumæ. The Pompeians fared poorly, and Menecrates committed suicide to avoid capture.

Menelaus, legendary king of Sparta, son of Atreus and Ærope. The abduction of Helen, his wife, by Paris (Alexander), prince of Troy, is asserted by Homer to have been the cause of the Trojan war. He spent his young life in exile with his brother Agamemnon, but with Tyndareus' help they expelled their uncle Thyestes from the throne of Mycenae. Menelaus wooed Helen, a much sought woman. To prevent disorder, a solemn oath was taken that Helen's choice would be respected and defended. She chose Menelaus and he became Tyndareus' heir. When Helen was abducted, this oath caused the union of the Greeks against Troy. He is not depicted as being as significant in the war as other heroes, but he acquitted himself well and was one of the men who entered Troy in the belly of the Trojan Horse. After the war he lived quietly in Sparta and the gods sent him to the Elysian Fields. *3H6 2.2.147:* Sh.'s comparison of Henry VI to Menelaus and Henry's queen, Margaret, to Helen, shifts the blame for England's War of the Roses from Henry and Edward IV to a hated foreign woman. By making Margaret a scapegoat, Sh. protects the reputations of two venerated English kings.

Tro: As in Homer, Menelaus is overshadowed by the powerful personalities around him. Some critics feel that his lack of assertiveness contributes to the impression that the war is being fought over nothing of consequence; however, since his character comes from the sources it may not be a thematic strategem. More obvious is the frequent ridiculing of Menelaus as a cuckold by referring to his 'horns,' for example: *1.1.112.*

Menenius Agrippa, *Cor,* Menenius Lanatus Agrippa, Roman consul for the year 503 BC. He successfully commanded Rome's armies in wars with the Sabines. He also brought the city internal peace by negotiating a truce between its rival social classes, the patricians and the plebeians. Plutarch ('Coriolanus' 6.3–4) says that he persuaded the common people to cooperate with the Senatorial aristocracy by telling them 'the fable of the belly.' The fable developed an analogy between the various classes in society and the organs of the human body: just as each organ has its appropriate function and the health of all depends on each acknowledging the value of the others, the well-being of the state requires each citizen to be content with his station.

Menon, *Tro 5.5.7,* Greek warrior king, cousin of Achilles. He is mentioned several times in Sh.'s primary source, William Caxton's *Recuyell of the Historyes of Troy* (1474). He was slain by Hector after having been beaten by him in several encounters. In the *Iliad* 12, the name is used for a Trojan killed by Leonteus, a possible source for Leontes (q.v.) Similarly, Plutarch ('Phocion') has a cavalry commander named Menon who takes over when Leonatus is slain. Menon also appears in Plutarch as a Greek general in the service of Cyrus. In Arrian's biography of Alexander the Great, there is a satrap with the name. *The Countess of Pembrokes Arcadia* by Sidney has a Memnon, a name which occurs frequently in the legends of Troy for an Ethiopian king.

Menteith, 1) area in south Perthshire between the Teith and the Forth in central Scotland. It became an earldom during the reign of Malcolm IV. *1H4. Mac*

2) *Mac,* F1 'Menteth,' thane who allies himself with Malcolm against Macbeth. The historical thane was named Walter Dalyell and Sh. got his name from Holinshed's *Chronicles* (1577).

Menteith, Earl of, *1H4 1.1.73,* see Mordake.

Mephistophiles, *MWW 1.1.121,* F1 'Mephostophilus,' the name of a demon which first appears in the 1587 version of the Faust legend by Johann Spies. It may have been concocted out of Greek words meaning, 'disliking the light,' but its origin is unknown. Sh. probably borrowed the name from Marlowe as the allusion to Doctor Faustus at *4.5.64* implies. Since *MWW* contains Sh.'s only uses of these names, it seems likely that Marlowe's play (or one of the prose versions of the legend) was on his mind as he wrote *MWW.*

Mercadé, *LLL,* F1 'Marcade,' messenger who abruptly changes the tone of the play when he brings the Princess of France word that her father has died. The name is a play on Mercury, messenger of the gods.

Mercatio, *TGV 1.2.12,* one of Julia's prospective husbands. His name suggests that he made his money as a merchant (It. *mercato,* 'market'). It is possible, also, that the name is linked to Mercutio, since Arthur Brooke's *Tragicall Historye of Romeus and Juliet* (1562) influenced the making of this play, and was later the source for *Rom.*

Mercurial, of or pertaining to the god Mercury. *Cym 4.2.312,* 'His foot Mercurial,' his quick foot.

Mercury, messenger of the Roman gods, originally a god of commerce, son of Jupiter and Maia. His functions were similar to those of Hermes, the Greek deity who was the guardian of travellers, ambassadors, and boundary markers. He served other gods as a messenger, and artists often depict him with winged feet. His staff was the Caduceus. He was considered very clever, a trickster, the patron god of craftiness.

Tit 4.1.65, 4.3.56, 4.4.14. R3 2.1.89, 4.3.55. LLL 5.2.913, 'words of M.,' Mercadé's message. *Jn 4.2.174. 1H4 4.1.107. MWW 2.2.79,* 'she-Mercury.'

H5 2.0.7, (pl.). *Ham 3.4.57,* 'herald M.' *TN 1.5.93,* the meaning seems to be a wish that the god of tricksters give Maria the skill of lying. *Tro 2.2.44, 2.3.11. Ant 4.16.36. WT 4.3.25,* Autolycus is born under Mercury which implies he is frivolous, 'mercurial,' a 'con man.'

Mercutio, *Rom,* mad companion to Romeo, killed by Tybalt. At *1.2.68,* Mercutio is invited to Capulet's feast along with his brother Valentine. Given his apparent intimacy with the Montagues, this is curious, especially since Tybalt is offended by Romeo's presence, though no other mention is made of Mercutio's presence. Perhaps Sh. had originally intended the killing of Mercutio to occur at the feast and later changed his mind. It stretches belief to think that Sh., often careless at replicating names, could have been so careless as to mean a second Mercutio. More likely he was thinking of the Mercutio in Arthur Brooke's *Tragicall Historye of Romeus and Juliet* (1562), Sh.'s source, who is not only present at the feast, but whose cold hand Juliet compares to Romeus' warm hand. Further, he is said to be courteous of speech and pleasant of devise. Some critics have pointed out the suggestion of Mercury in his behavior in Sh. and related it to astrology; however, the name goes a long way back into the sources of the story including Luigi da Porto's *Istoria novellamente ritrovata di due Nobili Amanti* (c. 1530) where the corresponding character is named 'Marcuccio Guertio.'

Merlin, magician associated with King Arthur. He was spawned by a demon in a plot to create an antichrist, but a prompt baptism saved him from being Satan's tool. He was discovered to have great powers of prophecy when he was brought to King Vortigern and became advisor to the royal house. By magic he brought from Ireland the stones to create Stonehenge and assisted king Uther Pendragon in his desire to seduce the wife of the duke of Cornwall. Arthur was conceived from this union and Merlin undertook the boy's education and saw to his inheritence of the throne. Merlin was then tricked into living imprisonment within a stone, or within the air, or within a thornbush. From the latter two, he can occasionally be heard speaking. Many of the stories of Merlin begin with Nennius' *Historia Britonem,* which calls the magician Ambrosius. Later Merlin's adventures were embellished most importantly by Geoffrey of Monmouth in his *Historia Regum Britanniæ* and then in his *Vita Merlini,* which earned him the bishopric of St. Asaph, though he died before assuming office. After Geoffrey's writings, Merlin becomes a major figure in the legends of Arthur. There was an historical bard of the 5th c. named Merlin who is supposed to have died in a battle fighting for Arthur. This obscure figure may have been merged with the Celtic mythology and Geoffrey's imagination, both of which provided much of the material for the Arthurian legends.

1H4 3.1.146,: the Arthurian myths had Welsh roots, and Owain Glyndŵr's followers circulated rumors of ancient oracles from Merlin that confirmed their hope that the Welsh war for independence would succeed. *Lr 3.2.95*: this seems to be a joke at the expense of Holinshed's chronology, which puts the play in the time of Joash, king of Judah. The Fool not only predicts the future existence of Merlin, but the exact nature of his prophecy. It also seems likely that this may mock something particular or common in other plays Sh. had seen.

Merops, king of Cos. As husband of Clymene, who gave birth to the ill-fated Phæthon out of Helios or Apollo, M. is called Phæthon's father. He became the 'eagle' constellation. *TGV 3.1.153,* Phæthon should have been content to claim M. as father, but aspired too high, says the Duke, as Valentine aspires to Silvia. This parallels a remark made in telling the story in Ovid's *Metamorphoses,* 1–2.

Merriman, *Shr Ind. 1.15,* a dog. The dog's names in this section seem to come from their physical or behavioral traits. In F1 the line begins 'Brach Merriman' which would mean 'the bitch M.'; however, this is usually thought to be a printing error since 'brach' also occurs in the next line. Another word, such as 'breathe' (meaning 'rest,' imperative) is usually substituted by editors.

Mesopotamia, *Ant 3.1.8,* 'land between the rivers,' name Greek geographers gave to the territory drained by the Tigris and the Euphrates. The Euphrates marked the frontier between the Roman and Parthian empires.

Messala, *JC,* Marcus Valerius Messala Corvinus, (d. c. 3 BC), youth who espoused the Republican cause in the war that erupted after Julius Cæsar's assassination. Although he was not in Rome when Cæsar was killed and took no part in the plot against Cæsar, he was devoted to Cassius, the leader of the coup. At the battle of Philippi he commanded a unit in Cassius' army, and he nearly succeeded in capturing Octavius. After the defeat of the Republican forces at Philippi, he joined Mark Antony's party. He did not approve of Antony's relationship with Cleopatra, and in 36 BC he defected to Octavius. He served in the army Octavius brought to Actium in 31 BC, and, following Antony's defeat at Actium, he was appointed to fill out Antony's term as consul. Once Octavius was firmly in control of the empire, M., who may have had poor health, abandoned politics for literary pursuits. He wrote voluminously in many genres and was one of his generation's notable patrons of the arts.

Messaline, *TN 2.1.15, 5.1.230,* home of Sebastian, father of Sebastian and Viola. No such place exists in geography. One suggestion is that it is a confusion of Mytilene, but it is probably Messina in Sicily which is intended. It is in sailing proximity of Illyria.

Messina, *Ado,* setting of the play, a city of northeast Sicily, opposite the Calabrian mainland. It has changed hands many times in its history. Greek colonists founded the city in the 8th c. BC, to take advantage of the trade passing through the Straits of Messina and originally called it Zancle because of its sickle shape around a circular harbor opening to the north. The name was changed about 488 BC when the Samians under Anaxilas took the city from King Skythes. The Carthaginians razed the city in 397 BC, but Dionysius of Syracuse recaptured and rebuilt it. In wars between Syracuse and Carthage, it sided with Carthage and subsequently appealed to Rome for help against Hiero II of Syracuse. The Romans seized the city in 264 AD, precipitating the First Punic War. It was made a free ally of Rome in 241 BC and ultimately gained Roman citizenship before the rest of Sicily. It sided with Sextus Pompeius against Octavius in the civil war and was sacked for its trouble in 35 BC. When the Roman Empire was split, Messina fell under the Eastern empire.

In 831 it was captured by the Saracens and in 1061 by the Normans. Richard the Lionheart passed half a year in the city on his way to the Crusades, then sacked it. The Hohenstaufens gained control of it in 1194, but nearly a hundred years later, after the death of Conradin, the last of the dynasty, it became a pawn in the struggle between Pedro III of Aragon (see Pedro) and Charles, duke of Anjou. Pedro defeated Charles and the city remained in Spanish control from 1282 until 1713. According to Matteo Bandello's *Novelle* (1554) upon which *Ado* is primarily based, Pedro moved his court from Palermo to Messina in order to be closer to his peninsular possessions in Calabria, the 'second Sicily.' The city flourished as a trading center until it became a bone of contention again between the French and Spanish in the 17th c. A sign of its prosperity in Sh.'s time is the founding of the University of Messina in 1548. Ultimately it was the last city of Sicily to be incorporated into Garibaldi's united Italy. The city has always been troubled by earthquakes and has suffered several major ones.

Metamorphoses, *Tit 4.1.42,* long poem by Ovid (Publius Ovidius Naso). Ovid, one of the great literary figures who clustered in Rome in the generation of Octavius Augustus, was the author of a number of important works. The *Metamorphoses,* his longest composition, was probably written about the time of the birth of Christ. It described numerous miraculous transformations that had supposedly taken place in the period between the creation of the world and the apotheosis of Julius Cæsar. Sh. drew very heavily from Arthur Golding's translation (1565–7) of the *Metamorphoses*—if not the original—for many of the references to classical mythology that are scattered through his poems and plays. Along with Holinshed's *Chronicles* and Plutarch's *Lives,* he relied upon it more than any other work.

Metellus Cimber, *JC,* Lucius Tillius Cimber, a friend of Cæsar's who joined the plot to assassinate him. Cimber's assignment was to give the assassins an excuse to cluster around Cæsar. His plan was to have them join him in pleading with Cæsar for the recall of Cimber's brother from exile. Cimber gave the signal for the murderers to strike by tugging at Cæsar's toga. After Cæsar's death Cimber assumed command of the province of Bithynia, which Cæsar had promised him, and helped the Republicans against Mark Antony and Octavius (Augustus). The Greek text of Plutarch's 'Cæsar' (66.3–4) calls him Tillius Cimber. Metellus Cimber is the name given in Sh.'s source, Sir Thomas North's English translation (1579) of a French version of Plutarch's work (1559).

Metheglin, drink made of fermented honey and spices, spiced mead. It comes from the Welsh *meddyglyn,* 'medicinal drink.' *LLL 5.2.233. MWW 5.5.157* (pl.).

Mexico, *MV 1.3.20, 3.2.266,* country in north America. Great native civilizations, such as the Mayan and the Aztec, had developed in the area before the Spanish arrived. The conquest of Mexico was a recent event in Sh.'s lifetime. Hernando Cortez arrived in 1519 and by 1521 had overturned the Aztec Empire at its capital Tenochtitlan, which became Mexico City. Mexico became the Viceroyalty of New Spain in 1535. As early as 1551, a university was established in the city. A Franciscan mission arrived in 1524 and the Jesuits in 1572. The Inquisition arrived in 1571. Renowned for its mineral riches, the country was plundered, particularly for its gold, and was the target of raiding by English privateers, including John Hawkins, who seized an island near Vera Cruz in 1568; Francis Drake (1572, 1578); and Thomas Cavendish, who raided the west coast in 1587 while circumnavigating the globe. His return to Plymouth in September 1588 with extraordinary wealth, particularly from the seizure off the coast of Mexico of the Spanish treasure ship the 'Great St. Anne' was a sensation. The fact that Cavendish was in financial difficulty within three years might have contributed to the portrayal of Bassanio's propensity for losing his wealth and Antonio's sudden bankruptcy.

Michael, Order of St., *1H6 4.7.69,* fraternity of knights established by Louis XI of France. This might be the order to which Sh. believed that John Talbot belonged. If so, he was incorrect. Talbot died in 1453, and the order was not established until 1469.

Michael, St., *1H6 4.7.69,* heaven's highest ranking angel, God's general in the fight against the forces of evil. He is also the protector of souls on their journey to paradise. His military attributes encouraged medieval soldiers to adopt him as their patron. He was thought to give prudence and was associated with the planet Mercury. He was usually depicted as a young warrior, usually fighting a dragon from the account in Revelation 7:7–9.

Michael, Sir, *1H4,* minor character for whom Sh. may have had no historical model. His profession is uncertain. Sh.'s contemporaries used the title 'sir' to address both priests and knights. Michael could have been either, for he brings a message to the archbishop of York during a military engagement.

Michaelmas, 29 September, the feast of St. Michael the Archangel. It marked the beginning of one of the quarters into which the medieval fiscal year was divided. A goose was the customary meal for the day. *1H4 2.5.53. MWW 1.1.188:* Simple has confused the dates and may mean Martlemas, November 11.

Midas, in mythology, son of Gordius and Cybele, king of Phrygia, and founder of Ankara. Silenus, companion of Bacchus (Dionysus), was brought to Midas in an extremely drunken state. Midas entertained him for ten days, then brought him to the god. Bacchus in gratitude gave Midas a wish, which was that anything Midas touched should turn to gold. After initial delight, he discovered he was unable to eat because when he touched his food it was transformed into gold. Bacchus showed mercy, however, and Midas rinsed away the curse in the river Pactolus. In another myth, Apollo gave him ass's ears because he favored Pan over Apollo in a musical competition. Both stories are in Ovid's *Metamorphoses,* 11. Midas was also said to be the discoverer of white and black lead. *MV 3.2.102,* 'hard food for M.'

Milan, Italian city on the plain of Lombardy 300 mi. northwest of Rome. The proximity of Alpine passes gave Milan military and commercial significance, and early in the Middle Ages the community became a powerful, self-governing city-state. In 1277 the Visconti family overthrew Milan's republican government and established a duchy. The Sforza succeeded the Visconti in 1450, and in 1535 the Hapsburg emperor Charles V occupied the city. In Sh.'s day Milan was still in the hands of the emperor's Spanish heirs. *TGV 1.1.61, 71; 2.5.1. 4.1.20:* The setting of the main action of the play is arguably either Milan, Padua, or Verona, illustrating the confusions of the F1 text. Only one line supports Padua and those supporting Verona are much weaker than those for Milan. The intended action of the play moves obviously from Verona to Milan to Verona.

Jn 3.1.64, 5.2.120. Tmp, F1 'Millaine,' the city or the duke of Milan. Milan is said to be the preeminent duchy of Europe by Prospero as he explains his history to Miranda, 'and for the liberal arts/ Without a parallel,' which suggests the reputation of the nearby University of Pavia (founded 1361) in Sh.'s time.

Milan, Duke of, 1) *TGV,* father of Silvia. The duke is often referred to, when he is offstage, as the Emperor. This is either the result of reassembling the play for F1 long after it was staged, or simply the careless confusion of titles one finds in the texts of Sh.'s plays. The setting itself is confusing, for the duke of Milan seems to be holding court in Verona (see Milan). In fact there was no duke of Verona. The references to the Emperor may have derived from John Lyly's *Euphues, the Anatomy of Wit* (1578) and *Euphues and His England* (1580), influential novels which have the Emperor hold court in Naples. *TGV* and many other works of the time owe much to Lyly's novels of Euphues. A likely possibility is that Sh. was thinking of Charles V, Holy Roman Emperor and ruler of Milan after 1535.

2) *Tmp:* Prospero is the rightful duke, but his office has been usurped by his brother Antonio.

Milan's gown, Duchess of, *Ado 3.4.14:* important people influenced fashion then as now, but there is no evidence that this refers to a particular dress known in Sh.'s London.

Mile End, *AWW 4.3.272,* see Mile End Green.

Mile End Green, field east of London where Lord Saye's son-in-law, James Cromer, had a home. It was there that Cade's rebels captured and beheaded Cromer. The green was also a drill field used by London's militia and a site for fairs and other public gatherings.

2H6 4.7.107–108. 2H4 3.2.276.

Milford, *R3 4.4.464,* town on the northern side of Milford Haven, a fjord that extends 10 mi. into Wales just north of Pembroke.

Milford Haven, *Cym,* a fjord and harbor in the southwest of Pembrokeshire, Wales, known in Welsh as Aberdaugleddau. On the north shore is a town of the same name. The harbor has served as the launching point for attacking and returning from Ireland, including Henry II's in 1172, and Richard II's return in 1399 to surrender to Bolingbroke. During his reign as Henry IV, a French fleet landed there to assist the rebellion of Glyndŵr. The Earl of Richmond, Henry Tudor, also landed there from France in 1485 to depose Richard III. In *Cym* 'Milford' is used interchangeably with 'Milford Haven,' sometimes for the harbor, sometimes the town. Posthumus lands there after his exile in Rome and intends to have Innogen murdered by Pisanio there. Lucius debarks for Rome from there and his invasion of Britain assembles there.

Miller, Ed, *MWW 1.1.144,* F1 'Yead Miller' (possibly meaning 'Yed' or 'Ned' also), person mentioned by Slender, possibly a contemporary of Sh.'s known to his audience.

Milo, *Tro 2.3.242,* 'Bull-bearing Milo,' M. of Crotona, famous Greek athlete of the 6th c. BC. At Olympia, he carried a four-year-old bull through the stadium, knocked it dead with one punch, then ate the whole thing. Ovid's *Metamorphoses* (15.229–231) has a meditation on aging that mentions him. Crotona, a Greek colony in the south of Italy, produced many celebrated athletes.

Minerva (Gr. Athena), virgin goddess of wisdom, war, handicrafts, horticulture, and agriculture. Jupiter impregnated Metis, then swallowed her. Minerva was born, fully armed, out of Jupiter's head. Usually depicted with helmet and spear, she also carried the Ægis, a shield adorned with the head of Medusa, the sight of which turned the viewer into stone. The owl was sacred to her, as well as the olive tree (which she created), the serpent, cock, and crow. As her Greek name implies, she was the protectress of the city of Athens. 'Minerva' is related to the L., Gr., and Sanskrit words for 'mind.' She has also been associated with the dawn as a metaphor for the coming of knowledge. She appears in numerous myths.

Shr 1.1.84. Cym 5.6.165, 'straight-pitched M.,' F1: 'straight-pight,' erect, or well-postured M.

Minola, Baptista, *Shr,* father of Katherine the shrew and Bianca. A rich widower, he tries to do his best by his daughters by marrying them to suitable men, but faced with Katherine's intemperate personality, he is forced to command that his younger daughter Bianca shall not be allowed to wed until her older sister is taken care of. Modern readers are often appalled by Baptista's mercenary negotiation of the wedding contract with Petruccio, but in a society in which an impoverished woman might face suffering, prostitution, and death by starvation, it was a good father's obligation to make certain that his daughters would be well cared for after his death. Love seems less important in potentially desperate circumstances. Although astonished by Petruccio's offer, he quickly accepts it—and not just to grasp at the first convenient straw. Petruccio makes handsome promises to provide for Katherine. His handling of Bianca's wooers seems even more calculating, but this, too, would guarantee the best financial arrangements—if not necessarily the best personal relationship. One may note that love triumphs between Lucentio and Bianca, and the ending is happy, only after Vincentio lubricates the relationship with his money. The taming of Katherine implies perhaps a more important deficiency of Baptista as a father. He has no spirit to match Kate's and if he had assumed his proper role as the teacher of his children, possibly she would be no shrew and Bianca would be less spoiled. Kate has little respect for her father, it seems, nor does Bianca—despite the way in which Baptista seems to favor her. Her eloping with Lucentio would have been seen as a blatantly disrespectful act in Sh.'s day. In a sense, Baptista is the ineffectual head of a dysfunctional family, responsible for his own vexations.

Minola, Bianca, *Shr,* daughter of Baptista Minola and younger sister of Katherine. Forbidden to marry until her elder sister has a husband, Bianca is seen at first as the opposite of her rough-and-tumble sister: sweet, innocent, and kind. Yet, as the play progresses, Sh. subtly introduces other aspects of her character, indicating that the purity which other characters have seen in her is an illusion. She torments her sister as she apparently has for years. Her father seems to side with her in conflicts with Kate and pamper her in ways he would never attempt with his older daughter. The sibling rivalry, we come to see, is ferocious and not all the nastiness comes from Kate. Later, too, she manipulates her suitors and has little concern for their feelings.

Despite our modern rapturizing of love, at the time her elopement would have been regarded as a severe insult to her father and an immoral act, redeemed only by Vincentio's wealth. In the final scene it becomes apparent that the spoiled brat will likely be a poor wife for Lucentio who was blinded by her superficial attractiveness. *Bianca* is Italian for 'white,' an ironic comment on her character. She is 'darker' than she appears. It can also be inferred that it implies 'fairness' and that the play is one of the typical Sh. pairings of a boy actor playing a light-complexioned woman with a darker one, though this is not fully developed (see Helena, Hermia, Celia, etc.). One of the final lines (*5.2.191*) plays on her name and the white bullseye of targets of the day.

Minola, Katherine, *Shr,* 'Katherina,' 'Kate,' the shrew tamed by Petruccio, daughter of Baptista Minola and sister of Bianca. Katherine has reacted to what appears to be an unhappy home life by rejecting society as a defense against its rejecting her. She is filled with anger. Her father dotes on Bianca, but is unable to gain Kate's respect. Although he intends to do well by her, she seems to think he is merely disposing of her. Bianca, the 'princess' of the household, torments her about her age and spinster status. Petruccio, however, sees beyond the superficial excesses of her character and in the manner of an idealized lover sees to her true self, which wants to be loved and included in society. He breaks down her defensive shell rather roughly, but her hide has gotten pretty thick over the years. Modern readers are often appalled by Katherine's final speech, in which Petruccio seems to be exploiting the broken spirit of his wife in order to strut himself as a big man.

Yet, even given the Renaissance conception that order and happiness could be maintained only in an acceptance of hierarchy, Katherine and Petruccio share an equality of temperament, respect, consideration, and spirit that is the ideal of marriage. Petruccio has not just shown that she is good enough to be a wife—something no one else was willing to allow—but that her strength and appearance can be valued. They have become so attuned to one another in the process of the taming that the last scene can be seen as almost conspiratorial in which he and she play a game on the foolish people around them. She is far from a humiliated and defeated creature, nor is she, as some have argued, merely playing a role in order to make Petruccio think that he has conquered her. Neither situation is worthy of Sh.'s ironic mind. Though the frame story of

Christopher Sly implies that the whole comedy is a fairy tale, both of them are deeper than the characters are usually played. Katherine is recognizable in her wit as the forerunner of heroines like Beatrice and Rosalind, sharp-tongued and intelligent. In contrast to Bianca, she also has the features of the dark woman opposed to the fair woman, a pairing Sh. used many times.

Minos, legendary king of Crete. Minos imprisoned the architect Dædalus for Dædalus' involvement in an escapade that resulted in Minos' wife (Pasiphæ) giving birth to a monster (the Minotaur). Dædalus fashioned wings of wax and feathers so that he and his son, Icarus, could escape the island of Crete. Icarus' wings disintegrated when he flew too close to the sun, and the boy plunged to his death in the sea. *3H6 5.6.22:* when Richard of Gloucester comes to kill Henry VI, Sh. has Henry compare himself to Dædalus, his murdered son to Icarus, and Richard's father, who began the war that led to these tragedies, to Minos.

Minotaur, *1H6 5.5.145,* mythical beast that combined the characteristics of a bull and a human male. Its title means 'bull of Minos' from Gr. *tauros* 'bull.' When Minos, king of Crete, refused to sacrifice an unusually handsome bull to Poseidon, Poseidon punished him by causing his queen, Pasiphaë, to conceive a passion for the animal. She had intercourse with the bull and gave birth to Asterion, the Minotaur. Minos had the labyrinth constructed to imprison the monster, and he fed it young men and women whom he extorted as tribute from the city of Athens. The Minotaur was tracked in its lair and killed by Theseus, a prince of Athens. The story is in Ovid, *Metamorphoses,* 8.132–169.

Miranda, *Tmp,* daughter of Prospero. Her name follows the pattern of girls in the late romances (Marina, Perdita) whose names' meanings represent their situations in the plays. M. comes from the L. gerundive *mirandus,* 'admirable,' 'a girl to be wondered at.' An Earl of Miranda was at the court of Spain in 1607. There is a Lord Galcot of Mirandala in Dent's translation of the *History of Philip de Comines* (1526), which has parallels to other characters' names (Prospero, Alonzo, Ferdinand). The lord's name might have been shortened into Miranda.

Misanthropos, *Tim 4.3.53,* what Timon calls himself after rejecting humankind. His adoption of the name may directly reflect a passage in one of the sources of the play, Lucian of Samosata's *Dialogue of Timon* (2nd c. AD). The word comes from Gr. *miseo* 'hate' and *anthropos* 'man.'

Misena, Mount, *Ant 2.2.167,* Misenum, promontory on the coast of Italy south of the ancient Campanian city of Cumæ. Octavius Augustus made it the principle naval base on Italy's western coast.

Mistress Tail-Porter, *WT 4.4.267,* 'Tale-Porter' (F1), mocking name for a gossip, or 'story carrier.' Since mid-wives have just been mentioned there may well be a pun intended on the homonym, or a risque implication.

Mithridates, *Ant 3.6.73,* king of Comagene (Commagene) and one of the men who Plutarch ('Antony' 61.2) says sided with Mark Antony against Octavius. M., 'Dedicated-to-the-god-of-the-sun,' was a fairly common name in eastern royal families. The line that ruled Comagene probably descended from the Seleucid dynasty that was established in Syria by a general who had served Alexander the Great.

Mitigation, Madam, *MM 1.2.43,* Lucio's mocking name for Mistress Overdone. She 'mitigates' a man's sexual desire.

M.O.A.I., *TN 2.5.106, 109, 118:* anagrams and other word games were particularly popular during Sh.'s lifetime. This one is probably exactly what it seems, a riddle on the name Malvolio, or it is possibly something the audience would recognize (like 'My Own Adored Idol') now lost to us. *Mare, orbis, ær, ignis,* the four elements (water, earth, air, and fire) and the name Montaigne have also been suggested as possibilities, but none of these seems persuasive. Malvolio's vanity, of course, leads him to interpret it as he does, but that hardly makes him more foolish than those anagram hawks who think they find 'I am Edward De Vere! No kidding!' in the initial letters of the sonnets.

Mockwater, Monsieur, *MWW 2.3.52–54,* the Host's nickname for Caius. He tells him it means 'valiant,' but the joke is that it must not. Exactly what is meant is unclear. 'Make-water' might refer to urinating out of fear. 'Muck water' is also possible. The most likely alternative is that it continues the joke on urinals at *2.3.31* and is based upon the physician's study of urine as an indicator of health.

Modena, *Ant 1.4.57,* Mutina, town in northern Italy (Cisalpine Gaul) that Mark Antony tried to take from Brutus, one of Julius Cæsar's assassins. Antony was attacked there by a Senatorial army led by the consuls Hirtius and Pansa, accompanied by Cæsar's adopted son, Octavius. Although Antony killed both consuls, he was compelled to retreat into Gaul.

Modo, *Lr 3.4.135 (Q 11.132), Q 15.58,* name of a demon, prince of murder, according to Edgar. Sh. borrowed it from Samuel Harsnett. See Flibbertigibbet for details. Harsnett describes M. as the grand Commander of the captains of the seven deadly sins.

Mohammed (571–632), Arab prophet whose sermons are collected in the *Koran,* the sacred book of the Islamic religion. He believed that Jews and Christians had distorted the messages of the prophets whom God had sent them and that the transcendent deity, Allah, had, therefore, commissioned him to transmit the final and complete revelation of his will to a new 'Chosen People,' the Arabs. Like most founders of major religions, his life is shrouded in legends. He was born at Mecca and began preaching at age 40. He didn't have much success, and when a plot was hatched to murder him, he fled to Medina. The Islamic world dates its beginning from this flight, called the Hegira. In Medina he converted the populace and established a theocracy that conquered the rest of the peninsula by 630. His followers later expanded across Africa, deep into Asia, and into Europe. His name derives from the Arabic 'praiseworthy.'

1H6 1.3.119: Sh.'s reference to a dove as the medium through which Mohammed received messages from God was a medieval slander. Hostile Christians claimed that Mohammed deceived his simpleminded followers with a cheap conjurer's trick. He trained an ordinary dove to light on his shoulder and feed on grain concealed in his ear. The people who witnessed this performance were told that the dove was the Holy Spirit delivering messages from God to the Prophet.

Monarcho, *LLL 4.1.98,* self-given title of an insane Italian who lived in London, hung about the court, and asserted he was emperor of the world.

Monday, *1H4 1.2.34,* second day of the week, named for the moon, which was considered the second of the great celestial bodies.

Monmouth, 1) county seat of Monmouthshire on the Wye river 130 mi. west of London. John of Gaunt acquired its castle, and his grandson, Henry V, was born there. Monmouth's location within the orbit of Welsh culture and influence permitted Henry, when convenient, to call himself a Welshman. *1H6 3.1.202, H5 4.7.11, 24, 26, 27, 51, 98,* 103

2) *2H4 2.3.45,* see Henry V.

Monmouth, Harry, *1H4 5.2.49, 5.4.58, 2H4 intro.28, 1.1.19, 1.1.109, 1.3.83,* see Henry V.

Monmouth, Henry, *1H6 2.5.23, 3.1.202,* see Henry V.

Monsieur the Nice, *LLL 5.1.325,* Biron's mocking name for Boyet. The meaning is 'Mr.

Fastidious,' or 'Mr. Ceremonious,' a scrupulous follower of formality.

Monster, Monsieur, *Tmp 3.2.18,* a nickname for Caliban.

Montague, *Rom,* one of the two feuding families, Romeo's surname. In Arthur Brooke's *Tragicall Historye of Romeus and Juliet* (1562), Sh.'s source, it is 'Montagew(e)' or 'Montague,' and the name goes far back into the sources. In Luigi da Porto's *Istoria novellamente ritrovata di due Nobili Amanti* (c. 1530), the family is called 'Montecchi.' The Montecchi of Verona are mentioned in Dante's *Purgatorio* 6.107, for causing disorder, along with the Capelletti, a family of Cremona. George Gascoigne wrote a masque (published 1575) for the double marriage of the son and daughter of the Viscount Montacute [sic] with the son and daughter of Sir William Dormer. In that masque a fictional connection is made between the Mountacutes and the 'noble House of the Mountacutes in Italie.' In this, however, a descendant of the Italian branch says that his family always sported their symbol in his cap in order to be recognized by the 'Capels' as they pass. Geoffrey Bullough also points out that Viscount Montague was high in court favor in 1591, just a few years before the usual date assigned for *Rom,* and possibly provided some impetus for its creation.

2) 'Old M.,' Romeo's father. He enters in *1.1* with sword drawn but is held back from attacking Capulet by his wife. After the Prince stops the brawl, he describes Romeo's melancholy mood. He also enters after the death of Tybalt and is usually attributed *3.1.182–84,* arguing for his son's life, as F1 inexplicably gives the lines to Capulet. He says nothing else in the scene. In the final act, he reveals that his wife has died of grief and is then shown Romeo's body. He then offers to raise a statue of pure gold in honor of Juliet. Although his character is not developed, the consequences of his irrational dispute are particularly heavy, even Lear-like.

Montague, Lord, *H8 1.1.217,* Henry Pole (1492–1538), eldest son of Margaret, countess of Salisbury, daughter of Edward IV's brother, the duke of Clarence. His connection with the royal blood of the Yorkist house made Henry VIII nervous. The Tudors' hereditary claim to the throne was tenuous, and Montague could have mounted a challenge to their authority. When Henry charged the duke of Buckingham with treason, he took the precaution of arresting Montague, the husband of Buckingham's granddaughter, Joan Abergavenny. He was cleared of suspicion of complicity, but he was less fortunate later in life. He and his family were ardent Catholics who protested Henry VIII's decision to sever England's ties with the papacy and to dissolve its monasteries. His brother Reginald, a cardinal, lived in exile on the continent and did everything that he could to stir up trouble for Henry. In August 1538 Henry interrogated a priest who had been Reginald's chaplain. Information the priest provided led to the arrest of Montague's brother Geoffrey, and Geoffrey confessed to conversations that implicated all the members of the Pole family in treason. Geoffrey was pardoned, but his brother Montague was beheaded. Reginald Pole remained safely abroad until Henry's daughter, Mary, restored England's allegiance to the papacy. Mary appointed him archbishop of Canterbury, and he encouraged her infamous persecution of Protestants.

Montague, Marquis of, *3H6,* Montacute, John Neville (d. 1471), younger brother of Richard Neville, the earl of Warwick. Edward IV owed his throne to the support the Nevilles had given him at the time of his father's death, and the Nevilles expected Edward to be their puppet. When Edward wriggled out from beneath the Neville thumb, Montague and Warwick were infuriated. He joined Warwick in a plot to restore the family's influence by overthrowing Edward and returning Henry VI to the throne. The brothers, who had spent their lives in the service of the house of York, died fighting for the Lancastrian cause at the battle of Barnet.

Montague, Romeo, *Rom,* star-crossed lover and husband of Juliet. He is shown as a frivolous young man, quick to fall in love, but is described admirably by his enemy Capulet, who refuses to let Tybalt forcibly remove Romeo from the feast. To what extent Sh. is implying that Romeo and Juliet are the victims of a mad passion is debatable. This would be very Classical in its theme and was definitely Arthur Brooke's intended moral in his *Tragicall Historye of Romeus and Juliet* (1562), Sh.'s source. The name 'Romeo' goes far back into the earlier sources. Brooke uses the Latinized 'Romeus,' mostly, but 'Romeo' at least once. Bandello's *Le Novelle del Bandello* (1554), Brooke's source, and the earlier Luigi da Porto's *Istoria novellamente ritrovata di due Nobili Amanti* (c. 1530) both use 'Romeo'. 'Romeo' means 'pilgrim,' more particularly ('a pilgrim to Rome') whence the punning in *1.5.94–101.* Others have argued that it is a contraction of Romualdo, a Lombard name that may have been a corruption of Romulus, but this is grasping at straws. The punning makes it obvious that Sh. was aware of the meaning, though he may merely have taken the name from his source.

Montague, Thomas, (1388–1428), Montacute, earl of Salisbury, among the most talented of the generals who assisted Henry V and the duke of Bedford in the later part of the Hundred Years' War. Henry IV had executed Salisbury's father for his support of Richard II, the king whom Henry deposed. It was some time before the new administration convinced itself of young Thomas' loyalty and confirmed him in his family's lands and titles, but Salisbury eventually became a trusted servant of the house of Lancaster. Salisbury fought for Henry V at Agincourt and Harfleur and enjoyed a succession of increasingly important commands. After Henry V's death, Salisbury became Bedford's chief assistant, and he was responsible for some of the most important campaigns England waged during the period of Henry VI's minority. Although he erred in advocating the controversial seige of Orléans where the fortunes of war turned against the English, he did not live to see the outcome of that venture. On the fourth day of the siege he was mortally wounded by cannon fire, and he died on 3 November 1428. His grandson, Warwick 'the Kingmaker,' played a major role in the dramatic events that ended Henry VI's reign.

1H6. H5.

Montague's Wife, *Rom,* often called Lady Montague by modern editors, though there is no particular indication that the family is a noble one. She prevents her husband from attacking Capulet, but in the last act is said to have died of grief at Romeo's exile.

Montano, *Oth,* governor of Cyprus replaced by Othello. He does not argue with his replacement, as perhaps a military leader is necessary in the circumstance of a threatened invasion. Later he is wounded in the drunken brawl that degrades Cassio. He is also present at play's end, catching Iago as he attempts to flee. The name may be related to the romance languages for 'mountain' as part of a nobleman's name, such as Mazzeo della Montagna in Boccaccio's *Decameron* 4.10.

Montanto, Signor, F1 'Mountanto,' *Ado 1.1.29,* Beatrice's mocking name for Benedick. She hides her interest in the young man by joking about his sharp tongue. The ribald implication is also obvious. In fencing a 'montant' was an upright blow or thrust. The addition of the 'o' turns it into mock Spanish or Italian. Montanto first appears in Ben Jonson's *Every Man in His Humour* (1598), while Sh. also uses 'montant' in *MWW 2.3.25.*

Montferrat, Marquis of, *MV 1.2.111,* man whom Bassanio once accompanied on a visit to Portia's father. Montferrat is a territory south of the Po and east of Torino. In the 12th c., the family that held it was one of the most powerful in northern Italy. Several of the nobles of Montferrat were deeply involved in the Second and Third Crusades, one marrying Sibylla, heiress to the kingdom of Jerusalem. Boniface of Montferrat was one of the leaders of the Fourth Crusade which attacked Constantinople.

Montgomery, John, *3H6,* (d. 1495), one of the men who induced Edward IV to claim the royal title—on the theory that more soldiers could be recruited to fight for a king than a duke. *3H6 4.7.49.* Holinshed (3.680) calls him Thomas Montgomery.

Montjoy, *H5,* French herald who negotiates with Henry before the battle at Agincourt and who brings him news of the surrender of France's army. His name recalls a battle cry used by the French.

Moonshine, *MND 3.1.56, 5.1.135, 234–300,* allegorical character presented by Robin Starveling. He carries a lantern, a thorn bush, and leads a dog. The man in the moon was equated with the man who violates the Sabbath in Numbers 15:32–36 by picking up firewood and is stoned to death. The thorn bush represents the sticks. Another tradition makes Cain the man in the moon. In this version the thorns represent the fall of man and the dog with him a devil. As with Wall, Sh. parodies the use of allegorical characters.

Moor, 1) Muslim of north Africa. Although often assumed to be a black race, in fact the Moors were of Berber and Arab descent, mixed with considerable Negroid and Iberian blood. The word probably derives from *Mauri,* L. by way of Gr. for 'dark men.' Their native lands constituted parts of Morocco, Algeria, and Mauritania. One theory is that the name originally derives from Berber *Amazigh,* 'free men,' referring to their nomadic existence, and in Greek times came to mean anyone with dark skin. By the Middle Ages the term came to be applied to any Muslim (similarly, all Europeans were called Franks in the Mohammedan world). Since Moors were thought of as being dark-skinned, the word was also used generally to apply to blacks, although light-skinned Moors were well known. The word 'blackamoor' was also common, which implies a distinction from lighter-skinned Moors.

In any case, attitudes to race were much different then because there had been so little direct contact between the population of England and the 'exotic' races. There was also no long history of the disgusting racist theories which still burden the modern world. There were celebrity Moors in London, but the overall awareness would be of a faraway people, who, to a greater or lesser degree, were allied with the enemies of Christendom. After their early history (see Mauritania), the Moors were overrun by the Arabs in the 7th c., who replaced their religion and language and formed a dynamic culture. In the 8th c. the Moors defeated the Visigoths and conquered Spain. Their attempt to move north into France was turned back by Charles Martel in 732, though they conquered Sicily in 827. Gradually the Christian reconquest drove them back until the only Moorish stronghold in Spain, Granada, fell in 1492. The Iberian Moors, who had considerably intermarried, returned to Africa where they were known as Andalusians, and scattered over the enormous range of the Moors, from the Mediterranean to the Senegal river, and from the Atlantic to Timbuktu.

MV 2.1 s.d., Morocco's description as a 'tawnie Moore' is often cited to demonstrate that Othello, or Moors in general, were not thought of as being black. This may be wishful thinking. *TNK 3.5.120,* Moors were common in morris dances.

2) *Tit,* see Aaron.

3) *MV 3.5.37, 38,* woman, otherwise unmentioned in the play who has been impregnated by Lancelot. The word 'Negro' is also used to refer to her.

4) *Oth,* Othello. In Sh.'s source for the plot, Giraldi Cinthio's *Hecatommithi* (1566), 3.7, Othello is unnamed and always called 'the Moor.' It is not clear how dark Sh. intends Othello to be and the role has been played in a range from an Arab to a member of the Negro race. Despite our modern obsessions, race is not the primary issue of the play and is relevant

only as a matter of physical description and Othello's status as an outsider.

Moor-ditch, *1H4 1.2.78,* part of a moat that spanned medieval London's northern wall between Moorgate and Bishopsgate. Sh. may have thought of it as a 'melancholy' place because of the quality of its water or because it was close to Bedlam hospital where the insane were housed.

Moorfields, *H8 5.3.31,* swampy field north of medieval London's wall between Cripplegate and Bishopsgate. It was a training ground for London's citizen soldiers.

Moorish, pertaining to the Moors. *Err 4.3.27* 'Moorish pike,' F1 'Moris Pike,' a pike whose design was thought to be Moorish in origin.

Moorship, his, *Oth 1.1.32,* Iago's insulting term for Othello.

Mopsa, *WT,* shepherdess. Hers is the only name Sh. retains from his main source (Robert Greene's *Pandosto, or the Triumph of Time,* 1588; rptd. 1607 as *Dorastus and Fawnia*); however, in the original, Mopsa is a shrew. There is also a Mopsa in Sir Philip Sidney's *Arcadia.*

Moray, Murray, one of the seven original Scottish earldoms. It encompassed the modern counties of Inverness and Ross. See Moray, Earl of, *1H4.*

Moray, Earl of, *1H4 1.1.73,* Murray, Thomas Dunbar, fourth earl, one of the Scottish nobles captured by the Percies at the battle of Holmedon Hill in 1402.

Mordake, *1H4 1.1.71, 2.5.360, 4.4.23,* Murdac Stewart (d. 1425), duke of Albany and earl of Fife and Menteith. He was the son of Robert Stewart, duke of Albany, not, as Sh. says, the son of Archibald, earl of Douglas. Sh.'s confusion rose from a punctuation error in the text from which he drew his historical information. Holinshed's *Chronicles* (3.520) read: 'Mordacke earle of Fife, son to the governor Archembald earle Dowglas.' There should have been a comma following 'governor' to indicate that 'governor' was not intended as a title for Archibald Douglas. Mordake's father Robert Stewart was at the time of Mordake's capture at Holmedon Hill regent (i.e., 'governor') for Scotland. Sh. replicates another of Holinshed's errors—listing his titles, Fife and Menteith, as if they referred to two men, not one.

More, Thomas, (1478–1535), successor to Cardinal Wolsey as Lord Chancellor in Henry VIII's government. He was one of Europe's leading humanists and the most famous English scholar of his generation. Although he was an advocate of social and educational reform, he had no sympathy with the Protestant Reformation sparked by his contemporary, Martin Luther. He was a religious conservative who enjoyed the opportunities made possible by the increasing secularization of his age. During the medieval era a man of his interests and ambitions would have entered the church. More, however, was a married layman who won appointment to offices traditionally reserved for clerics. He began his career on the staff of John Morton, archbishop of Canterbury. From there he, like many colleagues in holy orders, moved into government service. Increasing tensions between church and state and Cardinal Wolsey's failure to deliver on his promise to win papal approval for the annulment of Henry VIII's marriage with Katherine of Aragon opened a unique door for More. In 1529 Henry dismissed Wolsey as Lord Chancellor and gave the job to More—the first layman in English history to be so honored. His appointment may have been part of Henry's plan to bend the church to his will.

Henry was no religious reformer, but he was prepared to do whatever was necessary to force the church to permit him a marriage that would produce an indisputable heir to his throne. He believed that the pope's reluctance to grant him an annulment was motivated by self-interest, not by theological scruples, and he was eager not to prejudice his case by creating the impression that he differed with the pope's religion. In these circumstances, More was an ideal candidate for the chancellor's office. He was not part of the ecclesiastical establishment, but he was internationally respected as an orthodox scholar. He also supported Henry's policy of demonstrating England's hostility to heresy by tracking down and executing Protestants. By the time More took office, however, time was running out for diplomacy. Henry was impatient with the papacy, and the discovery of Anne Boleyn's pregnancy in January 1533 convinced him to take the fateful step of breaking England's ties with Rome. More was profoundly shaken by the king's decision and quickly concluded that he could not reconcile his conscience with the policies of the government he served. Since he had no wish for martyrdom, he tried to avoid a confrontation by resigning his office and dropping out of public life. The strategy was naive, for he was a prominent person. His resignation clearly, if silently, rebuked his king. In 1534 he was called before the royal council and forced to take a stand. When he refused to affirm the king's right to be head of the English church, he was convicted of treason. He and John Fisher, bishop of Rochester, were the most prominent victims of England's reformation.

STM: a portion of a manuscript in the British library, 'The Booke of Sir Thomas Moore,' which contains a heavily revised play of the life of More, is believed to be by Sh. The scene usually attributed to him consists of More, as Sheriff of London (actually he was undersheriff, but already knighted and on the Privy Council), persuading an angry crowd to submit to the king's mercy. These events were part of the 'Evil May Day' disorders of 1517, in which there was a riot against foreign laborers. Several were attacked. Forty rioters were hanged on May 4 despite a plea for mercy from London officials including More. Some believe *STM* to be the only extant scene in Sh.'s handwriting. Also believed to be by Sh. is a soliloquy which More gives after being appointed Lord Chancellor. The other authors believed to have worked on the manuscript are Anthony Munday, Henry Chettle, Thomas Dekker, and possibly Thomas Heywood. The subject of More may have been too politically explosive to be allowed on stage.

H8 3.2.394.

Morgan, 1) *AWW 4.3.111,* soldier in service to Florence with a common Welsh name of unknown derivation. In Old Welsh it was *Morcant.*

2) *Cym,* F1 'Mergen,' name assumed by Belarius in exile. There is a mention of a Morgan three times in Harrison's *Description of Britaine* (1587), very near a Cloten and an Arviragus, suggesting that Sh. may have been mining this source for names, but Morgan is common enough that there is no need for it to have a specific source.

Morisco, *2H6 3.1.365,* a Moor, a Muslim of north African or Spanish origin. Specifically, they were the Muslims who lived under Christian domination, as, for example, in Seville after 1248 or in Grenada after 1492. They were savagely deported from Spain by the end of the 1500s. The term is also used for a folk dancer of a type introduced to England from Spain in the 14th c. Portions of Spain were occupied by Muslims until the end of the 15th c., and Spanish culture was strongly influenced by the customs of Muslim Africa. The 'Morris' dance of the Morisco featured elaborate costumes, bells, and wild gyrations. See Morris.

Morocco, *MV,* a country in northwest Africa across the Straits of Gibraltar from Spain—*Maghreb-al-Aksa,* the 'country farthest west.' The ancient explorer Hanno mentions Carthaginian colonies there, and the original inhabitants the Berbers, supplied troops to the Romans in the 1st c. BC before falling under Roman rule in 1st c. AD as part of the province of Mauretania. After invasions by the Vandals and the Goths, the Arabs moved in around 682. The Berbers, though adopting Islam, revolted against their masters in 739 and an independent kingdom was created in 788. Conflict continued, however, until the country was unified under the Almoravids, whose empire stretched from Spain to Egypt to Senegal. In the 15th c. Portugal began to seize areas along the coast. The Moroccans engaged in a *jihad* against the European incursions with limited success until the battle of Alcazaquivir in 1578, at which three kings perished. Ahmed IV, the Golden, then revived relations with Queen Elizabeth and other kings, which may have had something to do with the inclusion of the Prince in *MV.* He also succeeded in expanding his territory and controlling the gold and tobacco of Timbuktu. Ahmed's successor, Zidan, even employed English troops, and continued the trend towards fairly open relations with Europe.

Morocco, Prince of, *MV 2.1, 2.7,* one of Portia's suitors. His comments about his own heroism and the outcome of his choice bear all the marks of the braggart, he nonetheless has many admirable qualities (if he did but half of what he claims). Portia's remarks to Nerissa about his skin seem, in the least, to be unbecoming—though in the context of the time they were more likely to have been taken as comment upon a non-English oddity than condemnation of a race. He is described upon his entry as 'a tawny Moor,' not a 'blackamoor,' and it is interesting that reference to Islamic faith is never made, though when he calls for help he calls on 'Some god,' *2.7.13.* His comments upon the redness of his blood echo Shylock's speech about the humanity of the Jew, and his point that chance may make the weaker man win a contest over a stronger (*2.1.31–38*) is a good one, though it may imply that he does not understand the fundamental basis of the choice of caskets: absolute trust in the divine will. His vanity is, interestingly enough, shared by Sh.'s other Moors, Aaron and Othello, and may be a part of Sh.'s conception of the Moors. See also 'Moor.'

Morris, dance brought to England from Spain during the reign of Edward III. Its name derives from its being originally a military dance of the Moors or Moriscos. It was popular during May Day celebrations and featured wild gyrations and elaborate costumes often adorned with bells. By the time of Henry VIII, it was a regular feature of village celebrations. Outlawed by the Puritans, it was revived at the Restoration but gradually declined until almost extinct by the 20th c. Stock characters were also part of the morris, including Robin Hood, Little John, Friar Tuck, Bavian or Babion ('baboon') the Fool, a hobby-horse, Tom Piper, a taborer, dragon, and others—including various ranks of society and outlandishly dressed Moors. At its height, it might be compared to the mummers' parades in Philadelphia, though the earliest versions seem to have only five men and a boy dressed as a lusty Maid Marian. As Queen of the May, Marian was one of the most important stock characters and she became a clown's role as 'Marykin' or 'Malkin the Clown.'

H5 2.4.25. AWW 2.2.23. TNK 2.2.277, 3.5.122, 5.4.51: a morris is arranged in *3.5* in which there are six male dancers (including the taborer) and six female. Likely the taborer was an accompanist and six countrymen are required for the scene. The nine characters mentioned by Gerald the Schoolmaster are the Lord and Lady of the May, The Serving-man and the Chambermaid, the Host and his wife, The Clown, the Fool, and the Babion. There would rather obviously be three more: the She-clown, the She-fool (the Jailer's Daughter replacing Cicely), and the She-Babion. This would then correspond to the antimasque in Francis Beaumont's *Masque of the Grayes Inne and the Inner Temple* (1613). Gerald would also correspond to Beaumont's Pedant.

Mort Dieu, *2H6 1.1.120,* Fr. 'by the death of God,' an oath on the crucifixion.

Mortimer, family of the earls of March and Ulster, descendants of Roger of Mortemer-sur-Eaulne, one of William the Conqueror's Norman vassals. Fr. *mortemer* 'dead sea,' probably referred to a stagnant marsh. The Mortimers acquired great estates in England and Ireland and wielded considerable influence at court. In 1326 a Roger Mortimer seized control of England's government. He joined Edward II's queen, Isabella, in a coup that forced the incompetent and unpopular Edward from the throne. For a brief period Roger and Isabella ruled England in the name of Edward's young son, Edward III. When Edward III staged a coup of his own, Isabella was imprisoned for life, Roger was beheaded, and the Mortimers suffered a period of disgrace. Roger's grandson (another Roger) restored the family's political fortune. He fought at Crécy, was invited to be a founding member of the Order of the Garter, and won the hand of Edward III's granddaughter for his son Edmund. The marriage of Edmund Mortimer with Philippa, heir to Edward III's second surviving son, produced Mortimers who were in line to inherit the throne. Richard II, who was childless, declared Edmund's son, Roger, heir presumptive. When Richard abdicated, there were many in England who considered the Mortimers to have a better claim to the crown than Henry IV, a descendant of Edward III's fourth son. *2H6 4.2.40. 1H6 2.5.91* (pl.)

Mortimer, Anne, *2H6 2.2.38,* (b. 1388), daughter of Roger, fourth earl of March and heir presumptive to Richard II. Anne was Richard of York's mother. Since none of her siblings had heirs, she passed the Mortimer claim to the throne to her son.

Mortimer, Dame, *1H4 2.5.110,* see Percy, Lady.

Mortimer, Edmund, 1) (1391–1425), fifth earl of March, and potential claimant to the throne of England. The Mortimers were descendants of Ralph of Mortemer-sur-Eauline, a Norman soldier in William the Conqueror's train. They were among England's strongest and wealthiest barons, for the protection of their fiefs on the Welsh border justified their maintenance of a large military establishment. Edmund's grandfather, Edmund (1351–1381), had married the heiress to the estate of Edward III's second son, Lionel, and King Richard II, who was childless, designated their son, Roger (1374–1398), heir to his throne. Since the Mortimers were scions of a branch of the royal family senior to the house of Lancaster, Roger's son, Edmund, was believed by many to have a stronger claim to the throne than the Lancastrian king, Henry IV, who forced Richard to abdicate in his favor. Although an attempt was made at the start of Henry V's reign to involve Edmund in a coup to overthrow the Lancastrians, he apparently had no desire to be king. He served Henry loyally in the French wars. When he died childless on 18 January 1425, his estate and claim to the throne passed to his sister's son, Richard, earl of Cambridge and (after 1426) duke of York. Richard started the War of the Roses that led to Henry VI's deposition and the establishment of Richard's son, Edward IV, as the first of England's Yorkist kings.

2H6 2.2.36, 39. 1H6.

2) *1H4.* Sh. confuses Edmund Mortimer fifth earl of March (d. 1424) with his uncle, Sir Edmund Mortimer (1376–1409), Hotspur's friend and ally. Sir Edmund was the second son of Edmund Mortimer, third earl of March. His brother Roger inherited their father's earldom, but Roger's early death left Sir Edmund head of the family and guardian of Roger's son, Edmund. Sir Edmund's sister married Hotspur, and Sir Edmund assisted his brother-in-law in efforts to subdue the Welsh rebel Owain Glyndŵr. In 1402 Glyndŵr captured Edmund, and Hotspur applied to Henry IV for help in arranging his ransom. Henry refused to cooperate in procuring Sir Edmund's liberty, for he did not trust the Mortimers. Sir Edmund's nephew, the fifth earl, had a claim to the English throne that had been recognized by Richard II, and Henry believed that Sir Edmund was less Glyndŵr's captive than his colleague in plotting trouble for England. Henry's suspicious behavior may have helped bring about the very thing he feared. Glyndŵr persuaded Sir Edmund to switch sides, and Sir Edmund married the Welsh leader's daughter. This wedding created a link between Glyndŵr and the Percies, and in 1403 Sir Edmund, Glyndŵr, and Hotspur pledged themselves to drive Henry from the throne. Henry nipped the revolt in the bud and

killed Hotspur at the battle of Shrewsbury. In 1405 Hotspur's father, Northumberland, proposed that Mortimer and Glyndŵr join him in a new scheme to depose Henry and partition England. This project, like the first, came to nothing, and Mortimer died four years later defending Harlech castle against Henry. Sh. blended into one both of the plots against Henry that involved Mortimer.

Mortimer, Eleanor, *2H6 2.2.38,* (d. 1418), second daughter of Roger, the fourth earl of March who was heir presumptive to Richard II. Eleanor married Edward Courtenay, the eleventh earl of Devonshire. Her death without issue left the Yorkist descendants of her sister Anne the only heirs to the Mortimer claim to the throne.

Mortimer, Hugh, *3H6 1.2.62,* Edward IV's uncle (d. 1460), brother of John Mortmer. The nature of his relationship to the king is unknown. He may have been Edward's mother's illegitimate brother. He died at the battle of Wakefield. He has no speaking lines, though he enters with his brother.

Mortimer, John, 1) *2H6 3.1.359, 3.1.372, 4.2.119 4.4.27, 4.6.6,* name assumed by Jack Cade to legitimate his rebellion. Many stories circulated about Cade, and scholars have had a hard time separating fact from fiction. Some authorities believe that Cade's rebellion was initiated by a Mortimer whose place Cade took, but Sh. claims that Cade and the duke of York started the rumor that Cade was a descendant of the twin brother of the Roger Mortimer (1374–1398) whom Richard II designated heir to the throne. A romantic tale was circulated to explain the absence of any record of the birth of Roger's twin. The boy was supposedly hidden and raised in ignorance of his ancestry.

2) *3H6 1.2.62,,* Edward IV's uncle, (d. 1460), brother of Hugh Mortimer. The nature of his relationship to the king is unknown. He may have been Edward's mother's illegitimate brother. He died at the battle of Wakefield.

Mortimer, Lady, *1H4,* daughter of Owain Glyndŵr and wife to Sir Edmund Mortimer (whom Sh. confuses with Sir Edmund's nephew Edmund, the earl of March). Sir Edmund fought at the side of his sister's husband, Hotspur (Henry Percy). Hotspur was Henry IV's lieutenant for Wales, and he had been commissioned by the king to subdue the Welsh nationalist leader Owain Glyndŵr. In 1402 Glyndŵr captured Sir Edmund, and Hotspur turned to Henry for help in arranging his brother-in-law's ransom. Henry infuriated the Percies by refusing to do anything for Sir Edmund. Sir Edmund's nephew, another Edmund Mortimer, had what many believed to be a stronger claim to the throne than Henry himself, and Henry distrusted the Mortimers. The Percies' sense of family honor proved to be greater than their allegiance to Henry—a king whom they had helped to the throne. Their determination to right the wrongs which they perceived the ungrateful Henry to have done them caused a dramatic shift in political allegiances. The Percies made peace with Glyndŵr, and Glyndŵr liberated Sir Edmund and gave him his daughter's hand in marriage. The family alliances forged by marriage facilitated cooperation among the Welsh, the Percies and the Mortimers in efforts to overthrow Henry.

Mortimer of Scotland, Lord, *1H4 3.2.164,* George, earl of Dunbar and March, (1388–1420). Sh. erroneously associates him with the Mortimer family. Sh. may have assumed that he was a Mortimer because of his title. The Mortimers were lords of the English march, and the earls of Dunbar were lords of the Scottish march. The borders separating their jurisdictions were as vague as their allegiances to their national governments. Dunbar led armies against England and then defected to England to seek revenge for an offense to his honor. In 1388 the heir to the Scottish throne had been engaged to marry Dunbar's daughter, but the commitment was broken in favor of an alliance with Archibald Douglas' family. Dunbar joined the Percies, and fought on their side at the battle of Holmedon Hill (1402). There he had the pleasure of seeing many of his countrymen killed or captured. Dunbar's primary allegiance was to Henry IV, not the Percies. When the Percies conspired against Henry IV, Dunbar warned the king of their pending rebellion, and in the battle that ensued between Henry and Hotspur at Shrewsbury, he rescued Henry from a charge led by Dunbar's nemesis, Archibald Douglas. He returned to Scotland in 1409 and lived out the rest of his life quietly on his estates.

Mortimer, Roger, (1374–1398), fourth earl of March, son of Edmund Mortimer and Phillipa of Clarence. His maternal grandfather was Edward III's son, Lionel of Clarence. From Lionel he inherited a claim to the throne, and Richard II, who had no children of his own, declared him heir presumptive. The Mortimers did not press their claim when Henry Bolingbroke, the son of Clarence's younger brother John of Gaunt, usurped Richard's crown. But three generations later the Mortimer right was asserted by its heir, Richard of York. Richard's challenge to the legitimacy of Henry VI's government began the War of the Roses.

2H6 2.2.37, 48. 3H6 1.1.106.

Morton, *2H4,* character invented by Sh. 'Morton' conjures up thoughts of the French *mort* 'death,' though it derives from a common place name meaning 'town by a moor.' It is, therefore, an appropriate name for the man whose only function in *2H4* is to bring the earl of Northumberland the news that his son Hotspur has been killed at the battle of Shrewsbury.

Moscows regiment, *AWW 4.1.70,* F1 'Muskos Regiment,' probably Muscovite troops in the service of Parolles' enemies. Contact with the Russians was common in the trading of England but the language must have seemed exotic. Mercenaries were common in Renaissance Italian wars. Possibly a regiment armed with muskets (a handgun named after the sparrow-hawk, It. *moschetto*) is meant, but it would not explain the language problem.

Moses, *TGV 5.3.7,* F1 'Moyses,', one of the outlaws who pursues Proteus.

Most Lamentable Comedy and Most Cruel Death of Pyramus and Thisbe, *MND 1.2.11–12,* the 'rude mechanicals' title for their play to be offered to the court of Athens. Its length is not unusual for the time, nor is its editorializing on the content. The contradiction is exaggerrated when the play is mentioned later. Sh. may again be mocking *Cambyses* by Thomas Preston (1569), whose full title runs *A Lamentable Tragedie Mixed Full of Pleasant Mirth, Containing the Life of Cambises, King of Percia.*

Mote, *LLL,* F1 and Q 'Moth,' Armado's page. A small, witty fellow, he plays Hercules 'in his minority,' in the pageant of the Nine Worthies. Editors vary on whether to use 'Mote' or 'Moth.' There was no difference in pronunciation of the two words in the Elizabethan period (similarly, 'nothing' sounded like 'noting'). Both words suggest small; a dust particle floats as erratically as a moth flutters. Several editors have decided that there are no jokes on his being insect-like, so prefer 'Mote.' Others point out Costard's 'most pathetical nit' (*4.1.147*) and assert Mote's activeness is more appropriate to an insect than a speck. This is a modern problem only, given contemporary spelling and pronunciation, 'Mote' or 'Moth' would have been moot. As with other characters in the play there have been attempts to make the page into a parody of an Elizabethan celebrity, in this case writer Thomas Nashe, and some of the inexplicable jokes of the play may refer to current controversies, such as the Marprelate pamphlet war between Nashe and Gabriel Harvey. These efforts are highly dubious given the stock nature of the comic characters, and the obscurity of the jokes.

Moth, *LLL,* see Mote.

Mother, the, 1) *MM 1.4.85,* mother superior, prioress of the order in which Isabella is a novice.

2) *Lr 2.2.231 (Q 7.225),* see *Histerica passio.*

Mouldy, Ralph, *2H4,* comic name that indicates the unsuitability of its owner for the military service into which Falstaff intends to draft him.

Mount, the, *Ant 2.4.6,* see Misena.

Mountague, *Rom,* variant sp. of Montague, particularly in Q2.

Mountain, *Tmp 4.1.254,* spirit in the shape of a hound. It is not clear what to make of the coincidence of the word also appearing in Jakob Ayrer's *Die Schöne Sidea* (published 1618, but Ayrer died in 1605). Ayrer adapted English plays which were acted in Germany for his own company and the resemblances between *Tmp* and *Die Schöne Sidea* have been listed by many scholars. Either Ayrer's play is a source or both are based on some earlier play, or it is all coincidence. A play called *Celinda and Sedea* played in Germany with English actors in 1604 and 1613, but the connection—if any—is not clear. In Ovid's *Metamorphoses* 3, there is a passage from which Sh. often borrowed in which Actaeon is torn to pieces by his hounds. In it there are two dogs Oribasus (Gr. 'Mountain-ranger') and Oresitrophus (Gr. 'Mountaineer'). Golding's translation gave them the names 'Scalecliffe' and 'Hylbred,' however.

Mousetrap, The, *Ham 3.2.226,* Hamlet's joking name for *The Murder of Gonzago,* set up to trap Claudius. There is a pun on the word 'Trapically' immediately following in Q1.

Mowbray, Thomas, *R2, 2H4 3.2.25, 4.1.109,* (1366–1399), earl of Nottingham, Earl Marshal of England, and duke of Norfolk. He was originally an ally of the 'lords appellant,' the men at Richard II's court who intended to curtail the king's freedom to rule as he pleased. Richard won him to his side in the struggle, and in 1397 he helped Richard engineer the arrests of the appellants' leaders: Gloucester, Arundel, and Warwick. Mowbray was warden of the castle at Calais where Gloucester was imprisoned, and Gloucester either died or was murdered while in his keeping. Richard's behavior, once he was free from the threat of opposition, may have alarmed Mowbray. He confided some private doubts about the king to Henry (IV) Bolingbroke, and Henry passed them on to his father, John of Gaunt. Gaunt, who may have been worried about the consequences of concealing information, reported everything to Richard, and Mowbray found himself under suspicion of treason. Since no one could prove who had said what to whom, the king proposed that Mowbray and Henry be tried by combat. A duel was scheduled to take place before the court at Coventry in September 1398, but at the last moment Richard called off the fight and banished both of them. Some scholars believe that Mowbray may have been in league with Richard to compromise Henry and that Richard intended, after a decent interval, to revoke Mowbray's banishment. If so, he never got the chance. Mowbray devoted his time away from home to the honorable profession of crusading, and died in Venice in 1399 while arranging for transportation to the Holy Lands.

Muliteus, *Tit 4.2.151,* pseudo-classical name that Sh. created for a character he invented, a countryman of Aaron the Moor's. Aaron proposes to conceal his affair with the emperor's wife, Tamora, by substituting Muliteus' fair-skinned newborn son for the darkly hued baby to which Tamora has given birth. Sh.'s source for *Tit* is unknown, but an 18th c. chapbook preserves a later version of a tale that may have been familiar to him. Since the chapbook says nothing about Tamora having a child by Aaron, it has no need for a character like Muliteus.

Mulmutius, *Cym 3.1.54, 58,* Donwallo Molmutius, a mythic king of Britain. According to Holinshed he was the Solon of ancient Britain, having written many good laws which were translated into Latin by Gildas Priscus and thence into English by Alfred the Great. At the urging of his advisors, he had a gold crown fashioned. His coronation was the first of a king of Britain, as opposed to areas of Britain. In

Spenser's *Færie Queene,* 2.10.37–40, Donwallo unites Britain by force after the line of Brutus' descendants ends and creates an era of law and order. In Geoffrey of Monmouth's history, he is a lawgiver and son of Cloten, king of Cornwall.

Murder, *Tit 5.2.45, 59, 62, 83, 100, 134, 155,* allegorical figure symbolizing the violence inspired by a desire for revenge.

Murder of Gonzago, The, *Ham,* play sponsored and modified by Hamlet to produce signs of guilt in his uncle Claudius. It may be based upon the story of a murder of 1538 which appealed to Renaissance Europe's fascination with poisons. Luigi Gonzaga was accused of killing the duke of Urbino, Francesco Maria della Rovere, by pouring poison in his ear. Gonzaga denied it vehemently and was never punished for the crime, though the duke's barber was tortured and executed. The duke's wife Eleanora was also a Gonzaga. She and the duke ('the Prefect') are mentioned in Baldassare Castiglione's *Book of the Courtier* (4.2 and 1.54ff., respectively). The murder is not mentioned, but it was a politically delicate matter given the Gonzagas and their allies. A Curzio Gonzaga was also the author of *Gl'Inganni* (1592) a play which may have contributed to the creation of *TN.*

Murellus, *JC,* Caius Epidius Marullus (Marillus), plebeian tribune deposed by Julius Cæsar (44 BC). Plutarch ('Cæsar' 51.1–5) says that on the feast of the Lupercalia Mark Antony offered Cæsar a crown and urged him to make himself king of Rome. When a crowd of bystanders failed to respond to the idea with enthusiasm, Cæsar took the hint and spurned Antony's gesture. Subsequent events suggest that Antony may have been acting with Cæsar's approval. Secret agents went through the city decking Cæsar's statues with crowns and again inviting Cæsar to overturn the Republic. M. and Flavius, two of the tribunes, removed the treasonous symbols of monarchy and arrested some of the men who had cheered Cæsar when Antony hailed him as king. There were Romans who considered M. and Flavius defenders of the Republic, but Cæsar was offended by their actions and removed them from office.

Muscadel, *Shr 3.2.174,* muscatel, a sweet wine made from the muscadine or muscat, a white grape so named for its musky flavor.

Muscovites, *LLL 5.2.122, 303,* natives of Muscovy, Russians. *265,* 'frozen M.' The men disguise themselves as Russians at the masked ball. This episode is believed to be influenced by the Christmas revels at Gray's Inn 1594/5 in which performers were costumed as Russians and the Emperor of Russia was mocked for his pomposity. A 'Comedy of Errors (like to Plautus his *Menæchmus*)' was performed which may mean that Sh. was present.

Muscovy, *LLL 5.1.393,* the princedom of Moscow. Russia was originally a confederation of princedoms dominated by different cities at different times—Kiev and Novgorod, for example. After the Mongol invasions of the 13th c. and Alexander Nevsky's defeat of the Swedes, Moscow gradually became the principal city of Russia because of its position on the trade routes and the cleverness of the descendants of Nevsky, who cultivated their Golden Horde overlords. Muscovy expanded as the Tatars weakened. When Constantinople fell to the Turks in 1452, Moscow was recognized by the Orthodox church as the new capital of Christianity. By 1480 the end of Tatar rule left it the most powerful principality of Russia and during the reign of Ivan the Terrible (1547–1584), the ruler of Muscovy was recognized as the czar of all the Russians.

Muse, one of the ancient Greek goddesses of the liberal arts, the daughters of Zeus and Mnemosyne (memory). The word 'music' derives from their name. Nine in number, each oversaw a particular art form: Erato (love lyrics and bridal songs), Calliope (epic poems), Euterpe (lyric poems), Melpomene (tragedy), Thalia (comedy), Polyhymnia (sacred poetry, rhetoric, and geometry), Clio (history), Terpsichore (choral dance and song), and Urania (astronomy). Since Homer's day, it has been a literary convention for writers to invoke the Muse's blessing and her assistance, usually without specifying by name the particular Muse responsible for the area of artistry. 'The Muse' then becomes a term for inspiration in the arts, particularly poetry, and 'my Muse' would imply the poet's well of inspiration. *MND 5.1.52* (pl.) *Son 21.1; 32.10; 38.1, 9,* 'tenth muse,' a new source of inspiration. *38.13; 78.1; 79.4; 82.1; 85.1, 4 (plural); 100.1, 5, 9; 101.1, 5, 13; 103.1.*

H5, pro. 1, 'muse of fire!' a Muse equal to the task of portraying the great events of the play. *Oth 2.1.130.*

Mustardseed, *MND,* fairy, likely played by a child, the name suggesting small size. To increase the humor, Bottom addresses the fairy deferentially as Master and Monsieur, makes reference to eating hot mustard, and gets Mustardseed to help Cobweb scratch him. See Cobweb.

Mutius, *Tit,* Titus Andronicus' youngest son. Titus kills him when he opposes Titus in an argument about whom to choose as a husband for Titus' daughter Lavinia. *Tit* is not a dramatization of historical events, and there is no historical figure that serves as a prototype. Sh.'s source for the tale is unknown, but a later version of a Titus story that might have been familiar to Sh. survives in an 18th c. chapbook. Since it makes no mention of M., it is likely that Sh. arbitrarily chose a Roman name for the character. Sh. drew on the biographies of Plutarch for material for many of his plays, and Plutarch mentions a number of men called Mutius (Mucius).

'My Heart is Full of Woe,' *Rom 4.5.131–2,* song also known as 'A Pleasant New Ballad of Two Lovers.' In it a woman laments separation from her lover.

Myrmidons, 1) troops of Achilles. According to Ovid's *Metamorphoses,* 7, Ægina, the kingdom of Æacus was depopulated by a nasty plague. The king prayed to Jupiter (his father) that his people be restored in numbers as large as a column of ants he saw upon an oak tree. Jupiter changed the ants into men who were loyal and hardworking subjects. He named them *myrmix,* 'ant people.' Later they emigrated to Thessaly. Æacus was grandfather of Achilles.

Tro 1.3.371, (sing.) 'the great M.,' Achilles. *5.5.34, 5.7.1, 5.9.13.*

2) *TN 2.3.27,* 'M. are no bottle-ale houses': M. is not a cheap bar. M. seems to have been an inn to which Feste intends to take his woman.

Mytilene, *Per,* city into which Marina is sold into white slavery, called Machilenta in Lawrence Twine's *Patterne of Painefull Adventures* (1594), a major source for the play. Mytilene is the ancient capital of Lesbos, a large island in the east Ægean. Often the island is called Mytilene, also. The city was originally built on the east end of an island facing the coast of Asia Minor, but as it grew it was connected by a causeway to Lesbos. After the collapse of the Mycenæan kingdoms, the island was colonized around 1000 BC by Æolian speaking Greeks whose nobility claimed descent from Orestes. It became an important and prosperous cultural center for the Greeks in the 7th and 6th c. BC and was the home of the philosophers Theophrastus, Aristotle, and Epicurus, the musician Terpander, and the poets Sappho and Alcæus. Mytilene became a naval power and founded colonies in Mysia and Thrace, though in the 6th c. a long struggle with Athens over Sigeum near the Hellespont weakened it. After the fall of Croesus, king of Lydia, the island submitted to Persian rule, later taking part in the Ionic revolt which stimulated the Persian Wars. It became part of the Delian League (the Athenian Empire), but tested Athens' power by attempting to withdraw in 428 BC during the Peloponnesian War. Mytilene was defeated in the following year and a judgment was passed that the inhabitants should be exterminated. Fortunately, the sentence was rescinded.

Sparta and its allies repeatedly attacked the island in the late phases of the war. In 334, the Persian admiral Memnon used the island as his base of operations against Alexander the Great. In 88 Mytilene fought against Rome as an ally of the king of Pontus, Mithridates VI, and went through a lengthy siege. Pompey nonetheless made it a free community and it continued to prosper for many centuries. Lesbos was part of the Ægean theme of the Byzantine Empire. It fell to the Seljuk Turks in 1091 AD, then was repeatedly occupied by the Venetians. The Byzantines recaptured it in 1224, but gave it as dowry to the Gattilusio family of Genoa. In 1462, it was absorbed by the Turks and remained in their hands until the 20th c., fading steadily in power and wealth.

N

Nan, nickname for Anne, deriving from the affectionate 'mine Anne.'

1) *TGV 2.3.21,* Lance's family's maid.

2) *MWW 4.4.47, 70, 73, 83, 4.6.20, 5.3.11,* Anne Page.

Naples, chief port on Italy's southwestern coast, originally Neapolis (Gr. 'new city'). The Greek colony there was conquered by the Romans in the 4th c. BC, but the culture was relatively unaffected as the Romans enjoyed the city as one of their resorts. It declined with the fall of Rome and was held by the Byzantines from the 6th to the 8th c. when it became independent. In the 11th c., it became a base for Norman adventurers who transformed conquests in southern Italy and Sicily into a kingdom known as 'the two Sicilies.' After 1282, it was the capital of the kingdom of Naples. In England in Sh.'s time, syphilis was sometimes called the Neapolitan disease.

2H6 5.1.116. 3H6 1.4.123, 5.7.39. Tmp. Oth 3.1.4: the joking may refer to the nasal twang of the Neapolitan accent. In *commedia dell'arte* Pulcinella was called the Neapolitan mask and the actor spoke through the nose, sometimes using a reed (as in a wind instrument) to change the voice. Pulcinella was a cruel jester very much like Punch in the puppet tradition.

Naples, King of, 1) Duke René of Anjou, father of Henry VI's queen, Margaret. The kingdom of N. was the creation of the Norman house of Hauteville. In the 11th c., the sons of Tancred of Hauteville passed through Italy on their way home from a pilgrimage to the Holy Lands. They enlisted as mercenaries in the service of feuding Italian barons, recruited friends and relatives to join them, and gradually succeeded in supplanting their employers. In 1059 they won papal recognition for their right to rule southern Italy, and in 1130 Roger de Hauteville evicted the Muslims from Sicily and added the island to his family's Italian domain. This created the 'kingdom of the two Sicilies,' of which the kingdom of Naples was part. In 1194 the heir to the imperial Hohenstaufen dynasty married the heiress to the Sicilian kingdoms. When the Hohenstaufens died out in 1252, the king of Aragon and a French duke, Charles of Valois, contested the Hohenstaufens' Italian legacy. The French had initial success, but by the 15th c., they had lost the power to intervene effectively in Italian affairs. René of Anjou inherited Charles of Valois' claim to the throne, but he was never able to establish himself in his nominal kingdom. See René, duke of Anjou, king of Naples.

2H6 1.1.45. 3H6 1.4.122. 1H6.

2) *Tmp,* Alonso.

Naps of Greet, John, *Shr Ind. 2.92,* 'J. N. of Greece' in F1, an old friend or acquaintance of Christopher Sly's. There may have been humor in telling Sly that the names in this section were of people that did not exist, when they were names of people familiar to the audience, particularly names from the Stratford area.

Narcissus, beautiful son of Cephisus the river god and the nymph Liriope. At N.'s birth, Tiresias the seer said he would live to a ripe old age if he did not come to know himself. At age sixteen N. attracted the love of many boys and girls, but he pridefully spurned their advances. His rejection of Echo resulted in her withering away to only a voice. Finally one of the males he scorned begged the gods that N. might fall in love and be unable to gain his loved one. Nemesis granted the prayer and Narcissus fell in love with his own reflection in a woodland pool. He died of lovesickness (or drowned trying to embrace himself in the water) and was transformed into the white flower called 'narcissus' that blooms on the banks of streams and lakes. The story is told in Ovid's *Metamorphoses,* 3.

Ven 160. Luc 265. Ant 2.5.97. TNK 4.2.32; flower named and myth alluded to at *2.2.119–21.*

Naso, *LLL 4.2.123, 124,* see Ovid. His full Latin name is used here to pun on 'nasal' and smelling.

Nathaniel, (Heb. 'God has given') one of the twelve apostles.

1) *Shr 4.1.79,* one of Petruccio's servants.

2) *LLL,* 'Sir N.,' 'Master Parson,' a curate. The companion of Holofernes, he mimicks the pedant's pomposity though he is not as overeducated. In the pageant of the Nine Worthies, he plays Alexander the Great and flees the nobles' mockery after being afflicted with stage fright. This incident makes him more pathetic than ridiculous, foreshadows Holofernes' humiliation, and is reminiscent of Malvolio's exit in *TN* in which the humor suddenly seems more cruel than intended.

Nature, goddess personification of the creative forces, what is given at birth as opposed to what is shaped by Fortune. The Roman goddess of nature was *Fauna* or *Bona Dea,* a feminine entity, which is how Sh. generally uses the term. For the Greeks Pan was god of nature, and the difference of attitude revealed in this is more than a matter of masculine and feminine attributes. Differentiating between when Sh. is using Nature as a personification or when he is using it as an abstract noun is often a difficult decision for editors. The word/name is scattered throughout the plays. A sampling: *AYLI 1.2.40–54. TN 1.5.229. Tro 3.3.122. Son 4.3, 11.9. Oth 4.1.38. AWW 1.2.74. Lr. 2.2.53 (Q 7.52), 2.2.320 (Q 7.305), 4.5.86 (Q 20.86). Cym 4.2.171.*

Navarre, *LLL 1.1.12, 217, 2.1.90.* former kingdom located mostly in the Pyrenees in what is now the Spanish province of Navarra and part of southern France. It was formed out of the region inhabited by the Vascones (Basques and Gascons), and, though the Visigoths put much pressure on these peoples, they maintained their independence as Vasconia. The origins of the royal line are obscure, but the first important Navarrese king was Sancho Garcia in the 10th c. who began the rise of Navarre to significant power in Iberia. By the 13th c., however, parts of it had been seized by Castile and Aragon. The crown was claimed by the kings of Aragon, but in 1234, Navarre went by marriage to a line of French rulers. In 1516, Ferdinand V annexed Spanish Navarre. French Navarre remained independent until Henry of Navarre became Henry IV of France in 1589 and began the Bourbon dynasty. Navarre derives from Sp. *nava,* 'flat valley surrounded by hills,' and Basque '*-erri,*' 'region of.'

2) Ferdinand, king of N., *LLL 2.1.7, 22, 81, 89, 2.1 230, 227.*

Nazarite, native of Nazareth, Jesus Christ. *MV 1.3.32,* Jesus is said by Shylock to have 'conjured the devil' into swine, thus tainting all pork, which, nonetheless, Shylock asserts, Christians continue to eat contrary to God's laws. Paul released Christians from the Hebraic injuncton against pork, as he released them from circumcision. Nazarite was also a term for a sect which had taken a vow of abstinence and separation, and this could suggest some confusion with Jesus' period in the wilderness and his temptation by the devil.

Neapolitan 1) *Shr 1.1.203, Tmp 1.2.161, 2.2.111,* native of Naples.

2) *2H6 5.1.115,* Queen Margaret. Since Margaret's father claimed to be king of Naples, but never succeeded in occupying its throne, Sh. has the duke of York mock Margaret's pretensions to royalty by calling her a 'Neapolitan.'

3) (adj.) of or pertaining to Naples. 'N. prince,' *MV 1.2.38, 56,* one of Portia's suitors. He is obsessed with his horse. *Tro 2.3.18,* 'N. bone-ache,' syphilis. Englishmen of the time thought the disease had originated among the Italians, though, in fact, its origin is unknown. Its effects in the New World indicate (despite its appearance in the 1490s after Columbus' voyage) that it was not native to America. One possibility is that syphilis was a mutation of the tropical disease known as yaws.

Nebuchadnezzar, *AWW 4.5.20,* N. II (d. 562 BC), the most powerful Babylonian king. As general of his father's army in 605 BC, he inflicted a major defeat on the Egyptians at Carchemish, Syria, and later that year succeeded to the throne. He continued his conquests in the Middle East, becoming a major figure in the Bible. He conquered Jerusalem in 597 and imprisoned Jehoiakim, king of Judah, and many of his people in Babylon. After a revolt in Judah in 588, even more of the Jews were made part of the 'Babylonian Captivity.' Among them was Daniel who interpreted Nebuchadnezzar's dreams and prophesied for him. The Clown's joke refers to Daniel 4:28–37, in which the king loses favor with God and loses his mind in a fever: '. . . he was driven from men and did eat grass as oxen, and his body was wet with the dew of heaven.' Later, Nebuchadnezzar is cured and praises the God of Israel.

Ned, nickname for Edward, deriving from the affectionate 'mine Edward.'

1) *3H6 5.4.19, 5.5.50,* see Edward, Prince.

2) *3H6 5.7.16,* see Edward V.

3) *1H4, 2H4 2.4.322, 327,* see Poins, Edward.

Nedar, *MND 1.1.107, 4.1.129,* deceased father of Helena. Source unknown.

Negro's belly, *MV 3.4.37,* womb of the Moor Lancelot has impregnated. There is no other reference to her in the play.

Nell, nickname deriving from the affectionate 'mine Eleanor' or 'mine Helen.' It is used in many contexts implying a low-class or sluttish woman.

1) *2H6,* Eleanor Cobham (q.v.), used affectionately by her husband Humphrey of Gloucester.

2) *Err,* Adriana's fat kitchen maid. She never appears on stage but is described in detail in a comic bit by Dromio of Syracuse (*3.2*). At play's end, he announces his intention to wed her. It has been debated whether Nell is the same as Luce (q.v.) with Nell being merely Dromio's nickname for a sluttish woman used by Dromio.

3) *Rom 1.5.9,* woman invited to the servants' part of Capulet's feast. One cannot help notice that the name is paired with Susan Grindstone, as, in the history plays, Nell Quickly is paired with Doll Tearsheet.

4) *2H4 2.2.120,* Ned Poins' sister. Falstaff warns Prince Harry that Poins presumes on the Prince's friendship and has gone so far as to say that Harry's affection for Poins will lead the Prince to make a most inappropriate marriage with Poins' sister, Nell.

5) *H5 5.1.77, 2.1.29,* see Quickly, Mistress.

6) *Tro 3.1.52, 134,* Paris' nickname for Helen. It was a common name and its use is cheapening here, rather than affectionate, capturing the dubiousness of fighting a war over her.

7) *TNK 3.5.27,* one of the morris participants.

Nemean lion, in Greek mythology a lion which terrorized the Nemea valley in Argolis. The first labor of Hercules was to kill it. Failing to do so with his club, the powerful hero caught it in his arms and crushed the breath out of it. Hercules is almost always depicted wearing the skin of the lion as his cloak.

LLL 4.1.87. Ham 1.4.60. TNK 1.1.68, 'Nemean hide.'

Nemesis, *1H6 4.7.78,* deity from Greek mythology. She was a virgin goddess, the daughter of Night. Her primary duty was to maintain the sense of moral obligation that is the chief sanction of the law. She was the principle of retributive justice that motivated the pursuit and punishment of law-breakers. She also guarded the boundaries between the human and the divine spheres. Whenever fortune favored a human being with so many blessings that he forgot his place in the scheme of things, Nemesis intervened to humble him and to teach him to respect the limits of his mortality.

Neoptolemus, *Tro 4.7.26,* see Pyrrhus Neoptolemus, son of Achilles by Deidanira. Sh.'s use of the name in this context is confused. He seems to mean Achilles himself and may have thought Neoptolemus was a family name from the full name of Achilles' son. At *3.3.202,* Pyrrhus is clearly said to be at home. John Lydgate's *Troy Book* (1412–20), a source, mentions a Neoptolemus at Achilles' side at Troy, but in Sh. there is no reason for Hector to be referring to anyone other than the 'great Myrmidon,' Achilles himself—neither his son, nor a third party. William Caxton's *Recuyell of the Historyes of Troy* (1474), Sh.'s primary source, also has Neoptolemus at home at this point in the action as Pyrrhus is fetched by Menelaus after the death of Achilles to lead his father's troops. In the *Iliad* 19, Achilles mourns Patroclus and touchingly says that he had wanted Patroclus to assume responsibility for Neoptolemus after his own death, which he had always assumed would precede Patroclus'.

Neptune, Roman god of the sea, originally a minor entity until he was associated with the Greek Poseidon, son of Cronos and Rhea. His name may have been borrowed from the Etruscan god Nethunus. In Sh., his name is often used as a substantive for the sea.

MND 2.1.126, 'N.'s yellow sands,' the shore. *3.2.393. R2 2.1.63. Jn 5.2.34. 2H4 3.1.50.*

Ham add. Q2 A.1.1.12 'N.'s empire.' *3.2.149,* 'N's salt wash.' *Tro 1.3.44,* 'made a toast for N.,' prayed or sacrificed to the sea god. *5.2.177. Tim 5.5.83.*

Mac 2.2.58, 'N.'s ocean.' *Ant 2.7.129, 4.15.58. Cor 3.1.256. Per 10.45,* 'N.'s billow,' the waves. *13.36,* 'masted N.': in Q 'mask'd' which has been explained as 'deceivingly calm,' but 'masted' would just refer to the masts on N.'s back. *20.17,* 'N.'s annual feast,' the god's festival day was July 23. *21.14* 'N.'s triumphs.'

WT 4.4.28, refers to N.'s abduction of Theopane daughter of Bisaltis. She bore a golden ram of the union, the fleece of which was the object of the Argonaut's quest. Ovid's *Metamorphoses* 6, describes Arachne's tapestry and contains a reference to Neptune as ram, to Apollo in peasant garb, and Jupiter as bull and is therefore the obvious source of the passage *4.4.25–31. 5.1.153.*

Cym 3.1.19, 'N.'s park,' an area enclosed by the sea. *Tmp 1.2.205, 5.1.35. TNK 5.1.49,* here in the sense of the sea: Mars (war) has turned the green sea purple with blood (see the similar image at *Mac 2.2.58–61*).

Nereides, *Ant 2.2.212,* (pl. of 'Nereis'), the fifty daughters of the sea god Nereus. According to classical mythology, a different group of nymphs inhabits each of the earth's great bodies of water. The Nereides live in the Mediterranean sea. The Oceanides dwell in the great ocean that surrounds the habitable earth, and the Naiades reside in the various bodies of fresh water.

Nerissa, *MV,* lady-in-waiting to Portia. It has been pointed out that she should not be mistaken for a servant in the usual sense. Her station allows her to be a suitable match for Graziano at the end of the play. Her name may derive from It. *nera* or *nericcia,* fem. 'black,' and refer to her hair, which would contrast with Portia's. In many of Sh.'s plays we find the pairing of a fair-haired woman with a darker one.

Nero, N. Claudius Cæsar Drusus Germanicus, (37–68 AD), last emperor of Rome's Julio-Claudian dynasty. He came to power under the guidance of his mother Agrippina, who persuaded emperor Claudius to adopt him. When Claudius died, he succeeded and rejected his mother's influence. She then began schemes to replace her son with Britannicus (Claudius' son). Britannicus was likely poisoned at Nero's behest and Nero then murdered both his mother and his wife Octavia. He later married Poppæa, another schemer. He conceived bold, but unrealistic, plans for the reform of Roman society. His hope was to accustom his Roman subjects to the values and institutions of Greek civilization. Toward this end he promoted athletic and artistic competitions in place of rougher Roman pastimes, championed new religions, and designed lavish buildings in highly original styles.

When the city of Rome was nearly destroyed by fire in 64, some people assumed that Nero set the blaze to clear land for his projects. Suetonius (*Lives of the Twelve Cæsars,* Nero, 38) says that Nero watched the city burn while singing a Homeric poem entitled 'The Fall of Ilium.' This story prompted the legend that Nero played (the harp, the lute, and, finally, the fiddle) while Rome burned. More bloody deaths, such as those of Seneca and Poppæa, bred more discontent. A revolt of legions stationed in Spain and Gaul panicked him into taking his own life. His alleged indifference to the suffering of his people made him a model of hard heartedness (*3H6 3.1.40*) and an archetype for wicked rulers (*Jn 5.2.152*). He made many mistakes, but his most foolish was to neglect the interests of the Roman army, the true source of imperial power.

1H6 1.6.73. Ham 3.2.383, reference to matricide. *Lr. 3.6.6 (Q 13,6),* 'N. is an angler': some critics have quibbled with this line claiming that Rabelais (whose works were translated before 1575) said Trajan was an angler for frogs in hell, and Nero was a fiddler there, but Nero was used so as not to use Trajan unfavorably. This is false erudition. Samuel Harsnett's *Declaration of Popish Impostures,* a source for *Lr.,* mentions Nero, who is said to have fished in the Tiber in Chaucer's *Monk's Tale.* The devil Fratteretto who is mentioned in this line is followed by a mention of a fiddler in Harsnett, which may have reminded Sh. of Nero.

Nervii, *JC 3.2.171,* barbarian tribe native to Gallia Belgica (the Ardennes). Cæsar slaughtered them in 58 BC.

Nessus, centaur who was the indirect cause of the near death and apotheosis of Hercules, the fabled strong man whose adventures are described in classical mythology. Hercules killed him with a poisoned arrow to prevent the centaur from carrying off Hercules' wife Deianira. As Nessus lay dying, he persuaded Deianira to collect his blood which, he said, was a powerful charm that would prevent Hercules' love for her from fading. Deianira, fearing that Hercules might leave her for Iole (whom Hercules had recently abducted) steeped her husband's robe in the centaur's blood (Sh.'s 'shirt of N.,' *Ant 4.12.43*). When Hercules put the garment on, the centaur's corrosive blood seeped into his skin and caused him such torment that he tried to kill himself. Zeus intervened and carried the hero off to Olympus to dwell with the gods. *AWW 4.3.255:* reference to Nessus' attempted rape of Deianira.

Nestor 1), mythical hero of the Trojan war, son of Neleus and Chloris, and king of Pylos, the fortress that commanded the southwestern corner of Mycenæan Greece. In classical mythology Nestor is linked with Hercules (who killed 11 of his brothers), Jason and the Argonauts, and the Lapiths who fought the Centaurs. By the time the Trojan war was fought Homer says that Nestor had reigned over three generations of his subjects. This made him the eldest of the warriors at Troy and, therefore, the man most respected in the council of chiefs. He led ninety ships against Troy. He was renowned for his age, wisdom, and courage.

3H6 3.2.188. 1H6 2.5.7. Luc 1401, 1420. LLL 4.3.167. MV 1.1.56: 'Nestor' is used for 'a sober old man.'

Tro: Sh. much demeans him. He supports Ulysses' scheme to force Achilles into fighting and describes Hector's fighting, but is a doddering old man prone to verbosity. Ovid's *Metamorphoses* mentions him several times and makes him over 200 years old (12.187–8), which probably contributed to Sh.'s portrayal.

2) *Per 11.64,* attendant of Pericles, name borrowed from the hero.

Netherlands, The, the Low Countries (Belgium, Holland, Utrecht, Brabant, and additional areas) or the country formed from them when the Dutch revolted against their Spanish rulers beginning in 1568. The nasty war lasted until 1648 when the Dutch Republic of United Provinces was formed, a beachhead of freedom, scientific inquiry, and republican government on a continent of increasingly absolutist monarchies. People of many nationalities, including the Pilgrims, sought freedom there. Many Englishmen, including Ben Jonson and Sir Philip Sidney, served in the wars in the Low Countries in the late 1580s, as a way of curbing the threat of Catholic Spain. It has been argued, on such slight evidence that Sh. portrays the life of a soldier well, that Sh. served there, too. This overlooks the fact that he portrays the lives of kings and women quite well, which only an addlepate would conclude came from direct experience, although there are, after all, those who have asserted that Sh. was really Queen Elizabeth. In common parlance, the Netherlands are equated with Holland, which is actually only the northwestern portion of the country. 'Netherlands' comes from the Dutch *neder* 'low' and *land* 'country.' *Err 3.2.143:* here the Low Countries, Belgium and the Netherlands, are equated, to make the pun that Dromio could not look so low on the 'globe' that is Nell.

Neville, 1) *2H6 1.1.197, 240, 1.3.76, 2.2.8, 3.2.215,* family of English nobles who first became prominent in the 12th c. Since many of their estates lay in northern England, the Nevilles were frequently involved in the border wars of the Scottish marches. Generations of judicious marriages allied the Nevilles with the most important families in England (in particular, the Percies, with whom the Nevilles were often at odds, and the houses of Lancaster and York). The Nevilles who feature in Sh.'s plays are usually, but not always, identified by their titles (i.e., Salisbury and Warwick) rather than their family name.

2) *2H4 3.1.61,* see Neville, Richard, earl of Warwick 2).

Neville, Richard, earl of Salisbury, (1400–1460), scion of one of England's strongest and most quarrelsome baronial families. The Nevilles and their neighbors, the Percies, thrived in the stormy environment of the Scottish marches. The two families shared responsibility for guarding England's frontiers with Wales and Scotland. The crown relied on their services, but the large military machines they headed and the important castles they held sometimes made it difficult for the royal government to control them. Neville was connected to both branches of the royal family, the houses of Lancaster and York. His mother, Joan Beaufort, was the daughter of John of Gaunt (duke of Lancaster), and his sister, Cecillia (Cecily), married Richard of York. Neville inherited the earldom of Salisbury from his wife's father, Thomas Montague (Montacute), a famous warrior who died at the siege of Orléans in 1428. At the start of his career as earl of Salisbury, Neville charted a middle course in the feud between Lancaster and York, but as King Henry VI's incapacities became more and more obvious, Neville drifted toward the Yorkist camp. At the first battle of St. Albans he sided with Richard of York. Richard won that engagement, but his political ascendancy was short lived. When Henry and Margaret regained the upper hand, Neville, Richard's ally, was indicted on a charge of treason and forced to flee to France. His son, Richard Neville, earl of Warwick ('Warwick the king-maker') accompanied him. They returned in 1460 to hold London for the Yorkists while Richard triumphed over Henry at the battle of Northampton. Neville did not long survive the resurgence of the Yorkist cause. A group of Lancastrians captured him during a raid, and, after a brief period of imprisonment, he was murdered at Pontefract Castle. *2H6. R3.*

Neville, Richard, earl of Warwick, 1) (1428–1471), 'the Kingmaker,' who held the balance of power between the houses of York and Lancaster at a crucial point in the War of the Roses. Richard Neville was the son of another Richard Neville, earl of Salisbury. In 1450 marriage brought him the Warwick title and estates, and further acquisitions eventually made him the largest landowner in England. In 1452 the two Richard Nevilles sided with Richard of York against Henry VI. Warwick fought for York at the first battle of St. Albans, and in 1455 he served as captain of Calais. Control of Calais, England's last possession in France, gave him leverage in domestic politics and a convenient retreat from court whenever schemes went awry. After an ill-fated Yorkist uprising in 1459, he took Edward, York's son and heir, to safety in Calais. In 1460 he helped the Yorkists organize an assault on England from the continent, and at the subsequent battle of Northampton King Henry fell into his enemies' hands. Warwick persuaded York to settle for parliamentary recognition of his right to be Henry's successor and not to press for the king's immediate deposition. He was watching over Henry in London when York was killed at the battle of Wakefield. When Warwick's assault on the Lancastrians at the second battle of St. Albans failed, Henry regained his freedom, but Warwick saved the day for York's son, Edward. He persuaded the Londoners to proclaim Edward king in Henry's place, and Henry fled from England. Edward owed Warwick a great deal, but he was determined not to be his puppet.

He and Warwick found it particularly difficult to agree on foreign policy. Warwick favored an alliance with France, while Edward preferred to side with Burgundy. The relationship between the king and his 'maker' deteriorated rapidly after Edward married Elizabeth Woodville in May of 1464. Warwick considered the king's alliance a diplomatic blunder and a personal embarrassment. (Edward secretly wed Elizabeth while Warwick was abroad negotiating a marriage for him with a French princess.) The queen and her relatives wanted to destroy Warwick to advance their own ambitions. Warwick was prepared to risk everything to maintain his position behind the throne. In 1469 he persuaded Edward's brother, Clarence, to marry his daughter, and he threatened Edward with deposition in favor of Clarence. In April of 1470 Edward rallied his supporters and drove Warwick and Clarence from England. Warwick turned to Louis XI of France for help. The price that Louis demanded was Warwick's conversion to the Lancastrian cause. Warwick made peace with his old enemy, Queen Margaret, and led a Lancastrian army into England. Edward fled to Burgundy, and Henry VI was restored to the throne as a front for Warwick's government. The Lancastrian revival was brief. Burgundy financed Edward's return to England in March of 1471, and Warwick died in the ensuing battle of Barnet on 14 April 1471. Warwick's daughter, Anne, married Edward's brother, the future Richard III, and the royal family took possession of the King-maker's huge estate.

2H6. 3H6. R3 1.1.153, 1.3.135, 1.4.49, 2.1.111, 4.1.86.

2) *2H4,* a case of mistaken identity. The only member of the Neville family to possess the earldom of Warwick was Richard Neville (1428–1471), the 'Kingmaker' who dominated the struggle between Henry VI and Edward IV for the throne of England. During the reigns of Henry IV, Henry V, and Henry VI the earldom belonged to Neville's father-in-law, Richard Beauchamp (1381–1439). Beauchamp fought for Henry IV against Owain Glyndŵr and helped put down Hotspur's revolt at Shrewsbury in 1405. He accompanied Henry V to France in 1415. After the fall of Harfleur Warwick was commissioned to convey the king's loot back to England. This assignment deprived him of a chance to witness the famous battle at Agincourt. Beauchamp returned to France to take part in Henry's later campaigns, and at Henry's death in 1422 he was charged with overseeing the education of the infant heir to the throne, Henry VI.

New Year's gift, *MWW 3.5.8:* dating back to the ancient Greeks, the custom of giving gifts on New Year's survived into modern times. Bribing magistrates on the day was outlawed in 1290, but the king continued to receive gifts until the reign of James II. New Year's was not 1 January in England until 1752 (in Scotland, 1600) and the adoption of the Gregorian calender. In Sh.'s time, the legal beginning of the year was March 25, called Lady Day to celebrate the Annunciation. Thus February 1595 *followed* March 1595.

Newgate, gate in London's western wall. In the 13th c., the jail over it became chief prison of the city of London and county of Middlesex. Executions were held in front on the street. The jail was closed in 1880, but its name became slang for all prisons. *1H4 3.3.90,* 'N. fashion,' side by side. It alludes to the custom of chaining prisoners in pairs when it was necessary to march them from one place to another.

Nicander, *Per 11.65,* attendant of Pericles. The name is a variant of Nicanor as in the early Roman grammarian known as Sevius Nicander or Sevius Nicanor. There is a Nicanor in Plutarch's 'Phocion.' Nicanor is also one of the seven deacons in Acts 6.5. Nicander, a Greek scholar of Alexandria, wrote a *Transformations* (c. 150 BC) which furnished much material to Ovid.

Nicanor, *Cor,* Roman who brings the Volscians the news that Coriolanus has been exiled from Rome. His name does not appear in Sh.'s primary source, Plutarch's 'Coriolanus,' but a Nicanor is found in Plutarch's 'Phocion' (32) and in his 'Eumenes' (17). See Nicander.

Nice, Monsieur the, *LLL,* see Monsieur the Nice.

Nicholas, *Shr 4.1.79,* one of Petruccio's servants.

Nicholas, St., Christian bishop of Myra (Lycia) martyred during the persecution of the emperor Diocletian. His veneration by western Christians dates from the 9th c. He was famous for acts of anonymous charity, and during the Middle Ages the custom developed of secretly giving gifts to friends on the eve of his feast day (December 6). From this the traditions associated with Christmas and 'Santa Claus' (Du. *Sinterklaas,* 'St. Nicholas') have evolved. In Sh.'s day robbers were called the 'clerks of St. Nicholas.' Several explanations have been proposed for the association of the saint with criminals. The link might have been an incident in one of Nicholas' legends where the saint miraculously causes thieves to restore stolen booty. More likely, since he was the patron of poor scholars, his reputation suffered from the antisocial behavior of the rowdy youths who were his clients. Or Nicholas may simply have been the victim of an unfortunate coincidence. His name was similar to the one by which the devil was popularly known: 'old Nick.'

TGV 3.1.292, humor based on Nicholas' being the patron saint of scholars. *1H4 2.1.64–65.*

Nightwork, Jane, *2H4 3.2.195,* woman nostalgically recalled by Justice Shallow. Her name suggests the reason Shallow has pleasurable memories of his youthful association with her.

Nightwork, old, *2H4 3.2.206,* Jane Nightwork's husband.

Nightwork, Robin, *2H4 3.2.205,* Jane Nightwork's son.

Nile, great river that sustained ancient Egypt. It originates in Lake Victoria and flows 3,500 mi. from the heart of Africa to the Mediterranean sea. The mystery of the great river's source was debated until well into Victorian times. Early Greek geographers may have given the river its name in an attempt to approximate the sound of an Egyptian word for water. Without the Nile and its annual flood bearing fertile mud no significant density of population would have been possible in Egypt—and no true civilization.

Ant 1.5.25, 2.5.78, 2.7.17, 3.13.169. Cym 3.4.35, 'worms of N.,' asps.

Nilus, L. 'Nile,' the river personified as a divinity. *Tit 3.1.71. Ant 1.2.44, 1.3.69, 2.7.20, 5.2.57, 5.2.239.*

Nim, Corporal, or 'Nym,' one of Falstaff's cronies. 'Nim' is an archaic verb from OE 'to take.' It fell out of use sometime after the 18th c. and is related to 'nimble.' It implies his pilfering. Sh.'s references to Nim's 'humour' may relate him to Ben Jonson's comedies of humour. *MWW:* he angers Falstaff by refusing to carry Falstaff's love notes to Mistress Ford, and makes trouble for Falstaff by telling Master Page that Falstaff is in pursuit of Page's wife.

H5: he joins Henry V's army, and he quarrels with Pistol, his comrade in arms and old friend. (Pistol had married Mistress Quickly to whom Nim claims that he was engaged.) The troublesome Nim comes to a bad end during the campaign. He is hanged for looting French churches in contradiction of Henry's orders. The incident illustrates Sh.'s contention that Henry's war was a holy crusade to vindicate England's rights, not a greedy grab for French territory. The character is thought to have been influenced by a similar character in George Chapman's *Blind Beggar of Alexandria* (1596).

Nine Men's Morris, game. A square in the turf would be set up with two smaller squares inside it with parallel sides. These squares would be joined at the corners and the center of each side by straight lines. At the intersections small circles would be cut. Alternately, opposite players would place stones or pegs. Whenever a player got three in a row, he removed one of his opponent's pieces. This continued until one side had lost all his men. The playing pieces were called 'merrells' (Fr. *merelles*) or 'morris,' and opponents each began with nine. *MND 2.1.98:* because the playing area was cut into the ground, heavy rains could ruin it, as mentioned by Titania.

Nine Worthies, heroes who made major contributions to the civilizations that were most important to medieval European scholars: Christian, Hebrew, Greek and Roman. In chronological order they were: Hector, the defender of Troy; Joshua, the general who led the Jews into the Promised Land; David, king of the Jews; Alexander the Great, conqueror of the world; Judas Maccabeus, the defender of the Jews from the gentiles; Julius Cæsar, founder of the Roman empire; Arthur, legendary king of prehistoric Britain; Charlemagne, founder of the medieval European empire; and Godfrey of Bouillon, the man the soldiers of the first crusade chose to be king of Jerusalem. *2H4 2.4.222. LLL:* in *5.2,* a scene similar to the Pyramus and Thisbe play of *MND,* the commoners present a pageant of the Worthies to the nobility, which mocks it throughout. Armado plays Hector; Costard, Pompey; Nathaniel, Alexander; Mote, the young Hercules; and Holofernes, Judas Maccabeus. They never finish the pageant, in which they were to change into the other Worthies. Two of the five Worthies the commoners list—Pompey and Hercules—were not on the traditional lists. This error may be the author's or is an attempt to point up the false erudition of Holofernes. This pageant is believed to be influenced by the Christmas revels at Gray's Inn 1594/5 described in the *Gesta Grayorum.* On December 28, the 'Night of Errors,' the play watchers became rowdy because too many people had shown up and the disorder forced the Temple Ambassador to withdraw. After the law students left, a 'Comedy of Errors (like to Plautus his *Menæchmus*)' was performed which may mean that Sh. was present.

Ninny, *MND 3.1.91, 5.1.201, 258,* Flute and Bottom's confusion with Ninus. The use of 'ninny' to mean fool is first cited by the *OED* to only 1593 and may derive from 'innocent.'

Ninus, *MND 3.1.92, 5.1.137,* 'N.'s tomb.' Ninus was a king of ancient Babylon, founder of Nineveh, son of Belus, husband of Semiramis. He was said to have conquered all of western Asia and to have founded the Assyrian empire. Semiramis was accused of causing Ninus' death, but she built an enormous tomb/temple in his honor outside Babylon. His name may be linked to one of the epithets of Ishtar or to a word meaning fish, relating to a place sacred to her.

Niobe, daughter of Tantalus and Dione (one of the Pleiades), wife of Amphion, and mother of seven sons and daughters. When she mocked a worship of the goddess Leto, mother of Apollo and Diana, Apollo struck down the prideful Niobe's children with arrows. In her grief she was transformed into marble and was set upon a mountain top (Mt. Sipylus in Lydia) where the stone continued to weep. Weeping Niobe has been a favorite subject of artists. Her story is recounted in Ovid's *Metamorphoses,* 6.146–312. *Tro 5.11.19. Ham 1.2.149.*

Noah, patriarch of the Bible; son of Lamech; the father of Shem, Ham, and Japheth; and savior of humankind and the animals of the earth. In the familiar story from Genesis 6–9, God was displeased with the wickedness and violence of the human race and he decided to destroy it. He instructed Noah to build an enormous ark and fill it with the many species of animals upon the earth, his sons and their wives, his own wife, and sufficient food to outlast the flood. When Noah became six hundred years old, it rained for forty days and nights, the waters rose and everything not in the ark was drowned. At the end of 150 days the waters began to retreat. Two months later the Ark settled in the mountains of Ararat. Three months later the mountaintops became visible. By sending out a raven and a dove, Noah found out the progress of the flood's retreat. The first dove returned unable to find a place to land, a week later the second returned with an olive branch, and after another week the third failed to return. The earth dried and all the creatures emerged from the Ark and spread over the earth. God then established a covenant with Noah that He would never destroy the earth by flood again and as symbol of the covenant, he placed his bow (the rainbow) in the sky. He also gave Noah and his descendants mastery over all things that move on the earth.

Noah then grew a vineyard and passed out naked and drunk from the wine. His son Ham looked on his nakedness and told his brothers, who covered their father without looking on him. He awoke and cursed Ham's descendants from Ham's son Canaan on, to be the servant of servants to his brothers, while Japheth and Shem were to prosper. (This passage was a traditional justification for the subjection of the black 'Hamitic' races). Noah died at age 950. His story appears quite early in English drama and the portrayal in plays performed at Wakefield and Chester of his wife as a shrew who will not cooperate with her husband's plans to escape the flood is often cited as an example of independent fictional characterization creeping into drama, since she is hardly mentioned and not characterized at all in the Bible. The slapstick involved in this marital relationship remained standard comic fare.

Err 3.2.108, 'N.'s flood.' *TN 3.2.16.*

Nob, Sir, *Jn 1.1.147,* nickname that Sh. has Philip the Bastard bestow on his half-brother, Robert Falconbridge. 'Nob' was slang for 'head,' and Sh. may have intended the term to be a bawdy play on 'Rob(ert).'

Non nobis, *H5 4.8.123,* 'Not to us,' title given Psalm 115 from its opening line: 'Not unto us, Lord, not to us, but to your name give the glory.' Holinshed (3.555) says that Henry V ordered his priests to sing this hymn while the English army knelt to thank God for its victory at Agincourt.

Norbery, John, *R2 2.1.285,* Norbury, a Lancastrian knight, one of Henry IV's life-long companions. He accompanied young Henry (IV) Bolingbroke on a crusade to Lithuania in 1390, and Henry chose him to share the exile to which Richard II condemned the Lancastrian heir in 1398. When Bolingbroke decided in 1399 to defy Richard, N. joined the small company of knights that returned to England with Henry to raise a revolution. Despite his comparatively humble rank, Henry IV chose him, at the start of his reign, to be the treasurer of England, and he served in this post, which was second only to the office of Lord Chancellor, until 31 May 1401. He remained at court for the rest of Henry's life, and the appearance of his name on the lists of witnesses appended to many documents suggests that he was often in the king's presence.

Norfolk, *3H6 1.1.157, 209, 4.9.12,* county on the eastern coast of England at the point where the English channel widens into the North Sea. The name means 'land of the northern folk' as opposed to Suffolk, 'land of the southern folk.' The earldom of Norfolk, which had existed since the days of the Norman conquest, was elevated to a dukedom in 1397 for Thomas Mowbray. See Norfolk, Duchess of, *H8*; Duke of, *3H6*; *R2, 2H4*; *R3*; *H8.*

Norfolk, Duchess of, Agnes, daughter of Sir Philip Tilney and wife of Thomas Howard. She was grandmother to Henry VIII's fifth wife, Catherine Howard, and godmother to his daughter, Elizabeth. *H8 4.1.53, 5.2.202.* When Catherine was brought to trial for adultery, the duchess of Norfolk was arrested and accused of destroying relevant evidence. She was convicted and sentenced to life imprisonment, but released after a few months incarceration.

Norfolk, Duke of, 1) *3H6,* John Mowbray (1415–1461), Earl Marshall of England. Since Richard of York married one of Mowbray's maternal aunts, Mowbray had a personal reason to prefer Richard to Queen Margaret when it became necessary to appoint a regent for the ailing Henry VI. He was careful, however, to maintain ties with both the Lancastrian and Yorkist factions during the opening phase of the War of the Roses. When Richard died and his son Edward declared himself king in Henry's place, Mowbray was forced to make a decision. He distinguished himself in the Yorkist cause at the battle of Towton, and, as hereditary Earl Marshall of England, he played an important role in the ceremonies surrounding Edward's coronation. He died shortly after Edward took the throne, and his son, John, succeeded him as the fourth duke. John was survived by a single daughter, Ann, whose hand was promised to Edward IV's younger son, Richard. Richard did not live to claim his bride.

2) *R3,* John Howard (d. 1485), courtier who adroitly threaded his way through the political complexities of the War of the Roses. Howard began his military career under the command of an earlier duke of Norfolk, his mother's kinsman, John Mowbray. Edward IV made him captain of Colchester Castle in 1461 and of Norwich Castle in 1462. Somehow he also earned Henry VI's favor and received a barony during Henry's brief restoration to the throne in 1470. A debt of gratitude to the Lancastrian king did not prevent him from helping the Yorkist contender topple Henry in 1471. Howard's conduct inspired no suspicions of disloyalty in Edward IV, for Edward appointed him to the crucial post of governor of Calais. The split that took place in the Yorkist camp after Edward's death required Howard, who had walked many a fine line, to make a fateful commitment. Although he had pledged to support Edward's son as heir to the throne, he joined forces with Richard of Gloucester against the boy. He also persuaded Edward's queen to surrender her younger son, so that he might be confined with his elder brother in the Tower. As soon as the impediment of the princes had been removed and Richard (III) had ascended the throne, Howard received his reward: the duchy of Norfolk. His tenure of the estate was as brief as his patron's reign. Howard was killed commanding the king's vanguard during the battle at Bosworth Field.

3) *R2, 2H4,* see Mowbray, Thomas.

4) *H8,* Thomas Howard (1443–1524), first earl of Surrey and second duke of Norfolk. Howard began his career in the service of Edward IV, for whom he fought at Barnet. He and his father John, the first Howard duke of Norfolk, accepted Richard III's usurpation of the crown and fought for Richard at Bosworth Field. The elder Howard died in the battle, and Henry VII, the victor, imprisoned the younger until he convinced the king of his trustworthiness. In 1489 he was restored to the earldom of Surrey and entered Henry's service. The earl commanded the defense of England's border with Scotland. Surrey negotiated peace with Scotland in 1501 and conducted Henry's daughter, Margaret, to Scotland for her marriage with James IV. The young Henry VIII made the earl his chief advisor until Wolsey drove him from court in 1512. The earl returned to military service on the Scottish frontier, and in 1513 he defeated James IV at the battle at Flodden Field. As a reward for his victory, he was permitted to succeed his father as duke. In 1520 Henry made him regent for England while the king was in France conferring with Francis I on the 'Field of the Cloth of Gold.' In 1521 Henry gave him the painful duty of passing a sentence of death on his friend Edward Stafford, duke of Buckingham. The historical Norfolk died in 1524, but Sh. keeps the character alive to wit-

ness Wolsey's downfall (1529) and the christening of Anne Boleyn's daughter, Elizabeth (1533).

Norman, 1) *Ham 4.7.76, 77,* Lamord, a native of Normandy.

2) Pl.: people from Normandy (q.v.). Norman vassals were subject to both the king of England and the king of France, and they were uncertain where their duty lay when their overlords quarreled. In the early 13th c., John, king of England, lost control of Normandy to Philip Augustus of France, but the English crown did not surrender title to its former continental domain. When Henry V embarked on the conquest of France, Normandy was, both historically and geographically, the appropriate place for him to begin his campaign. Since English kings won so many famous battles during the Hundred Years' War, Henry VI's subjects found it difficult to accept the outcome of that conflict. Rather than fault their king for the loss of the land their ancestors had occupied on the continent, Sh.'s characters tend to accuse the Normans of treachery. *2H6 4.1.87. H5 3.5.10.*

Normandy, province in the north of France. Its coast commands the central stretch of the English channel. The district's name derives from a French term for the Vikings (i.e., Normans or Norsemen) who conquered it in the 10th c. When efforts to evict the Viking invaders failed, the Carolingian king of France, Charles the Simple, put the best face on his losses by granting the Viking chief, Rollo, the title of duke and proclaiming Normandy a French fief. Rollo took an oath of allegiance to the French monarchy, but his promise meant little at the time. The kings of the Capetian dynasty, who succeeded the Carolingians, were no match for any of their major vassals, and the powerful Norman dukes ignored them. In 1066 the Normans embarked on a project that vastly increased the advantage they already enjoyed over their nominal sovereigns. William of Normandy invaded England and became William I, 'the Conqueror,' founder of England's Norman dynasty. The link William established between Normandy and England complicated the question of feudal allegiances. As dukes of Normandy the kings of England were vassals of the French kings, but as kings of England the dukes of Normandy were the equals of any monarch in Europe. For several generations the Capetians were cowed by the power of England/Normandy, and the English royal house acquired extensive holdings in France. Henry II (1154–1189) of England built a huge 'Angevin Empire' that sprawled over far more French territory than was ruled by the Capetian king of France.

The long process of driving England from France and separating the two nations began during the reign of the French king, Philip Augustus (1180–1223). Because Normandy lay between the English channel and Paris, the Capetian seat, it was the arena for battles between England and France. After King John of England lost a major engagement at Bouvines in 1215, Philip repossessed it and the other fiefs the English held in the north of France. The English made no serious effort to recoup their losses until July 1346, when Edward III launched an invasion. His subsequent triumph over Philip of Valois at Crécy began the drawn-out struggle known as the Hundred Years' War. During the war the English kings made a serious bid for the throne of France, and Normandy was the seat of their military operations. England won a number of famous battles in the early years of the war, but it lacked the resources to follow them up by occupying French territory. In 1415, however, a civil war broke out in France, and Henry V of England seized the opportunity to invade. His victory over the armies of the French Armagnac faction at the battle of Agincourt and his subsequent alliance with the duke of Burgundy enabled him to reclaim Normandy, take Paris, and win recognition as heir to the throne of France. Henry's premature death in 1422 halted England's advance, and, thereafter, the balance of power gradually shifted in favor of the French. With Joan of Arc's help, Charles VII, the young king of France, began to push the English back to the channel. Henry V's brother, the duke of Bedford, maintained England's hold on Normandy until his death in 1435. Revolts against the English armies of occupation erupted in Normandy, and England's grip on its conquered territory weakened. By 1450 all of it had again been lost to the French. England's only remaining base in northern France was the port of Calais in Artois on the channel coast north of Normandy.

In 1513 Henry VIII invaded French territory from Calais and won a much acclaimed victory at the 'Battle of the Spurs,' but France was, by then, far too powerful a nation for England to conquer. In 1521 Henry and his young colleague, Francis I of France, met near Calais at a temporary camp called the 'Field of the Cloth of Gold.' Their conference did not end quarrels between England and France, but the threat Spain posed to both kingdoms forced them to moderate their ancient feud. In 1558 Henry's heir, Mary, supported Spain against France, and her decision cost England its last outpost on the continent. The French took the city of Calais, and the fall of Calais finally divorced England's island kingdom from the continent and its ancient roots in Normandy.

2H6 1.1.84, 111, 215, 4.7.26. LLL 2.1.43. Ham 4.7.68.

North, The, *1H4 2.5.103, 338,* English counties lying north of the Humber river.

North Gate (of Milan), *TGV 3.1.257, 361,* where Valentine arranges to meet his servant Speed in fleeing for his life.

North Pole, northernmost point on the globe above and around which the stars appear to revolve. *LLL 5.2.686,* 'By the N.,' a humorously exotic oath by Armado. The fashion for such oaths was also mocked by Ben Jonson in his *Every Man in His Humour* (1598) in the person of Captain Bobadill, a similar cowardly braggart. Peculiar oaths have remained a stock ingredient of comedy all the way up to western movies and the *Batman* television series.

North Star, *Ado 2.1.234,* Polaris, a distant place, the end of the universe.

Northampton, city 65 mi. northwest of London and the administrative center of the county of Northamptonshire. One of the major battles of the War of the Roses (the engagement that resulted in Richard of York's capture of Henry VI in 1460) was waged near Northampton. *3H6 4.9.15. R3 2.4.1.* See Northampton, Earl of, *H8.*

Northampton, Earl of, *H8 1.1.200,* title held by Edward Stafford, duke of Buckingham. The earldom came to Stafford through the female line after the death of the last male of the deBohun family vacated the earldoms of both Hereford and Northampton.

Northamptonshire, *Jn 1.1.51,* county at the center of England between Cambridgeshire and Warwickshire. Its seat is the town of Northampton, which is situated 65 mi. northwest of London.

Northumberland, 1) the most northeastern of England's counties. It commands about two-thirds of England's border with Scotland. *H5 2.0.25, 2.2.65, 146. Mac 3.6.31,* 'the people of N.'

2) Pl.: *3H6 5.7.8,* see Northumberland, Earls of, 1) and 3).

3) *2H4 Ind.36,* see Northumberland, Earl of, (1).

Northumberland, Earl of, 1) *3H6 1.1.4, 2.1.3,* Henry Percy (1394–1455), Hotspur's son, member of the council of regents that governed England during Henry VI's minority. Percy spent much of his life fighting with the Scots and his family's traditional enemies, the Nevilles. When Richard of York took up arms against Henry VI in 1455, Percy died fighting for the king at the first battle of St. Albans.

2) *R3 1.3.184,* Henry Percy (1421–1461), third earl, grandson of the famous Hotspur. Like his warrior ancestor, he spent his life fighting the Scots. As warden of the east marches, he conducted numerous forays into Scotland. In

domestic politics, he was a firm supporter of the Lancastrian cause. He did Henry VI a great service by killing Richard of York at the battle of Wakefield in 1460. (Sh. says that he also witnessed the callous murder of York's young son, Rutland). At the second battle of St. Albans he helped Queen Margaret's troops rout the Yorkists and the earl of Warwick. He died at the battle of Towton as his party went down to defeat.

3) *R3 5.6.1,* Henry Percy (1446–1489), fourth earl and son of the third earl who died at the battle of Towton. The triumph of the Yorkist party at Towton in 1461 created a difficult situation for the Percy heir. His father was famous for having killed Richard of York, the father of Edward IV, the man who had just become England's king. Edward punished the Percies by depriving Henry of his patrimony and sending him to prison. In 1469 Percy made his peace with York, and Edward granted him his father's offices: the earldom of Northumberland and wardenship of the east marches. He served Edward well, but he may have found it difficult to muster enthusiasm for Edward's brother, Richard III. Sh. says that his reserve caused Richard to dub him the 'melancholy' earl (*R3 5.5.21*). He commanded the right wing of Richard's forces at Bosworth, but he never ordered his men into action. After Richard's death, the new king, Henry VII, reappointed him to his offices, and the change of dynasty made little difference to his career. He was killed quelling a riot on one of his manors.

4) Henry Percy (1342–1408), Henry (IV) Bolingbroke's chief ally in his campaign to win the crown from Richard II. Percy's domains lay along England's frontier with Scotland, and he spent most of his time skirmishing with the Scots. Politically he steered an independent course. In 1376 he supported the commons in a struggle to enhance the role played by parliament in the government of England. The commons wanted to establish the principle that the king had to correct problems parliament called to his attention before expecting parliament to authorize additional taxes, but John of Gaunt convinced Northumberland to change his mind, and by 1397 the earl was amenable to Richard II's argument that the king of England ought to be an absolute monarch. He was, however, openly critical of Richard, and he was not reluctant to condemn behavior that he considered excessive. In 1399 he ignored Richard's order to join an army being mustered for the invasion of Ireland, and Richard decreed his banishment. Richard soon had reason to regret offending the leader of the powerful Percy clan. In 1398 Richard had exiled Henry Bolingbroke, and, following the death of Henry's father John of Gaunt, Richard had confiscated the duchy of Lancaster. In July 1399, Henry defied the king by returning to England to demand the restoration of his estates. Henry had only a handful of knights at his disposal, but Northumberland came to his aid with enough soldiers to give his cause credibility. As more and more barons followed his lead, Richard was forced to surrender. Northumberland personally escorted Richard to the meeting at Flint Castle where Richard yielded to Henry.

After Richard's deposition, Henry IV rewarded Percy for his invaluable assistance. He became constable of England and returned to his favorite sport: war with Scotland. The vigorous campaigns he and his son, Henry 'Hotspur,' waged against the Scots served ultimately, however, to sour his relationship with the king he had helped create. The Percies believed that Henry, who was chronically short of cash, failed to provide them with the financial support that was their due. In 1403 Northumberland and the earl of Worcester joined forces to drive Henry from his newly won throne. Hotspur was killed in the fighting, and Worcester was captured and beheaded. Northumberland submitted to the king and was, after a brief period of imprisonment, pardoned. Conflict with his rivals, the Nevilles, involved him in another rebellion in 1405. When it failed, he fled to France. In 1408 he returned to England via Scotland and tried to stir up opposition to royal taxation. He was killed in a skirmish with the sheriff of Yorkshire, and his head was sent to London for public display.

R2. 1H4. 2H4 Ind.36.

5) *H8 4.2.12,* Henry Algernon Percy (1502–1537), suitor for Anne Boleyn's hand. In his youth he was a member of Cardinal Wolsey's household. When Anne Boleyn was introduced at court in 1522, he fell in love with her and proposed to her. Wolsey learned of the affair and forced him to end it. Northumberland did as he was told and wed the daughter of the earl of Shrewsbury. His marriage was unhappy, and the couple separated almost at once. It may have amused Henry VIII, who married Anne, to give him assignments that, in light of his history, were emotionally complicated. When Wolsey fell from power, Henry sent him to arrest the cardinal. He was also appointed to the court that condemned Anne Boleyn to death.

Northumberland's wife, *2H4,* Maud de Lucy, widowed countess of Angus, the earl of Northumberland's second wife and, therefore, Hotspur's step-mother.

Norway, 1) westernmost country in Scandinavia, a mountainous land with a long coastline split by famous fjords. The terrain made it difficult for a unified people to develop in the area until they turned their attention to the sea. Twenty-nine kingdoms are recorded there in the 8th c. and their subjects included some Finns, who were increasingly oppressed. Norway was not united as a nation until 872 during the reign of Viking king Harold I, but on his death it was divided among his 20 heirs, undoing his life's work. Olaf I came to the throne in 995 after having been converted in England. He attempted to Christianize the nation with English bishops and priests, but he was killed in battle against the Danes and Swedes in 1000. Olaf II expelled the enemies and reunited the nation. He also forced Christianity on his people during his reign (1015–1028), but he was driven from the throne by Canute, who briefly united Denmark, Norway, and England as his realm. On his death, Olaf's son, Magnus I, regained Norway and united it with Denmark. Despite some disorder, the country was enriched by its trading fleets. Magnus' successor Harold III was killed at Stamford Bridge during the invasion of England in 1066. The country suffered anarchy for many years until Sverre defeated the nobles in 1201 and centralized power. Norway grew and reached its greatest power in the reigns of Håkon IV (1217–63) and Magnus VI (1263–70). Håkon V (1270–1319) completed the royal centralizing of power by nearly obliterating the nobility. This, combined with the cities of the Hanseatic League cutting off its trade routes, and the depredations of the Black Death, brought a precipitous decline.

In 1319, Magnus II of Sweden was made king. In 1370 Olaf II of Denmark became Olaf IV of Norway. The nation lost its independent status in 1392 when Margaret officially joined the crown of Norway with that of Denmark. It remained a part of that nation until the Danes were forced to yield Norway to the Swedes in 1814. By the end of the century, Norway had separated from Sweden and was again independent. In the medieval period, Britain was subject to many assaults by the Vikings across the North Sea. By the time of the Renaissance, the result, however, was a curious kind of kinship with the Danes and Norwegians, as the English had absorbed the settlers, traded in the Baltic, and was no longer threatened by Norway except as part of the soon-to-decline Danish nation.

Ham 1.1.81, 96, 2.2.40, add. Q24.4.3: in the 16th c. Norway was in danger of being gobbled up by increasing Swedish power and Danish Lutheranism was imposed upon the Norwegians. By the mid-17th c. there was some counterbalance to Swedish designs in the influence of Dutch and British interference. Sh.'s N. is therefore an utter fiction. It could not have carried out a war against the Poles at the time in which *Ham* is set and certainly was no threat to the throne of Denmark. *Mac 1.2.59,* 'N's king,' Sweno.

2) *Ham,* king of N., Fortinbras.

3) *Mac 1.2.51, 1.3.110,* Sweno, king of N.

Norwegian, (adj.) *Mac, 1.2.31, 49, 1.3.93,* F1 'Norweyan,' of or pertaining to Norway or its people.

Norweyan, see Norwegian.

Numa, *Cor 2.3.239,* Numa Pompilius, legendary king of Rome (715–673 BC), successor to Rome's founder, Romulus. He was a Sabine and, unlike his Latin predecessor, a man of peace. Many of Rome's most ancient sacred institutions were alleged to have been the result of his legislation.

Numbers, Book of, *H5 1.2.98,* fourth book of the Torah. Sh. has the archbishop of Canterbury cite Numbers 27:8 to convince Henry V that God sanctioned the inheritance rights of women. The archbishop's point is that the Bible provides grounds for denying the validity of the 'Salic' law, an ancient tradition that the French said prohibited Henry from claiming the French throne through the female line of his family.

Nym, see Nim.

O

Oatcake, Hugh, *Ado 3.3.10,* 'Ote-cake' F1, one of Dogberry's constables.

Oberon, *MND,* king of the fairies. Angry at his wife Titania because she is withholding from him the possession of an Indian boy, he uses a love potion so that she falls in love with the ass-headed Bottom. Later, when she gives up the child, he returns her to normal. He then blesses the wedding of Theseus and Hippolyta. Although he enforces his will upon Titania, he does not greatly mistreat her, and in general he is depicted as being sympathetic and gently amused by the foibles of the lovers. Oberon was almost certainly taken from the Fr. romance *Huon of Bordeaux,* translated into English in 1533, though the name was in circulation in Sh.'s time. In *Huon,* he is the son of Julius Cæsar and Morgan La Fay, and only three feet tall. Oberon had also appeared in Robert Greene's *King James IV.* Spenser mentions him in *The Færie Queene* (2.1.6.9 and 2.10.75.8) also. 'Oberon' may be derived from Alberich, the elf king in Scandinavian mythology.

Obidicut, *Lr Q 15.57,* demon of lust. In Samuel Harsnett's *Declaration of Popish Impostures,* from which Sh. borrowed many demon's names, 'Haberdicut' is listed as one of the devils fraudulent priests claimed to exorcise from Sara Williams. The name may be a variant of Hobberdidance (see Hoppidance; Flibbertigibbet).

Occasion, *Jn 4.2.125,* personification of an inevitable event.

Octavia, *Ant,* (d. 11 BC) sister of Octavius and wife of Mark Antony. In 40 BC her marriage to Antony was arranged as part of a deal to renew the second triumvirate, a political alliance between Antony and her brother. She accompanied her new husband to his post in the eastern Mediterranean, and for several years they lived in apparent domestic harmony. Their union, however, became an instrument that Octavius used against Antony. In 37 BC Antony revived a dormant relationship with Egypt's queen, Cleopatra. He married Cleopatra and promised to bestow kingdoms on her sons. Although Antony's actions may have been essential to his military objectives in the east and were not intended as a repudiation of his Roman wife, Octavius publicized them in the worst light. Octavia's conspicuous virtue and unshaken loyalty to her errant husband won her the sympathy of the Roman people and increased the credibility of her brother's charge that Antony had become Cleopatra's puppet. Antony's hope was to rally Rome to his side against Octavius by first conquering the Parthian empire, but when his Parthian campaign foundered, his countrymen lost faith in him. In 31 BC Octavius dissolved the triumvirate and routed Antony's dispirited troops at the battle of Actium. Antony and Cleopatra committed suicide, and Octavius added Egypt to the Roman empire. Octavia assumed responsibility for all her husband's children: her own and those he had by Cleopatra and by his first wife, Fulvia. The two daughters she bore Antony had descendants who became Roman emperors. The elder Antonia was Nero's grandmother. The younger was the mother of Claudius and the grandmother of Caligula.

Octavius Cæsar, Gaius Octavius (63 BC–14 AD), commonly known by the title 'Augustus,' the first Roman emperor. Octavius (Octavianus) was the grandson of Julius Cæsar's sister. His public career began in 45 BC, when Cæsar won him a military commission from the Senate. In the fall of 45 BC Cæsar posted him to Greece to further his education. He was at school in the city of Apollonia when word of Cæsar's assassination reached him. He hastened back to Italy to discover that his deceased great-uncle, who was childless, had adopted him and made him heir to his estate. Cæsar's sudden death threw Rome into confusion and provided Octavius with an opportunity to rise quickly to a position of great power. Although he was only 19 years old, he skillfully outmaneuvered older, more experienced politicians. Since the Senators who assassinated Cæsar were not prepared to accept the fact that their traditional Republic was no longer a viable form of government, they naively and erroneously assumed that by killing Cæsar they could automatically trigger a rebirth of Republican government. But the Republic had no executive office efficient enough to run an empire, and Cæsar's murder only succeeded in creating a vacuum of power that drew forth another man like Cæsar.

The strongest contender for the job was Cæsar's second-in-command, Mark Antony. Cæsar's troops trusted Antony, and they spontaneously turned to him at news of Cæsar's death. Antony hoped to ease himself into Cæsar's position by quietly winning support from all sides. He gave Cæsar's followers a splendid funeral at which to vent their grief, but he also prevented the troops from going on a rampage to root out Cæsar's murderers in the Senate. If it had not been for Octavius, Antony might have emerged as the savior of the state and Rome's new dictator. Young Octavius 'Julius Cæsar' spoiled things for Antony by storming into Rome demanding vengeance for his adoptive father's murder. His rhetoric inflamed Cæsar's troops and caused them to think twice about Antony's policy of accommodation with the Senate. Antony tried to head off problems by removing the army from the city. He retreated to northern Italy to be closer to Gaul where Cæsar's military organization was based. Although Octavius called for the punishment of the Senators who had killed Cæsar, the Senate decided that he, an inexperienced youth, was a lesser danger to them than Antony. Persuaded in part by the orator Cicero, they gave him a military commission—in the expectation that he and Antony would lock horns to their mutual destruction. With the title 'prætor,' he accompanied the consuls Hirtius and Pansa in pursuit of Antony. Antony retreated from Italy into Gaul, but in the course of the fighting the consuls were killed and Octavius assumed command of their army. He marched on Rome, extorted a consulship from the Senate, and forced the Senators to condemn colleagues implicated in Cæsar's assassination.

Antony strengthened his position by coming to terms with another of Cæsar's men, Lepidus, commander of Cæsar's troops in Spain. Antony and Octavius may have hoped for a battle that would quickly establish one of them as Cæsar's heir, but their soldiers saw no reason for them to fight. Both armies were composed of men loyal to Cæsar's memory, and both blamed the Senate for Cæsar's death. Consequently he and Antony were compelled to join forces against the Senate. They combined their armies and announced the formation of a temporary corporate dictatorship (the second 'triumvirate') with a five year mandate to do whatever was necessary to restore the Republic. The triumvirs (Octavius, Antony, and Lepidus) published a list of enemies of the state, and the condemned fled to Greece to join a Republican army headed by the assassins, Brutus and Cassius. The issue between Cæsar's heirs and his murderers was decided at Philippi in 42 BC. The partial military victory of the triumvirs was enough to send Brutus and Cassius into fits of despair that led them to doom their cause by committing suicide. The triumvirs took command of the Roman empire, and each began promptly to plot the destruction of the others. Lepidus, the weakest of the three, was sent to Africa to deal with fugitives from Philippi. Octavius assumed responsibility for Italy and the settlement of Cæsar's veterans. Antony, the dominant member of the group, reserved the most promising assignment to himself. He went east to prepare for a war with the Parthian empire. Antony hoped that Parthia would do for him what Gaul had done for Cæsar. It would allow him to build a military organization with which to overwhelm his rivals.

Octavius understood Antony's intent and eagerly looked for means to frustrate his plans. His strategy was to turn the Roman people against Antony and to convince them that he was the true defender of their Republic. This was difficult to do, but Antony blundered into Octavius' hands. In 41 BC Antony summoned Cleopatra, queen of Egypt, to his headquarters in Tarsus. Antony intended to requisition the resources of Egypt for his Parthian campaign. Although Egypt was not part of Rome's empire, it was surrounded by Roman territory and its rulers understood that their survival as independent monarchs required them to stay on good terms with Rome. Cleopatra accepted the humiliation of being summoned to Tarsus, but, once there, she persuaded Antony to treat her as an ally, not a client. The two became lovers, but Antony was not so infatuated with Cleopatra that he lost sight of his political objectives. In 41 BC Antony's wife, Fulvia, and his brother, Lucius, raised a revolt against Octavius in Italy. He had little difficulty routing the troublemakers, but the incident imperiled the triumvirate. Antony, whose Parthian campaign was pending, did not want to be sidetracked by a squabble. Consequently, he repudiated all responsibility for what Fulvia had tried to do for him. She died while fleeing east to seek his protection, and he proposed a renewal of the triumvirate—to be sealed by a hasty marriage with Octavius' sister, Octavia. Antony returned to the east with a new wife, and Octavius concentrated on the elimination of other rivals.

In 39 BC Octavius defeated Pompey's son, Sextus, whose fleet had imperiled Rome's food supply. He then moved against the triumvir Lepidus. Lepidus was stripped of his titles and confined to his house in Rome for the rest of his life. In 37 BC Antony sent Octavia back to Italy, and he went to Egypt to make final arrangements for his Parthian campaign. To ratify the treaties guaranteeing Egypt's support of Rome's war, Antony married Cleopatra and promised the sons she had borne him and her previous Roman lover, Julius Cæsar, kingdoms in the lands he was about to conquer. Under Roman law Antony's marriage with Cleopatra did not abrogate his union with Octavia, and the ceremony may have been little more than a gesture for the benefit of Cleopatra's subjects, but it provided Octavius with the perfect opportunity to accuse Antony of selling Rome out to Egypt. Antony refused to return to Rome to defend himself. He did not want to delay the Parthian campaign that he believed would bring him the power he needed to sweep Octavius aside. In 36 BC Antony led his troops across the Euphrates river into Parthia. The Parthians drew him into their huge country, cut off his supplies, and nearly trapped him. Antony recognized the hopelessness of his situation and managed a brilliant retreat that preserved a remnant of his army. The venture severely damaged his reputation as a commander and undercut the morale of his men.

Octavius pounced on his weakened rival by declaring the triumvirate at an end and marshalling troops to defend the Republic against Antony and Cleopatra. The contest was decided in 31 BC by a minor naval battle off the western coast of Greece at Actium. According to reports that are strongly influenced by Octavius' propaganda, Antony lost the fight because of his infatuation with Cleopatra. Cleopatra, who had brought her own ship to Actium, was alleged to have panicked and fled at the start of the engagement. Antony, supposedly caring more for his woman than his men, abandoned his troops to follow her. It is more likely that the Parthian debacle had caused Antony's army to lose confidence in him and that Cæsar's veterans, on both sides, were not enthusiastic about shedding each other's blood. Octavius pursued Antony and Cleopatra to Egypt. When Antony failed to reorganize his forces in time to mount an effective defense for Egypt, he realized that the game was up and committed suicide. Cleopatra lingered in the hope of reaching an accommodation, but it soon became clear to her that the passions Octavius had raised against her in Rome made it impossible for him to allow her to escape unpunished. Cleopatra took her own life, and Octavius proclaimed Egypt a province within Rome's empire.

He returned to Rome to continue the job, he said, of restoring the Republic, but he had no intention of allowing Rome to revert to its archaic and unworkable constitution. Julius Cæsar's assassination had taught him the danger of openly exercising dictatorial or monarchical powers. Consequently, he had to face the problem of reconciling what Rome needed with what Rome would tolerate. His solution was the creation of an invisible monarchy. He preserved the forms of the Republic, but retained control of specific offices and resources that permitted him to run the empire from behind the scenes. As a result, struggles for power ceased, and the civil war that had dragged on for a century came quietly to an end. The Roman people declared their gratitude by hailing him as *princeps* 'first citizen,' *pater patriæ* 'father of the country,' and *augustus* 'nurturer' or 'consecrated one.' In later years, when reality overwhelmed fantasy, his family name (Cæsar) and his Republican agnomens became royal titles that openly proclaimed the true nature of his power.

JC. Ant. Cym: this is the only play in which Sh. uses the title 'Augustus' to refer to Octavius.

'Od, euphemism for God, intended to avoid censorship of oaths. *AYLI 4.3.19,* "Od's my will.' *MWW 3.4.55,* "Od's heartlings,' 'by God's heart.' *4.1.22,* "Od's nouns,' a pun on 'God's wounds.'

TN 5.1.182, "Od's lifelings,' God's little lives. *Cym 4.2.295,* "Od's pitykins,' God's little pities.

Old Comedy, *Lr 1.2.131 (Q 2.130),* here a general term meaning a highly structured form of play in which the 'catastrophe' (conclusion) appears predictably. Comedy was often used as a general term for drama. Probably Sh. has in mind early dramas which he saw in his youth. It is curious, however, that the literary term 'Old Comedy' refers to the patterned comedy of ancient Greece of which Aristophanes was the most famous practitioner. Aristotle may have first made the distinction. Henry Puttenham uses the term in his *English Poesie* (1589) describing the Old Comedy as 'bitter' and replaced by a more pleasant style.

Oldcastle, John, *1H4,* (d. 1417), Lord Cobham by right of his second wife, Joan, and a distant inspiration for Sh.'s character 'Falstaff.' He was a Herefordshire knight who served in Henry IV's Welsh campaigns. Henry's son, Prince Harry, was lieutenant for Wales, and Oldcastle's conduct in the Welsh wars probably brought the knight to the prince's attention. He received a commission in an army the prince convinced the royal council, over Henry's objections, to send to France in 1411. He seems to have been a dependable professional soldier. It was not profligate or cowardly behavior, but religious enthusiasm, that got him in trouble with his king. He joined the Lollards, a proto-Protestant sect spawned by the teachings of John Wycliffe. Wycliffe was an Oxford theologian whose fulminations against the sins of churchmen earned him John of Gaunt's ear and protection. Lollards were defined less by a common theology than by a determined opposition to the Catholic priesthood. They believed that each Christian had the right to read and interpret the Scriptures for him or herself, and they denied the church's claim to be specially sanctioned to interpret the word of God. Oldcastle first fell afoul of the authorities in 1410 when he was accused of allowing unlicensed preachers to work on his estates. In March 1413, he was charged with heresy, but his record of service to the young king, Henry V, delayed prosecution. On 23 September he appeared before an ecclesiastical court and gave an account of his faith. Although he professed to believe in the sacraments, the court questioned his interpretation of their meaning, and he was indicted for heresy for rejecting oral confession and claiming that the use of images in worship was idolatry. He was confined to the Tower and given forty days to correct his thinking. Instead of yielding or asking for mercy, he escaped from the Tower and conspired with other Lollards to capture the king.

Henry put down his hastily organized revolt, but the Lollard champion eluded capture until November 1417. He was executed by hanging and burning on 14 December 1417. His early friendship with Henry V caused a scandal in light of his subsequent behavior, but his sins were those of the spirit, not the flesh. Sh. modeled his cowardly, drunken, womanizing Oldcastle on a character of the same name found in an early, anonymous play, *The Famous Victories of Henry V.* The criminally inclined, but jolly, drunkard who appears in this piece may have owed less to a historical prototype than to a legend: the rumor that Prince Harry was a wild youth naturally attracted to riotous companions. Sh. denied any connection between his Oldcastle character and the historical Sir John.

2H4 epi. 30. In 1597 William Brooke, Lord Cobham (Elizabeth I's Lord Chancellor) brought a complaint against Sh. for the use of Oldcastle's name. Oldcastle was one of Lord Cobham's ancestors. Sh. promptly renamed the character Falstaff. See Falstaff, John.

Oliver 1) *1H6 1.3.9,* character from a French medieval epic poem, *Le Chanson de Roland* 'The Song of Roland.' It was written in ten syllable lines during the 12th c. Roland was a duke of Brittany who died in the battle of Roncevaux in 778, and Oliver, son of Regnier duke of Genoa, was his boon companion. Medieval poets depicted Oliver as the model of chivalry and the ideal knightly advisor. Oliver is more level-headed and cautious than the dashing Roland, but no less willing to die in defense of honor. They once fought each other for five days, with neither dominating. Their equality as noble warriors led to the expression 'a Roland for an Oliver,' meaning tit for tat.

2) *AYLI,* older brother of Orlando who, like Duke Frederick, misuses his brother, then undergoes a miraculous conversion to goodness. He also falls instantly in love with Celia, occasioning Rosalind's mocking of love at first sight. The name was likely suggested by Charlemagne's knight Olivor in Ariosto's *Orlando Furioso* (see Orlando).

Olivia, *TN,* 'Countess O.,' 'Lady O.,' niece or cousin of Sir Toby Belch. She is in mourning for the death of her brother and spurns Duke Orsino's advances, falling in love with the go-between, Viola disguised as Cesario. This difficult attraction resolves itself with the appearance of Sebastian, Viola's twin brother. As a character, she is not very intriguing except that she provokes such admiration among her suitors. She seems tolerant in allowing both Sir Toby and the upright Malvolio as important parts of her household. The name Olivia, like the rest in the play, does not appear in any of Sh.'s known sources. The corresponding character in *Gl'Ingannati* (1538) is Isabella, Niccolo Secchi's *Gl'Inganni* (1562) Portia, and in Barnabe Riche's 'Apolonius and Silla,' from *His Farewell to the Military Profession* (1581), Julina. There is a play from 1598, Emanuel Forde's *Parismus, the Renowned Prince of Bohemia* which has some superficial resemblances to *TN* and has an Olivia as well as a Violetta, but the name is too common to assert with much authority that Sh. got it there.

Olympian, *Tro 4.7.78,* inhabitant of Olympus, one of the gods of classical mythology. Wrestling was one of the favorite sports of the ancient Greeks.

Olympian games, *3H6 2.3.53,* best known of the athletic festivals celebrated by the ancient Greeks. The Greeks traditionally staged games as solemn religious events. The custom may have derived from mock battles fought at the funerals of early kings. No one knows when or why athletes first began to gather to compete at Olympia in southern Greece, but from 776 BC until 393 AD Olympia was the site of the most famous athletic contests in the world. The 'rewards as victors wear' that George, duke of Clarence, promises his men were simple crowns of laurel. The honor of the victory was highlighted by the fact that the prize had no innate worth.

Olympus, peak at the eastern end of a chain of mountains marking the northern frontier of ancient Greece (between Thessaly and Macedonia). In Greek myth it was home to Zeus and his divine family. *Tit 2.1.1. JC 3.1.74, 4.2.146. Tro 2.3.10,* 'thunder-darter of O.,' Jupiter. *Ham 5.1.250. Oth 2.1.189,* 'O.-high.' *Cor 5.3.30.*

Ophelia, *Ham,* sister of Lærtes, daughter of Polonius. She is drawn into a plot to expose Hamlet's madness as a fraud, but after Hamlet kills her father, she later goes mad herself and commits suicide. Her madness seems to have come from her unrequited love of Hamlet, as much as her father's death, though it is never quite clear whether Hamlet loves her or not. She is very much a victim of the rottenness in Denmark. Her name was unusual in Sh.'s day and where he got it is a mystery. It is a Greek name like her brother's, and was first used by poet Jacopo Sannazaro (1458–1530) as Ofelia in his *Arcadia,* which influenced Sir Philip Sidney and many other pastoral poets. The use of a beautiful woman to unmask Hamlet's madness is a plot element in Sh.'s sources Saxo Grammaticus *Historia Danica* (c. 1200) and François de Belleforest's *Histoires tragiques* (1576), but she is unnamed, not the old counsellor's daughter, and her suicide is not in the story. She does appear in *Der Bestrafte Brudermord* (1710) which seems to be a German rendition of an older version of the play, which might imply that she was in a Hamlet by Kyd (or someone else that Sh. reworked) and therefore he simply took the name from it, though her father's and brother's names are different in the German version. Her name would mean 'helpful' from Gr. *opheleia,* which tells us little even though John Ruskin thought Lærtes alludes to it when he calls her a 'ministering angel' (*5.1.236*). One theory is that Aphelia, meaning 'innocence' has been misspelled. A remote possibility is that it has been adapted from Ormilda or some other medieval Danish name. There is also an Ofellus in Horace. In Plutarch, Lucretius Ofella is murdered by Sulla.

Oracle, Sir, *MV 1.1.93,* Graziano's mocking name for men who try to pass off their seriousness or melancholy for wisdom.

Orator, *Tit 4.1.14,* a work by the Roman rhetorician Marcus Tullius Cicero. Sh.'s reference is probably to one or all of Cicero's essays on the subject of speech making: *De oratore* 'On Oratory,' *De Partitione Oratoria* 'On the Classification of Rhetoric,' *De Optimo Genere Oratorum,* 'On the Best Type of Orator,' or *Orator* 'The Orator.'

Orlando, *AYLI,* brother of Oliver, he learns about true love from Rosalind in disguise, after mooning about in the courtly manner of a lover. Physically strong and courageous, O. was likely borrowed as a familiar heroic name in a French context from the title character of Ludovico Ariosto's *Orlando Furioso* (1516, 1532, trans. John Harington 1591), containing the adventures of a French knight of Charlemagne's court, Roland. *Orlando Furioso* had a powerful effect on English Renaissance literature and art. Robert Greene had dramatized it in 1589 and Edmund Spenser used it as a source for *The Færie Queene* (1590, 1596). Sh. may or may not have known *Orlando Furioso* in the original, but he certainly knew it indirectly.

Orléans, *1H6,* French city situated on the Loire river about 75 mi. southwest of Paris. It is thought to have been a very ancient town and an important trading post. Known as Genabum when the Gauls revolted against Cæsar in 52 BC, it was renamed Aurelianum in the 5th c. AD. Attila the Hun and Odoacer the Saxon unsucessfully besieged it in the 5th c., before it fell to Clovis in 498. It was the capital from which the Merovingian dynasty ruled France before the royal government settled in Paris. A duchy of Orléans was created by Philip VI for his son Philip (d. 1375). It passed to Louis, duke of Orléans, brother to Charles VI, king of France. When Charles VI went mad, Louis quarreled bitterly with his uncle, Philip of Burgundy, over the office of regent for the incapacitated king. Shortly after the performance of a ceremony that was intended to reconcile Orléans and Burgundy, the duke of Burgundy assassinated Louis. Orléans' father-in-law (the count of Armagnac) assumed leadership of his faction (the Orléanists or Armagnacs), and France braced for civil war. The confusion in France tempted Henry V of England to invade Normandy and revive the Hundred Years' War. After Henry's victory at Agincourt in 1415 and his occupation of Paris, the city of Orléans became the chief stronghold of the Armagnac forces that carried on the struggle to liberate France from English occupation. *Cym*

1.4.34. See Orléans, Bastard of, *1H6*; Duke of, *H5, 1H6, 2H6, H8.*

Orléans, Bastard of, *1H6,* see John, count of Dunois.

Orléans, Duke of, 1) Charles (1391–1465), son of Louis of Orléans, who was the brother of King Charles VI of France. When Charles VI was incapacitated by mental illness, Louis and his uncle, Philip the Bold of Burgundy, quarreled over the issue of who had the right to rule for the mad king. In 1407 Louis was assassinated by Philip's son, John the Fearless, and Charles inherited the duchy of Orléans. The fight to avenge Louis was led by young Charles's father-in-law, Bernard VII, count of Armagnac. Charles himself was forced on to the sidelines for much of his life. In 1415 he was captured at the battle of Agincourt, and he spent the next twenty-five years as a hostage in England. Enforced retirement gave Charles time to develop his substantial talent as a poet. He was the last important author to observe the conventions of the medieval courtly style. Henry VI released him from captivity in 1440 in exchange for his promise to work for peace between England and France. When he returned to France, he found that he had little influence over his cousin, Charles VII. The duke of Burgundy had helped to arrange Orléans' release, and Charles may have considered him a Burgundian agent.

Orléans put pressure on the king by reviving the Armagnac party and proposing a marriage between Henry VI and a daughter of the count of Armagnac. Although Charles neutralized the threat posed by Orléans and his allies, the French king decided to allow his cousin to negotiate terms with England. Charles drove a hard bargain. In 1445 Henry, whose request for the hand of one of the king's daughters was denied, accepted a lesser match with Charles VII's niece, Margaret of Anjou. In exchange, France agreed to a truce of five years, not a permanent peace. Orléans, having done what he could to discharge his obligations to his former captor, retired to Blois. At his ducal court he amassed a large library and provided patronage for artists and scholars. He might have been content to spend the rest of his life at Blois enjoying the pleasures of a cultivated country gentleman, but he was repeatedly drawn back into politics. He had inherited a claim to the duchy Milan from his mother, Valentina Visconti. When the Visconti died out, he initiated a fruitless struggle to evict the Sforza family from Milan. The duke was frequently called to court to mediate disputes between his king and factions of the nobility. When Charles VII died, his heir, the dauphin, was in exile in Burgundy and it fell to Orléans, the king's senior relative, to preside at his funeral. His relationship with Charles's difficult and devious son, Louis XI, was never good. *2H6 1.1.6. 1H6 3.7.69. H5.*

2) *H8 2.4.171,* Henry of Valois (1519–1559), second son of Francis I, king of France. He was proposed as a husband for Henry VIII's daughter, Mary, but negotiations for their union were broken off. He and his elder brother, Francis, spent four years (1526–1530) as hostages in Spain, after Charles V turned back their father's invasion of Italy. In 1533 he married Catherine de Médicis, and in 1536 the death of his brother made him heir to the French throne. He succeeded his father in 1547 and reigned as Henry II until he was killed in a jousting accident in 1559. He had three sons, each of whom in turn inherited the throne. At the death of the last, Henry III, the Valois dynasty ended.

Orpheus, mythological poet who sang so sweetly that brooks ceased flowing in order to listen and trees bowed in respect. The son of Apollo and Calliope (one of the Muses) or of Oeagrus, king of Thrace, and either Clio or Polyhymnia (also Muses). He accompanied Jason on the quest for the Golden Fleece and saved the Argonauts several times with his music, once even blotting out the Sirens' song until the Argo had safely passed. In the most famous story, his wife Eurydice, whom he loved deeply, was killed by a snakebite. Using the power of his song, he entered the Underworld and sang for Pluto and Proserpine. They were so moved they released

Eurydice on one condition, that Orpheus not look back at her until she had stepped into the world of the living. He led her shade up, but as he stepped into the sunlight, he turned to embrace her. Since she was still beyond the portal, she faded away and he was not allowed to enter the Underworld again. Inconsolable, he settled in Thrace and made only boys his companions until he was torn apart by Ciconian women in a Bacchic frenzy. They flung his head into the river Hebrus which drifted to the shore of Lesbos where either the Muses (or Apollo) buried it. His body they buried at the bottom of Mt. Olympus. These burials were supposed to explain why so many poetic talents were from Lesbos and why the nightingales supposedly sang sweetest on the mountain. In an alternative story he was killed by a thunderbolt from Jupiter. Virgil, Apollonius of Rhodes, and Ovid tell the story quite similarly; *Metamorphoses* 10–11, however, is most likely the version most familiar to Sh.

TGV 3.2.77, 'O.'s lute.' *Luc 553. MV 5.1.80,* refers to Orpheus' effect on inanimate objects. *H8 3.1.3.*

Orsino, *TN,* 'Count O.,' 'the County,' duke of Illyria. He pines for the love of Olivia as the play opens, mooning about in a manner ridiculous to the other characters. He uses the page Cesario (Viola in disguise as a man) to court her. Viola, however, falls in love with him. Late in the play after Olivia falls for Viola's brother Sebastian, Orsino comes to his senses and turns his attention to Viola whom he decides to marry. The corresponding character in *Gl'Ingannati* (1538) is Flaminio, in Niccolo Secchi's *Gl'Inganni* (1562) Gostanzo, and in Barnabe Riche's 'Apolonius and Silla,' from *His Farewell to the Military Profession* (1581), Duke Apolonius of Constantinople. It is an attractive possibility that Sh. got this name from Gentile Virginio Orsini, duke of Bracciano, who visited London in the winter of 1600–01. He was entertained with great pomp by Queen Elizabeth. One of these celebrations took place on the evening of Twelfth Night (Epiphany, January 6), but it cannot be proved that *TN* was performed on this occasion. Using the name of a foreign ambassador could also be extremely sensitive. The Orsino of the play is a bit of a fool, after all. In addition, word of the Duke's coming did not reach England until December 26, 1600. Sh. worked miracles, it is obvious, but completing this play that quickly? As well as producing it? One might force the argument by imagining it is a revised earlier play, but that is grasping at straws.

The first definite record of a performance is in a law student's diary. John Manningham attended a performance at the Inns of Court on February 2, 1602. By then, perhaps, the name could have been borrowed from Bracciano, but other allusions make it likely the play was written a year or two earlier than Manningham's attendance.

In any case, the Orsinis were a very prominent family in Italian history since the 10th c. Other major figures from the family include Cardinal Napoleone Orsini and Niccolo Orsini, count of Pitigliamo. Their family crest is adorned with bears and the It. *orso* 'bear' is the derivation of the name. Some critics believe that Sh. may be playing on the legendary large appetites of bears in his selection of name for Orsino.

Osric, *Ham,* silly courtier provided for comic relief just before the climax of the play. He and Hamlet discuss the wager over the duel. Hamlet twists Osric's words back upon themselves and reveals the courtier's shallowness. Although Hamlet shows distaste for Osric's obsequiousness, he seems amused at toying with him. The scene may be based upon John Florio's *Second Frutes* (1591). Later Osric referees the duel and announces the coming of Fortinbras. The name Osric occurs in the source story by Saxo Grammaticus, where he is a foster brother of Amlethus (Hamlet). In *Der Bestrafte Brudermord* (1710) which seems to be a German rendition of an older version of the play, the equivalent character is Phantasmo, the court fool.

Ossa, *Ham 5.1.280,* mountain in Thessaly about 6400 ft. high. It is between Pelion and Olympus, from which it is separated by the vale of Tempe, a supposed paradise on earth. In mythology the Aloadæ, gigantic sons of Neptune, attempted to storm heaven by piling Ossa and Pelion on Olympus. Jupiter killed them with lightning. The story is told in Ovid's *Metamorphoses* 1.151–162 and is mentioned in Virgil's *Georgics* 1.281.

Ostler, Robin, *1H4 2.1.10–11,* see Robin Ostler.

Oswald, *Lr,* Goneril's steward. He insults Lear, who strikes him, provoking Goneril's anger. Later, Kent beats him and insults him for his aspirations to higher social status. Edgar kills him when he attempts to kill the blind Gloucester. Oswald has been seen as a parody of the social-climbing Elizabethan, as ridiculous as Malvolio or Osric and stupidly loyal to his evil mistress to achieve his ends. Sh.'s sympathy, as presented in the play, is clearly with the 'old money' against the *nouveau riche.* Some critics have tried to link him to William Ffarington, steward to Lord Strange, but this is highly conjectural. It is more likely Oswald is simply and directly inspired by the character of the favor-currying Skalliger in *The True Chronicle Historie of King Leir* (1605).

Othello, *Oth,* the Moor of Venice, husband and murderer of Desdemona. As a very great man, Othello is an appropriate subject for tragedy and is clearly intended to be so. His accomplishments as a warrior in service of Venice have overcome the hindrances which his outsider status in Venetian society have placed in his way. Even his 'falling sickness' is an indication of his martial greatness, as epilepsy was the disease of Julius Cæsar. His outsider status, however, also provides the germ for his inability to trust Desdemona while simultaneously relying too strongly on Iago. In a sense, his difficulties derive from an insecurity about his place in his adopted world, mingled with a considerably developed, perhaps compensatory, vanity about his achievements. Many passionless critics seem to find his explosive temperament inexplicable, as if spousal murder for little cause were an uncommon occurrence in the world, and interpret his behavior as an insulting characteristic of his race, when it may have been exactly Othello's temperament that has granted him success. The tragedy is that what makes him great undoes him.

As a Moor, Othello may or may not be played as a member of the Negroid race, though it is now generally the case that this is considered a black man's role. The insults against his appearance which are hurled by Iago and Rodcrigo are similar to the racial insults of our own time, but they are not unlike the imagery affectionately directed at the 'Dark Lady' of the sonnets, and could be consistent with the racial mixture called Moor. While several earlier critics seem to have wished that Othello were not black (for the reason that a great man could not be a Negro), contemporary critics seem to wish that the play provide insight into contemporary racial problems and turn Venice into Los Angeles. Yet it is plain that race is not the same issue to Sh. that it is to us, and is perhaps not an issue at all. The racial insults directed at Othello emphasize his outsider status, not the inferiority of the black race, and the imagery of darkness, blackness, etc. are convenient metaphors. The elaborate racist mythology of later times had not yet been developed. One of Sh.'s most common themes is that moving out of one's social station brings trouble upon society, whether that is a noble forcing himself into kingship (Henry IV) or a king descending to retirement (Lear). The greatness of the play lies not in Othello as a symbol of race or anything else, but Othello as man, provoking pity and terror because he is subject to the same weaknesses as other men.

There have been several attempts to link the sole extant source (Giraldi Cinthio's *Hecatommithi,* 1566) to a true story. One Christophal Moro, a lieutenant of Cyprus, returned from the island in 1508 after having lost his wife. Moro was married four times, and performed heroic military exploits against Cesare Borgia. Besides meaning 'Moor,' 'Moro' may also mean 'mulberry' (which was Moro's insignia) which has been related tenuously to the strawberries of Desdemona's handkerchief. Cinthio's story also resembles that of Sampiero, a leader in Corsica, who was an Italian in service to France. He distinguished himself militarily and married Vanina d'Ornano against her relatives' wishes. In 1563 he left France to beg assistance for Corsica from the Turks against Genoa. Enemies made him believe his wife was having an affair with his secretary Antonio. Sampiero strangled her at Aix with a handkerchief, and the story was well-known.

The origin of 'Othello' is unknown. Cinthio calls him simply, 'the Moor.' There are some slight indications, however, that another source has been lost. It is not typical of Sh. to be that inventive with names. It has been speculated that Othello is an Italianizing of Othman (Osman) the founder of the Ottoman empire. John Ruskin's argument that the name derives from Gr. *othomai* 'to be careful' is farfetched. Othello is anything but careful—that is the point of the play. Another possibility is Reynold's *God's Revenge Against Adultery* in which Othello is an old German soldier, there is also an Iago, and the eighth story is said to be an Italian one. Thee is also an Othello in *The first and second part of the History of the famous Euordanus, Prince of Denmark. With the strange adventures of Iago, Prince of Saxonie: and of both theyr severall fortunes in Love* (1605). In 1606, an M. A. Othelio replied to a papal bull excommunicating the Doge, Senate, and Republic of Venice. There is a curious set of coincidences in that Ludovico Sforza, ruler of Milan, was nicknamed 'the Moor,' had a mistress Bianca, and his first name is used for one of the minor characters.

Ottoman, *Oth 1.3.49,* follower of the Turkish empire established by Osman I (1288–1320), who began by seizing several cities from the Byzantines. Othman or Ottoman is an alternative spelling for Osman (Arabic *Usman*). The empire lasted until 1919 and for most of its history constituted the greatest Moslem threat to Christian Europe.

Ottomites, *Oth 1.3.34, 233, 2.3.164,* Ottoman Turks.

Out-talian, *2H6 4.7.57,* mispronunciation of 'Italian.' Sh. had no sympathy for Cade's rebellion. He depicts Cade's followers as ignorant fools who mistook Latin for a modern language of which they were equally ignorant.

Overdone, Mistress, *MM,* madam of a brothel. She appears in various scenes, mostly to point up the corruption of Vienna. She is accused of carrying venereal disease and when she is arrested complains that Lucio, whose child by Kate Keepdown she is rearing, has betrayed her. Her name, like those of Sh.'s other whores, reflects her characteristics: she has been well used. In Sh.'s sources the name is not used, but in George Whetstone's *Promos and Cassandra* (1578) there is a madam and her servant who correspond to her and Pompey.

Ovid, Publius Ovidius Naso (43 BC–c.17 AD) Roman poet, author of *Metamorphoses, Artis Amatoriæ, Amores, Fasti, Heroides, Remedia Amoris, Tristia,* and other works. Born in Sulmo (modern Sulmona, 90 mi. east of Rome), Ovid was trained in the law and completed his education in Athens. He also travelled in Asia and Sicily. By age fifty, he was a judge and leading citizen of Rome, but in 8 AD, Ovid was exiled to Tomi, now Constanta, Romania, on the Black Sea, because of a 'poem' and a 'mistake.' The first is generally thought to be the *Artis Amatoriæ* and the second to have something to do with a scandal connected with Julia, Cæsar Augustus' daughter. He died in exile. His works were a tremendous influence upon Sh., his predecessors, and his contemporaries.

Shr 1.1.33. Tit 4.1.42. AYLI 3.3.6, reference to Ovid's exile, indicating a familiarity with the *Tristia,* Ovid's appeal for Cæsar's clemency from his miserable life in Tomi.

Ovidius Naso, *LLL 4.2.123,* Latin name of Ovid, used to pun on 'nasal.'

Owl of death, *1H6 4.2.15,* bird of evil omen. Ovid (*Metamorphoses,* 10.453) refers to the owl as a messenger of death. The human imagination finds it easy to associate a bird that hunts at night with the darkness of death's realm. For example, the owl is also a death messenger among the Kiowa and many other native American tribes.

Oxford, seat of the county of Oxfordshire, situated on the Thames 45 mi. northwest of London. Its name obviously derives from its location as a place to ford oxen across the river, though some scholars believe 'ox' relates to a Celtic word which means 'water.' In the mid-12th c. it became a gathering place for English scholars who were prevented by war from studying in the schools of France. The university that evolved at Oxford is composed of many colleges, one of which, Queen's, was founded in 1340 by the chaplain of Philippa, queen-consort of Edward III and mother of the Black Prince, who was a student there. Henry V also studied there. Christ Church was begun in 1525 by Cardinal Wolsey.
R2 5.2.52, 99, 5.3.14, 139, 5.6.13, 16. 2H4 3.2.9. H8 4.2.59.

Oxford, Earl of, John de Vere (1443–1513), a loyal Lancastrian who played a major role in the fighting that brought down the house of York and inaugurated the Tudor era. Suspicions of disloyalty led Edward IV to imprison him in the Tower of London in 1468. Following his release in 1469, he fled to France. There, he joined an army that the earl of Warwick had raised to try to restore Henry VI to the throne. He fought with distinction at the crucial battle at Barnet, but the loss of that engagement doomed the Lancastrian cause and forced the earl once again to flee to France. In 1473 he led a raid across the channel to Cornwall. He seized the island of St. Michael's Mount and held it until a blockade forced him to surrender. Edward sent him back to France to imprisonment in Hammes Castle. After Richard III usurped the throne from Edward's heir, he escaped from Hammes and joined the army that the earl of Richmond, the Tudor pretender, assembled for the invasion of England. At the battle of Bosworth, he helped tip the balance in Richmond's favor, and he was richly rewarded for his service when Richmond became Henry VII, the first of the Tudor kings.
3H6. R3.

Oxfordshire, *3H6 4.9.18,* county in central England crossed by the upper reaches of the Thames river. The university city of Oxford, situated about 45 mi. northwest of London, is its administrative center.

P

Pabylon, *MWW 3.1.23,* Evans' dialect for Babylon.

Pace, Doctor, *H8 2.2.122,* Richard, (d. 1532), Henry VIII's secretary, predecessor in that office to Stephen Gardiner, bishop of Winchester. Pace also served Henry as an ambassador. His most important mission was an attempt in 1524 to persuade the college of cardinals to elect Wolsey pope. Sh. assumes that Pace was dead before the pope permitted a court to consider Henry's case for an annulment of his marriage with Katherine of Aragon, but Pace actually died some years after the hearing.

Pacorus, *Ant 3.1.4,* (d. 38 BC), son of Orodes, king of Parthia. He died battling a Roman army led by Ventidius, one of Mark Antony's men. Sh. has Ventidius make the claim that Pacorus' death was retribution for the Parthians' murder of Marcus Crassus. In 53 BC Orodes' general, Surenas, had killed Marcus Crassus, a member of the first triumvirate. Crassus had invaded Parthian territory. When his campaign foundered, he attempted to negotiate with the Parthians who invited him to a conference and killed him.

Paddock, *Mac 1.1.9,* name applied to a spirit who calls the witches. Paddock derives from the Anglo-Saxon *pada,* 'toad.' It is diminutive of 'pad,' as 'hillock' is of 'hill.' Witches were supposed to keep spirits in the form of a frog or toad.

Padua, (It. *Padova*) city in northern Italy, just 22 mi. west of Venice. It received its name from the L. *Padum,* the Po river, which was named from the Celtic *padi* 'pines,' which grew abundantly at the river's mouth. Padua is only about 30 mi. northwest of the Po delta. In Roman times the city was known as Patavium and was the most important town of Venetia. The university there, founded in 1222, was one of the most reputable in Europe: Galileo taught there and it also had Europe's first anatomy hall. Padua was generally a free city from the 12th to the 14th c., when it came under the control of the Carrera family. In 1405 the Venetians gained control and Padua became an important port because of the extensive network of canals in northern Italy.

Shr, setting for the play. Padua is shown as a prosperous merchant city (a good place for a man to marry money), and reputable for its learning ('nursery of arts'). *TGV 2.5.1:* according to F1, Launce meets Speed there. The confusion of the text is such that it is not clear whether the setting of the main action is Milan, Verona, or Padua, though this is the only line supporting the latter and is thus usually assumed to be a mistake and edited to Milan. An argument has been made that the mistake derives from *A Courtlie Controversy of Cupids Cautels* by Jacques d'Yver, trans. by Henry Wotton in 1578. This work has been supported as a source, though it is now usually considered an analogue.

MV 3.4.49, F1 'Mantua,' an obvious mistake for P., *4.1.108, 118, 400, 5.1.268,* residence of Bellario, wise doctor of laws. *Ado 1.1.34,* Benedick's home town. The Italians of the Two Sicilies generally supported Pedro III's efforts against their French conquerors. P., however, is far to the north. The use of it here might imply Benedick's intelligence, but probably Sh. chose it as a random detail to add verisimilitude.

Page, Anne, *MWW,* daughter of Margaret and George, sister of William. Margaret tries to arrange her marriage with Dr. Caius, while George Page pushes for Abraham Slender. Anne, however, loves Fenton. In the display put on in the woods to humiliate Falstaff, both Caius and Slender believe they are eloping with her in disguise as a fairy. To their dismay, they have eloped with boys while she marries Fenton. She is not a disobedient daughter, really, as she urges Fenton to persuade her father before they resort to elopement, and the Pages are not unreasonable, as Margaret agrees to listen to her daughter's opinions about her prospective husband. Both accept Fenton as their son-in-law. Anne serves primarily as a focus for the insane behavior of the characters around her. Her name reflects her ordinary, middle-class common sense. She is called 'Nan' several times late in the play.

Page, Master George, *MWW,* father of Anne and William, husband of Margaret. Middle-class, sensible, and generally cheerful, George shows only slight bad judgment when he tries to arrange a marriage between Anne and Slender, who, despite his ridiculousness, is a good financial choice. Fenton is poor, has kept bad companions, and is of a higher class—all ingredients for a potentially disastrous marriage. When the youngsters elope, however, George accepts the marriage with equanimity. Throughout the play this is his primary trait. He tries to talk Ford out of his mad jealousy, to stop the fight between Dr. Caius and Hugh Evans, and it is he who invites Falstaff to dinner after the knight has been punished, thus presiding over the reconciliations.

Page, Master Thomas, *MWW 1.1.41,* F1, George Page, the only time he is called Thomas. This is either Sh.'s usual carelessness, a text problem, or a printing error. There would be no comic justification for Evans misnaming him here. The confusion of the two names indicates his choice of a sturdy, ordinary name for not just the husband, but his family.

Page, Mistress Margaret, *MWW,* wife of George, mother of Anne and William, one of the two 'Merry Wives.' A sturdy middle-class woman, she is a bit more assertive than her husband. She is intent on Falstaff's humiliation upon receiving his romantic overtures and acts accordingly. She is not bullying, however. She tries to arrange her daughter's marriage to Dr. Caius, but accepts the marriage to Fenton quite easily. Her name reflects her sturdy, bourgeois character.

Page, Nan, see Page, Anne.

Page, William, *MWW 4.1,* brother of Anne, son of George and Margaret. His only appearance is in this scene, in which he is quizzed on his Latin by Hugh Evans and observed by Anne and Mistress Quickly. As in the French lesson of Katherine of France in *H5,* cheap puns and double entendre are the chief source of humor. The audience would have also identified readily with the situation, as Latin was the bane of many a schoolboy and William has a fool of a teacher, something which all students endure at some point.

Palamedes, *Tro 5.5.13,* Greek warrior. When Ulysses feigned madness to avoid serving in the Trojan War, Palamedes deliberately endangered Ulysses' infant son Telemachus, forcing Ulysses to reveal his sanity. In revenge Ulysses later placed stolen gold in Palamedes' tent, whereupon Palamedes was stoned to death. In William Caxton's *Recuyell of the Historyes of Troy* (1474), Sh.'s primary source, Palamedes arrives late for the war because of illness, speaks against Agamemnon's leadership, is made commander-in-chief, kills Deiphobus and Sarpedon, and is himself killed by one of Paris' poisoned arrows.

Palamon, *TNK,* 'Prince P.,' one of the two kinsmen of the title. Originally intending to leave corrupt Thebes, he stays to defend his homeland with his cousin Arcite. As a wounded prisoner of war, however, he falls into a love triangle with his cousin and duels over Emilia. To be beheaded upon losing the duel, he is saved when Arcite is killed by a runaway horse. Palamon is less of a leader than his cousin but is nastier in provoking the duel. He has a slight cynical streak and refers to his love as a burden imposed by his patron goddess Venus. The men are not terribly different, however, and both characters are vague in delineation—the result of multiple authorship or general carelessness. The name is borrowed from the source, Chaucer's *Knyghtes Tale.* Richard Edwards (c. 1523–1566) also wrote a play called *Palamon and Arcite,* which was performed in 1566, but is no longer extant.

Palestine, Gr. 'land of the Philistines,' the district the Bible calls Canaan or Judea. During the Middle Ages it was the Christian Holy Land that the crusaders hoped to free from Muslim domination. *Jn 2.1.4. Oth 4.3.37:* an allusion to pilgrimages.

Pallas, Athena, Greek goddess of wisdom and patron of the city of Athens (Roman Minerva). 'Pallas' is a Greek word meaning 'virgin,' and Athena was a virgin goddess. Some authorities, however, suggest that the epithet derives from the name of one of the Titans. *Tit 4.1.65, 4.3.56, 65. TNK 3.5.95.*

Pandar, 1) *Tro,* see Pandarus.

2) term for a pimp: *MWW 5.5.165, Ado 5.2.30* (pl.), *WT 2.1.48, Cym.*

Pandarus, Lycian ally of the Trojans, son of Lycaon of Zeleia. He was taught archery by Apollo. He wounded Menelaus to break a truce. Diomedes killed him. Homer makes him a cruel man, the son of Lycaon (from whom we get 'lycanthropy') who killed a child and was turned into a wolf. *Tro:* Sh. makes Pandarus into a major character, his role in events of the Trojan War having already grown during the Middle Ages, when the story of Troilus' ill-fated love first surfaced. In Boccaccio's *Filostrato* (1338), he becomes friend and ally of Troilus and much more significant, but in Chaucer's *Troilus and Criseyde* (c. 1385) he becomes the go-between for the lovers and develops into the character recognizable as Sh.'s. William Caxton's *Recuyell of the Historyes of Troy* (1474). Sh.'s primary source, does not, however, involve him in the Troilus love story. By the Elizabethan era, Pandarus' name had become equivalent with procurers, as it still remains. He is an amiable degenerate in Sh. His language is just tasteless enough to make one uncomfortable; his behavior annoying.

TN 3.1.50, 'Lord P. of Phrygia.' *MWW 1.3.69,* 'Sir P. of Troy.' He is alluded to at *AWW 2.1.97.*

Pandolf, Cardinal, *Jn,* (d. 1226), Pope Innocent III's delegate to the court of King John, an Italian cardinal dispatched to England in 1211 to persuade John to accept Stephen Langton as archbishop of Canterbury. When he failed to sway the king by rational argument, Pandolf tried to intimidate him with a sentence of excommunication. In 1213 a shift in John's political plans necessitated a change in his religious policy. He sought reconciliation with the church, and Innocent sent Pandolf back to England to handle the negotiations. John swore an oath of fealty to the pope, and Pandolf presided at the ceremony that made England a fief of the Roman church. John's status as papal vassal entitled him to Innocent's protection, and Innocent stood by his man. The pope, who believed that kings were accountable only to God, was appalled in 1215 when John's barons cornered him at Runnymede and forced him to agree to limit the use of his authority. Innocent instructed the cardinal to release John from the oath he took to abide by the terms of Magna Carta, and Pandolf excommunicated the lords who had presumed to challenge the divine right of their king. After John's death, Pandolf stayed on in England, and as the representative of the new king's papal overlord, he tried to dominate the regents who governed during the minority of Henry III. His arrogant behavior earned the church few friends, and in 1221 Stephen Langton arranged for his recall.

Pannonians, *Cym 3.1.73, 3.7.3,* ancient peoples of Pannonia. The nation was south and east of the Danube, north of Dalmatia and east of Noricum. The area covers much of modern Hungary, Austria, and parts of Yugoslavia, and Italy. The original Pannonians were probably an Illyrian people, but beginning in the 4th c. BC, Pannonia was invaded by Celts. In 35 BC, the Pannonians joined a revolt by the Dalmatians against the Romans, which Augustus put down. The area was incorporated into Illyria in 9 BC. In 7 AD, the Pannonians revolted again and were subdued by Tiberius and Germanicus. The Romans made Pannonia a province on its own, but later subdivided it. Ultimately it passed into the hands of the Huns, the Ostrogoths, the Lombards, the Avars, and the Magyars.

Pansa, *Ant 1.4.58,* Caius Vibius Pansa, (d. 43 BC), friend of Julius Cæsar's and consul of the Roman Republic for the year following Cæsar's death. Cæsar's heir, Octavius, was a member of the army that Pansa and his fellow consul, Hirtius, used to lift Mark Antony's siege of Brutus' camp at Mutina. Antony retreated, but both consuls fell in battle. The man who profited most from the affair was Octavius, who, despite his youth, assumed command of Pansa's men and demanded the consular title.

Pantheon, *Tit 1.1.242, 330,* Roman temple dedicated to all the gods. It was first erected during the reign of Octavius Augustus by his friend Marcus Agrippa (whose name is inscribed on its portico). The emperor Hadrian replaced all of the building except its porch in 120 AD. The temple was consecrated as a Christian church in 609 AD, and continuous use for Christian worship ensured its preservation. It is the only major ancient building in Rome to survive intact into the modern era.

Panthino, *TGV,* F1 'Panthion,' Antonio's servant and confidant. He advises him to send his son Proteus to the Emperor's court. Later he banters some with Lance. The name may have been adapted from Pandion, a character in John Lyly's *Sapho and Phaon* (1584), in Chaucer's 'Legend of Philomela' in *The Legende of Good Women*, or in Plutarch's 'Theseus' in which Pandion is the adoptive father of Ægeus. Pandion is also mentioned in Spenser's 'Virgil's Gnat,' line 401. He was the father of Philomela and Procne and died of grief when they were changed into birds.

Paphlagonia, *Ant 3.6.71,* ancient kingdom on the shore of the Black Sea between Bithynia and Pontus. During the reign of Augustus it became a client state dependent on the Roman empire.

Paphos, town sacred to Venus on the western side of Cyprus near where the goddess was born on the sea. It was named for the son of Pygmalion and Galatea. The name is also applied to the island itself, which was sacred to Venus. *Ven 1193. Per 15.32,* 'dove of P.,' Venus' chariot was drawn by doves. *Tmp 4.1.93.*

Papist, follower of the Pope, any adherent to the Roman Catholic rites. *AWW 1.3.52,* a reference to the Roman Catholic practice of avoiding meat (eating fish) on holy days. In general, the term is a pejorative one used by Protestants, and its single use in Sh. may reflect, as some have argued, his sympathy, or lack of disdain, for Catholicism. It is interesting that Sh. is very delicate about the great religious controversies of his day, but what that delicacy means is uncertain. Some have argued that Stratford contained many Catholic sympathizers and that Sh. himself may have been sympathetic. However, the clues produced to supporting theories of Sh.'s sectarian beliefs are very slight.

Paracelsus, *AWW 2.3.11,* Philippus Aureolus P., real name Theophrastus Bombastus von Hohenheim (c. 1493–1541), Swiss physician interested in alchemical and chemical means of dealing with illness. Born in Einsiedeln, he was likely educated at the University of Vienna. He attacked the prevalent theory of the imbalance of bodily humors causing illness and believed in curing by use of mineral compounds. A cranky antagonist who also believed in magic, his precepts foreshadowed scientific medicine in his belief that illness was invasive (coming from an external source) and in distinguishing the symptoms of specific illnesses such as goiter and syphilis. He also opposed the use of purging and bleeding to balance the humors.

Paradise, *Err 4.3.17,* here, the Garden of Eden.

Parca, *H5 5.1.19,* Parcæ (pl.), the three 'fates' or goddesses who in Greek myth weave the threads of human destiny. See Fates.

Pardie, F1 'perdy,' 'perdie,' an oath, 'By God!' from Fr. *par dieu. Err 4.4.72. H5 2.1.47. TN 4.2.76. Ham 3.2.281. Lr 2.2.258 (Q 7.251).*

Paris, 1) capital of France, located on the Seine river about 250 mi. inland from the English channel. It is named from a Celtic tribe called the Parisii who had their fortified capital Lutetia there. Cæsar mentions them in his *Gallic Wars.* The city owed its location and its subsequent importance as a center of trade and communications to an island in the Seine. Thanks to the *îsle de la cité,* the Seine was easier to bridge at Paris than elsewhere. Numerous paths converged at Paris, but it did not emerge as a politically important settlement until the 12th c. Its destiny was in part determined by the fact that it was the seat of Hugh Capet (987–996), whose descendants acquired an exclusive right to the French crown after the extinction of the western branch of the Carolingian dynasty. The Capetians were far poorer than many of the families who controlled great counties and duchies within their kingdom, and it was several generations before the Capetians could exercise authority over their chief vassals. Philip II Augustus (1180–1223) lay the foundations for a system of national government administered from Paris, but for most of the medieval period France remained a loose association of virtually independent fiefdoms. It was not until the end of the Hundred Years' War and the reign of Louis XI (1461–1483) that a French nation began to coalesce about the city.

2H6 1.1.91, 215, 1.3.175. 1H6 1.1.61, 65. H5 2.4.131, 2.4.132.

Ham 2.1.7, where Lærtes has gone—then, as now, a place to go for an education. *AWW 1.2.22, 1.3.215, 229, 231, 4.3.190.*

2) Alexandros, son of Priam and Hecuba, the Trojan prince whose abduction of the Greek queen, Helen, caused the war that inspired Homer's *Iliad.* He was brother of Hector, Troilus, Deiphobus, Helenus, Cassandra, and Polyxena. In Hecuba's pregnancy, Æsacus had prophesied that Paris would cause the downfall of Troy, but when he was exposed (like many mythic heroes) upon Mt. Ida, he was suckled by a bear for five days, then rescued by Æsacus' herdsman Agelaus who raised him as his own. In his maturity, he was compelled to make an impossible choice: the Judgment of Paris. While he was guarding flocks in the countryside, the goddesses Hera, Athena, and Aphrodite appeared before him to demand that he declare one of them more lovely than the others. Each offered a bribe: power, fame, or beauty. Paris decided in favor of Aphrodite, who promised him the most handsome mate in the world. This, unfortunately, turned out to be a married woman: Helen, wife of Menelaus of Sparta. When Paris abandoned his wife Œnone and abducted Helen, the Greeks declared war on Troy to avenge the wrong done to Menelaus. The spurned deities, Hera and Athena, sided with the Greeks in a ten year struggle that culminated in Troy's destruction. Paris plays a minor role in the military actions and the discussions whose descriptions constitute most of the *Iliad.* For Homer, he was a greater lover than soldier. He did, however, fight Menelaus after initially running in fear from him. During the war he challenged Menelaus to single combat to settle the conflict, but when the wronged husband gained the upper hand, Aphrodite helped him escape. The truce was broken, and the war continued. Later, when Achilles was charmed by Polyxena and went to the temple of Apollo to negotiate a marriage and an end to the war, Paris killed the hero with a poisoned arrow, which struck his only vulnerable spot, his heel. Later, Philoctetes wounded Paris with the arrows of Hercules. Paris returned to Œnone to be healed, but she rejected him and he went back to Troy and died. She regretted her rejection and hanged herself.

Shr 1.2.247. 1H6 5.7.104. Luc 1473.

Tro: 'Prince P.,' 'Lord P.,' *pro.10,* 'wanton P.': Sh.'s Paris is a decadent courtier, more interested in his sensual pleasures than in the war he has caused. He comments on other warriors on the battlefield at one point, but says to Pandarus that Helen preferred he stay with her. Paris is just another example of what is wrong in Sh.'s Trojan world. In William Caxton's *Recuyell of the Historyes of Troy* (1474),

Sh.'s primary source for *Tro,* Paris is killed by Ajax.

3) *Rom,* count, would-be husband of Juliet, a 'man of wax,' who has the misfortune to be betrothed to the wrong woman—for which error he is later killed by Romeo. The name is used in Arthur Brooke's *Tragicall Historye of Romeus and Juliet* (1562), Sh.'s source, and in Pierre Boaistuau's French adaptation of 1559, but an earlier version, Luigi da Porto's *Istoria novellamente ritrovata di due Nobili Amanti* (c. 1530) calls the corresponding character the Count of Lodrone. The mythological suggestion of 'Paris' fits nicely with his described attractiveness. Brooke interestingly makes allusion to the mythological seducer early in his poem when he says that Romeus saw a maid 'which Theseus, or Paris would have chosen to their rape,' a definitely unfavorable comparison for Romeus. Later, Juliet compares herself to 'the famous Grecian rape,' Helen of Troy, as she apologizes to her mother for resisting the arranged marriage with the county Paris. Sh. also follows Brooke in calling him both an 'earl' and a 'count.'

Paris Garden, *H8 5.3.2,* wooded area west of Southwark opposite London's Blackfriars and Baynard's Castle. During Henry VIII's reign it boasted an amphitheater where bear-baitings and other crude entertainments were staged.

Park, the, *MWW 1.4.105, 5.1.10, 5.3.4,* royal hunting preserve at Windsor, also known as Great Park. William the Conqueror originally moved his residence to there because of the hunting. *3.1.5,* 'the P. Ward,' F1 'Parke-ward,' in the direction of the Great Park.

Parliament, governing body of England. In Sh.'s day it exercised less power than it does now. The word 'parliament' evolved from a French term for 'colloquium' or 'conference.' (Since England's Norman ruling class spoke French, French expressions are common in English law.) Political assemblies of one kind or another were a fact of life in England from the start of the Middle Ages. The Anglo-Saxons who conquered Britain in the 6th c. held *folkmoots,* convocations of the free men who had the right to bear arms. Saxon kings were advised by aristocratic councils called *witans.* When the Normans brought continental feudalism to England in the 11th c., these older native institutions were confirmed by customs that were evolving with the new feudal order. Feudal monarchs kept their vassals mindful of oaths of obedience by regularly summoning them to court for consultation. A typical feudal council was composed of lay and clerical lords. In the early Middle Ages these people were the only ones who mattered to the government, for they controlled the land that was the primary source of wealth and provided most of the king's soldiers, but by the 13th c., when parliaments first began to be mentioned in English documents, the feudal aristocracy's monopoly of power had been challenged by a new urban middle class. Trade and industry provided non-agrarian sources of wealth that kings could not afford to ignore. Kings, therefore, summoned commoners (representatives from towns and rural administrative districts called shires) to their council meetings. Early parliaments were simply royal councils with expanded membership.

The first national assembly to bring the upper and middle classes (i.e., 'the lords' and 'the commons') together was called not by a king, but by a rebel. In 1265 Simon de Montfort captured King Henry III. Simon rallied national support for his highly irregular government by inviting men from the towns and shires to meet with him and the feudal barons. Henry's son, Edward I, restored royal authority, but he saw practical advantages in convening parliaments like the one Simon had invented and continued to call them. Edward had no reason to fear parliaments, for the early medieval assemblies were no threat to the power of the king. They met only at his pleasure, and they had no legislative authority. Their function was to respond to royal requests for grants of money—requests that medieval people considered extraordinary, for feudal kings were expected to meet the costs of government from the income of their estates. The monarch's private fortune was adequate when his nation was at peace, but it rarely stretched to the funding of wars. If kings got into financial difficulty, they had no choice but to turn to their propertied subjects for help. Since their subjects' well-being was linked to victory over the nation's enemies, the king could make a strong case for assistance. The men summoned to parliament found it an expensive honor, but they also sensed an advantage to themselves in the situation. If they stuck together, they could refuse to consent to the king's demand for levies of taxes until the king promised to make changes they wanted in the personnel or the policies of his government. Parliament's power over taxation was the instrument that won it a recognized place in English political tradition.

The Hundred Years' War hastened the evolution of parliament by creating fiscal emergencies that forced kings to summon parliaments on a regular basis. At the conclusion of the war the pace of parliament's development slowed. Sh. lived at a time when the Tudor and Stuart kings and queens enjoyed quasi-autocratic authority. During their reigns parliaments met infrequently and struggled hard to resist royal intimidation. A few decades after Sh.'s death in 1616 tension between the throne and parliament erupted in a civil war that abolished the monarchy and established a republic (1649–1660) in England. The experiment failed, but it taught the kings who were ultimately restored to England's throne to respect the parliamentary tradition. During the 18th c. parliament took the lead in governing England, and England's monarchs evolved into the figureheads they are today.

2H6 4.7.14, 5.5.30. 3H6, passim. 1.1.39: the 'bloody parliament' is a name Sh. proposes for the parliament of 1460 at which York put forth a claim to Henry VI's throne; York made separate bids for power in 1455 and 1460, but Sh. treats both as parts of one attempted coup.

1H6 2.5.127, 3.5.20. R2 5.2.44. MWW 2.1.27. 2H4 5.2.133.

Paroles, F1 'Parolles,' 'Monsieur P.,' 'Captain P.,' braggart soldier in the tradition of the *miles gloriosus* of Roman comedy. A bad influence on Bertram, he encourages Bertram's flight to Italy and the attempted seduction of Diana. Although everyone else seems to know what a dubious character he is, Bertram is blind to his faults and the relationship is reminiscent of that between Falstaff—another cowardly soldier—and Prince Hal. Paroles seems to have been an invention of Sh., as his equivalent does not appear in the sources. His name means 'words' in French, reflecting that he is not at all a man of deeds.

Parson, Master, *TN 4.2.12, 16, 28,* term of address for Sir Topas the Curate (Feste in disguise).

Parthia, territory south of the mountains that form the lower edge of the basin of the Caspian Sea. The Parthian people were related to the ancient Scythians and shared their fame as horse soldiers. After the death of Alexander the Great, a Parthian empire arose from the ruins of the old Persian empire. By the end of the 2nd c. BC the Parthians had claimed all the territory between the Euphrates and the Indus rivers and had become worthy rivals for Rome.

JC 5.3.36. Ant 2.2.15, 2.3.30, 39, 3.1.1, 33, 3.6.14.

Parthian, 1) inhabitant of Parthia. *Ant 3.1.7,* pl. *Cym 1.6.20,* the Parthians were reputed to be masters of feigning flight and raining arrows back upon the closed ranks of their pursuers, thereby effecting victory from what appeared defeat. They struck quickly from horseback, then withdrew in the manner of light cavalry. Their defeat of Crassus in 53 BC opened the way for the war between Cæsar and Pompey.

2) (adj.) of or pertaining to Parthia. *Ant 1.2.94, 3.1.6, 4.14.70. TNK 2.2.50,* 'like a P. quiver.'

Partlet, Dame, (Fr. *Partelote*) traditional name for a hen from the stories of Reynard the Fox. It is used by Chaucer in the *Nonnes Preestes Tale. WT 2.3.76,* Leontes is accusing Antigonus of being 'hen-pecked.' *1H4 3.3.51:*

though Falstaff is probably referring to the Hostess' henlike agitation or scolding, it has been suggested that this is a quibble based upon a covering for neck and throat also called a 'partlet.'

Patay, Battle of, *1H6 4.1.19,* major defeat for the English in the Hundred Years' War. The death of King Henry V in 1422 had slowed, but not halted, England's conquests of France. The English army continued to advance into territory held by the Armagnac defenders of France until May 1429, when Joan of Arc forced the English to give up the seige of Orléans. The English army fell back and waited for John Fastolf and John Talbot to bring reinforcements from Paris. On 18 June 1429, the French surprised Fastolf and Talbot at Patay, a French village about 15 mi. northwest of Orléans. Talbot was captured, and Fastolf escaped with a remnant of his company. The losses forced the English to retreat and made it possible for the Dauphin to occupy the city of Rheims and to be crowned king of France in its cathedral. This proved to be the last turning point of the war.

Patchbreech, *Per 5.52,* nickname for a fisherman that makes fun of his clothes.

Patience, 1) *H5 2.1.22,* personification of a human virtue. Sh.'s reference is to a proverb: 'Patience is a good nag, but she will buck.'

2) *H8 4.2.166,* Spanish noblewoman, Maria de Salinas, who accompanied Katherine of Aragon to England. She married Lord Willoughby de Eresby, but remained with Katherine after Katherine was dismissed from Henry VIII's court. She was at the queen's side when Katherine died.

Patrick, Friar, *TGV 4.3.43, 5.1.205, 5.2.40,* confessor of Silvia. She intends to meet Eglamour at his cell to make her escape. Though he never appears on stage, the mention of him suggests the collusion with Friar Lawrence in *Rom,* and the influence of Arthur Brooke's *Tragicall Historye of Romeus and Juliet* (1562).

Patrick, St. *Ham 1.5.140,* (c. 389–461), patron saint of Ireland. Most of his life is obscure. He was born at Bennavem, which was probably in Wales, to a Roman official named Calpurnius. His birth name was Succat. The Picts captured him and sold him into slavery in Ireland, but he escaped to Gaul. He studied at the monastery at Lérins on the Mediterranean, returned to Britain, then felt his call to convert the heathen. He prepared by studying for 14 years at Auxerre. He began his conversion of the Irish in 432, landing at Wicklow. There were already a few Christian communities in Ireland, but some had fallen into heresy. He first preached to the people of Ulster and built many churches, including the cathedral at Armagh. He may have travelled to Rome in 441 to gather relics. He retired several years before his death and is said to have been buried at Downpatrick. A few writings survive which are attributed to him, including the Confession, the Letter to Coroticus, and a strange hymn known as the Lorica of St. Patrick. The most famous legend about him is that he cleared Ireland of its snakes. His symbols include the shamrock leaf and St. Patrick's cross, a red 'X' on a white background. The latter is part of the Union Jack.

Patroclus, Greek warrior, son of Menœtius. He killed a man in a gambling dispute and was protected by Peleus, father of Achilles. In the *Iliad,* when Achilles refuses to fight, Patroclus borrows his armor to prevent a Greek defeat and momentarily routs the Trojan forces. Hector, however, cuts him down, provoking Achilles to return and avenge his friend's death with particular brutality to Hector's corpse. *Tro:* Patroclus negotiates between the Greek leaders and his friend, mocking the mannerisms of the leaders. He is not otherwise a much developed character, despite his pivotal role in the plot. Thersites calls him a 'masculine whore' (*5.1.17*), touching on the long established legend that Patroclus and Achilles were lovers, which would explain Achilles' extreme reaction to his friend's death. William Caxton's *Recuyell of the Histroyes of Troy* (1474), Sh.'s primary source for *Tro,* says that he was a 'moche noble duc and ryche and louyd so moche Achylles that they were bothe of one Allyance,' but the love is not explicitly sexual.

Paul, St., *R3 1.2.36, 41, 3.4.76; 5.5.170,* 'Apostle Paul,' (c. 10–68 AD), early Christian missionary and author of the most important of the New Testament's epistles. Paul, whose Hebrew name was Saul, was a Jew of the diaspora. He came from Tarsus, a town in Cilicia in southeastern Asia Minor. Nothing is known about his background but the fact that he was a student of Pharisaic Judaism. The Pharisees emphasized the study of scripture, the maintenance of ritual purity, and the scrupulous keeping of the laws of the Torah. He was about twenty when he came to Jerusalem to study with Gamaliel, the most famous rabbi of his day. Jesus had recently been crucified, and the first Christians were proclaiming their faith in his divinity. In Paul's opinion Christians blasphemed the Hebrew God by claiming that a man had shared God's transcendent nature, and he felt compelled to defend Judaism by exposing Christians and encouraging their prosecution. The Book of Acts says that he witnessed the execution of St. Stephen, the first Christian martyr, and that when Christians fled Jerusalem after Stephen's death, he pursued them.

Paul was on his way to Damascus to stir up trouble for its church when he was miraculously converted to the faith that previously had repelled him. A burst of light struck him temporarily blind, and he heard the voice of the resurrected Christ. The experience convinced him that, although he had never met the historical Jesus, Jesus had chosen him to rank with the apostles and to commit his life to spreading the Christian message. In particular, he devoted himself to the conversion of gentiles. His success was not pleasing to some of Jesus' companions who thought of their Christian faith as the continuation of the Judaism they had always practiced. Splits developed within churches when Christians from Jewish backgrounds insisted that gentile converts accept the full burden of the Hebrew law. Paul concluded that the law was a needless impediment to the Christian mission, and wrote letters expressing his conviction that Christ had fulfilled the law and inaugurated an era of grace. His letters, which predate the composition of the Gospels, are the earliest extant articulations of a Christian theology. They circulated beyond the churches to which they were originally addressed and acquired the authority of scripture. Internal evidence suggests that some of the 'Pauline' letters in the New Testament are anonymous works that have been erroneously ascribed, but the obviously authentic epistles are among the most important works of Christian literature. Apart from Jesus himself no one has had more influence on the development of the Christian faith than Paul.

Paul's, St. Paul's cathedral, seat of the bishop of London. It is situated in London's west end not far from Baynard Castle. The first building on the site was erected about 610 by missionaries to the pagan Saxons. The present church is the work of the famous English architect, Christopher Wren (1632–1723). The building Sh. knew was a Gothic structure that was completed about 1283 and destroyed by the great fire that devastated London in 1666. Like other medieval cathedrals, Paul's was both a house of worship and a community center where business of all kinds was conducted. The outdoor pulpit on its northeastern wall was a rallying point for large public meetings that were sometimes more political than religious. At various times during the Wars of the Roses sermons were preached from St. Paul's to solicit popular support for one or the other parties to the conflict.

R3 1.2.30, 3.6.3. 1H4 2.5.532. 2H4 1.2.51. H8 5.3.15.

Paulina, *WT,* wife of Antigonus who engineers Leontes' reunion with Hermione. She is courageous, loyal, wise, and caring, and her opposition to her monarch's foolishness is reminiscent of Kent's in *King Lear.* She has no equivalent in Sh.'s source, Robert Greene's *Pandosto, or the Triumph of Time* (1588; rptd. 1607 as *Dorastus and Fawnia*), although she has some correspondences with the jailer. Suggestive is Plutarch's life of Æmilius Paulus, which, with a little tinkering would provide the names of two female characters in the play. The name Paulinus also appears in Plutarch.

Paunch, John, *1H4 2.2.64,* see Oldcastle, John.

Peace, lady, *2H4 1.2.208,* personification of concord, the opposite of war.

Peascod, Master, *MND 3.1.179,* Bottom's joking name for Peaseblossom's father, 'the ripe pea pod.' Compare *TN 1.5.152.*

Peaseblossom, *MND,* fairy, likely played by a child. To increase the humor, Bottom addresses the fairy deferentially as Master P., Cavaliery P., and gets him to scratch his jackass head. The name comes from the flower of a pea plant. See Cobweb.

Pedascule, *Shr 3.1.48,* vocative for Latin *pedasculus,* 'little pedant,' a term of address coined by Hortensio for Lucentio in the disguise of a Latin teacher.

Pedro of Aragon, Don, *Ado,* 'Don P.,' 'the Prince,' 'Don Peter,' ruler of Sicily, brother of John. Pedro has just defeated a revolt against his rule by his brother and in the flush of victory amuses himself by playing Cupid with his followers Claudio and Benedick. The kindly ruler seems oblivious to the danger posed by John and seems to have forgiven the treason of his brother. Like the Duke of Vienna in *MM,* Pedro seems to enjoy manipulating his followers (though more frivolously), but unlike the Duke and most of the princes in Sh.'s comedies, however, Pedro is conspicuously wifeless at play's end. Benedick remarks on his serious expression and with a risqué joke urges him to get a wife, which is reminiscent of the urgings in the Sonnets. Sh. borrowed the name from his primary source, Matteo Bandello's *Novelle* (1554; there are many contemporary versions of the plot). The historical Pedro III of Aragon (1236–1286) was the son of James the Conqueror. After marrying Constance daughter of Manfred, king of Sicily, he became primary claimant to the Hohenstaufen thrones in Naples and Sicily in opposition to Charles I, king of the Two Sicilies and duke of Anjou, who had been granted Sicily by the Pope in his power struggle with Manfred. Charles's claims began a struggle of twenty-one years between the Angevins and the Aragonese in southern Italy. After the notorious 'Sicilian Vespers' of 1282, when the Sicilians rose against the French and butchered not only all the French they could locate, but even women pregnant by Frenchmen, Pedro seized control of the island. He held court first in Palermo, but after destroying Charles' fleet in a bloody battle, he moved to Messina, according to Bandello, to be closer to the Italian peninsula and the other half of his kingdom. Charles died shortly after his devastating defeat. Pedro also defeated an invasion of Catalonia by the king of France in support of Charles. Because of his conquest of Sicily, Pedro was known as Peter the Great in England.

Pegasus, 1) in ancient mythology a winged horse that (like his brother Chrysaor) rose from the blood of the Medusa after Perseus beheaded her. It was captured and tamed by Minerva, then given to the Muses on their mountain Helicon. There it kicked open the fountain of inspiration, Hippocrene. Minerva loaned the golden bridle of the horse to Bellerophon in order to do battle with the Chimera. After several successful conquests Bellerophon in his vanity attempted to fly to Olympus to join the gods. Jupiter sent a fly to sting Pegasus, which threw Bellerophon, leaving him crippled and blind. Because the winged horse was the Muses' it was said in ancient times that poets rode the Pegasus when inspired.

1H4 4.1.110. H5 3.7.14.

2) *Shr 4.4.5,* an inn, in the custom of the time having a sign with a winged horse. There was evidently a Pegasus in Cheapside, though not necessarily in Genoa. Sh.'s foreign lands often resemble his England.

Peg-o'-Ramsey, *TN 2.3.73,* mocking comparison to Malvolio. The insult is, however, lost, as we do not know who this person was. Ramsey was a town in Huntingdonshire. In the context, Toby is likely alluding to a song, and there are at least two songs of that time with the title, one of them risqué. How they might apply is mysterious, unless it is merely Toby's drunken musings.

Pelion, mountain in Thessaly about 5340 ft. high. It was the home of the Centaurs, and its wooded slopes provided the lumber for Jason's ship, the Argo. In mythology the Aloadæ, gigantic sons of Neptune, attempted to storm heaven by piling Ossa and Pelion on Olympus. Jupiter killed them with lightning, or, alternatively, imprisoned them beneath it. The story is told in Ovid's *Metamorphoses,* 1.151–162, and is mentioned in Virgil's *Georgics,* 1.281.

MWW 2.1.77, Mistress Page compares Falstaff's size to the mountain and alludes to the imprisonment of the giants (though there were no giantesses). *Ham 5.1.249.*

Peloponnesus, *Ant 3.10.30,* (Gr. 'Pelops' island'), the half of Greece that lies south of the Isthmus of Corinth. Greek legend claims that it was named for Pelops (q.v.).

Pelops, king of Lydia, son of Tantalus and Dione. Murdered by his father, he was cooked into a meal for the gods. Before the hideous crime was discovered, Demeter had bitten off a chunk of his shoulder. He was restored to life and his father sentenced to a torturous eternal punishment. *TNK 4.2.21,* 'Smoother than Pelops' shoulder!': his shoulder was repaired with shaped ivory and he was given a chariot with immortal, winged horses. The story is mentioned in Ovid's *Metamorphoses,* 6.

Pembroke, *R3, 4.5.7,* county seat of Pembrokeshire, most western county in south Wales. Its castle commands the fjord known as Milford Haven. Lying on a peninsula, Pembroke gets its name from the Welsh *pen* 'end' and *bro* 'land.' Henry VII was born at Pembroke, and it was via Milford Haven that he returned to England in 1485 to wrest the crown from Richard III at the battle of Bosworth Field.

Pembroke, Earl of, 1) *3H6,* William Herbert (d. 1469), soldier in the service of the house of York. He was a member of Edward IV's privy council, and his title was a reward for his success in taking Harlech Castle, the last Lancastrian fortress left in England in 1468. At Harlech he captured the young earl of Richmond (the future Tudor king, Henry VII) and became his guardian. He disliked Edward's patron, the earl of Warwick, and encouraged Edward to distance himself from the 'Kingmaker.' Warwick, however, had the last word. In 1469 Pembroke was captured and executed when he led an expedition to put down a rebellion Warwick had raised in northern England.

2) *R3 4.5.11, 5.4.5,* Jasper Tudor (1431–1495), second son of Owen Tudor by Henry V's widowed queen, Catherine of France. In 1453 Henry VI recognized Jasper as a legitimate half-brother and created him earl of Pembroke. Since Jasper was a prominent and belligerent Lancastrian, he fled England when the Yorkist leader, Edward IV, triumphed over Henry VI. He remained in exile until 1470, when he joined the army that the earl of Warwick recruited to force Edward IV from the throne. The Lancastrian resurgence was short lived, but it enabled him to regain control of his orphaned nephew, the earl of Richmond, the future Henry VII. When Edward IV returned to power in 1471, Pembroke carried Richmond to safety in Brittany. He and his nephew bided their time until 1485, when a split in the Yorkist party gave them a chance to wrest the crown from Richard III at the battle of Bosworth Field. Pembroke's popularity in Wales helped Richmond attract the soldiers he needed to win the throne, and the new king was generously grateful to the uncle to whom he owed so much. He was granted the duchy of Bedford, and he spent the remainder of his life in the field defending the interests of the Tudor dynasty.

3) *Jn,* William le Marshal (d. 1219), warrior and statesman who served four English

kings: Henry II, Richard the Lionhearted, John, and Henry III. William began his career under the tutelage of his mother's brother, Patrick, earl of Salisbury. Henry II appointed him to the household of his son Henry, the heir apparent. Although William took part in a rebellion organized by the prince, Henry bore him no grudge. After the prince's death in 1183, William enlisted as a crusader and made a pilgrimage to the Holy Lands. He returned to Europe in 1188 and entered Henry II's service. Henry gave him the hand of the wealthy heiress to the earldom of Pembroke. When Richard the Lionhearted became king and departed on the third crusade, he appointed the new earl to the council of regents charged with running the Angevin empire. Pembroke sided with Richard's brother, John, and helped him overthrow William Longchamp, a regent whose autocratic behavior offended the English barons. Pembroke was, however, loyal to Richard and did his best to block John's attempts to undercut Richard. Richard made him 'earl marshal' of England and custodian of the royal treasury. At Richard's death, the Marshal oversaw the transition from Richard's to John's administrations. William le Marshal did not always agree with John's policies, but he was scrupulously loyal to the throne John occupied. He stood by John in 1215 when the English barons rebelled against him, and John named him regent for his young heir, Henry III. The aged warrior died of natural causes early in Henry III's reign.

Pembroke, Marchioness of, *H8 2.3.63, 95, 3.2.91,* title that Henry VIII granted to Anne Boleyn in 1532, when she began to live with him. The honor of Pembroke had been held by ancestors of the Tudor dynasty, and Henry may have hoped that it would bestow an aura of royal dignity on the woman whom he hoped to make his wife and queen.

Pendragon, *1H6 3.5.54,* Utherpendragon, legendary king of Britain who sired its famous King Arthur. According to Geoffrey of Monmouth's fanciful 12th c. *Historia Regum Britanniæ,* Uther was the third son of Constantine II, a prince of Brittany who was summoned to England to be its king when the Romans withdrew their armies. Uther became king after the assassinations of his father and brothers. He avenged them and then proceeded, with the help of the sorcerer Merlin, to build Stonehenge and to defend England from Saxon invaders. He adopted the name Pendragon when an omen in the form of a dragon-shaped meteor foreshadowed his coronation. He became infatuated with Ygerna, wife of Gorlois, duke of Cornwall. He persuaded Merlin to bestow Gorlois' likeness on him so that he could seduce the virtuous Ygerna. He then conquered Cornwall, married Ygerna, and begot Arthur.

Penelope, *Cor 1.3.84,* wife of Ulysses and queen of Ithaca, classical mythology's paradigm for marital fidelity. She remained in Ithaca when Ulysses sailed away to fight the Trojan war. During the twenty years that it took him to find his way home she remained scrupulously faithful to him. Although almost everyone gave him up for dead and many men gathered to sue for her hand, she resisted pressure to remarry. She devised a peculiar strategy to stall for time. She claimed that she could not choose a new husband until she finished work on a robe she was weaving. She worked diligently at her task each day, and at night she secretly unravelled her work to delay its completion. Just as the suitors' patience neared an end, Ulysses appeared to reclaim his kingdom and his wife. The story is told in Homer's *Odyssey* and repeated elsewhere.

Pentapolis, *Per,* kingdom of Simonides, probably Bengazi. The name means five cities and was applied to a region dominated by five Greek colonies (Apollonia, Arsinoë, Berenice, Cyrene, and Ptolemais) in what is modern eastern Libya. Cyrene was the first of the five towns from which the district Cyrenaica (as it was called from the 4th c. BC to the 7th c. AD) eventually took its name and was the main Hellenic colony in Africa. It was founded in 631 BC by Battus and colonists from Thera. After seven kings a republic was established about 450. It fell under the control of Egypt when Berenice married Ptolemy III in the 3rd c. It became a Roman province in 74 BC and declined after the Emperor Trajan severely punished the city for its Jewish uprisings. In the decline of Rome it went over to local control. The Arabs seized it in 641 AD. Another Pentapolis was a group of five cities on the Adriatic coast of Italy (Rimini, Ancona, Fano, Pesaro, and Senigallia) which were outposts of Byzantine culture from the 5th c. AD to the 11th. Yet another Pentapolis (named for the five cities of Mytilene, Methymna, Antissa, Eresus, and Pyrrha) was the island of Lesbos. The Phrygian Pentapolis consisted of Eucarpia, Hieropolis, Otrous, Stectorium, and Bruzus. In *Per* neither Italy nor Phrygia is out of the question; however, because of Lysimachus, Ptolemy, and Cyrene appearing in Plutarch's Demetrius, it is likely Sh. was thinking of Cyrenaica. Berenice is mentioned in Plutarch's Pyrrhus. It is more likely Pericles fleeing Tarsus would shipwreck in Africa. The Lesbian Pentapolis does not fit, however, because Mytilene is a different kingdom from Simonides.' Pentapolis is also the name of the setting of the story in John Gower's *Confessio Amantis* (1390) and Lawrence Twine's *Patterne of Painefull Adventures* (1594), though the king's name is different.

Pentecost, seventh Sunday after Easter, set aside to celebrate the descent of the Holy Ghost upon the apostles (Acts 2:1–4.), also called Whitsunday. The word comes from the Greek for 'fiftieth day,' referring to the 50 days since the resurrection. It descends from a Jewish harvest festival, Shavuot, held 50 days after the second day of Passover in accordance with Leviticus 23: 15–16. *TGV 4.4.155,* the time of year when the miracle cycles were acted at Chester and some other places. *Err 4.1.1. Rom 1.5.36.* See Whitsun.

Penthesilea, *TN 2.3.171,* queen of the Amazons, daughter of Ares and Otrera. She brought her mighty female warriors to fight as Troy's ally. Achilles struck her dead and was so moved by her young and beautiful body that he wept. Thersites mocked Achilles at this moment and the great Myrmidon killed him with a single blow. According to Pausanias (5.11), Achilles mourning over her body was the subject of one of the art works in the temples at Olympia, as well as Hercules battling the Amazons (5.10). Virgil's *Æneid* 1.490–495 briefly mentions her. She is also mentioned in Spenser's *Færie Queene* 3.4.2.5. She does not appear in Homer.

Pépin, name of several men who contributed to the rise and prosperity of the Carolingian dynasty. There might be some confusion as to which is being referred to, but the most likely possibilities follow. 'King Pippin' was also apparently slang for 'penis' and would add much comedy to some of the lines. *LLL 4.1.119,* 'King P. of France': the name is invoked as an equivalent of ancient times (or as a penis joke). *H5 1.2.65, 87. AWW 2.1.75,* F1 'Pippin': another possible dirty joke. In 751 Pépin II's grandson, Pépin III, 'the Short' (c. 714–768) father of Charlemagne and Carloman, obtained papal permission to depose the Merovingian ruler Childéric and to assume the royal title. *H8 1.3.10:* Pépin I, 'the Elder,' 'of Landen' (d. 639?) was an advisor to the Merovingian king, Clotaire II (d. 628) and exercised near-monarchical power. His grandson Pépin II 'of Heristal' (d. 714) was only a royal official, but the increasing impotency of the Merovingian dynasty allowed him to exercise monarchical authority over their 'kingdom of the Franks.' He was father of Charles Martel.

Percy, 1) family of English knights descended from William de Percy (1030–1096), one of William the Conqueror's warriors. The male line of the house died out in 1175, but the husband of its heiress, Agnes de Percy, assumed her family name and founded a second Percy dynasty. It was to this lineage that the characters in Sh.'s plays belong. The original Percy estates were in Yorkshire, but territories acquired by Henry de Percy (1273–1314) made the family the largest landowner in Northumberland. The need to defend the properties they possessed along the volatile border between England and Scotland forced the Percies to maintain a large military establishment and invest a great deal of time in border warfare. The soldiers at their command also made them a force to be reckoned with in England's domestic politics. The Percies helped Henry (IV) Bolingbroke of Lancaster overthrow King Richard II. In 1403 they quarreled with Henry, and championed the right to the throne of young Edmund Mortimer, earl of March. Although Henry IV suffered several Percy rebellions, the Percies loyally supported his popular son, Henry V, and kept to the Lancastrian side during the War of the Roses. In addition to their involvement in national politics, the Percies had a private quarrel with the Neville family that complicated the royal government's attempts to maintain peace in England. *1H6 2.5.67. 1H4 1.1.88.*

2) *2H4 1.1.75, 93, 110, 2.3.12,* see Hotspur.

3) *2H4,* see Northumberland, Earl of.

Percy, Harry, *R2,* see Hotspur.

Percy, Henry, *1H4,* see Hotspur.

Percy, Lady, *1H4,* Elizabeth [called 'Eleanor' by Holinshed (3.521), and 'Kate' by Sh.], daughter of Edmund Mortimer, third earl of March, and wife of Henry Percy, 'Hotspur.' When her brother, Edmund Mortimer, was captured by the Welsh nationalist Owain Glyndŵr in 1402, the Percies tried to arrange his ransom. The event became the turning point in their relationship with their king, Henry IV. Henry feared the Mortimers, who had a strong claim to the English throne, and he refused to negotiate Edmund's release. This angered the Percies, who had helped Henry win the crown from Richard II. They allied themselves with Glyndŵr, who liberated Mortimer and joined them in a conspiracy to overthrow Henry. Henry attacked before his opponents could marshal their forces, and Hotspur was killed at the battle of Shrewsbury on 21 July 1403. Henry IV confiscated the Percy estates, but in 1414 Henry V restored the earldom of Northumberland to the only son Elizabeth bore Hotspur.

Perdita, *WT,* daughter of Leontes and Hermione, lost to him for many years, and reared as the child of the old shepherd. The name means 'she who was lost' (from L. *perdo*). Perhaps also it implies the word 'perdition' as Leontes must go through a great suffering before he can get her and her mother back. The child who is abandoned to die and later returns to claim its birthright is one of the major elements of various mythological tales, including that of Oedipus. In Sh.'s source Robert Greene's *Pandosto, or the Triumph of Time,* (1588; rptd. 1607 as *Dorastus and Fawnia*), her equivalent is Fawnia, whose name makes obvious allusion to the Roman goddess Fauna, and her reputed father is given the name Porrus, which Sh. drops, and Porrus is given a shrewish wife, Mopsa, whose character is dropped but whose name is given to a shepherdess.

Pericles, *Per,* prince of Tyre. The story of his long suffering is very ancient. As a folk tale it survived among Greek shepherds until this century, was transmitted through the works of Apollonius of Tyre, and in Greek manuscripts of the Middle Ages into Sh.'s time. By the 6th c., Latin versions existed. The story is told in the *Gesta Romanorum* (compiled late 13th to early 14th c., first printed in England about 1510 by Wynken de Worde) and versions of the story appeared in Italy, the Netherlands, Germany, France, and Spain. There is an Anglo-Saxon fragment (11th c.) with the story, and Chaucer refers to it. In the early versions, Pericles is called Apollonius of Tyre (Appolinus in Gower). Direct sources for the play include John Gower's *Confessio Amantis* and Lawrence Twine's *Patterne of Painefull Adventures* (1594). At what point Apollonius of Tyre became Pericles is not clear either, but it has been suggested that the name change is related to the words 'perils' (L. *pericula* or *pericla*) for what he suffered. A French ms., *Du noble roy apolonie,* has the hero say his name has been 'perillie' for two years, though he is called Apollonius in the rest of the text. For Sh. the name may have been a recent borrowing from Sir Philip Sidney's *Countess of Pembroke's Arcadia* (1590). The hero Pyrocles goes through adventures which bear comparison to, but not direct correspondence to Pericles'. *The Painfull Adventures of Pericles, Prince of Tyre* (1608) by George Wilkins is either a source for the play, a revision of it, or a preliminary prose version. All of the names in Wilkins (who may have been Sh.'s co-author) are the same as in *Per* (except for Boult, who is not named), but most of these are also in Gower and Twine. The suggestion that the name comes from Plutarch's Pericles, a model of perseverance, seems less persuasive in the presence of all the other evidence, but there are correspondences with other Greek names in Plutarch and some other similarities.

Périgord, Lord, *LLL 2.1.41,* someone whose wedding Maria attended. Périgord was one of the old provinces of east/central France. Its capital and ducal seat was Périgueux. The area is now predominantly encompassed by the department of Dordogne. It had its own dukes from the 8th c. and was allied with Aquitaine. For a long time the duke was also a vassal of the king of England. It was a Protestant stronghold in the 16th c.

Perigouna, *MND 2.1.78,* Perigone or Perigenia, daughter of Sinnis whom Theseus killed. She bore Theseus the son Melanippus, but was later handed over to Deioneus. Either she or her son was founder of a cult that worshipped the asparagus. Theseus' love life is recounted in Plutarch.

Perk, Gilbert, *H8 1.1.219,* priest who Holinshed (3.863) says was chancellor of the duke of Buckingham's household. When Henry charged Buckingham with treason, Perk was among the ducal officials taken into custody and questioned. There is debate about his name. The spelling 'Pecke,' which appears in some editions, may be a misreading for 'Perk.' Both may be corruptions of the title 'clerk,' for contemporary documents identify the duke's chancellor as a certain Robert Gilbert, 'clerk.'

Perks, Clement, *2H4 5.1.33,* character who brings a case to be tried by Justice Shallow. There may have been a family with the name Perkis (Purchase) at Stinchcombe Hill in Gloucestershire in Sh.'s day, but there is no reason to believe that Sh. had one of its members in mind when he wrote *2H4.*

Perseus, Greek hero who rode Pegasus on his adventures. He was son of Zeus by Danaë, a mortal. His name means 'from Zeus.' It had been prophesied he would kill his grandfather Acrisius, so he was set adrift in a wooden chest. Later he accidentally killed Acrisius with a discus. His most famous exploit was killing the Medusa in order to steal Atlas' gold. He rescued Andromeda from a monster she was being sacrificed to. The story is told, among other places, in Ovid's *Metamorphoses,* 4.604–5.249.

H5 3.7.21, 'beast for P.,' Pegasus (q.v.) *Tro 1.3.41,* 'P.'s horse,' Pegasus. *4.7.70.*

Persia, *Err 4.1.4,* modern Iran, Asian country bounded on the north by the Caspian Sea, the Caucasus, and Turkestan, on the east by Afghanistan and Pakistan, on the south by the Indian Ocean and Persian Gulf, and on the west by Iraq and Turkey. The territories of ancient Persia varied quite a bit and were the subject of many wars in S.'s lifetime involving the Turks, Uzbeks, and others. Persia's history was long and complex, and would have been known in England through the stories of the Persian Wars and other writings of Greek and Roman times. The reputation of the Persians would have been that of a great, wealthy, and warlike nation. The conflicts between Persians and Ottomans in Sh.'s time were largely based upon the Shi'ite-Sunni religious antipathies, and there were many in Europe who were grateful that the Persians distracted the Turks from their ambitions in Christendom. See Persian.

Persian, (adj.) of or pertaining to Persia. *MV 2.1.26,* 'P. prince,' someone slain by the Prince of Morocco, or so he says. Whether the next line means that the Persian had won three fields from Suleiman or Morocco's scimitar did has been argued. The former reading seems less awkward. It has been asserted that the line refers to Suleiman the Magnificent's campaign against the Persians in 1535 which was not notably successful. Ultimately a treaty was signed in 1555. However, Suleiman attacked Persia in 1533, 1534, 1535, 1548, 1553, and 1554. He won Baghdad through these struggles, but weather, terrain, and the ferocity of the Persians exacted great cost. In none of these conflicts was the Sophy (Shah Tahmasp, 1524–1576) killed. Later conflicts between the Sophy (Shah Abbas the Great, 1586–1628) and Sultans Murad III, Mohammed III, Ahmed I, and Osman II ultimately resulted in the restoration of Persian lands, but, again, the Sophy was not killed, Suleiman was long dead, and the dating would not correspond with the apparent date of the play.

Lr 3.6.38, as Persia was a land of fabled wealth, the adjective was synonymous with 'opulent' from the times of Horace and Cicero. *Q 13.74–5,* 'P. attire.'

Peter, 1) *Shr 4.1.120,* servant of Petruccio's, abused by his master (*4.2.145–66*) when he brings the mutton. He has two lines. At F1 *4.4.67.sd,* 'Enter Peter' appears. He seems to have no function here as Petruccio's servant, which leads some critics to believe that Peter is the name of an actor, not a character, though this person cannot be identified with the available information.

2) *Rom,* illiterate servant of the house of Capulet who asks Romeo to read a guest list for the feast at his master's. The part was played by William Kempe, whose name appears in the speech attributions in the Q. In Luigi da Porto's *Istoria novellamente ritrovata di due Nobili Amanti* (c. 1530), Peter is Giulietta's servant, who comes to tell Romeo about the arranged marriage. In Bandello's *Le Novelle del Bandello* (1554), Pietro is Romeo's servant. He provides a rope ladder and plays the role of Sh.'s Balthasar in telling Romeo of Juliet's 'death.' Peter is much the same in Sh.'s immediate source, Arthur Brooke's translation of Bandello, the *Tragicall Historye of Romeus and Juliet* (1562). Sh. obviously retains the common name but changes his role and adds Balthasar.

3) *Rom 3.5.116,* see St. Peter.

4) *Jn 1.1.186,* arbitrarily chosen male name.

5) *MM,* 'Friar P.,' a minor character and friend of the Duke of Vienna, who assists him in his disguise and in his plot to unmask Angelo. At his entrance in F1 1.4 (modern *1.3*) he is called 'Frier Thomas,' but never thereafter. At *4.5* he is called Peter. This kind of carelessness is common in early editions of the plays and likely derives from the use of original drafts or alternate versions of a play.

Peter, Don, F1 and Q, *Ado 1.1.1, 9,* Don Pedro. The name seems to have been given by mistake here or possibly Sh. initially intended to Anglicize the name in his first drafts of the play. Pedro III was known as Peter the Great in England at that time.

Peter of Pomfret, *Jn,* prophet whom Holinshed (3.180) says was tortured and executed for predicting that John would resign his crown in 1213. The prediction was correct in the sense that John yielded the crown to Innocent III and received it back as a fief of the papacy.

Peter, Saint, fisherman who became Jesus' first apostle. In Gethsemane, he defended Jesus by cutting off the ear of one of those arresting Christ. The sword is one of his symbols. He also denied that he was a Christian several times, as Jesus had predicted. According to tradition, in Rome in 65 AD he was crucified upside down—he felt he was not worthy to die in the same manner as his Lord. As the traditional first bishop of Rome, the papacy traces its origins to him. He is also considered the keeper of the keys to the Kingdom and is the gatekeeper of heaven.

Rom 3.5.116. Ado 2.1.42. Oth 4.2.95.

Peto, *2H4,* one of the gang of young rowdies with whom Falstaff and Prince Harry associated. The character is the same as the one called Harvey in *1H4.* Sh. changed several of the names of the characters he introduced in *1H4* after the family of Lord Cobham objected in 1597 to his use of the name of one of its ancestors, Sir John Oldcastle. Sh. turned Oldcastle into Falstaff and purged his work of other names that he feared might give offence to members of the nobility. Since the widowed mother of Sh.'s patron, the earl of Southampton, had married William Lord Harvey, Sh. may have assumed that it would be best to avoid the appearance of inviting a comparison between Harvey and Prince Harry's wild friends. John Florio's Italian-English dictionary of 1598, *A Worlde of Wordes*, says *peto* refers to someone who rolls his eyes, 'goat-eied,' or who has half-closed or squinting eyes. This may have told the actor how to play the part, or was characteristic of the actor himself. Perhaps more in tune with the earthy side of Renaissance England is the fact the It. *peto* means 'fart.'

Petrarch, *Rom 2.3.37,* Francesco Petrarca (1304–1374), one of the greatest literary figures of the Renaissance and a major force in reviving Classical learning. He was born in Arezzo but grew up in the village of Arno, near Florence, until his father moved the family to Avignon in 1313. The cosmopolitan society there opened Petrarch's eyes to the joys of scholarship and after his father died, he left the study of law in Bologna to return to Avignon, where he took minor orders with the church. After a period of solitude, he emerged as one of the most famous poets of Europe. He traveled widely and resided in several Italian cities, developing a conception of a unified Italy as the heir of the Romans. The Senate made him poet laureate in 1341. He wrote in both Latin and Italian, but his primary influence was in his use of the Tuscan idiom of his youth. He wrote an epic poem about Scipio Africanus, biographies of famous men, essays and eclogues. His letters are a wealth of information about his times. He had a long correspondence and friendship until death with Giovanni Boccaccio, whose *Decameron* provided sources for Sh.'s plays. In many ways, he has long been considered the founder of Renaissance humanism.

The most famous event of his life, however, occurred on Good Friday, 6 April 1327, when he saw Laura in the church of St. Clara in Avignon. His instant and lifelong romantic love for her became the subject of his *Canzoniere* ('Songbook') or *Rime in vita e morta di Madonna Laura.* These made the sonnet form predominate as the primary poetic invention of the Renaissance. In England this led to the great sonnets of Wyatt, Surrey, Sidney, Sh., and others. It may also be said that the particular use of the sonnet as a personal lyric expression of the poet is the beginning of modern poetry. Despite the powerful inspiration of Laura, Petrarch never had a personal relationship with her. He only loved from afar and remained uncured of his infatuation even though he had children by another relationship. A story of questionable provenance identifies Laura as the daughter of Audibert de Noves and wife of Hugh de Sade, yet the name Laura may well be a contrivance which obscures her true identity. As idealized as she is, some critics have maintained that she was not a real woman at all, but an imaginative creation representing the perfect and unavailable woman.

Petruccio, F1 'Petruchio.' 1) *Shr,* son of Antonio, wooer and husband of Katherine Minola. Too much has been made of his announcement early in the play that he intends to 'wive it wealthily.' He is not a fortune hunter who would marry anyone for her fortune. He says that his father left him wealth which he increased, and the number of his servants, etc., indicates he is already wealthy. A man of his station in the Renaissance would be expected to marry at his own economic level. He seems immediately attracted to Katherine as a kindred type, a high-spirited person of strong appetites—much too vigorous for his timid friend Hortensio. Furthermore, although his action in taming Katherine might seem cruel and insensitive by modern standards, it contrasts with the standard treatment advised for shrewishness in those days: regular, forceful thrashings. He puts on a demonstration of male shrewishness to demonstrate to his wife the consequences of her own actions, but he never beats her and his 'mistreatment' is always couched in terms of his care for her. Finally, the play has many layers. The story of Petruccio is a play presented to Christopher Sly, and therefore it must be seen as an artifice rather than an attempt to create a true tale of the creation of marital bliss. Petruccio's actions, we are aware at the very least from the point of his speech at *4.1.174–96* if not before, are calculated—not a genuine madness—thereby constituting a play within the play which is Sly's play. Also there is the distinct possibility in the last act, in which Kate demonstrates the depth of their relationship, that the two of them have conspired or at least have enough shared understanding to put on an act. She may be demonstrating her wifely role as a way of pleasing him, and he may be understanding that she is to a great extent wearing a mask. That she would do this for him and he would appreciate it, mutually enforces their love.

2) *Rom,* guest at Capulet's feast, identified for Juliet by her nurse.

Petty Ward, *MWW 3.1.5,* F1 'pittie-ward,' in the direction of 'the Petty,' or Little Park at Windsor, from the Fr. *petit,* 'little.'

Phaëthon, 'the shining one,' name for Helios, god of the sun, but also the name by which Helios' son was known. Sh.'s reference is to the son. *R2 3.3.177.* See Phaëton.

Phaëton, son of the Greek god of the sun, Helios. Youthful enthusiasm led Phæton to make a tragic error. He persuaded his father to let him drive the chariot of the sun in its daily course across the sky. The boy was unable to control the horses that pulled the fiery vehicle, and it slid from its path. To prevent it from setting the earth ablaze, Zeus hurled a bolt of lightening that killed Phaëton. *TGV 3.1.153:* the Duke implies that Valentine aspires too high. It may be an allusion to John Lyly's *Midas* or to *The Troublesome Raigne of John, King of England. 3H6 1.4.34, 2.6.12:* Sh. found the story such an apt simile for dramatic changes of fortune that he had Clifford mention it twice: once when he killed Richard of York, and again when Clifford himself met death in the battle that brought Richard's son, Edward, to power.

Pharamond, *H5 1.2.37, 41, 58,* legendary king of the Salian Franks and reputed author of the 'Salic' law which French authorities cited as grounds for rejecting Henry V's claim to the throne of France. Henry was tied to the French royal house through the female line, and the 'Salic' law allegedly denied women the right to inherit the French crown or transmit it to male relatives.

Pharaoh, title used by the kings of ancient Egypt. It derives from 'great house,' a metonymy probably employed much like the term 'the White House' is today. *1H4 2.5.478,* 'P.'s lean kine,' recalls Genesis 41:19, where a pharaoh asks the Hebrew patriarch Joseph for a prophetic interpretation of a dream. The pharaoh has had a vision in which seven fat and seven lean cows (i.e., kine) have come up from the Nile. *Ado 3.3.129,* 'P.'s soldiers,' a reference to some painting in which the clothing is like some young men's fashion of the time.

Pharsalia, *Ant 3.7.31,* territory in Thessaly belonging to the ancient Greek city of Pharsalus. It was the site of the battle at which Julius Cæsar won control of the Roman empire from Pompey in 48 BC. Plutarch ('Antony' 62.3) says that Antony challenged Octavius to single combat at Pharsalus because it was the place where their predecessors had settled an earlier fight for control of the empire.

Phebe, *AYLI,* F1 for Phoebe (q.v.).

Phibus'car, *MND 1.2.31,* Bottom's corruption of Phoebus' chariot.

Philadelphos, *Ant 3.6.70,* king of Paphlagonia and one of the monarchs who Plutarch ('Antony' 61.1) says sided with Antony against Octavius.

Philario, *Cym,* see Filario.

Philemon, 1) *Ado 2.1.88,* 'P.'s roof,' an inviting refuge. In mythology, Philemon was the devoted husband of Baucis. In one of Ovid's gentlest tales (*Metamorphoses,* 8) Jupiter and Mercury came to earth in human guise. In Bithynia they knocked upon door after door and were refused food and a place to rest. At the shabby home of Philemon, however, the old couple welcomed the gods and fed them what they could. As a reward they were made priests of Jupiter's temple and when they died were transformed into an oak and a linden that grew side by side. In *Færie Queene,* 2.4, (1590) Edmund Spenser uses the plot which also became *Ado.* He also uses the name Philemon for the character equivalent to Don John. This could have suggested the imagery to Sh.

2) *Per,* Cerimon's servant. The name Philominus is used in a German version of the story by Heinrich von Neustadt in the 14th c. In another analogue he is called Silemon. In the direct source, Lawrence Twine's *Patterne of Painefull Adventures* (1594), he is called Machaon, but Twine gives Dionyza's daughter the name Philomacia. The character is unnamed in John Gower's *Confessio Amantis* (1390). See Pericles.

Philharmonus, *Cym,* soothsayer who interprets the mysterious tablet sent by Jupiter in Posthumus' vision. The soothsayer is named only once at *5.6.434.* The use of the name, which implies harmony, peace, and the love of concord is particularly appropriate in the atmosphere of reconciliation at this point in the play.

Philip, 1) *Shr 4.1.79,* one of Petruccio's servants.

2) Philip (II) Augustus, *Jn,* (1165–1223), king of France. In 1180, when the 15-year-old Philip inherited the French throne, the Capetian dynasty was very weak. His father, Louis VII, had reigned over little more than Paris and its environs. In the course of a few years Philip charted a new path for the French monarchy, and by bringing great expanses of land into the royal domain he earned the cognomen 'Augustus' (i.e., 'augmenter'). The Capetians' new possessions were acquired at the expense of the kings of England. At the start of his reign the young king confronted the most powerful monarch in Europe, England's Henry II. Henry was master of the great 'Angevin empire' that included England and much more of France than Philip controlled. Although Henry was Philip's vassal for his French domains (not his English kingdom), Philip had no real power over him or the great dukes and counts of France. Part of Philip's genius lay in finding ways to turn his nominal rights as a feudal overlord to practical advantage. His opportunities to maneuver increased greatly when Henry died and Richard the Lionhearted became England's king. Richard was less interested in the practical business of governing than in the adventure of leading a crusade to the Holy Lands. Richard was astute enough to realize that he ought not to leave Philip at his back to prey on his possessions while he was fighting in the east. Consequently, Richard forced him to join the crusade, which was represented to the people of Europe as a joint venture for the glory of Christendom conducted by the kings of England, Germany, and France. Philip was too astute to waste his time on wars in distant lands. He remained in the east only long enough to fulfill his crusader vow. The crusaders departed Europe in 1190, and by Christmas 1191 Philip was home in Paris.

While Richard attacked the Muslims, Philip attacked Richard's fiefs and encouraged Richard's ambitious brother John to create as much confusion as possible. Richard was finally forced to give up his dream of conquering Jerusalem and hasten home to rescue his kingdom. Richard tried to save time by sneaking incognito through the territory of an enemy, Duke Leopold of Austria. This turned out to be a serious mistake. He was recognized, and Leopold threw him in prison. Philip and John did what they could to prolong Richard's captivity, but Richard's friends raised a huge ransom and won his release. In 1194 Richard returned to France and set about rebuilding his empire. Philip might have lost all he had won were it not for an accident that caused Richard's death in 1199. John, who succeeded to the Plantagenet throne, was not Richard's equal and no match for Philip. At first it appeared that France and England might coexist peacefully. In 1200 John gave his niece, Blanche of Castile, in marriage to Philip's heir, Louis (VIII). But by 1202 Philip was at war with John—claiming that John had reneged on feudal obligations and forfeited his fiefs. John's tyrannical behavior prompted many of his French vassals to defect to Philip, and the English quickly lost most of their French empire. All that remained by 1208 was a portion of the duchy of Aquitaine known as Gascony. John was slow to respond, but he conceived a grand plan for recouping his losses. In 1213 John ended a long quarrel with the papacy and swore an oath of fealty to Innocent III. In 1214 John recruited Otto of Brunswick, the German emperor, for a joint attack on France. John did not believe that Philip would be able to deal with a war on two fronts, particularly if dissident French barons joined the English-German coalition. The situation was very serious for Philip, but he and his son Louis mounted a vigorous defense of their territories. On 27 July 1214, at Bouvines in Flanders he dealt his enemies a decisive blow. John retreated to England to face the anger of his vassals, and Philip was left in peace to consolidate Europe's strongest feudal monarchy. By the time of his death on 14 July 1223, great progress had been made toward the creation of a centralized government for France.

Philip and Jacob, *MM 3.1.461,* feast of Sts. Philip and James, 1 May (Anglican rite; in the Roman, 3 May). Philip was one of the twelve apostles, but what little is known of him is recorded only in the book of John. He was present at the dividing of the fishes and loaves which fed the multitudes, and therefore, his symbol is a loaf. He is supposed to have died on the cross, which also became his symbol in medieval art. Jacob is the Hebrew equivalent for James and refers to St. James the Less. He was one of the twelve, also, but little is known about him other than that he was the son of Alpheus. See May Day.

Philip of Macedon, *H5 4.7.20,* (382–336 BC), Philip II, king of the most northern state on the Greek mainland. Philip took the throne from his brother's infant son in 359 and quickly became the strongest king in his nation's history. He subdued warring factions of nobles whose squabbles had retarded Macedon's evolution. He imported artists and intellectuals to bring his people the benefits of the culture for which their southern neighbors had become famous, and he turned Macedon's feudal levies into the most sophisticated army in Greece. Philip was a brilliant military strategist and politician. When he came to the throne, the Ægean world was in chaos. Endemic civil wars had halted the advance of Hellenic civilization and squandered the resources of the Greek city-states. Philip's skillful initiatives in diplomacy and his judicious use of force ended disputes among the Greeks and brought peace to the mainland. Philip knew that his achievements would not endure if he treated the Greeks with a heavy hand. The liberty-loving Hellenic city-states would resist permanent Macedonian occupation. Philip's strategy was to persuade the Greeks to accept his leadership voluntarily by enlisting them in the service of a dream. Philip invited the Greeks to forget the grudges they bore each other and to unite in an assault on their common enemy, Persia. The Golden Age in Greek history had begun in the 5th c. when the Greeks fought off repeated invasions from Persia. Philip convinced the Greeks that by attacking Persia they could halt their decline and restore their faded glory. Philip laid the military and political groundwork for a great campaign that he did not get a chance to fight. He was assassinated on the eve of his departure for the east, and history remembers his son, Alexander the Great, as the conqueror of Persia and the author of a new era in Greek civilization. Philip derives from the Gr. for 'lover of horses,' a trait appropriate to a conquering king, and shared by his empire-building son.

Philip the Bastard, *Jn,* illegitimate son whom Richard the Lionhearted allegedly fathered by a Lady Falconbridge. Holinshed (3.160) says that Richard had a son out of wedlock whom he named Philip and to whom he assigned the castle of Coinacke. When Richard was killed besieging the stronghold of the viscount of Limoges, this Philip supposedly avenged him by destroying the viscount. Holinshed does not suggest a link between Philip of Coinacke and the English Falconbridge family. Some scholars believe that Sh. derived that detail from an anonymous play, *The Troublesome Raigne of John, King of England.* The story's ultimate source may be a folk tradition that collapsed the name of Falcasius de Brente (Fawkes de Brent), a warrior of illegitimate birth who was one of King John's opponents, into 'Falconbridge.'

Philip the Good, *1H6,* (1396–1467), duke of Burgundy, holder of the balance of power in the closing phase of the Hundred Years' War between England and France. Philip's father, John the Fearless, and Louis of Orléans quarreled over which of them should be regent for the mad king of France, Charles VI. Their fight divided France and exposed it to the danger of invasion from England. The Burgundians stood aloof as Henry V of England decimated the Orléanists at the battle of Agincourt in 1415. An attempt was made to unite the two French factions against the English in 1419, but it failed when an Orléanist assassinated John. Philip reacted to the death of his father by joining forces with Henry V against the Orléanists. He recognized Henry V as regent for Charles VI and heir to the throne of France. The arrangement ignored the rights of Charles's son, the Dauphin, who took refuge with the Orléanists. For a brief time it looked like England, with Philip's help, would win the Hundred Years' War. The deaths of Henry and Charles in 1422 changed the picture and caused Burgundy to doubt the wisdom of an alliance with the regents who ruled England for Henry's infant heir, Henry VI. The duke of Bedford, who commanded the English forces in France, tried to bolster the alliance by marrying Philip's sister, Anne, but Bedford's brother, Gloucester, started a private feud with Burgundy over rights to the county of Hainaut. Burgundy and Bedford quarreled when the city of Orléans offered to surrender to Philip, but not to the English.

The series of defeats the English suffered after Joan of Arc entered the war at the siege of Orléans further sapped Philip's enthusiasm for his allies. In 1435 Philip broke with England and agreed to a separate truce with Charles VII of France. With Burgundy's help, Charles won Paris back from the English and regained the territories the English had been occupying in France. England's withdrawal from the continent ended the Hundred Years' War, and cleared the way for old problems between France and Burgundy to surface. Philip helped rebellious French nobles who tried unsuccessfully to trim Charles VII's power, and Philip provided asylum for Charles's overly ambitious son when young Louis plotted against his father. Two years before his death, Philip transferred the burdens of his office to his son, Charles the Bold. Charles was determined to add to his territory and transform Burgundy into an independent kingdom of the Rhineland. The danger he posed to Louis XI of France gave the English a bargaining chip in the game of continental politics. Neither Burgundy nor France wanted England to intervene on the side of its opponent. Consequently, when the War of the Roses broke out in England, both Burgundy and France were happy to supply money to the contenders for England's throne. Louis backed Henry VI, and Philip supported Edward IV. When the war ended, Edward, the victor, earned a good income by selling England's neutrality to France.

Philippan, *Ant 2.5.23,* sword with which Sh. says Antony won his decisive victory at Philippi over the Republican armies commanded by Brutus and Cassius. The custom of giving names to weapons developed during the Middle Ages, but there is no evidence for it in the ancient world. This detail is, therefore, probably Sh.'s invention.

Philippi, battlefield in Macedonia named for the nearby city of Philippi, which had been conquered, fortified, and renamed by Philip II of Macedon, who exploited the gold mines in the area. In 42 BC, Mark Antony and Octavius routed the Republican forces led by Cæsar's assassins, Brutus and Cassius. Later the city became the site of St. Paul's first church in Europe. He addresses an epistle to its inhabitants. The site lay between the modern Greek cities of Dráma and Kaválla, not far from the current borders with Bulgaria and European Turkey. *JC 4.2 (passim), 5.1.5, 82, 5.5.19. Ant 2.6.13, 3.2.57, 3.11.35.*

Phillida, *MND 2.1.68,* shepherdess with whom Oberon dallied. Phillida was a common name in pastoral poems and plays, and derived from the L. and Gr. genitive of 'Phyllis,' which means 'foliage.' The latter was the subject of a myth, who was supposedly transformed into a tree after dying of love. In *Tottel's Miscellany* (1557) is the pastoral poem 'Harpalus' Complaint of Phillida's Love bestowed on Corin that loved her not, and denied him that loved her,' which is perhaps the first English use of the name in this way.

Phillipe, *2H6 2.2.35, 2.2.49,* Phillipa, heiress to Lionel of Clarence, son of Edward III. Her marriage to Edmund Mortimer produced children who were in line to succeed to the English throne. Her daughter Anne was Richard of York's mother. Because of Anne and Phillipe, York claimed to have a better right to the throne than Henry VI, whose royal blood was inherited from one of Lionel's younger brothers.

Philo, *Ant,* friend of Mark Antony's. The character's name does not appear in the dialogue of Sh.'s play, but is supplied by F1, from which all extant texts of *Ant* derive. No friend of Antony's named Philo appears in the sources that Sh. is known to have used. Since Philo appears only in the opening scene of the play, has no development as a distinct character, and makes no contribution to the action of the plot, Sh. may have invented him and his colleague Demetrius. Sh. uses their conversation to illustrate the Roman attitude toward Antony's relationship with Cleopatra and to set the stage for the story he wants to tell. The name derives from Gr. *philos,* 'brotherly love.'

Philomel, see Philomela. *Luc 1079, 1128, Tit 2.3.43, 2.4.38, 2.4.43, 4.1.47, 5.2.193,* (pl.) *MND 2.2.13, 24. Son 102.7. Cym 2.2.46,* 'Where P. gave up': Innogen may be reading any number of sources for the tale including Ovid's *Metamorphoses,* 6.420 ff., John Gower's *Confessio Amantis,* 5, Chaucer's *Legende of Good Women,* or George Pettie's *A Petite Palace of Pettie His Pleasure* (1576) in which it is the second story. *TNK 5.5.124* (pl.), nightingales.

Philomela, (Gr. 'lover of song') mythological daughter of Pandion. Her sister Procne was given in marriage to Tereus and gave birth to Itys (Itylus). All was well until Procne asked her husband to bring Philomela to visit her. Upon seeing his sister-in-law Tereus was inflamed with passion. Taking her into the woods, he raped her. He then cut out her tongue to silence her and raped her again. He told Procne her sister was dead, but Philomela had a tapestry made which revealed her story. Procne rescued her during a Bacchic festival. The sisters then murdered Itys and cooked him up as a meal for his father. The angry gods then changed Philomela into a swallow (which is a tongueless bird) and Procne into a nightingale. Tereus was transformed into the red-crested hoopoe. This is the tale as told by Ovid in *Metamorphoses,* 6; however, in other versions from antiquity, Procne has her tongue cut out and becomes the swallow, Philomela becomes the nightingale, and Tereus was made into a hawk to harry the two throughout eternity. Sh. uses the name Philomela as a substitute for nightingale, which, given his frequent use of Ovid as a source, is curious. He also uses the name to represent the raped and mutilated Philomela, particularly in *Tit,* in which Lavinia is similarly brutalized and Titus cooks up his enemy's sons in a pie.

Tit 4.1.52. PP 14.17, a nightingale.

Philoten, *Per 15.18, 36,* daughter of Cleon and Dionyza. In comparison to her companion Marina, she seemed less wonderful, provoking Dionyza to arrange Marina's murder. John Gower explains this in his chorus, but Philoten never appears on stage. Her name is one of many that appear in Gower's *Confessio Amantis* (1390). See Pericles.

Philotus, *Tim 3.4,* creditor of Timon's. The name appears in Plutarch's life of Mark Antony which contains a passage about Timon. There is also a Philotus in Plutarch's 'Alexander,' and a servant—maid Philotis—in his 'Romulus.' A Filades is a character in another version of the story, M. M. Boiardo's *Timone* (c. 1487). A Philautus is the betrayed friend of the title character in *Euphues, The Anatomy of Wit* by John Lyly (1579). It is likely that this story was an important influence on *TGV.*

Phoebe, 1) (Gr. 'bright one') one of the epithets of Diana/Artemis, chaste goddess of the hunt who is inevitably evoked in pastoral romances. *Tit 1.1.313. LLL 4.2.39. MND 1.1.209.*

2) *AYLI,* shepherdess who falls in love with Ganymede, but marries Silvius. The name is taken from Sh.'s source, Lodge's *Rosalynde.*

Phoebus, (Gr. 'bright one') originally one of the epithets of the god Apollo. At a late period in the evolution of classical mythology Apollo was linked with the image of the sun, and his name, Phoebus, came to be used for the god of the sun (Helios).

3H6 2.6.11: Clifford pays Henry VI no compliment by comparing him to Phoebus. Henry, like Phoebus-Helios in the tale of Phaëton (q.v.), unwisely let another use his power. As a consequence, the world he should have nurtured was imperilled. *Rom 3.2.1–4,* possibly an allusion to Marlowe's *Edward II, 4.3.43–47.*

MV 2.1.5, 'P.'s fire.' *1H4 1.2.15. H5 3.0.6, 4.1.270. Ado 5.3.26,* 'the wheels of P.' *Ham 3.2.148,* 'P.'s cart,' his chariot. *Tro 1.3.228.*

Lr 2.2.106 (Q 7.104), 'P.'' front,' the sun's face. *Ant 1.5.28, 4.9.29, 5.2.311. Cor 2.1.215. WT 4.4.124. Cym 2.3.20. 5.6.190,* 'P.'s wheel.'

Tmp 4.1.30, 'P.'s steeds,' the horses that draw the sun's chariot. *TNK 1.1.46,* 'holy P.,' the sun. *1.2.85:* alludes to the death of Phaëton, which so angered Phoebus (according to Ovid's *Metamorphoses,* 2) he tormented and whipped the sun chariot's horses. *5.2.22.*

Phoenicia, *Ant 3.6.16,* coastal district of ancient Syria, roughly corresponding to the coast of modern Lebanon. Its ports, such as Sidon, Tyre, Tripolis, and Berytus, were major centers of commerce for the ancient world, though they never united to form a nation. The people of these city-states were among the ancient world's pioneer sailors and among its most adventurous traders. They established colonies throughout the Mediterranean, including Carthage and Tarshish. They had several periods of independence between subjugations by the Egyptians, Assyrians, and Persians. Ultimately, their area was Hellenized and absorbed into the Roman province of Syria. Their conquerors often had need of their expertise on the sea, but perhaps the greatest contribution of Phoenicia was the invention of the alphabet. The origin of the area's name is obscure. It is usually said to be from the son of Agenor of Tyre, Phoenix. Some think it may derive from Gr. *phoinix,* 'purple' the color of the Phoenician's most celebrated trading product, Tyrian purple, a dye. The etymology is further confused by the meaning 'date palm' and the immortal bird, Phoenix (q.v.), whose name may have an Egyptian origin.

Phoenicians, *Ant 3.7.64,* residents of the coastal district of Syria.

Phoenix, 1) bird from Egyptian myth often mentioned by ancient writers, including Ovid, one of Sh.'s favorite sources. Herodotus and Pliny provide detailed descriptions of the myth. Usually said to be an Arabian bird, the phoenix, when it would reach 500 years of age, would build a nest or pyre of aromatic twigs and immolate itself. A young phoenix would then be born from the ashes. The myth was a symbol of resurrection or immortality. In classical art the phoenix was depicted as an eagle; in Egyptian art as a heron. The name seems to have an Egyptian origin, but how that relates to Phoenicia (q.v.) is obscure. Only one Phoenix could exist at a time: *AYLI 4.3.18,* 'as rare as P.'; *Tmp 3.3.23–4.*

PhT: Phoenix's union with turtle (turtle dove) in this poem is obviously allegorical, but exactly what it refers to is unknown. Some have thought it alludes to the love of Elizabeth and Essex, but it is as likely to refer to some other less notable couple. Phoenix in the poem seems to symbolize beauty, as the turtle symbolizes loyalty. *AWW 1.1.164. TNK 1.3.70,* 'p.-like,' a reference to the fragrant wood of the fire.

2) *Err,* house (and presumably business location) of Antipholus of Ephesus. It was common to name a house after some exterior feature, such as a carving of a phoenix decorating the exterior. Such a decoration would also serve the purposes of the drama. Three entrances from supposedly different buildings were the rule in ancient Roman drama and this practice was imitated in the Renaissance. It is thought that the play may have been performed at the Christmas festivities at Gray's Inn on 28 December 1594, and the three houses would have been represented with painted canvas flats.

3) *TN 5.1.57,* name of a ship Antonio seized.

Photinus, *Ant 3.7.14,* Potheinus, one of Cleopatra's ministers. A Photinus was the guardian of Cleopatra's young brother and co-regent, Ptolemy. This Photinus was executed by Julius Cæsar for ordering the murder of Pompey. (When Pompey sought refuge in Egypt after his loss to Cæsar at Pharsalus, Photinus had expected to curry favor with Cæsar by sending him the head of his defeated enemy.) The Potheinus who Plutarch ('Antony' 60.1) lists in Cleopatra's service at a much later date could not have been the same man. Nor did Plutarch claim that this Potheinus was, as Sh. implies, a eunuch. Sh. may have misread a phrase in Plutarch's text that applies to the eunuch Mardian, another of Cleopatra's servants.

Phrygia, country in Asia Minor, roughly the land west of the central Anatolian plateau. It had indefinite boundaries, which may have been the result of its being associated with a people, rather than defining a geographic area, or of various expansions and contractions. Greater Phrygia, however, was landlocked. It was named for the Greek word for 'freemen.' It is possible that the Phrygians were immigrants from Europe. The ancients said that the Phrygians were the oldest people in the world and that their wealth was great—Midas was one of their kings. They were also said to build their cities with huge walls. There may have been linguistic connections between the Phrygian language and Greek. All of these elusive details may have connections with the myths of ancient Troy. Sh. equates the Trojan kingdom with Phrygia, which, indeed, may have been the case in Homeric times.

Tro pro. 7, 1.2.119, 4.7.70, 106, 5.11.24. TN 3.1.50, 'Lord Pandarus of P.'

Phrygian, (adj.) of or pertaining to Phrygia. *Luc 1502. Tro 4.7.70, 106, 5.11.24. MWW 1.3.83,* 'Phrygian Turk,' a phrase alluding to the legend of Pandarus at *1.3.69,* possibly meaning an ultimate heathen, but likely simply extravagant nonsense.

Phrynia, *Tim,* one of Alcibiades' camp followers. Timon gives her some of his treasure. The name comes from Phryne, a wealthy courtesan of 4th c. BC Athens. Born Mnesarete at Thespiæ in Boeotia, she was renamed for the word 'toad' because of her complexion. She played temptress to the philosopher Xenocrates. She once proposed rebuilding the walls of Thebes if they could be inscribed, 'Alexander destroyed them, Phryne the prostitute rebuilt them.' Another legend says that she was acquitted of the capital crime of profaning the Eleusian mysteries by exposing her magnificent breasts to the judges. She has been credited with having been the model for the Cnidian Aphrodite by Praxiteles and having inspired Apelles' painting of the Aphrodite Anadyomene when she disrobed to wade into the sea at the festival of Poseidon at Eleusis.

Pia mater, inner meninx of the brain, used figuratively for the intellect. Arab anatomists called the two membranes of the brain the 'mothers.' The outer, thicker one was the hard or tough mother (L. *dura mater*), while the inner, more delicate one directly against the brain itself was the 'meeke mother' (L. *pia mater),* which according to *Batman uppon Bartholome,* nourished and protected the delicate tissues. The third meningeal tissue lining the dura mater and covering brain and spinal cord is called the arachnoid, after Arachne, because of its resemblance to a cobweb. *Batman uppon Bartholomew* was John Trevisa's 1398 translation of *De Propietatibus Rerum* by Bartholomew de Glanville (mid. 13th c.), an encyclopedia. Though much of its information was grossly out of date or muddled in Trevisa's attempt to make it more readable than factual, it was a very influential book in the Renaissance. It was printed by Wynken de Worde in 1495.

LLL 4.2.70. TN 1.5.111.

Picardy, province in northern France defined by the basin of the Somme river. Its perimeter is marked by the channel coast and the borders of Hainaut, Champagne, Normandy, and the Île de France. Its inhabitants were celebrated for the use of the pike (Fr. *pique*). During the Middle Ages Picardy was a wealthy district famous for its weaving industry. The powerful dukes of Burgundy dominated it during the Hundred Years' War, but in 1477, following the death of Charles the Bold, the province was claimed by the French crown.

2H6 4.1.88. 1H6 2.1.10.

Pickbone, Francis, *2H4 3.2.19,* comical name Sh. invents for one of the youthful companions whom Justice Shallow recalls when he reminisces about his student days at Clement's Inn. Perhaps it refers to a hungry fellow who meticulously cleans bones at dinner, or there is some obscure ribald implication.

Pickpurse, *1H4 2.1.48,* pickpocket. The reference is to a comic proverb well known in Sh.'s day: 'Ready as a pickpocket.' Pickpockets had to keep themselves in a constant state of nimble fingered preparedness if they hoped to be able spontaneously to exploit the unpredictable opportunities on which their craft depended.

Pickt-hatch, *MWW 2.2.19,* Falstaff's insulting name for Pistol's home. A 'picked hatch' was a half door topped with spikes to prevent intruders from climbing over it. It has been argued that references in 1598 in John Marston's *Scourge of Villainy* and Ben Jonson's *Every Man in His Humour* show that a particular brothel may have been called this because of its door. These authors may refer to a 'red-light' district of London, which has been asserted to be Turnmill Street in Clerkenwell. Pickt-hatch is also mentioned in *A Woman is a Weathercock* (1612) and *Amends for Ladies* (1618), which were very popular and apparently performed earlier by at least two companies at Blackfriars. The latter play identifies 'Picked Hatch' with Turnbull Street.

Pie Corner, *2H4 2.1.25,* district in west Smithfield, London. It took its name from its bakery and butcher shops. Leather goods, like the saddle Sh. mentions, were made in the same neighborhood.

Pigmies, *Ado 2.1.252,* any small race of people, mysterious but fascinating to Renaissance Europeans as the world became more open to exploration. Based on fact, these people were regarded with much the same wonderment and credulity as such imaginary beings as the men whose heads grow between their shoulders and the men with tails. The ancient writers Homer and Herodotus described pygmies and several groups of them (which do not seem to be genetically related) still live in remote areas of the planet. The largest group is in central Africa, but there are also pygmies in various locations in Asia and the Pacific. Their name derives from the Gr. for 'cubit,' the distance from elbow to knuckles and refers to their height. See Pygmies, King of, *TNK.*

Pigrogromitus, *TN 2.3.22,* person of whom Sir Andrew Aguecheek says Feste spoke the previous night. It is possible that the name is a corrupted one (indicating Sir Andrew's weak mind) which was recognizable to Sh.'s audience, but no longer familiar. It is more likely that it is a nonsense name which the clown has devised to deceive the foolish Sir Andrew with false erudition.

Pilate, fifth Roman governor of Judea (26–36 AD), official who ordered the crucifixion of Jesus of Nazareth. The fact that the Roman government had executed the man whom the Christians claimed was the messiah was an embarrassment that complicated the early church's efforts to establish a good working relationship with the empire. When the Gospel accounts of Jesus' death were written, the church was breaking with Judaism, concentrating on the conversion of gentiles, and trying to avoid persecution by the Roman state. It was convenient, therefore, for Christian preachers to pin the blame for Jesus' fate on the Jews and to minimize Rome's involvement. The Gospels depict Pilate as a victim of Jewish pressure. The Jews seek Jesus out and bring him to Pilate to demand his execution. Pilate argues forcefully for Jesus' innocence, but when he concludes that he cannot avoid killing Jesus to appease the Jews, he calls for a basin, washes his hands, and transfers the guilt for Jesus' blood from Rome to the Jews. The story has encouraged Christian anti-Semitism and made Pilate a symbol of people who deny responsibility for their actions.
R3 1.4.267. R2 4.1.229, 230 (pl.)

Pilch, *Per 5.52,* nickname for a fisherman, probably referring to a leather or skin outer garment. Thomas Dekker made fun of Ben Jonson for having worn a pilch.

Pillicock, *Lr 3.4.72 (Q 11.69),* 'Pillicock sat on Pillicock Hill,' probably a line from a nursery rhyme or a nonsense song. 'Pillicock' meant 'penis,' in northern dialects and derived from Norwegian *pill.* Later it was also applied to young men as an affectionate term. Some think it may here mean 'pelican,' or 'male pelican,' as suggested in l. 71. 'Pillaloo' was an Irish and English dialect call of mourning, which seems appropriate to the tone of the play, but is likely only a coincidence.

Pimpernel, Henry, *Shr Ind. 2.93,* friend Christopher Sly called out for. Possibly the name came from a real person. See Sly, Stephen.

Pinch, Doctor, *Err,* schoolmaster and exorcist. He is described as a cadaverous conjurer and mountebank. He diagnoses Antipholus of Ephesus and his servant Dromio as possessed and recommends they be confined in darkness. This standard treatment of the time is similarly meted out to Malvolio by Sir Topas in *TN.* Exorcisms and the quackery they attracted were a frequent subject in Elizabethan and Jacobean times—as they are now. The name could imply that the doctor confines, squeezes, or torments his victims. It could also describe his face and nose. The use of 'pinch' to mean 'steal' seems to evolve later (*OED,* 1673), but since it is figurative, it could have been in slang use. Paul's epistle to the Ephesians makes allusions to Ephesus as a center for witchcraft, which perhaps contributes to the characterization of Pinch.

Pindarus, *JC,* one of Caius Cassius Longinus' freedmen. Plutarch ('Antony' 22.3) claims that he helped Cassius commit suicide after the Republican army lost to Antony and Octavius at the battle of Philippi.

Pirithous, *TNK,* 'Prince P.,' friend and aide of Theseus. The closeness of the friendship seems intended as a parallel to that of Arcite and Palamon. Otherwise, Pirithous, despite his frequency upon the stage, has little function. He appears in the source, Chaucer's *Knyghtes Tale,* and the friendship is described in Plutarch's 'Theseus' and Ovid's *Metamorphoses,* 12. The mythical friend of Theseus was son of Zeus or Ixion and Dia. He challenged Theseus by stealing his cattle, but they became devoted friends at first sight. At Pirithous' wedding, a terrible fight broke out between the Lapiths (of whom he was king) and the Centaurs. The battle was frequently depicted in ancient art. Pirithous also participated in the Calydonian boar hunt, which is mentioned in the play, and was made a prisoner in Hades for trying to abduct Persephone.

Pisa, city in north central Italy located on the Arno river 8 mi. from its mouth on the Tuscan sea. Originally an Etruscan town, it flourished under the Romans. In the 9th and 10th c. it became a powerful maritime republic and was a Mediterranean power by the 12th c., as a Ghibelline center. It declined in the 13th and 14th c. Florence seized the city in 1406, but Pisa regained its independence in 1493. Florence conquered it for good in 1509. The university of Pisa (founded 1338) is one of the oldest in the world, whence the remark 'P. renownèd for grave citizens' (*Shr 1.1.10*). Galileo was a professor at Pisa. In *Shr* it is the birthplace of Lucentio and home of Vincentio.

Pisanio, *Cym,* servant of Posthumus. He is ordered by his master to murder Innogen, but cannot bring himself to it. He helps her to flee in a disguise.

Pissing Conduit, *2H6 4.6.3,* water fountain in London's Stocks Market at the intersection of Lombard and Cornhill streets. By the 13th c. London had grown to the point where wells and springs could not provide enough water for its residents. Conduits were built to bring fresh water into the city from the countryside. The most important of these was the Standard in Cheapside. It was constructed in 1285. The Stocks Market was licensed by the government in 1282, and the conduit supplied water to the heart of a working class district. By having Jack Cade absurdly decree that for a year this fountain should flow with wine rather than water, Sh. belittles the motives of the men who followed Cade in rebelling against Henry VI's government.

Pistol, Ensign, comically appropriate name for the soldier who served as Falstaff's junior officer. The weapon for which he is named was inaccurate and often misfired until advances were made in its design in the 19th c. It has also had a phallic connotation from Sh.'s time to Mae West's. Bombastic and cowardly, Pistol may derive from a stock character of *commedia dell'arte,* Thrasio (from the Thraso of Terence's *Eunuchus*), as well as from an attempt to parody the style of Marlowe and the acting of Edward Alleyn of the Lord Admiral's Men. His creation also may have been influenced by the character Piston, the servant of Basilisco in *Solyman and Perseda* (c. 1588) by Thomas Kyd. Pistol shares Falstaff's punishment when Henry V turns against his old friends, but in *MWW* he becomes Falstaff's nemesis and thwarts his attempts to seduce Mistress Ford, though he does not play a significant role after informing Ford and Page of Falstaff's intentions on their wives. In *H5* Pistol appears as the husband of Nell Quickly, the hostess of the inn in Eastcheap at which Prince Harry and Falstaff held their revels in *1H4.* When Falstaff dies and Henry V declares war on France, Pistol leaves his wife in charge of their tavern, the Boar's Head, and enlists in Henry's army with his old companions. The compelled exit of Falstaff from the stage probably made Pistol a more important character than Sh. had originally intended.

2H4. MWW. H5.

Pius, *Tit 1.1.23,* agnomen accorded Titus Andronicus. A number of illustrious Romans were hailed as 'Pius' in recognition of their devotion to Rome's sacred traditions. There is, however, no historical prototype for Sh.'s Titus.

Pizzle, Captain, *2H4 2.4.157,* comic mispronunciation of Ensign Pistol's name.

Placentio, *Rom 1.2.67,* guest invited to Capulet's feast. Perhaps he is the kind of person invited only because of the 'lovely nieces' which are mentioned. His name may derive from the Roman town of Placentia (modern Piacenza). See Anselme.

Plack, Edward the, *H5 4.7.91–92,* see Edward the Black Prince.

Plantagenet, 1) the dynasty that ruled England from 1154 to 1485 (from Henry II to Richard III). Various explanations have been suggested for the name. The most popular traces it to a Latin term for the broom plant, *planta genista*—sprigs of which Henry II's father, Geoffrey, count of Anjou, habitually wore in his cap. The name was not used by the English royal family until Richard, duke of York, popularized it. He may have adopted it to remind the English people that he descended from an older branch of the royal family than his opponent, Henry VI. Sh. employed the name for the royal family in general (*2H6 2.1.39, 40, 4.2.43, 3H6 1.1.122, 1H6 1.6.73, 2.5.52, 3.1.176, R3 4.4.20, Jn 5.6.12, 1H4 1.1.88*) and for some of its individual members (see ff.)

2) *3H6 1.1.40, 95, 1.3.49, 1H6 2.4.36, 64, 69, 74, 77, 2.5.18, 34, 52,* see Richard of York.

3) *3H6 2.2.61, R3 4.4.19, 20,* see Edward (V), Henry VI's son.

4), pl., *R3 1.2.118,* see Henry VI; also Edward, Prince.

5) *R3 1.2.143, 3.7.100,* see Richard III.

6) *R3 1.4.216,* see, Edward, Prince.

7) *R3 4.1.1,* Margaret (1473–1540), second daughter of George, duke of Clarence, Edward IV's brother. Margaret and her children were the last of the Plantagenets. Since Margaret's brother, Edward, earl of Warwick, had been proposed as heir to the childless Richard III, Henry VII, who deposed Richard, protected his Tudor dynasty against rival claimants by imprisoning Edward. The boy was only ten when he entered the Tower of London following the battle of Bosworth Field in 1485. He stayed there until his execution in 1499. Sh. committed an anachronism when he had Richard III (*R3 4.3.37*) speak of Margaret's marriage. It was not until 1491, six years after Richard's death, that Henry VII arranged for Margaret to wed Sir Richard Pole (d. 1505) of Buckinghamshire, a knight whose mother was half-sister to Henry VII's mother. (Pole was not related to the Poles who were earls and dukes of Suffolk and earls of Lincoln.) Margaret's conduct under adversity won her the respect of the court, and Henry VIII may have felt some guilt about his father's treatment of her family. In 1513 Henry named her countess of Salisbury and charged her with the care of his daughter Mary. The improvement in Margaret's situation was not permanent. In 1536 her son, Reginald Cardinal Pole, angered the king by opposing his ecclesiastical policy. After a number of provocations, Henry ordered the execution of Margaret and her children.

8) Ned P., *R3 4.4.146,* see Edward V.

9) *Jn 1.1.167,* see Richard I.

10) *Jn 1.1.9, 2.1.238,* see Arthur, duke of Brittaine.

11) Henry P., *H5 5.2.237,* see Henry V.

Plautus, Titus Maccius, *Ham 2.2.402,* (d. 184 BC), Roman comic playwright. He was born in Sarsini, near Umbria. He came to Rome where he worked in theater, but invested his earnings in a merchant enterprise. This failed abysmally and he ended up pushing a millstone for a living. He somehow managed to write three plays in his spare time which were so successful he was able to spend the rest of his life writing. Only the works of Plautus and Terence are extant from Roman comedy. Twenty-one of Plautus' plays are still available in whole or in part. Most critics think his strength was his deftness with character despite using stock characters and the high spirited vigor of his plays. Although he adapted his plays from Greek New Comedy (especially Menander), he (like Sh.) worked freely and marked them as his own distinct works. He also used flute-accompanied solo songs in his plays. Whether he invented this element or borrowed it from someone else is unknown. None of the other extant plays use it in this way. Although he was nearly forgotten during the Middle Ages, his influence on Renaissance drama is quite pronounced. His *Menæchmi* (along with parts of *Amphitryon*) was revised as Sh.'s *Err,* and his *Miles Gloriosus* ('the Braggart Soldier') provided a model for the character of Falstaff and numerous other Renaissance characters in plays by Sh. and others. Sh. borrowed extensively from Plautus' *Mostellaria* for *Shr* and many other Plautine influences are scattered through Sh. One may also note the extensive, rather Plautine, use of song in Sh.'s comedies.

Plebeians, *JC,* lower of the two castes into which citizens of ancient Rome were born. The more distinguished was the aristocratic patrician class. No information has survived to explain the origin of the distinction between the two 'orders'—as they were called. In Rome's quasi-legendary histories the patricians are said, at the start of the Republic, to have monopolized all authority within the city. Plebeians who served in Rome's army rebelled at their disenfranchisement and staged military strikes to force the patricians to cede them rights. The offices of the Republic were divided between the orders, and a man's birth determined the kind of political career to which he aspired.

Pleshey, *R2 1.2.66, 2.2.90, 120,* castle in Essex that was the residence of Thomas of Woodstock, duke of Gloucester.

Pluto, Roman name for the Greek god Hades, lord of the underworld, also called Dis, a Latin abbreviation for *dives* 'rich man.' Gr. *ploutos* 'wealth' is the origin of the name. Because of his association with the earth, the resource that supplies all human needs—from grain to gold—he was sometimes considered the giver of prosperity, which contributes to his confusion with Plutus (q.v.). In classical mythology Pluto ruled all the dead, but not as their punisher. Sh. assimilated the pagan god to Christian images of Satan, a king of the damned who rides through the fires of hell in a blazing chariot. Sh. also often confuses the Greek god of riches (Plutus) with the lord of the Underworld.

2H6 Add'l ll. B.2. Tit 4.3.13, 38. Luc 553. 2H4 2.4.151. JC 4.2.156, 'P.'s mine,' see Plutus. *Tro 3.3.190,* 'P.'s gold,' see Plutus. *4.5.127, 5.2.105, 156. Cor 1.5.7.*

Plutus, minor god of riches and agricultural wealth, son of Iasion and Demeter, brother of Philomelus. His name derives from Gr. *ploutos* 'wealth.' He was honored in the Eleusinian Mysteries, the most well-known of ancient religious rites honoring Demeter and Persephone. According to Hesiod, he was born in Crete and he wanders over the earth giving wealth to whoever shakes his hand. Zeus supposedly blinded him so that he could not distinguish the good from the bad in his giving. His name survives in 'plutocrat.' Plutus should not be confused with Pluto, the Roman god of the Underworld, though he frequently is. *JC 4.2.156. Tro 3.3.190,* F1 'Plutoe's gold.' *AWW 5.3.102. Tim 1.1.279.*

Po, (L. *Padum,* from Celtic *padi* 'pines,' which were abundant at its mouth) Italian river originating in the Alps and flowing eastward to the Adriatic Sea. It is the longest river in Italy and its basin collects all of the waters in a 400-mile long plain flowing north from the Apennines and east or south from the Alps. Its basin corresponded to the province of Cisalpine Gaul during the Roman empire and was not part of what Rome considered the Italian homeland. *Jn 1.1.203. TNK Pro. 12.*

Poins, Edward or **Ned,** youthful friend of Prince Harry and the creator of various jokes played on Oldcastle. Sh. may have developed the character from a Ned who is the Prince's companion in an earlier, anonymous play, *The Famous Victories of Henry V.* A Poyntz family held the office of sheriff for Gloucestershire in Sh.'s day.

1H4. 2H4. MWW 3.2.67.

Poisson the papist, *AWW 1.3.52,* F1 'Poysam,' name for any Roman Catholic from Fr. *poisson* 'fish.' It refers to the ritual avoidance of meat on holy days and contrasts with Chairbonne (q.v.), the meat eater.

Poitiers, *1H6 1.1.61, 4.3.45,* French town about 50 mi. south of the Loire valley. It lay between territories England claimed in northern and southern France. In 1356 Edward the Black Prince won a decisive victory over France's King John the Good at Poitiers. John was taken captive and Poitiers passed into English hands until Charles V won it back for France in 1373. The battle of Poitiers was among the most significant of the campaigns of the Hundred Years' War.

Poitou, *Jn 1.1.11, 2.1.488, 529,* Poitiers, French province on the Bay of Biscay between Anjou and Angoulême. It was part of the dowry that Eleanor of Aquitaine brought Henry II of England when she married him in 1152. It remained under English control until Philip Augustus took it away from Henry's son, John.

Polack, 1) *Ham 2.2.63, 75; add't'l Q2 J. 4.4.14,* either the people or, more likely, the king of Poland. There is no insult implied in this word in Sh.'s time, with *Polaque* being a French equivalent. *Ham 5.2.329,* 'P. wars.'

2) *Ham 1.1.62,* pl., 'the sledded P.,' the people or army of Poland, on sleds. There has been some critical argument that this should be 'pole-axe' and refer to a weapon, but this is not a substantial opinion. Although there is no record of a victory over sledded Poles on a frozen lake, Christian II defeated a Swedish enemy on the ice in 1520, and there were apparently other such exotic engagements in the then-Danish territories of southern Sweden.

Poland, country in central Europe. It came into existence in the Dark Ages, founded by a group of people called the Lechici who had earlier been driven from the Danube by the Romans. The Poles under king Mieszko converted to Christianity in the late 10th c. as part of their resistance to the pressure from the Germanic tribes, who had used the Poles' paganism as an excuse to attack them. In succeeding centuries, Poland was either a mighty kingdom (as under Boleslaus I) or the spoils of foreign wars, divided among enemies to east and west, including Germans, Tartars, Russians, Lithuanians, and others. By Sh.'s time, it had coalesced under the Jagiellonian dynasty into a political unit of various nationalities and was a major power. After the short reigns of Henry of Valois and Stephen Báthory, Sigismund III held the throne from 1587 to 1632. This was a period of great opportunity, as most of Poland's enemies were weakened, but it became a period of lost opportunities—partly because Sigismund clung to his claims for the Swedish throne and engaged his country in a number of foolish wars against the Scandinavians. For a while, the English worried that a combined Swedish/Polish kingdom might conquer Denmark and unite with the Spanish against England, but Sigismund's costly conflicts prevented his consolidating power. These conflicts were fueled by Sweden's Protestantism and Poland's Catholicism, though the wars were not popular with the Poles. By the end of the 18th c., Poland had disappeared from the map and was not reestablished until the end of World War I.

Err 3.2.100, 'P. winter,' a long winter. Dromio is joking that there's enough grease in Nell's clothes to last through one. *Ham 5.2.301, Add. Q2 J.4.4.4, 6:* the Norwegians seek free passage through Danish territory in order to make war on Poland. *MM 1.3.14.*

Pole, 1) *Ham Add. Q2, J. 4.4.12,* king of Poland, or possibly its people.

2) *Oth 2.1.15,* Polaris, the North Star; 'guards of th' ever-fixe\d P.,' refers to the stars adjacent to Polaris in the tail of Ursa minor, 'the Little Dipper.'

Pole, William de la, (1396–1450), fourth earl of Suffolk, and Henry VI's chief advisor. The Poles were a family of merchants who won admission to the ranks of the nobility. The first Pole to occupy high office was William's grandfather, Michael (d. 1389), chancellor to Richard II. William's career began in 1415 when he inherited the earldom of Suffolk from his brother, Michael. Michael was one of the few English casualties of the battle at Agincourt. William took Michael's place in Henry V's army, and he served in France for fifteen years. He was Salisbury's chief aide at the siege of Orléans. When Salisbury was killed, Suffolk was appointed to take over his command. Suffolk returned to England in 1431 and entered politics. In 1443 he succeeded Cardinal Beaufort as the leader of the most influential group at Henry VI's court. Suffolk's party persuaded Henry to end the Hundred Years' War and make peace with France. In 1444 Suffolk arranged a truce with France that Henry hoped would blossom into peace, and a year later Suffolk arranged Henry's unpopular marriage with Margaret of Anjou. Humphrey of Gloucester, Henry's uncle, loudly objected to Suffolk's peace policy and to the royal marriage that was part of it, but Gloucester's death in 1447 left Suffolk without an effective opponent. In 1448 Henry granted Suffolk a duchy. This raised him to the rank enjoyed by the king's closest relatives. Suffolk may have had few friends who rejoiced at his success. His ambition and unprincipled tactics cost him popularity, and his position at court made it easy to blame him for the blunders of Henry's government.

One of Henry's most serious mistakes was the appointment of the incompetent Edmund Beaufort, duke of Somerset, to Richard of York's post as commander of England's armies in France. Although Henry sent Somerset to replace Richard because of Richard's opposition to the peace Henry wanted to make with France, Somerset himself broke that peace. France's response to Somerset's provocation was so forceful that Normandy was quickly lost and, with it, the Hundred Years' War. England's parliament vented its frustration by compelling Henry to banish Suffolk, whom it accused of corrupting the king's judgment. Suffolk did not survive to suffer the pain of exile. He was beheaded by unknown men who boarded the ship that was to carry him from England. His son, John (1442–1492), may have felt betrayed by the king, for John switched his family's allegiance from the house of Lancaster to the Yorkist camp. He married Richard of York's daughter, and their son, John (1462–1487), was designated heir to the throne by the childless Yorkist king, Richard III. When Henry Tudor killed Richard and usurped the throne, Henry's enemies organized plots centering on members of the Pole family. The threat the Poles had posed to the dynasty that ruled Sh.'s England may color his description of them.

2H6. 1H6.

Polemon, *Ant 3.6.74,* one of the eastern kings who Plutarch ('Antony' 61.2) says sided with Mark Antony against Octavius. Sh. misreads Plutarch and identifies Polemon as king of Mede (Media). Plutarch mentions the king of the Medes, but he does not name him. Plutarch's Polemon was king of Pontus. Polemon, the son of a Greek orator from Laodicea, became governor of Cilicia in 39 BC, and was subsequently translated by Antony to the kingdom of Pontus. Polemon accompanied Antony on his disastrous foray into Parthia in 36 BC and fought for him at Actium. After Antony's defeat at Actium, Polemon came to terms with Octavius and retained his throne. He died defending his lands from invasion by the Aspurgians.

Polixenes, 1) *Tro 5.5.11,* Greek warrior. Although there is a Polixenus, son of Agasthenes and co-commander of the Epeans, in the *Iliad* 2.716, some critics assert the name is adapted from the female Polyxena. In William Caxton's *Recuyell of the Historyes of Troy* (1474), Sh.'s primary source, he is a noble duke killed by Hector. There is also a king Polixenus (perhaps the same) slain by Hector and a Polixenus, a bastard son of Priam, who is killed by Dinadorus. Perhaps Sh. lumped this bastard with Margareton the bastard for the sake of this passage. Polyxena is mentioned in Sidney's *Arcadia* and in several works by Chaucer.

2) *WT,* king of Bohemia, close brother of Leontes, wrongly accused of seducing Hermione. In Sh.'s source Robert Greene's *Pandosto, or the Triumph of Time,* (1588; rptd. 1607 as *Dorastus and Fawnia*), Polixenes' equivalent is Egistus. The name Polyxemus appears in North's translation of Plutarch, from which Sh. got most of his names for *WT.*

Polonius, *Ham,* father of Ophelia and Lærtes, and an important noble in Claudius' government. Although Polonius is in large measure sympathetic, or at the least, endearing, he reveals himself to be a windy fool, boring and incapable of getting to the point. He also seems to spend a good deal of his time spying on people. He pays Reynaldo to spy on his son, he spies on the young lovers Ophelia and Hamlet, and is finally killed accidentally, because he conceals himself behind Gertrude's arras to listen in on Hamlet's conversation with her. It is an amusing irony that so many of Sh.'s 'wise sayings' come out of the mouth of this lovable windbag, who thinks himself clever but is hypocritical and misunderstands almost everything. Many of his characteristics may derive from the stock comic character of the *commedia dell'arte,* the aged Pantaloon. Where Sh. got the name is a mystery, but it seems to allude to Poland (Polonia) in some way. Although Norway's war with the 'Polacks' is in the background of the play, it seems to have nothing to do with the old man. Some think the name alludes to a minor source for the play *De Optimo Senatore* (1568) by Laurentius Grimalius Goslicius, translated into English as *The Counsellor* (1598). The author was Polish and there are some similarities in passages of both *Ham* and *MM* to his treatise. The mystery of Polonius' name is deepened by the fact that it seems to have been a deliberate change. In Q1 of the play the old man is called Corambis and this name is carried into the German curiosity *Der Bestrafte Brudermord* (1710) which seems to be a rendition of an older version of the play. In it, Polonius is called Corambus. Neither Claudius nor the Queen in the German version retain their names from the F1 *Ham* either, though there is no other evidence—as with Polonius—to suggest that their names are survivals from an older version. It has been suggested that Corambis had become associated with a buffoon in Sh.'s earlier version or in a lost play by Thomas Kyd (or someone else) which scholars have come to call the *Ur-Hamlet,* and maybe Sh. changed the name to give his royal minister a graver, or possibly more political quality. On the other hand, Sh. often handles his character's names in a peremptory manner which signifies nothing.

Polydamas, *Tro 5.5.6,* one of two Trojan warriors may be meant. The first possibility is the son of Panthous and Phrontis. He was a friend of Hector's and a seer. The second is the son of Antenor. He married one of Priam's daughters and was accused of being a traitor to Troy. The latter is frequently mentioned in William Caxton's *Recuyell of the Historyes of Troy* (1474), Sh.'s primary source. The former is not.

Polydore, *Cym,* name given to Guiderius by his foster father Belarius. In Holinshed's *Chronicles,* the ancient historian Polydore Virgil is often quoted in the margins of the story of Cymbeline. At F1 *Cym 3.3.86,* the name is spelled 'Paladour,' which is an ancient name for Shaftesbury, but there is no indication that this should be the correct version of the name throughout.

Polyxena, *Tro 3.3.201,* daughter of Priam and Hecuba. Achilles saw her and fell in love with her, possibly during Priam's mission to Achilles to claim Hector's body. After the fall of Troy, the ghost of Achilles demanded her, so she was sacrificed on his tomb by Neoptolemus. Sh. has Achilles in love with her before Hector's death.

Pomegranate, *1H4 2.5.36,* room in an inn. The fruit's name means 'apple with many seeds.' It is bright red inside which would have made it good for decorating the room. Further, it was associated with the myth of Proserpina (q.v.), who ate only a few seeds while forcibly held in the Underworld.

Pomfret, Pontefract, castle in Yorkshire belonging to the dukes of Lancaster. It was one of the favorite residences of Henry IV, the first Lancastrian king. Following his abdication Richard II was confined there, and he may have starved himself to death or been murdered in the dungeons of the castle. Pomfret is a Norman shortening of L. *pontus fractus* 'broken bridge,' presumably a local landmark.

2H6 2.2.26. R3 2.4.41, 3.1.180, 3.2.47, 79, 109, 3.4.90, 5.5.94. Jn 4.2.148. R2 5.1.52, 5.4.10. 2H4 1.1.204.

Pompeius, *Ant 1.2.175,* see Pompey, Sextus.

Pompey, 1) *MM,* F1 'Clown,' pimp and servant to Mistress Overdone. He produces much humor by showing the inability of the legal system to deal with him initially because of his verbal cleverness. He basically makes the argument that prostitution is a victimless crime. He continues to provide levity in jail, where he becomes the executioner Abhorson's assistant. His name obviously comes from the Roman hero and creates the humor of contrast. It has been argued because of Escalus' equation of Pompey to iniquity (*2.1.165*) that his character is intended to relate to the morality play character of Iniquity. At *2.1.207* he tells Escalus that his name is also Bum, probably meaning his last name, though possibly an alias or nickname. It provides a cheap joke on the British slang for 'buttocks' and then is abandoned. In Sh.'s sources this name is not used, but in George Whetstone's *Promos and Cassandra* (1578) there is a madam and her servant who correspond to Mistress Overdone and Pompey.

2) *Ant,* see Sextus Pompey.

3) *Ant 1.5.31,* see Pompey the Great.

Pompey the Great, Gnæus Pompeius Magnus (106–48 BC), Julius Cæsar's rival in the Roman civil wars. When Pompey began his career in the early 1st c. BC, Rome was struggling to adapt its antiquated republican institutions to the responsibilities of ruling a world empire. The limits that tradition set to the power of Rome's magistrates prevented them from abusing their offices, but made it difficult for them to oversee lengthy foreign campaigns. When Rome was faced with serious military situations, its Senate had no choice but to create 'special commands' that were free of constitutional restrictions. Pompey understood that these offices offered greater opportunities than the official magistracies. He therefore ignored the latter and pursued the former. Adroitly, he moved from one unique assignment to another, and each project brought him a larger following of soldiers. The crowning event of Pompey's military career was a campaign in Asia Minor and Palestine. Pompey marched beyond Rome's frontiers into new territories and nearly completed the empire's encirclement of the Mediterranean. In 61 BC he concluded that the time had come to return to Rome to claim the honors to which he was entitled. The subsequent course of events suggests that he was a better general than a politician.

Pompey underestimated the fear he inspired among his fellow senators. They knew that if he chose to use the army he had built, they could not prevent him from taking over the state. The Senate, therefore, devised a risky strategy to neutralize him. It awarded special commands to Julius Cæsar to permit him to create an army that was beyond Pompey's reach. The Senate hoped that Pompey's and Cæsar's military machines would check each other and prevent either man from stepping out of line. Pompey and Cæsar had no affection for each other, but they understood that it was in their mutual interest to cooperate. They enlisted the support of Crassus, one of the empire's wealthiest men, and formed the 'first triumvirate.' The triumvirate was an unstable coalition of individuals who, together, had the power to dominate Rome, but each of the triumvirs eagerly anticipated the day when he could dispense with the others. The delicate bonds of self-interest that restrained them began to unravel in 53 BC. Crassus' death in battle with the Parthians cleared the way for a showdown between Pompey and Cæsar. Pompey knew that Cæsar's plan was to build an army in Gaul to rival the force that Pompey had stationed in Asia Minor and Greece. Pompey decided to counter Cæsar's strategy by forcing Cæsar from the political offices that gave him the legal right to command Roman soldiers. Cæsar suggested compromise, but Pompey realized that time was not on his side and refused to back down.

In 49 BC Cæsar committed treason by leading an army into Italy from Gaul. Pompey retreated to Greece where he could marshal the men that he had stationed in the east. Cæsar had a much smaller contingent of soldiers, but he was the better commander. At the battle of Pharsalus Cæsar routed Pompey, and Pompey fled to Egypt, which was still outside Rome's jurisdiction. Advisors to the young pharaoh, Ptolemy, feared that the presence of Cæsar's enemy would tempt Cæsar to invade their country. To forestall this, they assassinated Pompey and sent his beautifully gift-wrapped head to Cæsar. The gesture did them no good. Cæsar invaded Egypt to punish it for an assault on a Roman citizen.

2H6 4.1.139–140: the reference to Pompey's murder by 'savage islanders' may derive from Elizabethan interpretations of Plutarch's account of Pompey's death. Plutarch ('Pompey,' 77.2) says that a Greek from the island of Chios persuaded the Egyptians to kill Pompey. *LLL 5.1.122, 5.2.504–5, 531, 541–558, 581, 675–700:* in the pageant of the Nine Worthies, Costard assumes the role of P. *H5 4.1.70, 72.*

JC 1.1.37, 42, 51, 2.1.215, 3.1.116, 3.2.186, 5.1.74. MM 2.1.209–10: the pimp Pompey (above) is compared to the Roman. *Ant 1.2.180, 1.5.31.*

Pompey's Porch, *JC 1.3.125, 147,* portico attached to the Pompey's Theater (q.v.).

Pompey's Theater, *JC 1.3.152,* first permanent theater constructed in Rome. Pompey gave it to the city in 55 BC. Julius Cæsar, who hounded Pompey to his death, was assassinated in Pompey's theater at the foot of a statue that commemorated the building's donor. Cæsar himself was partially responsible for the irony of the event. The Senate's regular meeting house had burned down in 52 BC. Cæsar had ordered its reconstruction, but, while the work was in progress, he convened the Senate under the porticos of Pompey's theater.

Pompion the Great, *LLL 5.2.501,* play on 'Pompey' and an old word for 'pumpkin,' perhaps alluding to Costard's size and shape.

Pont, *Ant 3.6.72,* kingdom of Pontus on the southern shore of the Black Sea. Plutarch ('Antony' 61.2) claims that its ruler, Polemon, sided with Mark Antony in his struggle with Octavius.

Pontic Sea, *Oth 3.2.456,* the Black Sea. *Pontus,* meaning 'sea,' was its Latin name, transferred from the Greek. Strabo tells us that ancient Greeks regarded it as a second Oceanus and, therefore, *the* sea was appropriate to its stature. He also remarks that sailing into it was a trip into the unknown. The Pontus was also known as the Euxine, or 'hospitable,' after the Ionians planted colonies, as a euphemism to encourage settlement. The old name, which Homer uses, is Axenus, 'inhospitable.' The image of the Black Sea ceaselessly flowing outward derives from Philemon Holland's translation of Pliny the Elder's *Naturalis Historia* 2, the source of several similes in the play.

Ponton, Lord, *1H6 1.6.6,* see Santrailles, Lord Ponton de.

Poor-John, see John 2).

Poor Tom, *Lr,* common name for a mad beggar, a Bedlam beggar, a Tom o' Bedlam, also called an Abram man from the 'Abraham ward,' where the mad lived who were composed enough to be released to beg for their sustenance. The situation is quite comparable to the many mentally ill homeless who were released from the asylums in recent times and who now sleep on the streets. Many beggars feigned madness to increase their alms, so the terms often became associated with fraud and theft. Edgar assumes the role to hide from his enemies. 'Tom' in this phrase is used in the sense of 'anyone.' See Bedlam.

Pope, bishop of Rome and, until the Reformation of the 16th c., the supreme spiritual leader of western Europe's Christians. The pope styled himself 'the vicar of Christ' by right of succession to St. Peter. Church tradition held that Peter was the first bishop of Rome and that he bequeathed to subsequent bishops of Rome the privilege of presiding over the church universal that Christ had bestowed on him in Matthew 16. The pope's ability to exercise the authority he claimed developed slowly. It was not until the 14th c. that the papacy was successful in asserting its right to oversee the appointment of clergy, levy taxes, and exercise jurisdiction over certain kinds of crimes in every nation in Europe. Henry VIII declared England independent of the papacy thirty years before Sh.'s birth, but England had in Sh.'s day not yet found its footing as a Protestant nation. Henry's son, Edward, promoted a more radical reformation than his father, but Edward's successor, his elder sister Mary, tried to return England to Catholicism. Her heir, her younger sister Elizabeth, favored a moderate Protestantism, and Elizabeth's successor, James I, was opposed to any strong religious organization that might compromise royal authority.

1H6 1.4.49, 51. 5.1.1: a reference to Eugenius IV who joined other international leaders in arranging the peace conference between the English and the French that led to the Treaty of Arras in 1442. *Jn. H8 2.4.117, 3.2.30, 288.*

Popillius Læna, *JC,* Popillius Lænas, Senator from a Roman plebeian family famous for its arrogance and cruelty. Plutarch ('Brutus' 15.3) says that Læna made a cryptic remark that frightened Brutus and Cassius. They feared that his comment meant that word of their plot to assassinate Julius Cæsar had leaked out.

Popp'rin' pear, *Rom 2.1.38,* pear of phallic shape named after the town of Poperingue in French Flanders.

Porcupine, *Err 3.1.117; 3.2.173; 4.1.49; 5.1.223, 276,* F1 'Porpentine,' the Courtesan's house. It is one of three entrances on stage with the Phoenix (q.v) and priory. Three doors were traditional in the backdrop of Roman theater.

Port le Blanc, *R2 2.1.278,* bay on the coast of Brittany from which Henry (IV) Bolingbroke may have launched his invasion of Richard II's England. Some authorities—citing the speed of Henry's passage and the place where he landed in England—believe, however, that Henry sailed from Boulogne. Henry may have tried to throw his opponent off guard by leaking the story that he was in Brittany rather than Flanders.

Porter, *1H6 2.3.1,* title for a servant who guards a door, from L. *porta,* 'gate.'

Portia, 1) *MV,* one of Sh.'s most admirable heroines. She rigorously adheres to the rules of selecting a husband that her father decreed on his deathbed and thus trusting to providence, but actively intervenes in the trial of Antonio for the sake of her fiancé Bassanio. She disguises herself as an attorney and attempts to persuade Shylock to exercise mercy in one of Sh.'s most beloved speeches. When this fails, she is able to spot a loophole in the contract which can be used to save Antonio, and despite the bitterness of all concerned, the tone of mercy she has set influences the Duke's treatment of Shylock.

Energetic and witty, she is also like Sh.'s other vigorous heroines Rosalind, Helena, and Beatrice, in that she helps make her beloved young man aware of his own weakness by putting him through some torment. Her mixture of nobility and youthful energy make her a complexly endearing, yet strong and intelligent character—much more admirable than the other characters in the play. Symbolically, she brings God's mercy and justice into an impossible situation rather like the *deus ex machina* of God, Gabriel, Michael, and the Virgin in the earliest extant dramatic version of the story (14th c.), *Le Miracle de un marchant et un juif* included in *Miracles de Nostre Dame par personnages* by the goldsmiths of Paris. Some critics have made connections between Portia and Elizabeth I in the queen's character and in that the queen's suitors correspond to Portia's. If so, there might be a parallel also between Bassanio and Essex, an implied suggestion that the Queen might forgive the young man's faults and proceed to a happy union.

Portia's name is borrowed from Cato's daughter (below). Relationships to L. *porta* 'gate,' *portio* 'a portion,' and *porto* 'to bring' are possible, but obscure.

2) Porcia, daughter of the hero of the Roman Republic, Marcus Porcius Cato Uticensis, and wife of Marcus Brutus, Cæsar's assassin. Her name derives from the Roman family name, which is related to the word *porcus,* 'pig.' It is doubtful this latter association provoked the spelling change as spelling would have had little influence in a theatrical production and little in what was essentially still an oral society. According to Plutarch ('Brutus' 13.3–5) Portia gave her husband vivid proof of the strong character she had inherited from her father, a man famous for his Stoic demeanor. She secretly inflicted a wound on herself. When she became ill from loss of blood, Brutus investigated and was told that she wished to show him her strength so that he would not fear to share his secrets with her. Brutus was impressed and promptly told her of the plot against Cæsar's life. When Mark Antony and Octavius defeated the Republican army and Brutus committed suicide, Portia resolved to die also. Plutarch ('Brutus' 53.4–5) says that several stories circulated about her death. According to the most famous, her friends, fearing that she might do violence to herself, kept all weapons away from her. She, however, outsmarted them by swallowing live coals. This seems improbable, but it may contain an element of truth. Suicidal Romans did sometimes asphyxiate themselves with fumes from charcoal fires, which are heavy with carbon monoxide.

MV 1.1.166. JC.

Portugal, *STM Add. II.D.143,* country located on the Iberian peninsula. It had been head of a worldwide empire and had just gone through its golden age of literature when it abruptly collapsed under the pressure of Spain about 1580. It did not reestablish its independence until 1640. Its name derives from L. *Portus cale* 'warm harbor,' 'ice-free harbor,' which the Romans called Oporto.

Portugal, Bay of, term used by sailors to refer to a stretch of water (not really a bay) in the Atlantic ocean between Oporto and the headland at Cintra, north of Lisbon. The bottom drops off very rapidly and would have been unfathomable in Sh.'s time. The term appears in a biography of Raleigh, but not in any geographies or on any maps. *AYLI 4.1.198,* reference to the supposed immeasurable depth of the bay. One commentator believes the attention in England to Portuguese affairs from 1578 to 1602 ought to date the simile, and therefore the play, to this period.

Posthumus Leonatus, *Cym,* husband of Innogen, son of Sicilius Leonatus. Posthumus secretly marries Innogen and is banished by Cymbeline. In Rome he makes a tasteless wager that Giacomo cannot seduce her. Giacomo deceives him and he instructs his servant to murder her. Grief-stricken, he fights with the Britons against Rome, then joins the Roman captives as a means of suicide. Later he discovers his wife is alive, and he is forgiven. Although he may be seen as a confusing character because Sh. had not yet discovered the proper form for his romances, he fits very well with the other young men who do reprehensible things and suffer to a new maturity or understanding of the nature of love. The irritating and often questionable behavior of Bassanio, Claudio, Orlando, and other young men endures through the range of Sh.'s plays from his early plays to his late. Sh.'s young women are almost always more admirable than their male leads who wager on faithfulness, fly into jealous rages, and so forth. Posthumus' name, which seems to have some hidden symbolic meaning in our time was, in fact, not unusual in Sh.'s, and indicates the son was born after his father's death. His mother also died in giving him birth. Leonatus, 'the lion's whelp,' as the play says, was an honorary name inherited from his father. Until he fights the Romans, there seems nothing particularly courageous about him. There may also be some implication that he is misguided because of his being orphaned. The story of Posthumus' wager on Innogen's chastity is from Boccaccio's *Decameron,* 2.9, though the corresponding character is Bernarbo Lomellini.

Potpan, *Rom 1.5.1, 9,* servant in Capulet's house, the nickname deriving from his kitchen duties.

Pots, *MM 4.3.17,* mocking name for one of the impoverished criminals Pompey knows. As prisoners paid for their own food, many were forced to beg passers by.

Prætor, *JC 1.3.143,* judicial office belonging to the Roman Republic. Both of Rome's chief executives, the consuls, had prætors who served as their assistants. The prætors were responsible for maintaining order within the city. Brutus held a prætorship when the plot against Cæsar was unfolding, and Plutarch ('Brutus' 10, 3–4) says that Cassius convinced Brutus that the office obligated him to defend Rome against Cæsar.

Prague, Praha, city on the Vltava (Moldau), traditional capital of Bohemia, now capital of the Czech Republic. The site of several 9th c. castles, it began to flourish under Wenceslaus I (1230–1253), who built extensive defenses. It had long attracted groups of German colonists, producing a cosmopolitan atmosphere, with various languages, and groups including a large community of Jews. Within a century it was the second largest city in Europe. During the reign of Emperor Charles IV, it grew even more spectacular. In 1348 Charles University (the U. of Prague) was founded with its faculty organized among the four nations: Czech, Polish, Saxon, and Bavarian. When the Czechs were given supremacy and reformer Jan Hus was elected rector, the Germans abandoned it and founded the university at Leipzig. Hus's ideas for reforming the Catholic church had been derived partly from John Wycliffe of England and took strong hold in Bohemia, anticipating the Reformation. Even after Hus was tricked and executed, Hussites gained control of the city in 1442. The Hussite wars caused considerable decline during the first half of the 16th c., but Prague recovered greatly after submission to the Habsburgs. The Thirty Years' War began there in 1618 when two imperial councillors were tossed from the windows of Hradcany castle (now the president's residence). After the war, Prague remained fairly quiet until the Austrian War of Succession and the Seven Years' War. The German character of the city grew, but in the late 19th c. and early 20th, the Bohemian nationalist movement developed. It led to the establishment of Czechoslovakia at the end of World War I. In Sh.'s time the city would have been known as one of the most prominent marketplaces of ideas, where learning and new ideas were highly valued. *TN 4.2.14,* 'the old hermit of P., that never saw pen and ink,' possibly a man known as Camaldoli in Tuscany, but there is no reason why anyone particular is in Sh.'s mind, any more than if he had written, 'the wise old man of the hills.'

Prat, Mother, *MWW 4.2.168,* Falstaff in disguise as the old woman of Brentford. Although Pratt is a common English name, 'prat' also meant a trick or, in slang, a buttock. The latter sounds like the kind of pun referring to Falstaff's anatomy to which Sh. was often enthusiastically equal.

Prester John, *Ado 2.1.250–1,* imaginary Christian king located in the remotest part of Asia or Africa. 'Prester' or 'presbyter' means priest, which the emperor supposedly chose to be called. He was reputedly a powerful and extremely wealthy monarch. The legend was persistent, seeming to begin in the 12th c. because of the appearance of an Indian priest who told miraculous stories about a shrine to St. Thomas in India. Later the story appears in a chronicle by Otto, bishop of Freisingen. A letter purporting to be from the priest king to the emperor Manuel in 1165 caused a sensation. It described the fabulous kingdom and its wonders. Pope Alexander III evidently wrote to John in 1177. Genghis Khan and Gur Khan, who founded Kara-Khitai in central Asia and threatened

Persia, were confused with an imaginary son or grandson of Prester John, named David, who was supposedly crushing Islam. Marco Polo identified him with Unc Khan, the chief of the Keraits, a Nestorian Christian tribe of Mongols. By the 14th c. the name is applied to the king of Abyssinia, a Coptic Christian state in Africa, though frequently said to be in the Indies. His dominions were said to embrace the Tropics from the Red Sea to the Ethiopic (Indian) Ocean. The persistence of the legend seems to be a way for Christians to deny the vast and mostly non-Christian expanses of Asia. The slightest shreds of confused evidence for John's existence were immediately seized.

Priam, king of Troy, son of Laomedon and either Strymo or Placia. Originally he was named Podarces, but was called Priam, 'ransomed,' because of his sister Hesione's ransom of him from Hercules. Laomedon had given his daughter Hesione to appease a sea monster sent by Neptune to ravage Troy. Priam became king of Troy when his father refused to give Hercules the horses of Neptune he had promised him for rescuing Hesione and Hercules conquered Troy, giving Hesione to Telamon and placing Priam on the throne. He was first married to Arisbe, but gave her away to marry Hecuba. By the time of the Trojan War, he was quite aged and unable to fight but had fifty sons and twelve daughters—some sources say fifty daughters as well. In *The Iliad* Homer shows him tenderly treating Helen of Troy and creates great pathos when Priam bravely goes to Achilles to ransom the mutilated body of his son Hector. Priam's death is described in Virgil's *Æneid* 2.470 ff. As the Greeks are sacking his city he struggles into his old armor, but Hecuba convinces him that their only salvation could come from the gods. While they kneel at the altar of Jupiter, Pyrrhus chases Priam's son Polites into the temple and kills him. Priam calls upon the gods to avenge the sacrilege, whereupon Pyrrhus stabs him in the side, then beheads him.

Shr 3.1.29, 34, 42: Priami . . . senis, 'old Priam,' quoted from a couplet in Ovid's *Epistolæ,* 1.33–4. *3H6 2.5.120. Tit 1.1.80, 5.3.83. Luc 1367, 1448, 1466, 1485, 1490, 1522, 1546, 1548, 1550, 1560. 2H4 1.1.72, 74:* Percy's misfortune is compared to Priam's. Since Priam witnesses the destruction of all his children, Sh. uses him as an archetype for grieving fathers.

Ham 2.2.450, 467, 475, 482, 495: the speech that Hamlet remembers is similar to one in Christopher Marlowe's *Dido, Queen of Carthage.* The original telling of Priam's death by Æneas to Dido occurs in Virgil's *Æneid.* It is possible that Sh. has a speech from a lost play in mind, but he could just as likely have fabricated it to poke fun at the overwrought style still popular with the Lord Admiral's Men.

Tro: Priam is relatively insignificant in the play, a victim of circumstance, as he is in the *Iliad.* Too old to fight, he ineffectually presides over the destruction of his kingdom, asking for advice on whether Helen should be given back to Menelaus and begging Hector not to fight. *AWW 1.3.71,* 'King P.'s joy,' Helen of Troy.

Priamus, *Tro 2.2.206, 5.3.56,* variant for Priam.

Priapus, son of Dionysus (or Hermes) and Aphrodite, Roman god of fertility, one of the Numina, protector of shepherds, fishermen, and farmers. Born at Lampsacus he was ugly and deformed and he was eventually regarded as a fomenter of obscenity and pornography. His lecherous pursuit of the nymph Lotis resulted in her being changed into the lotus tree. His statue of red-painted wood was often placed in gardens and he was represented as having an enormous, erect 'yard' (as Alexander Schmidt optimistically refers to it). *Per 19.13,* 'she's able to freeze the god Priapus,' even the god of the erection would be immobilized by Marina's saintliness.

Priest, Sir, *TN 3.4.264.* Since priests were also usually university graduates, they were called 'sir.' Bachelors of Arts were called 'Dominus' meaning 'sir' which was abbreviated as 'D.,' a practice still followed at Cambridge. Viola seems to be saying, 'I would rather engage in peaceful practices than warlike ones.'

Prince, from L. *princeps,* 'first citizen,' title granted the Roman emperor Augustus in gratitude for his achievements in allegedly restoring the Roman Republic. Since Augustus wielded the power of a monarch, his republican title acquired royal associations. In ordinary usage 'prince' can refer to an heir to a throne or to a reigning monarch. *The Prince* (It. *Il Principe*) was also the title of Machiavelli's controversial textbook on leadership which was so often discussed during the Renaissance (see Machiavel).

1) *Tit 2.2.5,* see Bassianus.

2) *1H6 1.4.67,* Henry VI (q.v.) in his minority.

3) *LLL 4.1.99,* see Ferdinand, king of Navarre.

4) *Rom,* see Escalus.

5) 'the wild P.,' *MWW 3.2.66,* Prince Hal, later Henry V (q.v.).

6) *WT,* Florizel or Mamillius (qq.v.).

7) *Tmp. 1.1.51,* see Ferdinand.

Prince of Cats, *Rom,* see Tybalt.

Prince of Darkness, *Lr 3.4.134 (Q 11.131),* the devil.

Prince of Wales, 1) title traditionally accorded the heir to the English throne. Edward I was the first English king to bestow it on his son, Edward II, who was born at the Welsh castle of Carnarvon in 1284, a year after his father had conquered Wales. The place of his birth gave Edward II a Welsh connection, and by granting the heir to the English throne the Welsh royal title Edward I planned to forestall its usurpation by the ambitious Welsh noblemen who hoped to restore the independence of Wales. The formal association of the Welsh title with the right of succession to the English throne began with Edward III's son, Edward the Black Prince.

R2 2.1.173. 2H6 2.2.11, see Edward, the Black Prince.

2) *2H4 2.1.136, 2.2.112, 4.3.184,* see Henry V.

Princess Dowager, *H8 3.2.70, 4.1.23,* title by which Henry VIII insisted that Katherine of Aragon be known after their separation. It signified that she and Henry had never been truly married and that her legal rank was that of her first and only husband, Arthur, prince of Wales. Katherine chose to suffer physical deprivation rather than comply with Henry's decree. If she had relinquished the royal title, she would have signaled acceptance of Henry's argument that her marriage was invalid and her daughter Mary illegitimate.

Princess of France, *LLL,* leader of an embassy to Ferdinand king of Navarre to settle a disagreement concerning the payment of a debt. This matter of state is sufficient to force Ferdinand to meet with her and he immediately falls in love, forgetting his vow of asceticism. Like many of Sh.'s heroines, the Princess is clever and intelligent, and, along with her ladies in waiting, makes her suitor jump through several humiliating hoops before he can gain promise of her affection. She and her ladies trick the lords as to their identities during a masked ball, for example. At the end of the play, her father dies and she swears Ferdinand to a monastic life during the year of her mourning, after which she will become his bride. 'Queen' is more frequently used in the old editions for her. It is thought that the Princess' embassy to Navarre was suggested by the visit in 1578 of Marguerite de Valois and her mother Catherine de Médicis to Henry of Navarre (Marguerite's estranged husband) or possibly a visit by Marguerite to Flanders in 1577. Another possibility considered much less likely was Catherine's attempt in October 1586 at St. Bris to negotiate with Henry an end to the religious civil war and a marriage to the Princess of Lorraine. See Ferdinand, king of Navarre.

Priscian, *LLL 5.1.29,* Priscianus Cæsariensis, Latin grammarian of the 6th c. Born in Cæsaria, Mauritania, he worked in Constantinople. He summed up the grammar of the previous centuries in 18 books called the *Institutiones Grammaticæ.* Its rich use of quotes which have not otherwise survived made it a valuable resource for scholars. As a grammar it was largely superseded by other works in the 13th c. Priscian also wrote on poetry, the emperor Anastasius, rhetoric, and other subjects.

Privy Council, *H8 4.1.114,* small group of royal agents who emerged during the period when Thomas Cromwell dominated Henry VIII's government. The full royal council was an amorphous group of advisors and administrators who were under oath to serve the king. Since it was not convenient to gather them all together to consult on every item of royal business, different groups convened for different purposes. Cardinal Wolsey relied most frequently on a committee that was known, from the place where it met, as the Council of the Star Chamber. Under Cromwell the Star Chamber specialized in judicial matters, and the Privy Council provided the arena for political discussions.

Procris, see Cephalus.

Procrus, *MND 5.1.197–8,* Procris, wife of Cephalus (q.v.).

Proculeius, *Ant,* Cornelius Proculeius, wealthy member of the Roman equestrian class and friend of Octavius. Plutarch ('Antony' 78.1–79.1) says that Proculeius handled the negotiations that took place between Octavius and Cleopatra after the battle of Actium. Proculeius was also known to the poet Horace, who mentioned him in one of his songs (*Carmina* 2.2).

Prodigal Son, character from the parable Jesus narrates in Luke 15:11–32. The prodigal squanders his inheritance in riotous living, repents, and is welcomed home by his father. The story illustrates God's mercy and his readiness to forgive sinners.

TGV 2.3.3: Lance confuses 'Prodigal' with 'prodigious.' *Err 4.3.18,* because the jailer was wearing a jerkin of calf's skin, the Prodigal Son (for whom the fatted calf was killed) is alluded to.

MWW 4.5.7. 2H4 2.1.47. WT 4.3.96.

Progne, *Tit 5.2.194,* Procne, sister of Philomel, daughter of Pandion of Attica and wife of Tereus, king of Phocis. See Philomela.

Prologue, spoken introduction to a play, directly addressed to the audience. It was a device of ancient drama, getting the audience's attention and preparing them for the tone and intention of the play to follow. Sh. infrequently used the device and parodies it in *MND.* Hamlet's players also use it. The speaker usually wore a distinctive costume of black velvet if he assumed an allegorical role, as in *Rom, H5,* and *TNK.* In *Tro,* he is described as being armed, perhaps an allusion to Ben Jonson's armed Prologue in *Poetaster* (1601). In *Per,* poet John Gower performs the function. The invocation of the Muses in the Chorus' prologue of *H5* may be intended to equate King Henry with the great warriors of antiquity.

Promethean, (adj.) pertaining to Prometheus, meaning 'life-giving,' or 'inspired from heaven.' It has been argued that Sh. got the word from George Chapman's *Shadow of Night* (1594), though it seems a simple invention. *LLL 4.3.327, add. l. 9,* 'P. fire.' *Oth 5.2.12,* 'P. heat.'

Prometheus, *Tit 2.1.17,* one of the Titans, the divine race that preceded the Olympian gods. His name means something like 'foresight.' The many myths that mention him are difficult to fit into a coherent story, but he is usually described as a friend of the human species whose services to humanity got him into serious trouble. He violated Zeus's orders by giving human beings fire and various technologies that permitted them to compete with the gods. Zeus responded by chaining the disobedient Titan to a rock (in Tartarus or Hades in some myths, in the Caucasus mountains at the edge of the earth in others). A gigantic eagle was dispatched at regular intervals to tear at Prometheus' liver. His fate is variously described. He may ultimately have been rescued by Hercules, another god may have volunteered to take his place, or Zeus may finally have forgiven him.

Propontic, *Oth 3.2.459,* the Sea of Marmora, a small body of water connecting the Black Sea to the Meditterranean. The name derives from its position *pro,* 'before,' the Pontus (L. 'Black Sea'). The image of the Black Sea ceaselessly flowing outward derives from Holland's translation of Pliny's *Natural History,* the source of several similes in the play.

Proserpina, Roman goddess (Gr. Persephone), daughter of Ceres and wife of Pluto. Pluto carried her off to the Underworld and Ceres begged for her return. He said he would allow her return to her mother if she had not eaten during her stay. As she had tasted only pomegranate seeds, he allowed her to visit her mother for part of each year. That part corresponded to spring and summer, symbolizing Ceres' joy; winter corresponded to her sorrow. Pirithous and Theseus attempted to free Proserpina for their mother. Pirithous became trapped in Hades because of it. *Tro 2.1.34. WT 4.4.116.*

Proserpine, *TNK 4.3.24,* Proserpina.

Prosper, *Tmp 2.2.2, 81; 3.3.99,* Prospero.

Prospero, *Tmp,* rightful Duke of Milan. A Neo-Platonist who studies the interrelationships of the universe, a scholar of divine things, he practices white magic as opposed to Sycorax's black magic. The distinction is important because of King James' antipathy to black magic, illustrated by his *Demonology.* 'Prospero' is used in Ben Jonson's *Every Man in his Humour* in which Sh. acted. One possible source for the play, Thomas' *History of Italy* (1549), contains a Prospero Adorno who is deposed as the Duke of Genoa and then restored to his throne as a lieutenant of the Duke of Milan. When he connived with Ferdinando, king of Naples, however, Milan set out to depose him. Prospero Adorno defeated them, but was later deposed and succeeded by Antony Adorno as governor under Milan. There is also a Prospero Calonne in Dent's Translation of the *History of Philip de Comines* (1526), along with some other coincidences of name, and there was a Prospero who was a riding master in London whom Sh. might have known. The name means 'favorable' (It. from L. *prosperus*). It has been popular to imagine that the character is an allegory for Sh. himself and that Sh.'s retiring from the theater is paralleled by Prospero's giving up magic. There is no real evidence for this view, despite its appeal. If a particular island must be chosen as the setting for Prospero's exile, Lampedusa, between Malta and Tunisia, is a likely candidate. It was famous for storms, firewood, caves, and was associated by the Jews with the supernatural. Another critic suggests Pantelleria, more to the west. More likely, as in Sh.'s Ardenne and Bohemia, the details of geography did not fret the playwright.

Protector, Lord, title granted the guardian of a young king. It implied something less than the post of regent. A regent had the right to act with the full authority of the king whom he represented. The protector governed with the cooperation of a powerful council of royal advisors. Humphrey, duke of Gloucester, bore this title (*2H6 1.1.37, 162, 175, 176, 1.2.44, 3H6 1.1.111, 1H6*) during Henry VI's minority and chafed under its restrictions. Sh. pokes fun at Jack Cade by claiming that he aspired to the office (*2H6 4.2.157*). Richard of Gloucester was 'protector' during young Edward V's brief reign (*R3 1.3.14, 3.1.141, 3.4.7, 3.7.133*).

Proteus, 1) *TGV,* F1 'Protheus,' one of the two gentlemen of the title. Sworn to Julia, he is sent to the Emperor's court by his father and there falls in love with his friend Valentine's beloved Silvia. He ruthlessly schemes against his friend and tries to force himself on Silvia. At play's end, however, there is a round of forgiving which results in his recommitment to Julia. His changeability obviously relates to the mythical creature mentioned many times in Ovid's *Metamorphoses,* in Homer's *Odyssey,* and other sources (see below). The opening of *TGV* resembles the duologue between the friends Endimion and Eumenides that opens John Lyly's *Endimion* (1591) and suggests Sh. may have been thinking of them in molding his characters Valentine and Proteus.

2) *3H6 3.2.192,* Greek sea deity who had the gifts of prophecy and shape-shifting. Proteus would foretell the future, but only for those who had the courage to hold on to him as he assumed a succession of frightening forms. Sh. has Richard of Gloucester (Richard III) profess to rival the god in shiftiness.

Provençal roses, *Ham 3.2.264–5,* F1 'Prouinciall r.' Editors are uncertain what is meant here. Some say that the roses of Provence, in the south of France, were especially large. Others think that Provins, about 40 mi. from Paris is meant, a place celebrated for its roses, supposedly imported from Syrie by the Comte de Brie. It has also been noted that the damask rose was called the 'Rosa provincialis.' It seems most likely, however, that a false rose placed upon the shoe strings as a decoration is what is meant and the implication is one of excesses in fashion, such as might be worn by a flamboyant actor.

Proverbs, *MWW 3.1.96,* book of the Old Testament, traditionally said to be written by Solomon. There are many allusions and echoes of the book of Proverbs throughout Sh.'s works. In this case, it is also possible that the Host of the Garter means proverbs in general. The word comes from L. *proverbium,* 'words put forth.'

Provost, *MM,* title of the chief officer of the prison. He is both merciful and yet is willing to carry out duties which he finds unpleasant. The title originates in L. *præpositus,* 'one placed before others,' and applied to various functions, such as the highest official of a cathedral or a chief magistrate in Scotland.

Prudence, Sir, *Tmp 2.1.291,* Antonio's mocking name for the conscience, which he perceives as an insignificant enemy.

Psalm, see Hundredth Psalm.

Psalmist, *2H4 3.2.36,* the author of the Bible's book of hymns, the Psalms. Medieval tradition credited the book to the Hebrew king, David. David's skill as a singer and harpist was greatly appreciated by his predecessor, King Saul.

Ptolemy, 1) *Ant 1.4.6, 17,* Cleopatra's younger brother and husband. Cleopatra's father, Ptolemy Auletes ('Flute-player'), had left his throne to her and her elder brother (also named Ptolemy). War broke out between their respective factions, and Rome intervened. Ptolemy, the elder brother, died fleeing an army led by Julius Cæsar. Cæsar restored order to Egypt by confirming Cleopatra's claim to the throne and wedding her to her younger brother, the Ptolemy to whom Sh. refers. Cleopatra put her nominal husband to death in 43 BC.

2) *Ant 3.6.15,* see Cæsarion.

3) Pl.: *Ant 2.7.33, 3.12.18,* ancient Egypt's last dynasty of pharaohs. The line was founded by Alexander the Great's general, Ptolemy Soter (323–285 BC). After Alexander's death in Babylon in 323 BC, Ptolemy detached Egypt from Alexander's empire and restored its independence. Ptolemy also hijacked Alexander's body from its funeral cortege and buried it in a lavish mausoleum in Egypt's new capital city, Alexandria. Cleopatra was the last of Ptolemy's descendants to rule Egypt. When she died, Egypt became a province of the Roman empire, and the title of pharaoh lapsed.

Publicola, 1) *Ant 3.7.73,* Lucius Gellius Publicola, consul for the year 36 BC. In the Roman civil wars he first sided with Julius Cæsar's assassins. He later repudiated the Republican party and offered his allegiance to Octavius and Mark Antony. When war broke out between them, he cast his lot with Antony. He commanded the right wing of Antony's fleet at Actium, and he may have died in that battle.

2) *Cor 5.3.64,* Publius Valerius Publicola, consul and co-founder of the Roman Republic with Junius Brutus. The cognomen 'Publicola' means 'People's friend.' It was awarded in recognition of the consul's liberal legislation. His most important law granted a citizen who was

condemned to death by a magistrate of the Republic the right of appeal to the assembly of the people.

Publius, 1) *Tit,* nephew of Titus Andronicus who assists him in avenging the wrongs done their family by Demetrius and Chiron, the sons of the wicked empress, Tamora. The plot of *Tit* is not derived from history, and there is no known source from which Sh. might have taken the character he calls 'Publius.' He may have liked the name for its Roman sound, for he used it for other characters for whom he had no historical prototypes or no recorded names.

2) *JC,* elderly Senator who is a member of the group that escorts Julius Cæsar to his assassination. Publius has no known historical prototype, and Sh. probably invented the character for dramatic purposes. Publius provides the excuse for a bit of action that shows Brutus, despite his participation in Cæsar's murder, to be a gentle, noble person. Publius is ignorant of the plot against Cæsar and greatly alarmed when it erupts. In the midst of the confusion surrounding Cæsar's murder, Brutus looks after Publius and assures him that he is safe. Sh. may have chosen the name 'Publius' for its Roman sound. He used it also for the brother of Metellus Cimber, whose name was not supplied by Sh.'s source, Plutarch's 'Cæsar.'

3) *Cor 2.3.241,* member of the Martian family who Plutarch ('Coriolanus' 1.1) says assisted Quintus Marcius Rex during the construction of the Aqua Marcia in 144 BC.

Publius Cimber, *JC 3.1.53, 57,* exiled brother whose recall Metellus Cimber begs from Julius Cæsar. Cæsar's assassins approached him under the guise of gathering at Metellus' side to support his suit. They had arranged to strike Cæsar when Metellus gave the signal by grabbing hold of Cæsar's toga (Plutarch, 'Cæsar' 66.3–4). Plutarch, Sh.'s chief source, does not name Metellus' brother. Sh.'s reason for calling him 'Publius' is uncertain. The Roman sound of the name may simply have appealed to him, for he used it for other characters for whom he had to supply names.

Pucelle, *1H6 1.3.89,* Fr. 'maid' or 'virgin,' see Joan of Arc.

Puck, type of mischievous fairy. It is mentioned in Spenser's *Epithalamion,* 341. See Goodfellow, Robin.

Puckey, *Mac 4.1.47,* spirit called forth by the witches in a song not appearing in F1, but which appears in Thomas Middleton's play *The Witch* (c. 1609, but not printed until the 18th c.). William Davenant's version of *Mac* (printed 1674), however, contains the song and it has been argued that he may have had access to an earlier text. It is most likely two spirits are being invoked rather than one, though this line is sometimes edited 'Firedrake Puckey,' as in Davenant. The name was taken from Reginald Scot's *Discoverie of Witchcraft* (1584), probably, though the puck was a well-known spirit.

Puckle, *Mac 3.5.43,* spirit called forth by the witches. The name came from Reginald Scot's *Discoverie of Witchcraft* (1584). This is probably the same as Puckey (q.v.).

Pudding, *MM 4.3.15,* 'lusty P.,' mocking name for one of the impoverished criminals Pompey knows. As prisoners paid for their own food, many were forced to beg passers by. 'Pudding' has long been slang for the sexual organs (L. *pudendus,* 'that which is shameful').

Puff of Bar'son, *2H4 5.3.90–91,* character with a name invented to poke fun at Falstaff's shape. Goodman Puff is the only person in England Justice Shallow claims to know who is larger than Falstaff.

Purgatory, place where departed souls are purged by fire of their venial sins, a place of temporary suffering. See Limbo. *Rom 3.3.18. Oth 4.3.76.*

Puritan, adherent to a number of Protestant beliefs becoming increasingly stronger during the Elizabethan period. By 1649, Puritans would be powerful enough to depose and execute Charles I and rule the nation until 1660. In America, they established and controlled the Plymouth and Massachusetts Bay colonies and importantly influenced a number of what are considered distinctly American attitudes. They were primarily middle class believers in the Protestant concepts developed by John Calvin of Geneva. Implicit in Calvin's teachings was a democratic notion of equality of all men in the eyes of God. A king was as worthless to the divinity as a peasant. Therefore, despite their often rigorous enforcement of religious principles when in power, their rise contributed significantly to democratic reform in a number of ways. Parliament was an important vehicle for airing their views. Cromwell, despite his dictatorial powers, refused to become a monarch. By the Restoration (of Charles II and partly due to his frivolous nature) the monarchy's power had been reduced and would continue to be eroded, particularly by the Glorious Revolution of 1688, but steadily thereafter, until today the ruling family of England are reduced to decorating stamps and feeding tourism and yellow journalism.

The word Puritan comes from the group's attempt to 'purify' Christianity by removing all of the corruptions that had been appended since apostolic times. These included clerical dress, the papacy, and the episcopal system. The Puritans were also opposed to a number of things they considered corrupting influences, believing that one's mind should be upon God and his grace rather than entertainment. They opposed the cruel sports of bull and bear baiting (though not really because of the animals' suffering), as well as the theater, which was often associated with those sports. Whenever Puritans appear in plays of the period, ridicule is heaped on them as melancholic, obsessive spoilsports, though it is to Sh.'s credit that, as usual, he grants them a humanity which makes them more than caricatures. In outlawing theater in 1642, Puritans broke the short tradition of Renaissance English theater and when theater came back with the Restoration, it was quite different, having women actors, for example.

WT 4.3.43: the Clown's singers have only one Puritan, and even he sings psalms to hornpipes. The use of elaborate music was opposed by Puritans, who preferred the simple human voice. *TN 2.3.135, 137, 141:* Malvolio is a 'kind of P.,' who opposes the raucous behavior of Sir Toby and his pals, but who is a fool in love and tortured unmercifully for it.

AWW 1.3.52, a reference to the rejection of the Roman Catholic practice of avoiding meat on holy days. *1.3.91. Per 19.18.*

Purr, *Lr Q 13.41,* possibly the name of a demon. If so, Sh. borrowed it from Samuel Harsnett's 'Purre' (see Flibbertigibbet) a fat devil who was conjured up for money in 1584, Harsnett observes wryly, and wouldn't go back to hell until good company came for him. The line alludes also to the fact that Sara Williams, one of the women exorcised, was tormented by cats. However, the word here is more likely merely the imitation of a cat's sound.

Pygmalion, *MM 3.1.313,* king of Cyprus and misogynist sculptor. He carved his ideal woman of ivory. The statue was so perfect he was obsessed with it and prayed to Venus to give it life. When the statue came to life, she was called Galatea. She married him and gave birth to Paphos, for whom a city sacred to Venus was named. The story is told in Ovid's *Metamorphoses,* 10.

Pygmies, see Pigmies.

Pygmies, King of, *TNK 3.4.15:* the Jailer's Daughter in her madness says that the King is an exceptional fortune-teller. Her land of the Pygmies would lie somewhere in the Black Sea, where many fantastic people and things supposedly dwelled.

Pyramus, mythological star-crossed lover from ancient Babylon. He fell for Thisbe, his neighbor's daughter, speaking to her through a crack in the wall between their houses. Their families, however, opposed the marriage. In planning to elope, the lovers made arrangements to meet at Ninus' tomb, but a lioness on the prowl chased Thisbe away and tore her veil in its bloodstained maw. Pyramus found the cloth and assumed the lion had killed her. He then committed suicide with his sword. When Thisbe returned, she found his body and threw herself on his sword. The parents of the two mingled their cremated remains in one urn and, as Pyramus' blood had stained the white mulberry tree, the gods made its berry a dark purple when ripe. The story is told in Ovid's *Metamorphoses,* 4, and is an obvious prototype for the story of Romeo and Juliet—though Sh.'s source for *Rom* is more direct.

Tit 2.3.231. MND: the rustics put on a play of Pyramus and Thisbe, with Bottom playing Pyramus. As *MND* was written in the same time period (1594–95) as *Rom,* it is refreshing that Sh. parodied his own play, or (if the sequence is reversed, a less likely possibility) made serious the story his rustics made ridiculous.

Pyrenean, *Jn 1.1.203,* Pyrenees, mountains that divide France from Spain. During the Middle Ages they were governed by the kings of Navarre and Aragon.

Pyrrhus, Neoptolemus, son of Achilles and Deidameia (or in some sources, Iphigenia). After the death of his father, he was brought to Troy by the Greeks in obedience to a prophecy that said that the war could not be won without his presence. He was one of the warriors who concealed himself in the wooden horse that brought Troy down. He cruelly slew Priam on the altar of Jupiter. He executed Polyxena on his father's tomb and took Andromache as his concubine. Later he was killed by Orestes at Delphi.

Luc 1449, 1467. Tro 3.3.202. 4.7.26, see Neoptolemus. *Ham 2.2.453, 454, 455, 466, 475, 480, 483, 490, 494, 516:* the speech that Hamlet remembers is similar to one in Christopher Marlowe's *Dido, Queen of Carthage.* Its source, Æneas' recounting of Priam's death to Dido, is in Virgil's *Æneid* 2.240 ff. It is possible that Sh. has a speech from a lost play in mind, but he could just as likely have fabricated it to poke fun at the overwrought style still popular with the Lord Admiral's Men.

Pythagoras, (c. 582–c. 507 BC) ancient philosopher, born in Samos, son of Mnesarchus, and possibly a follower of Pherecydes. What is known about his life was transmitted through his followers, who regarded him as a demigod and the son of Apollo. He supposedly travelled throughout the ancient world to Babylon, even India, but was significantly affected by a twenty-two year stay in Egypt. He was also influenced by the Greek, Egyptian, and Chaldean mystery cults. Ultimately he settled in Crotona, a Greek colony in southern Italy. There his antidemocratic political teachings and their opposition to traditional religious practices resulted in a revolt against the Pythagoreans, and their power was destroyed in Magna Græcia. He died shortly after in Metapontion (modern Metaponto). Aristotle said that Pythagoras had first worked at mathematics, then condescended to wonder-working. Bertrand Russell facetiously described him as a combination of Einstein and Mrs. Eddy in that he is credited largely with advancing interest in mathematics but also with organizing a religious cult with a number of curious beliefs and taboos, such as abstaining from beans in order to purify the soul. The Pythagoreans fascination with numbers led in two directions, one to pure mathematical thinking, the other to numerology. They believed the entire universe could be reduced to numbers. By applying numbers to music, the Pythagoreans made great advances in understanding musical tones. They also considered the earth to revolve around a fixed point in the universe. In modern times Pythagoras' name is mostly associated with the Pythagorean theorem used in calculating the sides of a right triangle, but in Sh. the name is always in reference to Pythagoras' belief in the transmigration of the immortal soul.

AYLI 3.2.173, 'P.'s time,' a long time ago, in a previous life. *MV 4.1.130. TN 4.2.50, 58.*

Q

Queen, 1) *LLL,* the Princess of France. Throughout F1, Queen is more frequently used than Princess and is used for all dialogue attributions. Perhaps this is an indication that Marguerite de Valois, estranged wife of Henry of Navarre, was in Sh.'s mind when creating the play.

2) *MND 2.1.17, 19, 3.2.376,* see Titania.

3) *MND 4.1.108,* see Hippolyta.

4) *R2,* Isabella of Valois (1390–1409), daughter of King Charles VI of France and second wife to Richard II. Her marriage with Richard in 1396 sealed a controversial treaty of peace between England and France. Given her extremely young age, Sh.'s description of her affectionate relationship with Richard would be more accurate as a depiction of the king's tie with his first wife, Anne of Bohemia. Anne and Richard often demonstrated their love for each other in public, and Richard was so grieved by her death in 1394 that he ordered the palace where she died dismantled. Richard's conduct with Isabella must have been quite different. She was less than seven years old at the time of their marriage and only twelve when Richard was deposed. Her last meeting with Richard took place as he left for his campaign in Ireland, and after his deposition she did not have an opportunity for a conversation with him like the one Sh. describes. Henry IV returned her to her father and requested her hand for his heir. His proposal was rejected, for France could not immediately recognize the legitimacy of the Lancastrian usurpation of a throne that had been occupied by Charles's son-in-law. In 1406 Isabella married her cousin, the count of Angoulême, and died in childbirth at the age of nineteen.

5) *2H4 epi.33,* see Elizabeth I.

6) *Ant,* see Cleopatra.

7) *H8 1.1.177,* see Katherine of Aragon.

Queen, First, *TNK,* widow who, with two others who are not identified precisely, pleads for Theseus to avenge the sacrilegious treatment of her husband King Capaneus, who has been killed besieging Thebes and whose body has been left to rot in the fields. This would identify her with the faithful Evadne of mythology who, at Capaneus' funeral rites, threw herself on the pyre. The mentioning of Capaneus alone among the Seven Against Thebes and the pleading of Evadne is directly from Chaucer's *Knyghtes Tale.*

Queen of the Fairies, 1) *MND,* see Titania.

2) *MWW,* 'the Fairy Queen,' a role assumed by Mistress Quickly. Since the characterization seems out of her depth, it is sometimes argued that Sh. intended only that the actor who played Quickly, also play the Queen, who, it is said, hates all 'sluts and sluttery.'

Queen of Troy, *Tit 1.1.136,* see Hecuba.

Queen o' th' Sky, *Tmp 4.1.70,* see Iris.

Queubus, *TN 2.3.23,* 'the equinoctial of Q.,' an imaginary location. Either Sir Andrew's has confused what Feste spoke of on the previous night, or Feste has gulled Sir Andrew with false erudition.

Quickly, Mistress Nell, hostess of the Boar's Head in Eastcheap frequented by Prince Harry and his rowdy friends. The character may have been suggested to Sh. by a phrase from an early anonymous play, *The Famous Victories of Henry V:* 'pretty wench in Eastcheap.' Her name may be from 'quick lay,' though 'quick,' meaning 'alive' was used often in sexual contexts, referring to genitalia, and would have been sufficiently suggestive. If it referred to her manner of doing business, it would serve as well.

1H4. 2H4. 2.1.97, 'Gossip Q.' *H5 2.1.17,* 'Nell Q.' *2.1.76.* In *MWW* she is Caius' housekeeper and later plays the Queen of the Fairies in the humiliation of Falstaff. In the Latin lesson, she makes ribald words out of the Latin. Many critics argue that this woman is not the same as the one who is hostess at the Boar's Head and who marries Pistol. She doesn't even know Falstaff as the play begins. Furthermore, she undergoes an apparent change of character when she assumes her fairy role, which may mean that the actor who played her was now to play a different role.

Quinapalus, *TN 1.5.32,* supposed authority invented by Feste to lend credence to the 'quotation.' The use of this name mocks all pompous speakers who invoke the names of dead authorities rather than using reason to support their contentions.

Quince, Peter, *MND,* carpenter who organizes the Pyramus and Thisbe play. He assumes a role much like Holofernes in *LLL* and Gerald the Schoolmaster in *TNK,* and occasionally overembellishes his speech as they do more frequently. He writes the play and later is mentioned by Bottom as the possible author of 'Bottom's Dream.' He also carefully handles the rambunctious Bottom and serves as the leader of the rustic troupe, though he does a particularly bad job with his own prologue, orally mispunctuating his speech so that it no longer says what it intends. This particular humorous bit was a common device of English comedy from the time of *Ralph Roister Doister* by Nicholas Udall (c. 1553). As with his comrades, his name is thought to derive from his occupation. 'Quoins' or 'quines' were wedges used for various purposes such as shimming. The word also meant the external angle of a wall. Much less likely is 'quinch' or 'quince' which meant to move or flinch. Holinshed uses it in this way, for example, and it may have been appropriate if this were part of the actor's characterization, say as a tic.

Quintus, 1) *Tit,* one of the sons of Titus Andronicus. He and his brother were falsely accused and executed for the murder of the emperor Saturninus' brother, Bassianus. An 18th c. chapbook preserves a later version of a tale that might have served as Sh.'s source for *Tit,* and it contains an episode dealing with the deaths of Titus' sons.

2) *Cor 2.3.241,* Martius Rex, Roman official who, about 144 BC, oversaw the construction of an aqueduct that bore his name, the Aqua Marcia.

R

Ragusine, *MM 4.3.68, 73, 97,* F1 'Ragozine,' pirate whose head, when Barnardine refuses to be executed, is substituted for that of Claudio's. The name likely derives directly or indirectly from Ragusa (modern Dubrovnik), the Adriatic seacoast town which was founded in the 7th c. BC as Ragusium. In Richard Knolle's *General Historie of the Turkes* (1603), which Sh. seems to have had some familiarity with in his writing of *Oth,* there is a 'Ragazonius' as well as an 'Hieronymus Ragazonius,' bishop of Famagusta.

Ralph, 1) *Shr 4.1.122,* one of Petruccio's servants.

2) *1H4 2.5.37,* fellow bartender whom the drawer Francis addresses offstage while Poins and Prince Harry plot a joke.

Ram, *Tit 4.3.72,* see Aries.

Rambures, French town on the Somme near Abbeville. See Rambures, Lord, *H5.*

Rambures, Lord, *H5,* (d. 1415), commander of a French crossbow unit that fought at Agincourt. Holinshed (3.555) includes him on the list of the most notable French casualties of that engagement.

Ramston, Thomas, *R2 2.1.284,* one of the faithful Lancastrian knights who accompanied Henry (IV) Bolingbroke into exile in 1398. He followed his lord back to England in 1399 and helped him wrest the crown from Richard II. He was well rewarded for his loyalty. Henry IV named him constable of the Tower of London and admiral of England's fleet.

Rape, *Tit 5.2.45, 62, 134, 155,* allegorical figure, a fit companion for the spirits of murder and revenge.

Rapine, *Tit 5.2.59, 83, 103,* see Rape.

Rash, Master, *MM 4.3.4,* mocking name for one of the impoverished criminals Pompey knows. As prisoners paid for their own food, many were forced to beg passers by. The name probably refers to the man's unwise behavior. His crime is usury. Although interest had been fixed at 10% by statute, his way of attempting to evade the law was to lend the money and then sell the client a worthless commodity for the excess. This is the brown paper and ginger referred to. There might be some obscure relationship to the 16th c. use of 'rash' to mean a type of smooth cloth. The use of the word to mean an eruption of the skin does not appear to have been in use until the 18th c., so the usual low-humor venereal disease joke can be eliminated in this rare instance.

Ratcliff, Richard, *R3,* (d. 1485), Lord Derwentwater and Keswick by right of his wife and one of Richard III's loyal followers. Ratcliff was knighted by Edward IV following the battle at Tewkesbury, but he disliked the king's marriage and belonged to the faction at court that opposed Queen Elizabeth and her Woodville relatives. After Edward's death, he helped Richard to the throne by assisting at the arrests and murders of William Lord Hastings and members of the Woodville party. Richard lavished gifts on Ratcliff, who repaid him by laying down his life at the battle of Bosworth Field.

Ratolorum, *MWW 1.1.7,* corruption of L. *rotulorum,* 'of the rolls.' See Custalorum.

Ravenspurgh, district at the mouth of the Humber estuary in northern England. Both Henry (IV) Bolingbroke and Edward IV used it as the staging area for the armies they brought from the continent to help them win their thrones. It sank beneath the sea during the 16th c. *3H6 4.8.8. R2. 1H4 1.3.245, 3.2.95, 4.3.79.*

Reading, *MWW 4.5.73,* F1 'Readins' (perhaps to reflect Evans' accent), important town upstream on the Thames west of Windsor at the confluence of the Kennet. The site was first settled by the Danes in 871. A Benedictine monastery was founded there in 1121 and Henry VIII converted the abbey there to a palace which did not survive the Civil War. Clothing was its chief industry in Sh.'s day, though it had begun to decline.

Reason, *MWW 2.1.5,* personification of logic opposed to the emotion of Love. Sh. may be alluding to Sir Phillip Sidney's sonnet 10 from *Astrophel and Stella.*

Recorder, *R3 3.7.30,* probably Thomas Fitzwilliam who occupied the office in 1483. The recorder of the city of London was a prominent judicial officer.

Regan, *Lr,* daughter of Lear, sister of Cordelia and Gonoril, and wife of Cornwall. After flattering Lear to gain her moiety, she mistreats him, encourages the blinding of Gloucester by her husband, becomes a widow, and seeks the hand of Edmund. Gonoril, also interested in Edmund, poisons Regan before stabbing herself. Regan is generally her big sister's follower in evil-doing, although in the blinding scene she kills a servant who tries to interrupt and is intensely involved in the orgy of violence. In John Higgin's *Mirror for Magistrates* (1574), she is Ragan and Regan in Spenser's *Færie Queene,* 2.10. The name is probably of Celtic origin, like Lear. Critics have linked the name to 'Rience' in the Holy Grail legends and Cornish *reian,* 'to give bounteously,' but there seems no significance for Sh. in these.

Regent, title for a person who exercises royal authority during the minority or incapacity of a king. John, duke of Bedford, was named regent for France during the minority of Henry VI (*1H6 1.1.84*). The conduct of affairs in Henry's English domain was the responsibility of a Great Council and Bedford's brother, Humphrey of Gloucester, Lord Protector. *2H6 1.1.63, 1H6 5.6.94:* Richard, duke of York succeeded on Bedford's death to the position of Henry VI's supreme commander in France.

2H6 1.1.195, see Neville, Richard. *1.3.109, 164, 208, 3.1.290, 294, 305:* Richard, duke of York and Edmund Beaufort, duke of Somerset (qq.v.) vie for the regency of France. *R2 2.3.77:* Edmund Langley (q.v.) is regent during Richard's absence in France.

Remorse, Monsieur, *1H4 1.2.112,* name that Ned Poins uses to mock Sir John Oldcastle. Poins's implication is that Oldcastle is devoid of concern for the moral implications of his actions.

René, duke of Anjou and king of Naples (1409–1480), great-grandson of King John of France. René succeeded to the duchy of Anjou upon the death of his brother, Louis III (1434). He tried to take possession of the duchy of Lorraine to which his wife had a claim, but her rights were challenged by another heir supported by Philip the Good, duke of Burgundy. In the ensuing struggle René was captured and confined for several years in Philip's prisons. The marriage of his eldest son to Philip's niece won his freedom and permitted him to undertake a new project. In 1438 he went to Naples to press a claim to its throne. Three years later Alphonse of Aragon forced him to return to France where he blundered into the only significant achievement of his career. René's sister, Mary of Anjou, was Charles VII's wife, and in 1444 Charles sealed a truce with Henry VI of England by persuading Henry to marry his niece, René's daughter Margaret. Henry had hoped for a French princess, and many in England believed that their king had made an inferior match. René retired from public life in 1454 to become a painter, a poet, and a patron of the arts.

3H6 5.7.38. 1H6.

Report, *MV 3.1.6,* female personification of rumor, Salerio's informant. Solanio then jokes that she is a liar.

Revenge, allegorical figure similar to the Eumenides or the avenging 'Furies' of classical mythology. *Tit 3.1.269,* 'R.'s cave' may be an allusion to a grotto near the Areopagus in

Athens that was sacred to the Furies. *5.2.3–184 (passim). 2H4 5.5.37.*

Reynaldo, 1) *Ham 2.1,* F1 'Reynoldo,' Polonius' servant. He is sent to Paris to check up on the mischief Lærtes may get into. He is a little hesitant about his instructions, as if to point up the immorality of a father engaging a paid informant against his son, but exits the stage and the play. In Q1, he is called Montano ('mountain') and he does not appear in *Der Bestrafte Brudermord* (1710) a German adaptation of an earlier version of the play. It has been weakly suggested that since Reynaldo is a steward, the name comes from the steward of Louis the Pious, Rinaldo. An interesting coincidence occurs in Ariosto's *Orlando Furioso* (5.88) in which Renaldo kills Polynesso. Could this have suggested Sh.'s replacement names for Corambis (Polonius) and Montano?

2) *AWW,* F1 'Rynaldo,' Countess of Rousillon's steward. His name is not used until his part has nearly ended in *3.4.* In his scenes, he reports on the activities of the other characters and serves little other function. Possibly the actor then assumed a role as one of the soldiers in the Tuscan war.

Rheims, Reims, French city 100 mi. east of Paris, built on the site of Durocortorum, the capital of the Remi, a tribe of Gauls. It became the seat of an archbishop in the 8th c. The 13th c. cathedral is considered one of the finest of Gothic structures and the Church of St. Rémi was associated with an important abbey. The support the archbishops of Rheims early gave to the struggling Capetian dynasty earned them the honor of presiding at the coronation of French kings. In 1429 Charles VII's claim to be the true king of France was much strengthened when he fought his way through the English lines to be crowned in the cathedral of Rheims. *Shr 2.1.80. 1H6 1.1.60.*

Rhenish 1) (n.), Rhine (white) wine. From the L. *Rhenus,* the Rhine. *Ham 1.4.11:* Hamlet seems to be referring to legendary drunken habits of the Danes. King Christian IV was once reported to have taken 35 toasts and was carried from the feast besotted in his chair. *5.1.175.*

2) (adj.) *MV 1.2.93, 3.1.37.*

Rhesus, *3H6 4.2.20,* son of the king of Thrace and Troy's ally in its war with the Greeks. In *The Iliad,* 10, Diomedes and Odysseus sneak into the Trojan camp at night to kill Rhesus and steal his horses. Sh. cites the story as the classic example of a military maneuver carried out under cover of darkness.

Rhodope of Memphis, *1H6 1.8.22,* prostitute about whom fantastic tales were told by the ancient Greeks. Rhodope ('Rosy-cheeked') was allegedly a Greek slave who worked in the Egyptian port of Naucratis. Herodotus (*Histories,* 2.135–136) mentions, but denies, the story to which Sh. alludes: i.e., that Rhodope used the proceeds from her trade to build the third of the great pyramids at Gizah. Popular tradition may have confused Rhodope of Memphis with Nitocris, an Egyptian queen whom legend also associated with the third pyramid. Herodotus claims that the real Rhodope was a slave named Doricha whose freedom was purchased by the poet Sappho's brother. Sappho devoted her poetic skills to convincing her brother that his association with the woman shamed his family. Herodotus reports that Rhodope left a memorial more modest than a pyramid. He says that she devoted a tenth of her fortune to the purchase of iron spits that were stored in the sanctuary of the Chians at Delphi.

Rhodes, *Oth 1.1.28 1.3.23, 27, 32, 35,* large island in the Ægean Sea just west of Turkey. Early in Greek history its cities Lindus, Camirus, and Ialysus were important trading centers and joined the Delian League in the 5th c. BC. The city of Rhodes was built in 408 BC and the earlier cities declined. The island submitted to Alexander in 332 BC, but revolted upon the great king's death in 323. Rhodes attained its greatest political and artistic influence in the 3rd and 2nd c. It was during this period the Colosus of Rhodes, a statue of Apollo 105 feet high and one of the Seven Wonders of the Ancient World, was built. An earthquake felled it in 224 BC, but fragments of it remained until the Saracens conquered Rhodes in 656 AD. A medieval myth said that the statue's legs bridged the harbor entrance, but this was not true. The Laocoön group was a Rhodian sculpture of the 1st c., also. Usually loyal to Rome, Rhodes sided with Julius Cæsar against Pompey, though the Rhodian navy had assisted Pompey earlier. Rhodes suffered under the invasion of Gaius Cassius Parmensis, one of Cæsar's assassins. The island never quite recovered from his looting. It remained part of the Byzantine Empire with some temporary occupations by the Saracens and Venetians until 1309, when it was taken by the Knights of St. John of Jerusalem. During the Middle Ages it was most successful in trading pottery and in engaging in piracy. After a failed assault in 1480, a bloody Turkish siege established Ottoman control over the island from 1522 until 1912. Sh.'s mention of a joint invasion of R. and Cyprus never happened. The attack upon Cyprus did not occur for half a century after the fall of Rhodes.

Rhys-ap-Thomas, *R3 4.5.12,* or Rice, son of Thomas (d. 1525), a wealthy landowner in southern Wales. He presided over a large militia recruited from his neighbors and the tenants of his estates. Although Richard III courted his favor by paying him a large retainer, Rhys joined his fellow Welshman, the earl of Richmond, when Richmond invaded Wales in 1485. Richmond (Henry VII) knighted Rhys after the battle of Bosworth Field and relied on him to defend the interests of the Tudor dynasty he had helped establish.

Rialto, *MV 1.3.19, 36, 106, 3.1.1, 41,* the exchange of Venice, located opposite San Jacobo's church originally built in the 5th c. just north of the Rialto bridge. It was likely so named from Riva Alta, a 'high shore' (the highest land in Venice), which was a good meeting place. In its heyday it was a square surrounded by arches and business was conducted under the shelter of the surrounding structures or in the open square. The Banco Giro was established here and the area was a hotbed of business activity. The Rialto bridge connected the area to the island which contains St. Mark's and the Doge's Palace. The bridge was originally built in 1178 and floated on pontoons, but was rebuilt from 1588–1592 by Antonio da Ponte. Like many bridges of the period, it was lined with shops and was also a business area, though Sh. is probably not referring to it in the play. In the fifth uses of the word, 'on' or 'upon' the R. is the preposition, but, for example, the expression 'on the Street' meaning Wall Street—America's Rialto—does not imply Wall Street is on a bridge. 'In' is used once, but up to the 19th c. at least, 'in' a street could mean the same thing as 'on,' as in the sentence, 'The newspaper publishers are in Fleet Street.'

Ribs, *1H4 2.5.111,* Prince Harry's joking allusion to Oldcastle. Harry also calls Oldcastle a 'brawn' or 'ox.' The terms are appropriate both to the man and the place. The fat old reprobate is meeting his young cronies in a tavern in Eastcheap, a district where London butchers turned oxen into ribs and tallow.

Richard I, *Jn 1.1.89, 267, 2.1.3,* 'the Lionhearted' (1157–1199), king of England, third son born to Henry II and Eleanor of Aquitaine. The share of his parents' 'Angevin Empire' that was first marked out for Richard was his mother's duchy of Aquitaine. The early deaths of his older brothers improved his prospects, but when his father ordered a redistribution of the family's possessions, Richard refused to cooperate. Henry wanted Richard, who had become heir to the throne, to surrender Aquitaine to his brother, John. Richard refused to comply and raised a revolt that weakened the kingdom and poisoned his father's remaining years. In 1189 Richard succeeded his father and immediately set about liquidating his assets in order to finance a crusade. Philip Augustus of France and Frederick Barbarossa of Germany joined him in what was touted to be the most significant enterprise of the century. The 'third crusade' failed to live up to the expectations of its participants. It achieved no notable military objective and served primarily to build the legend of Richard 'the Lionhearted.' In 1192 Richard faced up to the fact that his holy war was hopeless and that he had to go home to attend to the neglected affairs of his kingdom. His journey home took longer than expected, for he was spotted as he tried to slip through the territories of his enemy, Leopold of Austria. Leopold threw him into prison, and negotiations for his ransom were protracted by the meddling of a horde of interested persons that included the pope, the German emperor, the French king, Richard's mother Eleanor, and his brother John.

In 1194 Richard returned to the west, visited England briefly, and then concentrated his attention on recovering fiefs in France that had been occupied by Philip Augustus. Richard made steady progress toward the restoration of his empire, until the king, who had fought so many famous campaigns, was felled in an inconsequential squabble. Richard disputed the right of his vassal, the viscount of Limoges, to keep a buried treasure that had been found on his estate. While Richard was directing the siege of the viscount's castle at Châlus, he was struck in the shoulder by an arrow. The wound became infected and he died on 6 April.

Richard II, (1367–1400), king of England deposed by Henry IV. Richard was the son of Edward III's son, Edward the Black Prince. The death of his father in 1376 left him heir to his grandfather's throne, and in 1377, at the age of ten, he became king of England. Although he was not old enough to govern, no regent was appointed for him. During the last years of Edward III's reign, senility had rendered the old king incapable of ruling, and his councilors had stepped into the breach to assume responsibility for the government. They continued this arrangement through Richard II's minority and well into his adulthood. Richard resented these men who, in his opinion, had taken advantage of his grandfather's weakness and his youth to usurp power that belonged to the crown. Richard was eager to escape their tutelage and to exercise the autocratic prerogative that he assumed was the divine right of kings. As a youth, Richard showed talent for leadership. In 1381, when he was only fourteen, an unprecedented peasant uprising nearly toppled England's government. The Black Plague had wreaked economic havoc throughout Europe and increased the desperation of the poor. Abrupt demographic changes (the effect of mortality from the disease) disrupted markets and labor supplies and created inflation and shortages. The rich and powerful shifted much of the burden of adjusting to the new situation onto the backs of the disenfranchised peasantry.

Late in May 1381 the poor in Essex and Kent—lacking an alternative—spontaneously rose up and marched on London. They had no program of reform. They simply lashed out at the establishment. Since most of the government's soldiers were fighting abroad that spring, no defense could be organized for London. The peasants entered the city on 13 June, looted the houses of the wealthy, and slaughtered any officials unfortunate enough to fall into their hands. Richard and his advisors took refuge in the Tower of London and waited to see what would happen. When the peasants' spokesman, Wat Tyler, demanded face to face negotiations with the king, Richard twice confronted the angry mob and promised them everything they demanded. At his second meeting the mayor of London, who was in the king's party, nearly cost Richard his life. The mayor lost his temper, pushed Wat Tyler from his horse, and in the confusion the peasants' leader was killed. A riot would have ensued had Richard not intervened and persuaded the peasants to put their trust in their king. Such was their respect for the monarchy that they obediently dispersed. The last pockets of rebellion were cleaned up within a month, and the government, once its safety was assured, ignored all the promises it had made Tyler's followers. From the perspective of its authors, the revolt was a failure, but it had fateful consequences that they could not have anticipated. The peasants' obedience confirmed Richard's faith in the absolute power of his office and his right to rule alone.

A year after the revolt Richard married Anne of Luxemburg-Bohemia, the daughter of the Holy Roman Emperor Charles IV. This event signified the approaching end of his political minority, but his councilors were in no hurry to relinquish their authority. They delayed his assumption of personal rule until he turned twenty-two in 1389. Richard was very impatient with the lords who had been so slow to give him what was his, and, as soon as possible, he shoved them aside to make room for new friends, young favorites on whom he lavished lands and titles. These men—chiefly Michael de la Pole (Suffolk) and Robert de Vere (Oxford)—replaced the older nobility (many of whom were the king's relatives) in key offices. Richard's reorganization of the government angered many powerful men, and the king's uncle, John of Gaunt, the duke of Lancaster, stepped in to mediate between the young monarch and his growing horde of enemies. In 1386 Gaunt left England to pursue an old dream, the conquest of a kingdom in Spain, and his departure increased the likelihood of a confrontation between Richard and his barons. As the court filled with toadies on whom the king lavished gifts, the lords who did not profit criticized royal extravagance and joined the commoners in expressing horror at the king's demand for taxes. Normally the lords paid little attention to the commons, but a shared antagonism to the king motivated both groups to work together in the parliament of 1386. The 'Wonderful Parliament' forced Richard to dismiss the pliant advisors he had appointed and to govern through a council parliament established. He was incensed at the presumption of his subjects, and he persuaded a panel of royal judges to declare the acts of parliament an illegal infringement on the rights of kingship.

This infuriated the barons, who threatened to resort to force. Richard took refuge in the Tower of London, and Robert de Vere raised an army for the king's defense. The king's uncle, Thomas of Woodstock, duke of Gloucester, and the earls of Arundel, Warwick, Nottingham, and Derby (Richard's cousin, Henry Bolingbroke) defeated de Vere's men at Oxford, and de Vere, the king's closest friend, fled abroad to die in exile. Richard was forced to yield, and he might have been deposed had there been agreement on someone to succeed him. Gloucester wanted the crown, but Bolingbroke was the son of Gloucester's elder brother and would not yield his superior hereditary right. In February 1388, the 'Merciless Parliament' earned its name by taking vengeance on the king. Gloucester, Arundel, Warwick, Nottingham, and Derby 'appealed' (i.e., 'charged') the king's ministers with treason. For a brief period the 'lords appellant' dominated Richard's government, but their individual ambitions made it hard for them to stick together. Richard cleverly negotiated separate deals with some of them, split up their alliance, and wriggled out from under their control. On 3 May 1389, he proclaimed his independence and reorganized his government. Although Richard continued to be a wasteful and extravagant king whose fancy was caught by all kinds of unrealistic projects, no one opposed him directly for almost a decade.

Then in July 1397 the king learned that his uncle, Gloucester, was again plotting against him. Richard struck suddenly and decisively. He surprised Gloucester, Arundel, and Warwick, carted them off to prison, and convened a parliament—whose meeting place he surrounded with soldiers. The king 'appealed' the 'lords appellant' of treason. Warwick was banished, Arundel executed, and Gloucester sent to prison in Calais where he died promptly and mysteriously. There was little doubt that he had been murdered. Although Gaunt's son, Henry Bolingbroke, who had earlier sided with the 'lords appellant,' survived Richard's initial attack, his turn came quickly. In December 1397, Henry quarrelled with Thomas Mowbray, the duke of Norfolk. Henry claimed that Norfolk privately told him that they were both in danger and could not trust the king. Henry repeated Mowbray's words to his father, John of Gaunt, and Gaunt tried to head off suspicion of treason by reporting everything to the king. Richard ordered an inquest, and at its second sitting Henry levied additional charges against Norfolk. He accused the duke of misappropriation of funds and complicity in Gloucester's murder. Since there was inadequate evidence to reach a verdict, Richard authorized a trial by combat. Elaborate arrangements were made for a duel to be fought at Coventry on 16 September 1398, but at the last moment Richard called it off and banished both Norfolk and Bolingbroke. (It is possible that Norfolk was an agent provocateur working for Richard who wanted an excuse to rid himself of Bolingbroke. Richard may have intended, after a brief interval, to recall Norfolk from exile. If so, he never got a chance. Norfolk set out for the Holy Lands and died in Venice in 1399.)

Richard, in the absence of his most powerful opponents, had no difficulty cowing the parliament that met in 1398. It adjourned promptly—agreeing to vest its authority in a committee of the king's men. Richard, now freed of all restraints, decided to give his barons a lesson in autocracy. John of Gaunt died on 3 February 1399. On 18 March the sentence of exile that had been levied against his heir, Bolingbroke, was extended from ten years to life and Gaunt's estate was confiscated by the crown. Richard's assault on the rights of inheritance alarmed every person of property in England, for it was clear that no family was safe if the king could arbitrarily disinherit one of the greatest magnates in the land. Since Richard was feeling very strong and had a pressing need for Gaunt's money, he may have been inclined to underestimate the significance of the resentment stirred up by his attack on the house of Lancaster. The king was eager to mount an expedition to Ireland, and, with his opponents routed, he saw no reason to tarry longer in England. Richard had fought a nominally successful campaign in Ireland in 1395, and he had entrusted the island to Roger Mortimer, the kinsman who was to inherit his throne should Richard die childless. On 20 July 1398, the Irish ambushed and killed Mortimer, and Richard felt that his personal presence—the prestige of the crown—was required to restore order in Ireland. On 29 May 1399, Richard entrusted England to his uncle, the duke of York, and sailed for Ireland. Richard was aware of his lack of popularity, for he went to unusual lengths to ensure the loyalty of his subjects while he was abroad. Before he departed, Richard required men from all over England to send him 'blank charters.' A blank charter was a piece of paper bearing a man's seal, and it was the political equivalent of a signed blank check.

Richard's crass attempt at universal intimidation backfired by creating additional sympathy for his cousin, Henry Bolingbroke. Henry was in Paris when word reached him of his father's death, his permanent banishment, and the loss of his inheritance. He rallied all the men he could find (probably no more than 300) and set out for England. On 4 July 1399, Henry landed at the mouth of the Humber river in northern England and marched through districts that belonged to his family's duchy of Lancaster. The resources he brought with him would not have carried him far, but the great northern lords, the Percies and Nevilles, lent him their formidable family armies. The duke of York tried to organize resistance, but it was impossible. Richard had taken most of the mobilized soldiers to Ireland, and there was no groundswell of popular support for the king. On 27 July York yielded to the inevitable and came to terms with Henry. The next day Bristol surrendered, and Richard's most hated advisors, who had taken refuge in Bristol Castle, were executed. When Richard heard what was happening, he sent the earl of Salisbury to northern Wales to raise an army while he tried hastily to settle things in Ireland. On 27 July he sailed from Waterford for Milford Haven. He arrived too late. Rumors that he had been killed had disheartened his men, and many of them had deserted. Richard headed north to Conway to rendezvous with Salisbury, but Salisbury's troops had melted away.

Although Richard had nothing left with which to fight, he refused to flee. Henry moved to Chester and sent the earl of Northumberland and Archbishop Arundel to parley with the king. Richard was told that he could retain the crown and that all that Henry wanted was the restoration of his duchy. That may have been Henry's original plan, but, on reflection, he must have realized that it was unworkable. Richard could not be trusted, for he had once before overthrown a coalition of barons who thought that they could control him. If Richard had remained king, Henry would never have known a moment's peace. Henry sent Richard to London to the Tower, and a parliament was called for 30 September. When it convened, it was told that Richard had abdicated the day before and that the throne was vacant. This created a peculiar legal problem. Only a monarch had the power to open the parliament that had been called to acknowledge the fact that there was no monarch. It was decided to ignore the inconvenient legal conundrum—and the tradition governing right of succession. The person with the strongest claim to the throne was Roger Mortimer's son, Edmund. He was, however, only 8 years old and in no position to assert his prerogative. Parliament forgot him and acquiesced when Henry (IV) claimed the crown by right of royal descent and 'conquest.' Richard was sent far from London to Pontefract Castle in Yorkshire, but even in a distant prison he was a threat to the new dynasty.

On 17 December 1399, the earls of Rutland, Kent, and Huntingdon met with a group of Richard's friends to plan a coup that would restore him to the throne. Their plan was to take part in a tournament Henry was hosting at Windsor. As combatants they could bear arms into the king's presence—arms that could be used to kill the king. Henry got wind of the plot in time to flee to safety in London, and his would-be assassins retreated to Cirencester where the citizens captured and beheaded them. Henry had been lucky, but he knew that so long as Richard lived such things could continue to happen. A month after the defeat of the 'earls' plot' it was announced that Richard had died in captivity (about 14 February). His body was brought to London and exhibited before the people to prove that he was dead. The officially registered cause of death was self-starvation, but a story circulated in France that one of Henry's knights had acted on a hint from Henry and murdered Richard.

2H6 2.2.19. 3H6 1.1.139. 1H6 2.5.64. R3 3.3.11.

R2. 1H4 1.3.144, 153, 173, 240, 3.2.94, 5.1.35. 2H4 1.1.204, 1.3.98, 101, 3.1.53, 59, 62, 83, 4.1.58. H5 4.1.292, 299.

Richard III, (1452–1485), 'Crookback,' duke of Gloucester, last king of England from the house of York. The youngest of Cecily Neville and Richard of York's sons, he was only eight when the Lancastrians killed his father and his brother Rutland at the battle of Wakefield. While Richard's eldest brother, Edward, stayed in England under the tutelage of the earl of Warwick (the 'Kingmaker') to continue the family's fight, Richard and his remaining brother, George, were sent to safety in Utrecht. The fortunes of war shifted in their favor, and on 29 March 1461, at the battle of Towton, Edward wrested the crown from the Lancastrian king, Henry VI. The new monarch brought his brothers home and named George duke of Clarence and Richard duke of Gloucester. Richard was given a post in Warwick's household and forgotten. George enjoyed greater royal favor, but the attention lavished on him nourished ambition more than gratitude. In 1464 when Edward's secret wedding with Elizabeth Woodville Gray estranged him from his patron, Warwick, a test of strength developed between the king and his 'maker.' George was quick to take advantage of the situation. Until the birth of a son to Edward in March of 1469, George had been heir to the throne, and George was reluctant to relinquish his great expectations. In 1469 George married Isabel, Warwick's elder daughter, expecting that Warwick would depose Edward and enthrone him. Warwick discovered that there was little popular support for a campaign to replace an elder brother with a younger, and Louis XI of France persuaded him to drop George and take up the cause of his former enemy, Henry VI.

Warwick's coup took Edward by surprise. The Yorkist king fled England, and Warwick restored the Lancastrian monarchy. Since the allies to whom Edward appealed were initially reluctant to risk offending France by helping him, his fate was uncertain, but Richard remained loyal to his brother at the nadir of the king's career and shared his exile. By March of 1471 Edward had persuaded the duke of Burgundy to assist him, had regrouped his forces, and had returned to England to fight for his throne. George remained tied to Warwick until it dawned on him that he had nothing to gain from the restoration of the Lancastrian dynasty. On the eve of battle between Edward and Warwick, George reassessed the situation and returned to Edward's camp. George was welcomed back, but Richard made the most significant contribution to the campaign to restore the Yorkist monarchy. Warwick was killed in the fighting at Barnet and Henry's son, Edward, was captured and executed at Tewkesbury. In both campaigns Richard commanded the forward position in the army, and the story circulated that he personally arranged the murders of the Lancastrian heir and Henry VI. Edward rewarded Richard's services handsomely. He was assigned many of Warwick's offices and granted a free hand in the management of the northern counties of Cumberland and Westmorland. George was not pleased to see Richard's star ascending, and he was particularly reluctant to share any of his father-in-law's Warwick estates with him.

Richard undercut George's claim to be Warwick's sole heir by proposing marriage to Warwick's younger daughter, Anne. George did his best to prevent the union by carrying his wife's sister off to a hiding place in the country, but shortly after Easter 1472 Richard tracked Anne down and, with her consent and cooperation, abducted and married her. George's arrogant conduct and treasonous ambition culminated in his arrest and execution on 18 February 1478. Sh. assumed that Richard conspired to poison George's relationship with Edward and to bring about his death, but no contemporary source implicates Richard. At the time, if anyone was suspected of causing trouble between the king and his brother, it was Edward's queen—and her Woodville relatives. On 12 May 1480, Richard was appointed lieutenant-general of the north with primary responsibility for a campaign Edward contemplated in Scotland. Developments on the continent distracted Edward, and in 1482 he gave Richard a free hand in dealing with Scotland. Richard discharged his duties brilliantly. James III, king of Scots, lost control of his nation's fractious nobility. Scotland's defenses crumbled, and Richard occupied Edinburgh. The gentry of northern England were impressed by Richard's ability, and Northumberland and Stanley became his allies.

Unfortunately, Richard's success contributed to the polarization of the nobility. Those who resented the influence the queen and the Woodvilles enjoyed at court turned to Richard for leadership. Edward's premature death on 9 April 1483, left a royal household dangerously divided against itself. Since Edward's testament has not survived, it is not certain what arrangements he suggested for the government of England during the minority of his heir. Young Edward V had been committed to the care of his mother's relatives, but Richard, as the senior member of the house of York, was the obvious regent for the boy's kingdom. To strengthen their hand, the Woodvilles requested permission to raise an army to bring the young king to London for his coronation. Their enemies in the royal council blocked their proposal, and Richard used the soldiers already at his disposal to take charge. He captured Edward and ordered the execution of his guardians. Queen Elizabeth claimed sanctuary for herself and Edward's younger brother in Westminster Abbey. Richard had reason to believe that his safety depended on his ability to control the young king. His brother, George, had been the victim of a court maneuvered judicial murder, and history could have repeated itself. Edward V would have had little personal knowledge of or affection for his uncle, and Richard's prospects would not have been good in an England administered by the queen and the Woodvilles. Richard's intent may have been simply to depose Edward's sons and take their place. Edward himself had created a precedent for such an action, and Henry VI, whose throne Edward had seized, had survived a long time in Edward's custody. The transfer of the crown from one member of the royal family to another did not necessitate murder, but once the process began it was difficult to prevent events from unfolding with increasing violence. Richard was a military man who was accustomed to shedding the blood of his enemies.

When the most incorruptible of Edward IV's ministers, William, Lord Hastings, opposed him, Richard, who believed that he had no time to waste, dragged Hastings from a council meeting and beheaded him. When the queen, who realized that she had no support, was persuaded by the council and the archbishop of Canterbury to surrender her younger son to Richard, he confined both princes in the Tower. They were never seen again, and he launched a campaign to discredit their legitimacy. He charged that Edward IV's marriage to Elizabeth Woodville Gray had been invalid because Edward had previously engaged himself to wed another woman. (Richard may even have made an attempt to cast doubt on Edward IV's parentage.) The strategy did not meet with public approval, but on 25 June 1483, Buckingham convened a pliant parliament that petitioned Richard to take the throne. A few months later, Buckingham changed his tune. He sparked a rebellion in England's southern counties, where Richard's policy of rewarding loyal northern cronies with offices was deeply resented. Buckingham had royal blood, and he may have decided to make his own bid for the throne while people still had second thoughts about Richard's coup. If so, he misjudged the extent of Richard's unpopularity and the seductiveness of his own candidacy. The support he hoped for failed to materialize, and he was captured and executed. Some of Buckingham's accomplices fled to Brittany to join Henry Tudor, the earl of Richmond, and what was left of the Lancastrian party.

At the beginning of August, 1485, Richmond sailed from France with a small army of exiles and foreign mercenaries. He landed near Milford Haven and moved through Wales, his family's traditional base, recruiting followers. His success was modest, and the army he assembled to challenge Richard at Bosworth Field was only half the size of Richard's. Richard was an experienced warrior with a fine record for personal courage and vigorous action in battle, but the terrain at Bosworth Field made it difficult for him to deploy his men effectively. He chanced everything on a bold plan. He personally led a charge into the midst of the Lancastrian line in an attempt to cut down the earl of Richmond. He got close enough to kill the man who bore Richmond's standard, and he may have been on the point of victory when the tide of battle was turned by the defection of one of his own men, Lord Stanley. The king went down fighting, and even his enemies praised the manner of his death. Richmond (Henry VII) claimed the throne by right of conquest and Lancastrian inheritance, but it was not at all certain that the new Tudor dynasty had won a definitive victory. The royal house of York was not yet extinct. Richard's only child, one of many princes named Edward, had died in 1484 at the age of 8. After the boy's death, Richard considered designating his sister Elizabeth's son, John de la Pole, earl of Lincoln, heir to the throne. Richard's brother George also had a son, Edward, earl of Warwick, and a daughter, Margaret—who was to have sons. To secure their hold on the throne, the Tudors had to dispose of all these potential rivals. Henry VII confined Warwick in the Tower of London for fourteen years before ordering his execution. Lincoln died in battle with Henry VII, and Henry VIII rounded up and executed Margaret and her offspring. By 1540 the destruction of the house of York was complete and the Tudors' grip on the crown secure.

As the victors on the field, the Tudors promulgated the official interpretation of the events that ended the War of the Roses. They justified Henry VII's usurpation of the throne and legitimated their dynasty by charging that Richard III was totally unfit for royal office. Sh. followed Tudor sources in representing Richard as the chief of villains, but his portrait may not be historically accurate. Sh.'s claim that Richard was a hunchbacked monster with severe physical handicaps is hard to reconcile with reports of his prowess in battle. Sh. did not invent his picture, but he may have taken the sources from which he drew his image more literally than necessary. Sh. depended on historians (e.g., Hall and Holinshed) whose chronicles were colored by Tudor propaganda. Tudor apologists labored hard to justify Henry VII's appropriation of the crown, for his link with the Plantagenet dynasty that had ruled England for most of the medieval period was extremely tenuous. The most effective propagandistic strategy was to depict Richard III as a monster who was totally unfit to rule the kingdom. Henry VII's assault on Richard could then be explained as the work of a sainted knight commissioned by God to rescue his people from a Plantagenet dragon. The authors who developed this thesis followed the literary conceit of Renaissance writers who believed that the face ought to mirror the soul. They assumed that Richard's body would mirror the deformity of his soul, and they made him a monster in the physical as well as the moral sense.

There is, however, no contemporary evidence that Richard was 'crookbacked' or otherwise crippled. The tradition on which Sh. drew for his description of Richard may have originated in an essay that Sir Thomas More wrote in 1513. More's book contained a surprisingly detailed, but unsubstantiated, portrait of the last Plantagenet king. It is possible that More intended his piece to be read not as history, but as allegory. He may have planned it to compliment the book his friend and fellow humanist Erasmus was writing for the edification of Christian princes. Erasmus' work detailed the virtues that were to be found in ideal rulers; More's used Richard as a model for the evil that princes should avoid. Sh. accepted other unverifiable assertions made by Tudor historians—most significantly, the charge that Richard murdered Edward IV's sons. The evidence against Richard consists largely of imputations of motive and opportunity, but he shared these things with others at his court. The duke of Buckingham handled the arrest and confinement of the princes, and their disappearance was as convenient for his subsequent bid for the throne as it was for Richard's. There is little doubt that Richard was ruthless in pursuit of his goals, but in this respect he was not different from his contemporaries. He may have elicited little affection from his subjects, but there was never any question about his courage or his competence. Much of what Sh. says about Richard must be taken with a grain of salt, but in making Richard a complex and darkly witty character Sh. was probably not far off the mark.

2H6. 3H6. R3. H8 1.2.197, 2.1.109.

Richard Coeur-de-lion, *Jn 1.1.253,* see Richard I.

Richard Conqueror, *Shr Ind. 1.4,* a confounding by the drunken Sly of Richard the Lion Heart and William the Conqueror. He is attempting to claim descent for the Slys from the 11th c. Norman lords.

Richard Crookback, *2H6, 3H6,* see Richard III.

Richard du Champ, *Cym 4.2.379,* false name given by Innogen to Lucius for the headless body of Cloten, which she has mistaken for Posthumus. Why it is necessary to conceal Posthumus' identity is unclear. The name means 'Richard of the Field' in French, compounding the linguistic mishmash of the play.

Richard, duke of York, 1) (1411–1460), leader of the Yorkist faction in the English civil war, the 'War of the Roses.' He descended from King Edward III through both paternal and maternal lines. His father, Richard of Cambridge (d. 1415), was the son of Edmund Langley, Edward III's fourth son. His mother, Anne Mortimer, was the great-granddaughter of Lionel, Edward III's second son. The advantages of Richard of York's blood were augmented by an inheritance from his uncle, Edmund Mortimer, which made him the largest landowner in England. Although his father was executed in 1415 for plotting to overthrow Henry V, young Richard made his peace with his father's executioner. Henry V's victories in France made Henry so popular that coups against him were unthinkable. Richard was knighted by Henry VI in 1426, and he saw military service in France. Following the death of the duke of Bedford in 1435, he took command of England's war with France. A year later he concluded that there was insufficient support from England for the French campaign, and he resigned the post. He returned to England and joined the party of malcontents headed by Henry's uncle, Humphrey of Gloucester. He was reappointed lieutenant for France in 1440 and remained in Normandy until his enemies arranged for his recall in 1445. At Gloucester's death in 1447 Richard became Henry VI's closest living male relative, and, so long as Henry remained childless, he was the obvious heir to Henry's throne. Henry tried to prevent him from complicating life at court by appointing him lieutenant for Ireland, but he delayed taking up the post until 1449 and returned to England after a brief tour of duty.

When Henry suffered his first bout with mental illness in 1453, parliament appointed Richard his 'protector.' Richard probably believed that Henry's reign was virtually finished and that his own succession to the throne was assured, but at the end of 1453 Queen Margaret bore Henry a son who dashed Richard's hope of a quick and easy path to the throne. Henry's recovery at the end of 1454 ended York's protectorate, but York refused to step aside and allow Henry's old friend, the duke of Somerset, to return to power at court. On 22 May 1455, he killed Somerset at the first battle of St. Albans, the opening engagement in the War of the Roses. Henry relapsed into madness, and York reclaimed the office of protector. Henry recovered in February 1456, and Queen Margaret persuaded him to banish York and his supporters from court. York wanted to fight, but since his soldiers were not yet ready to take up arms against their king, he retreated once more to Ireland. His hand was soon strengthened by the acquisition of a powerful ally, Richard Neville, earl of Warwick, son of Richard Neville, earl of Salisbury. Warwick commanded the port of Calais and headed a fleet of privateers that preyed on shipping in the English channel. In 1460 Warwick invaded England and captured Henry at the battle of Northampton. Warwick's goal was to become the power behind the throne, and it served his purpose to keep Henry alive as a check on Richard. Richard agreed to an arrangement whereby Henry was to continue as king for the remainder of his life, but disinherit his son in Richard's favor. Richard did not live to claim the prize that was promised him. Two months after his proclamation as heir apparent he was killed in a skirmish at Wakefield. It was Richard's son, Edward, who, with Warwick's help, realized the Yorkist dream of driving the Lancastrians from the throne.

2H6. 3H6. 1H6.

2) *R3 4.4.43,* (1472–1483), second son of Edward IV and Elizabeth Woodville Gray, brother to Edward V. Richard was eleven years old when his father died and his uncle, Richard III, usurped his brother's throne. His mother tried to protect him by taking him with her to sanctuary in Westminster Abbey. When she released him to Richard's custody, he and Edward disappeared into the Tower of London and were never seen again.

Richard, earl of Cambridge, (d. 1415), the second son of Edmund Langley, first duke of York and fifth son of Edward III. Richard began his career campaigning in Wales, and in 1414 he succeeded to the earldom of Cambridge, an honor previously enjoyed by his father. He married Anne, daughter of Roger Mortimer and granddaughter of Edward III's third son, Lionel, duke of Clarence. Richard schemed to put his wife's brother, Edmund Mortimer, earl of March, on Henry V's throne. The plotters planned to spring into action in 1415 as soon as Henry had left England to begin his war with France, but before Henry left the country, Mortimer himself exposed the plans to the king. Mortimer was acquitted of all responsibility for the actions of his supporters, and Richard was executed for treason on 5 August. Richard's son, Richard duke of York (q.v.), inherited his uncle Mortimer's claim to the throne. He asserted it unsuccessfully against Henry VI, but his son,

Edward (IV), realized the family's dream by deposing Henry and winning the crown.
2H6 2.2.45. 1H6 2.4.90, 2.5.54, 84. H5.

Richard Gloucester, *R3,* see Richard III.

Richard of Bordeaux, *R2 5.6.33,* see Richard II. Richard was born in the city of Bordeaux on 6 January 1367. Bordeaux was a port from which his father, Edward the Black Prince, managed England's continental possessions.

Richard Plantagenet, 1) *1H6, 3H6,* see Richard, duke of York; Plantagenet 2).

2) *Jn,* Philip the Bastard assumes the name when he renounces his mother's wedded name (Falconbridge) and is acknowledged as the illegitimate son of King Richard (I) the Lion-hearted.

Richmond, *Jn 2.1.553,* town in Yorkshire about 45 mi. northwest of the city of York. The earldom of Richmond was granted by William the Conqueror to an Alan Rufus who began construction of the castle. Henry VII's father, Edmund Tudor, received the title in 1452, and Henry bore it before ascending the throne. See Richmond, Countess of, *R3*; Earl of, *Jn*; *3H6.*

Richmond, Countess of, *R3 1.3.20,* Margaret Beaufort (1441–1509), wife of Edmund Tudor, earl of Richmond and half-brother to Henry VI. She was a descendant of Edward III via his son, John of Gaunt. The blood she bequeathed her son, Henry (VII), helped him establish a claim to England's throne and made him the head of the house of Lancaster after the deaths of Henry VI and Henry's son, Edward. Her husband died two months before her son's birth, and she put herself under the protection of her brother-in-law, Jasper Tudor, the earl of Pembroke. Jasper took her son to Brittany for safety in 1471, but she remained in England to look after the family's interests. She secured her position by marrying Thomas Stanley, the future earl of Derby, one of Edward IV's chief advisors. Stanley acquiesced to Richard III's usurpation of the crown, but Richard was never sure of the sincerity of his commitment. Richard's reluctance to offend Stanley prevented him from interfering too directly with Margaret's schemes to win the throne for her son. When Henry made his move and invaded England, Stanley stayed on the fence as long as possible. He commanded a portion of Richard's army at the battle of Bosworth Field, and his decision to defect in the midst of the fight was probably the chief reason for Richard's defeat. Margaret chose retirement rather than life at her son's court, but she corresponded with him frequently and took a deep interest in affairs of state. She was also interested in the intellectual movements of her day and was a generous patron of colleges at Cambridge and Oxford.

Richmond, Earl of, 1) *3H6 4.7.67, 93, 100, R3,* see Henry VII.

2) *Jn 2.1.553,* one of the honors John of England promised his nephew Arthur of Brittany when John and Philip Augustus negotiated a peace between England and France in 1200. Holinshed reports (3.161) that Arthur did homage to John for Brittany and Richmond.

Ringwood, *MWW 2.1.114,* one of Actæon's dogs. Since dog's names in Sh. seem to be based on physical or behavioral characteristics, this name might imply a dog that circles the woods or sniffs along the periphery instead of going into it. The name appears in Arthur Golding's translation (3.270) of Ovid's *Metamorphoses* (3.233, *Hylactor* 'barker'). The Roman poet names the hounds and Golding substituted common English names for them. Most of Golding's translations approximate the original names for the thirty-six dogs mentioned by Ovid—for example, 'Kildeere' for *Theridamas* 'beast-killer' and 'Hylbred' for *Oresitropus* 'mountaineer.'

'Riot of the Tipsy Bacchanals Tearing the Thracian Singer in their Rage, The.' *MND 5.1.48–49 (add. 31–32),* one of the entertainments offered to Theseus on his wedding day. He rejects it as being done before, as indeed it was, from Euripides on down. See Bacchanals and Orpheus.

Rivers, Earl, *3H6, R3,* Anthony Woodville (1442–1483), brother to Edward IV's queen, Elizabeth Woodville Gray. Rivers fought for the Lancastrians at the battle of Towton, but he ingratiated himself with the Yorkists once the Lancastrian cause was lost. By right of his wife's estate he enjoyed the title 'Lord Scales,' and in 1469 he succeeded his father to the earldom of Rivers. Edward IV richly rewarded his brother-in-law and employed him on important missions. Rivers helped arrange the marriage of Edward's sister Margaret to the duke of Burgundy. He served as lieutenant of Calais and was one of Edward's staunch supporters in his final, desperate fight with Warwick. In 1473 Edward made him guardian of his sons, and Rivers was a key player in the drama that determined their fate. After Edward's death, he asked permission of the government to raise an army with which to bring the royal heir to London. Edward's brother, Richard of Gloucester, frustrated this plan, entrapped Rivers and his half-brother, Richard Gray, and beheaded them without the formality of a trial. The young princes, whom the Woodvilles had failed to protect, were sent to the Tower by their Yorkist uncle and robbed of their inheritance and, probably, their lives.

Rivo, *1H4 2.5.111,* drinker's chant. It may derive from Sp. *arriba,* 'upwards' (i.e., 'up with your glasses').

Robert, *MWW,* servant of the Fords. It is an old Norman name that means 'bright-famed.'

Robin, 1) *2H6 2.3.78,* companion for Peter Thump, an armorer's apprentice who accused his master of treason. See Thump, Peter.

2) *MWW,* Falstaff's page who joins in the plot against his master. The remarks about his smallness may indicate the physique of a particular actor, as with Slender. He is sometimes thought to be the same page who accompanies Falstaff in *2H4* and Bardolph, Nim, and Pistol in *H5.* As R. is diminutive of Robert, it may reflect his size, or may be a typical Sh. confusion with the Ford servant, Robert.

3) *Ham 4.5.185,* name in a song sung by the mad Ophelia. It may refer to Robin Hood in 'Robin Is to the Greenwood Gone' or some other song, but is more often thought to be the same as 'Bonny Robin' (q.v.). 'R.' was probably a reference to the penis then, as 'John Henry,' and 'Dick' are today.

4) *TN 4.2.73,* name mentioned in a song sung by Feste. It may refer to the bird, or the jolly R. of Sherwood whose Maid Marian in medieval tradition was anything but a maid. It may simply be a R. in the sense of any Tom, Dick, or Harry, or 'penis,' see above 3). The song predated Sh. and was attributed to Sir Thomas Wyatt in one manuscript, though it is likely older.

5) *Mac 4.1.48,* spirit called forth by the witches in a song not appearing in F1, but which appears in Thomas Middleton's play *The Witch* (c. 1609, but not printed until the 18th c.). William Davenant's version of *Mac* (printed 1674), contains the song and it has been argued that he may have had access to an earlier text. Robin Goodfellow was a well-known spirit famous for trickery; therefore, Middleton's text is usually adapted to 'Liar R.,' as was done by Davenant. Another possibility is 'Laird R.,' 'Lord Robin.' A *liard* was also a tiny French coin worth ¼ of a sou. It may, therefore, mean something like 'tiny R.' That this is an invocation of two different spirits, however, is obvious given what Hecate says in *The Witch 1.2.1 ff.* The names are taken from Reginald Scot's *Discoverie of Witchcraft* (1584).

Robin Hood, legendary medieval folk hero who lived in Sherwood Forest with his band of outlaws. Scholars have proposed many theories to account for the origin of his myth and suggested several historical persons who might have been his prototype. There is no historical evidence for his existence, but he, his men, and Maid Marian were popular figures in May Day celebrations. Likely some local legend became mixed with the belief in Robin Goodfellow, the trickster forest sprite. Robin Hood is part of numerous literary works including Langland's *Piers Plowman,* and as vehicles for roisterous and bawdy comedy Robin Hood plays were common by the 16th c., so much so the general assembly of Scotland in 1577 and 1578 asked that they be forbidden on the sabbath. *A Mery Geste of Robyn Hoode* published sometime between 1553 and 1569 has Robin offering Friar Tuck a woman whom he accepts with lusty joy.

Such action would be typical of the tone and nature of the May plays. George Peele's *Edward I* has the rebel Lluellen go into the woods, dress in Kendall green, and live with his men in the roles associated with Robin Hood. Lluellen describes his role as Robin Hood as being 'the Master of Misrule' which is a good summing up of the Renaissance attitude. Another example is in *Cambises, King of Percia* by Thomas Preston (c. 1569), a popular play of the period, the rustic Hob (q.v., an old nickname for Robin) is the husband of Marian-May-Be-Good, for example, an obvious allusion to the lowlife version of Robin Hood. There is more serious treatment of Robin Hood in Anthony Munday and Henry Chettle's *Downfall of Robert, Earl of Huntingdon, Otherwise called Robin Hoode of merrie Sherwodde* (1601), foreshadowing the chivalric romanticism which would be attached to the character as May Day rituals declined. In later ages Robin practiced virtues that were traditionally associated with knighthood. He was generous, a protector of women and defenseless persons, and a footloose adventurer. The stories of his escapades mirror the tensions and illustrate the sensitivities to issues of class that developed in late medieval English society. In the 16th c., however, the name Robin Hood was associated with freedom from ordinary mores and social obligations and with sexual comedy, slapstick, and pastoral holidays.

TGV 4.1.35, 'R.H.'s fat friar,' Friar Tuck. He appears in *The Downfall of Robert, Earl of Huntingdon* and *The Death of Robert Earl of Huntingdon* (1598). It has been suggested that *TGV* derives some of its greenwood material from these plays, but the early dating makes it more likely that it comes from common sources.

AYLI 1.1.111, the exiled Duke lives like 'old R.H. of England.' The citing of R.H. implies the kind of things which will transpire in the pastoral setting. *2H4 5.3.104. TNK pro. 21,* the tales of R.H. are mocked for their vulgar appeal in comparison to the noble works of Chaucer.

Robin Ostler, *1H4 2.1.10–11,* recently deceased owner of the inn in Rochester where Gadshill goes to spy on persons he and Oldcastle hope to rob. Robin is said to have succumbed from the effects of shock brought on by a rise in the price of oats. The story would have struck members of Sh.'s audience as black humor, for there had been a dramatic increase in the cost of commodities used to feed horses between 1594 and 1596.

Rochester, *1H4 1.2.128,* cathedral city on the pilgrim route between London and Canterbury about 30 mi. east of London. See Rochester, Bishop of, *H8.*

Rochester, Bishop of, *H8,* John Fisher (1459–1535), politician and intellectual active at the court of Henry VIII. Fisher was a learned humanist who associated with Thomas More and who helped bring the famous continental scholar Erasmus to England. Like Erasmus and More, he opposed the Reformation and wrote several treatises to refute what he perceived to be Martin Luther's errors. He spoke against the proposals for the reform of the English church that originated in parliament, and he refused to accept either Henry VIII's annulment of his marriage with Katherine of Aragon or the king's claim to be head of the English church. Fisher was the most prominent of the small number of English clerics who refused to acquiesce in Henry's decision to remove England from the jurisdiction of the papacy. He was beheaded, his head exposed on London Bridge and then thrown in the river. His body was later buried beside More's. The Roman church beatified him in 1886.

Rochford, town in the county of Essex about 40 mi. northeast of London. It was the country seat of the Boleyn family. See Boleyn, Thomas (Viscount Rochford), *H8.*

Rochford, Viscount, *H8 1.4.96,* see Boleyn, Thomas.

Roderigo 1) F1 'Rodorigo,' *TN 2.1.15,* Sebastian seems to be saying it is another name he has been using for himself, but why he is saying this is a mystery. It is never again used. Possibly it refers to incidents in an unknown source for the play.

2) *Oth,* 'gulled gentleman,' who believes his approaches to Desdemona are being furthered by Iago. In this he is similar to Sir Andrew Aguecheek of *TN*; however, the consequences are more serious. Not only are his lavish gifts stolen by Iago, but he becomes involved in a plan to disgrace Cassio and is wounded first by Cassio, then killed by Iago. Iago's attempt to silence R. fails because of the letters in R.'s pocket.

Roger, earl of March, *2H6 2.2.37,* see Mortimer, Roger.

Rogero, *WT,* see Ruggiero.

Roland, hero of a medieval French epic poem, *Chanson de Roland* 'Song of Roland.' Although most of the poem is fantasy, it commemorates a real event. In 777 Charlemagne took advantage of a quarrel among Muslim chiefs to invade Spain. The campaign did not go well. Charlemagne ordered a retreat, and Roland, the duke of Brittany who commanded Charlemagne's rear guard, died in an ambush. For medieval poets Roland personified the impetuous valor that was both the strength and the weakness of young knights. He, like the heroes who gathered at King Arthur's round table, embodied the ideals of chivalry that were the aspirations of real soldiers. Roland was a popular figure, and his story was familiar to Sh.'s audience. A poem by Lodovico Ariosto (1474–1533), *Orlando Furioso,* was the basis for a play by the same name written by Robert Greene in 1589. The medieval French poem was translated into English in 1591 by Sir John Harington. Sh. may have known this version and have drawn material from it for *Ado* and *Oth.*

1H6 1.3.9. Lr 3.4.170 (Q 11.167), 'Childe Rowland.' Child (*Infans*) was a term for the highest level of apprentice knight, derived from the Fr. *enfant* and Sp. *infante.*

Rolls, Master of the, *H8 5.1.34–35,* head of the clerks who worked in medieval England's office of the chancery. The 'master' kept the rolls of parchment on which government records were entered and served as the chancellor's assistant.

Roman, Romans, 1) (n.) native(s) of Rome or its empire. *Tit. Luc 1811, 1828, 1854. 2H4 2.2.115:* Romans, like Spartans (the other race of exemplary warriors described in classical literature), were reputed to be masters of terse speech. An excellent example is Julius Cæsar's often quoted description of his campaign against Pharnaces of Pontus: 'I came, I saw, I conquered.'

H5 3.3.27. JC. Ham 5.2.292: Horatio is saying he has the courage to commit suicide. *Oth 4.1.117:* Othello compares Cassio to a conqueror. He cannot mean that Cassio is a native of Rome because he has already been identified as Florentine. There is also a play on 'triumph,' the parade of the conquerors held in Rome after each victory.

Ant 3.2.37. Cor. Cym: the Britains resist Roman demands for tribute and war with them. *2.4.70,* 'her R.,' Mark Antony. *5.6.81,* 'R.'s heart, a heart of courage.

2) *Ant 1.3.84, 1.5.42, 4.16.59,* see Antony, Mark.

3) (adj.) of or pertaining to Rome or its people. *Shr 2.1.291. 2H6 4.1.137. Tit. Luc 3, 51505,1628, 1831. LLL 5.2.607,* 'face of a R. coin,' a metaphor of worn shapelessness.

MV 3.2.293, 'ancient R. honour,' describes Antonio.

JC. AYLI 4.2.4. H5 2.4.37, 3.3.18. Ham add. Q2 A.1.1.9.

Mac 5.10.1, 'R. fool,' a suicide. *Ant. Cor. Cym 4.2.350, 5.6.471,* 'R. eagle,' the eagle was a symbol of Rome; *4.4.17,* 'R. horses,' the cavalry.

4) (adj,) an Italian style of handwriting which was coming into vogue among the aristocracy. It had been developed from Carolingian models and was replacing the 'secretary' style. After the first manual of the style was published by papal secretary Ludovici degli Arrighi in 1522, it spread rapidly through Europe. Modern handwriting and Italic type-faces derive from it. *Tit 5.1.139,* 'R. letters.' *TN 3.4.26,* 'R. hand.'

Romanos, *2H6 1.4.59,* L. 'Romans,' from the text of an oracle the Pythian Apollo gave Pyrrhus when he asked the god if he would conquer Rome (Cicero, *De Divinatione,* 2.56). Apollo's oracles were famous for their ambiguity.

Rome, city on the Tiber river, capital of the modern nation of Italy, seat of the leader of the Catholic church, and center of an ancient empire that encompassed Europe, the Middle East and North Africa. The city of Rome was founded in the middle of the 8th c. BC by Italic peoples from the plain of Latium and the Apennine hills. They were attracted to Rome by the strategic significance of its site. From Rome west to the sea the Tiber river was a broad expanse of water that was difficult to cross, but at the city the river's channel narrowed enough to permit bridges to be built. Most of Italy's north-south trade routes converged at Rome. Their importance increased in the 8th c. as the Greek colonies of southern Italy and the Etruscan cities of the north extended their spheres of influence. Rome was pulled into the Etruscan orbit, and the Etruscans had a powerful influence on the development of Roman culture. During the 6th c. Rome was ruled by Etruscan monarchs. At the start of the 5th c. a rebellion by the Roman upper classes drove the Etruscan kings from the city. The Romans repudiated the concept of monarchy and established a republican government. The Republic was not a democracy. It was dominated by aristocracies of blood and wealth and was severely strained by internal tensions among its classes. The Republic did, however, have remarkable success in preserving the city and guiding it toward empire.

At the start of the republican period, Rome was a small, landlocked city-state surrounded by enemies bent on its destruction. Rome no sooner weathered one war than it was faced with another: Rome's Latin neighbors organized a league that was sometimes Rome's ally, but often its opponent; Etruscans tried to regain control of the city; Celtic tribes crossed the Alps, marauded through Italy, and looted Rome; and the Samnite tribes that inhabited the Apennine mountains raided Roman and Latin territory. The Romans were by no means invincible in all these campaigns, but by one means or another they survived, subdued, or assimilated those who attacked them. Rome steadily accrued importance to the point where the balance of power in the Italian peninsula shifted in its favor. In 285 the defeat of the Greek colony of Tarentum enabled Rome to organize Italy as a federation of city-states united for mutual defense. The shores of Italy failed to provide the federation with an adequate defensive frontier, for the Greek cities of Italy were involved with the Greeks of Sicily. They dragged Rome into war with their enemies, the Carthaginians. Carthage, a Phoenician empire based on Africa's northern coast, was a major sea power well situated to block Rome's expansion. The Romans and Carthaginians clashed on three occasions (the Punic Wars of 264–241, 218–202, and 149–146), and it was only at great cost in men and resources that Rome obliterated Carthage to emerge as the master of the western Mediterranean.

Rome's conquest of Carthage's territory alarmed the nations of the east and caused new wars that drew Rome's armies far from home and nearer to world dominion. Rome's military success imposed tremendous burdens on its government. The Republic had been designed for the management of a city-state, not an empire, and the tensions between rich and poor that had always complicated Roman politics became intolerable as Rome experienced the consequences of its empire. The soldiers who fought Rome's wars were impoverished by long terms of military service; the loot from their victories enriched the few families who had the clout to monopolize the Republic's magistracies. The situation deteriorated rapidly until competition among generals and powerful family organizations erupted in a civil war that nearly lost Rome all that it had won. Much of the difficulty sprang from Rome's reluctance to face the fact that its antiquated Republic was incapable of handling the responsibilities of empire. Given the primitive means of communication available to the ancient world, monarchies were the only political systems efficient enough to maintain order in large territories. Romans cherished the image of themselves as a free people who had thrown off the yoke of kings, and national pride prevented them from accepting the form of government that their circumstances required. For a century Roman politicians experimented with a variety of economic, social, political, and military reforms, but nothing slowed Rome's drift toward autocracy. Armies grew larger as competitors for power eliminated each other and consolidated their gains.

By 48 BC, two generals, Julius Cæsar and Pompey, were locked in a struggle for control of the world. Cæsar was victorious in war, but defeated by peace. It was clear to him that the Republic could not maintain order in the empire and that Rome needed a powerful executive at the helm. The Roman people, however, were not yet convinced that the time had come to yield to a king. In 44 BC, a group of idealistic nobles assassinated Cæsar. They saw themselves as defenders of the Republic and assumed that once Cæsar was dead the Republic would automatically rise to the challenge of governing the empire. This romantic illusion quickly faded. The Republic did not revive, but the civil war did. Mark Antony, Cæsar's second-in-command, and Octavius (commonly known by the honorary title 'Augustus'), Cæsar's nephew and personal heir, began a long, bloody contest for control of Rome. Octavius, who triumphed in 31 BC, profited from Cæsar's mistakes. He avoided all the trappings of monarchy, posed as the savior of the Republic, and contented himself with the private exercise of a power whose existence he publicly denied. Octavius created a kind of invisible monarchy behind the facade of the old Roman Republic. The Roman Senate continued to meet and the officers of the Republic continued to be elected, but effective governmental authority shifted to the household of the *imperator* (commander-in-chief) or the *princeps* (the 'first citizen' of the Republic). Since the monarchy was never openly acknowledged, no constitutional arrangement could be made to pass the office from one man to another. Octavius simply bequeathed it to his natural heirs as part of his private estate. This established a dynasty that was soon strong enough to disregard the trappings of the Republic and adopt a royal style. Emperors fostered or heaped contempt on republican traditions according to their whims, but none halted the evolution of autocracy.

For several centuries Rome maintained peace and order in the civilized west, but in the 5th c. the empire began to weaken. Rome's simple agrarian economy could not support the elaborate bureaucratic and military machinery needed for management and defense of the empire. Pressures on the Rhine and Danube frontiers from barbarian migrants exacerbated internal difficulties and caused Rome's rulers to conclude that no one man could cope with all the challenges the state faced. The eastern and western halves of the empire were given separate governments, and the city of Rome was abandoned for locations that had better communications with the military hot spots. The Roman empires of the east and west quickly diverged. The east, which evolved a powerful government seated in the city of Constantinople, continued stable and prosperous for several generations. The west bore the brunt of the barbarian invasions and deteriorated very rapidly. The last Roman emperor of the west was deposed in 476 AD, and the provinces of the western empire became independent states under the control of German warriors.

The imperial title lapsed until 800, when the church revived it for Charlemagne, a king from the tribe of the Franks. Throughout the Middle Ages the 'Roman' emperors were all German kings, and most of them were based in lands that had never been part of ancient Rome's empire. The medieval city of Rome never recovered its position as the seat of a secular empire, but it acquired compensatory significance. In the 7th c. Rome came under the control of its highest ranking religious leader, its Christian bishop. The man responsible for the Roman diocese was more than an ordinary bishop. According to medieval tradition, the apostle Peter, whom Christ had appointed head of the church (Matthew 16), had founded Rome's Christian congregation. When Peter was martyred in Rome, he bequeathed the power Christ had given him to the Roman bishops who were his successors. This gave them a precedence over all other bishops that, during the Middle Ages, developed into the institution of the papacy. For Sh. and his contemporaries Rome was first the seat of the pope and only secondarily a symbol for secular empire. The city's ecclesiastical associations were so strong that 'Rome' often signified not the city, but the leadership of the international church.

Shr 4.2.76. Tit. 1H6 3.1.52. Luc 715, 1644, 1818, 1833, 1838, 1851.

LLL 5.2.705. Jn 3.1.106, 3.1.120, 3.1.131. MV 4.1.152: Portia in disguise is supposedly from R. *H5 5.0.26. JC. Ham 2.2.393, add. Q2 A.1.1.6. MM 3.1.355.*

Ant. Cor. Cym: the city is portrayed both as the mighty imperial city and as a Renaissance Italian city. *H8.*

Rome, Court of, *H8 2.2.105,* see Rome.

Romish stew, *Cym 1.6.153,* Roman brothel. 'The stews' originally meant 'bath houses.' Romish was occasionally used as a substitute for Roman, but it shows much more contempt, as does, for example, 'Popish,' as opposed to 'papal.'

Rosalind, *AYLI,* witty and intelligent heroine, beloved by Orlando, who disguises herself as Ganymede. She is played as the taller, fairer of the two female friends (Celia the darker). This pairing is similar to that in *MND,* and is likely because of particular boy actors. Sh. got the name from his source, Thomas Lodge's *Rosalynde* (1590). The name would mean 'beautiful rose' in Spanish, reflecting her grace and femininity.

Rosalinda, *AYLI 3.2.134,* Rosalind, the extra syllable to show Orlando's forcing the meter in his love poetry.

Rosaline, 1) *LLL,* object of Biron's affections, one of the ladies attendant to the Princess of France. She is witty and enjoys the power she has over men, although she is not as fully formed as the later more strikingly intelligent and assertive women, like Rosalind and Beatrice. She is described as dark, a recurrent feature of a female character in several plays. It was likely a characteristic of one of the Lord Chamberlain's Men's boy actors.

2) *Rom,* niece of Capulet and beloved of Romeo in the beginning of the play though she is sworn to chastity. Her fairness is lengthily discussed by Romeo at *1.1.203–234,* she is identified as such at *1.2.70,* and Mercutio calls her 'pale,' at *2.3.4.* The fact that Romeo is twice shown enamored of a Capulet perhaps bears on the meaning of the play. He falls in love with women he cannot reasonably have and when he does get his Juliet, a girl even closer to his father's enemy, the result is disaster.

Roscius, Quintus R. Gallus, (126–62 BC), most famous actor in the history of the ancient Roman theater. He polished his skills by studying the performances of the orators who argued cases before Rome's courts. Despite his birth as a slave and the general contempt in which his profession was held, Roscius earned the respect of the most important men in Rome, grew rich, and founded an acting school. He also wrote a book on his profession. Cicero studied with him, regarded him as a friend, and wrote a speech

(*Pro Roscio Comœdo*) to support him in a law suit of 68 BC. Plutarch mentions him, Catullus composed a poem in his honor, and the dictator Sulla admitted him to the equestrian order. It was a compliment to an Elizabethan performer to compare him with Roscius.
3H6 5.6.10. Ham 2.2.392.

Rose, *AYLI 1.2.21,* 'sweet R.,' nickname for Rosalind.

Rose, The, *H8 1.2.153,* house in London belonging to Edward Stafford, duke of Buckingham, in the parish of St. Lawrence Poultney.

Rosencrantz, *Ham,* boyhood friend of Hamlet now in the service of Claudius. Along with Guildenstern, he is an opportunistic courtier who cannot be trusted by his old friend. How guilty he and Guildenstern are in Claudius' plots is never clear; however, they are certainly guilty of acquiescing to the general corruption of the state. When Hamlet switches papers on them, they go unknowingly to their deaths. R. was a noble name common at the Danish court in the late 16th c. and at the university of Wittenberg. An ambassador sent to England at the start of James I's reign had the name.

Ross, 1) *Mac,* domain in northern Scotland, including only the area between Moray and Dornoch firths, which was frequently harassed by the Vikings. The Celts held it as part of the large county of Moray, but David I weakened them by diminishing Moray. The first earl of Ross received his title from Malcolm IV. At present it is part of the county of Ross and Cromarty.

2) *Mac,* thane who mainly serves as the bearer of news throughout the play. Sh. got the name from Holinshed's *Chronicles* (1577) where it was mistakenly listed among the enemies of Macbeth. In fact, Macbeth was the thane of Ross and Moray during the time setting of the play.

Ross, Lord, *R2,* William Roos, (1394–1414), one of the first English barons to declare for Henry (IV) Bolingbroke when he returned to England in 1399 to challenge the authority of Richard II. Ross served on the commission that received Richard's abdication, and Henry IV appointed him treasurer of England.

Rouen, capital of the French province of Normandy. It commanded the Seine valley west of Paris and was of great strategic importance in the medieval wars between the English and the French. The trial and execution of Joan of Arc took place in Rouen, which was the seat of the English high command in France. *1H6. H5 3.5.54, 64.*

Roussi, *H5 3.5.44, 4.8.99,* (d. 1415), soldier whom Holinshed (3.555) lists among the many notable French casualties of the battle at Agincourt.

Roussillon, *AWW,* F1 'Rossillion,' 'Rosignoll,' old province of France. The Pyrenees formed its southern border and the Mediterranean the eastern. Foix lay to the west and Languedoc to the north. Its name derived from Ruscino or Rosceliona, a small place near Perpignan, the capital of the province. After the Roman Empire, the area was controlled by the Visigoths. The Saracens held it briefly in the 8th c., but fell back before Pépin. In 893 Suniaire II became the first hereditary count of Roussillon, but the province was never strong enough to become much more than a bone of contention between French and Spanish rulers. In 1258, it went by treaty to Aragon and remained in Spanish hands pretty much until 1659 when it went by treaty to France and remained French until the present. In Sh.'s day it had gone through a period of suffering at the hands of both sides because of the French/Spanish war of 1496–98 and the dauphin's siege of Perpignan in 1542, in which the natives remained loyal to Spain. Sh. overlooks the Spanish orientations of the Roussillonais. In Sh.'s source, William Painter's *Palace of Pleasure* (1566), an adaptation of a tale in Boccaccio's *Decameron,* 3.9, the area is called 'Rossiglione.'

Roussillon, Count of, *AWW* see Bertram.

Roussillon, Countess of, *AWW,* widowed mother of Bertram. She opens the play by turning her son over to the wardship of the king, which is symbolic of Bertram's movement from childhood to adulthood. But as Bertram does not make the change easily, his mother sympathizes with Helen and is dismayed at Bertram's behavior. Her kindliness is rewarded as she watches the reconciliation at the end. Although a minor role, she watches over all with a gentle righteous presence which contrasts with the sordidness of the others.

Rowland, 1) *MM 4.5.8,* friend or vassal of the duke.

2) *Lr,* see Roland.

Rowland de Bois, Sir, *AYLI,* deceased father of Orlando and Oliver. His counterpart in Sh.'s source, Lodge's *Rosalynde,* is Sir John of Bordeaux, indicating Sh. is patching together a French name. In a possible source, the 14th c. *Tale of Gamelyn,* the corresponding man is named Sir Johan de Boundrys. Fr. *bois* means 'forest' perhaps suggested by the setting, though it seems to have little significance.

Rudesby, any crude, barbarous person. *Shr 3.2.10. TN 4.1.50.*

Ruffian, *1H4 2.5.459,* Prince Harry's characterization of Oldcastle. The word was sometimes used as a synonym for Satan. In the late 16th c. and especially in the Romance languages it was used as a term for a man who protected prostitutes. Its origin is unknown. Sh. otherwise uses the term generically throughout the plays for a rough and tumble person. Occasionally he uses it as a verb.

Rugby, Jack, *MWW 1.4.54,* see Rugby, John. It has been argued that the meaning here is 'knave Rugby,' as when he calls Evans the 'jack-priest' (*1.4.113*), but Caius may just be showing wonderment at the English language in which Jack and John are equivalent, something not true of Jacques and Jean. Later in the play there seems no insult intended when he calls him Jack.

Rugby, John, *MWW,* Caius' servant, described as honest and discreet by Mistress Quickly, but given to prayer. Rugby is, of course, a town in Sh.'s Warwickshire where the famous school was founded in 1567 and may be John's hometown or an allusion to his religious education. The name of the town has Danish origins. There is no reason to accept the argument that Rudesby was the servant's intended name. His character is not sufficiently defined.

Ruge-mount, *R3 4.2.107,* or Rougemont (Fr. 'red castle'), Norman castle north of the city of Exeter. It was destroyed during the English civil wars.

Ruggiero, *WT 5.2.21,* F1 'Rogero,' name of the Second Gentleman, another of those Shakespearean characters like Salerio in *MV* whose function is to carry transitions, describe offstage action, and, possibly, to allow more important actors time to change costume. The name may have come from a popular tune. It is also prominent in Ariosto's *Orlando Furioso,* which was very popular in Sh.'s time in the translation by Sir John Harington (it uses the spelling 'Rogero'). It is also found in Boccaccio's *Decameron* (Ruggieri d'Aieroli). Although it does not seem to fit the play and the contexts in which Ruggiero/Rogero appears, there may be some humor in 'roger,' which was slang for the male organ and used a verb meaning to have sex (though the *OED* first cites this use in the mid-17th c.). There was an earlier use (mid-16th c.) of 'roger,' possibly with a hard 'g' which derived from 'rogue' and meant a vagabond. These kinds of jokes are certainly not beneath Sh. in many other instances. See also Camillo.

Rumour, *2H4,* an allegorical character who represents the unsubstantiated stories that circulated immediately after the battle of Shrewsbury—the battle at which Henry IV killed Hotspur and ended the rebellion raised by the Percies. He is described as wearing a costume covered with tongues, a tradition that goes back to the description in Virgil's *Æneid,* 4.173 ff.

Russell, *1H4,* one of the men who joins Oldcastle in an attempted robbery at Gadshill. In 1597 Lord Cobham, one of Oldcastle's descendants, objected to Sh.'s use of Oldcastle's name in his plays. Sh. promptly changed his character's name to Falstaff and purged his work of other references that might have offended powerful courtiers. Since the earls of Bedford were Russells, Sh. headed off possible problems with them by transforming his Russell into 'Peto,' a name with no aristocratic English associations.

Russia, country in easternmost Europe. Nomadic tribes inhabited the area in ancient times, but the vast plains which are characteristic of these parts of Europe and Asia resulted in numerous migrations of peoples into the area, including Huns, Magyars, Avars, and others. Ultimately the Slavs dominated and, as skilled traders, exploited the river networks. They were a tribal people, however, and in an attempt to maintain order around Novgorod, they invited Rurik, a Scandinavian, to become ruler in 862. As the Scandinavians were called the Rus, the kingdom became known as the 'land of the Rus.' Orthodox Christianity became established in 988. There was often dissension in the kingdom and stress between the commercial centers of Kiev and Novgorod. There were also threats from invaders such as the Lithuanians, Poles, and Teutonic Knights. In 1242 the Mongols founded the Khanate of the Golden Horde and forced what was left of Russia to submit to the Tartars. Gradually, Moscow became more important, and the duke of Muscovy began to consider himself the prince of all Russia. In 1480 Ivan III refused to submit tribute to the Golden Horde, and the domain of Muscovy began to expand. Ivan the Terrible became the first czar in 1547 and substantially expanded the kingdom during his reign. He also made many trading overtures to the west, and Englishmen became regular traders in Baltic ports. Ivan even once, like most single European monarchs, proposed a marriage with Elizabeth I. After his death, however, the kingdom began to unravel and was in anarchy until the election of Michael Romanov as czar in 1613. The Romanovs would rule the country until 1917. In Sh.'s day, Russia was an exotic place, but somewhat familiar because of extensive trade relations with England.

MM 2.1.129, reference to the lengthy winter nights in the higher latitudes.

Russia, Emperor of, the czar, though technically Russia was not an empire until Peter the Great was proclaimed emperor in 1721. 'Czar' derives from 'Cæsar,' used in the sense of 'emperor.' *MM 3.1.354,* rumor has it that Vincentio is meeting with the czar, possibly because he told Angelo he was travelling to Poland.

WT 3.2.118, Hermione's father. In Sh.'s source Robert Greene's *Pandosto, or the Triumph of Time,* (1588; rptd. 1607 as *Dorastus and Fawnia*), the emperor is father of Egistus' (Polixenes') wife, not Bellaria (Hermione).

Russian, 1) (n.) a native of Russia. *LLL 5.2.443,* (sing.) *LLL 5.2.122, 361, 157, 362* (pl.): the noblemen disguise themselves as Russians. This episode is believed to be influenced by the Christmas revels at Gray's Inn 1594/5 in which performers were costumed as R. and the Emperor of Russia was mocked for his pomposity. A 'Comedy of Errors (like to Plautus his *Menæchmus*)' was performed which may mean that Sh. was present. There may be punning on the Fr. *roussiner* 'to mount a mare.'

2) (adj.) of or pertaining to Russia. *LLL, 5.2.368,* F1 'Russia,' *401,* 'R. habit,' in R. costumes. See Russians. *H5 3.7.140,* 'R. bear,' a ferocious wild beast, a reference to bear baiting. *Mac 3.4.99,* 'R. bear.'

Rutland, Earl of, 1) Edmund, (1443–1460), second son of Richard, duke of York. Rutland is a tiny English county between Lincolnshire and Leicestershire. An earldom of Rutland was granted to the duke of York's heir in 1386. Lord Clifford captured Edmund at the battle of Wakefield where Richard was killed. Although the boy was only twelve years old, Clifford put him to death to avenge the death of Clifford's father at the first battle of St. Albans.

3H6. R3 1.3.175, 4.4.45, 261.

2) *R2 5.2.43, 5.3.94,* title to which Henry IV demoted the duke of Aumerle in 1399 as punishment for his allegedly criminal services to Richard II. William Bagot, one of Richard's closest advisors, accused Aumerle of complicity in the murder of the duke of Gloucester. See Aumerle.

Rycas, *TNK 2.3.39,* country man coming to the fair, described as a fine dancer.

S

Saale, *H5 1.2.45, 52, 63,* F1 'Sala,' tributary of the Elbe River. It flows northward from northeast Bavaria past Halle and joins the Elbe between Dessau and Magdeburg.

Saba, *H8 5.4.23,* queen of Sheba. 'Saba' was the spelling used until 1611 when the publication of the King James Version of the Bible popularized the current form. Saba was the country in southwestern Arabia now called Yemen. The trade routes that connected the Indian Ocean and the Red Sea made ancient Saba a prosperous land. 1 Kings 10:1, 4, 10, 13, and 2 Chronicles 9:1, 3, 9, 12, tell the story of a queen of the Sabæans who journeyed to the court of the Hebrew king, Solomon, to test his reputation for wisdom. The royal house of Ethiopia claimed descent from a son that legend says the queen conceived by Solomon during her visit.

Sack, Spanish or Canary island wines such as sherries. The name derives from the Fr. *vin sec* or Sp. *vino seco,* 'dry wine,' although some of the sacks were sweet. There seem to be some confusions in the etymology such as the combining of a local patois word with 'dry.' *Passim* throughout the plays.

MWW 2.1.200–01, 'burnt s.,' mulled sack.

Sackerson, *MWW 1.1.275,* celebrated bear used for bear-baiting, a sport in which a bear was tied to a post and several dogs were released to attack it. Wagers were taken on the survivors. Unlike bull-baiting, the bear was usually saved from death so that it could be used again. S. appeared at the Paris Garden near the Globe. He is also mentioned in Sir John Davies' *Epigrams* (c. 1598).

Sacrament, The, *R2 1.1.139,* the Eucharist, the offering of the body and blood of Christ in the Mass. The Catholic church recognizes seven sacraments, but the Eucharist is the centerpiece of its worship and the sacrament most frequently witnessed by its people.

Safe, Sergeant, man mentioned by Doll. *STM Add. II.D.50,* 'Sergeant S.'s yeoman,' Arthur Watchins. Holinshed mentions that a sergeant at arms, Nicholas Downes, was injured in the arm at the May Day riots depicted in this manuscript.

Sagittary, 1) *Tro 5.5.14,* medieval name for the centaur, whose sparkling eyes could kill. In Sh.'s play, the Sagittary wreaks havoc among the Greek troops. In William Caxton's *Recuyell of the Historyes of Troy* (1474), the Sagittary is a 'meruallyous beste' brought by king Epistrophus of Eliane, a kingdom beyond that of the Amazons. The Sagittary is later killed by Diomedes. In discussion of the sources of Sh.'s play it has been noted that in the printed version of John Lydgate's *Troy Book* (1412–20) the Sagittary is not named. In Lydgate's manuscript, the name is used. The Sagittary is not mentioned in the *Iliad.*

2) *Oth 1.1.160, 1.3.115,* an inn or some other building. As an inn it would have had a sign illustrating the centaur archer, but it may have been a building decorated with the mythological creature. Some critics asserted that the Sagittary was the residence, at the arsenal, of the commanding officers of the navy and army. It had supposedly an archer over the gates, a statue, but not of a centaur. Most critics dismiss this claim. Lists of inns of Othello's time do not mention a Sagittary, either, though that may mean that Sh. borrowed it from something more contemporary, as he often does.

Saint Albans, town about 20 mi. northwest of London near the site of Roman Verulamium. During the Middle Ages it was renamed for its monastery, one of the oldest and richest in England. See Saint Albans, First battle of, Second battle of, and Alban, St.

2H6 1.2.57, 83, 1.4.62, 2.1.140. 1H4 4.2.46. 2H4 2.2.160.

Saint Albans, First battle of, *2H6 5.5.35,* the event that marks the beginning of the War of the Roses. The fight between the partisans of the houses of York and Lancaster that broke out in the streets of Saint Albans on 22 May 1455, was little more than a skirmish, but it had major political ramifications. During the fight York slaughtered his nemesis, Somerset, the earl of Northumberland, and the elder Lord Clinton. Henry VI was captured by the Yorkists, and the fragile monarch lapsed into insanity for the second time in his reign. This permitted York to reclaim the role of royal protector that had been his during Henry's first attack of mental illness. The historical events are not entirely consistent with the plot of *2H6,* for Sh. condenses the course of the war for dramatic purposes. Sh. has Henry flee to safety at the end of *2H6,* but in reality Henry remained York's puppet until he recovered his reason in February 1456. Queen Margaret then forced York from court, and for four years York and the queen engaged in a sparring match. On 10 July 1460 at Northampton, York again captured Henry. Henry remained a prisoner until Margaret liberated him at the second battle of Saint Albans. A month later the Lancastrians suffered a decisive defeat at Towton, and Henry and Margaret fled to Scotland.

Saint Albans, Second battle of, major battle in the War of the Roses. Late in December 1460 a Lancastrian army, led by Somerset, Clifford, and Northumberland, delivered a challenge to Richard of York at his castle at Sandal. Richard met his opponents near the town of Wakefield and suffered a disastrous defeat. Richard, his young son Edmund, and perhaps as many as 2,000 of their soldiers were killed. The events at Wakefield emboldened Henry VI's queen, Margaret, who had been raising troops in Scotland, to join her Lancastrian allies in a march on London. It fell to York's eldest son, Edward, who was in the west of England at the time, to reorganize the Yorkist party. Edward raised troops in the Welsh borderlands and set off for London. He was compelled, however, to change his objective when news reached him that a Lancastrian force assembled in France and Ireland had landed in Wales. On 3 February 1461, Edward triumphed over the invaders at the battle of Mortimer's Cross. While he fought in the west, his mentor, the earl of Warwick, tried to deal with the threat Margaret posed to London. Warwick had a very large army, which included a contingent of Burgundians skilled in the use of exotic firearms. Warwick also held an important hostage. Henry VI had fallen into Yorkist hands in July of 1460 after a battle at Northampton.

On 17 February 1461, Warwick took a stand north of London at Saint Albans, where, despite ample supplies and a good strategic position, he fared badly. Poor intelligence and communications may have caused him to fail to support a portion of his army when it was surprised by a sudden Lancastrian attack. In the confusion, the Yorkist troops lost confidence in their leaders and fled. Warwick and other lords escaped, but had to leave behind their illustrious prisoner, Henry VI. The Lancastrians, once again in possession of the person of the king, should have advanced on London to secure the city's allegiance, but Margaret ordered a retreat to Dunstable. The queen may have been afraid of the consequences if the Scots and other northerners in her army turned on London. The city was desperate for a protector, and on February 26 it opened its gates to Warwick and young Edward of York. A few days later the Yorkists took the decisive step of proclaiming the 19-year-old Edward king in Henry's place. After years of Lancastrian misrule, many in England were eager for a fresh start with a new leader. Margaret and Henry retreated farther to the north, and the Yorkists had an opportunity to make a full recovery from Richard's losses at Wakefield.

3H6 2.1.114, 120, 3.2.1. R3 1.3.130.

Saint Asaph, Bishop of, *H8,* Henry Standish (d. 1535), Franciscan friar who was one of Henry VIII's favorite preachers and an advocate appointed to represent Katherine of Aragon before the court that inquired into the validity of her marriage to Henry. Katherine did not believe that Standish had her interests at heart, and subsequent events suggest that he was very much the king's man. He assisted at Anne Boleyn's coronation and joined two other bishops in consecrating Thomas Cranmer archbishop of Canterbury. The diocese of Saint Asaph was one of the four medieval sees of Wales. It encompassed northeastern Wales.

Saint Bennet, *TN 5.1.35,* F1 'the belles of S Bennet.' Either an allusion to a song of this title or to a church in London whose bells rang out in some pattern of threes. There were several churches in London dedicated to St. Bennet (Benedict). It has been speculated that this refers to the one at Paul's Wharf that burned in the Great Fire of 1666.

Saint Colum's inch, *Mac 1.2.61,* island, now known as Inchcolm, about a half mile long and a third wide in the firth of Edinburgh and the county of Fife. 'Inch' means a small island. There was an abbey there dedicated to St. Columba, the Irish saint who converted the Picts.

Saint Crispin's day, *H5 4.3.67,* 25 October, see Crispian, Feast of.

Saint Cupid, *LLL,* see Cupid.

Saint Davy's day, *H5 4.1.56, 5.1.2,* 1 March, feast day of the patron saint of Wales. St. David (d. 589) is credited with beginning the mission that converted Wales to Christianity.

Saint Edmundsbury, *Jn 4.3.11, 5.4.18,* see Bury.

Saint Francis, *AWW 3.5.36,* inn for pilgrims near one of the gates of Florence.

Saint George's field, extensive meadow on the southern shore of the Thames between the suburb of Southwark and the archbishop of Canterbury's palace at Lambeth. It was named for a neighboring church dedicated to St. George the Martyr. Soldiers often used it as a training ground. *2H6 5.1.46. 2H4 3.2.192.*

Saint Gregory's Well, *TGV 4.2.82,* well near Milan, where Proteus is to meet Thurio. A print of the city showing the well appeared in Braun's *Civitates Orbis Terrarum* (1582). The accuracy of the reference is surprising and suggests a possible source of which scholars are unaware or the less likely theory of Sh.'s travels in Italy during the 'lost years.' The name of the well might, however, be an invention based upon the church of St. Gregory by St. Paul's in London. The church was in existence by 1070 and survived until the 19th c. Inigo Jones almost demolished it when constructing the portico of St. Paul's in 1637, but the parishioners protested loudly and Jones was summoned to the House of Lords. The stones intended for the cathedral were used to repair St. Gregory's. This incident indicates the importance of the church to the people in that area.

Saint Jaques le Grand, *AWW 3.5.34, 96, 4.3.52,* Santiago de Compostela, shrine of St. James the Great in northwest Spain. His body was supposedly translated there after his death and the relics were discovered by Theodomir, bishop of Iria, in 835. The bishop was supposedly guided to them by a star. A chapel was immediately erected on the site. In 997, the Moors destroyed the buildings, but did not harm the relics, and after Bermudo III reconquered the city for the Christians, it became one of the most important European sites to which to make a pilgrimage. Flocks of pilgrims choked the roads to the city, which formerly was capital of Galicia and the ecclesiastical rival of Toledo. A cathedral was begun in 1078 and was consecrated in 1211. It has been substantially added to in following centuries. Helen's posing as a pilgrim would be one of the few credible explanations for a woman undertaking a journey in Renaissance times and would afford some theoretical protection.

Saint Lambert's day, *R2 1.1.199,* commemoration of the martyrdom of Lambert of Maastrict, 17 September. Lambert was a bishop of Liège who was martyred on that date in 705/6 by one of the vassals of Pépin II of Heristal.

Saint Lawrence Poutney, *H8 1.2.154,* or Poultney, London parish church that stood at the corner of Candlewick Street and Lawrence Poultney Lane. The district took its name from Sir John Poultney, mayor of London, who in the 14th c. endowed a chantry in the church of Saint Lawrence and converted his neighboring townhouse into a college.

Saint Luke's, 1) *MM 3.1.266,* location of Mariana's 'moated grange.' There is no Saint Luke's near Vienna, but the parish church of Chelsea, which was a country church near the Thames, was built in the 14th c. It had a chapel added by Thomas More, and both More and John Fletcher's mother were buried there.

2) *Shr 4.5.15, 28,* church at which Biondello arranges for Lucentio's and Bianca's wedding. There is no such church in Padua or London. See *MM* above.

Saint Magnus' Corner, *2H6 4.7.155,* junction of Thames Street and Bridge Street near the city entrance to London Bridge. The church of St. Magnus was the most notable public building at the site in the 15th c. Since Jack Cade's headquarters were in Southwark and he entered London via London Bridge, this was an area through which Cade's men would have marched and where they might have rioted.

Saint Mary's chapel, *Jn 2.1.539,* probably the Lady Chapel of the cathedral of Angers.

Saint Tavy's day, *H5 4.7.101,* see Saint Davy's day.

Saint Valentine's day, 14 February, according to legend the day on which birds begin to mate and lovers seek each other. *MND 4.1.138. Ham 4.5.47.* See Valentine, St.

Sala, F1 for Saale (q.v.)

Salanio, *MV,* F1 'Solanio,' Venetian gentleman, who (with Salerio) serves a chorus-like purpose by commenting on the offstage action and defining the characters of Antonio and Shylock. They also, importantly, establish the attitude of the dominant culture of Sh.'s Venice toward the Jew and other characters. Salanio is not much developed as an individual, even to the extent of the merciless Graziano, and is not really active in the plot. The indefinite character of Salanio and Salerio/Salarino (q.v.) is reflected by the careless spellings of their names. They could be played by a minimum of two actors, but are often done as more. They could as well be called 'First and Second Kibbitzer.'

Salarino, *MV,* also F1 'Slarino' an obvious misspelling. Most contemporary editors believe that this is the same character as Salerio and edit to reflect it.

Salerio, *MV,* F1 'Salarino' (q.v.), also F1 'Salino' an obvious misspelling, Venetian gentleman, who [with Salanio (q.v.)] comments on the offstage action and defines the characters. The name could be related to the L. *salarius,* 'salt,' or the annual revenue from salt paid to Roman soldiers (from which we get 'salary'). If he is thought to be a wealthy merchant, rather than a gentleman, the L. *salarius,* 'dealer in salted fish,' might apply. See Salanio.

Salic land, *H5 1.2.39, 40, 44, 51, 52, 56,* area of Germany from which the tribe of the Salian Franks (cousins of the Ripuarian Franks of the Rhineland) was thought to have come. In Sh.'s sources it was the district drained by the Saale and Elbe rivers. Modern scholars have suggested other possible points of origin for the Salians.

Salic law, *H5 1.2.11, 54, 91,* Salian law, a collection of edicts that medieval scholars believed reflected the customs of the early inhabitants of France. The Salian Franks, Germanic immigrants, settled in the Rhine region of the Netherlands in the 4th c. They occupied the Roman provence of Gaul in the 5th c. and laid the foundations for the feudal kingdom of

France. Modern scholars believe that the oldest sections of the Salic law evolved during the Merovingian period, not Frankish prehistory. (The law addresses the concerns of a land-owning people, and the Salians were nomads before they settled in France.) The portions of the Salic law that survive constitute a criminal code, but there are passages dealing with property rights. In the late Middle Ages one of these, which declared daughters ineligible to inherit land from their fathers, was given a controversial interpretation. The archaic text was invoked to justify passing Louis X's throne to his brother rather than his daughter. The Salic law was accepted in France, but its validity was challenged by the kings of England. They believed that their descent from Philip IV's daughter, Isabella, mother of Edward III, gave them a claim to the French throne. The dispute was one of the causes of the Hundred Years' War.

Salisbury, or New Sarum (New Saresbury), county seat of Wiltshire and administrative center for the diocese of Salisbury. The town grew up around the cathedral which was begun in 1220, after relocating from Old Sarum which had been occupied by Celts, Romans (as *Sorbiodunum*), Saxons and Normans. The Anglo-Saxons replaced the Celtic *dunum* 'fort' with their equivalent, *burh.* The initial part of the name, *sorbio,* is of unknown origin, but evolved into *saris* (as in Saresbury) and after the Norman invasion into Salisbury. 'Sarum' is Latinized 'Saris.' An earldom of Salisbury was bestowed for the first time on a Patrick of Salisbury (c. 1149), a descendant of an Edward of Salisbury who appears in the *Domesday* survey as 'vicecomes of Wiltshire.' The heiress of William (d. 1196), the second earl, married William de Longespée (d. 1226), Henry II's illegitimate son. The Montague (Montacute) family acquired the earldom in 1301, and in 1400 it passed to the Nevilles. *R3 4.4.375, 382, 466, 469. H8 1.2.197.* See Salisbury, Earl of.

Salisbury, Earl of, 1) *2H6,* see Neville, Richard.
2) *1H6, H5,* see Montague, Thomas.

3) *R2,* John Montacute (1350–1400), English magnate conspicuous for his loyalty to Richard II. Salisbury earned Richard's favor by helping him overthrow the 'lords appellant,' the royal councilors who wanted to set limits to the monarch's power to act without the consent of his barons. In 1398 Salisbury did the king a further service by accepting appointment to a special royal commission to which Richard had persuaded parliament to cede its authority. Salisbury was also a member of the expedition Richard led to Ireland in 1399. When news reached Richard in Ireland that Henry (IV) Bolingbroke had defied his decree of banishment and landed in England, Richard sent Salisbury to Wales to raise the army the king needed to put down the revolt. Salisbury's soldiers deserted before Richard arrived, and the earl advised Richard to flee. Richard, however, refused to leave England, and Salisbury stayed to be captured with him. After Richard's deposition, Henry IV pardoned Salisbury, but the gesture failed to win the earl to the new regime. Late in 1399 Salisbury joined a conspiracy to kill Henry and restore Richard to the throne. When Henry got wind of the plot, Salisbury fled to Cirencester where he was captured and beheaded.

4) *Jn,* William de Longsword (d. 1226), illegitimate son of Henry II. Longsword was highly regarded by his royal half-brothers, Richard the Lionhearted and John. Richard arranged for him to marry the heiress to the earldom of Salisbury. When John came to the throne, the earl was entrusted with important military posts. He was a gifted soldier, who was prepared to carry out whatever orders he was given. After John's catastrophic defeat at Bouvines in 1215, he led the assault that drove a French fleet from England's shores. He was one of the English barons who stood by John at Runnymede, and he may have played a part in convincing John to agree to the terms of Magna Carta. Sometime early in 1216 Longsword had a change of heart and of allegiance. He turned against John and joined the English lords who invited Louis (VIII), heir to the French throne, to assume England's crown. Salisbury surren-

dered his castle to the French and tried to arrange Dover's capitulation. John's sudden and unexpected death on 18 October 1216, altered his perception of events. He rallied to young Henry III's side and was welcomed by the boy king's regents. In later years he fought in the Holy Lands and in defense of what was left of England's possessions in France. He died of injuries sustained in a ship wreck and was buried at Canterbury in the great cathedral whose construction he helped finance.

Samingo, *2H4 5.3.76,* jesting name quoted from a drinking song. It derives from 'Sir Mingo' (L. *mingo,* 'urinate').

Samson, 1) Hebrew strongman whose story is told in the Book of Judges 13–16. Samson was invincible so long as he remained dedicated to God, and the pledge of his allegiance was an oath not to cut his hair. The Philistines, the enemies of the Jews, bribed a beautiful woman named Delilah to seduce Samson and learn the secret of his strength. After several attempts to mislead her, Samson told her the truth, and she betrayed him by cutting his hair while he slept. When Samson's strength deserted him, his enemies put out his eyes and imprisoned him. In the end his power returned, and he avenged himself by pulling down his captors' temple on their heads.

1H6 1.3.12. LLL 1.2.68, 71, 73, 84, 165. H8 5.3.21.

2) *Rom,* member of the house of Capulet. This may be a Biblical borrowing, or, as many editors prefer, 'Sampson,' a common English surname.

Sandal, *3H6 1.2.63,* castle belonging to Richard, duke of York, 2 mi. southeast of the village of Wakefield.

Sands, Lord, William, *H8,* (d. 1540), soldier and bureaucrat who served the first two Tudor kings. Sands was one of the officials who arranged the meeting between Henry VIII and Francis I at the 'Field of the Cloth of Gold.' Henry appointed him Lord Chamberlain and relied on him for help in implementing his religious program. He participated in Anne Boleyn's coronation and sat with the judges who condemned Anne to death.

Santrailles, Lord Ponton de, *1H6 1.6.6,* John, (1400–1461), one of the more important members of the party of French nobles called the 'Armagnacs.' He assisted Joan of Arc in lifting the seige of Orléans, and he helped win the battle at Patay where John Talbot, who was then England's most famous soldier, was taken prisoner. The ransom that Santrailles demanded for the English officer was so high that it could not be raised. Talbot, therefore, remained a captive until Santrailles himself fell into English hands and agreed to exchange his own freedom for Talbot's (July 1433). Santrailles led the armies that evicted the English from Gascony (1451–1453), and in 1454 he became marshal of France. Sh. considered Santrailles to be France's best warrior—a Gallic version of England's Talbot.

Saracens, *R2 4.1.86,* term commonly applied in the early Middle Ages to all of Christian Europe's Muslim enemies. It derives from the Latin name for the Arab nomads who raided the Syrian frontier of the Roman empire: the Saraceni. It ultimately derives from an Arabic word meaning 'easterner.'

Sardians, *JC 4.2.55,* citizens of Sardis, a city in Asia Minor. See Sardis.

Sardinia, *Ant 2.6.35,* second largest island in the Mediterranean, located between Sicily and Corsica off the western coast of Italy. It is a mountainous island known for its hardy inhabitants and their banditry. It has many ruins of Bronze Age structures, a time when it was already rather well populated. There appear to have been a few Greek colonies, but Carthage had conquered the island by the early 5th c. BC. It became an important grain-growing center and Rome seized the island in 238 BC. The Romans thought little of the wild island, ruling both Corsica and Sardinia under the same administration. They thought the place unhealthy and often exiled people there. At the decline of Rome in the 5th c. AD it fell to the Vandals, then to the Byzantines in the 6th c. AD. The Saracens threatened it from 720 to 1022, but it never totally fell under their sway. Pisa and Genoa fought over it from the 11th to the 14th c., then it became part of Aragon. It remained in Spanish hands until 1713. The origin of the name is obscure, though a form of it was used by the Phoenicians. The sardine may have been so named by the Romans because of the schools of fish found near the island.

Sardis, *JC 4.2.28, 5.1.79, 5.5.18,* ancient city in western Turkey. In the 6th c. BC, Sardis was the capital of a kingdom of Lydia that encompassed most of Asia Minor. Thereafter it declined in importance, but it was still the seat of a provincial administrator in the Roman era.

Sarum Plain, *Lr 2.2.83 (Q 7.81),* Salisbury Plain, a bare upland covering about 300 sq. mi. north of the city of Salisbury. Stonehenge is located on it.

Satan, 'Sathan,' the devil, God's opponent. It derives from a Hebrew term for 'adversary' or 'accuser' (in the legal sense of prosecutor). *Err 4.3.48, 49,* 'Mistress S.': Antipholis of Syracuse equates the courtesan with the tempting Satan. The first line is a direct quote from the Geneva Bible, Matthew 4:10, in which Jesus is tempted in the wilderness. Dromio then seems to play on 'light' and 'Lucifer,' *4.3.51–57,* and the passage in 2 Corinthians 11:14 in which Satan seems to be transformed into an angel of light.

1H4 2.5.468. MWW 5.5.153. TN 3.4.115, 4.2.32. AWW 5.3.263.

Saturday, seventh day of the week, named after the Roman god Saturn, who led a golden age. *LLL 4.1.6. AYLI 4.1.108.*

Saturn, 1) Roman god of agriculture (equated very roughly with the Gr. Cronos), husband of Ops (Rhea) father of Jupiter, Juno, and the other Olympian gods. Myth had it that he was dethroned by Jupiter and fled to Italy, which under his rule enjoyed a golden age. In winter the Romans celebrated Saturnalia to commemorate this age, suspending executions and declarations of war, closing businesses, giving gifts, and having masters serve feasts to slaves. A number of Christmas customs have their roots in the Saturnalia.

Tit 4.3.57. Son 98.4: even cold Saturn could be joyous in the presence of April and the beloved one. *TNK 5.6.62,* 'Cold as old S.': in the source, Chaucer's *Knyghtes Tale* (A 2684–91), S. requests that Pluto send 'a fyr,' a fury, to frighten Arcite's horse in order to secure Emelye for Palamon.

2) sixth planet from the sun, named for the Roman god. *Tit 2.3.31. 2H4 2.4.265:* Sh.'s comparison of the elderly Falstaff's seduction of Doll Tearsheet to a conjunction of the planets Saturn and Venus is comical, for medieval astrologers considered the two heavenly bodies to be so opposed in spirit that they never came together. Their orbits do occasionally cross, but so low on the horizon of Europe's skies as rarely to be observed.

Ado 1.3.11, 'born under Saturn,' in astrology, of a sluggish and morose character, 'saturnine.' *Cym 2.5.12.*

Saturnine, *Tit 1.1.208, 225, 233,* see Saturninus.

Saturninus, *Tit,* mythical Roman emperor whose marriage to a Gothic queen, Tamora, leads to disaster for him and most of the members of the family of Titus Andronicus. Titus kills Tamora to avenge a series of wrongs she and her cohorts do him and his children. Saturninus executes Titus, and Titus' son, Lucius, kills Saturninus. Sh.'s source for *Tit* is uncertain, but an 18th c. chapbook preserves a later version of a tale he may have known. Since it does not name the emperor, it is possible that Sh. invented this detail. *Tit* is set in the period of the later Roman empire when the Romans began to have difficulty with the Goths. During the turbulent era of the 'Barracks Emperors' (235–285 AD), two men named 'Saturninus' made bids for the throne. One was a general serving the emperor Valerian (253–260 AD). The other challenged the emperor Probus (276–282 AD). 'Saturninus,' therefore, accurately evokes the disturbed period in Roman history that is the context for *Tit,* but the play does not dramatize real events or describe real people.

Savoy, *2H6 4.7.1,* palace built by John of Gaunt on the Strand in London's west end. The district was popular with England's bishops, many of whom had residences there.

Sawyer, *2H6,* humble laborer who does the rough and dirty work of sawing logs into timbers. Sh. claims that men of this rank made up most of Cade's followers. In reality, Cade had solid support from the propertied classes who resented royal taxation and the inability of Henry VI's government to protect English merchant ships from raids by the French fleet.

Saxons, Germanic tribe whose migrations hastened the collapse of the Roman empire. During the 6th c. groups of Saxons and their allies, the Angles, took over the Roman province of Britain and transformed it into the medieval kingdom of England (i.e., Angleland). The Saxons Sh. refers to in *H5 1.2.46, 1.2.62,* were not English Saxons, but a related group that established themselves in Germany just south of Denmark (see Saxony).

Saxony, (Ger. *Sachsen*) region of Germany, named for the tribe of Saxons which are first recorded in the 2nd c. AD. It was this same tribe who invaded Britain after the Roman withdrawal. In the 8th c. Charlemagne devoted much of his reign to a protracted war in Saxony. Drastic measures involving forced relocations of large numbers of people eventually brought the district under the control of the Carolingian monarchy and the Christian church. Subsequently, it became a powerful duchy and at times its domain stretched from the Rhine to the Oder, though originally it was bordered by the Rhine to the west, Eider on the north, and Elbe and Saale on the east. In the 16th c. Maurice, the duke of Saxony, although a Protestant, first sided with Charles V (the Holy Roman emperor) against the Protestants, but in 1552 he switched sides, marched on Innsbruck, and forced Charles out. He compelled a religious peace and became regarded as a hero of German nationalism and religious freedom. As Saxony contained the city and university of Wittenberg (q.v.) it was a hotbed of radical thinking and the area then became a Protestant bulwark, though it was extremely intolerant of Calvinism in the late 16th c. The publication of Martin Luther's translation of the Bible resulted in the Saxon dialect predominating as the national language. Other important cities of Saxony were Dresden and Leipzig.

MV 1.2.81–82 'D. of S.'s nephew,' suitor of Portia described as the sterotypical German drunk. It us interesting that this is emphasized and the Protestant policies which accord with England's are not hinted at.

Saye, Lord, *2H6,* James Fiennes, Baron Saye (Say, Sele), (d. 1450), soldier in Henry V's army who rose to high office under Henry VI. Saye served in France during Henry VI's minority and attended the young king when he went to Paris for his coronation. In 1437 Saye became sheriff for Kent. Ten years later he was entrusted with the responsibility of guarding the port of Dover. Saye was the duke of Suffolk's political ally, and he endorsed Suffolk's controversial policy of trading Maine and Anjou to the French in exchange for a truce. Saye assisted at the arrest of Suffolk's enemy, the duke of Gloucester, and Suffolk may have persuaded Henry to appoint Saye Lord Treasurer in October of 1449. Possession of the treasury office made Saye a target for those who disapproved of Henry's fiscal policies, and parliament signaled its discontent by forcing Henry to dismiss Saye and banish Suffolk. When Cade's rebellion broke out, Cade's followers accused Saye of extortion, and Saye's enemies at court convinced Henry to send him to the Tower of London. On 4 July 1450, Lord Scales, who held the Tower for Henry, turned Saye over to Cade, and Cade beheaded him at the Standard in Cheapside. Saye's corpse was stripped and dragged to Southwark, where it was hanged and quartered. Saye's head and the head of his son-in-law, James Cromer, were paraded through the streets of London on poles.

2H6 4.7.33, an anachronism. Cade's men accuse Saye of introducing printed books to England. At the time of Saye's death, Gutenberg was at work on his press, and the flood of printed books had not yet begun. The intent of Sh.'s charge was to brand Cade's men as louts, ignoramuses, and enemies of civilization.

'Sblood, an oath, 'by God's (Christ's) blood!' It was regarded as blasphemous and edited out of some editions. *1H4 1.2.73, 1.3.244, 2.2.35, 2.5.248, 448, 3.3.48, 86, 5.4.112. MWW 3.5.8. Ham 2.2.366. Oth 1.1.4. H5 4.8.10,* 'God's plood,' Fluellen's version.

Scales, Lord, Thomas, (c. 1399–1460), soldier under the duke of Bedford who campaigned at the side of Sir John Fastolf. He was among the officers whom the French captured at the battle of Patay (1429). After the English cause in Normandy was lost, Scales returned to his home in Norfolk. In 1450, he gathered a company of soldiers to help put down the rebellion Jack Cade raised against Henry VI's government. He met Cade's men in bloody combat on London Bridge on the night of 5 July 1450. Scales came from a part of England where Yorkist sympathies were strong, but he was a loyal Lancastrian. In 1460, when Richard of York made a bid for the throne, Scales tried, but failed, to hold London for Henry. Scales was murdered as he attempted to retreat from his command post in the Tower of London. His daughter and heiress, Elizabeth, married Anthony Woodville, Edward IV's brother-in-law. Thereafter, the lords of Scales were Woodvilles and Yorkist partisans.

2H6. 3H6 4.1.51. 1H6 1.1.146.

Scarlet, Will S., one of the band of merry men led by Robin Hood. He is also called 'Scarlok,' 'Scathlock,' 'Scarlett' in older writings. He appears in one of the earliest printed texts dealing with the outlaw, *A Gest of Robyn Hode* printed by Wynken de Worde around the beginning of the 16th c. The poem may have been composed as early as 1400. He usually plays a minor role, warning Robin of the possibility of danger, but sometimes participates in brawls with him. There have been attempts to link him with various persons in the historical records, including William Schirelock or Shyrelock, a religious novice ejected from an abbey in York, and William Schakelock who, as a former soldier, was given a maintenance allowance in 1316, and may appear in other records. If Scarlet was indeed based upon a historical person, he, like Robin Hood, has been long lost in his legends. For the purposes of the colorful May festivities, the opportunity for a bright costume may have settled Scarlet's name. Scarlet has long had the connotation of sin, which may relate this character to the more mischievous Robin Hood and sluttish Marian of the oldest folklore.

MWW 1.1.158: the joke refers to Bardolph's red nose, also. *2H4 5.3.104.*

Scarus, *Ant,* Marcus Æmilius Scaurus, son of Pompey the Great and half-brother of Sextus Pompey. In 48 BC Julius Cæsar routed an army led by Pompey at Pharsalus. Pompey fled to Egypt, where he was murdered. His death left Cæsar uncontested master of the Roman empire. Sextus assembled a band of soldiers to continue his father's fight, and he developed into a serious problem for Cæsar and Cæsar's successors. In 36 BC Octavius destroyed Sextus' fleet off Sicily, and Sextus and his brother Scaurus fled east. The following year Scaurus betrayed Sextus into Mark Antony's hands, and Antony ordered Sextus' execution. Scaurus enlisted in Antony's army and fought at Actium in 31 BC. After Antony's defeat at Actium, Octavius condemned Scaurus to death. The sentence was commuted when Scaurus' mother begged for his life.

Schoolmaster, *TNK,* see Gerald the Schoolmaster.

Scoggin, *2H4 3.2.29,* man who, as Justice Shallow recalls, lost a fight with the young Falstaff. The name of Edward IV's court jester, John Scoggin, had in Sh.'s day become a synonym for a buffoon or fool.

Scone, *Mac 2.4.36, 5.1.41,* traditional site for the crowning of Scottish kings, near the river Tay a couple of mi. north of Perth. It was a capital for the Picts in the 8th c. and their first recorded national council was held there in 906. The conversion of the Picts was proclaimed here and the site was long an ecclesiastical center. The Stone of Destiny, on which Celtic kings were crowned, was supposedly brought to Scone by Kenneth I in 843, but was removed to Westminster Abbey in 1296 by Edward I of England. In 1559 the abbey and temporary residence for kings was burned by the Protestant reformers incited by John Knox. At the time of *Mac* the palace was being rebuilt by Sir David Murray, who had received the property after its seizure from the Gowries, who had plotted against King James. The last king crowned there was Charles II (January 1651), though the outcome of the conflict between him and the Puritans was at the time still in doubt.

Scot, Scots, native(s) of Scotland. Whenever an English king committed himself to a war on the continent, he had reason to worry that the Scots would avail themselves of his absence to raid northern England. Until the 17th c. the Scots vigorously defended their independence from England. But following the death of Elizabeth I in 1603, the crowns of both England and Scotland passed to James VI of Scotland, a descendant of Henry VII of England. James began a long process of reconciliation that eventually brought both nations under one government.

1H4. 2H4, 4.3.98. H5 1.2.138, 144, 148, 170.

2) *2H4 1.1.126,* see Douglas, Earl of.

Scotch jig, *Ado 2.1.66, 68,* rapid dance, first mentioned in the 16th c., said to originate in Scotland. 'Jig' may derive from the name of a fiddle (Fr. *gigue*) but this is disputed. Another theory is that it is onomatopoeic.

Scotland, part of the island of Great Britain that lies north of the Tweed river and the Solway Firth. Throughout the ancient and medieval periods its people were politically independent and culturally distinct from those who occupied the lands to the south. Celts originally dominated all of prehistoric Britain, but by the end of the Middle Ages migrations and invasions had established a mix of peoples on the island. Julius Cæsar twice led Roman armies across the channel, but it was not until the reign of the emperor Claudius that Rome made a serious attempt to conquer Britain (43 AD). The southern portion of the island capitulated to the invaders, but the Picts and Scots of the north resisted repeated Roman incursions into their territories. In 123 AD the emperor Hadrian resolved the situation by taking steps to shut the northerners out rather than continue the struggle to bring them in. He constructed a great wall to divide the civilized Roman province of the south from the wild Gælic tribal lands of the north. The wall separated cultures that, during the medieval era, became distinct nationalities. In 410 Rome withdrew its troops from Britain and concentrated its military resources on a futile attempt to defend Gaul and Italy from Germanic invaders. As the empire crumbled, groups of Germans found their way to the shores of Britain. The old Roman province passed into the hands of the Saxons and Angles—from whom it took the name 'England.' Germans also penetrated Scotland, establishing themselves in the southeastern lowlands (the district of Lothian). Germans won the fight for Rome's territory, but they lost the struggle to preserve Rome's institutions.

As the empire collapsed, western civilization declined precipitously. England and Scotland owed the reconstruction of their culture to the Celts of Ireland. Since Ireland had never been part of the Roman empire, it did not suffer politically or militarily from the empire's decline. Ireland's location protected it from the

Germanic migrations that overwhelmed Gaul and Britain, and the island became a refuge for a civilization that elsewhere was in full retreat. By the 6th c. conditions had stabilized enough in Europe for the Irish to undertake the task of restoring the Christian religion and literacy to the old Roman lands. Irish monks, operating from the island of Iona, rooted Christianity in Scotland and began the conversion of the Saxon kingdoms that had sprung up across Britain. Although both the Scots and Saxons were successfully Christianized by the Irish, their religious practices soon diverged. In the 7th c. the Saxons of Britain opted to conform to the customs of Roman Christianity, while the Scots and Irish clung to native traditions. Disagreements about religion complicated an already difficult political situation. The Saxon kings of Northumbria, the most northern of the British kingdoms, brought a large part of Scotland under control, but in 685 a defeat at the hands of the Picts sent Northumbria into a decline from which it never recovered. The Picts were soon robbed of the fruits of victory. Norseman or 'Vikings' descended on the coasts of the British Isles late in the 8th c.

In order to protect their lands the tribes of the Scottish highlands had to pool their resources and unite behind a single leader. In 1018 their king, Malcolm II, conquered Lothian. His successor and grandson, Duncan I (1033–1040), ruled most of the territory that has come to be thought of as Scotland, after his having been named successor over the objection of many of the Celtic lords. Duncan's throne was usurped by one of his generals, Macbeth, and Macbeth was in turn unseated by Duncan's son, Malcolm III Canmore. It appears that Macbeth represented adherence to Celtic traditions and was protecting the claims of Lulach, Macbeth's wife's Gruach's son, to the crown. The Anglicization of Scotland accelerated after Malcolm's crowning. Following the Norman conquest of England in 1066, Malcolm wed a refugee Anglo-Saxon princess, Margaret. Queen Margaret and her sons introduced the Scots to Saxon (English) culture, and Edinburgh became the seat for a royal court. The use of the English language was encouraged, and the old Celtic system of a church run by the abbots of monasteries yielded to the common European practice of setting up geographically defined dioceses administered by bishops. Intermarriage between the Scottish and Norman royal families inched Scotland closer to the mainstream of medieval feudal culture, and, despite sporadic outbreaks of violence aimed at reviving ancient Celtic custom, a program of Anglicization was largely successful. Converging cultures and the meshing of ties among royal families helped communications between England and Scotland, but they did not guarantee peaceful relations. Neither government had much control over its subjects, and there was no agreement on the location of the borders of the two nations. The baronial families in the disputed territories headed large military establishments and lived by raiding the lands of their neighbors.

For much of the medieval period a state of war existed between England and Scotland. In 1286, the death of Alexander II precipitated a succession crisis in Scotland that Edward I, the king of England, saw as an opportunity to bring the two nations closer together. Alexander's only living descendant was an infant granddaughter, Margaret, a child born to his daughter, the wife of the king of Norway. Scotland was not eager to be dominated by Norway, but the alternative was unattractive. A John Balliol and a Robert Bruce, both descendants of Alexander's great-great-grandfather, David (1124–1153), were the other claimants to the throne. If Margaret's rights had been voided, a contest between the two male heirs would have plunged Scotland into civil war. Edward championed Margaret's cause, for he proposed to marry her to his son and heir, Edward II. Margaret's death at a very early age put an end to Edward's scheme for uniting the dynasties that ruled England and Scotland and forced him to devise a new policy. Edward tried to make a deal with John Balliol, the stronger claimant to the throne according to the rules of primogeniture that were emerging in feudal law. Edward offered Balliol his support in exchange for Balliol's oath of vassalage. The plan did not work. The Scots were offended by the arrangement, and Balliol was forced to rebel against Edward in order to preserve the loyalty of his subjects. When the powerful Bruce clan refused to back Balliol, he was unable to defend his nation. In 1296 Edward made an armed progress through Scotland and at the monastery of Scone took possession of an important symbol of Scots sovereignty, a stone on which Scottish monarchs sat to be crowned. The 'stone of Scone' was enshrined within England's coronation chair.

Edward's expedition inflamed Scottish nationalism and created a following for a popular leader. William Wallace emerged to mount attacks on the English garrisons stationed in Scotland. Edward led two more expeditions into Scotland, but he died in 1307 before achieving anything of lasting significance. England's relations with Scotland continued to deteriorate in the next generation. Edward's heir, Edward II, was an incompetent, but the man whom the Scots acknowledged as their king, Robert I, grandson of Robert Bruce, was not. At the battle of Bannockburn Robert destroyed the English army and wiped out Edward I's achievements. Scotland also found an ally who proved very troublesome for England. England and France were inching toward the Hundred Years' War, and France was eager to help England's enemies. In 1371 the house of Bruce died out, and the crown of Scotland passed to the Stewart/Stuart family. The Stuarts sought spouses from the ranks of the French nobility and won financial and military aid from France. In 1542 the death of James V left an infant, named Mary, heir to Scotland's throne. Henry VIII of England tried to obtain her hand for his son, but the Scots pledged her to France's dauphin. Mary was raised at the French court and reigned as queen of France for about a year. The premature death of her young husband, Francis II, sent her home to a Scotland she had never known. During her youth the Protestant Reformation had made headway in her kingdom, and many of her dour subjects were not in sympathy with her Catholic faith or her cultivated French manners. Mary quickly fell afoul of the power struggles that were the chief preoccupation of the Scots nobility. Her barons tolerated her until she gave birth to a son, James.

Once the future of the dynasty was secure, Mary ceased to be necessary to her people and her situation became untenable. In 1568 she fled to England to ask for help from her cousin, Elizabeth I. Mary was a potential rival for Elizabeth's throne, for Mary was the granddaughter of Henry VIII's sister, the wife of Scotland's James IV. Catholics, who did not recognize the legitimacy of the Protestant marriage between Elizabeth's parents, believed that Mary was the rightful heir to the English throne. Elizabeth's security necessitated Mary's confinement, and Elizabeth's suspicion that Mary was involved in plots against her prompted her to order the Scottish queen's execution in 1587. Sh.'s generation witnessed this drama and the final denouement of the long struggle between England and Scotland. In 1603 Elizabeth, the 'virgin queen,' died and the Tudor dynasty ended with her. Her heir was Mary's son, James VI of Scotland and James I of England. England and Scotland both acknowledged the sovereignty of the same king, but their parliaments remained separate until 1707. Scotland's distinctive church successfully resisted attempts to bring it within the confines of England's Anglican establishment.

Err 3.2.122, a location on the 'globe' of Nell, alluding to the country's barrenness, or possibly to a 'barren ness.'

3H6 3.1.13, 3.3.26, 34, 151. R3 3.7.15. 1H4 1.3.258, 261, 274, 3.1.43, 3.2.164, 4.1.85. 2H4 2.3.50, 67, 4.1.14. H5 1.2.168.

Mac, the setting. *Mac* is often called 'the Scottish play' because of a superstition in the theater world that saying 'Macbeth' in a theater is bad luck.

Scots, King of, *H5 1.2.161,* David II (1329–1371), whom the English captured at Neville's Cross on 17 October 1346. David was not, as Sh. says, taken to France to be presented to Edward III. That bit of misinformation appears in a contemporary play, *The Raigne of Edward III*

(1596, printed for 'Cuthbert Burby'/Burbage), which was once attributed to Sh., but now is thought to have been written by someone else. Some scholars consider it possible that Sh. may have been one of a group of authors who worked on it. If he did not, then he was certainly aware of the play and likely got the historical error from it. Throughout the historical David's life he was a pawn of political forces beyond his control. He was only five years old when he inherited the throne of a nation torn by civil war and threatened with invasion. King Edward III of England was the source of his greatest concern. Edward's grandfather had nearly conquered Scotland, but in one humiliating battle Edward's father had lost everything. Edward was determined to restore the family honor by bringing his nation's long standing dispute with Scotland to a successful conclusion. His first strategy was to assist Scottish exiles to invade their homeland and set up a government friendly to England. When this failed, Edward led troops into Scotland. The Scots reacted by turning for help to England's enemy, France. Edward considered the Franco-Scottish alliance a provocative act, and it was one of the things that persuaded him to invade France and begin the Hundred Years' War. As Edward's involvement on the continent deepened, he lost interest in Scotland. But David, who had fled to France for safety in 1334, returned home in 1341 to help his French allies by putting pressure on England.

The battle at Neville's Cross was David's attempt to force Edward to send troops back to England that the English king needed to follow up a stunning victory he had recently won over the French at Crécy. David was captured at Neville's Cross and condemned to a long period of nominal incarceration at the English court (1346–1357). The experience proved pleasant, and David found it difficult to return to his impoverished kingdom. David had little affection for the boisterous Scots nobles who made his nation virtually ungovernable. He had no children of his own, and he hated the remote relative who was his heir designate. Since he regarded Edward as his friend, he decided to try to convince the parliament of Scotland to accept one of Edward's sons as his successor on Scotland's throne. The Scots refused a proposal that struck them as outrageous, and David's crown went to the son of his half-sister, Scotland's first king from the family of the Stewarts/Stuarts.

Scottish, (adj.) of or pertaining to Scotland. *MV 1.2.74,* 'S. lord,' suitor of Portia. His disagreement with the English baron Falconbridge is mocked. *1H4 1.3.255.*

Scribe, *H8,* person charged with making an official transcript of judicial proceedings.

Scripture, the Bible. The King James translation was not published until 1611, so it is worth remembering that the English translations preceding it that could have influenced Sh.'s plays were Tyndale's (1525–35), Miles Coverdale's (1535), Thomas Matthew's (1537), the Great Bible (1539), the Geneva Bible (1560), and the Catholic Douai New Testament (1582).

MV 1.3.97. R3 1.3.332. Ham 5.1.36. Cym 3.4.83, used figuratively.

Scrivener, *R3,* professional copyist or scribe. He was an important professional in societies with low literacy and no mechanical methods of reproduction. Every legal document could require a scrivener's services.

Scrope, *1H4 4.4.3,* cousin whom Richard Scrope, archbishop of York, summons to help Hotspur at the battle of Shrewsbury (1403). The man in question may have been Stephen (d. 1408), brother of William Scrope, earl of Wiltshire (d. 1399). Stephen was the archbishop's cousin. Confusion about the identity of the character is created by the fact that earlier in the play (*1H4 1.3.265*) Sh. refers to Stephen's brother, Wiltshire, as the archbishop's brother. This mistake originated in Sh.'s source: Holinshed (3.23).

Scrope, archbishop of York, *1H4, 2H4,* Richard, (1350–1405), fourth son of Henry, first baron Scrope of Masham. (Henry was the cousin of the first baron Scrope of Bolton who was the father of William Scrope, earl of Wiltshire.) Richard owed his appointment to the see of York to the patronage of Richard II, but he was not conspicuously loyal to Richard. He followed his kinsmen, the Percies, when they sided with Henry (IV) Bolingbroke's against Richard. He was one of the commissioners chosen to witness Richard's abdication, and he took part in Henry IV's coronation. When the Percies turned against Henry, Scrope again followed their lead. Henry killed Henry Percy ('Hotspur') at the battle of Shrewsbury in 1403, but in 1405 the archbishop rallied the king's opponents for a second challenge to his authority. Scrope foolishly mismanaged the campaign. The earl of Westmorland, the commander of Henry's forces, convinced Scrope that Henry was prepared to yield to Scrope's demands for governmental reforms, and Scrope dismissed his soldiers. As soon as the archbishop was defenseless, Henry arrested him and arranged for his execution. The king's vengeful act was controversial, for medieval custom granted clergy immunity from trial or punishment by the state.

Scrope, Lord, 1) *1H4 1.3.265,* William, see Wiltshire, earl of. Sh. follows an error in Holinshed (3.23) and identifies Wiltshire as the brother of Richard Scrope, the archbishop of York, who took part in a rebellion against Henry IV. In reality, William was Richard's cousin.

2) *H5,* see Henry, Lord Scrope of Masham.

Scrope, Stephen, *R2,* (d. 1408), seasoned soldier who was scrupulously loyal to Richard II, but who also enjoyed the confidence of Richard's successor, Henry IV. Scrope died fighting for Henry in Ireland, and his widow married Sir John Fastolf.

Scylla, *MV 3.5.14,* beautiful young maiden whom Circe in a fit of jealousy over Glaucus' attraction transformed into a monster. She lived in a cave above a narrow strait opposite the whirlpool Charybdis (q.v.). Her upper body was normal, but her lower body was the necks and heads of a pack of vicious dogs. In *The Odyssey,* Odysseus lost six men to the ravenous Scylla trying to sail past her and avoid Charybdis. Her story is also told in Ovid's *Metamorphoses,* 13–14. In classical times Scylla and Charybdis were said to have lived on the straits of Messina, with Scylla on the Italian side.

Scythia, name the ancient Greeks applied to various districts in southeastern Europe and Russia. The Scythians were nomads with a reputation for ferocity, and the Greeks had great respect for their skill as warriors, but they were regarded as uncivilized, which is the primary Renaissance implication of their name.

Tit 1.1.131, 132. 1H6 2.3.6. Lr 1.1.116 (Q 1.109), 'barbarous Scythian.'

Seacoal, George, *Ado 3.3.10, 12,* or Francis, *Ado 3.5.54,* 'Sea-coale' F1, one of Dogberry's constables. It is possible that Francis and George were intended to be different characters, though that would serve no purpose. More likely this is just another instance of the carelessness with names which is characteristic of the text of this play. Some critics argue that Francis is the Sexton in 4.2 and a distinct character.

Sebastian 1) *TGV 4.4.40, 61,* name assumed by Julia in disguise as a man. The use of this name is a link to *TN,* in which the disguised Viola is mistaken for Sebastian her brother. The name comes from the saint who was martyred by Roman arrows in the 3rd c. He was from the town of Sebastia (modern Sivas, in Turkey). The Greek root of the name is *sebastos,* 'revered,' 'august.'

2) *TN,* twin brother of Viola. Shipwrecked on the shore of Illyria, he assumes Viola has drowned. He is several times mistaken for Viola in disguise as Cesario, wounds Sir Andrew and is betrothed to Olivia before it all can be sorted out. The corresponding character in *Gl'Ingannati* (1538) is Fabrizio, in Niccolo Secchi's *Gl'Inganni* (1562) Fortunato, and in

Barnabe Riche's 'Apolonius and Silla,' from *His Farewell to the Military Profession* (1581), Silvio.

3) *AWW 4.3.167,* commander in the Duke of Florence's army.

4), *Tmp,* brother of Alonso and co-conspirator with Antonio. He is a nasty man but shows his true evil when he agrees to kill his sleeping brother to inherit the throne. Antonio, however, persuades him to kill Gonzalo (Antonio's brother) while Antonio kills Alonso. Ariel, however, maddens both men and prevents the crimes.

Sebastian of Messaline, *TN 2.1.15, 5.1.230,* father of Sebastian and Viola, not otherwise mentioned. The corresponding character in *Gl'Ingannati* (1538) is Virginio Bellenzini, in Niccolo Secchi's *Gl'Inganni* (1562) Anselmo, and in Barnabe Riche's 'Apolonius and Silla,' from *His Farewell to the Military Profession* (1581), Pontus, the governor of Cyprus.

See of Rome, strictly, the Italian diocese over which the pope presides as bishop of Rome. In context the term may imply the wider responsibilities of the papacy. *Jn 5.2.72. MM 3.1.477.*

Seely, Bennet, *R2 5.6.14,* (d. 1400), conspirator executed for plotting to assassinate Henry IV and restore Richard II to the throne. There is much scholarly debate about the spelling of his surname (e.g, Cilie, Scheveley, Shelley), and some sources list him as John, not Bennet (Benedict). Little is known about the historical person who lies behind this character.

Seleucus, *Ant,* Cleopatra's steward. Plutarch ('Antony' 83.3) says that after the battle of Actium, when diplomats negotiated Cleopatra's surrender, Seleucus told the Roman authorities that Cleopatra was not making a full disclosure of her assets.

Semiramis, mythical Assyrian queen renowned for her voluptuousness and cruelty. Daughter of Dercetis of Ascalon, a fish goddess, S. was exposed as an infant, but was fed by doves until discovered by the usual kindly shepherd of mythology, this one of the royal house. Onnes (or Menones), governor of Ninevah, was attracted to her beauty, married her, and took her with him to the siege of Bactra, where she advised King Ninus. Ninus soon desired her, but Onnes refused to give her up and under Ninus' threat, hanged himself. Upon marriage to Ninus, he abdicated in favor of her. She supposedly was the founder of Babylon, which Ovid mentions in telling the story of Pyramus and Thisbe (q.v.) in *Metamorphoses,* 4, and of Ninevah. She was also credited with using her army of 3,000,000 infantry, 500,000 cavalry, and 100,000 chariots in the conquests of Persia, Libya, and Ethiopia. After a 42-year reign, she was defeated on the Indus by Stabrobates and either was killed or forced to abdicate by Ninyas, her son. She vanished in the form of a dove and was thereafter worshipped as a deity. The story is likely based upon Sammuramat, regent of Assyria from 810–805 BC. She is mentioned several times by Chaucer (*Man of Lawe his tale,* 359; Parlement of Foules, 288; and 'The Legend of Thisbe of Babylon' in *The Legende of Good Women,* 707).

Shr Ind. 2.38, 'the lustful bed. . .trimmed up for S.' *Tit 2.1.22, 2.3.118:* Tamora is compared to Semiramis, in the former line for her sensuality and in the latter for her cruelty.

Sempronius, 1) *Tit,* one of Titus Andronicus' relatives. Sh. did not take the plot of *Tit* from history, and his sources for the play are uncertain. Since the Sempronii were an illustrious and numerous family in ancient Rome, Sh. may have given their name to a fictional character so as to provide Titus with an appropriately noble kinsman. Sh. may have been familiar with the Sempronii from his reading in the works of Plutarch (e.g., the biographies of Tiberius Sempronius Gracchus and Caius Sempronius Gracchus).

2) *Tim,* friend to whom Timon appeals for help. He refuses, using the excuse that he is offended because Timon did not ask him first.

Senate, 1) most prestigious of the political assemblies belonging to the Roman Republic.

The Romans believed that the Senate (i.e., 'house of elders') preceded the establishment of the Republic. It was said to have been created by Romulus when he founded the city. During the period of the monarchy, the Senate served as a royal council. When the Romans expelled their kings and abolished monarchy, the Senate assumed the responsibility of running the nation. Although a popular assembly eventually wrested legislative and judicial authority from the Senate, the Senate remained nominally at Rome's head until the collapse of the empire in the early Middle Ages.

Tit 1.1.27, 41, 4.4.17. JC 2.2.72, 93, 98. Cor 3.1.73. Cym 4.2.339, 4.3.26.

2) *Oth 3.2.2,* ruling body of Venice. It served above the Great Council (which consisted of all who enjoyed the right to vote—the patricians) and decided matters of finance, war and peace, commerce, and foreign affairs. Its decisions could be overridden by the Council of Ten, which dealt with all cases of conspiracy and public morals. The Council also played a role in foreign affairs. A matter such as that of the complaint against Othello would have been heard by the *Collegio* and not the Senate. The *Collegio* was the administrative branch of the constitution and initiated action in all matters, determining what should go before the Council of Ten and the Senate. One might liken it to the legislative committees of Congress or the Speaker of Commons, who makes the decision which legislative matters will reach the floor. The *Collegio* was theoretically under the Doge and his council in the hierarchy; however, the doge and his councillors had power based more on prestige than legality. The constitutional power lay more in the *Collegio.*

3) *Tim,* ruling body of Athens. This is a confusion: the ruling body of Rome, not Athens, was called the Senate. Athens' assembly was the Boule or the Council of Areopagus. It uncharitably rejects Alcibiades' plea for mercy for a soldier and then exiles him for lodging an appeal. A Senator is one of Timon's creditors.

Senate House, *JC 2.2.52, 59, 2.4.1,* building in the northwestern corner of the Roman forum where Rome's Senate met. The Senators in *JC* speak of going to the Senate House, but the place where they convene is Pompey's theater. The Senate House, or Curia, had burned down in 52 BC, and the civil war had delayed its reconstruction. Work did not begun until 44 BC (shortly before Cæsar's death). The new Curia was not finished until 29 BC.

Senator, *Oth,* member of the ruling council of Venice, the *pregadi.* An unspecified number of senators hear Brabanzio's plea against Othello.

Seneca, Lucius Annæus S., 'the Younger,' *Ham 2.2.401,* (d. 65 AD), great Roman playwright, politician, and Stoic philosopher. His are the only Roman tragedies which are extant. He was born in Cordova (now in Spain), but educated in Rome. After a sickly childhood, he entered legal practice and received a government post. When Claudius became emperor in 43 AD, Seneca was banished to Corsica on an adultery charge which was arranged by Messalina, the emperor's wife. In 51, however, Messalina was replaced by Agrippina and Seneca became tutor to her son Nero, who treated him well in the first few years of his emperorship. Seneca was prætor and nearly ruler with Sextus Afranius Burrus. He was also a leader in what is called the Silver Age of Roman literature. When Nero murdered his mother, Seneca was given the unenviable task of defending the act to the Senate. Nero also attempted to poison his former tutor out of jealousy for his wealth. Seneca retired shortly thereafter, but Nero used the conspiracy of Gaius Calpurnius Piso as an excuse to place Seneca on the proscription list, which gave him the choice of immediate suicide or a miserable execution. Seneca sliced open his arms and dictated his sensations as he bled to death. To the Romans his was the epitome of a courageous death. Nine of his plays exist, and though they were not prominent in his life or during the Middle Ages, he became the very essence of the tragedian to the Renaissance. His ornate style, sensational horror, and fatalism became part of a style called 'Senecan tragedy.' Most of his writings are not dramatic, however: there are dialogues, letters, essays on philosophy and science. The amount of his writings surviving is exceeded only by that of Cicero. Stoicism informs all of his works.

Sennois, *TNK 2.3.39,* country man coming to the fair, described as a fine dancer. The name resembles 'Senoys' (Sienese, q.v.), but that makes no particular sense in the context unless it relates to some Italian dance. Given the alternatives, it seems the best possibility. 'Sinews,' for a thin man, is possible. Even more of a reach, Plutarch mentions a tribal neighbor of the Gauls named 'Senones.'

Senoys, *AWW,* see Sienese.

Servilius, *Tim,* one of Timon's servants. A Servilius is mentioned in Plutarch's biography of Pompey. The name would also imply his role in Timon's household. Another possibility for the selection of the name is from Cato's sister Servilia, mother of Marcus Brutus. She had a boy by Lucullus, which is another name Sh. uses in *Tim.* In Plutarch's Lucullus, Servilius the augur brings down Lucullus' father, only to be brought down by the son.

Servingman, *TNK 3.5.128,* character in the morris dance performed before Theseus.

Sessa, obscure exhortation. At *Lr 3.6.32* some critics have thought the F1 'sese' is from an old song and means the names 'Cissy' or 'Sessy' (which is also reported as a way of calling a dog). Much more likely judging from *Lr 3.4.93,* F1 '*Sesey,*' is that the Fr. *cessez,* 'stop!' is meant. *Q 11.90,* Q1 'caese' (obviously 'cease') would seem to verify this and its meaning would not contradict the meaning of the other passages in which it appears (*Shr Ind. 1.5*). Some have thought that there may be more than one word intended by the variant spellings.

Sestos, *AYLI 4.1.99,* ancient town on the Thracian (northern) side of the Hellespont, opposite Abydos. Hero was from here. In the Persian Wars, it is also where Xerxes' army crossed to the Greek mainland on a bridge of boats.

Setebos, *Tmp 1.2.375, 5.1.264,* Caliban's god. The name comes from Robert Eden's *History of Travaile* (1577). During his great voyage, Magellan is said to have seen the Patagonians roaring like bulls and beseeching their god Setebos for help.

Severn, England's second largest river. It drains the western counties that border on Wales, and it empties into the Bristol channel. *1H4 1.3.97, 102, 3.1.63, 71, 73. Cym 3.5.17:* in order to reach Milford Haven and his ship to Rome (or to meet the army from Gaul), Lucius must cross the Severn and is given safe-passage to its shores. For much of history it has served as the frontier of Wales or Cambria.

Sextus Pompeius, *Ant 3.6.25,* L. for 'Sextus Pompey' (q.v.)

Sextus Pompey, *Ant,* (75–35 BC), younger son of Pompey the Great by his third wife, Mucia. Sextus survived the battle of Pharsalia where his father was decisively defeated by Julius Cæsar. The senior Pompey was murdered by the Egyptians to whom he fled for protection after his loss at Pharsalia, and Sextus escaped to Spain to continue the fight against Cæsar and his successors. He raised an army from the ranks of his father's veterans and embarked on a successful career as a soldier of fortune. Sextus was a thorn in Octavius' side. Sextus built a fleet that threatened shipments of food to Rome, and by 39 BC he was strong enough to force Octavius to agree to peace on his terms. In 38 BC hostilities resumed, and in 36 BC Octavius' general, Agrippa, destroyed Sextus' fleet at the battle of Naulochus. Sextus fled to the east, where he was betrayed into Mark Antony's hands and executed.

Seymour, Lord, *R2 2.3.55,* Richard de St. Maur (i.e., Seymour), one of the barons in the company of the duke of York when York came to Berkeley Castle in 1399 to make his peace with Henry (IV) Bolingbroke. In May 1399 Richard II had charged his uncle, York, with the defense of England while Richard led an army to Ireland. Two months later York failed to organize a response to Henry's landing in Yorkshire. A revolution developed, and York advised Richard to come to terms with Henry. York retired from court after Richard's deposition, and Seymour's name does not appear among those summoned to parliament after 1400.

Seyton, *Mac,* Macbeth's servant who informs him of Lady Macbeth's death and helps him with his armor. The Seytons (Setons or Seatouns) were the hereditary armor bearers and squires of the body of the Scottish kings beginning with King Edgar, the son of Malcolm III. The family traces its descent from Douglas Seton of the court of Alexander I and is said to derive from the Anglo-Norman family of Say, supposedly leading to Sey-toun as the name of the lands granted to an ancestor in East Lothian. The Setons are related to the royal family of Scotland. If this family is what Sh. had in mind, which seems probable, it would not be an untypical anachronism for him. Some critics assert 'Seyton' is a pun on 'Satan' to illustrate Macbeth's final end, but this notion seems a bit forced.

Shadow, Simon, *2H4,* character whose comical name suggests his shortcomings as a soldier and Falstaff's lack of principles in drafting him. Sh. may have chosen the name to poke fun at an abuse of the treasury for which military men were notorious. 'Shadow soldiers' were listed on company rolls so that officers could claim pay for more men than they actually had in their units.

Shallow, Robert, *2H4,* uncle of Slender, justice of the peace to whom Sh. gives a name that proclaims his inadequacy for his profession. Sh. provides Shallow with a shape as ludicrous as his name. The justice's extreme emaciation makes him the perfect foil for the rotund Falstaff. In *2H4* S. entertains Falstaff and waxes nostalgic about their youthful escapades, giving him a nostalgic quality which balances his foolishness. In *MWW* he lacks this depth of character. He quarrels with Falstaff and accuses the knight of having cheated him and abused his hospitality. It has been suggested that Sh. created the character of Shallow in order to lampoon Sir Thomas Lucy (1532–1600), a Stratford gentleman who may once have prosecuted Sh. for poaching. In *MWW* Shallow, 'Esq.' makes a fool of himself by threatening Falstaff with indictment before the highest court in the land—for the crime of poaching. Sh. also gave Shallow a coat of arms that featured a dozen 'luces' or fish-emblems that appeared on the Lucy family shield. Despite these passages, some scholars doubt that Sh. intended a connection between S. and Thomas Lucy. They argue that Lucy was in physical form, social condition, and personality, nothing like S., and Sh.'s audience, ignorant of the details of his personal history, could not have gotten the joke that some modern readers think they see. A similar claim has been raised on behalf of William Gardiner (1531–1597), a dubious character who bought his judgeship, was involved in several legal altercations, and whose coat-of arms also resembled Shallow's.

Shaphalus, *MND 5.1.197–8,* Bottom and Flute's corruption of Cephalus (q.v.)

She-wolf of France, *3H6 1.4.112,* uncomplimentary nickname for Henry VI's queen, Margaret of Anjou. Given the nationalistic passions raised by the Hundred Years' War, Henry's French marriage was never popular. Margaret's comparative poverty and her father's never more than nominal claim to be a king (of Naples and Sicily) were held against her by her enemies. As Henry's health and government deteriorated, Margaret became the scapegoat blamed for her husband's failings. As a foreign woman she had few defenders in England, and by attacking her, critics of her husband's government could express their displeasure and avoid the treasonous implications of a direct confrontation with their king. Her reputation worsened with the fading of the Lancastrian cause, while public opinion transformed Henry's weakness into saintliness. See Margaret, Queen.

Sheffield, *1H6 4.7.66,* a town in Yorkshire about 160 mi. north of London. It has been noted for the manufacture of iron and steel as far back as its history can be traced.

Sheffield, Lord Furnival of, *1H6 4.7.66,* one of the titles that Sh. lists as belonging to John Talbot. Talbot married his mother's stepdaughter, Maud Neville, the only child of Thomas Neville and Joan of Furnival. Through Joan the family acquired the barony of Furnival and the fief of Hallamshire in Sheffield.

Shepherd, *1H6,* see James of Arc.

Sheriff, an official charged with representing the king's interests in a shire. The word 'sheriff' is a contraction for 'shire reeve.' Shires were the administrative districts into which medieval England was divided, and reeves were servants who supervised manors for their owners. The office of 'shire reeve' evolved in England during the Anglo-Saxon period, and it was one of several Anglo-Saxon institutions that the Norman kings were careful to preserve. Sheriffs were commoners with no hereditary right to the offices to which the king appointed them. They reduced the king's dependence on the nobility by providing him with agents who were not part of the feudal hierarchy.

2H6 2.4.18 (pl.), 75, 101. TN 1.5.143, 'S.'s post,' a large post set up in front of a sherriff's door as symbol of his office. Possibly proclamations were affixed to them, but most critics doubt this as the posts were carefully painted and carved. *1H4 2.4.67, 2.5.486–532.*

Sheriff of Yorkshire, *2H4 4.3.99,* Thomas de Rokeby (d. 1418), sheriff from 1407–1408 and from 1411–1412. After successfully leading the attack at Branham Moor on 19 February 1408, he was rewarded by the duke of Northumberland with several manors. Holinshed calls him 'Sir Thomas, or (as other copies have) Rafe Rokesbie.' He may have been related to a justiciar of Ireland named Thomas Rokeby (d. 1356), but this is uncertain.

Sherry, *2H4 4.2.99, 102, 109, 114, 117,* F1 'Sherris,' Spanish wines named after their town of origin, Xeres (Jerez de la Frontera, near Cadiz). The original spelling was mistaken for a plural and later made into a false singular. See Sack.

Sherry-sack, *2H4 4.2.93,* F1 'Sherris-Sack,' a redundant expression, like 'sherry-wine.' See Sherry, and Sack.

Shirley, *1H4 5.4.40,* Hugh, (d. 1403), Master of the Hawks to Henry IV. Holinshed (3.524) lists him among the king's men who fell at Shrewsbury.

Shoe-tie, Master, *MM 4.3.16,* F1 'Shootie the great traueller,' mocking name for one of the impoverished criminals Pompey knows. As prisoners paid for their own food, many were forced to beg passers by. Fancy decorations on shoes were a sign of foreign decadence.

Shore, *R3 3.5.30,* William S., London goldsmith and husband of Edward IV's mistress, Jane (Elizabeth) Warnstead.

Shore, Mrs., *R3 1.1.73, 93, 99, 3.1.182, 3.4.71, 3.5.49,* Jane (Elizabeth) Warnstead Shore (d. 1527), daughter of a textile merchant, wife of a London goldsmith, and Edward IV's mistress. Sir Thomas More claims that she was a kindly, responsible woman who used her influence with the king to soothe his violent moods and to make peace between him and his opponents. After Edward's death, the marquis of Dorset protected her until Richard III charged her with witchcraft and sent her to the Tower. Richard confiscated her large fortune, humiliated her in a public trial for harlotry, and left her to die in poverty.

Shortcake, Alice, *MWW 1.1.186–7,* woman mentioned by Simple. Probably she was an earlier object of Slender's affections. The name may have some obscure ribaldry in it.

Shrewsbury, 1) the county seat of Shropshire, situated on the Severn river about 140 mi. northwest of London. Shrewsbury was a frontier post used as a base for England's campaigns in Wales. Henry IV killed Henry Percy ('Hotspur') in a battle that took place at Shrewsbury on 21 July 1403.

1H4 3.1.83, 3.2.166, 4.2.53, 4.4.10, 5.4.145.

2H4 ind. 24, 34. 1.1.12, 24, 40, 64, 65. 1.2.63, 104, 149. 1.3.26.

2) earldom created by William the Conqueror for his principal counselor, Roger de Montgomery. The lands comprising the earldom lay in the county of Shropshire at the mid-point on the border between England and Wales. The title derived from the earl's castle at Shrewsbury on the Severn river in Shropshire. Roger's son, Robert of Belesme, was deprived of the earldom in 1102, and the title was not conferred again until 1442 when it was granted to John Talbot. See Talbot, Lord, *1H6.*

Shrewsbury, Earl of, 1) *1H6 4.7.61,* see Talbot, Lord.

2) *STM:* George Talbot (1468–1538), direct descendant of the warrior John Talbot. He inherited the title in 1473. His mother was the daughter of Katherine, fifth daughter of Humphrey Stafford, earl of Stafford and duke of Buckingham. He was firmly loyal to the Lancastrian (and therefore Tudor) cause, fighting for Henry VII at Stoke and serving him on diplomatic missions to France, and Henry VIII as Lord Steward, privy councilor, and chamberlain of the exchequer. He fought in France and was involved with various missions to Rome. He supported Henry's decision to divorce Katherine of Aragon totally. He testified against Katherine at the trial and profited from the dissolution of the monasteries. Although he signed the articles condemning Wolsey, he treated the fallen cardinal humanely, welcoming him into his house at Sheffield when Wolsey was being transported to London as a state prisoner. One of Shrewsbury's most important roles for Henry was his raising an army to respond to the spontaneous uprising in the north of England known as the Pilgrimage of Grace, a reaction against Henry's assumption of power over the church in England. Ironically, one of the rebel complaints was that Henry had appointed two many low-born councilors, and that only the duke of Surrey (earl of Norfolk) and Shrewsbury were 'worth calling noble.' Norfolk brutally suppressed the revolt. Perhaps the authors of *STM* were recalling Shrewsbury's role in the Pilgrimage of Grace as they portrayed him attempting to persuade the commoners to give up their intention to riot in 1517.

Shrove Tuesday, *AWW 2.2.22,* Mardi Gras, day before Ash Wednesday and Lent. As it was the last day before fasting, it was custom to eat well and in England to eat pancakes.

Shrovetide *2H4 5.3.36,* 'merry s,' see Shrove Tuesday.

Shylock, *MV,* Jewish moneylender of Venice and one of Sh.'s most fascinating characters. Apparently in reaction to the popular success of Christopher Marlowe's *Jew of Malta* (performed c. 1592), Sh. developed his own version of a 'Jewe play,' but instead of repeating Marlowe's comic evil-doer who poisons a nunnery and sets a trap for the Christian governor of Malta, he blended just enough humanity with Shylock's evil to make him credible. The usual prejudices of the age are, of course, present in the portrayal. Shylock is more concerned with his money than anything else, including his daughter and his immortal soul. On the other hand, the treatment he receives at Christian hands is generally quite unChristian. He speaks of being spat upon, his daughter Jessica rejects him and steals from him, and, in the final scene, were it not for the mercy which Portia has urged upon Shylock himself, but which is practiced by the duke, Shylock would be executed. Modern readers are appalled by Shylock's forced baptism;

however, in Renaissance belief, the free will or cooperation of the baptized was not necessary to provide the possibility of salvation. Therefore, even this humiliation upon Shylock would have been seen as an act of mercy.

To emphasize the modern sense of Shylock's brutalization and to justify his attempted vengeance upon Christian society, modern performances of the play have often trimmed his more vicious lines about hating Christians and played up his speech 'Hath not a Jew eyes?' It is very hard to be certain how inclined the Renaissance audience was to regard Shylock as a comic devil. The speeches in which he arouses sympathy may have been seen as more of the 'devil quoting Scripture' for his own ends and usually he rouses sympathy while justifying to himself the act of murdering Antonio. It is known that there was a very popular performing baboon in late 16th c. London named 'Gew' or 'Gue.' For Sh.'s audience, this might have turned 'Hath not a Jew eyes?' into a comic double entendre. Also abroad was the hysteria over the converted Jew Dr. Roderigo Lopez' alleged plot to poison Elizabeth. At least one critic thinks Shylock is a deliberate parody of Lopez, immediately recognizable to the audience.

Finally, since the practice of Judaism was a crime in the Christian country of England (especially so in an age of religious conflict) Sh. could not have drawn upon anything other than the exotic reputation created for the Jews, and his Jews of Venice may have been more symbolic of hardheads who reject Christ's grace, rather than an attempt to denigrate the religion. If Marlowe's play had popularized an Islamic or a Tartar heathen, perhaps Sh. would have exploited prejudices about those instead and we would have a play entitled 'The Merchant of Aleppo.' It is a reflection of the Holocaust that the fact of the play's being about a Jew is profoundly disturbing. That it can still be seen as worthwhile of performance after the Nazis gleefully used it for their own propaganda purposes is a credit to the quality of 'negative capability' which Keats admired in Sh.—the ability to hold contrary thoughts. One, in any case, must be cautious in reading modern evils into historical contexts in works such as *MV* and *Oth.* To use 'antisemitic'—implying persecution of a faith—to describe the play may be less accurate than 'anti-non-Christian.' That *MV* helped create the appalling caricature of the Jew should not be laid solely at Sh.'s feet.

The tale of a Jew unreasonable about collecting on a debt is an ancient folk tale that appeared many places before Sh. The earliest dramatic analogue is *Le Miracle de un marchant et un juif* in the *Miracles de Nostre Dame par personnages,* prepared in the 14th c. by the goldsmiths of Paris. Sh.'s direct sources seem to have included Giovanni Fiorentino's *Il Pecorone* (1558), Anthony Monday's *Zelauto* (1580), John Gower's *Confessio Amantis,* and the *Gesta Romanorum,* a collection of medieval tales translated by Richard Robinson in 1577. In no source is the name Shylock or anything like it, which has led to an enormous number of theories for its origin. The simplest of these theories are most credible. In Genesis 11:12–15, Salah (Shelah) is the forefather of Iscah (Gen. 11:29), who is thought to be the source of the name Jessica (q.v.) because of its spelling 'Jesca' in earlier Bibles. It is quite like Sh. to pluck names out of sources in this manner.

An appealing source might also be the word 'shullock,' 'shallock,' or 'shullok' a term of contempt for an idler or wastrel. Though the earliest *OED* citation for it is 1603, it may have been in oral use much earlier. Another theory is that Shylock is based on Shiloh, a town in the Bible. The reference to Shiloh and the allusion to the Messiah at Gen. 49.10 is supposed to support this view. Other theories include Heb. *shallach* 'cormorant,' the fishing bird which was used to describe usurers, and 'shacklock,' a term for a jailer. This latter term is related to the name of Robin Hood's outlaw Will Scarlet (q.v.) in early texts, and as he was a featured character in May Day festivities, may have had a comic association which contributed to the formation of 'Shylock.'

Sibyl, 1) *Shr 1.2.69:* several ancient prophetesses were called sibyls, but the most famous was the Cumæan Sibyl who guided Æneas to the underworld. Her name was either Amalthea, Deiphobe, Demo, Demophile, Herophile, or Phemonoe. Beloved by Apollo she did not give in to him. He tempted her by offering her anything she might wish. She raised a handful of dust and asked for as many birthdays as there were grains of dust. This he granted her, but she still refused to become his lover. She had forgotten, however, to ask for perpetual youth, and she aged eternally. The story is in Virgil's *Æneid,* 6 and Ovid's *Metamorphoses,* 14.

2) Pl.: female prophets (see above). Some sources accord the title to women in only four lineages (the Erythræan, Samian, Egyptian, and Sardian) and others, ten (the Babylonian, Libyan, Delphian, Cimmerian, Erythræan, Samian, Cumæan, Hellespontian, Phrygian, and Tiburtine). *Tit 4.1.104. 1H6 1.3.35,* 'the nine sibyls of old Rome' may be an extrapolation from a story told about the Cumæan sibyl. She offered Tarquinius, king of Rome, a set of nine books that contained oracles foretelling the future of his people.

Sibylla, *MV 1.2.103,* L. the Sybil (q.v.) of Cumæ.

Sicil, *2H6 1.1.6,* see Sicily.

Sicilia, 1) *2H6 1.1.45, WT,* see Sicily.

2) *WT 1.1.21, 1.2.148, 218,* Leontes, king of Sicily.

Sicilius Leonatus, *Cym,* father of Posthumus. Dead before the play opens, S. appears in Posthumus' vision of Jupiter. Sicilius earned his sobriquet of *leo-natus,* 'lion-born,' through his heroism with Cassibelan and Tenantius against the Romans. He died broken hearted over the death of his first two sons, and his wife died giving birth to Posthumus. *Cym 5.5.145,* 'S.'s heir.'

Sicils, *3H6 1.4.123, 5.7.39,* 'kingdom of the two Sicilies,' see Naples.

Sicily, 'Sicilia,' large island (nearly 10,000 square mi.) in the center of the Mediterranean between the peninsula of Italy and the coast of Africa. It is mountainous but very fertile. A rich land at one time, it is now associated with poverty. Currently part of Italy, during the Middle Ages it was an independent nation. The kingdom of Sicily was established in the 12th c. by Norman adventurers. In the 13th c. it passed by marriage to the Hohenstaufen emperors. When their line was exterminated following the death of Frederick II in 1250, Spain and France contested control of Sicily and the allied kingdom of Naples. Sicily was occupied briefly by Charles of Anjou and then seized by Aragon. René of Anjou, father of Henry VI's queen, was a descendant of Charles of Anjou and claimed to be the king of Sicily, Naples, and Jerusalem.

Tit 3.1.240. Ant 2.6.7, 35, 45, 3.6.24.

WT: Sicily is the traditional setting for Arcadia in the many Arcadian tales of the Renaissance. Arcadia itself was an area in central Greece with a pastoral lifestyle, but it became generalized to include any idealized rustic setting. As the setting for the first part of *WT* the island has become the nonpastoral location of Sh.'s play, however. Exactly why he chose to make Bohemia the 'Arcadia' and Sicily not, reversing the geography of his source Robert Greene's *Pandosto, or the Triumph of Time,* (1588; rptd. 1607 as *Dorastus and Fawnia*) is speculative. Since he had renamed all of Greene's characters, perhaps this was another way of adding variation to his adaptation.

Sicinius Velutus, *Cor,* companion of Junius Brutus who, Plutarch ('Coriolanus' 7.1) says, helped Rome's plebeian citizens extract political concessions from the city's patrician class. Each Roman citizen family was designated either patrician or plebeian. The origin of the distinction between them is unknown, but in the early days of the Republic only members of the patrician order could hold office or vote. Plebeians resented their exclusion from public life, but the patricians had no reason to care until they discovered that they had to field larger armies than they could staff from members of their own class. Military service gave plebeians currency with which to negotiate enfranchisement. When crises loomed, plebeian soldiers refused to fight until patrician authorities granted them some right or privilege. In this way the plebeians acquired their own political assembly chaired by 'tribunes,' magistrates who had the power to protect plebeians from abuse by patricians. Brutus and Sicinius Velutus were the first men elected to the tribunate. Coriolanus resented the novelty of their intrusion into affairs that he believed were no business of the common man. His open contempt for the populist trend in Republican government angered the masses and prompted the people to banish him from the city.

Sicyon, *Ant 1.2.106, 107, 112,* city in the Peloponnese south of Corinth. It was one of the most ancient in Greece. Plutarch ('Antony' 30.3) says that it was the place where Mark Antony's wife, Fulvia, died. At the time of her death Fulvia was on her way from Italy to her husband's eastern headquarters. She must have been anxious about the reception she was to receive, for she had caused Antony severe political embarrassment. Fulvia and Antony's brother, Lucius, had taken events into their own hands and tried to overthrow Antony's competitor, Octavius. Their attack on Octavius failed, but it threatened the survival of the second triumvirate, the legal arrangement that provided Antony with legitimacy. Antony had more to gain from a war he was preparing against Parthia than from a squabble with Octavius. Consequently, he took the opportunity of Fulvia's fortuitous death to repudiate responsibility for her actions, to renew the terms of the triumvirate, and to propose marriage to Octavius' sister.

Siena, city in Tuscany about 30 mi. south of Florence. The Etruscans founded it, but it fell under Roman rule and was called Sæna Julia. By the 12th c. AD it had become a republic and in 1203 founded a university. For several centuries it was a powerful and important state, but in 1557 it was annexed to Florence by Cosimo de' Medici. *Cym 4.2.343,* F1 'Syenna's Brother,' Giacomo. This should mean brother of the duke of Siena, though Siena was a republic. That quibble is, however, irrelevant since the play is supposedly set in Roman times. It might possibly mean that Giacomo is of the city, or it may be that Sh. meant it as merely another Italian name without reference to the city.

Sienese, *AWW 1.2.1,* F1 'Senoys,' from Fr. *Siennois,* the people of Siena.

Sigeia tellus, L. 'Sigeian land,' the Troad. Sigeum was the name of a promontory and seaport at the extreme northwest of Turkey, at the opening of the Hellespont into the Ægean. Achilles was supposedly buried here. *Shr 3.1.28, 32, 41:* mentioned in a couplet quoted from Ovid's *Heroides* 1.33–4.

Signor Junior, *LLL 3.1.175,* Cupid, who was considered to be both the youngest god and the oldest—'Senior Junior.' He was a child but had caused the creation of the universe by introducing love into Chaos.

Silence, Justice, *2H4,* Robert Shallow's cousin and fellow justice of the peace. Shallow entertains Silence and Falstaff at a party at which Silence mocks his own name by getting drunk and singing snatches of raucous songs.

Silius, *Ant,* officer who Sh. says served in an army led by Ventidius, one of Mark Antony's generals. Plutarch claims that Ventidius was the only Roman ever to triumph over the Parthians, but that he failed to exploit his opportunities for fear that he would make his commander jealous ('Antony' 34). Plutarch does not report a conversation between Ventidius and any member of his staff on this subject. Sh. probably invented the character of Silius so that he could dramatize Plutarch's narrative. There was a 1st c. poet, Silius Italicus, whose work Sh. may have known and whose name Sh. might have appropriated.

Silver 1) *Shr Ind. 1.17,* a dog. The dog's names in this section seem to come from their physical (in this case color) or behavioral traits.

2) *Tmp 4.1.254,* spirit in the form of a hound. It is not clear what to make of the coincidence of the word and 'Mountain' (q.v.) also appearing in Jakob Ayrer's *Die Schöne Sidea.* The connection—if any—is not clear.

Silvia, *TGV,* daughter of the Duke of Milan, beloved of Valentine and Proteus. Her name (L. for 'forest' or 'woods') suggests the pastoral heroine, but Silvia is a pale comparison to later Sh. women with neither the depth nor intelligence of Rosalind or Viola. She is merely the object of love and is passed from Proteus to Valentine at the end of the play as an indication of her role. The song in her honor (*4.2*) is one of Sh.'s most famous.

Silvius, 1) *AYLI,* a shepherd; from L. *silva,* 'woods.' His counterpart in the source (Lodge's *Rosalynde*) is Montanus, 'mountaineer,' or 'mountain.'

2) *Ant 2.1.18,* man from whom Menecrates says he learned that Octavius and Lepidus had assembled an army with which they hoped to take Sextus Pompeius. This could be a misspelling of Silius.

Simois (Gr. *Simoeis*), small river in the region of ancient Troy. It begins on the slopes of Mt. Ida (according to Homer) and flows east to west, joining the Scamander just north of Troy. Homer's *Iliad* mentions the river seven times, as well as many other ancient authors. *Shr 3.1.28, 31, 41,* mentioned in a couplet quoted from Ovid's *Heroides Epistolæ* 1.33–34. *Luc 1437, 1442.*

Simonides, *Per,* king of Pentapolis. He holds a competition for his daughter Thaisa's hand in marriage, which the scruffy-looking Pericles wins. His main thematic role is to wisely warn against judging people by their outward appearance. He is called Artestrates in John Gower's *Confessio Amantis* (1390) and Altistrates in Lawrence Twine's *Patterne of Painefull Adventures* (1594). Simonides of Ceos, a prominent Greek poet of 6th c. BC, is mentioned in Plutarch's 'Themistocles' and in many other ancient authors. There was also a Simonides of Amorgos, poet of the 7th c.

Simpcox, Simon, Saunder Simcox, *2H6,* charlatan who tried to exploit Henry VI's credulity and piety by claiming to be the beneficiary of one of St. Alban's miracles. Simpcox said that a dream directed him to leave his home in Berwick and come to St. Albans. There, just as Henry arrived in town, the saint cured Simpcox's blindness. Gloucester, the king's uncle, was not impressed by the tale and arrested Simpcox for vagrancy. Sh.'s source for the story was a chronicle written by Richard Grafton (1513–1572). Grafton credited the anecdote to Sir Thomas More.

Simpcox's wife, *2H6:* she is punished along with her husband for their fraud. See Simpcox, Simon.

Simple, Peter, *MWW,* Slender's servant. As with his master and his master's uncle, his name reflects his clownish character.

Sincklo, John, also 'Sinklo' and 'Sincler,' an actor whose name appears in speech attributions and stage directions in several of the earliest texts. These identify him as having assumed the role of one of the players in *Shr,* a keeper in *3H6,* and the beadle in *2H4.* Based on these three characters and the remarks about the beadle's thinness, critics have assumed that Sincklo played other skinny parts, such as Starveling in *MND.* Not much else is known about the man, except that he seems to have been acting for about fifteen years.

Sinel, *Mac 1.3.69,* Macbeth's father. Sh. got the name from Holinshed ('Sinell'), who got it from Hector Boece ('Synele'). It had been corrupted because Macbeth's father was named Finleg, Findlæch, or Finel. He was *mormaor* ('ruler') of Moray and Ross and was murdered by his nephews in 1020.

Sinon, son of Sisyphus and, significantly in Renaissance thought, related to the crafty Ulysses. He was a Greek prisoner of the Trojans who Virgil (*Æneid,* 2.79) says convinced the Trojans to accept a fatal gift: a great wooden statue of a horse. Sinon told the Trojans that the Greeks who had been besieging Troy had built the horse as an offering to the gods and that, if the Trojans honored the sacred object, it would bring them divine favor and victory over the Greeks. The Trojans trusted him and dragged the image into their city. Late at night he opened a secret door in the belly of the horse and liberated a band of soldiers. When the Greek army suddenly reappeared, the men who had infiltrated the city rendered Troy defenseless by opening its gates. As one of mythology's great deceivers he is in Sh.'s opinion, an excellent role model for Richard III.

3H6 3.2.190. Tit 5.3.84. Luc 1521, 1529, 1541, 1549, 1556, 1560, 1564.

Cym 3.4.59, 'S.'s weeping,' crocodile tears.

Sir, title prefix given to a minor nobleman, such as a knight or baronet. It was followed by the name of the person. In Sh.'s day it was also applied to recipients of the Bachelor of Arts, who were called 'Dominus,' or educated clergymen, who often now prefer to be called 'Doctor,' whether they have the doctor of divinity degree or not.

Sisters Three, *2H4 2.4.196,* see Fates.

Siward, *Mac,* 'old S.,' 'warlike S.,' 'good S.,' earl of Northumberland who comes to the aid of Malcolm in unseating Macbeth. A courageous and forthright military man, Siward shows pride that his son has died in battle which makes an interesting comparison to the several other moments in the play when someone is informed of the death of a dear one, such as Macduff's hearing of the deaths of his children or Macbeth hearing of the death of Lady Macbeth. This characterization of Siward also seems appropriate for a Viking warrior. Sh. mistakenly identifies Siward as Malcolm's uncle, although the source for the play, Holinshed's *Chronicles* (1577) mistakenly calls him Malcolm's grandfather. Several Scottish kings, including the founder of the Stuart line, descended from Siward. Neither King James himself nor Sh. seems to have known that, for Banquo gets all the credit as the forefather of kings. The historical Siward (or Sigurd the Dane, as he was also called) was born in Denmark the son of Beorn, earl of Northumberland. He likely came to England with Canute. Around 1038 he became earl of Deira on the death of Eadwulf Cutel, earl of Northumbria, and assumed the full title of Northumbria in 1041 by murdering Eadwulf, earl of Bernicia. He fought for King Hardecanute and later sided with Edward the Confessor against Earl Godwine in 1051 and was rewarded with the earlship of Huntingdon. Siward allied himself with Malcolm (either his brother-in-law or nephew) in 1054 and invaded Scotland with 10,000 men, losing his son Osbeorn in the battle with Macbeth. He succeeded in placing Malcolm on the throne of Cumbria, not all of Scotland. It was two years after Siward's death that Malcolm became king of Scotland. Said to be physically large and powerful, Siward was said in Northumbrian legend to have had a bear for a grandfather. In 1055 he faced death by rising from his bed in York and dressing in full armor. He was buried in York in a minster he had dedicated to St. Olaf.

Siward, Young, *Mac,* Osbeorne, son of Siward. He dies in single combat with Macbeth and seems little more than a dramatic device to show that Macbeth is still dangerous and that Siward is a formidable warrior, because of the controlled way he receives news of Osbeorne's death (this is a detail from Holinshed's history). The historical son of Siward indeed died in the battle against Macbeth in 1054, though not necessarily at the hand of Macbeth. Nothing else is known about Osbeorne.

Slender, Master Abraham, *MWW,* nephew of Shallow, a foolish and awkward suitor of Anne Page. His name implies both his physique and his mental capacity. When George Page arranges for him to elope with Anne, Fenton and Anne trick S. into running off with a boy in disguise. It has been argued that Slender is a parody of William Wayte, the stepson of William Gardiner, who married an heiress Gardiner swindled. Sh. was involved in a legal imbroglio with Wayte and may be lampooning him in revenge. It has also been suggested that Slender may be a parody of Ben Jonson. In neither case is the evidence particularly convincing. See Shallow.

Sly, *Shr Ind. 2.17,* 'old Sly's son,' F1 'Sies sonnes,' Christopher Sly's father.

Sly, Christopher. *Shr,* F1 'Christophero Sly,' 'Christopher Slie,' drunkard tinker who is discovered unconscious. A lord arranges that when he awakes he will be in place as a lord with servants, a wife, and all the pleasures of the upper class. As part of his privileges as a lord, he is presented the play of Petruccio and Katherine. As the play now exists, Sly appears only in the Induction and in a brief scene ending *1.1.* The frame story is thus incomplete and most scholars believe that the original performances were more like *The Taming of A Shrew,* an anonymous quarto of 1594, which some scholars believe to be a source of *Shr,* while others believe it to be a bad quarto or pirated edition, stolen by actors who played in it, probably William Sly and Alexander Cooke, though the names and many details of plot do not match. W. Sly is believed to have played his namesake. In this version of the story, C. Sly's role continues to the end when he is returned to his drunkard's sleeping place and sets out to go home to his angry wife, whom he says he now knows how to handle. *A Shrew* is no help in reconstructing *Shr,* however, because it is so inferior, and many productions simply eliminate the Sly frame story altogether. Sly's character is vivid, however. He has the pretension of many another low-life Sh. character and he describes himself as a knockabout, having worked as a peddlar, a cardmaker, a bear-herd, and a tinker. Ready for anything, he accepts his life as a lord quite easily, immediately ready, for example, to bed his 'wife.' In the lord's manipulation of Sly, there is the suggestion of the main plot in which Katherine is manipulated and deceived for her own good. The name may simply have been borrowed from William Sly, who may have been related to Stephen Sly (q.v.) and therefore have come from the area near Stratford. There are several allusions to that area in the Induction.

Sly, Stephen. *Shr Ind. 2.92,* someone Christopher Sly mentions. There was a Stephen Sly living in Stratford in Sh.'s time. The playwright seems to be using the names of people from his home area in this passage.

Smalus, *WT 5.1.156,* warrior of Libya. In Plutarch Dion sails from Africa to the town of Minoa in Sicily which is governed by Synalus, a Carthaginian and friend. Since Sh. borrowed so many names from North's translation of Plutarch, it is likely that typography made him mistake the 'yn' for an 'm.' Less likely is that Smalus is a variant on Ishmael of the Bible.

Smile, Jane, *AYLI 2.4.45,* peasant woman Touchstone has wooed.

Smile, Sir, *WT 1.2.197,* name given by Leontes to a man who fishes in his neighbor's pond, a cuckolder. It refers to Polixenes' pleasant manner as he, in Leontes' irrational jealous imaginings, is betraying him.

Smith the weaver, *2H6 4.2.30,* character Sh. invents to illustrate the kind of working class men whom he says were attracted to Jack Cade's rebellion. Many of Cade's supporters were, in reality, men of property.

Smithfield, Smoothfield, meadow north of London outside Aldersgate. Londoners found it useful for many purposes. Horse and cattle markets (*2H4 1.2.49, 1.2.52*) were held there, and the field was a staging ground for public entertainments—like tournaments and executions. Margery Jordan, who was condemned for witchcraft in the service of the duchess of Gloucester, was burned at the stake at Smithfield (*2H6 2.3.7, 4.5.10, 4.6.12*). Since Elizabeth I's sister, Mary, created large numbers of Protestant martyrs in the fires of Smithfield, the place would have had powerful, recent associations for Sh.'s audience.

Smooth, Master, *2H4 2.1.29,* appropriate name Sh. invents for a fictional character who is a dealer in silk.

Smulkin, *Lr 3.4.132,* demon. Sh. borrowed the name from Samuel Harsnett's 'Smolkin,' 'a punie spirit.' See Flibbertigibbet.

Snare, Sergeant, *2H4,* descriptive name that Sh. invents for a policeman who tries to take Falstaff into custody.

Sneak, *2H4 2.4.11, 19,* musician who leads a band hired to play for Doll Tearsheet, Falstaff, and their friends. Sh. may have chosen the name as a comical way to describe all musicians who work in taverns, or he may have selected it because it was the name of a real artist known to his London audiences.

Snout, Tom, *MND,* F1 'Snowt,' a tinker. In the performance before Theseus, he presents the role of Wall (q.v.). His name refers to his trade as a tin worker, in which he would frequently repair the snouts or nozzles of containers. There might also be a joke about the facial features of the actor, as there would have been with the features of Starveling.

Snug, *MND,* joiner and amateur actor. In the performance before Theseus, he presents the role of Lion (q.v.). His name refers to his trade as the maker of furniture or other small items involving wood, in which tightness is essential.

Socrates, *Shr 1.2.70,* here the husband of the legendary shrew Xanthippe. Generally regarded as one of the most important philosophers in history, Socrates (469–399 BC) left no writings himself and is only known from the writings of Plato, his best student, and Xenophon, who does not seem to understand him completely. Socrates neglected his own affairs in the pursuit of self-knowledge and developed the Socratic method in which each student was forced to examine the implications of his own statements through the give and take of question and answer. He was lampooned by the comic playwright Aristophanes and he developed many enemies. Ultimately he was arrested and tried for corrupting the youth of Athens, something perhaps largely based on his instruction of Alcibiades and Critias who betrayed the city. In truth the Peloponnesian War was a more significant contributor to cynicism among youth. Socrates was convicted and condemned to death. He was given the opportunity to flee Athens, but he steadfastly refused to do so because it would have gone against his principles. He voluntarily drank a cup of hemlock. It is not clear how much Sh. may have known of Plato's dialogues and Socratic philosophy. The tradition which began with Socrates and passed on to Plato, Aristotle, and the schools of Athens (which continued until Justinian closed them) permeates western civilization, but beyond this general influence, there seems to be no particular mark of Plato's dialogues on Sh. Of Greek philosophers, Pythagoras (probably because of his being mentioned in Ovid) is cited more than Socrates or Aristotle. Plato is never mentioned by Sh.

Sol, *Tro 1.3.89,* name for the sun in astrology, from Latin.

Solinus, *Err,* Duke of Ephesus. Early in the play he listens to the merchant Egeon's account of the separation of the twins, but despite his sympathy he cannot overrule the law that requires the merchant to be put to death if he cannot raise the ransom. He does, however, release Egeon for a day to borrow or beg it. He does not reappear until the final act, when he is overseeing the execution of Egeon and is petitioned by different characters to resolve the confusions brought about by the two sets of twins. When that is straightened out, he joins the characters at the feast in the priory. The name Solinus is only used once in F1 in the opening line. It may have come from Caius Julius Solinus of the 3rd c. AD, a geographer whose *Collectanea Rerum Memorabilium* was translated into English in 1587. Having gathered all of his information from Pliny the Elder and Pomponius Mela, his primary distinction is in having been the first to use 'Mediterranean' for that sea. The duke's name might also have been suggested from Solon, the lawgiver of Athens, who Plutarch says began his career as a merchant.

Solomon, F1 'Salomon,' king of Israel, son of David. He became king after defeating his elder brother Adonijah and ruled during the 10th c. BC. His name has become synonymous with wisdom and wealth. He built the great temple in Jerusalem and magnificent palaces. His reputation reached to the kingdom of Sheba (see Saba) at the far end of the Arabian peninsula in what is now Yemen, and its queen travelled to Jerusalem to see him. Perhaps as equally famous as the story of Sheba is the story of the judgment of Solomon. Faced with two women claiming ownership of a child, he ordered the infant divided. The woman who immediately abandoned her claim out of concern for the child was declared by Solomon to be the true mother. In Sh.'s time Solomon was credited with having written the apocryphal Wisdom of Solomon, Proverbs, Ecclesiastes, and the Song of Songs (Song of Solomon). The latter two are perhaps the most unusual in the Bible and have required elaborate interpretation. Ecclesiastes may have been attributed to Solomon because of its deep philosophical musings, often nearly existential, which would seem appropriate to a king of his intellectual capacity, and the Song of Songs, an erotic masterpiece, because of his legendary 700 wives and 300 concubines, and his opulent lifestyle. These features also led to his being a favorite subject for medieval and Renaissance artists. His story is told in 1 Kings 1–11, 1 Chronicles 22–23, 28–29, and 2 Chron. 1–9.

LLL 1.2.166, 4.3.166: The double mention of S., who otherwise, curiously, is not mentioned in Sh., may reflect P. de la Primaudaye's *Académie française* (1577, trans. 1586) and its dedication to Henry III, which compares Francis I to Solomon.

Solon, (638–558 BC), Athenian sage and lawgiver. When tension between the rich and the poor threatened Athens with civil war, the city tried to head off bloodshed by granting Solon dictatorial powers and commissioning him to create a new form of government that would be tolerably just to everyone. Solon made radical changes in Athens' institutions and then exiled himself to prove that he had not acted in his own interest.

Tit 1.1.177, 'S.'s happiness,' alludes to a legend about a conversation between Solon and Croesus, the richest of Solon's contemporaries. Croesus displayed his wealth and boasted of his happiness to Solon, but Solon warned him that no man could be safely judged happy until he died a happy death.

Somerset, Duchy of, *1H6,* honor created in 1443 for John Beaufort, grandson of John of Gaunt. Somerset is a county in southwestern England on the Bristol channel. See Somerset, Duke of, *1H6, 2H6, 3H6.*

Somerset, Duke of, 1) *2H6, 3H6, 1H6,* see Beaufort, Edmund.

2) Pl.: *3H6 5.7.5,* 'Dukes of S.,' the three who died in the War of the Roses. Edmund, second duke, was killed at the first battle of St. Albans in 1455, *3H6 1.1.18.* Henry, the third duke, Edmund's son, died as a result of the fighting at Hexham in 1464. Edmund, the fourth duke, Henry's brother, was executed following Tewkesbury in 1471. See Beaufort, Edmund (1404–1455), second duke; Beaufort, Henry (1436–1464), third duke; Beaufort, Edmund (1438–1471), fourth duke. Also see Beaufort, John (1403–1444), first duke.

Somerville, *3H6,* John, possibly a knight from the Gloucestershire family of Aston-Somerville. Early editions of the play do not give his first name. A Sir Thomas Somerville, who was the son of a Sir John, died about 1500.

Somme, *H5 3.5.1,* French river that flows past Amiens and empties into the English channel south of Calais.

Songs and Sonnets, *MWW 1.1.181:* Slender is likely referring to a specific book here, *Songs and Sonnets by the Right Honourable Lord Henry Howard Late Earl of Surrey and Others,* collected by Richard Tottel. Better known as *Tottel's Miscellany,* it contains love poems by Surrey, Sir Thomas Wyatt, Thomas Vaux, Nicholas Grimald, and others. A very popular book, it was first published in 1557 and republished several times through 1587. By its final edition it contained 310 poems and was an enormous literary influence. It may be possible that Slender is speaking generically or that this is the same book he means when he asks about the 'book of riddles,' but these possibilities seem less likely.

Sooth, Signor, *Per 2.49,* 'sooth' as in 'soothing,' here meaning Sir Sycophant, Sir Appeasement, a name for a flatterer.

Soothsayer, fortune teller. 'Sooth' is an Old English word for 'truth,' as in 'forsooth.' *JC. Ant.*

Sophy, emperor or shah of Persia. The first to use the title *Safi* was Ismail I (1500–1524) who founded the Safavid Dynasty (1500–1736). The word comes from the name of this dynasty, which in Arabic means 'purity of religion.' It seems that the Europeans also conflated the title with the Greek *sophos* and assumed the meanings 'wise' and 'learned' were included in it.

MV 2.1.25, see Persian prince.

TN 2.5.174, 3.4.271: references to an expedition to Persia which was the talk of London in 1600. The three Shirley brothers set out with a party in 1597 for Persia. They had many adventures on the way, were graciously received by the Sophy, and amply rewarded. Those of the mission who returned to England in September 1600 did so by crossing the Caspian Sea, Russia, and sailing out of Archangel. Sir Robert Shirley lived lavishly following his return. In 1611 Sir Thomas Shirley turned up in London as an ambassador of the Sophy, married to a niece or sister of the potentate. Sir Anthony Shirley, the leader, did not return with his brothers. He had been a follower of the Earl of Essex (whose attempted coup d'état resulted in his execution in 1601) and his loyalties were questioned. The first account of Shirley's expedition was seized and burnt upon publication, but William Parry, one of Shirley's comrades, later published another. A play *The Travells of Three Brothers* (1607) by John Day, William Rowley, and George Wilkins (who may have collaborated with Sh. on *Per*) was written about the adventure.

Sossius, *Ant 3.1.17,* Caius Sossius, one of Antony's generals. Plutarch ('Antony' 24.6) says that Sossius achieved great things for Antony in Syria, and in 38 BC Antony sent him to replace Ventidius as governor of Syria and Cilicia. Antony rewarded Sossius by arranging for him to celebrate a triumph in 34 BC and receive a consulship in 32 BC. Sossius held a command in the fleet that fought for Antony at Actium in 31 BC. He survived his party's loss at Actium and was pardoned by Octavius. Sh. has Ventidius name Sossius as an example of a servant who overreaches himself and forfeits the favor of his patron. There is, however, no record of a breach between Sossius and Antony.

Soto, *Shr Ind. 1.86,* character in a play which the Lord favorably remembers. In John Fletcher's *Women Pleased* there is a Soto which meets his description; however, the play was acted around 1620 which means either that this is a late interpolation into *Shr* or that the name is drawn from a much earlier play which is Fletcher's source.

South-Fog, *Cym 2.4.128,* south wind, *Notus* or *Auster.* Its heat and moisture were supposed to disrupt the balance of the humours, causing slowness of wit, gout, epilepsy, itch, and the ague.

South Sea, *AYLI 3.2.193:* Rosalind compares Celia's talk to an endless voyage on the southern oceans.

Southam, *3H6 5.1.9, 12,* town in Warwickshire, 11 mi. southeast of Coventry.

Southampton, *H5 2.0.30, 35, 42, 2.3.43,* port at the center of England's southern coast just south of Winchester and Salisbury.

Southwark, *2H6 4.4.26, 4.7.178,* district that borders London on the south side of the Thames river. It commanded the entrance to London Bridge, the only bridge that provided access to medieval London from the south. Southwark was a convenient site for inns serving travellers. Since it was outside London, it came under the jurisdiction of the sheriff of Surrey, not the city aldermen. The sheriff's duties elsewhere may have prevented him from keeping a close eye on what was functionally a London suburb, for Southwark was a rough neighborhood noted for its brothels.

Southwell, John, *2H6,* priest accused of helping the duchess of Gloucester plot Henry VI's death by witchcraft. Sh. has Henry condemn Southwell to die by hanging (*2H6 2.3.8*). The chronicles of Edward Hall (202) and Holinshed (3.623) report that Southwell died in the Tower the night before he was to be executed. Hall gives his name as Thomas, not John.

Spain, nation that, not long before Sh.'s birth, was formed by the union of the ancient Christian kingdoms of the Iberian peninsula. Throughout most of the medieval period Spaniards wrestled with a unique problem that complicated their political evolution. They were the only Europeans to share a frontier with the Muslim world and the only western Christians to endure a sustained threat of Muslim invasion. Early in the 8th c. Muslim armies from Africa had overrun Spain and crossed the Pyrenees into southern France. The Franks, under the leadership of the Carolingian dynasty, forced the Muslims back to Spain, but it was not until the 11th c. that a concerted effort was made to reclaim Spain for Christendom. Once begun, the crusade lasted a very long time. Granada, the last Muslim state on the peninsula, was not taken until 1492. Christian victory was due largely to the efforts of Ferdinand, king of Aragon and the Mediterranean coastal district of Catalonia, and Isabella, queen of the interior plateau of Castile. Their wedding in 1469 laid the foundation for a Spanish nation, and an astute marriage for their heiress, Juana, created a mammoth legacy for their grandson, Charles V. Charles fell heir to Spain, its possessions in the New World, Flanders, and the titles and vast territories of the Hapsburg emperors in Germany, Italy, and Central Europe. Charles's empire proved to be too large for efficient government, and, when he retired, he divided it between his brother, Ferdinand, and his son, Philip.

Philip, king of Spain and its wealthy dependencies, was the most powerful monarch in western Europe and a man whom Sh.'s contemporaries learned to fear. England's relations with Spain throughout the Middle Ages had largely been determined by England's policy toward France. From the 12th through the 15th centuries England ruled a portion of southern France and occasionally yielded to the temptation to involve itself in Spain's dynastic wars. Edward the Black Prince fought in Spain. His brother, John of Gaunt, married a Spanish heiress and took an army into Spain in a fruitless attempt to win himself a throne. England's hope of developing a continental empire evaporated at the end of the Hundred Years' War with the loss of England's bases in France. Continuing enmity toward France generally encouraged the English to ally with Spain, but in the 16th c. unexpected developments made Spain a greater threat to England than France had ever been. The second Tudor king, Henry VIII, chose his first wife, Katherine of Aragon, to foster England's customary policy of siding with Spain against France. The friendly relationship she symbolized between England and her homeland ended when Henry decided that he had to terminate their marriage. The only living child Katherine bore Henry was a daughter, Mary. England had never been ruled by a woman, and Henry was convinced that unless he had a son to succeed him his country would come apart. Since Katherine was older than Henry and at the end of her child-bearing years, Henry asked her to agree to an annulment.

Katherine refused, and her nephew, the emperor Charles V, exerted pressure on her behalf. The presence of his army in Italy made it impossible for the pope to grant Henry a dissolution of his marriage. From Henry's point of view, it seemed probable that Spain was intervening in the internal affairs of his kingdom with the intention of increasing England's vulnerability. A female succession to the English throne might have rekindled the recently ended War of the Roses and exposed England to attack by the large army that Charles had stationed in the Netherlands. Henry concluded that Rome had leagued with Spain against England and that the pope was no longer an impartial spiritual leader. Parliament agreed with him, and England declared itself a Protestant nation. England's newly created Protestant church gave Henry a divorce and blessed a series of remarriages for the king, one of which produced a male heir. Edward VI succeeded to Henry's throne without opposition, but he did not live long enough to sire a child of his own. His heir was the elder of his two sisters, Katherine's daughter, Mary. England accepted its first reigning queen, but Mary's record was not encouraging. Mary was a fervent Catholic committed to doing everything in her power to reverse her father's Protestant revolution. She also felt a debt of gratitude to Spain which had been the only nation that had tried to help her and her mother in their difficulties. To reward Spain and strengthen her hand against Protestant dissidents, Mary decided to wed Charles's son, Philip.

The marriage was extremely unpopular in England, for tiny England feared that it would be absorbed into Philip's empire. Philip's plans for England were severely disrupted when Mary died childless. As her husband, Philip laid claim to her estate, but the English people ignored him and turned instead to the last of Henry VIII's children, his Protestant daughter, Elizabeth. Elizabeth showed great skill in navigating a course through dangerous diplomatic waters. For a long time she successfully played her enemies off against each other and avoided commitments. Philip eventually lost patience with politics and opted for a military solution. A revolt broke out against the Spaniards in the Netherlands, and Philip decided to solve two problems at once. He built a great armada of military transports, and in 1588 his admirals departed for the Netherlands. They intended to secure the situation there, to embark soldiers, and to invade England. Elizabeth had no navy and no standing army with which to defend her nation, but she improvised a fleet and relied on a combination of foul weather and English seamanship to disperse the 'Spanish Armada.' The venture impoverished Philip, who, after one more attempt, was forced to give up the hope of ever conquering England. Elizabeth emerged from the crisis with the full confidence and deep affection of her people. Sh. was twenty-four when these events took place, and his plays reflect the nationalistic pride that was one of Elizabeth's gifts to his generation.

3H6 3.3.82. LLL 1.1.161. 1.1.171, 'tawny S.,' sunburnt S. *Jn 2.1.424.*

H5 3.6.57, 'fig of S.,' obscene gesture made by inserting the thumb through the fingers. It was used to challenge a man's honor and invite him to a fight. Commonly people name obscenities and diseases for their enemies, although the gesture may have been borrowed from the Spanish. The opened fig's resemblance to female genitalia is also referred to.

JC 1.2.121. STM Add. II.D.143. Oth 5.2.260, 'sword of S.': Spanish swords were considered the best. The one referred to here was tempered in ice-water. *H8 2.4.46, 53.*

2) *Err 3.2.133, 139,* a location on the 'globe' of Nell.

Spain, King of, *H8 2.4.46,* see Ferdinand.

Spaniard, 1) citizen of Spain. *LLL 1.2.169,* 'S.'s rapier.' *4.2.97. 2H4 5.3.120:* the warrior's *machismo* from the long history of war in Iberia and the rigidly orthodox Catholicism that evolved in Spain earned Spaniards a reputation for arrogance and belligerence that explains Sh.'s allusions to 'bragging' Spaniards. *Ado 3.2.33:* the passage mocks the fashionable Englishman's mixing of national fashions. *Per 16.96,* 'S.'s mouth,' the S. is mocked for his lechery and his ruff.

2) *Cym 1.4.sd,* non-speaking gentleman whose costume adds a worldly flavor to the first scene in Rome, for the sake of ethnic parody, or possibly to show Filario's hospitality to people of all nations. The character appears in one of Sh.'s sources *Frederyke of Jennen* (anonymous, 1560). Unidentified gentlemen are present at the wager in Boccaccio's *Decameron,* 2.9, the major source of the love plot. There is also a Catalan, Señor Encarach, who hires Ginevra in disguise as Lucius hires Innogen.

Spanish, (adj.) of or pertaining to Spain or its people. *Rom 1.4.85,* 'S. blades': the Spanish were reputed the best swordmakers. *1H4 2.5.70,* 'S. pouch': either this refers to the bartender's body shape in a S. leather jerkin or to a leather pouch characteristic of his attire. *AWW 4.1.47,* 'S. sword': Paroles mention of it might also betray his ostentation.

Sparrow, Philip, *Jn 1.1.231,* self-mocking reference that Sh. has the character, Philip the Bastard, make to his birth name (Philip Falconbridge) when he renounces it to assume the name of his natural father, King Richard I Plantagenet. In Sh.'s day pet birds were often called 'Philip,' and the Bastard finds the appellation too tame for a man of his mettle.

Sparta, powerful city-state of ancient Greece located on the west bank of the Eurotas river in the southern Peloponnesian peninsula. The city was founded by Dorian Greeks who conquered the area in the early 8th c. BC, though in mythology it was said to be founded by Lacedæmon, son of Zeus. The city expanded its control over all of Laconia and made war on the Messenians, Argives, and the Arcadians. In the Mycenæan period Sparta was already one of the major cities of Greece, with its most famous king being Menelaus of the *Iliad.* The Spartans cultivated the art of war after 600 BC and the sternness of the city's regime was so legendary that the word 'Spartan' has become synonymous with 'rigorous,' 'harsh,' and 'tough.' The city was built simply, with few notable structures, and was scattered in five separate quarters, so it has left little interesting in the way of ruins—unlike Athens and other ancient cities. Xenophon lived and wrote in exile there; otherwise, of all the great Greek cities, it was the least distinguished culturally. It had an unusual form of government, deriving from a constitution supposedly received from Lycurgus. The society was sharply divided between the aristocracy and their subjects. Any Spartan, for example, could kill a helot (serf) without repercussion. There were two co-ruling hereditary kings and five elected ephors who held the most power. There was also a senate of 28 elders.

Under king Leonidas, 300 Spartans famously defended the pass at Thermopylæ in 480 BC and died rather than surrender. They also fought at Platæa in 479, bringing an end to the Persian Wars. Athens' attempt to exploit its new power after the wars and to dominate S.'s neighbors eventually led to the Peloponnesian War (431–404), which at first went badly for the Spartans because Athens refused to face their troops on land. Eventually, however, the Spartans with Persian aid learned the techniques of naval warfare and the Athenian Empire collapsed. The Spartans, however, failed as rulers of the old Athenian Empire, turned Ionian territories over to the Persians in 387, and were harried by opposition financed out of Persia. In 394 at Cnidus the Athenian general Conon destroyed Sparta's fleet. Defeated by Thebes at Leuctra in 371, the myth of Spartan invincibility on land was broken. Sparta weakened and fell to Philip of Macedon who took over the mainland in 338. There were subsequent attempts to bring the city back to prominence, particularly by Cleomenes III (236–222), but by his day the number of citizens had been decimated and those left were largely impoverished. In 146, it became a Roman city and prospered, but in 395 AD, it fell to the Goths and faded into legend, until Greek independence in the 19th c. when modern Sparta was then built near the ruins of the old city.

MND 4.1.113, 'hounds of S.': these bloodhounds were known for their ferocity and quiet stalking, as the men of S. were also known for their stoicism and hard-heartedness. In the scene in Ovid's *Metamorphoses* in which Actæon is attacked by his dogs, the Spartan and Cretan breeds are mentioned for their ferocity. *4.3.125. Tro 2.2.182,* 'S.'s king,' Menelaus. *Per 6.18,* 'a knight of S.,' one of Thaisa's suitors.

Spartan, 1) (n.) a native of Sparta. *Tro 5.8.3,* 'double-horned S.,' Menelaus is a cuckold and therefore 'horned' in Renaissance parlance.

2) (adj.) of or pertaining to Sparta. *MND 4.1.118,* 'S. kind' and *Oth 5.2.371,* 'S. dog': see 'Sparta, hounds of,' *MND.*

Speed, *TGV,* servant of Valentine. The clown who is a quick-witted master of wordplay is typical of the Italian style of comedy to which the play owes so much. Perhaps his name suggests his agility with words. The jesting between Lance and Speed may have been suggested by that between Daris and Samias in John Lyly's *Endimion* (1591). Stephano, the servant of the two friends in *The excellent Comedy of two the moste faithfullest Friendes, Damon and Pithias* (1571, performed 1565) by Richard Edwards (c. 1523–1566), speaks of his hunger in much the same way as Speed does in *TGV 2.1.162–165.* Edwards also wrote a play called *Palamon and Arcite,* which was performed in 1566, but is no longer extant.

Spencer, *R2 5.6.8,* Thomas le Despenser (1373–1400), son-in-law of Edmund Langley, duke of York, and one of the men who conspired in January, 1400, to assassinate Henry IV and restore Richard II to the throne. In 1397 Spencer had sided with Richard against the 'lords appellant,' and he served with the army that Richard took to Ireland in 1399. When Richard surrendered to the revolution led by Henry (IV) Bolingbroke, he bargained for Spencer's safety. Spencer seemed to make his peace with the new king, Henry IV, for he was one of the parliamentary commissioners who carried out Richard's formal deposition, but Spencer quickly got into trouble. He was accused of having taken part in the murder of one of the 'lords appellant,' Thomas of Woodstock, duke of Gloucester. Henry deprived him of the earldom of Gloucester, and he joined other disaffiliated men in a plan to kill Henry. When the plot was revealed, Spencer fled to Bristol where he was captured and executed.

Sphinx, *LLL 4.3.318,* riddle-asking monster, half woman and half lion. The creature was sent to Thebes by Hera to punish Laius. It perched outside the city and asked each traveller 'What travels on four legs in the morning, two legs in midday, and three legs in the evening?' When the traveller couldn't answer, she consumed him. Oedipus, however, answered, 'Man' (crawling as a baby, upright as an adult, on a cane in old age) and the Sphinx in despair flung herself off a cliff.

Spinii, *AWW 2.1.41,* group involved in the Tuscan wars. Possibly it derives from Spinello in Ariosto's *Orlando Furioso* 13; however, this victim of Rodomonte is not named in Harington's English translation of 1591. Possibly, too, 'Spaine' was meant (which does appear in Harington).

Spurio, Captain, *AWW 2.1.41 4.3.166,* supposed officer in the armies in Tuscany. Because his name means 'spurious' in Italian, he is a fabrication of Paroles, who brags he wounded him—something he's quite unlikely to have ever done.

Squash, Mistress, *MND 3.1.178,* Bottom's joking name for Peaseblossom's mother, 'an unripe pea pod.' Compare *TN 1.5.152.*

Squeal, Will, *2H4 3.2.19–20,* one of the youthful companions whom Justice Shallow recalls when he reminisces about his riotous student days at Clement's Inn. Squeal's comic name suggests that he, like all of Shallow's friends, had a flawed character.

Stadlin, *Mac 3.5.43,* spirit called forth by the witches in a song named but not appearing in F1, but which appears in Thomas Middleton's play *The Witch* (c. 1609, but not printed until the 18th c.). William Davenant's version of *Mac* (printed 1674) and Q (1673), however, contains the song, and it has been argued that Davenant may have had access to an earlier text. In his version, the spirit is 'Stadling.' In Middleton's play, Stadlin is a witch character. The name came from Reginald Scot's *Discoverie of Witchcraft* (1584).

Stafford, seat of the county of Staffordshire, situated about 125 mi. northwest of London.

1) *2H6,* see Humphrey, earl of Stafford and duke of Buckingham; also see Stafford's brother.

2) *2H6,* see Stafford, Humphrey.

3) *3H6,* see Stafford, Lord 1).

4) *1H4,* see Stafford, Lord 2).

5) *H8,* see Edward, earl of Stafford and duke of Buckingham.

Stafford, Earl of, *H8 1.1.200,* one of the titles inherited by Edward Stafford, duke of Buckingham.

Stafford, Humphrey, *2H6* (d. 1450), sheriff of Gloucester and governor of Calais. He died attempting to put down Jack Cade's rebellion against Henry VI's government. His son and namesake sided with the house of York in the War of the Roses and was executed by Henry VII for assisting Richard III at the battle of Bosworth Field. Neither the father nor the son was the Humphrey Stafford who became duke of Buckingham.

Stafford, Lord, 1) *3H6,* Humphrey (1439–1469), cousin of the Staffords (Humphrey and William) who died in Cade's rebellion, heir to their estates. He sided with the house of York and earned his knighthood at the battle of Towton. In 1469 his defection in battle prompted Edward to order his execution.

2) Edmund (d. 1403), fifth earl of Stafford and husband of Edward III's granddaughter, Anne. He was killed at the battle of Shrewsbury on 21 July 1403. *1H4 5.3.7, 13, 5.4.40. 2H4 1.1.18:* the rumor, which Sh. repeats, that Stafford fled the field at Shrewsbury was false.

Stafford's brother, *2H6,* William, (d. 1450), brother of Sir Humphrey Stafford. He and Humphrey were both killed by Jack Cade's rebels, and Sh. implies that their deaths gave Cade's men the confidence to commit atrocities.

Staffordshire, *2H4 3.2.18,* county in the English midlands, north of Sh.'s home town, Stratford-on-Avon.

Staines, *H5 2.3.2,* town in the county of Middlesex on the northern bank of the Thames about 15 mi. west of London.

Stamford, *2H4 3.2.37,* market town in Lincolnshire about 90 mi. north of London. In February, March/April, and August it hosted the livestock fairs to which Sh. refers.

Standard in Cheapside, The, *2H6 4.7.106,* outlet for a conduit that supplied water to the shops and residences of Cheapside, London. It was a common place of assembly and occasionally a site for public executions.

Stanley, *Var,* subject of an epitaph or two epitaphs at the opposite ends of the Stanley tomb at Tong. The verses are attributed to Sh. in a manuscript of the 1630's and by William Dugdale in 1664. Sir Thomas Stanley died in 1576 and is thought to be praised on the east end of the tomb. Sir Edward Stanley died in 1609 and is praised on the west. There is an argument that only Sir Edward Stanley who died in 1632 is buried in the tomb, and that would make it impossible that Sh. wrote the poems. Sh. did have a connection to the Stanley family. *Tit* and *1H6* were both performed by the

Earl of Derby's Men, and Lord Strange's Men (Henry Stanley, Lord Strange, was the fourth Earl of Derby; his son Ferdinando was also a patron and known as Lord Strange). Another odd and silly theory makes William Stanley, sixth Earl of Derby, the author or partial author of Sh.'s works.

Stanley, George, *R3 4.4.426, 4.5.3, 4, 5.5.14, 48, 5.6.74, 76, 5.8.9,* (d. 1497), son of Thomas Stanley, earl of Derby. Richard III held him hostage to guarantee Thomas' loyalty while Richard struggled with Henry Tudor. When the elder Stanley held aloof from the battle of Bosworth Field, Richard ordered George's execution. Only the press of more urgent business and Richard's death in that battle saved the younger Stanley's life. Henry VII granted Thomas Stanley the earldom of Derby to reward him for his contribution to the Tudor victory. George's life had been risked to help his father earn this honor, but George did not live to inherit it. George died seven years before his father, and the heir to the estate was George's son, Thomas.

Stanley, John, *2H6,* man Sh. says was given the responsibility of overseeing Eleanor Cobham's incarceration on the Isle of Man. Sh. may have confused John with his father Thomas. Thomas governed Man until his death in 1458 and is identified by Holinshed (3.623) as the duchess of Gloucester's jailor.

Stanley, Lord, earl of Derby, *R3,* Thomas (1435–1504), pivotal figure in the last phase of the War of the Roses. Stanley married the earl of Warwick's sister, and, like 'the Kingmaker,' fought on both sides in the war. When Richard of York captured his Lancastrian opponent, Henry VI, at the battle of Northampton in 1460, Stanley was with the king. In the year that followed, the political situation in England changed rapidly, and Stanley changed with it. The Lancastrians liberated Henry and killed Richard, but Warwick forced Henry from England and helped Richard's son, Edward IV, to the throne. Warwick dominated the government of the young Yorkist king, and he saw to it that Stanley, his brother-in-law, had an honorable post at Edward's court. Stanley profited from Warwick's patronage, but he must also have been a man of ability and integrity. Edward came to trust him and forgave him a major transgression. In 1470 Warwick broke with Edward and joined the Lancastrians in an attempt to restore Henry VI to the throne. Edward was forced to flee England, and it took him a year to raise an army and claw his way back to power. Edward may have understood the conundrum of being caught between duty to family and to party. Although Stanley had participated in Warwick's revolution, Edward pardoned him and appointed him steward of the royal household.

In 1482 Stanley was sent to assist Edward's brother, Richard of Gloucester, in a war with Scotland, and shortly after that he made a portentous second marriage. He wed Margaret Beaufort, the widowed countess of Richmond, and Henry Tudor's mother. Her descent from the house of Lancaster made her son its leader after Henry VI and Prince Edward were killed in 1471. Margaret was preoccupied with schemes for winning the throne for Henry, but although Stanley became the young earl of Richmond's step-father (*R3 5.2.5*), he was not immediately reconverted to the Lancastrian cause. After Edward IV's death, Stanley risked his life by opposing Richard of Gloucester's plans to dispossess Edward's sons. When parliament sided with Gloucester, Stanley acquiesced to the inevitable and took part in Richard III's coronation. Stanley may not have been enthusiastic about Richard, but he avoided the temptation of enlisting in the duke of Buckingham's ill-fated rebellion, and he kept a tight reign on his wife's plots on behalf of Richmond. Stanley's scrupulously correct behavior may in part have been guaranteed by the fact that Richard, who did not entirely trust him, held his son, George, hostage. In 1485, when Richmond threw down the gauntlet and challenged Richard to a battle for the throne of England, Stanley faced hard choices. At Bosworth Field he and his men took up a position between the opposing armies, and Stanley avoided committing himself to the battle until it appeared that Richard might win. His sudden intervention probably carried the day for Henry. It is said that he found Richard's crown amid the debris of battle and personally placed it on Henry's head.

R3 1.3.17: since Henry VII appointed Stanley to the earldom of Derby, it is anachronistic for Sh.'s characters at Richard's court to address him by that title.

Stanley, William, (1435–1495), soldier whose shifting loyalties illustrate the strategies some men adopted to survive the War of the Roses. Henry VI's repeated bouts with mental illness brought on the war, which began as a contest for control of the government between Henry's cousin, Richard of York, and Henry's queen, Margaret. In 1459 York took up arms against Margaret. Warwick and the Nevilles were solidly on his side, but most of the English nobility stood by the king or tried to retain good relations with both York and Lancaster. Thomas Stanley, the earl of Derby and William's brother, pledged his support to the queen, but procrastinated when ordered to bring troops to her camp. William was bolder. He openly committed himself by joining the Yorkists in a skirmish with a Lancastrian force at Blore Heath. The Lancastrians were routed, but the engagement proved inconsequential. A few weeks later at Ludlow Richard was compelled to accept the fact that he had not been able to attract a sufficient following to continue to oppose the queen. He and those who had supported him retired into exile. When fortune turned and Richard's son, Edward, won the throne, he rewarded the loyalty of early allies like William Stanley. Stanley was given lands that once belonged to the Yorkist nemesis, Lord Clifford. When Warwick turned against Edward and rallied the Lancastrian army in 1470, Stanley stuck by Edward and may have helped him on his flight to safety in Flanders. Events proved this to be a good decision, for Edward regained the throne and Stanley profited from the king's gratitude. When Edward died and his brother Richard III usurped the throne, Stanley was compelled to make another difficult decision. Richard courted his support, but Stanley chose to hedge his bets by making overtures to the Tudor leader, Henry, earl of Richmond. This aroused Richard's suspicions, and his accusations of treason drove Stanley into Henry's camp. At the battle of Bosworth Stanley's timely arrival with reinforcements may have tipped the balance in Henry's favor. Stanley's political perspicacity and martial daring saw him through perilous times, but in the end he blundered fatally. In 1495 he was convicted of plotting against the Tudor dynasty he had helped bring to power, and he was beheaded.

3H6. R3 4.5.10.

Star Chamber, *MWW 1.1.1–2,* high court with legal jurisdiction, but controlled by the monarch. Founded in 1487 by Henry VII, it consisted of the King's Council and two judges. It met in a room in the palace of Westminster, the ceiling of which was decorated with stars. Although the punishments it might hand down now seem barbaric, it did not have the power of the death sentence and operated publicly during the Tudor period, most significantly being used to try individuals beyond the reach of lower courts. The Stuarts, however, used it to suppress opposition and closed its proceedings to outside scrutiny. Its power came to be resented and its name became synonymous with tyrannical power. It was disbanded in 1641 by Parliament. See Council.

Starve-lackey, Master, *MM 4.3.13,* 'tho rapier and dagger man,' mocking name for one of the impoverished criminals Pompey knows. As prisoners paid for their own food, many were forced to beg passers-by for their sustenance.

Starveling, Robin, *MND,* tailor and amateur actor. In the performance before Theseus, he badly presents the role of Moonshine (q.v.), forgetting his lines. Tailors do not require robustness for their trade and traditionally have been thought of as small, as in the expression, 'nine tailors make a man.' The name then probably indicates both the trade and the emaciated look of the character. John Sincklo specialized in this type of role for the Lord Chamberlain's men.

Statillius, *JC 5.5.2,* Statilius Taurus, general in the service of Octavius. In 31 BC he commanded Octavius' infantry at Actium. He was chosen consul in 26 BC, and in 16 BC he became præfect charged with responsibility for the government of Rome and Italy while Octavius toured Gaul.

Stefano, 1) *MV 5.1.28, 51,* F1 'Stephano,' messenger and servant of Portia. The accent is on the second syllable. See 2) below.

2) *Tmp,* F1 'Stephano,' drunken butler of Alonso. The accent is on the first and last syllables. Stephano is used for a character in Ben Jonson's *Every Man in his Humour* (1598) in which Sh. acted and in which Sh. supposedly learned this pronunciation after using the other pronunciation in *MV.* There is a Stephano who is the servant of the two friends in Ralph Edward's *Excellent Comedy of two the moste faithfullest Friendes, Damon and Pithias* (1571, performed 1565) upon which Sh. borrowed for his *TGV.* Stephano speaks of his hunger in much the same way as Speed does in *TGV 2.1 162–165.* Benedetto Croce wrote there may be a pun on the Neapolitan slang for 'stomach' (*stefano*) at *Tmp 5.1.289* deriving from the *commedia dell'arte,* so perhaps there is some deep connection, since *TGV* has a number of *commedia* elements. John Florio's Italian-English dictionary of 1598, *A Worlde of Wordes,* says *stefano* is a jesting word for the belly, and may have indicated the characters' appearance. Sh. may have had the name in mind from early in his career. Warburton's suggestion that there is a pun on 'whipped man' (*staffilato*) seems farfetched. *4.1.221, 225,* 'King S.,' a play on a ballad about King Stephen and his clothes: 'Take thy old cloak about thee,' in Thomas Percy's collection *Reliques of Ancient English Poetry.*

Stephen, King, *Oth 2.3.82,* king mentioned in a popular ballad, 'Bell My Wife.' The ballad appears in Percy's *Reliques.* See Stefano, *Tmp.*

Stephen, Saint, *Tit 4.4.42,* the first Christian martyr. He was a member of the church that the apostles founded in Jerusalem immediately following Christ's resurrection. He was named to the board of deacons that managed the financial affairs of the community, but he was also a missionary preacher. His sermons on the streets of Jerusalem offended the Hebrew authorities. They arrested him, convicted him of blasphemy against their faith, and stoned him to death. His story is told in Acts 6–7.

Steward, High, *H8 4.1.18, 41,* official charged with provisioning the royal household and presiding over state functions. The steward also had judicial duties. See Suffolk, Duke of, *H8.*

Stockfish, Samson, *2H4 3.2.31,* fruit merchant with whom Justice Shallow had a fight in his student days. The scrap was a youthful escapade the nostalgic old man recalled with great pleasure, but the names Sh. gave his adversary suggest that the duel was something less than a noble contest. Samson is, of course, the strong man from the Bible's Book of Judges, but Stockfish is a strip of dried cod that has to be pounded to tenderize it for cooking.

Stoics, *Shr 1.1.31,* group of ancient Greek philosophers who believed they should strive to be immune to bodily sensations such as pain, passion, and pleasure. They also held that one should be primarily concerned with virtue and ethics, accepting all occurrences as matters of divine will. The school was founded by Zeno in the early 4th c. BC and derived its name from the *stoa* 'porch' or 'portico' where he taught. The word soon came to be applied to anyone with strong self-control who could endure discomfort or great suffering without complaint.

Stokesley, bishop of London, *H8 4.1.103,* John (1475–1539), one of Henry VIII's chaplains and a scholar who marshaled support for the king's decision to separate from Katherine of Aragon. Stokesley handled negotiations with Italy's universities when Henry sought the support of Europe's intellectuals for the arguments he used against Katherine. Stokesley was consecrated bishop of London in 1530, and, like most of the other English bishops, he accepted the parliamentary legislation that curtailed the pope's authority in England. Although he acknowledged the king's right to be the head of the English church, he opposed Protestant doctrines and the translation of the Bible into the vernacular. In 1533 he baptized Anne Boleyn's daughter, Elizabeth.

Stony Stafford, *R3 2.4.2,* or Stony Stratford, a town in Buckinghamshire about 50 mi. northwest of London. It was a rest station on the route travelled by the party that conveyed young Edward V from Ludlow to London for his coronation.

Strachey, Lady of the, *TN 2.5.37.* An enormous amount of debate surrounds this name. If it is a topical allusion, we have no definite evidence as to whom Malvolio refers. One may suppose that whenever someone married below his or her station much gossip was provoked, especially if a woman did so. Whether a woman of the Strachey family did so is unknown. Speculation has given us theories that it is a misspelling of *satrape* 'governor'; *Trachy,* 'Thrace'; *starchy,* the room in which starching went on; *Austrasia,* an old name for Lorraine; *Strozzi,* a Florentine family; and even *Sophy,* the Persian potentate mentioned several times elsewhere. In the possible source for the play *Gl'Ingannati* (1538) there is a servant named Stragualcia which may have lingered in Sh.'s mind; in Niccolo Secchi's *Gl'Inganni* (1562) there is a servant named Straccia. The drift of Malvolio's remark is obvious, however, and it seems most sensible to read it as a reference to some scandal of the Strachey family now lost in time.

Strand, *H8 5.3.51,* street that connected London and Westminster. It ran from Temple bar to Charing Cross and paralleled the 'strand' or 'bank' of the Thames river.

Strange, Lord, *1H6 4.7.65,* see Blackmere, Lord Strange of.

Strato, *JC,* Greek who was a life-long friend of Brutus. The two men had been school boys together and were companions in arms at Philippi. Strato agreed to help Brutus commit suicide at Philippi when Brutus concluded that the Republican cause was lost. Plutarch ('Brutus' 53.1–2) says that Octavius was so impressed by Strato's loyalty to Brutus, that Octavius recruited Strato for his service. Strato distinguished himself for his new master at the battle of Actium.

Styga, *Tit 2.1.136,* L. accusative form of Styx.

Stygian, (adj.) *Tro 3.2.8,* of or pertaining to the river Styx.

Styx, one of five rivers that originate in Hades. In Greek myth the Styx was the dividing line between the realms of the living and the dead. The river was sacred to the gods, who swore oaths by its name. The Styx was a deadly stream whose waters were so corrosive that they could be carried only in a horse's hoof. The ferryman Charon greeted souls at the shore and rowed them to Hades, if they had the fee. The name derives from the Greek for 'hateful,' 'obnoxious.'

Tit 1.1.88. Tro 5.4.18. 2H6 Add'l B.4. R3 1.4.45: Clarence alludes to the river but does not name it.

Sueno, see Sweno.

Suffolk, *3H6 1.1.157, 4.9.12,* county at the northern end of England's channel coast, south of Norfolk and east of Cambridge. Its name means 'land of the southern folk.' Robert of Ufford (1298–1369) was named first earl of

Suffolk in 1337. The Ufford family died out in 1382, and in 1385 Richard II transferred the Ufford lands and title to Michael de la Pole. Suffolk's chief port in Sh.'s day was Ipswich. See Suffolk, Duke of, *H8*; Earl of, *H5*; *2H6, 1H6.*

Suffolk, Duke of, *H8,* Charles Brandon (d. 1545), Henry VIII's childhood friend and lifelong companion. He courted disaster by secretly marrying Henry's sister Mary, immediately following the death of her first husband, Louis XII, king of France. After a brief period of penance for his presumption in acting without royal permission, he was restored to Henry's favor. He was with Henry while Henry conferred with Francis I on the 'Field of the Cloth of Gold.' He supported Henry's decision to separate from Katherine of Aragon and to repudiate the authority of the pope. He was a member of the tribunal that convicted the men accused of committing adultery with Henry's fifth wife, Catherine Howard, and he took Catherine to the Tower to await execution. His daughter, Frances, married Henry Gray, and their daughter was the Lady Jane Gray who laid claim to the throne after the death of Edward VI.

Suffolk, Earl of, 1) see Pole, William de la, *1H6, 2H6.*

2) *H5 4.6.10, 11, 15, 4.8.103,* Michael de la Pole (1394–1415), third earl. Suffolk succeeded to the earldom when his father died of dysentery at the seige of Harfleur. He had little time to enjoy the title, for he died a few weeks later at the battle of Agincourt.

Sugarsop, *Shr 4.1.80,* servant of Petruccio. His name comes from a dish, bread soaked in a syrup and sometimes spiced.

Suleiman, 'the Magnificent' (1494–1566), son of Selim I, and sultan of Turkey from 1520. He ruled the Ottoman Empire at the height of its power and prestige. His conquests included Belgrade, most of Hungary, Baghdad, Armenia, Georgia, the Arabian coastlines, Algiers, and Rhodes. His fleet threatened the entire Mediterranean and his armies besieged Vienna (1529) in the deepest incursion by the Turks into Europe. It is entirely possible that had he not been harassed by the Persians, all of Christendom might have fallen. He was not uniformly successful, however, and lost several important naval engagements against Holy Roman Emperor Charles I and the Venetian Republic. His reforms give him stature in Turkish history as a lawgiver, and he was even known as a poet. He relieved some of the sufferings of his Christian subjects and allied himself with Francis I of France against the Hapsburgs, something which more narrow-minded Moslems found irreligious. Art and architecture prospered during his reign. He lived in extraordinary splendor and ultimately contributed to the voluptuous atmosphere around the sultanate which contributed centuries later to its downfall. He died during the siege of Szigetvár, in southern Hungary near Pecs. The city fell three days later.

MV 2.1.26: Morocco claims to have been in his service, which might be appropriate considering the conquests in north Africa by Barbarossa (Khair-ed-Din). See Persian prince.

Sunday, first day of the week, the Christian Sabbath, a day on which work was supposed to cease to provide time for spiritual contemplation. Since Christ rose from the dead on Sunday it was considered the Lord's day and the luckiest day of the week.

Shr 2.1.293, 294, 318, 320, 389, 391: Petruccio and Katherine's wedding day. *1H4 3.1.252,* 'S. citizens,' people in their fanciest outfits. *Ado 1.1.190,* 'sigh away Sundays,' spend the day without work, bored with one's wife.

Tro 1.1.76, day on which one would appear at her best. *Ham 1.1.75,* people are working even on Sunday. *4.5.181:* Ophelia seems to be saying that sorrow and repentance is called grace on Sunday, or that when people are on their best behavior—speaking most properly—they call rue 'herb-grace.'

Surecard, Master, *2H4 3.2.85,* name by which Falstaff erroneously remembers Justice Silence. A 'surecard' was a safe bet. Sh. doubtless intended this bit of word play to be a joke, but its point is no longer obvious. Perhaps Falstaff was implying that Silence was a fool and an easy mark for deceivers.

Surgeon, see Dick Surgeon.

Surrey, 1) English county situated south of the Thames river opposite the city of London and west of the county of Kent. Its name derives from an OE word for 'southerly.' See Surrey, Duke of, and Surrey, Earl of.

2) *R3 5.5.17,* horse that Richard III rode into battle at Bosworth Field. Sh.'s claim that at the crux of the battle Richard would have traded his kingdom for a horse did not imply cowardice, but an ardent desire to have the equipment needed to continue the fight. Holinshed (3.759–760) claims that Richard's men brought him a horse on which to flee, but the king chose to stay and accept what fate had in store.

Surrey, Duke of, *R2,* Thomas Holland (1375–1400), earl of Kent, Richard II's lieutenant for Ireland. He stayed with Richard until the king surrendered to Henry (IV) Bolingbroke, and he was imprisoned for a short time as punishment for his participation in Richard's plan to confiscate Bolingbroke's duchy of Lancaster. In October 1399 Surrey was accused of involvement in the murder of one of the 'lords appellant,' Thomas of Woodstock, duke of Gloucester. When Henry stripped him of his duchy, he joined his uncle, the duke of Exeter, in a plot to assassinate Henry IV and restore Richard II. The scheme was exposed, and he fled to Cirencester where he was murdered by a mob of angry citizens.

Surrey, Earl of, 1) Thomas Howard (1443--1524), second duke of Norfolk. Thomas became earl of Surrey when his father, John, was created the first Howard duke of Norfolk in 1483. Although Surrey had served Edward IV loyally, he supported Richard III when Richard disinherited Edward's sons. Richard trusted Surrey and gave him an important command at the battle of Bosworth Field. Surrey fought vigorously for the doomed king and paid for his choice of the losing side with five years imprisonment in the Tower of London. His conduct as a prisoner must have impressed Henry VII, for in 1489 Henry set Surrey free, restored his title and properties, and assigned him the job of guarding England's northern frontier. Surrey served his former captor well. He put down uprisings against the Tudor king and fended off the Scots, and in 1501 Surrey negotiated the peace with Scotland that was sealed by the marriage of James IV of Scotland and Henry VII's sister, Margaret. Surrey lived to serve four kings. After Henry VII's death, he continued as one of Henry VIII's advisers. Despite his advancing age he retained responsibility for the defense of northern England, and in 1513 he won a decisive victory over the Scots at Flodden Field. Henry rewarded him with the duchy of Norfolk, which his father had held, and in 1520 the duke governed England for Henry while Henry travelled to the continent. The elderly warrior remained active at court until the year before his death in 1524. *R3 5.5.22, 5.6.3, 5.6.26. STM:* he attempts to persuade the commoners to give up their intention to riot in 1517, see More, Thomas.

2) *2H4,* Thomas Fitzalan (1381–1415), eleventh earl of Arundel and Surrey. In 1397 Richard II executed Fitzalan's father on a charge of treason, and Fitzalan, at the age of 16, joined his uncle, Archbishop Arundel, in exile. A year later the two men acquired an important companion in misfortune. Richard banished John of Gaunt's son, Henry (IV) Bolingbroke. In 1399 Henry led Fitzalan, Arundel and other exiles home to England to force Richard's abdication. Once Henry secured the throne, he restored Fitzalan's family estates and took the young earl into his service. Fitzalan fought in Henry's Welsh wars and sided with the king against the rebellious Percies. In 1405 Fitzalan proved his loyalty to the king by presiding at the execution of Archbishop Scrope. The event was controversial, for although Scrope was guilty of treason, clerical orders had traditionally protected a man from capital punishment. At court Fitzalan became a member of Prince

Harry's circle, and he supported the Prince's plan to renew war with France. When the Prince (Henry V) succeeded to the throne, he appointed Fitzalan treasurer of England and took him to France with the army that besieged Harfleur. Shortly after the fall of Harfleur the earl returned to England to die of dysentery.

3) *H8,* Thomas Howard (1473–1554), eldest son of Thomas Howard, second duke of Norfolk, and, in due course, the third duke. When Surrey inherited his father's title in 1524, his son Henry became earl of Surrey. Thomas' son Henry Howard is considered one of the most important of the early English Renaissance poets because of his sonnets and translations of Virgil and he was more popular than Sir Thomas Wyatt in the time period, though he was executed for treason at age 30. From *H8 2.1* to the end, Sh.'s play deals with events that took place after 1524, but the character he continues to call Surrey is Thomas duke of Norfolk, not Henry Howard, earl of Surrey. Thomas was the duke of Buckingham's son-in-law and friend. He was not implicated in Buckingham's treason, but after the duke's execution he led the party that opposed Buckingham's nemesis, Cardinal Wolsey. When Wolsey lost the king's confidence, Norfolk relished the privilege of being the messenger sent to strip the cardinal of his civil offices. Wolsey's disgrace was only the beginning for Norfolk, who hounded Henry's fallen servant into his grave. Norfolk endorsed Henry's decision to separate from Katherine of Aragon, and he profited from the king's shifting domestic arrangements. Anne Boleyn, Henry's second wife, was Norfolk's niece. When Henry turned against Anne, Norfolk saved himself by presiding at her adultery trial and seeing to it that Henry got the guilty verdict that he wanted.

After Anne's execution, Norfolk added to his reputation by brutally punishing persons implicated in the revolt called the Pilgrimage of Grace. Norfolk hated Cromwell as much as he had Wolsey. And in 1540, when Henry abandoned Cromwell, Norfolk again had the pleasure of removing a fallen royal favorite from office. Norfolk's position at court was enhanced when Henry married Catherine Howard who, like Anne Boleyn, was one of Norfolk's nieces. Catherine, even more quickly than Anne, turned political advantage into liability. Multiple and flagrant adulteries led to her execution and the disgrace of the Howard family. In 1547 Norfolk's son, Henry, was executed for treason, and the same fate was decreed for Norfolk. Henry VIII died before the sentence could be carried out. Norfolk remained in the Tower of London throughout Edward VI's reign, but in 1553 Mary restored his liberty and returned him to government service. In January 1554 she ordered him to put down a rebellion raised by Thomas Wyatt. Norfolk's army deserted him, and the failure of his mission prompted his retirement from public life. He died a few months after leaving the court.

Surveyor, see Buckingham's Surveyor, *H8.*

Susan, *Rom 1.3.20, 21,* Juliet's nurse's daughter, who died young, probably as an infant, allowing her mother to become Juliet's wet-nurse, although wet-nurses often fed more than one child.

Sutton Coldfield, *1H4 4.2.3,* town about 25 mi. northwest of Warwick and Coventry.

Sweetheart, *Lr 3.6.21 (Q 13.57),* a dog whom Lear imagines barking at him, or a formerly faithful dog that has turned against him. The comparison to his three daughters is obvious. Perhaps there is a suggestion in the name of Cordelia, 'heart.'

Sweno, *Mac 1.2.59,* king of the Norwegian forces arrayed against Duncan. A monument near Forres that has runic inscriptions and is locally thought to celebrate his defeat is known as 'Sweno's stone.' Vikings made several invasions of the British isles and Svein I ruled in England beginning in 1013. Svein, a Dane and son of Knut the Great, was king of the Norwegians from 1030 to 1035, when he was replaced by Magnus the Good.

Swineshead, *Jn 5.3.8, 16,* coastal village in Lincolnshire, site of a monastery where Sh. says that King John died. Sh. claims that the king was poisoned by one of the monks of Swineshead and died of the abbey's perfidious hospitality. In reality, John sought refuge at Swineshead after a difficult crossing of the Lincoln Washes and, while there, came down with a fever. He journeyed on to Newark Castle, where he died, probably of dysentery, on 18 October 1216.

Swithin, *Lr 3.4.113 (Q 11.109),* F1 'Swithold,' saint known as St. Withold, Swithun, or Swithin (d. 862), bishop of Winchester. During the church reforms of Dunstan and Ethelwold, he became patron saint of Winchester cathedral, supplanting Peter and Paul. His body was moved there in 971 and many miracles supposedly resulted, although he himself had said he was to be buried in a humble place. In the Reformation his special status at the cathedral was ended and his shrine destroyed. Most of the material on his pious life is legendary. One legend is that if it rains on his saint's day (July 15) it will rain for forty more. If it doesn't, the weather will be fair. The rhyme in *Lr* refers to the story that he always journeyed on foot, even when he accompanied Alfred to Rome in 856. He subdued demons and was supposed to protect against disaster. This chant was supposed to protect horses from nightmares, as they were believed to be caused by demons. Swithold is mentioned in *The Troublesome Raigne of John, King of England,* a likely source for Sh., though it may be a coincidence.

Switzers, *Ham 4.5.95,* Swiss guards. The Swiss were celebrated mercenaries of the Renaissance. They were very active in Italian wars and gained a military reputation which is still strong, despite Switzerland's neutrality in all wars since the early 19th c. The Pope still has Swiss guards who wear colorful uniforms designed by Michelangelo.

'Swounds, or 'Zounds,' oath meaning 'by God's (Christ's) wounds.' It is scattered throughout the plays. As it was thought indecent, it was often removed from early editions.

Sycorax, *Tmp,* mother of Caliban, a blue-eyed witch banished from Algiers, who imprisoned Ariel in a cloven pine. She never appears on stage and her description owes much to Ovid's portrayal of Medea in *Metamorphoses,* 7. The name is not found in any source. It most likely derives from the Greek words for sow (*sys*) and raven (*corax*), both animals associated with witchcraft. The name may derive from a description of the raven in *Batman uppon Bartholome his booke De proprietatibus rerum* (1582), an encyclopedia, which suggests the wording of Caliban's first speech at *1.2.324.* Heartbreaker (*psychorrhax*) has also been suggested, as well as the Greek words for fig (*sukon*) and spider (*rax*). Another possibility is from Arabic, *shokoreth* 'deceiver.' The Coraxi were a tribe in Colchis, a center for witchcraft, where Circe, the famous witch of mythology, was born. Pliny locates the Chalybeates (who have been proposed as the source for Caliban) as living near the Coraxi. Circe was exiled to an island in the Mediterranean (like S.) and her name derived from a bird (hawk, *kikros*), also. Oddly, there was a town in Sardinia called Alghero which in ancient times was Corax. If a particular island must be chosen as the site of S.'s exile and Prospero's magic, Lampedusa, between Malta and Tunisia, is a likely candidate. It was famous for storms, firewood, and caves, and was associated with the supernatural. Another critic suggests Pantelleria, which has a town named Seiaxghihir, a possible origin for Sycorax. More likely, as in Sh.'s Ardenne and Bohemia, the details of geography did not concern the playwright.

Sylla, *2H6 4.1.84,* Lucius Cornelius Sulla (138–78 BC), first man to lead a Roman army in an assault on the city of Rome. Sh.'s 'gobbets of thy mother's bleeding heart' is an elaborate reference to the violence that Sulla did to his motherland in the process of rooting out his enemies.

Syracusa, *Err 1.1.3, 36; 5.1.327, 330,* Syracuse. *5.1.322,* 'S. bay.' In the first act it fits the pentameter, and may have been used for that purpose. In the fifth, it fits only at *327.* This may be a small indication of the state of the ms. used to set F1. This variant would also approximate the Italian and Latin pronunciations. Evidence such as this has also been used to adduce the presence of multiple authorship.

Syracuse, *Err,* powerful ancient city on the southeastern coast of Sicily about 80 mi. south of Messina. Corinthian colonists founded the city about 733 BC on the island of Ortygia which extends to the southeast from the shore and eventually became a peninsula. The colony rapidly grew as a trade center and by the 6th c. was sending out its own colonies. Around 485 the ruling families were expelled by the lower classes; however, Gelon, tyrant of Gela, restored the aristocracy and took the city for himself. Under him its power and prosperity increased and he scored a great victory in 480 at Himera over the Carthaginians. His successor, Hiero I, was a celebrated patron of the arts, who had such poets at his court as Æschylus, Bacchylides, Epicharmus, Pindar, and Simonides of Ceos. In 467, the despot Thrasybulus was overthrown and the city entered a democratic phase during which it prospered as never before. Syracuse was dragged into the Peloponnesian war because of its conflict with Segesta. However, the ill-fated Athenian expedition against Syracuse in 415–414 urged by Alcibiades (and later betrayed by him) was easily defeated. In 405, a tyranny was restored by Dionysius the Elder, who increased the city's strength and influence and resisted the formidable Carthaginian threat. In 343, democracy was re-established, but Agathocles, a soldier of fortune, reintroduced despotism in 317, which continued without interruption under Hiero II, who was an ally of Rome. After his death in 215, a faction favoring the Carthaginians took charge. In 212 BC the Romans conquered the city after a two year siege, killing in the process the great thinker Archimedes (who had helped in engineering the defenses). Under Roman rule Syracuse slowly declined, though it remained the most important city of Sicily because of culture. The Saracens looted the city in 878 AD, and it lost all importance after that. Modern Siracusa is a small city of about 75,000, with little left of its glorious past.

Syracusian, 1) *Err 1.1.14 (pl.), 28, 5.1.286, 328,* (n.), a native of Syracuse.
2) *Err 1.1.17, 1.2.3, 5.1.125,* (adj.), of or pertaining to Syracuse.

Syria, ancient name for the district between Asia Minor and Egypt that extends from the shore of the Mediterranean to the Tigris River.
Ant 1.2.95, 3.1.18, 3.6.10, 16, 5.2.196. Per 1.19.

T

Taborer, *TNK,* see Timothy the Taborer.

Tail-Porter, see Mistress T.

Talbonites, *1H6,* men loyal to John Talbot and the English cause in France. The spelling reflects a Latinization of Talbot's name.

Talbot, Gilbert, 1) *R3 4.5.10,* (d. 1517), third son of John Talbot, first earl of Shrewsbury. In 1485, when Henry Tudor landed in Wales to make his bid for the throne, Talbot was guardian for his nephew, the heir to the earldom of Shrewsbury. Talbot and the men of Shrewsbury sided with Henry, and Sir Gilbert was assigned command of the right wing of the Lancastrian forces at the battle of Bosworth Field. He was well rewarded for his services with grants from estates forfeited by Richard's followers. Henry VII also made him a knight of the Garter and governor of Calais.

2) *H5 4.3.54,* (1383–1419), elder brother of John Talbot. Gilbert was made a knight of the Garter as a reward for his service in England's battles with Owain Glyndŵr of Wales. After Agincourt Henry V gave Gilbert a military command in Normandy, and he died during the seige of Rouen.

Talbot, John, *1H6,* (d. 1454), viscount Lisle, son of John Talbot, earl of Shrewsbury. He died at his father's side in the battle at Pas de Rozen. The earl, John Talbot senior, had two sons named John. The elder was his first son by his first marriage (to Maud Neville). This John died at the battle of Northampton fighting for Henry VI (1460). The younger John was the eldest son of the earl of Shrewsbury's second marriage (to Margaret Beauchamp). Estates inherited from his mother brought him the title 'viscount Lisle.'

Talbot, Lord, *1H6,* John (c. 1384–1453), earl of Shrewsbury, one of the most famous of Henry V's soldiers. He inherited the baronies of Talbot and Strange from his brother, and his first wife, Maud Neville, was heiress to Furnival. His second wife, Margaret Beauchamp, daughter of the earl of Warwick, held a share in the barony of Lisle. Talbot began his military career in Wales in 1404. He served as lieutenant for Ireland from 1414 to 1419. In 1419 he joined the English army on the continent. Talbot's penchant for daring exploits won him a large popular following at a time when England's declining fortunes of war made the nation desperate for heroes. Talbot was, however, more courageous than clever. In 1428 he advocated an ill-fated assault on the city of Orléans, and impetuousness may have contributed to his defeat at Patay in 1429. In 1433, after he was ransomed from his French captors, he threw himself back into the war and became England's most aggressive campaigner. When Normandy was lost, Talbot mounted an expedition to rescue what remained of England's possessions in southern France. He had some early successes, but on 17 July 1453, he stretched his resources to try to lift the French siege of Castillon. A gallant, but foolish, charge into the teeth of the French artillery squandered his men. He fell back to Pas de Rozan, a ford on the Dordogne, and made a last, futile stand. He and his son died side by side, and with them passed England's hold on Gascony. Talbot was one of the few dashing officers in Henry VI's army, and in him the people of England believed they saw the last flash of the spirit shown by Henry V's courageous soldiers.

1H6 1.1.128, 2.1.39, 79, 81: Talbot's name became England's battle cry.

Tale-Porter, see Mistress Tail-Porter.

Tallow, *1H4 2.5.112,* Prince Harry's jibe at Oldcastle. The prince also calls his fat friend 'brawn' and 'ox.' The abuse draws an extra dimension from the fact that it is delivered in a tavern in Eastcheap, the district where medieval London's butcher shops rendered tallow from animal carcasses.

Tamora, *Tit,* mythical queen of the Goths, empress of Rome, and Titus Andronicus' implacable enemy. Before her marriage to Saturninus, the Roman emperor, Tamora's people were at war with Rome. Titus Andronicus, the leader of the Roman forces, lost a son during the campaign, and he avenged his boy by sacrificing one of Tamora's sons. *Tit* tells the tale of Tamora's attempt to destroy Titus and his family—and Titus' efforts to expose and punish the villainy of the empress, her sons, and her wicked aide, Aaron. Sh.'s source for *Tit* is unknown, but an 18th c. chapbook preserves a later version of a tale that might have been familiar to him. The chapbook calls the queen Attava, not Tamora. The name Sh. used has several possible derivations. It might be an allusion to Tomyris, a queen of the Massagetæ who avenged the death of her son by killing the Persian emperor, Cyrus the Great. (Sh. mentions Tomyris in *1H6 2.3.6.*) Since Tamora's lover and henchman, Aaron, has a Jewish name, it is also possible that Tamora is intended to call the Hebrew scriptures to mind. In Genesis 38:6ff a widowed Tamar assumes the guise of a harlot in order to fulfill religious law and conceive sons for her dead husband. In 2 Samuel 13:1–32 and 1 Chronicles 3:9ff King David's daughter, Tamar, is raped by her half-brother Ammon. The event inaugurates a sequence of bloody acts of vengeance.

Tamworth, *R3 5.2.13,* town on the border between Warwickshire and Staffordshire about 110 mi. northwest of London. The earl of Richmond camped there before his confrontation with Richard III at Bosworth Field.

Tantalus, king of Phrygia, Lydia, or Sipylus (depending on the source). The son of Zeus, he alone among mortals was allowed to eat with the gods, but he abused his privilege. There are different versions how—stealing a dog or the ambrosia and nectar of the gods, or divulging Zeus' secrets. The most common version is that driven by hatred against the gods, he killed his son Pelops and served him to the gods to trick them into becoming cannibals. The gods were not deceived. They punished him by placing him in a pool which drained each time he stooped to satisfy his thirst. Above him, abundant fruit hung, but each time he reached for it a wind raised it out of his reach. Thus through eternity he was doomed to be 'tantalized.' The only mention of his pausing in his desperate, eternal reaching for food and drink is upon his hearing Orpheus play in the Underworld. All of his descendants, the house of Atreus, also suffered greatly. He is mentioned in Ovid's *Metamorphoses,* 4. In the Renaissance Tantalus was often accused of usury.

Ven 599. Luc 858.

Tapster, Master, *MM 2.1.203, 204,* Escalus' manner of addressing Pompey. A tapster was a bartender (one who taps kegs).

Tapster, Thomas, *MM 1.2.104, Add. 1.2.29,* Overdone's mocking name for Pompey.

Tarentum, *Ant 3.7.21,* city that Greek colonists founded in southern Italy on the western coast of the Apulian peninsula, the heel of Italy's 'boot.' The large gulf that dominates Italy's southern coast is named for Tarentum.

Tarpeian rock, *Cor 3.1.212, 266, 3.2.3, 3.3.107,* ledge of stone forming part of the Capitoline hill, the hill that marks the western end of the Roman forum. According to Roman legend, it owed its name and its use as a place of execution to a girl called Tarpeia. Sabine warriors used the gold jewelry they wore to persuade Tarpeia to open the gates of the Capitoline citadel to them. When they stormed into the fort, they crushed Tarpeia beneath their shields and buried her with the baubles she had coveted.

Tarquin, 1) Lucius Tarquinius Superbus, last king of Rome and a tyrant whose behavior prompted the Romans to abolish monarchy and establish a republic. He acquired the throne by murdering his father-in-law. He then recruited a loyal bodyguard and from a position of personal security freely terrorized his subjects. He ruled Rome with an iron hand and extended his power over the city's neighbors. He was besieging the town of Ardea when his son, Sextus (see below) raped Lucretia. She committed suicide, and the Romans drove Tarquin and his sons from the city in 510 BC. He fled to the Etruscan state of Cære and sought help from his allies. The Romans resolved never again to submit to a king and improvised a form of popular government. Tarquin's attacks put the infant Republic to a severe test, but Rome successfully defended its independence. Its deposed king lost all his sons in battles to regain the throne and spent a lonely old age as a pensioner at the court of Aristobulus of Cumæ.

Tit 3.1.297. JC 2.1.54. Cor 2.1.146, 2.2.88, 94.

2) Sextus Tarquinius, son of the last Roman king, Lucius Tarquinius Superbus. Sextus was a son to delight the heart of a father renowned for cruelty and guile. He and his father worked smoothly and deviously to build their tyrannical regime. Typical was the ploy by which they won control of the Latin city of Gabii. Tarquinius Superbus feigned a quarrel with his son. Sextus showed the people of Gabii wounds on his back that he claimed were the result of a whipping ordered by his father. They believed his claim that he was eager for vengeance, and they appointed him to lead them in an assault on Rome. Instead, Sextus killed the leaders of Gabii and surrendered the town to his father. The Tarquini were assaulting the city of Ardea when Sextus committed an atrocity that brought down the royal house. He raped Lucretia, the wife of one of his fellow officers. She denounced him and committed suicide. Sextus' abuse of a woman renowned for her virtue roused the people of Rome to drive out the Tarquins and abolish monarchy. A legend claims that Sextus fled from Rome to Gabii in the hope of retaining control of that city, but friends of citizens he had previously murdered seized the opportunity to kill him. Another story gives Sextus a different fate. He may have fallen in the battle at Lake Regillus where the deities Castor and Pollux helped Rome defeat a coalition of states that hoped to restore the Tarquins to power.

Tit 4.1.62. Luc. Mac 2.1.55, 'T.'s ravishing strides.' *Cym 2.2.12.*

3) Pl., *Cor 5.4.44,* Etruscan family that became the last royal dynasty of Rome. The people of Rome initially welcomed the Tarquins and chose them to be kings, but the tyrannical conduct of some members of the family created disillusionment and the people of Rome drove them out (see above).

Tarsus, wealthy city spanning the Cydnus river about 12 mi. from the sea in Cilicia, now part of Turkey. The city was sacred to the god Baal Tars and was thought to have been founded by Sennacherib, the Assyrian king, in 690 BC. It soon became a major market for trade among Anatolia, Syria, and Egypt. Weaving goat hair was its primary industry. It is mentioned for the first time in history by Xenophon in his *Anabasis* (4th c. BC), where it is a wealthy and populous city under Persian rule. In Alexander's time it was ruled by a Persian satrap and then by the Seleucids. In 66 BC it became capital of Roman Cilicia. Cleopatra was summoned there by Mark Antony who was using the city as headquarters for his Parthian campaign in 41 BC. Under the early emperors it was renowned for its learning, and Strabo, the ancient geographer, ranked it even above Athens and Alexandria. It was also the birthplace of St. Paul. The inhabitants were reputed to be vain and voluptuous. It declined after the Roman Empire decayed and by Sh.'s time was under the Turks. *Per:* like a number of things in the play, Tarsus appears in Plutarch's life of Demetrius. It is spelled 'Tharsus' in Q, and Sh. may have mixed this city with Thasos and thought both were the same. Tharsus is also used in Lawrence Twine's *Patterne of Painefull Adventures* (1594).

Tartar, 1) Tartarus, lowest region of the land of the dead, the dismal underworld of classical mythology. It resembles the Christian vision of Hell. Only the most heinous criminals were punished there. Uranus sent the Hecatonchires there; Zeus sent the Titans and the Typhon there, etc. Tartarus is also used by many authors as a Roman name for Hades, god of the Underworld, but not by Sh.

Err 4.2.32, 'T. limbo, worse than hell.' *H5 2.2.120. TN 2.5.199.*

2) Mongol, a person from Tartary. In the Renaissance, the Tartars were considered savage heathens who threatened Christianity and thus, civilization. The association of their kingdom with Hades was inevitable. Sweeping out of Siberia and central Asia, they overran parts of Asia and Europe in the 13th c. crushing Russia, Poland, Hungary, and the Christian knights who defied them, reaching almost to Vienna, as well as conquering Persia and the Middle East almost to Egypt, terrifying Islam as well. Gradually the Turkic and Mongol peoples of the invading forces merged and became known as the Tartars. They ruled and dominated Russia and Siberia for some time after and Tartary was the general name given their dominions. In the late 15th c. the Empire of the Golden Horde which had been founded by the grandson of Genghis Khan, Batu Khan, broke up into several khanates (Crimea, Kazan, Astrakhan, and Siberia) which were conquered by Czar Ivan IV and the Ottoman Turks. The last Tartar state, Crimea, was annexed by Russia in 1783.

MND 3.2.101, 'T.'s bow,' the Mongol bow of laminated wood and bone was one of the most potent weapons of the Middle Ages. Reverse bent against the natural curve, it could penetrate armor. What's more, Mongol warriors could fire twelve arrows a minute, aimed, while at full speed on horseback. *3.2.264,* 'tawny T.,' dark savage.

Rom 1.4.5, 'T.'s painted bow of lath': the T. bow was shorter than the English bow and therefore more resembled Cupid's (or the Romans') bow as we see it in ancient art.

MV 4.1.31 (pl). *MWW 4.5.18,* 'Bohemian T.,' see Bohemian. *AWW 4.4.7,* 'T.'s bosom.' *Mac 4.1.29.*

Taurus, 1) mountain range in southern Turkey. It parallels the Mediterranean for about 200 mi. The highest peak rises to 12,251 feet above sea level. *MND 3.2.142,* 'T.'s snow.'

2) 'the bull,' one of the signs of the zodiac and a constellation of the northern hemisphere between Aries and Orion.

Tit 4.3.69. TN 1.3.133, 134: according to astrology, each sign governs a particular area of the body. Both Sir Andrew and Sir Toby are wrong, Taurus governed neither legs and thighs nor heart and sides, but neck, throat, and voice.

3) *Ant,* see Statillius.

Te Deum, Latin hymn of thanksgiving. *H5 4.8.123. H8 4.1.94.*

Tearsheet, Doll, colorful name Sh. invents for the prostitute who keeps company with Falstaff and his friends. The name may have been suggested to Sh. by a passage in a Robin Hood play, but scholars are uncertain about the reading of the relevant text. Doll was a common name for prostitutes. Some editions of *H5* have Pistol report Doll's death (*H5 5.1.77*), but the context suggests that the name should be read 'Nell,' not 'Doll,' and that Pistol is referring to his wife, Nell Quickly, not Doll Tearsheet.

2H4. H5 2.1.75.

Tedious Brief Scene of Young Pyramus And His Love Thisbe: Very Tragical Mirth, A, *MND 5.1.56–57 (add. 39–40),* revised title of the play by the 'rude mechanicals' or a description of it. Its length is not unusual for the time, nor is its editorializing on the content. The contradiction is exaggerated from its earlier mention and delights the nobility. Sh. may be making fun of the full title of Thomas Preston's popular bombastic play, *A Lamentable Tragedie, Mixed Full of Plesant Mirth, containing the Life of Cambises, King of Percia* (1569).

Telamon, *Ant 4.14.2,* Ajax 'Telamoniades' (i.e., 'son of Telamon'), reference to a son by his father's name. See Ajax.

Tellus, Roman earth-goddess also known as Terra (Gr. Gæa or Gaia), born from Chaos, wife of Uranus, and mother of numerous beings including Oceanus, the Cyclops, and the Titans.

Ham 3.2.149, 'T.' orbèd ground.' *Per 15.65.*

Temple Hall, *1H4 3.3.201,* refectory of the New Temple on Fleet Street. See Temple.

Temple, The, *1H6 2.4.3, 125, 2.5.19,* complex of buildings in London where lawyers congregated. Young Englishmen who wished to acquire a knowledge of the law studied as apprentices with members of four guilds of lawyers that in the early 14th c. were granted the legal right to argue cases in English courts. Lawyers and their students took over a number of London inns (the 'inns of court'), but some occupied 'the Temple,' a facility that had been constructed as headquarters for the order of Knights Templar. The Templars were a fraternity of crusading monks whose organization was suppressed by the papacy in 1313. The crown confiscated the Templars' property and rented their London buildings to a group of lawyers. The part of the Temple precinct that lay on the bank of the Thames inside the city wall was known as the Inner Temple. The idea that plaintiffs lodge pleas before the 'bar' recalls the fact that the Temple was located near one of the 'bars' or gates of the city of London.

Ten Commandments, F1 'Commandements' (possibly to indicate four syllables), the prohibitions Moses brought down from Mount Sinai. Two versions of them, only slightly different, appear in the Bible at Exodus 20:1–17 and Deuteronomy 5:6–21. They were written on two tablets by God's finger according to Exod. 31:18, then remade by God in the same manner (Exod. 34:4) after Moses shattered them in anger at the Hebrews' worship of the Golden Calf. They were afterward kept in the Ark of the Covenant, which one recent journalist very speculatively suggests was ultimately removed to Ethiopia. *2H6 1.3.145,* a joke for the ten fingers. *MM 1.2.8.*

Tenantius, *Cym 1.1.31,* youngest son of king Lud, brother to Androgeus (and, in some versions, Cassibelan), father of Cymbeline. In Spenser's *Færie Queene,* Lud dies before his son's minority, and Cassibelan, Lud's brother, takes the throne. Androgeus later betrays Cassibelan to the Romans, and Tenantius succeeds Cassibelan. Holinshed usually calls him Theomantius, and he is father to Kymberline or Cimbeline. *5.5.167,* 'T.'s right,' his claim to the throne.

Tenedos, *Tro pro. 11,* small island of about 15 sq. mi. in the north Ægean, opposite the Troad and southwest of Troy. The Greeks used it as a staging area for their attack upon the city. Xerxes also headquartered his fleet there in his invasion of Greece in the 5th c. BC.

Tereus, 1) son of the god Mars and king of the Thracians. Pandion, king of Athens, concluded a military alliance with Tereus by giving him his daughter Procne in marriage. After a few years Tereus told Pandion that Procne had died, and he demanded the hand of her sister, Philomela. When Philomela learned that Procne was still alive, Tereus cut out her tongue to prevent her from revealing what she knew. She managed to explain what was happening to Procne by weaving a message into a cloth. Procne took savage revenge by killing her son and preparing his flesh as a feast for his father. The sisters escaped Tereus' wrath by beseeching the gods to change them into birds.

Luc 1134. Tit 2.4.26, 41, 4.1.48.

2) *Cym 2.2.45,* 'the tale of T.': Innogen may be reading any number of sources for the tale including Ovid's *Metamorphoses,* 6.420 ff., John Gower's *Confessio Amantis,* 5, and George Pettie's *A Petite Palace of Pettie His Pleasure* (1576) in which it is the second story.

Termagant, name given by the Crusaders and in romances to the god of the Saracens. In Italian romances he was called *Trivigante* and in French *Tervagant.* Presumably it is based upon some word the Saracens used, but we have no way of knowing. *Ramazan* has been offered, but with little certainty. As T. was introduced into morality plays, he wore long, flowing robes and the quality of the actor's performance was measured by how violently and loudly he could rant. Later, because of the clothing, the name survived for a shrewish woman.

1H4 5.4.112. Ham 3.2.14.

Tewkesbury, town in Gloucestershire 125 mi. west of London. It was the site of the battle on 4 May 1471, at which Edward IV killed Henry VI's son and captured his wife, Margaret. The earl of Warwick, their chief ally, had previously gone down to death and defeat at the battle of Barnet. Tewkesbury doomed Henry VI. He had survived for years as Edward's prisoner, but the death of his heir extinguished his line and meant that the Yorkist king no longer had any reason to allow him to live. Apart from its historical significance, Tewkesbury was apparently known to Sh.'s audience for a kind of mustard it marketed.

3H6 5.3.19. R3 1.2.228, 1.3.120, 1.4.56, 2.1.112, 5.5.74. 2H4 2.4.243.

Thaisa, *Per,* daughter of Simonides, wife of Pericles, mother of Marina. She is restored to her husband in a manner much like Hermione is in *WT.* Thaisa is one of many of Sh.s character names that appears in John Gower's *Confessio Amantis* (1390), although she corresponds to Marina in that play, not Thaisa. She is called Lucina in Lawrence Twine's *Patterne of Painefull Adventures* (1594). See Pericles.

Thaliart, *Per,* assassin told by Antiochus to kill Pericles. He is called 'Taliarcus' in Lawrence Twine's *Patterne of Painefull Adventures* (1594).

Thames, largest river in England. It flows eastward 170 mi. from the Cotswold hills in Gloucester past Oxford, Windsor, and London to the North Sea, where it is over 5 mi. wide. The source of its name is lost in antiquity. The Romans called it *Tamesis,* presumably from some local name. From Oxford and upstream it is often called Isis, a shortening of the Latin name.

2H6 4.7.156. MWW 3.3.14, 3.5.5, 19, 111, 118: the river winds east past Windsor and Eton, then turns southeast direction. It is about 600 feet wide in this area. *H5 4.1.115.*

Thasos, *JC 5.3.103,* island in the northern Ægean not far from the coast of Thrace and the battle field at Philippi where Mark Antony and Octavius triumphed over Cæsar's assassins in 42 BC.

Theban, *Lr 3.4.147 (Q 11.144),* person from Thebes—in this context, a philosopher. Though Thebes was a major city in ancient times, it was not particularly famous as a center of philosophy. The main claimant in this regard would be a certain Philolaus (late 5th c. BC), a Pythagorean who took refuge in Thebes and taught Simmias and Cebes, who were present at Socrates' death. He was apparently the first to argue that the earth moved around the sun. It is unlikely Sh. has anyone particular in mind, however, and he may be using 'Theban' as a synonym for 'ancient Greek.' There is no reason to assume that the reference is to the ancient Egyptian city of Thebes.

2) (adj.) *TNK 2.2.46,* 'T. hounds,' Palamon laments that death will mean no more hunting. Compared to Arcite's lament for no wife or children, it may be taken as a reflection of character, though inconsistant with Palamon's worship of Venus and Arcite's of Mars.

Thebes, city of ancient Greece, located in Boeotia north of Mount Kithairon. In legend it was founded by Cadmus. It was the location for the myths of Oedipus, Antigone, and Hercules, and home of the poet Pindar. A bitter enemy of Athens, it sided with Xerxes in the Persian War after a contingent of Thebans died with the Spartans at Thermopylæ, and, initially, with Sparta in the Peloponnesian War. The city broke the Spartan hold on the peninsula in 371 BC and enjoyed a short period of domination until 362, when the city was defeated by Philip II of Macedon. After a revolt against his son Alexander, it was leveled and the inhabitants sold into slavery. Though rebuilt in 315 BC, it quickly declined to village size and was so described by Strabo. The small town of Thebai now occupies the site.

MND 5.1.51 (add. 34), reference to Theseus' conquest of the city when he hears of Creon's not allowing the burial of the seven who tried to depose him. *TNK,* home of Palamon and Arcite.

Thersites, ugliest and most vicious-mouthed of the Greek warriors attacking Troy. He was lame and deformed. In the *Iliad,* 2, he is beaten by Ulysses for saying Agamemnon was lengthening the war for his own purposes. In another legend, when he ridiculed Achilles' grief over the fallen Amazon queen, Penthesilea, Achilles struck him with his fist and killed him.

Tro: Sh. uses Thersites as a kind of Caliban, deformed and subhuman, but his railings point up the corruption of the world of the Trojan conflict. Some critics seem willing to accept him as a humorous voice of satiric insight, but his viciousness works against this interpretation. He is no 'wise fool,' like Lear's jester. He is as sick as the society he inveighs against, a coward and a weasel who more than deserves the beating Ajax gives him. Although Sh.'s primary source for his play was William Caxton's *Recuyell of the Historyes of Troy* (1474), T. is not a character in it. *Tro 2.1.36,* 'Mistress T.' Ajax' insult. *Cym 4.2.253,* 'T.'s' body.'

Theseus, mythological king of Athens, greatest hero of Attica, son of Ægeus and Æthra. His name derives from Gr. *tithanai* and means 'orderer' or 'settler' presumably because of his role in establishing the independent Athenian city-state. According to myth, Ægeus placed his sword and sandals under a stone and told his wife not to send Theseus to him until the boy was strong enough to get them. Reared at Troezen by Æthra's father Pittheus, Theseus rolled back the stone and had a series of adventures upon returning to Athens, defeating Cercyon, Periphetes, Procrustes, Sciron, Sinis, and the Crommyonian sow. When he arrived in Athens, Medea, wife of Ægeus, tried to poison him. She was discovered, however, and fled to Asia. The city was under the power of King Minos of Crete who exacted a tribute of young men and women who would be sent into the Labyrinth to be consumed by the Minotaur. Theseus volunteered to face the monster, and with the help of a thread supplied by Ariadne, Minos' daughter, who had fallen in love with him, he was able to go into the maze, kill the Minotaur, and find his way out again. He married Ariadne, but deserted her and sailed home. He was supposed to fly white sails on his ship should the expedition succeed, but he forgot, and Ægeus, seeing the black sails, committed suicide.

As king, Theseus gathered the residents of Attica into the city, coined money, and initiated a number of religious festivals. He voyaged into the Black Sea on an expedition against the Amazons, who had not yet recovered from Hercules' attack. He seized Antiope (Melanippe, or Hippolyta) and took her with him. The Amazons retaliated by attacking Attica. They succeeded in entering Athens, but he ultimately defeated them. At age fifty, he also attempted to carry off the very young Helen, but was forced to give her back. After Antiope died, he married Phædra. She developed a passion for her stepson Hippolytus (or Demophon), but the young man refused her advances. She killed herself and left a note accusing Hippolytus. Theseus called down Poseidon's wrath and Hippolytus' chariot went over a cliff after the horses were frightened by a sea monster. He became friends with Pirithous, king of the Lapiths, and participated with them in the war against the Centaurs. He accompanied his friend into the Underworld to help Pirithous in his designs on Persephone (L. Proserpina), wife of Hades. They were both caught and chained to a rock on the palace gate, where they remained until Hercules freed Theseus (or begged his release). Pirithous was not freed. In Plutarch, Pirithous is said to have been torn to pieces by dogs.

Upon Theseus' return to Athens, he could not recover his power because of vicious infighting. He cursed Athens and retired to Scyros, where he had lands. There he either fell to his death while strolling along the cliffs on the shore or was pushed by king Lycomedes.

The bones were returned to Athens and his burial place became a place of sanctuary for those persecuted by people in power. At the battle of Marathon, some of the Athenians saw his ghost leading them into battle. His story is told in numerous sources. Plutarch devotes a life to him and compares him with Romulus. He appears several times in Ovid's *Metamorphoses,* also. Sh. knew both of these authors extremely well.

TGV 4.4.165, 'T.'s perjury,' reference to his desertion of Ariadne. *MND:* T. is in the process of wedding Hippolyta. He is depicted as the wise duke of Athens, having the qualities of Vincentio of *MM* and the duke in *MV.* He sympathizes with Hermia, for example, and tries to use his influence to prevent tragedy, but he will not arbitrarily reverse the process of law. He is generous, graciously receiving the inept homage of the 'rude mechanicals' and their play—something for which Elizabeth I was renowned. He is also quite responsive to his fiancée. Altogether, he is the embodiment of the chivalrous ruler.

Per 9.73, 'straggling T.,' a reference to young Theseus' return to Athens from Troezen. *TNK:* as in *MND,* T. is in the process of marrying Hippolyta. This may be no coincidence as the sections dealing with T. are usually thought to be parts of the play written by Sh. instead of his collaborator John Fletcher. The situation is borrowed directly from Chaucer's *Knyghtes Tale.* T. is depicted as the quintessential man of honor. He is similarly portrayed in *The Compleynt of feire Anelida and fals Arcite.*

Thessalian bulls, *MND 4.1.121,* breed of bull with a pendulous flap of skin (dewlap) at the neck.

Thessaly, largest plain in the northern half of ancient Greece and a state that lay directly to the south of Macedon. *MND 4.1.125:* Sh. seems to have in mind the Calydonian boar hunt in which Atalanta, Theseus, Meleager, Pirithous, and others participated. The hunt caused a quarrel and a war between the Calydonians and the Curetes. Sh. probably knew the tale from Ovid's *Metamorphoses,* 8. *Ant 4.14.2:* 'boar of T.' See Althæa.

Thetis, daughter of Nereus and Doris, sister of the Nereids, wife of Peleus, and mother of Achilles. As a sea-goddess, she lived under the ocean. She appears in a number of myths. When the lame Hephæstus (Vulcan) was rejected by his mother Hera (Juno), she and Eurynome cared for him for nine years under the sea. Ovid (*Metamorphoses,* 11) and many other ancient authors tell how Zeus was enamored of her, but Proteus (or Prometheus) prophesied that the son of Thetis would be greater than the father, so Zeus ordered Peleus, son of Æacus, to win her. On first encounter, he seized her but she assumed a variety of shapes and escaped. Finally, however, he trapped her with the assistance of Proteus. Eris, goddess of discord, was not invited to the wedding. In anger, she rolled a golden apple into the festivities. On it was inscribed 'To the fairest.' Hera, Aphrodite, and Athena each claimed it and the subsequent controversy caused the judgment of Paris and eventually the Trojan War. She attempted to confer invulnerability on her son Achilles by dipping him in the river Styx. Because she held him by the ankle, however, his heel was covered by her hand and it remained his single spot of weakness. As the Trojan War began to develop, she concealed Achilles disguised as a girl at the court of King Lycomedes of Scyros. Odysseus, however, discovered him there. In the dispute between Agamemnon and Achilles which begins the *Iliad* Thetis intercedes with Zeus on behalf of her son to give temporary success on the battlefield to the Trojans. She also procured from Hephæstus the armor of Achilles so that he could face Hector. After Achilles abused the body, Zeus called on her to persuade her son to return it to Priam, Hector's father. Often Thetis is confused by Sh. with Tethys, the Titan goddess of the sea, and sister/wife of Oceanus.

Tro 1.3.38, 'gentle T.,' the sea. *1.3.212, 3.3.88,* 'T.'s son,' Achilles. *Ant 3.7.60. Per, Add'l from Q, l. 6,* the sea. *l. 8,* 'T.'s birth-child,' Marina.

Thidias, *Ant,* Thyrsus, a freedman whom Octavius sent to persuade Egypt's queen, Cleopatra, to surrender to Rome. Plutarch ('Antony' 73.1–3) says that the long, private conversations Thidias held with Cleopatra aroused Mark Antony's jealousy. Antony ordered Thidias to be whipped and sent him back to Octavius with an insulting message.

Thisbe, *MV 5.1.7,* the beloved of Pyramus (q.v.)

Thoas, *Tro 5.5.12,* Greek warrior and king of Ætolia. He contributed 40 ships to the Trojan War and was among those concealed in the Trojan horse. Several other 'Thoas' appear in mythology—three are mentioned in the *Iliad* including a Trojan—but Agamemnon must mean this one. He is frequently mentioned in William Caxton's *Recuyell of the Historyes of Troy* (1474), Sh.'s primary source. Chaucer also mentions him in *The Legende of Good Women* and 'Toas' in *Troilus and Criseyda.*

Thomas, 1) *R2 2.1.281,* (1381–1415), earl of Arundel, son of Richard, earl of Arundel, the 'lord appellant' whom Richard II executed in 1397. After Thomas' father's death, he fled abroad to the protection of his uncle, Thomas, the archbishop of Canterbury. Both Arundels joined Henry (IV) Bolingbroke in Paris where he lived after Richard banished him from England in 1398. In 1399 they joined the expedition that Henry raised to force Richard from the throne. Henry IV trusted Arundel and relied on his help to maintain discipline among the English barons. Henry's son, Henry V, made Arundel treasurer of England and warden of the Cinque Ports. When Henry invaded France in 1415, Arundel helped capture Harfleur. An attack of dysentery, which sent him home to die, prevented him from taking part in Henry's famous battle at Agincourt.

2) *R2 1.2.16,* see Gloucester, Duke of, Thomas of Woodstock.

Thomas, duke of Clarence, *2H4,* (1388–1421), Henry IV's second son. Thomas was only 12 years old when his father appointed him lieutenant for Ireland. That post and later assignments in Wales and with the navy prepared him for a busy military career that earned him a reputation as a good soldier. When Henry IV fell sick near the end of his reign, a quarrel between the king and his eldest son Prince Harry briefly thrust Thomas into the center of things. The prince wanted to attack France and bring on a war of which Henry disapproved. The king was too weak to put up much resistance, and Harry swayed the royal council to his point of view. Thomas kept his distance from Harry's faction, because it included the king's Beaufort relatives who were contesting Thomas' rights to some property. Henry IV ultimately asserted himself, dismissed Prince Harry and the Beauforts, and appointed Thomas to his council. Henry commissioned Thomas to lead an army to the continent to help France's Orléanist party against its Burgundian enemies. The campaign was cut short by the king's death, and as soon as Prince Harry (Henry V) ascended the throne, it was called off. Thomas acquiesced gracefully to the change in England's foreign policy, and Henry bore his brother no grudge. Thomas participated in the seige of Harfleur that began the war with France of which Henry had dreamed. But having been ordered to take the wounded home to England, he missed the famous battle at Agincourt. He was with his brother when the English entered Paris in 1420, and thereafter France was entrusted to his care whenever Henry was in England. Thomas died in battle shortly before Henry's premature death from disease in 1422.

Thomas, Friar, *MM,* see Peter.

Thomas, Lord Mowbray, *2H4,* (1386–1405), hereditary Earl Marshal of England and duke of Nottingham. Mowbray was the elder son of the Thomas Mowbray, duke of Norfolk, whom Richard II banished from England for quarrelling with Henry (IV) Bolingbroke (1398). Mowbray's father died in exile in 1399 while Mowbray was still a page assigned to the court of Richard's queen, Isabella of Valois. After Henry IV became king, Mowbray continued his father's feud by conspiring to unseat the man who had forced Richard from the throne. In 1405 he, Archbishop Scrope of York, and the earl of Northumberland, tried to spark a rebellion. The venture failed when Scrope allowed himself to be persuaded that they had frightened the king into coming to terms. When the archbishop lay down his arms, Henry ignored the promises he had made and arrested the rebels. Scrope and the 19-year-old Lord Mowbray were promptly executed.

Thomas of Woodstock, *2H6 2.2.16,* (1355–1397), duke of Gloucester, Edward III's youngest surviving son. He and John of Gaunt, the eldest of the royal siblings after the death of the Black Prince, were driven into an uneasy alliance by the autocratic behavior of their nephew, Richard II. Gloucester was a leader among the 'Lords Appellant,' a coalition of nobles that worked together to curtail the power of the king. Richard deeply resented the Lords' assault on his prerogatives—particularly when the situation deteriorated to the point where they threatened him with deposition. Fortunately for Richard, English barons were unable to maintain a united front for very long. When the Lords began to squabble among themselves, Richard gained the upper hand and avenged himself on his enemies. In 1397 Richard arrested his uncle Gloucester and imprisoned him in Calais. The first parliament held by Richard's successor, Henry IV, was informed that Gloucester had been murdered by jailers acting on Richard's orders.

Thomas Tapster, see Tapster.

'Thou Canst Not Hit It,' *LLL 4.1.124–127,* song sung by Rosalind and Boyet. Versions of this song can be found in several contemporary lute books.

Thrace, *3H6 4.2.21,* district bordering the northern rim of the Ægean Sea. At the start of the classical period in Greek history, it was peopled by nomadic tribes famous for their horses. In Homer's *Iliad* Rhesus of Thrace fights for the Trojans and is killed in a night raid organized by Diomedes and Odysseus.

Thracian, (adj.) of or pertaining to Thrace. *Tit 1.1.138,* 'T. tyrant,' Polymestor, king of Chersonesus in Thrace. According to Greek legend, Priam, king of Troy, entrusted his son Polydorus and a great treasure to Polymestor at the start of the Trojan war. Polymestor confiscated the treasure, slew the boy, and threw his body into the sea. The corpse washed ashore and was recognized by Polydorus' mother, Hecuba. Hecuba avenged her son by murdering Polymestor's children and blinding him.

MND 5.1.49 (add. 32), 'T. singer,' Orpheus. His death and mutilation at the hands of the Bacchantes is described in Ovid's *Metamorphoses,* 11.

Thrasonical, (adj.) in the manner of Thraso, a character in the Roman playwright Terence's *Eunuchus* (161 BC), and thus, bombastic and arrogant. Thraso developed into the *commedia dell'arte* character Thrasio.

LLL 5.1.12, describing Don Adriano de Armado. *AYLI 5.2.30,* 'Cæsar's t. brag': *Veni, vidi, vici.*

Threepile, Master, *MM 4.3.9,* 'the mercer,' mocking name for one of the impoverished criminals Pompey knows. As prisoners paid for their own food, many were forced to beg passers by. Threepile is a cloth with a triple nap.

Thrice-three Muses Mourning for the Death Of Learning, Late Deceased in Beggary, The, *MND 5.1.52–53 (add't'l ll. 35–36),* play offered for the nuptial celebrations of Theseus and Hippolyta. It is refused as unsuitable satire. This title has been asserted to relate to the death of Robert Greene in abject poverty on September 2, 1592, or, possibly, to Edmund Spenser's poem of 1591, *The Teares of the Muses.* Some think that the rewriting of the play may set it as late as January 1599, when Spenser died. This is not necessarily a topical allusion, however. Satires about the failure of society to appreciate genius were common (and still are), frequently written by authors who feel they have been unjustly ignored.

Thump, Peter, *2H6,* all-too-appropriate name that Sh. invents for an armorer's apprentice who was anonymous in his source (Hall, 207–208). The apprentice accused his master of committing treason by saying that York and not Henry VI should be king of England. Sh. has him vindicate his charge in a trial by combat.

Thurio, *TGV,* cowardly suitor of Silvia. He is initially the duke's choice for his daughter, but when he shows his faintheartedness at the prospect of fighting Valentine, the duke offers her to Valentine. Thurio's character owes much to the style of Italian comedy which seems to have been a model for the play and particularly to the *miles gloriosus,* the braggart soldier character type originally invented by Terence. The name may have been suggested by Curio in John Lyly's *Euphues* and his character has some similarities to Sir Tophas in Lyly's *Endimion.* Thyreus in North's Plutarch is a possibility, or Thurii, mentioned in Plutarch's 'Timoleon.'

Thursday, fifth day of the week, named for the Norse god Thor, who, like the Roman Jove or Jupiter and the Greek Zeus, commanded the lightning bolt. *Rom:* the planned wedding day for Juliet and Paris. *1H4 2.5.65, 3.2.174. 2H4 2.4.277.*

Tib, name for a common woman of low character. *AWW 2.2.21,* 'Tib's rush,' a ring made of twisted rush for a mock marriage. *Per 19.191.*

Tiber, (It. *Tevere*) river on whose southern bank the city of Rome was founded. It begins in the Apennines and flows south and southwest until it empties into the Tyrrhenian sea.

JC 1.1.45, 58, 1.2.103, 116, 3.2.242. Ant 1.1.35. Cor 2.1.48, 3.1.261.

Tiberio, *Rom 1.5.128,* man whose son and heir is pointed out by Juliet's nurse at Capulet's feast. Probably the name was suggested by the emperor Tiberius.

Tiffin, *Mac 4.1.46,* spirit called forth by the witches in a song not appearing in F1, but which appears in Thomas Middleton's play *The Witch* (c. 1609, but not printed until the 18th c.). William Davenant's version of *Mac* (printed 1674) contains the song and it has been argued that he may have had access to an earlier text. A 'tiffin' is a small drink in some later uses, but it is not clear that it was so used in Middleton's time. The name was taken from Reginald Scot's *Discoverie of Witchcraft* (1584).

Tiger, 1) *Err 3.1.96,* an inn.

2), *TN 5.1.58,* ship that Antonio seized. It was a common name at the time (see below).

3) *Mac 1.3.6,* a ship. Sh. seems to have borrowed the name from Hakluyt's *Voyages,* which has an account of a ship called the Tiger in 1583 sailing to Tripoli, where the crew continued to Aleppo by caravan; or Sh. may well have known of the voyage himself, firsthand from the sailors.

Tike, Sir, *MWW 4.5.51.* F1 reads 'I Sir: like who more bold' with the apparent meaning 'who could be more bold?' or 'bold as the boldest.' However, at *H5 2.1.28,* Pistol calls Nim a 'Base Tyke,' which seems to parallel the *MWW* quarto's 'I tike': 'Ay, tyke.' 'Tyke' could mean 'tick,' the parasitic arachnid, or, more likely, an ill-bred dog, the word deriving from Old Norse *tik,* a bitch, or Old Welsh *taiawc,* a churl or inferior.

Timandra, *Tim,* one of Alcibiades' camp followers. Timon gives her some of his treasure. She is mentioned as Alcibiades' mistress in Plutarch's biography.

Timbria, *Tro pro. 16,* one of the six gates of Troy. These are not in the *Iliad* which appears to give Troy only one double gate, though a city near Troy is named Thymbra. In William Caxton's *Recuyell of the Historyes of Troye,* 3 (c. 1474), the first English printed book and Sh.'s major source for the play, the six gates are listed, Timbria being the second.

Time, 1) the personification of time, Father Time. *Err 2.2.70–111,* humor based on Time's baldness ('Father T.' *2.2.70*), see below. *Jn 3.1.250. R2 2.1.195.*

Per 15.47 'winged T.' *AYLI 4.1.189–90. Tro 3.3.159, 4.5.41, 4.7.108. TNK 2.2.104,* 'old T.'

2) *WT,* chorus opening act 4. He provides a transition for a sixteen-year gap in the action, but thematically he relates to the power of time in overcoming injustice and suffering. Despite his single speech, his importance in Sh.'s mind could be indicated by the prominence in the title of Sh.'s source, Robert Greene's *Pandosto, or the Triumph of Time* (1588; rptd. 1607 as *Dorastus and Fawnia*). How Time was represented on stage may be assumed from emblems of the period or drawing books which describe Time as winged, old, bald, and carrying an hourglass and a scythe, little different from how he is usually represented now.

Timon, notorious misanthrope of ancient Athens about the time of the Peloponnesian War. He was the son of Echecratides and born in the 5th c. BC in a district northeast of the Acropolis called the Collytos. He became a hermit and refused to see anyone except Alcibiades, with whom he was very affectionate. Asked why, he answered that he knew Alcibiades would one day do infinite mischief to the Athenians. Timon first came to literature in the comedies of Aristophanes (c. 445–c.385 BC), his contemporary. He is referred to in *The Birds* and in *Lysistrata.* He was also a character in Phrynichus' *Monotropos* (*The Hermit*) in the 5th c. and in a play by Antiphanes in the 4th. A Neanthes of Cyzicus (3rd c.) compiled a biography and many other poets and writers mentioned him, including Plato (so Plutarch says), Pausanias, and the geographer Strabo. Plutarch in his life of Mark Antony tells of Timon's relationship with Alcibiades (this is also mentioned in his life of Alcibiades) and with Apemantus. Celebrating the feast of the dead with him, Apemantus said what a grand party the two of them were having. Timon responded 'It would be, if you were away.' Plutarch also tells how Timon, before cutting down a fig tree, offered it to whoever in Athens might wish to hang themselves. After his burial at Halæ, the sea wore away the shore and surrounded his tomb, thus preventing anyone from coming near. Plutarch records two epitaphs for Timon and claims that much more could be said about the man, but never writes more.

Some of Plutarch's lines are closely mirrored in *Tim.* Sh.'s Timon is believed by some critics to have been a 'dry run' for King Lear which was abandoned because the character lacked sufficient depth. The situations a hermit might get into lack dramatic possibility, and if the play was abandoned, as its manuscript might indicate, this might be a likely cause. In any case, a connection to Lear seems rather tenuous. Given the nature of the play as it exists, it is more a play of ideas, almost an allegory, of the sort favored by sophisticated nobility. Timon is, therefore, less a human character than a representative of a conception. The play may not have been intended to be included in F1 because of its incomplete state and because of the possibility that Thomas Middleton wrote large parts of it. It seems to have been included, however, because of some problem in using *Tro.*

LLL 4.3.168, 'critic T.,' this line indicates that Sh. was familiar with the story of Timon very early in his career. An anonymous play on Timon was written in the 1580s. It has notable resemblances to Sh.'s, making it a likely source. *Tim.*

Timothy the Taborer, *TNK,* country man participating in the morris performed for Theseus. A tabor is a small drum, and therefore easy to carry in the dance. The player usually accompanied himself with a fife, also, and is so depicted in contemporary art such as the Betley stained glass window in the Victoria and Albert

Museum in London. 'Tabor' is an Old Fr. word which derives from Arabic, making it especially appropriate to the morris, 'Moorish,' dance.

Tirrel, James, *R3,* see Tyrrell, Sir James.

Tisick, Master, *2H4 2.4.83,* deputy before whom Nell Quickly was arraigned for keeping a disorderly public house. His name is a comic imitation of the sound of an asthmatic wheeze.

Titan, Helios, god of the sun, son of Hyperion and Theia, father of Circe and King Aietes. He rode across the sky daily in his chariot drawn by four horses. The Colossus of Rhodes was dedicated to him. More correctly, Helios is the son of a Titan, but Sh. does not make the distinction. He never uses the term to mean anything other than the sun. In Greek mythology the Titans were the generation of gods, including Hyperion, removed from power in a great war with the Olympian gods. When Zeus took over the world, he confined them to the depths of Hades, but some of their descendants survived in the terrestrial realm.

Tit 2.4.31. Ven 177. Rom 2.2.4, 'T.'s fiery wheels,' the sun, from Helios' chariot. In Arthur Brooke's *Tragicall Historye of Romeus and Juliet* (1562), Sh.'s source, the image of Titan's steeds loitering is used to convey Romeus' feeling that time passed slowly in exile in Mantua (l. 1756). *1H4 2.5.119, 120. Cym 3.4.164,* 'common-kissing Titan,' the sun (which comes into contact with everyone).

Titania, *MND,* queen of the fairies. She argues with her husband Oberon over the possession of an Indian boy, the son of a deceased friend. Later, misled by a love potion, she dotes on Bottom, who has been translated into an ass. She gives the Indian boy to Oberon, and he releases her from the spell. Titania is an epithet of the goddess Diana which relates her to the Titans. Ovid uses the name at *Metamorphoses* 3.173, for Diana, but Arthur Golding did not in the translation on which Sh. so commonly relied. This could mean that Sh. read Ovid's original Latin text. Ovid also uses Titania for Latona, Circe, Pyrrha, and Tethys.

Titinius, *JC,* (d. 42 BC), soldier loyal to Cæsar's assassins, Cassius and Brutus. During the battle of Philippi, Plutarch says ('Brutus' 43.4–7) that Cassius sent Titinius to reconnoiter a cavalry unit that Cassius thought was pursuing him. Cassius did not realize that the soldiers were friendly and were bringing news of a victory won by his colleague Brutus. Cassius witnessed the boisterous greeting the soldiers gave Titinius, interpreted it as an attack, assumed all was lost, and retreated to his tent to commit suicide. Titinius returned to camp too late to prevent Cassius' death. He blamed himself for the tragedy and took his own life.

Titty, *Mac 4.1.46,* spirit called forth by the witches in a song not appearing in F1, but which appears in Thomas Middleton's play *The Witch* (c. 1609, but not printed until the 18th c.). William Davenant's version of *Mac* (printed 1674), contains the song and it has been argued that he may have had access to an earlier text. 'Titty' is a Scottish term of affection for 'little sister.' Possibly 'Sister T.,' is meant (as in Davenant's version) or it is supposed to be a repetition of T., but either of these alternatives ignores Hecate's use of the names separately in *The Witch 1.2.1 ff.* The name was taken from Reginald Scot's *Discoverie of Witchcraft* (1584).

Titus, 1) *Tit,* see Titus Andronicus.

2) *TN 5.1.59,* a nephew of Orsino's. He lost his leg in a sea battle with Antonio. He is otherwise unmentioned.

3) *Tim 3.4,* a creditor of Timon's.

Titus Andronicus, *Tit,* Roman general who engages in a bloody feud with his emperor's wife. Titus wins a victory over the Goths and avenges the death in battle of one of his sons by sacrificing a son of Tamora, queen of the Goths. Tamora weds the Roman emperor, Saturninus, and she and her lover, Aaron, plot a gruesome revenge on Titus. They bring about the deaths of two more of Titus' sons, the rape and mutilation of his daughter, and his own self-mutilation. In the end Titus destroys Tamora, her sons, and Aaron. (Titus also kills his much abused daughter.) The emperor, Saturninus, kills Titus, and is destroyed and succeeded by yet another of Titus' sons. There is no historical prototype for Sh.'s Titus, and the sources from which Sh. drew the plot for *Tit* are uncertain. An 18th c. chapbook in the collection of the Folger Library contains a later version of a tale that might have been known to Sh., and Sh. probably derived some of the incidents in the play from classical mythology (e.g., the tale of Philomela and Procne, Ovid's *Metamorphoses,* 6).

Titus Lartius, *Cor,* see Lartius, Titus.

Toby, Sir, *TN,* see Belch, Sir Toby.

Toledo, Archbishopric of, Spanish diocese seated in Toledo, a town 40 mi. southwest of Madrid. For much of the medieval period it was the center of Spanish politics and culture. Toledo's cathedral was the seat of the primate of Spain. The city had a university that exploited the intellectual opportunities created by Spain's unique mix of Christian, Hebrew and Muslim cultures. Toledo's craftsmen were famous throughout Europe for the quality of their steel. Sh.'s claim that Wolsey was angered by the refusal of Charles V to appoint him to the see of Toledo is consistent with a practice that helped precipitate the Reformation. Medieval clergy could obtain licenses to hold more than one 'living' at a time, and some churchmen grew wealthy by piling up numerous offices. Exemptions from canon law permitted clergy who did not reside in their parishes or dioceses to siphon off the income from their posts while delegating their duties to poorly paid assistants. *H8 2.1.164.*

Tom, 1) any common man. *LLL 5.2.899. AWW 2.2.22,* 'T.'s forefinger,' any man's finger.

2) *2H6 2.3.80,* apprentice whom Sh. invents to be a companion for Peter Thump. See Thump, Peter.

3) *1H4 2.1.5, 2.5.8,* one of three bartenders whom Prince Harry acknowledged as personal friends.

4) *Lr,* see Poor Tom, and Bedlam.

Tom Drum, *AWW 5.3.323,* Lafeu's mocking name for Paroles, who deserves a good beating.

Tom o' Bedlam, *Lr 1.2.132–3,* madman released to beg. Compare *Q 2.131,* 'them of B.' See Poor Tom and Bedlam.

Tomyris, *1H6 2.3.6,* queen of the Massagetæ who killed the Persian emperor, Cyrus the Great. Herodotus (*Histories* 1.214) claims that Tomyris blamed Cyrus for her son's death in battle. Tomyris routed the Persian army and devised an appropriate humiliation for the corpse of its commander. She tossed Cyrus' head into a bucket filled with human blood and invited him to drink his fill.

Tong, *Var,* location of a Shropshire parish church where the epitaph or epitaphs at opposite ends of the Stanley tomb have been attributed to Sh. since the 1630's.

Tongue, Lady, *Ado 2.1.257,* Benedick's mocking name for Beatrice, referring to her wit.

Topas the curate, Sir, *TN 4.2.2,* identity assumed by Feste when he torments Malvolio, who has been caged as a lunatic. The topaz was believed to have a curative effect on madness, and the tests which the 'curate' applies were also used in the diagnosis and treatment of mental illness. Both were about equally ineffective. It has been argued that Sh. drew from an altercation revolving around a Puritan exorcist named John Darrell and his account of his treatment of Nicholas Starkey's children (*True Narration,* 1600) because of the use of 'bibble babble' by the posessing demons. Samuel Harsnett's *Discovery of the Fraudulent Practices of John Darrell* (1599) had exposed the exorcist. It has also been argued that there are many other instances of the use of this wording. It does seem, however, in the context that using a Puritan exorcist to humiliate Malvolio well fits the logic of the humor. Besides the jewel topaz, the comic knight of Chaucer's *Tale of Thopas* has been suggested as source of the name, as well as a character in John Lyly's *Endimion.*

Toryne, *Ant 3.7.23, 3.7.55,* Torone, bay on the western coast of Greece (Epirus) where Octavius gathered the fleet he took to Actium in 31 BC to defeat Mark Antony.

Touchstone, *AYLI,* the Clown. It is not clear that Sh. intended T. to be his name, as it appears in F1 in a stage direction (*2.4*): 'Enter Rosaline for Ganimed, Celia for Aliena, and Clowne, alias Touchstone.' This could mean he is in disguise as T., but this seems to make no difference in the play. The name might refer to the touchstone, a hard piece of black stone, such as jasper or basalt, that was used to test the quality of precious metals by streaking them across it (*Per 6.41* refers to this). Touchstone often fulfills the function of Sh.'s best 'wise fools' by commenting on the action in ways that reveal the fundamental truths of the situation. A less plausible, but not impossible, suggestion is that there is also an obscene connotation. Some critics who find a great difference between the Clown as played by William Kempe and the Clown as played by Robert Armin consider Touchstone to exhibit traits of both actors and the part as possibly transitional or revised.

Touraine, French province in the center of the Loire valley, administered from the city of Tours. It was bordered by Anjou, Maine, Berry, Poitou, and Orléans. *1H6 1.3.79. Jn 1.1.11, 2.1.488, 527.*

Tours, French city on the Loire river about 150 mi. southwest of Paris. It was the seat of an archbishop, and its cathedral housed the shrine of one of Europe's most famous saints (Martin, a 4th c. missionary to the Gauls). During the early phase of the Hundred Years' War it found itself in a dangerous location. It lay between districts where England based armies for its war with France. *2H6 1.1.5, 1.3.53. 1H6 4.3.45.*

Tower Hill, *H8 5.3.60,* rise of land on the northwestern side of the Tower of London that, until 1747, was used as a place to stage executions of state prisoners.

Tower, the, 'Tower of London,' castle on the bank of the Thames river at London's eastern end. The legend that claims that it was built by Julius Cæsar is fictitious, for Cæsar did not establish a permanent base in Britain. The Tower's oldest extant components are Norman structures begun by William the Conqueror shortly after his victory over the Saxons. The Tower was an impregnable stronghold to which government officials retreated when dangerous situations developed within the city. It was also the government's favorite place for the incarceration of important prisoners.

2H6 4.5.5, 4.6.14. 3H6. 1H6 1.1.167, 1.4.1. R3. R2 4.1.306, 5.1.2, 52. H8.

Tranio, *Shr,* Lucentio's servant. He disguises himself as his master so that Lucentio can gain access to Bianca in the disguise of a Latin teacher. Clever and intelligent, he not only pulls off his impersonation of a young nobleman, he adapts quickly to unforeseen circumstances, such as tricking the Pedant into playing Vincentio, then carrying out the fraud even when the true Vincentio appears. The name is borrowed from a clever servant in Plautus' *Mostellaria* ('The Haunted House').

Transylvanian, *Per 16.20,* customer of the brothel who dies from his sexual dalliance. Transylvania is an area now located in central Romania separated from Walachia by the Transylvanian Alps and from Moldavia and Bukovina by the Carpathians. Settled by various ethnic groups, it has been disputed between Hungary and Romania for centuries. In Sh.'s England this would have been a remote and obscure place, so it is likely that Sh. is merely drawing on the common knowledge of Latin in which T. means 'across the forest.'

Traveller, Monsieur, *AYLI 4.1.31,* mocking name applied to Jaques by Rosalind, perhaps satirizing gentlemen who travelled on the Continent for their education.

Travers, *2H4,* servant who informs the earl of Northumberland of the disaster that befell the earl's son, Hotspur, at the battle of Shrewsbury. There is no obvious historical prototype for the character and the name is a common one meaning a family or person that lived near a ford. It is related to 'traverse' (derived from Fr.).

Tray, *Lr 3.6.21 (Q 13.57),* dog whom Lear imagines barking at him, or of a formerly faithful dog that has turned against him. The comparison to his three daughters is obvious. Although 'tray' as a dog's name may have referred to the third of a litter, another use recorded in the 16th c. is as a synonym for 'pain' and 'suffering,' which is certainly appropriate to the context.

Trebonius, *JC,* Caius Trebonius, (d. 43 BC), one of the ringleaders of the conspiracy to assassinate Julius Cæsar. At the start of his career Trebonius was allied with Rome's aristocratic party, but in 55 BC he changed affiliations and won election as a plebeian tribune. He used his office to help the first triumvirate enact its legislative program, and Cæsar rewarded him with a military appointment in Gaul. Trebonius remained loyal to Cæsar during the struggles with Pompey, and in 45 BC Cæsar sponsored Trebonius for a consulship and a lucrative proconsular appointment as governor of the province of Asia. Despite the debt Trebonius owed Cæsar's patronage, Trebonius entered enthusiastically into the plot to assassinate Cæsar. Plutarch ('Antony' 13.1) says that Trebonius convinced his colleagues not to invite Mark Antony to join their conspiracy. Trebonius had once confided to Antony his belief that Cæsar was a danger to the Republic. Antony was not sympathetic, but he did not report the conversation to Cæsar. Sh. expanded Plutarch's story by having Trebonius support Brutus in arguing that Antony should not be killed with Cæsar. If Trebonius did share Brutus' leniency, he made a fatal mistake. After Cæsar's murder, Trebonius claimed the Asian governorship Cæsar had promised him, and Antony's general Dolabella captured and killed Trebonius at the latter's headquarters at Smyrna in 43 BC.

Trent, river originating in Staffordshire and flowing east across England to the Humber. It marks the border between northern and southern England. *1H4 3.1.71, 76, 99, 132. TNK pro. 12,* 'silver T.': between the Po and the T. would encompass nearly all of the civilized world in Renaissance English thinking.

Tressell, *R3 1.2.209,* gentleman at Edward IV's court. Since Sh. has invented the story of Anne Neville presiding at the funeral of Henry VI, it is impossible to identify with any certainty the men whom he says accompanied her on that occasion. A Sir William Trussel served as sheriff of Warwickshire in 1477. Either he or his brother, Edmund, might be assumed to have been in the service of Warwick's daughter.

Tribune(s), officer(s) of the Roman Republic charged with guarding the interests of the plebeian order. The Roman Republic was founded by a party of aristocratic revolutionaries who overthrew monarchy and vested all authority in the members of a patrician Senate. In 471 BC Rome's plebeian citizens rose up to express their discontent with a skewed political system that barely recognized their existence. The plebeians staged a military strike and refused to serve in Rome's armies until the Senate granted them some rights. A plebeian assembly was established, and plebeian executives called tribunes were appointed to be its spokesmen. Their primary duty was to protect plebeians from abuses of authority by patrician magistrates. Their most effective weapon was a 'veto' that gave them the power to forbid any action proposed by any assembly or officer of the Republic. *Tit. Cor. Cym 3.7.8.*

Trigon, *2H4 2.4.267,* one of the four groups into which astrologers divide the twelve signs of the zodiac. The 'fiery Trigon' is composed of the three fire signs: Sagittarius, Aries, and Leo. Each of the other elements postulated by classical physics (air, earth and water) has its own Trigon of compatible signs.

Trinculo, *Tmp,* Alonso's jester. The name has been suggested to be an echo of Neapolitan slang but its Romance language root clearly refers to the character's propensity for drink, Neapolitan or not.

Tripoli, F1 'Tripolie,' city located in what is now Libya on the coast of the Mediterranean, believed to be the Oea of antiquity. It began as a colony of Tyre (c. 7th c. BC) and was ultimately part of the Carthaginian domain. During the Punic Wars it was captured by the Romans in the 1st c. BC. The Vandals seized it in the 5th c. AD, the Byzantine Empire in the 6th and the Arabs in the 7th. In the 12th c. the Normans of Sicily looted the area. It became a Spanish possession in 1510, but King Ferdinand V of Castile then gave it to the Knights of St. John of Jerusalem. The city was taken by the Ottomans in 1551, who retained it with varying degrees of authority until 1912.

Shr 4.2.77, possible destination of the Pedant. He intends to go to Rome, then to Tripoli. This would make the African T. in the right direction; however, he may be going from Rome to the Holy Land, doing some sort of religious pilgrimage, which would mean he is sailing to Tripolis (q.v.) in the Middle East.

Tripolis, or Tripoli, city in what is now northern Lebanon, located on the Mediterranean. Founded after 700 BC it became capital of a Phoenician federation (the 'tri-polis' or 'three cities' with Sidon and Tyre) and a major ancient trade center. It prospered under the Seleucids and Romans after Pompey the Great's conquest of 64 BC, then was captured by the Arabs in 638 AD. The Crusaders took it in 1109. The Sultan of Egypt sacked it in 1289. Afterwards it was rebuilt and became part of the Ottoman Empire.

MV 1.3.18, 3.1.94, 3.2.266, Antonio's trading ventures to T. miscarry. Although he could be trading with the Tripoli in North Africa, the mention of another ship's going to Barbary in the last citation probably means that the Middle East is what is in mind. Furthermore, Venetian trade was very much directed to the east.

Triton, *Cor 3.1.92,* son of the sea god, Neptune, and one of the Nereids named Amphitrite. Some ancient myths speak of a class of Tritons, creatures whose forms are partially human and partially piscine. Tritons accompanied Neptune's processions, blowing horns made from conch shells.

Troien, *Tro pro. 16,* one of the six gates of Troy. These are not in the *Iliad* which appears to give Troy only one double gate, but in William Caxton's *Recuyell of the Historyes of Troye,* 3 (c. 1474), the first English printed book and Sh.'s major source for the play, the six gates are listed. 'Troyenne' is the fifth.

Troilus, 1) member of the Trojan royal family, youngest son of Priam and Hecuba, brother of Hector, Paris, Cassandra, Deiphobos, Æsacus, Polyxena, Creusa, and Helenus. He fell in love with Cressida, and fulfilled his passion for her with the help of Pandarus (the first 'panderer'), but she betrayed him with Diomedes. It had been prophesied that Troy would not fall if Troilus reached the age of twenty. Achilles killed him before he reached that age. Troilus appears in the *Iliad,* which was available to Sh. in Hall's (1581) and Chapman's translations (1598) into English, among others in French and Latin. Chaucer had treated the love story in *Troilus and Criseyde* (based on Boccaccio's *Filostrato*), but Sh.'s main source seems to have been William Caxton's *Recuyell of the Historyes of Troy* (1475), based on Guido delle Colonne's *Historia Troiana* (1287). Benoît de Saint-Maure's 12th c. *Roman de Troie,* which seems to be the first account of a love affair between Troilus and Briseida (Cresida), was the source of Boccaccio's and Colonne's versions. Other possible sources include John Lydgate's *Troy Book* (1412–20), Robert Henryson's *Testament* *of Cresseid* (1532) and possibly George Whetstone's *Rock of Regard.* After Chaucer, Cressida becomes a debased character and Troilus a proud young warrior who is misled by a degenerate woman. Oddly, too, the Greeks are regarded as uncouth, unchivalric killers, while the Trojans are elevated to noble status. This is undoubtedly related to the English legend that the first king of Britain was Brut, a descendant of the Trojan Æneas.

Luc 1486. MV 5.1.4. Ado 5.2.30. AYLI 4.1.91, Rosalind says T. was killed by a club, not love.

TN 2.5.51. Tro: F1 'Troylus,' 'Prince T.' Most of Sh.'s treatment of Troilus in love, derives from Chaucer, as Caxton is more interested in other characters.

2) *Shr 4.1.136,* Petruccio's spaniel.

Trojan, 1) (n.) native of Troy. *Luc 1551. LLL 5.2.629,* a common man. *5.2.668. 1H4 2.1.69 (pl.). H5 5.1.18, 30,* slang for a man of low mindedness and dishonesty. *Tro.*

2) *1H6 5.7.106,* Paris, Alexandros.

3) *MND 1.1.174,* 'false T.,' Æneas.

4) (adj.) of or pertaining to Troy. *Luc 1431. MV 5.1.4,* 'T. walls': *The Iliad* describes them as being slanted and therefore possible to climb. *2H4 2.4.164,* 'T. Greeks,' an apparent contradiction in terms. The people of the ancient city of Troy were destroyed by the Greeks and were culturally distinct from them. But since Homer's *Iliad* describes the heroes on both sides of the Trojan war in identical terms, Sh. may have thought that the warriors at Troy were a single people engaged in a fratricidal conflict. The passage might also be read as referring to Greeks exclusively. Because of their involvement in a 'Trojan' war, the Greek soldiers could be said to be the 'Trojan' Greeks. *Tro. Per 4.92,* 'T. horse': according to mythology, the Greeks resorted to trickery to conquer Troy. After ten years of siege, Ulysses advised the Greeks to feign a withdrawal after constructing a large wooden horse with several warriors concealed inside. The city's inhabitants rushed outside, giddy with victory. Bewildered by the huge horse, a Greek who was supposedly abandoned, Sinon, told them it was an offering to Athena made large to prevent its being dragged inside the city as a trophy. Laocoön warned it was a trick but was attacked and killed with his two sons by huge serpents. Taken as an omen, the serpents were the final thing which convinced the Trojans to drag the horse inside the walls. Late at night, as the city dwellers snored from all their celebrating, Sinon released the warriors. They opened the gates and the waiting Greek army sacked Troy. The story was widely told and Sh. would have read it in Virgil's *Æneid* as well as other places.

Troy, ancient city that commanded the western entrance to the Hellespont, the waterway linking the Ægean and Black seas. It was the site of the battle described in Homer's epics, the *Iliad* and the *Odyssey.* Homer describes it as rich, bustling, elegant, and with huge walls which were, according to myth, built by Poseidon and Apollo. The mythical Teucer built the first town there, calling it Sminthium, for the mice (*sminthos,* Cretan or Mysian 'mouse') which had gnawed his bowstring. Dardanus (whose name survives in the Dardanelles, the entrance to the Black Sea) later built a city there, and then Ilus (see Ilium). The cities merged and became known as Ilium or Troy—after Dardanus' grandson Tros. The patron goddess of the city was Athena. A wooden statue of the seated goddess protected the city from invaders. Hercules besieged the city on one occasion, then Paris seduced Helen, provoking the Greek destruction of the city. By the Middle Ages, many of the western Europeans were claiming descent from the dispersed Trojans and the sympathy of Europe had turned from the Greeks. The British claimed ancestry from Brutus, a grandson of Æneas, who entered Britain when it was inhabited only by giants. He supposedly built Troynovant ('New Troy') on the site which is now London. Actually, 'Troynovant' seems to be a confusion of Trinobant, a tribe Cæsar encountered in his invasion. For many years scholars doubted the existence of Troy, but it is now generally conceded that the mound that the archæologist Heinrich Schliemann located and excavated at Hissarlik, Turkey, in 1870 contains the remains of the city Homer describes. It was later excavated by Wilhelm Dorpfeld and Carl Blegen. The seventh city built on the site is thought to be the basis for the Homeric Troy, which according to tradition was destroyed in 1184 BC. Archaeology supports the razing of one of the Troys about 1200. There were attempts to rebuild the city in the Hellenistic and Roman periods, mainly as a tourist attraction, but it had disappeared by the fall of the Roman empire. Sh. describes Troy as having six gates, though Homer names only one, the Scæan (possibly implying 'northern') or Dardanian gate. Since Homer uses the plural, however, it has been thought that this was a double gate.

2H6 1.4.17: Sh. lists the fall of Troy as one among several famous nocturnal disasters that support his contention that the night is the appropriate time for evil deeds. *3.2.118. 3H6 2.1.51,* 'hope of T.,' Hector. *2.1.52, 3.2.190, 4.9.25.*

Tit 1.1.136, 3.1.69, 3.2.28, 4.1.20, 5.3.83, 5.3.85. Luc.

LLL 5.2.530, 'Hector of T.' *5.2.867,* 'worthy knight of T,' Hector. *R2 5.1.11. MV 3.2.56. 2H4 1.1.73, 2.4.220.*

JC 1.2.115. Tro. AWW 1.3.70.

Tubal, *MV,* Jewish friend of Shylock's. He reveals gossip about Jessica's wasting of Shylock's money and tells him about Antonio's financial reverses, thus setting up the motives and means for Shylock's revenge. In Sh.'s day the name was thought to mean 'slanderer.' Tubal is one of the sons of Noah's son Japheth in Genesis 10:2. Strangely, medieval historians made Japheth an ancestor of Alfred the Great. There is also Tubal-cain in Genesis 4. He is one of the sons of Lamech, the descendant of Cain. This latter unfavorable blood line may be more thematically suitable to Sh.'s Tubal. Dr. Tubal Holofernes is also a character in François Rabelais' *Gargantua et Pantagruel,* whose name and character traits Sh. adopted for Holofernes of *LLL.*

Tuelygod, *Lr 2.2.183 (Q 7.186),* 'Poor T.,' F1 'Turlygod,' what mad beggars are called, or what they cry out. This may be related to 'Turlupin' a 14th c. group of French heretics who lived in the fields and survived on lupins, or lived with wolves (Fr. *loup*). Old It. also has *turlupino* and *turluru.* The word survives in Fr. for a cheap punster. Unfortunately there are no English usages of these words. It may also be related to 'tirl,' an old word meaning 'to strip off (clothing, for example) and expose,' or the uses of 'spinning,' or 'making noise.' It might also be a corruption of 'thoroughly good.' 'Tewly' also meant 'sickly, weak,' but why a 'sickly god'? None of these explanations seems quite satisfying. After wrestling with the problem, Wells and Taylor elected to use the earliest reading from Q, simply because it is the earliest.

Tuesday, third day of the week, named for Tiu, a German god who corresponds to the Roman Mars. *1H4 1.2.35. MM 5.1.227. Oth 3.3.61, 62.*

Tullus Aufidius, *Cor,* see Aufidius, Tullus.

Tully, Marcus Tullius Cicero (106–43 BC), orator who rose to a position of leadership in the Roman Senate as Pompey and Julius Cæsar inched the empire toward civil war. Sh. lists him among the great men of history who have been murdered by their inferiors. Cicero's involved schemes landed him on the wrong side in the struggle that erupted for control of Rome after Cæsar's assassination. Cicero was condemned to death by Cæsar's heirs, and Plutarch ('Cicero,' 68.48) says that his execution was carried out by a man whom Cicero had successfully defended on a charge of patricide.

2H6 4.1.138. Tit 4.1.14, 'T.'s *Orator.*'

Tunis, *Tmp,* town in north Africa. Like nearby Carthage, Tunis was a Phoenician settlement. Founded in the 6th c. BC, it did not grow as rapidly as its neighbor and soon fell under its sway. At the end of the Punic Wars, when Carthage was destroyed, Tunis was conquered by the Romans and remained a minor port of the province of Africa. The Vandals ruled the area from 430 to 534 AD, when it was conquered by Belisarius, the Byzantine general. After the Arab conquests of the 7th c., despite a period of conflict in the 10th c., the city grew and was of considerable importance, particularly under the Hafsite dynasty (1228–1574). The pirate Khair ad-Din ('Barbarossa,' 1466?–1546) captured Tunis in 1534, but the Spanish expelled him and briefly ruled until the Ottoman conquest of 1574. A stable Turkish dependency was established which lasted until 1881. Tunis continued to be a safe harbor for piracy, which helped assure its prosperity for several centuries. Most trading nations paid a bribe to the bey of Tunisia to secure safe shipping. This did not end until the early 1800s, however, when the United States attacked the Barbary Coast pirates with several naval expeditions. At *2.1.87–90,* Gonzalo wrongly insists that Tunis and Carthage are the same places. It has been noted, however, that Æneas' voyage in Virgil goes from Carthage to Cumæ (Naples) as does that of Alonso's party, with a visit to the underworld midway.

Tunis, King of, *Tmp 2.1.76,* ruler who married Claribel, daughter of Alonso, from whose wedding the Neapolitans are returning when they wreck on Prospero's island, which (if a particular island must be chosen), would seem to be Lampedusa, between Malta and Tunisia.

Tunis, Queen of, *Tmp 2.1.260,* Claribel, Alonso's daughter.

Turf, Peter, *Shr Ind. 2.93,* F1 'Turph,' old friend of Christopher Sly. Possibly this was the name or nickname of a real person in the Stratford area. Several names in this scene appear to be.

Turk, 1) native of Turkey, synonymous with 'heathen.' In Sh.'s day the Ottoman Turks were the leaders of the Muslim world. Since they were the chief threat to Christendom, their name was given to all the devil's minions. The Ottoman Turks first appeared in history as mercenary soldiers in the employ of the Muslim rulers of Asia Minor. The Ottomans quickly learned the ways of their masters and in the 13th c. took over the states they had been hired to protect, assuming the name of their first great leader Osman (1248–1326) or Othman, whose name may explain the origin of Othello. With the passion of new converts, the Ottomans awakened the crusading spirit of Islam. They opened campaigns on many fronts, and in 1453 they scored a coup. They took the Christian city of Constantinople, a stronghold that had successfully resisted assault for nearly a thousand years. The Ottomans renamed Constantinople Istanbul and made it the capital of a rapidly expanding empire. They charged across the Balkans and up the Danube valley into Central Europe. By the end of the 15th c. the Hapsburg fortress at Vienna was all that stood between them and the heart of Christendom. The Ottomans restored political unity to the Islamic world and confronted Europe in the 16th c. with the most formidable threat it had faced since the days of old Rome. Sh. was about seven years old when a Hapsburg naval victory at Lepanto broke the momentum of Ottoman expansion, but the battle did little to diminish the threat that Sh. and his contemporaries felt.

H5 5.2.206. Ado 3.4.52, 'turn T.,' go heathen, change my nature. *2H4 3.2.303:* When Sh. had Henry V talk of evicting the Turk from Constantinople, he committed an anachronism. Constantinople did not fall to the Turks until 1453, long after Henry V's death in 1422. The Muslim conquest was a fairly recent memory for people of Sh.'s generation. Their rulers were still proposing schemes for the reclamation of the ancient Christian city, and such a project would have been just the kind of thing to cap the career of a worthy Christian knight like Henry.

AYLI 4.3.34. Ham 3.2.264. Mac 4.1.29. Oth.

Pl.: synonymous with 'heathens.' *R3 3.5.39. R2 4.1.86, 4.1.130. MV 4.1.31. Oth.*

2) 'the Turk,' the sultan of Istanbul who reigned over the Ottoman empire. *1H6 4.7.73.*

AWW 2.3.89. Lr 3.4.86, 'out-paramoured the T.,' had more women than the Sultan.

Turk Gregory, *1H4 5.3.46,* anyone noted for reckless behavior. For Sh. and his contemporaries a 'Turk' might be a Muslim or anyone whose temperament reflected the violence for which Christendom's enemies were infamous. Since 'Gregory' is a Christian name and Oldcastle's comparison of himself to a 'Turk Gregory' is intended to be funny, the reference is probably not to a Muslim warrior. The Gregories best known to Sh.'s audience were both popes—and both were alleged to have behaved like Turks. John Foxe's widely read *Booke of Martyrs* had publicized Gregory VII's fits of temper. Gregory (d. 1085) did not perform 'deeds in arms' in the military sense, but he was said to have assaulted his predecessor, Alexander II. Gregory XIII (d. 1585) was another violent pope whom Sh. might have had in mind. On St. Bartholomew's Day, 24 August 1572, the French monarchy had stunned Europe by inaugurating a massive slaughter of defenseless Protestants. Protestant England was particularly incensed when Pope Gregory congratulated the French on their foray into genocide. Gregory's reputation as a 'Turk' was enhanced when he offered a spiritual reward to anyone who succeeded in assassinating England's queen, Elizabeth.

Turkey, (adj.), *Shr 2.1.349,* 'T. cushions.' Turkish traders introduced a number of things into Renaissance Europe, such as the guinea fowl (which was first called a 'turkey,' then the name was reapplied incorrectly to the North American bird). Anything identified as 'Turkish' or with 'Turkey' (used as an adjective) would therefore be regarded as exotic, expensive, or special.

Turkish, *Err 4.1.104,* 'T. tapestry.' *Oth.* See Turkey.

Turnbull Street, *2H4 3.2.302,* London street that paralleled the Fleet river. It was part of a disreputable neighborhood inhabited by whores and thieves.

Tuscan, *AWW 1.2.14, 2.3.270,* of or pertaining to Tuscany, a region in northwest Italy bordering the Tyrrhenian sea. The cities of the region (Siena, Pisa, Florence) became independent communes in the 11th–12th c. and strong republics. There were many conflicts among the city-states in Italy, with much foreign interference, which is what Sh. has in mind in the play. The struggle for dominance among the Tuscans was won by Florence and the grand duchy of Tuscany was created by the Medicis in 1569. Tuscany was the center of the Italian Renaissance. Its dialect became Italy's literary language, and the duchy hosted a great flowering of art and science. The name of the region derives from the Etruscans who ruled it in the early days of the Roman republic.

Twelve Celestial Signs, *LLL 5.2.789,* the Zodiac.

Tybalt, *Rom,* man of the house of Capulet, nicknamed Prince or King of Cats from 'Tybert' in 'Reynard the Fox.' 'Tibert' was even used as a synonym for cats. A strutting young man, he taunts Mercutio into a fight and kills him. Tybalt is later killed by Romeo. The name appears in Arthur Brooke's *Tragicall Historye of Romeus and Juliet* (1562), Sh.'s source, as 'Tibalt' or 'Tybalt,'and goes well back into the sources, though in many variations: 'Thibault' (Boaistuau, 1559), 'Tibaldo' (Bandello, 1554), 'Tebaldo,' (Clizia, 1553), and 'Theobaldo Capilletti,' (Da Porto, c.1530). All of this seems to disprove the assertion that the name derives from Girard Thibault, a fencing master who wrote a manual describing the Spanish style of the sport.

Tyburn, the name of a tributary of the Thames which became applied to an execution site of Middlesex at the corner of Edgware and Bayswater roads. First called Tyburn gate, it was later renamed Cumberland gate. The gallows site was marked by three brass triangles in the pavement. The last execution there was held in 1783. Marble Arch is its current site. Marylebone was formerly the village of Tyburn. *LLL*

4.3.51, 'love's Tyburn,' an allusion to a triangle, either the shape of the gallows or of the site of the gallows.

Typhon, Typhoëus, one of the Titans, the monstrous sons of Tartarus and Gæa that made war on the Olympian deities. A giant, he battled the gods until Zeus smote him with a lightning bolt and buried him under Mt. Ætna. His mouth roars from the volcano's crater, spewing flame and ashes, says Ovid's *Metamorphoses,* 5.346–358, and his struggles to escape cause earthquakes. Pindar also locates Typhoëus under Ætna. Hesiod's *Theogony,* 820 ff. describes him as a hundred-headed dragon, each head issuing different noises. After Zeus's victory, Typhoëus ruled the violent winds of great storms. The name means 'to smoke,' or 'to burn.' Some sources (Hesiod) make Typhon the son of Typhoëus, but overall the names are used interchangeably. Curiously, the modern word 'typhoon' does not derive from the Typhon myth, but from a Chinese word.

Tit 4.2.93. Tro 1.3.160.

Tyrant, *Tmp 4.1.255* spirit in the shape of a hound. It either implies the dog's behavior among other dogs or a general fierceness. Sh. uses 'tyrant' frequently elsewhere in the usual meaning of pitiless ruler. The derivation, Gr. *turannos,* seems to come from Asia Minor and may imply a usurper.

Tyre, important Phoenician trading city in ancient times, located on an island just off the coast of what is now southern Lebanon. The first city was built on the mainland, but the second was relocated on the island, which is about a mile long, parallel to the shore, with a strait a half to a mile wide. The whole island was surrounded by a wall 150 feet high. With two large harbors, it was one of the most important and wealthy of the Phoenician cities. It is frequently mentioned in the Old Testament for its beauty, prosperity, power, and arrogance. The Tyrian king Hiram assisted Solomon in the rebuilding of the Temple. Tyre was particularly famous for its dyes. The expensive Tyrian purple was worn in the ancient world as a show of wealth. Founded as early as 2800 BC, it had already established distant colonies by 1100 BC, the most famous being Carthage, founded about 850—by Dido, according to legend. It was captured by a succession of conquerors, the Assyrians, the Babylonians, the Persians. After a long siege, it was sacked by Alexander the Great in 332 BC who connected it to the mainland, creating a peninsula. In 64 AD it became part of the Roman Empire. The Crusaders made it a Christian enclave. It was destroyed by the Moslems in 1291. Ultimately Tyre's wealth was destroyed by the conquest of Syria by the Turks in 1516, and it has declined into another of the torn cities fought over by the various factions in Lebanon.

Per: like a number of things in the play, Tyre appears in Plutarch's life of Demetrius.

Tyre, Prince of, *Per,* Pericles.

Tyrian, (adj.) of Tyre. *Per 20.18. Shr 2.1.345,* 'T. tapestry,' an expensive tapestry.

Tyrrell, James, *R3,* (d. 1502), commander of Richard III's bodyguard who, Sh. says, Richard ordered to arrange the murder of Edward IV's sons. Sh.'s story derives ultimately from a prejudiced account of Richard's life written by Sir Thomas More. Historians are not agreed on what if any guilt Tyrrell bears for the deaths of the princes. More admits that Tyrrell was a man of good reputation. He stood by Richard III through his defeat at Bosworth Field, and Henry VII pardoned him and restored him to the offices he had held during Richard's reign. He enjoyed Henry's favor until 1501 when he was implicated in a plot to restore the Yorkist monarchy. More reports that Henry convicted him of treason for the crime of giving aid to Henry's enemy, the earl of Suffolk. Tyrrell was promptly beheaded, and his son was condemned for the same cause. The younger Tyrrell was not executed and soon earned a parliamentary reversal of the writ of attainder levied against him and his father. More says that Henry mentioned, after Tyrrell's death, that Tyrrell had confessed to the murder of Edward's sons. The story is suspect, for such a confession would have been very useful to the king and, if it had been available, it would have been widely publicized. The future of Henry's dynasty was uncertain, and he was eager to squelch rumors that the Yorkist heirs were still alive. If Tyrrell had been prepared to give a public account of their deaths, the king would have given him every opportunity to do so. No such confession was published, however, and no new information emerged to warrant a search for the bodies of the princes. There is another peculiarity that casts doubt on More's indictment of Tyrrell. More says that John Dighton, one of the servants Tyrrell sent to murder the boys, confirmed Tyrrell's confession and admitted his own role in the crime. Nothing, however, was done to punish Dighton, who was still a free man when More published his account of Richard's reign in 1513.

Tyrus, *Per,* L. Tyre. The source of Sh.'s play, Lawrence Twine's *Patterne of Painefull Adventures* (1594), uses this form only.

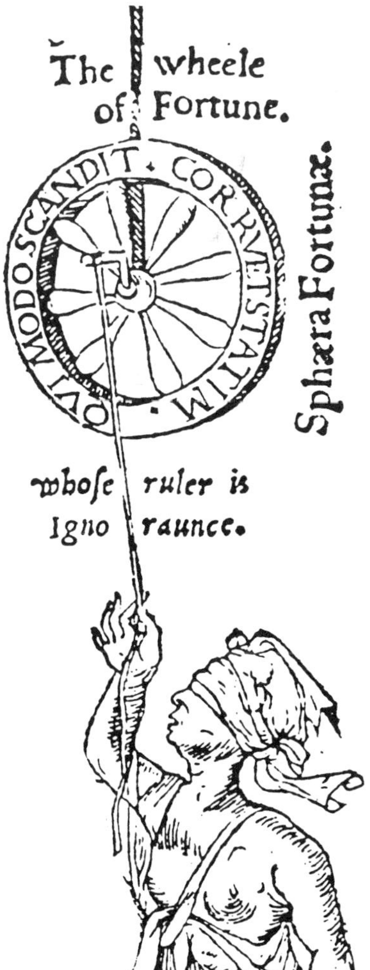

U

Ulysses, (Gr. Odysseus), son of Lærtes and Anticleia, one of the warriors whose exploits are narrated in Homer's epics. As one of the suitors of Helen, he brought 12 ships against Troy, although he feigned madness to avoid it. He was swift: he won a race at the funeral games for Patroclus. With Diomedes he also undertook a raid to capture Rhesus' horses, and one to steal the Palladium. The most subtle thinker in the Greek camp, he was a fluent liar when need be. He is credited with conceiving the strategy that won the war. Since his plan involved tricking the Trojans into dragging a large wooden horse filled with Greek soldiers into their city, it earned him a reputation for deviousness. His reputation suffered during the Middle Ages when European sympathies favored the Trojans (the mythological forebears of the Romans and the British), and idolized purer heroes than the ancient Greeks. After the war Ulysses became lost on the way home to Ithaca and wandered for ten years. His adventures are chronicled in the *Odyssey*—encountering the Cyclops, the witch Circe, the Sirens, and visiting the Underworld. Once home, he was killed accidentally by a spear thrown by his son Telegonus. The origin of his name is lost but the Greeks themselves associated it with *odyssesthai* 'to hate.' It is also a mystery why the Latin form is so different from the Greek, leading some scholars to argue that it came into Latin by way of the Etruscan language, changing the 'd' to 'l.'

3H6 3.2.189: Ulysses' gift for treachery made him, Sh. claims, an inspiration to Richard III. *4.2.19. Tro:* 'Lord U.': Sh. has Ulysses speak better than anyone else among the Greeks. His warning about the neglect of proper hierarchy seems to pin down why there is so much disorder. On the other hand, in practice he shows himself to be the wily Ulysses of legend who manipulates Achilles and resorts to cheap expedience. In creating his character, Sh. borrows strongly from Ovid's *Metamorphoses,* 13, in which Ulysses argues with Ajax over Achilles' armor.

Urchinfield, Lord of, *1H6 4.7.64,* title that Sh. lists as belonging to John Talbot. Urchinfield is a district in southeastern Herefordshire. The castle, now called Urishay, has been there since 1242.

Ursa Major, *Lr 1.2.127 (Q 2.125),* constellation, the 'Big Bear' or 'Big Dipper.' It was also known as 'Charles' Wain' (q.v.), 'the Wagon,' and 'the Plow.'

Ursula, the name derives from L. *ursa* 'bear,' possibly hinting at the woman's size and shape.

1) *TGV 4.4.115,* servant of Silvia, mentioned only once.

2) *2H4 1.2.242,* woman whom Falstaff says that he has often promised to wed. Mistress Quickly claims that Falstaff once offered to marry U. and cites the date of his proposal (*2H4 2.1.86–90*). Since Falstaff was probably generous with his proposals, there is no need to assume that Sh. intended Mistress Ursula and Mistress Quickly to be taken for the same person.

3) *Ado,* gentlewoman attendant of Hero. A pleasant character, she has an amusing flirtation with old Antonio (*2.1.101–113*) and happily plays Cupid to Beatrice and Benedick. She has no other function in the play. 'Ursley,' in Q may indicate a common pronunciation.

V

Valdes, *Per 15.145,* pirate leader. His men kidnap Marina and sell her into a brothel. In the Spanish Armada a Don Diego Flores de Valdés acted as chief of staff for the Duke of Medina Sidonia on the *San Martin.* Also, Diego Flores' cousin Don Pedro de Valdés commanded a squadron of Andalusians, and surrendered his flagship, the *Nuestra Señora del Rosario,* without a struggle to Sir Francis Drake after it had become accidentally immobilized after running into another Spanish ship. This ship was the greatest prize captured in the battle.

Valence, Earl of, *1H6 4.7.63,* title that Sh. reports as belonging to John Talbot. Valence is a French town on the Rhône, about 60 mi. south of Lyons. Aymer of Valence was the last earl of Pembroke in the direct male line. His sister, Johanna, married John Comyn. Their heir, Elizabeth, married Talbot's father, Richard.

Valentine, Roman priest beaten to death about 270 AD for helping persecuted Christians. There was also a martyred bishop of Terni of the same name. There is no apparent reason why either of these saints should be associated with lovers. It seems rather to be a survival of customs of the Roman Lupercal (Feb. 15) in which gifts were given and partners chosen for a year. There are a number of other St. Valentines but the previous two are honored by the feast day. 'Valentine' derives from the L. *valere* 'to be strong.' See Saint Valentine's Day.

1) *TGV,* one of the two gentlemen who loves Silvia. He remains loyal to his friend Proteus even when the latter has caused his exile. In one of the perplexities of this play he gives up all his claim for her in the final act, basically tossing her to the man who has just attempted to force himself on her. It is clumsy, but not that bizarre within the extremely abstract concept of renunciation for the sake of a friend, part of the Neoplatonic fad of the period. Gisippus' giving away his bride to Titus in Sir Thomas Elyot's *Governour* (1531) seems to be the source of the scene. Julia's fainting, however, results in Proteus' rebetrothal to her, so Valentine ends up with Silvia nonetheless. Obviously St. Valentine is suggested, making Valentine the perfect name for a lover. The *OED* cites uses of 'a Valentine' many years before Sh., meaning someone who is chosen as a sweetheart for the ensuing year. When Lance jokes, 'There's not a hair on's head/ but 'tis a Valentine' (*3.1.191, 192*), he could mean either 'but 'tis a lover,' or 'but 'tis himself.' A similar line is at *3.1.211* and could mean either the character or 'a lover.' The opening of *TGV* resembles the duologue between the friends Endimion and Eumenides that opens John Lyly's *Endimion* (1591) and suggests Sh. may have been thinking of them in molding his characters Valentine and Proteus. Valentine becoming chief of the outlaws has also been compared with Pyrocles appearing as the captain of the Helots in Sir Philip Sidney's *Countesse of Pembrokes Arcadia* (1590).

2) *Tit,* Titus Andronicus' kinsman. He does not have a speaking part. He merely accompanies Titus while Titus feigns madness by shooting arrows at the sky. Since *Tit* does not dramatize historical events or depict real people, Sh. doubtless invented the character of Valentine and gave him a name that sounded appropriately Roman. Roman emperors named Valens and Valentinian reigned during the 4th and 5th centuries AD, a period compatible with the action imagined in the play.

3) *Rom 1.2.68,* guest invited to Capulet's feast, brother of the Mercutio who is also invited.

4) *Ham 4.5.50,* loved one, chosen in celebration of Saint Valentine's day.

5) *TN,* attendant to Orsino. Before the appearance of Viola disguised as Cesario, he serves as the Duke's go-between to Olivia. He mainly serves to convey the exposition and to tell Viola that she is in the Duke's favor. His name reflects his role as carrier of messages of love.

Valentinus, 1) *TGV 1.3.67,* variation of 'Valentine,' perhaps to hint at Antonio's formality. It is not metrical.

2) *MM 4.5.8,* F1 'Valencius,' friend or vassal of the duke.

Valentio, *Rom 1.2.71,* cousin of Tybalt invited to Capulet's feast.

Valeria, *Cor,* sister of one of the early Roman Republic's most eminent statesmen, Publius Valerius Publicola. Plutarch ('Coriolanus' 33.1–6) claims that she persuaded Coriolanus' mother, Volumnia, to go to Coriolanus' camp and persuade him to withdraw the troops with which he was besieging Rome.

Valerius, 1) *TGV 5.3.7,* one of the outlaws who pursues Proteus. This is the name adopted by Felismena (the equivalent of Julia) when she disguises herself as a page in Jorge de Montemayor's *Diana Enamorada* (1559), which was a source for Sh., probably through a lost play of 1585. Barnaby Googe's *Eglogs, Epytaphes, and Sonnettes* (1563) drew on Montemayor and had a page named Valerius who is used by a knight to woo a lady.

2) *TNK,* nobleman of Thebes. He tells Palamon and Arcite about the war with Athens, which provokes them to do their duty and stand by their country. Poplicola (Publius Valerius Publicola) is discussed in Plutarch, the most likely possibility. Valerianus was an emperor, and Gaius Valerius Flaccus was a Roman poet. There are others. Valerius was a common Roman name. Chaucer does not use the name in the *Knyghtes Tale* (from which Sh. derived *TNK*) or *Compleynte of feir Anelida and fals Arcite,* but he does use it in *Wyves Tale of Bath* and *Monkes Tale,* and 'Valerye' in *Legende of Good Women.*

Valour, Sir, *Tro 1.3.176,* personification of courage.

Valtemand, *Ham 1.2, 2.2,* Danish ambassador to Norway. Young Fortinbras is raising an army to restore the lands taken from his father by King Hamlet, so Claudius sends Cornelius and Valtemand to request that Fortinbras' uncle, the king, restrain his nephew. The peace mission succeeds, though it is difficult to see why, if Fortinbras is a threat, he would be allowed passage with his armies through Denmark to engage the Poles.

Vanity, *Lr 2.2.34 (Q 7.33),* 'V. the puppet,' Goneril, here equated with one of the evil characters of the morality plays, such as Pride, Wrath, and Envy in *The Castle of Perseverance* (c. 1425). Vanity personified was a part of puppet shows well into Sh.'s time, also.

Vanity in Years, *1H4 2.5.460,* Prince Harry's characterization of Oldcastle. The prince suggests that Oldcastle has failed to learn the lessons of age that help a good man redeem the vices of his youth. A morality play character is also suggested by the phrase.

Vapians, *TN 2.3.22,* imaginary people of whom Sir Andrew says that Feste spoke the previous night. Either the name is corrupted by Andrew's weak recollection and was recognizable to Sh.'s audience, or Feste has deceived him with false erudition. Either proves Sir Andrew's foolishness.

Varrius, 1) *MM 4.5.11, 13, 5.1 sd,* friend or vassal of the duke.

2) *Ant,* Lucius Varius Cotyla, one of Mark Antony's most trusted companions. He was with Antony at Mutina when Antony fought the consuls Hirtius and Pansa (43 BC). Plutarch ('Antony' 18.4) says that Antony left Varrius in charge of his base in Gaul while Antony and Lepidus negotiated the formation of the second triumvirate with Octavius.

Varro, *Tim,* one of Timon's creditors. Marcus Terentius Varro (116–c. 27 BC) was one of Rome's most prolific writers. A Varro who is allied with Pompey is mentioned in Plutarch's Julius Cæsar. Terentius Varro, a Roman consul, fights Hannibal in Plutarch's Fabius and a

Cingonius Varro is mentioned in his Galba. The name would have been very familiar in the Renaissance.

Varrus, *JC,* one of Brutus' soldier-servants. He is a minor character with a common Latin name. Sh. may have had no historical prototype in mind for him.

Vaudemont, Earl of, *H5 3.5.43, 4.8.100,* (d. 1415), noble whom Holinshed (3.555) lists among the notable French casualties of the battle at Agincourt. The Vaudemonts were a cadette branch of the ducal house of Lorraine. The title comes from a district in the Lorraine near Nancy.

Vaughan, Thomas, *R3,* (d. 1483), possibly an illegitimate son of Sir Roger Vaughan of Tretower. He was a soldier from the Welsh marches who was ardently loyal to Edward IV. As early as 1460 Henry VI listed him among those who were to be censured for their encouragement of Richard of York's political ambitions. Edward IV rewarded Vaughan's loyalty to the Yorkist house by appointing him one of the prince of Wales' tutors. Vaughan was a member of the party that tried to bring young Edward V to London to claim his crown in 1483. The company got as far as Stony Stafford, where Richard of Gloucester ordered the arrest of Vaughan and Lords Gray and Rivers. The three guardians of the young prince were taken to Pontefract castle and executed.

Vaumond, *AWW 4.3.170,* commander in the Duke of Florence's army, probably from Vaudemond.

Vaux, Nicholas, *H8,* (d. 1523), wealthy landowner and popular Tudor courtier whose family was conspicuous for its loyalty to the Lancastrian cause. Vaux's father, William, died fighting for Henry VI at Tewkesbury (1471). When the victorious Yorkists confiscated his estates, young Nicholas was taken into the household of Henry Tudor's mother, Margaret, countess of Richmond. Henry's triumph over Richard III at Bosworth Field returned the Lancastrians to power, and William Vaux's fidelity to the Lancastrian cause was ultimately rewarded. Henry VII, who made much of his tenuous Lancastrian connections, restored Nicholas' patrimony, and Nicholas held posts at Henry VIII's court. Although Cardinal Wolsey tried to convince Henry VIII that Vaux was privy to the treasonous conversations of Edward Stafford, duke of Buckingham, Vaux retained Henry's confidence. He was governor of Guisnes at the time of his death. The name Vaux derives the Fr. pl. of *val* 'valley' or 'dale' from place-names in northern France. Another less likely possibility is that it is a version of Falkes, a Norman name meaning 'falcon,' which goes back many centuries.

Vaux, William, *2H6 3.2,* (d.1471), member of an old Norman family (see Vaux, Nicholas) with estates in Northamptonshire. He served Henry VI with unswerving loyalty in the War of the Roses. After Henry's Lancastrian army was routed at Towton in 1461, Vaux accompanied Queen Margaret into exile. He returned to England with Margaret's army in 1471 and met his death at the battle of Tewkesbury. Although the Yorkist victor, Edward IV took posthumous revenge on Vaux by depriving Vaux's son, Nicholas (q.v), of his father's legacy.

Velutus, *Cor,* see Sicinius Velutus.

Venetian, 1) (n.) native or subject of Venice. *MV 1.2.110,* Bassanio; *2.9.86,* B's servant *Oth 1.3.355, 4.1.132* (pl.), *5.2.363.*

2) (adj.) of or pertaining to Venice or its peoples. *MV 3.2.217, 4.1.175. Oth 5.2.346.*

Venezia, *LLL 4.2.96,* (It. Venice), here quoted from a proverb: 'O Venice, Venice, he who has not seen you, cannot appreciate you.'

Venice, major cultural and economic city in Sh.'s time, located at the northern end of the Adriatic. The city is built upon piles driven into about 120 islands and most movement within the city utilizes the 117 canals that crisscross it.

The city was first built in the 5th c. AD as a refuge from the barbarian invasions of Italy. The Venetians began bringing goods from Constantinople and sent them over the Alps into Europe's interior. Developing a government and lifestyle that was distinctive, by the 9th c. Venice became a major power as the capital of a commercial and maritime state, the Venetian Republic, and signed a trade treaty with the Saracens, giving Venice unequaled access to Eastern goods. For many centuries, Venice controlled all the trade in glass in Europe. By the 13th c. Venice was taking chunks of the weakened Byzantine Empire for its own, and at the end of the century Marco Polo, a Venetian merchant, made his famous journey to China. In the 13th and 14th c. Venice also engaged in a series of wars with Genoa, which eventually led to Venetian supremacy. Venice became not just the major Christian naval power, but also a center for Renaissance culture, producing such greats as Titian, Tiepolo, and Veronese in art, and Andrea and Giovanni Gabrieli in music. In the 15th c. the Ottoman Turks seized many of the republic's Greek and Ionian islands, particularly Cyprus, which figures so largely in *Oth.* Moslem power also began to close eastern Mediterranean ports to commerce. The final major destructive blow to Venetian commerce occurred when the route to India via the Cape of Good Hope was discovered by Vasco da Gama and exploited by the Portuguese. In 1508 the League of Cambrai divided Venetian possessions among the Holy Roman Empire, the papacy, France and Spain, but V. regained the territories through diplomacy in 1516. Although it was already in decline in Sh.'s day, it was still playing a major role by being on the frontlines between the Ottomans and Europe, and through its financial power. It would have been difficult for anyone of Sh.'s time to imagine V. in humiliation, but by 1797 it had declined to the point that it did not even resist Napoleon and allowed itself to be given to Austria.

Shr 2.1.310, 318, 350; 4.2.84; 4.4.15. LLL 4.2.95.

Ado 1.1.253–254, 'if Cupid have not spent all his quiver in V.': if Cupid hasn't wasted all his arrows in the city of love. Venice was regarded in much the same way as moderns regard Paris.

MV, setting for most of play. *R2 4.1.88. Oth:* the setting for the early part of the play. The credibility of having Othello as an important general for the city is made more credible by the assertion of several Italian sources that the Venetians preferred mercenary generals so that there could be no Cæsar-like control over the state.

Ventidius, *Ant,* Publius Ventidius Bassus, talented man of obscure origin who, with Julius Cæsar's assistance, won great honors. Ventidius worked as a kind of transportation agent supplying vehicles to Roman magistrates who were heading to assignments in the empire's provinces. He came to Cæsar's attention in his professional capacity, and Cæsar recruited him for service with Cæsar's army in Gaul. Cæsar backed Ventidius for election to a tribunate in 43 BC. Following Cæsar's assassination, Ventidius threw in his lot with Mark Antony. He fought for Antony at Mutina against the consuls Hirtius and Pansa, and in 39 BC Antony sent Ventidius east to make war on the Parthians. Plutarch ('Antony' 34.5) claims that Ventidius was the only Roman general ever to earn a triumph by winning battles with the Parthians (38 BC), but Plutarch also says (34.2–3) that Ventidius' fear of Antony's jealousy prevented him from exploiting his victories.

2) *Tim,* F1 'Ventigius' and 'Ventidgius.' Imprisoned for debt, he is ransomed by Timon, but later, after inheriting his father's estate, he refuses to help his benefactor. The name appears in Plutarch's life of Mark Antony which contains a passage about Timon.

Venus, 1) (Gr. Aphrodite) Roman goddess of sensual love and beauty, daughter of Jupiter and Dione or born of the foam of the sea when Uranus was castrated by Saturn (Cronos) and the male organs were cast into the sea (hence 'foam-born' Aphrodite). She was married to Vulcan in an ironic pairing of ugliness and beauty. She was mother of Cupid by Mars, and

Æneas by Anchises. The islands of Cythera and Cyprus were sacred to her, as were doves. She was associated with gardens, the rose, the myrtle, and the linden. Numerous myths involve her, particularly her love for Adonis, her role in the Judgement of Paris, and her bringing Galatea to life for Pygmalion.

Ven. Luc 58, 'V.'s doves.' *LLL 2.1.256. MND 1.1.171,* 'V.'s doves.' *Rom 2.1.11. MV 2.6.5,* 'V.'s pigeons': the dove is a type of pigeon. *Ado 4.1.60. AYLI 4.1.201,* 'Wicked bastard of V.,' Cupid.

Tro 3.1.32, 'mortal V.,' the human incarnation of the goddess. *4.1.23,* 'V.'s hand,' Æneas is swearing by his mother. *4.6.50, 4.7.63,* 'V.'s glove,'a play on Mars' gauntlet. *5.2.168.*

Ant 1.5.18, 2.2.207. Cym 5.6.164, 'shrine of V.,' the image or essence of the goddess. *Tmp 4.1.87. TNK 5.2.6, 5.6.45.*

2) second planet from the sun, named for the goddess. Its proximity to the sun and the reflective attributes of its cloud cover make it an unusually lustrous heavenly body. When it is visible in the east just before sunrise, it is called the 'morning star.'

1H6 1.3.123. Tit 2.3.30. MND 3.2.61, 107. 3.2.381, alluded to but not mentioned.

2H4 2.4.265: the comparison of the elderly Falstaff's seduction of Doll Tearsheet to a conjunction of the planets Saturn and Venus was comical, for medieval astrologers considered the two heavenly bodies to be so opposed in spirit that they never came together. Their orbits do cross, but so low on the horizon of Europe's skies as rarely to be observed.

Ver, (L. 'spring') a personification. *LLL 5.2.877–78:* V. sings a song of the cuckoo. *TNK 1.1.7.*

Verdun, Lord, *1H6,* see Alton, Lord Verdun of.

Vere, *3H6 3.3.102,* Ver, village near the French city of Bayeux, Normandy, which gave its name to one of the aristocratic families established in England by William the Conqueror.

Vere, Lord Aubrey de, *3H6 3.3.102,* (d. 1462), eldest son of John de Vere, twelfth earl of Oxford. Since he and his father were both executed at the same time for their support of the Lancastrian party, the family title passed to Aubrey's brother, John, the 'Oxford' who is on stage in both *3H6* and *R3.*

Verges, *Ado,* 'Goodman V.,' second in command to Dogberry on the watch. His role is pretty much to be Dogberry's straight man as are the other characters of the watch; however, he may be named simply because of the popularity of the comic pair who played the role. In F1 *4.2,* he is called 'Cowley' in two speech prefixes, indicating the part was at one time acted (probably originated) by Richard Cowley (q.v.). Dogberry describes his comrade as old, a bit thick, and honest, to which Verges himself remarks he is 'as honest as any man living that is an old man and no honester than I' (*3.5.16–17*). It is easy to imagine this pair as Lancelot Gobbo and his father (*TGV*). The name's origin is not clear and it may depend on punning associations. One theory holds that it is a pronunciation of the word 'verjuice' or 'vergeus' meaning the sour juice of crab apples, unripe grapes, or other green fruit. This might imply how his character should be played or have some wispy connection to his comrade's plant name. Various kinds of planting peripheries are also called verges. Another argument is that a 'verge' or 'verger' was a rod symbolising authority or the carrier of same who preceded the justices or the dignitaries of a cathedral, church, or university. There may have been an opportunity for physical humor if Verges carries such a staff, or the inappropriate carrying of the staff another sign of Dogberry's pomposity. Verges may thus be a simple designation of his office, like 'ancient,' rather than a name. Finally, 'verge' was also used to mean the male organ, which might provide additional humor for Sh.'s audience.

Vernon, John, *1H6,* (d. 1451), knight who served with Henry V in France. Hall's chronicle puts him in the company of Lord Talbot at the siege of Bordeaux and with Talbot and his son at their last battle. He was a member of Henry VI's first parliament. He served as speaker of the house and in 1450 was appointed treasurer for Calais. Sh. places him on York's side against Henry in the War of the Roses.

Vernon, Richard, *1H4,* (d. 1403), descendant of a family that came to England with William the Conqueror and acquired extensive lands in the nation's northern districts. He was implicated in Hotspur's plot to overthrow Henry IV and was beheaded after the battle of Shrewsbury.

Veroles, Monsieur, *Per 16.102,* French knight, customer of the brothel to which Marina is sold. Used for nationalistic humor like the Spaniard mentioned before him, his name is French for 'pox,' or 'syphilitic sores.'

Verona, city in northeast Italy on both banks of the Adige river, 72 mi. northwest of Venice. One of the oldest towns in Italy, it was first settled by either the Euganei or the Celtic Cenomani. Located on the Brenner road to central Europe, it has had strategic and commercial importance since it began flourishing as a Roman colony. In 249 Decius defeated the Emperor Philip here, in 312 Constantine beat the army of Maxentius, and in 405 Stilicho repelled the armies of Alaric. In the 5th and 6th c. it was a barbarian base. In the 12th it became a free commune. In the 13th and 14th c. it was the site of the Guelph and Ghibelline struggle, and it suffered as a result. It joined a league of towns which allied with the Lombard League against the Hohenstaufen emperors, but it fell under Ezzelino da Romano, a Ghibelline, in 1277. It prospered under the Scaliger family from 1262 to 1387, when it fell to Milan, as well as under the Visconti and Carrara rulers which succeeded them. By transferring itself to Venetian rule in 1405 it avoided the tyranny of hereditary rulers and remained under that city until 1797. Besides its importance historically, Verona is rich in art history, particularly as the birthplace of Paolo Veronese, and classical and medieval architecture. Many of these buildings still survive, though the Roman stone bridge and the Ponte Scaligero were blown up by the retreating Germans in 1945.

TGV 3.1.82, 4.1.18, 45: Valentine goes to Milan, perhaps implying the period of Milanese rule. It is curious that Verona is not mentioned early in the play as the setting or in order to identify the two gentlemen. The setting of the main action of the play is either Milan, Padua, or Verona, illustrating the confusions of the F1 text. Only one line supports Padua and those suggesting Verona (*3.1.81, 4.1.45, 5.4.127*) are weaker than those for Milan.

Shr 1.2.1, 1.2.22, 48, 189; 2.1.47: Petruccio's hometown.

Rom, setting for most of the play. It is described as an ancient town of great respectability. Popular traditions, perhaps sustained by the tourist industry, have located Juliet's home and asserted that the couple was buried in the catacombs of the Franciscan monastery of S. Fermo Maggiore. When the monastery was burned and rebuilt in 1313, the supposed sarcophagus of Juliet was taken from the ruins and put on display. Using Verona as the setting suggests the period of Guelph-Ghibelline conflict.

Verona, Duke of, *TGV 4.1.46–47,* an outlaw tells Valentine he was exiled for actions similar to Valentine's by 'practising to steal away a lady, an heir, and near allied unto the Duke.' This has been taken to refer to a duke of Verona. Historically, there was none—the city was under the control of the Venetian Republic from 1405. Also, it well could be that such a woman would be attached to a duke of another city. Perhaps Sh. concocted a duke or he imagined Verona under the sway of the duke of another city.

Veronessa, *Oth 2.1.27,* F1 'Verenessa,' apparently a ship of Verona in service to Venice. It may refer to a ship of a particular design of Veronese origin. It is also possible that this word does not derive from Verona at all, but is an obscure word for a particular design of ship. It. *verrinare* 'to cut, penetrate, pierce' might be similar in implication to the term 'cutter' for a ship.

Vice, character in the morality plays. He was the clown of the plays, wearing jackass ears, a long coat and carrying a wooden dagger. He mocked and played with the Devil until he roared, then the Devil usually carried Vice off to Hell on his back. Vice often played at being the gentleman, luring people into sin. These traits carried past the age of morality plays and into the drama of subsequent times. For example, Ambidexter in *Cambises, King of Percia* by Thomas Preston is called the Vice. The Vice has been recognized as influencing the creation of a number of Sh.'s characters, particularly Falstaff, Toby Belch, Iago, and Richard III.

TN 4.2.127. 1H4 2.5.458, 'reverend Vice,' one of Prince Hal's characterizations of Oldcastle. When Falstaff carries off Hotspur's body, it may suggest the Devil's carrying off Vice, though Falstaff is most like Vice himself. *2H4 3.2.309,* 'V.'s dagger,' the lath dagger of Vice in the morality plays. An annoying, but not dangerous weapon.

Vienna, 1) capital of Austria, located on the Danube. The Romans called it Vindobona after they seized it from the Celts in 1 AD. At that time it was the city protecting the empire from the tribes beyond the Danube. Later it fell to Attila, the Avars, and to Charlemagne. The duke of Austria made it his capital in 1156. During the Crusades it was an important center for traffic to the Holy Land, increasing in wealth and size. In 1276, it became the capital of the Habsburgs. They founded its university in 1365. The Hungarians beseiged it in 1477 and Matthew Corvinus captured it in 1485. In many ways, it was the city at the door of Asia, as the Hungarians remained fairly Asiatic through much of the Middle Ages. For some centuries Vienna was at the front of resistance to the conquest of Europe by the Ottomans. One Turkish siege failed in 1529, a more dangerous one was repulsed in 1683 by Polish troops under John Sobielski. In modern times Vienna evokes the Austro-Hungarian city with its lively cultural and intellectual life. The collapse of the empire in World War I and the extermination of the dynamic Jewish community in World War II have reduced the city to secondary status. In Sh.'s time, it was not a city of the rank of Paris, London, or Rome, but was important for its location.

Ham 3.2.227: in Q1 V. becomes 'Guiana,' a mishearing by whoever was stealing the play. *MM,* the setting. According to the play the brothels are located in the suburbs, which was the situation in London.

2) *MM 1.1.44,* possible substantive for the Duke, but as the only such use in the play it seems more likely to mean the city.

Vienna, Duke of, *MM,* see Vincentio 2).

Vincentio, 1) *Shr,* father of Lucentio, a grave and reverend old man. Petruccio and Katherine encounter him on the road to Padua and their odd behavior befuddles him. He travels on with them to see Lucentio, only to discover that Tranio is impersonating his son and the Pedant impersonating Vincentio. Mistaken identity was one of Sh.'s favorite devices for humor.

2) *MM,* wily duke of Vienna. His name is only given in the *dramatis personæ* and never used in the play. He puts Angelo in charge and orders him to curb the excesses of vice in his city, then returns in disguise as a Friar to curb Angelo's excesses. In the conclusion he marries Isabella. His manipulations to effect a greater righteousness are utterly fantastic, but the play operates more as a morality play than anything realistic. It has also been pointed out that if he hadn't let things get so out of hand, he would not have been forced to bring in the hatchetman Angelo. The name does not appear in Sh.'s sources for this play and descends through French from L. *vinco, vincere,* 'to conquer.'

Viola, *TN,* twin sister of Sebastian who disguises herself as Cesario and finds herself the go-between for Orsino and Olivia, both of whom fall in love with her. Her name does not appear in any of the main sources of the story. The corresponding character in *Gl'Ingannati* (1538) is Lelia, in Niccolo Secchi's *Gl'Inganni* (1562) Ginevra, and in Barnabe Riche's 'Apolonius and Silla' (from *His Farewell to the Military Profession,* 1581), Silla. Emanuel Forde's *Parismus, the Renowned Prince of Bohemia* (1598) has some superficial resemblances to *TN* and has a Violetta who disguises herself as a page, as well as an Olivia. There is also a Viola in John Gower's *Confessio Amantis* but the name (L. 'violet') is too common to assert with much authority that Sh. took it from any particular source.

Violenta, *AWW 3.5 s.d.,* F1, name which appears only here. The scene gives no indication of this character. Possibly this was Sh.'s original intention for the name of Diana.

Virgilia, *Cor,* Vergilia, Coriolanus' virtuous wife. She assists her mother-in-law in persuading Coriolanus to cease his attacks on Rome. There is confusion in the ancient Roman sources about the names of Coriolanus' female relatives. Some authorities record his mother's name as Veturia and his wife's as Volumnia. Sh. follows Plutarch ('Coriolanus' 34.1) in saying that Volumnia was Coriolanus' mother and Virgilia his wife.

Virginius, *Tit 5.3.36, 49,* paterfamilias in Roman legend who preferred to kill his daughter, Virginia, rather than permit her to be sexually exploited. Virginius was serving in the Roman army when Appius Claudius, a 'decemvir' (a member of a board of ten men to whom the Roman people had granted dictatorial powers), decided to abduct his daughter. Appius Claudius instructed one of his henchmen to challenge Virginia's legal status as a freely born woman. Her case was to be heard in Appius Claudius' court, and, after Appius Claudius decided against her, his agent was to claim her as a slave and secretly deliver her to Appius Claudius' house. Virginius discovered the plot and realized that he had no hope for justice. Rather than submit to the authorities, Virginius stabbed his daughter to death at her trial and accused her judge of villainy. The people of Rome, inspired by Virginius' determination to resist tyranny, rose up against the decemvirs and restored Rome's Republic.

Virgo, *Tit 4.3.65,* 'the Virgin,' astrological sign for a constellation near the equator. It represents Ceres, and the star Spica marks an ear of grain which she holds.

Virtue, feminine personification of the quality of moral goodness. Arete was the Greek goddess of virtue. The Roman Virtus, however, was masculine, a personification of bravery and manliness. *Ham 3.2.22. Ant 4.9.17. Cym 5.5.221.*

Visor, William, *2H4 5.1.32, 35,* possibly a member of the Visor or Vizard family that resided in Woodmancote, Gloucestershire. The character is sued in Justice Shallow's court by Clement Perks. Sh. may have used real or plausible names without having an actual historical event in mind.

Vitruvio, *Rom 1.2.66,* man whose widow is invited to Capulet's feast. Vitruvius was author of a 1st c. AD Roman book on architecture. See Anselme.

Volquessen, *Jn 2.1.527,* the Vexin, a district in Normandy near Gisors. During the high Middle Ages it had great strategic significance, for it was on the border between lands claimed by England and France and commanded a route to Paris.

Volsces, *Cor,* Volsci, Italian people who lived on the coast of ancient Latium. They were frequently at war with their Latin neighbors and with Rome. *Cor 1.4.28, 1.11.5* (sing.)

Volumnia, *Cor,* Caius Marcius Coriolanus' mother. When Coriolanus attacks Rome seeking revenge for wrongs that he believes his fellow citizens have done him, Volumnia reminds him of his duty to his homeland and persuades him to withdraw. Sh. follows Plutarch's account ('Coriolanus' 33.2). Livy's history of Rome

(2.40.1) says that Volumnia was Coriolanus' wife and that his mother's name was Veturia.

Volumnius, *JC,* Publius Volumnius, life-long friend of Brutus' who served in his army. After the loss of the battle of Philippi, Volumnius refused Brutus' request for help in committing suicide. Sh. found this story in Plutarch ('Brutus' 52.2), who was well informed about Volumnius. Volumnius was an author whose works were among Plutarch's acknowledged sources ('Brutus' 48.1).

Vulcan, (Gr. Hephaistos), Roman god of fire and smithing, son of Jupiter and Juno, husband of Venus, and father of Cupid. He was deformed and was deserted by his mother to be reared in the sea by Eurynome and Thetis. He had a forge within Mt. Ætna, where he was assisted by the Cyclops. The ultimate craftsman, he created Achilles,' Mars,' and Æneas' armor and the shield of Hercules.

Tit 2.1.89, 'V.'s badge,' the sign of the cuckold. In a memorable story in the *Odyssey,* 8, Hephaistos creates an invisible net to catch Ares (Mars) with his wife. He then displays them in their adulterous position for the other Olympians' raucous amusement.

Ado 1.1.174–5, 'V. a rare carpenter?' (see Cupid *Ado 1.1.174*): Vulcan worked in metal, not wood. *TN 5.1.49. Tro 1.3.168,* 'V. and his wife,' a great physical mismatch. *5.2.173. Ham 3.2.82,* 'V.'s stithy,' his forge (see Mars, *Tro 4.7.139*).

W

Wakefield, *3H6 2.1.107,* town in Yorkshire, 175 mi. north of London. In the area are fields upon which 'wakes' or holidays were celebrated. In 1203, the local ruler William, Earl Warenne, received the right to hold a fair there on the eve, day, and following day of All Saint's. The bank of the Calder river just outside of the town was the site of the skirmish between the Yorkists and Lancastrians that cost Richard of York his life on 30 December 1461. The result of the engagement was not the defeat of the Yorkist cause, but a shift of its leadership to the earl of Warwick and to Richard's son, Edward. Edward dropped his father's plan to win control of England as Henry VI's guardian and declared himself the nation's rightful king.

Wales, mountainous western edge of the island of Great Britain, called Cambria by the Romans, which for much of the medieval period functioned as an independent nation. The name derives from the Anglo-Saxon *wealas* 'the foreigners,' though the Celtic inhabitants called themselves *Cymru.* The district that became Wales was annexed to the Roman province of Britain in 78 AD, but the Roman presence in Wales was little more than a military occupation. Wales never evolved the urban and villa institutions that characterized Roman civilization in England. When the Roman troops were withdrawn from Britain in the 5th c., the island, like the rest of Europe, was overrun by migrating German tribes. Angles and Saxons established kingdoms in the old Roman province, but they did not penetrate the mountains of Wales. Hostilities between the Germans of 'England' (Angle-land) and the Celts of Wales prompted a Saxon king, Offa of Mercia (757–796), to construct a long earthwork ('Offa's dike') to separate the two peoples. Mountainous terrain made it difficult to unite Wales under one ruler, but from time to time great warriors appeared and rallied large followings. One of the most powerful leaders was Gruffydd ap Llewelyn (1039–1063). His raids into England convinced William I, the Norman conqueror, that the security of his newly won nation required the containment of the Welsh. William established military bases (marches) along England's western frontier and encouraged fortune hunting Norman knights to prey on the Welsh.

Wales was overrun, but an English civil war in the early 12th c. gave the Welsh an opportunity to regain their independence. When Henry II (1154–1189) restored order in England, he found it expedient to reach a peaceful agreement with a native prince who had appeared in southern Wales, Rhys ap Gruffydd. After Rhys' death the leadership of the Welsh passed to Llewelyn ap Iorwerth (1194–1240), and his descendant, Llewelyn ap Gruffydd was the first man whom the English officially recognized as the prince of all Wales. Llewelyn's government collapsed when Edward I attacked Wales. A dispute among Welsh leaders frustrated attempts to organize a response to Edward's invasion, and the English captured key territories. In 1284 the English monarchy tried to set up an administrative system in Wales similar to England's. Distant royal authority proved, however, no match for the power of the entrenched nobility. In 1400 Owain Glyndŵr, a Welsh warrior from an ancient line, revived the fight for national independence. He found an important ally in France, whose king was eager to stir up trouble for Henry IV of England. Henry beat back the rebels, and Wales was devastated. However, the Hundred Years' War and the War of the Roses prevented the English from pressing their advantage.

The latter conflict brought a surprising conclusion to the ancient struggle between Wales and England. In 1471 Henry Tudor, descendant of the Welsh adventurer Owen Tudor and the Gaunt-Beaufort line of the English royal house, inherited leadership of the Lancastrian faction. In 1485 he brought the War of the Roses to an end by wresting the English crown from Richard III at the battle of Bosworth Field. The acquisition of the English throne by a Welshman established close ties between England and Wales, and the nations were finally joined by parliamentary Acts of Union legislated between 1536 and 1542.

R3 4.5.7. 1H4 1.1.37, 2.5.339, 3.1.43, 73, 4.3.97, 5.5.40.

2H4 1.2.106, 2.1.178, 2.4.296. H5 2.4.56, 4.7.92. Cym 3.2.60.

Wales, Prince of, 1) *R3 1.3.196,* Edward (V), son of Edward IV. Edward I was the first English king to grant the Welsh title to his son. Edward (II) was born at the Welsh castle of Cærnarvon while his father was in the process of conquering Wales. The custom of using the Welsh royal title for the heir to the English throne (which was established by the reign of Edward III) encouraged the Welsh to identify with the English monarchy.

2) *1H4,* see Henry V.

Wall, *MND,* part played by Snout in the rustics' presentation before Theseus. In the myth, a wall with a chink in it separated Pyramus and Thisbe and on Bottom's suggestion this bit of architecture is represented by some loam, roughcast, and stone. Wall satirizes the extremes of personification, a too-common device of writers and players of the period.

Wallon, *1H6 2.1.10,* district in southeastern Belgium occupied by people of Celtic descent. The Romance language spoken there (a dialect of French) distinguished the area from neighboring territories to the north and east where German dialects prevailed. The name has the same origin as Wales and means 'land of the foreigners,' probably originally implying 'land of the Celts.'

Walloon, *1H6 1.1.137,* native of Wallon.

Walter, *Shr 4.1.80,* one of Petruccio's servants. The name was very popular in medieval England, having been brought in by the Normans. Its meaning is 'ruler of an army.'

Ware, Bed of, *TN 3.2.46,* an enormous oak bed, 10' 9" square and 7½' high. The date 1460 was on its back as the date of construction, but it is first mentioned in 1596 by Ludwig Anhalt-Köthen, a German prince, in his itinerary of a visit to England. Where it was kept in Sh.'s day is unknown. After many years of use at an inn called The Saracen's Head it was auctioned in 1864.

Wart, Thomas, *2H4,* comical name suggesting physical blemishes or small stature. Tom Wart was one of several unlikely candidates whom Falstaff recruited for the army.

Warwick, *3H6 5.1.13,* county seat of Warwickshire. It is 8 mi. north of Sh.'s birth place, Stratford-on-Avon. During the War of the Roses, its castle belonged to the Nevilles and was an important Yorkist stronghold. The place-name derives from 'weir buildings,' referring to a dam or weir that must have once been prominent in the area.

Warwick, Earl of, earldom created by William II, son of William the Conqueror. It was first held by the Beaumonts, descendants of the Norman counts of Meulan. When the Beaumont male line died out in 1268, the earldom passed through an heiress to William de Beauchamp. The Beauchamp family became extinct in 1449, and its lands passed by marriage to the Nevilles.

1) *2H6, 3H6, R3,* see Neville, Richard.

2) *1H6, 2H4, H5,* see Beauchamp, Richard, earl of Warwick.

Warwickshire, county at the center of England just north of Oxford and situated on the Avon river. Warwickshire was Sh.'s home county. *2H6 3.2.201. 3H6 4.9.9. 1H4 4.2.51.*

Watchins, Arthur, *STM Add. II.D.50, 67,* brother of Doll, yeoman of Sergeant Safe. Holinshed does not mention this person, so it is not clear where the name comes from. He does mention that a Nicholas Downes, a sergeant at arms, was hurt in the civil disorder depicted in the manuscript.

Waterford, Earl of, *1H6 4.7.63,* title that Sh. lists as belonging to John Talbot. Waterford is the name of a county on the southern coast of Ireland between Cork and Wexford, and also of a port on Ireland's southern coast. In 1445 Talbot was posted from France to Ireland, where on 17 July 1446, Henry VI created him earl of Waterford and lord of Dungarvan. In 1448 Talbot resigned the governorship of Ireland to his brother Richard and went back to France to join the English forces in Normandy.

Waterton, Robert, *R2 2.1.286,* Lancastrian knight in Henry (IV) Bolingbroke's household. He accompanied Henry on his crusades to Lithuania in 1390 and 1392. In 1399, when Henry defied Richard II's decree of exile and returned to England, Waterton brought him 200 men-at-arms. Waterton's career blossomed after Henry deposed Richard and ascended the throne. He served Henry in many capacities at home and abroad, and he had the honor of witnessing Henry's will.

Weald of Kent, *1H4 2.1.55,* wilds of Kent. Merchants, pilgrims, and government officials had to pass through Kent to reach London from the south, and they were vulnerable to attack from highwaymen when travelling through desolate areas.

Wednesday, fourth day of the week. The word derives from an Old English term meaning 'Woden's Day.' Woden or Odin was a Germanic god. In the ancient Roman calendar the fourth day of the week was named for Mercury. *Err 1.2.55. Rom 3.4.17, 19. R2 4.1.309. MV 1.3.124.*

1H4 1.1.102, 3.2.173, 5.1.37. 2H4 2.1.91, 2.4.85. Cor 1.3.61. Oth 3.3.62

WT 4.4.274, perhaps a reference to a real ballad, like the one entered in the Stationers Register of 1604, 'The most true and strange report of A monstruous fishe that appeared in the forme of A woman from the wast upward Seene in the sea.' Editors argue over which fish monstrosity ballad Sh. had in mind. Obviously it could now be lost.

Welcome, *Tro 3.3.162,* personification of greeting.

Welsh, 1) *1H4 3.1.48, 117, 189, 196, 204, 226, 231,* native language of the people of Wales (q.v.). It evolved from the ancient Celtic tongue of the pre-Roman people of Britain. During the period of the Anglo-Saxon invasions of the 5th and 6th centuries, the residents of the old Roman province of Britain (medieval England) adopted the German dialects of the newcomers. The older Celtic languages survived only in Cornwall and Wales where Anglo-Saxon influences were slight.

2) (n.) natives of Wales. *MWW 3.1.89, 2H4 1.3.83,* see Welshmen.

3) (adj.) of or pertaining to the people and nation of Wales. *MWW 2.1.190, 5.3.12, 5.5.80., 5.5.136,* 'ridden with a W. goat,' to be harassed. *5.5.161,* 'W. flannel,' a rustic cloth, suggesting the rough life in Wales.

Welshman, 1) *MWW 2.2.292,* native of Wales (q.v.)

2) *1H4 1.1.41,* see Glyndŵr, Owain.

3) *H5 4.1.84,* see Fluellen.

4) Pl.: residents of Wales. The unsettled politics of Wales gave its men plenty of opportunities to acquire military experience, and Welsh soldiers were employed in England's armies at home and abroad. At the start of the War of the Roses, Richard of York, earl of the Welsh marches, recruited troops in Wales, but Wales later acquired a Lancastrian connection. Henry V, born at Monmouth, styled himself a Welshman (*H5 4.1.52*), and his widow, Catherine, married a Welsh gentleman of the court, Owen Tudor. Their son, Edmund Tudor, earl of Richmond, wed John of Gaunt's great-granddaughter, Margaret Beaufort. Their son, Henry Tudor, was, after the deaths of Henry VI and his son, heir to the leadership of the Lancastrian party. He wrested the crown from Richard III and founded the Tudor dynasty.

3H6 2.1.180. R3 4.4.407. R2 2.4.5, 3.2.69, 3.3.2. H5 4.7.96.

Welshwomen, *1H4 1.1.45,* women who accompanied Owain Glyndŵr's soldiers when they captured Sir Edmund Mortimer in 1402. Holinshed (3.520) claims that they committed unspeakable atrocities on the bodies of fallen Englishmen.

West Indies, *MWW 1.3.64,* islands of the Caribbean, famously mistaken by Columbus and other early explorers for the islands of Asia. Falstaff here means a place in which to get rich: Mistresses Ford and Page shall serve this purpose as his Indies.

Western Isles, *Mac 1.2.12,* Ireland and the nearby islands. The 'kerns and gallowglasses' referred to in the next line are types of Irish soldiers.

Westminster, 1) *2H6 1.2.37, 4.4.30,* urban district west of London that has always been regarded as having an independent identity. (Despite its immediate proximity to London, in 1900 it was granted the legal status of a separate city.) It is home to many government buildings and the ancient church, Westminster Abbey, which is the burial place of English kings and other notables. The name means 'minster' or monastery, to the west. A palace, Westminster Hall, was built by the early Norman kings and extensively reconstructed by Richard II. During the 14th c. so many parliaments convened in the royal complex that it came to be thought of as the appropriate place for parliament to meet. Most of these medieval buildings were destroyed by fire in 1834 and replaced by the present Houses of Parliament.

2) Westminster Abbey, or the church of St. Peter at Westminster. The first church on the Abbey's site, a spot on the northern bank of the Thames river west of the walls of medieval London, was built in the 7th c. Edward the Confessor constructed a wholly new edifice in 1065, but between 1245 and 1502 different portions of Edward's building were torn down and replaced. The present abbey contains almost nothing of his work. The church that Sh. knew lacked the prominent western towers Westminster now sports. These were erected in the 18th c. Since the days of Edward the Confessor, the abbey has served as England's coronation church.

R3 4.1.32. 2H4 2.4.358.

Westminster, Abbot of, *R2 4.1.143,* William of Colchester (d. 1420), churchman who served both Richard II and Henry IV. William was with Richard in Ireland during Richard's last campaign, but he quickly made his peace with Henry after Richard's fall. He was one of the official witnesses to Richard's abdication. In 1414 Henry appointed him England's delegate to the international meeting at Constance that negotiated an end to the papal schism. Since William had a long, distinguished career in Henry's service, it is hard to believe Holinshed's claim (3.514–515) that in 1399 William organized a conspiracy to assassinate Henry and restore Richard to the throne.

R2 5.6.19: the sources on which Holinshed (and Sh.) drew may have confused William, abbot of Westminster, with Thomas Merke, a bishop of Carlisle who was once a monk at Westminster. Contrary to Sh.'s report, it was the bishop who died in 1400, not the abbot.

Westmorland, county in northwestern England between Cumberland and Yorkshire. It was the seat of the powerful Neville family. See Westmorland, Earl of.

Westmorland, Earl of, 1) *3H6,* Ralph Neville (d. 1484), was the second earl to bear the title of the county of Westmorland. He married Elizabeth Percy, daughter of the family that was his family's chief rival for power in northern England. Sh. numbers him among Henry VI's staunch supporters, but he was not particularly active in the military campaigns that determined the fate of the house of Lancaster.

2) Ralph Neville (1364–1425), most powerful baron in northern England after Henry IV's defeat of the Percies. Westmorland's mother was a Percy, and he was Hotspur's cousin. But Westmorland married Henry IV's sister and found that it served his interests to help Henry

subdue the Percies. Before Henry's rise to power, Westmorland had had a good relationship with his predecessor, Richard II. Richard had permitted Westmorland's son to marry one of the king's nieces. When Richard exiled Henry (IV) Bolingbroke and confiscated his duchy of Lancaster, the king's autocratic behavior alarmed Westmorland and convinced him to follow the lead of his Percy relatives and back Henry against Richard. Westmorland was one of the commissioners appointed to witness Richard's abdication, and he took part in Henry IV's coronation ceremony. Henry made him Earl Marshal of England and retained him in an office that he had occupied under Richard: warden of the Scottish marches. Westmorland's military experience and influence in northern England increased his importance to Henry in 1403 when the Percies rebelled. After Hotspur's death at the battle of Shrewsbury, Henry sent Westmorland to deal with Hotspur's father, Northumberland. Westmorland forced the elder Percy to come to terms, but only temporarily.

In 1405 Northumberland, Archbishop Scrope, and Thomas Mowbray plotted a second uprising. Westmorland intervened before the rebels consolidated their forces and persuaded Archbishop Scrope to lay down his arms. Henry captured and executed Scrope and Mowbray, but Northumberland escaped to France. The defeat of the Percies left Westmorland unopposed in northern England where he, as marshal and warden, bore responsibility for guarding England's frontier with Scotland. Although Sh. follows Holinshed (3.553) in reporting that Westmorland took part in the battle at Agincourt in 1415, he was not in France at that time. Henry V had left him at home to guard against an attack from Scotland while the king was abroad. The reservations that Sh. has Westmorland express about Henry's wars on the continent may be authentic in spirit if not in detail. A man who had devoted his life to protecting northern England against the Scots might have preferred his nation to invest its military resources in wars closer to home. He survived Henry V and was named executor of the king's will.

1H4. 2H4. H5.

Wexford, Earl of, *1H6 4.7.63,* title that Sh. lists as belonging to John Talbot. Wexford (Washford) is a port on the southeastern Irish coast between Dublin and Waterford. The Talbots claimed the honor as part of the estate of the earls of Pembroke. Talbot's father, Richard, inherited it from his wife's mother, Johanna, sister and heir to Aymer de Valence, earl of Pembroke.

Wheeson week, *2H4 2.1.191,* week that begins with the Christian festival of Whitsund (q.v.) or Pentecost.

White Hart, *2H6 4.7.178,* inn in Southwark where Jack Cade established headquarters for the rebellion he raised against Henry VI's government.

Whitehall, *H8 4.1.99,* royal residence in London in use between the reigns of Henry VIII and William III. It was located near the present Westminster Bridge and St. James Park, not far from Buckingham Palace. The first building on the site was erected in the early 13th c. by Hubert de Burgh. He left it to the Dominicans, who sold it to the archbishop of York. Thereafter it was known as York House or York Place. Cardinal Wolsey, who held the archdiocese of York, vastly enlarged the complex, and in 1530 Henry VIII confiscated it from the disgraced Wolsey. It replaced a royal accommodation at Westminster that had been damaged by fire. The court frequented Whitehall until a large portion of it burned in 1698. Of the royal buildings, only a 17th c. banqueting hall remains.

Whitmore, Walter, *2H6,* man who, Sh. claims, boarded the vessel that was to take the duke of Suffolk into exile and who assassinated Suffolk. According to Edward Hall's *Union of the Two Noble and Illustre Famelies of Lancastre and Yorke* (219), however, a Nicholas 'of the Tower,' the captain of a war ship belonging to the duke of Exeter, captured Suffolk and brought him to Dover. There he was beheaded and his body discarded on the beach.

Whitsun, Whitsunday, Pentecost, festival commemorating the descent of the Holy Spirit on Christ's disciples (Acts 2:1–4). It falls seven Sundays after Easter and Whitsuntide was a time of the May games, dancing, and plays. 'White Sunday' was named for the white robes that newly baptized persons wore to services. The spring season has always been a time of rejoicing, and the church's celebration of the new life of Christ's resurrection merged smoothly with customs whose roots were in ancient pagan fertility rites.

H5 2.4.25: the 'Whitsun morris-dance' to which Sh. refers was a popular rural custom of obscure origins. Dancers, who may sometimes have painted their faces black like Moors, donned costumes and acted out the stories of Robin Hood, Maid Marian, and other folk heroes. *WT 4.4.134,* 'W. pastorals': as the plays, etc., were ribald, Perdita is surprised to be talking in the manner of these plays and blames it on her costume.

Widow Capilet, *AWW,* see Capilet, Widow.

Will, nickname for William. 1) *2H6 2.3.79,* character Sh. invents to be Peter Thump's second in a duel with his master, Thomas Horner.

2) *Son. 57.13. 135. 136.2, 14:* the poet plays on his own name, and the other meanings of 'will.' These are the only times in his entire corpus of work that he mentions himself. Even his epitaph says nothing about him.

William, common English name of Germanic origins through Norman French. It seems to mean something like 'desiring protection.' It was, for many centuries after the Conquest, the most common English name, though by Sh.'s day it had fallen second to John.

1) *2H4 3.2.8,* Justice Silence's son, a student at Oxford following in his father's footsteps and preparing for admission to the Inns of Court and the practice of law.

2) *AYLI,* young rustic who lays claim to Touchstone's Audrey. The part is so small it is possible that the character's name was the actor's. The role provides, however, an opportunity for a squabble over a common woman such as was seen in many Robin Hood plays.

William of Hatfield, *2H6 2.2.12,* Edward III's second son. He died in infancy.

William of Windsor, *2H6 2.2.17,* Edward III's seventh and last son. He died in infancy.

Williams, Michael, *H5,* fictional character, soldier who quarrels with Henry V as he moves incognito among his troops on the eve of the battle at Agincourt. The two men exchange tokens so that they can recognize each other and finish their fight after the battle. Henry gives his token to the hot-tempered Fluellen who is infuriated when Williams recognizes it and, seemingly without grounds, attacks him. Henry steps forward at the crucial moment to straighten out the comic confusion.

Williamson, *STM,* one of the commoners working himself up to riot. Holinshed does not mention such a person.

Willoughby, Lord, *R2,* William, (1396–1409), scion of a family that had a long history of loyalty to the house of Lancaster. William accompanied Henry (IV) Bolingbroke on his crusades to Lithuania in 1390 and 1392. He travelled with him to the Holy Lands, and he was one of the soldiers who enlisted in Henry's service in 1399 when Henry defied a decree of banishment and returned to England to confront Richard II. Willoughby was a witness to Richard's abdication, and he became a member of Henry IV's council. He remained at the center of things at court until his death.

Wiltshire, Earl of, 1) *3H6 1.1.14,* James Butler (1420–1461), heir to the Irish earldom of Ormond. During the War of the Roses he campaigned actively for the Lancastrians. He administered Ireland for Henry VI and served a term as England's treasurer. The Yorkists beheaded him after capturing him at the battle of Towton. Edward IV confiscated his estates and allowed the Wiltshire title to lapse. Wiltshire is the county in southwestern England containing the great Salisbury plain. The name derives from the town of Wilton, which is named after the Wylye river, so-called because it is 'wily,' breeching its banks unpredictably.

2) *R2 2.1.216, 157, 2.2.136, 3.2.118, 137, 3.4.54,* William Scrope (d. 1399), one of Richard II's favorites. As a young man Scrope saw considerable military action in Edward III's wars in France, and for about a decade he served as seneschal of Gascony. He became vice-chamberlain of Richard's court in 1393 and helped the king destroy the faction of nobles known as the 'lords appellant.' Richard appointed him treasurer of England, and he earned notoriety by exploiting the office for personal profit. In 1399 Wiltshire was left in England to assist Richard's regent, his uncle the duke of York, while Richard led an expedition to Ireland. Shortly after Richard's departure, Henry (IV) Bolingbroke raised a revolt. York promptly capitulated, and Wiltshire and Richard's other unpopular advisors fled to Bristol to avoid capture. They found no sanctuary. The people of Bristol defected to Henry's camp, and Henry executed Wiltshire and his companions without benefit of trial.

Winchester, seat of Wessex, one of the kingdoms of the Anglo-Saxons set up in Britain at the start of the Middle Ages. 'Chester' (L. *castra*) indicates it was a Roman camp, but the 'win' is obscure. It possibly comes from 'Venta of the Belgæ' (place of the Belgæ) as the Romans called it, from the tribe which gave its name to Belgium. Gwent in Wales may have similarly derived. During the 9th c., when Viking invaders overran all of Britain except for Wessex, the Anglo-Saxons rallied behind Wessex's king, their last surviving native leader. Alfred the Great recovered a portion of Britain from the Vikings and established the dynasty that, with the exception of a period of Viking resurgence, ruled England until the eve of the Norman conquest. Although London's superior location helped it evolve as the nation's capital, important administrative offices, like the royal treasury, lingered at Winchester long after the arrival of the Normans. The diocese was the wealthiest in England, and its cathedral was used for royal baptisms, coronations, and burials. See Winchester, Bishop of, *1H6*; Lord of, *H8.*

1H6 1.4.52, 'Winchester goose'; *Tro, Q ending not in F1, l. 22,* 'goose of W.,' a prostitute. The brothels of Southwark were located in the jurisdiction of the Bishop of Winchester.

Winchester, Bishop of, *1H6,* see Beaufort, Henry, bishop of Winchester.

Winchester, Lord of, *H8 3.2.232, 4.1.105,* see Gardiner, Stephen.

Wincot, *Shr Ind. 2.20,* a village about 4 mi. from Stratford. Parish records note that several Hackets lived there in the 1590s.

Windmill in Saint George's Field, *2H4 3.2.192,* possibly an allusion to a brothel in Southwark. Southwark bordered on St. George's Field and boasted a large number of disorderly houses.

Windsor, town on the southern bank of the Thames river about 20 mi. west of London. Originally, there may have been a Roman settlement upon which the Anglo-Saxon kings built a residence that Edward the Confessor donated to Westminster Abbey. William the Conqueror persuaded the Abbey to return the gift to the crown, and he fortified the site. The original village where the residence of Edward was located is about 2 mi. southeast of the castle built by the Conqueror. It declined so much that 'New W.' was soon simply called Windsor. Henry II began the construction of the castle for which Windsor is now famous. Edward III remodeled the fortress for use as a palace and made its chapel the headquarters for the Order of the Garter because of a legend that Arthur's

Knights of the Round Table met atop the hill. The Tudors, who ruled England in Sh.'s day, greatly expanded the complex of buildings at Windsor, and the castle is now one of the chief residences for the English monarch. Its name derives from the Anglo-Saxon *Wyndeshour* or *Wyndsore,* referring to a windlass used to pull carts up the slope from the shore, perhaps after they were loaded from boats.

2H6 2.2.17. 1H4 1.1.103. 2H4 2.1.93, 4.2.14, 4.3.50.

MWW, the setting. *3.1.5,* 'old W.' *5.5.1,* 'W. bell.' *5.5.42,* 'W. chimneys,' the castle chimneys. *3.3.207, 5.5.55,* 'W. Castle.' *4.4.28,* 'W. forest': William the Conqueror acquired the land from Westminster Abbey because of the good hunting. The enormous woods encompassed nearly 60,000 acres to the south as late as 1790, but was legally reduced to unprotected land from forest status in 1813. *5.5.12,* 'W. stag,' a stag of the forest.

Wingfield, Lord Cromwell of, *1H6 4.7.66,* one of the titles that Sh. lists as belonging to John Talbot. Wingfield is a village in Derbyshire about 15 mi. north of the county seat at Derby. Talbot's first wife was Maud Stanhope, niece of Ralph, lord Cromwell (d. 1456), Henry VI's chamberlain and treasurer.

Wingham, *2H6 4.2.24,* village in the county of Kent about 7 mi. east of Canterbury.

Wittenberg, *Ham 1.2.113, 119, 164, 167,* German city on the Elbe, seat of a university founded in 1502. The city was in existence as early as the 12th c. AD, but its importance begins with the 16th. The Lutheran Reformation began there when Martin Luther nailed his 95 theses to the church door in 1517, and he publicly burned the papal bull against him in the town square in 1520. In 1534 the first Lutheran Bible was printed there. Both Luther and Melanchthon are buried there. Charles V captured the city in 1547, ending its life as a hotbed of radicalism. The capital of Saxony was moved to Dresden and Wittenberg declined. Hamlet and Horatio's university was absorbed by the university of Halle in 1817. Their studying there would indicate they were at the forefront of thinking at their time.

Wolsey, Cardinal, *H8,* (1473–1530), archbishop of York and chief advisor to Henry VIII. Wolsey was a man of humble origins—allegedly the son of a butcher from the town of Ipswich. The early flowering of his extraordinary intellect won him a place at Oxford where he served as tutor to the sons of Thomas Grey, marquess of Dorset. Henry Deane, archbishop of Canterbury, made Wolsey his secretary, and in 1506 Wolsey entered the royal service. Henry VIII liked Wolsey, for Wolsey encouraged the young king's dream of winning glorious battles with England's ancient foes, France and Scotland. The campaigns that followed were not all clear victories, but Wolsey's skill as diplomat and administrator brought Henry through crises with credit. In 1514 Henry made Wolsey archbishop of York. A year later, he became a cardinal and chancellor of England. He was a hard working administrator. He overhauled the royal government and improved the king's ability to police his subjects. A group of Henry's councilors routinely gathered at Wolsey's behest in the 'Star Chamber' (a room with a ceiling painted to resemble the heavens) to inquire into the conduct of the nobility and to prosecute those who were not keeping the 'king's peace.'

As his usefulness to Henry increased, so did his power. He dominated England's national government, and an appointment as papal legate made him *de facto* primate of England's ecclesiastical establishment. Wolsey was more interested in tapping the wealth of the church than improving its spiritual condition. The cardinal revelled in the abuses of clerical power decried by his contemporary, Martin Luther. He accumulated many church offices, amassed a staggering fortune, lived lavishly, entertained extravagantly, and had a son—to whom he gave properties that belonged to the church. His ultimate ambition was to become pope, but that dream and his fortunes foundered on the rock of England's foreign policy. Hoping for the support of Charles V in the papal elections, he pushed

England into an unpopular war with Charles's enemy, France. His plan was to use an English army to distract the king of France while Charles made himself master of Italy. In 1525 Charles won a victory over France, but England did not profit from it. Charles concluded that England's contribution to his success had been minimal and that England no longer had much importance as an ally. When Charles broke a promise to marry Henry's daughter, Mary, Henry began to worry about the problems England might someday have with its powerful neighbors. Henry's concern for England's stability and security increased his desperation to have a male heir.

Wolsey promised Henry that he would win papal approval for an annulment of the king's barren marriage with Katherine of Aragon. The pledge raised expectations that were doomed to disappointment. Katherine fought the annulment, and her nephew, Charles V, was positioned to give her decisive support. Charles's army occupied Italy and prevented Clement VII from acting on Henry's request. In desperation Wolsey suggested that Henry join the French in a war to liberate the pope. That improbable venture failed in 1529, and Henry took out his frustration on Wolsey. Deprived of royal protection, Wolsey was attacked from all quarters. His courts had infuriated the nobles, his taxes had angered the propertied classes, his high-handed conduct and personal greed had alienated the clergy. Worst of all, he had earned the hatred of the woman with whom his king was infatuated, Anne Boleyn. On 9 October 1529, he was stripped of his civil offices and exiled to his diocese. Wolsey continued to correspond with Rome, France, and the empire in the hope of finding some way to recoup his position, but this proved to be a mistake. Word of the cardinal's letters leaked out, and his enemies convinced Henry that Wolsey was plotting treason. Henry ordered him to London for trial, but he was spared this final humiliation by a death from natural causes on 29 November 1530.

Wo'ncot, *2H4 5.1.33,* slurred pronunciation of Woodmancote, a village in Gloucestershire.

Woodeville, Anthony, *R3 1.1.67,* Woodville; see Rivers, Earl.

Woodstock, *2H6 2.2.16,* royal forest preserve and hunting lodge in Oxfordshire that was a favorite retreat for England's kings throughout the Middle Ages. The Anglo-Saxon monarchs held court there. Henry I, the third of the Norman rulers, often resided there—as did his grandson, Henry II. Edward the Black Prince was born there, and 'Bloody' Mary held her sister Elizabeth under house arrest there. Woodstock's medieval buildings were destroyed during the English civil war, and early in the 18th c. the crown relinquished the property to John Churchill, duke of Marlborough. It is now the site of one of England's most imposing country houses, Blenheim palace.

Woodville, Richard, *1H6,* (d. c. 1440/42), lieutenant of the Tower of London and grandfather of Edward IV's queen. Woodville (Wydeville) served in the campaigns that Henry V and the duke of Bedford conducted in France. He was Bedford's chamberlain. After Bedford's death, he returned to England and sided with Bishop Beaufort in the quarrels that raged among Henry VI's regents. In 1425 when Humphrey, duke of Gloucester, attempted a *coup d'état,* Beaufort entrusted the crucial Tower of London to Woodville. Woodville helped restore order by courageously refusing to allow Gloucester to enter and assume command of the Tower. In 1429 he was appointed lieutenant of England's most important continental possession, the port of Calais. He returned to England in 1435 and served a term as sheriff of Northamptonshire. His granddaughter, Elizabeth Woodville, married Edward IV in 1464, and her Woodville relatives were a powerful faction at the court of the Yorkist king.

Worcester, county seat of Worcestershire and the administrative center for the diocese. Its name indicates that it was a Roman camp ('chester,' L. *castra*), and the initial syllable is thought to refer to the Weogoran, a Celtic tribe that 'lived by the winding river.' It is situated on the Severn about 100 mi. west of London. King John and Henry VIII's elder brother Arthur are buried in its cathedral. *Jn 5.7.99. 1H4 4.1.126.*

Worcester, Earl of, Thomas Percy (1344–1403), brother of Henry Percy, the earl of Northumberland, and uncle to Henry's son Henry 'Hotspur.' In his youth Worcester fought in Edward III's French wars, and he was a member of John of Gaunt's expedition to Spain (1386). He was steward of the royal household at the court of Richard II, and he enlisted in the army Richard took to Ireland in 1399. After his Percy relatives sided with Henry (IV) Bolingbroke against Richard, Worcester resigned his offices and joined the rebellion that forced Richard's abdication. Worcester participated in Henry IV's coronation, but he, like the other Percies, soon turned against the king the Percies had helped to the throne. In 1403 he joined the conspiracy Hotspur organized to unseat Henry. By sabotaging Henry's efforts to negotiate a settlement, Worcester may have hastened the start of the battle at Shrewsbury. If so, he did himself and his allies no favor. Hotspur was forced to rush into action before his confederates arrived. His men were routed; he was killed; and Worcester was captured and beheaded.

R2 2.2.58, 2.3.22. 1H4. 2H4 1.1.125.

Worm, Lady, *Ham 5.1.86,* mocking name for one of the dead the gravedigger unearths.

Worthy, (n.) or Worthies, see Nine Worthies.

Wye, river flowing from southern Wales through Herefordshire and Gloucestershire to the Bristol channel. Its name is Celtic for 'conveyor,' perhaps referring to its use as a trade artery, or 'moving one.'

1H4 3.1.62. H5 4.7.27, 104.

X

Xanthippe, *Shr 1.2.70,* F1 'Zentippe,' wife of the ancient Athenian philosopher Socrates. According to gossip among the ancients she was extremely shrewish. This folklore is easy to accept given the exasperations of living with her husband. His seemingly careless attitudes are lampooned in Aristophanes' *Clouds*—and responding accordingly. Diogenes Lærtius in his *Lives and Opinions of the Eminent Philosophers* (c. early 3rd c. AD) reports that Aristotle says that Socrates had two wives, Xanthippe was the first and Myrto the second. Also, though, Lærtius reports that both Satyrus and Hieronymus of Rhodes wrote that Socrates had two wives simultaneously because of a law designed to increase the birth rate in Athens—perhaps another thing provoking her. Lærtius also reports that Socrates, to maintain his integrity, never accepted any fees and that Xanthippe once complained of the poorness of a meal they were offering to rich guests. He goes on to describe arguments in which Xanthippe scolded Socrates and even dumped water on him, but that the philosopher laughed off her outbursts and said to his friends that he had gotten used to her rantings and liked her as a horseman likes a spirited horse. Lærtius must have gotten the latter story from Xenophon's *Symposium* 2.10, and the attitude expressed by it sounds curiously like Petruccio's to the untamed shrew Katherine.

Y

Yorick, *Ham 5.1.176, 180,* jester who played with Hamlet when the prince was a child. Hamlet contemplating the skull of Yorick is the most famous image of the play, indeed one of the most famous images in literature. The source of the name is mysterious. It may be an adaptation of Erik, a common enough Danish name. Claudius, in fact, is called Erico in *Der Bestrafte Brudermord* (1710) a German adaptation of an earlier version of the play. Another theory is that it is an adaptation of the German Georg or Danish Jörg. Another idea is that it is from Rorik, Amleth's maternal grandfather in Saxo Grammaticus' original version of the story and in Belleforest's. It has also been suggested that the discussion of Yorick may be an allusion to Richard Tarleton, one of the first 'stars' of the English theater. He was a very popular comedian, even with queen Elizabeth. He died in 1589 but his memory lingered well into the Jacobean period with many jokes, joke books and stories attributed to him. In one such book, *News Out of Purgatory,* Tarleton appears to the editor as a satirical, anti-Catholic ghost. Maybe in some strange way this influenced the creation of Hamlet's father.

York, 1) seat of the county of Yorkshire and of the archdiocese of York. The city of York, which was one of medieval England's largest, was situated on the Ouse and Foss rivers about midway between London and Edinburgh. Its location made it a convenient place for negotiations between Scottish and English rulers. The city of York has been an important site since ancient times. The Romans established a military camp there and named it Eburacum, related to a Celtic word for 'yew.' The final form of the name is a Norse corruption of OE *Eoforwic,* 'boar farm.' The emperors Hadrian and Severus visited the city and the latter died there. Also, Constantine the Great was inaugurated there. A bishop of York is recorded as early as the 4th c. AD and by the 8th c. it was one of the centers of learning in Europe. It was also a major bone of contention between Edgar Ætheling and William the Conqueror, who burnt the city and devastated the countryside to suppress the revolt of 1068. During the reign of Richard I, in one of the most hideous incidents in its history, there was a riot against the Jews, who were pursued into the castle and murdered.

Although the archbishop of Canterbury was usually acknowledged to be the primate, or the highest ranking clergyman in England, some of the medieval archbishops of York were strong enough to challenge Canterbury's authority. The county of Yorkshire is the largest county in England and comprises the northeastern part of the nation. The duchy of York was created for Edmund Langley (1341–1402), the fifth son of Edward III. It passed to Langley's grandson, Richard, whose rebellion against Henry VI started the War of the Roses. York's emblem was a white rose. The red rose was the heraldic symbol used by the house of Lancaster, whose duke usurped Richard II's throne.

3H6 1.4.180, 181, 4.8.8. 1H4 5.5.37. 2H4 1.2.65, 2.1.68, 4.2.71. H8 4.2.13.

2) *R3 1.4.230, 3.5.85, 4.4.40* see Richard, duke of York, son of Richard of Cambridge.

3) *R3 1.1.2, 3.1.27,* see Richard, Duke of York, son of Edward IV.

4) *1H4 1.3.243,* see Edmund Langley.

York, Archbishop of, 1) *3H6 4.4.26,* George Neville (1433–1476), brother of Warwick 'the Kingmaker.' After Richard of York's death at Wakefield, George assisted Warwick in obtaining the throne for Richard's son, Edward. George's sermon to the people of London defending Edward IV's title was one of the crucial events that won young Edward recognition as England's king. Edward promoted George to high ecclesiastical office and employed him as chancellor of England for the first seven years of the reign. The archbishop's influence declined as Edward wriggled out from under Warwick's thumb, and George joined his brother in plots to restore the Neville family's power. In 1469 he presided at the marriage of Edward's brother, Clarence, to Warwick's daughter, Isabel. This forged an alliance that brought Clarence into the Neville camp for possible use as a rival for Edward's crown. In 1470 France, to whom Warwick had turned for aid, persuaded him to take up the Lancastrian cause and restore Henry VI to the throne. Edward was captured and placed in the archbishop's custody at Middleham Castle. The king escaped to Flanders, but no blame accrued to his jailor. Archbishop Neville was appointed chancellor in Henry VI's short-lived government, and he was in charge of both London and Henry's person when Edward regained control of the city in 1471. Edward imprisoned the archbishop briefly in England and, after a short period of liberty, arrested him once again and sent him to France. When Neville's health failed in 1475, he was allowed to return to England to die.

2) *1H4,* see Scrope, archbishop of York.

York, Cardinal of, *H8 1.1.51, 2.2.106,* see Wolsey, Cardinal.

York, Duchess of, 1) *R3,* Cecily Neville (d. 1495), great-granddaughter of Edward III via the Beaufort descendants of his son, John of Gaunt. In 1438 Cecily married Richard, duke of York, the man who aspired to Henry VI's throne. Richard died before achieving his objectives, but two of his sons wore England's crown: Edward IV and Richard III. Cecily outlived all of her children but one—Margaret, duchess of Burgundy.

2) *R2,* Isabel of Castile (d. 1393), wife of Edmund Langley and the mother of the duke of Aumerle (Rutland). Sh. takes some dramatic liberties with the marital history of the house of York. Isabel died long before Richard II's deposition and her son's alleged involvement in a plot to assassinate Henry IV. Aumerle (Rutland) was also not, as Sh. implies, her only son. She was mother to Richard, earl of Cambridge, and she had a daughter Constance, who married Thomas le Despenser (Spencer). In 1395 her husband remarried. He wed Joan, the daughter of Thomas Holland, earl of Kent. They had no children, and in 1400 Joan would not have been the aged matron whom Sh. describes as York's wife. Joan died in 1434.

York, Duke of, 1) *R2,* see Edmund York.

2) *H5,* Edward, see Aumerle, Duke of.

York, Heirs of, *R3. 5.5.91* see York, House of.

York, House of, branch of the royal family that took the throne of England away from the Lancastrian kings during the War of the Roses. Richard, duke of York, advanced his claim to the throne in 1460, after Henry VI had demonstrated incompetence and mental illness. Richard enjoyed double descent from King Edward III—from whom his Lancastrian opponents also derived their royal blood. Richard's father, Richard of Cambridge, was the son of Edmund Langley, the first duke of York and Edward III's fifth son. Richard of Cambridge married Anne Mortimer, a descendant of Edward III's third son, Lionel of Clarence. The death of Anne's brother, Edmund Mortimer, brought Anne's son, Richard of York, the Mortimer estates and the Mortimer claim to the throne. Since the Lancastrians were scions of Edward III's fourth son, John of Gaunt, Richard argued that his Mortimer lineage (deriving from Gaunt's elder brother) constituted the superior right to the royal estate.

2H6 4.1.94. 3H6. 1H6 3.1.169.
R3 1.4.15, 4.4.402, 403, 5.8.27.

York, Lord of, *H8 3.1.61; 2.2.122,* see Wolsey, Cardinal.

York Place, *H8 4.1.96, 97,* see Whitehall.

Yorkshire, England's largest county. It faces the North Sea between the counties of Durham and Lincoln. *R3 4.4.450. 2H4 4.3.99.*

Z

Z, *Lr 2.2.63 (Q 7.62),* F1 'Zed.' Kent calls Oswald 'whoreson Z, thou unnecessary letter.' It did not appear in many dictionaries of Sh.'s time because it was not used in Latin, and its sound can be represented by 'S,' as it more frequently is in British English. Noah Webster's reforms of spelling made more prominent in American spelling.

Zed, see Z.

Zenelophon, *LLL 4.1.66,* Penelophon, beggar maid king Cophetua fell in love with and married. See Cophetua.

Zentippe, see Xanthippe.

Zounds, or 'Swounds,' 'God's wounds,' oath scattered through the plays. As it was considered indecent it was edited from F1 and editions after 1608. The printing of indecency and use of oaths on stage was outlawed by Parliament in the early 17th c.

Works Consulted

Editions of the Works

Allen, Michael J. B. and Kenneth Muir, eds. *Shakespeare's Plays in Quarto.* Berkeley: Univ. Of California Press, 1981.

Barnet, Sylvan, gen. ed. *The Complete Signet Classic Shakespeare.* San Diego: Harcourt Brace Jovanovich, 1972.

Bevington, David, ed. *The Complete Works of Shakespeare.* Glenview, IL: Scott, Foresman, 1980.

Brockbank, Philip, gen. ed. *The New Cambridge Shakespeare.* New York: Cambridge Univ. Press.

Brooks, Harold F. and Harold Jenkins, gen. eds. *The Arden Edition of the Works of William Shakespeare.* London: Methuen.

Campbell, Oscar James, Alfred Rothschild, and Stuart Vaughan. *The Bantam Shakespeare.* New York: Bantam.

Evans, C. Blakemore, textual ed. *The Riverside Shakespeare.* Boston: Houghton Mifflin, 1974.

Furness, H. H., ed.; H. H. Furness, Jr.; and the Modern Language Association. *A New Variorum Edition of Shakespeare.*

Harbage, Alfred, gen. ed. *The Pelican Shakespeare.* New York: Viking Penguin.

Kökeritz, Helge. *Mr. William Shakespeare's Comedies, Histories, and Tragedies.* Intro. Charles Tyler Prouty. New Haven: Yale Univ. Press, 1954.

Spencer, T. J. B., gen. ed. *The New Penguin Shakespeare.* New York: Viking Penguin.

Wells, Stanley, gen. ed. *The Oxford Shakespeare.* New York: Oxford Univ. Press.

Wright, Louis B., gen. ed. *The Folger Library General Reader's Shakespeare.* New York: Washington Square Press.

Secondary Sources

Adams, Joseph Quincy, ed. *Chief Pre-Shakespearean Dramas.* Boston: Houghton Mifflin, 1924.

Alighieri, Dante. *The Divine Comedy.* Trans. Charles Singleton. Princeton: Princeton Univ. Press, 1982.

Allmand, Christopher. *Henry V.* Berkeley: Univ. of California Press, 1992.

______. *Lancastrian Normandy 1415–1450: The History of a Medieval Occupation.* New York: Oxford Univ. Press, 1983.

Anderson, Bernhard W. *Understanding the Old Testament.* 2nd ed. Englewood Cliffs, NJ: Prentice-Hall, 1966.

Aristophanes. *The Complete Plays of Aristophanes.* Ed. Moses Hadas. New York: Bantam, 1962.

Ariosto, Ludovico. *Orlando Furioso.* Trans. Sir John Harington. Ed. Robert McNulty. London: Oxford Univ. Press, 1972.

Arrian. *Arrian.* Trans. E. Iliff Robson. Cambridge: Harvard Univ. Press, 1966.

Ashley, Maurice. *The Life and Times of King John.* London: Weidenfeld & Nicholson, 1972.

Attwater, Donald. *The Penguin Dictionary of Saints,* 2nd ed. Harmondsworth, Middlesex: Penguin Books, 1983.

Baker, Arthur E. *A Shakespeare Commentary.* 2 vols. New York: Ungar, 1938; rptd. 1971.

Becker, George Joseph. *Shakespeare's Histories.* New York: Ungar, 1977.

Bellamy, John. *Robin Hood: An Historical Inquiry.* Bloomington: Indiana Univ. Press, 1985.

Bentley, Gerald. *Shakespeare: A Biographical Handbook.* New Haven: Yale Univ. Press, 1961.

Besant, Walter. *London in the Time of the Tudors.* London: A. & C. Black, 1904.

Blake, N. F. *Shakespeare's Language: An Introduction.* London: Macmillan Press, 1983.

Blom, Eric. *Everyman's Dictionary of Music.* Rev. Jack Westrup. New York: St. Martin's, 1971.

Bloom, Allan, and Harry V. Jaffa. *Shakespeare's Politics.* New York: Basic Books, 1964.

Boardman, John, *et al.* eds. *The Oxford History of the Classical World.* Oxford: Oxford Univ. Press, 1986.

Boccaccio, Giovanni. *Decameron.* 3 vols. Trans. John Payne. Rev. Charles S. Singleton. Berkeley: Univ. of California Press, 1982.

Boris, Edna. *Shakespeare's English Kings, the People, and the Law.* Rutherford, NJ: Fairleigh Dickinson Univ. Press, 1978.

Bourne, Frank. *A History of the Romans.* Boston: Heath, 1966.

Boyce, Charles. *Shakespeare A to Z.* New York: Facts on File, 1990.

Bradbrook, Muriel. *Muriel Bradbrook on Shakespeare.* Totowa, NJ: Barnes and Noble Books, 1984.

Bradley, A. C. *Shakespearean Tragedy.* 2nd ed. London: Macmillan, 1971.

Brewer, Ebenezer Cobham. *Brewer's Dictionary of Phrase and Fable.* Centenary ed. Revised by Ivor H. Evans. New York: Harper and Row, 1981.

Bromley, John. *The Shakespearean Kings.* Boulder: Colorado Associated Univ. Press, 1971.

Brooke, Nicholas, *Shakespeare's Early Tragedies.* London: Methuen, 1968.

Brownlow, F. W. *Shakespeare, Harsnett, and the Devils of Denham.* Newark: Univ. of Delaware Press, 1993.

Bulfinch, Thomas. *Bulfinch's Mythology.* New York: Thomas Y. Crowell, 1970.

Bullough, Geoffrey, ed. *Narrative and Dramatic Sources of Shakespeare.* 8 vols. New York: Columbia Univ. Press, 1957–75.

Butler, E. M. *Ritual Magic.* Hollywood, CA: Newcastle, 1971.

Calvocoressi, Peter. *Who's Who in the Bible.* New York: Viking, 1987.

Campbell, Oscar James. *Shakespeare's Satire.* New York: Gordian Press, 1971.

______, ed. *The Reader's Encyclopedia of Shakespeare.* New York: Thomas Y. Crowell, 1966.

Cardozo, Jacob Lopes. *The Contemporary Jew in the Elizabethan Drama.* New York: Burt Franklin; rptd. Paris, 1925.

Castiglione, Baldassare. *The Book of the Courtier.* Trans. Charles S. Singleton. Garden City, NY: Anchor, 1959.

Caxton, William. *The Fables of Aesop.* Joseph Jacobs, ed. London: D. Nutt, 1889.

______. *The History of Reynard the Fox.* Donald B. Sands, ed. Cambridge: Harvard Univ. Press, 1960.

______. *The Recuyell of the Historyes of Troy.* H. Oskar Sommer, ed. London: D. Nutt, 1894.

Chambers, E. K. *The Elizabethan Stage,* 4 vols. Oxford: Clarendon Press, 1923.

Chappell, William. *A Collection of Ancient Songs, Ballads and Dance Tunes.* London: Cranmer, Beall, and Chappell, 1859.

Chaucer, Geoffrey. *The Riverside Chaucer.* Ed. Larry D. Benson. 3rd ed. Boston: Houghton Mifflin, 1987.

Chaucer. *The Works of Chaucer.* Ed. Alfred W. Pollard, et al. New York: Macmillan, 1904.

Chrimes, Stanley. *Henry VII.* Berkeley, CA: Univ. of California Press, 1972.

Chute, Marchette. *Shakespeare of London.* New York: E. P. Dutton, 1949.

Cicero, Loeb Classical Library, 38 vols. Cambridge: Harvard Univ. Press.

Clark, Sandra, ed. *The Hutchinson Shakespeare Dictionary.* 2nd ed. London: Arrow Books, 1991.

Clarke, C. P. S. *Everyman's Book of Saints.* Rev. Rosemary Edisford. New York: Philosophical Library, 1968.

Clout, Hugh. *The Times London History Atlas.* New York: HarperCollins, 1991.

Combe, William. *History and Antiquities of the City of York.* A. Ward, 1785.

Cunliffe, Richard John. *A New Shakespeare Dictionary.* London: Blacke and Son, 1910.

Daiches, David, ed. *The Penguin Companion to English Literature.* New York: McGraw-Hill, 1971.

Davis, Michael Justin. *The England of William Shakespeare.* New York: E. P. Dutton, 1987.

Dean, Leonard F., ed. *A Casebook on* Othello. New York: Thomas Y. Crowell, 1961.

De Felice, Emidio. *Dizionario dei cognomi italiani.* Milano: Mondadori, 1978.

Delaney, John. *Dictionary of Saints.* Garden City, NY: Doubleday, 1980.

Dictionary of National Biography, 22 vols. Oxford: Oxford Univ. Press, 1885-1911.

Diogenes Lærtius. *Lives of Eminent Philosophers.* Trans. R. D. Hicks. 2 vols. Cambridge: Harvard Univ. Press, 1966.

Dobson, R. B., and J. Taylor. *Rymes of Robyn Hood.* Pittsburgh: Univ. of Pittsburgh Press, 1976.

Donadoni, Eugenio. *A History of Italian Literature.* 2 vols. Trans Richard Monges. New York: New York Univ. Press, 1969.

Eccles, Mark. *Shakespeare in Warwickshire.* Madison: Univ. of Wisconsin Press, 1961.

Ekwall, Eilert. *The Concise Oxford Dictionary of English Place-Names.* 4th ed. Oxford: Oxford Univ. Press, 1960.

______. *Street Names of the City of London.* Oxford: Oxford Univ. Press, 1954.

Encyclopædia Britannica, 13th ed.–15th ed.

Erasmus, Desiderius. *The Colloquies of Erasmus.* Trans. Craig R. Thompson. Chicago: Univ. of Chicago Press, 1965.

Forse, James H. *Art Imitates Business: Commercial and Political Influence in Elizabethan Theatre.* Bowling Green, OH: Bowling Green State University Popular Press, 1993.

Frankforter, A. Daniel. *Civilization and Survival.* Vol. 1. Lanham, MD: University Press of America, 1988.

Fripp, E. I. *Shakespeare: Man and Artist.* Oxford: Oxford Univ. Press, 1938.

Froissart, John. *The Chronicles of England, France and Spain.* Trans. by Thomas Johnes, ed. by H. P. Dunster. New York: E. P. Dutton, 1961.

Gay, Peter, and R. K. Webb. *Modern Europe to 1815.* New York: Harper & Row, 1973.

Gayley, Charles Mills. *The Classic Myths in English Literature and in Art.* 1911; rptd. Waltham, MA: Blaisdell, 1968.

Gesner, Carol. *Shakespeare and the Greek Romance: A Study of Origins.* Lexington: Univ. of Kentucky Press, 1970.

Glanville, Philippa. *London in Maps.* London: The Connoisseur, 1972.

Grafton, Richard. *Sir Richard Grafton's Chronicle, or History of England. To which is added his table of the bailiffs, sheriffs, and mayors, of the city of London, from the year 1189 to 1558.* London: Printed for J. Johnson (etc.), 1809.

Grant, Michael, and Rachel Kitzinger, eds. *Civilization of the Ancient Mediterranean*, 3 vols. New York: Charles Scribner's Sons, 1988.

______. *History of Rome.* New York: Scribner's, 1978

Greg, W. W., ed. *Gesta Grayorum 1688.* Oxford: Oxford Univ. Press, 1915.

Grose, Francis. *A Classical Dictionary of the Vulgar Tongue.* Ed. Eric Partridge. New York: Dorset, 1992.

Gross, John. *Shylock: A Legend and Its Legacy.* New York: Simon and Schuster, 1992.

Hall, Edward. *Union of the Two Noble Families of Lancaster and York, 1550.* Memston, England: Scolar Press, 1970.

Hallam, Elizabeth M. *Chronicles of the Wars of the Roses.* London: Weidenfield and Nicholson, 1988.

Halley, Henry H. *Halley's Bible Handbook.* 23rd ed. Minneapolis: Zondervan, 1962.

Halliday, F. E. *Shakespeare in His Age.* London: G. Duckworth, 1956.

______. *A Shakespeare Companion.* Baltimore: Penguin, 1969/64.

Hamilton, Edith. *Mythology.* New York: Mentor, 1942.

Hammond, N. G. L., ed. *Atlas of the Greek and Roman World in Antiquity.* Park Ridge, NJ: Noyes Press, 1981.

______, and H. H. Scullard, eds. *The Oxford Classical Dictionary.* Oxford: Clarendon Press, 1970.

Hanham, Alison. *Richard III and his Early Historians 1483-1535.* Oxford: Clarendon Press, 1975.

Hanks, Patrick, and Flavia Hodges. *A Concise Dictionary of First Names.* New York: Oxford Univ. Press, 1992.

Hankins, John Erskine. *Backgrounds of Shakespeare's Thought.* Hamden, CT: Archon, 1978.

Harris, Mary Dormer, ed. *The Coventry Leet Book.* Early English Text Society, vols. 134–135, 138, 146. London: Kegan, Paul, Trench, and Trübner, 1907.

Harrison, G. B. *The Elizabethan Journals.* Ann Arbor: Univ. of Michigan Press, 1955.

Harrison, William. *Harrison's Description of England in Shakespeare's Youth.* Ed. by F. J. Furnivall. Chicago: Library Resources, 1970/1871-81.

Harsnett, Samuel. *A Declaration of Egregious Popish Impostures,* etc., in Brownlow (above).

Harvey, John Hooper. *The Black Prince and His Age.* NJ: Rowman & Littlefield, 1976.

Harvey, Paul, ed. *The Oxford Companion to Classical Literature.* Oxford: Clarendon Press, 1974/37.

Hastings, James. *Encyclopedia of Religion and Ethics,* 12 vols. New York: Charles Scribner's Sons, 1961.

Hathorn, Richmond Y. *Crowell's Handbook of Classical Drama.* New York: Thomas Y. Crowell, 1967.

Hazlitt, W. Carew, ed. *A Select Collection of Old English Plays.* 4th ed. 15 vols. New York: Benjamin Blom, 1964 (rptd. from 1874–76).

______. *Shakespeare Jest-books,* 3 vols. London: Willis and Sotheran, 1864.

______. *Shakespeare's Library: A Collection of the Plays, Romances, Novels, Poems and Histories Employed by Shakespeare in the Composition of His Works.* Chicago: Library Resources, 1970.

Hesiod. *Hesiod, the Homeric Hymns and Homerica.* Ed. and trans. Hugh G. Evelyn-White. Cambridge: Harvard Univ. Press, 1970.

______. *Hesiod.* Trans. Richard Lattimore. Ann Arbor: Univ. of Michigan Press, 1959.

Hewitt, Herbert James. *The Black Prince's Expedition of 1355-1357.* Manchester: Manchester Univ. Press, 1958.

Holinshed, Raphael. *Chronicles of England, Scotland and Ireland.* 6 vols. London: J. Johnson, 1807-8; rptd. New York: AMS, 1965.

______. *Holinshed's Chronicle as used in Shakespeare's Plays.* Ed. by Allardyce and Josephine Nicoll. London: Dent, 1959.

Homer. *The Iliad.* Trans. Robert Fagles. New York: Viking, 1990.

Holt, J. C. *Robin Hood.* London: Thames and Hudson, 1982.

Holzknecht, Karl Julius. *The Backgrounds of Shakespeare's Plays.* New York: American Book Co., 1950.

Holweck, F. G. *A Biographical Dictionary of the Saints.* St. Louis: B. Herder, rptd. Detroit: Gale, 1969.

Horace. *Satires, Epistles and Ars Poetica.* Trans. Henry Rush Fairclough. Loeb Classical Library. New York: Putnam's, 1929.

Hotson, J. Leslie. *Shakespeare's Motley.* London: R. Hart-Davis, 1952.

______. *Shakespeare's Sonnets Dated and Other Essays.* London: R. Hart-Davis, 1949.

Irvine, Theodore. *A Pronouncing Dictionary of Shakespearean Proper Names.* New York: Barnes and Noble, 1945.

Jacob, Ernest Frazer. *Henry V and the Invasion of France.* New York: Macmillan, 1950.

______. *The Fifteenth Century, 1399-1485.* Oxford: Clarendon Press, 1961.

Jorgensen, Paul. *Shakespeare's Military World.* Berkeley: Univ. of California Press, 1973/56.

Joseph, Bertram. *Shakespeare's Eden: The Commonwealth of England, 1158-1629.* New York: Barnes and Noble, 1971.

Jump, John, ed. *Shakespeare:* Hamlet. Casebook Series. London: Macmillan, 1968.

Juvenal. *Juvenal and Persius.* Trans. George Gilbert Ramsay. Loeb Classical Library. Cambridge: Harvard Univ. Press, 1940.

Keen, Maurice. *The Outlaws of Medieval Legend.* Toronto and Buffalo: Univ. of Toronto Press, 1977.

Kelly, J. N. D. *The Oxford Dictionary of Popes.* New York: Oxford Univ. Press, 1986.

Kendall, Paul. *Richard the Third.* Garden City, NY: Doubleday, 1965.

______. *The Yorkist Age.* Garden City, NY: Doubleday, 1962.

Kent, William, ed. *An Encyclopedia of London.* New York: Macmillan, 1951.

Kermode, Frank. *Shakespeare:* King Lear. Casebook Series. Nashville: Aurora, 1970.

Kirby, John Lavan. *Henry IV of England.* London: Constable, 1970.

Kökeritz, Helga. *Shakespeare's Names: A Pronouncing Dictionary.* New Haven: Yale Univ. Press, 1966.

Kravitz, David. *Who's Who in Greek and Roman Mythology.* New York: Clarkson N. Potter, 1975.

Leggatt, Alexander. *Shakespeare's Political Drama: The History Plays and the Roman Plays.* New York: Routledge, 1988.

Leishman, J. B. *Themes and Variations in Shakespeare's Sonnets.* London: Hutchinson, 1961.

Levith, Murray J. *What's in Shakespeare's Names.* Hamden, CT: Archon, 1978.

Livy. *The Early History of Rome.* Tr. by Aubrey de Selincourt. Baltimore, MD: Penguin Books, 1960.

Mahood, M. M. *Bit Parts In Shakespeare's Plays.* Cambridge: Cambridge Univ. Press, 1992.

Malory, Thomas. *The Works of Sir Thomas Malory.* 3rd ed. 3 vols. Ed. Eugène Vinaver. Rev. P. J. C. Field. Oxford: Oxford Univ. Press, 1990.

Manley, L. *London in the Age of Shakespeare: An Anthology.* London: Croom Helm, 1986.

Mantinband, James H. *Dictionary of Latin Literature.* Paterson, NJ: Littlefield Adams, 1964.

Markham, Clements. *Richard III, His Life and Character Reviewed in Light of Recent Research.* New York: Russell & Russell, 1968/06.

Marlowe, Christopher. *The Complete Plays of Christopher Marlowe.* Ed. Irving Ribner. Indianapolis: Odyssey Press, 1963.

Martin, Michael Rheta, and Richard C. Harrier. *Concise Encyclopedic Guide to Shakespeare.* New York: Horizon, 1971.

Matthew, Donald. *Atlas of Medieval Europe.* New York: Facts on File, 1983.

Mattingly, Garrett. *The Armada.* Boston: Houghton Mifflin, 1959.

______. *Catherine of Aragon.* Boston: Little, Brown, 1941.

______. *Renaissance Diplomacy.* New York: Russell and Russell, 1970.

McKisack, May. *The Fourteenth Century, 1307-1399.* Oxford: Clarendon Press, 1959/63.

Menke, Frank G. *The Encyclopedia of Sports.* Rev. ed. New York: A. S. Barnes, 1953.

Miller, Madelein, and J. Lane Miller. *Harper's Bible Dictionary.* New York: Harper and Brothers, 1961/52.

Miller, Hellen. *Henry VIII and the English Nobility.* New York: Blackwell, 1986.

Millett, Fred B. and Gerald Eades Bentley. *The Art of the Drama.* New York: Appleton Century Crofts, 1963.

Mills, A. D. *A Dictionary of English Place Names.* New York: Oxford Univ. Press, 1991.

Miracles de Nostre Dame par personnages. Societé des Anciens Textes Français, ed. Gaston Paris and Ulysse Robert. Paris: Librairie de Firmin Didot, 1881.

Montaigne, Michel de. *The Essays of Michael, Lord of Montaigne.* 3 vols. Trans. John Florio. London: J. W. Dent, 1923.

Muir, Kenneth. *The Sources of Shakespeare's Plays.* New Haven: Yale Univ. Press, 1978.

Murray, Peter and Linda. *The Penguin Dictionary of Art and Artists.* 4th ed. New York: Penguin, 1976.

Myers, Alec. *London in the Age of Chaucer.* Norman, OK: Univ. of Oklahoma Press, 1972.

New Catholic Encyclopedia. New York: McGraw-Hill, 1967-89.

Noble, Richmond. *Shakespeare's Biblical Knowledge and Use of the Book of Common Prayer.* New York: Octagon, 1970.

North, Thomas, trans. *Plutarch's Lives of the Noble Greeks and Romans.* George Wyndham, ed. The Tudor Translations 1st ser. vol. 7-12. London: D. Nutt, 1895-96.

Nungezer, Edwin. *A Dictionary of Actors and Other Persons Associated with the Public Representation of Plays in England Before 1642.* Cornell Studies in English XIII. New Haven: Yale Univ. Press, 1929.

Oizumi, Akio, ed. *A Complete Concordance to the Works of Geoffrey Chaucer.* 10 vols. New York: Olms-Weidman, 1991.

Onions, C. T. *A Shakespeare Glossary.* Oxford: Clarendon Press, 1968/11.

Osgood, Charles Grosvenor, ed. *A Concordance to the Poems of Edmund Spenser.* Carnegie Institution of Washington, 1915.

Ovid. *The Art of Love and Other Poems.* J. H. Mozley, ed. Loeb Classical Library. Cambridge: Harvard Univ. Press, 1969.

______. *Metamorphoses.* 2 vols. Ed. and trans. Frank Justus Miller. Cambridge: Harvard Univ. Press, 1936.

______. *Ovid's* Metamorphoses: *The Arthur Golding Translation.* Ed. John Frederick Nims. New York: Macmillan, 1965.

______. *Shakespeare's Ovid, Being Arthur Golding's Translation of the Metamorphosis.* Ed. by W. H. D. Rouse. London: De la More Press, 1904.

Oxford English Dictionary, compact ed. New York: Oxford Univ. Press, 1971.

Painter, Sidney. *The Reign of King John.* Baltimore: Johns Hopkins Press, 1949.

Partridge, Eric. *Shakespeare's Bawdy.* Rev. London: Routledge and Kegan Paul, 1968.

Pausanias. *Description of Greece.* 5 vols. Trans. W. H. S. Jones and Henry A. Ormerud. London: W. Heineman, 1918-35.

Percy, Thomas. *Reliques of Ancient English Poetry; Consisting of Ballads, Songs, and Other Pieces.* Philadelphia: C. DeSilver and Boston: Phillips, Sampson and Co., 1855.

Perroy, Edouard. *The Hundred Years' War.* New York: Capricorn Books, 1965.

Pierce, Robert. *Shakespeare's History Plays, the Family and the State.* Columbus: Ohio State Univ., 1971.

Plutarch. *Plutarch's Lives.* 11 vols. Trans. Bernadotte Perrin. Cambridge, MA: Harvard Univ. Press, 1959-59.

______. *Plutarch's Lives.* 4 Vols. Trans. Aubrey Stewart and George Long. London: G. Bell, 1913-16.

Pollard, A. F. *Henry VIII.* New York: Harper and Row, 1966.

Pollard, A. J. *Richard III and the Princes in the Tower.* New York: St. Martin's, 1991.

Poole, Adrian. *Coriolanus.* New York: Harvester-Wheatsheaf, 1988.

Powicke, Frederick. *The Thirteenth Century, 1216-1307.* Oxford: Clarendon Press, 1962.

Preminger, Alex, ed. *Princeton Encyclopedia of Poetry and Poetics.* Princeton: Princeton Univ. Press, 1965.

Quennell, Peter. *Shakespeare: A Biography.* New York: Avon, 1963.

Quennell, Peter, and Hamish Johnson. *Who's Who in Shakespeare.* New York: Morrow, 1973.

Rabelais, François. *Gargantua and Pantagruel.* Trans. Sir Thomas Urquhart and Peter le Motteux. London: Oxford Univ. Press, 1934.

Ridley, Jasper. *Elizabeth I.* London: Constable, 1987.

______. *Henry VIII.* New York: Viking, 1985.

Riggs, David. *Shakespeare's Heroical Histories: Henry VI and Its Literary Tradition.* Cambridge, MA: Harvard Univ. Press, 1971.

Rollason, David. *Saints and Relics in Anglo-Saxon England.* Oxford: Basil Blackwell, 1989.

Room, Adrian. *Brewer's Dictionary of Names.* New York: Cassell, 1992.

Roper, William. *The Lyfe of Thomas More, Knighte.* New York: Swallow Press, 1950.

Ross, Charles. *Richard III.* Berkeley, CA: Univ. of California Press, 1981.

Rowse, A. L. *The England of Elizabeth: The Structure of Society.* New York: Macmillan, 1951.

Rubinstein, Frankie. *A Dictionary of Shakespeare's Sexual Puns and Their Significance.* 2nd ed. London: Macmillan, 1989.

Russell, Bertrand. *A History of Western Philosophy.* New York: Simon and Schuster, 1945.

Saccio, Peter. *Shakespeare's English Kings, History, Chronicle, and Drama.* New York: Oxford, 1977.

Sannazaro, Jacopo. *Arcadia and Piscatorial Eclogues.* Trans. Ralph Nash. Detroit: Wayne State Univ. Press, 1966.

Schmidt, Alexander. *Shakespeare Lexicon and Quotation Dictionary.* 3rd ed. Revised by Gregor Sarrazin. Berlin: George Reimer, 1902; rptd. New York: Dover, 1971.

Schoenbaum, Samuel. *William Shakespeare: A Compact Documentary Life.* Rev. New York: Oxford Univ. Press, 1987.

Scholes, Percy. *The Concise Oxford Dictionary of Music.* 2nd ed. Ed. John Owen Ward. London: Oxford Univ. Press, 1964.

Scot, Reginald. *The Discoverie of Witchcraft.* Carbondale: Southern Illinois Univ. Press, 1965.

Scullard, Howard. *From the Gracchi to Nero: A History of Rome from 133 BC to AD 68*, 2nd ed. London: Methuen, 1965/63.

Shakespeare's England: An Account of the Life and Manners of His Age. 2 vols. Oxford: Clarendon Press, 1916.

Shepherd, William. *Atlas of Medieval and Modern History.* New York: Holt & Co., 1932.

Sidney, Philip. *The Countesse of Pembrokes Arcadia.* Ed. Albert Feuillerat. Cambridge: Cambridge Univ. Press, 1922.

Smith, Al. *Dictionary of City of London Street Names.* New York: Arco, 1970.

Smith, Lacey Baldwin. *Henry VIII: The Mask of Royalty.* Boston: Houghton Mifflin, 1971.

______. *Treason in Tudor England: Politics and Paranoia.* Princeton: Princeton Univ. Press, 1986.

Smith, William, and Charles Anthon. *A New Classical Dictionary of Greek and Roman Biography, Mythology and Geography.* New York: Harper and Brothers, 1868.

Somerset, Anne. *Elizabeth I.* New York: Knopf, 1991.

Source Book, The. Chicago: Perpetual Encyclopedia Corp., 1930.

Spencer, Christopher. *The Genesis of Shakespeare's* Merchant of Venice. Lewiston, NY: Edwin Mellen, 1988.

Spenser, Edmund. *Edmund Spenser's Poetry.* Ed. Hugh Maclean. New York: W. W. Norton, 1968.

______. *The Works of Edmund Spenser: A Variorum Edition.* 9 vols. Eds. Edwin Almiron Greenlaw, Charles Grosvenor Osgood, and Frederick Morgan Padelford. Baltimore: Johns Hopkins Univ. Press, 1932–49.

Spurgeon, Caroline F. E. *Shakespeare's Imagery.* 1935.

Stokes, Francis Griffin. *A Dictionary of the Characters and Proper Names in the Works of Shakespeare.* Boston: Houghton Mifflin, 1924.

Strabo. *The Geography of Strabo.* 8 vols. Ed. and trans. Horace Leonard Jones. Cambridge: Harvard Univ. Press, 1960.

Strayer, Joseph, ed. *Dictionary of the Middle Ages.* 12 vols. New York: Charles Scribner's Sons, 1982.

Sugden, Edward H. *A Topographical Dictionary to the works of shakespeare and His Fellow Dramatists.* Manchester: Manchester Univ. Press, 1925.

Thomson, Wilfred W. *Shakespeare's Characters: A Historical Dictionary.* Folcroft, PA: Folcroft Library Editions, 1951/72.

Tierney, Brian, and Sidney Painter. *Western Europe in the Middle Ages, 300-1475*, 4th ed. New York: Alfred A. Knopf, 1983/70.

Tilliott, P. M. *A History of York: The City of York.* Victoria History of the City of York. London: Oxford Univ. Press, 1961

Tillyard, E. M. W. *The Elizabethan World Picture.* New York: Vintage, 1959.

Times Encyclopedia and Gazetteer. Chicago: Consolidated Book Publishers, 1935.

Traversi, Derek. *An Approach to Shakespeare.* 3rd ed. Garden City, NY: Anchor, 1969.

______. *Shakespeare: The Roman Plays.* Stanford, CA: Stanford Univ. Press, 1963.

Tuck, Anthony. *Richard II and the English Nobility.* New York: St. Martin's Press, 1974.

Virgil. *Virgil.* 2 vols. Trans. Henry Rushton Fairclough. Loeb Classical Library, Cambridge: Harvard Univ. Press, 1967.

Wain, John. *Shakespeare:* Macbeth. Casebook Series. Nashville: Aurora, 1970.

Warren, Wilfred. *King John.* Berkeley: Univ. of California Press, 1978.

Warrington, John. *Everyman's Classical Dictionary.* London: J. M. Dent & Sons, 1961.

Weekley, Ernest. *The Romance of Words.* 1911; rptd. New York: Dover, 1961.

Wells, Stanley, and Gary Taylor. *William Shakespeare: A Textual Companion.* Oxford: Oxford Univ. Press, 1987.

Wilders, John. *The Lost Garden: A View of Shakespeare's English and Roman History Plays.* Totowa, NJ: Rowman and Littlefield, 1979.

Willen, Gerald, and Victor B. Reed, eds. *A Casebook on Shakespeare's Sonnets.* New York: Thomas Y. Crowell, 1964.

Wilson, David. *A History of England.* Hinsdale, IL: Dryden Press, 1972/67.

Withycombe, E. G. *The Oxford Dictionary of English Christian Names.* Oxford: Oxford Univ. Press, 1973.

Wolffe, Bertram. *Henry VI.* London: Eyre Methuen, 1981.

Woolf, Rosemary. *The English Mystery Plays.* Berkeley and Los Angeles: Univ. of California Press, 1972.

Xenophon. *The History of Xenophon.* 5 vols. Trans. Henry Graham Dakyns. New York: Tandy-Thomas, 1909.

FINIS.